AN EXPOSITION OF HEBREWS

by

ARTHUR W. PINK

BAKER BOOK HOUSE
GRAND RAPIDS, MICHIGAN

Library of Congress Catalog Card Number: 54-11076

ISBN: 0-8010-6857-6

First printing, September 1954
Second printing, December 1963
Third printing, January 1967
Fourth printing, June 1968
Fifth printing, September 1970
Sixth printing, October 1971
Seventh printing, March 1974
Eighth printing, July 1975
Ninth printing, December 1976
Tenth printing, March 1979
Eleventh printing, July 1981
Twelfth printing, January 1984
Thirteenth printing, February 1986
Fourteenth printing, January 1988
Fifteenth printing, June 1989

PHOTOLITHOPRINTED BY CUSHING - MALLOY, INC.
ANN ARBOR, MICHIGAN, UNITED STATES OF AMERICA

FOREWORD

This is perhaps the most complete and exhaustive exposition of the Epistle to the Hebrews produced in this century available to the preacher, teacher, and Bible student. Pink's EXPOSITION OF HEBREWS unfolds, verse by verse and passage by passage, the rich teachings of this Epistle, and indicates how these eternal truths apply also to the age in which we live. It makes the Scriptures shine with clearer light. It is packed with helpful sermon material. It is a helpful guide to assist you to mine the inexhaustible wealth of God's Word.

—The Publishers

CONTENTS

CHAPTER ONE

Introduction

Before taking up the study of this important Epistle let writer and reader humbly bow before its Divine Inspirer, and earnestly seek from Him that preparation of heart which is needed to bring us into fellowship with that One whose person, offices, and glories are here so sublimely displayed. Let us personally and definitely seek the help of that blessed Spirit who has been given to the saints of God for the purpose of guiding them into all truth, and taking of the things of Christ to show unto them. In Luke 24:45 we learn that Christ opened the understanding of the disciples "*that* they might understand the Scriptures." May He graciously do so with us, then the entrance of His words will "give light" (Psa. 119:130), and in *His* light *we* shall "see light."

In this opening article we shall confine ourselves to things of an introductory character, things which it is necessary to weigh ere we take up the details of the Epistle. We shall consider its addressees, its purpose, its theme, its divisions, its characteristics, its value, and its writer. Before doing so, let us say that we expect to quote freely from other expositors, and where possible name them. In some cases we shall not be able to do so owing to the fact that extensive and long-distance travelling has obliged the writer to break up five libraries during the last twenty years. During those years he has read (and owned most of them) between thirty and forty commentaries on Hebrews, from which he has made notes in his Bible and taken helpful extracts for his own use when lecturing on this Epistle. As most of these commentaries have been disposed of, we can now do no more than make a general acknowledgement of help received from those written by Drs. J. Owen, J. Gill, Moses Stewart, Andrew Bonar, Griffith-Thomas, and Messrs. Pridham, Ridout, and Tucker. Let us now consider:—

1. *Its Addressees.*

In our English Bibles we find the words "The Epistle of Paul the Apostle to the Hebrews" as the address. Perhaps some of our readers are not aware that the titles found at the head of the different books of the Bible are *not* Divinely inspired, and therefore are not accounted canonical as are the contents. No doubt these titles were originated by the early scribes, when making copies of the original manuscripts—manuscripts, all traces of which have long since disappeared. In some instances these titles are unsatisfactory; in a few, glossly erroneous. As an example of the latter, we may refer to the final book of Scripture. Here the title is "The Revelation of St. John the Divine," whereas the opening sentence of the book itself designates it "The Revelation of Jesus Christ!"

While treating in general with the titles of the books of Scripture, we may note that in almost all of the Epistles there is a Divinely-named addressee in the opening verses. But we may add, the contents of each Epistle are *not* to be restricted to those immediately and locally addressed. It is important that the young Christian should grasp this firmly, so that he may be fortified against ultra-dispensational teaching. There are some, claiming to have great light, who would rob the saints to-day of the Epistle of James because it is addressed to "the Twelve Tribes which are scattered abroad." With equal propriety they might take from us the Epistles to the Philippians and Colossians because they were addressed only to the saints in those cities! The truth is that what Christ said to the apostles in Mark 13:17—"What I say unto *you,* I say unto *all*"—may well be applied to the whole of the Bible. *All* Scripture is needed by us (2 Tim. 3:16, 17), and all Scripture is God's word to us. Note carefully that while at the beginning of his Epistle to Titus Paul *only* addresses Titus himself (1:4), yet at the close of this letter he expressly says, "Grace be with you *all*" (3:15)!

Ignoring then the man-made title at the head of our Epistle, we are at once struck by the *absence* of any Divinely-given one in the opening verses. Nevertheless, its first sentence enables us to *identify* at once those to whom the Epistle was originally sent: see 1:1, 2. They to whom God spake through the prophets were the children of Israel, and it was also *unto them* He had spoken through His Son. In 3:1 we find a word which, however, *narrows* the circle to which this Epistle was first sent. It was not the Jewish nation at large which was addressed, but the "holy brethren, partakers of the heavenly calling" among them. Clear confirmation of this is supplied in the Epistles of Peter. His first was addressed, locally, to "the elect sojourners of the Dispersion (1:1—Gk., "eklektois parepidenois diasporas"). His second Epistle (see 3:1) was addressed, locally and immediately, to the same company. Now in 2 Peter 3:15 the apostle makes specific reference to "our beloved brother Paul also according to the wisdom given unto him hath written *unto you*." Thus all doubt is removed as to whom our Epistle was first sent.

The Epistle itself contains further details which serve to identify the addressees. That it was written to saints who were by no means young in the faith is clear from 5:12. That it was sent to those who had suffered severe persecutions (cf. Acts 8:1) is plain from what we read in 10:32. That it was addressed to a Christian community of considerable size is evident from 13:24. From this last reference we are inclined to conclude that this Epistle was first delivered to the church in Jerusalem (Acts 11:22), or to the churches in Judea (Acts 9:31), copies of which would be made and forwarded to Jewish Christians in foreign lands. Thus, our Epistle was first addressed to those descendants of Abraham who, by grace, had believed on their Saviour-Messiah.

2. *Its Purpose.*

This, in a word, was to instruct Jewish believers that Judaism had been superceded by Christianity. It must be borne in mind that a very considerable proportion of the earliest converts to Christ were Jews by natural birth, who continued to labour under Jewish prejudices. In his early Epistles the apostle had touched several times on this point, and sought to wean them from an undue and now untimely attachment to the Mosaic institutions. But only in *this* Epistle does he deal fully and systematically with the subject.

It is difficult for us to appreciate the position, at the time this Epistle was written, of those in Israel who had believed on the Lord Jesus. Unlike the Gentiles, who, for long centuries past, had lost all knowledge of the true God, and, in consequence, worshipped idols, the Jews *had* a Divine religion, and a Divinely-appointed place of worship. To be called upon to *forsake* these, which had been venerated by their fathers for over a thousand years, was to make a big demand upon them. It was natural that even those among them who had savingly believed on Christ should want to retain the forms and ceremonies amid which they had been brought up; the more so, seeing that the Temple still stood and the Levitical priesthood still functioned. An endeavour had been made to link Christianity on to Judaism, and as Acts 21:20 tells us there were many thousands of the early Jewish Christians who were "zealous of the law"—as the next verses clearly show, the *ceremonial* law.

"Instead of perceiving that under the new economy of things, there was neither Jew nor Gentile, but, that, without reference to external distinctions, all believers in Christ Jesus were now to live together in the closest bonds of spiritual attachment in holy society, they dreamed of the Gentiles being admitted to the participation of the Jewish Church through means of the Messiah, and, that its external economy was to remain unaltered to the end of the world" (Dr. J. Brown).

In addition to their natural prejudices, the *temporal circumstances* of the believing Jews became increasingly discouraging, yea, presented a sore temptation for them to abandon the profession of Christianity. Following the persecution spoken of in Acts 8:1, that eminent scholar, Adolph Saphir—himself a converted Jew—tells us: "Then arose another persecution of the believers, especially directed against the apostle Paul. Festus died about the year 63, and under the high priest Ananias, who favoured the Sadducees, the Christian Hebrews were persecuted as transgressors of the law. Some of them were stoned to death; and though this extreme punishment could not be frequently inflicted by the Sanhedrim, they were able to subject their brethren to sufferings and reproaches which they felt keenly. It was a small thing that they confiscated their goods; but they banished them from the holy places. Hitherto they had enjoyed the privileges of devout Israelites: they could take part in the beautiful and God-appointed services of the sanctuary; but now they were treated as unclean and apostates. Unless they gave up faith in Jesus, and forsook the assembling of themselves together, they were not allowed to enter the Temple, they were banished from the alter, the sacrifice, the high priest, the house of Jehovah.

"We can scarcely realise the piercing sword which thus wounded their inmost heart. That by clinging to the Messiah they were to be severed from Messiah's people, was, indeed, a great and perplexing trial; that for the hope of Israel's glory they were banished from the place which God had chosen, and where the divine Presence was revealed, and the symbols and ordinances had been the joy and strength of their fathers; that they were to be no longer children of the covenant and of the house, but worse than Gentiles, excluded from the outer court, cut off from the commonwealth of Israel. This was indeed a sore and mysterious trial. Cleaving to the promises made unto their fathers, cherishing the hope in constant prayer that their nation would yet accept the Messiah, it was the severest test to which their faith could be put, when their loyalty to Jesus involved separation from all the sacred rights and privileges of Jerusalem."

Thus the *need* for an authoritative, lucid, and systematic setting forth of the real relation of Christianity to Judaism was a pressing one. Satan would not miss the opportunity of seeking to persuade these Hebrews that their faith in Jesus of Nazareth was a mistake, a delusion, a sin. Were *they* right, while the vast majority of their brethren, according to the flesh, among whom were almost all the respected members of the Sanhedrim and the priesthood, wrong? Had God *prospered* them since they had become followers of the crucified One? or, did not their temporal circumstances evidence that He was most displeased with them? Moreover, the believing remnant of Israel had looked for a speedy return of Christ to the earth, but thirty years had now passed and He had not come! Yes, their situation was critical, and there was an urgent need that their faith should be strengthened, their understanding enlightened, and a fuller explanation be given them of Christianity in the light of the O.T. It was to meet this need that God, in His tender mercy, moved His servant to write this Epistle to them.

3. *Its Theme.*

This is, the superabounding excellence of Christianity over Judaism. The sum and substance, the centre and circumference, the light and life of Christianity, is *Christ*. Therefore, the method followed by the Holy Spirit in this Epistle, in developing its dominent theme, is to show the immeasurable superiority of Christ over all that had gone before. One by one the various objects in which the Jews boasted are taken up, and in the presence of the superlative glory of the Son of God they pale into utter insignificance. We are shown First, His superiority over the prophets 1:1-3. Second, His superiority over angels in 1:4 to 2:18. Third, His superiority over Moses in 3:1-19. Fourth, His superiority over Joshua 4:1-13. Fifth, His superiority over Aaron in 5:14 to 7:18. Sixth, His superiority over the whole ritual of Judaism, which is developed by showing the surpassing excellency of the new covenant over the old, in 7:19 to 10:39. Seventh, His superiority over each and all of the O.T. saints, in 11:1 to 12:3. In the Lord Jesus, Christians have the substance and reality, of which Judaism contained but the shadows and figures.

If the Lord permits us to go through this Epistle—O that He may come for us before—many illustrations and exemplifications of our definition of its theme will come before us. At the moment, we may note how frequently the comparative term "better" is used, thus showing the *superiority* of what we have in Christianity over what the saints of old had in Judaism. In Heb. 1:4 Christ is "better than angels;" in 7:19 mention is made of a "better hope;" in 7:22 of a "better testament" or "covenant; in 8:6 of "better promises;" in 9:23 of "better sacrifices;" in 10:34 of a "better substance;" in

11:16 of a "better country;" in 11:35 of a "better resurrection," and in 11:40 of the "better thing." So, too, we may observe the seven *great* things mentioned therein, namely: the "great salvation" (2:3), the "great High Priest" (4:14), the "great Tabernacle" (9:11), the "great fight of afflictions" (10:32), the "great recompense" (10:35), the "great cloud of witnesses" (12:1), the "great Shepherd of the sheep" (13:20).

Again; in contrast from what the believing Hebrews were called upon to *give up,* they were reminded of what they had *gained.* Note how frequently occurs the "we *have*"—a great High Priest (4:14, 8:1), an anchor of the soul (6:19), a better and enduring substance (10:34), an altar (13:10). Once more, we may note how these Hebrews were encouraged to forget the things which were behind and to press toward those which were before. All through this Epistle the *forward look* is prominent. In 1:6 and 2:5 mention is made of a "world (or 'habitable earth') to come;" in 6:5 of an "age to come;" in 8:10 of a "new covenant," yet to be made with the house of Israel; in 9:11 and 10:1 of "good things" to come; in 9:28 of a "salvation" to be revealed; in 10:37 of the coming Redeemer, in 11:14 and 13:14 of a "city" yet to be manifested.

Throughout this Epistle great prominence is given to the *Priesthood* of Christ. The centre of Judaism was its temple and the priesthood. Hence the Holy Spirit has here shown at length how that believers now have in Christ the substance of which these supplied but the shadows. The following passages should be carefully weighed:—2:17; 3:1; 4:14, 15; 5:6, 10; 6:20; 7:26; 8:1; 9:11; 10:21. "Though deprived of the temple, with its priesthood and altar and sacrifice, the apostle reminds the Hebrews, 'we have' the real and substantial temple, the great High Priest, the true altar, the one sacrifice, and with it all offerings, the true access into the very presence of the Most Holy" (A. Saphir).

4. *Its Divisions.*

These have been set forth so simply by Dr. J. Brown we cannot do better than quote from him: "The Epistle divides itself into two parts—the first, doctrinal; the second, practical—though the division is not so accurately (closely, A.W.P.) observed, that there are no duties enjoined or urged in the first part, and no doctrines stated in the second. The first is by far the larger division, reaching from the beginning of the Epistle down to the 18th verse of the 10th chapter. The second commences with the 19th verse of the 10th chapter, and extends to the end of the Epistle. The superiority of Christianity to Judaism is the great doctrine which the Epistle teaches; and constancy in the faith and profession of that religion, is the great duty which it enjoins."

5. *Its Characteristics.*

In several noticeable respects Hebrews differs from all the other Epistles of the New Testament. The name of the writer is omitted, there is no opening salutation, the ones to whom it was first specifically and locally sent are not mentioned. On the positive side we may note, that the typical teachings of the O.T. are expounded here at greater length than elsewhere; the priesthood of Christ is opened up, fully, only in this Epistle; the warnings against apostasy are more frequent and more solemn, and the calls to steadfastness and perseverance are more emphatic and numerous than in any other N.T. book. All of these things are accounted for by the fleshly nationality of those addressed, and the circumstances they were then in. Unless we keep these features steadily in mind, not a little in this Epistle will necessarily remain obscure and dark. Much of the language used, the figures employed, the references made, are only intelligible in the light of the O.T. Scriptures, on which Judaism was based. Except this be kept before us, such expressions as "*purged* our sins" (1:3), "there remaineth therefore a *sabbath-keeping* to the people of God" (4:9), "leaving the principles of the doctrine of Christ, let us go on unto perfection" (6:1), "our bodies washed with pure water" (10:22), "we have an altar" (13:10), etc., will remain unintelligible.

The first time that *Christ* is referred to in this Epistle it is as seated at "the right hand of the Majesty on high" (1:3), for it is with a *heavenly* Christ that Christianity has to do: note the other reference in this Epistle to the same fact—1:13, 8:1, 10:12, 12:2. In perfect accord with 1:3, which strikes the keynote of the Epistle, in addition to the heavenly Christ, reference is made to "the heavenly calling" (3:1), to "the heavenly gift" (6:4), to "heavenly things" (8:5), to "the heavenly Country" (11:16), to the "heavenly Jerusalem" (12:22), and to "the church of the First-born, whose names are written in Heaven" (12:23). This emphasis is easily understood when we remember that our Epistle is addressed to those whose inheritance, religious relationships, and hopes, had been all *earthly*.

In 13:22 there is a striking word which defines the *character* of this Epistle: "And I beseech you, brethren, suffer the word *of exhortation,* for I have written a letter unto you in few words." Upon this verse Saphir has well said, "The central idea of the Epistle is the glory of the New Covenant, contrasted with and excelling the glory of the old covenant; and while this idea is developed in a systematic manner, yet the aim of the writer throughout is eminently and directly practical. Everywhere his object is exhortation. He never loses sight of the dangers and wants of his brethren. The application to conscience and life is never forgotten. It is rather a sermon than an exposition. . . . In all his arguments, in every doctrine, in every illustration, the central aim of the Epistle is kept prominent—the exhortation to *steadfastness.*" This is, indeed, a peculiarity about Hebrews. In his other Epistles, the apostle rarely breaks in on an argument to utter an admonition or exhortation; instead, his well-nigh uniform method was to open with doctrinal exposition, and then base upon this a series of practical exhortations. But the unusual situation which the Hebrews were in, and the peculiar love that the writer bore to them (cf. Rom. 9:3) explains this exception.

What has just been said above accounts for what we find in Heb. 11. Nowhere else in the Bible do we find such a lengthy and complete description of *the life of faith.* But here a whole chapter, the longest in the Epistle, is devoted to it. The reason for this is not far to seek. Brought up in a system with an elaborate ritual, whose worship was primarily a matter of *outward* symbols and ceremonies; tempted as few ever have been to walk by sight, there was a special and most pressing need for a clear and detailed analysis and description of what it means to "walk by faith." Inasmuch as "example is better than precept," better because more easily grasped and because making a more powerful appeal to the heart, the Holy Spirit saw well to develop this important theme by an appeal to the history of saints recorded in the Scriptures of the Hebrews.

But it is most important that we recognize the fullness of the term *faith.* As Saphir well said, "Throughout Scripture faith means more than trust in Jesus for personal safety. This *is* the central point, but we must take care that we understand it in a true and deep manner. Faith, as the apostle explains in the Epistle to the Corinthians, is looking at the things which are not seen and temporal: it is preferring spiritual and eternal realities to the things of time, sense, and sin; it is leaning on God and realising His Word; it is the substance of things hoped for, the evidence of things not seen. Thus every doctrine and illustration of this Epistle goes straight to the heart and conscience, appeals to life, addresses itself to faith. It is one continued and sustained fervent and intense appeal to cleave to Jesus, the High Priest; to the substantial, true, and real worship. A most urgent and loving exhortation to be steadfast, patient, hopeful, in the presence of God, in the love and sympathy of the Lord Jesus, in the fellowship of the great cloud of witnesses."

Another prominent characteristic, concerning which there is no need for us now to enlarge upon, is the repeated *warnings* in this Epistle *against apostasy*. The most solemn and searching exhortations against the danger of falling away to be found anywhere in Holy Writ were given to these Hebrews. 2:1-3, most of the third and fourth chapters, 6:4-6, 10:26-29, 12:15-17 will at once occur to all who are familiar with the contents of this Epistle. The occasion for and the need of them has already been pointed out: the disappointing of the hopes the Hebrews had cherished, the persecutions they were then enduring, and the Divine judgment which was on the very eve of falling on Jerusalem (in A.D.70) made them imperative.

6. *Its Value.*

Let us mention first its *evidential* value. The Epistle is particularly rich in proofs of the *verbal* inspiration of Scripture. This is seen in the way the apostle refers to the O.T., and the use he makes of it. Mark how in 1:5-9 when quoting from the Psalms, 2nd Samuel, Deuteronomy, he refers these utterances to God Himself—"He saith," vv. 6, 7, 8. So in 3:7 "the Holy Spirit saith." Observe how when quoting from the O.T. the apostle attentively weighs *every word,* and often builds a fundamental truth on a single expression. Let us cite a few from the many examples of this:

See how in 2:8 the apostle argues from the authority of the word "all." In 2:11, when quoting from Psalm 22, he deduces the conclusion from the expression "My brethren" that the Son of God took to Himself human nature. Observe that in 3:7-19 and 4:2-11, when quoting from Psalm 95, he builds on the words "To-day," "I have sworn." and "My rest;" also in 3:2-6 how his conclusions there are drawn from the words "servant," and "My house" in Numbers 12:7. His whole argument in chapter 8 is based on the word "new" found in Jer. 31:31. How blessedly he makes use of the words "My son" from Prov. 3:11 in 12:5-9! How emphatically he appeals in 12:26, 27 to the words "once more" in Hag. 2:6,7. Is it not abundantly clear that in the judgment of the apostle Paul the Scriptures were Divinely inspired even to the *most minute* expression?

The *evangelical* value of this Epistle has been recognised by Christians of all schools of thought. Here is set forth with sunlight clearness the preciousness, design, efficacy and effects of the great Sacrifice offered once and for all. Christ has Himself purged our sins (1:3); He is able to save "to the uttermost" (7:25); by His one offering He has "perfected forever the sanctified" (10:14); by

His blood a new and living way has been opened for His people into the Holiest (10:19, 20): such are some of its wondrous declarations. Emphasising the inestimable worth of His redemptive work, it is here that we read of an "eternal salvation" (5:9), "eternal redemption" (9:12), and of the "eternal inheritance" (9:15).

The *doctrinal* importance of this book is exceeded by none, not even by the Roman Epistle. Where its teachings are believed, understood, and embodied in the life, ritualism and legalism (the two chief enemies of Christianity) receive their death-blow. In no other book of Scripture are the sophistries and deceptions of Romanism so clearly and systematically exposed. So fully and pointedly are the errors of Popery refuted, it might well have been written *since* that Satanic system became established. Well did one of the Puritans say, "God foreseeing what poisonous heresies would be hatched by the Papacy, prepared this antidote against them."

But perhaps its chief distinctive value lies in its exposition of the O.T. types. It is here we are taught that the Tabernacle and its furniture, the priesthood and their service, the various sacrifices and offerings, all pointed to the person, offices, and glories of the Lord Jesus. Of Israel's priests it is said, "who served unto the example and shadow of heavenly things" (8:5); the first tabernacle was "a figure for the time then present" (9:9); the ceremonial law had "a shadow of good things to come" (10:1). Melchizedec was a type of Christ (7:15), Isaac was a figure of Him (11:9), and so on. The details of these will be considered, D. V., in due course.

7. *Its Writer.*

This, we are fully assured, was the apostle Paul. Though he was distinctively and essentially the "apostle of the Gentiles" (Rom. 11:13), yet his ministry was by no means confined to them, as the book of Acts clearly shows. At the time of his apprehension the Lord said, "He is a chosen vessel unto Me, to bear My Name before the Gentiles, and kings, and the children of Israel" (Acts 9:15). It is significant that Israel is there mentioned *last,* in harmony with the fact that his Epistle to the Hebrews was written *after* most of his others to Gentile saints. That this Epistle *was* written by Paul is clear from 2 Peter 3:15. Peter was writing to saved Jews as the opening verses of his first Epistle intimates; the first verse of chapter 3 in his second Epistle informs us that this letter was addressed to the same people as his former one had been. Then, in vv. 15 he declares that his beloved brother Paul "also according to the wisdom given unto him hath written *unto you.*" If the Epistle to the Hebrews be not *that* writing, where is it?

CHAPTER TWO

The Superiority of Christ over the Prophets.

(1:1-3)

Before taking up the study of the opening verses of our Epistle, let us adduce further evidence that the apostle Paul was the writer of it. To begin with, note its Pauline *characteristics*. First, a *numerical* one. There is a striking parallel between his enumeration in Rom. 8:35-39 and in Heb 12:18-24. In the former he draws up a list of the things which shall not separate the saint from the love of God which is in Christ Jesus. If the reader will *count* them, he will find they are seventeen in number, but divided into a seven and a ten. The first seven are given in v. 35, the second ten in vv. 38, 39. In Heb. 12:18-23 he draws a contrast between Mount Sinai and Mount Sion, and he mentions seventeen details, and again the seventeen is divided into a seven and a ten. In vv. 18, 19 he names seven things which the saints are *not* "come unto"; while in vv. 22 to 24 he mentions ten things they *have* "come unto," viz., to Mount Sion, the City of the living God, the heavenly Jerusalem, an innumerable company of angels, the general Assembly, the Church of the Firstborn, to God the Judge of all, to the spirits of just men made perfect, to Jesus the Mediator, to the Blood of sprinkling. Compare also Gal. 5:19-21, where the apostle, when describing the "works of the flesh," enumerates *seventeen*. So far as we are aware, no other Epistle writer of the N.T. used this number seventeen in such a manner.

Again; the *terms* which he used. We single out one only. In Heb. 2:10 he speaks of the many *sons* which Christ is bringing to glory. Now Paul is the *only* N.T. writer that employs the term "sons." The others used a different Greek word meaning "children."

For *doctrinal* parallelisms compare Rom. 8:16 with Heb. 10:15, and 1 Cor. 3:13 with Heb. 5:12-14, and who can doubt that the Holy Spirit used the *same* penman in both cases?

Note a *devotional* correspondency. In Heb. 13:18 the writer of this Epistle says, "Pray for us." In his other Epistles we find Paul, more than once, making a similar request; but *no other* Epistle-writer is placed on record as soliciting prayer!

Finally, it is to be noted that *Timothy* was the companion of the writer of this Epistle, see 13:23. We know of no hint anywhere that Timothy was the fellow-worker of anyone else but the apostle Paul: that he companied with *him* is clear from 2 Cor. 1:1, Col. 1:1, 1 Thess. 3:1, 2.

In addition to the many Pauline characteristics stamped on this Epistle, we may further observe that it was written by one who had been in "bonds" (see 10:34); by one who was now sundered from Jewish believers (13:19)—would not this indicate that Paul wrote this Epistle while in his hired house in Rome (Acts 28:30)? Again; here is a striking fact, which will have more force with some readers than others: if the Epistle to the Hebrews was *not* written by the apostle Paul, then the N. T. contains only *thirteen* Epistles from his pen—a number which, in Scripture, is ever associated with evil! But if Hebrews was also written by him, this brings the total number of his Epistles to fourteen, i.e., 7 x 2—seven being the number of perfection and two of witness. Thus,*a perfect witness* was given by this beloved servant of the Lord to Jew and Gentile!

In the last place, there is one other evidence that the apostle Paul penned the Hebrews' Epistle which is still more conclusive. In 2 Thess. 3:17-18 we read, "The *salutation* of Paul with mine own hand, which is the token in *every* Epistle, so I write, the *grace* of our Lord Jesus Christ *be with you all.*" Now, if the reader will turn to the closing verse of each of the first thirteen Epistles of this apostle, it will be found that this "token" is given in each one. Then, if he will refer to the close of the Epistles of James, Peter, John and Jude, he will discover a noticeable *absence* of it. Thus it was a *distinctive* "token" of the apostle Paul. It served to identify *his* writings. When, then at the close of Hebrews we read *"grace be with you all"* the proof is conclusive and complete that none other than Paul's hand originally wrote this Epistle.

Ere passing from this point a word should be added concerning the distinctive *suitability* of Paul as the penman of this Epistle. In our little work "Why Four Gospels" (pages 20-22), we have called attention to the *wisdom* of God displayed in the selection of the four men He employed to write the Gospels. In each one we may clearly perceive a special personal fitness for the task before him. Thus it is here. All through the Epistle of Hebrews Christ is presented as the glorified One in Heaven. Now, it was *there* the apostle Paul first saw the Lord (Acts 26:19); who, then, was so well suited, so experimentally equipped, to present to the Hebrews the rejected Messiah at God's right hand! *He* had seen Him there; and with the exceptions of Stephen, and later, John of Patmos, he was the only one who had or has!

Should it be asked, *Why* is the apostle Paul's *name* omitted from the preface to this Epistle? a threefold answer may be suggested. First, it is addressed, primarily, to converted "Hebrews," and Paul was not characteristically or essentially an apostle *to them:* he was the apostle to the Gentiles. Second, the inscribing of his name at the beginning of this Epistle would, probably, have prejudiced many Jewish readers against it (cf. Acts 21.27, 28; 22:17-22). Third, the supreme purpose of the Epistle is to exalt Christ, and in this Epistle *He* is the "Apostle," see 3:1. Therefore the impropriety of Paul making mention of his own apostleship. But let us now turn to the contents of the Epistle:

VV. 1-3. These verses are not only a preface, but they contain a summary of the doctrinal section of the Epistle. The keynote is struck at once. Here we are shown, briefly but conclusively, the superiority of Christianity over Judaism. The apostle introduces his theme in a manner least calculated to provoke the antipathy of his Jewish readers. He begins by acknowledging that Judaism was of Divine authority: it was *God* who had spoken to their fathers. "He confirms and seals the doctrine which was held by the Hebrews, that unto them had been committed the oracles of God; and that in the writings of Moses and the prophets they possessed the Scripture which could not be broken, in which God had displayed unto them His will" (A. Saphir). It is worthy of note that the Gospels open with a summary of O.T. history from Abraham to David, from David to the Captivity, and from the Captivity to Jesus, the Immanuel predicted by Isaiah (see Matt. 1), and that the Epistles also begin by telling us that the Gospel expounded by the prophets had been "promised afore by God's prophets in the Holy Scriptures" (Rom. 1:1-3).

Having affirmed that God *had* spoken to the fathers by the prophets, the apostle at once points out that God has now spoken to us by His Son. "The great object of the Epistle is to describe the contrast between the old and new covenants. But this contrast is based upon their unity. It is impossible for us rightly to understand the contrast unless we know first the resemblance. The new covenant is contrasted with the old covenant, not in the way in which the light of the knowledge of God is contrasted with the darkness and ignorance of heathenism, for the old covenant is also of God, and is therefore possessed of Divine glory. Beautiful is the night in which the moon and the stars of prophecy and types are shining; but when the sun arises then we forget the hours of watchfulness and expectancy, and in the clear and joyous light of day there is revealed to us the reality and substance of the eternal and heavenly sanctuary" (A. Saphir). Let us now examine these opening verses word by word.

"God" (v. 1). The particular reference is to the Father, as the words "by (His) Son" in v. 2 intimate. Yet the other Persons of the Trinity are not excluded. In O.T. times the Godhead spoke by the Son, see Exodus 3:2, 5; 1 Cor. 10:9; and by the Holy Spirit, see Acts 28:26, Heb. 3:7, etc. Being a Trinity in Unity, one Person is often said to work by Another. A striking example of this is found in Gen. 19:24, where Jehovah the Son is said to have rained down fire *from* Jehovah the Father.

"God . . . . spake " (v. 1). Deity is not speechless. The true and living God, unlike the idols of the heathen, is no dumb Being. The God of Scripture, unlike that absolute and impersonal "first Cause" of philosophers and evolutionists, is not silent. At the beginning of earth's history we find Him speaking: "*God said,* Let there be light: and there was light" (Gen. 1:4). "He spake and it was done, He commanded and it stood fast" (Psa. 33:9). To men He spake, and still speaks. For this we can never be sufficiently thankful.

"God who at sundry times . . . . spake" (v. 1). Not once or twice, but many times, did God speak. The Greek for "at sundry times" literally means "by many parts," which necessarily implies, some at one time, some at another. From Abraham to Malachi was a period of fifteen hundred years, and during that time God spake frequently: to some a few words, to others many. The apostle was here paving the way for making manifest the superiority of Christianity. The Divine revelation vouchsafed under the Mosaic economy was but *fragmentary*. The Jew desired to set Moses against Christ (John 9:28). The apostle acknowledges that God *had* spoken to Israel. But *how?* Had He communicated to them the fulness of His mind? Nay. The O.T. revelation was but the refracted rays, not the light unbroken and complete. As illustrations of this we may refer to the *gradual* making known of the Divine character through His different titles, or to the prophesies concerning the coming Messiah. It was "here a little and there a little."

"God who . . . . in divers manner spake" (v. 1). The majority of the commentators regard these words as referring to the *various ways* in which God revealed Himself to the prophets—sometimes directly, at others indirectly—through an angel (Gen. 19:1, etc.); sometimes audibly, at others in dreams and visions. But, with Dr. J. Brown, we believe that the particular point here is *how* God spake *to the fathers* by the prophets, and not how He has made known His mind to the prophets themselves. "The revelation was sometimes communicated by typical representations and emblematical actions, sometimes in a continued parable, at other times by separate figures, at other times—though comparatively rarely—in plain explicit language. The revelation has sometimes the form of a narrative, at other times that of a prediction, at other times that of an argumentative discourse; sometimes it is given in prose, at other times in poetry" (Dr. J. B.). Thus we may see here an illustration of the *sovereignty* of God: He did not act *uniformly* or confine Himself to any one method of speaking to the fathers. He spake by way of promise and prediction, by types and symbols, by commandments and precepts, by warnings and exhortations.

"God . . . . spake in times past unto the fathers by the prophets" (v. 1). Thus the apostle sets his seal upon the Divine inspiration and authority of the O.T. Scriptures. The "fathers" here goes right back to the beginning of God's dealings with the Hebrews—cf. Luke 1:55. To "the fathers" God spake "by," or more literally and precisely, *"in"* the prophets. This denotes that God possessed their hearts, controlled their minds, ordered their tongues, so that they spake not their own words, but *His* words—see 2 Peter 1:21. At times the prophets were themselves conscious of this, see 2 Sam. 23:2, etc. We may add that the word "prophet" signifies the mouthpiece of God: see Gen. 20:7, Ex. 7:1, John 4:19—she recognised *God* was speaking to her; Acts 3:21!

"God . . . . hath in these last days spoken unto us by"—better "in (His) Son" (v. 2). "Having thus described the Jewish revelation he goes on to give an account of the Christians, and begins it in an antithetical form. The God who spake to 'the fathers' now speaks to 'us.' The God who spake in 'times past,' now speaks in these 'last days.' The God who spake 'by the prophets,' now speaks 'by His Son.' There is nothing in the description of the Gospel revelation that answers to the two phrases 'at sundry times,' and 'in divers manners'; but the ideas which they necessarily suggest to the mind are, the *completeness* of the Gospel revelation compared with the imperfection of the Jewish, and the *simplicity* and clearness of the Gospel revelation compared with the multiformity and obscurity of the Jewish" (Dr. J. Brown).

"This manifesting of God's will by parts ('at sundry times,' etc.), is here (v. 1) noted by way of distinction and difference from God's revealing His will under the Gospel; which was all at one time, viz., the times of His Son's being on earth; for then the whole counsel of God was made known so far as was meet for the Church to know it while this world continueth. In this respect Christ said, '*All* things that I have heard of My Father, I have made known to you' (John 15:15), and 'the Comforter shall teach you all things, and bring to your remembrance whatsoever I have said unto you' (14:26). The woman of Samaria understood this much: 'When the Messiah is come, He will tell us *all* things' (John 4:25). Objection: the apostles had many things revealed to them later. Answer: those were no other things than what Christ had revealed before, while He lived" (Dr. Gouge).

The central point of contrast here is between the O.T. "prophets" and Christ "the Son." Though the Holy Spirit has not here developed the details of this contrast, we can ourselves, by going back to the O.T., supply them. Mr. Saphir has strikingly summarised them under seven heads. "First, they were many: one succeeded another: they lived in different periods. Second, they gave out God's revelation in 'divers manners'—similitudes, visions, symbols. Each prophet had his peculiar gift and character. Their stature and capacity varied. Third, they were sinful men—Isa. 6:5, Dan. 10:8. Fourth, they did not possess the Spirit constantly. The 'word' came to them, but they did not *possess* the Word! Fifth, they did not understand the heights and depths of their own message—1 Peter 1:10. Sixth, still less did they comprehend the whole of God's revelation in O.T. times. Seventh, like John the Baptist they had to testify 'I am not the Light, I am only sent to bear witness of the Light.' " Now, the very opposite was the case in all these respects with the "Son." Though the revelation which God gave the prophets is equally inspired and authoritative, yet that through His Son possesses a greater dignity and value, for *He* has revealed all the secrets of the Father's heart, the fulness of His counsel, and the riches of His grace.

"In these last days" (v. 2). This expression is not to be taken absolutely, but is a contrast from "in time past." The ministry of Christ marked "the last days." That which the Holy Spirit was pressing upon the Hebrews was the *finality* of the Gospel revelation. Through the "prophets" God had given predictions and foreshadowings; in the Son, the fulfilment and substance. The "fulness of time" had come when God sent forth His Son (Gal. 4:4). He has nothing now in reserve. He has no further revelation to make. Christ is the *final* Spokesman of Deity. The written Word is now complete. In conclusion, note how Christ *divides history*: everything before pointed toward Him, everything since points back to Him; *He* is the Centre of all God's counsels.

"Spoken unto us" (v. 2). "The pronoun *us* refers directly to the Jews of that age, to which class belonged both the writer and his readers; but the statement is equally true in reference to all, in every succeeding age, to whom the word of this salvation comes. God, in the completed revelation of His will, respecting the salvation of men through Christ Jesus, is still speaking to all who have an opportunity of reading the N.T. or of hearing the Gospel" (Dr. J. Brown).

"In (His) Son" (v. 2). Christ is the "Son of God" in two respects. First, eternally so, as the second Person in the Trinity, very God of very God. Second, He is also the "Son as incarnate." When He took upon Him sinless human nature He did not cease to be God, nor did He (as some blasphemously teach) "empty" Himself of His Divine attributes, which are inseparable from the Divine Being. "*God* was manifest in flesh" (1 Tim. 3:16). Before His Birth, God sent an angel to Mary, saying, "He (the Word become flesh) shall be called the Son of God" (Luke 1:35). The One born in Bethlehem's manger was the *same* Divine Person as had subsisted from all eternity, though He had now taken unto Him another, an additional nature, the human. But so perfect is the *union* between the Divine and the human natures in Christ that, in some instances, the properties of the one are ascribed to the other: see John 3:13, Rom. 5:10. It is in the *second* of these respects that our blessed Saviour is viewed in our present passage—as the Mediator, the God-man, God "spake" in and through Him: see John 17:8, 14, etc.

Summarising what has been said, we may note how that this opening sentence of our Epistle points a threefold contrast between the communications which God has made through Judaism and through Christianity. First, in their respective *characters*: the one was fragmentary and incomplete; the other perfect and final. Second, in the *instruments* which He employed: in the former, it was sinful men; in the latter, His holy Son. Third, in the *periods* selected: the one was "in time past," the other in "these last days," intimating that God has now fully expressed Himself, that He has nothing in reserve. But is there not here something deeper and more blessed? We believe there is. Let us endeavor to set it forth.

That which is central and vital in these opening verses is God *speaking*. A silent God is an unknown God: God "speaking" is God expressing, *revealing* Himself. All that we know or can now know of God is what He has revealed of Himself through His Word. But the opening verse of Hebrews presents a contrast between God's "speakings." To Israel He gave a revelation of Himself in "time past"; to them He also gave another in "these last days." *What,* then, was the *character* of these two distinct revelations?

As we all know, God's Word is divided into two main sections, the Old and the New Testaments. Now, it is instructive to note that the distinctive character in which God is revealed in them strikingly corresponds to those two words about Him recorded in the first Epistle of John; "God is light" (1:5); "God is love" (4:8). Mark attentively the order of these two statements which make known to us what God actually is in Himself.

"God is light." It was in this character that He was revealed in Old Testament times. What is the very first thing we hear Him saying in His Word? This: "Let there be light" (Gen. 1:3). In what character does He appear to our fallen first parents in Gen. 3? As "light," as the holy One, uncompromisingly judging sin. In what character was He revealed at the flood? As the "light," unsparingly dealing with that which was evil. How did He make Himself known to Israel at Sinai? As the One who is "light." And so we might go on through the whole Old Testament. We do not say that His love was entirely unknown, but most assuredly it was not fully revealed. That which was *characteristic* of the revelation of the Divine character in the Mosaic dispensation was God as *light.*

"God is love." It is in this character that He stands revealed in New Testament times. To make known His love. God sent forth the Son of His love. It is only in Christ that love is fully unveiled. Not that the light was absent; that could not be, seeing that He was and is God Himself. The love which he exercised and manifested was ever an holy love. But just as "God is light" was the characteristic revelation in Old Testament times, so "God is love" is characteristic of the New Testament revelation. In the final analysis, *this* is the contrast pointed to in the opening verses of Hebrews. In the prophets God "spoke" (revealed Himself) as *light:* the requirements, claims, demands of his holiness being insisted upon. But in the Son it is the sweet accents of *love* that we hear. It is the *affections* of God which the Son has expressed, appealing to ours; hence, it is by the heart, and not the head, that God can be known.

"God . . . . hath in these last days spoken unto us by (His) Son." It will be noted that the word "His" is in italics, which means there is no corresponding word in the original. But the omission of this word makes the sentence obscure; nor are we helped very much when we learn that the preposition "by" should be "in." "God hath spoken in Son." Yet really, this is not so obscure as at first it seems. Were a friend to tell you that he had visited a certain church, and that the preacher "spoke in Latin," you would have no difficulty in understanding what he meant: "spoke *in* Latin would intimate that that particular language marked his utterance. Such is the thought here. "In Son" has reference to that which *characterised* God's revelation. The thought of the contrast is that God, who of old had spoken *prophetwise,* now speaks *sonwise.* The thought is similar to that expressed in 1 Tim. 3:16, "God was manifest in flesh," the words "in flesh" referring to that which characterised the Divine manifestation. God was not manifested in intangible and invisible ether, nor did He appear in angelic form; but "in flesh." So He has now spoken "in Son," Sonwisely.

The whole revelation and manifestation of God is now in Christ; He alone reveals the Father's heart. It is not only that Christ declared or delivered God's message, but that He *himself* was and is God's message. All that God has to say to us is in His Son: all His thoughts, counsels, promises, gifts, are to be found in the Lord Jesus. Take the perfect life of Christ, His deportment, His ways; *that* is *God* "speaking"—revealing Himself—to us. Take His miracles, revealing His tender compassion, displaying His mighty power; they are *God* "speaking" to us. Take His death, commending to us the love of God, in that while we were yet sinners, He died for us; that is *God* "speaking" to us. Take His resurrection, triumphing over the grave, vanquishing him who had the power of death, coming forth as the "first fruits of them that slept"—the "earnest" of the "harvest" to follow; that is *God* "speaking" to us.

That which is so blessed in this opening sentence of the Hebrews' Epistle, and which it is so important that our hearts should lay hold of, is, that God has come out in an entirely new character—*Sonwise*. It is not so much that God speaks to us in *the* Son, but God addresses Himself to us in Sonlike character, that is, in the character of *love*. God might have spoken "Almightywise," as He did at Sinai; but that would have terrified and overwhelmed us. God might have spoken "Judgewise," as He will at the great white Throne; but that would have condemned us, and forever banished us from His presence. But, blessed be His name, He has spoken "Sonwise," in the *tenderest* relation which He could possibly assume.

What was the announcement from Heaven as soon as the Son was revealed? "Unto you is born"—what? Not a "Judge," or even a "Teacher," but "a Saviour, which is Christ the Lord" (Luke 2:11). There we have the *heart* of God revealed.

It is the *character* in which God "spoke" or revealed Himself which this opening sentence of our Epistle emphasises. He has appeared before us in the person of His beloved Son, to bring us a knowledge of the Divine affections, and this in order to engage our affections. In the very nature of the case there can be nothing higher. Through Christ, God is now fully, perfectly, finally revealed.

We lose much if we fail to keep constantly in mind the fact that Christ is *God*—"God *manifest* in flesh." We profess to believe that *He is* Divine, the second person of the blessed Trinity. But it is to be feared that often we forget this when reading the record of His earthly life or when pondering the words which fell from His lips. How necessary it is when taking up a passage in the Gospels to realise that there it is God "speaking" to us "Sonwise," God's affections made known.

Take the familiar words of Luke 19:10, "The Son of man is come to seek and to save that which is lost." But who was this "Son of man?" It was *God* "manifested in flesh"; it was God revealing Himself in His "Son" character. Thus, this well-known verse shows us the *heart* of God, yearning over His fallen creatures. Take, again, that precious word of Matt. 11:28, "Come unto Me all ye that labour and are heavy laden, and I will give you rest" Those words were uttered by "Jesus of Nazareth," yet they illustrate what is said in Heb. 1:2: it was God "speaking" Sonwisely, i.e., bringing to poor sinners a knowledge of Divine affections. Let us re-read the four Gospels with this glorious truth before us.

Cannot we now discern the wondrous and blessed contrast pointed in the opening verses of Hebrews? How different are the two revelations which God has made of His character. In Old Testament times God "spoke," revealed Himself, according to what He is as *light;* and this, in keeping with the fact that it was "in the prophets"—those who made known His *mind*. In New Testament times God has "spoken," revealed Himself, according to what He is as *love;* and this, in keeping with the fact that it was "in Son" He is now made known. May we not only bow before Him in reverence and godly fear, but may our hearts be drawn out to Him in fervent love and adoration.

CHAPTER THREE

The Superiority of Christ over the Prophets.

(1:1-3)

That which distinguishes the Hebrews' Epistle from all other books is that it has for its subject the superiority of Christianity over Judaism. Its theme is the superabounding excellency of the new covenant. The method followed by the Holy Spirit in developing His theme is to take Him who is the centre and circumference, the life and light of Christianity, even Christ, and hold before Him one object after another. As he does so, elevated, important, venerated, as some of those objects are, yet, in the presence of the "Son" their glories fade into utter insignificance.

Someone has suggested an analogy with what is recorded in Matthew 17. There we see Christ upon the holy Mount, transfigured before His disciples; and, as they continue gazing on His flashing excellency, they saw no man "save Jesus only." At first, there appeared standing with Him, Moses and Elijah, and so real and tangible were they, Peter said, "If Thou wilt, let us make here three tabernacles; one for Thee, one for Moses, and one for Elijah." But as they looked "a bright cloud overshadowed them." and a Voice was heard saying, "This is My Beloved Son: hear *Him*" (Luke 9:35). How significant are the words that immediately followed: "And when the Voice was passed, Jesus was found *alone.*" The glory associated with Moses and Elijah was so eclipsed by the infinitely greater glory connected with Christ, that they faded from view.

Now it is something very much like this that we see here all through the Hebrews' Epistle. The Holy Spirit takes up one object after another, holds each one up as it were in the presence of the all-excellent "Son," and as He does so, their glory is eclipsed, and the Lord Jesus is "found *alone.*" The prophets, the angels, Moses, Joshua, the Levitical priesthood, the Old Testament men of faith, each come into view; each is compared with Christ, and each, in turn, fades away before His greater glory. Thus, the very things which Judaism most highly esteemed are shown to be far inferior to what God has now made known in the Christian revelation.

In the opening verses the keynote of the Epistle is at once struck. As is usual in Scripture, the Spirit has placed the key for us over the very entrance. There we see an antithesis is drawn. There we behold a contrast between Judaism and Christianity. There we are shown the immeasurable superiority of the latter over the former. There we have brought before us the "Son" as the Speaker to whom we must listen, the Object on which to gaze, the Satisfier of the heart, the One through whom God is now perfectly and finally made known. God hath, in these last days, "spoken unto us in Son." As God is the *Source* from which all blessings flow, *He* is set before us in the very first word of the Epistle. As Christ is the *Channel* through which all blessing comes to us, *He* is mentioned next, and that, in His highest character, as "Son." The more these opening verses are prayerfully pondered, the more will their wondrous depths, exhaustless contents and unspeakable preciousness be made apparent.

In the preceding article we pointed out how that in the first two verses of Hebrews a contrast is drawn between Christ and the prophets. Israel regarded them with the highest veneration, and justly so, for they were the instruments Jehovah had condescended to employ in the giving forth of the revelation of His mind and will in Old Testament times. But Divine as were their communications, they were but introductory to something better and grander. The revelation which God made through them was neither complete nor final, as was hinted at in its fragmentary character: "in many parts and in many ways" God, of old, spake to the fathers in the prophets. Over against this, as transcending and excelling the Old Testament revelation, God has, in these last days "spoken to us in Son," i.e., in Christianity has given a new, perfect, final revelation of Himself.

Thus, the superiority over Judaism of Christianity is here denoted in a twofold way: First, by necessary implication the latter, not being diverse and fragmentary, is one and complete; it is the grand consummation toward which the other was but introductory; it is the substance and reality, of which the former furnished but the shadows and types. Second, by the instruments employed: in the one God spoke "in the prophets," in the other "in (His) Son." Just as far as the personal glory of the Son excells that of the prophets, so is the revelation God made through Christ more sublime and exalted than that which He made under Judaism. In the one He was made known as *light*—the requirements, claims, demands of His holiness. In the other, He is manifested as *love*—the affections of His heart are displayed.

Now, to prevent the Hebrews from concluding that Christ was nothing more than another *instrument* through which God had "spoken," the Holy Spirit in the verses which we are now to take up, brings before us some of the highest and most blessed of our Saviour's personal excellencies. He there proceeds to exalt the Hebrews' conception of the Divine Prophet and Founder of the new economy. This He does by bringing into view seven of His wondrous glories. To the contemplation of those we now turn. Let us consider.

1. *His Heirship.*

"Whom He hath appointed Heir of all things" (v. 2). There are three things here claiming attention. First, the character in which Christ is viewed. Second, His appointment unto the inheritance. Third, the scope of the inheritance.

First, this declaration that God has appointed the Saviour "Heir of all things" is similar in scope to that word of Peter's on the day of Pentecost. "Therefore let all the house of Israel know assuredly, that God hath made that same Jesus, whom ye have crucified, both Lord and Christ" (Acts 2:36). In both passages the reference is to the honour which has been conferred upon the Mediator, and in each case the design of speaker or writer was to magnify the Christian revelation by showing the exalted dignity of its Author and Head.

That the title "Heir" is similar in force to "Lord" is clear from Gal. 4:1, "The heir, as long as he is a child, differeth nothing from a servant, though he be *lord* of all." Yet though there is a similarity between the terms "Heir" and "Lord," there is also a clear distinction between them; not only so, we may admire the Divine discrimination in the one used in Heb. 1:2. Strikingly does it follow immediately after the reference to Him as "Son," in fact furnishing proof thereof, for the son *is* the father's heir.

The word "heir" suggests two things: dignity and dominion, with the additional implication of legal title thereto. For its force see Gen. 21:10, 12; Gal. 4:1, etc. "An 'heir' is a successor to his father in all that his father hath. In connection with the Father and the Son, the supreme sovereignty of the One is nowise infringed upon by the supreme sovereignty of the Other—cf. John 5:19. The difference is only in the manner: the Father doeth all *by* the Son, and the Son doeth all *from* the Father" (Dr. Gouge). The title "Heir" here denotes Christ's proprietorship. He is the Possessor and Disposer of all things.

Second, unto an inheritance Christ was "appointed" by God. This at once shows us that the "Son" through whom God has revealed Himself, is here viewed not in His abstract Deity, but mediatorially, as incarnate. Only as such could He be "*appointed*" Heir; as God the Son, essentially, He could not be deputed to anything.

This "appointment" was in the eternal counsels of the Godhead. Two things are hereby affirmed: certainty and valid title. Because God has predestined that the Mediator should be "Heir of all things," His inheritance is most sure and absolutely guaranteed, for "the Lord of hosts hath purposed, and who shall disannul?" (Isa. 14:27); hath He not said, "My counsel *shall* stand, and I will do all My pleasure" (Isa. 46:10)! Again: because God has "appointed" the Mediator "Heir" we are assured of His indubitable *right* to this supreme dignity. That which is said of Christ's being made priest, in Heb. 5:5, may also be applied to this other dignity: Christ glorified not Himself to be an Heir, but He that saith to Him, "Thou art My Son, to-day have I begotten Thee," also "appointed" Him Heir.

Above we have said, This appointment was in the eternal counsels of the Godhead. With our present passage should be compared Acts 2:23, "Him, being delivered by the determinate counsel and foreknowledge of God, ye have taken, and by wicked hands have crucified and slain." Thus there were two chief things to which the Mediator was "appointed": sufferings (cf. also 1 Pet. 1:19, 20), and glory—cf. 1 Pet. 1:11. How this shows us that, from the beginning, *Christ* was the Centre of all the Divine counsels. Before a single creature was called into existence, God had appointed an "Heir" to all things, and that Heir was the Lord Jesus. It was the predestined *reward* of His voluntary humiliation; He who had not where to lay His head, is now the lawful Possessor of the universe.

This appointment of Christ to the inheritance was mentioned in O.T. prophecy: "Also I will make Him My Firstborn, higher than the kings of the earth" (Psa. 89:27). "Firstborn" in Scripture refers not so much to primogeniture, as to dignity and inheritance: see Gen. 49:3 for the first occurance. It is remarkable to observe and most solemn to discover that, in the days of His flesh, Israel recognised Him as such: "*This is* the Heir come let us kill Him, and the inheritance shall be ours" (Mark 12:7), was their terrible language.

Third, a few words now on the extent of that Inheritance unto which the Mediator has been deputed: "Whom He hath appointed Heir of *all* things." The *manifestation* of this is yet future, but confirmation of it was made when the risen Saviour said to the disciples, "All power is *given* unto Me in heaven and earth" (Matt. 28:18). At that time we will recall God's words, "I will declare the decree (i.e., the "appointment"), Thou art My Son; this day have I begotten Thee. Ask of Me, and I shall give Thee the heaven for Thine inheritance, and the uttermost parts of the earth for Thy possession" (Psa. 2:7, 8). His proprietorship of mankind will be

That which is in view in this third item of our passage so far transcends the grasp of the finite mind that it is impossible to give it adequate expression in words. Christ is the irradiation of God's glory. The Mediator's relation to the Godhead is like that of the rays to the sun itself. We may conceive of the sun in the firmament, yet shining not: were there no rays, we should not see the sun. So, apart from Christ, the *brightness* of God's "glory" could not be perceived by us. Without Christ, man is in the dark, utterly in the dark concerning God. It is in Christ that God is *revealed.*

4. *His Being.*

"The express image of His person," or, more literally, "the impress of His substance" (v. 3). The Greek for "express image" is a single word, and the verb from which it is derived signifies "to engrave," and in its noun form "that which is engraved," as the stamp on a coin, the print pressed on paper, the mark made by a seal. Nothing can be more like the original mold or seal than the image pressed out on the clay or wax, the one carrying the very form or features of the other. The O.T. saints did not perfectly "express" God, nor can angels, for they are but finite creatures; but Christ, being Himself God, could, and did. All that God is, in His nature and character, is expressed and manifested, absolutely and perfectly, by the incarnate Son.

"And the very impress of His substance." Here again we are faced with that which is difficult to comprehend, and harder still to express. Perhaps we may be helped to get the thought by comparing 1 Tim. 6:16 with Col. 1:15: "Dwelling in the light which no man can approach unto; whom no man hath seen, nor can see," "Who is the image of the invisible God." All true knowledge of God must come from His approach unto us, for we cannot by "reaching" find Him out. The approach must come from *His* side, and it *has* come, "the only begotten Son, which is in the bosom of the Father, He hath declared Him" (John 1:18).

"The very impress of His substance." This is the nearest approach to defining God's essence or essential existence. The word "substance" means essential being or essential existence; but how little we know about this! God—self-existent: One who never had a beginning, yet full of all that we know of blessed attributes. And Christ, the incarnate Son, is the very "impress," as it were, of that substance. As we have said, the original term is taken from the impress of a seal. Though we had never seen the seal we might, from beholding the impress of it (that which is exactly like it), form a true and accurate idea of the seal itself. So Christ is the

Impress of the substance of God, the One in whom all the Divine perfections are found. Though essentially Light, He is also the Outshining of the "Light"; though in Himself essentially God, He is also the visible Representation of God. Being "with God" and being God, He is also the Manifestation of God; so that by and through Him we learn what God is.

"The very impress of His substance." It is not enough to *read* Scripture, nor even to compare passage with passage; nor have we done all when we have prayed for light thereon; there must also be meditation, *prolonged meditation.* Of whom were these words spoken? Of the "Son," but as incarnate, i.e., as the Son of man; of Him who entered this world by mysterious and miraculous conception in the virgin's womb. Men doubt and deny this, and no wonder, when they have nothing but a corrupt reason to guide them. How can a sin-darkened understanding lay hold of, believe, and *love* the truth that the great God should hide Himself in a frail human nature! That Omnipotence should be concealed in a Servant's form! That the Eternal One should become an Infant of days! This is the "great mystery" of godliness, but to the family of God is "without controversy."

But if the human mind, unaided, is incapable of grasping the fact of the great God hiding *Himself* in human form, how much less can it apprehend that that very hiding was a *manifestation,* that the concealing was a revealing of Himself—the Invisible becoming visible, the Infinite becoming cognisible to the finite. Yet such it was: "And the very impress of His substance." *Who was?* The incarnate Son, the Man Christ Jesus. Of *whose* "substance?" Of God's! But how could that be? God is *eternal,* and Christ *died!* True, yet He manifested His Godhead in the very way that He died. He died as none other ever did: *He* "laid down" His life. More, He manifested His Godhead by rising again: "destroy this temple" (His body) said He, "And I will raise it again"; and He *did.* His Godhead is now manifested in that "He is alive forever more."

But God is *immutable* and *self-sufficient,* and Christ *hungered and thirsted!* True; because He was made "in all things like unto His brethren," and because that from actual experience of these things, He might be able to "succor them that are tempted." Moreover, He manifested *His* self-sufficiency by miraculously feeding the five thousand, and by His absolute power over all Nature—ruling the winds and waves, blasting the fig tree, etc.

But God is *Lord of all,* and Christ was "Led as a lamb to the slaughter": He seemed so helpless when arrested and when hanging upon the cross! But appearances are deceptive; sometimes it is a greater thing to withhold the putting forth of power than to exert it! Yet glimpses of *His* Lordship flashed forth even then. See Him in the Garden, and those sent to apprehend Him prostrate on the ground (John 18:6)! See Him again on the Cross, putting forth His power and "plucking a brand from the burning": it was the power of God, for nothing short of *that* can free one of Satan's captives! Yes, Christ *was,* ever was, the "very impress of His substance," "for in Him dwelleth all the fulness of the Godhead bodily" (Col. 2:9).

5. *His Administration.*

"Upholding all things by the word of His power" (v. 3). The Spirit of truth continues to describe the dignity and majesty of Him in whom God now "speaks" to us. Here is a declaration that is unequivocal in meaning and unlimited in its scope. Against the statement "by whom" *God* "made the worlds," it might be argued that, after all, the "Son" was only a minister, an agent whom God employed for that great work. In reply it would be sufficient to point out that there is no hint in Scripture of God ever having assigned to a mere creature, no matter how exalted his rank, a work which was in any wise comparable with the stupendous task of "making the worlds." But as if to anticipate such an objection, to show that the "Son" is high above the noblest and most honoured of God's ministers, it is here affirmed that "He upholdeth all things by the word of His power," that is, His *own* power; we may add that the Greek reads "His own" as in Matt. 16:26—"his own soul"; and "His own house" (Heb. 3:6). The "upholding" of all things is a *Divine* work.

We have said that the term "Heir" connotes two things: dignity and dominion. In the opening clauses of v. 3 the dignity of the Mediator is set forth; here, it is His dominion which is brought before us. As it was said that He is appointed Heir of "all things," so are we now told that He upholds "all things" — all things that are visible or invisible, in heaven or earth, or under the earth: "all things" not only creatures, but all events.

The Greek word for "upholding" means to "carry or support," see Mark 2:3; it also signifies "to energise or impel," see 2 Pet. 1:21. It is the word used in the Sept. for "moved" in Gen. 1:2. That which is in view in this fifth glory of Christ is His Divine *providence.* "The term 'uphold' seems to refer both to preservation and government. 'By Him the worlds were made'—their materials were called into being, and arranged in comely order; and by Him, too, they are preserved from running into confusion, or reverting back into nothing. The whole universe hangs on His arm; His unsearchable wisdom and boundless power are manifested in governing and directing the complicated movements of animate and inanimate, rational, and irrational beings, to the attainment of His own great and holy purposes; and He does this by the word of His power, or by His powerful word. All this is done without effort or difficulty. He speaks, and it is done; He commands, and it stands fast" (Dr. J. Brown). What a proof that the "Son" is *God!*

He who appeared on earth in *servant* form, is the Sustainer of the universe. He is Lord over all. He has been given "power over all flesh" (John 17:2). The Roman legions who destroyed Jerusalem were "*His* armies" (Matt. 22:7). The angels are "*His* angels," see Matt. 13:41; 24:31. Every movement in heaven and earth is directed by Jesus Christ: "by Him all things consist" (Col. 1:17). He is not only at the head of the spiritual realm, but he "upholds *all things.*" All movements, developments, actions, are borne up and directed by the word of His power. Glimpses of this flashed forth even in the days of His flesh. The winds and the waves were subservient to His word. Sickness and disease fled before His command. Demons were subject to His authoritative bidding. Even the dead came forth in response to His mighty fiat. And all through the ages, to-day, the whole of creation is directed by the will and word of its Heir, Maker, and Upholder.

6. *His Expiation.*

"When He had by Himself purged our sins" (v. 3). Here is something still more wondrous. Striking is it to behold the point at which this statement is introduced. The cross was the great stumbling-block unto the Jews; but so far was the apostle from apologising for the death of the "Son," he here includes it as among His highest glories. And such indeed it was. The putting away of the sins of His people was an even greater and grander work than was the making of the worlds or the upholding of all things by His mighty power. His sacrifice for sins has brought greater glory to the Godhead and greater blessing to the redeemed than have His works of creation or providence.

"Why has this wonderful and glorious Being, in whom all things are summed up, and who is before all things the Father's delight and the Father's glory; why has this infinite light, this infinite power, this infinite majesty come down to our poor earth? For what purpose? To shine? To show forth the splendour of His majesty? To teach heavenly wisdom? To rule with just and holy right? No. He came to *purge our sins.* What height of glory! what depths of abasement! Infinite in His majesty, and infinite in His self-humiliation, and in the depths of His love. What a glorious Lord! And what an awful sacrifice of unspeakable love, to purge our sins by Himself"! (Saphir).

"By Himself purged our sins." This has reference to the atonement which He has made. The metaphor of "purging" is borrowed from the language of the Mosaic economy—cf. 9:22. The Greek word is sometimes put for the *means* of purging (John 2:6), sometimes for the *act* itself (Mark 1:44). Both are included here: the *merits* of Christ's sacrifice, and the *efficacy* thereof. The tense of the verb, the aorist, denotes a *finished* work, literally, "having purged." Another has suggested an additional and humbling thought which is pointed by this metaphor—the *filth* of our sins, which needed "purging" away. The contrastive and superlative value and efficacy of Christ's sacrifice is thus set before us. *His* blood is here distinguished from that of the legal and ceremonial purifications. None of them could purge away sins—10:4. All they did was to sanctify to "the purifying of the flesh" (9:13), *not* to the "purifying of the *soul!*"

"The manner and power of this purification form the subject of this whole Epistle. But in this short expression, 'by Himself He purged our sins,' all is summed up. By Himself; the Son of God, the eternal Word in humanity. Himself: the priest, who is sacrifice, yea, altar, and everything that is needed for full and real expiation and reconciliation. Here is fulfilled what was prefigured on the day of atonement, when an atonement was made for Israel, to cleanse them from all sins, that they may be clean from all their sins before the Lord (Lev. 16:30). Thus our great High Priest saith unto us, Ye are clean this day before God from all your sins. He is the fulfillment and the reality, because He is the Son of God. 'The blood of Jesus Christ His Son cleanseth us from all sin' (1 John 1:7). The church is purchased by the blood of Him who is God (Acts 20:28, with His own blood). Behold the perfection of the sacrifice in the infinite dignity of the incarnate Son. Sin is taken away. Oh, what a wonderful thing is this!" (Saphir).

7. *His Exaltation.*

"Sat down on the right hand of the Majesty on high" (v. 3). Unspeakably blessed is this. The One who descended into such unfathomable depths of shame, who humbled Himself and became "obedient unto death, even the death of the cross," has been highly exalted above all principality and power, and dominion, and every name which is named, not only in this world, but also in that which is to come. All-important is it, too, to mark carefully the connection between these two wondrous statements: "*when* He had by Himself purged our sins, *sat down* on the right hand of the Majesty on high." We cannot rightly think of the God-man as *where* He now is, without realising that the very circumstance of His being there, shows, in itself, that "our sins" are put away for ever. The present possession of glory by the Mediator is the conclusive evidence that my sins *are* put away. What blessed connection is there, then between our peace of soul, and His glory!

"Sat down on the right hand of the Majesty on high." Three things are here denoted. First, high honour: "sitting," in Scripture, is often a posture of dignity, when superiors sit before inferiors: see Job 29:7, 8; Dan. 7:9, 10; Rev. 5:13. Second, it denotes settled continuance. In Gen. 49:24 Jacob said to Joseph that his "bow *sat* in strength," fittingly rendered "abode in strength." So in Lev. 8:35 "abode" is literally "sit." Though He will vacate that seat when He descends into the air (1 Thess. 4:16) to receive His blood-bought people unto Himself, yet it is clear from Rev. 22:1 that this position of highest honour and glory belongs to Christ for ever and ever. Third, it signifies rest, cessation from His sacrificial services and sufferings. It has often been pointed out that no provision was made for Israel's priests to sit down: there was no chair in the Tabernacle's furniture. And why? Because their work was never completed —see Heb. 10:1, 3. But Christ's work of expiation *is* completed; on the cross He declared, "It is *finished*" (John 19:30). In proof of this, He is now seated on High.

The term "the Majesty on high" refers to God Himself. "Majesty" signifies such greatness as makes one to be honoured of all and preferred above all. Hence it is a delegated title, proper to kings, cf. 2 Pet. 1:16. In our passage it denotes God's supreme sovereignty. It is brought in here to emphasise and magnify the exaltation of the Saviour—elevated to the highest possible dignity and position. The "right hand" speaks of power (Ex. 15:6), and honour (1 Kings 2:19). "On high" is, in the Greek, a compound word, used nowhere else in the N.T.; literally, it signifies, "the highest height," the most elevated exaltation that could be conceived of or is possible. Thus we are shown that the highest seat in the universe now belongs to Him who once had not where to lay His head.

It is to be observed that in vv. 2, 3 the Holy Spirit has, briefly, set forth the three great offices of the Mediator. First, His *prophetic*: He is the final Spokesman of God. Second, His *kingly*: His royal majesty—upholding all things, and that, by the word of His power, which affirms His absolute sovereignty. Third, His *priestly*: the two parts of which are expiation of His people's sins and intercession at God's right hand.

In conclusion, it should be pointed out how that everything in these opening verses of Hebrews is in striking contrast from what Israel enjoyed under the old economy. They had prophets; Christ is the final Spokesman of Diety. They were His people; He, God's "Son." Abraham was constituted "heir of the world" (Rom. 4:13); Christ is the "Heir" of the universe. Moses made the tabernacle; Christ, "the worlds." The law furnished "a shadow of good things to come"; Christ is the Brightness of God's glory. In O.T. times Israel enjoyed theophanic manifestations of Christ; now, He is revealed as the Image of God's person. Moses bore the burden of Israel (Num. 11:11, 12); Christ, "upholds *all* things." The sacrifices of old took not sins away; Christ's sacrifice did. Israel's high priests never sat down; Christ has.

CHAPTER FOUR

Christ Superior to Angels.

(1:4-14)

One of the first prerequisites for a spiritual workman who is approved of God, is that he must prayerfully and constantly aim at a "rightly dividing" of the Word of Truth (2 Tim. 2:15). Pre-eminently is this the case when he takes up those passages treating of the person of the Lord Jesus Christ. Unless we "rightly divide" or definitely distinguish between what is said of Him in His essential Being, and what is predicated of Him in His official character, we are certain to err, and err grievously. By His "essential Being" is meant what He always was and must ever remain as God the Son. By His "official character" reference is made to what may be postulated of Him as Mediator, that is, as God incarnate, the God-man. It is the *same* blessed person in each case, but looked at in different relationships.

It is failure to thus rightly divide what is said in the Word of Truth concerning the Lord Jesus which has caused unregenerate men to entertain most dishonouring and degrading views of Him, and has led some regenerate men to err in their interpretation of many passages. As illustrations of the former we may cite some of the more devout unitarians, who, appealing to such statements as "My Father is greater than I" (John 14:28), "when all things shall be subdued unto Him, then shall the Son also Himself *be subject* unto Him that put all things under Him" (1 Cor. 15:28), etc., have argued that though the Son be superior to all creatures, yet is He inferior to the Father. But the passages cited do not relate to the "essential Being" of Christ, but speak of Him in His Mediatorial character. As an example of the latter we may mention how that such an able exegete as Dr. John Brown interprets the second half of Heb. 1:4 as referring to the essential Being of the Saviour.

Thus it will be seen that that to which we have drawn attention above is something more than an arbitrary theological distinction; it vitally affects the forming of right views of Christ's person and a sound interpretation of many passages of Holy Writ. Now in His

Word God has not drawn the artificial lines which man is fond of making. That is to say, the essential and the official glories of Christ are often found intermingling, rather than being separately classified. A case in point occurs in the first three verses of Heb. 1. First we are told that, at the close of the Mosaic dispensation, God spoke to the Hebrews by (in) His Son. Obviously this was upon earth, *after* the Word had become flesh. Thus the reference is to Christ in His *Mediatorial* character. Second, "whom He hath appointed Heir of all things" manifestly views Him in the same character, for, in His essential Being no such "appointment" was needed—as God the Son "all things" *are* His. But when we come to the third clause, "by whom also He made the worlds" there is clearly a change of viewpoint. The worlds were made long before the Son became incarnate, therefore *this* postulate must be understood of Him in His eternal and essential Being.

The inquiring mind will naturally ask, *Why* this change of viewpoint? Why introduce this higher glory of the Son in the midst of a list of His Mediatorial honours?—for it is clear that the Holy Spirit *returns* to these in the clauses which follow in v. 3. The answer is not far to seek: it is to *exalt* the Mediator in our esteem; it is to show us that the One who appeared on earth in Servant form was possessed of a dignity and majesty which should bow our hearts in worship before Him. He who "by Himself purged our sins" is the same that "made the worlds." The crucified was the Creator! But this is not the wonder set forth in this passage. In order to be crucified it was needful for the Creator to become man. The Son of God (though never ceasing to be such) became the Son of man, and this Man has been exalted to the right hand of the Majesty on high. So beautifully has the late Mr. Saphir written on this point we transcribe from him at length:—

"Is it more wonderful to see the Son of God in Bethlehem as a little babe, or to see the Son of man at the right hand of the Father? Is it more marvelous to see the Counsellor, the Wonderful, the Mighty God, the Prince of Peace, the Everlasting Father, a child born unto us, and a Son given unto us—or to see the Son of man, and in Him the dust of earth, seated at the right hand of God? The high priest entered once a year into the holy of holies, but who would have ventured to abide there, or take up his position next to the cherubim, where the glory of the Most High was revealed? But Jesus, the Son of man, ascended, and by His own power, and in His own right, as well as by the appointment of the Father, He is enthroned, crowned with glory and majesty. On the wings of omnipotent love He came down from heaven, but to return to heaven, omnipotence and love were not sufficient. It was comparatively easy (if I may use this expression of the most stupendous miracle) for the Son of God to humble Himself, and to come down to this earth; but to return to heaven, it was necessary for Him to be baptized with the baptism of suffering, and to die the death upon the accursed tree. Not as He came down did He ascend again; for it was necessary that He who in infinite grace had taken our position should bow and remove our burden and overcome our enemies. Therefore was His soul straightened to be baptized with His baptism; and therefore, from the first moment that He appeared in Jerusalem, He knew that the temple of His sacred body was to be broken, and He looked forward to the decease which He should accomplish on that mount. Not as He came did He ascend again; for He came as the Son of God; but He returned not merely as the Son of God, but as the Son of God *incarnate,* the Son of David, our brother and our Lord. Not as He came did He ascend again; for He came alone, the Good Shepherd, moved with boundless compassion, when He thought of the lost and perishing sheep in the wilderness; but He returned with the saved sheep upon His shoulders, rejoicing, and bringing it to a heavenly and eternal home. He went back again, not merely triumphing, but He who had gone forth weeping, bearing precious seed, who Himself had been sown, by His sacrifice unto death, returned, bringing His sheaves with Him. . . . It was when He had by Himself purged our sins that He sat down at the right hand of God; by the power of His blood He entered into the holy of holies; as the Lamb slain God exalted Him, and gave Him a name which is above every name."

Thus that which is prominent, yea dominant, in this opening chapter in Hebrews is the *Mediatorial* glories of the Son. True, His essential glory is referred to in v. 2: "By whom also He made the worlds," but, as already stated, this is introduced for the purpose of exalting the Mediator in our esteem, to prevent us forming an unworthy and erroneous conception of His person. The One who "by Himself purged our sins" is the same person as made the worlds, it is He who is "the Brightness of God's glory, and the express Image of His substance." What ground, what cause have we for exclaiming, "Worthy is the Lamb that was slain to receive power and riches, and wisdom and strength, and honour and glory, and blessing" (Rev. 5:12)! To this the God-man is entitled. Because of this, God exalted Him to His own right hand. Having shown His infinite elevation above the prophets we have next revealed His immeasurable superiority over the angels.

"Being made so much better than the angels, as He hath by inheritance obtained a more excellent name than they" (v. 4). Before attempting to expound the details of this verse, it may be well for us first to enquire, *Why* does the Holy Spirit here introduce the "angels?" What was His particular purpose in showing Christ's superiority over them? To these questions a threefold answer, at least, may be returned:—

First, because the chief design of the Holy Spirit in this Epistle is to exalt the Lord Jesus, as the God-man, far above every name and dignity. In the next section (chapter 3) He shows the superiority of Christ over Moses. But to have commenced with Moses, would not have gone back far enough, for Moses the mediator, received the law by "the disposition of angels" (Acts 7:53). Inasmuch as angels are described in Holy Writ as "excelling in strength," and thus as far raised in the scale of being above man, it was necessary, in order to establish Christ's superiority over *all* created beings, to show that He was much better than they. To prove that God the Son was superior to angels were superfluous, but to show that the Son of man has been exalted high above them was essential if the Hebrews were to ascribe to Him the glory which is His due.

Second, the object before the Holy Spirit in this Epistle in presenting the supreme dignity and dominion of the Mediator was to demonstrate the immeasurable superiority of Christianity over Judaism. The method He has followed here is very striking and convincing. The old order or economy was given by "the disposition of *angels*" (Acts 7:53). Exactly what this means perhaps we cannot be quite sure, though there are several scriptures which throw light thereon, for in Deut. 33:2 we read: "The Lord came from Sinai, and rose up from Seir unto them; He shined forth from Mount Paran, and He came with ten thousand of saints"—"holy ones," i.e., "angels." Again, Psa. 68:17 tells us, "The chariots of God are twenty thousand, even thousands of angels: the Lord is among them, as in Sinai." Finally, Gal. 3:19 says, "Wherefore then serveth the law? It was added because of transgressions, till the Seed would come to whom the promise was made; and it was ordained *by angels* in the hand of a mediator." Thus, the glory of Jehovah at Sinai (the beginning of the Mosaic economy) was an angelic one, and the employment of angels in the giving of the law stamped a dignity and importance upon it. But the legal dispensation has been set aside by a new and higher glory revealed in "the Son," and Heb. 1 shows us the angels subservient to Him, and not only so, closes with the statement that they are now the *servants* of the present "heirs of salvation!"

Third, it is necessary to show the superiority of Christ (the Centre and Life of Christianity) over the angels, because the Jews regarded them as the most exalted of all God's creatures. And rightly so. It was as "the Angel of the covenant" (Mal. 3:1), the

"Angel of the Lord" (Ex. 3:2), that Jehovah had appeared most frequently unto them. From earliest times angelic ministration had been a chief instrument of Divine power and medium of communication. It was "the Angel of the Lord" who delivered Hagar (Gen. 16:7), and who appeared to Abraham. Angels delivered Lot (Gen. 19:1). It was the Lord's "angel" who protected Israel on the passover-night (Num. 20:16). Thus the Jews esteemed angels more highly than man. To be told that the Messiah Himself, God the Son incarnate, had become *man* made Him, in their eyes, *inferior* to the angels. Therefore, was it necessary to show them from their own Scriptures that the Mediator, God manifest *in flesh,* possessed a dignity and glory as far excelling that of the angels as the heavens are higher than the earth.

"Being made so much better than the angels." This verse may be termed the text, and the remainder of the chapter, the sermon — the exposition and application of it. The first key to its meaning and scope lies in its first two words (which are but one in the Greek), "being made." Grammatically it seems almost a blemish to open a new paragraph with a participle; in truth, it demonstrates the perfections of the Spirit's handiwork. It illustrates a noticeable difference which ever distinguishes the living works of God from the lifeless productions of man—contrast the several parts of a chair or table with the various members of the human body: in the one the several sections of it are so put together that its pieces are quite distinct, and the joints between them clearly perceptible; in the other, the ending of one member is lost in the beginning of the next. Our analogy may be commonplace, but it serves to illustrate one of the great differences between the writings of men and the Scriptures of God. The latter is a *living* organism, a body of truth, vitilised by the breath of God!

Though v. 4 begins a distinct section of the Epistle it is closely and inseparably united to the introductory verses which precede, and more especially to the final clauses of v. 3. Unless this be kept in mind we are certain to err in our interpretation of it. At the close of v. 3 Christ is presented as the One who has purged the sins of His people, in other words, as the Son of man, God incarnate, and it was *as such* He has been exalted to the right hand of the Majesty on high. There is now a Man in the glory. And it is this *Man,* the "second Man (1 Cor. 15:47) who has been made better than the angels," and who has obtained "a more excellent name than they." It is *this* which the opening participle makes clear, being designed to carry our thoughts back to what has been said at the close of v. 3.

"Being made so much better than the angels." To appreciate the force of this we must, briefly, consider the *excellency* of the "angels." Angels are the highest of all God's creatures: heaven is their native home (Matt. 24:36). They "excel in strength" (Psa. 103:20). They are God's "ministers" (Psa. 104:4). Like a king's gentlemen-in-waiting, they are said to "minister *unto* the Ancient of days" (Dan. 7:10). They are "holy" (Matt. 25:31). Their countenances are like "lightning," and their raiment is as white as snow (Matt. 28:3). They surround God's throne (Rev. 5:11). They carry on every development of nature. "God does not move and rule the world merely by laws and principles, by unconscious and inanimate powers, but by living beings full of light and love. His angels are like flames of fire; they have charge over the winds, and the earth, and the trees, and the sea (the book of Revelation shows this—A.W.P.). Through the angels He carries on the government of the world" (Saphir).

But glorious as the angels are, elevated as is their station, great as is their work, they are, nevertheless, in subjection to the Lord Jesus *as Man;* for in His human nature God has enthroned Him high above all. "The apostle in the former verses proves Christ to be more excellent than the excellentest of men; even such as God extraordinarily inspired with his holy Spirit, and to whom he immediately revealed his will that they might make it known to others. Such were the priests, prophets, and heads of the people. But these, as well as all other men, notwithstanding their excellencies, were on earth mortal. Therefore he ascendeth higher, and culleth out the celestial and immortal spirits, which are called angels. Angels are of all mere creatures the most excellent. If Christ then be more excellent than the most excellent, He must needs be the most excellent of all. This excellency of Christ is so set out, as thereby the glory and royalty of His kingly office is magnified. For this is the first of Christ's offices which the apostle doth in particular exemplify: in which exemplification He giveth many proofs of Christ's divine nature, and showeth Him to be man as He is God also; and in the next chapter, so to be God as He is man also: 'like to his brethren' (2:17)" (Dr. Gouge).

"Being made so much better than the angels." Through Isaiah God had promised that the "Man of sorrows" who was to be "cut off out of the land of the living" for the transgression of His people, should be richly rewarded for His travail: "Therefore, will I divide Him a portion with the great and He shall divide the spoil with the strong" (53:12). In Psa. 68:18 He is represented as ascending "on high," and that, as a mighty conqueror leading captives in His train and receiving gifts for men. In Phil. 2 we learn that He who took upon Him the form of a servant and was made in the likeness of men, who became obedient unto death, even the death of the cross, "God also hath highly exalted Him and given Him a name which is above every name, that at (in) the name of Jesus (given to Him at His incarnation) *every* knee should bow, of things *in heaven* and in earth, and under the earth" (vv. 9-11). He has been "made so much better than the angels" first of all, by the *position* accorded Him—He is seated on the right hand of the Majesty on High: angels are "*round about* the throne" (Rev. 5:11), the Lamb is *on* the Throne!

"As He hath by inheritance obtained a more excellent name than they" (v. 4). "We who live in the West think a name of slight importance: but God always taught His people to attach great importance to names. The first petition in the Lord's prayer is, 'Hallowed be Thy name;' and all the blessings and privileges which God bestowed upon Israel are summed up in this, that God revealed unto them His name. The name is the *outward expression* and the pledge and seal of all that a person really and substantially is; and when it says that the Son of God has received a higher name than angels, it means that, not only in dignity, but in kind, He *is* high above them" (A. Saphir). "The descriptive designation given to Christ Jesus, when contrasted to that given to angels, marks Him as belonging to a higher order of beings. Their name is created spirits; His name is the only-begotten Son of God" (Dr. J. Brown).

"As He hath by inheritance obtained a more excellent name than they" (v. 4). When commenting on the first part of this verse we endeavoured to show that the reference is to the Father rewarding the Mediator for His sacrificial work, and attention was directed to the parallel supplied in Phil. 2:9-11. That passage begins by saying: "Wherefore God also hath highly exalted Him," and this finds its counterpart here in "being made so much better than the angels." Then follows the statement "and hath given Him a name which is above every name," the parallel being found in "a more excellent name than *they*," i.e., the highest of all created beings. Finally, His *right* to this exalted name is to be owned by every knee bowing before it; so also the last clause of Heb. 1:4 affirms Christ's right to His more excellent name. Is it not more than a coincidence that the corresponding passage to *Heb.* 1:4 is found in one of the apostle *Paul's* Epistles!

"He hath by inheritance obtained a more excellent name than they." This affirms the right of Christ to His more excellent name. The English rendering here seems slightly misleading. The Greek for "He hath by inheritance obtained" is a single word. It is a technical term relating to legal title, secure tenure. The right of inheritance which Sarah would not that the son of the bondwoman should have, is expressed by this word: "shall not the heir" (Gal. 4:30) — "Shall not by inheritance obtain," or, "shall not inherit." Christ's right to His supreme dignity is twofold: first, because of the union between His humanity and essential Deity; Second, as a reward for His mediatorial sufferings and unparalleled obedience to His Father.

"For unto which of the angels said He at any time, Thou art My Son?" (v. 5). Having affirmed the superiority of Christ over angels, the Holy Spirit now supplies proof of this, drawing His evidence from the O.T. Scriptures. The first passage appealed to is found in the second Psalm, and the manner in which it is introduced should be noted. It is put in the form of a question. This was to stir up the minds of those who read the Epistle. It is worthy of remark that this interrogative form of instruction is found quite frequently in the Pauline Epistles—e.g., 1 Cor. 9:4-10, Gal. 3:1-5—and much more so than any other N.T. writer. This method of teaching was often employed by the Lord Jesus, as a glance at the Gospels will show. Observe, too, how the question asked in our text assumes that the Hebrews were *familiar* with the entire contents of Scripture. The interrogative way of presenting this quotation was tantamount to saying: Judge for yourselves whether what I say be true — where in the Sacred Writings is there any record of God's addressing an angel as His "Son"? They could not thus judge unless they were well versed in the Word.

"Unto which of the angels said He at any time, Thou art My Son"? The answer is, To none of them. Nowhere in the O.T. Scriptures is there a single instance of God's addressing an angel as "My Son." It is true that in Job 38:7 the angels are termed "sons of God," but this simply has reference to their *creation*. Adam is termed a "son of God" (Luke 3:38) in the same sense. So, regenerated saints are "sons of God" by virtue of new creation. But no *individual* angel was ever addressed by the Father as "My Son." The Lord Jesus *was*, both at His baptism and His transfiguration. Herein we perceive not only His pre-eminence, but His uniqueness.

"Unto which of the angels said He at any time, Thou art My Son, this day have I begotten Thee" (v. 5)? This latter expression has occasioned not a little difficulty to some of the commentators, and, in the past, has been made the battleground of fierce theological fights. The issue raised was "the eternal *Sonship* of Christ." Those affirming understood "this day (or "to-day") — the Greek is the same as in Luke 23:43—to be *timeless,* and "this day have I begotten Thee" to refer to the eternal generation of the Son by the Father. Much of the fighting was merely a strife "about *words,*" which was to no profit. Though Scripture clearly teaches the Godhead and absolute Deity of the Son (Heb. 1:8, etc.) and affirms His eternality (John 1:1, etc.), it nowhere speaks of His eternal "sonship," and where Scripture is silent it behooves us to be silent too. Certainly *this* verse does not teach the eternal sonship of Christ, for if we allow the apostle to define his own terms, we read in Heb. 4:7, "He *limiteth* a *certain* day, saying in David, *To-day,*" etc. This, it appears to us, illustrates the Spirit's foresight in thus preventing "to-day" in 1:5 being understood as a timeless, limitless "day"—eternity.

Further proof that the Spirit is not here treating of the essential Deity or eternal sonship of Christ is seen by a glance at the passage from which these words are taken. Heb. 1:5 contains far more than the mere quotation of a detached sentence from the O.T. The reference is to the second Psalm, and if the reader will turn to and read through it, he should at once see the striking propriety in the apostle's reference to it here. This is the *first* O.T. passage quoted in Hebrews, and like the first of anything in Scripture claims special attention because of its prime importance. Coming as it does right after what has been said in v. 4, namely, that He who, positionally, had been made lower than the angels, is now exalted above them, an appeal to the 2nd Psalm was most appropriate. That has two divisions and treats of the humiliation and exaltation of the Messiah! In v. 3 counsel is taken against Him; In vv. 10-12 kings and judges are bidden to pay homage to Him.

Now it is in this 2nd Psalm that the Father is heard saying to the Messiah, "Thou art My Son, this day have I begotten Thee" (v. 7). The whole context shows that it is the Father addressing the Son in time, not eternity; on earth, not in heaven; in His mediatorial character, not His essential Being. Nor is there any difficulty in the "to-day have I begotten Thee," the Holy Spirit having explained its force in Acts 13:33. There the apostle declared to the Jews that God had fulfilled *the* promise made unto the fathers, namely, that He had "raised up Jesus," i.e. had sent the Messiah unto them. Acts 13:33 has no reference to Christ's resurrection, but relates to His incarnation and manifestation to Israel—cf. Deut. 18:18, "I will *raise them up* a Prophet"; also Acts 3:26. It was not until Acts 13:34, 35 that the apostle brought in His resurrection "raised Him up *from the dead.*" Thus in Acts 13 Psalm 2 is cited to prove the Father had sent the Saviour to Israel and His promise so to do had been fulfilled in the Divine incarnation. We may add that the word "again" in Acts 13:33 is not found in the Greek and is omitted in the R.V.! If further proof be needed that the "*This day* have I begotten Thee" refers to the *incarnation* of Christ, Luke 2:11 supplies it, "unto you is born *this day* in the city of David a Saviour, which is Christ the Lord"—could so much be said of any but the only-begotten Son of God? Thus "this day" is here, by an angel's voice expressly referred to the day of the Saviour's birth.

"This day have I begotten Thee." This, then, is another verse which teaches the *virgin-birth* of Christ! His humanity was "begotten" by God the Father. Though the Son of man, He was not begotten by a man. Because His very humanity was begotten by the Father it was said unto His mother, "That holy thing which shall be born of thee shall be called the Son of God" (Luke 1:35).

"And again, I will be to Him a Father, and He shall be to Me a Son" (v. 5). The opening "and" connects this second quotation with the first; what follows clearly and conclusively fixes the scope of the first part of this verse. Here is indubitable proof that the Holy Spirit is speaking of Christ not according to His essential glory, but in His mediatorial character, as incarnate. Had the first part of v. 5 referred to the *eternal* relationship of the Son of the Father as practically all of the older (Calvinistic) commentators insist, it would surely be meaningless to add the quotation which follows — "I *will be*" does not take us back into the timeless past! Nor was there any occasion for the first Person of the Trinity to assure the Second that He would be "a Father unto Him." Clearly, it is the Father accepting and owning as His Son the One whom the world had cast out.

"And again, I will be to Him a Father and He shall be to Me a Son." This second quotation is from 2 Sam. 7:12-17, which forms part of one of the great Messianic predictions of the O.T. Like all prophecy it had a minor and major scope and receives a partial and ultimate fulfilment. Its first reference was to Solomon, who, in many respects, was a remarkable type of the Lord Jesus. But its chief application was to Christ Himself. That Solomon did not exhaust its fulfilment is clear enough from the language of v. 13 itself, for, as Dr. Brown has pointed out, "It refers to a son to be *raised up* after David had gone to be with his fathers, whereas Solomon was not only born but crowned before David's death; and the person to be raised up, whosoever he is, was to be settled 'in God's house and kingdom,' and his throne was to be 'established forevermore',—words certainly not applicable, in their full extent, to Solomon." Doubtless none would have argued for an exclusive reference to Solomon had it not been for the words which follow in 2 Sam. 7:14. But competent Hebrew scholars tell us that "if he commit iniquity" may fairly be rendered "whosoever shall commit iniquity" and find their parallel in Psalm 89:30-33.

"I will be to Him a Father, and He shall be to Me a Son." This was God's promise concerning the Messiah, David's Son a thousand years before He appeared on earth. "I will be to Him a Father." I will *own* Him as My Son, I will *treat* Him accordingly. This He did. In death He would not suffer Him to see corruption. He raised Him from the dead. He exalted Him to His own right hand. "And He shall be to Me a Son": He shall act as such. And He did. He ever spake of Him as "Father," He obeyed Him even unto death. He committed His spirit into His hands.

"And again, when He bringeth in the Firstbegotten into the world, He saith, 'And let all the angels of God worship Him' " (v. 6). This is a quotation from Psalm 97:7, which in the Sept. reads, "Worship Him, all ye His angels." What a proof was this that the Son *had* been "made *so* much better than the angels": so far were these celestial creatures from approaching the glory of the incarnate Son, they are commanded to worship Him! But before we enlarge upon this, let us mark attentively the special character in which Christ is here viewed. Many are His titles, and none of them is without its distinctive significance. It is as "Firstbegotten" or "Firstborn" that the angels are bidden to render Him homage. As many are far from clear as to the precise value and meaning of this name, let us look at it the more closely. The Greek word, "protokokos," is found nine times in the N.T., eight of them referring to the Lord Jesus. It is manifestly a title of great dignity.

This N.T. title of Christ, like many another, has its roots in the O.T. Its force may be clearly perceived in Gen. 49:3, where Jacob says of Reuben, "Thou art my firstborn, my might, and the beginning of my strength, the *excellency of dignity,* and the excellency of power." Thus, the primary thought in it is not primogeniture, but dignity, honour, dominion. Note in Ex. 4:22 God calls Israel His "firstborn" because to them belonged the high honour of being His favoured people. In the great Messianic prediction of Psa. 89, after promising to put down His foes and plague them that hate Him (v. 23), and after the perfect Servant says "Thou art My Father, My God, and the Rock of My salvation" (v. 26), the Father declares, "I *will make Him* My Firstborn, higher than the kings of the earth" (v. 27). Clearly, then, this title has no reference whatever to the eternal origin of His Being, i.e. His "eternal Sonship," still less does it intimate His creation in time, as Russellites and others blasphemously affirm; but relates to the high position of honour and glory which has been conferred upon the Son of man because of His obedience and suffering.

The first occurrence of this term in the N.T. is in Matt. 1:25, "she brought forth her firstborn Son," and the second is parallel —

Luke 2:7. That Mary had other sons is clear from Matt. 13:55. The Lord Jesus was not only the first in time, but the Chief, not only among but over them. In Romans 8:29 we read, that God has predestinated His elect to be conformed to the image of His Son in order that He might be the Firstborn among many brethren, i.e. their Chief and most excellent Ruler. In Col. 1:15 He is designated the "Firstborn of every creature," which most certainly *does not* mean that He was Himself the first to be created, as many today wickedly teach, for never does Scripture speak of Him as "the Firstborn of God," but affirms that He is the Head and Lord of every creature. In Col. 1:18 He is spoken of as "the Firstborn from the dead," which does not signify that He was the first to rise again, but the One to whom the bodies of His saints shall be conformed — see Phil. 3:21. In Heb. 11:28 this term is applied to the flower and might of Egypt. In Heb. 12:23 the Church in glory is termed "the Church of the Firstborn." This title then is synonymous with the "appointed Heir of all things." It is, however, to be distinguished from "Onlybegotten" in John 1:18, 3:16. This latter is a term of *endearment*, as a reference to Heb. 11:17 shows — Isaac was not Abraham's *only* "begotten," for Ishmael was begotten by him too; but Isaac was his *darling*: so Christ is God's "Darling" — see Psalm 22:20, 35:17.

"Under the law the 'firstborn' had authority over his brethren (cf. Rom. 8:29, A.W.P.), and to them belonged a double portion, as well as the honour of acting as priests; the firstborn in Israel being holy; that is to say, consecrated to the Lord. Reuben, forfeiting his right of primogeniture by his sin, his privileges were divided, so that the dominion belonging to it was transferred to Judah and the double portion to Joseph, who had two tribes and two portions in Canaan by Ephraim and Manasseh (I Chron. 5:1, 2); while the priesthood and the right of sacrifice was transferred to Levi. The word 'firstborn' also signifies what surpasses anything as of the same kind, as 'the firstborn of the poor' " (Isa. 14:30); that is to say, the most miserable of all; and 'firstborn of death' (Job 18:13), signifying a very terrible death, surpassing in grief and violence. The term 'firstborn' is also applied to those who were most beloved, as Ephraim is called 'the firstborn of the Lord' (Jer. 31:9), that is, His 'dear son.' In all these respects the application of 'firstborn' belongs to the Lord Jesus, both as to the superiority of His nature, of His office, and of His glory" (Robert Haldane).

"And again when He bringeth in the Firstbegotten into the world," etc. Commentators are divided as to the meaning and placing of the word "again," many contending it should be rendered,

"When He shall bring in again into the habitable earth the Firstborn." There is not a little to be said in favour of this view. First, the Greek warrants it. In the second part of v. 5 the translators have observed the order of the original—"and again, I will be unto Him," etc. But here in v. 6 they have departed from it — "And again, when He bringeth in" instead of "when He shall bring in again." Secondly, we know of nothing in Scripture which intimates that the angels worshipped the infant Saviour. Luke 2:13, 14 refers to them adoring God in heaven, and not His incarnate Son on earth. But Rev. 5:11-14 shows us all heaven worshipping the Lamb on the eve of His return to the earth, when He comes with power and glory. Scriptures which mention the angels in connection with Christ's second advent are Matt. 13:41; 16:27; 24:31; 25:31; 2 Thess. 1:7.

That v. 6 has reference to the second advent of Christ receives further confirmation in the expression "when He *bringeth* in the Firstbegotten into the world." This language clearly looks back to Jehovah putting Israel into possession of the land of Canaan, their promised inheritance. "Thou shalt *bring them in*, and plant them in the mountain of Thine inheritance" (Ex. 15:17). "To drive out the nations from before thee, greater and mightier than thou art, to *bring thee in*, to give thee their land for an inheritance" (Deut. 4:38). In like manner, when Christ returns to the earth, the Father will say to Him, "Ask of Me, and I shall give Thee the heathen for Thine *inheritance*, and the uttermost parts of the earth for Thy *possession*" (Psa. 2:8).

In addition to what has just been said on "when He *bringeth* in the firstborn" into the world we would call attention to what we doubt not, is a latent contrast here. It is set over against His *expulsion* from the world, at His first advent. Men, as it were, drove Him ignominiously from the world. But He will re-enter it in majesty, in the manifested power of God. He will be "brought into it" in solemn pomp, and the same world which before witnessed His reproach, shall then behold His Divine dominion. Then shall He come, "in the glory of His Father" (Matt. 16:27), and then shall the angels render gladsome homage to that One whose honour is the Father's chief delight. Then shall the word go forth from the Father's lips, "Let all the angels of God worship Him."

Our minds naturally turn back to the first advent and what is recorded in Luke 2. But there the angels praised the Sender, not the Sent: God in the highest was the object of their worship though the moving cause of it was the lowly Babe. But when Christ comes back to earth it is the Firstborn Himself who shall be worshipped by them. It was to this He referred when He said, "When He shall come in His own glory, and in His Father's *and* of the holy angels." The "glory of the angels," i.e. the glory they will bring to Him, namely, their worship of Him. Then shall be seen "the angels of God ascending and descending upon the Son of man" (John 1:51). May we who have been sought out and saved by Him "worship" Him *now* in the time of His rejection.

CHAPTER FIVE

Christ Superior to Angels.

(1:7-9)

The verses which are now to be before us continue the passage begun in our last article. As a distinctive section of the Epistle this second division commences at 1:4 and runs to the end of the second chapter. Its theme is the immeasurable superiority of Christ over the angels. But though the boundaries of this section are clearly defined, yet is it intimately related to the one that precedes. The first three verses of chapter one contain a summary of that which is afterwards developed at length in the Epistle, and, really, 1:4-14 is a setting forth of the proofs for the various affirmations made in vv. 2, 3. First, in v. 2, the One whom the Jewish nation had despised and rejected is said to be "Son," and in v. 5 we are shown that He against whom the kings of the earth did set themselves and the rulers take counsel together, is addressed by Jehovah Himself as "Thou art My Son." Second, in v. 2 the One who had been crucified by wicked hands is said to be "the Heir of all things," and in v. 6 proof of this is given: God affirmed that He is the "Firstborn" — the two titles being practically synonymous in their force.

Thus is will be seen that the method followed here by the Holy Spirit, was in moving the apostle to first make seven affirmations concerning the exalted dignity and dominion of Christ, and then to confirm them from the Scriptures. The proofs are all drawn from the Old Testament. From it He proceeds to show that the Messiah *was to be* a person superior to the angels. Psalm 2 should have led the Jews to *expect* "the Son" and Psalm 97:7 ought to have taught them that the promised Messiah was to receive the adoration of all the celestial hierarchies. In vv. 5, 6 the Spirit has established the superiority of Christ both in name and dignity; in the verses which follow He shows the inferiority of the angels in nature and rank.

"And of the angels He saith, Who maketh His angels spirits" (v. 7). This is a quotation from Psalm 104, the opening verses of which ascribe praise unto Jehovah as Creator and Governor of the universe. Its second and third verses apparently relate to the intermediary heavens, and the fourth verse to their inhabitants; verse five and onwards treats of the earth and its earliest history. The fact that the earth is mentioned right after the angels suggests that they are there viewed as connected with mundane affairs, as the servants God employs in regulating its concerns.

The Spirit's purpose in quoting this verse in Heb. 1 is evident: it was to point a contrast between the *natures* of the angels and the Son: they were "made"—created; He is uncreated. Not only were the angels created, but they were created by Christ Himself—"*Who* maketh" which looks back to the last clause of v. 2, "He (The Son) made the worlds:" it is the making of the worlds that Psalm 104 speaks of. Moreover, they are here termed not merely "the angels," but "*His* angels!" They are but "spirits," He is "God;" they are "His ministers," He is their Head (Col. 2:10).

"Who maketh His angels spirits." The Hebrew word for "spirits" in Psalm 104:4 and the Greek word rendered "spirits" in Heb. 1:7 has both a primary and secondary meaning, namely, spirits and "winds." It would seem from the words which follow—"and His ministers a flame of fire"—that God is not only defining the nature of these celestial creatures, but is also describing their qualities and activities. Thus we are inclined to regard the words before us as having a double force. A threefold reason may be suggested why the angels are likened unto "winds." First, their power to render themselves invisible. The wind is one of the very few things in the natural world which is unseen by the eyes of man; so the angels are one of the very few classes of God's creatures that are capable of passing beyond the purview of man's senses. Second, because of their great power. Like as the wind when commissioned by God, so the angels are able to sweep everything before them (2 Kings 19:35). Third, because of the rapid speed at which they travel. If the reader will ponder carefully Dan. 9:21, 23, he will find that during the brief moments the prophet was engaged in prayer, an angel from the highest heaven reached him here on earth! Other analogies will be suggested by prayerful meditation.

"And His ministers a flame of fire" (v. 7). Here, as always in Scripture, "fire" speaks of Divine judgment, and the sentence as a whole informs us that the angels are the executioners of God's wrath. A number of passages supply us with solemn illustrations of this fact. In Gen. 19:13 we read that the two angels said to Lot concerning Sodom, "*We* will destroy this place, because the cry of them is waxen great before the face of the Lord: and the Lord hath sent *us* to destroy it." Referring to God's judgments which fell upon Egypt we are told, "He cast upon them the fierceness of His anger, wrath and indignation, and trouble, *by* sending evil angels" (Psa. 78:49), by which we do not understand fallen angels, but "angels of evil," i.e. angels of judgment—compare the word "evil" in Isa. 45:7, where it is contrasted *not* with "good" but "peace." Again, in Matt. 13:41:42 we read, "The Son of man shall send forth His angels, and they shall gather out of His kingdom all things that offend, and them which do iniquity; and shall *cast* them into a furnace of fire; there shall be wailing and gnashing of teeth." Does not this passage throw light on Rev. 20:15? — "And whosoever was not found written in the book of life was *cast* into the lake of fire" — by whom, if not the angels, the executioners of God's wrath!

"And His ministers a flame of fire." Doubtless these words refer also to the brilliant brightness and terrifying appearance of the angels, when manifested in their native form to mortal eyes. A number of scriptures confirm this. Note how when Baalam saw the angel of the Lord that he "fell flat on his face" (Num. 22:31). Note how it is said of the angel who rolled back the stone of the Saviour's sepulchre that "his countenance was like lightning," and that "for fear of him the keepers did shake and become as dead men" (Matt. 28:3:4). This accounts for the "fear not" with which angels so frequently addressed different ones before whom they appeared on an errand of mercy: see Matt. 28:5; Luke 1:30; 2:10. Note how in proof the angels are "a flame of fire," we are told that when the angel of the Lord came to Peter, "*a light shined* in the prison" (Acts 12:7)! Yea, so resplendent is an angel's brightness when manifested to men, that the apostle John fell at the feet of one to worship (Rev. 19:10) — evidently mistaking him for the Lord Himself, as He had appeared on the mount of transfiguration.

"But unto the Son He saith, Thy throne, O God, is forever and ever" (v. 8). Here the Holy Spirit quotes from still another Psalm, the 45th, to prove the superiority of Israel's Messiah over the angels. How blessed and marked is the contrast presented! Here we listen to the Father addressing His incarnate Son, owning Him as "God." "Unto the Son He *saith,*" that others might hear and know it. "Thy throne, O God." How sharp is the antithesis! How immeasurable the gulf which separates between creature and Creator! The angels are but "spirits," the Son is "God." They are but "ministers," His is the "throne." They are but "a flame of fire," the executioners of judgment, He the One who commands and commissions them.

"But unto the Son He saith, Thy throne, O God." This supplies us with one of the most emphatic and unequivocal proofs of the Deity of Christ to be found in the Scriptures. It is the Father Himself testifying to the Godhead of Him who was despised and rejected of men. And how fittingly is this quotation from Psalm 45 introduced at the point it is in Heb. 1. In v. 6 we are told that all the angels of God have received command to "worship" the Mediator, now we are shown the *propriety* of them so doing — He is "God!" They must render Divine honours to Him because of His very nature. Thus we may admire, once more, the perfect *order* of Scripture.

"But unto the Son, He saith, Thy throne, O God, is forever and ever." Difficulty has been experienced by some concerning the identity of the "throne" here mentioned. It is clear from what precedes and also from what follows in v. 9. — "Thy God," that the Son is here addressed in His mediatorial character. But is it not also clear from 1 Cor. 15:24-28 that there will be a time when His mediatorial kingdom will come to an end? Certainly not. Whatever the passage in 1 Cor. 15 may or may not teach, it certainly does not contradict other portions of God's Word. Again and again the Scriptures affirm the *endlessness* of Christ's mediatorial kingdom: see Isa. 9:7; Dan. 7:13, 14; Luke 1:33; etc. Even on the new earth we read of "The *throne* of God *and* of the Lamb" (Rev. 22:1)!

If then it is not the mediatorial kingdom which Christ shall deliver up to the Father, *what* is it? We answer, His *Messianic* one, His kingdom on *this* earth. In Luke 19:12 (the Gospel which, distinctively, sets forth His perfect humanity) Christ speaks of Himself as a "Nobleman" going into a far country to "receive for Himself a *kingdom* and to return," after which He added, "when He was returned, having received the kingdom," etc. (v. 15). It is to this Matt. 25:31 refers, "When the Son of man shall come in His glory, and all the holy angels with Him, then shall He sit upon the throne of *His* glory." As in the days of His first advent, the second Person of the Trinity (incarnate) was more dishonoured than the Father or the Spirit, so, following His second advent *He* shall, for a season, be more honoured than They. Following this, then He shall, still in His character as "Son of man" (see John 5:27) "execute judgment," i.e., on His enemies. Then, having put down (by power, *not* having reconciled by grace) all opposing forces, He shall "*deliver up* the kingdom to God" (1 Cor. 15:24) — observe that it is *not* "taken from" Him!

That it is *not* the mediatorial kingdom which Christ shall deliver up to the Father is clear from 1 Cor. 15:28, where we are expressly told "then shall the Son also Himself be subject unto Him." As the Godman, the Mediator, He will be officially subservient to the Father. This should be evident. Throughout eternity the mediation of Christ will be needed to preserve fellowship between the Creator and the creature, the Infinite and the finite, hence five times over (the number of *grace*) in Holy Writ occur the words, "Thou art a Priest forever after the order of Melchisedek." But in His essential Being the Son will *not* be in subjection to His Father, as is clear from John 17:5.

Thus we trust it has been made clear that whereas the Messianic kingdom of the Son will be but temporal, His Mediatorial kingdom will be eternal. His kingdom on this earth will continue only for a limited time, but His kingdom on the new earth will last forever. Blessed is it to observe that, even as Mediator, Christ is thus owned by the Father "Thy throne, *O God,* is forever and ever." How far above the angels that puts Him!

"A sceptre of righteousness is the sceptre of Thy kingdom" (v. 8). The apostle is still quoting from the 45th Psalm, and continuing to advance proofs of the proposition laid down in 1:4. There is no difficulty in perceiving how the sentence here cited contributes to his argument. The "sceptre" is the badge of royalty and the emblem of authority. An illustration of this is furnished in the book of Esther. When Ahasuerus would give evidence of his authoritative favour unto Esther, he held out his sceptre to her (see Esther 5:2; 8:4). So here the "sceptre" is the emblem of royal power. "The Son is the King; the highest dignity belonging to the angels is that they hold the first rank among His subjects" (Dr. J. Brown). The suffering Saviour is now the supreme Sovereign; the mighty angels are His servants.

"A sceptre *of righteousness* is the sceptre of Thy kingdom." This is very blessed. The sceptre of Christ's kingdom then is one not merely of power, arbitrarily exercised, but a "righteous" one. "The Greek word joined by the apostle to the sceptre signifieth rectitude, straightness, evenness; it is opposed to wickedness, roughness, unevenness. So doth the Hebrew word also signify; it is fitly applied to a sceptre, which useth to be straight and upright, not crooked, not inclining this way or that way; so as that which is set out by a sceptre, namely, government, is hereby implied to be right and upright, just and equal, not partially inclining to either side" (Dr. Gouge).

Of old the Triune God declared, "He that ruleth over men must be just, ruling in the fear of God" (2 Sam. 23:3). This has never yet been perfectly exemplified on earth, but ere long it will be. When the Lord Jesus shall return to Jerusalem and there establish His throne, He will order all the affairs of His kingdom with impartial equity, favouring neither the classes nor the masses. As the Antitype of Melchizedek, He will be both "King of righteousness" and "King of peace" (Heb. 7:2). These are the two qualities which will characterize His reign. "Of the increase of His government and peace there shall be no end, upon the throne of David and upon His Kingdom, to order it and to establish it with judgment and with justice from henceforth even forever" (Isa. 9:7). Then will be fulfilled that ancient oracle. "Behold the days come, saith the Lord, that I will raise unto David a *righteous* Branch, and a king shall reign and prosper, and shall execute judgment and justice in the earth." (Jer. 23:5). The rewards He will bestow, the judgments He will execute, will be administered impartially. But let it not be forgotten that this is equally true of His government even now, though faith alone perceives it; in all dispensations it remains that "justice and judgment are the habitation of Thy Throne" (Psa. 89:14).

"Thou hast loved righteousness, and hated iniquity" (v. 9). The past tense of the verbs is to be carefully observed. It is still the Father addressing His Son, owning on high the moral perfections He had manifested here upon earth. The reference is to the Lord Jesus in the days of His humiliation. The words before us furnish a brief but blessed description both of His character and conduct. First, He loved righteousness. "Righteousness" signifies the doing of that which is right. The unerring standard is the revealed will of God. From that standard the incarnate Son never deviated. As a Boy of twelve He said, "Wist ye not that I must be about My Father's business?" (Luke 2:49)—perform His pleasure, respond to His wishes. When replying to John's demur against baptizing Him, He replied, "Suffer it to be so now: for thus it becometh us to fulfil all righteousness" (Matt. 3:15). When tempted by the Devil to follow a course of selfwill, He answered, "It is written, Man shall not live by bread alone, but by every word that proceedeth out of the mouth of God" (Matt. 4:4). So it was all through: He "became *obedient* unto death, even the death of the cross" (Phil. 2:8).

"Thou hast loved righteousness." This is much more than *doing* righteousness. These words reveal to us the spring of all Christ's actions, even devotedness and affection unto the Father. "I *delight* to do Thy will, O God" (Psa. 40:8), was the confession of the perfect One. "O how love I Thy law! it is My meditation all the day" (Psa. 119:97), revealed His attitude toward the precepts and commandments of Holy Writ. Herein we perceive His uniqueness. How often *our* obedience is a reluctant one! How often God's will crosses ours; and when our response is an obedient one, frequently it is joyless and unwilling. Different far was it with the Lord Jesus. He not only performed righteousness, but "loved" it. He could say, "Thy law is within My *heart!*" (Psa. 40:8) — the seat of the affections. When a sinful creature is said to have God's law in his heart it is because He has *written* it there (see Heb. 8:10).

Because He loved righteousness, Christ "hated iniquity." The two things are inseparable: the one cannot exist without the other (Amos 5:15). Where there is true love for God, there is also abhorrence of sin. Illustrations of the Saviour's hatred of iniquity are found in His action at the close of the Temptation and in His cleansing of the Temple. Observe how, after meeting the vile solicitations of the Devil with the repeated "it is written," He, with holy abhorrence said, "Get thee hence, Satan" (Matt. 4:10). See Him, as the Vindicator of His Father's house, driving before Him its profane traffickers and crying, "Make not My Father's house an house of merchandise" (John 2:16). What must it have meant for One who thus loved righteousness and hated iniquity to tabernacle for thirty-three years in such a world as this! And what must it have meant for such an One to be "numbered with the transgressors" and "made sin" for His people!

"Thou hast loved righteousness and hated iniquity." This is true of Him still, for He changes not. "He that hath My commandments, he it is that loveth Me: and he that loveth Me shall be loved of My Father, and I will *love him,* and will manifest Myself to him" (John 14:21). So He still "hates": "So hast thou also them that hold the doctrine of the Nicolaitans which thing *I hate*" (Rev. 2:15). To what extent do these two things characterize you and me, dear reader? To the extent that we are really walking with Christ; no more, no less. The more we enjoy fellowship with Him, the more we are conformed to His image, the more shall *we* love the things He loves, and hate the things He hates.

"Therefore, God, Thy God, hath anointed Thee with the oil of gladness" (v. 9). The Spirit is still quoting from the 45th Psalm. The enemies of God's truth would discover here a "flat contradiction." In v. 8 the One spoken to is hailed as "God," on the throne. But here in v. 9 He is addressed as an inferior, "*Thy* God hath anointed Thee." How could the same person be both supreme and subordinate? If He Himself had a God, how could He at the same time be God? No wonder Divine things are "foolishness to the natural man!" Yet is the enigma easily explained, the seeming contradiction readily harmonized. The Mediator was, in His own person, both Creator and creature, God and man. Once we see it is *as* Mediator, as the God-man, that Christ is here spoken to, all difficulty vanishes. It is this which supplies the key to the whole passage. Much in Heb. 1 cannot be understood unless it be seen that the Holy Spirit is there speaking not of the essential glories of Christ, but of His mediatorial dignities and honours.

"Therefore, God, Thy God, hath anointed Thee." Concerning this Dr. Gouge has well said, "Christ is God-man, God may be said to be His God three ways: 1. As Christ's human nature was created of God, and preserved by Him like other creatures. 2. As Christ is mediator, he is deputed and sent of God (John 3:34), and he subjected himself to God and set himself to do the will of God, and such works as God appointed him to do (John 4:34; 9:4). In these respects also God is his God. 3. As Christ, God-man, was given by God to be an head to a mystical body, which is the church (Eph. 1:22, 23); God, therefore, entered into covenant with him in the behalf of that body (Isa. 42:6; 49:8). Thus he is called the messenger (Mal. 3:1) and the mediator of the covenant (Heb. 8:6). Now, God is in an especial manner their God, with whom he doth enter into covenant; as he said unto Abraham, 'I will establish my covenant between me and thee,' etc., 'to be a God unto thee' (Gen. 17:7). As God made a covenant with Abraham and his seed, so also with Christ and His seed, which are all the elect of God. This is the 'seed' mentioned in Isa. 53:10. So by special relation between God and Christ, God is his God in covenant with him. God also is, in especial manner, the God of the elect through Christ."

"Therefore, God, Thy God, hath anointed Thee." While here on earth the Mediator owned that God *was* His God. He lived by His Word, He was subject to His will, He was entirely dependent on Him. "I will put My trust in Him" was His avowal (Heb. 2:13); yea, did He not declare, "I was cast upon Thee from the womb: Thou art My God from My mother's belly" (Psa. 22:10)! Many similar utterances of His are recorded in the Psalms. On the cross He owned His subjection, crying, "My God, why hast Thou forsaken Me?" Even after His resurrection we hear Him saying, "I ascend unto My Father and to your Father; and *My God,* and your God" (John 20:17). So now: though seated at the right hand of the Majesty on high, He is there making "intercession." So when He returns to this earth in glory, He will "ask" for the inheritance (Psa. 2:8). How this brings out the truth of His humanity, real Man, though true God. Mysterious, wondrous, blessed Person; upholding all things by the Word of His own power, yet in the place of intercession; Himself the "Mighty God" (Isa. 9:6), yet owning God as *His* God!

"Thy God hath anointed Thee with the oil of gladness." There is a plain reference here to the ancient method, instituted by God, whereby the kings of Israel were established in their office. Their coronation was denoted by the pouring of oil upon their heads: see 1 Sam. 10:1; 16:13; 1 Kings 1:39, etc. It was in allusion to this the kings were styled "anointed" (2 Sam. 19:21) and "the anointed of the Lord" (Lam. 4:20). "The apostle and Psalmist are both speaking of the Messiah as a prince, and their sentiment is 'God, even Thy God, hath raised Thee to a kingdom far more replete with enjoyment than that ever conferred on any other ruler. He has given Thee a kingdom which, for extent and duration, and multitude and magnitude of blessings as far exceeds any kingdom ever bestowed on man or angels as the heaven is above the earth' " (J. Brown).

Though we are assured that this anointing of Christ with the "oil of gladness" (following the mention of His "sceptre" and "kingdom" in v. 8) is a reference to His investiture on High with royal honours — the "blessing of the Lord" which the King of glory received at the time of His ascension (Psa. 24:5, and note carefully the whole Psalm) — yet we do not think this exhausts its scope. In addition, we believe there is also a reference to His being honoured as our great High Priest, for it is written, "He shall be a Priest upon His throne" (Zech. 6:13). Thus there is also a manifest allusion in our verse to what is recorded in Psa. 133. There we read, "Behold, how good and how pleasant it is for brethren to dwell together in unity! It is like the precious ointment upon the head, that ran down upon the beard, Aaron's beard: that went down to the skirts of his garments — cf. Ex. 30:25, 30. This is most precious, though its beauty is rarely perceived. How few see in these verses of Psa. 133 anything more than a word expressing the desirability and blessedness of saints on earth dwelling together in concord. But is *this* all the Psalm teaches? We trow not. What then is the analogy pointed between what is said in v. 1 and v. 2? What is the meaning of "how good and how pleasant it is for brethren to dwell together in unity. *It is like* the precious ointment upon the head," etc?

What resemblance is there between brethren dwelling together in unity and the precious anointing-ointment which ran down from Aaron's head to the skirts of his garments? It seems strange that so many should have missed this point. As the high priest of Israel, Aaron foreshadowed our great High Priest. The anointing of his "head" prefigured the anointing of our exalted Head. The running down of the fragrant unguent even to the skirts of Aaron's garments, adumbrated the glorious fact that those who are members of the body of Christ partake of His sweet savor before God. The analogy drawn in Psa. 133 is obvious: the dwelling together of brethren in unity is "good and pleasant" not simply for the mere sake of preserving peace among them, but because it illustrates the spiritual and mystical union existing between Christ and His people. Our dwelling together in unity is "good and pleasant" not only, nor primarily, for our own well-being, but because it gives an outward manifestation, a concrete example of that invisible and Divine *one-*

ness which exists between the Head and the members of His body.

"Anointed Thee with the oil of gladness." As ever in the Old Testament, the "oil" was an emblem of the Spirit, and the anointing both of Aaron and of David were typifications of the enduement of Christ with the Holy Spirit. But the reference here is not (as some of the commentators suppose) to the coming of the Spirit upon Christ at the time of His baptism. This should be apparent from the structure of v. 9. The words "Thou hast loved righteousness and hated iniquity" look back to the earthly life of the Lord Jesus, as the past tense of the verbs intimate; the *"therefore,* God, even Thy God, hath anointed Thee," shows that this was the reward for His perfect work, the honouring of the humbled One. It is closely parallel with what we are told in Acts 2:36, "God hath made that same Jesus, whom ye have crucified, both Lord and Christ;" and Acts 5:31, "Him hath God exalted with His right hand to be a Prince and a Saviour."

"Anointed Thee with the oil of gladness" refers, we believe, to the Holy Spirit's being made officially subordinate to the Mediator. Just as the incarnate Son was subject to the Father, so is the Spirit now subject to Christ. Just as the Saviour when here glorified not Himself, but the Father, so the Spirit is here to glorify Christ (John 16:14). There are several scriptures which plainly teach the present official subordination of the Spirit to Christ: "But when the Comforter is come, whom *I will send* unto you from the Father" (John 15:26). That which took place on the day of Pentecost manifested the same fact: as His forerunner announced, "I indeed baptize with water, but *He* (Christ) shall baptize you with the Holy Spirit" (Mark 1:8). In Rev. 3:1 the Lord Jesus is referred to as "He that *hath* the seven Spirits of God," i.e. the Holy Spirit in the fulness of His perfections and the plentitude of His operations; "hath" to minister the Spirit unto His people. It is further proof that the suffering Saviour has been exalted to the place of supreme Sovereignty.

"Above Thy fellows." Opinion is divided among the commentators as to whether the reference be to angels or to Christians. Both the Hebrew word in Psa. 45:7 and the Greek word here signify "such as partake of one and the same condition." If it be borne in mind that the Holy Spirit is speaking here of Christ in His Mediatorial character, we are less likely to be stumbled by the thought of angels being termed His "fellows."

"They are styled His fellows in regard of that low degree whereunto the Son of God, Creator of all things, humbled Himself by assuming a creature nature; so that as He was a creature (Man), angels are His fellows" (Dr. Gouge). Nor must we overlook the fact that the chief design of the whole of this passage is to evidence the Mediator's superiority over the angels.

As already pointed out, the central thought of v. 9 is the investiture of Christ with *royal* honours, following right after the mention of His "sceptre" and "kingdom" in v. 8. Angels are also rulers; great powers are delegated to them; much of the administration of God's government is committed into their hands. But the Man Christ Jesus has been exalted high above them in this respect too. A close parallel is found in Col. 1:18, where it is said of the Lord Jesus, "that in all things He might have the pre-eminence." It is important to note that in the immediate context there, *angels* are mentioned in connection with "thrones, dominions, principalities and powers" (v. 16)! But Christ has been given a "sceptre" and royal honours which exalt Him high above them all.

But what has been said above does not exhaust the scope of these closing words of Heb. 1:9. As is so often the case in Scripture (evidencing the exhaustless fulness of its words) there is at least a *double* reference in the term "fellows:" first to the angels, second to Christians— thus supplying a *link* with v. 14, where the "heirs of salvation" are more directly in view. That the term "fellows" applies also to believers is clear from Heb. 3:14 where "metochos" is specifically used of them: "For we are made *partakers* (fellows) of Christ," if we hold the beginning of our confidence steadfast unto the end.

Though the wondrous grace of God has so united His people to His beloved Son that "he that is joined unto the Lord is one spirit" (1 Cor. 6:17), yet we must carefully bear in mind that He is "the Firstborn (Chief) among many brethren" (Rom. 8:29). Though members of His body, He is nevertheless the Head. Though joint-heirs with Him, He is our Lord! So, too, though Christians have been "anointed" with the Spirit (1 John 2:20; 27), yet our blessed Redeemer has been "anointed with the oil of gladness *above* His fellows." The Spirit is now subject to His administration; not so to ours. Christ is the one who is "glorified," the Spirit is the Agent, we the vessels through which He works. Thus in *all* things Christ *has* "the pre-eminence."

It is indeed striking to see how much was included in the ancient oracle concerning the Messiah which the Spirit here quoted from Psa. 45. Let us attempt to summarise the content of that remarkable prophecy. First, it establishes His Deity, for the Father Himself owns Him as "God." Second, it shows us the exalted position He now occupies: He is on the throne, and there for ever. Third, it makes mention of His Kingship, the royal "sceptre" being wielded by Him. Fourth, it tells of the impartiality of His government and the excellency of His rule: His sceptre is a "righteous" one. Fifth, it takes us back to the days of His flesh and makes known the perfections of His character and conduct here on earth: He "loved righteousness and hated iniquity." Sixth, it reveals the place which He took when He made Himself of no reputation, as Man in subjection to God: "Thy God." Seventh, it announces the reward He received for such condescension and grace: "*Therefore*. . . . God hath anointed Thee." Eighth, it affirms He has the pre-eminence in all things, for He has been anointed with the oil of gladness "*above* His fellows." May the Spirit of God stir us up to search more prayerfully and diligently the volume of that Book in which it is written of Him.

CHAPTER SIX

Christ Superior to Angels.

(Heb. 1:10-13)

The closing verses of Heb. 1 present a striking climax to the apostle's argument. They contain the most touching and also the most thrilling references to be found in this wondrous chapter. In it the Holy Spirit completes His proof for the superiority of the Mediator over the angels, proof which was all drawn from Israel's own Scriptures. Five times He had cited passages from the Old Testament which set forth the exalted dignities and glories of the Messiah. A sixth and a seventh is now quoted from the 102nd and the 110th Psalms, to show that He who had passed through such unparalleled humiliation and suffering, had been greeted and treated by God as One who was worthy of supremest honour and reward. The details of this will come before us in the course of our exposition.

It is very striking to observe how that the *character* of these seven quotations made by the Holy Spirit from the O.T. agree perfectly with the *numerical* position of each of them. One is the number of *supremacy*: see Zech. 14:9—there will be none other in that day to dispute the Lord's rule for Satan will be in the Pit. So the first quotation in Heb. 1 brings out the supremacy of Christ over the angels as "Son" (v. 5). Two is the number of *witness*: see Rev. 11:3, etc. So the force of the second quotation in Heb. 1 is the unique relation of the Son to the Father borne witness to. Three is the number of *manifestation*, and in the third quotation we see the superiority of the Mediator manifested by the angels "worshipping" Him (v. 6). Four is the number of the *creature*, and in the fourth quotation the Holy Spirit significantly turns from Christ, who is more than creature, and dwells upon the inferiority of the angels (v. 7) who are "made." Five is the number of *grace*, and the fifth quotation brings before us the "throne" of the Saviour (v. 8), which *is* "the throne of Grace" (Heb. 4:16). Six is the number of *man*, and the sixth quotation (vv. 10-12) contains God's response to the plaint of the Son of Man's being taken away "in the midst of His days." Seven is the number of completion and of *rest* after a finished work: see Gen. 2:3; and so the seventh quotation views Christ as now seated at God's right hand (v. 13), as the reward of His finished work. How perfect is every detail of Holy Writ!

The final verse of Heb. 1 furnishes the fullest demonstration of the superiority of Christianity over Judaism and the exaltation of Christ above the celestial hierarchies. So far are the angels below the Saviour, they are sent forth by Him to minister unto His people. The fact of this ministry, as well as the nature and value of it, are known to but few to-day. The subject is a most interesting as well as important one, and will well repay much fuller study than our limited space here permits us to indulge in. May the bare outline we attempt stimulate our readers to fill it in for themselves.

"And Thou, Lord, in the beginning, hast laid the foundation of the earth" (v. 10). The opening "and" shows that the apostle is continuing to advance proof of the proposition laid down in v. 4. This proof of Christ's excellency is taken from a work peculiar to God, creation. The argument is based upon a Divine testimony found in the Old Testament. The argument may be stated thus: The Creator is more excellent than creatures; Christ is the Creator, angels are creatures; therefore Christ is more excellent than angels. That Christ *is* Creator is here proved; that angels are creatures, has been shown in v. 7. This verse also completes the answer to a question which v. 4 may have raised in the minds of some, namely, what is the "more excellent name" which the Mediator has obtained? The reply is "Son" (v. 5), "God" (v. 8), "Lord" (v. 10).

"And Thou, Lord, in the beginning, hast laid the foundation of the earth." The Psalm from which this is quoted is a truly wondrous one; in some respects it is, perhaps, the most remarkable of the whole series. It lays bare before us the Saviour's very soul. Few, if any, of us would have thought of applying it to Christ, or even dared to, had not the Spirit of God done so here in Heb. 1. This Psalm brings before us the true and perfect humanity of Christ, and depicts Him as the despised and rejected One. It reveals Him as One who *felt,* and felt deeply, the experiences through which He passed. It might well be termed the Psalm of the Man of Sorrows. In it He is seen opening His heart and pouring out His grief before God. We lose much if we fail to attend carefully to the context of that portion which the Spirit here quotes. Let us go back to its opening verses:

"Hear My prayer, O Lord, and let My cry come unto Thee. Hide not Thy face from Me, in the day when I am in trouble; incline Thine ear unto Me: in the day when I call answer Me speedily. For My days are consumed like smoke, and My bones are burned as an hearth. My heart is smitten, and withered like grass; so that I forget to eat My bread. By reason of the voice of My groaning

My bones cleave to my skin. I am like a pelican of the wilderness; I am like an owl of the desert. I watch, and am as a sparrow alone upon the housetop, Mine enemies reproach Me all the day, and they that are mad against Me are sworn against Me. For I have eaten ashes like bread, and mingled My drink with weeping. Because of Thine indignation and Thy wrath: for Thou hast lifted Me up, and cast Me down. My days are like a shadow that declineth; and I am withered like grass" (vv. 1-11).

The above quotation is a longer one than we are accustomed to make, but it seemed impossible to abbreviate without losing its pathos and its moving effects upon us. There we are permitted to behold something of the Saviour's "travail of soul." How it should bow our hearts before Him! These plaintive sentences were uttered by our blessed Redeemer either amid the dark shadows of Gethsemane, or under the more awful darkness of Calvary. But notwithstanding His awful anguish, mark the perfect confidence in God of this suffering One:

"But Thou, O Lord, shalt endure forever, and Thy remembrance unto all generations. Thou shalt arise and have mercy upon Zion: for the time to favour her, yea, the set time, is come. For Thy servants take pleasure in her stones, and favour the dust thereof. So the heathen shall fear the name of the Lord, and all the kings of the earth Thy glory. When the Lord shall build up Zion, He shall appear in His glory. He will regard the prayer of the destitute, and not despise their prayer. This shall be written for the generation to come: and the people which shall be created shall praise the Lord. For He hath looked down from the height of His sanctuary; from heaven did the Lord behold the earth; to hear the groaning of the prisoner, to loose those that are appointed to death; to declare the name of the Lord in Zion and His praise in Jerusalem; when the people are gathered together, and the kingdoms to serve the Lord" (vv. 12-22). Blessed is it to behold here the Saviour looking away from the things seen to the things unseen: from the dark present to the bright future.

"He weakened My strength in the way; He shortened My days. I said O My God, take Me not away in the midst of My days" (vv. 23, 24). Here again we are permitted to hear the "strong crying" (Heb. 5:7) of Him who was "acquainted with grief" as none other ever was. Few things recorded in the Word are more affecting than this: that the Lord Jesus, the perfect Man, should, at the age of thirty-three, be deemed by men as unfit to live any longer. He had hardly entered upon man's estate when they crucified Him. Do you think *that* was nothing to Christ? Ah, brethren, He felt it deeply. Who can doubt it in the light of this awful plaint: "He weakened My strength in the way; He shortened My days. I said, O My God, take Me not away in the midst of My days." As Man He felt acutely this "cutting off" in His very prime.

Those words of the Saviour make manifest what He suffered in His soul. He was perfect Man, with all the sinless sensibilities of human nature. A very touching type of Christ's being cut off in the early prime of manhood is found in Lev. 2:14. Each grade of the meal-offering described in Lev. 2 pointed to the *humanity* of the Redeemer. Here in v. 14 Israel was bidden to take "*green* ears of corn dried by the fire" and offer it to the Lord as an offering. The "green ears of corn" (compare John 12:24 where Christ speaks of Himself under this figure) had not fully ripened, and so, were "dried by the fire"—symbol of being subjected to God's judgment. So it was with Christ. Man's sickle went over the field of corn and He was "cut off" in the midst of His days: when He was barely half of the "three score years and ten" (Psa. 90:10).

And what was Heaven's response to this anguished cry of the Saviour? The remainder of the Psalm records God's answer: "Thy years are throughout all generations. Of old hast Thou laid the foundation of the earth. And the heavens are the work of Thy hands. They shall perish, but Thou shalt endure, yea, all of them shall wax old like a garment; as a vesture shalt Thou change them, and they shall be changed: But Thou art the same, and Thy years shall have no end" (vv. 24-27).

"How marvellous is this! How incomprehensible this union of divine and human, of eternity and time, sadness and omnipotence! Do not wonder that such language of anguish, faintness and sorrow, of agonising faith, is attributed by the Holy Spirit to Jesus. Remember the life of Jesus was a life of faith, a real, true, and earnest conflict; and that, although He constantly took firm hold of the promises of God, yet His feelings of sorrow, His sense of utter dependence on God, His anxious looking forward to His last suffering, all this was a reality. He gained the victory by faith; He knew that He was, through suffering, returning to the Father. He knew that as Son of Man and Redeemer of His people He would be glorified with the glory which He had with the Father before the foundations of the world were laid" (Saphir).

Let us examine closely the blessed reply of the Father to the plaintive petition of His suffering Son. "And, Thou, Lord." Before His incarnation, David, by the Spirit, called Him "Lord" (Matt. 22:43). At His birth, the angels who brought the first glad tidings of His advent to this earth, hailed Him as "Christ the Lord" (Luke 2:11). During His earthly ministry the disciples owned Him as "Lord" (John 13:13). So, too, is He often referred to in the Epistles

(Rom. 1:3, etc.). But here, it is none other than the Father Himself who directly addresses as "Lord" that suffering Man, as He lay on His face in the Garden, sweating as it were great drops of blood. Thus may, and thus should, every believer also say of Him, "My Lord, and my God" (John 20:28), and *worship* Him as such.

"Thou, Lord, in the beginning." This phrase sets forth the *eternity* of the being of Him who became the Mediator. If Christ "in the beginning" laid the foundation of the earth, then *He* must be without beginning, and thus, eternal; compare (Prov. 8:22, 23).

"Hast laid the foundation of the earth." We have been deeply impressed with the fact that God has some good reason for referring in His Word to "the foundation" and "foundations" of the earth or world more than twenty-five times. We believe it is to safeguard His people from the popular delusion of the day, namely, that the earth revolves on its axis, and that the heavenly bodies are stationary, only *appearing* to our sight to move, as the banks and trees seem to be doing to one seated in a rowing-boat or sailing ship. This theory was first advanced (so far as the writer is aware) by Grecian heathen philosophers, echoed by Copernicus in the fifteenth century, and re-echoed by science "falsely so called" (see 1 Tim. 6:20) to-day. Alas, that so many of God's servants and people have accepted it. Such a conceit cannot be harmonised with "a *foundation*" so often predicated of the earth; which, necessarily, implies its *fixity!* Nor can such a theory be squared with the repeated statements of Holy Writ that the "sun moves" (Joshua 10:12), etc. The writer is well aware that this paragraph may evoke a pitying smile from some. But that will not move him. Let *God* be true and every man a liar. We are content to believe what *He* has said. Paul was willing to be a fool for Christ's sake (1 Cor. 4:10), and we are willing to be thought a fool for the Scripture's sake.

"And the heavens are the work of Thine hand" (v. 10). This seems to bring in an additional thought. In the preceding clause creation is ascribed to Christ; here the greatness of His power. The heavens being of so far vaster dimensions than the earth, suggests the omnipotency of their Maker.

"They shall perish, but Thou remainest" (v.11). This verse makes mention of still another perfection of Christ, namely, His *immutability*. The earth and the heavens shall perish. The apostle John, in prophetic vision, saw "a new heaven and a new earth, for the first heaven and the first earth were passed away" (Rev. 21:1). But Christ "remaineth." He is "the same yesterday, and to-day, and forever."

"And they all shall wax old as doth a garment, and as a vesture shalt Thou fold them up, and they shall be changed" (vv. 11:12).

This emphasizes the mutability of the creature. Two resemblances are employed: first the earth may be said to "wax old as doth a garment" in that it is not to last forever, but is appointed to an end: see 2 Pet. 3:10. The longer, therefore, it has continued, the nearer it approaches to that end; as a garment, the longer it is worn, the nearer it is to its end. May not the increasing number of earthquakes evidence that "old age" is fast coming upon it? Second, the heavens may be said to be "folded up as a vesture," inasmuch as Scripture declares "the heavens shall be rolled together as a scroll" (Isa. 34:4).

"*Thou* shall fold them up." This intimates Christ's absolute control over all creation. He that made all hath an absolute power to preserve, alter, and destroy all, as it pleaseth Him. He is the Potter, we are but the clay, to be moulded as He will. Our Lord Jesus Christ, being true God, is the Most High and supreme Sovereign over all, and He doeth all "that man may know that Thou, whose name is *Jehovah,* art the Most High over all the earth" (Psa. 83:18). "By the word of the Lord were the heavens made" (Psa. 33:6); by the same word shall they be folded up. The practical value of this for our hearts is plain; such a Lord may be safely trusted; such a Lord should be revered and worshipped. In what holy awe should He be held!

"But Thou art the same, and Thy years shall not fail" (v. 12). "The mutability of creatures being distinctly set out, the apostle returneth to the main point intended, which is Christ's immutability. It was before generally set down in the phrase, 'Thou remaineth.' Here it is illustrated in two other branches. Though all these three phrases in general intend one and the same thing, namely, immutability, yet, to show that there is no tautology, no vain repetition, of one and the same thing, they may be distinguished one from another:

" 'Thou remaineth,' pointeth at Christ's eternity before all times; for it implieth his being before, in which he still abides. 'Thou art the same' declares Christ's constancy. There is no variableness with him; thus, therefore, he says of himself, 'I am the Lord, I change not' (Mal. 3:6). 'Thy years shall not fail' intendeth Christ's everlastingness; that he was before all times, and continueth in all ages, and will beyond all times so continue" (Dr. Gouge).

"But Thou art the same, and Thy years shall not fail." *This* was God's answer to the plaint of Christ's being "cut off" in the midst of His days. As man, *His* "years" should have no end! As God the Son He *is* eternal in His being; but as Man, in resurrection, He received "life for evermore" (cf. Heb. 7:14-17). Do we really grasp this? For nineteen hundred years since the Cross, men have been born, have lived, and then died. Statesmen, emperors, kings have appeared on the scene and then passed away. But there is one glorious Man who spans the centuries, who in His own humanity bridges those nineteen hundred years. He has not died, nor even grown old; He is *"the same* yesterday, and to-day, and forever!"

"But Thou art the same, and Thy years shall not fail." What assurance was this for the believing of Israel who had been sorely perplexed at the "cutting off" of the Messiah, in the midst of His days! Humbled as He had been, yet was He the Creator. In servant form had He appeared among them, but He was and is the sovereign Disposer of all things. Died he had on the cross, but He was now "alive for evermore." Their own Scriptures bore witness to it: God Himself affirmed it!

And what is the practical application of this wondrous passage for us to-day! Surely this: first, such a Saviour, who is none other than Him who made heaven and earth, is a mighty Redeemer, "Able also to save them to the uttermost that come unto God by Him." Second, such an One, who is immutable and eternal, may be safely and confidently trusted; none can pluck out of *His* hand! Third, such an One, who is "Lord" over all, is to be held in holy awe and given the worship, submission, and service which are His due.

"But to which of the angels said He at any time, Sit on My right hand until I make Thine enemies Thy foostool?" (v.13). This completes the proof of what the apostle had said in vv. 2, 3. The O.T. itself witnessed to the fact that the rejected Messiah is now seated at God's right hand, and this by the word of the Father Himself. The quotation is from the 110th Psalm, a Psalm quoted more frequently in the N.T. than any other.

Verses 13 and 14 belong together. In them another contrast is pointed between Christ and the angels. As an argument it may be stated thus: He that sitteth at God's right hand is far more excellent than ministers: Christ sitteth at God's right hand, and angels *are* "ministers;" therefore, Christ is far more excellent than they. The former part is proved in v. 13, the latter is shown in v. 14.

As D.V. the subject of v. 13 will come before us again in our studies in this Epistle, we will now offer only the briefest comment. The Speaker here is the Father; the One addressed is the Son, but in His mediatorial character, for it was as the Son of Man that God exalted Him. Further proof of this is supplied by "until *I* make Thine enemies Thy footstool." As mediatorial King and Priest, Christ is subservient to the Father; He is subject to Him who has "put all things under Him" (1 Cor. 15:27).

"*Until* I make." Christ is not to sit at God's right hand forever. 1 Thess. 4:16 says, "The Lord Himself shall descend from heaven with a shout," etc. He remains there throughout this present Day of Grace. Then, following a brief interval, His enemies shall be made His footstool. This will be at His return to the earth: see Rev. 19:11-21; Isa. 63:1-3, etc. Then Christ *Himself* will subdue His enemies: note the "He" in 1 Cor. 15:25; but it will be by the Father's decree, see Psa. 2:6-9.

"Are they not all ministering spirits, sent forth to minister for them who shall be heirs of salvation?" (v. 14). This verse presents a fact which should awaken in every Christian varied and deep emotions. Alas that, through lack of diligence in searching the Word, so many of the Lord's people are largely in ignorance of much that is said therein, and here referred to.

It should awaken within us a sense of *wonderment*. The angels are portrayed as *our* attendants! When we remember who and what they are—their exalted rank in the scale of being, their sinlessness, their wondrous capacities, knowledge and powers — it is surely an astonishing thing to learn that they should minister unto us. Think of it, the unfallen angels waiting upon the fallen descendants of Adam! The courtiers of Heaven ministering to worms of the earth! The mighty angels, who "excel in strength," taking notice of and serving those so far beneath them! Could you imagine the princes of the royal family seeking out dwellers in the slums and ministering to them, not once or occasionally, but constantly? But the analogy altogether fails. The angels of God are sent forth to minister unto redeemed sinners! Marvel at it.

It should awaken within us *fervent praise to God*. What an evidence of His grace, what a proof of His love that He sends forth His angels to "minister" unto us! This is another of the wondrous provisions of His mercy, which none of us begin to appreciate as we should. It is another of the blessed consequences of our *union* with Christ. In Matt. 4:11 we read, "angels came and ministered unto Him." Therefore, because Divine grace has made us one with Him, they do so to us too. What a proof is this of our oneness with Him! Angels of God are sent forth to minister unto redeemed sinners! Bow in worship and praise.

It should deepen within us *a sense of security*. True, it may be abused, but rightly appropriated, how it is calculated to quiet our fears, counteract our sense of feebleness, calm our hearts in time of danger! Is it not written, "The angel of the Lord encampeth round about them that fear Him, and delivereth them;" then *why* be afraid? We doubt not that every Christian has been "delivered" many more times from the jaws of death by angelic interposition, than any of us imagine. The angels of God are sent forth to minister unto redeemed sinners. Then let the realization of this deepen within us a sense of the Lord's protecting care for entrusting us to His mighty angels.

"Are they not all ministering spirits sent forth to minister for them who shall be the heirs of salvation?" (v. 14). Three things are to be considered: those to whom the angels minister, why they thus minister and the form their ministry takes.

Those to whom the angels minister are here termed "heirs of salvation," an expression denoting at least four things. There is an Estate unto which God has predestined His people, an inheritance —*willed* to them by God. This Estate is designated "salvation," see 1 Thess. 5:9, where our appointment unto it is mentioned. It is the consummation of our salvation which is in view, Heb. 9:28; 1 Pet. 1:3, 4. Well may this estate or inheritance be called "Salvation," for those who enter it are forever delivered from all danger, freed from all enemies, secured from all evils. This expression "heirs of salvation" also denotes our *legal rights* to the inheritance: our title is an indefeasable one. Further, it presupposes the coming in of *death,* Christ's death. Finally, it implies the *perpetuity* of it —"to him and his heirs forever."

It is to these "heirs of salvation" that the angels minister. To enable us the better to grasp the *relation* of angels to Christians, let us employ an illustration. Take the present household of the Duke of York. In it are many servants, honoured, trusted, loved. There are titled "ladies" and "lords" of the realm, yet they are serving, "ministering," to the infant Princess Elizabeth. At present, she is inferior to them in age, strength, wisdom and attainments; yet is she superior in rank and station. She is of the royal stock, a princess, possibly heir to the throne. In like manner, the heirs of salvation are now in the stage of their infancy; they are but babes in Christ; this is the period of their minority. The angels far excel us in strength, wisdom, attainments; yet are they our servants, they "minister" unto us. Why? Because we are high above them in birth, rank, station. We are children of God, we are joint-heirs with Christ, we have been redeemed with royal blood, yea, we have been made "kings and priests unto God" (Rev. 1:6). O how wonderful is our rank—members of the Royal family of Heaven, therefore are we "ministered" unto by the holy angels. What a calling is ours! What provision has Divine love made for us!

Let us now inquire, Why do they thus "minister" unto us? For what reason or reasons has God ordained that the angels should be our attendants? All His ways are ordered by perfect wisdom. Let us then reverently enquire as to His purpose in this arrangement.

First, is it not to exercise the graces of obedience and benevolence in the angels themselves? Such a task being assigned them constitutes a real test of their fidelity to their Maker. They are bidden to leave the glories of Heaven and come down to this poor sin-cursed earth; yes, oftentimes to seek out children of God in hovels and workhouses. What a test of their loyalty to God! Not only so, but what an opportunity is thus afforded for the exercise in them of the spirit of benevolence! As the frail and suffering children of God, how their sympathies must be drawn out. There are no such objects in Heaven, there is no distress or suffering there; and methinks, that were the angels to be confined to that realm of unclouded bliss, they would be stoics—unable to sympathise with us poor afflicted creatures. Therefore, to cultivate both the spirit of obedience and of benevolence, God has commissioned them to "minister for them who shall be heirs of salvation."

Second, has not God assigned to them this ministry in order to give them a closer acquaintance with His own wondrous grace and matchless love for poor sinners? The angels are not simply far-distant spectators of the out-working of God's wondrous purpose of mercy, but have been made, in part, the actual administrators of it! Thus, by virtue of this commission which they have received from Him, they learn in a practical way how much He cares for us.

Third, has not God assigned to them this ministry in order that there might be a closer bond between the different sections of His family? That word in Eph. 3:15, refers, we believe, not only to the redeemed of Christ, but to all of Heaven's inhabitants—"of whom the whole family in heaven and earth is named." Yes, the angels are members of God's "family" too. Note how in Heb. 12:22, 23 the two great sections of it are placed side by side: "to an innumerable company of angels, to the general assembly and Church of the Firstborn." Thus, the angels are commissioned to minister for those who shall be heirs of salvation in order that there may be formed a closer bond of intercourse and sympathy between the two great sections of God's family.

Fourth, has not God assigned them this ministry in order to magnify the work of the Lord Jesus? The angels are not only subject to Christ as their Lord, are not only called on to worship Him as God, but they are also employed in watching over the safety and promoting the temporal interests of His redeemed. No doubt this fourth named reason is both the primary and ultimate one. How this magnifies the Saviour! Commissioning them to "minister for those who shall be heirs of salvation" is God's putting His imprimature upon the cross-work of Christ.

Let us now consider *how* the angels "minister" to us. First, in *protecting from temporal dangers.* A striking example of this is found in 2 Kings 6:15-17. Elisha and his servant were menaced by the king of Syria. His forces were sent out to capture them. An host compassed the city where they were. The servant was terrified; then the prophet prayed unto the Lord to open his eyes, "and the Lord opened the eyes of the young man; and he saw: and, behold, the mountain was full of horses and chariots of fire round about Elisha," which, in the light of Psa. 68:17 and Heb. 1:7, we know were the protecting angels of God. In the sequel we learn that the enemy was smitten with blindness, and thus the servants of God escaped. This was a concrete illustration of Psa. 34:7, "The angel of the Lord encampeth round about them that fear Him, and delivereth them."

Second, in *delivering from temporal dangers.* A case in point is that which is recorded of Lot: "And when the morning arose, then the angels hastened Lot, saying, Arise, take thy wife and thy two daughters which are here; lest thou be consumed in the iniquity of of the city. And while he lingered, the men laid hold upon his hand, and upon the hand of his wife, and upon the hand of his two daughters; the Lord being merciful unto him, and they brought him forth, and set him without the city." How often angels have "hastened" us when in the place of danger, and "laid hold" of us while we lingered, perhaps the Day will reveal.

Another example is found in the case of Daniel. We refer to the time when he was cast into the lions' den. All Bible readers are aware that the prophet was miraculously preserved from these wild beasts, but what is not generally known is the particular instrumentality which God employed on that occasion. This is made known in Dan. 6:22: "My God hath sent His *angel,* and hath shut the lions' mouths, that they have not hurt me." What an illustration is this of Psa. 34:7, "The angel of the Lord encampeth round about them that fear Him, and delivereth them!"

Nor is angelic deliverance of God's people confined to Old Testament times. In Acts 5:17-19 we read, "Then the high priest rose up, and all they that were with him (which is the sect of the Sadducees) and were filled with indignation, and laid their hands on the apostles, and put them in the common prison, But the angel of the Lord by night opened the prison doors, and brought them forth." Again, in Acts 12:6-9 we read, "The same night Peter was sleeping between two soldiers, bound with two chains; and the keepers before the door kept the prison. And, behold, the angel of the Lord came upon him, and a light shined in the prison: and he smote Peter on the side, and raised him up, saying, Arise up quickly. And his chains fell off from his hands. . . . And he went out, and followed him."

One other form which the ministry of angels takes in connection with their custody of God's children is brought before us in Luke 16:22: "And it came to pass, that the beggar died, and was carried by the angels into Abraham's bosom." To our natural feelings, a death-bed scene is often a most painful and distressing experience. There we behold a helpless creature, emaciated by disease, convulsed with pain, panting for breath; his countenance pallid, his lips quivering, his brow bedewed with a cold sweat. But were not the spiritual world hidden from us by a veil of God's appointing we should also see there the glorious inhabitants of Heaven surrounding the bed, waiting for God's summons, to convoy that soul from earth, through the territory of Satan, up to the Father's House. There they are, ready to perform their last office in ministering for those who shall be heirs of salvation. Then, Christian, why fear death?

It should be carefully noted that angels are mentioned in the plural number in Luke 16:22, so also are they in Psa. 91:11, 12: "For He shall give His *angels* charge over thee, to keep thee in all thy ways. *They* shall bear thee up in their hands, lest thou dash thy foot against a stone." There is nothing whatever in Scripture to support the Romish tradition of a single guardian angel for each person or Christian: the plural number in the above passages make directly against it.

"Are they not all ministering spirits, sent forth to minister for them who shall be heirs of salvation?" (v. 14). "This text wears an interrogative form; but it is just equivalent to a strong affirmation. It is certain that no angel sits on the throne of God; it is certain that they are all *ministering* spirits. A minister is a servant—a person who occupies an inferior place, who acts a subordinate part, subject to the authority and regulated by the will of another. The angels are '*ministering* spirits,' they are not *governing* spirits. Service, not dominion, is their province. In the first phrase there is an expression of their being God's ministers or servants; in the second, that He *sends forth,* commissions these servants of His to minister to those who shall be heirs of salvation. They are His servants, and He uses their instrumentality for promoting the happiness of His peculiar people. There is a double contrast. The Son is the co-ruler—they are servants; the Son sits — they are sent forth" (Dr. J. Brown).

Finally, it should be observed that "ministering spirits" is a title or designation. Not only do the angels render service to God's saints, but they have an *office* so to do. It is not simply that they "go forth" to minister for them, but they are "sent forth." They do not take this work upon themselves, but have received a definite charge or commission from their Maker. How this evidences, once more, the preciousness to Christ of those whom He purchased with

His blood! O that our hearts may be bowed in wonderment and worship for this blessed provision of His love toward us while we are left in this wilderness scene. O that our fears may be removed, and our hearts strengthened by the realization that, amid the dangers and perils with which we are now surrounded, the angels of God are guarding and ministering both for and to us.

CHAPTER SEVEN

Christ Superior to Angels.

(2:1-4)

The title of this article is based upon the fact that the opening verses of Heb. 2 contains an exhortation based upon what has been said in chapter 1. Thus, our present portion continues the second section of the Epistle. Inasmuch as it opens with the word "Therefore" we are called upon to review that which has already been before us.

The first section of the Epistle, contained in its first three verses, may be looked at in two ways: both as forming an Introduction to the Epistle as a whole, and as a distinct division of it, in which is set forth the superiority of Christ over the prophets. In what follows, to the end of the chapter, we are shown the superiority of Christ over angels. This is affirmed in v. 4, and the proofs thereof are found in vv. 5 to 14. These proofs are all drawn from the O.T. Scriptures, and the completeness and perfection of the demonstration thus afforded is evidenced by their being *seven* in number. Thus, centuries before He appeared on earth, the Word of Truth bore witness to the surpassing excellency of Christ and His exaltation above all creatures.

As an analysis and summary of what these seven passages teach concerning the superiority of Christ over the angels, we may express it thus: 1. He has obtained a more excellent name than they vv. 4, 5. 2. He will be worshipped by them as the Firstborn v. 6. 3. He made them v. 7. 4. He is the Divine throne-sitter vv. 8, 9. 5. He is anointed above them v. 9. 6. He is the Creator of the universe, immutable and eternal vv. 10-12. 7. He has a higher place of honour vv. 13-14.

It is striking to note that these same seven quotations from the O.T. also furnish proof of the sevenfold glory of the Mediator affirmed in vv. 2, 3. There He is spoken of, first as the "Son:" proof of this is supplied in v. 5, by a quotation from the 2nd Psalm. Second, He is denominated the "Heir:" proof of this is given in v. 6, where He is owned as the "Firstborn." Third, it is said in v. 2 that He "made the worlds:" proof of this is given in v. 10 by a quotation from the 104th Psalm. Fourth, He is called "the Brightness of God's glory:" in v. 9 an O. T. Scripture is quoted to show that He has been "anointed with the oil of gladness above His fellows." Fifth, He is the "express Image" of God's person: in v. 8 Scripture is quoted to show that the Father owned Him as "God." Sixth, in v. 3 it is said that He has "purged our sins": in v. 14 we have mention of "the heirs of salvation." Seventh, in v. 3 it is affirmed that He has "sat down on the right hand of the Majesty on high"; in v. 13 the 110th Psalm is quoted in proof of this. What an example is this of "proving all things" (1 Thess., 5:21), and that, by the Word of God itself!

Having set forth the excellency of Christ's Divine nature and royal function, the apostle now, in chapter 2, proceeds to show the reality and uniqueness of His humanity. In passing from one to the other the Holy Spirit moves him to make a practical application to his hearers of what he had already brought before them, for the two things which ever concern and the two ends at which the true servant of God ever aims, are, the glory of the Lord and the spiritual good of those to whom he ministers. God's truth is not only addressed to our understanding, but to our conscience. It is designed not only to instruct, but to move us and mould our lives.

In one sense the first four verses of chapter 2 form a parenthesis, inasmuch as they interrupt the apostle's discussion of Christ's relation to angels, which is resumed in v. 5 and amplified in v. 9. But this digression, so far from being a literary blemish, is very beautiful. When is it that a well-trained mind ceases to think logically? or an instructed preacher to speak in orderly sequence? Is it not when his heart is moved? when his emotions are deeply stirred? So was it here with the apostle Paul. His great heart yearned for the salvation of his brethren according to the flesh; therefore, did his mind turn for a moment *from* the theme he was pursuing, to address himself to their consciences. He who said to the saints at Rome, "Brethren, my heart's desire and prayer to God for Israel is, that they might be saved" (10:1), could not calmly write to the Hebrews without breaking off and making an impassioned appeal to them. This, we shall, D.V., find he does again and again.

That which is central in our present parenthesis is an exhortation to give good heed to the Gospel. This admonition is first propounded in v. 1, and then enforced in vv. 2-4. Two points are noted for the enforcing of this duty; one is the danger; the other, the vengeance, which is certain to follow on the neglect of the Gospel. The danger is intimated in the word, "Lest we should let them slip."

The vengeance is hinted in the question. "How shall we escape"? This is emphasised by a solemn warning, namely, despisers of God were summarily dealt with under the law; therefore, those who shut their ears to the Gospel, which is so much more excellent, are, without doubt, treasuring up unto themselves wrath against the day of wrath (Rom. 2:4-5). We are now ready to attend to the details of our present portion.

"Therefore, we ought to give the more earnest heed to the things which we have heard, lest at any time we should let them slip" (v. 1). In this verse, and in those which immediately follow, the apostle specifies a duty to be performed in regard of that most excellent Teacher which God sent to reveal His Gospel unto them. This duty is to give more than ordinary heed unto that Gospel. Such is the force of the opening, "Therefore," which signifies, for this cause: because God has vouchsafed so excellent a Teacher, He must be the more carefully attended unto. The "therefore" looks back to all the varied glories which set forth Christ's excellency named in the previous chapter. Because He is God's "Son," therefore give heed. Because He is "the Heir of all things," therefore give heed. Because He "made the worlds," therefore give heed; and so on. These are so many grounds on which our present exhortation is based.

"*Therefore* is equivalent to,'Since Jesus Christ is as much better than the angels, as He hath received by inheritance a more excellent name than they — since He is both essentially and officially inconceivably superior to these heavenly messengers, His message has paramount claims on our attention, belief, and obedience'," (Dr. J. Brown).

The eminency of an author's dignity and authority, and the excellency of his knowledge and wisdom, do much commend that which is spoken or written by him. If a king, prudent and learned, takes upon himself to instruct others, due attention and diligent heed should be given thereunto. "The Queen of the South came from the uttermost parts of the earth to hear the wisdom of Solomon" (Matt. 12:42), and counted those of his servants who stood continually before him and heard his wisdom, to be happy (1 Kings 10:8). But a greater than Solomon is here referred to by the apostle: therefore, we *ought* "to give the more earnest heed." It was usual with the prophets to preface their utterances with a "Thus saith the Lord," and thereby arrest the attention and awe the hearts of their hearers. Here the apostle refers to the person of the Lord Himself as the argument for hearing what He said.

"Therefore *we* ought." "It is striking to see how the apostle takes the place of such as simply had the message, like other Jews, from those who personally heard Him; so completely was he writing, not as the apostle magnifying his office, but as one of Israel, who were addressed by those who companied with Messiah on earth. It was confirmed 'unto *us,*' says he, again putting himself along with his nation, instead of conveying his heavenly revelations as one taken out from the people and the Gentiles to which he was sent. He looks at what was their proper testimony, not at that to which he had been separated extraordinarily. He is dealing with them as much as possible on their own ground, though, of course, without compromise of his own" (Wm. Kelly).

"We *ought* to give the more earnest heed." Here the apostle addresses himself to the *responsibility* of his readers. Here is an exhortation to the performing of a specific duty. The Greek verb is very strong and emphatic; several times it is translated "must." Thus, in 1 Tim. 3:2, "A bishop must be blameless"; that is, it is his duty so to be. That to which the apostle here pointed was a necessity lying upon his readers. It is not an arbitrary matter, left to our own caprice to do or not to do. "Give the more earnest heed," is something more than a piece of good advice; it is a Divine precept, and God has commanded us "to keep His precepts diligently" (Ps. 119:4). Thus, in view of His sovereignty, and His power and rights over us, we *"ought* to give the more earnest heed" to what He has bidden us do. Descending to a lower level, it is the part of wisdom so to do, and that for our own good; we "ought to earnestly heed the things which we hear" in order to our own happiness.

"To 'give heed' is to apply the mind to a particular subject, to attend to it, to consider it. It is here opposed to 'neglecting the great salvation.' No person can read the Scriptures without observing the stress that is laid on *consideration,* and the criminality and hazards which are represented as connected with inconsideration. Nor is this at all wonderful when we reflect that the Gospel is a moral remedy for a moral disease. It is by being believed it becomes efficacious. It cannot be believed unless it is understood; it cannot be understood unless it is attended to. Truth must be kept before the mind in order to its producing an appropriate effect; and how can it be kept before the mind, but by our giving heed to it" (Dr. J. Brown).

"The duty here intended is a serious, firm, and fixed settling of the mind upon that which we hear; a bowing and bending of the will to yield unto it; an applying of the heart to it, a placing of the affections upon it, and bringing the whole man into conformity thereunto. Thus it comprises knowledge of the Word, faith therein, obedience thereto, and all other due respects that may any way concern it" (Dr. Gouge).

"To the things which we have heard." To "hear" is not sufficient, there must be prayerful meditation, personal appropriation. No doubt the wider reference was to the Gospel, which these Hebrews had heard; though the more direct appeal was concerning that which the apostle had brought before them, in the previous chapter concerning the person and work of God's Son. To us, to-day, it would include all that God has said in His Word.

"Lest at any time we should let slip." There is a difficulty here in making quite sure of the Spirit's precise meaning. The expression "we should let slip" is one word in the Greek, and it occurs nowhere else in the N.T. The absence of the pronoun seems to be designed for the allowing of a *double* thought: lest we "let slip" the things we have heard, and, or, lest we ourselves slip away — apostatize.

"Lest at any time we let them slip." The danger is real. The effects of sin are stamped on our members; it is easy to recall the things of no value, but the things of God slip out of our mind. The fault is our own, through failing to give "the more earnest heed." Unless we "keep in memory" (1 Cor. 15:2), and unless we are duly informed by them, they slip away like water out of a leaky utensil.

"Lest haply we drift away." Understood thus, these words sound the first warning-note of this Epistle against apostasy, and this verse is parallel with 3:14; 4:1; 12:25. Perseverance in the faith, continuance in the Word, is a prime pre-requisite of discipleship, see John 8:31; Col. 1:23, etc. Many who heard, and once seemed really interested in spiritual things, "concerning the faith *have* made shipwreck" (1 Tim. 1:19).

Thus, in the light of the whole context four reasons may be memtioned *why* we should give the more earnest heed to the things which God has spoken unto us: First, because of the glory and majesty of the One by whom He has communicated His mind and will, the Son. Second, because the message of Christianity is final. Third, because of the infinite preciousness of the Gospel. Fourth, because of the hopeless perdition and terrible tortures awaiting those who reject or let slip the testimony of God's wondrous grace.

"For if the word spoken by angels was stedfast, and every transgression and disobedience received a just recompense of reward" (v. 2). The apostle here advances another reason why the Hebrews ought to attend diligently to the Gospel. Having shown that such attention should be given because of the excellency of its Author and Publisher, and because of the benefits which would be lost through negligence, he now announces the certain vengeance of Heaven on its neglecters, a vengeance sorer than even that which was wont to be executed under the Law.

The opening "for" indicates that what follows gives a reason for persuading the Hebrews. The "if" has the force of "since," as in John 8:46; 14:3; Col. 3:1, etc. The "word spoken by angels" seems to refer to the Mosaic law, compare Acts 7:53; Gal. 3:19. "The only difficulty seems to arise out of the express declaration made by the sacred historian, that Jehovah spake all the words of the law. But the difficulty is more apparent than real. What lies at the foundation of the apostle's whole argument is *God* spake both the Law and the Gospel. Both the one and the other are of Divine origin. It is not the origin, but the *medium* of the two revelations which he contrasts. 'He made known His will by the ministry of angels in the giving of the law; He made known His will by the Son in the revelation of mercy.' It seems probable from these words that the audible voice in which the revelation from Mount Sinai was made, was produced by angelic ministry" (Dr. J. Brown).

Because the word spoken, ministerially, by angels was the Word of the Lord, it was "stedfast"—firm, inviolable, not to be gainsaid. Proof of this is furnished in the "and every transgression," etc. The distinction between "transgression" and "disobedience" is not easy to define. The one refers more to the outward act of violating God's law; the other, perhaps, to the state of heart which produced it. The words "receive a just recompense of reward" signify that every violation of God's law was punished according to its demerits. The term "reward" conveys the thought of "that which is due." Punishment for the breaking of God's law is not always administered in this life, but is none the less sure: see Rom. 2:3-9.

This verse sets out a most important principle in connection with the governmental dealings of God: that principle is that the Judge of all the earth will be absolutely just in His dealings with the wicked. Though the direct reference be to His administration of the Law's penalty in the past, yet, inasmuch as He changes not, it is strictly applicable to the great assize in the Day to come. There will be degrees of punishment, and those degrees, the sentence meted out to each rebel against God, will be on this basis, that every transgression and disobedience shall receive "a *just* recompense of reward." In brief, we may say that punishment will be graded according to light and opportunity (Matt. 11:20-24; Luke 12:47, 48), according to the nature of the sins committed (John 19:11; Mark 12:38-40; Heb. 10:29), according to the number of the sins committed (Rom. 2:6, etc.).

"How shall we escape, if we neglect so great salvation?" (v. 3). This verse evokes a number of questions to which, perhaps, no conclusive and final answers may be furnished. Who are referred to by the "we"? How shall we escape—*what*? Exactly what is in view in the "so great salvation?" In pondering these questions several considerations need to be steadily kept before us. First, the people to whom this Epistle was directly addressed and the circumstances in which they were then placed. Second, the central purpose of the Epistle and the character of its distinctive theme. Third, the bearing of the context on this verse and its several expressions. Fourth, light which other passages in this Epistle may shed upon it.

The relation between this verse and the preceding ones is evident. The apostle had just been pressing upon his brethren the need of their more earnestly giving heed unto the things which they had heard, which is more or less defined in the second half of v. 3: "which at the first began to be spoken by the Lord" — the reference being to His preaching of the Gospel. By a metonymy, the Gospel, that reveals and proclaims God's salvation, is here meant. In Eph. 1:13 it is styled "The gospel of your salvation," in Acts 13:26 the "word of this salvation," in Rom. 1:16 it is called "the power of God unto salvation to every one that believeth," and in Titus 2:11, "the grace of God which bringeth salvation." The Gospel dispensation is denominated "the Day of Salvation" (2 Cor. 6:2). Ministers of the Gospel are they "which show unto us the way of salvation" (Acts 16:17).

That under this word "salvation" the Gospel be meant, is also evident from the contrastive expression in v. 2 — "the word spoken by angels." That word was spoken before the time of the Gospel's publication (note that the term "Gospel" is never once found in the O.T.), and obviously signified the Law. Fitly may the Gospel be styled "salvation:" first, because in opposition to the Law (which was a "ministration of condemnation" 2 Cor. 3:9), it is a ministration of salvation. Second, because the Author of the Gospel *is* "salvation" itself: see Luke 2:30, John 4:22, etc., where "salvation" is synonymous with "the Saviour." Third, because whatever is needful to a knowledge of salvation is contained in the Gospel. Fourth, because the Gospel is God's appointed means of salvation: see 1 Cor. 1:21. True, in O.T. times God's elect had and knew the Gospel — Gal. 3:16; Heb. 4:2 — yet it was not publicly proclaimed and fully expounded. They had it under types and shadows, and in promises and prophecies.

The excellency of this salvation is denoted by the words "so great." The absence of any co-relative implies it to be so wondrous that its greatness cannot be expressed. Upon this Dr. J. Brown has well said: "The 'salvation' here, then, is the deliverance of men through the mediation of Jesus Christ. This salvation is spoken of by the Apostle as unspeakably great: not merely a great salvation, nor even *the* great salvation but, 'so great salvation' — an expression peculiarly fitted to express his high estimate of its importance. And who that knows anything about that deliverance can wonder at the Apostle using such language?

"What are the *evils* from which it saves us? The displeasure of God, with all its fearful consequences in time and eternity; and 'who knows the power of His anger?' We must measure the extent of infinite power, we must fathom the depths of infinite wisdom, before we can resolve the fearful question. We can only say, 'According to Thy fear, so is Thy wrath.' The most frightful conception comes infinitely short of the more dreadful reality. A depravity of nature ever increasing, and miseries varied according to our varied capacities of suffering—limited in intensity only by our powers of endurance, which an almighty enemy can enlarge indefinitely, and protracted throughout the whole eternity of our being—these are the evils from which this salvation delivers.

"And what are the *blessings* to which it raises? A full, free, and everlasting remission of our sins—the enjoyment of the paternal favour of the infinitely powerful, and wise, and benignant Jehovah—the transformation of our moral nature—a tranquil conscience—a good hope down here; and in due time, perfect purity and perfect happiness for ever in the eternal enjoyment of God.

"And *how* were these evils averted from us?—how were these blessings obtained for us? By the incarnation, obedience, suffering, and death of the Only-begotten of God, as a sin-offering in our room! And how are we individually interested in this salvation? Through the operations of the Holy Spirit, in which He manifests a power not inferior to that by which the Saviour was raised from the dead, or the world was created. Surely such a deliverance well merits the appellation, a 'so great salvation!'"

But this great salvation, which is made known in the Gospel, may be "neglected." While it is true that salvation is not only announced, but is also secured to and effectuated in God's elect by the Holy Spirit, yet it must not be forgotten that the Gospel addresses the *moral responsibility* of those to whom it comes. There is not only an effectual call, but a general one, which is made unto "the sons of men" (Prov. 8:4). The Gospel is for the sinner's *acceptance,* see 1 Tim. 1:15; 2 Cor. 11:4! The Gospel is more than a publication of good news, more than an invitation for burdened souls to come to Christ for relief and peace. In its first address to those who hear, it is a Divine mandate, an authoritative command, which is disregarded at the sinner's imminent peril. That it *does* issue a "command" is clear from Acts 17:30; Rom. 16:25, 26. That disobedience to *this* "command" will be punished, is clear from John 3:18, 1 Peter 4:17, 2 Thess. 1:8.

The Greek word here rendered "neglect" is translated "made light of" in Matt. 22:5. In this latter passage the reference is to the King making a marriage for His Son, and then sending forth his servants to call them which were bidden to the wedding. But they "made light of" the King's gracious overtures and "went their ways, one to his family, another to his merchandise." The parable sets forth the very sin against which the apostle was here warning the Hebrews, namely, failure to give earnest heed to the things which were spoken by the Lord, and neglecting His great salvation. To "neglect" the Gospel, is to remain inattentive and unbelieving. How, then, asks the apostle, shall such "escape?" "Escape" what? Why, the "damnation of Hell" (Matt. 23:33)! Such, we take it, is the first meaning and wider scope of the searching question asked in v. 3. Should it be objected, This cannot be, for in the "we" the apostle Paul manifestly included himself. The answer is, so also does he in the "we" of Heb. 10:26! That the "we" includes more than those who had really believed the Gospel will be clear from v. 4.

Coming now to the narrower application of these words and their more direct bearing upon the regenerated Hebrews whom the Holy Spirit was specifically addressing, we must consider them in the light of the chief design of this Epistle, and the circumstances in which the Hebrews were then placed; namely, under sore temptation to forsake their espousal of Christianity and to return to Judaism. Looked at thus, the "so great salvation" is only another name for Christianity itself, the "better thing" (Heb. 11:40) which had been brought in by Christ. Judaism was about to fall under the unsparing judgment of God. If, therefore, they turned from their allegiance to Christ and went back to that which was on the eve of being destroyed, how could they "escape" was the question which they must face?

Heb. 2:3 must be interpreted in harmony with its whole context. In the opening verse of chapter 2 the apostle is making a practical and searching application of all he had said in chapter 1, where he had shown the superiority of Christianity over Judaism, by proving the exaltation of Christ — the Center and Substance of Christianity — over prophets and angels. In 1:14 He had spoken of the "*heirs* of salvation" which, among other things, pointed to their salvation as being yet future. In one sense they had been saved (from the penalty of sin), in another sense they were still being saved (from the power of sin), in still another sense they were yet to be saved (from the presence of sin). But God ever deals with His people as *accountable* creatures. As moral beings, in contrast from stock and stones, He addresses their responsibility. Hence, God's saints are called upon to give diligence to make their "calling and election sure" (2 Peter 1:10) — sure unto themselves, and unto their brethren. This, among other things, is done, by using the Divinely-appointed means of grace, and by perseverance and continuance in the faith: see John 8:31; Acts 11:23; 13:43; 14:22; 2 Tim. 3:14, etc.

The Christian life is likened unto a "race" set before us: 1 Cor. 9:24; Phil. 3:13, 14; 2 Tim. 4:7; Heb. 12:1. A "race" calls for self-discipline, personal exertion, perseverance. The Inheritance is set before us in promise, but it is written, "Ye have need of patience, that, after ye have done the will of God, ye might receive the promise" (Heb. 10:36). The "promise" is secured by faith and patience, by actually "running" the race set before us. In the light of this, "neglect" would signify failure to "give diligence" to make our calling and election sure, failure to "press forward" and "run the race." If then we "neglect," how shall we "escape?" Escape *what*? Ah, note how abstractly the apostle worded it. He did not *specify* the "what." It all depends upon the state of the individual. If he be only a lifeless professor and continues neglecting the Gospel, Hell will be his certain portion. But if he be a regenerated believer, though a careless and worldly one, then lack of assurance and joy, profitless and fruitlessness, will be his portion; and then, how shall he "escape" the chastening rod of the holy Father? Thus, the question asked in our verse addresses itself to *all* who read the Epistle.

"Which at the first began to be spoken by the Lord, and was confirmed unto us by them that heard" (v. 3). This need not detain us long. Its central design is to emphasize the importance and need of heeding that which had been spoken by Christ: with it should be carefully compared Deut. 18:18, 19: Luke 9:35. Incidentally, the words "at the first *began*" intimates that Christ was the first Gospel-Preacher! The reference is to that which was preached first by Christ Himself, recorded in the Gospels; then, to that which was proclaimed by His apostles, reported in the book of Acts. The title here given to the Saviour, "Lord," emphasizes both His dignity and authority, and intimates that the responsibility of the Hebrews was being addressed. Till Christ came and preached, "the people sat in darkness and in the shadow and region of death;" and when He began to preach, they "saw great light" (Matt. 4:16). With the "confirmed unto us" compare Luke 1:1, 2. The apostle was calling the Hebrews' attention to the *sureness* of the ground on which their faith rested.

"God also bearing witness, both with signs and wonders, and with divers miracles, and gifts of the Holy Spirit, according to His own will" (v. 4). The reference here is to the miracles wrought by God through the apostles in the early days of the Christian era. The book of Acts records many examples and illustrations of what is here said: see 5:9, 10; 13:11; 3:7; 9:40; 19:12, etc. The Gospel was first preached by the Lord Himself, then it was confirmed by the apostles, and then again by God Himself in such works as could not be performed by a Divine power. "Bearing witness with" is a single word in the Greek, but a double compound. The simple verb signifies to witness to a thing as in John 1:7; the compound, to add testimony to testimony, or to add a testimony to some other confirmation; the double compound, to give a joint-testimony or to give-witness-together with one another. A similar compound is used in Rom. 8:16.

The means employed by God in thus confirming the witness of His servant are described by four terms: signs, wonders, miracles, gifts. The first three refer to the same things, though under different aspects. "Signs" denote the making more simple and evident that which otherwise could hardly be discerned; compare the use of the terms in Matt. 12:38; 16:1, and note the "see" and "show." "Wonders" points both to the striking nature of the "signs" and to the effects produced in those who beheld them: compare Acts 2:19; 7:36. "Miracles" refers to the supernatural power which produced the "signs" and "wonders." The Greek word is rendered "mighty deeds" in 2 Cor. 12:12. Thus, "miracles" are visible and wondrous works done by the all-mighty power of God, above or against the course of nature. Our text speaks of "*divers* miracles": many sorts of supernatural interpositions of God are recorded in the Acts.

An additional means employed by God in confirming the Gospel was "gifts of the Holy Spirit." The Greek word here rendered "gifts" means "divisions" or "distributions"; in the singular number it occurs in Heb. 4:12, where it is translated "dividing asunder." In its verbal form it is found in 1 Cor. 7:17, "God hath distributed to every man." Because these distributions of the Holy Spirit originated not in those by whom they were exercised and through whom they were displayed, they are not unfitly translated "gifts"; the reference being to the gifts extraordinary, manifested through and by the apostles. These "gifts" may also be seen in the book of Acts — the day of Pentecost, e.g., also in 1 Cor. 12:4 and what there follows. We may add that these "divers miracles and gifts of the Holy Spirit" were given by God *before* the N.T. was written. Now that the Scriptures are complete they are no longer needed, nor given.

"According to His own will." The forementioned divers miracles and distributions of gifts were ordered and disposed according to the sovereign pleasure of Deity. The act of distributing is attributed to God the Father in 1 Cor. 7:17, to the Son in Eph. 4:7, to the Spirit in 1 Cor. 12:11. The Greek signifies, "according to *His own* will." The will of God is the one rule by which all things are ordered that He Himself doeth, and whereby all things ought to be ordered that His creatures do. Scripture distinguishes between the secret and revealed will of God, see Deut. 29:29, where both are referred to. The secret will of God is called His "counsel" (Isa. 46:10), the "counsel of His will" (Eph. 1:11), His "purpose" (Rom. 8:28), His "good pleasure" (Eph. 1:9). The revealed will of God is made known in His Word, and is so called because, just as the ordinary means by which men make known their minds is by the word of their mouth, so the revelation of God's will is called "His Word." This revealed will of God is described in Rom. 12:2, and is primarily intended in the second clause of the Lord's prayer. Here in our text it is the secret will of God which is meant.

In these days of creature-pride and haughtiness, we need reminding that God is sovereign, conferring with none, consulting none; doing as *He* pleases. God's will is His only rule. As He creates, governs, and disposes all things, so He distributes the gifts of His Spirit "according to His own will." Should any murmur, His challenge is "Is it not lawful for Me to do what I will with Mine own?" (Matt. 20:15). It is important to note that these gifts of the Spirit were distributed *not* "according to the faith" of those who received them — just as in the parable of the talents the supreme Sovereign distributed them unequally, according to His own good pleasure. May Divine grace bring both writer and reader into complete subjection to the secret will of God and obedience to His revealed will.

What has been before us in vv. 2, 3 tells us how firm and sure is the foundation on which our faith rests. In giving earnest heed to the Gospel, notwithstanding its unique and amazing contents, we are not following cunningly devised fables, but that which comes to us certified by unimpeachable witnesses. First, it began to be spoken by the Lord Himself. Though this was sufficient to make the Gospel "worthy of all acceptation," God mercifully, because of our weakness, caused it to be "confirmed" by those who had heard the Lord for themselves. The witness of these men was, in turn, authenticated by Divine displays of power through them such as was never seen before or since. Finally, additional attestation was furnished in supernatural outpourings of the Holy Spirit. Thus, God has graciously added witness to witness and testimony to testimony. How thankful we should be for these many infallible proofs! May this consideration of them result in the strengthening of our faith to the praise of the glory of God's grace.

CHAPTER EIGHT

Christ Superior to the Angels.

(2:5-9)

The scope, the order of thought, and the logical bearings of our present passage are not so easily discerned as those we have already gone over. That it, the first part at least, picks up the thread dropped in 1:14 and continues to exhibit the superiority of Christ over angels, is clear from v. 5; but when we reach v. 9 we read of Jesus being "made a little *lower* than the angels." At first glance this seems to present a real difficulty, but, as is generally the case with such passages, in reality v. 9, taken as a whole, supplies the key to our present portion.

In 1:4-14 the Holy Spirit, through the apostle, has furnished a sevenfold proof of the superiority of Israel's Messiah over the angels. This proof, taken from their own Scriptures, was clear and incontrovertible. In 2:1-4 a parenthesis was made, opportunity being taken to give a solemn and searching application to the consciences and hearts of the Hebrews of what had just been brought before them: the authority of the Gospel was commensurate with its grace, and God would avenge the slightings of that which was first proclaimed by His Son, as surely as He had the refractions of that law which he had given by the mediation of angels. Now here in 2:5 and onwards an objection is anticipated and removed.

The objection may be framed thus: How could supremacy be predicated of One who became Man, and died? As we have shown in a previous article, the Jews actually regarded the angels with a higher veneration than the greatest of the "fathers"—Abraham, Moses, Joshua, and David. And rightly so; their own Scriptures declared that they "excel in strength." Thus a real difficulty was presented to them, in the fact that He whom the apostle affirmed had, by inheritance, obtained "a more excellent name" than angels, was known to them as "the Son of man," for man was a creature *inferior* to angels. Moreover, angels do not die, Christ had; how, then, could He be their superior?

The method followed by the Holy Spirit in meeting this objection and removing the difficulty is as follows: He shows (in v. 9) that so far from the humiliation and suffering endured by Christ tarnishing His glory, they were the meritorious cause of His exaltation. In support of this a remarkable quotation is made from the 8th Psalm to prove that God has placed *man,* and not angels, at the head of the future economy — the "world to come." The design of God in that economy is to raise "man" to the highest place of all among His creatures, and that design has been secured by Christ's becoming Man and dying, and thus obtaining for Himself and His people that state of transcendent dignity and honour which the Psalmist prophesied should be possessed by man in the Age to come.

Thus, those commentators are mistaken who suppose that in Heb. 2:5 the apostle begins to advance *further proof* of Christ's superiority over angels. Complete demonstration of this had been made in chapter 1, as the *seven* O.T. passages there cited go to show. True it is that what the apostle says in v. 5 makes manifest the exaltation of the Saviour above the celestial hierarchies, yet his purpose in so doing was to meet an objector. What we have in our present section is brought in to show that the evidence supplied in chapter 1 could not be shaken, and that the very objection which a Jew might make against it had been duly provided for and fully met in his own Scriptures. Thus may we admire the wisdom of Him who knoweth the end from the beginning, and maketh even the wrath of man to praise Him.

"For unto the angels hath He not put in subjection the world to come, whereof we speak" (v. 5). In taking up this verse three questions need to be duly pondered: What is here referred to in "the world to come?" What is meant by its being "put in subjection?" What bearing has this statement upon the apostle's argument? Let us endeavor to deal with them in this order.

Commentators are by no means agreed on the signification of this term "the world to come." Many of the older ones, who were post-millennarians, understood by it a reference to the present Gospel dispensation, in contrast from the Mosaic economy. Others suppose that it refers to the Church, of which Christ, and not angels, is the Head. Others look upon it as synonymous with the Eternal State, comparing it with the Lord's words in Matt. 12:32, "Whosoever speaketh against the Holy Spirit, it shall not be forgiven him, neither in this world, neither in the world to come." The objection against this last view is that the Greek word for "world" is quite different in Heb. 2:5 from that which is used in Matt. 12:32.

We believe the first key to the right understanding of this expression is to be found in the particular term used here by the Holy

Spirit, translated "world." It is neither "kosmos," the common one for "world," as in John 3:16, etc.; nor "aion," meaning "age," in Matt. 13:35, Heb. 9:26, etc. Instead, it is "oikoumene," which, etymologically, signifies "habitable place"; but this helps us nothing. The word is found fifteen times in the N.T. In thirteen of them it appears to be used as a synonym for "earth." But in the remaining passage, namely, Heb. 1:6, light is cast upon our present verse. As we sought to show in our exposition of that verse, the words "when again He brings in the Firstborn into the world" (oikoumene) refer to the second advent of Christ to this earth, and point to His millennial kingdom. This, we are satisfied, is also the reference in 2:5.

The "world to come" was a subject of absorbing interest and a topic of frequent conversation among all godly Jews. Unlike us, the object of hope set before them was not Heaven, but a glorious kingdom on earth, ruled over in righteousness by their Messiah. This would be the time when Jerusalem should be no more "trodden down by the Gentiles," but become "a praise in all the earth"; when heathen idolatry should give place to "the knowledge of the glory of the Lord," filling the earth as the waters do the sea. In other words, it would be the time when the kingdom-predictions of their prophets should be fulfilled. Nor had there been anything in the teachings of Christ to show these expectations were unwarranted. Instead, He had said, "Ye which have followed Me, in the regeneration (Millennium) when the Son of Man shall sit in the throne of His glory, ye also shall sit upon twelve thrones, judging the twelve tribes of Israel. And every one that hath forsaken houses, or brethren . . . . for My name's sake, shall receive an hundredfold," etc. (Matt. 19:28-30). Those who had believed in Him as the Saviour from sin, eagerly awaited the establishing of His kingdom on earth: see Acts 1:6.

The "world to come" is the renovated earth under the reign of the Messiah. In the spiritual arithmetic of Scripture the number of the earth is *four*, a number plainly stamped upon it: note the four seasons of the year, the four points to its compass. How striking is it to note, then, that the Word speaks of exactly *four* earths, namely, the pre-Adamic, the present, the Millennial (delivered from the curse), the new earth. The "world to come" is the time when Israel shall dwell in their own land in peace and blessing, when wars shall be made to cease, when oppression and injustice shall end, when all the outward creation shall manifest the presence of the Prince of peace.

Not unto the angels hath God "put in subjection" this world to come. "Put in subjection" is the translation of a single compound

Greek word, meaning "to put under." In its simple form it signifies to appoint or ordain; in its compound, to appoint over. Note the relative "He": God places in subjection whom He will and to whom He will. Because God hath not put the world to come in subjection to angels, therefore angels have no authority over it. "It is the good pleasure of God to use an angel where it is a question of providence, or law, or power; but where it comes to the manifestation of His glory in Christ, He must have other instruments more suited for His nature, and according to His affections" (W. Kelly). To whom, then, hath God subjected the world to come? Instead of supplying a categorical answer, the apostle leaves his readers to draw their answer from what an O.T. oracle had said.

Ere taking up the point last raised, let us now consider the bearing which the contents of this 5th verse has upon the apostle's argument. It opens with the word "for," which intimates that there is a glance backwards to and now a continuation of something said previously. This casual particle connects not with the first four verses of our chapter, for, as we have shown, they are of the nature of a parenthesis. The backward glance is to what was said in 1:14, where we are told, "Are they not all ministering spirits sent forth to minister for them who shall be heirs of salvation?" The Inheritance will not be governed by angels; they are but *ministers* to its "heirs." "*For* He (God) hath not put in subjection to angels the world to come" (the earthly inheritance) whereof we speak. Thus the connection is clear. The "whereof we speak" takes us back to 1:14, and is amplified in 2:6-9.

Before turning to that which follows, let us summarize that which has been before us in v. 5. In 1:14 the apostle had affirmed that the angels are in a position of *subjection to* the redeemed of Christ; now he declares that, in the Millennial era also, not angels, but the "heirs of salvation," shall occupy the place of governmental dominion. The "world to come" is mentioned here because it is in the next Age that the Inheritance of salvation will be entered into and enjoyed. In view of what follows from Psa. 8, Heb. 2:5 may possibly set forth a designed contrast from the pre-Adamic earth, which, most probably, was placed under the dominion of unfallen Satan and his angels. The *practical* bearings of this verse on the Hebrews was: Continue to hold fast your allegiance to Christ, *for* the time is coming when those who do so shall enter into a glory surpassing that of the angels.

"But one in a certain place testified, saying, 'What is man, that Thou art mindful of him? or the son of man, that Thou visitest him?' " (v. 6). In seeking to discover the relevancy of this quotation and its bearing upon the apostle's argument, the scope and details of this remarkable and little-understood Psalm from which it is taken, need to be carefully studied. But observe, first, *how* the quotation is introduced, "But one in a certain place testified, saying." It suggests that the Hebrews were so familiar with the Holy Scriptures that it was not necessary to give the reference! The "But" intimates that the apostle is about to point a contrast from the angels: not "and," but "but!"

Before proceeding further, let us ponder the doctrinal teaching of Psa. 8. Upon this we cannot do better than reproduce the summary of it given by Dr. Gouge: "The main scope of the Psalm is, to magnify the glory of God: this is evident by the first and last verses thereof. That main point is proved by the works of God, which in general He declares to be so conspicuous, as very babes can magnify God in them to the astonishment of His enemies, v. 2. In particular He first produceth those visible glorious works that are above; which manifest God's eternal power and Godhead, v. 3. Then He amplifieth God's goodness to man (who had made himself a mortal miserable creature, v. 4), by setting forth the high advancement of man above all other creatures, not the angels excepted, vv. 5-7. This evidence of God's greatness to man so ravished the prophet's spirit, as with an high admiration he thus expresseth it, 'What is man?' etc. Hereupon he concludeth that Psalm as he began it with extolling the glorious excellency of the Lord."

The force of the 4th verse of Psalm 8, the first here quoted in Heb. 2, may be gathered from the words which immediately precede: "When I consider Thy heavens, the work of Thy fingers, the moon and the stars which Thou hast ordained — What is man, that Thou are mindful of him? and the son of man, that Thou visitest him?" In view of the magnitude of God's creation, in contrast from the heavenly bodies, What is *man!* This is confirmed by the particular word which the Holy Spirit has here employed. In the O.T. He has used four different words, all rendered "man" in our English version. The one used here is "enosh," which signifies "frail and fallen man." It is the word used in Psalm 9:20! What is man, fallen man, that the great God should be mindful of him? Still less that He should crown him with "glory and honour?" Ah, it is *this* which should move our hearts to deepest wonderment, as it *will* fill us with ever-increasing amazement and praise in the ages yet to come.

"What is man that Thou art mindful of him? or the son of man that Thou visitest him?" (v. 6). The latter clause seems to be added in order to emphasize the preceding thought. "Son of man" is added as a *diminution* for "man": compare Job 25:6 for a parallel. Another reason why this second clause may be added to v. 6

is to show that it is *not* Adam who is here spoken of. From the contents of vv. 5, 6, 7 many have thought that Psalm 8 was referring to the father of the human family (see Gen. 1:26); but this second part of its fourth verse seems to have been brought in designedly to correct us. Certainly Adam was not a "*son* of man!"

"Thou madest him a little lower than the angels" (v. 7). This supplies additional proof that it is not Adam who is here in view. Both the Hebrew word used in Psa. 8:5 and the Greek word in Heb. 2:7 signify the failing or falling of a thing from that which it was before. "The word 'made lower' does not signify to be created originally in a lower condition, but it signifies to be brought down from a higher station to a lower" (Dr. J. Brown). The Hebrew word is used to denote the failing of the waters when Noah's flood decreased (Gen. 8:4); and, negatively, of the widow's oil that did not fail (1 Kings 17:14, 16). The Greek word is used of the Baptist when he said, "I must decrease" (John 3:30).

But to what is the Holy Spirit here referring in our 7th verse? First, it should be pointed out that both the Hebrew and Greek word here for "little" has a double force, being applied both to time and degree. In 1 Peter 5:10 it is rendered "a while," that is, a short space of time; so also in Luke 22:58 and Acts 5:34. Such, we believe, is in force here, as it certainly is in the 9th verse. Now in what particular sense has God made frail and fallen man a "little while" lower than the angels? With Dr. J. Brown we must answer, "We cannot doubt that man, even in his best estate, was in some respects inferior to the angels; but in some points he was on a level with them. One of these was immortality; and it deserves consideration, that this is the very point referred to when it is said of the raised saints, the children of the resurrection, 'Neither can they die any more: for they are equal unto the angels' " (Luke 20:36). Thus, for a season, man, through being subject to *death*, has been made "lower than the angels."

"Thou madest him a little lower than the angels; Thou crownedst him with glory and honour, and didst set him over the works of Thy hands" (v. 7). Just as in the first part of this verse reference is made to the humiliation of man, so the second part of it speaks of God's exaltation of man. "The verbs being expressed, not in the Future, but in the Past tense, will not be felt as an objection to its being considered as a prediction, this being quite common in the prophetic style. Most of the predictions, for example, in the 53rd chapter of Isa. are expressed in the Past tense" (Dr. J. Brown). To this we may add, all prophecy speaks from the standpoint of God's eternal purpose, and so certain is this of accomplishment, the Past tense is used to show it is as sure as if it were already wrought out in time: compare "glorified" in Rom. 8:30, and see Rom. 4:17. Thus we understand the second part of this 7th verse as referring to the coming glorification of Christ's redeemed.

"Thou crownedst him with glory and honour, and didst set him over the works of Thy hands." This is applied by the Spirit to the redeemed, the "heirs" of 1:14, "whereof we speak" (2:5). That the redeemed *are* to be "crowned" is clearly taught in the N.T. For example, in 2 Tim. 4:7, 8 the apostle says, "I have fought a good fight, I have finished my course, I have kept the faith: Henceforth there is laid up for me a *crown* of righteousness, which the Lord, the righteous Judge, shall give be at that day: and not to me only, but unto all them also that love His appearing." So also James declares, "Blessed is the man that endureth temptation; for when he is tried, he shall receive the *crown* of life, which the Lord hath promised to them that love Him" (1:12).

They are to be crowned with "glory and honour." In Scripture "glory" is put for the excellency of a thing: hence, what is here predicted is, that the dignity which God will place upon His saints will be the most excellent they could be advanced unto. The Hebrew word means that which is real and substantial, in contrast from that which is light and vain. The word for "honour" implies that which is bright: and in Psa. 110:3 is rendered "beauty." Its distinctive thought is that of being esteemed by others. Thus we have here a striking word upon the glorification of the redeemed. First, they are to be "crowned," that is, they are to be elevated to a position of the highest rank. Second, they are to be crowned with "glory," that is, they will be made supremely excellent in their persons. Third, they are to be crowned with "honour," that is, they will be looked up to by those below them.

"And didst set him over the works of Thy hands." This has reference to the rule and reign of God's saints in the Day to come. In Dan. 7:18, 27 we read, "But the saints of the Most High shall take the kingdom, and possess the kingdom forever, even forever and ever. . . . . And the kingdom and dominion, and the greatness of the kingdom under the whole heaven, shall be given to the people of the saints of the Most High, whose kingdom is an everlasting kingdom, and all dominions shall serve and obey Him." So also in Rev. 2:26 we are told, "And he that overcometh and keepeth My works unto the end, to him will I give power over the nations."

"Thou hast put all things under his feet" (v. 8). The language here employed shows plainly the connection between this quotation from the 8th Psalm and what the apostle had declared in v. 5. There he had said, "For unto the angels hath He not put in subjection the world to come whereof we speak." Here we learn that unto "man" will the world to come be placed in subjection. Here we learn that "man," frail and fallen, but redeemed and exalted by the Lord, will have, in the world to come, "all things" put under his feet. It is the blessed sequel to Gen. 1:26 — the earthly Paradise regained. The *absoluteness* of this "subjection" of the world to come unto redeemed man, is intimated by the figure which is here used, "under his feet"; lower a thing cannot be put. It is not simply "*at* his feet," but "under." The *scope* of the subjection is seen by the "*all* things." This goes beyond the terms of Psa. 8:7, 8, for the last Adam has secured for His people more than the first Adam lost. All creation, even angels, will then be "in subjection" to man.

"For in that He put all in subjection under him, He left nothing that is not put under him" (v. 8). This is the apostle's comment on his quotation from Psa. 8. "Thou hast bestowed on man such honours as Thou hast bestowed on none of Thy creatures. Thou hast set him at the head of the created universe. From this passage it appears that, with the single exception of Him who is to put all things under him, i.e., God, all things are to be put under man. In the world to come even angels are subordinate to them. Man is next to God in that world" (Dr. J. Brown). In Rev. 21:7 we read, "He that overcometh shall inherit *all things*; and I will be his God, and he shall be My son." Our joint-heirship with Christ (Rom. 8:17) will be *manifested* in the world to come. What a prospect! O for faith to lay hold of it and *enjoy* it, even now. Were it more real to us, the trifling baubles of this world would fail to attract us. Were it more real to us, the trials and troubles of this life would be unable to sadden or move us. May the Lord enable each of His own to look away from the things seen to the things unseen.

"But now we see not yet all things put under him" (v. 8). This is the language of an hypothetical objector, which confirms and establishes what was said in the opening paragraphs of this article. The "him" here is the "man" of v. 6. Anticipating the objection that Jesus of Nazareth could not be superior to the angels, seeing that He was Man, the apostle met it by showing that one of God's ancient oracles declared that he who, for a short season, was made lower than the angels, has been crowned with glory and honour and set over the works of His hands; yea, that *all* things, and therefore angels, have been "put in subjection under him." But how can this be? says the objector: "Now we *see not* yet all things put under him." What you have said is belied by the testimony of our senses; that which is spread before our eyes refutes it. Why, so far from "all things" being in subjection to man, even the wild beasts will not perform his bidding! Unanswerable as this difficulty might appear, solution, satisfactory and complete, is promptly furnished. This is given in our next verse.

"But we see Jesus, who was made a little lower than the angels . . . . crowned with glory and honour" (v. 9). It is most blessed to observe how the apostle meets the objector: he does so by pointing at once and directly to Him who is the Centre of all our hopes and in whose Person all our interests and blessings are bound up. "The following appears to me to be the track of the apostle's thoughts: 'In the world to come, men, not angels, are to occupy the first place. An ancient oracle, which refers to the world to come, clearly proves this. The place to be occupied by man in that world is not only a high place, but is the first place among creatures. The words of the oracle are unlimited. With the exception of Him who puts all things under man, everything is to be subjected to him. This oracle must be fulfilled. In the exaltation of Christ, after and in consequence of His humiliation, we have the begun fulfilment of the prediction, and what, according to the wise and righteous counsels of heaven, were necessary, and will be the effectual means of the complete accomplishment of it in reference to the whole body of the redeemed from among men" (Dr. J. Brown).

"But we see Jesus." What is meant by this? To what was the apostle referring? *How* do we "*see* Jesus?" Not by means of mysterious dreams or ecstatic visions, not by the exercise of our imagination, nor by a process of visualization; but by *faith.* Just as Christ declared, in John 8:56, "Abraham rejoiced to see My day, and he *saw* it, and was glad." Faith is the eye of the spirit, which views and enjoys what the Word of God presents to its vision. In the Gospels, Acts, Epistles, Revelation, God has told us about the exaltation of His Son; those who receive by faith what He has there declared, "*see* Jesus crowned with glory and honour," as truly and vividly as His enemies once saw Him here on earth "crowned with thorns."

It is this which distinguishes the true people of God from mere professors. Every real Christian has reason to say with Job, "I have heard of Thee by the hearing of the ear: but *now* mine eye *seeth* Thee" (42:5). He has "seen" Him leaving Heaven and coming to earth, in order to "seek and to save that which was lost." He has "seen" Him as a sacrificial Substitute on the cross, there bearing "our sins in His own body on the tree." He has "seen" Him rising again in triumph from the grave, so that because He lives, we live also. He has "seen" Him highly exalted, "crowned with glory and honour." He has "seen Him *thus* as presented to the eye of faith in the sure Word of God. To Him the testimony of Holy Scripture is infinitely more reliable and valuable than the testimony of his senses.

The name by which God's Son is here called is that of His humiliation. "Jesus" is *not* a title; "Saviour" is an entirely different word in the Greek. "Jesus" was His human name, as Man, here on earth. It was as "Jesus of Nazareth" that His enemies ever referred to Him. But not so His own people: to the apostles He said, "Ye call Me Master and Lord: and ye say well; for so I am" (John 13:13). Only once in the four Gospels do we ever find any of His own speaking of Him as "Jesus of Nazareth" (Luke 24:19). and that was when their faith had completely given way. It was the language of unbelief! That He is referred to in the narratival form in the Gospels as "Jesus" is to emphasise His humiliation.

When we come to the Acts, which treats of His exaltation, we read there, "God hath made this same Jesus . . . . both Lord and Christ" (2:36). So in the Epistles: God has "given Him a name which is above every name," and that name is "Lord" (Phil. 2:9, 10). Thus, it is either as "Christ" which *is* a title, or as the Lord Jesus Christ, that He is commonly referred to in the Epistles: read carefully 1 Cor. 1:3-10 for example. It is thus that His people should delight to own Him. To address the Lord of glory in prayer simply as "Jesus," or to speak of Him to others thus, breathes an unholy familiarity, a vulgar cheapness, an irreverence which is highly reprehensible.

After the four Gospels the Lord Christ is never referred to in the N.T. simply as "Jesus" save for the purpose of historical identification (Acts 1:11, e.g.), or to stress the humiliation through which He passed, or when His enemies are speaking of Him. Here in Heb. 2:9 "Jesus" rather than "the Lord Jesus" is used to emphasise His humiliation: it was the One who had passed through such unparalleled shame and ignominy that had been "crowned with glory and honour." May Divine grace enable both writer and reader to entertain such exalted views of this same Jesus that we may ever heed the exhortation of 1 Peter 3:15: "But sanctify in your hearts Christ as Lord" (R.V.).

Now that which it is of first importance for us to observe is the *use* which the apostle here makes of the Saviour's glorification. The exaltation of Jesus is both the proof and pledge of the coming exaltation of His redeemed. The prophecy of Psa. 8 has already begun to receive its fulfilment. The crowning of Jesus with glory and honour is the ground and guarantee of the ultimate glorification of all His people. Christ has entered Heaven as the "First-fruits," the earnest of the coming harvest. He passed within the veil as the "Forerunner" (Heb. 6:20), so that there *must be* others to follow.

Here, then is, we believe, the true interpretation and application of Psa. 8. The verses quoted from it in Heb. 2 refer not to Adam, not to mankind as a whole, nor to Christ Himself considered alone, but to His redeemed. The Holy Spirit, through the Psalmist, was looking forward to a *new order of man,* of which the Lord Jesus is the Head. In the Man Christ Jesus, God has brought to light a new order of Man, One in whom is found not merely innocence, but *perfection.* It is of *this* "man" that Eph. 2:15 speaks: "To make in Himself of twain (redeemed from among the Jews and from the Gentiles) one *new man*"*;* and also Eph. 4:13: "Till we all come in the unity of the faith, and of the knowledge of the Son of God unto *a perfect man,* unto the measure of the stature of the fulness of Christ." As God looks at His incarnate Son He sees, for the first time, a perfect Man, and us in Him. And as we, by faith, "see Jesus crowned with glory and honour," we discover both the proof and pledge of ourselves yet being "crowned with glory and honour."

"But we see Jesus, who was made a little lower than the angels . . . . crowned with glory and honour," as the ground and guarantee of our approaching exaltation. Here then is the Divine answer to the question asked by the Psalmist long ago: "When I consider Thy heavens, the work of Thy fingers, the moon and the stars which Thou hast made—What is man, that Thou art mindful of him?" Ah, brethren in Christ, when you go out at night and view the wondrous heavens, and then think of your own utter insignificance; when you meditate upon the glory of God's majesty and holiness, and then think of your own exceeding sinfulness, and are bowed into the dust; remember that up there is a Man in the glory, and that that Man is the measure of God's thoughts concerning *you.* Remember, that by wondrous and sovereign grace, you have been not only predestined to be conformed to His image, but that you should, as a joint-heir with Him, share *His inheritance.* May the Lord grant each Christian reader that faith which will enable him to grasp that wonderful and blissful prospect which the Word of God sets before him.

CHAPTER NINE

Christ Superior to Angels.

(Heb. 2:9-11)

In our last article we were obliged, through lack of space, to break off our exposition of Heb. 2 in the middle of a verse; to have continued further would have required us to go to the end of v. 11, and this would have made it much too long. However, the point at which we left off really completed the first thought which the apostle establishes in our present section. As we sought to show, at v. 5 the apostle begins meeting an objection which might be, and most probably was, made against what he had set forth in chapter one, namely, the immeasurable superiority of the Mediator, Israel's Messiah, above the angels. Over against this, two difficulties stood in the way, which needed clearing up.

First, How could Christ be superior to angels, seeing that He was *Man?* Second, How could He possess a greater excellency than they, seeing that He had died? The difficulty was satisfactorily removed by an appeal to Psalm 8, where God had affirmed, in predictive language, that He had crowned "man" with glory and honour and put "all things in subjection under his feet." To this the objector would rejoin, "But now we see not yet all things put under him" (v. 8), how, then, does Psalm 8 prove your point? In this way, answers the apostle, In that even now, "we see (by faith) *Jesus* crowned with glory and honour," and in *His* exaltation we find the ground and guarantee, the proof and pledge, of the coming exaltation of all His people.

In the remainder of this most interesting portion of Heb. 2, we shall see how the Holy Spirit enabled the beloved apostle to meet and dispose of the second difficulty of the Jews in a manner equally convincing and satisfactory as He had dealt with their first objection. Though it be true that angels do not and cannot die (Luke 20:36), and though it be a fact that Jesus had died, yet this by no means went to show that He was inferior to them. *This* is the particular point which the apostle is here treating of and which it will now be our object to consider.

First, he shows *why* it was necessary for Christ to die, namely, in order that He should taste death for every son, or, as it reads in the A.V., "for every man" (v. 9). Second, he declares that God had a benevolent design in suffering His Son to stoop so low: it was by His grace that He so "tasted death" (v. 9). Third, he affirms that such a course of procedure was *suited* to the nature and honouring to the glory of Him who orders all things: it "became Him" (v. 10). Fourth, he argues that this was inevitable because of Christ's oneness with His people (v. 11). Fifth, he quotes three O.T. passages in proof of the union which exists between the Redeemer and the redeemed. Let us now turn to our passage and attentively weigh its details.

"But we see Jesus, who was made a little lower than the angels, for the suffering of death, crowned with glory and honour; that He, by the grace of God, should taste death for every man" (v. 9). The central thought of this verse was before us in the preceding article, namely, the exaltation of the once-humbled One. Now we must examine its several clauses and note their relation to each other. Really, there are five things in this verse, each of which we shall consider. First, the humiliation of the Mediator: "But we see Jesus, who was made a little lower than the angels." Second, the character of His humiliation: "For," or much better "by the suffering of death." Third, the object of His humiliation: to "taste death for every man," better "every son." Fourth, the moving cause of His humiliation: "by the grace of God." Fifth, the reward of His humiliation: "crowned with glory and honour."

"But we see Jesus, who was made a little lower than the angels." How these words should melt our hearts and move our souls to profoundest wonderment! That He, the Creator of angels, the Lord of them, the One who before His incarnation had been worshipped by them, should be "made lower" than they; and this for *our* sakes! Our hearts must indeed be dead if they are not thrilled and filled with praise as we ponder that fathomless stoop. As was pointed out under our exposition on v. 7, the Greek word here for "little" is used in the N.T. in two senses: sometimes where it is a matter of degree, at others where it is a case of time. Here it is the latter, for "a little season." In what particular sense the apostle is here contemplating Christ's being "made lower" than the angels, the next clause tells us.

"For the suffering of death." Many have experienced difficulty with this clause. That which has exercised them is whether the words "for the suffering of death" state the *purpose for which Christ* was "made a little lower than the angels," or, whether "for the suffering of death" gives the *reason why* He has been "crowned with glory and honour." Personally, we are fully satisfied that neither of these give the real thought.

The difficulty mentioned above is self-created. It is occasioned by failure to rightly define the reference to Christ's being made "a little lower than the angels." As already stated, we believe this signified "for a little while." If the reader will turn back again to our comments on 2:7 he will see we have adopted the suggestion of Dr. J. Brown to the effect that the specific reference is to *mortality*, the angels being incapable of dying. This, we are assured, is the meaning of the verse now before us. All ambiguity concerning this clause of v. 9 disappears if the first word be rendered "by" instead of "for." The English translators actually give "by" in the margin. The Greek preposition is "dia," and is translated "by" again and again, both when it governs a noun in the accusative or the genitive case.

Thus by altering "for" to "by" it will be seen that in this third clause the Holy Spirit has graciously defined His meaning in the second. (1) "But we see Jesus;" (2) "who was made a little season lower than the angels;" (3) "by the suffering of death." It was in *this* particular that Jesus was made for a season lower than the angels, namely, by His passing through a death of sufferings—an experience which, by virtue of the constitution God had given them, they were incapable of enduring. Therefore, the point here seized by the Holy Spirit in affirming that Jesus had been made lower than the angels, was *His mortality*. But here we must be very careful to explain our terms. When we say that Christ, by virtue of His incarnation, became "mortal," it must not be understood that He was subject to death in His body as the fallen descendants of Adam are. His humanity was holy and incorruptible: no seed or germ of death was in it, or could attack it. He laid down His life of Himself (John 10:18). No; what we mean is, and what Scripture teaches is, that in becoming man Christ took upon Him a nature that was *capable of* dying. This the angels were not; and in *this* respect He was, for a season, made lower than they.

"By the suffering of death." This expression denotes that Christ's exit from the land of the living was no easy or gentle one, but a death of "suffering"; one accompanied with much inward agony and outward torture. It was the "death of the cross" (Phil 2:8). It was a death in which He suffered not only at the hands of men and of Satan, but from God Himself. It was a death in which He fully satisfied the demands of infinite holiness and justice. This was a task which no mere creature was capable of performing. Behold here, then, the wonder of wonders: Christ undertook a work which was far above the power of all the angels, and yet to effect it He was made lower than them! If ever power was made perfect in weakness, it was in this!

"Crowned with glory and honour." This is the dominant clause of the verse. Concerning it we cannot do better than quote from Mr. C. H. Welch: "The crowning with glory and honour is the consecration of Christ as the Priest after the order of Melchizedek. 'And no man taketh this *honour* unto himself. . . . So also Christ *glorified* not Himself' (Heb. 5:4,5). We shall find an allusion to this in 3:3, 'for this man was counted worthy of more *glory* than Moses, inasmuch as He who builded the house hath more *honour* than the house. Thus we find Christ superior in honour and glory to both Moses and Aaron; and when we see Him crowned with honour and glory we are indeed considering Him who is the Apostle (Moses) and High Priest (Aaron) of our profession."

Here, then, is the first part of the apostle's answer to that which was, for the Jews, the great "stumbling block" (1 Cor.1:23). He who by the suffering of death had been made, for a little season, lower than the angels, has, because of His humiliation and perfect atoning sacrifice, been "highly exalted" by God Himself. He has been "raised far above all principality and power, and might and dominion, and every name that is named, not only in this world, but also in that which is to come" (Eph. 1:21). It is not simply that this exaltation followed the Mediator's suffering and death, but, as the "therefore" in Isa. 53:12 and the "wherefore" of Phil. 2:9 plainly denote, were the meritorious reward thereof. Thus, so far from the Cross needing an apology, it has magnified the Saviour. So far from Christ's degradation and death being something of which the Christian need be ashamed, they are the very reason why God has so signally rewarded Him. The "crown of thorns" which man gave Him, has been answered by the "crown of glory and honour" that God has bestowed upon Him. The humbled Christ is humiliated no longer; the Throne of the Universe is where He is now seated.

Ere passing on to the next verse, let us ask the reader, Have *you* "crowned with glory and honour" Him whom the world has cast out? Do you, in a practical way, own Him as your Lord and Master? Is *His glory* and honour ever the paramount consideration before you? Is He receiving from you the devotion and adoration of a worshipping heart? "*Worthy* is the Lamb." O may He, indeed, occupy the throne of our hearts and reign as King over our lives. In what esteem does the Father hold His once humiliated Son: He has crowned Him with glory and honour; then what *must* He yet do with those who "despise and reject" Him?

"That He by the grace of God should taste death for every man." Here is the second part of the apostle's answer to the Jew's objection. God had a benevolent design in permitting His Son, for a season, to become lower than the angels. The end in view fully justified the means. Only by the Son tasting death could the sons of God be delivered from the ruins of the fall; only thus could the righteousness and mercy of God be reconciled. This, we take it, indicates the relation of this final clause to the remainder of the verse: God's *design* in making His Son lower than the angels was that He might become the Redeemer of His people. The opening conjunction "that" (hopos, meaning "to the end that"), expressing purpose, is conclusive.

There has been considerable discussion as to the precise import of the expression "tasted death." Here, as ever in Scripture, there is a fulness in the language used which no brief definitions of man can ever embrace. The first and most obvious thought suggested by the language is, that the Saviour consciously, sensibly, experienced the bitterness of death. "The death of our Lord Jesus Christ was a slow and painful death; He was 'roasted with fire' as was prefigured by the Paschal lamb. But it was not merely that it lasted a considerable time, that it was attended with agony of mind as well as pain of body; but that He came, as no finite creature can come, into contact with death. He tasted death in that cup which the Lord Jesus Christ emptied on the cross" (Saphir).

He tasted that awful death *by anticipation*. From the beginning of His ministry (yea, before that, as His words in Luke 2:49 plainly show), there was ever present to his consciousness the Cross, with all its horror, see Matt. 16:21, John 2:4, 3:16, etc. At Calvary He actually drained the bitter cup. The death He tasted was "The curse which sin brings, the penalty of the broken law, the manifestation of the power of the devil, the expression of the wrath of God; and in all these aspects the Lord Jesus Christ came into contact with death and tasted it to the very last" (Saphir).

"That He by the grace of God should taste death for every man." The opening words of this clause set forth the efficient cause which moved the Godhead in sending forth the Son to submit to such unparalleled humiliation: it was free favour of God. It was not because that the ends of Divine government required mercy should be shown to its rebels, still less because that they had any claim upon Him. There is nothing whatever outside God Himself which moves Him to do anything: He "worketh all things after the counsel of His *own* will" (Eph. 1:11). It was solely by the grace and good pleasure of God, and not by the violence of man or Satan, that the Lord Jesus was brought to the Cross to die. The appointment of that costly sacrifice must be traced back to nothing but the sovereign benignity of God.

"For every man." This rendering is quite misleading. "Anthropos," the Greek word for "man" is *not* in the verse at all. Thus, one of the principal texts relied upon by Arminians in their unscriptural contention for a general atonement vanishes into thin air. The R. V. places the word "man" in italics to show that it is not found in the original. The Greek is "panta" and signifies "every one," that is, every one of those who form the subjects of the whole passage —every one of "the heirs of salvation" (1:14), every one of the "sons" (2:10), every one of the "brethren" (2:11). We may say that this is the view of the passage taken by Drs. Gouge and J. Brown, by Saphir, and a host of others who might be mentioned. Theologically it is demanded by the "tasted death *for* every one," i.e., substitutionally, in the room of, that *they* might not. Hence, every one for whom He tasted death shall themselves never do so (see John 8:52), and this is true *only* of the people of God.

What we have just said above is confirmed by many Scriptures. "For the transgression of *My people* was He stricken" said God (Isa. 53:8), and all mankind are not His "people." "I lay down My life *for the sheep,*" said the Son (John 10:10), but every man is not of Christ's sheep (John 10:26). Christ makes intercession on behalf of those for whom He died (Rom. 8:34), but He prays not for the world (see John 17:9). Those for whom he died are redeemed (Rev. 5:9), and from redemption necessarily follows the forgiveness of sins (Col. 1:14), but all have not their sins forgiven.

"For it became Him, for whom are all things, and by whom are all things, in bringing many sons unto glory, to make the captain of their salvation perfect through sufferings" (v. 10). This gives the third part of the apostle's reply to the objection which he is here rebutting, and a most arresting statement it is: he now takes still higher ground, advancing that which should indeed bow our hearts in worship. The word "became" means suited to, in accord with, the character of God. It was consonant with the Divine attributes that the Son should, for a season be "made lower than the angels" in order to "taste death" for His people. It was not only according to God's eternal purpose, but it was also suited to all His wondrous perfections. Never was God more Godlike than when, in the person of Jesus, He was crucified for our sins.

"For it became Him, for whom are all things, and by whom are all things, in bringing many sons unto glory, to make the captain of their salvation perfect through sufferings." There are five things in this verse claiming our reverent and diligent attention. First, the particular character in which God is here viewed; as the One "for whom are all things and by whom are all things." Second, the manner in which it "became" the Most High to bring many sons unto glory by giving up His beloved Son to the awful death of the cross. Third, the particular character in which the Son Himself is here viewed: as "The Captain of our salvation." Fourth, in what sense He was, or could be, "made perfect through sufferings." Fifth, the result of this Divine appointment: the actual conducting of many sons "unto glory."

First, then, the special character in which God is here viewed. "For it became Him, for whom are all things, and by whom are all things." This expression sets forth the high sovereignty of God in the most unqualified and absolute manner: "all things" without exception, that is, all creatures, all events. "For whom are all things" affirms that the Most High God is the Final Cause of everything: "The Lord hath made all things *for* Himself" (Prov. 16:4), i.e., to fulfill His own designs, to accomplish His own purpose, to redound to His own glory. So again we read in Rev. 4:11, "Thou art worthy, O Lord, to receive glory and honour and power: for Thou hast created all things, and *for* Thy pleasure they are and were created." This blessed, basic, yet stupendous truth is to be received with unquestioning and unmurmuring faith. He who maketh the wrath of man to praise Him (Psa. 76:10) will not only vindicate His broken law in the punishment of the wicked, but His justice and holiness shall be magnified by their destruction. Hell itself will redound to His glory.

"And by whom are all things." Every creature that exists, every event which happens, is by God's own appointment and agency. Nothing comes to pass or can do so without the will of God. Satan could not tempt Peter without Christ's permission; the demons could not enter the swine till *He* gave them leave; not a sparrow falls to the ground apart from His decree. This is only another way of saying that God actually *governs* the world which He has made. True, there is much, very much in His government which *we* cannot understand, for how can the finite comprehend the Infinite? He Himself tells us that His ways are "past finding out," yet His own infallible word declares, "For of Him, and through Him, and to Him are all things: to whom be glory forever" (Rom. 11:36).

"For whom are all things, and by whom are all things." Nothing so stirs up the enmity of the carnal mind and evidences the ignorance, the sin, and the high-handed rebellion of fallen man as the response which he makes when this great fact and solemn truth is pressed upon him. People at once complain, if this be so, then we are mere puppets, irresponsible creatures. Or worse, they will blasphemously argue, If this be true, then God, and not ourselves, is to be charged with our wickedness. To such sottish revilings, only one reply is forthcoming, "Nay but, O man who art thou that repliest against God? Shall the thing formed say to Him that formed it, Why hast Thou made me thus?" (Rom. 9:20).

Consider now the *appropriateness* of this title or appellation of Deity. The varied manner in which God refers to Himself in the Scriptures, the different titles He there assumes are not regulated by caprice, but are ordered by infinite wisdom; and we lose much if we fail to attentively weigh each one. As illustrations of this principle consider the following. In Rom. 15:5 He is spoken of as "The God of patience and hope": this, in keeping with the subject of the four preceding verses. In 2 Cor. 4:6 He is presented thus: "God who commanded the light to shine out of darkness hath shined in our hearts," which is in beautiful keeping with the theme of the five preceding verses. In Heb. 13:20 it is "The God of Peace" that brought again from the dead our Lord Jesus. Why? Because His holy wrath had been placated at the cross. So in Heb. 2:10 the apostle would silence the proud and wicked reasoning of the Jews by reminding them that they were replying against the Sovereign Supreme. For Him are all things and by Him are all things: His glory is the end of everything, His will the law of the universe; therefore, to quarrel with *His method* of bringing many sons unto glory was insubordination and blasphemy of the worst kind.

And what are the *practical bearings* upon us of this title of God? First, an *acknowledgement* of God in this character is due from us and required by Him. To believe and affirm that "for Him are all things, and by Him are all things" is simply owning that He *is* God—high above all, supreme over all, directing all. Anything short of this is, really, atheism. Second, *contentment* is the sure result to a heart which really lays hold of and rests upon this truth. If I really believe that "all things" are for God's glory and by His invincible and perfect will, then I shall receive submissively, yea, thankfully, whatsoever He ordains and sends me. The language of such an one must be, "It is the Lord: let Him do what seemeth Him good" (1 Sam. 3:18). Third, *confidence and praise* will be the outcome. God only does that which "becomes" Him; therefore, whatsoever He does must be right and best. Those who truly recognise this "*know* that all things work together for good to them that love God" (Rom. 8:28). True it is that our short-sighted and sin-darkened vision is often unable to see *why* God does certain things, yet we may be fully assured that He always has a wise and holy reason.

"For it became Him." More immediately, the opening "for" gives a reason for what has been advanced at the close of v. 9. Should it be reverently inquired why God's "grace" chose *such* a way for the redeeming of His elect, here is the ready answer: it "became Him" so to do. The Greek term signifies the answerableness or agreement of one thing to another. Thus, "speak thou the things that *become* sound doctrine" (Titus 2:1), i.e., that are agreeable thereto. So, too, the Greek term implies the *comeliness* of a thing. Thus, "which *become* women professing godliness (1 Tim. 2:10). The adorning of Christian women with good works is a comely thing, yea, it is the beauty and glory of their profession. In like manner the grace of God which gave Christ to taste death for His people, answered to the love of His heart and agreed with the holiness of His nature. Such an appointment was suited to God's character, consonant with His attributes, agreeable to his perfections. Never did anything more exhibit, and never will anything more redound to the glory of God than His making the Son lower than the angels in order to taste death for His people. A wide field of thought is here set before us. Let us, briefly, enter into a few details.

It "became" God's *wisdom*. His wisdom is evidenced in all His works, but nowhere so perspicuously or conspicuously as at Calvary. The cross was the masterpiece of Omniscience. It was there that God exhibited the solution to a problem which no finite intelligence could ever have solved, namely, how justice and mercy might be perfectly harmonized. How was it possible for righteousness to uphold the claims of the law and yet for grace to be extended to its transgressors? It seemed impossible. These were the things which the angels desired to look into, but so profound were their depths they had no line with which to fathom them. But the cross supplies the solution.

It "became" the *holiness* of God. What is His holiness? It is impossible for human language to supply an adequate definition. Perhaps about as near as we can come to one is to say, It is the antithesis of evil, the very nature of God hating sin. Again and again during O.T. times God manifested His displeasure against sin, but never did the white light of God's holiness shine forth so vividly as at Calvary, where we see Him smiting His own Beloved because the sins of His people had been transferred to Him.

It "became" His *power*. Never was the power of God so marvelously displayed as it was at Golgotha. Wherein does this appear? In that the Mediator was enabled to endure within the space of three hours what it will take an eternity to expend upon the wicked. All the waves and billows of Divine wrath went over Him (Psa. 42:7). Yet was He not destroyed. There was concentrated into those three hours of darkness that which the lost will suffer forever and ever, and nothing but the power of God could have upheld the suffering Saviour. Yea, only a Divine Saviour could have stood up under that storm of outpoured wrath; that is why God said, "I have laid help upon One that is *mighty*" (Psa. 89:19).

It "became" His *righteousness*. He can by no means clear the guilty. Sin must be punished where ever it is found. God's justice would not abate any of its demands when sin, through imputation, was found upon Christ: as Rom. 8:32 says, He "spared not His own Son." Never was the righteousness of God more illustriously exhibited than when it cried, "Awake O sword against My Shepherd, and against the Man that is My Fellow saith the Lord of hosts: smite the Shepherd" (Zech. 13:7).

It "became" the *love* and *grace* of God. Innumerable tokens of these have and do His children receive, but the supreme proof of them is furnished at the cross. "Herein is love, not that we loved God, but that He loved us, and sent His Son to be the propitiation for our sins" (1 John 4:10). The mercy of God is over all His works, but never so fully and so gloriously was it manifested as when Christ became Man and was made a curse for His people, that theirs might be the blessing.

We must next consider the special character in which the Saviour Himself is here contemplated: "The Captain of their salvation." This is one out of more than three hundred titles given to the Lord Jesus in the Scriptures, each of which has its own distinctive meaning and preciousness. The Greek word is "Archegos," and is found four times in the N.T. It signifies the "Chief Leader." It is the word rendered "Author" in Heb. 12:2, though that is an unhappy rendition. It is translated "Prince" in Acts 3:15 and 5:31. Thus, it is a title which calls attention to and emphasises the dignity and glory of our Saviour, yet, in His mediatorial character.

It needs to be borne in mind that in N.T. days the "captain" of a regiment did not remain in the rear issuing instructions to his officers, but took the lead, and by his own personal example encouraged and inspired his soldiers to deeds of valour. Thus the underlying thoughts of this title are, Christ's going before His people, leading His soldiers, and being in command of them. He has "gone before" them in three respects. First, in the way of obedience, see John 13:15. Second, in the way of suffering, see 1 Peter 2:21. Third, in the way of glory: He has entered heaven as our forerunner, so that faith says, "Thanks be unto God which giveth us the victory through our Lord Jesus Christ." Thus it will be seen that v. 10 continues the same thought as v. 9.

"The Captain of their salvation." The plain and necessary implication of this title is that we are passing through a country full of difficulties, dangers, oppositions, like Israel in the Wilderness on their way to the promised inheritance; so that we need a Captain,

Guide, Leader, to carry us safely through. This title of Christ's, then, is for the *encouragement* of our hearts: the grace, the faithfulness, and the power of our Leader guarantees the successful issue of our warfare. It teaches us once more that the *whole* work of our salvation, from first to last, has been committed by God into the hands of Christ.

"To make the Captain of their salvation perfect through suffering." This sentence has occasioned real trouble to many: how can a perfect person be "made perfect?" But the difficulty is more imaginary than real. The reference is not to the person of Christ, but to a particular office which He fills. His character needed no "perfecting." Unlike us, no course of discipline was required by Him to subdue faults and to develop virtues. We believe that Heb. 5:9 supplies the key to the words we are now considering: "being made perfect, He became the author of eternal salvation unto all them that obey Him." The previous verse speaks of Christ "learning obedience by the things which He suffered," which does not mean that He learned to obey, but rather that He learned by experience what obedience is. In like manner it was by the experiences through which He passed that Christ was "perfected," not experimentally, but officially, to be "the Captain" of our salvation. A striking type of this is furnished by the case of Joshua, who, as the result of his experiences in the wilderness, became experimentally qualified to be Israel's "captain," leading them into Canaan.

"To make the Captain of their salvation perfect through sufferings." Two other things need to be borne in mind: the particular design of this passage, and the special purpose and aim of the Epistle as a whole. The special design of the apostle was to remove the scandal of Christ's humiliating death, which was such a stumbling-block to the Jews. Therefore, he here affirms that the sufferings of Christ eventuated not in ignominy but glory: they "perfected" His equipment to be the "Captain" of His people, v. 18 amplifies. In regard to the scope of the Epistle as a whole, this word of the apostle's was well calculated to *comfort* the afflicted and sorely-tried Hebrews: their own Captain had reached glory via sufferings—sufficient for His soldiers to follow the same path. Thus, this word here is closely parallel with 1 Peter 4:1.

It should be added that the Greek word for "perfected" is rendered "consecrated" in 7:28. By His sufferings Christ became qualified and was solemnly appointed to be our Leader. It was *by* His sufferings that He vanquished all His and our foes, triumphing gloriously over them, and thus He became fitted to be our "Captain." What reason have we then to *glory* in the Cross of Christ! The eye of faith sees there not only consummate wisdom, matchless mercy, fathomless love, but victory, triumph, glory. By dying He slew death.

"In bringing many sons unto glory." This is both the Captain's work and reward. The term "glory" is one of the most comprehensive words used in all the Bible. It is almost impossible to define; perhaps "the sum of all excellency" is as near as we can come to it. It means that the "many sons" will be raised to the highest possible state and position of dignity and honour. It is *Christ's own* "glory" into which they are brought: "And the glory which Thou gavest Me I have given them; that they may be one, even as we are one" (John 17:22, and see Col. 3:4).

Into this "glory" *many* sons are to come. Some have difficulty in harmonizing this word with "many be called, but *few* chosen" (Matt. 20:16). In contrast from the vast multitudes which perish, God's elect are indeed "few" (Matt. 7:14); His flock is only a "little" one (Luke 12:32). Yet, considered by themselves, the redeemed of all generations will constitute "many."

Into this "glory" the many sons do not merely "come," but are "*brought*." It is the same word as in Luke 10:34 where the Good Samaritan "brought" the poor man that was wounded and half dead, and who could not "come" of himself, to the "inn." Let the reader consult these additional passages: Song of Sol. 2:4; Isa. 42:16; 1 Peter 3:18. This "bringing" of the many sons "unto glory" is in distinct stages. At regeneration they are brought from death unto life. At the Lord's return they will be brought to the Father's House (1 Thess. 4:16, 17). The whole is summarised in the parable of the lost sheep; see Luke 15:4-6.

In closing, let us ask the reader, "Are *you* one of these many "sons" whom Christ is bringing "unto glory"? Are you quite sure that you are? It is written, "As many as are led by the Spirit of God, they are the sons of God" (Rom. 8:14). Is *this* true of you? Can others see the *evidences* of it? Is your daily life controlled by self-will, the ways of the world, the pleasing of your friends and relatives, or by the *written Word,* for that is what the Spirit uses in leading His sons.

Above we have contemplated that which "became" God; let our final consideration be that which "becomes" His favoured children. "Let your conversation (manner of life) be as it *becometh* the Gospel of Christ" (Phil. 1:27). If we are now light in the Lord, let us "walk *as* children of light" (Eph. 5:8). Let us seek grace to "walk worthy of the vocation wherewith we are called" (Eph. 4:1).

CHAPTER TEN

Christ Superior to Angels.

(Heb. 2:11-13)

Inasmuch as we feel led to break up the second half of Heb. 2 into shorter sections than is our usual habit (so that we may enter more in detail), it will be necessary to begin each chapter with a brief summary of what has already been before us. Though we dislike using valuable space for mere repetitions, yet this seems unavoidable if the continuity of thought is to be preserved and the scope of the apostle's argument intelligently followed. Moreover, as we endeavor to study the holy Word of God, it is ever the part of wisdom to heed the Divine injunction, "he that believeth shall not make haste" (Isa. 28:16). To pause and review the ground already covered, serves to fix in the memory what otherwise might be crowded out. As said the apostle to the Philippians, "to write the *same* things to you, to me indeed is not grievous, but for you it is safe" (3:1).

In the opening chapter of our Epistle, from vv. 4 to 14, seven O.T. passages were quoted for the purpose of showing the superiority of Israel's Messiah over the angels. The first four verses of chapter 2 are parenthetical, inasmuch as the argument of that section is broken off in order to make a searching application to the conscience of what has already been said. At 2:5 the discussion concerning the relative positions of the Mediator and the celestial creatures is resumed. Two objections are now anticipated and dealt with—this is made clear by the last clause of v. 8, which is the interjecting of a difficulty. The objections are: How could Christ be superior to angels, seeing that He was *Man?* and, How could He possess a greater excellency than they, seeing that He had *died?*

In meeting these objections appeal was first made to the 8th Psalm, which affirmed, in predictive language, that God has crowned "man" (redeemed man) with "honour and glory," and that He has put "all things under *his* feet"; and in the exaltation of Jesus faith beholds the ground and guarantee, the proof and pledge, of the coming exaltation of all His people (v. 9). Second, the necessity for the Mediator's humiliation lay in the fact that He must "taste death," as the appointed Substitute, if "every son" was to receive eternal life (v. 9). Third, the apostle affirmed that God had a benevolent design in suffering His Son to stoop so low: it was by His "grace" that He tasted death (v. 9). Fourth, it is announced that such a course of procedure was suited to the nature and honouring to the glory of Him who ordains all things: it "became Him" (v. 10). Fifth, the Divine love and wisdom in causing the Captain of our salvation to be perfected "through sufferings" was fully vindicated, for the outcome from it is that many sons are brought "unto glory."

In Heb. 2:11, which begins our present portion, the needs-be for the Son's humiliation is made still more evident: "For both He that sanctifieth and they who are sanctified, are all of one: for which cause He is not ashamed to call them brethren." The opening "for" at once intimates that the Holy Spirit is still advancing confirmation of what He had said previously, and is continuing to show *why* the Lord of angels had been made Man. It may help the reader to grasp the force of this verse if we state it thus: It was imperative that Christ should be made, for a season, "lower than the angels" if ever He was to have ground and cause to call *us* "brethren." *That* is a title which presupposes a *common* state and standing; for this He must become "one" with them. In other words, the Redeemer must identify Himself with those He was to redeem.

We may add that the opening "for" of v. 11 supplies an immediate link with v. 10: a further reason is now advanced why it "became" God to make the Captain of His people perfect through sufferings, even because He and they are "all of one." Herein lies the *equity* of Christ's sufferings. It was not that an innocent person was smitten in order that guilty ones might go free, for that would be the height of injustice, but that an innocent Person, voluntarily, out of love, *identified Himself with* trangressors, and so became answerable for their crimes. Therefore, "in all things it behooved Him to be made like unto His brethren" (Heb. 2:17). How this should endear Him to us!

"All of one," is very abstract, and for this reason not easy to define concretely. "Observe that it is only of sanctified persons that this is said. Christ and the sanctified ones are all of one company, men together in the same position before God; but the idea goes a little further. It is not of one and the same Father; had it been so, it could not have been said, 'He is not ashamed to call them brethren.' He could not then do otherwise than call them brethren. If we say 'of the same mass' the expression may be pushed too far, as though He and others were of the same nature as children of Adam, sinners together. In this case Jesus would have to call every man His brother; whereas it is only the children whom God hath given Him, 'sanctified' ones, that He so calls. But He and the sanctified ones are all as men in the same nature and position together before God. When I say 'the same' it is not in the same state of sin, but the contrary, for they are the Sanctifier and the sanctified, but in the same proof of human position as it is before God as sanctified to Him; the same as far forth as man when He, as the sanctified One is before God" (Mr. J. N. Darby).

Though the above quotation is worded somewhat vaguely, nevertheless we believe it approximates closely to the thought of the Spirit. They, Christ and His people, are "all of one." Perhaps we might say, All of one class or company. If Christ were to be the Saviour of men, He must Himself be Man. This is what the quotations from the O.T., which immediately follow, go to show. We do believe, however, that the "all of one" is a little fuller in scope than that brought out by Mr. Darby's comments. The remainder of Heb. 2 seems to show it also has reference to the oneness in *condition* between the Sanctifier and the sanctified, i.e., in this world. The Shepherd went before the sheep (John 10:4): the path they follow is the same He trod. Thus, "all of one" in position, in sufferings, in trials, in dependency upon God.

"For both He that sanctifieth and they who are sanctified are all of one." Many of the commentators have quite missed the meaning of this "all of one." Had sufficient attention been given to the context they should have seen that the apostle is *not* here treating of the oneness of Christians with Christ in acceptance before God and in glory—that, we get in such passages as Eph. 1 and 2; instead, he is bringing out the oneness of Christ with His people in their humiliation. In other words, the apostle is not here speaking of our being lifted up to Christ's level, but of His coming down to ours. That which follows clearly establishes this.

But what is meant by "He that sanctifieth and they who are sanctified"? The Sanctifier is Christ Himself, the sanctified are the many sons who are being brought to glory. "The source and power of sanctification are in the Son of God our Saviour. We who were to be brought unto glory were far off from God, in a state of condemnation and death. What could be more different than our natural condition and the glory of God which we are awaiting? Condemned on account of our transgressions of the law, we lived in sin, alienated from God, and without His presence of light and love. We were dead; and by 'dead' I do not mean that modern fancy which explains death to mean cessation of existence, but that continuous, active, self-developing state of misery and corruption into which the sinner has fallen by his disobedience. Dead in trespasses and sins, wherein we *walked;* dead while living in pleasing self (Eph. 2:1, 2, 1 Tim. 5:6). What can be more opposed to glory than the state in which we are by nature? and if we are to be brought into glory, it is evident we must be brought into holiness; we must be delivered and separated from guilt, pollution, and death, and brought into the presence of God, in which is favour, light, and life — that His life may descend into our souls, and that we may become partakers of the Divine nature.

"Christ is our sanctification. 'By one offering He hath perfected forever them that are sanctified' (Heb. 10:14). By the offering of His body as the sacrifice for sin, He has sanctified all that put their trust in Him. To sanctify is to separate unto God; to separate for a holy use. We who were far off are brought nigh by the blood of Christ. And although our election is of God the Father (who is thus the Author of our sanctification, Jude 4), and the cleansing and purification of the heart is generally attributed to the Holy Spirit (Titus 3:4, 5), yet is it in Christ that we were chosen, and from Christ that we receive the Spirit, and as it is by the constant application of Christ's work and the constant communication of His life that we live and grow, Christ is our sanctification.

"We are sanctified through faith that is in Him (Acts 26:18). By His offering of Himself He has brought us into the presence of God. By the Word, by God's truth, by the indwelling Spirit, He continually sanctifies His believers. He gave Himself for the church, 'that He might sanctify and cleanse it by the washing of water by the Word' (Eph. 5:26). 'Sanctify them through Thy truth' (John 17:17; 15:3).

"Christ Himself is the foundation, source, method, and channel of our sanctification. We are exhorted to put off the old man and to put on the new man day by day, to mortify our members which are upon the earth. But in what way or method can we obey the apostolic exhortations, but by our continually beholding Christ's perfect sacrifice for sin as our all-sufficient atonement? In what other way are we sanctified day by day, but by taking hold of the salvation which is by Him, 'The Lamb that is slain'? Jesus is He that sanctifieth. The Holy Spirit, the Comforter, is sent by Christ to glorify Him, and to reveal and appropriate to us His salvation. We are conformed to the image of Christ by the Spirit as coming from Christ in His glorified humanity" (Saphir).

"For which cause He is not ashamed to call them brethren" (v. 11). Because Christ became Man, He is not ashamed to own as "brethren" those whom the Father had given to Him. The community of nature shared by the Sanctifier and the sanctified furnishes ground for Him to call them "brethren." That He did so in the days of His humiliation may be seen by a reference to Matt. 12:49; John 20:17. That He will do so in the Day to come, appears from Matt. 25:40. That He is "not ashamed" to so own them, plainly intimates an act of condescension on his part, the condescension arising out of the fact that *He* was more than Man, none other than "the Lord of glory." There is, no doubt, a latent contrast in these words: the world hated them, their brethren according to the flesh despised them, and called them "apostates"; but the Son of God incarnate was not ashamed to call them "brethren." So, too, He owns us. Therefore, if *He* is "not ashamed" to own us, shall *we* be "ashamed to confess Him!" Moreover, let us "not be ashamed" to own as "brethren" the poorest of the flock!

"For which cause He is not ashamed to call them brethren." Ere passing from these blessed words, it needs to be said, emphatically, that this grace on the part of Christ *does not* warrant His people becoming so presumptuous as to speak of Him as their "Brother." Such a thing is most reprehensible. "Question, May we by virtue of this relation, call the Son of God our Brother? Answer, We have no example of any of the saints that ever did so. They usually gave titles of dignity to Him, as Lord, Master, Saviour. Howsoever the Son of God vouchsafes this honour unto us, yet we must retain in our hearts an high and reverent esteem of Him, and on that ground give such titles to Him as may manifest as much. Inferiors do not use to give like titles of equality to their superiors, as superiors do to their inferiors. It is a token of love in superiors to speak to their inferiors as equals; but for inferiors to do the like, would be a note of arrogancy" (Dr. Gouge). The same principle applies to John 15:15. Christ in His condescending grace may call us His "friends," but this does *not* justify us in speaking of Him as our "Friend"!

"Saying, I will declare Thy name unto My brethren" (v. 12). Once more the apostle appeals to the written Word for support of what he had just affirmed. A quotation is made from Psa. 22, one which not only substantiated what had been said in v. 11, but which also made a further contribution towards removing the objection before him. As is well known, the 22nd is the great Cross Psalm. In vv. 20, 21, the suffering Saviour is heard crying, "Deliver My soul from the sword (of Divine justice, cf. Zech. 13:7), My darling from the power of the dog (the Gentiles, cf. Matt. 15:24-26). Save Me from the lion's (the Devil's, cf. 1 Peter 5:8) mouth." Then follows faith's assurance, "For Thou *hast* heard Me from the horns of the unicorn." This is the turning point of the Psalm: the cries of the Sufferer are heard on High.

What a conclusive and crushing reply was this to the objecting Jew! God's own Word had foretold the humiliation and sufferings of their Messiah. There it was, unmistakably before them. What could they say? The Scriptures *must* be fulfilled. No reply was possible.

But more: not only did the 22nd Psalm announce beforehand the sufferings of the Messiah; it also foretold His victory. Read again the last clause of v. 21: "Save Me from the lion's mouth: for Thou *hast* heard Me." Christ *was* "saved," not from death, but out of death, cf. Heb. 5:7. Now what is the very next thing in Psalm 22? This: "I will declare Thy name unto My brethren" (v. 22). Here the Saviour is seen on resurrection ground, victorious over every foe. It is *this* which the apostle quotes in Heb. 2:12.

Now that which it is particularly important to note is that in this verse from Psa. 22 Christ is heard saying He would declare the Father's name unto His "brethren." *That* could only be possible on resurrection ground. Why? Because by nature they were "dead in trespasses and sins." But as "quickened together with Christ" (Eph. 2:5) they were made sons of God, and therefore the "brethren" of the risen Son of God. Hence the great importance of noting carefully the very point at which v. 22 occurs in the 22nd Psalm. The Lord Jesus never called His people "brethren" on the other side of the Cross! He spoke of them as "disciples," "sheep," "friends," but never as "brethren." But as soon as He was risen from the dead, He said to Mary, "Go to My brethren, and say unto them, I ascend unto My Father and to your Father" (John 20:17). Here, then, was the unanswerable reply to the Jews' objection: Christ could reach *resurrection* ground only by passing through death, cf. John 12:24.

"I will declare Thy name unto My brethren." Here the Son is heard addressing the Father, promising that He would execute the charge which had been given Him. The Greek word for "declare" is very emphatic and comprehensive. It means, To proclaim and publish, to exhibit and make known. To declare God's "Name" signifies to reveal what God is, to make known His excellencies and counsels. This is what Christ came here to do: see John 17:6, 26. None else was competent for such a task, for none knoweth the Father but the Son (Matt. 11:27). But only to His "brethren" did Christ do so. They are the "babes" unto whom heavenly things are revealed (Matt. 11:25); they are the ones unto whom are made known the "mysteries of the kingdom of heaven" (Matt. 13:11). From all others these blessed revelations are "hid," to those "without" they are but "parables."

"In the midst of the church will I sing praise unto Thee" (v. 12). This completes the quotation from Psalm 22:22. No doubt the first fulfilment of this took place during the "forty days" of Acts 1:3: mark how Acts 1:4 brings in the assembly; though its ultimate fulfilment is yet future. The *position* in which Christ is here viewed is very blessed, "in the midst": it is the Redeemer leading the praises of His redeemed. Strangers to God may go through all the outward forms of mere "religion," but they never *praise* God. It is only upon resurrection ground that worship is possible. A beautiful type of this is found in Ex. 15:1: it was only after Israel had crossed the Red Sea, and the Egyptians were dead upon the shore, that "Then sang Moses and the children of Israel this song." Note how Moses, the typical mediator, *led* their praises!

"And again, I will put My trust in Him" (v. 13). The apostle is still replying to the Jews' objection, How could Jesus of Nazareth be the superior of angels, seeing that He was Man and had died? Here, in vv. 12, 13, he quotes Messianic passages from the O.T. in proof of the statements made in vv. 10, 11. First, Psalm 22:22 is cited, in which Christ is heard addressing His redeemed as "brethren." The implication is unmistakable: that is a title which presupposes a common position and a common condition, and in order to do that the Lord of glory had to be abased, come down to their level, become Man. Then, in the same passage, the Saviour is heard "singing praise" unto God. This also views Him as incarnate, for only as Man could He sing praise unto God! Moreover, it is not as Lord over the church, but as One "in the midst" of it He is there viewed. Thus "all of one" is illustrated and substantiated.

A second quotation is now made, from Isa. 8:17, according to the Septuagint version. The passage from which this is taken is a very remarkable one. Beginning at v. 13 the exhortation is given, "Sanctify the Lord of Hosts Himself; and let Him be your fear, and let Him be your dread." This means, give Him His true place in your hearts, recognize His exalted dignity, bow before His ineffable majesty, submit to His high sovereignty, tremble at the very thought of quarreling with Him.

Then, in v. 14, the Lord of Hosts is brought before us in a twofold character: "And He shall be for a sanctuary; but for a stone of stumbling and for a rock of offence to both the houses of Israel, for a gin and for a snare to the inhabitants of Jerusalem." These expressions, Sanctuary and Stone of stumbling, define the relation of the Lord to the elect and to the non-elect. To the one He is Refuge, a Resting-place, a Centre of worship; to the other, He is an offence. "The Stone" is one of the titles of

Christ, and it is most interesting and instructive to trace out the various references, the first being found in Gen. 49:24. Here in Isa. 8 it is Christ in His *lowliness* which is in view. Israel was looking for One who would be high among the great ones of the earth, therefore when One who was born in a manger, who had toiled at the carpenter's bench, who had not where to lay His head, appeared before them, they "despised and rejected" Him. The figure used here is very affecting. How *low* a place must the Lord of glory have taken for Israel to "stumble" over Him, like a stone lying at one's feet! Thus, once more, the Holy Spirit refers to an O.T. passage in which the Messiah was presented in humiliation, as it were "a stone" lying on the ground.

It is scarcely necessary to add that the very lowliness into which the Saviour entered, coming here not to be ministered unto but to minister, and give His life a ransom for many, is that which makes Him a "precious Stone" (1 Peter 2:6) to all whose faith sees the Divine glory shining beneath the humiliation. What is more moving to our hearts, what is more calculated to bow them in worship before God as we behold His Son in John 13? — verily, "a Stone" at the feet of His disciples, washing them! Blessed is it to know that the very Stone which the builders rejected "is become the head of the corner" (Psa. 118:22), that is, has been exalted.

Returning now to Isa. 8, v. 15 amplifies what was said in the previous one: "And many among them shall stumble, and fall, and be broken, and be snared, and be taken." How solemnly and how literally this was fulfilled in the history of the Jews we all know. Then, in v. 16, we have stated the *consequences* of Israel's rejection of their Messiah: "Bind up the testimony, seal the law among My disciples." Ever since there has been a veil over Israel's heart, even when reading the Holy Scriptures (2 Cor. 3:15).

Now comes the word in Heb. 2:13, "I will put My trust in Him" (Isa. 8:17, Sept. version). A most blessed word is this. It reveals the implicit confidence of the Saviour in God. Notwithstanding the treatment which He met with from both the houses of Israel, His trust in Jehovah remained unshaken; He looked away from the things seen to the things unseen. The *relevancy* of this citation in Heb. 2 is obvious: such a thing could not have been unless Christ had become Man — considered simply as God the Son, to speak of Him "trusting" was unthinkable, impossible. Wonderful proof was this of what had been affirmed in 2:11 concerning the oneness which exists between Christ and His people: He, like they, was called on to tread the path of faith.

"I will put My trust in Him." This is indeed a word which should bow our hearts in wonderment. What a lowly place had the Maker of heaven and earth taken! How these words bring out the reality of His humanity! The Son of God had become the Son of Man, and while here on earth He ever acted in perfect accord with the place which He had taken. He lived here a life of faith, that is, a life of trust in and dependence upon God. In John 6:57 we hear Him saying, "I live by the Father." *This* is what He pressed on Satan when tempted to manufacture bread for Himself.

Isa. 8:17 is not the only O.T. passage which speaks of Christ "trusting" in God. In Psalm 16:1 He cries, "Preserve Me, O God: for in Thee do I put My trust." As Man it was not fitting that He should stand independent and alone; nor did He. The whole of this Psalm views Him in the place of entire dependency — in life, in death, in resurrection. Strikingly will this appear if vv. 10 and 11 be compared with John 2:19 and 10:18. In the passages in John's Gospel, where His *Divine* glory shines forth through the veil of His humanity, He speaks of raising Himself from the dead. But here in Psa. 16, where the perfections of His manhood are revealed, He is seen trusting in God to raise Him again. How important it is to get the Spirit's viewpoint in each passage!

"I will put My trust in Him." This perfection of our Lord is not sufficiently pondered by us. The life which Jesus Christ lived here for thirty-three years was a life of faith. That is the meaning of that little-understood word in Heb. 12:2: "Looking off unto Jesus (His name, as Man), the Author (Greek, same as "Captain" in 2:10) and Perfecter of faith." If these words be carefully weighed in the light of their context, their meaning is plain. In Heb. 11 we have illustrated, from the O.T. saints, various aspects of the life of faith, but in Jesus we see *every* aspect of it *perfectly* exemplified. As our Captain or Leader, He has gone before His soldiers, setting before them an inspiring example. The path we are called on to tread, is the same He trod. The race we are bidden to run, is the same He ran. And we are to walk and run as He did, by faith.

"I will put my trust in Him." This was ever the expression of His heart. Christ could say, and none but He ever could, "I was cast upon Thee from the womb: Thou art My God from My mother's belly" (Psa. 22:10). Never did another live in such complete dependence on God as He: "I have set the Lord always before Me; because He is at My right hand, I shall not be moved" (Psa. 16:8) was His language. So evident was His faith, even to others, that His very enemies, whilst standing around the Cross, turned it into a bitter taunt: "He trusted on the Lord that He would deliver Him, let Him deliver Him, seeing He delighted in Him" (Psa. 22:8). How blessed to know that when *we* are called on to walk by faith, to submit ourselves unto and live in dependency on God, to look away from the mists of time to the coming inheritance, that Another has trod the same path, that in putting forth His sheep, the Good Shepherd went before them (John 10:4), that He bids us to do nothing but what He has Himself first done.

"I will put My trust in Him." This is *still* true of the Man Christ Jesus. In Rev. 1:9 we read of "the kingdom and *patience* of Jesus Christ": that is the patience of faith, cf. Heb. 11:13. Heb. 10:12, 13 interprets: "But this Man, after He had offered one sacrifice for sins forever, sat down on the right hand of God; from henceforth *expecting* till His enemies be made His footstool." That is the expectation of *faith,* awaiting the fulfilment of God's promise. Ah, dear reader, fellowship with Christ is no mystical thing, it is intensely practical; fellowship with Christ means, first of all, walking by faith.

"And again, behold I and the children which God hath given Me" (v. 13). This completes the quotation made from Isa. 8:17, 18. The pertinency of these words in support of the apostle's argument is evident: it is Christ's taking His place before God as Mediator, owning the "children" as His gift to Him; it is Christ as Man confessing His oneness with them, ranking Himself with the saints — "I and the children," compare "My Father and your Father" (John 20:17). It is the Lord Jesus presenting Himself to God as His Minister, having faithfully and successfully fulfilled the task committed to Him. He is here heard addressing the Father, rejoicing over the fruits of His own work. It is as though He said, "Here am I, O Father, whom Thou didst send out of Thine own bosom from Heaven to earth, to gather Thine elect out of the world. I *have* performed that for which Thou didst send Me: behold I and the children which Thou hast given Me." Though He had proved a stone of stumbling and a rock of offence to both the houses of Israel, yet was He not left without a people; "children" had been given to Him, and these He owns and solemnly presents before God.

Who are these "children?" First, they are those whom the Mediator brings to God. As we read in 1 Peter 3:18, "For Christ hath also once suffered for sins, the Just for the unjust, that He might *bring us to God.*" This is what Christ is seen doing here: formally presenting the children to God. Second, they are here regarded as the "children" of *Christ.* In Isa. 53:10, 11 it was said, "He shall see His seed, He shall prolong His days, and the pleasure of the Lord shall prosper in His hands. He shall see *of the travail* of His soul, and shall be satisfied." In John 13:33 and 21:5 He is actually heard *owning* His disciples as "children." Nor was there anything incongruous in that. Let the reader ponder 1 Cor. 4:14,

15: if they who are converted under the preaching of God's servants may be termed *their* "children," how much more so may they be called "children" of Jesus Christ whom *He* has begotten by His Spirit and by His Word!

"Behold I and the children which God hath given Me." Those whom God hath given to Christ were referred to by Him, again and again, during the days of His public ministry. "All that the Father giveth Me shall come to Me" (John 6:37). "I have manifested Thy name unto the men which Thou gavest Me out of the world: Thine they were, and Thou gavest them Me. . . . . I pray for them: I pray not for the world, but for them which Thou hast given Me" (John 17:6, 9). They were given to Christ before the foundation of the world (Eph. 1:4). These "children" are God's elect, sovereignly singled out by Him, and from the beginning chosen unto salvation (2 Thess. 2:13). God's elect having been given to Christ "before the foundation of the world," and therefore from all eternity, throws light upon a title of the Saviour's found in Isa. 9:6: "The everlasting Father." This has puzzled many. It need not. Christ is the "everlasting Father" because from everlasting He has had "children!"

Why were these "children" given to Christ. The first answer must be, For His own glory. Christ is the Centre of all God's counsels, and His glory the one object ever held in view. Christ will be eternally glorified by having around Him a family, each member of which is predestined to be "conformed to His image" (Rom. 8:29). The second answer is, That He might save them: "All that the Father giveth Me shall come to Me, and him that cometh to Me I will in no wise cast out" (John 6:37).

"Behold I and the children which God hath given Me." We doubt not that the ultimate reference of these words looks forward to the time anticipated by that wonderful doxology found at the close of Jude's Epistle: "Now unto Him that is able to keep you from falling, and to *present* you faultless before the presence of His glory with exceeding joy, to the only wise God our Saviour, be glory and majesty, dominion and power, both now and ever." When the Lord Jesus shall, in a soon-coming Day, gather the company of the redeemed unto Himself and "*present* it to Himself a glorious church, not having spot, or wrinkle, or any such thing" (Eph. 5:27), then shall He triumphantly exclaim, "Behold I and the children which God hath given Me." In the meantime let us seek to take unto our hearts something of the blessedness of these words that, even now, the "joy of the Lord" may be our strength (Neh. 8:10).

"Behold I and the children which God hath given Me." Let us endeavour to point out one or two plain implications. First, *how dear,* how precious, must God's elect be unto Christ! They are the Father's own "gift" unto Him. The value of a gift lies not in its intrinsic worth, but in the esteem and affection in which the giver is held. It is in this light, first of all, that Christ ever views His people — as the expression of the Father's own love for Himself. Second, how certain it is that Christ will continue to care for and minister unto His people! He cannot be indifferent to the welfare of one of those whom the Father has given to Him. As John 13:1 declares, "having loved His own which were in the world, He loved them unto the end." Third, *how secure* they must be! None of His can possibly perish. Beautifully is this brought out in John 18:8, 9, where, to those who had come to arrest Him, Christ said, "If therefore ye seek Me, let these go their way: that the saying might be fulfilled, which He spake, Of them which Thou gavest Me have I lost none."

Inexpressibly blessed is that which has been before us in Heb. 2:12, 13. The Lord's people are there looked at in a threefold way. First, Christ owns them as His "brethren." O the wonder of it! The ambitious worldling aspires to fleshly honours and titles, but what has he which can, for a moment, be compared with the honoured title which Christ confers upon His redeemed? Next time you are slandered by men, called some name which hurts you, remember, fellow-Christian, that *Christ* calls you one of His "brethren." Second, the entire company of the redeemed are here denominated "the church," and Christ is seen in the midst singing praise. There, they are viewed corporately, as a company of worshippers, and He who is "a Priest forever" leads their songs of joy and adoration. Third, the Lord Jesus owns us as His "children," children which have been given to Him by God. This speaks both of their nearness and dearness to Himself. Surely the contemplation of these wondrous riches of grace must impel us to cry, "To Him be glory and dominion for ever and ever. Amen" (Rev. 1:6).

CHAPTER ELEVEN

Christ Superior to Angels.

(Heb. 2:14-16)

The closing verses of Heb. 2 are so rich and full in their contents and the subjects with which they deal are of such importance that we feel the more disposed to devote extra space for the exposition of them. More and more we are learning for ourselves that a short portion of Scripture prayerfully examined and repeatedly meditated upon, yields more blessing to the heart, more food to the soul, and more help for the walk, than a whole chapter read more or less cursorily. It is not without reason that the Lord Jesus said in the parable of the Sower, "that on the good ground are they, which in an honest and good heart, having heard the Word, keep, and bring forth fruit with *patience*" (Luke 8:15). The only way in which the Word is "kept" or held fast is through prolonged meditation and patient or persevering study.

The verses which are to be before us on this occasion form part of the apostle's inspired explanation of "the Son's" becoming Man and suffering the awful death of the cross. If the reader will turn back to the third paragraph of the preceding article he will there find five reasons (substantiated in vv. 9, 10), as to why Christ endured such humiliation. In vv. 11 to 13 four more are advanced. It was necessary for the second Person of the holy Trinity to be made lower than the angels if He were to have ground and cause for calling us "brethren" (vv. 11, 12), for that is a title which presupposes a common ground and standing. Then, it was necessary for the Lord of glory to become "all of one" with His people if, in the midst of the church, He should "sing praise" unto God (v. 12); and this, the O.T. scriptures affirmed, He would do. Again, it was necessary for Him who was in the form of God to take upon Him "the form of a servant" if He was to set before His people a perfect example of the life of faith; and in Isa. 8:17 He is heard saying, by the Spirit of prophecy, "I will put My trust in Him" (v. 13). Finally, His exclamation "Behold I and the children which God hath given Me" (v. 13), required that He should become Man and thus rank Himself alongside of His saints.

In vv. 14 to 16 we have one of the profoundest statements in all Holy Writ which treats of the Divine incarnation. For this reason, if for no other, we must proceed slowly in our examination of it. Here too the Holy Spirit continues to advance further reasons as to why it was imperative that the Lord of angels should, for a season, stoop beneath them. Three additional ones are here given, and they may be stated thus: first, that He might render null and void him who had the power of death, that is, the Devil (v. 14); second, that He might deliver His people from the bondage of that fear which death had occasioned (v. 15); third, Abraham's children could only be delivered by Him laying hold of Abraham's seed (v. 16).

"Forasmuch then as the children are partakers of flesh and blood He also Himself likewise took part of the same; that through death He might destroy him that had the power of death, that is, the devil" (v. 14). "The connection between this verse and the preceding context may be stated thus: Since it became Him for whom are all things and by whom are all things, in bringing many sons unto glory, to make the captain of their salvation perfect through suffering; and since, according to Old Testament prophecies, the Sanctifier and the sanctified, the Saviour and the saved, must be of the same race; and since the saved are human beings, — the Son of God, the appointed Saviour, assumed a nature capable of suffering and death — even the nature of man, when He came to save, that in that nature He might die, and by dying accomplish the great purpose of His appointment, the destruction of the power of Satan, and the deliverance of His chosen people" (Dr. J. Brown).

The opening words of our verse denote that the Holy Spirit is drawing a conclusion from the proof-texts just cited from the O.T. The Greek words for "forasmuch then" are rendered "seeing therefore" in 4:6, and their force is, "it is evident hereby" that the Son of God became the Son of Man for the sake of those whom God had given Him.

"Forasmuch then as the children are partakers of flesh and blood He also Himself likewise took part of the same; that through death He might destroy him that had the power of death, that is, the devil" (v. 14). Here we have the eternal Word becoming flesh, the Son of God becoming the Son of man. Let us consider, first, the Wonder of it; second, the Needs-be of it; third, the Nature of it; fourth, the Perfection of it; fifth, the Purpose of it.

The tragic thing is that, for the present, our minds are so beclouded and our understandings so affected by sin, it is impossible for us to fully perceive the *wonder* of the Divine incarnation. As the apostle wrote, "But now we see through a glass darkly" (1 Cor. 13:12). But thank God this condition is not to last for ever; soon, very soon, we shall see "face to face." And when by God's marvellous grace His people behold the King in His beauty, they will not, we think, be bewildered or dazed, but instead, filled with such wonderment that their hearts and whole beings will spontaneously bow in worship.

Another thing which makes it so difficult for us to grasp the wonder of the Divine incarnation is that there is nothing else which we can for a moment compare with it; there is no analogy which in any wise resembles it. It stands unique, alone, in all its solitary grandeur. We are thrilled when we think of the angels sent forth to minister for those who shall be heirs of salvation: that those wondrous creatures, which so far excel us in wisdom and strength, should have been appointed to be our attendants; that those holy creatures should be commissioned to encamp round about poor sinners; that the courtiers of Heaven should wait upon worms of the earth! Truly, that *is* a great wonder. But O my brethren, that wonder pales into utter insignificance and, in comparison, fades away into nothingness, before this far greater wonder — that the Creator of angels should leave His throne on High and descend to this sin-cursed earth; that the very One before whom all the angels bow should, for a season, be made lower than they; that the Lord of glory, who had dwelt in "light unapproachable," should Himself become partaker of "flesh and blood"! *This* is the wonder of wonders.

So wonderful was that unparalleled event of the Divine incarnation that the heavenly hosts descended to proclaim the Saviour newly-born. So wonderful was it that the "glory of the Lord," the ineffable Shekinah, which once filled the temple, but had long since retired from the earth, appeared again, for "the glory of the Lord shone round about" the awe-struck shepherds on Bethlehem's plains. So wonderful was it that chronology was revolutionized, and anno mundi became anno domini: the calendar was changed, and instead of its dating from the beginning of the world, it was re-dated from the birth of Christ; thus the Lord of time has written His very signature across the centuries. Passing on now, let us consider the *needs-be* for the Divine incarnation.

This is plainly intimated both in what has gone before and in what follows. If the "children" which God had given to His Son were to be "sanctified" then He must become "all of one" with them. If those children who are by nature partakers of flesh and blood were to be "delivered from him that had the power of death, that is the devil," then the Sanctifier must also "likewise take part of the same." If He was to be a merciful and faithful High Priest in things pertaining to God, He must in all things "be made like unto His brethren." If He is to be able to "succor them that are tempted," then He must Himself, "suffer, being tempted"; and, as God Himself "cannot be tempted," He had to become Man in order to that experience.

The needs-be was real, urgent, absolute. There was no other way in which the counsels of God's grace towards His people could be wrought out. If ever we were to be made "like Him," He first had to be made like us. If He was to give us of His Spirit, He must first assume our flesh. If we were to be so joined unto the Lord as to become "one spirit" (1 Cor. 6:17) with Him, then He must first be joined with our flesh, so as to be "all of one" with us. In a word, if we were to become partakers of the Divine nature, He must be made partaker of human nature. Thus we perceive again the force of the apostle's reply to the objection which he is here removing — How could it be that a Man was superior to angels? He has not only shown from the Jews' own scriptures that the Man Christ Jesus had been given a name more excellent than any pertaining to the celestial hierarchies, but here he shows us the needs-be for the Lord of glory to become Man. If we were to be "conformed to His image" then He must be "made in the likeness of sin's flesh." If the children of Abraham were to be redeemed, then He must take on Him the "seed of Abraham."

The *nature* of the Divine incarnation is here referred to in the words "flesh and blood." That expression speaks of the frailty, dependency, and mortality of man. This is evident from the other passages where it occurs. The words "flesh and blood" are joined together five times in the N.T.: Matt. 16:17, 1 Cor. 15:50, Gal. 1:16, Eph. 6:12, Heb. 2:14. It is a humbling expression emphasizing the weakness of the flesh and limitations of man: note how in Eph. 6:12 "flesh and blood" is contrasted from the mightier foes against which Christians wrestle.

"Flesh and blood" is the present state in which is found those children whom God has designed to bring unto glory. By their natural constitution and condition there is nothing to distinguish the elect from the non-elect. The Greek noun for "partakers" is derived from the root signifying "common": in Rom. 15:27 Gentile believers are said to be "partakers" of Israel's spiritual blessings, that is, they enjoy them in common, one with another. So God's children are "partakers," equally with the children of the Devil, of "flesh and blood." Nor does our regeneration effect any change concerning this: the limitations and infirmities which "flesh and blood" involve still remain. Many reasons for this might be suggested:

that we may not be too much puffed up by our spiritual standing and privileges; that we might be rendered conscious of our infirmities, and made to feel our weakness before God; that we might abase ourselves before Him who is Spirit; that the grace of compassion may be developed in us — our brethren and sisters are also partakers of "flesh and blood," and often we need reminding of this.

In the words "He also Himself likewise took part of the same" we have an affirmation concerning the *reality* of the Saviour's humanity. It is not merely that the Lord of glory *appeared* on earth in human form, but that He actually became "flesh and blood," subject to every human frailty so far as these are freed from sin. He knew what hunger was, what bodily fatigue was, what pain and suffering were. The very fact that He was "the Man of sorrows" indicates that "He also Himself likewise took part of the same." Thereby we see the amazing condescension of Christ in thus conforming Himself to the condition in which the children were. How marvellous the love which caused the Lord of glory to descend so low for us sons of men! There was an infinite disparity between them: He was infinite, they finite; He omnipotent; they frail and feeble; He was eternal, they under sentence of death. Nevertheless, He refused not to be conformed to them; and thus He was "crucified through weakness" (2 Cor. 13:4), which refers to the state into which He had entered.

The *perfection* of the Divine incarnation is likewise intimated in the words "He also Himself likewise took part of the same." These words emphasize the fact that Christ's becoming Man was a *voluntary* act on His part. The "children" were by nature subject to the common condition of "flesh and blood." They belonged to that order. They had no say in the matter. That was their state by the law of their very being. But not so with the Lord Jesus. He entered this condition as coming from another sphere and state of being. He was the Son who "thought it not robbery to be equal with God." He was all-sufficient in Himself. Therefore it was an act of condescension, a voluntary act, an act prompted by love, which caused Him to "take part of the same."

These words also point to the *uniqueness* of our Lord's humanity. It is most blessed to observe how the Spirit here, as always, has carefully guarded the Redeemer's glory. It is not said that Christ was a "*partaker* of flesh and blood," but that "He likewise took part of the same." The distinction may seem slight, and at first glance not easily detected; yet is there a real, important, vital difference. Though Christ became Man, real Man, yet was He different, radically different, from every other man. In becoming Man He did not "partake" of the foul poison which sin has introduced into the human constitution. *His* humanity was not contaminated by the virus of the Fall. Before His incarnation it was said to His mother, "That *Holy* Thing which shall be born of thee" (Luke 1:35). It is the sinlessness, the uniqueness of our Lord's humanity which is so carefully guarded by the distinction which the Holy Spirit has drawn in Heb. 2:14.

The *purpose* of the Divine incarnation is here intimated in the words that "through death He might destroy him that had the power of death, that is, the devil." It was with *this* end in view that the Son of God took part in "flesh and blood." In the several passages where the Divine incarnation is referred to in the New Testament different reasons are given and various designs are recorded. For example, John 3:16 tells us that one chief object in it was to reveal and exhibit the matchless love of God. 1 Tim. 1:15 declares that "Christ Jesus came into the world to save sinners." But here in Heb. 2:14 it is the destroying of him that had the power of death that is mentioned.

The object of the Holy Spirit in our present passage is to display the glorious and efficacious side of that which was most humbling — the infinite stoop of the Lord of glory. He is pointing out to those who found the Cross such a stumbling-block, how that there was a golden lining to the dark cloud which hung over it. That which to the outward eye, or rather the untaught heart and mind, seemed such a degrading tragedy was, in reality, a glorious triumph; for by it the Saviour stript the Devil of his power and wrested from his hands his most awful weapon. Just as the scars which a soldier carries are no discredit or dishonour to him if received in an honourable cause, so the cross-sufferings of Christ instead of marking His defeat were, actually, a wondrous victory, for by them He overthrew the arch-enemy of God and man.

"That through death He might destroy him that had the power of death, that is, the devil." It is most blessed to note the bearing of this statement upon the special point the apostle was discussing. The Jews were stumbled by the fact that their Messiah had died. Here the Holy Spirit showed that so far from that death tarnishing the glory of Christ, it exemplified it, for by death He overthrew the great Enemy and delivered His captive people. "Not only is He glorious in heaven, but He hath conquered Satan in the very place where he exercised his sad dominion over men, and where the judgment of God lay heavily upon men" (Mr. J. N. Darby).

"That through death He might destroy him that had the power of death, that is, the devil." Three things here claim attention: First, what is meant by the Devil having "the power of death"? Second, what "death" is here in view? Third, in what sense has Christ "destroyed" the Devil? From the words of the next verse it is clear that the reference is to what particularly obtained before Christ became incarnate. That it does not mean the Devil had absolute power in the infliction of physical death in O.T. times is clear from several scriptures. Of old Jehovah affirmed, "See now that I, even I, am He, and there is no god with Me: I kill, and I make alive" (Deut. 32:39). Again, "the Lord killeth, and maketh alive; He bringeth down to the grave, and bringeth up" (1 Sam. 2:6). And again, "unto God the Lord belong the issues from death" (Psalm 68:20). These passages are decisive, and show that even during the Mosaic economy the giving of life and the inflicting of death were in the hands of God only, no matter what instruments He might employ in connection therewith.

The particular kind of "death" which is here in view is explained for us in the words "that through death He" etc. The death which Christ died was "the wages of sin" — the penal infliction of the law, suffering the wrath of a holy God. The point raised here is a deeply mysterious one, yet on it Scripture throws some light. In John 8:44 Christ declared that the Devil was "a murderer" (literally "man-slayer") from the beginning. In Zech. 3:1 we are shown Satan standing at Jehovah's right-hand to resist Israel's high priest. Upon the subject Saphir has said, "But which death did Christ die? That death of which the Devil had the power. Satan wielded that death. He it was who had a just claim against us that we should die. There is justice in the claim of Satan.

"It is quite true that Satan is only a usurper; but in saving men God deals in perfect righteousness, justice, truth. According to the Jewish tradition the fallen angels often accuse men, and complain before God that sinful men obtain mercy. Our redemption is in harmony with the principles of righteousness and equity, on which God has founded all things. The prince of this world is *judged* (John 16:11); he is conquered not merely by power, but by the power of justice and truth. . . . He stood upon the justice of God, upon the inflexibility of His law, upon the true nature of our sins. But when Christ died our very death, when He was made sin and a curse for us, then all the power of Satan was gone. . . . And now what can Satan say? The justice, majesty, and perfection of the law are vindicated more than if all the human race were lost forever. The penalty due to the broken law Jesus endured, and now, as the law is vindicated, sin put away, death swallowed up, Christ has destroyed the Devil."

Inasmuch as the Devil is the one who brought about the downfall of our first parents, by which sentence of death has been passed upon all their posterity (Rom. 5:12); inasmuch as he goeth about as a roaring lion "seeking whom he may devour" (I Peter 5:8); inasmuch as he challenged God to inflict upon the guilty the sentence of the law (Zech. 3:1); and, inasmuch as even the elect of God are, before their regeneration, under "the power of darkness" (Col. 1:13 and cf. Acts 26:18), dead in trespasses and sins, yet "walking according to the Prince of the power of the air"; the Devil may be said to have "the *power* of death."

The word "*destroy* him that had the power of death" does not signify to annihilate, but means to make null and render powerless. In 1 Cor. 1:28 this same Greek word is rendered "bring to nought"; in Rom. 3:3 "without effect"; in Rom. 3:31 "make void." Satan has been so completely vanquished by Christ the Head that he shall prevail against none of His members. This is written for the glory of Christ, and to encourage His people to withstand him. Satan is an enemy bespoiled. Therefore is it said, "Resist the Devil, and he will flee from you" (James 4:7). To such as believe there is assurance of victory. If the Devil gets the upper hand of us, it is either because of our timidity, or lack of faith. "To 'destroy him that had the power of death' is to strip him of his power. It is said by the apostle John, 'for this purpose was the Son of God manifested, to destroy the works of the Devil,' i.e. ignorance, error, depravity, and misery. In the passage before us, the destruction is restricted to the peculiar aspect in which the Devil is viewed. To destroy him, is so to destroy him as having 'the power of death'—to render him, in this point of light, powerless in reference to the children; i.e., to make death cease to be a penal evil. Death, even in the case of the saints, is an expression of the displeasure of God against sin; but it is not—as but for the death of Christ it must have been—the hopeless dissolution of his body; it is not the inlet to eternal misery to his soul. Death to them for whom Christ died consigns, indeed, the body to the grave; but it is 'in the sure and certain hope of a glorious resurrection,' and it introduces the freed spirit into all the glories of the celestial paradise" (Dr. J. Brown).

This stripping Satan of his power of death was accomplished by the laying down of the Saviour's life, "that through death He might destroy." "The means whereby Christ overcame Satan, is expressly said to be death. To achieve this great and glorious victory against so mighty an enemy, Christ did not assemble troops of angels, as He could have done (Matt. 26:53), nor did He array Himself with majesty and terror, as in Exodus 19:16; but He did it by taking part of weak flesh and blood, and therein humbling Himself to death. In this respect the apostle saith, that Christ 'having spoiled principalities and powers, made a show of them openly, triumphing over them in the cross' (Col. 2:15), meaning thereby, His death. The apostle there resembleth the cross of Christ to a trophy whereon the spoils of enemies were hanged. Of old conquerors were wont to hang the armour and weapons of enemies vanquished on the walls of forts and towers." (Dr. Gouge.)

"That through death He might destroy him that had the power of death, that is, the devil." A striking type of this is furnished in Judges 14:12-19 — will the reader please turn to this, before considering our brief comments. The riddle propounded by Samson prefigured what is plainly declared here in Heb. 2:14. The greatest "eater" (Judges 14:14), or "consumer," is Death. Yet out of the eater came forth meat: that is, out of death has come life; see John 12:24. Note in Judges 14 how, typically, the natural man is, of himself, utterly unable to solve this mystery. The secret of the death of Christ, the Lion of the tribe of Judah, must be *revealed.* Finally, note how that a change of raiment was provided for those to whom the riddle was explained — a foreshadowment of the believer's robe of righteousness!

"And deliver them who through fear of death were all their life-time subject to bondage" (v. 15). It needs to be carefully borne in mind that throughout this passage the apostle has in view a particular class of persons, namely, the "heirs of salvation," the "sons" of God, the "brethren" of Christ. Here they are described according to their unregenerate condition: subject to bondage; so subject, all their unregenerate days; so subject through "the fear of death." It was to deliver them from this fear of death that Christ died. Such we take it is the general meaning of this verse. 2 Tim. 1:7 gives the sequel: "For God hath not given us the spirit of fear; but of power, and of love, and of a sound mind."

The opening "And" and the verb "deliver" (which is in the same mood and tense as "destroy" in the previous verse) intimate that Christ's death had in view these two ends which cannot be separated, namely, destroying the Devil, delivering us. Just as Abraham destroyed those enemies who had taken Lot captive together with the other inhabitants of Sodom, that he might "deliver" them (Gen. 14:14), and as David destroyed the Amalekites, that he might "deliver" his wives and children and others out of their hands (1 Sam. 27:9), so Christ vanquished the Devil, that he might "deliver" those who had (by yielding to his temptations) fallen captive to him. What thanks is due unto Christ for thus overthrowing our great adversary!

To the "fear of death," *i.e.,* that judgment of God upon sin, all men are in much greater bondage than they will own or than they imagine. It was this "fear" which made Adam and Eve hide themselves from the presence of God (Gen. 3:8), which made Cain exclaim, "my punishment is greater than I can bear" (Gen. 4:13), which made Nabal's heart to die within him (1 Sam. 25:37), which made Saul fall to the ground as a man in a swoon (1 Sam. 28:20), which made Felix to tremble (Acts 24:25), and which will yet cause kings and the great men of the earth to call on the mountains to fall on them (Rev. 6:15, 16). True, the natural man, at times, succeeds in drowning the accusations of his conscience in the pleasures of sin, but "as the crackling of thorns under a pot, so is the laughter of the fool" (Ecc. 7:6). It is from this fearful bondage that Christ delivered His people: through His grace, by His spirit filling them "with all joy and peace in believing" (Rom. 15:13).

A beautiful and most complete type of the truth in our present verse is to be found in 1 Sam. 17. Will the reader turn to that chapter and note carefully the following details: First, in vv. 4-8 there we have, in figure, Satan harassing the O.T. saints. Second, where was David (type of Christ) during the time Goliath was terrifying the people of God? Verses 14, 15 answer: In his father's house, caring for his sheep. So through the Mosaic economy Christ remained on High, in the Father's house, yet caring for His sheep. Third, Goliath defied Israel for "forty days," v. 16 — figure of the forty centuries from Adam to Christ, when the O.T. saints lived in fear of death, for "life and immortality" were only brought "to light through the Gospel" (2 Tim. 1:10). Fourth, next we see David leaving his father's house, laden with blessings for his brethren, vv. 17, 18. Note the "early in the morning," v. 20, showing his *readiness* to go on this mission. Fifth, mark the sad reception he met with from his brethren, v. 28: his efforts were unappreciated, his purpose misunderstood, and a false accusation was brought against him. Sixth, in vv. 32, 38-49, we have a marvellous type of Christ defeating Satan in the wilderness: note how David went forth in his *shepherd* character (v. 40 and compare John 10). He took "five" stones out of the brook (the place of running water—figure of the Holy Spirit) but used only one of them; so Christ in the Wilderness selected the Pentateuch (the first five books of Scripture) as His weapon, but used only one of them, Deuteronomy. Note David *slew* him not with the stone! He stunned him with that, but slew him with his *own* sword: so Christ vanquished him that had the power of death *"through death."* Read again v. 51 and see how accurate is the figure of Christ "bruising" the Serpent's *head*. Finally, read v. 52 and see the typical climax: those "in fear" *delivered*. What a marvelous Book is the Bible!

"For verily He took not on angels; but He took on the seed of Abraham" (v. 16). This verse, which has occasioned not a little controversy, presents no difficulty if it be weighed in the light of its whole context. It treats not of the Divine incarnation, that we have in v. 14; rather does it deal with the purpose of it, or better, the consequences of Christ's death. Its opening "for" first looks back, remotely to vv. 9, 10; immediately, to vv. 14, 15. The Spirit is here advancing a *reason* why Christ tasted death for every son, and why He destroyed the Devil in order to liberate His captives; because not angels, but the seed of Abraham, were the objects of His benevolent favour. The "for" and the balance of the verse also, looks forward, laying a foundation for what follows in v. 17: the ground of Christ's being made like to His brethren and becoming the faithful and merciful High Priest was because He would befriend the seed of Abraham.

The Greek verb here translated "He took on" or "laid hold" is found elsewhere in some very striking connections. It is used of Christ's stretching out His hand and rescuing sinking Peter, Matt. 14:31, there rendered "caught." It is used of Christ when He "took" the blind man by the hand (Mark 8:23). So of the man sick of the dropsy. He "took" and healed him (Luke 14:4). Here in Heb. 2:16 the reference is to the almighty power and invincible grace of the Captain of our salvation. It receives illustration in those words of the apostle's where, referring to his own conversion, he said, "for which also I am (was) *apprehended* (laid hold) of Christ Jesus" (Phil. 3:12). Thus it was and still is with each of God's elect. In themselves, lost, rushing headlong to destruction; when Christ stretches forth His hand and delivers, so that of each it may be said, "Is not this a brand *plucked* from the burning" (Zech. 3:2). "Laid hold of " so securely that none can pluck out of His hand!

But not only does our verse emphasise the invincibility of Divine grace, it also plainly teaches the absolute sovereignty of it. Christ lays hold not of "the seed of Adam," all mankind, but only "the seed of Abraham"—the father of God's elect people. This expression, "the seed of Abraham," is employed in the N.T. in connection with both his natural and his spiritual seed. It is the latter which is here in view: "Now to Abraham and his seed were the promises made. He saith not, And to seeds, as of many, but as of one, And to thy seed which is Christ" (Gal. 3:16)—not only Christ personal, but Christ mystical. The last verse of Gal. 3 shows that: "And if ye be Christ's then are ye Abraham's seed, and heirs according to promise."

This verse presents an insoluble difficulty to those who believe in the *universality* of God's love and grace. Those who do so deny the plain teaching of Scripture that Christ laid down His life for "the sheep," and for them alone. They insist that justice as well as mercy demanded that He should die for all of Adam's race. But why is it harder to believe that God has provided no salvation for part of the human race, than that He has provided none for the fallen angels? They were higher in the scale of being; they, too, were sinners needing a Saviour. Yet none has been provided for *them!* He "laid not on" angels.

But more: Our verse not only brings out the truth of election, it also presents the solemn fact of reprobation. Christ is not the Saviour of angels. "And the angels which kept not their first estate, but left their own habitation, He hath reserved in everlasting chains under darkness unto the judgment of the great day" (Jude 6). On this Dr. J. Brown has well said:

"What an overwhelming subject of contemplation is this! He is not the Saviour of angels, but of the elect family of men. We are lost in astonishment when we allow our minds to rest on the number and dignity of those whom He does not lay hold of, and the comparative as well as real vileness of those of whom He does take hold. A sentiment of this kind has engaged some good, but in this case not wise men, in an inquiry why the Son of God saves men rather than angels. On this subject Scripture is silent, and so should we be. There is no doubt that there are good reasons for this, as for every other part of the Divine determinations and dispensations; and it is not improbable that in some future stage of our being these reasons will be made known to us. But, in the meantime, I can go no further than, 'even so, Father, for so it hath seemed good in Thy sight.' I dare not 'intrude into things. which I have not seen,' lest I should prove that I am 'vainly puffed up by a fleshly mind.' But I will say with an apostle, 'Behold the goodness and severity of God; on them that fell, severity'—most righteous severity; 'but to them who are saved, goodness'—most unmerited goodness." (Dr. J. Brown.)

May the Lord add His blessing to what has been before us.

CHAPTER TWELVE

Christ Superior to Angels.

(2:17-18)

The verses which are now to be before us complete the second main division of the Epistle, in which the apostle has set forth the superiority of Christ over angels, and has met and removed a double objection which might be made against this. In showing that it was necessary for the Son of God to become Man in order to save His people from their sins, the Holy Spirit took occasion to bring out some striking details concerning the real and perfect humanity of Christ. In 2:11 He affirms that Christ and His people are "all of one." This receives a sevenfold amplification, which is as follows: First, they are one in sanctification, v. 11. Second, they are one in family relationship, vv. 11, 12a. Third, they are one in worship, v. 12b. Fourth, they are one in trust, v. 13. Fifth, they are one in nature, v. 14. Sixth, they are one in the line of promise, v. 16. Seventh, they are one in experiencing temptation, v. 18.

It is remarkable to notice, however, that in this very passage which sets forth Christ's identification with His people on earth, the Holy Spirit has carefully guarded the Saviour's glory and shows, also in a sevenfold way, His uniqueness: First, He is "the Captain of our salvation" (v. 10), we are those whom He saves. Second, He is the "Sanctifier," we but the sanctified (v. 11). Third, the fact that He is "not ashamed to call us brethren" (v. 11), clearly implies His superiority. Fourth, He is the Leader of our praise and presents it to God (v. 12). Fifth, mark the "I, and the children" in v. 13. Sixth, note the contrast between "partakers" and "took part of" in v. 14. Seventh, He is the Destroyer of the enemy, we but the delivered ones vv. 14, 15. Thus, here as everywhere, *He* has the pre-eminence in all things."

Another thing which comes out strikingly and plainly in the second half of Heb. 2 is the distinguishing grace and predestinating love of God. Christ is His "Elect" (Isa. 42:1), so called because His people are "chosen in Him" (Eph. 1:4). Mark how this also is developed in a sevenfold manner. First, in "bringing many *sons* unto glory" (v. 10). Second, "the Captain of *their* salvation" (v.

10). Third, "they who are sanctified," set apart (v. 11). Fourth, "in the midst of the church" (v. 12). Fifth, "the children which God hath given me" (v. 13). Sixth, "He took on Him the seed of Abraham" (v. 16), not Adam, but "Abraham," the father of God's chosen people. Seventh, "to make reconciliation for the sins of *the* people" (v. 17).

If the reader will turn back to the third paragraph in article 10, and the second and third in article 11, he will find that we have called attention to twelve distinct reasons set forth by the apostle in Heb. 2:9-16, which show the meetness and necessity of Christ's becoming man and dying. In the verses which we are now to ponder, two more are advanced: First, the incarnation and death of the Saviour were imperative if He was to be "a merciful and faithful High Priest" (v. 17). Second, such experiences were essential that He might be able to "succor them that are tempted" (v. 18). Thus, in the fourteen answers given to the two objections which a Jew would raise, a *complete* demonstration is once more given of the two leading points under discussion.

Though our present portion consists of but two verses yet are they so full of important teaching that many more pages than what we shall now write might well be devoted to their explication and application. They treat of such weighty subjects as the incarnation of Christ, the priesthood of Christ, the atoning-sacrifice of Christ, the temptation of Christ, and the succour of Christ. Precious themes indeed are these; may the Spirit of truth be our Guide as we prayerfully turn to their consideration.

"Wherefore in all things it behooved Him to be made like unto His brethren, that He might be a merciful and faithful High Priest in things pertaining to God, to make reconciliation for the sins of the people" (v. 17). The Holy Spirit here adduces a further reason why it was necessary for the Son of God to become incarnate and lay down His life for His people: it behooved Him so to do that He might be an effectual High Priest. As the priesthood of Christ will come before us again and again in the later chapters, D.V., we shall not here discuss it at length. Let us now ponder the several words and clauses of our present verse.

"Wherefore" is the drawing of a conclusion from what has been said in the previous verses. "It behooved Him": the Greek word is not the same as for "it became" Him in 2:10. There the reference is to the Father, here to the Son; that signified a comeliness or meetness, this has reference to a necessity, though not an absolute one, but in conjunction with the order of God's appointment in the way sinners were to be redeemed, and His justice satisfied, cf.Luke 24:46. "To be made like unto His brethren" is parallel with "all of one" in v. 11 and "He also Himself likewise took part" in v. 14. The expression goes to manifest the reality of Christ's human nature: that He was Man, such a man as we are.

The words "it behooved Him in all things to (His) brethren to be made like" are not to be taken absolutely. When the writer points out that, in view of other scriptures, the word "all" must be limited in such passages as John 12:32, 1 Tim. 2:4, 6, etc., some people think we are interpreting the Bible so as to suit ourselves. But what will *they* do with such a verse as Heb. 2:17? Can the words "in all things it behooved Him to be made like unto His brethren" be understood *without* qualification? Was He made like unto us in the depravity of our natures? Did He suffer from physical sicknesses as we do? Emphatically no. How do we know this? From other passages. Scripture needs to be compared with Scripture in order to understand any verse or any expression. The same Greek words here rendered "all things" (kapa panta) occur again in Heb. 4:15, where we are told that Christ "was in all points (things) tempted like as we are sin *excepted*" for thus the Greek word should be rendered. Thus the Holy Spirit expressly declares that the "all things" is *not* universal!

What then does the "all things" signify and include? We answer, everything which Scripture does not except or exclude. "When people saw Him, they did not notice in His outward appearance anything super-human, glorious, free from earthly weakness and dependency. He did not come in splendor and power. He did not come in the brightness and strength which Adam possessed before he fell. 'In all things He became like unto us' In His body, for He was hungry and thirsty; overcome with fatigue, He slept; in His mind, for it developed. He had to be taught. He grew in wisdom concerning the things around Him; He increased, not merely in stature, but in mental and normal strength. In His affections, for He loved. He was astonished; He marvelled at men's unbelief. Sometimes He was glad, and 'rejoiced in spirit'; sometimes He was angry and indignant, as when He saw the hypocrisy of the Jews. Zeal like fire burned within Him: 'The zeal for the house of God consumed Me'; and he showed a vehement fervor in protecting the sanctity of God's temple. He was grieved; He trembled with emotion; His soul was straitened in Him. Sometimes He was overcome by the waves of feeling when He beheld the future that was before Him.

"Do not think of Him as merely *appearing* a man, or as living a man only in His body, but as Man in body, soul, and spirit. He exercised faith; He read the Scriptures for His own guidance and encouragement; He prayed the whole night, especially when He had some great and important work to do, as before setting apart the apostles. He sighed when He saw the man who was dumb; tears fell from His eyes when at the tomb of Lazarus He saw the power of death and of Satan. His supplications were with strong crying and tears; His soul was exceeding sorrowful" (Saphir). Thus, the Son of God was made like unto His brethren in that He became Man, with a human spirit, and soul and body; in that He developed along the ordinary lines of human nature, from infancy to maturity; and, in that He passed through all the experiences of men, sin, and sickness excepted.

"That He might be a merciful and faithful High Priest in things pertaining to God, to make reconciliation for the sins of the people." The Son of God became the Son of Man in order that He might be an High Priest. There was an absolute necessity for this. First, because of the infinite disparity there is between God and men: He is of infinite glory and majesty, and dwells in that light which no man can approach unto (1 Tim. 6:16); they are but dust and ashes (Gen. 18:27). Second, because of the contrariety of nature between God and men: He is most pure and holy, they most polluted and unholy. Third, because of the resultant enmity between God and men (Rom. 5:10; Col. 1:21). Hence we may observe: there is no immediate access for any man to God without a priest; there is no priest qualified to act for men in things pertaining to God, but Jesus Christ, the God-man. Thus has He been appointed "Mediator between God and men" (1 Tim. 2:5, 6).

Because of the perfect union between His two natures, the Lord Jesus is "a merciful and faithful High Priest": "merciful" manwards, "faithful" Godwards. To be "merciful" is to be compassionate, ever ready, under the influence of a tender sympathy, to support, comfort, and deliver. Having trod the same path as His suffering and tried people, Christ is able to enter into their afflictions. He is not like an angel, who has never experienced pain. He is Man; nor are His sympathies impaired by His exaltation to heaven. The same human heart beats within the bosom of Him who sits at God's right hand as caused Him to weep over Jerusalem! To be "faithful" means that His compassions are regulated by holiness, His sympathies are exercised, according to the requirements of God's truth. There is a perfect balance between His maintenance of God's claims and His ministering to our infirmities.

"To make reconciliation for the sins of the people." It is a pity that the translators of the A.V. rendered this clause as they did. The Revisers have correctly given: "to make *propitiation* for the sins of the people." The Greek word here is "Hilaskeothai," which is the verbal form of the one found in 1 John 2:2 and 4:10. The word for "reconciliation" is "katallage," which occurs in 2 Cor.

5:18, 19, and Rom. 5:11, though the word is there wrongly rendered "the atonement." The difference between the two terms is vital though one which is now little understood. Reconciliation is one of the effects or fruits of propitiation. Reconciliation is between God and us; propitiation is solely Godward. Propitiation was the appeasing of God's holy anger and righteous wrath; reconciliation is entering into the peace which the atoning sacrifice of Christ has procured.

"To make propitiation for the sins of the people." Here is the climax of the apostle's argument. Here is his all-conclusive reply to the Jews' objection. Atonement for the sins of God's elect could not be made except the Son became Man; except He became "all of one" with those who had, from all eternity been set apart in the counsels of the Most High to be "brought unto glory"; except He took part in "flesh and blood," and in all things be "made like unto His brethren." Only thus could He be the *Redeemer* of the "children" which God had given Him.

In Scripture the first qualification of a redeemer was that he must belong to the same family of him or her who was to be redeemed: "If thy brother be waxen poor, and hath sold away of his possession, and if any of his kin come to redeem it, then shall he redeem that which his brother sold" (Lev. 25:25). The redeemer must be a "kinsman": this fact is fully and beautifully illustrated in the book of Ruth (see 2:20; 3:12, 13; 4:1, 4, 6). Neither pity, love, nor power were of any avail till *kinship* was established. The important bearing of this on what immediately follows we shall now endeavor to show.

"To make propitiation for the sins of the people." This word, in the light of its setting, is one of the most vital to be found in all Holy Writ on the subject of the Atonement, bringing out, as it does, the absolute righteousness of God in connection therewith. At the back of many minds, we fear, there lurks the suspicion that though it was marvellous grace and matchless love which moved God to give His Son to die for sinners, yet that, strictly speaking, it was an act of *un*-righteousness. Was it really just for an *innocent* person to suffer in the stead of the guilty? Was it right for One who had so perfectly honoured God and kept His law at every point, to endure its awful penalty? To say, It *had* to be, there was no other way of saving us, supplies no direct answer to our question; nay, it is but arguing on the jesuitical basis that "the end justifies the means."

Sin must be punished; a holy God could not ignore our manifold transgressions; therefore, if we are to escape the due reward of our iniquities a sinless substitute must be paid the wages of sin in our stead. But will not the Christian reader agree that it had been infinitely better for all of us to be cast into the Lake of Fire, than that God should act *un*-righteously to His Own Beloved? Has, then our salvation been secured at the awful price of a lasting stigma being cast upon the holy name of God? This is how the theological schemes of many have left it. But not so the Holy Scriptures. Yet, let us honestly face the question: Was God *just* in taking satisfaction from His spotless Son in order to secure the salvation of His people?

It is at this point that so many preachers have shown a zeal which is *not* "according to knowledge" (Rom. 10:2). In their well-meant but carnal efforts to simplify the things of God, they have dragged down His holy and peerless truth to the level of human affairs. They have sought to "illustrate" Divine mysteries by references to things which come within the range of our senses. God has said, "The natural man receiveth not the things of the Spirit of God: for they are foolishness unto him: neither can he know, because they are spiritually discerned" (1 Cor. 2:14). Why not believe what He has said? You cannot teach a corpse, and the natural man is dead in sin. If the Word of God does not bring him life and light, no words of ours can or will. And to go outside of Holy Writ for our "illustrations" is a piece of impertinency, or worse. When a preacher attempts to simplify the mystery of the three Persons in the Godhead by an illustration from "nature" he only exhibits his foolishness, and helps nobody.

Thus it has been with the sacred truth and holy mystery of the Atonement. Good men have not hesitated to ransack the annals of history, both ancient and modern, to discover examples of those who, themselves innocent of the crime committed, volunteered to receive the penalty due to those who were guilty. Sad, indeed, is it to behold this unholy cheapening of the things of God; but what is far worse, most reprehensible is it to observe their *mis*-representations of the greatest transaction of all in the entire history of the universe. An innocent man bearing the punishment of a guilty one may meet the requirements of a human government, but such an arrangement could never satisfy the demands of the righteous government of God. Such is *its* perfection, that under it no innocent person ever suffered, and no guilty person ever escaped; and so far from the atonement of the Son of God forming an exception to this rule, it affords the most convincing evidence of its truth.

Once we perceive that the Atonement is founded upon the *unity* of Christ and His people, a unity formed by His taking part in flesh and blood, the righteousness of God is at once cleared of the aspersion which the illustrations of many a preacher has, by necessary implication cast upon it. The propitiation rendered unto God was made neither by a stranger, nor an intimate friend, undergoing what another merited; but by the Head who was responsible for the acts of the members of His spiritual body, just as those members had been constituted guilty because of the act of their natural head, Adam—when "by the offence of one, judgment came upon all men to condemnation" (Rom. 5:18). It is perhaps worthy of notice in this connection that, in the over-ruling providence of God, it is the *head* of a murderer's body which is dealt with when capital punishment is inflicted—either decapitation as in France, hanging by the neck as in England, or being gassed as in some parts of U.S.A. Thus the head is held responsible for the feet, which were swift to shed blood, and the hand which committed the lethal crime.

However great the dignity of the substitute, or however deep his voluntary humiliation, atonement for us would not have been possible unless that substitute became actually, as well as legally, one with us. In order to ransom His church, in order to purge our sins, Christ must so unite Himself with His people, that their sins should become His sins, and that His sufferings and death should become their sufferings and death. In short, the union between the Son of God and His people, and theirs with Him, must be as real and as intimate as that of Adam and his posterity, who all sinned and died in him. Thus did He, in the fulness of time, assume their flesh and blood, bear their sins in His own body on the tree, so that they, having died to sin, may live unto righteousness, being healed by His stripes. Therefore, no human transaction can possibly illustrate the suretyship and sacrificial death of Christ, and any attempt to do so is not only to darken counsel by words without knowledge, but is, really, to be guilty of presumptuous impiety. Probably more than one preacher will be led to cry with the writer, "Father, forgive me, for I knew not what I did."

Here, then, is the answer to our question: so far from the salvation of God's elect having been procured at the unspeakable price of sullying the holy name of Deity, the manner in which it was secured furnishes the supremest demonstration of the inexorable justice of God; for when sin was found upon Him, God "spared not His own Son" (Rom. 8:32). But it was against *no* "innocent Victim" that God bade His sword awake. It was against One who had graciously condescended to be "numbered *with* transgressors," who not only took their place, but had become one with them. Had He not first had a real and vital relation to our sins, He could not have undergone their punishment. The *justice* of God's imputation of our sins to the Saviour's account rested upon His *oneness* with His people.

It is this fact which is iterated and reiterated all through the immediate context. "Both He that sanctifieth and they who are sanctified are all of one" (v. 11), "Behold I and the children which God hath given Me" (v. 13), "Forasmuch then as the children are partakers of flesh and blood, He also Himself likewise took part of the same" (v. 14), "Wherefore in all things it behooved Him to be made like unto His brethren" (v. 17). Why? Why? Here is the inspired answer: "*To* make propitiation for the sins of the people." That was only possible, we say again, because of His union with them. When Christ became one with His people their guilt became His, as the debts of a wife become by marriage the debts of the husband. This itself is acknowledged by Christ, "For innumerable evils hath compassed Me about: *Mine* iniquities have taken hold upon Me, so that I am not able to look up; they are more than the hairs of Mine head: therefore My heart faileth Me" (Psa. 40:12).

"To make propitiation for the sins of the people." In the light of all that has gone before in the Epistle, this statement is luminous indeed. The whole context shows us His *qualifications* for this stupendous work, a work which none but He could have performed. First, He was Himself "the Son," the brightness of God's glory and the very impress of His substance. Thus it was the dignity or Deity of His person which gave such infinite value to His work. Second, His moral perfections as Man, loving righteousness and hating iniquity (1:9), thus fulfilled every requirement of the law. Third, His union with His people which caused him "made sin for us, that we might be made the righteousness of God in Him."

The "propitiation" (which is the N.T. filling out of the O.T. "to make an atonement") which Christ made, was the perfect satisfaction that He offered to the holiness and justice of God on behalf of His people's sins, so that they could be righteously blotted out, removed for ever from before the face of God, "as far as the east is from the west." This sacrificial work of the Saviour's was a priestly act, as the words of our present verse clearly enough affirm.

For "the sins of *the* people" is parallel with Matt. 1:21; John 10:11. They plainly teach that atonement has been made for the sins of God's elect only. "The people" are manifestly parallel with the "heirs of salvation" (1:14), the "many sons" (2:10), the "brethren" (2:12), the "seed of Abraham" (2:16). It is with them alone Christ identified Himself. The "all of one" of 2:11 is expressly defined as being only between "He that sanctifieth and they who are sanctified." He laid hold of "the seed of Abraham," and not "the seed of Adam." He is the "Head" not of mankind, but of "the church which is His body" (Eph. 1:21—23). A *universal* atonement, which largely fails of its purpose, is an invention of Satan, with the design of casting dishonour upon Christ, who would thus be a defeated Saviour. A *general* atonement, abstractedly offered to Divine justice, which is theoretically sufficient for everybody, yet in itself efficient for nobody, is a fictitious imagination, which finds lodgment only in those who are vainly puffed up by a fleshly mind. A *particular* atonement, made for a definite people, all of whom shall enjoy the eternal benefits of it, is what is uniformly taught in the Word of God.

"For in that He Himself hath suffered being tempted He is able to succour them that are tempted" (v. 18). Here is the final reason given why it was necessary for the Son to become Man and die: He is the better able to succour His tried people. It was not simply His having been "tempted" that qualified Him, for God Himself may be tempted (Num. 14:22), though not with evil (James 1:13). So men may be tempted, yet as to be moved little or nothing thereby. But such temptations as make one *suffer,* do so work on him, as to draw out his pity to other tempted ones, and to help them as far as He can. It is *this* point which the Spirit has here seized.

"For in that He Himself hath suffered, being tempted." The subject of Christ's being tempted is an important one, for erroneous conceptions thereof necessarily produce a most dishonouring conception of His peerless Person. If the Lord wills, we hope to discuss it more fully when we come to 4:15, yet feel we must offer a few remarks upon it now. That the temptations to which our blessed Lord was subjected were *real* ones is evidenced from the inspired declaration that He "suffered" from them, but that they involved a conflict *within* Him, or that there was any possibility of His yielding thereto, must be emphatically denied. That He became Man with a human spirit and soul and body, and therefore possessed a human will, we fully believe; but that there was the slightest inclination for His heart or will to yield to evil solicitations, is wicked to so much as imagine. Not only was *His* humanity sinless, but it was "holy" (Luke 1:35), and His inherent holiness repelled all sin as water does fire.

The temptations or trials which Christ suffered here on earth must not be limited to those which came upon Him from Satan, though these are included. First, Christ suffered bodily hunger (Matt. 4:1, 2), etc. Second, His holy nature suffered acutely from the very presence of the foul Fiend, so that He said, "Get thee hence" (Matt. 4:10). Third, the temptations from the Pharisees and others "grieved" Him (Mark 3:5). Fourth, from the words of His own disciples, which were an "offence" unto Him (Matt. 16:23). Fifth, His greatest sufferings were from His Father's temptings or tryings of Him. (See John 12:27; Matt. 26:38, 39; 27:46). Note how in Luke 22:28, "My temptation," the Saviour spoke of His whole life as one unbroken experience of trial! How real and deep His "sufferings" were, many of the Messianic Psalms reveal.

The very fact that He *suffered* when "tempted" manifests His uniqueness. "He suffered, never yielded. *We* do not 'suffer' when we yield to temptation: the flesh takes pleasure in the things by which it is tempted. Jesus suffered, being tempted. It is important to observe that the flesh, when acted upon by its desires, does not suffer. Being tempted it, alas, enjoys. But when, according to the light of the Holy Spirit and fidelity of obedience, the spirit resists the attacks of the enemy, whether subtle or persecuting, then one suffers. This the Lord did, and this we have to do" (Mr. J. N. Darby).

"He is able to succour them that are tempted." Having passed through this scene as the Man of sorrows, He can, experimentally, gauge and feel the sorrows of His people, but let it be clearly understood that it is not the "flesh" in us which needs "succouring," but the new nature, the faithful heart that desires to please Him. We need "succour" *against* the flesh, to enable us to mortify our members which are upon the earth. Not yet has the promised inheritance been reached. We are still in the wilderness, which provides nothing which ministers to us spiritually. We are living in a world where everything is opposed to true godliness. We are called upon to "run the race which is set before us," to "fight the good fight of faith," and for this we daily need His "succour."

The Greek word for "He is able" implies both a fitness and willingness to do a thing. Christ is both competent and ready to undertake for His people. If we have not, it is because we ask not. The Greek word for "succour" here is very emphatic, and signifies a running to the cry of one, as a parent responding to the cry of distress from a child. A blessed illustration of Christ's "succouring" one of His own needy people is found in Matt. 14:30, 31, where we read that when Peter saw the wind was boisterous he was afraid, and began to sink, and cried "Lord save me." And then we are told, "And *immediately* Jesus stretched forth His hand and caught him."

On one occasion the Lord Jesus asked His disciples, "Believe ye that I am able to do this" (Matt. 9:28). And thus He ever challenges the faith of His own. To Abraham He said, "Is anything too hard for the Lord?" (Gen. 18:14). To Moses, who doubted whether the Lord would give flesh to Israel in the wilderness, He asked, "Is the Lord's hand waxed short?" (Num. 11:23). To Jeremiah the searching question was put, "Is there anything too hard for Me?"

(Jer. 32:27). So He still asks, "Believe *ye,* that I am able to do this?" Do *what?* we may ask. Whatever you are really in need of—give peace, impart assurance, grant deliverance, supply succour.

"He is able to succour them that are tempted." Remember who He is, the God-man. Remember the experiences through which He passed! He, too, has been in the place of trial: He, too, was tempted—to distrust, to despondency, to destroy Himself. Yes, He was tempted "in all points like as we are, sin excepted." Remember His present position, sitting at the right hand of the Majesty on high! How blessed then to know that He *is* "able" both to enter, sympathetically, into our sufferings and sorrows, and that He has power to "succour."

"As Man, a man of sorrows,
Thou hast suffered every woe,
And though enthroned in glory now,
Canst pity all Thy saints below."

Oh, what a Saviour is ours! The all-mighty God; yet the all-tender Man. One who is as far above us in His original nature and present glory as the heavens are above the earth: yet One who can be "touched with the feeling of our infirmities." One who is the Creator of the universe; yet One who became Man, lived His life on the same plane ours is lived, passed through the same trials we experience, and suffered not only as we do, but far more acutely. How well-fitted is such a One to be our great High Priest! How self-sufficient He is to supply our every need! And how completely is the wisdom and grace of God vindicated for having appointed His blessed Son, to be made, for a season, lower than the angels! May our love for Him be strengthened and our worship deepened by the contemplation of what has been before us in these first two chapters of Hebrews.

CHAPTER THIRTEEN

Christ Superior to Moses.

(3:1-6).

Our present portion introduces us to the third division of the Epistle, a division which runs on to 4:6. The first division, comprising but the three opening verses of the first chapter, evidences the superiority of Christ over the prophets. The second division, 1:4 to the end of chapter 2, sets forth the superiority of Christ over the angels. The one we are now commencing treats of the superiority of Christ over Moses. "The contents of this section may be stated briefly thus: That the Lord Jesus Christ, the mediator of the new covenant, is high above Moses, the mediator of the old dispensation, inasmuch as Jesus is the Son of God, and Lord *over* the house; whereas Moses is the servant of God, who is faithful *in* the house. And upon this doctrinal statement is based the exhortation, that we should not harden our hearts lest we fail to enter into that rest of which the possession of the promised land was only an imperfect type. This section consists of two parts—a doctrinal statement, which forms the basis, and an exhortation resting upon it" (Saphir).

Of all the godly characters brought before us in the O.T. scriptures, there is not one who has higher claims on our attentive consideration than the legislator of Israel. Whether we think of his remarkable infancy and childhood, his self-sacrificing renunciation (Heb. 11:24-26), the commission he received from God and his faithfulness in executing it, his devotion to Israel (Ex. 32:32), his honoured privileges (Ex. 31:18), or the important revolutions accomplished through his instrumentality; "it will be difficult to find," as another has said, "in the records either of profane or sacred history, an individual whose character is so well fitted at once to excite attachment and command veneration, and whose history is so replete at once with interest and instruction."

The history of Moses was remarkable from beginning to end. The hand of Providence preserved him as a babe, and the hand of God dug his grave at the finish. Between those termi he passed through the strangest and most contrastive vicissitudes which, surely, any mortal has ever experienced. The honours conferred upon him by God were much greater than any bestowed upon any other man, before or since. During the most memorable portion of their history, all of God's dealings with Israel were transacted through him. His position of nearness to Jehovah was remarkable, awesome, unique. He was in his own person, prophet, priest and king. Through him the whole of the Levitical economy was instituted. By him the Tabernacle was built. Thus we can well understand the high esteem in which the Jews held this favoured man of God—cf. John 9:28, 29.

Yet great as was Moses, the Holy Spirit in this third section of Hebrews calls upon us to consider One who so far excelled him as the heavens are above the earth. First, Christ was the immeasurable superior of Moses in His own *person*: Moses was a man of God, Christ was God Himself. Moses was the fallen descendant of Adam, conceived in sin and shapen in iniquity; Christ was sinless, impeccable, holy. Again; Christ was the immeasurable superior of Moses in His *Offices*. Moses was a prophet, through whom God spake; Christ was Himself "the Truth," revealing perfectly the whole mind, will, and heart of God. Moses executed priestly functions (Ex. 24:6; 32:11); but Christ is the "great High Priest." Moses was "king in Jeshurun" (Deut. 33:5); Christ is "King of kings." To mention only one other comparison, Christ was the immeasurable superior of Moses in His *work*. Moses delivered Israel from Egypt, Christ delivers His people from the everlasting burnings. Moses built an earthly tabernacle, Christ is now preparing a place for us on High. Moses led Israel across the wilderness but not into the Canaan itself; Christ will actually bring many sons "unto glory." May the Holy Spirit impress our hearts more and more with the exalted dignity and unique excellency of our Saviour.

"Wherefore, holy brethren, partakers of the heavenly calling, consider the Apostle and High Priest of our profession, Christ Jesus" (v. 1). There are three things in this verse which claim our attention: the exhortation given, the people addressed, the characters in which Christ is here contemplated. The exhortation is a call to "consider" Christ. The people addressed are "holy brethren, partakers of the heavenly calling." The characters in which the Saviour is viewed are "the Apostle and High Priest."

"Wherefore." This word gives the connecting link between the two chapters which precede and the two that follow. It is a perfect transition, for it looks both ways. In regard to that which goes before, our present verse makes known the *use* we are to make of it; we are to "consider" Christ, to have our hearts fixed upon Him who is "altogether lovely." In regard to that which follows, this basic exhortation lays a foundation for the succeeding admonitions: if we render obedience to *this* precept, then we shall be preserved from the evils which overtook Israel of old—hardening of the heart, grieving the Lord, missing our "rest."

The exhortation given here is, "Wherefore. . . consider the Apostle and High Priest of our profession." Three questions call for answers: what is meant by "considering" Him; why we should do so; the special characters in which He is to be considered. There are no less than eleven Greek words in the N.T. all rendered "consider," four of them being simple ones; seven, compounds. The one employed by the Holy Spirit in Heb. 3:1 signifies to thoroughly think of the matter, so as to arrive at a fuller knowledge of it. It was the word used by our Lord in His "consider the ravens, consider the lilies" (Luke 12:24, 27). It is the word which describes Peter's response to the vision of the sheet let down from heaven: "I considered and saw fourfooted beasts" (Acts 11:6). It is found again in Matt. 7:3, Rom. 4:19, Heb. 10:24. In Acts 7:31 "katanoeo" is rendered "to behold." In Luke 20:23 it is translated "perceived." In all, the Greek word is found fourteen times in the N.T.

To "consider" Christ as here enjoined, means to thoroughly ponder who and what He is; to attentively weigh His dignity, His excellency, His authority; to think of what is *due* to Him. It is failure to thoroughly weigh important considerations which causes us to let them "slip" (Heb. 2:1). On the other hand, it is by diligently pondering things of moment and value that the understanding is enabled to better apprehend them, the memory to retain them, the heart to be impressed, and the individual to make a better use of them. To "consider" Christ means to *behold* Him, not simply by a passing glance or giving to Him an occasional thought, but by the heart being fully occupied with Him. "Set Me as a seal upon thine heart" (Song of Sol. 8:6), is His call to us. And it is our failure at this point which explains why we know so little about Him, why we love Him so feebly, why we trust Him so imperfectly.

The motive presented by the Spirit here as to *why* we should so "consider" Christ is intimated in the opening "Wherefore." It draws a conclusion from all that precedes. Because Christ is the One through whom Deity is now fully and finally manifested, because He is the Brightness of God's glory and the very Impress of His substance; because, therefore, He has by inheritance obtained a more excellent name than the angels; because He, in infinite grace, became "all of one" with those that He came to redeem, having made propitiation for the sins of His people; because He is now seated at the right hand of the Majesty on High, and while there is "a merciful and faithful High Priest;" because He has Himself suffered being tempted and is able to succor them who are tempted;—therefore, He is infinitely worthy of our constant contemplation and adoration. The opening "Wherefore" is also an anticipatory inference from what follows: because Christ is worthy of more honour than Moses, therefore, "consider" Him.

There are two special characters in which the Holy Spirit here bids us contemplate Christ. First, as "the Apostle." This has reference to the *prophetical* office of Christ, the title being employed because an "apostle" was the highest minister appointed in N.T. times. An apostleship had more honours conferred upon it than any other position in the church (Eph. 4:11): thus the excellency of Christ's prophetic office is magnified. The term apostle means one "sent forth" of God, endowed with authority as His ambassador. In John's Gospel Christ is frequently seen as the "Sent One," 3:34, 5:36, etc. The general function of Christ as a prophet, an apostle, a minister of the Word, was to make known the will of His Father unto His people. This He did, see John 8:26 etc. His special call to that function was immediate: "as My Father hath sent Me, so send I you" (John 20:21).

Christ is more than an apostle, He is *"the* Apostle," that is why none others, not even Paul, are mentioned in this Epistle. He eclipses all others. He was the *first* apostle, the twelve being appointed by Him. His apostolic jurisdiction was more extensive than others; Peter was an apostle of the circumcision. Paul of the Gentiles; but Christ preached both to them that were nigh *and* to them that were far off (Eph. 2:17). He received the Spirit more abundantly than any other (John 3:34). With Him the Messenger was the message: He was Himself "the Truth." The miracles He wrought (the "signs of an apostle" II Cor. 12:12) were mightier and more numerous than those of others. Verily, Christ is "the Apostle," for in *all* things He has the pre-eminence. The special duty for us arising therefrom is, "Hear ye Him" (Matt. 17:5)—cf. Deut. 18:15, 18.

The second character in which we are here bidden to "consider" Christ Jesus, is as the "High Priest of our profession." As the priesthood of Christ will come before us, D.V., in detail in the later chapters, only a few remarks thereon will now be offered. As we have already been told, the Lord Jesus is "a merciful and faithful High Priest in things pertaining to God" (2:17). This at once gives us the principal feature which differentiates His priestly from His prophetic office. As Prophet, Christ is God's representative to His people; as "Priest," He is their representative before God.

As the Apostle He speaks *to* us from God, as our High Priest He speaks *for* us to God. The two offices are conjoined in John 13:3, "He was from God, and went to God." Thus He fills the whole space between God and us: as Apostle He is close to me; as Priest, He is close to God.

"Of our profession." The Greek word here is a compound and properly signifies "a consent." In the N.T. it is used for the confession of a thing (1 Tim. 6:12, 13), and to set forth the faith which Christians profess (Heb. 4:14). Here it may be taken either for an act on our part—the confessing Christ to be "the Apostle and High Priest," or, the subject matter *of* the faith we profess. Christians are not ashamed to own Him, for He is not ashamed to own them. The apostleship and priesthood of Christ are the distinguishing subjects of our faith, for Christianity centers entirely around the person of Christ. The confession is that which faith makes, see Heb. 10:23. The cognate of this word is found in Heb. 11:13 and 13:15, "giving thanks:" these two references emphasizing the "stranger and pilgrim" character of this profession, of which Christ Jesus is the Apostle and High Priest.

It remains now for us to notice the people to whom this exhortation is addressed: they are denominated "holy brethren, partakers of the heavenly calling." These Hebrews were addressed as "brethren" because they belonged spiritually to the family of God. "He evidently refers to the blessed truth just announced, that Jesus, the Son of God, is not ashamed to call us brethren" (2:11). He means therefore those who by the Spirit of God have been born again, and who can call God their Father. He addresses those of God who are in Christ Jesus, who were quickened together with Him; for when He rose from the dead He was 'the first-born among many brethren'. He calls them 'holy brethren,' because upon this fact of brotherhood is based their sanctification: 'He that sanctifieth and they who are sanctified are all of one' " (Saphir). No doubt the "holy brethren" was also designed to distinguish them from their brethren according to the flesh, the unbelieving Jews. By his use of this appellation the apostle to the Gentiles evidenced his interest in and love for the Hebrews: he acknowledged and esteemed them as "brethren."

"What an interesting and delightful view is thus presented to our minds of genuine Christians scattered all over the earth — belonging to every kindred, and people, and tongue, and nation — distinguished from one another in an almost infinite variety of ways, as to talent, temper, education, rank, circumstances, yet bound together by an invisible band, even the faith of the truth, to the one great object of their confidence, and love, and obedience, Christ

Jesus — forming one great brotherhood, devoted to the honor and service of His Father and their Father, His God and their God! Do *you* belong to this holy brotherhood? The question is an important one. For answer, note Christ's words in Matt. 12:50" (Dr. J. Brown).

"Partakers of the heavenly calling." This at once serves to emphasize the superiority of Christianity over Judaism, which knew only an earthly calling, with an earthly inheritance. The word "partakers" signifies "sharers of." The calling wherewith the Christian is called (Eph. 4:1) is *heavenly,* because of its origin — it proceeds from Heaven; because of the means used — the Spirit and the Word, which have come from Heaven; because of the sphere of our citizenship (Phil. 3:20); because of the end to which we are called — an eternal Heaven. Thus would the Holy Spirit press upon the sorely-tried Hebrews the inestimable value of their privileges.

Finally, the whole of this appellation should be viewed in the light of the relation between those addressed and Christ. How is it possible for sinful worms of the earth to be thus denominated? Because of their union with the incarnate Son, whose excellency is imputed to them, and whose position they share. We are partakers of the heavenly calling because He, in wondrous condescension, partook of our earthly lot. What He has, we have; where He is, we are. He is the Holy One of God, therefore are we holy. He has been "made higher than the heavens," therefore are we "partakers of the heavenly calling!" Just so far as our hearts really lay hold of this, shall we walk as "strangers and pilgrims" here. Where our "Treasure" (Christ) is, there will our hearts be also. That is why we are here bidden to "consider" Him.

"Who was faithful to Him that appointed Him, as also Moses was in all His house" (v. 2). "To speak of Moses to the Jews was always a very difficult and delicate matter. It is hardly possible for Gentiles to understand or realize the veneration and affection with which the Jews regard Moses, the man of God. All their religious life, all their thoughts about God, all their practices and observances, all their hopes of the future, everything connected with God, is with them also connected with Moses. Moses was the great apostle unto them, the man sent unto them of God, the mediator of the old covenant" (Saphir). Admire then the perfect wisdom of the Holy Spirit so plainly evidenced in our passage. Before taking up Christ's superiority over Moses, He points first to a resemblance between them, making mention of the "faithfulness" of God's servant. Ere taking this up let us dwell on the first part of the verse.

"Who was faithful to Him that appointed Him." The chief qualification of an apostle or ambassador is, that he be *faithful*. Faithfulness signifies two things: a trust committed, and a proper discharge of that trust. "Our Lord had a trust committed to Him . . . this trust He faithfully discharged. He sought not His own glory, but the glory of Him that sent Him; He ever declared His message to be not His own, but the Father's; and He declared the whole will or word of God that was committed unto Him" (Dr. J. Owen). Christ was ever faithful to the One who sent Him. This was His chief care from beginning to end. As a boy, "I must be about My Father's business" (Luke 2:49). In the midst of His ministry, "I must work the works of Him that sent Me" (John 9:4). At the finish, "Not as I will, but as Thou wilt" (Matt. 26:39).

"As also Moses was faithful in all His house." "The key to the whole paragraph is to be found in the meaning of the figurative term 'house,' which so often occurs in it (just seven times, A.W.P.). By supposing that the word 'house' here is equivalent to *edifice*, the whole passage is involved in inextricable perplexity. 'House' here signifies a family or household. This mode of using the word is an exemplification of a common figure of speech, by which the name of what contains is given to what is contained. A man's family usually resides in his house, and hence is called his house. This use of the word is common in the Bible: 'The House of Israel,' 'the House of Aaron,' 'the House of David,' are very common expressions for the children, the descendants, the families of Israel, Aaron and David. We have the same mode of speech in our own language, 'the House of Stuart,' 'the House of Hanover.' Keeping this remark in view, the verse we have now read will be found, short as it is, to contain in it the following statements: — Moses was appointed by God over the whole of His family: Moses was faithful in discharging the trust committed to him. Jesus is appointed by God over the whole of His family: Jesus is faithful in the discharge of the trust committed to Him" (Dr. J. Brown).

"The house, the building, means the children of God, who by faith, as lively stones, are built upon Christ Jesus the Foundation, and who are filled with the Holy Ghost; in whom God dwells, as in His temple, and in whom God is praised and manifested in glory. The illustration is very simple and instructive. We are compared unto stones, and as every simile is defective, we must add, not *dead* stones, but *lively* stones, as the apostle in his epistle to the Ephesians speaks of the building *growing*. The way in which we are brought unto the Lord Jesus Christ and united with Him is not by *building*, but by *believing*. The builders rejected the 'chief corner-stone' (Psa. 118:22); but 'coming unto Christ' (1 Peter 2:4, 5), simply believing, 'ye also, as lively stones, are built up a spiritual house.' When we go about the works of the law we are trying to build, and as long as we build we are not built. When we give up working, then by faith the Holy Ghost adds us to Christ, and grafts up into the living Vine, who is also the Foundation. We are rooted and grounded. The house is one, and all the children of God are united in the Spirit" (Saphir).

That which the Spirit has here singled out for mention in connection with Moses, the typical "apostle," is that he was *faithful* in all God's house, faithful in the discharge of his responsibilities concerning the earthly family over which Jehovah placed him. Although he failed personally in his faith, he was faithful as an "apostle." He never withheld a word which the Lord had given him, either from Pharaoh or from Israel. In erecting the tabernacle all things were made "according to" the pattern which he had received in the mount. When he came down from Sinai and beheld the people worshipping the golden calf, he did not spare, but called for the sword to smite them (Ex. 32:27, 28). In all things he conformed to the instructions which he had received from Jehovah (Ex. 40:16).

"For this Man was counted worthy of more glory than Moses, inasmuch as He who hath builded the house hath more honour than the house" (v. 3). The apostle now proceeds to present Christ's superiority over Moses. But ere considering this, let us admire again the heavenly wisdom granted him in the method of presenting his argument. In the previous verse he has acknowledged the greatness of Moses, and here he also allows that he was worthy of glory, or praise. This would at once show that Paul was no enemy of Judaism, seeking to disparage and revile it. Equally striking is it to note how, in now turning the eyes of the Hebrews to One who is infinitely greater than Moses, he does not speak of his *failures* — his slaying of the Egyptians (Ex. 2), his slowness in responding to the Lord's call (Ex. 3, 4), his angered smiting of the rock (Num. 20); but by presenting the *glories* of Christ.

This third verse presents to us the first of the evidences here furnished of the superiority of Christ over Moses: He is the Builder of God's house; this, Moses never was. Its opening "For" looks back to the first verse, advancing a reason or argument *why* the Hebrews should "consider" the Apostle and High Priest of their confession, namely, because He is worthy of more glory than Moses the typical apostle. "The phrase, 'to build the house,' is equivalent to, be the founder of the family. This kind of phraseology is by no means uncommon. It is said, Ex. 1:21, that God 'made houses' to those humane women who refused to second the barbarous policy of Pharaoh in destroying the infants of the Israelites: i.e. He established their families, giving a numerous and flourishing offspring. In Ruth 4:11, Rachel and Leah are said to have built the house of Israel. And Nathan says to David, 2 Sam. 7:11: 'Also the Lord telleth thee that He will make thee a house;' and what the meaning of that phrase is, we learn from what immediately follows, v. 12" (Dr. J. Brown).

The contrast thus drawn between Christ and Moses is both a plain and an immense one. Though officially raised over it, Moses was not the founder of the Israelitish family, but simply a member of it. With the Apostle of our confession it is far otherwise. He is not only at the head of God's family (Heb. 2:10, 13 — His "sons," His "children"), but He is also the Builder or the Founder of it. As we read in Eph. 2:10, "for we are His workmanship, created in (or "by") Christ Jesus." Moses did not make men children of God; Christ does. Moses came to a people who were already the Lord's by covenant relationship; whereas Christ takes up those who are dead in trespasses and sins, and creates them anew. Thus as the founder of the family is entitled to the highest honor from the family, so Christ is worthy of more glory than Moses.

"For every house is builded by some man; but He that built all things is God" (v. 4). Here the Spirit brings in a yet higher glory of Christ. The connection is obvious. In the preceding verse it has been argued: the builder is entitled to more honor than the building; as then Christ is the Builder of a family, and Moses simply the member of one, He must be counted worthy "of more glory." In v. 4 proof of this is given, as the opening "for" denotes. The proof is twofold: Christ has not only built "the house," but "all things." Christ is not only the Mediator, "appointed" by God (v. 2), but He *is* God. To how much greater glory then is He justly entitled!

"For every house is builded by some one," should be understood in its widest signification, regarding "house" both literally and figuratively. Every human habitation has been built, every human family has been founded, by some man. So "He that built all things" is to be taken without qualification. The entire universe has been built ("framed," Heb. 11:3) by Christ, for "all things were made by Him" (John 1:3), all things "that are in heaven, and that are in earth, visible and invisible" (Col. 1:16). Therefore Christ made Moses, as the whole family of Israel. "He that built all things is *God*." The Holy Spirit here designedly uses the Divine title because the work attributed to Christ (building the family of God) is a Divine work: because it proves, without controversy, that Christ is greater than Moses; because it ratifies what was declared in the first chapter concerning the Mediator, that He is true God. Therefore should all "honor the Son even as they honor the Father" (John 5:23).

"And Moses verily was faithful in all His house, as a servant, for a testimony of those things which were to be spoken after; but Christ as a Son over His own house" (vv. 5, 6). These words bring before us the next proofs for the superiority of Christ over Moses: the typical apostle was but a servant, Christ is "Son;" the one was but a testimony unto the other. The position which Divine grace allotted to Moses was one of great honor, nevertheless he ministered before Jehovah only as a "servant." The words "in all His house" should be duly pondered: other servants were used in various parts of the family, but the glory of Moses was that he was used in every part of it; that is to say, he was entrusted with the care and regulation of the whole family of Israel. Still, even this, left him incomparably the inferior of the Lord Jesus, for He was a Son not "*in* all His house," but "*over* His own House."

"And Moses verily was faithful in all His house, as a servant." Here again the apostle would subdue the prejudices of the Jews against Christianity. He was not discrediting the greatness of Moses. So far from it, he *repeats* what he had said in v. 2, emphasizing it with the word "verily." Yet the faithfulness of Moses was as a "servant," a reminder to all, that this is the quality which should ever characterize all "servants." The word "*as* a servant" has the same force as in John 1:14, "we beheld His glory, the glory *as* of the Only-begotten of the Father:" thus the "as" brings out the *reality* of the character in view. Moses faithfully conducted himself *as* a "servant," he did not act as a lord. This was evidenced by his great reverence for God (Ex. 3:6), his earnestly desiring an evidence of God's favour (Ex. 34:9), his preferring the glory of the Lord to his own glory (Heb. 11:24-26, Ex. 32:10-12), and in his meekness before men. (Num. 12:3).

"For a testimony of those things which were to be spoken after." This was a word much needed by the Jews. So far from the revelation of Christianity clashing with the Pentateuch, much there was an anticipation of it. Moses ordered all things in the typical worship of the house so that they might be both a witness and pledge of that which should afterwards be more fully exhibited through the Gospel. Therefore did Christ say, "For had ye believed Moses, ye would have believed Me: for he wrote of Me" (John 5:46). And on another occasion we are told, "And beginning at *Moses* and all the prophets, He expounded unto them in all the Scriptures the things concerning Himself" (Luke 24:27).

"But Christ as a Son over His own house." Here is the final proof that Christ is "counted worthy of more glory than Moses." The proofs presented in this passage of our Lord's immeasurable superiority are seven in number, and may be set forth thus: Moses was an apostle, Christ "the Apostle" (v. 1). Moses was a member of an "house:" Christ was the Builder of one (v. 3). Moses was connected with a single house, Christ "built *all* things," being the Creator of the universe (v. 4). Moses was a man; Christ, God (v. 4). Moses was but a "servant" (v. 5); Christ, the "Son." Moses was a "testimony" of things to be spoken after (v. 5), Christ supplied the substance and fulfilment of what Moses witnessed unto. Moses was but a servant in the house of Jehovah, Christ was Son over His *own* house (v. 6). The Puritan Owen quaintly wrote, "Here the apostle taketh leave of Moses; he treats not about him any more; and therefore he gives him, as it were, an honourable burial. He puts this glorious epitaph on his grave: "Moses, a faithful servant of the Lord in His whole house."

"But Christ as a Son over His own house, whose house are we" (v. 6). Here the "house" is plainly defined: it is a spiritual house, made up of believers in Christ. Not only are the "brethren" of v. 1 partakers of the heavenly calling, but they are members of the spiritual family of God, for in them He dwells. How well calculated to comfort and encourage the sorely-tried Hebrews were these words "whose house are we!" What compensation was this for the loss of their standing among the unbelieving Jews!

"If we hold fast the confidence and the rejoicing of the hope firm unto the end" (v. 6). Do these words weaken the force of what has last been said? In nowise; they contained a much-needed warning. "There were great difficulties, circumstances calculated especially to effect the Jew, who, after receiving the truth with joy might be exposed to great trial, and so in danger of giving up his hope. It was, besides, particularly hard for a Jew at first to put these two facts together: a Messiah come, and entered into glory; and the people who belonged to the Messiah left in sorrow, and shame, and suffering here below" (W. Kelly). The Hebrews were ever in danger of subordinating the future to the present, and of forsaking the invisible (Christ in heaven) for the visible (Judaism on earth), of giving up a profession which involved them in fierce persecution. Hence their need of being reminded that the proof of *their* belonging to the house of Christ was that they remained steadfast to Him to the end of their pilgrimage.

"If we hold fast the confidence and the rejoicing of the hope firm unto the end." As the same thought is, substantially, embodied again in v. 14, we shall now waive a full exposition and application of these words. Suffice it now to say that the Holy Spirit is here pressing, once more, on these Hebrews, what had been affirmed in 2:1, "Therefore we ought to give the more earnest heed to the things which we have heard, lest at any time we should let them slip." Let each Christian reader remember that our Lord has said, "If ye *continue* in My word, then are ye My disciples indeed" (John 8:31).

CHAPTER FOURTEEN

Christ Superior to Moses.

(Heb. 3:7-12)

In the first six verses of our present chapter four things were before us. First, the call to "consider" the Apostle and High Priest of our profession. Of old, Moses was God's apostle or ambassador to Israel, Aaron, the high priest. But Christ combines both these offices in His own person. Second, the superiority of Christ over Moses: this is set forth in seven details which it is unnecessary for us to specify again. Third, the one thing which the Spirit of God singles out from the many gifts and excellencies which Divine grace had bestowed upon Moses, was his "faithfulness" (vv. 2, 5); so too is it there said of Christ Jesus that He was "faithful to Him that appointed Him" (v. 2). Fourth, the assertion that membership in the household of Christ is evidenced, chiefly, by holding fast the confidence and rejoicing of the hope firm unto the end (v. 6). That there is an intimate connection between these four things and the contents of our present passage will appear in our exposition thereof.

"If we hold fast the confidence and the rejoicing of the hope firm unto the end." The "hope" mentioned here is that made known by the Gospel (Col. 1:23), the hope which is laid up for God's people in Heaven (Col. 1:5), the hope of glory (Col. 1:27). Christians have been begotten unto a living hope (1 Peter 1:3), that "blessed hope" (Titus 2:13), namely, the return of our God and Saviour Jesus Christ, when He shall come to take us unto Himself, to make us like Himself, to have us forever with Himself; when all God's promises concerning us shall be made good. The reference to the holding fast the "confidence" of this hope is not subjective, but objective. It signifies a fearless profession of the Christian faith. It is to be "ready *always* to give an answer to every man that asketh you, a reason of the hope that is in you, with meekness and fear" (1 Peter 3:15). Stephen is an illustration. Then, this hope is also to be held fast with "rejoicing" firm unto the end: Paul is an example of this, Acts 20:24.

What follows in our present portion contains a solemn and practical application of that which we have briefly reviewed above. Here the apostle is moved to remind the Hebrews of the *un*-faithfulness of Israel in the past and of the dire consequences which followed their failure to hold fast unto the end of their wilderness pilgrimage the confidence and rejoicing of the hope which God had set before them. A passage is quoted from the 95th Psalm which gives most searching point to both that which precedes and to that which follows. The path in which God's people are called to walk is that of faith, and such a path is necessarily full of testings, that is, of difficulties and trials, and many are the allurements for tempting us to wander off into "By-path meadow." Many, too, are the warnings and danger-signals which the faithfulness of God has erected; unto one of them we shall now turn.

"Wherefore" (v. 7). This opening word of our present passage possesses a threefold force. First, it is a conclusion drawn from all that precedes. Second, it prefaces the application of what is found in 3:1-6. Third, it lays a foundation for what follows. The reader will observe that the remaining words of v. 7 and all of vv. 8 to 11 are placed in brackets, and we believe rightly so, the sentence being completed in v. 12: "Wherefore take heed, brethren, lest there be in any of you an evil heart of unbelief, in departing from the living God."

The reasons for this exhortation have been pointed out above. First, because of the supreme excellency of our Redeemer, exalted high above all Israel's prophets, and given a name more excellent than any ever conferred on the angels; therefore, those who belong to Him should give good heed that they harden not their hearts against Him, nor depart from Him. Second, because the Apostle, Christ Jesus, is worthy of more honour than Moses, then how incumbent it is upon His people to be especially watchful that they be not, by any means, turned from that obedience which He requires and which is most certainly due Him. Third, in view of the lamentable history of Israel, who, despite God's wondrous favours to them, hardened their hearts, grieved Him, and so provoked Him to wrath, that He sware they should not enter into His rest, how much on our guard we need to be of "holding fast" the confidence and rejoicing of our hope "firm unto the end!"

"As the Holy Spirit saith." Striking indeed is it to mark the way in which the apostle introduces the quotation made from the O.T. It is from the 95th Psalm, but the human instrument that was employed in the penning of it is ignored, attention being directed to its Divine Author, the One who "moved" the Psalmist — cf. 2 Peter 1:20, 21. The reason for this, here, seems to be because Paul would press upon these Hebrews the weightiness, the Divine authority of the words he was about to quote: consider well that what follows are the words of the Holy Spirit, so that you may promptly and unmurmuringly submit yourselves thereunto.

"As the Holy Spirit saith." Striking indeed is it to mark the way it links up with Heb. 1:1 and 2:3. In the former it is God, the Father, who "spake." In 2:3, "How shall we escape if we neglect so great salvation, which at the first began to be *spoken* by the Lord?:" there it is the Son. Here in 3:7 the Speaker is the Spirit; thus, by linking together these three passages we hear all the Persons of the Godhead. Observe, next, the tense of the verb used here; it is not "the Holy Spirit said," but "saith:" it is an ever-present, living message to God's people in each succeeding generation. "Whatever was given by inspiration from the Holy Ghost, and is recorded in the Scripture for the use of the Church, He continues therein to speak it unto us unto this day" (Dr. J. Owen). Let the reader also carefully compare the seven-times-repeated, "he that hath an ear to hear, let him hear what the Spirit *saith* unto the churches" in Rev. 2 and 3.

"As the Holy Spirit saith." Dr. Gouge has pointed out how that this sentence teaches us four things about the Holy Spirit. First, that He is true God: for "*God* spake by the mouth of David" (Acts 4:25). " God" spake by the prophets (Heb. 1:1), and they "spake as they were moved by the Holy Spirit" (2 Peter 1:21). Second, the Holy Spirit is a distinct person: He "saith." An influence, a mere abstraction, cannot speak. Third, the Holy Spirit subsisted before Christ was manifested in the flesh, for He spake through David. True, He is called, "the Spirit of Christ," yet that He was before His incarnation is proven by Gen. 1:2 and other scriptures. Fourth, He is the Author of the O.T. Scriptures, therefore are they of Divine inspiration and authority.

"To-day if ye will hear His voice, harden not your hearts" (vv. 7:8). Here begins the apostle's quotation from Psa. 95, the first portion of which records a most fervent call (vv. 1, 6) for the people of God to be joyful, and come before Him as worshippers. Most appropriate was the reference to this Psalm here, for the contents of its first seven verses contain, virtually an amplification of the "consider" of 3:1. There the Hebrews were enjoined to be occupied with Christ, and if their hearts were engaged with His surpassing excellency and exalted greatness, then would they "come before His presence with thanksgiving, and make a joyful noise unto Him with psalms" (Psa. 95:2).

Their Apostle and High Priest had "built all things" (Heb. 3:4), being none other than God. The same truth is avowed in Psalm 95:3-5, "For the Lord is a great God, and a great King above all gods. In His hand are the deep places of the earth: the strength of the hills is His also. The sea is His, and He made it: and His hands formed the dry land." The apprehension of this will prepare us for a response to what follows, "O come, let us worship, and bow down: let us kneel before the Lord our Maker. For He is our God; and we are the people of His pasture, and the sheep of His hand" (Psa. 95:6, 7).

The next thing in the Psalm is, "To-day, *if* ye will hear His voice harden not your heart." So the next thing in Heb. 3 is, "whose house are we *if* we hold fast the confidence and the rejoicing of the hope firm unto the end." Thus the Psalmist admonished those addressed in his day to hearken to the voice of the Lord, and not to harden their hearts against Him as had their ancestors before them. By quoting this here in Heb. 3, the apostle at once intimated what is the *opposite* course from holding fast their confidence.

"To-day" signifies the time present, yet so as to include a continuance of it. It is not to be limited to twenty-four hours, instead, this term sometimes covers a present interval which consists of many days, yea years. In Heb. 3:13 it is said, "But exhort one another daily, while it is called To-day." So in Heb. 13:8 we read, "Jesus Christ the same yesterday, and to-day and forever." So in our text. As that present time wherein David lived was to him and those then alive "to-day", so that present time in which the apostle and the Hebrews lived was to them "to-day," and the time wherein we now live, is to us "to-day." It covers that interval while men are alive on earth, while God's grace and blessing are available to them. It spans the entire period of our wilderness pilgrimage. Thus the "end" of Heb. 3:6 is the close of the "to-day" in v. 7.

"If ye will hear His voice." "Unto you, O men I call; and My voice is to the sons of man" (Prov. 8:4). But no doubt the immediate reference in our text is unto those professing to be God's people. The "voice" of God is the signification of His will, which is the rule of our obedience. His will is made known in His Word, which is a *living* Word, by which the voice of God is now uttered. But, alas, we are capable of closing our ears to His voice. Of old God complained, "The ox knoweth his owner, and the ass his master's crib: but Israel doth not know. My people doth not consider" (Isa. 1:3). To "hear" God's voice signifies to attend reverently to what He says, to diligently ponder, to readily receive, and to heed or obey it. It is the hardening of our hearts which prevents us, really, hearing His voice, as the next clause intimates. To it we now turn.

"If ye will hear His voice, harden not your hearts." It is to the *heart* God's Word is addressed, that moral centre of our beings out of which are the issues of life (Prov. 4:23). There may be conviction of the conscience, the assent of the intellect, the admiration of understanding, but unless the heart is moved there is no response. A tender heart is a pliable and responsive one; a hard heart is obdurate and rebellious. Here hardening of the heart is attributed to the creature: it is due to impenitency (Rom. 2:5), unbelief (Heb. 3:12), disobedience (Psa. 95:8).

"It appears that unto this sinful hardening of the heart which the people in the wilderness were guilty of, and which the apostle here warns the Hebrews to avoid, there are three things that do concur: 1. A *sinful neglect,* in not taking due notice of the ways and means whereby God calls any unto faith and obedience. 2. A *sinful forgetfulness and casting out* of the heart and mind such convictions as God by His word and works, His mercies and judgments, His deliverances and afflictions, at any time is pleased to cast into them and fasten upon them. 3. An *obstinate cleaving of the affections* unto carnal and sensual objects, practically preferring them above the motives unto obedience that God proposeth unto us. Where these things are so, the hearts of men are so hardened, that in an ordinary way, they cannot hearken unto the voice of God. Such is the nature, efficacy and power of the voice or word of God, that men cannot withstand or resist it without a sinful hardening of themselves against it. Every one to whom the word is duly revealed, who is not converted of God, doth *voluntarily* oppose his own obstinancy unto its efficacy and operation. If men will add new obstinacy and hardness to their minds and hearts, if they will fortify themselves against the word with prejudices and dislikes, if they will resist its work through a love to their lusts and corrupt affections, God may justly leave them to perish, and to be filled with the fruit of their own ways" (Dr. J. Owen).

"Harden not your hearts, as in the provocation, in the day of temptation in the wilderness" (v. 8). The reference here is to what is recorded in the early verses of Ex. 17. There we are told that the congregation of Israel journeyed to Rephidim, where there was "no water for the people to drink." Instead of them counting on Jehovah to supply their need, as He had at Marah (Ex. 15:25) and in the wilderness of Sin (16:4), they "did chide with Moses" (v. 2), "and when they thirsted, the people murmured against Moses, and said, Wherefore is this that thou hast brought us up out of Egypt, to kill us and our children and our cattle with thirst?" (v. 3). Though Moses cried unto the Lord, and the Lord graciously responded by bringing water out of the rock for them, yet God's servant was greatly displeased, for in v. 7 we are told, "And he called the name of the place Massah (Temptation) and Meribah (Strife), because of the chiding of the children of Israel and because they tempted the Lord, saying, Is the Lord among us, or not".

Once more we would point out the oppositeness of this quotation to the case of the Hebrews. "The thought of Moses (in vv. 1 to 5 A. W. P.) naturally suggests Israel in the wilderness. Faithful was the mediator, through whom God dealt with them; but was Israel faithful? God spake: did they obey? God showed them wonder signs: did they trust and follow in faith? And if Israel was not faithful unto Moses, and their unbelief brought ruin upon them, how much more guilty shall we be, and how much greater our danger, if we are not faithful unto the Lord Jesus" (Saphir).

It is not only true that the difficulties and trials of the way test us, but these testings reveal the state of our hearts — a crisis neither makes nor mars a man, but it does *manifest* him. While all is smooth sailing we appear to be getting along nicely. But are we? Are our minds stayed upon the Lord, or are we, instead, complacently resting in His temporal mercies? When the storm breaks, it is not so much that we fail under it, as that our habitual lack of leaning upon God, of daily walking in dependency upon Him, is made evident. Circumstances do not change us, but they do *expose* us. Paul rejoiced in the Lord when circumstances were congenial. Yes, and he also sang praises to Him when his back was bleeding in the Philippian dungeon. The fact is, that if we sing only when circumstances are pleasing to us, then our singing is worth nothing, and there is grave reason to doubt whether we are rejoicing "in *the Lord*" (Phil. 4:4) at all.

The reason Israel murmured at Meribah was because there was no water; they were occupied with their circumstances, they were walking by sight. The crisis they then faced only served to make manifest the state of their hearts, namely, an "evil heart *of unbelief*." Had their trust been in Jehovah, they would at once have turned to Him, spread their need before Him, and *counted* on Him to supply it. But their hearts were hardened. A most searching warning was this for the Hebrews. Their circumstances were most painful to the flesh. They were enduring a great fight of afflictions. How were they enduring it? If they were murmuring that would be the outward expression of unbelief within. Ah, it is easy to *profess* we are Believers, but the challenge still rings out, "What doth it profit, my brethren, though a man say he hath faith, and have not works?" (James 2:14).

"When your fathers tempted Me, proved Me, and saw My works forty years" (v. 9). The "when" looks back to what is mentioned in the previous verse. The "Day of Temptation in the wilderness" covered the whole period of Israel's journeyings from the Red Sea to Canaan. "The history of the Israelites is a history of continued provocation. In the wilderness of Sin they murmured for the want of bread, and God gave them manna. At Rephidim they murmured for the want of water, and questioned whether Jehovah was with them and He gave them water from the rock. In the wilderness of Sinai, soon after receiving the law, they made and worshipped a golden image. At Taberah they murmured for want of flesh and the quails were sent, followed by a dreadful plague. At Kadesh-barnea they refused to go up and take possession of the land of promise, which brought down on them the awful sentence referred to in the Psalm; and after that sentence was pronounced, they presumptuously attempted to do what they had formerly refused to do. All these things took place in little more than two years after they left Egypt. Thirty-seven years after this, we find them at Kadesh again, murmuring for want of water and other things. Soon after this, they complained of the want of bread, though they had manna in abundance, and were punished by the plague of fiery flying serpents. And at Shittim, their last station, they provoked the Lord by mingling in the impure idolatry of the Moabites. So strikingly true is Moses' declaration: 'Remember, and forget not, how thou provoked the Lord thy God to wrath in the wilderness: from the day that thou didst depart out of the land of Egypt, until ye came unto this place ye have been rebellious against the Lord', Deut. 9:7" (Dr. J. Brown).

"When your fathers tempted Me, proved Me, and saw My works forty years" (v. 9). Israel's terrible sins in the wilderness are here set forth under two terms: they "tempted" and "proved" Jehovah, the latter being added as an explanation of the former. To tempt one is to try or prove whether he be such as he is declared to be, or whether he can or will do such and such a thing. By tempting God Israel found out by experience that He was indeed the God He had made Himself known to be. In this passage the tempting of God is set down as a sin which provoked Him, and so is to be taken in its worst sense. Instead of believing His declaration, Israel acted as though they would discover, at the hazard of their own destruction, whether or not He would make good His promises and His threatenings.

"In particular men tempt God by two extremes: one is presumption, the other is distrustfulness. Both these arise from unbelief. That distrustfulness ariseth from unbelief is without all question. And however presumption may seem to arise from overmuch confidence, yet if it be narrowly searched into, we shall find that men presume upon unwarrantable courses, because they do not believe that God will do what is meet to be done, in His own way. Had the Israelites believed that God in His time and in His own way would have destroyed the Canaanites, they would not have presumed, against an express charge, to have gone against them without the ark of the Lord and without Moses, as they did, Num. 14:40 etc. Alas, what is man!

"Men do presumptuously tempt God, when, without warrant, they presume on God's extraordinary power and providence; that whereunto the devil persuaded Christ when he had carried Him up to a pinnacle of the temple, namely, to cast Himself down, was to tempt God; therefore, Christ gives him this answer, 'Thou shalt not tempt the Lord thy God,' Matt. 4:5-7. Men distrustfully tempt God when in distress they imagine that God cannot or will not afford sufficient succor. Thus did the king of Israel tempt God when he said, 'The Lord hath called these three kings together, to deliver them into the hand of Moab,' 2 Kings 3:13. So that prince who said 'Behold, if the Lord would make windows in heaven, might this thing be', 2 Kings 7:2" (Dr. W. Gouge).

"And saw My works forty years." This brings out the inexcusableness and heinousness of Israel's sin. It was not that Jehovah was a Stranger to them, for again and again He had shown Himself strong on their behalf. The "works" of God mentioned here are the many and great wonders which He did from the time that He first took them up in Egypt until the end of the wilderness journey. Some of them were works of *mercy*. In delivering them from enemies and dangers, and in providing for them things needful. Others were works of *judgment,* as the plagues upon the Egyptians, their destruction at the Red Sea, and His chastening of themselves. Still others were *manifestations* which He made of Himself, as by the Cloud which led them by day and by night, the awesome proofs of His presence on Sinai, and the Shekinah glory which filled the tabernacle. These were not "works" done in bygone ages, or in far-distant places, of which they had only heard; but were actually performed before them, upon them, which they "saw." What clearer evidence could they have of God's providence and power? Yet they tempted Him! The clearest evidences God grants to us have no effect upon unbelieving and obdurate hearts.

An unspeakably solemn warning is this for all who profess to be God's people to-day. A still more wonderful and glorious manifestation has God now made of Himself than any which Israel ever enjoyed. God has been manifested in flesh. The only-begotten Son has declared the Father. He has fully displayed His matchless grace and fathomless love by coming here and dying for poor sinners. When He left the earth, He sent the Holy Spirit, so that *we* now have not a Moses, but the third Person of the Trinity to guide us. God made known His laws unto Israel, but His complete Word is now in our hands. What more can He say, than to us He has said! How great is our responsibility; how immeasureably greater than Israel's is our sin and guilt, if we despise Him who speaks to us!

A further aggravation of Israel's sin is that they saw God's wondrous works for "forty years." God continued His wonders all that time: despite their unbelief and murmuring the manna was sent daily till the Jordan was crossed! Man's incredulity cannot hinder the workings of God's power: "What if some did not believe? shall their unbelief make the faith of God without effect? God forbid" (Rom. 3:3). An incredulous prince would not believe that God could give such plenty as He had promised when Samaria by a long siege was famished; yet, "it came to pass as the man of God had spoken" (2 Kings 7:18). Nor would the Jews, nor even the disciples of Christ, believe that the Lord Jesus would rise again from the dead: yet He did so on the third day. O the marvelous patience of God! May the realization of it melt and move our hearts to repentance and obedience.

"Wherefore I was grieved with that generation" (v. 10). In these words, and those which follow, we learn the fearful consequences of Israel's sin. "When God says He 'was grieved' He means that He was burdened, vexed, displeased beyond that forbearance could extend unto. This includes the judgment of God concerning the greatness of their sin with all its aggravations and His determinate purpose to punish them. Men live, speak and act as if they thought God very little concerned in what they do, especially in their sins; that either He takes no notice of them, or if He do, that He is not much concerned in them; or that He should be grieved at His heart — that is, have such a deep sense of man's sinful provocations — they have no mind to think or believe. They think that, as to thoughts about sins, God is altogether as themselves. But it is far otherwise, for God hath a *concernment of honour* in what we do; He makes us for His glory and honour, and whatsoever is contrary thereunto tends directly to His dishonour. And this God cannot but be deeply sensible of; He cannot deny Himself. He is also concerned as a God of *Justice.* His holiness and justice is His nature, and He needs no other reason to punish sin but Himself" (Dr. J. Owen).

"And said, They do alway err in their heart" (v. 10). To err in the heart signifies to draw the wicked and false conclusion that sin and rebellion pay better than subjection and obedience to God. Through the power of their depraved lusts, the darkness of their understandings, and the force of temptations, countless multitudes of Adam's fallen descendants imagine that a course of self-will is preferable to subjection unto the Lord. Sin deceives: it makes men call darkness light, bitter sweet, bondage liberty. The language of men's hearts is, "What is the Almighty, that we should serve Him? and what profit should we have, if we pray unto Him?" (Job 21:15). Note Israel "*alway* erred in their hearts," which evidenced the hopelessness of their state. They were radically and habitually evil. As Moses told them at the end, "Ye have been rebellious against the Lord from the day that I knew you" (Deut. 9:24).

"And they have not known My ways" (v. 10). The word "ways" is used in Scripture both of God's dispensations or providences and of His precepts. A way is that wherein one walks. It is not God's secret "ways" (Isa. 55:9, Rom. 9:33), but His manifest ways are here in view. His manifest ways are particularly His *works,* in which He declares Himself and exhibits His perfections, see Psa. 145:17. The works of God are styled His "ways" because we may see Him, as it were, walking therein: "they have seen Thy goings, O God" (Psa. 68:24). Now it is our duty to meditate on God's works or "ways" (Psa. 143:5), to admire and magnify the Lord in them (Psa. 138:4, 5), to acknowledge the righteousness of them (Psa. 145:17). God's precepts are also termed His way and "ways" (Psa. 119:27, 32, 33, 35), because they make known the paths in which He would have us walk. Israel's ignorance of God's ways, both His works and precepts, was a wilful one, for they neglected and rejected the means of knowledge which God afforded them; they obstinately refused to acquire a practical knowledge of them, which is the only knowledge of real value.

"So I sware in My wrath, They shall not enter into My rest" (v. 11). This was the fearful issue of Israel's sin. The patience of God was exhausted. Their inveterate unbelief and continued rebellion incensed Him. The sentence He pronounced against them was irrevocable, confirmed by His oath. The sentence was that they should not enter into Canaan, spoken of as a "rest" because entrance therein would have terminated their wilderness trials and travels; "God's rest," because it would complete His work of bringing Israel into the land promised their fathers, and because His sojournings (*see* Lev. 25:23) with His pilgrims would cease.

"We may observe, 1. When God expresseth great indignation in Himself against sin, it is to teach men the greatness of sin in themselves. 2. God gives the same stability unto His threatenings as unto His promises. Men are apt to think the *promises* are firm and stable, but as for the threatenings, they suppose some way or other they may be evaded. 3. When men have provoked God by their impenitency to decree their punishment irrevocably, they will find severity in the execution. 4. It is the presence of God alone that renders any place or condition good or desirable, 'they' shall not enter into My rest" (Dr. J. Owen).

"Take heed, brethren, lest there be in any of you an evil heart of unbelief, in departing from the living God" (v. 12). Here the apostle begins to make a practical application to the believing Hebrews of the solemn passage which has just been quoted from the 95th Psalm. He warns them against the danger of apostatising. This is clear from the expression "in departing from the living God." The same Greek verb is rendered "fall away" in Luke 8:13, and in its noun form signifies "apostasy" in 2 Thess. 2:3. Such apostasy is the inevitable outcome of giving way to an "evil heart of unbelief," against which the apostle bids those to whom he was writing to "take heed."

Thus the contents of this verse at once bring before us a subject which has been debated in Christendom all through the centuries— the possibility or the impossibility of a true child of God apostatising and finally perishing. Into this vexed question we shall not here enter, as the contents of the verses which immediately follow will oblige us taking it up, D.V. in our next article. Suffice it now to say that what is here in view is the *testing of profession*; whether the profession be genuine or spurious, the ultimate outcome of that testing makes evident in each individual's case.

"Take heed brethren." The introducing here of this blessed and tender title of God's saints is very searching. Those unto whom the apostle was writing, might object, "The scripture you have cited has no legitimate application to *us*; that passage describes the conduct of unbelievers, whereas *we* are believers." Therefore does the apostle again address them as "brethren;" nevertheless, he bids them "take heed." They were not yet out of danger, they were still in the wilderness. Those mentioned in Psa. 95 began well, witness their singing the praises of Jehovah on the farther shores of the Red Sea (Ex. 15). They too had avowed their fealty to the Lord: "all the people answered together, and said, All that the Lord hath spoken we will do" (Ex. 19:8); yet the fact remains that many *of them* apostatised and perished in the wilderness. Therefore the searching relevancy of this word, "take heed brethren lest there be in any *of you* an evil heart of unbelief."

"In departing from the living God." The reference here is plainly to the Lord Jesus Himself. In Matt. 16:16 the Father is denominated "the living God," here and in 1 Tim. 4:10 the Son is, in 2 Cor. 6:16 (cf. 1 Cor. 3:16) the Holy Spirit is. The reason for the application of this Divine title to the Saviour in this verse is apparent: the temptation confronting the Hebrews was not to become atheists, but to abandon their profession of Christianity. The unbelieving Jews denounced Jesus Christ as an impostor, and were urging those who believed in Him to renounce Him and return to Judaism, and thus return to the true God, Jehovah. That Christ is God the apostle had affirmed here, in v. 4, and he now warns them that so far from the abandonment of the Christian profession and a return to Judaism being a going back to Jehovah, it would be the "*departing from* the living God." That Christ was the true and living God had been fully demonstrated by the apostle in the preceding chapters of this epistle.

The extent to which and the manner in which the warning from Psa. 95 and the admonition of Heb. 3:12 applies to Christians today, we must leave for consideration till the next chapter. In the meantime let us heed the exhortation of 2 Peter 1:10, "Wherefore the rather, brethren, give diligence to make your calling and election sure," and while attending to this duty, let us pray the more frequently and the more earnestly for God to deliver *us* from "an evil heart of unbelief."

CHAPTER FIFTEEN

Christ Superior to Moses.

(Heb. 3:13-19)

There are two great basic truths which run through Scripture, and are enforced on every page: that God is sovereign, and that man is a responsible creature; and it is only as the balance of truth is preserved between these two that we are delivered from error. The Divine sovereignty should not be pressed to the exclusion of human responsibility, nor must human responsibility be so stressed that God's sovereignty is either ignored or denied. The danger here is no fancied one, as the history of Christendom painfully exhibits. A careful study of the Word, and an honest appropriation of all it contains, is our only safeguard.

We are creatures prone to go to extremes: like the pendulum of a clock in motion, we swing from one side to the other. Nowhere has this tendency been more sadly exemplified than in the teachings of theologians concerning the security of the Christian. On the one hand, there have been those who affirmed, Once saved, always saved; on the other hand, many have insisted that a man may be saved today, but lost tomorrow. And both sides have appealed *to the Bible* in support of their conflicting contentions! Very unwise and unguarded statements have been made by both parties. Some Calvinists have boldly declared that if a sinner has received Christ as his Saviour, no matter what he does afterward, no matter what his subsequent life may be, he cannot perish. Some Arminians have openly denied the efficacy of the finished Work of Christ, and affirmed that when a sinner repents and believes in Christ he is merely put in a salvable state, on probation, and that his own good works and faithfulness will prove the deciding factor as to whether he should spend eternity in Heaven or Hell.

Endless volumes have been written on the subject, but neither side has satisfied the other; and the writer for one, is not at all surprised at this. Party-spirit has run too high, sectarian prejudice has been too strong. Only too often the aim of the contestants has been to silence their opponents, rather than to arrive at the truth. The method followed has frequently been altogether unworthy of the "children of light." One class of passages of Scripture has been pressed into service, while another class of passages has been either ignored or *explained away.* Is it not a fact that if some Calvinists were honest they would have to acknowledge there are some passages in the Bible which they wish were not there at all? And if some Arminians were equally honest, would they not have to confess that there are passages in Holy Writ which they are quite unable to fit into the creed to which they are committed? Sad, sad indeed, is this. There is nothing in the Word of God of which any Christian needs be afraid, and if there is a single verse in it which conflicts with his creed, so much the worse for his creed.

Now the subject of the Christian's security, like every other truth of Scripture, has *two* sides to it: into it there enters both God's sovereignty and human responsibility. It is failure to recognize and reckon upon this which has wrought such havoc and created so much confusion. More than once has the writer heard a renowned Bible-teacher of orthodox reputation say, "I do not believe in the perseverance of saints, but I do believe in the preservation of the Saviour." But that is to ignore an important side of the truth. The N.T. has much to say on the *perseverance* of the saints, and to deny or ignore it is not only to dishonour God, but to damage souls.

There have been those who boldly insisted that, if God has eternally elected a certain man to be saved, that man *will be* saved, no matter what he does or does not do. Not so does the Word of God teach. Scripture says, "God hath from the beginning chosen you to salvation, through sanctification of the Spirit *and belief of the truth*" (2 Thess. 2:13), and if a man *does not* "believe the truth" he will never be saved. The Lord Jesus declared, "Except ye repent, ye shall all likewise perish" (Luke 13:3); therefore, if a sinner, *does not* "repent," he will not be saved. In like manner, there are those who have said, If a man is *now* a real Christian, no matter how he may live in the future, no matter how far or how long he may backslide, no matter what sins he may commit, he is sure of Heaven. Put in *such* a way, this teaching has wrought untold harm, and, at the risk of our own orthodoxy being suspected, we here enter a solemn and vigorous protest against it.

The writer has met many people who profess to be Christians, but whose daily lives differ in nothing from thousands of non-professors all around them. They are rarely, if ever, found at the prayer-meeting, they have no family worship, they seldom read the Scriptures, they will not talk with you about the things of God, their walk is thoroughly worldly; and yet they are quite sure *they* are bound for heaven! Inquire into the ground of their confidence, and they will tell you that so many years ago they accepted Christ as their Saviour, and "once saved always saved" is now their comfort. There are thousands of such people on earth today, who are nevertheless, on the Broad Road, that leadeth to destruction, treading it with a false peace in their hearts and a vain profession on their lips.

It is not difficult to anticipate the thoughts of many who have read the above paragraphs: "We fully agree that there are many in Christendom resting on a false ground of security, many professing the name of Christ, who have never been born again; but this in nowise conflicts with the declaration of Christ that no sheep of His shall ever perish." Quite true. But what we would here point out and seek to press on our readers is this: I have no right to appropriate to myself the blessed and comforting words of the Saviour found in John 10:28, 29, *unless I answer to* the description of His "sheep" found in John 10:27; and I have no warrant for applying His promise to those who give no evidence of being conformed to the characters of those He there has in view. Let no man dare separate what God Himself has there joined together.

The passage begins with, "My sheep *hear* My voice, and I know them, and they *follow Me*." That is the Lord's own description of those whom *He* owns as His "sheep." Now if, to the contrary, I am "hearkening" to the seductive voice of this world, if I am "following" a course of self-will, self-seeking, self-gratification, what right have I to regard myself as one of the "sheep" of Christ? None at all. And if, notwithstanding, I do profess to be one of His, then my walk gives the lie to my profession. And any one who comes to me with words of comfort, pressing upon me the *promises* of God to His people, is only encouraging me in a course of wrong-doing and bolstering me up in a false hope.

It may be replied, "Yet a real Christian may leave his first love." True, and before a church that had done so, the Lord Jesus appeared and said — not, "It will be alright in the end," but — "Repent, and do the first works, or else I will come unto thee quickly, and will remove thy candlestick" (Rev. 2:5). "But a real Christian may backslide, and in a large measure become worldly again." Then if he does, *his* need is *not* to hear about the eternal security of God's saints, but the eternal and fearful consequences of giving way to an evil heart of unbelief if such a course be continued in. "Yes, but if he *is* one of God's people, he will be chastened, and grace will restore him; and therefore I cannot see the need or propriety of giving him to believe there is a danger of his being lost."

Ah, it is not without reason that the Lord Jesus declared, more than once, "he that *endureth to the end* shall be saved." And let it not be forgotten that in Matt. 13:20, 21, He spoke of some who "but dureth *for a while*"! Again it may be objected, "Such a pressing of the need of perseverance of God's elect is uncalled for: if a man *be* a Christian, he *will* persevere, and if he persevere then there is no need of urging him *to* persevere." Not so did the apostles think or act. In Acts 11:22, 23 we read, "they sent forth Barnabas, that he should go as far as Antioch. Who when he came, and had seen the grace of God, was glad and *exhorted* them all, that with purpose of heart they would *cleave unto* the Lord." Again, in Acts 13:43 we read, "Paul and Barnabas: who, speaking to them, persuaded them to *continue* in the grace of God." Once more, in Acts 14:21, 22 we are told "And when they had preached the Gospel to that city, and had taught many, they returned again to Lystra, and Iconium, and Antioch, Confirming the souls of the disciples, *exhorting them to continue* in the faith, and that we must through much tribulation enter into the kingdom of God."

According to the views of some, such earnestness on the part of the apostles was quite unnecessary. But the impartial Christian reader will gather from the above passages that the apostles believed in no *mechanical* salvation, wherein God dealt with men as though they were stocks and stones. No, they preached a salvation that needed to be *worked out* with "fear and trembling" (Phil. 2:12); in a salvation which calls human responsibility into exercise; in a Divine salvation effectuated by the *use* of the means of grace which God has mercifully provided for us. True we *are* "kept by the power of God," but the very next words afford us light on *how* God keeps—"*through* faith" (1 Peter 1:5). And not only does faith feed on the promises of God, but it is stirred into healthful exercise and directed by the solemn *warnings* of Scripture.

A real need then is there for such words as these, "But Christ as a Son over His own house; whose house are we, *if* we hold fast the confidence and rejoicing of the hope firm unto the end" (Heb. 3:6). "Oh, blessed word and promise of God, that *He* will keep us unto the end. But *how* is it that we are kept? Through faith, through watchfulness, through self-denial, through prayer and fasting, through our constant taking heed unto ourselves according to His Word. 'Hold fast' if you desire it to be manifested in that day that you are not merely outward professors, not merely fishes existing in the net, but the true and living disciples of One Master." (Saphir).

"But exhort one another daily, while it is called Today; lest any of you be hardened through the deceitfulness of sin" (v. 13).

"There is need of constant watchfulness on the part of the professors of Christianity, lest under the influence of unbelief they 'depart from the living God.' 'Take heed,' says the apostle. There is nothing, I am persuaded, in regard to which professors of Christianity fall into more dangerous practical mistakes than this. They suspect everything sooner than the soundness and firmness of their belief. There are many who are supposing themselves believers who have no true faith at all, — and so it would be proved were the hour of trial, which is perhaps nearer than they are aware, to arrive; and almost all who have faith suppose they have it in greater measure than they really have it. There is no prayer that a Christian needs more frequently to present than, 'Lord, increase my faith'; 'deliver me from an evil heart of unbelief.'

"All apostasy from God, whether partial or total, originates in unbelief. To have his faith increased — to have more extended, and accurate and impressive views of 'the truth as it is in Jesus' — ought to be the object of the Christian's most earnest desire and unremitting exertion. Just in the degree in which we obtain deliverance from the 'evil heart of unbelief' are we enabled to cleave to the Lord with full purpose of heart, to follow Him fully, and, in opposition to all the temptations to abandon His cause, to 'walk in all His commandments and ordinances blameless.' To prevent so fearful and disastrous a result of apostasy from the living God, the apostle calls on them to strengthen each other's faith by mutual exhortation, and thus oppose those malignant and deceitful influences which had a tendency to harden them in impenitence and unbelief" (Dr. J. Brown).

To "exhort one another daily" is to call attention to and stir up one another for discharging our mutual duties. But in performing this obligation we are sadly lax: like the disciples upon the mount of transfiguration (Luke 9:32) and in Gethsemane (Luke 22:45), we too are very dull and drowsy and in constant need of both exhortation and incitation. As fellow pilgrims in a hostile country, as members of the same family, we ought to have "care for one another" (1 Cor. 12:25), to "love one another" (John 13:34), to "pray one for another" (James 5:16), to "comfort one another" (1 Thess. 4:18), to "admonish one another" (Rom. 15:14), to "edify one another" (1 Thess. 5:11), to have "peace one with another" (Mark 9:50). Only thus are we really helpful one to another. And, note, the exhorting is to be done "daily," for we must not be weary in well doing. *While* it is called "To-day" warns us that our sojourn in this scene is but brief; the night hastens on when no man can work.

"Lest any of you be hardened" adds force to the duty enjoined. In v. 8 the terrible damage which hardness of heart produces had been pointed out; here it is warned against. The implication is unmistakable: hardness of heart is the consequence of neglecting the means for softening it—"lest." Clay and wax which are naturally hard, melt when brought under a softening power, but when the heat is withdrawn they revert again to their native hardness. The same evil tendency remains in the Christian. The flesh is "weak," our heart "deceitful"; only by the daily use of means and through fellowship with the godly are we preserved. Oftentimes the failure of a Christian is to be charged against his brethren as much as to his own unfaithfulness. How often when we perceive a saint giving way to hardness of heart we go about mentioning it to others, instead of faithfully and tenderly exhorting the offending one!

"Through the deceitfulness of sin." Here is the cause of the evil warned against and upon which we need to be constantly upon our guard. It is the manifold deceits of sin which prevail over men so much. The reference here is to the corruption of our nature, with which we are born, and which we ever carry about with us. It is that which, in Scripture, is designated the "flesh," the lustings of which are ever contrary to the Spirit. God's Word speaks of "deceitful lusts" (Eph. 4:22), the "deceitfulness of riches" (Matt. 13:22), for their innate depravity causes men to prefer material wealth to vital godliness and heavenly happiness. So we read of the "deceivableness of unrighteousness" (2 Thess. 2:10); philosophy (the proud reasoning of that carnal mind which is enmity against God) is termed "vain deceit" (Col. 2:8); and the lascivious practices of formal professors are called "their own deceivings" (2 Peter 2:13). This is one of the principal characteristics of sin: it deceives. "All the devices of sin are as fair baits whereby dangerous hooks are covered over to entice silly fish to snap at them, so as they are taken and made a prey to the fisher" (Dr. Gouge).

This deceitfulness of sin should serve as a strong inducement to make us doubly watchful against it, and that because of our foolish disposition and proneness of nature to yield to every temptation. Sin presents itself in another dress than its own. It lyingly offers fair advantages. It insensibly bewitches our mind. It accommodates itself to each individual's particular temperament and circumstances. It clothes its hideousness by assuming an attractive garb. It deludes us into a false estimate of ourselves. One great reason why God has mercifully given us His Word is to expose the real character of sin. By the deceitfulness of sin the heart is *hardened.* "To be hardened is to become insensible to the claims of Jesus Christ, so that they do not make their appropriate impression on the mind, in producing attention, faith, and obedience. He is hardened who is careless, unbelieving, impenitent, disobedient" (Dr. J. Brown).

In the light of the whole context the specific reference in the exhortation of v. 13 constitutes a solemn caution against apostasy. What we particularly need to daily exhort one another about is to cleave fast to Christ, lest something else supplant Him in our affections. The whole trend of our sinful natures is to depart from the living God, to grasp at the shadows and miss the substance. This was the peculiar danger of the Hebrews. Sin was trying to deceive them. It was seeking to draw them back to Judaism as the one true and Divinely-appointed religion. To guard against the insidious appeals being made, the apostle urges them to "exhort one another daily," that is, promptly and frequently. The importance of taking heed to this injunction is placed in its strongest light by what immediately follows.

"For we are made partakers of Christ, if we hold the beginning of our confidence steadfast unto the end" (v. 14). These words complete the exhortation commenced at v. 12. They are added as a motive to enforce the dissuasion from apostasy (v. 12), and also the warning against that which occasions it (v. 13). The contents of this verse are similar in their force to that which was before us in v. 6: in both instances it is profession which is being put to the proof. There are two classes on which such exhortations have no effect: the irreligious who are dead in trespasses and sins, and have no interest in such matters; and the self-righteous religionist, who, though equally dead spiritually, yet has an intellectual interest. Many a professing Christian, who is infected by the Laodicean spirit of the day, will shrug his shoulders, saying, Such warnings do not concern me, there is no danger of a real child of God apostatising. Such people fail to get the good of these Divine warnings, their conscience never being reached. But where there is a heart which is right with God, there is always self-distrust, and such an one is kept in the place of dependency through taking heed to the solemn admonitions of the Spirit. It is these very warnings against departure from God which *curb* the regenerate.

"Persistency in our confidence in Christ unto the end is a matter of great endeavour and diligence, and that unto all believers. It is true that our persistency in Christ doth not, as to the issue and event, depend absolutely on our own diligence. The *unalterableness of union with Christ,* on the account of the faithfulness of the covenant of grace, is that which doth and shall eventually secure it. But yet our own diligent endeavour is such an indispensable means for that end as that without it it will never be brought about.

Hence are many warnings given us in this and other epistles, that we should take heed of apostasy and falling away; and these cautions and warnings are given unto all true believers, that they may know how indispensably necessary, from the appointment of God, and the nature of the thing itself, is their watchful diligence and endeavour unto their abiding in Christ" (Dr. J. Owen).

But it should be pointed out that these solemn warnings of Scripture ought not to be pressed upon weak Christians, who though anxious to walk acceptably before God, are lacking in assurance. "Observe here—for Satan, and our own conscience when it has not been set free often make use of this epistle—that doubting Christians are not here contemplated, or persons who have not yet gained entire confidence in God: to those who are in this condition its exhortations and warnings have no application. These exhortations are to preserve the Christian in a confidence *which he has,* and to persevere, not to tranquillise fears and doubts. This use of the epistle to sanction such doubts is but a device of the enemy. Only I would add here that, although the full knowledge of grace (which in such a case the soul has assuredly not yet attained) is the only thing that can deliver and set it free from its fears, yet it is very important in this case practically to maintain a good conscience, in order not to furnish the enemy with a special means of attack" (J. N. D.).

For the right understanding of this verse it is of first importance that we should note carefully the tense of the verb in the first clause: it is *not* "we shall be made partakers of Christ if"—that would completely overthrow the gospel of God's grace, deny the efficacy of the finished Work of Christ, and make assurance of our acceptance before God impossible before death. No, what the Spirit here says is, "We *are* made partakers of Christ," and in the Greek it is expressed even more decisively: "For partakers we have become of the Christ." The word "partakers" here is the same as in 3:1, "partakers of the heavenly calling," and at the end of 1:9 is rendered, "fellows." Perhaps, "companions" would be a better rendering. It means that we are so "joined unto the Lord," as to be "one spirit" with Him (1 Cor. 6:17). It is to be so united to Christ that we are "members of His body, of His flesh, and of His bones" (Eph. 5:30). It is to be made by grace, "joint-heirs" with Him (Rom. 8:17). The word "*made* partakers of Christ" shows there was a time when Christians were not so. They were not so born naturally; it was a privilege conferred upon them when they "received" Him as their Saviour (John 1:12).

"If we hold the beginning of our confidence steadfast unto the end." This does not express a condition of our remaining partakers of Christ in the sense of its being a contingency. "What is the one thing which the Christian desires? What is the one great thing which he does? What is the one great secret which he is always endeavouring to find out with greater clearness and grasp with firmer intensity? Is it not this: 'my Beloved is mine, and I am His'? The inmost desire of our heart and the exhortation of the Word coincide. To the end we must persevere; and it is therefore with great joy and alacrity that we receive the solemn exhortations: 'He that endureth unto the end shall be saved'; 'No man, having put his hand to the plow, and looking back, is fit for the kingdom of God.' We desire to hear constantly the voice which saith from His Heavenly throne, 'To him that overcometh will I grant to sit with Me in My kingdom, even as I also overcame, and am set down with My Father in His throne' " (Saphir).

To hold fast the beginning of our confidence firm unto the end is to furnish evidence of the genuineness of our profession, it is to make it manifest both to ourselves and others that we have been made "partakers of Christ." Difficulties in the path are presupposed, severe trials are to be expected: how else could faith show itself? Buffetings and testings do but provide occasions for the manifestation of faith, they are also the means of its exercise and growth. The Greek word for "confidence" here is not the same as in v. 6: there the "confidence" spoken of is to make a bold and free confession of our faith; here, it is a deep and settled assurance of Christ's excellency and sufficiency, which supports our hearts. The one is external, the other is internal. To "hold fast the beginning of our confidence" signifies to "continue in the faith, grounded and settled" (Col. 1:23). It is to say with Job, "Though He slay me, yet will I trust in Him,"(Job13:15).

"Firm unto the end." This is the test. At the beginning of our Christian course, our confidence in Christ was full and firm. We knew that He was a mighty Saviour, and we were fully persuaded that He was able to keep that which we have committed unto Him against that day. But the roughness of the way, the darkness of the night, the fierceness of the storm into which, sooner or later, we are plunged, tends to shake our confidence, and perhaps (much to our sorrow now) we cried, "Lord, carest Thou not"? Yet, if we were really "partakers of Christ" though we fell, yet were we not utterly cast down. We turned to the Word, and there we found help, light, comfort. In it we discovered that the very afflictions we have experienced were what God had told us *would be* our portion for "we are appointed thereunto" (1 Thess. 3:3). In it we learned that God's chastenings of us proceeded from His love (Heb. 12). And now, though we have proved by painful experience to have less and less confidence in ourselves, in our friends, and even in our brethren, yet, by grace, our confidence in the Lord has grown and become more intelligent. Thus do we obtain experimental verification of that word, "Better is the end of a thing than the beginning thereof" (Eccl. 7:8).

"While it is said, To-day if ye will hear His voice, harden not your hearts, as in the provocation" (v. 15). The apostle continues to make practical application of the solemn passage he had been quoting from Psalm 95, pressing upon them certain details from it. That which is central in this verse is its directions for cleaving fast to Christ. Two things are to be observed: the duty to be performed, positively to "hear His voice," negatively not to "harden their hearts." This duty is to be performed promptly, "To-day," and is to be persevered in—"*whilst* it is said today" i.e. to the end of our earthly pilgrimage. The opportunity which grace grants us is to be eagerly redeemed, the improvement of it is to be made as long as the season of opportunity is ours. The admonition is again pointed by the warning of Israel's failure of old. Thus the sins of others before us are to be laid to heart, that we may avoid them.

"When we hear God's voice—and, oh, how clearly and sweetly does He speak to us in the person of His Son Jesus, the Word incarnate, who died for us on Golgotha!—the *heart* must respond . . . By this expression is meant the centre of our spiritual existence, that centre out of which thoughts and affections proceed, out of which are the issues of life, that mysterious fount which God only can know and fathom. Oh that Christ may dwell *there*! God's voice is to *soften* the heart. This is the purpose of the divine word —to make our hearts tender. Alas, by nature we are *hard*-hearted; and what *we* call good and soft-hearted is not so in reality and in *God's* sight . . . . When we receive God's word in the heart, when we acknowledge our sin, when we adore God's mercy, when we desire God's fellowship, when we see Jesus, who came to save us, to wash our feet and shed His blood, for our salvation, the heart becomes soft and tender. For repentance, faith, prayer, patience, hope of heaven, all these things make the heart tender: tender towards God, tender towards our fellow-men" (Saphir).

"For some, when they had heard, did provoke: howbeit not all that came out of Egypt by Moses" (v. 16). The apostle here begins to describe the kind of persons who sinned in the provocation, amplification being given in what follows. His purpose in making mention of these persons was to more fully evidence the need for Christian watchfulness against hardness of heart, even because those who of old yielded thereto provoked God to their ruin. The opening "for" gives point to what has preceded. The unspeakably solemn fact to which He here refers is that out of six hundred thousand men who left Egypt, but two of them were cut off in the wilderness, Caleb and Joshua.

The Greek word "provoke" occurs nowhere else in the N.T., but the Sept. employs it in Psalm 78:17, 40; 106: 7, 33; Jer. 44:8, etc. They "vexed" Him (Isa. 63:10), and this because of their contempt of His word. Hereby they showed they were not of God, see John 8:47, 1 John 4:6. Should any unsaved man or woman read these lines, we would say, Beware of provoking God by *thine* obstinacy. To them that believe not, the gospel becomes "a savor of death unto death."

"But with whom was He grieved forty years"? (v. 17). This being put in the form of a question was designed to stir up the conscience of the reader, cf. Matt. 21:28, James 4:5, etc. "Was it not with them that had sinned, whose carcases fell in the wilderness"? (v. 17). "He doth not say 'they died,' but their 'carcases fell,' which intimates contempt and indignation. God sometimes will make men who have been wickedly exemplary in sin, righteously exemplary in their punishment. To what end is this reported? It is that we may take heed that we 'fall not after the same example of unbelief' (4:11). There is then an example in the fall and punishment of unbelievers" (Dr. J. Owen).

"And to whom sware He that they should not enter into His rest, but to them that believeth not"? (v. 18). Having reminded the Hebrews in the previous verse that sin was the cause of Israel's destruction of old, he now specifies the character of that sin, Unbelief. The order is terribly significant: they harkened not to God's voice; in consequence, their hearts were hardened; unbelief was the result; destruction, the issue. How unspeakably solemn! The Greek word here rendered "believed not" may, with equal propriety, be rendered "obeyed not"; it is so translated in Rom. 2:8; 10:21. It amounts to the same thing, differing only according to the angle of view-point: looked at from the mind or heart, it is "unbelief"; looked at from the will, it is "disobedience." In either case it is the sure consequence of *refusal* to heed God's voice.

"So we see that they could not enter in because of unbelief" (v. 19). "The apostle does not single out the sin of making and worshipping the golden calf; he does not bring before us the flagrant transgressions into which they fell at Beth-peor. Many much more striking and to our mind more fearful sins could have been pointed out, but God thinks the one sin greater than all is *unbelief*. We are saved by faith; we are lost through unbelief. The heart is purified by faith; the heart is hardened by unbelief. Faith brings us nigh to God; unbelief is departure from God" (Saphir).

There is no sin so great but it may be pardoned, if the sinner believe; but "he that believeth not shall be damned."

The application of the whole of this passage to the case of the sorely-tried and wavering Hebrews was most pertinent and solemn. Twice over the apostle reminded them (vv. 9, 17) that the unbelief of their fathers had been continued for "forty years." Almost that very interval had now elapsed since the Son had died, risen again, and ascended to heaven. In Scripture, forty is the number of probation. The season of Israel's testing was almost over; in A.D. 70 their final dispersion would occur. And God changeth not. He who had been provoked of old by Israel's hardness of heart, would destroy again those who persisted in their unbelief. Then let *them* beware, and heed the solemn warning, "Take heed, brethren, lest there be in any of you an evil heart of unbelief, in departing from the living God." May God grant us hearts to heed the same admonitory warning.

CHAPTER SIXTEEN

Christ Superior to Joshua.

(Heb. 4:1-3).

The exhortation begun by the apostle in Heb. 3:12 is not completed till 4:12 is reached, all that intervenes consisting of an exposition and application of the passage quoted from Psa. 95 in Heb. 3:7-11. The connecting link between what has been before us and that which we are about to consider is found in 3:19, "So we see that they could not enter in because of unbelief." These words form the transition between the two chapters, concluding the exhortation found in vv. 12, 13, and laying a foundation for the admonition which follows. Ere proceeding, it may be well to take up a question which the closing verses of Heb. 3 have probably raised in many minds, namely, seeing that practically all the adults who came out of Egypt by Moses perished in the wilderness, did not the promises of God to bring them into Canaan fail of their accomplishment?

In Ex. 6:6-8 Jehovah said unto Moses, "Wherefore say unto the children of Israel, I am the Lord, and I will bring you out from under the burdens of the Egyptians, and I will rid you out of their bondage, and I will redeem you with a stretched out arm, and with great judgments: and I will take you to Me for a people, and I will be to you a God . . . and I will bring you in unto the land, concerning the which I did sware to give it to Abraham, to Isaac, and to Jacob, and I will give it you for an heritage: I am the Lord." We quote now from the helpful comments of Dr. J. Brown upon these verses:

"This is a promise which refers to Israel *as a people,* and which does not by any means necessarily infer that all, or even that any, of *that* generation were to enter in. No express condition was mentioned in this promise—not even the believing of it. Yet, so far as that generation was concerned, this, as the event proved, was plainly implied; for, if it had been an absolute, unconditional promise to *that* generation, it must have been performed, otherwise He who cannot lie would have failed in accomplishing His own word. There can be no doubt that the fulfillment of the promise *to them* was suspended on their believing it, and acting accordingly. Had they believed that Jehovah was indeed both able and determined to bring His people Israel into the land of Canaan, and, under the influence of this faith, had gone up at His command to take possession, the promise would have been performed to them.

"*This* was the tenor of the covenant made with *them*: 'Now therefore, *if* ye will obey My voice indeed, and keep My covenant, *then* ye shall be a peculiar treasure unto Me above all people: for all the earth is Mine: and ye shall be unto Me a kingdom of priests, and an holy nation' (Ex. 19:5, 6). 'Behold, I send an Angel before thee, to keep thee in the way, and to bring thee into the place which I have prepared. Beware of Him, and obey His voice, provoke Him not; for He will not pardon your transgressions: for My name is in Him. But *if* thou shalt indeed obey His voice, and do all that I speak; *then* I will be an Enemy unto thine enemies, and an Adversary unto thine adversaries' (Ex. 23:20-22).

"Their unbelief and disobedience are constantly stated as the reason why they did not enter in. 'Because all those men have seen My glory, and My miracles, which I did in Egypt and in the wilderness, and have tempted Me now these ten times, and have not harkened to My voice; surely they shall not see the land which I sware unto their fathers, neither shall any of them that provoked Me see it' (Num. 14:22, 23), cf. Josh. 5:6. God promised to bring Israel into the land of Canaan; but He did not promise to bring them in whether they believed and obeyed or not. No promise was broken to *those* men, for no absolute promise was made to them.

"But their unbelief did not make the promise of God of none effect. It was accomplished to the next generation: 'And the Lord gave unto Israel all the land which He sware to give unto their fathers; and they possessed it, and dwelt therein' (Josh. 21:43). Joshua appealed to the Israelites themselves for the completeness of the fulfilment of the promise, see Josh. 23:14. *That* generation believed the promises that God would give Canaan, and under the influence of this fact, went forward under the conduct of Joshua, and obtained possession of the land for themselves."

This same principle explains what has been another great difficulty to many, namely, Israel's actual tenure of Canaan. In Gen. 13:14, 15 we are told, "And the Lord said unto Abraham, after that Lot was separated from him, Lift up now thine eyes, and look from the place from where thou art northward, and southward, and eastward, and westward: For all the land which thou seest, to thee will I give it, and to thy *seed for ever.*" This promise was repeated again and again, see Gen. 7:8, etc. How then came it that the children of Israel occupied the land only for a season?

Their descendants, for the most part are not in it to-day. Has, then, the promise of God failed? In no-wise. In His promise to Abraham God did not specify that any particular generation of his descendants should occupy the land "for ever" and herein lies the solution to the difficulty.

God's promise to Abraham was made on the ground of pure grace; no condition whatever was attached to it. But grace only superabounds where sin has abounded. Sovereign grace intervenes only after the responsibility of man has been tested and his failure and unworthiness manifested. Now it is abundantly clear from many passages in Deut., e.g. 31:26-29, that Israel entered Canaan not on the ground of the unconditional covenant of grace which Jehovah made with Abraham, but on the ground of the conditional covenant of works which was entered into at Sinai (Ex. 24:6-8). Hence, many years after Israel had entered Canaan under Joshua, we read, "And an Angel of the Lord came up from Gilgal to Bochim, and said, I made you to go up out of the land of Egypt, and have brought you unto the land which I sware unto your fathers; and I said, I will never break My covenant *with you*. And ye shall make no league with the inhabitants of this land; ye shall throw down their altars; *but ye have not obeyed* My voice: Why have ye done this? *Wherefore* I also said, I will not drive them out from before you; but they shall be a thorn in your sides, and their gods shall be a snare unto you" (Judges 2:1-3).

The same principles are in exercise concerning God's fulfilment of His *gospel* promises. "The gospel promise of eternal life, like the promise of Canaan, is a promise which will assuredly be accomplished. It is sure to all 'the seed.' They were 'chosen in Christ before the foundation of the world.' Eternal life was promised in reference to them before the times of the ages, and confirmed by the oath of God. They have been redeemed to God by 'the blood of the Lamb,' and are all called in due time according to His purpose. Their inheritance is 'laid up in heaven' for them, and 'they are kept for it by the mighty power of God, through faith unto salvation.' And they shall all at last 'inherit the kingdom prepared for them from the foundation of the world.'

"But the Gospel revelation does not testify directly to anyone that Christ so died for him in particular, that it is certain that *he* shall be saved through His death: neither does it absolutely promise salvation to all men; for in this case all must be saved,—or God must be a liar. But it proclaims, 'he that believeth shall be saved—he that believeth not shall be damned.' It is as believers of the truth that we are secured of eternal life; and it is by holding fast this faith of the truth, and showing that we do so, that we can alone enjoy the comfort of this security. 'The purpose of God according to election must stand,' and all His chosen will assuredly be saved; but they cannot know their election—they cannot enjoy any absolute assurance of their salvation—independent of their continuance in the faith, love, and obedience of the Gospel, *see* 2 Peter 1:5-12. And to the Christian, in every stage of his progress, it is of importance to remember, that he who turns back, turns 'back to perdition'; and that it is he only who believes straight onward—that continues in the faith of the truth—that shall obtain 'the salvation of the soul' " (Dr. J. Brown).

Our introduction for this article has already exceeded its legitimate limits, but we trust that what has been said above will be used of God in clearing up several difficulties which have exercised the minds of many of His beloved people, and that it may serve to prepare us for a more intelligent perusal of our present passage. The verses before us are by no means easy, as any one who will really study them will quickly discover. The apostle's argument seems to be unusually involved, the teaching of it appears to conflict with other portions of Scripture, and the "rest" which is its central subject, is difficult to define with any degree of certainty. It is with some measure of hesitation and with not a little trepidation that the writer himself now attempts to expound it, and he would press upon every reader the importance and need of heeding the Divine injunction of 1 Thess. 5:21, "Prove all things; hold fast that which is good."

It should be evident that the first thing which will enable us to understand our passage is to attend to the *scope* of it. The contents of this chapter are found not in Romans or Corinthians or Ephesians, but in Hebrews, the central theme of which is the superiority of Christianity over Judaism, and there is that in each chapter which exemplifies this. The theme is developed by the presentation of the superlative excellencies of Christ, who is the Centre and Life of Christianity. Thus far we have had Christ's superiority over the prophets, the angels, Moses. Now it is the glory of Christ which excels that attaching to Joshua.

Our next key must be found in noting the *connection* between the contents of chapter four and that which immediately precedes. Plainly, the context begins at 3:1, where we are bidden to "consider the Apostle and High Priest of our profession." All of chapter 3 is but an amplification of its opening verse. Its contents may be summarized thus: Christ is to be "considered," attended to, heard, trusted, obeyed: first, because of His exalted personal excellency:

He is the Son, "faithful" over His house; second, because of the direful consequences which must ensue from not "considering" Him, from despising Him. This second point is illustrated by the sad example of those Israelites who hearkened not unto the Lord in the days of Moses, and in their case the consequence was that they failed to enter into the rest of Canaan.

In the first sections of Heb. 4, the principal subject of chapter 3 is *continued*. It brings out again the superiority of our "Apostle," this time over Joshua, for he too was an "apostle" of God. This is strikingly brought out in Deut. 34:9, "And Joshua the son of Nun was full of the spirit of wisdom; *for* Moses had laid hands upon him; and the children of Israel hearkened unto him, and did as the Lord commanded Moses"—the prime thought of the "laying on of hands" in Scripture being that of *identification*. Let the reader compare Josh. 1:5, 16-18. The continuation of the theme of Heb. 3 in chapter 4 is also seen by the repeated mention of "rest," *see* 3:11, 18 and cf. 4:1, 3, etc. It is on this term that the apostle bases his present argument. The "rest" of 3:11 and 18 refers to Canaan, and though Joshua actually conducted Israel into this (see marginal rendering of 4:8), yet the apostle proves by a reference to Psalm 95 that Israel never really (as a nation) entered into the rest *of God*. Herein lies the superiority of the Apostle of Christianity; Christ *does* lead His people into the true rest. Such, we believe, is the line of truth developed in our passage.

"Let us therefore fear, lest a promise being left us of entering into His rest, any of you should seem to come short of it" (v. 1). The opening words of this chapter bid us seriously take to heart the solemn warning given at the close of 3. God's judgment upon the wicked should make us more watchful that we do not follow their steps. The "us" shows that Paul was preaching to himself as well as to the Hebrews. "Let us therefore *fear*" has stumbled some, because of the "Fear thou not" of Isa. 41:10, 43:1, 5, etc. In John 14:27 Christ says to us, "Let not your heart be troubled, neither let it be afraid." And in 2 Tim. 1:7 we read, "For God hath not given us the spirit of fear; but of power, and of love, and of a sound mind." On the other hand, believers are told to "Fear God" (1 Peter 2:17), and to work out their own salvation "with fear and trembling" (Phil. 2:12). How are these two different sets of passages to be harmonized?

The Bible is full of paradoxes, which to the natural man, appear to be contradictions. The Word needs "rightly dividing" on the subject of "fear" as upon everything else of which it treats. There is a fear which the Christian is to cultivate, and there is a fear from which he should shrink. The fear of the Lord is the beginning of wisdom, and in Prov. 14:26, 27 we read, "In the fear of the Lord is strong confidence. . . . The fear of the Lord is a fountain of life"; so again, "Happy is the man that feareth always" (Prov. 28:14). The testimony of the New Testament inculcates the same duty: Christ bade His disciples, "Fear Him who is able to destroy both soul and body in Hell" (Matt. 10:28). To the saints at Rome Paul said, "Be not high-minded, but fear" (Rom. 11:20). To God's people Peter wrote, "Pass the time of your sojourning here in fear" (1 Pet. 1:17). While in Heaven itself the word will yet be given: "Praise our God all ye His servants, and ye that fear Him both small and great" (Rev. 19:5).

Fear may be called one of the disliking affections. It is good or evil according to the object on which it is placed, and according to the ordering of it thereon. In Heb. 4:1 it is placed on the right object—an evil to be shunned. That evil is unbelief, which, if persisted in, ends in apostasy and destruction. About this the Christian needs to be constantly on his guard, having his heart set steadily against it. Our natural proneness to fall, the many temptations to which we are subject, together with the deceitfulness of sin, the subtlety of Satan, and God's justice in leaving men to themselves, are strong enforcements of this duty. Concerning God Himself, we are to fear Him with such a reverent awe of His holy majesty as will make us careful to please Him in all things, and fearful of offending Him. This is ever accompanied by a fearsome distrust of ourselves. The fear of God which is evil in a Christian is that servile bondage which produces a distrustful attitude, kills affection for Him, regards Him as a hateful Tyrant. This is the fear of the demons (James 2:19).

"Let us therefore fear." "It is salutary to remember our tendency to partiality and one-sidedness in our spiritual life, in order that we may be on our guard, that we may carefully and anxiously consider the 'Again, it is written'; that we may be willing to learn from Christians who have received different gifts of grace, and whose experience varies from ours; above all, that we may seek to follow and serve the Lord Himself, to walk with God, to hear the voice of the Good Shepherd. Forms of godliness, types of doctrine, are apt to become substitutes instead of channels, weights instead of wings.

"The exhortations of this epistle may appear to some difficult to reconcile with the teachings of Scripture, that the grace of God, once received, through the power of the Holy Spirit by faith, can never be lost, and that they who are born again, who are once in Christ, are in Christ for ever. Let us not blunt the edge of earnest and piercing exhortations. Let us not pass them over, or treat them with inward apathy. 'Again it is written.' We know this does not mean that there is any real contradiction in Scripture, but that various aspects of truth are presented, each with the same fidelity, fulness and emphasis. Hence we must learn to move freely, and not to be cramped and fixed in one position: we must keep our eyes clear and open, and not look at all things through the light of a favourite doctrine. And while we receive fully and joyously the assurance of our perfect acceptance and peace, and of the unchanging love of God in Christ Jesus, let us with the apostle consider also our sins and dangers, from the lower yet most real earthly and time-point of view.

"When Christ is beheld and accepted, there is peace; but is there not also fear? 'With Thee is forgiveness of sin, that Thou mayest be feared' (Psa. 130:4). Where do we see God's holiness and the awful majesty of the law as in the cross of Christ? Where our own sin and unworthiness, where the depths of our guilt and misery, as in the atonement of the Lord Jesus? We rejoice with fear and trembling. . . . It is because we know the Father, it is because we are redeemed by the precious blood of the Saviour, it is as the children of God and as the saints of Christ, that we are to pass our earthly pilgrimage in fear. This is not the fear of bondage, but the fear of adoption; not the fear which dreads condemnation, but the fear of those who are saved, and whom Christ has made free. It is not an imperfect and temporary condition; it refers not merely to those who have begun to walk in the ways of God. Let us not imagine that this fear is to vanish at some subsequent period of our course, that it is to disappear in a so-called 'higher Christian life.' No; we are to pass the time of our sojourn here in fear. To the last moment of our fight of faith, to the very end of our journey, the child of God, while trusting and rejoicing, walks in godly fear" (Saphir).

"Lest a promise being left us." It is very striking to observe how this is expressed. It does not say, "lest a promise being made" or "given." It is put thus for the searching of our hearts. God's promises are presented *to* faith, and they only become ours individually, and we only enter into the good of them, as we appropriate or lay hold of them. Of the patriarchs it is said concerning God's promises (1) "having seen them afar off, (2) and were persuaded of them, (3) and *embraced* them" Heb. 11:13). Certain promises of Jehovah were "left" to those who came out of Egypt. They were not "given" to any particular individuals, or "made" concerning that specific generation. And, as the apostle has shown in Heb. 3, the majority of those who came out of Egypt *failed* to "embrace" those promises, through hearkening not to Him Who spake, and through hardening their hearts. But Caleb and Joshua "laid hold" of those promises and so entered Canaan.

When the apostle here says, "Let us fear therefore lest a promise being left"—there is no "us" in the Greek—he addresses the *responsibility* of the Hebrews. He is pressing upon them the need of walking by faith and not by sight; he is urging them to so take unto themselves the promise which the Lord has "left," that they might not seem to come short of it. But to what is the apostle referring when he says, "lest *a promise* being left"? Surely in the light of the context the primary reference is clear: that which the Gospel makes known. The Gospel proclaims salvation to all who believe. The Gospel makes no promise to any particular individuals. Its terms are "whosoever believeth shall not perish." That promise is "left," left on infallible record, left for the consolation of convicted sinners, "left" for faith to lay hold of. This promise of salvation looks forward, ultimately, to the enjoyment of the eternal, perfect, and unbroken rest of God in heaven, of which the "rest" of Canaan, as the terminal of Israel's hard bondage in Egypt and their wearisome journeyings in the wilderness, was the appropriate figure.

"Any of you should seem to come short of it." Passing over the word "seem" for a moment, let us inquire into the meaning of "to come short of it." Here again the language of Heb. 11:13 should help us. As pointed out above, that verse indicates three distinct stages in the faith of the patriarchs. First, they saw God's promises "afar off." They seemed too good to be true, far beyond their apprehension. Second, they were "persuaded of them" or, as the Revised Version renders it, "*greeted* them," which signifies a much closer acquaintance of them. Third, and "embraced them"; they *did not* "come short," but took them to their hearts. It is thus the awakened and anxious sinner has to do with the Gospel promise. Wondrous, unique, passing knowledge as it does, that promise is "left" him, and the Person that promise points to is to be "greeted" and "embraced." "That which was from the beginning (1), which we have heard (2), which we have seen with our eyes (3), which we have looked upon (4), and our hands *have handled* of the Word of Life" (1 John 1:1).

At this stage perhaps, the reader is ready to object against what has been advanced above, "But how can the 'promise' here refer to that presented in the Gospel before poor sinners, seeing that the apostle was addressing believers? Is not the 'promise' plainly enough defined in the 'of entering into His rest'?" Without attempting now to enter into a fuller discussion of God's "rest," it should be clear from the context that the primary reference is to the eternal sharing of His rest in heaven. *This* is the believer's hope which is laid up for you in heaven, "whereof ye heard before in the Word of the truth *of the Gospel*" (Col. 1:5). At first this "hope" appears "afar off," but as faith grows it is "greeted" and "embraced." But only so as faith is in exercise. If we cease hearing and heeding the Voice which speaks to us from heaven, and our hearts become hardened through the deceitfulness of sin, the brightness of our hope is dimmed, we "come short" of it; and if such a course be continued in, hope will give way to despair.

The whole point of the apostle's exhortation here is a pressing upon Christians the imperative need of persevering in the faith. Israel left Egypt full of hope, as their song at the Red Sea plainly witnessed, *see* Ex. 15:13-18. But, alas, their hopes quickly faded. The trials and testings of the wilderness were too much for them. They walked by sight, instead of by faith; and murmuring took the place of praising, and hardness of heart instead of listening to the Lord's voice. So too the Hebrews were still in the wilderness: their profession of faith in Christ, their trust in the Lord, was being tested. Some of their fellows had already departed from the living God, as the language of 10:25 clearly implies. Would, then these whom the apostle had addressed as "holy brethren" fail, finally, to enter into God's rest? So it is with Christians now. Heaven is set before them as their goal: toward it they are to daily press forward, running with perseverance the race that is set before them. But the incentive of our hope only has power over the heart so long as faith is in exercise.

What is meant by "*seeming* to come short" of the Gospel promise of heaven? First, is not this word inserted here for the purpose of modifying the sharpness of the admonition? It was to show that the apostle did not positively conclude that any of these "holy brethren" were apostates, but only that they might appear to be in danger of it, as the "lest" warned. Second, was it not to stir up their godly fear the more against such coldness and dulness as might hazard the prize set before them? Third, and primarily, was it not for the purpose of showing Christians the *extent* to which they should be watchful? It is not sufficient to be assured that we shall never utterly fall away; we must not "seem" to do so, we must give no occasion to other Christians to think we have departed from the living God. The reference is to our *walk*. We are bidden to "abstain from all *appearance* of evil" (1 Thess. 5:22). Note how this same word "seem" signifies "appeared" in Gal. 2:9. The very appearance of backsliding is to be sedulously avoided.

"For unto us was the Gospel preached, as well as unto them: but the word preached did not profit them, not being mixed with faith in them that heard" (v. 2). The contents of this verse unequivocally establish our definition of the "promise" in v. 1, namely, that it has reference to the Gospel promise, which, in its ultimate application, looks forward to the eternal rest in heaven. Here plain mention is made of the "gospel." The obvious design of the apostle in this verse is to enforce the admonition of us fearing a like judgment which befell the apostate Israelites, by avoiding a like course of conduct in ourselves—unbelief.

The Gospel preached unto Israel of old is recorded in Ex. 6:6-8, and that it was *not* "mixed with faith in them that heard it" is seen from the very next verse, "And Moses so spake unto the children of Israel, but they *hearkened* not unto Moses for anguish of spirit, and for cruel bondage." We need hardly say that was not the only time a gospel message was proclaimed to them, *see* Num. 13:26, 27, 30; and for their unbelief, 14:1-4. "But the word preached did not profit them." "They were none the better for it. They did not obtain the blessing in reference to which a promise was given them: they did not enter into Canaan: they died in the wilderness" (Dr. J. Brown). The reason for this was, because they did not receive the good news in faith. The mere hearing of the Gospel is not enough: to profit, it must be believed. Thus Heb. 4:2 is parallel with 2:3.

"For we which have believed do enter into rest" (v. 3). Failure to rightly understand these words led many of the commentators right off the track of the apostle's argument in this passage. It pains us to have to take issue here with some eminent expositors of Scripture, but we dare not call any man, however spiritual or well-instructed, our "father." We must follow the light which we believe God has granted us, though we would again press upon the reader *his* responsibility for "proving all things" for himself.

"For we which have believed do enter into rest." Many have taken these words as referring to a spiritual rest into which believers enter here and now. But we believe this is a mistake. The apostle did not say, "We which believe *have entered* into rest." To which it may be replied, "Nor did he say, 'We which have believed *shall* enter into rest.'" True, for to have put it thus would have weakened his argument. Moreover, it would be to evacuate the exhortation of v. 11 of its significance, "Let us labour therefore *to* enter into that rest, lest any man fall after the same example of unbelief." If then v. 3 does not refer to a spiritual rest into which believers now enter, what is its meaning?

Bagster's Interlinear (and we know of no English translation which is its equal) gives, "For we enter into the rest, who believe." This is a literal word for word rendering of the Greek into English. Put thus, the historical tense is avoided, and we have simply an abstract statement of a doctrinal fact. This verse gives us the positive side of v. 2, defining the characters of those who *will* enter God's rest, namely, Believers. Unbelieving Israelites did not, believing Christians shall. It is important to remember that the "rest" of this whole passage is as yet only "promised," v. 1.

"For we which have believed do enter into rest." "The apostle speaks of believers of all ages as a body, to which he and those to whom he was writing belonged, and says, 'It is we who believe, and we alone, who under any dispensation can enter into the rest of God' " (Dr. J. Brown). The opening "for" signifies that what follows is added as a reason to confirm what has been previously stated. The reason is drawn from the law of contraries, the inevitable opposites. Of contraries there must be opposite consequences. Now faith and unbelief are contraries, therefore their consequences are contraries. As then unbelievers cannot enter into God's rest (3:18), believers must (4:3), *that* is *their* privilege. Such we believe is the force of this abstract declaration.

"The qualification of such as reap the benefit of God's promise is thus set down, 'Which have believed.' To believe is to yield such credence to the truth of God's promise, as to rest on Him for participation of the thing promised. We can have no assurance of the thing promised till we do believe the promise: 'After that ye believed, ye were sealed with the Holy Spirit of promise' (Eph. 1:13). 'I know whom I have believed,' saith the apostle, and thereupon maketh this inference, 'and I am persuaded that He is able to keep that which I have committed unto Him against that day' (2 Tim. 1:12). This, Christ manifested by the condition which He required of those whom He cured, thus, 'If thou canst believe, all things are possible,' Mark 9:23." (Dr. Gouge).

The second half of v. 3 we must leave for the next chapter. In the meantime, "Let *us* therefore fear." "The absolute safety, the fixed and unchanging portion of the chosen people of God can never be doubted. From the eternal, heavenly, divine point of view, saints can never fall; they are seated in heavenly places with Christ; they are renewed by the Spirit, and sealed by Him unto everlasting glory. But who sees the saints of God from this point of view? Not the world, not our fellow-Christians. They only see our character and walk . . . From our point of view, as we live in time, from day to day, our earnest desire must be to continue steadfast, to abide in Christ, to walk with God, to bring forth fruit that will manifest the presence of true and God-given life. Hence the apostle, who says to the Philippians, 'Being confident of this very thing, that He which hath begun a good work in you will perform it until the day of Jesus Christ' (1:6), adds to a similar thought in another epistle, '*If* ye continue in the faith grounded and settled, and be not moved away from the hope of the gospel.' In the one passage Paul's point of view is the heavenly, eternal one; in the other he looks from earth heavenwards, from time to eternity. And in what other way could he think, speak, exhort, and encourage both himself and his fellow-Christians but in this manner? For it is by these very exhortations and warnings that the grace of God keeps us. It is in order that the elect may not fall, it is to bring out in fact and time the (ideal and eternal) impossibility of their apostasy, that God in His wisdom and mercy has sent to us such solemn messages and such fervent entreaties, to watch, to fight, to take heed unto ourselves, to resist the adversary" (Saphir).

CHAPTER SEVENTEEN

Christ Superior to Joshua.

(Heb. 4:3-10)

There has been so much confusion in the minds of commentators, so many conflicting interpretations of Heb. 4 in the past, that we deem it the more necessary to go slowly, and endeavor to supply full proof of the exposition which we are here advancing. That which appears to have occasioned the most difficulty for many is the statement made at the beginning of v. 3, "For we which have believed do enter into rest," or, more literally, "for we enter into the rest, who believed." Having regarded this verse as setting forth a spiritual rest into which believers now enter, they have altogether failed in their understanding of the second part of v. 1. That sinners do enter into rest upon believing is clear from the promise of Christ in Matt. 11:28. That the measure in which this is *enjoyed,* subsequently, will be determined by the degree and frequency with which faith is kept in exercise, we fully allow. But these things are not the subjects of which Paul is treating here in Heb. 4.

Considering that Heb. 4:3 speaks of the believer's present rest, many expositors have read this into the opening verse of the chapter, and have regarded its admonition as meaning, Let Christians be on their guard lest, through carelessness and backsliding, they "seem to come short" in their experimental enjoyment of Christ's rest. In other words, they look upon the "rest" of the opening verses of Heb. 4 as signifying *communion* with the Lord. They argue that this *must* be what was in the apostle's mind, for he was not addressing the unconverted, but "holy brethren, partakers of the heavenly calling." With considerable ingenuity they have appealed to the context, the contents of the closing verses of Heb. 3, as supporting their contention. Those who failed to enter into Canaan (which they consider was a figure of the saints' present portion) were not heathen, but Israelites, the covenant-people of God. We must therefore expose the error of this interpretation before proceeding farther.

First, we would remind the reader once more that the apostle was not here writing to Gentile Christians, but to Hebrews, whose circumstances and temptations were peculiar, unique. There was a very real and grave danger menacing them, not so much of interrupting their spiritual fellowship with Christ, but of shaking their faith in Him altogether. The temptation confronting them was the total abandonment of their Christian profession, of their faith in Jesus of Nazareth, now exalted at the right hand of God; and returning to Judaism. This fact must be kept in mind as we take up the study of each chapter of this Epistle. To lose sight of it, courts certain disaster in our interpretation.

Second, while it is true that the apostle's warning in Heb. 3 is taken from the history of Israel, the covenant people of God, it needs to be borne in mind that in connection with Israel there was an election within an election, a spiritual one within the national. Rom. 9:7, 8 distinctly affirms, "Neither because they are the seed of Abraham, are they all children: but, In Isaac shall thy seed be called. That is, They which are the children of the flesh, these are not the children of God: but the children of the promise are counted for the seed." Unless this fact be steadily remembered, much misunderstanding and error will ensue. The fact is that Israel *as a Nation,* in O.T. times, is *not* a type of God's elect in this N.T. dispensation (as so many have wrongly supposed), but a figure of *Christendom* as a whole. It was only the spiritual remnant, the elect of God within the nation, who foreshadowed His saints of today.

Third, close attention to what is said of the Israelites in Heb. 3 shows conclusively that they were an illustration not of true Christians out of communion with God, but instead, of nominal professors who were never born again. In proof of this note in 3:10 it is said of them, "They do alway err in heart;" now though believers err frequently they do not so "alway;" then it is added, "they have not known My ways"—could this be said of the spiritual election of God? Surely not. Again, in v. 11, We are told, "So I sware in My wrath, They shall not enter into My rest:" but God is never wrathful with His own children. Further, in v. 17 it is not simply said that "they died" but that their "carcases fell" in the wilderness, sure proof is such language that they were not children of God, for "precious in the sight of the Lord is the death of His saints" (Psa. 116:15). Finally, the words of the apostle in 3:19 admit of no misunderstanding, "So we see that they could not enter in because of unbelief." Thus, they were "children in whom is *no* faith" (Deut. 32:20).

Now at the beginning of chapter 4 the apostle applies this solemn warning to *test* the profession of those who were in danger of "departing from the living God." First he says, "Let us *therefore* fear." The "therefore" would have no real force if after referring to *un*-believers he should apply their example to warn believers, of the tendency and danger of ceasing to have *communion* with the Lord; in such a case his illustration would be strained and irrevelant. No, when he says, "Let us therefore *fear*" he obviously has in mind the danger of an empty profession, and sets them to a testing of their faith, which test is answered by perseverance. "*Lest* a promise being left us *of* entering into His rest, any of you should seem to come short of it." It was *not* a "rest" of communion into which they *had* entered but were warned against leaving, or failing to enjoy; but instead, a rest that was *promised*. What follows clearly defines "His rest" and confirms what we have said above. It has to do with the Gospel, and not with precepts to saints! And the point insisted on is the presence or absence of *faith*.

The order of thought in Heb. 4, so far as we discern it, is as follows: First, there is a searching exhortation made (v. 1) to all who profess to be Christians, that they should work out their salvation with fear and trembling, and that their walk should be such as to give no one the impression that they "seem" to be departing from Christ. This is followed by a solemn warning (v. 2) that, the mere hearing of the Gospel is not enough; to profit us, it must be received by faith. Third, this is followed by the declaration that only believers enter into the rest of God. In the remainder of our passage the Spirit makes further comment on Psalm 95 and shows (by negative inference) what the "rest" of God is, and how that the believer's entrance into it is yet future.

"For we which have believed do enter into rest, as He said, As I have sworn in My wrath, if they should enter into My rest" (v. 3). The relation of these two clauses the one to the other, is denoted by "as He said," what follows being a quotation from the 95th Psalm; their connection with the opening words of the verse being that they supply proof of what is there said. As pointed out in the previous article, "For we enter into the rest, who believed," simply informs us *who* are privileged to enter God's rest, namely, Believers. Corroboration of this is now furnished. Upon the second clause of this verse we cannot do better than quote from Dr. Gouge:

"These words 'as He said' may have a double reference. One immediate, to the words next before. Considered thus, they furnish a proof by the rule of contraries. The force of the argument resteth on that ruled case, which the apostle taketh for granted, v. 6, namely, that 'some *must* enter' into that rest which God hath promised. Hereupon this argument may be made: If some 'must enter,' then believers or unbelievers: But not unbelievers, for God by oath hath protested against them; Therefore believers shall enter."

"The other reference is more remote to the latter part of the former verse. If the first clause of v. 3 be included in a parenthesis, the reference of this unto the former verse will appear to be the more fit. For it showeth unbelievers reap no benefit by the word of promise, because God hath sworn that such shall not enter His rest. The relative 'He' is to God. That which He said was in and by David, in Psa. 95:11." Upon the words here quoted from the Psalm, Dr. J. Brown said, "According to the Hebrew idiomatical elliptical mode of expressing an oath, '*they* shall not enter into My rest'."

"Although the works were finished from the foundation of the world" (v. 3). It is at this point the real difficulty of our passage begins, due in part to its peculiar grammatical structure. "The passage that follows wears a peculiarly disjointed appearance, and has occasioned perplexity to interpreters. I apprehend that the last clause of the 3rd verse should be disconnected from the words immediately preceding, and should be connected with those which immediately follow. Along with the 4th and 5th verses, it appears to be a kind of explanatory note on the expression, 'the rest of God'." With this explanation the writer is in full accord, indeed, it seems to him impossible to see in the passage any connected sense unless it be taken thus. Continuing to quote from Dr. Brown:

"A promise is left us of entering into *His rest*. The 'rest' of God, in its primary use in the Old Testament scriptures, is descriptive of that state of cessation from the exercise of creating energy, and of satisfaction in what He hath created, into which God is represented as entering on the completion of His six days' work, when in the beginning 'He formed the heavens and the earth, and all their hosts.' In this sense the phrase was plainly not applicable to the subject which the apostle is discussing; but in these words he shows that the phrase, the *rest of God* is not in the scriptures so appropriated to the rest of God after the creation as not to be applicable, and indeed applied, to other subjects.

"Vv. 4, 5, Although the works were finished from the foundation of the world (for He spake in a certain place of the seventh day on this wise, 'And God did rest the seventh day from all His works'), yet in this place again, 'If they shall enter into My rest.' In this way the three apparently disjointed members are formed into one sentence; and that one sentence expresses a sentiment calculated to throw light on the language which the apostle has employed."

"Although the works were finished from the foundation of the world." This sentence is introductory to what immediately follows, in which the apostle, step by step, leads the Hebrews to the consideration of an higher and better rest than ever was enjoyed in this world. There were two "rests" frequently mentioned in the O.T. as special pledges of God's favour: the sabbath and the land of Canaan: the former being styled "the sabbath of rest to the Lord" (Ex. 35:2), and "the sabbath of the Lord" (Ex. 20:10); the latter, "the rest which the Lord gave them" (Deut. 12:9; Josh. 1:15). In view of these the Hebrews might well say, We have always enjoyed the Lord's sabbath, and our fathers have long occupied Canaan, why then do you speak so much about entering into God's rest? The verses which follow meet this objection, showing that neither of those "rests" was meant by David in Psa. 95, nor by himself here in Heb. 4.

The "rest" to which the apostle was pointing the Hebrews was so blessed, so important, so far surpassing anything that Judaism had known, that he was the more careful they should not be mistaken in connection with *its* nature and character. First, he clears the way for a definition of it by pointing out what it *does not* consist of. He begins with the sabbath which is the first "rest" mentioned in Scripture. Second, he passes on to the rest of Canaan. The rest of the sabbath *did* foreshadow the heavenly rest, and Canaan *was,* in an important sense, a figure of it too; but Paul would turn them from types and shadows to contemplate and have them press forward to the antitype and substance itself.

This reference to "the works" being "finished from the foundation of the world" takes us back to Gen. 2:1, 2. It is the works of creation and restoration, detailed in Gen. 1. The word "foundation" here carries with it a double thought: stability and beginning. As pointed out in our remarks upon Heb. 1:10, "foundation" denotes the fixity of that which is reared upon it: it is the lowest part of an edifice, upon which the whole of the structure rests. As the "foundation" is the first thing attended to in connection with a building, so this term is used here to denote the *beginning* of this present world system.

"For He spake in a certain place of the seventh day on this wise, And God did rest the seventh day from all His works" (v. 4). God's rest on that primitive seventh day possesses at least a fourfold significance. First, it denoted His own complacency, His satisfaction in what He had made: "And God saw everything that He had made and, behold, it was *very good.*" Second, it was the Creator setting before His creatures an example for them to follow. Why had God taken "six days" to make what is described in Gen. 1? Had He so pleased, all could have been done in one day, yea, in a moment! Obviously it was for the purpose of teaching *us.* Just as the great God employed in works of usefulness, in providing for the temporal necessities of His creatures, so should we be. And just as God has ceased from all the works of those six days and on the seventh day "rested," so must we. Third, that primitive sabbath was the prophetic pledge of the "rest" which this earth shall enjoy during the reign of Christ. Fourth, it was a foreshadowing and earnest of the eternal sabbath, when God shall "rest in His love" (Zeph. 3:17).

Perhaps it needs to be added that the words "and God did rest" do not signify, absolutely, that He remained in a state of inactivity. The "rest" of Scripture is never a condition of inertia. The words of our Saviour in John 5:17 respecting the sabbath day, "My Father worketh hitherto" in nowise conflict with Gen. 2:3. God's "rest" there was from creating new kinds of creatures; what Christ speaks of is His work in doing good to His creatures; it concerns God's providences, which never cease day or night, preserving, succoring, governing His creatures. From this we learn that *our* keeping of the sabbath is not to consist of a state of idleness, but is forebearing from all the ordinary works of the preceding six days. The Saviour's own example in the Gospels teaches us that works of absolute necessity are permissible, and works of mercy proper. Isa. 58:13, 14 informs us *how* the sabbath is to be kept. John 5:17 linked to Gen. 2:3 also contains a hint of the eternal "rest" of heaven: it will be a ceasing from all the carnal works in which we were engaged here, yet it will not be a state of idleness as Rev. 22:3 proves.

"And in this again, If they shall enter into My rest" (v. 5). The line of argument which the apostle is here pursuing will the more readily be perceived if due attention be paid to the word "again". He is proving that there was *another* "rest" of God beside that which followed upon His works of creation. This is evident from the language of Psa. 95, upon which he comments in the next verse. Thus the Holy Spirit warns us that each expression used in Holy Writ must be interpreted strictly in harmony with its context. A great deal of unnecessary confusion had been avoided if expositors heeded this simple but fundamental rule. Take the oft-quoted words of James 5:16, "The effectual fervent prayer of a righteous man available much." How often the "righteous man" here is regarded as synonymous with "Christian," one who is "righteous" *in Christ*. But such a view ignores the context. This statement is found not in Romans, but James. The epistle of James does not give us the believer's standing, so much as his state. The prayers of a Christian whose ways are *not* "right" before God, "avail" little or nothing. So all through the book of Proverbs the "righteous" man is not regarded there as one who is righteous imputatively, but practically.

Take again the believer's present experimental "rest." There are numbers of passages in the N.T. where the *same* word "rest" is found, but they by no means all refer to the same thing or experience. Each reference needs to be studied in the light of its immediate context, in the light of the particular book in which it is found, (remembering the special theme of that book), and in connection with what is predicated of that "rest". "Come unto Me, all ye that labour and are heavy-laden, and I will give you rest. Take My yoke upon you, and learn of Me; for I am meek and lowly in heart: and ye shall find rest unto your souls" (Matt. 11:28, 29). Here it is obvious, almost at first glance, that two distinct "rests" are before us. The first may be designated rest *of conscience,* which the convicted sinner, groaning beneath the intolerable load of his conscious sins, obtains when he casts himself on the mercy of Christ. The second is rest *of soul,* which alas, many professing Christians know very little, if anything, about. It is obtained by *taking* Christ's "yoke" upon us and "learning" of Him.

"Seeing therefore it remaineth that some must enter therein, and they to whom it was first preached entered not in because of unbelief" (v. 6). The first words give intimation of an inference being drawn from what has gone before. In v. 5 God's protestation against unbelievers is recorded, here the apostle infers therefrom that there is a rest for believers to enter into. Since God has made promise of some entering into His rest, then they *must* do so: if no unbelievers, then believers. The words, "it remaineth" here signify "it followeth," for no word of God can fall to the ground. No promise of His can be utterly made void. Though many reap no good thereby, yet others shall be made partakers of the benefit of it. Though the vast majority of the adult Israelites perished in the wilderness, yet Caleb and Joshua entered Canaan.

"And they to whom it was first preached entered not in because of unbelief." The word "preached" here means "evangelize." The same rootword is rendered "gospel" in v. 2. This shows us, first, that God has employed only one instrument in the saving of sinners from the beginning, namely, the preaching of the gospel, cf. Gal. 3:8. Second, that the demand of the Gospel from those who hear it is *faith,* taking God at His word, receiving with childlike simplicity and gladness the good news He has sent us. Third, that "unbelief" shuts out from God's favour and blessing. In Heb. 11:31 we are told, "By faith the harlot Rahab perished not with them that believed not." It was not because the others were Canaanites, heathen, wicked people, but because they *believed not* that they "perished." Solemn warning was this for the Hebrews whose faith was waning.

"Again, He limiteth a certain day, saying in David, Today" (v. 7). It is evident that v. 6 is an incomplete sentence, finished, we apprehend, in v. 11. What follows in vv. 7 to 10 is a parenthesis, and to its consideration we must now turn. The purpose of this parenthesis is to *establish* the principle on which the exhortation is based, namely, that since there is a "rest of God" for believers to enter, and seeing that Israel of old failed to enter therein, it behooves us today to give the more earnest heed to the word of the Gospel which we have heard, and to "labour to enter into that rest, lest any man fall after the same example of unbelief."

"Again He limiteth a certain day, saying, in David, Today, after so long a time, as it is said, Today if ye will hear His voice, harden not your hearts" (v. 7). This may be called the text which the apostle goes on to expound and apply. The R.V. rendering of it is much to be preferred: "He again defineth a certain day, Today, saying in David, so long a time afterward (even as hath been said before), Today if ye will hear" etc. Having drawn an argument from Psa. 95:11 to show that the promise of rest which is "left" (v. 1) Christians, is not the same as that mentioned in Gen. 2:3, the apostle now proceeds to point out that there is another "rest" to be sought after than the land of Canaan — let us not deem the demonstration of this *needless,* lest we be found impugning the wisdom of the Holy Spirit.

The apostle's argument here turns on the word "Today" found in Psa. 95:7. *This* was what was "limited" or "defined." The "after so long a time" refers to the interval which elapsed after the Israelites perished in the wilderness and the writing of that Psalm, which contained a Divine exhortation for God's people living then. Betwixt Moses and David was a period of five centuries (Acts 13:20). "The apostle's argument may thus be framed: That rest wherewith men are invited to enter four hundred and fifty years after a rest possessed, is another rest than that which Israel possessed. But the rest intended by David is a rest wherein he inviteth men to enter four hundred and fifty years after Canaan was possessed. Therefore Canaan is not that rest" (Dr. Gouge).

"For if Joshua had given them rest, then would He not afterward have spoken of another day" (v. 8). It is plain that the apostle is here anticipating a Jewish objection, which may be stated thus: Though many of the Israelites which were in the wilderness entered not into Canaan, yet others did; for Joshua conducted their children thither. To obviate this, the apostle proves that the O.T. Scriptures spoke of another "rest" besides that. He does not deny Canaan to be a rest, but he denies that it was the only rest, the rest to be so rested in as no other was to be sought after. The "then would he have not afterward have spoken of another day" is the proof that Joshua did not settle God's people in the "rest" which David mentioned.

It is right here that we may discern the point to which the apostle would direct the Hebrews' attention, though to spare their feelings he does not state it explicitly. It was a glorious thing when Joshua led Israel's hosts out of the wilderness, across the Jordan, into the promised land. Truly that *was* one of the outstanding epochs in their national history. Nor would the apostle, directly, deprecate it. Yet if the Hebrews would but meditate for a moment on the *nature* of that rest into which the illustrious successor of Moses led their fathers, they must see that it was very far from being the perfect state. It was only an earthly inheritance. It was filled with enemies, who had to be dispossessed. Its continued tenure was dependent on their own faithfulness to God. It was enjoyed comparatively only a short time. Different far is the rest of God into which the Apostle of Christianity will yet lead His people. Listen to His own words, "In My Father's house are many mansions: if it were not so I would have told you. I go to prepare a place for you. And if I go and prepare a place for you, I will come again, and receive you unto Myself; that, where I am, there ye may be also" (John 14:2, 3). Here, then, we may see the superiority of Christ over Joshua, as the rest into which He brings His people excels that into which Joshua conducted Israel.

"There remaineth therefore a rest to the people of God" (v. 9). This verse gives the conclusion drawn from the preceding argument. The apostle had shown that the "rest" mentioned by David was neither the rest of the primitive sabbath in Gen. 2 nor the rest of Canaan into which Joshua had conducted the second generation of Israel. *Therefore* there "remaineth a rest to the people of God:" that is, there is some other rest for God's people to look forward to. Thus, the "therefore" here is, first of all, a general inference drawn from all that precedes. A "promise is left" of entering into God's rest (v. 1). That promise must be appropriated, "mixed with faith" in those who hear it (v. 2). Only believers will enter that rest, for God hath sworn that unbelievers shall not enter therein (v. 3). Although there is a rest of God mentioned in Gen. 2 (vv. 2, 3), and although Joshua led Israel into the rest of Canaan (v. 8), yet neither of these "rests" was what is promised Christians (v. 8). Hence, we can only conclude there is *another* "rest" for God's people (v. 9).

That the Christian's perfect "rest" is yet future is clear from the language of v. 11, where the Hebrews were admonished to "labour therefore to enter into that rest." Thus, regarding v. 9, first, as a general conclusion drawn from the whole of the context, we understand it to mean: "Thus it is evident there is a rest for the people of God." These words were designed to *re-assure* the hearts of the Hebrews. In turning their backs on Judaism the "rest" of Canaan was relinquished, but this did not mean that they had, because of their faith in Christ, *ceased to be* "the people of God," nor did it involve the forfeiture of all privileges and blessings. Nay, the apostle had warned them in 3:6, 12, 14 that it was impossible to retain the privilege of belonging to the people of God except through faith in Christ. Now he assures them that only for such people was there a rest of God remaining.

Above, we have pointed out that the "therefore" of v. 9 denotes, first of all, that the apostle is here drawing a general conclusion from all he had said in the context. We would now call attention to a more specific inference pointed by that word. It needs to be most carefully observed that in this verse the Holy Spirit employs an entirely different word for "rest" than what he had used in vv. 1, 3, 4, 5 and 8. There the Greek word is rightly rendered "rest," but here it is "sabbatismos" and its meaning has been properly given by the translators in the margin — "keeping of a Sabbath." The R.V. gives the text itself, "There remaineth therefore a sabbath rest for the people of God."

The purpose of the Holy Spirit in employing this term here is not difficult to discover. He was writing to Hebrews, Jews who had professed to become Christians, to have trusted in the Lord Jesus. Their profession of faith involved them in sore trials at the hands of their unbelieving brethren. They denounced them as apostates from the faith of their fathers. They *disowned* them as the "people of God." But as we have said the apostle here re-assures them that now only believers in Christ had any title to be numbered among "the people of God." Having renounced Judaism for Christ the question of the "sabbath" must also have exercised them deeply. Here the apostle sets their minds at rest. A suitable point in his epistle had now been reached when this could be brought in: he was speaking of "rest," so he informs them that under Christianity also, "there *remaineth* therefore a sabbath-keeping for the people of God." The *specific* reference in the "therefore" is to what he had said in v. 4: *God* did *rest* on the seventh day from all His works, *therefore* as believers in Christ are the "people of God" they must rest too.

"There *remaineth* therefore a sabbath-keeping for the people of God." The reference is not to something future, but to what is present. The Greek verb (in its passive form) is never rendered by any other English equivalent than "remaineth." It occurs again in Heb. 10:26. The word "remain" signifies "to be left after others have withdrawn, to continue unchanged." Here then is a plain, positive, unequivocal declaration by the Spirit of God: "There remaineth therefore a sabbath-keeping." Nothing could be simpler, nothing less ambiguous. The striking thing is that this statement occurs in the very epistle whose theme is the superiority of *Christianity* over Judaism; written to those addressed as "holy brethren, partakers of the *heavenly* calling." Therefore, it cannot be gainsaid that Heb. 4:9 refers directly to *the Christian Sabbath.* Hence we solemnly and emphatically declare that any man who says there is no Christian Sabbath takes direct issue with the *N.T.* scriptures.

"For he that is entered into his rest he also hath ceased from his own works, as God from His" (v. 10). In this verse the apostle expressly defines the *nature* of that excellent rest of which he had been speaking: it is a cessation from our works, as God from His. The object in thus describing our rest is to show that it is not to be found in this world, but is reserved for the world to come. The argument of this verse — its opening "for" denotes that further proof is being supplied to confirm what has been said — is taken from the self-evident principle that rest is not enjoyed till work is ceased from. This world is full of toil, travail and trouble, but in the world to come there is full freedom from all these.

"Thy commandment is exceedingly broad" (Psalm 119:96). There is a breadth and fullness to the words of God which no single interpretation can exhaust. Just as v. 9 has at least a double application, containing both a general conclusion from the whole preceding argument, and also a specific inference from what is said in v. 4, so is it here. Not only does v. 9 state a general principle which serves to corroborate the apostle's inference in v. 9, but it also has a specific reference and application. The change in number of the pronoun here is not without meaning. In v. 1 he had used a plural, "us," so in v. 3 "we," and again in v. 11 he uses "us," but here in v. 10 it is "he and his." "It appears to me that it is the rest of Christ from His works, which is compared with the rest of God from His works in creation." (Dr. J. Owen).

The reference to Christ in v. 10 (remember the section begins at 3:1 and concludes with 4:14-16) completes the positive side of the apostle's proof of His superiority over Joshua. In v. 8 he had pointed out that Joshua *did not* lead Israel into the perfect rest of God; now he affirms that Christ, our Apostle, *has* entered it, and *His* entrance is the pledge and proof that His people shall —

"whither the Forerunner is *for us entered*" (Heb. 6:20). But more: what is said of Christ in v. 10 clinches our interpretation of v. 9 and gives beautiful completeness to what is there said: "There remaineth therefore a sabbath-keeping to the people of God. *For* He that is entered into His rest, He also hath ceased from his own works, *as* God from His."

Thus, the Holy Spirit here teaches us to view Christ's rest from his work of Redemption as parallel with God's work in creation. They are spoken of as parallel in this respect: the relation which each "work" has to *the keeping of a sabbath*! The opening "for" of v. 10 shows that what follows furnishes a reason *why* God's people, now, must keep the sabbath. That reason invests the sabbath with a fuller meaning than it had in O.T. times. It is now not only a memorial of God's work of creation, and a recognition of the Creator as our Proprietor, but it is also an emblem of the rest which Christ entered as an eternal memorial of His finished work; and inasmuch as Christ ended His work and entered upon His "rest" by rising again on the *first* day of the week, we are thereby notified that the Christian's six work-days must run from Monday to Saturday, and that his sabbath must be observed on Sunday. This is confirmed by the additional fact that the N.T. shows that after the crucifixion of Christ the first day of the week was the one set apart for Divine worship. May the Lord bless what has been before us.

CHAPTER EIGHTEEN

Christ Superior to Joshua.

(Heb. 4:11-16)

The verses which are to be before us complete the present section of our Epistle, a section which begins at 3:1 and which has two main divisions: the first, setting forth the superiority of Christ over Moses; the second, His superiority over Joshua. In the last six verses of chapter 4 a practical application is made of what had previously been said. That application begins with an exhortation for Christians to "labour therefore to enter into that rest." Both the nature and the place of this "rest" have been defined in the earlier verses. As the opening verse of the chapter shows, it is the "rest of God" which is, in promise, set before us. Beautifully has another said:

"But what did God mean by calling it *His* rest? Not they enter into *their* rest, but His own. Oh, blessed distinction! I hasten to the ultimate and deepest solution of the question. God gives us *Himself*, and in all His gifts He gives us Himself. Here is the distinction between all religions which men invent, which have their origin in the conscience and heart of man, which spring up from the earth; and the truth, the salvation, the life, revealed unto us from above, descending to us from heaven. All religions seek and promise the same things: light, righteousness, peace, strength, and joy. But human religions think only of creature-light, creature-righteousness, of a human, limited, and imperfect peace, strength and blessings. They start from man upwards. But God gives us Himself, and in Himself all gifts, and hence all His gifts are perfect and divine.

"Does God give us righteousness? He Himself is our righteousness, Jehovah-Tsidkenu. Does God give us peace? Christ is our peace. Does God give us light? He is our light. Does God give us bread? He is the bread we eat. As the Son liveth by the Father, so he that eateth Me shall live by Me (John 6). God Himself is our strength. God is ours, and in all His gifts and blessings He gives Himself. By the Holy Spirit we are one with Christ, and Christ the Son of God is our righteousness, nay, our life. Do you want any other real presence? Are we not altogether 'engodded,' God dwelling and living in us, and we in Him? What more real presence and indwelling, awful and blessed, can we have than that which the apostle described when he said: 'I live; yet not I, But Christ liveth in me?' Or again, 'I can do all things through Christ which strengtheneth me.' Thus God gives us *His* rest as our rest" (Saphir).

Following the exhortation to labour to enter into God's rest, reference is made to the living, powerful, and piercing character of the Word of God, and the effects it produces in regeneration. In the light of the solemn warning which follows in v. 13, the contents of v. 12 seem to be brought in for the purpose of enabling the Hebrews to test the genuineness of their Christian profession: sufficient is there said for them to discover whether or not they had been born again. Then the chapter closes with one of the most precious passages to be found in our Epistle, or indeed in the whole of the N.T. It makes known the gracious provisions which God has made for His poor people while they are yet in the place of testing. It brings before us the sufficiency and sympathy of our great High Priest, in view of which Christians are bidden to "come boldly unto the throne of grace," that they "may obtain mercy, and find grace to help in time of need." May the Spirit of God condescend to open up to us this portion of His Word.

"Let us labour therefore to enter into that rest, lest any man fall after the same example of unbelief" (v. 11). As pointed out in the preceding article, this verse completes the sentence begun at v. 6. It is in view of the solemn fact that the great majority of those Israelites to whom the Gospel of Rest was first preached did not receive it in faith, and so perished in the wilderness, and hence because that only true believers will enter into God's rest, the Hebrews were now enjoined to spare no efforts in making sure that they would not fail and miss it. This 11th verse is also the complement to v. 1.

The verb for "let us labour" is derived from another verb meaning "to make haste." It is designed to point a contrast from "any of you should seem to come short of it" in v. 1. There the word is derived from a root meaning "afterwards," and some able linguists declare that the word for "come short of" means, literally, "be a day late." We believe the Spirit's designed reference is to what is recorded in Num. 14. Israel had already crossed the wilderness, and had reached Kadesh-barnea. From thence Moses had sent the twelve spies to view the land of Canaan. They had returned with a conflicting report. Ten of them magnified the difficulties which lay ahead, and discouraged the people but Caleb said, "Let us go up *at once,* and possess it" (Num. 13:30). The congregation listened only to the ten, and "wept that night" and "murmured against Moses and against Aaron: and the whole congregation said unto them, Would God we had died in the land of Egypt! or would God we had died in this wilderness! And wherefore hath the Lord brought us into this land, to fall by the Sword, that our wives and children should be a prey? were it not better for us to return into Egypt? And they said one to another, Let us make us a captain and let us return into Egypt" (Num. 14:1-3).

Then it was that the wrath of Jehovah was kindled against His unbelieving people, saying, "How long shall I bear with this evil congregation which murmur against Me? I have heard the murmurings of the children of Israel, which they murmur against Me. Say unto them, As truly as I live, saith the Lord, *as* ye have spoken in Mine ears, *so* will I do to you: Your carcases shall fall in this wilderness" (Num. 14:27-29). But instead of bowing to the Lord's solemn sentence, we are told, "And they rose up early in the morning, and gat them up into the top of the mountain, saying, Lo, we be here, and *will* go up unto the place which the Lord hath promised" (v. 40). Moses faithfully expostulated with them, "Wherefore now do ye transgress the commandment of the Lord? but it shall not prosper. Go not up, for the Lord is not among you; that ye be not smitten." But they heeded him not: "They presumed to go up unto the hill top . . . Then the Amalekites came down, and the Canaanites which dwelt in that hill, and smote them, and discomfited them, even unto Hormah" (vv. 44, 45). *They were a day late!* They had delayed, they had failed to trust the Lord and heed His voice through Caleb the previous day, and now they "came short" of entering the promised rest of Canaan.

It was in view of Israel's procrastination at Kadesh-barnea that the apostle admonished the Hebrews, "Let us therefore fear, lest a promise being left of entering into His rest, any of you should seem to come short of it." As we pointed out the word "seem" regarded their *walk*: let there be nothing in their ways which gave the appearance that they were halting, wavering, departing from Christ. For Christians to *seem* to come short, be a day late, in laying hold of the promise "left" them of entering into God's rest, means to sink to the level of the ways of the world, to settle down *here,* instead of going forward as "strangers and pilgrims." It means to look back to and long for the flesh-pots of Egypt. Ah, my reader, to which does your daily life witness? to the fact that you have *not yet* entered your "rest," or that you *have* found a substitute for it *here*? If so, heed that solemn word, "Arise ye, and depart for *this* is not your rest: because it is polluted, it shall destroy, even with a sore destruction" (Micah 2:10).

Having then warned the Hebrews in v. 1 what to *avoid*, the apostle now tells them in v. 11 what to *essay*. They were to "labour" to enter into that rest. As stated above, the Greek word is derived from another verb meaning "to make haste;" the one used here signifies to "give diligence" and is so rendered in the R.V. In 2 Tim. 2:15 it is translated "study." "The word 'labour' is equivalent to 'eagerly and perseveringly seek.' The manner in which the Hebrew Christians were to 'labour to enter unto that rest,' was by believing the truth, and continuing 'steadfast and unmoveable' in the faith of the truth, and in the natural results of the faith of the truth" (Dr. J. Brown). It is human responsibility which is here being addressed again, and Heb. 4:11 is closely parallel with the exhortations of 1 Cor. 10:10-12 and 2 Pet. 1:5-10.

Our real "rest" is yet to come, it is but "promised" (v. 1); in the meantime we are to press forward to it. "This world is not a fit place, nor this life a fit time, to enjoy such a rest as is reserved in heaven. Rest here would glue our hearts too much to this world, and make us say, 'It is good to be here' (Matt. 17:4). It would slack our longing desire after Christ in heaven. Death would be more irksome, and heaven the less welcome. There would be no proof or trial of our spiritual armour, and of the several graces of God bestowed on us. God's providence, prudence, power, mercy, could not be made so well discerned. This rest being to come, and reserved for us, it will be our Wisdom, while here we live, to prepare for trouble, and to address ourselves to labour: as the soldiers in the field and as the labourers in the daytime. Yet withal to have our eye upon this rest to come; that thereby we may be the more encouraged and incited to hold out to the end" (Dr. Gouge).

"Lest any man fall after the same example of unbelief." To enforce the previous exhortation the apostle points out the danger and damage that would follow a neglect thereof. The "rest" is a word of caution and calls for circumspection as a preventative against apostasy. The "lest any man" intimates that this care and circumspection is not to be restricted to one's own self, but extended to our fellow-pilgrims. The word "fall" signifies to fall utterly: it is used in Rom. 11:22. Professors may fall away; many have done so (see 1 John 2:19 etc.); then let *us* be on our guard. The "example" of others having fallen through unbelief should make us wary.

"We may well observe from this exhortation, 1. That great oppositions will and do arise against men in the work of entering into God's rest . . . But notwithstanding all these difficulties, the promise of God being mixed with faith will carry us safely through them all. 2. That as the utmost of our endeavour and labours are required to our obtaining an entrance into the rest of Christ, so it doth very well deserve that they should be laid out therein. Men are content to lay themselves out to the utmost and to spend their strength for the 'bread that perisheth,' yea 'for that which is not bread.' But the rest of the Gospel deserves our utmost diligence and endeavour. To convince men thereof is one of the chief ends of the preaching of the Gospel" (Dr. J. Owen).

As was the case with the contents of vv. 9 and 10, so we are assured there is a *double* reference to the words of v. 11: a general and a specific. The general, refers to the future and perfect rest of the Christian in heaven; the specific, being to that which is the emblem and type of it, namely, the weekly sabbath. This, we believe, is why the Holy Spirit here says, "Let us give diligence therefore to enter into *that* rest," rather than "into *His* rest," as in v. 1. "*That* rest" designedly includes both the eternal rest of God, and the sabbath rest, spoken of in v. 10. This we are to "give diligence" to enter, not only because the sabbath-desecration of worldlings is apt to discourage us, but also because there are professing Christians who loudly insist that there is no such thing *as* a "Christian sabbath." Beware lest we fail to heed this word of God, and "fall through the same example of unbelief" as Israel in the wilderness, who failed to listen to God.

"For the Word of God is quick, and powerful, and sharper than any two edged sword, piercing even to the dividing asunder of soul and spirit, and of the joints and marrow, and is a discerner of the thoughts and intents of the heart" (v. 12). The first word of this verse (which has the force of "because") denotes that the apostle is here furnishing further reason *why* professing Christians should give diligence in pressing forward to the rest which is set before them. That reason is drawn from the nature of and the effects produced by the Word of God. This verse and the one which follows appear to be brought in for the purpose of *testing* profession and enabling exercised souls to discover whether or not they have been born again.

"Let us give diligence therefore to enter into that rest . . . *For* the Word of God is quick and powerful, and sharper than any two-edged sword, piercing even to the dividing asunder of soul and spirit, and of the joints and marrow, and is a discerner of the thoughts and intents of the heart." It should be evident that the first thing emphasized here is that Christianity consists not so much of external conduct, as the place which the Word of God has *within* us. The Word of God "piercing even to the dividing asunder of soul and spirit" is the effect which it produces, under the application of the Lord, when a sinner is regenerated. Man is a tripartite being, consisting of spirit and soul and body. This, we believe, is the first and deepest meaning of Gen. 1:26, "And God said, Let *us* make man in Our image, after Our likeness." God Himself is a Trinity in Unity, and such He made man to be.

The "spirit" is the highest part of man, being the seat of God-consciousness. The "soul" is the ego, the individual himself, and is the seat of self-consciousness; man *has* a "spirit," but he *is* "a living soul." The "body" is his house or tabernacle, being the seat of sense-consciousness. In the day that man first sinned, he died spiritually. But in Scripture "death" never means extinction of being; instead, it always signifies *separation* (see Luke 15:24). The nature of man's spiritual "death" is intimated in Eph. 4:18, "*alienated from* the life of God." When Adam disobeyed his Maker, he became a fallen creature, separated from God. The first effect of this was that his "spirit" no longer functioned separately, it was no more in communion with God. His spirit *fell* to the level of his soul.

The "soul" is the seat of the emotions (1 Sam. 18:1, Judges 10:16, Gen. 42:21, etc.). It is that part of our nature which stirs into exercise the "lust of the flesh, the lust of the eyes, and the pride of life." The unregenerate man is termed "the *soulical* man" (1 Cor. 2:14), the Greek word there being the adjectival form of "psuche" or "soul." That is to say, the unregenerate man is entirely dominated by his soul, his lusts, his desires, his emotions. Spiritual considerations have no weight with him whatsoever, for he is "alienated from the life of God." True, he *has* a "spirit," and by means of it he is capable of perceiving all around him the evidences of the "eternal power and godhead" of the Creator (Rom. 1:20). It is the "candle of the Lord" (Prov. 20:27) within him; yet has it, because of the fall, *no* communion with God. Now at regeneration there is, literally, a "dividing asunder of soul and spirit." The spirit is restored to communion with God, made *en-rapport* with Him, "reconciled." The spirit is raised from its immersion in the soul, and once more functions separately: "For God is my witness, whom I serve with my *spirit*" (Rom. 1:9); "my *spirit* prayeth" (1 Cor. 14:14) etc.

The first consequence of this is intimated in the closing words of v. 12, "And is a discerner of the thoughts and intents of the heart." The Word of God now exposes his innermost being. Having eyes to see, he discovers, for the first time, what a vile, depraved and hell-deserving creature he is. Though, in the mercy of God, he may have been preserved from much outward wickedness in his unregenerate days, and so passed among his fellows as an exemplary character, he now perceives that there dwelleth "*no* good thing" in him, that every thought and intent of his desperately-wicked heart had, all his life, been contrary to the requirements and claims of a holy God. The Word has searched him out, and discovered him to himself. He sees himself a lost, ruined, undone sinner. This is ever the first conscious effect of the new birth, for one who is still "dead in trespasses and sins" has *no* realization of his awful condition before God.

Ere passing on let us earnestly press upon the reader what has just been before us, and ask, has the Word of God thus "pierced" you? Has it penetrated, as no word from man ever has, into your innermost being? Has it exposed the workings of your wicked heart? Has it detected to you the sink of iniquity which dwells within? Make no mistake about it, dear friend, the thrice holy God of Scripture "requireth truth in the *inward* parts" (Psa. 51.6). If the Word of God *has* searched you out, then you cried with Isaiah "Woe is me! for I am undone" (6:5); with Job, "I abhor myself" (42:6); with the publican, "God be merciful to me the sinner" (Luke 18:13). But if you are a stranger to these experiences, no matter what your profession or performances, no matter how highly you may think of yourself or Christians think of you, *God* says you are still *dead* in sin.

Let it not be supposed that we have attempted to give above a *complete* description of all that takes place at the new birth; not so, we have confined ourself to what is said in Heb. 4:12. Nor let it be thought that the language of this verse is to be *restricted* to what occurs at regeneration, not so, that is only in initial reference. The activities of the Word of God therein described are repeated whenever a Christian gets out of communion with Him, for then he is dominated to a large extent by his soul rather than his spirit. It should not need pointing out, yet the terrible ignorance of Scripture prevailing today makes it necessary, that when a child of God is walking in communion with Him, His word does not come to *him* as a "sword"; rather is it "a lamp" unto his feet. If the reader will compare Rev. 2:12 and 19:15 he will obtain confirmation of this.

The relation of this 12th verse to the whole context is very striking, and its contents divinely appropriate. It brings out the dignity and Deity of "The Apostle" of our profession. It shows the *sufficiency* of His Word. It is striking to note that just *seven* things are here said of it. First, it is the "Word of God." Second, it is living, or "quick." Third, it is mighty, "powerful." Fourth, it is effectual, "sharper than any two edged sword." Fifth, it is penetrating, "piercing." Sixth, it is regenerative, "even to the dividing asunder of soul and spirit." Seventh, it is revealing and exposing, bringing to light the "thoughts and intents of the heart, etc." The reference to the Word piercing to the dividing asunder of "the joints (external) and marrow" (internal) tells of its discriminating power over every part of our being. The more we submit ourselves unto its searching and convicting influence the more shall we be blest.

"Neither is there any creature that is not manifest in His sight: but all things are naked and opened unto the eyes of Him with whom we have to do" (v. 13). The rendering of the A.V. here is faulty, the opening "Neither" being quite misleading. The R.V. gives "And there is no creature that is not manifest in His sight" etc. Thus the first word denotes that a reason is being given for the power and efficacy of the Word, a reason which is drawn from the nature of Him whose Word it is, namely, God; who being Himself the Searcher of the heart and the Discerner of all things, is pleased to exercise that power in and by the ministry and application of His Word. The two verses taken together supply a further reason why Christ's voice should be heeded, even because, as God, He is the omniscient One.

"Seeing then that we have a great High Priest, that is passed into the heavens, Jesus the Son of God, let us hold fast our profession" (v. 14). The connection between this and what has gone before is most blessed. The closing verses of our chapter contain precious words of encouragement. They tell of the wondrous provisions of God's grace for His people while they are still in the place of testing. They assure us that none of those who are really the people of God shall, finally, miss the perfect and eternal rest.

The R.V. reads, "Having then a great High Priest"; Bagster's interlinear gives, "Having therefore a High Priest, great." The general reference is back to what was said in 1:3, 2:17, 3:1: the Divine sonship, the incarnation, the exaltation of Jesus, our High Priest, is the supreme motive for holding fast our profession. The particular reference is to the apostle's main point in this chapter: if the question be asked, What hope have we poor sinners got of entering into *God's* rest? The answer is, Because Christ, our High Priest, has already entered heaven, and we also must do so in and by Him. The immediate reference is to what had been said in vv. 12, 13: we shall be assuredly found out if we fall from our profession, therefore it becomes us to hold it fast.

As the priesthood of Christ will, D.V., come before us more fully in the chapters that follow, we shall offer here only a few brief remarks on the verse now before us. First, it is to be noted that the Holy Spirit here designates Christ the "*great* High Priest";

no other, neither Aaron nor Melchizedek, is so denominated. Its use emphasises the supreme dignity, excellency, and sufficiency of our High Priest. Second, He has "passed in (Greek "through") the heavens." "This word signifies to pass through notwithstanding any difficulties that may seem to hand. Thus it is said that an angel and Peter '*passed* the first and second wards' (Acts 12:10). Our Lord Christ having assumed our nature, passed through the virgin's womb; and being born, in His infancy, childhood, and manhood, passed through many difficulties, temptations, afflictions, persecutions, yea, death itself and the grave; after His resurrection He passed through the air and the stellar heavens, entering the heaven of heavens. Thus we see that nothing could hinder Him from that place where He intended to appear as our Priest before His Father" (Dr. Gouge).

"For we have not an High Priest which cannot be touched with the feeling of our infirmities; but was in all points tempted like as we are, yet without sin" (v. 15). Most blessed is this. The third thing said in v. 14 of our exalted High Priest is that He is "the Son of God." Well may poor sinners, conscious of their unworthiness and vileness, ask, How may we, so weak and worthless, approach unto and seek the mediation of *such* an One? To re-assure our poor hearts, the Holy Spirit at once reminds us that albeit Christ *is* such a great and glorious Priest, yet, withal, He is full of sympathy and tender compassion for His afflicted people. He is "merciful" (2:17), as well as omnipotent. He is Man, as well as God. He has Himself been tempted in all things, like ourselves, sin excepted.

"But was in all points tempted like as we are, yet without sin," or literally, "who has been tempted in all things according to our likeness, apart from sin" i.e. in spirit, and soul, and body. "He was tempted— tried, exercised—for no more doth the word impart. Whatever is the moral evil in temptation is due to the depraved intention of the tempter, or from the weakness and sin of the tempted. In itself, it is but a trial, which may have a good or bad effect. He was tempted like as we are, yet without sin. Sin may be considered as to its principle, and as to its effect. Men are tempted to sin by sin, to actual sin by habitual sin, to outward sin, by indwelling sin. And this is the greatest source of sin in us who are sinners. The apostle reminds us of the holiness and purity of Christ, that we may not imagine that He was liable unto any such temptations unto sin from within as we find ourselves liable unto, who are never free from guilt and defilement. Whatever temptation He was exposed unto or exercised withal, as He was with all and of all sorts that can come from without, they had none of them in the last degree any effect unto Him. He was absolutely in all things 'without sin'; He neither was tempted by sin, such was the holiness of His nature; nor did His temptation produce sin, such was the perfection of His obedience" (Dr. J. Owen).

The Man Christ Jesus was the Holy One of God, and therefore He *could not* sin. But were not Satan and Adam created without sin, and did not they yield to temptation? Yes; but the one was only a created angel the other merely man. But our Lord and Saviour was not a created being; instead, He was "God manifest in flesh." In His humanity He was "holy" (Luke 1:35) and, as such, as high above unfallen Satan or Adam as the heavens are above the earth. He was not only impeccable God, but impeccable Man. The prince of this world came, but found *nothing* in Him (John 14:30). Thus, He is presented before us not only as an example to be followed, but as an Object upon which faith may rest with unshaken confidence.

"Let us therefore come boldly unto the throne of grace, that we may obtain mercy, and find grace to help in time of need" (v. 16). This verse sets before us the second use we are to make of the priesthood of Christ. The first is named in v. 14, to "hold fast our profession"; here, to "come boldly unto the throne of grace." In relation to the whole context this verse makes known the wondrous and blessed provision God has made for His wilderness people. Herein, too, we may behold again the immeasurable superiority of Christianity over Judaism. The Israelites were confined to the outer court; none at all save the high priest was permitted to draw near to God within the vail. But all Christians, the youngest, weakest, most ignorant, have been "made nigh" (Eph. 2:13); and in consequence, freedom of access to the very throne of Deity is now their rightful and blessed portion.

"And having such a High Priest in heaven, can we lose courage? Can we draw back in cowardice, impatience, and faintheartedness? Can we give up our profession, our allegiance, our obedience to Christ? Or shall we not be like Joshua and Caleb, who followed the Lord fully? Let us hold fast our profession; let us persevere and fight the good fight of faith. Our great High Priest in the highest glory is our righteousness and strength. He loves, He watches, He prays, He holds us fast, and we shall never perish. Jesus is our Moses, who in the height above prays for us. Jesus our true Joshua, who gained the victory over our enemies. Only be strong, and of a good courage; be not afraid, neither be thou dismayed. In that mirror of the Word in which we behold our sin and weakness, we behold also the image of that perfect One who has passed through the conflict and temptation, who as the High Priest bears us on His loving heart, and as the Shepherd of the flock holds us in safety forever more. Boldly we come to the throne of grace. In Jesus we draw near to the Father. The throne of majesty and righteousness is unto us a throne of grace. The Lord is our God. There is not merely grace on the throne, but the throne is altogether the throne of grace. It is *grace* which disciplines us by the sharp and piercing Word, it is grace which looks on us when we have denied Him, and makes us weep bitterly. Jesus always intercedes: the throne is always a throne of grace. The Lamb is in the midst of the throne. Hence we come boldly.

"Boldly is not contrasted with reverently and tremblingly. It means literally 'saying all,' with that confidence which begets thorough honesty, frankness, full and open speech. 'Pour out your heart before Him.' Come as you are, say what you feel, ask what you need. Confess your sins, your fears, your wandering thoughts and affections. Jesus the Lord went through all sorrows and trials the heart of man can go through, and as He felt affliction and temptation most keenly, so in all these difficulties and trials He had communion with the Father. He knows therefore, how to succor them that are tempted, how fully and unreservedly, then, may we speak to God in the presence and by the mediation of the man Christ Jesus!

"The Lord Jesus is filled with tender compassion and the most profound, lively, and comprehensive sympathy. This belongs to the perfection of His high-priesthood. For this very purpose He was tempted. He suffered. Our infirmities, it is true, are ultimately connected with our sinfulness; the weakness of our flesh is never free from a sinful concurrence of the will; and the Saviour knows from His experience on earth how ignorant, poor, weak, sinful, and corrupt His disciples are. He loved them, watched over them with unwearied patience; prayed for them that their faith fail not; and reminded them the spirit was willing, but the flesh is weak. He remembers also His own sinless weakness; He knows what constant thought, meditation, and prayer are needed to overcome Satan, and to be faithful to God. He knows what it is for the soul to be sorrowful and overwhelmed, and what it is to be refreshed by the sunshine of Divine favour, and to rejoice in the Spirit. We may come in to Him expecting full, tender, deep sympathy and compassion. He is ever ready to strengthen and comfort, to heal and restore, He is prepared to receive the poor, wounded, sin-stained believer; to dry the tears of Peter weeping bitterly; to say to Paul, oppressed with the thorn in the flesh, 'My grace is sufficient for thee.'

"We need only understand that we are sinners, and that He is High Priest. The law was given that every mouth may be shut, for we are guilty. The High Priest is given that every mouth may be opened. . . . We come in faith as sinners. Then shall we obtain mercy; and we always need mercy, to wash our feet: to restore to us the joy of salvation, to heal our backslidings, and bind up our wounds. We shall obtain help in every time of need. For God may suffer Satan and the world, want and suffering, to go against us; but He always causes all things to work together for our good. He permits the time of need, that we may call upon Him, and, being delivered by Him, may glorify His name" (Saphir).

"We should come therefore with boldness to the throne of grace" (Bagster). Then let us do so, in the full confidence of our acceptance before God in the person of His Beloved (Eph. 1:6). The verb in 4:16 is not in the aorist tense, but the present—let us "come" constantly, continually; let us form the habit of doing so. This is the first of seven occurrences of this blessed word in our epistle: the other references are 7:25; 10:1, 22; 11:6; 12:18, 22, To "*obtain* mercy" is passive, and refers to past failures. "*Finding* grace" is active, and signifies that we humbly, earnestly, and believingly seek it. To "help in time of need:" this is daily, yea, hourly. But whenever the need may be, spiritually or temporal, grace all-sufficient is ever-available. May it be ours to constantly *seek* it, for the unchanging promise is, "Seek, and ye shall find."

CHAPTER NINETEEN

Christ Superior to Aaron.

(Heb. 5:1-4).

We are now to enter upon the longest section of our Epistle (5:1-10:39), and a section which is, from the doctrinal and practical viewpoints, perhaps the most important of all. In it the Holy Spirit treats of our Saviour's *priesthood.* Concerning this most blessed and vital subject the utmost confusion prevails in Christendom today. Yet this is scarcely to be wondered at. For not only has the time now arrived when the majority of those who profess the name of Christ "will not endure sound doctrine," who after their own fleshly and worldly lusts have heaped to themselves teachers that tickle their itching ears with God-dishonoring novelties, but they have turned away their ears from the truth, and are "turned unto fables" (2 Tim. 4:3, 4). Never was there a time when true God-fearing Christians more needed to heed that Divine admonition, "*Prove* all things, hold fast that which is good" (1 Thess. 5:21). Our only safeguard is to emulate the Bereans and search the Scriptures daily to ascertain whether or not the things we hear and read from men—be their reputation for scholarship, piety, and orthodoxy never so great—are according to the unerring Word of God.

Romanists, and with them an increasing number of Anglicans (Episcopalians), virtually set aside the solitary grandeur of the Priesthood of Christ and the sufficiency of His Atonement, by bringing in human priests to act as mediators between God and sinful men. Arminians are in fundamental error by representing the priestly office and ministry of Christ as having a relation to and a bearing upon the whole human race. Most of the leaders among the Plymouth Brethren have wrested the Scriptures by denying the *priestly* character of Christ's death by insisting that He only entered upon His priestly office after His ascension, and by affirming that it bears no direct relation to sin or sins, but is only a ministry of sympathy and succor for weakness and infirmities. But as it will serve no profitable purpose to deal with the errors of others, let us turn to the positive side of our subject.

Three references to the High Priesthood of Christ have already been before us in the preceding chapters of our Epistle. First, in 2:17 we read, "Wherefore, in all things it behoved Him to be made like unto His brethren, that He might be a merciful and faithful High Priest in things pertaining to God, to make propitiation for the sins of the people." This, of itself, is quite sufficient to expose the sophistries of those who teach that the priestly work of Christ has nothing to do with "sins." Second, in 3:1 we have been exhorted to, "consider the Apostle and High Priest of our profession, Christ Jesus." Third, in 4:14 we are told, "We have a great High Priest, that is passed into the heavens, Jesus the Son of God." Here again is a single statement which is alone sufficient to prove that our Saviour entered upon His priestly office *before* His ascension, for it was *as* the "great High Priest" He "passed into the heavens."

Supplementing our previous comments on Heb. 4:14 and introducing what is to be before us, let us note that the Lord Jesus is designed a "*great* High Priest." This word at once emphasises His excellency and pre-eminency. Never was there, never can there be another, possessed of such dignity and glory. The "greatness" of our High Priest arises, first, from the dignity of His person: He is not only Son of man, but Son of God (4:14). Second, from the purity of His nature: He is "without sin" (4:15), "holy," (7:26). Third, from the eminency of His order: that of Melchizedek (5:6). Fourth, from the solemnity of his ordination: "with an oath" (7:20, 21)—none other was. Fifth, from the excellency of His sacrifice: "Himself, without spot" (9:14). Sixth, from the perfection of His administration (7:11, 25)—He has satisfied divine justice, procured Divine favour, given access to the Throne of Grace, secured eternal redemption. Seventh, from the perpetuity of His office: it is untransferable and eternal (7:24). From these we may the better perceive the blasphemous arrogancy of the Italian pope, who styles himself "pontifex maximus"—the *greatest* high priest.

"No part of the Mosaic economy had taken a stronger hold of the imaginations and affections of the Jews than the *Aaronical High-priesthood,* and that system of ritual worship over which its occupants presided. The gorgeous apparel, the solemn investure, the mysterious sacredness of the high priest, the grandeur of the temple in which he ministered, and the imposing splendour of the religious rites which he performed,—all these operated like a charm in riveting the attachment of the Jews to the now overdated economy, and in exciting powerful prejudices against that simple, spiritual, unostentatious system by which it had been superceded.

In opposition to those prejudices, the apostle shows that the Christian economy is deficient in nothing excellent to be found in the Mosaic; on the contrary, that it has a more dignified High Priest, a more magnificent temple, a more sacred altar, a more efficacious sacrifice; and that, to the spiritually enlightened mind, all the temporary splendours of the Mosaic typical ceremonial, wax dim and disappear amid the overwhelming glories of the permanent realities of the Christian institution" (Dr. John Brown).

But once more we could fain pause and admire the consummate wisdom of the Spirit of God as exhibited in the method pursued in presenting the truth in this Epistle. Had it opened with the declaration of Christ's superiority over Moses and Aaron, the prejudices of the Jews had been at once aroused. Instead, the personal dignity of the mediatorial Redeemer has been shown (from their own Scriptures) to be so great, that the glory of the angels was so far below His, it follows as a necessary consequence that, the honour attaching to the illustrious of earth's mortals must be so too. Moreover, at the close of chapter 4 the High Priesthood of Christ is presented in such a way that every renewed heart must be won by and to it. There the apostle had announced not only that our High Priest is Divine (v. 14), holy, (v. 15), and had passed into the heavens, but also that He is One filled with tender sympathy toward our infirmities, having Himself been tempted in all points like as we are (sin excepted); and, moreover, that through Him we have obtained free access to God's throne of grace, so that there we may obtain mercy (the remitting of what *is* due us) and find grace (the receiving that to which we are *not* entitled) to help in time of need. How we should *welcome* such a Priest! How thankful we should be for Him!

Having thus comforted the hearts of God's children by assuring them of the tender compassion of Christ as the pledge of His effectual intercession for them on high, the apostle now proceeds to set forth more precisely the nature and glory of the priesthood of the Incarnate Son. He pursues the same method as was followed in the previous sections. As in chapters 1 and 2 He has been compared and contrasted with angels, and in chapters 3 and 4 with Moses and Joshua, so now in the present and succeeding chapters the order and functions of the Aaronic priesthood are examined, that the way may be paved for a setting forth of the more excellent order to which *our* High Priest belongs. "In the course of the section he makes it evident that whatever was essential to the office of a high priest was to be found in Christ Jesus, that whatever imperfections belonged to the Aaronical high priesthood were not to be found in Him, and that a variety of excellencies were to be found in Him of which none of the Aaronical priests were possessed," (Dr. J. Brown).

"For every high priest taken from among men is ordained for men in things pertaining to God, that he may offer both gifts and sacrifices for sins: Who can have compassion on the ignorant, and on them that are out of the way, for that he himself also is compassed with infirmity. And by reason hereof he ought, as for the people, so also for himself, to offer for sins. And no man taketh this honour unto himself, but he that is called of God, as was Aaron" (vv. 1-4). Here we have defined the intrinsic nature of the priestly office.

The verses just quoted above contain a general description of the Levitical high priests. Five things are here said concerning them. First, he must be "taken from among men," that is, he must partake of the nature of those on whose behalf he acts. Second, he acted not as a private individual, but as a public official: "is ordained for men." Third, he came not empty-handed before God, but furnished with "gifts and sacrifices for sins." Fourth, for he himself was not exempt from infirmity, so that he might the more readily succour the distressed (vv. 2, 3). Fifth, he did not presumptuously rush into his office of himself, but was chosen and approved of God (v. 4). Let us look at each of these more closely.

"For every high priest taken from among men." First, then, his humanity is insisted upon. An angel would be no fitting priest to act on behalf of men, for he possesses not their nature, is not subject to their temptations, and has no experimental acquaintance with their sufferings; therefore is he unsuited to act on their behalf: therefore is he incapable of having "compassion" upon them, for the motive-spring of all real intercession is heart-felt sympathy. Thus, the primary qualification of a priest is that he must be personally related to, possess the same nature as, those for whose welfare he interposes.

"For every high priest taken from among men." Bearing in mind to whom this Epistle was first addressed, it is not difficult for us to discern why our present section opens in this somewhat abrupt manner. As was pointed out so frequently in our articles upon Heb. 2, that which so sorely perplexed the Jews was, that the One who had appeared and tabernacled in their minds in human form should have claimed for Himself divine honours (John 5:23, etc.). But if the Son of God had never become *man,* He could never have officiated as priest, He could never have offered that sacrifice for the sins of His people which Divine justice required. The Divine Incarnation was an imperative necessity if salvation was to be secured for God's elect. "It was necessary for Christ to become a real man, for as we are very far from God, we stand in a manner before Him in the person of our Priest, which could not be were He not one of us. Hence, that the Son of God has a nature in common with us does not diminish His dignity, but commends it the more to us; for He is fitted to reconcile us to God, because He is man" (John Calvin).

"Is ordained for men." This tells us the reason why and the purpose for which the high priest was taken "from among men:" it was that he might transact on behalf of others, or more accurately, in the stead of others. To this position and work he was "ordained" or appointed by God. Thereby, under the Mosaic economy, the Hebrews were taught that men could not directly and personally approach unto God. They were sinful, He was holy; therefore was there a breadth between, which they were unable to bridge. It is both solemn and striking to observe how at the very beginning, when sin first entered the world, God impressed this awful truth upon our fallen parents. The "tree of life," whose property was to bestow immortality (Gen. 3:22), was the then emblem and symbol of God Himself. Therefore when Adam transgressed, we are told, "So He drove out the man; and He placed at the east of the garden of Eden cherubim, and a flaming sword which turned every way, to keep the way of the tree of life" (Gen. 3:24). Thereby man was taught the awful fact that he is "*alienated from* the life of God." (Eph. 4:18).

The same terrible truth was pressed unto the Israelites. When Jehovah Himself came down upon Sinai, the people were fenced off from Him: "And thou shalt set bounds upon the people round about, saying, Take heed to yourselves, that ye go not up into the mount, or touch the border of it: whosoever toucheth the mount shall be surely put to death" (Ex. 19:12). There was the Lord upon the summit, there were the people at the base: separated the One from the other. So too when the Tabernacle was set up. Beyond the outward court they were not suffered to go; into the holy place, the priests alone were permitted to enter. And into the holy of holies, where God dwelt between the cherubim, none but the high priest, and he only on the day of atonement, penetrated. Thus were the Hebrews, from the beginning, shown the awful truth of Isa. 59:2—"Your iniquities have *separated* between you and your God."

But in the person of their high priest, through his representing of them before God, Israel might approach within the sacred enclosure. Beautifully is that brought out in the 28th chapter of Exodus, that book whose theme is *redemption.* There we read, "And thou shalt take two onyx stones, and grave on them the names of the children of Israel . . . and thou shalt put the two stones upon the shoulders of the ephod for stones of memorial unto the children of Israel: and Aaron shall bear their names before the Lord . . . And thou shalt make the breastplate of judgment . . . and thou shalt set in it setting of stones . . . and the stones shall be with the names of the children of Israel . . . And Aaron shall bear the names of the children of Israel in the breast-plate of judgment upon his heart when he goeth in unto the holy, for a memorial before the Lord continually" (vv. 9, 12, 15, 17, 21, 29). Concerning the high priest being "ordained for men" we are told, "Aaron shall lay both his hands upon the head of the live goat, and confess over him all the iniquities of the children of Israel, and all their transgressions in all their sins, putting them upon the head of the goat, and shall send him away by the hand of a fit man into the wilderness" (Lev. 16:21).

"Is ordained for men." The application of these words to the person and work of Christ is patent. He not only became Man, but had received appointment from God to act on behalf of, in the stead of, men: "Lo I come, to do Thy will, O God" (Heb. 10:9), announce both the commission He had received from God and His own readiness to discharge it. What that commission was we learn in the next verse: "By the which will we are sanctified through the offering of the body of Jesus Christ once for all." He came to do what men could not do—satisfy the claims of Divine justice, procure the Divine favour. Note, in passing "ordained for *men*," not mankind in general, but that people which God had given Him—just as Aaron, the typical high priest, confessed not the sins of the Canaanites or Amalekites over the head of the goat, but those of Israel only.

"In things pertaining to God," that is, in meeting the requirements of His holiness. The activities of the priests have God for their object: it is His character, His claims, His glory which are in view. In their application to Christ these words, "in things pertaining to God" distinguishes our Lord's priesthood from His other offices. As a prophet, He reveals *to us* the mind and will of God. As the King, He subdues *us* to Himself, rules over and defends *us*. But the object of His priesthood is not us, but *God*.

"That He may offer both gifts and sacrifices for sins." To "offer" is the chief function of the high priest. He offers to God for men. He offers both gifts and sacrifices; that is, eucharistic or thanksgiving offerings, and sacrificial or propitiatory sacrifices. "The first word includes, as I think, various kinds of sacrifices, and is therefore a general term; but the second denotes especially the sacrifices of expiation. Still the meaning is, that the priest without a sacrifice is no peace-maker between God and man, for without a sacrifice sins are not atoned for, nor is the wrath of God pacified. Hence, whenever reconciliation between God and man takes place this pledge must ever necessarily precede. Thus we see that angels are by no means capable of obtaining for us God's favour, because they have no sacrifice" (John Calvin).

"That He may offer both gifts and sacrifice for sins." The application of these words to the Lord Jesus, our great High Priest, calls attention to a prominent and vital aspect of His death which is largely lost sight of today. The sacrificial death of Christ was a *priestly* act. On the Cross Christ not only suffered at the hands of men, and endured the punitive wrath of God, but He actually "accomplished" (Luke 9:31) something: He *offered* Himself as a sacrifice to God. At Calvary the Lord Jesus was not only the Lamb of God bearing judgment, but He was also His Priest officiating at the altar. "For every high priest is ordained to offer gifts and sacrifices: wherefore it is of necessity that this Man have somewhat also *to offer*" (Heb. 8:3). As Heb. 9:14 also tells us, He "*offered* himself without spot to God."

Christ on the Cross was far more than a willing victim passively enduring the stroke of Divine judgment. He was there *performing* a work, nor did He cease until He cried in triumph, "It is finished." He "loved the Church and *gave* Himself for it" (Eph. 5:25). He "*laid down* His life" for the sheep (John 10:11, 18)—which is the predicate of an active agent. He "*poured out* His soul unto death" (Isa. 53:12). He "dismissed His spirit" (John 19:30). "Hell's utmost force and fury gathered against Him: heaven's sword devouring Him, and heaven's God forsaking Him: earth, and hell, and heaven, thus in conspiring action against Him, unto the uttermost of heaven's extremest justice, and earth's and hell's extremest injustice:—what is the glory of the Cross if it be not *this*: that with such action conspiring to subdue *His* action, His action outlasted and outlived them all, and He did not die subdued and overborne in the dying, He did not die till He *gave* Himself in death" (H. Martin on "The Atonement").

"Who can have compassion on the ignorant, and on them that are out of the way; for that he himself is compassed with infirmity" (v. 2). Passing now from the design of the Levitical priesthood, we have a word upon their qualifications, the first of which is *compassion* unto those for whom he is to act. "The word here translated 'have compassion' is rendered in the margin 'reasonably bear with.' A person could not be expected to do the duties of a high priest aright if he could not enter into the feelings of those whom he represented. If their faults excited no sentiments in his mind but disapprobation—if they moved him to no feeling but anger, he would not be fit to interpose in their behalf with God—he would not be inclined to do for them what was necessary for the expiation of their sins, and the accomplishment of their services. But the Jewish high priest was one who was capable of pitying and bearing with the ignorant and erring; for 'he himself also was compassed with infirmity.' 'Infirmity,' here, plainly is significant of sinful weakness, and probably also of the disagreeable effects resulting from it. The Jewish high priest was himself a sinner. He had personal experience of temptation, and the tendency of man to yield to it—of sin, and of the consequences of sin; so that he had the natural capacity, and ought to have had the moral capacity, of pitying his fellow-sinners" (Dr. J. Brown).

And what, we may enquire, was the Spirit's design in here making mention of this personal qualification in the Levitical high priest? We believe His purpose was at least fourfold. First, implicitly, to call attention to the failure of Israel's high priests. It is very solemn to mark how that the last of them failed, most signally, at this very point. When poor Hannah was "in bitterness of soul," and while she was in prayer, weeping before the Lord, Eli, because her lips moved not, thought that she was drunken, and spoke roughly to her (1 Sam. 1:9-14). Thus, instead of sympathizing with her sorrows, instead of making intercession for her, he cruelly misjudged her. True, it is "human to err;" equally evident is it that the ideal priest would never be found among the sons of men. Second, was not the Spirit of God here paving the way for a contrast of the superiority of our great High Priest over the Aaronical? Third, does not this statement of v. 2 show, once more, that the value and efficacy of his work was inseparably connected with the *personal* qualifications of the priest himself, namely, his moral perfections, his human sympathy? Fourth, thus there was emphasized again the necessity for the Son of God becoming man, only thus could He acquire the requisite human compassion.

"This compassionate, loving, gentle, all-considerate and tender regard for the sinner can exist in perfection only in a sinless one. This appears at first sight paradoxical; for we expect the perfect man to be the severest judge. And with regard to *sin,* this is doubtless true. God charges even His angels with folly. He beholds sin where we do not discover it. And Jesus, the Holy One of Israel, like the Father, has eyes like a flame of fire, and discerns everything that is contrary to God's mind and will. But with regard to the *sinner,* Jesus, by virtue of His perfect holiness, is the most merciful, compassionate, and considerate Judge. For we, not taking a deep and keen view of sin, that central essential evil which exists in all men, and manifests itself in various ways and degrees, are not able to form a just estimate of men's comparative guilt and blameworthiness. Nay, our very sins make us more impatient and severe with regard to the sins of others. Our vanity finds the vanity of others intolerable, our pride finds the pride of others excessive. Blind to the guilt of our own peculiar sins, we are shocked with another's sins, different indeed from ours, but not less offensive to God, or pernicious in its tendencies. Again, the greater the knowledge of Divine love and pardon, the stronger faith in the Divine mercy and renewing grace, the more hopeful and the more lenient will be our view of sinners. And finally the more we possess of the spirit and heart of the Shepherd, the Physician, the Father, the deeper will be our compassion on the ignorant and wayward.

"The Lord Jesus was therefore most compassionate, considerate, lenient, hopeful in His feelings toward sinners, and in His dealings with them. He was infinitely holy and perfectly clear in His hatred and judgment of sin; but He was tender and gracious to the sinner. Beholding the sinful heart in all, esteeming sin according to the Divine standard, according to its real inward character, and not the human, conventional, and outward measure; Jesus, infinitely holy and sensitive as He was, saw often less to shock and pain Him in the drunkard and profligate than in the respectable, selfish, and ungodly religionists. He looked upon sin as the greatest and most fearful evil, but on the sinner as poor, lost, and helpless. Thus, while Jesus, in perfect holiness, judges most truly, lovingly, and tenderly of us, He knows by experience the weakness of the flesh, and the difficulty and soreness of the struggle. What a marvelous fulfilment of the Priest's requisite, that he should be taken from men! one to whom we can look with full and calm trust, our Representative, the Man Christ Jesus, possessed of perfect, Divine love and compassion" (Abbreviated from A. Saphir).

Those for whom the high priest was deputed to act are here described as "the ignorant and them that are out of the way." These are not two different classes of people, instead, those words give a twofold description of sinners. It has been rightly said that "in the Bible all sin is represented as the result of ignorance, but of blameable ignorance." "The way of the wicked is as darkness: they know not at what they stumble" (Prov. 4:19). "There is none that understandeth, there is none that seeketh after God" (Rom. 3:11). Every sinner is a fool. "Out of the way" means that men have turned aside from the path which the Word of God has marked out for them to walk in: "All we like sheep have gone astray, we have turned every one to *his own* way" (Isa. 53:6).

"And by reason hereof he ought, as for the people, so also for himself, to offer for sins" (v. 3). "There was none who could offer sacrifice for the sins of the high priest; therefore, he must do it for himself. He was to offer for himself in the same way and for the reasons as he offered for the people, and this was necessary, for he was encompassed with the same infirmities and was obnoxious as to sin, and so stood in no less need of expiation or atonement than did the people" (Dr. John Owen). For scriptures where the high priest was bidden to present an offering for his own sin, let the reader consult Lev. 4:3, 9:7, 16:6, 24.

"And by reason hereof he ought, as for the people, so also for himself, to offer for sins" (v. 3). Here again we may observe the Spirit of God calling attention to the imperfections of the Levitical priests that the way may be prepared for presenting the infinitely superior perfections of Christ. But that is not all we have in this verse. It is the personal *qualifications* of the one who exercises his office which is now before us. Before Aaron could present an offering on behalf of Israel, he must first bring a sacrifice for his own sins, that he might be purified and stand accepted before Jehovah. In other words, the one who was to come between a holy God and a sinful people must himself have no guilt resting upon him, and must be an object of Divine favour. Thus, personal fitness was an essential qualification of the priest: in the case of the Levitical, a ceremonial fitness; with Christ, a personal and inherent.

"And no man taketh this honour unto himself, but he that is called of God, as was Aaron" (v. 4). "The foregoing verses declare the personal functions of a high priest, but these alone are not sufficient to invest any one with that office; for it is required that he be lawfully called thereunto. Aaron was called of God immediately, and in an extraordinary way. He was called by the command of God given to Moses, and entrusted to him for execution; he was actually separated and consecrated unto the office of high priest, and this was accomplished by special sacrifices made by another for him; and all these things were necessary unto Aaron, because God, in his person, erected a new order of priesthood" (Dr. J. Owen).

"And no man taketh this honour to himself." The expression "this honour" refers to the high priestly office, for one to approach unto the Most High, to have personal dealings with Him, to transact on behalf of others before Him, obtaining His favour toward them, is a signal privilege and great favour indeed. To mark this distinguishing honour, Aaron was clothed in the most gorgeous and imposing vestments (Ex. 28). Looking beyond the type to the Antitype, we may discern how that the Spirit is, once more, bringing before the Hebrews that which was designed to remove the offence of the Cross. To carnal reason the death of Christ was a humiliating spectacle; but the spiritually enlightened see at Calvary One performing the functions of an office with high "honour" attached to it.

"But he that is called of God, as was Aaron." This was the ultimate and most important qualification: no man could legitimately act as high priest unless he was Divinely called to that office. "The principle on which the necessity of a Divine calling to the legitimate exercise of the priesthood rests is an obvious one. It depends entirely on the will of God whether He will accept the services and pardon the sins of men; and suppose again that it is His will to do so, it belongs to Him to appoint everything in reference to the manner in which this is to be accomplished. God is under no obligation to accept of every one, or of any one who, of his own accord, or by the choice of his fellow-men, takes it upon him to offer sacrifices or gifts for himself or for others; and no man in these circumstances can have reason to expect that God will accept of his offerings, unless He has given him a commission to offer them, and a promise He will be appeased by them. This, then, from the very nature of the case, was necessary to the legitimate discharge of the functions of a high priest" (Dr. J. Brown). What the apostle is here leading up to was the proof that *God* was the Author of Christ's Priesthood. As that will come before us in the verses which follow, we pass it by now.

"But he that is called of God, as was Aaron." That which makes an office lawful is the personal call of God. A most important principle is this to recognize, but one which, in these days of abounding lawlessness, is now flagrantly ignored. The will of man is to be entirely subordinated to the will of God. Everything connected with His work is to be regulated by the Divine appointments. Expediency, convenience, popular customs, are ruled out of court. Nor is any one justified in rushing into a holy office uncalled of God. To elect myself, or to have no higher authority than the election of fellow-sinners, is to usurp the authority of God.

All ministry is in the hand of Christ (Rev. 2:1). He appointed the twelve apostles, and later the seventy disciples, to go forth. He bids us "Pray ye therefore the Lord of the harvest, that *He* send forth labourers into His harvest" (Matt. 9:38). When He ascended on high *He* "gave some, apostles; and some, prophets; and some, evangelists; and some, pastors and teachers" (Eph. 4:11). In the days of Paul it was said, "How shall they preach, except they be sent?" (Rom. 10:15). But in these days, how many there are who run *without* being "sent!" Men have taken it upon themselves to be evangelists, pastors, teachers, who have received no call from God to such a work. The *absence* of His call, is evidenced by the absence of the qualifying gift. When God calls, He always equips.

Returning to the call of Aaron, we may observe that a time came when his official authority was challenged (Num. 16:2). The manner in which God vindicated His servant is worthy of our most thoughtful attention. The record of it is found in Num. 17: Aaron's rod budded and brought forth almonds. *Supernatural fruit* was the sign and pledge that he had been called of God. Let this be laid well to heart. Judged by *this* standard, how many today stand accredited as God's sent-servants? When God calls a man, He does not send him forth on any fruitless errand.

It is a solemn thing for one to obtrude himself into a sacred office. The tragic case of Uzzah (2 Chron. 26:16-21) is a lasting warning. Alas, how rarely is it heeded; and how grievously is God dishonored! There are those who decry a "one-man ministry," and cut themselves off from many an edifying message from God's true servants; but after twenty years' experience on three continents, the writer much prefers that which some so unchristianly condemn, to the lawlessness and fleshly exhibitions of an "everyman ministry" which is their alternative. Again: how many are urged to become Sunday School teachers and open-air speakers who have received neither call nor qualification from God to such work! Again: how many go forth as missionaries, only a few years later, at most, to abandon the work: what a proof that they were not "sent" or "called by God!" Let every reader weigh well Heb. 5:4. Unless *God* has called you, enter not into any work for Him. Let restless souls seek grace to heed that Divine command, "Be swift to hear, *slow to speak*" (James 1:19).

CHAPTER TWENTY

Christ Superior to Aaron.

(Heb. 5:5-7)

The central design of the Holy Spirit in this Epistle needs to be kept steadily before the mind of the reader: that design was to prove the superiority of Christianity over Judaism. The centre and glory of Judaism was the divinely appointed priesthood: what, then, had Christianity to offer at this point? "The unbelieving Jews would be apt to say to their Christian brethren, 'your new religion is deficient in the very first requisite of a religion—you have no high priest. How are your sins to be pardoned, when you have none to offer expiatory oblations for you? How are your wants to be supplied, when you have none to make intercession for you to God?' The answer to this cavil is to be found in the apostle's word 'We *have* a High Priest' 4:14," (Dr. J. Brown).

That God has provided His people with a High Priest is the fulfilment of His own promise. On the demonstrated failure of the Aaronical priesthood in the days of Eli and his sons (1 Sam. 1:14, 2: 12-17, 22), the Lord declared, "And I will raise Me up a faithful Priest, that shall do according to that which is in Mine heart and in My mind: and I will build Him a sure house" (1 Sam 2:35). The fulfilment of this is found in the person and work of the Lord Jesus Christ. But in taking up the study of the priesthood of Christ it is of the greatest possible importance to perceive that *both* the typical persons of Aaron and Melchizedek were required to prefigure the varied actions, and excellencies of the great High Priest who is the centre and heart of Christianity. It was failure to recognize this which has resulted in so many inadequate and faulty treaties on the subject.

Both Aaron and Melchizedek were needed to set forth the various phases of Christ's priestly ministry. But before the apostle could take up the latter, he had first to show that Christ fulfilled all which was adumbrated by the former: before he could dwell upon the points in which Christ's excelled the Levitical priesthood, he must first establish its parallels and similarities. This the apostle does in Heb. 5. In its first four verses we have a description of the

Levitical high priest: first with respect to his nature (v. 1), second his employment (v. 1), third his qualification (v. 2), fourth his duty (v. 3), fifth his call (v. 4). In the verses which immediately follow, an application of this is made, more directly, to Christ. In so doing the Holy Spirit had before Him a double design:

He first shows the *fulfilment of the type.* God's purpose in appointing Israel's high priests was to foreshadow the person and work of the Lord Jesus. Thus, there must be some resemblance between the one and the other. Second, that the Hebrews might know that the ministry and service of the Levitical order had *terminated.* Their purpose having been served, they were no longer needed; now that the Substance had come, the shadows were superfluous. Nay, more, their very retention would repudiate the design of their institution: they were *prefigurative,* therefore to perpetuate them would deny that the Reality had come. For the Levitical priesthood to go on functioning would argue that it had a value and a use apart from Christ. Hence the necessity of showing the relation of Aaron's priesthood to Christ's, that it might the more plainly appear that a continuance of the former was not only useless but pernicious.

That there *was* a close connection between the priesthood of Aaron and that of Christ is evident from the opening verse of our present passage. Having stated, "No man taketh this honour unto himself, but he that is called of God, as Aaron," the apostle now adds, "*So also* Christ" (v. 5), or, "In like manner Christ." Thus, unmistakably, a parallel is here drawn. *As* it was with the Levitical high priests in all things necessary to that office, *so,* in like manner, was it with the Christ. In vv. 5-10 the same five things (personal sin excepted) predicated of Aaron and his successors were found in our great High Priest. That there were, also, dissimilarities was inevitable from the personal imperfections that appertained to Aaron and his descendants: had there been anything in Christ which corresponded to their blemishes and failures, He had been disqualified.

"So also Christ glorified not Himself to be made an high priest" (v. 5). In 2:17, 3:1, 4:14 it had been affirmed that Christ *is* High Priest. A difficulty is now anticipated and met. Considering the strictness of God's law, and the specified requirements for one entering the priestly office, and more especially seeing that Jesus did not belong to the tribe of Levi, *how* could He be said to be "Priest?" In meeting this difficulty, the apostle emphasises the fact that the *chief* requirement and qualification was a Divine *call:* "No man taketh this honour unto himself, but he that is called of God" (v. 4): applying that rule the apostle now shows, from Scripture itself, our Lord's right and title to this office. Ere weighing the proof for this, let us note that He is here designated "the Christ": the apostle's design was to demonstrate that the promised Messiah, the Hope of the fathers, was to be High Priest forever over the house of God. The "Anointed One" signified His unction unto this office.

"So also Christ glorified not Himself to be made an high priest." He did not take this dignity unto Himself; He did not obtrude Himself into office. As He declared, "If I honour Myself, My honour is nothing: it is My Father that honoureth Me." (John 8:54). No, He had made Himself of no reputation; He had taken upon Him the form of a servant (Phil. 2:7), and He ever acted in perfect subjection to the Father. Nor was there any need for Him to exalt Himself: He had entered into a covenant or compact with the Father, and He might be safely trusted to fulfill His part of the agreement. "He that shall humble Himself shall be exalted" (Matt. 23:12) was no less true of the Head than of His members.

"So also Christ glorified not Himself to be made an high priest." He to whom the authority belonged, invested Christ with the honours of priesthood, as He had Aaron. An ellipsis needs supplying to complete the implied antithesis: "But *He* glorified Him," or *He* (God) made Him to be High Priest." That Christ was *glorified* by being invested with the high priesthood is here plainly inferred. It was a high honour bestowed upon His mediatorial person, that is, upon His *humanity* (united unto His deity). Scripture plainly teaches that His mediatorial person was capable of being glorified, with degrees of glory, by augmentation of glory: see John 17:1; 1 Peter 1:21. This honour appears more plainly when we come to consider the *nature* of the work assigned Him as Priest: this was no less than healing the breach which sin had made between God and men, and this by "magnifying the law and making it honourable." It appears too when we contemplate the *effects* of His work: these were the vindicating and glorifying of the thrice holy God, the bringing of many sons unto glory, and the being Himself crowned with glory and honour. By that priestly work Christ has won for Himself the love, gratitude, and worship of a people who shall yet be perfectly conformed to His image, and shall praise Him world without end.

How wonderful and blessed it is to know that the honour of Christ and the procuring of our salvation are so intimately connected that it was His *glory* to be made our Mediator! There are three chief offices which Christ holds as Mediator: He is prophet, priest and potentate. But there is an importance, a dignity and a blessedness (little as carnal reason may be able to perceive it) attaching to His *priestly* office which does not belong to the other two. Scripture furnishes three proofs of this. First, we never read of "our *great* prophet," or "our *great* King," but we do *of* "our great High Priest" (Heb. 4:14)! Second, the Holy Spirit nowhere affirms that Christ's appointment to either His prophetic or His kingly office "glorified" Him; but this *is* insisted upon in connection with His call to the sacerdotal office (5:5)! Third, we read not of the dread solemnity of any divine "oath" in connection with His inauguration to the prophetic or the kingly office, but we *do* His priestly—"The Lord hath sworn, and will not repent, thou art a priest forever." (Psa. 110:4)! Thus the priesthood of Christ is invested with supreme importance.

"So also Christ glorified not Himself to be made an high priest; but he that said unto Him, Thou art My Son, today have I begotten Thee." (v.5). The apostle here cites the testimony of the 2nd Psalm: but *how does* this quotation confirm the priesthood of Christ or prove His "call" to that office? That the quotation here *is* adduced as proof-text is clear from the next verse—"As He saith *also* in *another* Psalm," which is given as further confirmation of His call. In weighing carefully the purpose for which Psalm 2:7 is here quoted, observe, first, it is not the priesthood but His *call* thereunto which the apostle has before him. Second, his object was simply to show that it was from *God* Christ had all His mediatorial authority. Third, in Psalm 2:7 God declares the incarnate Christ to be His Son. The proclamation. "Thou art My Son," testified to the Father's *acceptance* of Him in the discharge of all the work which had been committed to Him. This solemn approbation by the Father intimated that our Redeemer undertook nothing but what God had appointed. The Father's owning of Christ in human nature as "My Son," acclaimed Him Mediator—Priest for His people. In other words, Christ's "call" by God consisted of the formal and public owning of Him as the incarnate Son. Ps. 2:7 describes the "call."

It is to be observed that Psa. 2:7 opens with the words, "I will *declare* the decree," which signifies a public announcement of what had been eternally predestinated and appointed in the everlasting covenant. It was God making known that the Mediator had received a Divine commission, and therefore was possessed of all requisite authority for His office. The deeper meaning, in this connection, of the proclamation, "Thou art My Son," tells us that Christ's sufficiency as Priest lies in His *Divine* nature. It was the dignity of His person which gave value to what He did. Because He was the Son, God appointed Him High Priest: He would not give this glory to another. Just as, because He is the Son, He has made Him "Heir of all things." (Heb. 1:2.)

"Thou art My Son." The application of these words to the call which Christ received to His priestly office, refers, historically, we doubt not to what is recorded in Matt. 3:16-17. There we behold a shadowing forth on the lower and visible plane of that which was to take place, a little later, in the higher and invisible sphere. There we find the antitype of what occurred on the occasion of Aaron's induction to the priestly office. In Lev. 8 we find three things recorded of the type: First, his call (v. 1, 2). Second, his anointing (v. 12). Third, his consecration, (v. 22). These same three things, only in inverse order again (for in *all* things He has the pre-eminence) are found on the occasion of our Saviour's baptism, which was one of the great crises of His earthly career. For thirty years He had lived in retirement at Nazareth. Now the time had arrived for His public ministry. Accordingly, He consecrates, dedicates Himself to God—presenting Himself for baptism at the hands of God's servant. Second, it was at the Jordan He was anointed for His work: "God *anointed* Jesus of Nazareth with the Holy Spirit" (Acts 10:38). Third, it was there and then He was owned of God. "This is my beloved Son in whom I am well pleased." That was the Father's attestation to His acceptance of Christ for His priestly office and work.

Above, we have pointed out the first historical fulfilment of the prophetic word recorded in Psa. 2:7. As all prophecy has at least a double accomplishment, we find, accordingly, this same word of the Father's approbation of the Son recorded a second time in the Gospel narratives. In Matt. 17:5 we again hear the Father saying, "Thou art my Son," or "This is My Beloved Son." Here it was upon the mount, when Christ stood glorified before His disciples. It was then that God provided a miniature tableau of Christ's glorious kingdom. As Peter says, "We are eye-witnesses of His *majesty*" (2 Peter 1:16). And no doubt this is the profounder reference in Heb. 5:5, for the 2nd Psalm, there quoted, foretells the setting up of Christ as "King." Yet, let it not be forgotten that the priesthood of Christ is the basis of His kingship: "He shall be a priest upon His throne." (Zech. 6:13). It is as the "Lamb" He holds His title to the throne (Rev. 22:1)—cf. the "wherefore" of Phil. 2:9. He is a Priest with royal authority, a King with Priestly tenderness.

"As He saith also in another, Thou art a priest forever after the order of Melchizedek" (v. 6). A further proof of God's call of Christ to the priestly office is now given, the quotation being from the 110th Psalm, which was owned by the Jews as a Messianic one.

There the Father had by the Spirit of prophecy, said these words to His incarnate Son. Thus a double testimony was here adduced. The subject was of such importance that God deigned to give unto these Hebrews confirmation added to confirmation. How graciously He bears with our dullness: compare the "twice" of Psalm 62:11, the "again" of the Lord Jesus in John 8:12, 21 etc., the "many" proofs of Acts 1:3. "As *He* saith" is another evidence that God was the Author of the Old Testament. Here, the Father is heard speaking through David; in Psalm 22:1, the Son; in Heb. 3:7 the Spirit. "As He *saith,*" namely unto the Son. The Father's here *speaking* to Him was His "call," just as in 7:21 it is His "oath." *"Thou art* a priest" was declarative of His eternal decree, of the everlasting covenant between the Father and the Son, wherein He was designated unto this office. Thus was Christ "called of God as was Aaron."

"Who in the days of His flesh, when He had offered up prayers and supplications with strong crying and tears unto Him that was able to save Him from death, and was heard in that He feared." (v. 7) In seeking to expound this verse three things require attention. To ascertain its scope, or theme, to discover its relation to the context and its own contribution unto the apostle's argument, and to define its solemn terms. Its theme is the priestly ministry of Christ: this is evident from the expression "offered up." "As the theme of vv. 4-6 is, 'Jesus Christ has been divinely appointed to the priestly office, so the theme of vv. 7-9 is Jesus Christ has successfully executed the priestly office.' " (Dr. J. Brown). Its relation to the context is that the apostle was here showing the "compassed with infirmity" (v. 2) is found in the Antitype: the "strong crying and tears" being the proof. Its terms will be weighed in what follows. Ere submitting our own interpretations, we first subjoin the helpful analysis of Dr. Brown.

"The body of the sentence (vv. 7-10) divides itself into two parts: 1. 'He' Christ in the character of a Priest 'learned obedience by the things which He suffered.' 2. 'He', in the same character, 'has become the Author of eternal salvation to all that obey Him.' The clauses, 'In the days of his flesh,' and 'though He were a Son,' qualify the general declaration, 'He learned obedience by the things which He suffered,' and the clauses, 'when *He* had offered up,' 'prayers and supplications with strong crying and tears, unto Him that was able to save Him from death,' and 'when He had heard' —or having been heard—'in that He feared,' contain in them illustrations both of the nature and extent of those sufferings by which Christ learned obedience; whilst the clause, 'being made perfect,' qualifies the second part of the sentence, connecting it with the first, and showing how His 'learning obedience by the things which He suffered,' led to His being 'the Author of eternal salvation to all who obey Him.' "

In this 7th verse two other of the qualifications of Israel's high priest are accommodated to Christ. First, his being "compassed with infirmity" (v. 2) so as to fit him for having compassion on those for whom he transacted. In like manner was the Son, when He entered upon the discharge of His office, compassed with sinless infirmity. This is here exemplified in a threefold way. First, the time when He fulfilled the Aaronic type, namely, *"in the days of* His flesh," which was before He was "crowned with glory and honour." Second, from His condition, "in the days of His *flesh,"* which signifies a state of weakness and humiliation. Third, from the manner of His deportment: "with strong crying and tears," for these proceed from the "infirmity" of our nature—angels do not weep. Second, Israel's high priest was appointed to "offer." (v. 1, 2). This is what Christ is here seen doing: *offering* up to God—*"to* Him that was able to save Him." This was a sacerdotal act, as is clear from the fact that the declaration of v. 7 is immediately preceded (v. 6), and succeeded (v. 10) by a reference to His *priesthood.* Let us now examine our verse clause by clause.

"Who in the days of His flesh." "Flesh as applied to Christ, signifies human nature not yet glorified, with all its infirmities, wherein He was exposed unto—hunger, thirst, weariness, labour, sorrow, grief, fear, pain, death itself. Hereby doth the apostle express what he had before laid down in the person of the high priest according to the law—he was 'compassed' with infirmity." (Dr. J. Owen.) The word "flesh" is often used in Scripture of man as a poor, frail, mortal creature: Psalm 78:39, 65:2. The "days of His flesh" is antithetical to "made perfect." They cover the entire period of our Lord's humiliation, from the manger to the grave—cf. 2 Cor. 5:16. During that time Christ was "a man of sorrows," filled with them, never free from them; "and acquainted with grief," as a companion that never departed from Him. No doubt there is special reference to the close of those days when His sorrows and trials came to a head.

"The 'days of His flesh' mean the whole time of His humiliation —that period when He came among men as one of them, but still the Son of God, whose majesty was hid. As applied to Christ 'flesh' intimates that He put on a true humanity, but a humanity under the weight of imputed guilt, with the curse that followed in its train—a sinless, yet a sin-bearing humanity. The Lord felt the weakness of the flesh in His whole vicarious work, and though personally spotless, was in virtue of taking our place, subjected to all that we were heir to. We do not, indeed, find in Him the personal consequences of sin, such as sickness and disease, but the consequences which could competently fall to the sinless substitute; for He never was in Adam's covenant, but was Himself the last Adam. As He took flesh for an official purpose, He submitted to the consequences following in the train of sin-bearing—hunger and thirst, toil and fatigue in the sweat of His brow, persecution and injustice, arrest and sufferings, wounds and death." (Prof. Smeaton on the Atonement.)

"When He had offered up prayers and supplications." The Greek word for "offer up" signifies "to bear toward." It occurs in this Epistle sixteen times, and always as a *priestly* act. See 8:3, 9:7, 14, 10:11, 14, 18, etc. Prayers and supplications are expressive of the frailty of human nature, for we never read of angels praying. "Prayers" are of two kinds: petitions for that which is good, requests for deliverance from that which is evil: both are included here. The Greek word for "supplications" occurs nowhere else in the New Testament; in its classical usage it denotes an olive bough, lifted up by those who were supplicating others for peace. What is here in view is Christ "offering" *Himself* unto God (9:14), His offering being accompanied with priestly prayers and supplications. These are mentioned to exemplify His "infirmity," and to impress upon us how great a work it was to make expiation for sin. These prayers and supplications are not to be restricted to the agony of Gethsemane, or the hours of torture on the Cross; they must be regarded as being offered by Him through the entire period of His humiliation. "The pressure of human guilt habitually weighed down His mind and He was by way of eminence a Man of prayer, as well as a Man of sorrows." (Dr. Brown.)

"With strong crying and tears." These words not only intimate the intensity of the sufferings endured by our Priest, but also the extent to which He felt them. The God-man was no stoic, unmoved by the fearful experiences through which He passed. No, He suffered acutely, not only in body, but in His soul too. The curse of the law, under which He had spontaneously placed Himself, smote His soul as well as His body, for *we* had sinned in both, and He redeemed both. These crying and tears were evoked not by what He received at the hands of man, but what imputed guilt had brought down upon Him from the hand of God. He was overwhelmed by the pressure of horror and anguish, caused by the Divine anger against sin.

"With strong crying and tears." These were, in part, the fulfilment of that prophecy in Psa. 22:1: "the words of My roaring." A part of those "strong cryings" are recorded in the Gospels. To

His disciples He said, "My soul is exceeding sorrowful, even unto death" (Matt. 26:38). To the Father He prayed, "If Thou be willing, remove this cup from Me" (Luke 22:42). There we read of Him "being in an agony," that "He prayed more earnestly," that "His sweat was as it were great drops of blood falling down to the ground." Such was the "*travail* of His soul" that He cried for deliverance. He voluntarily entered the place into which sin had brought us: one of misery and wretchedness. No heart can conceive the terribleness of that conflict through which our Blessed Substitute passed. "Jesus cried with a loud voice, My God, My God, Why hast Thou forsaken Me?" (Matt. 27:46): here again we witness the "strong crying" accompanying His sacrifice. And what is the application of this to us? If His sacrifice was offered to God with "strong crying and tears" let none of us imagine we are savingly interested therein if our hearts are unmoved by the awfulness of sin, and are in the coldness of impenitence and the sloth of unbelief. Let him who would approach unto Christ ponder well how He approached unto God on behalf of sinners.

"Unto Him that was able to save Him from death." The particular character in which our suffering Surety here viewed God, calls for close attention. These words reveal to us how Christ contemplated Deity at that time: "unto Him that is able." Ability or power is either natural or moral. Natural power is strength and active efficacy; in God, omnipotence. Moral power is right and authority; in God, absolute sovereignty. Christ looked toward both. In view of God's omnipotence He sought deliverance; in view of His sovereignty, He meekly submitted. The former was the object of His faith; the latter, of His fear. These two attributes of God should ever be before us when we approach unto His footstool. A sight of His omnipotence will encourage our hearts and strengthen our faith: a realization of His high sovereignty will humble us before Him and check our presumption.

"Unto Him that was able to save Him from death." This also makes known the *cause* of His "strong crying and tears:" it was His sight of death. What "death?" Not merely the separation of the soul from the body, but the "wages of sin," that curse of the law which God, as a just judge, inflicts on the guilty. As the Surety of the covenant, as the One who had voluntarily taken upon Himself the debts of all His people, the wrath of a holy God must be visited upon Him. To this Christ referred when He said, "I am afflicted and ready to die from youth up; I suffer Thy terrors, I am distracted" (Psa. 88:15). Fiercer grew the conflict as the end was neared, and stronger were His cries for deliverance: "The sorrows of death compassed Me, and the pains of hell gat hold upon Me: I found trouble and sorrow. Then called I upon the name of the Lord; O Lord, I beseech Thee, deliver My soul" (Psa. 116:3, 4).

But what was the "deliverance" which He sought? Exemption from suffering this death? No, for He had received commandment to endure it (John 10:18, Phil. 2:8). What then? Note carefully that Christ prayed not to be delivered from *dying*, but from "death." We believe the answer is twofold. First, He sought to be *sustained* under it. When death as the penal visitation of God's anger upon Him for our sins was presented to His view, He had deep and dreadful apprehension of the utter inability of frail human nature bearing up under it, and prevailing against it. He was conscious of His need of Divine succour and support, to enable Him to endure the incalculable load which was upon Him. Therefore it was His duty, as perfect yet dependent Man, to pray that He might not be overwhelmed and overborne. His confidence was in "Him that is able." He declared, "For the Lord God will help Me, therefore shall I not be confounded" (Isa. 50:17).

"And was heard in that He feared." The best commentators differ in their understanding of these words. Two interpretations have been given, which, we believe, need to be combined to bring out the full meaning of this clause. Calvin gave as its meaning that the object of Christ's "fear" was the awful judgment of God upon our sins, the smiting of Him with the sword of justice, His desertion by God Himself. Arguing against the "fear" here having reference to Christ's own piety, because of which God answered Him, this profound exegete points out the *absence* of the possessive "His fear;" that the Greek preposition "apo" (rather than "huper") signifies "from," not "on account of;" and that the word "fear" means, for the most part, anxiety—"consternation" is its force as used in the Sept. His words are, "I doubt not that Christ was 'heard' *from that* which He feared, so that He was not overwhelmed by His evils or swallowed up by death. For in this contest the Son of God had to engage, not because He was tried by unbelief (the source of all our fears), but because He sustained as a man in the flesh the judgment of God, the terror of which could not have been overcome without an arduous effort"—and, we may add, without a Divine strengthening.

The sufferings of Christ wrung His soul, producing sorrow, perplexity, horror, dread. This is shown by His exercises and agony in Gethsemane. While He suffered God's "terrors," He was "distracted" (Psa. 88:15). "I am poured out like water," He exclaimed, "and all My bones are out of joint: My heart is like wax, it is melted in the midst of My bowels. My strength is dried up like a potsherd; and My tongue cleaveth to My jaws" (Psa. 22:14, 15).

And again, He cried, "Save Me, O God; for the waters are come in unto My soul. I sink in deep mire, where there is no standing. . . . . Let not the waterflood overflow Me, neither let the deep swallow Me up" (Psa. 69:1, 2, 15). Fear, pain, torture of body and soul, were now His portion. He was then enduring that which shall yet cause the damned to weep and wail and gnash their teeth. He was deserted by God. The comforting influences of His relation to God were withdrawn. His relation to God as *His* God and Father were the fount of all His comfort and joy. The sense of this was now suspended. Therefore was He filled with heaviness and sorrow inexpressible, and, "and with strong crying and tears" He prayed for deliverance.

"And was heard." This means, first of all, God's approval or acceptance of the petitioner himself. Christ's prayer here was answered in the same way as was Paul's request for the removal of the thorn in his flesh—not by exemption, but by Divine succour which gave enablement to bear the trial. In Gethsemane "There appeared an angel unto Him from heaven, *strengthening* Him" (Luke 22:43). So too on the Cross. "His mind and heart were fortified and sustained against the dread and terror which His humanity felt, so as to come to a perfect composure in the will of God. He was heard insofar as He desired to be heard; for although He could not but desire deliverance from the whole, as He was man, yet He desired it not absolutely as the God-man, as He was wholly subject to the will of the Father" (Dr. J. Owen).

"And was heard in that He feared." Other commentators have rightly pointed out that the Greek word for "fear" here signifies godly reverence or piety: cf. Heb. 12:28, where it is found in its noun form. Having from godly fear offered up prayers and supplications, He was heard. His personal perfections made His petition acceptable. This was His own assurance, at the triumphant completion of His sufferings: "Thou hast heard Me from the horns of the unicorns" (Psa. 22:21). This brings us to the second and ultimate meaning of the Saviour's petition to be delivered "from death," and the corresponding second response of the Father. "To 'save from death' means, to deliver from death after having died. God manifested Himself as 'Him who was able to save Him from death,' when, as 'The God of peace'—the pacified Divinity—'He brought again from the dead our Lord Jesus that great Shepherd of the sheep, by the blood of the everlasting covenant'. Heb. 13:20" (Dr. J. Brown).

Thus, to summarise the contents of this most solemn and wonderful verse, we here learn: First, that our blessed Substitute, in the discharge of His priestly work, encountered that awful wrath of

God which is the wages of sin—"death." Second, that He encountered it in the frailty of human nature, compassed with infirmity—"in the days of His flesh." Third, that He felt, to an extent we are incapable of realizing, the visitation of God's judgment upon sin—evidenced by His "strong crying and tears." Fourth, that He cried for deliverance: for strength to endure and for an exodus from the grave. Fifth, that God answered by bestowing the needed succour and by raising Him from the dead.

Many are the lessons which might be drawn from all that has been before us. Into what infinite depths of humiliation did the Son of God descend! How unspeakably dreadful was His anguish! What a hideous thing sin must be if such a sacrifice was required for its atonement! How real and terrible a thing is the wrath of God! What love moved Him to suffer so on our behalf! What must be the portion of those who despise and reject such a Saviour! What an example has He left us of turning to God in the hour of need! What fervour is called for if our prayers are to be answered! Above all, what gratitude, love, devotion and praise are due Him from those for whom the Son of God died!

CHAPTER TWENTY-ONE

Christ Superior to Aaron.

(Heb. 5:8-10).

The first ten verses of Heb. 5 present to us a subject of such vast and vital importance that we dare not hurry over our exposition of them. They bring to our view the person of the Lord Jesus and His official work as the great High Priest of God's people. They set forth His intrinsic sufficiency for the discharge of the honourous but arduous functions of that office. They show us His right and title for the executing thereof. They reveal His full qualifications thereunto. They make known the nature and costliness of His sacrificial work. They declare the triumphant issue thereof. Yet plain as is their testimony, the subject of which they treat is so dimly apprehended by most Christians today, that we deem it necessary to devote a lengthy introduction to the setting forth of the principal features belonging to the Priesthood of Christ.

Let us begin by asking the question, Why did God ordain the office of priesthood? Wherein lay the *necessity* for it? The first and most obvious answer is, Because of sin. Sin created a breech between a holy God and His sinful creatures. Were God to advance toward them in His essential character it could only be in judgment, involving their sure destruction; for He "will by no means clear the guilty" (Ex. 34:7). Nor was the sinner capable of making the slightest advance toward God, for he was "alienated from the life of God" (Eph. 4:18), and thus, "dead in trespasses and sins" (Eph. 2:1); and as such, not only powerless to perform a spiritual act, but completely devoid of all spiritual aspirations. Looked at in himself, the case of fallen man was utterly hopeless.

But God has designs of *grace* unto men, not unto all men, but unto a remnant of them chosen out of a fallen race. Had God shown grace to all of Adam's descendants, the glory of His grace had been clouded, for it would have looked as though the provisions of grace were something which were due men from God, because of His having failed to preserve them from falling into sin. But grace is *unmerited* favour, something to which no creature is entitled, something which he cannot in any wise *claim* from God.

Therefore it must be exercised in a *sovereign* manner by the Author of it (Ex. 33:19), that grace may appear to be grace (Rom. 11:6).

But in determining to show grace unto that people whom He had chosen in Christ before the foundation of the world (Eph. 1:4, 2 Tim. 1:9), God must act in harmony with His own perfections. The sin of His people could not be ignored. Justice clamoured for its punishment. If they were to be delivered from its penal consequences, it could only be by an adequate satisfaction being made for them. Without blood shedding there is no remission of sins. An Atonement was a fundamental necessity. Grace could not be shown at the expense of justice; no, grace must "reign through righteousness" (Rom. 5:21). Grace could only be exercised on the ground of accomplished redemption (Rom. 3:24).

And *who* was capable of rendering a perfect satisfaction unto the law of God? Who was qualified to meet all the demands of Divine holiness, if a sinful people were to be redeemed consistently with its claims? Who was competent both to assume the responsibilities of that people, and discharge them to the full satisfaction of the Most High? Who was able both to honour the rights of the Almighty, and yet enter sympathetically into the weakness and needs of those who were to be saved? Clearly, the only solution to this problem and the only answer to these questions lay in a *Mediator,* one who had both ability and title to act on God's behalf and on theirs. For this reason was the Son of God appointed to be made in the likeness of sin's flesh, that as the God-man He might be a "merciful and faithful High Priest" (Heb. 2:17); for *mediatorship* is the chief thing in priesthood.

Now this is what is brought before us in the opening verse of Heb. 5. There we are shown three parties: on the one side God, on the other side men, and the high priest as the connecting link between: "For every high priest taken from among men is ordained for men in things pertaining to God, that he may offer both gifts and sacrifices for sins" (v. 1). No correct conception of priesthood can exist where this double relation and this double service are not perceived. In Christ alone is this perfectly made good. He is the one connecting link between Heaven and earth, the only Mediator between God and "men" (1 Tim. 2:5). From Deity above, He is the Mediator downward to men beneath; and from men below, He is the Head upward to God. Priesthood is the *alone channel* of living relationship with a holy God. Solemn and awful proof of this is found in the fact that Satan, and then Adam, fell because there was *no Mediator* who stood between them and God, to maintain them in their standing before Him.

Above we have said, that Christ is the one connecting link between Heaven and earth, that He alone bridges the chasm between God and His people, considered as fallen and ruined sinners. Our last sentence really sums up the whole of Heb. 1 and 2. There we have a lengthy argument setting forth the relation between the two natures in Christ, the Divine and the human, and the needs-be of both to fit Him for the priestly office. He must be the Son of God in human nature. He must "in all things be made like unto His brethren" in order that He might be "a merciful and faithful High Priest;" in order that He might "make propitiation for the sins of the people;" and in order that He might be "able to succour them that are tempted." Heb. 2:17, 18 brings us to the climax of the apostle's argument in those two chapters.

The priestly work of Christ was to "make propitiation for the sins of the people." It was to render a complete satisfaction to God on behalf of all their liabilities. It was to "magnify the law and make it honourable." (Isa. 42:21). In order to do this it was necessary for the law to be kept, to be perfectly obeyed in thought, word and deed. Accordingly, the Son of God was "made under the law" (Gal. 4:4), and "fulfilled" its requirements (Matt. 5:17). And this perfect obedience of Christ, performed substitutionally and officially, is now imputed to His people: as it is written, "By the obedience of One shall many be (legally) made righteous" (Rom. 5:19). But "magnifying *the* law" also involved His enduring its penalty on the behalf of His peoples' violation of its precepts, and this He suffered, and so "redeemed us from the curse of the law" by "being made a curse for us" (Gal. 3:13).

To sum up now the ground we have covered. 1. The *occasion* of Christ's priesthood was sin: it was this which alienated the creature from the Creator. 2. The *source* of Christ's priesthood was grace: rebels were not entitled to it; such a wondrous provision proceeded solely from the Divine favour. 3. The *function* of Christ's priesthood is mediation, to come between, to officiate for men Godwards. 4. The *qualification* for perfect priesthood is a God-man: none but God could meet the requirements of God; none but Man could meet the needs of men. 5. The *work* of priesthood is to make propitiation for sin. To these we may add: 6. The *design* of priesthood is that the claims of God may be honoured, the person of Christ glorified, and His people redeemed. 7. The *outcome* of His priesthood is the maintaining of His people in the favour of God. Other subsidiary points will come before us, D.V., in the later chapters.

Verses 8, 9 of Heb. 5 complete the passage which was before us in the preceding article. That we may the better perceive their scope and meaning, let us recapitulate the teaching of the earlier verses. In this first division of Heb. 5 the apostle's design was to show how that Christ fulfilled the Aaronic type. First, He had been Divinely called or appointed to the priestly office (vv. 4-6). Second, to fit Him for compassion on behalf of those for whom He officiated, He was "compassed with (sinless) infirmity" (vv. 3, 7). Third, He had "offered" to God, as Priest, "as for the people so also for himself" (v. 3), "strong crying and tears" (v. 7). That which is now to be before us, brings out still other perfections of Christ which qualified Him to fill the sacerdotal office, and also makes known the happy issues therefrom.

"Though He were a Son, yet learned He obedience by the things which He suffered" (v. 8). In view of His unspeakable humiliation, portrayed in the previous verse, the Divine dignity of our High Priest is here mentioned both to guard and enhance His glory. "The things discoursed in the foregoing verse seem to have an inconsistency with the account given us concerning the person of Jesus Christ at the entrance of this Epistle. For He is therein declared to be the Son of God, and that in such a glorious manner as to be deservedly exalted above all the angels in heaven. Here He is represented as in a low, distressed condition, humbly, as it were, begging for His life, and pleading with 'strong crying and tears' before Him who was able to deliver Him. These things might seem unto the Hebrews to have some kind of repugnancy unto one another. And, indeed, they are a 'stone of stumbling, and a rock of offence,' unto many at this day; they are not able to reconcile them in their carnal minds and reasonings. . . . .

"The aim of the apostle in this place is, not to repel the objections of unbelievers, but to instruct the faith of those who do believe in the truth of these things. For He doth not only manifest that they were all possible, upon the account of His participation of flesh and blood, who was in Himself the eternal Son of God; but also that the whole of the humiliation and distress therein ascribed unto Him was necessary, with respect unto the office which He had undertaken to discharge, and the work which was committed unto Him. And this he doth in the next ensuing and following verses" (Dr. J. Owen).

"Though He were a Son, yet learned He obedience by the things which He suffered" (v. 8). First, what relation does this statement bear to the passage of which it is a part? Second, what is the particular "obedience" here referred to? Third, in what sense did the Son "learn obedience"? Fourth, how did the things "which He suffered" teach Him obedience? Fifth, what are the practical lessons here pointed for us? These are some of the questions raised by our verse which call for answer.

"Though He were a Son" looks back more immediately to v. 5, where a part of Psa. 2:7 is quoted. "That quotation has also reminded us of the Divine dignity and excellence of Christ as the ground of His everlasting priesthood. Jesus had a Divine commission; He was appointed by the Father because He was the Son; and thus He was possessed of all requisite qualifications for His office. Nevertheless the Son had to 'learn obedience.' He must not only possess authority and dignity, but be able to sympathize with the condition of sinners. By entering the circle of human experience He was made a merciful and faithful High Priest, and through suffering fitted for compassionately guiding our highest interests, as well as conducting our cause. The bond of brotherhood, the identity of suffering and sorrow, fitted Him to be touched with the feeling of our infirmities. He was made like unto His brethren (2:17); He suffered, that He might be in a position to succour them that are tempted (2:18); He was made in all respects like us, with the single exception of personal sinfulness (4:15); and He learned obedience by what He suffered. The design of all this was, that He might be a compassionate and sympathizing High Priest" (Prof. Smeaton).

Here then is the answer to our first question. In the 8th verse the Holy Spirit is still showing how that which was found in the type (v. 3), is also to be seen in the Antitype. What could more emphatically exemplify the fact that our High Priest was "compassed with infirmity" than to inform us that He not only felt acutely the experiences through which He passed, but also that He "learned obedience" by those very experiences? Nor need we hesitate to go as far as the Spirit of truth has gone; rather must we seek grace to believe all that He has said. None were more jealous of the Son's glory than He, and none knew so well how His glory had been displayed by His voluntary descent into such unfathomable depths of shame. While holding firmly to Christ's absolute deity, we must not (through a false conception of His dignity) shrink from following Him in thought and affection into that abyss of humiliation unto which, for our sakes, He came. When Scripture says, "He learned obedience" we must not whittle down these words to mean anything less than they affirm.

"Yet learned He obedience" brings out, very forcibly, the *reality* of the humanity which the Son assumed. He became true Man. If we bow to the inspired statement that "Jesus increased in wisdom and stature, and in favour with God and man" (Luke 2:52), why balk—as many have—at He "learned obedience?" True, blessedly true, these words do not signify that there was in Him a will which resisted the law of God, and which needed severe discipline to bring it into subjection. As Calvin well says, "Not that He was driven to this by force, or that He had need of being thus exercised, as the case is with oxen or horses when their ferocity is to be tamed; for He was abundantly willing to render to His Father the obedience which He owed." No, He declared, "I *delight* to do Thy will, O God" (Psa. 40:8). And again, "My *meat* is to do the will of Him that sent Me" (John 4:34).

But what is "obedience?" It is subjection to the will of another: it is an owning of the authority of another; it is performing the pleasure of another. This was an entirely new experience for the Son. Before His incarnation, He had Himself occupied the place of authority, of supreme authority. His seat had been the throne of the universe. From it He had issued commands and had enforced obedience. But now He had taken the place of a servant. He had assumed a creature nature. He had become man. And in this new place and role He conducted Himself with befitting submission to Another. He had been "made under the law," and its precepts must be honoured by Him. But more: the place He had taken was an official one. He had come here as the Surety of His people. He had come to discharge their liabilities. He had come to work out a perfect righteousness for them; and therefore, as their Representative, He must obey God's law. As the One who was here to maintain the claims of God, He must "magnify the law and make it honourable," by yielding to it a voluntary, perfect, joyous compliance.

Again; the "obedience" of Christ formed an essential part of His priestly oblation. This was typified of old—though very few have perceived it—in the animals prescribed for sacrifice: they were to be "without spot, without blemish." That denoted their excellency; only the "choice of the flock" (Ezek. 24:5) were presented to God. The antitype of this pointed to far more than the sinlessness of Christ—*that* were merely negative. It had in view His positive perfections, His active obedience, His personal excellency. When Christ "offered Himself without spot to God" (Heb. 9:14), He presented a Sacrifice which had already fulfilled every preceptive requirement of the law. And it was as Priest that He thus offered Himself to God, thereby fulfilling the Aaronic type. But in all things *He* has the pre-eminence, for at the cross He was both Offerer and Offering. Thus there is the most intimate connection between the contents of v. 8 and its context, especially with v. 7.

"Yet learned He obedience." The incarnate Son actually entered into the experience of what it was *to* obey. He denied Himself, He renounced His own will, He "pleased not Himself" (Rom. 15:3). There was no insubordination in Him, nothing dis-inclined to God's law; instead, His obedience was voluntary and hearty. But by being "made under the law" as Man, He "learned" what Divine righteousness required of Him; by receiving commandment to lay down His life (John 10:18), He "learned" the extent of that obedience which holiness demanded. Again; as the God-man, Christ "learned" obedience experimentally. As we learn the sweetness or bitterness of food by actually tasting it, so He learned what submission is by yielding to the Father's will. "But, moreover, there was still somewhat peculiar in that obedience which the Son of God is said to learn from His own sufferings, namely, what it is for a *sinless person* to suffer for sinners, 'the Just for the unjust.' The obedience herein was peculiar unto Him, nor do we know, nor can we have an experience of the ways and paths of it" (Dr. J. Owen).

"By the things which He suffered" announces the *means* by which He learned obedience. Everything that Christ suffered, from first to last, during the days of His flesh, is here included. His entire course was one of suffering, and He had the experience of obedience in it all. Every scene through which He passed provided occasion for the exercise of those graces wherein obedience consists. Meekness and lowliness (Matt. 11:29), self-denial (Rom. 15:3), patience (Rev. 1:9), faith (Heb. 2:13), were habitually resident in His holy nature, but they were only capable of exercise by reason of His suffering. As His suffering increased, so His obedience grew in extent and intensity, by the very pressure brought to bear upon it; the hotter the conflict grew, the more His inward submission was manifested outwardly (compare Isa. 50:6, 7). There was not only sufferings passively endured, but obedience in suffering, and that the most amazing and unparalleled.

To sum up now the important teachings of this wonderful verse: He who personally was high above all obedience, stooped so low as to enter the place of obedience. In that place He learned, by His sufferings, the actual experience of obedience—He obeyed. Hereby we learn what was required to the right discharge of Suretyship: there must needs be both an active and a passive obedience vicariously rendered. The opening word "though" intimates that the high dignity of His person did not exempt Him from the humiliation which our salvation involved. The word "yet" is a note of exclamation, to deepen our sense of wonderment at His infinite condescension on our behalf, for in His place of servitude He never ceased to be the Lord of glory. "He was no less God when He died, than when He was 'declared to be the Son of God with power, by the resurrection from the dead,' Rom. 1:4" (Dr. J. Owen).

And what are the practical lessons here pointed for us? First, our Redeemer has left us an example that we should follow His steps. He has shown us how to wear our creature nature: complete and unquestioning subjection to God is that which is required of us. Second, Christ has hereby taught us the extent to which God ought to be submitted unto: He was "obedient unto death." Third, obedience to God cost something: "Yea, and all that will live godly in Christ Jesus shall suffer persecution" (2 Tim. 3:12). Fourth, sufferings undergone according to the will of God are highly instructive. Christ Himself learned by the things which He suffered; much more may we do so, who have so much more to learn (Heb. 12:10, 11). Fifth, God's love for us does not exempt from suffering. Though the Son of His love, Christ was not spared great sorrows and trials: sufficient for the disciple to be as his Master.

"And being made perfect, He became the Author of eternal salvation unto all them that obey Him" (v. 9). "The apostle having declared the sufferings of Christ as our High Priest, in His offering of Himself, with the necessity thereof, proceeds now to declare both what was effected thereby, and what was the especial design of God therein. And this in general was that, the Lord Christ, considering our lost condition, might be every way fitted to be a 'perfect cause of eternal salvation unto all that obey Him,' There are, therefore, two things in the words, both which God aimed at and accomplished in the sufferings of Christ. 1. On His own part, that He might be 'made perfect;' not absolutely, but with respect unto the administration of His office in the behalf of sinners. 2. With respect unto believers, that He might be unto them the 'Author of eternal salvation' " (Dr. J. Owen). This is a good epitome of the teaching of the 9th verse, but a number of things in it call for fuller elucidation.

"And being made perfect." The word, "perfect" is one which is found frequently in this Epistle. It signifies "to consummate" or "complete." It also means "to dedicate" or "fully consecrate." Our present passage contains its second occurrence, the first being in 2:10, to which we must refer the reader. There the verb is used actively with respect to the Father: it became Him to "make perfect" the Captain of our salvation. Here it is used passively, telling of the *effect* of that act of God on the person of Christ; by His suffering He was "perfected." It has reference to the setting apart of Christ as Priest. "The legal high priests were consecrated by the sufferings and deaths of the beasts which were offered in sacrifice at their consecration (Ex. 29). But it belonged unto the perfection of the priesthood of Christ to be consecrated in and by His *own* sufferings" (Dr. J. Owen). It is most important to note that the reference here is to what took place in "the days of His flesh," not at His resurrection or ascension—vv. 7-9 form one complete statement. The Greek is even more emphatic than the A.V.: "And having been perfected became to those that obey Him all, the Author of salvation eternal." It was not in heaven that He was "perfected," but *before* He "became the Author of salvation"—cf. 10:14, which affirms our oneness with Him in His approved obedience and accomplished sacrifice.

"And being made perfect" does not contemplate any change wrought in His person, but speaks of His being fully qualified to officiate as Priest, to present Himself to God as a perfect sacrifice for the sins of His people. His official "perfecting" was accomplished in and by means of His sufferings. By His offering up of Himself He was consecrated to the priestly office, and by the active presentation of His sacrifice to God He discharged the essential function thereof. Thus, the inspired declaration we are now considering furnishes another flat contradiction (cf. 2:17) of those who affirm that Christ was not constituted and consecrated High Priest till His resurrection. True, there were other acts and duties pertaining to His sacerdotal office yet to be performed, but these depend for their efficacy on His previous sufferings; those He was now made meet for. The "being made perfect" or "consecrated" to the priestly office at the Cross, finds a parallel in our Lord's own words, "For their sakes I sanctify (dedicate) Myself" (John 17:19). "Here is the ultimate end why it was necessary for Christ to suffer: that He might thus become initiated into His priesthood" (J. Calvin).

"He became the Author of eternal salvation." "Having thus been made perfect through such intense, obediental, pious suffering—having thus obtained all the merit, all the power and authority, all the sympathy, which are necessary to the discharge of the high priestly functions of Saviour, 'He is become the Author of eternal salvation.' This is the second statement which the apostle makes in illustration of the principle, that our Lord has proved Himself qualified for the office to which He has been divinely appointed by a successful discharge of its functions, the subsidiary clause, 'being made perfect,' connects this second statement with the first; showing how our Lord's 'learning obedience by the things which He suffered in the days of His flesh'—His humbled state—led to His being now, in His exalted state, 'the Author of salvation to all who obey Him' . . . . 'Being made perfect' is just equivalent to 'having thus obtained' every necessary qualification for actually saving them" (Dr. J. Brown).

The "Author of salvation" conveys a slightly different thought than the "Captain of salvation" in 2:10. There it is Christ actually conducting many sons, by the powerful administration of His Word and Spirit, unto glory. Here it is the work of Christ as the meritorious and efficient Cause of their salvation. It was the perfect satisfaction which He rendered to God, the propitiatory sacrifice of Himself, which has secured the eternal deliverance of His people from the penal consequences of their sins. By His expiation He became the purchaser and procurer of our redemption. His intercession and His gift of the Spirit are the effects and fruits of His perfect oblation. "He has done everything that is necessary to make the salvation of His people consistent with, and illustrative of, the perfections of the Divine character and the principles of the Divine government; and He actually does save His people from guilt, depravity and misery—He actually makes them really holy and happy hereafter" (Dr. J. Brown).

The salvation which Christ has procured and now secures unto all His people, is here said to be an *"eternal"* one. First of all, none other was suited unto us. By virtue of the nature which we have received from God, we are made for eternal duration. But by sin we made ourselves obnoxious to eternal damnation, being by nature "the children of wrath, even as others" (Eph. 2:3). Therefore an eternal salvation was our deep and dire need. Second, the merits of our Saviour being infinite, required from the hand of Justice a corresponding salvation, one infinite in value and in duration: cf. 9:12. Third, the salvation procured by our great High Priest is here contrasted with that obtained by the Levitical high priest: the atonement which Aaron made, held good for one year only (Lev. 16); but that which Christ has accomplished, is of eternal validity.

"To all them that obey Him" describes those who are the beneficiaries of our High Priest's atonement. "The expression is emphatical. To all and every one of them that obey Him; not any one of them shall be exempted from a share and interest in this salvation; nor shall any one of any other sort be admitted thereunto" (Dr. J. Owen). It is not all men universally, but those only who bow to His sceptre. The recipients of His great salvation are here spoken of according to the terms of human accountability. All who hear the Gospel are commanded to believe (1 John 3:23); such is their responsibility. The "obedience" of this verse is an evangelical, not a legal one: it is the "obedience *of faith*" (Rom. 16:26). So also in Acts 5:32 we read of the Holy Spirit "whom God hath given to them that obey Him." But this "obedience" is not to be restricted to the initial act, but takes in the whole life of faith. A Christian, in contradistinction from a non-Christian, is one who *obeys* Christ (John 14:23). The "all them that obey Him" of Heb. 5:9 is in opposition to "yet learned He obedience" in the previous verse: it identifies the members with their Head!

Before taking up the next verse, let us seek to point out how that the passage which has been before us, not only shows Christ provided the substance of what was foreshadowed by the Levitical priests, but also how that He excelled them at every point, thus demonstrating the immeasurable superiority of Christ over Aaron. First, Aaron was but a man (v. 1); Christ, the "Son." Second, Aaron offered "sacrifices" (v. 1); Christ offered one perfect sacrifice, once for all. Third, Aaron was "compassed with infirmity" (v. 2); Christ was the "mighty" One (Psa. 89:19). Fourth, Aaron needed to offer for his own sins (v. 3); Christ was sinless. Fifth, Aaron offered a sacrifice external to himself; Christ offered Himself. Sixth, Aaron effected only a temporary salvation. Christ secured an eternal one. Seventh, Aaron's atonement was for Israel only; Christ's for "*all* them that obey Him."

"Called of God an high priest after the order of Melchizedek" (v. 10). This verse forms the transition between the first division of Heb. 5, and its second which extends to the end of chapter 7—the second being interrupted by a lengthy parenthesis. In the first section treating of our Lord's priesthood, the apostle has amplified his statement in 2:17, 18, and has furnished proof that Christ fulfilled the Aaronic type. In the second section wherein he treats of our Lord's sacerdotal office, he amplifies his declaration in 4:15, and shows that in Christ we have not only an High Priest, but "a *great* High Priest." The different aspects of his theme treated of in these two divisions of Heb. 5 is intimated by the variation to be noted in vv. 6, 10. In the former he says, "Thou art a priest forever after the order of Melchizedek," but in v. 10 he adds, "Called of God an High Priest after the order of Melchizedek."

The Greek word for "called" in v. 10 is entirely different from the one used in v. 4, "called of God." The former signifies to ordain or appoint; the latter to salute or greet. To the right understanding of the purport of v. 10, it is essential to observe carefully the exact point at which this statement is introduced: it is not till *after* the declarations that Christ had "offered up" (v. 7), had "learned obedience" (v. 7), had been "made perfect," and had become "the Author of salvation" (v. 9), we are told that God saluted Christ as "High Priest after the order of Melchizedek." What is found in v. 6 does not in any wise weaken the force of this, still less does it clash with it. In vv. 5, 6 the Spirit is not treating of the *order* of Christ's priesthood, but is furnishing proof that He had been called to that office by God Himself.

We do not propose to offer an exposition of the contents of this 10th verse on the present occasion, but content ourself with directing attention to the important fact that it was consequent upon His being officially "made perfect" and becoming "the Author of eternal salvation," that Christ was saluted by God as "High Priest after the order of Melchizedek." This act of God's followed the Saviour's death and resurrection. It was God's greeting of the glorious Conqueror of sin and death. Hence the propriety of His new title. If the reader refers to Gen. 14 he will find that the historical Melchizedek first comes on the scene to greet Abraham after his notable conquest of Chedorlaomer and his allies. It was upon his "return from the slaughter" of the kings, that Melchizedek appeared and blessed him. Thus he owned Abraham's triumph. In like manner, God has greeted the mighty Victor. May the Spirit of God fit our hearts and minds for a profounder insight of His living oracles.

CHAPTER TWENTY-TWO

Christ Superior to Aaron.

(Heb. 5:11-14)

At the close of our last article we pointed out that the 10th verse of Heb. 5 forms the juncture of the two divisions of that chapter. In the first section, vv. 1-9, the apostle has shown how Christ fulfilled that which was typified of Him by the Levitical high priests, and also how that He excels Aaron in His person, His office, and His work. The second section, which begins at 5:10 and extends, really, to the end of chapter 10, continues to display the superiority of Christ over Aaron, principally by showing that the Lord Jesus exercises a priesthood pertaining to a more excellent order than his. In substantiation of this the apostle, in 5:10, makes reference to Psa. 110:4. His purpose in so doing was twofold: first, to allow that Christ was not a high priest according to the constitution, law, and order of the Aaronic priesthood; second, to remind the Hebrews there was a priesthood antecedent unto and diverse from that of Aaron; which had also been appointed of God, and that for the very purpose of prefiguring the person of our great High Priest.

But at this point a difficulty has been presented to many students. We might state it thus: Seeing that this Epistle expressly declares, again and again, that Christ is priest "after the order of Melchizedek," how can it be true that Aaron, who belonged to a totally different order, could pre-figure His priestly office and work? This difficulty has largely resulted from failure to observe that the Holy Spirit has not said Christ is "an high priest *of* the order of Melchizedek," but, "*after* the order of," etc. The difference between the two expressions is real and radical. The word "of" would have necessarily *limited* His priesthood to a certain order. For when we say, as we must, that Phineas and Eli were "high priests *of* the order of Aaron," we mean that they had the very same priesthood that Aaron had. But it is not so with Christ. *His* priesthood is not restricted to any human order, for no mere man could possibly sustain or perform the work which pertains to Christ's priesthood.

As we have pointed out on previous occasions, it is of the very greatest importance, in order to a clear understanding of the priesthood of God's Son, to perceive that *both* Aaron and Melchizedek were needed to foreshadow His sacerdotal office.The reason for this was, that the priestly work of Christ would be performed in two distinct stages: one in the days of His humiliation, the other during the time of His exaltation. Aaron prefigured the former, Melchizedek the latter. In perfect keeping with this fact Christ is not said to be a high priest "after the order of Melchizedek" in 2:17; 3:1, or 4:15. It was not until *after* the apostle has shown in 5:5-9 that Christ fulfilled that which Aaron typified (5:1-4), that He is "saluted of God" as an high priest after the order of *Melchizedek.* And, we would here point out again that, this was wondrously and blessedly adumbrated in Gen. 14, where Melchizedek is seen coming to meet and greet the *victorious* Abraham.

There were various things, peculiar to the person of Melchizedek, above and beyond what appertained to Aaron, which rendered him an illustrious type of our great High Priest; and when Christ is designated Priest "after the order of Melchizedek," the meaning of that expression is, according to the things revealed in Scripture concerning that O.T. character. "Because of the especial resemblance there was between what Melchizedek was and what Christ was to be, God called His priesthood Melchizedekecian" (Dr. Owen). "After the order of Melchizedek" does not mean a limitation of His priesthood to that order—else it had said "of the order of Melchizedek"—but points to the particulars in which his priesthood also prefigured that of Christ's. The various details of which that resemblance consisted are developed in Heb. 7; all that we would now call attention to is, that nowhere in Scripture is Melchizedek ever seen offering a sacrifice, instead, we read, he "brought forth bread and wine" (Gen. 14:18)—typically, the *memorials* of the great Sacrifice already offered, once for all.

It was in death that Christ fulfilled the Aaronic type, making a full and perfect atonement for the sins of His people. It is in resurrection that He assumed the character in which Melchizedek foreshadowed Him—a *royal* Priest. It was after He had been officially "perfected" and had become "the Author of eternal salvation unto all them that obey Him" that the Lord Jesus announced, "All power is *given* unto Me in heaven and in earth" (Matt. 28:18). There was first the Cross and then the Crown: first He "offered up Himself" (7:27), then He entered "into heaven itself, now to appear in the presence of God for us" (9:24); and there He is seated "a Priest upon His throne" (Zech. 6:13).

"Called of God an high priest after the order of Melchizedek" (v. 10). A most important point had now been reached in the apostle's argument, the central design of which was to exhibit the immeasurable superiority of Christianity over Judaism. The very center of the Jewish economy was its temple and priesthood; so too, the outstanding glory of Christianity, is its Priest who ministers in the heavenly sanctuary, officiating there in fulfillment of the Melchizedek type. But though the apostle had now arrived at the most important point in this treatise, it was also one which required the most delicate handling, due to the fleshly prejudices of his readers. To declare that, following His exodus from the grave, God Himself had greeted Christ as priest "after the order of *Melchizedek*," was tantamount to saying that the Aaronic order was thus Divinely set aside, and with it, all the ordinances and ceremonies of the Mosaic law. This was the hardest thing of all for a Hebrew, even a converted one, to bow to; for it meant repudiating everything that was seen, and cleaving to that which was altogether invisible. It meant forsaking that which their fathers had honoured for fifteen hundred years, and following that which the great majority of their brethren according to the flesh denounced as Satanic. In view of the difficulty created by this prejudice, the apostle interrupts the flow of his argument, and pauses to make a lengthy parenthesis.

"The apostle has scarcely entered on the central and most important part of his epistle, when he feels painfully the difficulty of explaining the doctrine of the heavenly and eternal priesthood of the Son, and this not merely on account of the grandeur and depth of the subject, but on account of the spiritual condition of the Hebrews, whom he is addressing. He had presented to their view the Lord Jesus, who after His sufferings was made perfect in His exaltation to be the High Priest in heaven. When he quotes again the 110th Psalm, 'Thou art a priest, forever after the order of Melchizedek,' the solemn and comprehensive words which are addressed by the Father to the Son, he has such a vivid and profound sense of the exceeding riches of this heavenly knowledge, of the treasures of wisdom and consolation which are hidden in the heavenly Priesthood of our ascended Lord, that he longs to unfold to the Hebrews his knowledge of the glorious mystery; especially as this was the truth which they most urgently needed. Here and here alone could they see their true position as worshippers in the true tabernacle, the heavenly sanctuary. Here and here alone was consolation for them in the trial which they felt on account of their excision from the temple and the earthly service in Jerusalem; while from the knowledge of Christ's heavenly priesthood they would also derive light to avoid the insidious errors, and strength to overcome the difficulties which were besetting their path" (A. Saphir).

In the course of his parenthesis which we are now about to begin, the apostle strikes two distinct notes: first he sounds a solemn warning, and then he gives forth a gracious encouragement. The warning is found in 5:11 to 6:8, the encouragement is contained in 6:9-20. Just so long as Christians have the flesh in them and are subject to the assaults of the Devil, do they need constant warning; and just so long as they are harassed by indwelling sin and are left in an hostile world, do they stand in need of heavenly encouragement. All effective ministry to the saints proceeds along these two lines, alternating from the one to the other. Preachers will do well to make a careful note of this fact, fully exemplified in all the Epistles of the apostles; and every Christian reader will do well to take to heart the solemn and searching passage we are now to take up.

"Of whom we have many things to say" (v. 11). "Of whom:" concerning Christ as the fulfiller of the Melchizedek type, the apostle had much in mind, much that he desired to bring before his brethren. There were many things pertaining to this order of priesthood which were of deep importance, of great value, and most necessary to know; things which concerned the glory of Christ, things which concerned the joy and consolation of His people. But these things were "hard to be uttered," or as the R. V. has, "hard of interpretation." This does not mean that the apostle himself found it difficult to grasp them; nor does it mean they were of such a nature that he laboured to find language for expressing himself clearly. No, it was because the things themselves were *unpalatable* to the Hebrews, that the spirit of the apostle was straitened. This is seen from the next clause.

"And hard to be uttered, seeing ye are dull of hearing" (v. 11). "To be 'dull of hearing' is descriptive of that state of mind in which statements may be made without producing any corresponding impression, without being attended to, without being understood, without being felt. In a word, it is descriptive of mental listlessness. To a person in this state, it is very difficult to explain anything; for, nothing, however simple in itself, can be understood if it be not attended to" (Dr. J. Brown). The R. V. is again preferable here; "ye are *become* dull of hearing." They were not always so. Time was when these Hebrews had listened to the Word with eagerness, and had made diligent application thereof. "When the Gospel was first preached to them, it aroused their attention, it exercised their thoughts; but now with many of them it had become a common thing. They flattered themselves that they knew all about it. It had become to them like a sound to which the ear had been long accustomed—the person is not conscious of it, pays no attention to it" (Dr. J. Brown).

The Greek word for "dull" is translated "slothful" in 6:12. It signifies a state of heaviness or inertia. These Hebrews had become mentally and spiritually what loafers are in the natural world—too indolent to bestir themselves, too lazy to make any effort at improvement. They were spiritual sluggards; slothful. Let the reader turn to Prov. 12:27, 19:24, 21:25, 24:30-34, 26:13-16, and remember these passages all have a *spiritual* application. To become, "dull of hearing" or "slothful," is the reverse of "giving diligence" in 2 Peter 1:5, 10. In such a condition of soul, the apostle found it difficult to lead the Hebrews on to the apprehension of higher truth. He had many things to say unto them, but their coldness, lethargy, prejudice, restrained him. And this is recorded for *our* learning; it has a voice for *us*; may the Spirit grant us an hearing ear.

"Ye are become dull of hearing." Of how many Christians is this true today! "Ye did run well; who did hinder you?" (Gal. 5:7). This is a cause of mourning unto all the true servants of God. Because iniquity abounds, the love of many waxes cold. Affections are set upon things below, rather than upon things above. Many who are deluded into thinking their eternal salvation is secure, evidence no concern over their present relationship to God. And Christians who mingle with these lifeless professors are injuriously affected, for "evil communications corrupt good manners" (1 Cor. 15:33). There is little "reaching forth unto those things which are before" (Phil. 3:13) and, consequently, little *growth* in grace and in the knowledge of the Lord. By the very law of our constitution, if we do not move forward, we slip backward.

There are few who seem to realize that truth has to be "bought" (Prov. 23:23), purchased at the cost of subordinating temporal interests to spiritual ones. If the Christian is to "increase in the knowledge of God" (Col. 1:10), he has to give himself whole-heartedly to the things of God. It is impossible to serve God and mammon. If the heart of the professing Christian be set, as the heart of the nominal professor is, upon earthly comforts, worldly prosperity, temporal riches, then the "true riches" will be missed—sold for "a mess of pottage" (Heb. 12:16). But if, by Divine grace, through the possession of a new nature, there is a longing and a hungering for spiritual things, that longing can only be attained and that hunger satisfied by giving ourselves entirely to their ceaseless quest. "The loins of our minds" (1 Peter 1:13) have to be girded, the Word has to be "studied" (2 Tim. 2:15), the means of grace have to be used with "all diligence" (2 Peter 1:5). It is the diligent soul which "shall be made fat" (Prov. 13:4).

How many who sit under the ministry of a true servant of God are "dull of hearing!" There is little waiting upon God, little real exercise of heart, before the service, to prepare them for receiving His message. Instead, the average hearer comes up to the house of God with a mind full of worldly concerns. We have to *"lay aside* all filthiness and superfluity of naughtiness" if we are to "receive with meekness the engrafted Word" (James 1:21). We have to listen unto God's Word with a right motive; not out of idle curiosity, not merely to fulfill a duty, still less for the purpose of criticizing; but that we "may *grow* thereby" (1 Peter 2:2)—grow in practical godliness. And, if what we have heard is not to be forgotten, if it is really to profit the soul, it must be meditated upon (Psa. 1:2), and accompanied with earnest prayer for grace to enable us to "heed" what has been heard.

"For when for the time ye ought to be teachers, ye have need that one teach you again which be the first principles of the oracles of God; and are become such as have need of milk, and not of strong meat" (v. 12). The opening "for" intimates that the apostle is here substantiating the charge which he had preferred against the believing Hebrews at the close of the preceding verse. His reproof was with the object of emphasizing the sad state into which their inertia had brought them. Their condition was to be deplored from three considerations. First, they had been converted long enough to be of help to others. Second, instead of being useful, they were useless, needing to be grounded afresh in the A.B.C. of the Truth of God. Third, so far from having the capacity to masticate strong food, their condition called for that which was suited only to a stunted babyhood.

"For when for the time ye ought to be teachers." This, it seems to us, is only another way of saying, Consider how long you have been Christians, how long you have known the Truth, and what improvement of it ought to have been made! It was a rebuke for their having failed to "redeem the time" (Eph. 5:16). Most probably among these Hebrews were some who had been called during the days of Christ's public ministry, others no doubt were among the three thousand saved on the day of Pentecost, since which, about thirty years had passed. During that time they had the O.T. Scriptures which clearly testified to all they had been taught concerning Christ. The Gospel had been preached and "confirmed" unto them (2:1-3). Moreover, as the book of Acts shows, the apostles had laboured hard and long among them, and much of the N.T. was now in their hands. Hence, in 6:7 they are likened to the earth which drinketh in the rain that "cometh *oft* upon it." Thus, every privilege and opportunity had been theirs.

"Ye ought to be teachers." This tells us the improvement which should have been made of, and the use to which they ought to have put, the teaching they had received. The Gospel is given by God to the Christian, not only for his own individual edification and joy, but as a "pound" to be traded with for Christ's glory (Luke 19:13), as a "light" for the illumination of others (Matt. 5:15, 16). "You *ought* to be teachers" shows that this was a duty required of them. How little is this perceived by Christians today! How few listen to the ministry of the Scriptures with an ear not only for their own soul's profit, but also with the object of being equipped to help others. Instead, how many attend the preaching of the Word simply as a matter of custom, or to satisfy their conscience. Two aims should be prayerfully sought by every Christian auditor: his own edification, his usefulness to others.

"Ye ought to be *teachers*." Let not the searching point of this be blunted by saying, God does not want all His people to be public preachers. The N.T. does not limit "teaching" to the pulpit. One of the most important spheres is *the home,* and that should be a Christian seminary. Under the law God commanded the Israelite to give His words to the members of his household: "And Thou shalt teach them diligently unto thy children, and shalt talk of them when thou sittest in thine house, and when thou walkest by the way, and when thou liest down, and when thou risest up" (Deut. 6:7). Does God require less from us now, in this dispensation of full light? No, indeed. Note, again, how in Titus 2:3-5 the older sisters are bidden to *"teach* the young women:" never was there a greater need for this than now. So in 2 Tim. 2:2 the brethren are to "teach others also." Yes, every Christian "ought to be" a teacher.

"Ye have need that one teach you again." The apostle continues his reproof of the listless Hebrews, and presses upon them the inevitable consequence of becoming "dull of hearing." Spiritual sloth not only prevents practical progress in the Christian's life, but it produces retrogression. It was not that they had lost, absolutely, their knowledge of Divine truth, but they had failed to lay it to heart, and live in the power of it. In 2 Peter 1 Christians are called on to *add* to their faith "virtue, and to virtue, knowledge; and to knowledge, temperance; and to temperance, patience; and to patience, godliness; and to godliness, brotherly kindness; and to brotherly kindness, love;" and then the apostle adds, "For if these things be in you, and abound, they make you that ye shall neither be barren nor unfruitful in the knowledge of our Lord Jesus Christ."

On the other hand, we are solemnly warned, "But he that lacketh these things is blind, and cannot see afar off, and hath forgotten that he was purged from his old sins." This was the condition of the Hebrews.

"Which be the first principles of the oracles of God." Because of their unresponsiveness of heart, they had gone back so far that they were only fit to be placed in the lowest form of learners; they needed to be re-taught their A.B.C. Clear proof was this of their dullness and lack of proficiency. The *"first principles* of the oracles of God" signify the rudiments of our faith, the first lessons presented to our learning, the elementary truths of Scripture. Until these are grasped by faith, and the heart and life are influenced by them, the disciple is not ready for further instructions in the things of God. In the case of the Hebrews, those "first principles" or elementary doctrines were, that the O.T. economy was strictly a typical one, that its ordinances and ceremonies foreshadowed the person and work of God's Son, who was to come here and make an atonement for the sins of His people. He had thus come: the types had given place to the great Antitype, and therefore the shadows were replaced by the Substance itself. True, he had left this scene, gone into heaven, itself, there to appear in the presence of God for His people. Thither their faith and affections should have followed Him. But instead, they wanted to go back again to the temple-services in Jerusalem. They were setting their hearts upon the now effete types and figures, which the apostle hesitated not to call "the weak and beggarly elements" (Gal. 4:9).

Instead of walking by faith, the Hebrews were influenced by the things of sight. Instead of looking forward to an ascended and glorified Saviour, they were occupied with a system which had foreshadowed His work in the days of His humiliation. Thus they needed to be taught afresh the "first principles of the oracles of God." They needed to be reminded that that which is perfect had come, and therefore that which was in part had been done away. And what is the present-day application of this expression to Christians? This: the elementals of our faith are, that Christ Jesus came into this world to save sinners; that His salvation is perfect and complete, leaving nothing for us to add to it; that the only fitness He requires from sinners is the Spirit's discovery to them of their *need* of Him. The greater the sinner I know myself to be, the greater my need of Christ, and the more I am *suited* to Him, for He died for "the ungodly" (Rom. 5:6). It was the realization of my ruin and wretchedness which first drew me to Him. If I cast myself, in all my want and poverty, upon Him, then He *has* received me, for His declaration is, "him that cometh to Me, I will in no wise cast out." Believing this, I go on my way rejoicing, thanking Him, praising Him, living on Him and for Him.

But instead of living in the joyous assurance of their acceptance in the Beloved, many give way to doubting. They question their "interest in Christ;" they wonder, "Am I His, or am I not?" They are continually occupied with self, either their good self or their bad self. And thus their peace is at an end. Instead of affections set upon Christ, their attention is turned within, occupied with their faith or their lack of it. Instead of walking in the glorious sunshine of the conscious favour of God, they dwell in "Doubting Castle," or flounder in the "Slough of Despond." Thus, instead of themselves being teachers of others, they have need that one teach them again "which be the first principles of the oracles of God." They are fit only for the kindergarten. They require to be told once more that faith looks away from self, and is occupied entirely with Another. They need to be told that Christ, not faith, is the sinner's Saviour; that faith is simply the empty hand extended to receive from Him.

This clause is susceptible of various legitimate applications. Let us consider its bearing upon another class of Christians, among which may be numbers of our readers. Time was when, in the "far country," you sought to be filled with the husks which the swine fed on (Luke 15). But you found your quest was in vain. To change the figure, you sampled one after another of the world's cisterns, only to find that "whosoever drinketh of this water shall thirst again" (John 4:13). You discovered that the things of the world could not meet your deep need. Then, weary and heavy-laden, you were brought to Christ, and found in Him that "altogether lovely" One. O the joy that was now yours! "Thou O Christ art all I want," was your confession. But is this the language of your heart today? Alas, "thou hast left thy first love" (Rev. 2:4), and with it, peace and contentment are also largely a thing of the past. Like a sow that returns to her wallowing in the mire, many go back to the world for recreation, then for satisfaction. Ah, have not you, my reader, need to be taught again "which be the first principles of the oracles of God?" Do you not need reminding that nothing in this scene can minister to the new nature, a nature which has been created for heaven? Do you not need to relearn that Christ alone can satisfy your heart?

The "oracles of God" is one of many names given to the Holy Scriptures. Stephen called them the "living oracles" (Acts 7:38). "They are so in respect of their Author,—they are the oracles of 'the living God;' whereas the oracles with which Satan infatuated the world were most of them at the shrines and graves of dead men. They are so in respect of their use and efficacy: they are 'living' because life-giving oracles unto them that obey them (Deut. 32:47). Because they are 'the oracles of God,' they have supreme authority over the souls and consciences of us all. Therefore are they also infallible truth" (Dr. J. Owen).

"And are become such as have need of milk, and not of strong meat." Here the apostle continues to rebuke the Hebrews for their laxity, and sets before them their deteriorated condition under a figure designed to humble them: he likens them to infants. The same similitude is used in 1 Cor. 3:1, 2. "Milk" here signifies the same thing as the "first principles of the oracles of God." The "strong meat" had reference to the offices of Christ, especially His priesthood, as suited to our needs and affections. "Milk" is appropriate for babes, but Christians ought to grow and become strong in the Lord. They are exhorted to "be not children in understanding" (1 Cor. 14:20). They are bidden to "quit ye like men" (1Cor. 15:13).

"For every one that useth milk is unskillful in the word of righteousness: for he is a babe" (v. 13). "Useth milk" means, lives on nothing else. By the "word of righteousness" is meant the Gospel of God's grace. In 1 Cor. 1:18 it is termed "the Word of the Cross," because that is its principal subject. In Rom. 10:8 it is designated "the Word of Faith," because that is its chief requirement from all who hear it. Here, the Word of Righteousness, because of its nature, use and end. In the Gospel is "the righteousness of God revealed" (Rom. 1:16, 17), for Christ is "the end of the law for righteousness unto every one that believeth" (Rom. 10:4). Now the Hebrews are not here said to be ignorant of or utterly without the Word of Righteousness, but "unskillful" or "inexperienced" in the use of it. They had failed to improve it to its proper end. Did they clearly apprehend the Gospel, they had perceived the needlessness for the perpetuation of the Levitical priesthood with its sacrifices.

The one unskilled in the Word of Righteousness is a "babe." This term is here used by way of reproach. A "babe" is weak, ignorant.

A spiritual "babe" is one who has an inadequate knowledge of Christ, i.e. an experimental knowledge and heart-acquaintance with Him. Let the reader note that a state of infancy was what characterized God's people of old under Judaism (Gal. 4:1-6). They were looking forward to the Christ that was to come, and whose person and work was represented to their eyes by typical pictures and persons. Such was the ground to which these Hebrews had well-nigh slipped back. Earthly things were engrossing their attention. So it is still. A person may have been a Christian twenty or thirty years, but if he is not forgetting the things which are behind, and constantly pressing to the things before, he is, in actual experience and spiritual stature, but "a babe."

"But strong meat belongeth to them that are of full age, those who by reason of use have their senses exercised to discern both good and evil" (v. 14). Here the apostle completes the antithesis begun in the preceding verse, and describes the character of those to whom strong meat is suited. By necessary implication his statement explains to us *why* the Hebrews had become "dull of hearing." There is much here of deep practical importance. "Strong meat" is contrasted from "milk" or the "first principles" of God's Word, which we have defined above. This "strong meat" is the appropriate portion of those who have left infancy behind, who have so assimilated the "milk" of babyhood they have "grown thereby," grown in faith and love. This growth is produced and promoted by *using* our spiritual "senses" or faculties. Infants *have* "senses," but they know not how to exercise them to advantage. The proper use of our spiritual faculties enables us to distinguish between "good and evil". It was here the Hebrews had failed so lamentably.

"A child is easily imposed upon as to its food. Its nurse may easily induce it to swallow even palatable poison. But a man, 'by reason of use,' has learned so to employ his senses as to distinguish between what is deleterious and what is nourishing" (Dr. J. Brown). The same holds good in the spiritual realm. There is in the new man that which corresponds to our "five senses" naturally, namely, understanding, conscience, affections. But these have to be trained and developed. It is only by the constant and assiduous exercise of minds upon spiritual things, by the diligent study of the Word, by daily meditation thereon, by the exercise of faith therein, by earnestly supplicating the Spirit for light, that we acquire the all-important discernment to distinguish between good and evil, Truth and error. "Senses *exercised*" means ability or fitness acquired, as a disciplined soldier is equipped for his duty, or a trained athlete is for his work. Such capacity is only attained by the Christian through a constant and sedulous application of himself to the things of God. "By reason of use" refers not to spasmodic effort, but to a regular practice, a confirmed habit. The outcome is a spiritual ability to judge rightly of all that is presented to his notice.

It was here the Hebrews had failed, as, alas, so many Christians do now. "Their senses had not been exercised; that is, they had not walked closely with God, they had not followed the Master, listening earnestly to His voice, and proving what is that good, and acceptable, and perfect will of God. They had not conscientiously applied the knowledge which they had, but allowed it to remain dead and unused. If they had really and truly partaken of the milk, they would not have remained babes" (A. Saphir). Because of their slothfulness, they were unable to distinguish between "good and evil," i.e., between Truth and error, the promptings of the Spirit and the solicitations of Satan, the desires of the new nature and the lustings of the old. They were like babes are in the natural world, unable to discriminate between what is wholesome and what is hurtful; therefore were they unable to see the difference between what was right under the Judaic economy, and what was now suited to Christianity.

"Senses trained to discern both good and evil" has reference to what is set before a believer as food for his soul. The "good" is that which is nutritious and suited to his nourishment, "evil" is that which tends not to his edification, but to his destruction. Scripture itself is "evil" when wrongly divided and misapplied. This is seen in Satan's misuse of Scripture with Christ (Matt. 4:6). Truth becomes "evil" when it is not presented in its due and Divine *proportions.* The enemies of the Hebrews were appealing to the O.T. Scriptures, as Romanists now do to favour their elaborate form of worship and priesthood. In many other ways is Satan active today in setting before God's people both "good and evil," and unless their spiritual faculties have been diligently trained, through much waiting upon God, they fall easy victims to his half-lies.

"If people really *loved and cherished* what they so fondly called 'the simple gospel,' their knowledge and Christian character would deepen, and all the truths which are centered in Christ crucified would become the object of their investigation and delight, and enrich and elevate their experience. . . . There are no doctrines more profound than those which are proclaimed when Christ's salvation is declared. All our progress consists in learning more fully the doctrine which at first is preached unto us" (A. Saphir). It is *using* the light we already have, putting into *practice* the truth already received, which fits us for more. Unless this *is* done, we retrograde, and the light which is in us becomes darkness. Manna not used breeds worms (Ex.16:20)! Milk undigested—not taken up into our system—ferments. A backslidden state deprives us of a sound judgment. The secret of "senses trained to discern good and evil" is revealed in Hos. 6:3, "Then shall we know, if we *follow on* to know the Lord." May His grace stir us up so to do.

CHAPTER TWENTY-THREE

Infancy and Maturity.

(Heb. 6:1-3)

The interpretation which we shall give of the above verses is not at all in accord with that advanced by the older writers. It differs considerably from that found in the commentaries of Drs. Calvin, Owen and Gouge, and more recently, those of A. Saphir, and Dr. J. Brown. Much as we respect their works, and deeply as we are indebted to not a little that is helpful in them, yet we dare not follow them blindly. To "prove all things" (1 Thess. 5:21) is ever our bounden duty. Though it is against our natural inclination to depart from the exposition they suggested (several, with some diffidence), yet we are thankful to God that in later years He has granted some of His servants increased light from His wondrous and exhaustless Word. May it please Him to vouchsafe us still more.

The writers mentioned above understood the expression "the principles of the doctrine of Christ," or as the margin of the R. V. more accurately renders "the word of the beginning of Christ," to refer to the elementary truths of Christianity, a summary of which is given in the six items that follow in the second half of v. 1 and the whole of v. 2; while the "Let us go on unto perfection," they regarded as a call unto the deeper and higher things of the Christian revelation. But for reasons which to us seem conclusive, such a view of our passage is altogether untenable. It fails to take into account the central theme of this Epistle, and the purpose for which it was written. It does not do justice at all to the immediate context. It completely breaks down when tested in its details.

As we have repeated so often in the course of this series of articles, the theme of our Epistle is the immeasurable superiority of Christianity over Judaism. Unless the interpreter keeps this steadily in mind as he proceeds from chapter to chapter, and from passage to passage, he is certain to err. This is the key which unlocks every section, and if attempt be made to open up any portion without it, the effect can only be strained and forced. The importance of this consideration cannot be overestimated, and several striking exemplifications of it have already been before us in our survey of the previous chapters. Here too it will again stand us in good stead, if we but use it. The apostle is not contrasting two different stages of Christianity, an infantile and a mature; rather is he opposing, once more, the substance over against the shadows. He continues to press upon the Hebrews their need of forsaking the visible for the invisible, the typical for the antitypical.

That in taking up our present passage it is also of first importance to study its *connection* with the immediate context, is evident from its very first word, "Therefore." The apostle is here drawing a conclusion from something said previously. This takes us back to what is recorded in 5:11-14, for a right understanding of which depends a sound exposition of what immediately follows. In these verses the apostle rebukes the Hebrews for their spiritual sloth, and likens them to little children capacitated to receive nothing but milk. He tells them that they have need of one teaching them again "*which* be the first principles of the oracles of God," which denoted they had not yet clearly grasped the fact that Judaism was but a temporary economy, because a typical one, its ordinances and ceremonies foreshadowing Him who was to come here and make an atonement for the sins of His people. Now that He had come and finished His work the types had served their purpose, and the shadows were replaced by the Substance.

The spiritual condition in which the Hebrew saints were at the time the Holy Spirit moved the apostle to address this Epistle to them, is another important key to the opening of its hortatory sections. As we showed in our last article, the language of 5:11-14 plainly intimates that they have gone backward. The *cause* of this is made known in the 10th chapter, part of which takes us back to a point in time prior to what is recorded in chapter 5. First in 10:32 we read, "But call to remembrance the former days, in which, after ye were illuminated, ye endured a great flight of afflictions." This "great flight of afflictions" they had, as v. 34 tells us, taken "*joyfully.*" Very remarkable and rare was this. How was such an experience to be accounted for? The remainder of v. 34 tells us, "*Knowing* in yourselves that ye have in heaven a *better* and an enduring substance."

But this blessed and spiritual state which characterized the Hebrews in the glow of "first love" had not been maintained. While affections were set upon things above where Christ is seated at the right hand of God, whilst faith was in exercise, they realized that their real portion was on High. But faith has to be tested, patience has to be tried, and unless faith be maintained "hope deferred maketh the heart sick" (Prov. 13:12). Alas, their faith had wavered, and in consequence they had become dissatisfied to have *nothing* down here; they became impatient of waiting for an *unseen* and *future* inheritance. It was for this reason that the apostle said to them, "Cast not away therefore your confidence, which hath great recompence of reward. For ye have need of *patience,* that, after ye have done the will of God, ye might receive the promise" (10:35, 36).

Now it was this discontented and impatient condition of soul into which they had fallen, which accounts for the state in which we find them in 5:11, 12. So too it explains the various things referred to in chapter 6. That is why the apostle was moved to set before them the most solemn warning found in vv. 4-6. That is why we find "hope" so prominent in what follows: see vv. 11, 18, 19. That is why reference is made to "patience" in v. 12. That is why Abraham is referred to, and why *his* "patience" is singled out for mention in v. 15. And that is why in our present passage the Hebrews are urged to "go on unto perfection," and why the apostle interposes a doubt in the matter: "This will we do, *if* God permit" (v. 3), for there was good reason to believe that their past conduct had provoked Him. Thus we see again how wondrously and how perfectly Scripture interprets itself, and how much we need to "compare spiritual things with spiritual" (1 Cor. 2:13).

The sixth chapter of Hebrews does not commence a new section of the Epistle, but continues the digression into which the apostle had entered at 5:11. In view of the disability of those to whom he was writing receiving unto their edification the high and glorious mysteries which he desired to expound, the apostle goes on to set before them various reasons and arguments to excite a diligent attention thereunto. First, he declares his intention positively: to "go on unto perfection" (v. 1). Second, he names, what he intended to "leave," namely, "the word of the beginning of Christ" (vv. 1-3). Third, he warns of the certain doom of apostates (vv. 4-8). Fourth, he softens this warning in the case of the converted Hebrews (v. 9-14). Fifth, he gives an inspiring encouragement to faith, taken from the life of Abraham (vv. 15-21).

"Therefore leaving the principles of the doctrine of Christ" (v. 1). As already pointed out, the first word of this verse denotes that there is a close link between what has immediately preceded and what now follows. This will appear yet more clearly if we attend closely to the exact terms here used. The word "principles" in this verse is the same as rendered "first" in 5:12. The word "doctrine" is found in its plural form and is translated "oracles" in 5:12. The word "perfection" is given as "of full age" in 5:14. Thus it is very evident that the apostle is here *continuing* the same subject which he began in the previous chapter.

"Therefore leaving the principles of the doctrine of Christ." The rendering of the A. V. of this clause is very faulty and misleading. The verb is in the past tense, not the present. Bagster's Interlinear correctly gives "Wherefore *having left*." This difference of rendition is an important one, for it enables us to understand more readily the significance of what follows. The apostle was stating a positive fact, not pleading for a possibility. He was not asking the Hebrews to take a certain step, but reminding them of one they had already taken. They *had* left the "principles of the doctrine of Christ," and to them he did not wish them to return.

"Therefore leaving the principles of the doctrine of Christ." More accurately, "Wherefore having left the word of the beginning of Christ." Bagster's Interlinear, which gives a literal word for word translation of the Greek, renders it, "Wherefore, having left the of the beginning of the Christ discourse." This expression is parallel with the "first principles of the oracles of God" in 5:12. It has reference to what God has made known concerning His Son under Judaism. In the O.T. two things are outstandingly prominent in connection with Christ: first, prophecies of His coming into the world; second, types and figures of the work He should perform. These predictions had now received their fulfilment, those shadows had now found their substance, in the incarnation, life, death, resurrection and ascension of the Son of God. This, the "holy brethren" (3:1) among the Jews had acknowledged. Thus they had "left" the a.b.c. for the Word Himself, the pictures for the Reality.

"Let us go on unto perfection." There is the definite article in the Greek, and "The Perfection" is obviously set in apposition to "The word of the beginning of Christ:" note, not of "the Lord Jesus," but of "Christ," i.e., the Messiah. It is the contrast, once more, between Judaism and Christianity. That which is here referred to as "The Perfection" is the full revelation which God now made of Himself in the person of His incarnate Son. No longer is He veiled by types and shadows, His glory is seen fully in the face of Jesus Christ (2 Cor. 4:6). The only begotten Son has "declared" Him here on earth (John 1:18); but having triumphantly finished the work which was given Him to do, He has been "received up into glory" (1 Tim. 3:16), and upon an exalted and enthroned Christ the affection of the believer is now to be set (Col. 3:1).

"*Wherefore* having left . . . let us go on unto perfection." The first word looks back to *all* that the apostle had said. It is a conclusion drawn from the contents of the whole preceding five chapters. Its force is: In view of the fact that God has now spoken to us in His Son; in view of who He is, namely, the appointed Heir of all things, the Maker of the worlds, the Brightness, of God's glory, and the very Impress of His substance, the One who upholds all things by the word of His power; in view of the fact that He has by Himself "purged our sins," and, in consequence, has sat down at the right hand of the Majesty on high, having been made so much better than angels, as He hath by inheritance obtained a more excellent name than they; in view of the further fact that He was made in all things like unto His brethren, that He might be a merciful and faithful High Priest in things Godward, to make propitiation for the sins of the people, and having, in consequence of His successful prosecution of this stupendous work been "crowned with glory and honour;" and, seeing that He is immeasurably superior to Moses, Joshua and Aaron;—let us give Him His due place in our thoughts, hearts and lives.

"Let us go on unto perfection" has reference to the apprehension of the Divine revelation of the full glory of Christ in His person, perfections, and position. It is, from the practical side, a "perfection" of *knowledge,* spiritually imparted by the Holy Spirit to the understanding and heart. It refers to the mysteries and sublime doctrine of the Gospel. It is a perfection of knowledge in revealed truth. Yet, of course, it is only a relative "perfection," for an absolute apprehension of the things of God is not attainable in this life. Now "we know in part" (1 Cor. 13:9). "If any man think that he knoweth anything, he knoweth *nothing* yet as he ought to know" (1 Cor. 8:2). Even the apostle Paul had to say, "Brethren, I count not myself to have apprehended: but this one thing I do, forgetting those things which are behind, and reaching forth unto those things which are before, I press toward the mark for the prize of the high calling of God in Christ Jesus" (Phil. 3:13, 14).

"Let *us* go on unto perfection." Students are not agreed as to the precise force of the plural pronoun here. Some consider it to be the apostle linking on the Hebrews to himself in the task immediately before him; others regard the "us" as the apostle graciously joining himself with them in their duty. Personally, we think that both these ideas are to be combined. First, "let us go on:" it was his resolution so to do, as the remaining chapters of the Epistle demonstrate; then let *them* follow him. Thus considered it shows that the apostle did not look upon the condition of the Hebrews as quite hopeless, notwithstanding their "dullness" (5:11)—I shall therefore go on to set before you the highest and most glorious things concerning Christ. Second, the apostle condescends to unite himself with them in their responsibility to press forward. "Wherefore:" in view of the length of time we have been Christians, let us be diligent to grow in grace and in the knowledge of our Lord Jesus Christ. It was, thus, a call to stir them up.

"Let us go on" is passive, "be carried on." It is a word taken from the progress which a ship makes before the wind when under sail. Let us, under the full bent of our will and affections be stirred by the utmost endeavours of our whole souls, be borne onwards. We have abode long enough near the shore, let us hoist our sails, pray to the Spirit for His mighty power to work within us, and launch forth into the deep. This is the duty of God's servants, to excite their Christian hearers to make progress in the knowledge of Divine truth, to urge them to pass the porch and enter the sanctuary, there to behold the Divine glories of the House of God. Though the verb is passive, denoting the effect—"Let us be carried on"—yet it included the active use of means for the producing of this effect. "All diligence" is demanded of the Christian (2 Pet. 1:5). Truth has to be "bought" (Prov. 23:23). That which God has given us must be put into practice (Luke 8:18).

"Let us go on unto perfection." What, we may ask, is the application of this to Christians today? To the Hebrews it meant abandoning the preparatory and earthly system of Judaism, (which occupied their whole attention before believing in Christ as the sent Saviour) and, by faith, laying hold of the Divine revelation which has now been made in and through Him: set your affection on an ascended though invisible Christ, who now serves in the Heavenly Sanctuary on your behalf. For Christians it means, Turn away from those objects which absorbed you in the time of your unregeneracy, and meditate now on and find your joy and satisfaction in things above. Lay aside every weight and the sin which so easily besets, and run with perseverance the race that is set before us, "looking off unto Jesus"—the One who while here left us an example to follow, the One who is now enthroned on High because of the triumphant completion of His race.

To the Hebrews, this much-misunderstood exhortation of Heb. 6:1 was exactly parallel with the word which Christ addressed to the eleven immediately prior to His death: "Ye believe in God, believe also in Me" (John 14:1): Ye have long avowed your faith in "God," whom, though invisible, ye trust; now "believe *also* in Me," as One who will speedily pass beyond the range of your natural vision. I am on the point of returning to the Father, but I shall still have your interests at heart, yea, I am going to "prepare a place for you;" therefore, trust Me implicitly: let your hearts follow Me on high: walk by faith: be occupied with an ascended

Saviour. For us today, the application of this important word signifies, Be engaged with your great High Priest in heaven, dwell daily upon your portion in Him (Eph. 1:3). By faith, behold Christ, now in the heavenly sanctuary, as your righteousness, life, and strength. See in God's acceptance of Him, His adoption of you, that you have been reconciled to Him, made nigh by the precious blood. In the realization of this, worship in spirit and in truth; exercise your priestly privileges.

Thus, the "perfection" of Heb. 6:1 is, strictly speaking, scarcely doctrinal or experimental, yet partakes of both. "The law made nothing perfect, but the bringing in of a better hope did" (Heb. 7:19). It is Christ who has ushered in that which is "perfect." It is in Him we now have a full revelation and manifestation of the eternal purpose and grace of God. He has fully made known His mind (Heb. 1:2). And, by His one all-sufficient offering of Himself, He has "*perfected* forever" (10:14), them whom God set apart in His everlasting counsels. Christ came here to fulfill the will of God (10:9). That will has been executed; the work given Him to do, He finished (John 17:4). In consequence, He has been gloriously rewarded, and in His reward all His people share. This is all made known to us for "the hearing of faith."

"Not laying again the foundation of repentance from dead works" (v. 1). It is most important to see that the contents of the second half of v. 1. and the whole of v. 2 are a parenthesis. The "Let us be carried on to perfection" is completed in "*this* will we do if God permits" in v. 3. That which comes in between is a definition or explanation of what the apostle intended by his "Having left the word of the beginning of Christ." The six items enumerated—"repentance from dead works," etc.—have nothing to do with the "foundations of Christianity," nor do they describe those things relating to the elementary experiences of a Christian. Instead, they treat of what appertained to Judaism, considered as a rudimentary system, paving the way for the fuller and final revelation which God has now made in and by His beloved Son. Unless the *parenthetical* nature of these verses is clearly perceived, interpreters are certain to err in their exposition of the details.

"Not laying again the foundation," etc. It is to be remarked that there is no definite article in the Greek here, so it should be read, "a foundation," which is one of several intimations that it is not the "fundamentals of Christianity" which are here in view. Had these verses been naming the basic features of the new and higher revelation of God, the Holy Spirit had surely said, "*the* foundation;" that He did not, shows that something less important was before Him. As said above, this "foundation" respects Judaism. Now there are two properties to a "foundation," namely, it is that which is first laid in a building; it is that which bears up the whole superstructure. To which we may add, it is generally lost to sight when the ground-floor has been put in. Such was the relation which Judaism sustained to Christianity. As the "foundation" precedes the building, so had Judaism Christianity. As the "foundation" bears the building, so the truth of Christianity rests upon the promises and prophecies of the O.T., of which the N.T. revelation records the fulfillment. As the "foundation" is lost to sight when the building is erected on it, so the types and shadows of the earlier revelation are superceded by the substance and reality.

"Not laying again a foundation," etc. This is exactly what the Hebrews were being sorely tempted to do. To "lay again" this foundation was to forsake the substance for the shadows; it was to turn from Christianity and go back again to Judaism. As Paul wrote to the Galatians, who were being harassed by Judaisers, "Wherefore the law was our schoolmaster unto Christ, that we might be justified by faith" (3:24). To which he at once added, "But after that faith is come, we are no longer under a schoolmaster." Thus, under a different figure, he was here in Heb. 6:1 simply saying, Let us be carried on to maturity, and not go back again to the things which characterized the days of our childhood.

"Not laying again a foundation," etc. It will be noted that the apostle here enumerates just *six* things, which is ever the number of man in the flesh. Such was what distinguished Judaism. It was a system which appertained solely to man in the flesh. Its rites and ceremonies only "sanctified to the purifying of the flesh" (Heb. 9:13). Had the fundamentals of Christianity been here in view, the apostle had surely given seven, as in Eph. 4:3-6. The first which he specifies is "repentance from dead works." Observe that it is not "repentance from *sins*." That is not what is in view at all. This expression "dead works" is found again in Heb. 9:14 (and nowhere else in the N.T.), where a contrast is drawn from what is said in v. 13: the blood of bulls and goats sanctified to the purifying of the flesh, then much more should the blood of Christ cleanse their conscience from dead works. Where *sins* are in question the N.T. speaks of them as "wicked works" (Titus 1:16), and "abominable works" (Col. 1:21). The reference here was to the unprofitable and in-efficacious works of the Levitical service: cf. 10:1, 4. Those works of the ceremonial law are denominated "dead works" because they were performed by men in the flesh, were not vitalized by the Holy Spirit, and did not satisfy the claims of the living God.

"And of faith toward God." Of the six distinctive features of Judaism here enumerated, this one is the most difficult to define with any degree of certainty. Nevertheless, we believe that if due attention be given to the particular people to whom the apostle was writing all difficulty at once vanishes. The case of the Jew was vastly different from that of the Gentiles. To the heathen, the one true God was altogether "unknown" (Acts. 17:23). They worshipped a multitude of false gods. But not so was it with Israel. Jehovah had revealed Himself to their fathers, and given to them a written revelation of His will. Thus, "faith toward God" was a national thing with them, and though in their earlier history they fell into idolatry again and again, yet were they purified of this sin by the Babylonian captivity. Still, their faith was more of a form than a reality, a tradition received from their fathers, rather than a vital acquaintance with Him: see Matt. 15:8, 9, etc.

Israel's national faith "toward God" had, under the Christian revelation, given place to faith in the Lord Jesus Christ. A few references from the N.T. epistles will establish this conclusively. We read of "the faith of Jesus Christ," and "the faith of the Son of God" (Gal. 2:16, 20); "your faith in the Lord Jesus" (Eph. 1:15); "by faith of Jesus Christ" (Phil. 3:9). "your faith in Christ" (Col. 2:5); "the faith which is in Christ Jesus" (1 Tim. 3:13). As another has said, "All the blessings of the gospel are connected with 'faith,' but it is faith which *rests in Christ.* Justification, resurrection-life, the promises, the placing of sons, salvation, etc., are all spoken of as resulting from faith which rests upon Christ . . . 'Hebrews' reveals Christ as the 'one Mediator between God and men.' It reveals Christ as 'a Priest forever after the order of Melchizedek,' and urges the divine claim of the Son of God. The apostle is directing his readers to look away from self to Christ, the Center, the Sum of all blessing. This is not merely 'faith toward God,' but it is faith which comes to God by the way of the mediation and merits of His Son."

"Of the doctrine of baptisms" (v. 2). Had the translators understood the scope and meaning of this passage it is more than doubtful if they had given the rendering they did to this particular clause. It will be observed that the word "baptism" is in the plural number, and if scripture be allowed to interpret scripture there will be no difficulty in ascertaining what is here referred to. It is neither Christian baptism (Matt. 28:19), the baptism of the Spirit (Acts 1:5), nor the baptism of suffering (Matt. 20:23), which is here in view, but the carnal ablutions which obtained under the Mosaic economy. The Greek word is "baptismos." It is found but four times on the pages of the N. T.: in Mark 7:4, 5 and Heb.

6:2; 9:10. In each of the other three instances, the word is rendered "washings." In Mark 7 it is the "washing of cups and pans." In Heb. 9:10 it is "meats and drinks and divers washings and carnal (fleshly) ordinances," concerning which it is said, they were "imposed until the time of reformation."

It is to be noted that our verse speaks of "the *doctrine* of baptisms." There was a definite teaching connected with the ceremonial ablutions of Judaism. They were designed to impress upon the Israelites that Jehovah was a holy God, and that none who were defiled could enter into His presence. These references in Heb. 6:2 and 9:10 look back to such passages as Ex. 30:18, 19; Lev. 16:4; Num. 19:19, etc. Typically, these "washings" denoted that all the defiling effects of sin must be removed, ere the worshipper could approach unto the Lord. They foreshadowed that perfect and eternal cleansing from sin which the atoning blood of Christ was to provide for His people. They had no intrinsic efficacy in themselves; they were but figures, hence, we are told they sanctified only "to the purifying of the flesh" (Heb. 9:13). Those "washings" effected nought but an external and ceremonial purification; they "could not make him that did the service perfect as pertaining to the conscience" (Heb. 9:9).

"And of laying on of hands." The older commentators quite missed the reference here. Supposing the previous clause was concerned with the Christian baptisms recorded in the Acts, they appealed to such passages as Acts 8:17; 19:6, etc. But those passages have no bearing at all on the verse before us. They were exceptional cases where the supernatural "gifts" of the Spirit were imparted by communication from the apostles. The absence of *this* "laying on of hands" in Acts 2:41; 8:38; 16:33, etc., shows plainly that, normally, the Holy Spirit was given by God altogether apart from the instrumentality of His servants. The "laying on of hands" is not, and never was, a distinctive Christian ordinance. In such passages as Acts 6:6; 9:17; 13:3, the act was simply a mark of *identification,* as is sufficiently clear from the last reference.

"And of laying on of hands." The key which unlocks the real meaning of this expression is to be found in the O.T., to which each and all of the six things here mentioned by the apostle look back. Necessarily so, for the apostle is here making mention of those things which characterized Judaism, which the Hebrews, upon their profession of their personal faith in Christ had "left." The "laying on of hands" to which the apostle refers is described in Lev. 16:21, "And Aaron shall lay both his hands upon the head of the live goat, and confess over him all the iniquities of the children of Israel, and all their transgressions in all their sins, putting them on the head of the goat, and shall send him away by the hand of a fit man into the wilderness." This was an essential part of the ritual on the annual Day of Atonement. Of this the Hebrews would naturally think when the apostle here makes mention of the "*doctrine* (teaching) . . . of laying on of hands."

"And of resurrection of the dead." At first glance, and perhaps at the second too, it may appear that what is here before us will necessitate an abandonment of the line of interpretation we are following. Surely, the reader may exclaim, you will not ask us to believe that these Hebrews had "left" the doctrine of the resurrection of the dead! Yet this is exactly what we do affirm. The difficulty which is seemingly involved is more imaginary than real, due to a lack of discrimination and failure to "rightly divide the Word of Truth." The resurrection *of* the dead was a clearly revealed doctrine under Judaism; but it is supplanted by something far more comforting and blessed under the fuller revelation God has given in Christianity. If the reader will carefully observe the preposition we have placed in italic type, he will find it a valuable key to quite a number of passages. "We make a great mistake when we assume that the resurrection as taught by the Pharisees, held by the Jews, believed by the disciples, and proclaimed by the apostles, was one and the same" (C. H. W.). The great difference between the former and the latter may be seen by a comparison of the scriptures that follow.

"After the way which they call heresy, so worship I the God of my fathers, believing all things which are written in the law and in the prophets: and have hope toward God, which they themselves also allow, that there shall be a resurrection *of* the dead, both of the just and unjust" (Acts 24:14, 15). That was the Jewish hope: "Martha saith unto Him, I know that he shall rise again in the resurrection at the last day" (John 11:24). Now in contrast, note, "He charged them that they should tell no man what things they had seen, till the Son of man were risen *from* the dead. And they kept *that* saying with themselves, questioning one with another what the rising *from* the dead should mean" (Mark 9:9, 10). It is this aspect of resurrection which the N. T. epistles emphasize, an elective resurrection, a resurrection of the redeemed before that of the wicked: see Rev. 20:5, 6; 1 Cor. 15:22, 23; 1 Thess. 4:16.

"And of eternal judgment." In the light of all that has been before us, this should occasion no difficulty. The Jewish church, and most of Christendom now, believed in a General Judgment, a great assize at the end of time when God would examine every man's life, "For God shall bring every work into judgment with every secret thing, whether it be good or whether it be evil" (Ecc. 12:14). This is described in fullest detail in the closing verses of Rev. 20. It is the Great White Throne judgment.

Let us now, very briefly, summarize what has just been engaging our attention. The Hebrews had confessed their faith in Christ, and by so doing had forsaken the shadows for the Substance. But hope had been deferred, faith hath waned, persecutions had cooled their zeal. They were being tempted to abandon their Christian profession and return to Judaism. The apostle shows that by so doing they would be laying *again* "a foundation" of things which had been left behind. Rather than this, he urges them to be carried forward to "perfection" or "full growth." That meant to substitute "repentance unto life" (Acts 11:18), for "repentance from dead works;" trust in the glorified Saviour, for a national "faith toward God;" the all-cleansing blood of the Lamb, for the inefficacious "washings" of the law; God's having laid on Christ the iniquities of us all, for the Jewish high-priest's "laying on of hands;" a resurrection "from the dead," for "a resurrection of the dead;" the Judgment-seat of Christ, for the "eternal judgment" of the Great White Throne. Thus, the six things here mentioned belonged to a state of things before Christ was manifested.

"And this will we do if God permit" (v. 3). Here we learn of the apostle's resolution as to the occasion before him, and the limitation of his resolution by an express subordination of it to the good pleasure of God. The "*this* will we do" has reference to "Let us go on unto perfection." The use of the plural pronoun is very blessed. Though a spiritual giant when compared with his fellow Christians, the apostle Paul never imagined he *had* "attained" (Phil. 3:12). "This will *we do*" means, I in teaching, you in learning. In the chapters that follow, we see how the apostle's resolution was carried out. In 5:10 he had said, "an High Priest after the order of Melchizedek, of whom we *have* many things to say." By comparing 6:3 with 5:11, 12 we learn that no discouragement should deter a servant of God from proceeding in the declaration of the mystery of Christ, not even the dullness of his hearers.

"And this will we do, *if* God permit." This qualifying word may have respect unto the unknown sovereign pleasure of God, to which all our resolutions must submit: "I trust to tarry a while with you, if the Lord permit" (1 Cor. 16:7 and cf. James 4:13-15). Probably the apostle also had before him the sad state into which the Hebrews had fallen (5:11-14), in view of which this was a solemn and searching word for their conscience: because of their sloth and negligence there was reason to fear they had provoked God, so that He would grant them no further light (Luke 8:18). Finally, we believe the apostle looked to the Divine enablement of himself; were He to withdraw His assistance the teacher would be helpless: see 2 Cor. 3:5. To sum up: in all things we must seek God's glory, bow to His will, and recognize that all progress in the Truth is a special gift from Him (John 3:27).

CHAPTER TWENTY-FOUR

Apostasy.

(Heb. 6:4-6)

The passage which is now to occupy our attention is one of the most solemn in the Hebrews' epistle, yea, to be met with anywhere in the New Testament. Probably few regenerate souls have read it thoughtfully without being moved to fear and trembling. Careless professors have frequently been rendered uneasy in conscience as they have heard its awe-inspiring language. It speaks of a class of persons who had been highly privileged, who had been singularly favored, but who, so far from having improved their opportunities, had wretchedly perverted them; who had brought shame and reproach on the cause of Christ; and who were in such a hopeless condition that it was "impossible to renew them again unto repentance." Well does it become each one of us to earnestly lift up his heart to God, beseeching Him to prevent us making such a shipwreck of the faith.

As perhaps the majority of our readers are aware, the verses before us have proved one of the fiercest theological battlegrounds of the centuries. It is at this point that the hottest fights between Calvinists and Arminians have been waged. Those who believe that it is possible for a real Christian to so sin and backslide as to fall from grace and be lost eternally, have confidently appealed to these verses for proof of their theory. It is much to be feared their theory prejudiced them so much, that they were incapable of examining impartially and weighing carefully its varied terms. With their minds so biased by their views of apostasy, they have rather taken it for granted that this passage describes a true child of God, who, through turning his back upon Christ, ultimately perishes. But Scripture bids us "*Prove* all things" (1 Thess. 5:21), and this calls for something more than a superficial and hurried investigation of what is, admittedly, a difficult passage.

If on the one hand, Arminians have been too ready to read into this passage their unscriptural dogma of the apostasy of a Christian, it must be confessed that many Calvinists have failed to grapple successfully with and interpret satisfactorily the most knotty points in these verses. They are right in affirming that Scripture teaches, most emphatically and unequivocably the Divine preservation and the human perseverance of the saints, as they have also wisely pointed out that the Word of God does not and cannot contradict itself. If our Lord asserted that His sheep should "never perish" (John 10:28), then certainly Heb. 6 will not teach that some of them do. If through the apostle Paul the Holy Spirit assures us that nothing can separate the children from the love of their Father (Rom. 8:35-39), then, without doubt, the portion now before us does not declare that something will. It may not always be easy to discover the perfect consistency of one scripture with another, yet we must hold fast to the unerring harmony and integrity of God's Truth.

The chief difficulty connected with our passage is to make sure of the class of persons who are there in view. Is the Holy Spirit here describing regenerated or unregenerated souls? The next thing is to ascertain what is meant by, "If they shall *fall away*." The last, what is denoted by "It is *impossible* to renew them again unto repentance." Anticipating our exposition, we are fully assured that the "falling away" which is here spoken of signifies a deliberate, complete and final repudiation of Christ—a sin for which there is no forgiveness. So too we understand the "impossible" to renew them again to repentance, announces that their condition and case is beyond hope of recovery. Because of this, Calvinists have, generally, affirmed that this passage is treating of mere professors. But over against this there are two insuperable objections: first, mere professors have nothing from which to "fall away"; second, mere professors have *never* been "renewed" unto repentance.

In addition to the controversy which these verses have occasioned, not a few have turned them unto an unwarrantable use. "Misapprehension of this passage has also, I believe, in many cases occasioned extreme distress of mind to two classes of persons,—to nominal professors, who, after falling into gross sin, have been awakened to serious reflection; and to real Christians, on their falling under the power of mental disease, sinking into a state of spiritual languor, or being betrayed into such transgressions of the Divine law as David and Peter were guilty of: and this has thrown all but insurmountable obstacles in the way of both 'fleeing for refuge, to lay hold on the hope set before them' in the Gospel. All this makes it the more necessary that we should carefully inquire into the meaning of the passage. When rightly understood, it will be found to give no countenance to any of the false conclusions which have been drawn from it, but to be like every other part of inspired Scripture, 'profitable for doctrine, for reproof, for correction, for instruction in righteousness',—well-fitted to produce caution, no way calculated to induce despair" (Dr. J. Brown).

Before attempting an elucidation of the above-mentioned difficulties, and to prepare the way for our exposition of these verses, the contents of which have so sorely puzzled many, let us recall, once more, the condition of soul into which these Hebrew Christians had fallen. They had "become dull of hearing" (5:11), "unskilful in the Word of Righteousness" (5:13), unable to masticate "strong meat" (5:14). This state was fraught with the most dangerous consequences. "The Hebrews had become lukewarm, negligent, and inert; the gospel, once clearly seen and dearly loved by them, had become to them dull and vague; the persecutions and contempt of their countrymen a grievous burden, under which they groaned, and under which they did not enjoy fellowship with the Lord Jesus. Darkness, doubt, gloom, indecision, and consequently a walk in which the power of Christ's love was not manifest, characterized them. Now, if they continued in this state, what else could be the result but apostasy? Forgetfulness, if continued, must end in rejection, apathy in antipathy, unfaithfulness in infidelity.

"Such was their danger. And if they succumbed to it their state was hopeless. No other gospel remains to be preached, no other power to rescue and raise them. They had heard and known the voice which saith, 'Come unto Me, and I will give you rest'. They had professed to believe in the Lord who died for sinners, and to have chosen Him as their Saviour and Master. And now they were forgetting and forsaking the Rock of their Salvation. If they deliberately and wilfully continued in this state, they were in danger of final impenitence and hardness of heart.

"The exhortation must be viewed in connection with the special circumstances of the Hebrews. After the rejection of the Messiah by Israel, the gospel had been preached unto the Jews by the apostles, and the gifts and power of the Holy Spirit had been manifested among them. The Hebrews had accepted the gospel of the once crucified and now glorified Redeemer, who sent down from heaven the Spirit, a sign of His exaltation, and a pledge of the future inheritance. Having thus entered *into the sphere of new covenant manifestation,* any one who wilfully abandoned it could only relapse into that phase of Judaism which crucified the Lord Jesus. There was no other alternative for them, but either to go on to the full knowledge of the heavenly priesthood of Christ, and to the believer's acceptance and worship through the Mediator in the sanctuary above, or fall back into the attitude, not of the godly Israelites before Pentecost, such as John the Baptist and those who waited for the promised redemption, nor even into the condition of those for whom the Saviour prayed, 'for they know not what they do'; but into a state of wilful conscious enmity against Christ, and the sin of rejecting Him, and putting Him to an open shame" (A. Saphir).

"The danger to which this spiritual inertness exposed the Hebrews was such as to justify the strongest language of expostulation and reproof. Apostasy from Christ was a step more easy and natural to a Jewish than to a Gentile believer, because the way was always open and inviting them, as men, to return to those associations which once carried with them the outward sanctification of Jehovah's name, and which only the *power* of grace had enabled them to renounce. When heavenly realities became inoperative in their souls, the visible image was before them still, and here was the danger of their giving it the homage of their souls. If there were not an habitual exercise of their spiritual senses, the power of discernment could not remain: they would call evil good, and good evil. The ignorance which springs from spiritual neglect begins its own punishment of apathetic dulness on the once clear mind, and robs the spirit of its power to detect the wily methods of the Devil. It is in the presence of God alone that the Christian can exert his spiritual energies with effect. Abiding in Christ, maintains us in that presence. A more unhappy error cannot befall a believer than to separate, in the habit of his mind, acquired knowledge from the living Christ. Faith dies at once when separated from its object. Knowledge indeed is precious, but the knowledge of God is a progressive thing (Col. 1:10), whose end is not obtained this side of the glory (1 Cor. 8:2). The extreme experience of an advancing Christian is that of continual initiation. With a prospect ever-widening he has a daily deepening apprehension of the grace wherein he stands, and in which he is more and more established, by the word of righteousness. . . . .

"A clear and *growing* faith, in *heavenly* things was needed to preserve Jewish Christians from relapse. To return to Judaism was to give up Christ, who had left their house 'desolate' (Matt. 23:38). It was to fall from grace, and place themselves not only under the general curse of the law, but that particular imprecation which had brought the guilt of Jesus' blood on the reprobate and blinded nation of His murderers" (A Pridham). It should be pointed out, however, that it is just as easy, and the attraction is just as real, for a Gentile Christian to return to that world out of which the Lord has called him, as it was for a Jewish Christian to go back again to Judaism. And just in proportion as the Christian fails to walk with God daily, so does the world obtain power over his heart, mind and life; and a continuance in worldliness is fraught with the most direful and fatal consequences.

"For it is impossible for those who were once enlightened" etc. (v. 4). Here the apostle continues the digression which he began at 5:11. The parenthesis has two divisions: the first, 5:11-14 is reprehensory; the second, 6:1-20 is hortatory. In chapter 6 he exhorts the Hebrews unto two duties: to *progress* in the Christian course (vv. 1-11); to *persevere* therein (vv. 12-20). The first exhortation is proposed in vv. 1, 2 and qualified in v. 3. The *motive* to obedience is drawn from the danger of apostasy (vv. 4-6). The opening "For" of v. 4 intimates the close connection of our present passage with that which immediately precedes. It draws a conclusion from what the apostle had been saying in 5:11-14. It amplifies the "if" in v. 3. It points a most solemn warning against their continuance in their present sloth. It draws a terrible contrast from the possibility of v. 3. "The apostle regards the retrogression of the Hebrews with dismay. He sees in it the danger of an entire, confirmed, wilful, and irrecoverable apostasy from the truth. He beholds them on the brink of a precipice, and he therefore lifts up his voice, and with vehement yet loving earnestness he warns them against so fearful an evil" (A. Saphir).

Three things claim our careful attention in coming closer to our passage: the persons here spoken of, the sin they commit, the doom pronounced upon them. In considering the persons spoken of it is of first importance to note that the apostle does *not* say, "*us* who were once enlightened", nor even "you", instead, he says "those". In sharp contrast from them, he says to the Hebrews, "Beloved, we are persuaded better things of you". "Afterwards, when the apostle comes to declare his hope and persuasion concerning these Hebrews that they were not such as those whom he had before described, nor such as would fall away unto perdition, *he doth* it upon three grounds whereon they were differenced from them as: 1. That they had such things as did 'accompany salvation'; that is, such as salvation is inseparable from. None of these things therefore had he ascribed unto those whom he describeth in this place (vv. 4-6); for if he had so done, they would not have been unto him an argument and evidence of a contrary end, that these should not fall away and perish as well as those. Wherefore he ascribes nothing to these here in the text that *doth* peculiarly 'accompany salvation'. 2. He describes them by their *duties of obedience* and fruits of faith. This was their 'work and labor of love' towards the name of God, v. 10. And hereby, also, doth he differentiate them from those in the text, concerning whom he supposeth that they may perish eternally, which these fruits of saving faith and sincere love cannot do. 3. He adds, that, in the preservation of those there mentioned, the *faithfulness of God* was concerned: 'God is not unrighteous to forget'. For they were such he intended as were interested in the covenant of grace, with respect whereunto alone there is any engagement on the faithfulness or righteousness of God *to* preserve men from apostasy and ruin; and there is so with an equal respect unto all who are so taken into the covenant. But of those in the text he supposeth no such thing; and thereupon doth not intimate that either the righteousness or faithfulness of God was anyway engaged for their preservation, but rather the contrary" (Dr. J. Owen).

It is scarcely accurate to designate as "mere professors" those described in vv. 4, 5. They were a class who had enjoyed great privileges, beyond any such as now accompany the preaching of the Gospel. Those here portrayed are said to have had *five* advantages, which is in contrast from the *six* things enumerated in vv. 1, 2, which things belong to man in the flesh, under Judaism. Five is the number of *grace,* and the blessings here mentioned pertain to the Christian dispensation. Yet were they not true Christians. This is evident from what is *not* said. Observe, they were not spoken of as God's elect, as those for whom Christ died, as those who were born of the Spirit. They are not said to be justified, forgiven, accepted in the Beloved. Nor is anything said of their faith, love, or obedience. Yet *these* are the very things which distinguish a real child of God. First, they had been "enlightened". The Sun of righteousness had shone with healing in His wings, and, as Matt. 4:16 says, "The people which sat in darkness saw great light, and to them which sat in the region and shadow of death light is sprung up". Unlike the heathen, whom Christ, in the days of His flesh, visited not, those who came under the sound of His voice were wondrously and gloriously illumined.

The Greek word for "enlightened" here signifies "to give light or knowledge by teaching". It is so rendered by the Sept. in Judges 13:8, 2 Kings 12:2, 17:27. The apostle Paul uses it for "to make manifest", or "bring to light" in 1 Cor. 4:5, 2 Tim. 1:10. Satan blinds the minds of those who believe not, lest "the light of the gospel should shine unto them" (2 Cor. 4:4), that is, give the knowledge of it. Thus, "enlightened" here means to be instructed in the doctrine of the gospel, so as to have a clear apprehension of it. In the parallel passage in 10:26 the same people are said to have "received the knowledge of the truth", cf. also 2 Peter 2:20, 21. It is, however, only a *natural* knowledge of spiritual things, such as is acquired by outward hearing or reading; just as one may be enlightened by taking up the special study of one of the sciences. It falls far short of that spiritual enlightenment which *transforms*

(2 Cor. 3:18). An illustration of a *un*-regenerate person being "enlightened", as here, is found in the case of Balaam; Num. 24:4.

Second, they had "tasted" of the heavenly gift. To "taste" is to have a personal experience of, in contrast from mere report. "Tasting does not include eating, much less digesting and turning into nourishment what is so tasted; for its nature being only thereby discerned it may be refused, yea, though we like its relish and savour, on some other consideration. The persons here described, then, are those who have to a certain degree understood and relished the revelation of mercy; like the stony-ground hearers they have received the Word with a transcient joy" (J. Owen). The "tasting" is in contrast from the "eating" of John 6:50-56.

Opinion is divided as to whether the "heavenly gift" refers to the Lord Jesus or the person of the Holy Spirit. Perhaps it is not possible for us to be dogmatic on the point. Really, the difference is without a distinction, for the Spirit is here to glorify Christ, as He came from the Father by Christ as His ascension "Gift" to His people. If the reference be to the Lord Jesus, John 3:16, 4:10, etc., would be pertinent references: if to the Holy Spirit, Acts 2:38, 8:20, 10:45, 11:17. Personally, we rather incline to the latter. This Divine Gift is here said to be "heavenly" because from Heaven, and leading to Heaven, in contrast from Judaism—cf. Acts 2:2, 1 Peter 1:12. Of this "Gift" these apostates had "tasted", or had an experience of: compare Matt. 27:34 where "tasting" is opposed to actual drinking. Those here in view had had an acquaintance with the Gospel, as to gain such a measure of its blessedness as to greatly aggravate their sin and doom. An illustration of this is found in Matt. 13:20, 21.

Third, they were "made partakers of the Holy Spirit". First, it should be pointed out that the Greek word for "partakers" here is a different one from that used in Col. 1:12 and 2 Peter 1:4, where real Christians are in view. The word here simply means "companions", referring to what is external rather than internal. It is to be observed that this item is placed in the center of the five, and this because it describes the animating principle of the other four, which are all effects. These apostates had never been "born of the Spirit" (John 3:6), still less were their bodies His "temples" (1 Cor. 6:19). Nor do we believe this verse teaches that the Holy Spirit had, at any time, wrought *within* them, otherwise Phil. 1:6 would be contravened. It means that they had shared in the benefit of His supernatural operations and manifestations: "The place was shaken" (Acts 4:31) illustrates. We quote below from Dr. J. Brown:

"It is highly probable that the inspired writer refers primarily to the miraculous gifts and operations of the Holy Spirit by which the primitive dispensation of Christianity was administered. These gifts were by no means confined to those who were 'transformed by the renewing of their minds'. The words of our Lord in Matt. 7:22, 23 and of Paul in 1 Cor. 13:1, 2 seem to intimate, that the possession of these unrenewed men was not very uncommon in that age; at any rate they plainly show that their possession and an unregenerate state were by no means incompatible".

Fourth, "And have tasted the good Word of God". "I understand by this expression the promise of God respecting the Messiah, the sum and substance of all. It deserves notice that this promise is by way of eminence termed by Jeremiah 'that good word' (33:14). To 'taste', then, this 'good Word of God', is to experience that God has been faithful to His promise—to enjoy, so far as an unconverted man can enjoy the blessings and advantages which flow from that promise being fulfilled. To 'taste the good Word of God', seems, just to enjoy the advantages of the new dispensation" (Dr. J. Brown). Further confirmation that the apostle is here referring to that which these apostates had witnessed of the fulfilment of God's *promise* is obtained by comparing Jer. 29:10, "After seventy years be accomplished at Babylon I will visit you, and perform My *good word* toward you, in causing you to return to this place".

Observe how studiously the apostle still keeps to the word "taste", the better to enable us to identify them. They could not say with Jeremiah, "Thy words were found and I did *eat* them" (15:16). "It is as though he said, I speak not of those who have received nourishment; but of such as have so far tasted it, as that they ought to have desired it as 'sincere milk' and grown thereby" (Dr. J. Owen). A solemn example of one who merely "tasted" the good Word of God is found in Mark 6:20: "for Herod feared John, knowing that he was a just man and an holy, and observed him; and when he heard him, he did many things, and heard him *gladly*".

Fifth, "And the powers of the world to come," or "age to come." The reference here is to the new dispensation which was to be ushered in by Israel's Messiah according to O. T. predictions. It corresponds with "these last days" of Heb. 1:2, and is in contrast from the "time past" or Mosaic economy. Their Messiah was none other than the "mighty God" (Isa. 9), and wondrous and glorious, stupendous and unique, were His miraculous works. These "powers" of the new Age are mentioned in Heb. 2:4, to our comments on which we would refer the reader. Of these mighty "powers" these apostates had "tasted", or had an experience of. They had been personal witnesses of the miracles of Christ, and also of the wonders that followed His ascension, when such glorious manifestations of the Spirit were given. Thus they were "without excuse". Convincing and conclusive evidence had been set before them, but there had been no answering faith in their hearts. A solemn example of this is found in John 11:47, 48.

"If they shall fall away". The Greek word here is very strong and emphatic, even stronger than the one used in Matt. 7:27, where it is said of the house built on the sand, "and great was the fall thereof". It is a complete falling away, a total abandonment of Christianity which is here in view. It is a wilful turning of the back on God's revealed truth, an utter repudiation of the Gospel. It is making "shipwreck of the faith" (1 Tim. 1:19). This terrible sin is not committed by a mere nominal professor, for he has nothing really to fall away from, save an empty name. The class here described are such as had had their minds enlightened, their consciences stirred, their affections moved to a considerable degree, and yet who were never brought from death unto life. Nor is it backsliding Christians who are in view. It is *not* simply "fall into *sin*", this or that sin. The greatest "sin" which a regenerated man can possibly commit is the personal denial of Christ: Peter was guilty of this, yet was he "renewed again unto repentance". It is the total renunciation of all the distinguishing truths and principles of Christianity, and this not secretly, but openly, which constitutes apostasy.

"*If* they shall fall away". "This is scarcely a fair translation. It has been said that the apostle did not here assert that such persons *did* or *do* 'fall away'; but that if they did—a supposition which, however, could never be realized—then the consequence would be they could not be 'renewed again unto repentance'. The words literally rendered are, 'And have fallen away', or, 'yet have fallen'. The apostle obviously intimates that such persons might, and that such persons did, 'fall away'. By 'falling away', we are plainly to understand what is commonly called apostasy. This does not consist in an occasional falling into actual sin, however gross and aggravated; nor in the renunciation of some of the principles of Christianity, even though those should be of considerable importance; but in an open, total, determined renunciation of all the constituent principles of Christianity, and a return to a false religion, such as that of unbelieving Jews or heathens, or to open infidelity and open godlessness" (Dr. J. Brown).

"It is impossible . . . . if they fall away, to renew them again unto repentance". Four questions here call for answer. What is meant by "renewed unto repentance"? What is signified by "renewed *again* unto repentance"? *Why* is such an experience "impossible"? To whom is this "impossible"? Repentance signifies a change of mind: Matt. 21:29, Rom. 11:29 establish this. It is more than a mental act, the conscience also being active, leading to contrition and self-condemnation (Job. 42:6). In the unregenerate, it is simply the workings of nature; in the children of God it is wrought by the Holy Spirit. The latter is evangelical, being one of the things which "accompany salvation". The former is not so, being the "sorrow of the world", which "worketh death" (2 Cor. 7:10). This kind of "repentance" or remorse receives most solemn exemplification in the case of Judas: Matt. 27:3, 5. Such was the repentance of these apostates. The Greek verb for "renew" here occurs nowhere else in the N. T. Probably "restore" had been better, for the same word is used in the Sept., for a Heb. verb meaning to renew in the sense of restore: Psa. 103:5; 104:30; Lam. 5:21. Josephus applies it to the renovation of the Temple!

But what is meant by "renewing unto repentance"? "To be 'renewed' is a figurative expression for denoting a change, a great change, and a change for the better. To be 'renewed' so as to change a person's mind is expressive of an important and advantageous alteration of opinion, and character and service. And such an alteration the persons referred to had undergone at a former period. They were once in a state of ignorance respecting the doctrines and evidences of Christianity, and they had been 'enlightened'. They had once known not of the excellency and beauty of Christian truth, and they had been made to 'taste of the heavenly gift'. They once misunderstood the prophecies respecting the Messiah, and were unaware of their fulfillment, and, of course, were strangers to that energetic influence which the N. T. revelation puts forth; and they had been made to see that that 'good word' was fulfilled, and had been made partakers of the external privileges and been subjected to the peculiar energies of the new order of things. Their view, and feelings, and circumstances, were materially changed. How great the difference between an ignorant, bigoted Jew, and the person described in the preceding passage! He had become as it were a different man. He had not, indeed, become, in the sense of the apostle, a 'new creature', His mind had not been so changed as unfeignedly to believe 'the truth as it is in Jesus'; but still, a great and so far as it went, a thorough change had taken place" (Dr. J. Brown).

Now it is impossible to "renew again unto repentance" those who have totally abandoned the Christian revelation. Some things are "impossible" with respect unto the *nature* of God, as that He cannot lie, or pardon sin without satisfaction to His justice. Other things which are possible to God's nature are rendered "impossible" by His *decrees* or purpose: see 1 Sam. 15:28, 29. Still other things are "possible" or "impossible" with respect to the *rule or order* of all things God has appointed. For example, there cannot be faith apart from hearing the Word (Rom. 10:13-17). "When in things of duty God hath neither expressed command thereon, nor appointed means for the performance of them, they are to be looked upon then as impossible [as, for instance, there is no salvation apart from repentance, Luke 13:3. (A.W.P.)]; and then, with respect unto *us,* they are so absolutely, and so to be esteemed. And this is the 'impossibility' here principally intended. It is a thing that God hath neither commanded us to endeavor, nor appointed means to attain it, nor promise to assist us in it. It is therefore that which we have no reason to look after, attempt, or expect, as being not possible by any law, rule, or constitution of God.

"The apostle instructs us no further in the nature of future events but as our own duty is concerned in them. It is not for us either to look or hope, or pray for, or endeavor the restoration of such persons unto repentance. God gives a law unto *us* in these things, not unto Himself. It may be possible with God, for aught we know, if there be not a contradiction in it unto any of the holy properties of His nature; only He will not have us to *expect* any such thing from Him, nor hath He appointed any means for *us* to endeavour it. What *He* shall do we ought trustfully to accept; but our own duty toward such persons is absolutely at an end. And indeed, they put themselves wholly out of *our* reach" (Dr. J. Owen).

It needs to be carefully observed that in the whole of this passage from 5:11 onwards the apostle is speaking of *his own ministry.* In God's hands, His servants are instruments by which He works and through whom He accomplishes His evangelical purpose. Thus Paul could properly say "I have *begotten you* through the gospel" (1 Cor. 4:15). And again, "My little children, of whom I travail in birth again until Christ be formed in you" (Gal. 4:19). So the servants of God had, through the preaching of the Gospel, "renewed unto repentance" those spoken of in Heb. 6:4. But they had apostatised; they had totally repudiated the Gospel. It was therefore "impossible" for the *servants* of God to "renew them *again* unto repentance", for the all-sufficient reason that they had no other message to proclaim to them. They had no other Gospel in reserve, no further motives to present. Christ crucified *had been* set before them. Him they now denounced as an Imposter. There was "none other name" whereby they could be saved. Their public renunciation of Christ rendered their case hopeless so far as God's servants were concerned. "Let them alone" (Matt. 15:19) was now their orders: compare Jude 22. Whether or not it was possible for God, consistently with His holiness, to shame them, our passage does not decide.

"Seeing they crucify to themselves the Son of God afresh" (v. 6). This is brought in to show the aggravation of their awful crime and the impossibility of their being renewed again unto repentance. By renouncing their Christian profession they declared Christ to be an Imposter. Thus they were irreclaimable. To attempt any further reasoning with them, would only be casting pearls before swine. With this verse should be carefully compared the parallel passage in 10:26-29. These apostates had "received the knowledge of the truth", though *not* a saving knowledge of it. Afterward they sinned "wilfully": there was a deliberate and open disavowal of the truth. The nature of their particular sin is termed a "treading under foot the Son of God (something which no real Christian ever does) and counting (esteeming) the blood of the covenant an unholy thing", that is, looking upon the One who hung on the Cross as a *common* malefactor. For such there "remaineth no more sacrifice for sins". Their case is hopeless so far as man is concerned; and the writer believes, such are abandoned by God also.

"Seeing they crucify to themselves the Son of God afresh, and put Him to an open shame". "They thus identify themselves with His crucifiers—they entertained and avowed sentiments which, were He on earth and in their power, would induce them to crucify Him. They exposed Him to infamy, made a public example of Him. They did more to dishonour Jesus Christ than His murderers did. *They* never professed to acknowledge His divine mission; but these apostates had made such a profession—they had made a kind of trial of Christianity, and, after trial, had rejected it" (Dr. J. Brown).

Such a warning was needed and well calculated to stir up the slothful Hebrews. Under the O. T. economy, by means of types and prophecies, they had obtained glimmerings of truth as to Christ, called "the word of the beginning of Christ". Under those shadows and glimmerings they had been reared, not knowing their full import till they had been blessed with the full light of the Gospel, here called "perfection". The danger to which they were exposed was that of receding from the ground where Christianity placed them, and relaxing to Judaism. To do so meant to re-enter that House which Christ had left "desolate" (Matt. 23:38), and would be to join forces with His murderers, and thus "crucify *to themselves* the Son of God afresh", and by their apostasy "put Him to an open (public) shame". We may add that the Greek word here for "crucify" is a stronger one than is generally used: it means to "crucify up". Attention is thus directed to the erection of the cross on which the Saviour was held up to public scorn.

Taking the passage as a whole, it needs to be remembered that all who had professed to receive the Gospel were not born of God: the parable of the Sower shows that. Intelligence might be informed, conscience searched, natural affections stirred, and yet there be "no root" in them. All is not gold that glitters. There has always been a "mixt multitude" (Ex. 12:38) who accompany the people of God. Moreover, there is in the real Christian the old heart, which is "deceitful above all things and desperately wicked", and therefore is he in constant need of faithful *warning*. Such, God has given in every dispensation: Gen. 2:17; Lev. 26:15, 16; Matt. 3:8; Rom. 11:21; 1 Cor. 10:12.

Finally, let it be said that while Scripture speaks plainly and positively of the perseverance of the saints, yet it is a perseverance of *saints,* not unregenerate professors. Divine preservation is not only in a safe state, but also in a *holy* course of disposition and conduct. We are "kept by the power of God *through faith*". We are kept by the Spirit working in us a spirit of entire dependency, renouncing our own wisdom and strength. The only place from which we cannot fall is one down in the dust. It is there the Lord brings His own people, weaning them from all confidence in the flesh, and giving them to experience that it is when they are weak they are strong. Such, and such only, are saved and safe forever.

CHAPTER TWENTY-FIVE

The Twofold Working of the Spirit

(Heb. 6:4-6)

In our last article we attempted little more than an explication of the terms used in Heb. 6:4-6. Lack of space prevented us from throwing upon these verses the light which other portions of God's Word affords, yet this is necessary if we are to form anything like a true and adequate conception of the particular characters which are there in view. One chief reason why students of Scripture continue to experience difficulty in ascertaining the meaning of any verse therein, is because they fail to prayerfully and *patiently* compare "spiritual things with spiritual" (1 Cor. 2:13). All of us are in far too much a hurry, and for this reason miss the best of what God has provided—true both of temporal and spiritual things. Probably few of our readers considered that we had succeeded in clearing away all the difficulties raised by this solemn passage, therefore the need of a further article thereon.

On the present occasion we propose to take up our passage more from a topical viewpoint than an expository, seeking (as God may be pleased to graciously enable) to open up more fully that in it which has caused the most trouble, namely, the precise relation of the Holy Spirit to the characters therein mentioned. They who "fall away" and whom it is "impossible to renew again unto repentance", are said to have been "made partakers of the Holy Spirit". We ask now, On what has the Spirit wrought? What was the character of His work toward them? *How* had they been made "partakers" of Him? To what extent? This leads us to point out that Scripture reveals a twofold working of God's Spirit with men: with the elect, *and* with the non-elect. It is of the latter we shall here treat.

Concerning the Spirit's work with the non-elect, we begin by enquiring, Upon what does He work? We answer, Upon the faculties of men's souls. First, He works upon the *understanding*. There are in all men natural faculties of understanding, will, and affection. A man could not love God unless he had in him the faculty of affection—a stone could never love God! So a man could never understand spiritual things unless he had the faculty of understanding. With the elect, the Holy Spirit "renews" the understanding (Rom. 12:2 compared with Titus 3:5); but with the non-elect, He only enlightens or educates it. The understanding of fallen and unregenerate men, which is enlightened by the Spirit, *is* capable of knowing, in some measure, both the Godhead, and parts of His law. Let us give Scripture proof of this.

In Rom. 1:18 we read of men who "hold the truth in unrighteousness", and what is there referred to is explained in what follows: "Because that which may be known of God is manifest in them; for God hath showed unto them. For the invisible things of Him from the creation of the world are clearly seen, being understood by the things that are made: His eternal power and Godhead" (vv. 19, 20). The reference there, as the later verses show, is to the Heathen. Now what we would press upon the attention of the reader is, that in addition to poor fallen nature, God has granted to men a manifestation of Himself; that which "may be known of God", which He "hath *showed* unto them". It is not merely that creation reveals a Creator, but that the Creator *has revealed Himself*—"when they *knew* God" (v. 21), and that must have been by the Spirit's enlightening their natural understanding.

Again, in Rom. 2:14, 15 we read, "For when the Gentiles, which have not the law, do by nature the things contained in the law, these, having not the law are a law unto themselves: Which show the work of the law written in their hearts, their conscience also bearing witness". The Holy Spirit is speaking here of men according to "nature", not grace. In his natural heart there is *written* "the work of the law"—by whom but by the finger of God! Except for this, man would be destitute of moral light, for the Fall robbed him of all light.

The understanding in man, or the principle of reason, may, by education and contact with others, be developed to a considerable extent, so that a man may become exceeding wise; nevertheless, his knowledge and wisdom is only *natural,* even though his understanding be exercised upon super-natural objects. But let now the light of reason and the light of conscience be brought to the Scriptures for instruction, and man's knowledge will be much further increased, yet still his light is but *natural,* it rises not to the level of what grace produces. Proof of this is seen in the case of the Jews: "Behold, thou art called a Jew, and restest in the law, and makest thy boast of God; and knowest His will, and approvest the things that are more excellent, being instructed out of the law; and are confident that thou thyself art a guide of the blind, a light of them which are in darkness" (Rom. 2:17-19). How like thousands of unregenerate souls in Christendom today!

From the last-quoted passage we learn what is the effect of the light of nature (reason) being brought to the law of God: it is increased and improved. As we have seen above, a man has some light by nature that there is a God; let that light be brought to Scripture, and he becomes "confident" there is. A man by nature has some light about the duties which God requires of him; let him bring that light to the Scriptures and he will have "the *form* (systematised) of knowledge, and of the *truth* in the law" (Rom. 2:20). When the understanding of the natural man is illumined by the Scriptures, his light is both rarified and added unto, yet is it still *natural* light which he has; it is but the educating of his natural reason.

Second, the Holy Spirit works upon the *affections* of the natural man. There is in fallen man a natural devotion to a deity. This is evidenced by the fact that practically all of the heathen worship some god or other. In Acts 13:50 we read of "devout women" being stirred up against Paul and Barnabas: they had a devotion in them which is common to mankind. Now let men bring their natural devotion to the Scriptures and they will come to know of the true God, and learn to reverence Him too; yet is that only nature improved. Through the Word, the Holy Spirit may (usually, does) convince its reader that the Maker of heaven and earth is the true God, and therefore worthy of honour and homage. The fact is, though very few indeed recognize it, the identical principle which causes a Hindoo to worship Buddha, causes an Anglo-Saxon to worship the Father of Jesus Christ.

Again; there is in every sinner the natural recognition that his sins deserve eternal death, and that God, unless He be appeased, will punish him. Doubtless many of our readers will feel inclined to call into question this last statement; let our appeal again be to the Word of Truth. There we read, "Who, *knowing* the judgment of God, that they which commit such things are *worthy of death*" (Rom. 1:32). That, be it noted, is said of the heathen. Now bring one having such knowledge to the law of God, and what will follow? This, "But we *are sure* that the judgment of God is according to truth against them which commit such things" (Rom. 2:2). There it is the Jews speaking. The natural man enlightened from the Word has his conviction deepened.

Again; if a man is conscious of his sins, and realizes that the justice of God calls for their punishment, is it not natural for him to think next of a *mediator*, to desire someone to intercede for him with God? Such a concept is by no means a sure evidence of regeneration.

This too is found in mere nature. Every heathen religion, with the propitiatory offerings which are brought to their gods, exemplifies it. Romanism with its mediating priests demonstrates the same fact in this land. Illustrations are also to be found in the Holy Scriptures. When Pharaoh was convicted of his sins, he entreated Moses to intercede for him (Ex. 10:16, 17). So too wicked Simon Magus desired Peter to pray for him (Acts 8:24).

Once more; there is in the heart of every natural man a desire for happiness, and for a greater happiness than this poor world can provide. It is plainly evident that man rests not in anything down here, for like a bee which goes from one flower to another, so the heart of man cannot be satisfied with any earthly object. When Balaam saw the blessedness of God's people, he exclaimed, "Let *me* die the death of the righteous" (Num. 23:10). The most abandoned wretch does not want to go to hell, and to the very end he hopes that he will be taken to heaven.

So, likewise, in the matter of believing that a man really *is* a child of God. There is such self-love and self-flattery in the fallen heart that if an unregenerate man hears, out of the Word of God, the good news that Christ Jesus came into the world to save sinners, he at once concludes that *he* is the man God will honour, as wicked Haman imagined that *he* was the man king Ahasuerus would honour. So when the Holy Spirit has terrified a man's conscience, by giving it a sight of sin as it is before a holy God, when he learns about remission of sins through Christ, he at once fondly imagines that his own sins are pardoned. Alas, in the vast majority of cases it has to be said, "the pride of thine heart hath deceived thee" (Obad. 3).

Now let us take note of how the Holy Spirit may work upon these *natural* principles of the human soul, mightily raising them, and yet *not* changing a man's heart. Just as the rays of the sun shining upon plants in a garden adds no new nature to them, but serves to aid their best development, so the Holy Spirit when He deals with the reprobate communicates nothing new to them, yet raises their natural faculties to their highest point. The principles or faculties of man's soul *are* capable of being wrought upon *without* the impartation of regenerating grace. As we have seen, man's understanding is illuminated by the light of conscience, but let the Holy Spirit—*without* imparting a new eye—still further enlighten that conscience, bring before it the exalted claims of the thrice holy God, and its knowledge will be greatly increased. Nevertheless, this educated conscience falls far below the level of the spiritual discernment possessed by one who has been brought out of death into life. Let us particularise:

1. The Spirit restrains the Corruptions of men.

In Gen. 20:6 we read of how God bound the lust of Abimeleck when Sarah was at his mercy, "I also withheld thee from sinning against Me: therefore suffered I thee not to touch her". So in 2 Peter 2:20 we read of some "having escaped the pollutions of the world through the knowledge of our Lord and Saviour Jesus Christ", yet from what follows in the next two verses it is clear they were never regenerated. There the apostle uses the similitude of a sow being washed from her filth, and being kept for a while, after she is washed, from going back again into the mire; yet is there no changing or "renewing" of the swine's nature.

Contrast now what is said of the Lord's people in 2 Peter 1:3, 4, "According as His Divine power hath given unto us all things that pertain unto life and godliness, through the knowledge of Him that hath called us to glory and virtue: Whereby are given unto us exceeding great and precious promises; that by these ye might be partakers of the Divine nature, having escaped the corruption that is in the world through lust". In 2 Peter 2:20 the Greek word for the "pollutions" of the world, signifies the gross and outward defilements into which the irreligious run; but in 2 Peter 1:4 the regenerated are said to have escaped "the *corruption*" that is in the world *through lust* or "desire", i.e. the inward disposition toward evil. Moreover, the Lord's people are made "partakers of the Divine nature", which means, the Divine image is stamped upon them: "life and godliness" are seen in them.

Again; in the similitude used in 2 Peter 2:20 the apostle likens those who have known "the way of righteousness" to a dog that has been made sick, but which turns to its own vomit again. The figure is very striking and forcible. When the Holy Spirit brings the Word of God to bear upon an unregenerate man's conscience, he is made sick at heart. Of Christians it is said, "For ye have not received the Spirit of bondage again to fear" (Rom. 8:15), but to the non-elect He often becomes a Spirit *of* "bondage" by binding their sins upon their conscience. Whereas before they had a glimmering light that the judgment of God is against sinners, their conscience now is set on fire, and the temporary consequence is that sins are refused with loathing, vomitted out. Yet, like a dog, such a one loves them still, and ultimately returns thereto.

2. The Spirit causes men to turn naturally toward the Redeemer.

When conscience is wrought upon by a few sparks of God's wrath falling upon it, what saith the soul next? This, O for a physician! There is, as we have pointed out above, a natural principle in men which causes them to make use of a mediator unto God—a witch-doctor, a priest, or a preacher, as the case may be. Now a man who has lived under the sound of the Gospel learns that Christ is the one Mediator. Scriptural education has taught him this, just as the heathen education teaches a Turk that Mahomet is the one mediator. And, by the same principle that Agrippa believed Moses and the prophets, the unregenerate "Christian" (?) *believes* in Christ. Nay further, the light of the Spirit shining upon him, as the sun on the plants, develops his natural understanding and causes him to now remember that Redeemer which before he ignored.

A scripture clearly to the point of what we have just said above is Psa. 78:34, 35, "When He slew them, then they sought Him: and they returned and enquired early after God. And they remembered that God was their Rock, and the high God their Redeemer". Yet what immediately follows? This, "Nevertheless they did flatter Him with their mouth". And what signifies this "flattering"? Why, they sought Him merely out of *self-love,* simply because they felt their very lives were in imminent danger. There is a seeking out of friendship, out of love to the object. But if one seek unto an enemy because he hath need of him, *that* is but "flattery" or self-love. So if sinful man feels he is in extremity, if his conscience remains sick, mere nature will call for the Physician.

Self-love is the predominant principle in the natural man: he loves himself more than he loves God; it is this which lies at the root of depravity and sin. Now when a man's conscience is convicted so that he perceives his need of a physician, and recognizes that happiness comes from Christ, such good news appeals to his self-love. Satan, who knows human nature so well was right when he said, "skin for skin yea, all that a man hath will he give for his life" (Job 2:4). Make the self-love of the natural man conscious of the wrath of God, and he is ready to "accept Christ", or do anything else which the preacher bids him; yet that is only the workings of nature, he is still unregenerate.

When the storm arose and threatened to sink the ship in which Jonah lay asleep we read, "Then the mariners were afraid, and cried every man unto his god"; then the captain awoke Jonah and said. "Arise, call upon thy God, if so be God will think upon us that we perish not" (1:5, 6). So a conscience terrified by the prospect of Hell, will cause a man to seek Christ after a natural way. It is but the instinct of self-preservation at work. Add to this, the craving for happiness which self-love ever seeks, and hearing that such happiness is to be found only in Christ, little wonder that multitudes seek Him now for what they can get *from* Him, as of old they sought Him for the sake of the loaves and fishes.

In John 6:33 we are told that Christ announced, "For the bread of God is He which cometh down from heaven, and giveth life unto the world". What was their response? This, "Then they said unto Him, Lord, evermore *give us* this bread". Yet their eager request sprang not from a renewed heart, but from the corrupt spring of self-love. Proof of this is found in the immediate sequel. In v. 36 the Lord tells them plainly, ye "believe not". In v. 41 we are told that they "murmured at Him". Yet that very same people said to the Lord, "Evermore give us this Bread"! Ah, all is not gold that glitters.

An enlightened understanding, moved by self-love, is prepared to take up Divine duties never practiced before, yea, to walk in the commandments of God. This was demonstrated plainly at Sinai. When Jehovah appeared before Israel in His awesome majesty, and their conscience was smitten by His manifested holiness, they said to Moses, "Go thou near, and hear all that the Lord our God shall say; and speak thou unto us *all* that the Lord our God shall speak unto thee; and we will hear and *do*". They were prepared to receive and obey the Lord's statutes. Yet mark what God said of them, "Oh, that there were such a heart in them, that they would fear Me, and keep all My commandments always". They still lacked the principle of regeneration!

3. The Spirit elevates the natural faculties of man.

Just as the shining of the sun causes plants to grow higher and fruits to be sweeter than would be the case were the heavens to remain cloudy and overcast, so the Spirit works upon the faculties of the unregenerate and causes them to bring forth that which left to themselves they would not produce. Or, just as fire will raise the temperature and level of water, causing it to bubble up and ascend in steam, though the principle of heat is in the fire and not in the water, for when the fire is withdrawn the water returns to its natural coldness again; so the Spirit enlightens the understandings of the non-elect, stirs their affections, and moves their wills to action, without communicating a new principle to them, without regenerating them.

He elevates the *understanding*. In Num. 24:2 we read that the Spirit of God came upon Balaam, the consequence of which he has told us: "The man who had his eyes shut, but now opened, hath said: he hath said, which heard the words of God, which saw the vision of the Almighty, falling but having his eyes opened: How goodly are thy tents, O Jacob, thy tabernacles, O Israel!" (vv. 3-5).

Thus Balaam had a vision of the Almighty, and perceived the blessed estate of His people; yet was he still unregenerate!

He elevates the *affections.* In 1 Sam. 11:1-3 we read of how the enemies of Jehovah insulted His people. Then we are told, "And the Spirit of God came upon Saul when he heard these tidings, and his *anger was kindled* greatly" (v. 6). That was holy indignation, yet it proceeded from a reprobate! As the winds blowing upon the sea will, at times, raise its waters to a great height, so the Spirit, under a faithful sermon, will blow upon the affections of the unregenerate, and elevate them to nobler objects and occupations. Yet, He stops short of making them new creatures in Christ Jesus.

Again; as we have seen, there is in man a natural desire for real happiness, hence, when Christ is presented in the Gospel, many receive Him "with joy"; yet, are they, for the most part, but *stony-ground* hearers, destitute of any root of vital godliness (Matt. 13:20, 21). Nature may be so raised by the light which the Holy Spirit brings to it, that unregenerate men may taste of the heavenly gift, Christ, see John 4:10. So too they are enabled to *taste* of the "powers of the world to come". As in their conscience, they get a taste of Hell, and so know for a certainty that there is a Hell, the same natural principle which desires a happiness which is beyond this world, is *confirmed* and comforted when they have a "taste" of what belongs to the world to come.

He elevates the *will* and sets it to work in the way of obedience to God. The Holy Spirit is the Author of all moral and civil righteousness which there is in the world. The Lord stirred up the spirit of Cyrus to issue a proclamation for the building of His house (Ezra 1:1, 2); and He also moved Caiaphas to prophesy of Christ (John 11:51). Of wicked Herod we read that, when he heard John "he *did* many things, and heard him gladly" (Mark 6:20). And God will be no man's Debtor: every act of obedience, performed by him in obedience to His Word, shall be rewarded: a temporary joy shall be the portion of such. The tragic thing is that so many conclude from such an experience that they are in a state of grace, and therefore become loud in their professions of assurance, being fully persuaded that *they* are really born-again persons.

Now we trust that what has been said will enable some of our readers to understand the better what is found in Heb. 6:4-6. One eminent commentator suggested that these verses describe neither the regenerate nor the unregenerate, but a third condition, midway between; because there must be a third state between that of mere nature and that of supernatural grace. Nor are we at all surprised that he arrived at this conclusion. Few indeed have perceived the force of

1 Cor. 12:6, "And there are *diversities of operations,* but it is the same God which worketh all in all".

There *are* operations of the Spirit upon men's hearts which are above nature, which are works of Divine power, which produces that in and from unregenerate men which leads multitudes of them to fondly imagine that they have been actually born again, and yet *this* work of the Spirit falls far short of that *"exceeding greatness* of His power to usward who believe" (Eph. 1:19). Heb. 6:4-6 supplies a most striking example of this, for there we have men who are made "partakers of the Holy Spirit". There we see a work which is above nature, for they taste of the "heavenly Gift". It is a work of power, for they taste of the *"powers* of the world to come". As 1 Cor. 12:4 tells us, "There are diversities of gifts, but the same Spirit". And why is this? I Cor. 12:11 answers, "But all these worketh that one and the self-same Spirit, dividing to every man severally *as He will*": He proportions His power as He pleases, to an inferior or a superior work. Note carefully, there are "good gifts" from above, as well as "perfect gifts" (James 1:17)!

Of old Jehovah said, "My Spirit shall not always strive with man" (Gen. 6:3). There we find the Spirit putting forth power upon man, for He "strives" with him; yet, not in the fulness of His power, or it had not been resisted. In other cases He puts forth power and men yield thereto (as did Balaam), yet is that power simply directed to the winding up of man's natural faculties to their greatest height, and comes far short of regenerating them. This is clearly illustrated in the parable of the Sower. There is the stony-ground hearer, who received the Word with joy, yet falls away in time of persecution. There is also the thorny-ground hearer, who withstands persecution, and brings forth fruit, yet *not* "to perfection". And both of them represent unregenerate souls.

And *why* does God put forth His power upon the reprobate, yet not the "exceeding greatness" of His power? God has seen well to *test* men in various ways. First, He gave them the light of nature, the work of the law written in their hearts, augmented by the light of conscience—a light which enabled men to know there was a God and of their duties toward Him. And Socrates, who knew nothing of the Scriptures, went so far as to die for the truth that there was One God. But this light of nature did not regenerate men, nor enable them to bring forth the fruit of the Spirit.

Again; He tried the Jews with His Law. He would make it evident how far the light of nature, improved by the light of His Law, would go. And let it not be forgotten that of Israel under the Law it is said. "Thou gavest *also* Thy good Spirit to instruct them" (Neh. 9:20). Nevertheless, the law was "weak through the flesh"

(Rom. 8:3): it could not bring forth that which was truly spiritual. And just as God gave Socrates as the highest product of what the light of nature could produce, so He gave Saul of Tarsus—a man who walked *blamelessly* (Phil. 3:6)—as the highest product under the Law.

But now He is trying men with the Gospel, to show how far human nature as such can go. That Gospel is accompanied with the Spirit, and Heb. 6:4-6 shows us the highest point which can be attained under it, by man in the flesh. He may be enlightened, renewed unto repentance, enjoy the Word of God, be made a partaker of the Holy Spirit, and yet apostatise and perish forever. So too the same characters are said to have "done despite unto the Spirit of grace" (Heb. 10:26). The tragic thing is that the vast majority in Christendom look upon these inferior workings of the Spirit as evidence of His new-creating grace.

And *what,* we may enquire, *is God's purpose* in these secondary operations of His Spirit? It is manifold. We can barely mention the leading designs. First, it is *to exhibit the excellency of Grace.* Every thing in nature hath either its counterfeit or counterfoil. If there are stationary stars, there are also shooting stars. If there are precious stones, there are pebbles which closely resemble yet differ widely from them. The one serves to set off the other. So there is a natural faith—"Many believed in His name when they saw the miracles which He did. But Jesus did not commit Himself unto *them*" (John 2:23, 24); "The demons believe" (James 2:19)—and there is a supernatural faith, "the faith of God's elect" (Titus 1:1), called "*precious* faith" (2 Peter 1:1)! So there are common operations of the Spirit, and special operations; inferior workings upon the flesh, and superior workings that beget "spirit" (John 3:6). By virtue of this contrast, God says to each of His elect, See how much I have wrought on mere nature in the reprobate! yet it was not grace; I might have done no more for you, but I showed the "exceeding greatness of My power" (Eph. 1:19) toward *you.*

Second, to show *the depravity of human nature.* No matter under what trial God places man, that which is born of the flesh remains naught but flesh. The Law was weak through the flesh; so too is the Gospel, notwithstanding the shining of God's Spirit upon men. The conscience may be convicted, the understanding enlightened, the affections raised, and the will moved, yet it still remains true that "every man at his *best* state is altogether *vanity*" (Psa. 39:5). Men may be instructed in the truth, believe in the living God, "accept Christ as their personal Saviour", contend for the faith once delivered to the saints, and pass among men for devout Christians, yet be no better than "whited sepulchres, full of dead men's bones".

Third, to *place bounds upon sin.* The general workings of God's Spirit upon the reprobate serve to curb the risings of man's corrupt nature. As it is His presence here upon earth which hinders the full manifestation of the mystery of iniquity in the appearing of the Anti-Christ (2 Thess. 2), so His operations upon the non-elect prevent many outbursts of wickedness. In the time of Israel's apostasy the Holy Spirit (the "glory") withdrew gradually, stage by stage (Ezek. 11), so as the apostasy of Christendom increases, the restraining operations of the Spirit are decreasing and hence the rising tide of lawlessness.

Fourth, to *afford protection for the elect.* God's flock is only "the *little*" one (Luke 12:32), very, very much smaller than is commonly supposed. Christ Himself declared that only "FEW" are in the *Narrow* Way which leadeth "unto life" (Matt. 7:14). Nor must Rev. 7:9 be made to contradict these clear passages; instead, the "great multitude which no man could number" is to be compared with and interpreted by the expressions found in Judges 6:5, 7:12; 2 Chron. 12:3; Joel 1:6. Now suppose that only the elect had been reformed by the Gospel, and all the rest of the world had remained in utter enmity against it, then the fruits of the Gospel had been too bare, being without leaves. The leaves of a tree, though not fit for the table, *are* serviceable to the fruit, and ornamental to the tree, for without them the fruit would be exposed to ripen on bare twigs.

An acknowledgement of the doctrine of the Gospel, where it is not accompanied by regeneration of heart, may indeed be suitably compared to the leaves of a tree which shelter and protect the fruit. Thus they are serviceable, though not valuable in God's account. The leaf of the vine does more good to the grapes against a scorching sun, than the leaf of any other fruit tree—how much we may learn from God's creatures if only we have eyes to see! So God's elect have been outwardly shaded by the multitude of nominal christians around them. For this we may well thank the kind providence of our Lord. Moreover, God has rewarded the doctrinal faith of the great crowd of unregenerate professors by preserving our public liberties, which the little handful of the regenerate could never, humanly speaking, have enjoyed, without the others.

Again; the operations of the Spirit upon the reprobate have shamed the wicked, increased sobriety, promoted morality, and caused nominal professors to support externally the preaching of the Gospel, the carrying on of the ministry, and thus providing for the benefit of common hearers. This is all useful in its season, but will reap no reward in eternity. The writer most seriously doubts if there be a single church on earth today, having in it sufficient of God's elect to support a preacher, were all the unregenerate in it excluded.

Yea, most probably, most of God's own sent-servants, would be so completely dismayed if they could but see into the hearts of those who have a name to live and are dead, that they would be in despair. Yet though we cannot see into the hearts of professors, we *can* form an accurate idea of what is in them, for "out of the abundance of the heart the mouth speaketh". And the worldliness and emptiness of the ordinary speech of the majority shows plainly *Who* is *not* in their hearts.

We sincerely trust and earnestly pray that it may please our God to strike terror into the souls of many who read this article, that their false peace may be disturbed, and their worthless profession be exposed. Should some of the more thoughtful exclaim with the apostles, "Who then can be saved"? we answer in the words of our Lord, "With men this is *impossible*" (Matt. 19:26). Conclusive proof is this, my reader, that no sinner can be saved by *any* act of his own; and faithfulness requires us to tell you frankly that if your hope of Heaven is resting upon *your* act of "accepting Christ", then your house is built upon the sand. But blessed be His name, the Redeemer went on to say, "But with God all things *are* possible". "Salvation is of the Lord" (Jonah 2:9), not of the creature (Rom. 9:16). Then marvel not that Christ said, "Except a man be *born again,* he cannot see the kingdom of God" (John 3:3).

CHAPTER TWENTY-SIX

The Two Classes of Professors

(Heb. 6:7, 8)

Our preceding article was entitled "The Twofold Working of the Spirit". This was suggested by the contents of the first six verses of Heb. 6. In them we find persons belonging to two entirely different classes are spoken of. The former, one in whom a work of Divine grace had been wrought, effectually applying to them the "great salvation" of God. The latter, one upon whom a work of Divine grace was also wrought, transforming its objects to a considerable degree, yet falling short of actually regenerating them. "The Lord is good to all: and His tender mercies are over all His works" (Psa. 145:9), but the *richness* of His "mercy" is reserved for the objects of His great love (Eph. 2:4). So too God puts forth His power in *varying* degrees, proportioned to the work which He has before Him. Thus, Christ referred to His casting out of demons "with the *finger* of God" (Luke 11:20). Speaking to Israel, Moses said, "With a strong *hand* hath the Lord brought thee out of Egypt" (Ex. 13:9). When referring to the amazing miracle of the Divine incarnation Mary said, "He hath showed strength with His *arm*" (Luke 1:51). But when Paul prayed that God would enlighten His saints to apprehend His stupendous miracle of grace in salvation, it was that they might know "the *exceeding greatness* of His power to usward".

God's power was put forth and is displayed in the natural creation (Rom. 1:20). It will be made known in Hell, upon the vessels of wrath fitted to destruction (Rom. 9:22). It is exercised upon the reprobate in this life (in some more than in others, according to His sovereign pleasure) in subduing their corruptions, restraining their sins, reforming their characters, causing them to receive the doctrine of the Gospel. But the greatest excellency and efficacy of His power is reserved for His beloved people. His power toward *them* is such that it exceedeth all our thoughts: "Now unto Him that is able to do exceeding abundantly above all that we ask or think, *according to the power* that worketh *in us*" (Eph. 3:20).

The recognition of only one of the two distinct operations of God's Spirit upon men has divided theologians into two opposing camps. On the one hand, are the Arminians, who insist that Scripture teaches a *common* grace of God toward all men, a grace which may be despised. So far they are right, for Jude 4 expressly speaks of a class who turn "the *grace* of our God into lasciviousness". But they err when they teach there is no special grace, which is always efficacious upon those in whom it works. On the other side, the majority of modern Calvinists (the older ones did not) deny a common grace of God to all men, and insist in *distinguishing* grace to the elect only. In this they are wrong, and hence their unsatisfactory interpretations of Heb. 6:4-6 and 10:26.

Now as we have shown in our last article, James 1:17 tells us "Every good gift and every perfect gift is from above" etc. Two distinct "gifts" are here referred to. Scripture draws a clear line of distinction between that which God calls "good", and that which He designates "perfect". The main difference between them being that, usually, "good" is applied to something which is temporal, "perfect" to that which is spiritual. The operations of the Spirit upon the non-elect produces that which is "good", that which accomplishes a useful purpose in time, that which is serviceable to God's elect. But His operations upon the children of God produces that which is "perfect", i.e. spiritual, supernatural, eternal. The difference between these two classes and their relation to God in time, was clearly foreshadowed in the Old Testament. The commonwealth of Israel was the type of Christendom as a whole; the "remnant according to the election of grace" in Israel (Rom. 11:5), represented the regenerated people of God now. Hence in both the Tabernacle and the Temple there were two distinct grades of worshippers; so there are today. Those who are merely nominal christians are the outer-court worshippers; the regenerated Christians, who have been made "kings and *priests* unto God" (Rev. 1:6), worship in the holy place (Heb. 10:19). Both classes are contemplated in Heb. 6.

In the short passage which is to be before us on this present occasion, the apostle sums up and makes a searching application of all that he has been writing about in the preceding verses, and this in the form of a parable or similitude. In the context two different classes of people are viewed, though at first it is by no means easy to distinguish between them, the reason for this being that they have so much in common. They had both enjoyed the same external privileges, had been enlightened under the same Gospel ministry, had alike been made "partakers of the Holy Spirit", and had all made a good profession. Yet, of the second class it had to be said, as Christ said to the young ruler, "One thing thou lackest", namely, the shedding abroad of God's love in their hearts, evidenced by *leaving all* and following Christ.

The first class is addressed in the opening verses of our chapter, where the apostle bids the truly regenerated people of God "Go on unto perfection", i.e. having left the temporal shadows, seek to apprehend that for which they had been apprehended—live in the power and enjoyment of the spiritual, supernatural, and eternal. This, the apostle had said, "will we do, if God permit" (v. 3). Divine enablement was needed if they were to "possess their possessions" (Obad. 17), for the regenerate are just as dependent upon God as are the unregenerate. The second class are before us in vv. 4-6, where we have described the principal effects which the common operations of the Spirit produce upon the natural faculties of the human soul. Though those faculties be wound up to their highest pitch, yet the music which they produce is earthly not heavenly, human not Divine, fleshly not spiritual, temporal not eternal. Consequently, they are still liable to apostatise, and even though they should not, they are certain to perish eternally.

The apostle's design in this 6th chapter was to exhort the Hebrews to *progress* in the Christian course (vv. 1-3), and to *persevere* therein (vv. 12-20). The first exhortation is presented in v. 1 and qualified in v. 3. The *motive* to obedience is drawn from the danger of apostacy: (vv. 4-6, note the opening "for"). His purpose in referring to this second class (of unregenerate professors, who apostatise) was, to warn against the outcome of a continuance in a state of slothfulness. Here in the similitude found in vv. 6, 7, he continues and completes the same solemn line of thought, showing what is the certain and fearful doom of all upon whom a regenerating work of grace is not wrought. First, however, he describes the blessedness of the true people of God.

"For the earth which drinketh in the rain that cometh oft upon it and bringeth forth herbs meet for them for whom it is dressed, receiveth blessing from God; But that which beareth thorns and briers is rejected, and is nigh unto cursing; whose end is to be burned" (vv. 7, 8). In taking up these verses we shall endeavour to give, first, an interpretation of them; second, make an application of their contents. The interpretation respects, in its direct and local reference the *Jews,* or rather, two classes among the Jews; the application belongs to all who come under the sound of the Gospel.

The two verses quoted above are designed to illustrate and confirm the solemn admonition found in the six preceding verses, therefore are they introduced with the word "for". In the context two classes of people are in view, both of which were, according to the flesh, Jews. This we have sought to establish in our previous expositions. With the first class the apostle identified himself, note the "we" in v. 3; from the second class Paul dissociates himself, note the words "those" in v. 4 and "they" in v. 6. So, too, two different pieces of ground are now described: first, fruitful ground, which depicts those who have been truly regenerated, and who in consequence, had received the Word into good and honest hearts. Second, unfruitful ground, which represents that class against whose sin and doom the apostle was warning the Hebrews; namely, those who, however great their privileges and fair their professions, bring forth only thorns and briers, who, being rejected by God, are overtaken with swift and terrible destruction.

"For the earth which drinketh in the rain". The prime reference is to the Jewish nation. They were God's vineyard (see Isa. 5:7, 8; Jer. 2:21 etc.). It was unto them God had sent all His servants, the prophets, and last of all His Son (see Matt. 21:35-37). The "rain" here signifies the Word, or Doctrine which the Lord sent unto Israel: "My doctrine shall drop as the rain" (Deut. 32:2 and cf. Isa. 55:10, 11). Note how when Ezekiel was to prophesy or preach, his message would "drop" as the rain does (21:2 and cf. Amos 7:16). The figure is very beautiful. The rain is something which no man can manufacture, nor is the Word of human origin. Rain comes down from above, so is the Gospel a heavenly gift. The rain refreshes vegetation, and causes it to grow, so too the Doctrine of God revives His people and makes them fruitful. The rain quickens living seeds in the ground, though it imparts no life to dead ones; so the Word is the Spirit's instrument for quickening God's elect (John 3:5; James 1:18), who previously had (federal) life in Christ.

There is nothing in nature that God assumes the more into His own prerogative than the giving of rain. The first reference to it in Scripture is as follows, "For the Lord God had not caused it to rain upon the earth" (Gen. 2:5). All rain is from God, who gives or withholds it at His pleasure. The sending of rain He appeals to as a great pledge of His promises and goodness: "Nevertheless He left not Himself without witness, in that He did good, and gave us rain from heaven" etc. (Acts 14:17). Whatever conclusions men may draw from the commonness of it, and however they may imagine they are acquainted with its causes, nevertheless God distinguishes Himself from all the idols of the world in that none of them can give rain: "Are there any among the vanities of the Gentiles that can cause rain?" (Jer. 14:22). Hence the prophet said, "Let us now fear the Lord our God, that giveth rain" (Jer. 5:24).

The high sovereignty of God is also exhibited in the manner of His bestowal and non-bestowal of rain: "Also I have withholden the rain from you, when there were yet three months to the harvest:

and I caused it to rain upon one city, and caused it not to rain upon another city: one piece was rained upon, and the piece whereon it rained not withered" (Amos 4:7). Thus it is absolutely in connection with His providential sending of the Gospel to nations, cities, and individuals: it is of God's disposal alone, and He exercises a distinguishing authority thereon. "Now when they had gone throughout Phrygia and the region of Galatia, and were *forbidden* of the Holy Spirit to preach the Word in Asia, After they were come to Mysia, they assayed to go into Bithynia: *but* the Spirit suffered them not" (Acts 16:6, 7). God sends His Gospel to one nation and not to another, to one city and not to another—there are many large towns both in England and U. S. A. where there is no *real* Gospel preached today—and at one season and not at another.

The natural is but a shadowing forth of the spiritual. What a contrast was there between Egypt (figure of the world), and Canaan (type of the Church)! "For the land, whither thou goest in to possess it, is not as the land of Egypt, from whence ye came out, where thou sowedst thy seed, and waterest with thy foot, as a garden of herbs. But the land, whither ye go to possess it, is a land of hills and valleys, and drinketh water of the rain of heaven: A land which the Lord thy God careth for; the eyes of the Lord thy God are always upon it, from the beginning of the year unto the end of the year . . . I will give you the rain of your land in his due season, the first rain and the latter rain" (Deut. 11:11, 12, 14). Thus, there were two special wet seasons: the first in October (the beginning of Israel's year), when their seed was cast into the ground: the other in March when their corn was nearly grown. Hence we read, "Jordan overfloweth all his banks all the time of harvest" (Josh. 3:15, and cf. 1 Chron. 12:15). Besides these, were many "showers" (Psa. 65:10).

"The rain that cometh oft upon it". The reference is to the repeated and frequent ministerial showers with which God visited Israel. To them He had called, "O earth, earth, earth, hear the Word of the Lord!" (Jer. 22:29). It was looking back to these multiplied servants which Jehovah had sent to His ancient people that Christ said, "O Jerusalem, Jerusalem, that killest the prophets, and stonest them which are sent unto thee, *how often* would I have gathered thy children together" (Matt. 23:37). This then was the "earth" in which were the plants of God's husbandry.

In what follows to the end of the passage the apostle distributes the plants into two classes: "herbs" (v. 7), "thorns and briers" (v. 8). The former, represent those who, having believed and obeyed the Gospel, brought forth the fruits of practical godliness. These constituted that "remnant according to the election of grace" (Rom. 11:5), which obtained mercy, when the rest of their brethren according to the flesh were blinded. These still continued to be the vineyard of the Lord, a field which He cared for. They formed the first Gospel church, gathered out from the Hebrews, which brought forth fruit to the glory of God, and was blessed by Him. The latter, were made up of obstinate unbelievers on the one hand, who persistently rejected Christ and His Gospel; and on the other hand, of those who embraced the profession of the Gospel, but after a season returned again to Judaism. These were rejected of God, fell under His curse and perished.

"And bringeth forth herbs". Several have noted the close resemblance which our present passage bears to the parable of the Sower, recorded in the Gospels. There are some notable parallels between them; the one of most importance being, to observe that in both places we have men looked at, not from the standpoint of God's eternal counsels (as for example, Eph. 1:3-11), but according to *human responsibility*. The earth which receives the rain, is a figure of the hearts and minds of the Jews, to whom the Word of God had been sent, and to whom, in the days of Christ and His apostles, the Gospel had been preached. So our Lord compared His hearers unto several sorts of ground into which the seed is cast—observe how the word "dressed" or "tilled" presupposes the seed. What response, then, will the earth make to the repeated rains? or, to interpret the figure, What fruit is brought forth by those who heard the Gospel? That is the particular aspect of truth the Holy Spirit here has before Him.

"And bringeth forth herbs". The verb here properly signifies the bringing forth of a woman that hath conceived with child, cf. Luke 1:31. So here the earth is said to bring forth as from a womb impregnated, the rains causing the seeds to issue in fruit. The Greek word for "herbs" occurs nowhere else in the N.T. It appears to be a general term for vegetables and cereals. It is found frequently in the Sept. as the equivalent of the Heb. "eseb", which has the same extensive meaning. Now just as the cultivator of land has a right to expect that, under the providential blessings of God, his toils shall be rewarded, that the seed he has sown and the ground he has tilled, should yield an increase, so had Jehovah the right to expect fruit from Israel: "And He looked that it (His vineyard) *should* bring forth grapes" (Isa. 5:4).

"Meet for them by whom it is dressed". The Greek may be rightly rendered thus: equally so, as in the margin, "for whom" it is dressed: either makes good sense. "By whom" would look to the actual cultivator; "for whom," the proprietor. The apostle's design here is to show the importance of making a proper use of receiving God's Word: a "meet" or suitable response should be forthcoming.

The ministry of the Gospel tests the state of the hearts of those to whom it comes, just as the fallen rain does the ground which receives it; tests it by exhibiting its character from what is brought forth by it. As it is in nature, so it is in grace; the more frequently the rain falls, and the more the ground be cultivated, the better and heavier should be the yield. Thus it is with God's elect. The more they sit under the ministry of the Word, and the more they seek grace to improve what they hear, the more fruit will they yield unto God. Thus it had been with the godly in Israel.

"Receiveth blessing from God." The "blessing" here is not antecedent in the communication of mercies, for that we have at the beginning of the verse; rather is it a consequent upon the bringing forth of "herbs" or fruit. What we have here is God's acceptation and approbation, assuring His care unto a further improvement: "A vineyard of red wine: I the Lord do keep it; I will water it every moment; lest any hurt it, I will keep it night and day" (Isa. 27:2, 3). Three things then are included in God's blessing of this fruitful field: first, His owning of it: He is not ashamed to acknowledge it as His. Second, His watchcare over it, His pruning of the branches that they may bring forth more fruit (John 15:2). Third, His final preservation of it from evil, as opposed to the destruction of barren ground. All this was true of that part of Israel spoken of in Rom. 11:5.

"But that which beareth thorns and briers is rejected" (v. 8). It is important to note that in the similitude there is a common subject of the whole, which is then divided into two parts, with very different events ascribed unto each. The common subject is "the earth," of the nature whereof both parts are equally participant. Originally, and naturally, they differ not. On this common subject, on both parts or branches of it, the "rain" equally falls. And too both are equally "dressed." The difference between them lies, first, in what each part of "the earth" (Israel) produced; and secondly, God's dealings with each part. As we have seen, the one part brought forth "herbs" meet for the dresser or owner: a suitable response was made to the rain given and the care expended upon it. The other, which we are now to look at, is the very reverse.

"But that which beareth thorns and briers is rejected." Everything here is in sharp antithesis from the terms of the preceding verse. There, the good ground, "bringeth forth", the Greek word signifying a natural conception and production of anything in due order and season. But the evil ground "*beareth*" thorns and briers, the Greek verb signifying an unnatural and monstrous production, a casting out in abundance of that which is not only without the use of means, but actually against it. As God said of His Israelitish vineyard, "He looketh that it should bring forth grapes, and it brought forth *wild* grapes" (Isa. 5:2). The Greek for "thorns and briers" is identical with the Sept. rendering of Gen. 3:18, which, in our Bibles, is rendered, "thorns and thistles". Three thoughts seem suggested by the term here given to the product of this evil ground. First, it brought forth that which was of no profit to its owner, that which promoted not the glory of God. Second, "thorns and briers" are of a hurtful and noxious nature: see Ezek. 28:24 etc. Third, these terms tell us that all which is brought forth by the natural man is under the *curse* of God: Gen. 3:18, 4:11, 12.

"But that which beareth thorns and briers is rejected". Land which, after cultivation, brings forth only such products, is abandoned by the farmer as worthless. The Greek word here for "rejected", signifies the setting aside as useless after trial has been made of a thing. The application of it here is to by far the greater part of the Jewish people. First, Christ had warned them "the kingdom of God shall be taken from you and given to a nation bringing forth the fruits thereof" (Matt. 21:43). Second, after their full and open rejection of Himself and His Gospel, Christ told them, "Behold, your house is left unto you desolate" (Matt. 23:38). Third, proof that the Nation as a whole *had been* "rejected" by God, is found in Acts 2:40, when, on the day of Pentecost, Peter bade the believing remnant, "Save yourselves from this untoward generation".

"And is nigh unto cursing". This is in sharp contrast from what was said of the good ground: "receiveth blessing from God". The word "cursing" here, means, "given over to execration", or "devoted to destruction". It was given over to be "burned", which, according to the analogy of faith, means, it would be visited with Divine judgment. Israel had become a barren tree, a cumberer of the ground, and the word had gone forth, "Cut it down" (Luke 12:7,9). Further proof that Israel as a nation *was* given over to "execration", is found in the solemn incident of Christ's *cursing* of the "fig tree" (Matt. 21:19), figure of the Jews, see Matt. 24:32. True, a short respite had been granted—another "year" (Luke 13:8)—hence the "*nigh* unto cursing".

"Whose end is to be burned". In Eastern lands, when a husbandman discovers that a piece of ground is worthless, he neglects it, abandons it. Next, he breaks down its fences, that it may be known it is outside the bounds of his possession. Finally, he sets fire to its weeds, to prevent their seeds being blown on to his good ground. Thus it was with Israel. In the last chapter of Acts we see how the apostle Paul warned the Jews how that God had set them aside (Acts 28:25-28), and shortly after, the solemn words of Christ in Matt. 22:7 were fulfilled, "He sent forth His armies, and destroyed those murderers, and *burned up* their city".

The contents of Heb. 6:7, 8 are not to be restricted to the regenerated and unregenerated Jews, for "as in water face answereth to face, so the heart of man to man" (Prov. 27:19). "This is a similitude most appropriate to excite a desire to make progress in due time; for as the earth cannot bring forth a good crop in harvest except it causes the seed as soon as it is sown to germinate, so if we desire to bring forth good fruit, as soon as the Lord sows His Word, it ought to strike roots in us without delay; for it cannot be expected to fructify, if it be either choked or perish. But as the similitude is very suitable, so it must be wisely applied to the design of the apostle.

"The earth, he says, which be sucking in the rain produces a blade suitable to the seed sown, at length by God's blessing produces a ripe crop; so they who receive the seed of the Gospel into their hearts and bring forth genuine shoots, will always make progress until they produce ripe fruit. On the contrary, the earth, which after culture and irrigation, brings forth nothing but thorns, affords no hope of a harvest; nay, the more that grows which is its natural produce, the more hopeless is the case. Hence the only remedy the husbandman has is to burn up the noxious and useless weeds. So they who destroy the seed of the Gospel, either by their indifference or by corrupt affections, so as to manifest no sign of good progress in their life, clearly show themselves to be reprobates, from whom no harvest can be expected. The apostle then, not only speaks here of the fruit of the Gospel, but also exhorts us promptly to embrace it, and he further tells us, that the blade appears presently after the seed is sown, and that grain follows the daily irrigations". (Dr. John Calvin).

The Lord Jesus completed His parable of the Sower by saying, "Take heed therefore *how ye hear*" (Luke 8:18): how you profit by it, what use you make of it; be sure that *you* are a good-ground hearer. *Such*, are those in whom, first, the Word falls, as into "an honest and good heart" (Luke 8:15) i.e. they bow to its authority, judge themselves by it, are impartial and faithful in applying it to their own failures. Second, they "receive" the Word (Mark 4:20): they make personal appropriation of it, they take it home to themselves, they apply it to their own needs. Third, they "understand" it (Matt. 13:23): they enter into a spiritual and experimental acquaintance with it. Fourth, they "keep" it (*Luke 8:15*): they retain, heed, obey, practice it. Fifth, they "bring forth fruit with patience" (*Luke 8:15*), they persevere, overcome all discouragements, triumph over temptations, and walk in the paths of obedience. Upon such the "blessing" of God rests.

Now in contrast from the good-ground hearer, are the wayside, stony, and thorny-ground hearers. These, we believe, are they who come under the common or inferior operations of the Holy Spirit, spoken of in our last article. Let it be carefully noted, first, that even of the wayside hearer (the lowest grade of all) Christ said the Seed was "sown in his *heart*" (Matt. 13:19). Second, that of the stony-ground hearers it is said, "the same is he that heareth the Word, and anon with joy receiveth it" (Matt. 13:20), and "for a while believeth, and in time of temptation falls away" (Luke 8:13). Third, that of the stony-ground hearer Christ said, "Which when they have heard, go forth, and are choked with cares and riches and pleasures of this life, and bring no fruit to perfection" (Luke 8:14). Yet none of them had been born of the Spirit. All that they had brought forth, under His gracious operations, was but the works of the flesh—"thorns and briers".

Above, in our interpretation, we called attention to the difference between the "bringeth forth" of herbs in v. 7, and the "beareth" thorns in v. 8. There is a like producing, but an unlike manner and measure. The former "Bring forth in their lives what was before conceived and cherished in their hearts. They had the *root* in themselves of what they bring forth. So doth the word here used signify, viz., to bring forth the fruit of an inward conception. The doctrine of the gospel as cast into their hearts, is not only rain but seed also. This is cherished by grace, as precious seed, and as from a spiritual root or principle in their hearts, bringeth forth precious fruit. And herein consists the difference between the fruitbearing of the true believers, and the works of hypocrites or false professors. These latter bring forth fruit *like mushrooms,* they come up suddenly, have oft-times great bulk and goodly appearance, but are merely a forced excrescence, they have no natural seed or root in the earth. They do not proceed from a living principle in the heart". (Dr. John Owen).

Thus, it should be most carefully borne in mind that the "thorns and briers" of v. 8 have reference not to sins and wickedness as men view things, but to the *best* products of the flesh, as cultivated by "religion", and that, as instructed out of the Scriptures, and "enlightened" by the Holy Spirit. This is evident from the fact that the thorns and briers, equally with the "herbs", are occasioned by the same "rain" which had come oft upon the earth, and from which they sprang. However fair the professions of the unregenerate may appear in the eyes of their fellows, no matter what proficiency they may reach in an understanding of the letter of

Scripture, nor what their zeal in contending for the faith, loyalty to their church, self-sacrifice in their service; yet, in the sight of Him who searcheth the heart and taketh note of the *root* from which things spring, all is worthless. These products or works are only the fruits of a nature which is under the curse of a holy God.

"But that which beareth thorns and briers is *rejected*" i.e. of God. Little did the Jews believe this when Paul penned those words. Their great boast was that they *were* God's people, that He preferred *them* above all others. Nevertheless, though He yet withheld His wrath for a little space, He *had* disowned them. The sad analogy to this is found everywhere in Christendom today. Countless thousands who bear the name of Christ, and who have no doubts but that *they* are among the true people of God, are yet "rejected" by Him. Are you, my reader, among them?

What need is there for every professing Christian to heed that word in 2 Peter 1:10, "*Give diligence* to make *your* calling and election *sure*"! Those who sit under the ministry of God's Word are upon trial, and it is high time that many of us who have been so long privileged, should call on ourselves to a strict account with respect to our improvement thereof. *What* are we bringing forth? Are we producing "the fruits of righteousness which are by Jesus Christ, unto the glory and praise of God" (Phil. 1:11)? If so, all praise to Him who has made us fruitful. Or are we, though not notoriously wicked persons, yet so far as fruit for God is concerned, cumberers of the ground? If upon inquiry we find ourselves at a loss to be sure of which sort of ground we belong unto, and this because of our barrenness and leanness, unless we are hardened by the deceitfulness of sin, we shall give ourselves no rest until we have better evidences of our bearing spiritual fruit.

O let these solemn words search our hearts: "And is nigh unto cursing, whose end is to be burned". Such is the awful fate confronting multitudes of professing Christians in the churches today, who resist all exhortations to produce the fruit of godly living. Corrupt desires, pride, worldliness, covetousness, are as plainly to be seen in their lives, as are thorns and briers on abandoned ground. O what a thought! professing *Christians*, "nigh unto *cursing*"! Soon to hear their last sermon. Soon to be cut off out of the land of the living. Afterwards to hear from the lips of Christ the fearful sentence, "Depart from Me, ye cursed, into everlasting fire, prepared for the Devil and his angels" (Matt. 25:41).

CHAPTER TWENTY-SEVEN

Two Christians Described

(Heb. 6:9-11)

The passage which is to be before us is in strong and blessed contrast from what we found in vv. 4-6. There we beheld a class of people highly favoured, blest with grand external privileges, richly gifted, and wrought upon by the Holy Spirit. There we see the faculties of the natural man's soul wound up to their highest pitch: the conscience searched, the understanding enlightened, the affections drawn out, and the will moved to action. There we have described the character of a class which constitutes a very large proportion of those who profess the name of Christ. Yet, though they have never been born again, though they are unsaved, though their end is destruction, nevertheless, it is by no means an easy matter for a real child of God to identify them. Oftentimes their head-knowledge of the truth, their zeal for religion, their moral qualities, put him to shame. Still, if he weigh them in the balances of the sanctuary, they will be found wanting.

The careful reader of the four Gospels, will discover that in the days of His flesh, the Lord Jesus healed those concerning whom nothing is recorded of their faith. The blessings which He dispensed were not restricted to His disciples. Temporal mercies were bestowed upon natural men as well as upon spiritual. And, be it carefully noted, this was something more, something in addition to, the providential goodness of the Creator, which is extended to all of Adam's race: "He maketh His sun to rise, on the evil and on the good, and sendeth rain on the just and on the unjust" (Matt. 5:45). Rather did those gracious acts of Christ unto the unbelieving, foreshadow that which we designated in the preceding article, the inferior operations of His Spirit. On a few Christ bestowed spiritual blessings, saving mercies; to others, He imparted temporal blessings, mercies which came short of saving their recipients.

In our last article we made reference to James 1:17: "Every good gift and every perfect gift is from above". We believe that, in keeping with the character, theme and purpose of that epistle, those words have reference to two distinct classes of gifts, for two different classes of people: the "good" referring to those bestowed, under Gospel-ministry on the non-elect; the "perfect" imparted to God's own people. A scripture which we believe supplies strong corroboration of this is found in Psa. 68:18. There, in a Messianic prophecy concerning the ascension of Christ, we read, "Thou hast received gifts for men; yea, for the rebellious also": gifts are bestowed by Christ on two distinct classes. It is to be particularly observed that a part of this verse is quoted by the Spirit in Eph. 4:8; part of it we say, for its closing words, "the rebellious also" are there omitted. And why? Because in Ephesians it is the elect of God (see 1:3, 4 etc.) who are in view. Yet, in addition to them, Christ has received "gifts" for the "rebellious also"; that is, for the non-elect too.

Few indeed have perceived that there is *a double work of* GOD being prosecuted under the ministry of the Gospel. Plain intimation of this is found in the words of Christ in Matt. 22:14, "For many are called, but few chosen." Half of the human race has never heard the Gospel; those who have, are divided into four classes, as Christ has taught us in His parable of the Sower. The "wayside" hearers are those upon whom the preaching of the Gospel produces no effect. The "stony" and the "thorny" ground hearers are they which form a very large percentage of "church members" or who are "in fellowship" with those known as "the Brethren". Of these it is said that they "for a while believe" (Luke 8:13); nor are they unproductive, yet they "bring no fruit to perfection" (Luke 8:14). In them the "enmity" of the carnal mind is, to a considerable extent, subdued; yet it is not vanquished. There is a work of the Spirit upon them, yet it falls short of the new creation. They are "called" but not "chosen".

Only as due attention is paid to the distinction just noted, are we really able to appreciate the point and meaning of the qualifying language which the Spirit of God has used when speaking of the saving call of God's elect. For example, in Rom. 8:28 they are denominated the called "according to His purpose", which notes a distinction from others who receive an inferior "call" according to His providence, under the general proclamation of the Gospel. So too in 2 Tim. 1:9 we read of those "called with a holy calling . . . according to His own purpose and grace", which is the language of discrimination, signifying there are others called yet not with "a holy calling". So again in 1 Peter 5:10, "The God of all grace, who hath called *us* unto His eternal glory", is in antithesis from the many who are only called unto a temporal righteousness in this world.

It needs to be very carefully noted that the "us" of the Epistles is frequently used with a far narrower discrimination than from all the rest of the world: very often the "us" is in contrast from the great crowd of lifeless professors which ever surrounds the little handful of God's true people—professors which, though spiritually lifeless, are yet to be distinguished from the vast multitudes of non-professors; distinguished by a real work of the Holy Spirit upon them, but still an abortive work. Of this class the Epistle of James has much to say. Concerning them John, in his first Epistle, declares "They went out from *us*, but they were not of *us*; for if they had been of *us*, they would have continued with *us*" (2:19). A work of "calling" must have been wrought upon them, for they had once separated from the world, and united themselves with the true people of God. Moreover, that work of "calling" must have produced such a change in them that *they* had been accounted real Christians, or otherwise they had not been admitted among such.

The occasion of Christ's uttering those words "For many are called, but few chosen" (Matt 22:14) is exceedingly solemn and searching. The context records the parable of the wedding-feast of the King's Son. First, the invitation to it had been given to the Jews, but they despised it, mistreated God's servants, and, in consequence, their city was destroyed. Then God's servants are sent forth into the Gentile highways to bring in others. But when the King inspects the guests, He sees a man "which had not on a wedding-garment". The awful sentence goes forth, "Bind him hand and foot, and take him away, and cast him into outer darkness." Immediately after, Christ said, "*For* many are called, but few chosen".

Now in sharp and blessed contrast from the many professing the name of Christ who have received only the inferior call of God through the Gospel—a call which, yet, leads them to assent to the doctrine of His word, which brings them to espouse the outward cause of Christ in this world, which produces a real reformation in their ways, so that they become respectable and useful members of their community, as well as provide a measure of protection to the *few* of God's "chosen" from the openly antagonistic world;—our present passage treats of "the *remnant* according to the election of grace" (Rom. 11:5). This is clear from its opening words, "But, beloved, we are persuaded better things of you." The "But" sets these "beloved" ones in opposition from those mentioned in v. 8. The "better things" also points an antithesis. "Better" is an adjective in the comparative degree, set over against something which is merely "good". Those described in vv. 4, 5 had good things, yet these possessed something far better. Mark how this confirms what we have said on James 1:17!

In vv. 9-12 we find the apostle doing three things: first, he expresses his good will towards the Hebrew saints; second, he declares his judgment concerning their state; third, he gives the grounds upon which his judgment was based. His aim was that they should make a proper use of what he had set before them in the first eight verses, so that on the one hand they might not be discouraged, and on the other hand not become careless. We subjoin Dr. J. Brown's summary of our passage. "The general meaning of this paragraph, all the parts of which are closely connected together, plainly is: The reason why I have made these awful statements about apostates, is not because I consider you whom I am addressing as apostates for your conduct proves that this is not your character, and the promise of God secures that this doom shall not be yours; but that you may be stirred up to persevering steadiness in the faith, and hope, and obedience of the truth, by a constant continuance in which alone you can, like those who have gone before you, obtain in all their perfections the promised blessings of the Christian salvation."

"But, beloved" (v. 9). This term testified to the apostle's good will toward and affection in the Hebrew saints. Such an expression was more than the formal language of courtesy; it revealed the warmth of Paul's heart for God's people. Though he had spoken severely to them in 5:11-14, it was not because he was unkindly disposed toward them. Love is faithful, and because it seeks the highest good of its objects, will reprove, rebuke, admonish, when occasion calls for it. Spiritual love is regulated not by impulse, but by principle. Herein it differs from the backboneless amiability and affability of the flesh, and from the maudlin sentimentality of the day. "We hence conclude, that not only the reprobates ought to be reproved, severely, and with sharp earnestness, but also the elect themselves, even those whom we deem to be children of God" (J. Calvin).

"The apostle hastens to comfort and encourage, lest the Hebrews should be overwhelmed with fear and sorrow, or lest they should think that their condition was regarded by him as hopeless. The affection of the writer is now eager to inspire hope, and to draw them with the cords of love. The word 'beloved' is introduced here most appositely, a term of endearment which occurs frequently in other epistles, but only once in ours; not that the apostle was not filled with true and fervent love to the Hebrew Christians, but that he felt obliged to restrain as it were his feelings, by reason of the prejudices against him. But here the expression bursts forth, as in a moment of great danger or of anxious suspense the heart *will* speak out in tender language (A. Saphir).

"But, beloved, we are persuaded better things of you". In these words the apostle sets forth his judgment concerning the spiritual state of the Hebrews (cf. 3:1). The "persuasion" here did not amount to an infallible certitude, but was a strong confidence based on good grounds. It is similar to what we find in Rom. 15:14, "I myself also am persuaded of you my brethren, that ye also are full of goodness, filled with all knowledge, able also to admonish one another". So again in 2 Tim. 1:5, "When I call to remembrance the unfeigned faith that is in thee, which dwelt first in thy grandmother Lois, and thy mother Eunice; and I am persuaded that in thee also." However low the spiritual condition of these Hebrews (5:11-14), there had been, and still was found in them, fruit, such as manifested them to be truly regenerated souls. It ever holds good that a tree is known by its fruits, hence, the genuineness of my Christian profession is evidenced by what I bring forth, or its worthlessness by what I fail to produce. There may be a "form of godliness" (2 Tim. 3:5), but if the power thereof be "denied" by my works (Titus 1:16) then is it profitless and vain.

"But, beloved, we are persuaded better things of you." It is the bounden duty of every pastor to ascertain the spiritual condition of his people: "Be thou diligent to know *the state* of thy flocks" (Prov. 27:23). This is very necessary if the servant of God is to minister suitably and seasonably. While he is ignorant of their state, he knows not when or how to rebuke or console, to warn or encourage. A general preaching at random is little more than a useless formality. A physician of bodies must acquaint himself with the condition of his patients, otherwise he cannot prescribe intelligently or effectually. Equally so it is with a physician of souls. The same principle holds good in the fellowship of Christians one with another. I cannot really love a brother with the Gospel-love which is required of me, unless I have a well-grounded persuasion that he *is* a brother.

"And things that accompany salvation" (v. 9). The word "accompany" signifies "conjoined with", or inseparable from, that which has a sure connection with "salvation". The principal things that "accompany salvation" are sorrow for and hatred of sin, humility or self-abnegation, the peace of God comforting the conscience, godly fear or the principle of obedience, a diligent perseverance in using the appointed means of grace and pressing forward in the race set before us, the spirit of prayer, and a joyous expectation of being conformed to the image of Christ and spending eternity with Him. True Gospel faith and sincere obedience are far "better things" than the most dazzling gifts ever bestowed on unregenerate professors.

To believe on Christ is very much more than my understanding assenting and my will consenting to the fact that He is a Saviour for sinners, and ready to receive all who will come to Him. To be received by Christ, I must come to Him renouncing all my righteousness (Rom. 10:3), as an empty-handed beggar (Matt. 19:21). But more; to be received by Christ, I must come to Him forsaking my self-will and rebellion against Him (Psa. 2:11, 12; Prov. 28:13). Should an insurrectionist and seditionist come to an earthly king seeking his sovereign favour and pardon, then, obviously, the very law of his coming to him for forgiveness requires that he should come on his knees, laying aside his hostility. So it is with a sinner who comes to Christ for pardon; it is against the law of faith to do otherwise.

An "unfeigned faith" (2 Tim. 1:5) in Christ, is one which submits to His yoke and bows to His authority. There is no such thing in Scripture as receiving Christ as Saviour *without also* receiving Him as Lord: "As ye have therefore received Christ Jesus *the Lord,* walk ye in Him" (Col. 2:6). If it be an honest and genuine faith, it is inseparably connected with a spirit of obedience, a desire to please Him, a resolve to not henceforth live unto self, but unto Him which died for me (2 Cor. 5:15). The man who really thinks he has a saving faith in Christ, but yet has no concern for His glory and no heart for His commandments, is blinded by Satan. There are things which "*accompany* salvation", that have a certain connection therewith. As light is inseparable from the shining of the sun, as heat is inseparable from fire, so good works are inseparable from a saving faith.

"Though we thus speak" (v. 9). The reference is to what the apostle had said about apostates in vv. 6, 8, and which had been written to these Hebrews as a solemn and searching warning for them to take to heart. "In the visible professing church, all things outwardly seemed to be equal. There are the same ordinances administered unto all, the same profession of faith is made by all, the same outward duties are attended unto, and scandalous offences are by all avoided. But yet things are not internally equal. In a great house, there are vessels of wood and stone, as well as of gold and silver. All that eat outwardly of the bread of life, do not feed on the hidden manna. All that have their names enrolled in the church's book, may yet not have them written in the Lamb's book. There are yet better things than gifts, profession, participation of ordinances and whatever is of the like nature. And the use hereof in one word is to warn *all* sorts of persons, that they rest not in, that they take not up with an interest in, or participation of the privileges of the church, with a common profession, which may give them a name to live; seeing they may be dead or in a perishing condition in the meantime" (Dr. J. Owen).

"For God is not unrighteous to forget your work" (v. 10). Here the apostle makes known the ground on which his "persuasion" rested, and that was, the unchanging faithfulness of God toward His covenant promises unto His people, and why he believed that these Hebrews were numbered among them. The foundation on which confidence should rest concerning my own security unto eternal glory, as that of my fellow-Christians, is nothing in the creature. "It is of the Lord's mercies that we are not consumed" (Lam. 3:22). The believer's perseverance is not the cause but the consequence of God's preservation.

"For God is not unrighteous to forget your work". A scripture which enables us to understand the force of these words is 1 John 1:9, "If we confess our sins, He is faithful and just to forgive us our sins". God is "faithful" to His covenant engagements with us in the person of His Son; "just", to the full satisfaction which He rendered unto Him. The very justice of God is engaged on the behalf of those whom Christ redeemed. His veracity towards us is pledged: "In hope of eternal life, which God, that cannot lie, *promised* before the world began" (Titus 1:2). And because God is immutable, without variableness or shadow of turning, He cannot go back on His own oath: "For I am the Lord, I change not; *therefore* ye sons of Jacob are not consumed" (Mal. 3:6). Therefore have we the absolute assurance that "He which hath begun a good work in you will *finish it*" (Phil. 1:6).

"For God is not unrighteous to forget your work". Some have found a difficulty here, because these words seem to teach that heaven is a reward earned by good works. But the difficulty is more seeming than real. What God rewards is only what He Himself hath wrought in us: it is the Father's recognition of the Spirit's fruit. "The act of a benefactor in entering into engagements with his beneficiary may be wholly gratuitous, and yet, out of his act, rights may grow up to the beneficiary. The advantages thus acquired are not the less gracious, because they have become rights; for they originated in free grace" (Dr. Sampson, 1857). It may look now as though God places little value on sincere obedience to Him, that in this world the man who lives for self gains more than he who lives for Christ; yet, in a soon-coming day it shall appear far otherwise.

"For God is not unrighteous to forget your works". "God does not pay us a debt, but performs what He has of Himself freely promised, and not so much on our works, as on His own grace in our works; nay, He looks not so much on our works, as on His own grace in our works. And this is to be 'righteous', for He cannot deny Himself. . . God is righteous in recompensing works, because He is true and faithful; and He has made Himself a debtor to us, not by receiving anything from us, but, as Augustine says, by freely promising all things" (John Calvin). They who imagine there is an inconsistency between the God of all grace "rewarding" His people, will do well to ponder carefully the Reformer's words.

"Your work". We believe the reference here is to their *faith.* First, because he is here speaking of the "things that accompany salvation", and faith is inseparable therefrom. Second, because faith "worketh by love" (Gal. 5:6), and the very next thing mentioned in our verse is their "labour of love". Third, because in 1 Thess. 1:3 we read of the "work of faith, and labour of love, and patience of hope", and in Heb. 6:11, we have their "hope" mentioned. Should it be inquired, Why did the apostle omit the express mention of "faith" here? We answer, Because their faith was so small and feeble. To have commended their faith directly, would have weakened the force of his repeated exhortations in 3:12, 4:1, 2, 6:12, 12:1 etc. "Your work" refers not to any single work, but to a course of working, i. e. the whole course of obedience to God, of which faith is the principle moving thereunto. Evangelical obedience is thus denominated "your work" because this is what they had been regenerated unto (see Eph. 2:10), and because such a course calls for activity, pains, toil; cf. "all diligence" (2 Peter 1:5).

A living faith is a *working* faith (James 2:17). Two things are plainly and uniformly taught throughout the N. T. Justification is by faith, and not by works, (Rom. 4 etc.). Yet, such justifying faith is a living, operative, fruitful faith, evidencing itself by obedience to the commands of God (1 John 2:4 etc.). Christ gave Himself for us that "He might redeem us from all iniquity, and purify unto Himself a peculiar people, *zealous of good works*" (Titus 2:14). This greatly needs emphasising today and pressing repeatedly upon those professing to be believers in the Lord Jesus, for multitudes of these have a name to live, but "art dead" (Rev. 3:1). Their faith is not that of God's elect (Titus 1:1), but nothing better or different than that which the demons have (James 2:19).

"Your faith and the labour of love", for so the Greek reads. These were the evidences upon which the apostle grounded his confidence concerning the Hebrew saints. Five things are to be noted. First this distinguishing grace, their "labour of love": let the reader turn to and ponder carefully 1 John 3:16-19; 4:7-12. "Mutual love among believers is a fruit of the Spirit of holiness, and an effect of faith, whereby being knit together in the bond of entire spiritual affection, on the account of their joint interest in Christ; and participation of the same, new, divine, spiritual nature from God, they do value, delight and rejoice in one another, and are mutually helpful in a constant discharge of all those duties whereby their eternal, spiritual and temporal good may be promoted" (Dr. J. Owen). Note "*labour* of love": a lazy love, like that of James 2:15, 16, is no evidence of saving faith. True love is active, diligent, untiring.

"Which ye have showed". This gives us the second feature of their love. It was not a secret and unmanifested love: but one that had been plainly evidenced in a practical way. In James 2:18 the professor is challenged to "show" his faith, today it would also be pertinent to ask many of those who bear the name of Christ to "show" their love, especially along the line of 1 John 5:2. "Which ye have showed toward His name," defines, third, the *end before them* in the exercise of their ardent love in ministering to the saints. The words last quoted have a threefold force. *Objectively,* because God's name is upon His people (Eph. 3:15). It is both blessed and solemn to know that whatever is done unto the people of God, whether it be good or evil, is done toward the name of Christ: Matt. 25:34-45. *Formally:* they ministered to the saints *as* the people of God. This it is which gives spiritual love its distinctive character: when it is exercised to souls *because* God's name is on them. *Efficiently:* the "name of God" stands for His authority. God requires His people to love one another, and when they do so out of obedience to Him, it is, necessarily, done "toward His name", having respect to His will.

"In that ye have ministered to the saints, and do minister". This tells us, fourth, the *manner* in which their love had been exercised: in an untiring service. Fifth, it announces, the objects of their love, God's "saints". Many of God's people are in various kinds of temporal distress, and one reason why their loving Father permits this is, that their brethren and sisters in Christ may have the holy privilege of ministering to them: see Rom. 15:25-27, 2 Cor. 8:21, 9:11-15. But let such ministry be rendered not from sentimental considerations, nor to satisfy an uneasy conscience, still less with the object of vain glory, to gain a reputation for benevolence; rather let it be "*shown toward* His name". It is the owning of His authority, the conscious performance of His will, which alone gives life, spirituality and acceptance unto all those duties of love which we are able to perform to others.

In summing up the teaching of vv. 9, 10, let us observe *how* the apostle justified the Hebrews according to his Master's rule in Matt. 7:15-20. Genuine Christians give plain evidence that *their* profession of the Gospel *is* accompanied by transforming grace. The obedience of faith and the labour of love toward the saints—not from human instincts, but out of submission to the revealed will of God—both in the past and in the present, were the visible ground of Paul's good persuasion concerning them. It is important to note *what* were the particular graces singled out for mention. The apostle says nothing about their clear views of the truth, their missionary activities, zeal for "their church"—which are the things that many formal professors boast in.

"And we desire that every one of you do show the same diligence to the full assurance of hope unto the end" (v. 11). The apostle looks back to the exhortation of v. 1 and also the solemn warning pointed in vv. 4-8. His purpose had been to excite them unto a diligent persevering continuance in faith and in love, with the fruits thereof. All he had said was unto this end. The closer connection of this verse with the preceding one is: having expressed his conviction about their spiritual state, and having assured them of a blessed issue of their faith from the fidelity of God, he now presses upon them their responsibility to answer to the judgment he had formed of them, by diligent progress unto the end.

In this verse (11) the apostle, with heavenly wisdom, makes known the proper use and end of Gospel threatenings (vv. 6-8), and Gospel promises (vv. 9, 10): either may be, and often are, abused. Many have looked upon threatenings as serving no other purpose than a terrifying of the minds of men, causing them to despair; as if the things threatened must inevitably be their portion. Few have known how to make a right application of them to their consciences. On the other hand, many have abused the promises of God: those who had no title to such have suffered themselves to be deceived, and to be so falsely comforted by them to lie down in a carnal security, imagining that no evil could befall them. But here the apostle reveals the proper end of each, both to believers and unbelievers: the threatenings should stir up to earnest examination of the foundation of our hope; the promises should encourage unto a constant and patient diligence in all the duties of obedience. What wisdom is needed by a minister of the Gospel to make a proper and due use of both upon his hearers!

"And", or rather (Greek) "But we desire". In vv. 9, 10 the apostle had told them what was *not* his object in making to them the statements of vv. 4-8; now he tells them what it *was*. The word "desire" here signifies an intense longing; without this, preaching is cold, formal, lifeless. "That every one of you": the loving care and untiring efforts of the minister should be extended to all the members of his flock. The oldest, as much as the youngest, is in need of constant exhortation. "Do show the same diligence . . . unto the end". Unless this be done, our profession will not be preserved nor God glorified. Paul knew nothing of that half-heartedness and sluggish neglect of the means of grace which today satisfies the generality of those bearing the name of Christ. "Give thyself *wholly* to them" (1 Tim. 4-15).

Many are very "diligent" in their worldly business, still more are most punctual in prosecuting their round of pleasure and fleshly gratification; but there are very few indeed who exercise a godly concern for their souls. To an earnest endeavor after personal holiness, the work of faith and labour of love, the vast majority of professors are strangers, nor can they be persuaded that any such things are required or expected from them. They may be regular attenders of "church" from force of custom; they may perform certain acts of charity for the sake of their reputation; but to be really exercised in heart as to how they may please and honour God in the details of their lives, they know nothing and care still less. Such are *destitute* of those things which "accompany salvation"; they are deluded and lost souls. Make no mistake, my reader, unless there is in you a work of faith in keeping God's commandments, and a labour of love toward His saints as such, then "the root of the matter" (Job 19:28) is *not* in you. This is the test of profession, and the rule whereby each of us shall be measured.

Nor can this work of faith and labour of love be persisted in without studious diligence and earnest endeavour. It calls for the daily searching of the Scriptures, and that, not for intellectual gratification, but to learn God's will for my walk. It calls for watchfulness and prayer against every temptation which would turn me aside from following Christ. It requires that I should rightly abstain from "fleshly lusts that war against the soul" (1 Peter 2:11), yielding myself unto God as one that is passed from death unto life, and my members "as instruments of righteousness unto God" (Rom. 6:13). It requires that I "lay aside every weight" (whatever hinders vital godliness) and the sin which doth so easily beset (the love of self), and run (which calls for the putting forth of all our energies) the race that is set before us" (Heb. 12:1, 2), and that race is a fleeing from the things of this doomed world, with our faces set steadfastly towards God. Those who despise, or even continue to neglect such things, are only nominal Christians.

This "diligence" is to be shown "to the full assurance of hope". Full assurance here signifies a firm conviction or positive persuasion. "Hope" in the N. T. means an ardent desire for and strong expectation of obtaining its object. Faith looks to the Promiser, hope to the things promised. Faith begets hope. God has promised His people perfect deliverance from sin and all its troubles, and full enjoyment of everlasting glory with Himself. Faith rests on the power and veracity of God to make good His word. The heart ponders these blessings, and sees them as yet future. Hope values and anticipates the realization of them. Like faith, "hope" has its degrees. "Full assurance of hope" signifies a steady prevailing persuasion, a persuasion which issues from faith in the promises made concerning "good things to come". The "diligence" before mentioned, is God's appointed *means* toward this full assurance: compare 2 Peter 1:10, 11. To cherish a hope of Heaven while I am living to please self is wicked presumption. "Unto the end": no furloughs are granted to those called upon to "fight the good fight of faith" (1 Tim. 6:12); there is no discharge from that warfare as long as we are left upon the field of battle. No spiritual state is attainable in this life, where "reaching forth unto those things which are before" (Phil. 3:13) becomes unnecessary.

CHAPTER TWENTY-EIGHT

Christian Perseverance

(Heb. 6:12-15)

Two exhortations were set before the Hebrew Christians in the 6th chapter of this epistle. First, they were bidden to turn their backs upon Judaism and go on unto a full embracing of Christianity (v. 1). The application to God's people today of the principle contained in this exhortation is, Abandon everything which enthralled your hearts in your unregenerate days, and find your peace, joy, satisfaction in Christ. In contemplating the peculiar temptation of the Hebrews to forsake the Christian position and path for a return to Judaism, let us not lose sight of the fact that a danger just as real menaces the believer today. The flesh still remains within him, and all that Satan used in the past to occupy his heart, still exists in the present. Though Israel came forth from the House of Bondage, passed through the Red Sea, and started out joyfully (Ex. 15:1) for the promised land, yet it was not long ere their hearts went back to Egypt, lusting after its fleshpots (Ex. 16:3).

It is worse than idle to reply to what has been pointed out above by saying, Real Christians are in no "danger", for God has promised to preserve them. True, but God has promised to preserve His people in a way of holiness, not in a course of sinful self-will and self-gratification. Those whom Christ has declared shall "never perish" are they who "hear His voice and follow Him" (John 10:27, 28). The apostles were not fatalists, neither did they believe in a mechanical salvation, but one that required to be worked out "with fear and trembling" (Phil. 2:12). Therefore Paul, moved by the Holy Spirit, did not hesitate to refer to the Israelites who were "overthrown" in the wilderness, and say, "Now these things were *our* examples to the intent that *we* should not lust after evil things as they also lusted. Neither be ye idolators, as were some of them; . . . Neither let us tempt Christ, as some of them also tempted, and were destroyed of serpents. . . Now all these things happened unto them for ensamples: and they are written for *our admonition*. . . Wherefore let him that thinketh he standeth *take heed* lest he fall" (1 Cor. 10:6-12).

The second exhortation of Heb. 6 is found in vv. 11, 12, the first part of which was before us at the close of our last chapter. There the apostle says, "And we desire that everyone of you do show the same diligence". This, together with the verses that follow, is a call to perseverance in the path of godliness. To a church which had left its "first love" Christ said, "Repent, and do the first works" (Rev. 2:4, 5). What are these "first works"? A submitting of ourselves unto God, an humbling of ourselves before Him, a throwing down of the weapons of our hostility against Him. A turning unto Christ as our only hope, a casting of ourselves upon Him, a trusting in the merits of His precious blood. A taking of His yoke upon us, bowing to His Lordship, owning His authority, earnestly seeking grace to do His commandments.

Now the Christian is to continue as he began. He is to daily own his sins before God. He is to daily renew the same acts of faith and trust in Christ which he exercised at the first. Instead of counting upon some experience in the past, he is to maintain a *present* living upon Christ. If he continues to cast himself upon the Redeemer, putting his salvation wholly in His hands, then He will not, cannot, fail him. But in order to cast myself upon Christ, I must be *near* Him; I cannot do so while I am following Him afar off. To be near Him, I must be in separation from all that is contrary to Him. Communion is based upon an obedient walk: the one cannot be without the other. For the maintenance of this, I must "show the *same* diligence" I did when I was first convicted of my lost estate, saw Hell yawning at my feet ready to receive me, and fled to Christ for refuge.

This same diligence which marked my state of heart and regulated my actions when I first sought Christ, is to be continued "unto the end". This means persevering in a holy living, and unto this the servants of God are to be constantly urging their hearers. "Ministerial exhortation unto duty, is needful even unto them who are sincere in the practice of it, that they may abide and continue therein. It is not easy to be apprehended how God's institutions are despised by some, neglected by others, and by how few, duly improved; all for want of taking right measures for them. Some there are, who, being profoundly ignorant, are yet ready to say, that they know as much as the minister can teach them, and therefore, it is to no purpose to attend unto preaching. These are the thoughts, and this is too often the language, of persons profane and profligate, who know little, and practise nothing of Christianity. Some think that exhortations unto duty, belong only unto them who are negligent and careless in their performance; and unto them, indeed they do belong, but not unto them only, as the whole Scripture testifieth. And some, it may be, like well to be exhorted unto what they do, and do find satisfaction therein, but *how few are there* (it was the same then! A. W. P.) who look upon it as a means of God whereby they are enabled for, and kept up unto their duty, wherein, indeed, their use and benefit doth consist. They do not only direct unto duty, but through the appointment of God, they are means of communicating grace unto us, for the due performance of duties" (Dr. J. Owen, 1680).

"Do show the same diligence to the full assurance of hope unto the end". Hope is a spiritual grace quite distinct from faith or love. Faith casts me upon God. Love causes me to cleave to and delight in pleasing Him. Hope sustains under the difficulties and discouragements of the way. It supports the soul when the billows of trouble roll over it, or when we are tempted to despair, and give up the fight. That is why, in the Christian's armour, Hope is called "the helmet" (1 Thess. 5:8), because it wards off the sharp blows or bears the weight of those strokes which befall the saint in trials and afflictions. Hope values the things promised, looks forward to the day of their realization, and thus is nerved to fresh endeavour. Hope views the Promised Land, and this gives alacrity to the weary pilgrim to continue pressing forward. Hope anticipates the welcome and the glorious fare awaiting us at the Heavenly Port, and this gives courage to go on battling against adverse winds and waves. There is the test.

Many pretend to the possession of a good hope who yet have no faith. Others make a profession of faith who yet have no real hope. But real faith and real hope are inseparable. A spiritual faith eyes the Promiser, and is assured that He cannot lie. A spiritual hope embraces the promises, esteems them above all silver and gold, and confidently anticipates their fulfillment. But between the present moment and the actual realization of our hope lies a rugged path of testing, in which we encounter much that wearies, disheartens and retards us. If we are really walking in the path of God's appointment, there will be oppositions to meet, fierce persecutions to be endured, grievous troubles to be borne. Yet, if our valuation of God's promises be real, if our anticipation of their fulfilment be genuine, the comfort and joy they afford will more than offset and over-balance the effects of our trials. The exercise of hope will alone deliver from fainting and despondency under continued afflictions.

Now to be in the enjoyment of "the full assurance of hope unto the end", the Christian must continue giving "the *same* diligence" to the things of God and the needs of his soul, as he did at the beginning. When the terrors of God first awakened him from the sleep of death, when he was made to feel his own awful danger of being cast into the eternal burnings, when he learned that Christ was the only Refuge, no half-hearted seeker was he. How diligently he searched the Word! How earnestly he cried unto God! How sincere was his repentance! How gladly he received the Gospel! How radical was the change in his life! How real did Heaven seem unto him, and how he longed to go there! How bright was his "hope" then! Alas, the fine gold has become dim; the manna has lost much of its sweetness, and he has become as one who "cannot see afar off" (2 Peter 1:9). Why? Ah, cannot the reader supply the answer from his own experience?

But we dare not stop short at the point reached at the close of the preceding paragraph. Backsliding is dangerous, so dangerous that if it be persisted in, it is certain to prove fatal. If I continue to neglect the Divine means of grace for spiritual strength and support, if I go back again into the world and find my delight in its pleasures and concerns, and if I am not recovered from this sad state, then that will demonstrate that I was only the subject of the Holy Spirit's *inferior* operations, that I was not really regenerated by Him. The difference between thorny-ground and the good-ground hearers is, that the one brings forth no fruit "to perfection" (Luke 8:14), whereas the other brings forth fruit "with patience" or perseverance (Luke 8:15). It is *continuance* in Christ's word which proves us His disciples indeed (John 8:31). It is *continuing* in the faith, grounded and settled, and being "not moved away from the hope of the Gospel" (Col. 1:23) which demonstrates the reality of our profession.

"He said *to the end* that they might know they had not yet reached the goal, and were therefore to think of further progress. He mentioned *diligence* that they might know they were not to sit down idly, but to strive in earnest. For it is not a small thing to ascend above the heavens, especially for those who hardly creep on the ground, and when innumerable obstacles are in the way. There is, indeed, nothing more difficult than to keep our thoughts fixed on things in heaven, when the whole power of our nature inclines towards, and when Satan by numberless devices draws us back to earth" (John Calvin).

Once more would we press upon our hearts that it is only as "diligence" in the things of God is continually exercised that a scriptural "hope" is preserved, and the full assurance of it attained. First, because there is an inseparable connection between these two which is of Divine institution: God Himself has appointed "diligence" as the means and way whereby His people shall arrive at this assurance: cf. 2 Peter 1:10, 11. Second, because such "diligence" has a proper and necessary tendency unto this end. By diligence our spiritual faculties are strengthened, grace is increased in us, and thereby we obtain fuller evidence of our interest in the promises of the Gospel. Third, by a faithful attention to the duties of faith and love we are preserved from sinning, which is the principal evil that weakens or impairs our hope.

"That ye be not slothful, but followers of them who through faith and patience inherit the promises" (v. 12). These words confirm what we have said above concerning the force of the exhortation found in v. 11. There the apostle is giving a call to perseverance in the path of practical holiness. But there are multitudes of professing Christians that cherish a hope of heaven, who nevertheless continue in a course of self-will and self-pleasing. "There is a generation that are pure in their own eyes, and yet is not washed from their filthiness" (Prov. 30:12). Christ came here to save His people "*from* their sins" (Matt 1:21) not in them. No presumption is worse than entertaining the idea that I am bound for Heaven while I live like a child of Hell.

"That ye be not slothful, but followers of them who through faith and patience inherit the promises". This verse forms the connecting link between the preceding section and the closing one of this chapter. The apostle here warns against any evil, indolence and inertia, which stands opposed to giving "diligence": they are the opposite virtue and vice. Slothfulness persisted in would effectually prevent the performance of the duty just enjoined. In 5:11 Paul had charged the Hebrews with being "dull (slothful—the same Greek word) of hearing", not absolutely, but relatively; they were not as industrious in heeding "the word of *righteousness*" (5:13) as they ought to have been. Here he bids them be not slothful in good works, but emulators of the saints who had gone before.

"That ye be not slothful". "He knew that the utmost intention of our spirits, the utmost diligence of our minds, and endeavours of our whole souls, are required unto a useful continuance in our profession and obedience. This, God requireth of us; this, the nature of things themselves about which we are conversant, deserveth; and necessary it is, unto the end which we aim at. If we faint or grow negligent in our duty, if careless or slothful, we shall never hold out unto the end; or if we do continue in such a formal course as will consist with this sloth, we shall never come unto the blessed end which we expect or look for. The oppositions and difficulties which we shall assuredly meet with, from within and without, will not give way unto feeble and languid endeavours. Nor will the holy God prostitute eternal rewards unto those who have no more regard unto them, but to give up themselves unto sloth in their pursuits. Our course of obedience is called running in a race, and fighting as in a battle, and those who are slothful on such occasion will never be crowned with victory. Wherefore, upon a due compliance with this caution, depends our present perseverance, and our future salvation" (Dr. J. Owen).

The slothfulness against which the apostle warns, is in each of us by nature. The desires of the "old man" are not toward, but away from the things of God. It is the "new man" which is alone capacitated to love and serve the Lord. But in addition to the two natures in the Christian, there is the individual himself, the possessor of those natures, the "I" of Rom. 7:25, and *he* is held responsible to "make not provision for the flesh" (Rom. 13:14) on the one hand, and to "desire" the sincere milk of the Word that he may grow thereby" (1 Peter 2:2) on the other. It is the consciousness of this native sloth, this indisposition for practical holiness, which causes the real saint to cry out, "Draw me, we will run after Thee" (Song of Sol. 1:4); "Make me to go in the path of Thy commandments, for therein do I delight"; "Order my steps in Thy Word, and let not any iniquity have dominion over me" (Psa. 119:35, 133). It is *this* which distinguishes the true child of God from the empty professor—his wrestling with God in secret for grace to enable him to press forward in the highway of holiness.

"But followers of them who through faith and patience inherit the promises". The reference here is to the believing forefathers of the Hebrews, who, by continuing steadfast in faith and persevering in hope amidst all the trials to which they were exposed, had now entered into the promised blessings—Heaven. Dr. J. Brown has pointed out that there is no conflict between this declaration and what is said in 11:13. Though during their lives they had "not received the promises", yet at death, they *had* entered into their rest, and are among "the spirits of just men made perfect" (12:23). The word "inherit" denotes their right thereto.

The example which the apostle here sets before the Hebrews was that of the O. T. patriarchs. Just as in the 3rd chapter he had appealed to one portion of the history of their fathers in warning, so now he makes reference to another feature of it in order to encourage. Two things are here to be taken to heart: the happy goal reached by the patriarchs and the path of testing which led thereto. Two things were required of them: faith and patience. Their faith was something more than a general faith in God and the inerrancy of His Word (James 2:19); it was a special faith which laid hold of the Divine promises concerning the covenant of grace in Christ Jesus. Nor was this a mere notional faith, or bare mental assent to the Truth: it was marked by a practical and influential acknowledgement that they were "strangers and pilgrims on the earth" see 11:13. Such is the faith which God requires of us today.

The second grace ascribed unto the patriarchs is their "patience" or "longsuffering" as the word is usually rendered. A different word is employed in 10:36 and 12:1, where an active grace is in view. Here it is more of a passive virtue, hence it is used of the "longsuffering" of God in Rom. 9:22, 1 Peter 3:20 etc. "It is a gracious sedate frame of soul, a tranquility of mind on holy grounds with faith, not subject to take provocation, not to be wearied with opposition" (Dr. J. Owen). It is a spirit which refuses to be daunted by the difficulties of the way, which is not exasperated by trials and oppositions encountered, so as to desert the course or flee from the path of duty. In spite of man's hatred, and of the seeming slowness of God's deliverance, the soul is preserved in a quiet waiting upon Him.

"These were the ways whereby they came to inherit the promises. The heathen of old fancied that their heroes, or patriarchs, by great, and, as they were called, heroic actions, by valour, courage, the slaughter and conquest of their enemies, usually attended with pride, cruelty and oppression, made their way into heaven. The way of God's heroes unto their rest and glory, unto the enjoyment of the Divine promises, was by faith, longsuffering, humility, enduring persecution, self-denial, and the spiritual virtues generally reckoned in the world unto pusillanimity, and so despised. So contrary are the judgments and ways of God and men even about what is good and praiseworthy" (Dr. J. Owen).

As reasons *why* the apostle was moved to set before the Hebrews the noble example of their predecessors, we may suggest the following. First, that they might know he was exhorting them to nothing but what was found in those who went before them, and whom they so esteemed and admired. This, to the same end, he more fully confirms in chapter 11. Second, he was urging them to nothing but what was needful to all who shall inherit the promises. If "faith and patience" were required of the patriarchs, persons who were so high in the love and favour of God, then how could it be imagined that these might be dispensed with as *their* observance! Third, he was pressing upon them nothing but what was practicable, which others had done, and which was therefore possible, yea, easy for them through the grace of Christ.

Ere turning from this most important verse, we will endeavour to anticipate and dispose of a difficulty. Some of our readers who have followed attentively what has been said in the last few paragraphs, may be ready to object, but this is teaching salvation by works; you are asking us to believe that Heaven is a wage which we are required to earn by *our* perseverance and fidelity. Observe then how carefully the Holy Spirit has, in the very verse before us, guarded against such a perversion of the gospel of God's grace. First, in the preposition He used: it is *not* "who *for* faith and patience inherit the promises", but "through". Salvation is not bestowed because of faith and patience, in return for them; yet it *does* come "through" them as the Divinely appointed *channel,* just as the sun shines into a room through its windows. The windows are in no sense the cause of the sun's shining; they contribute nothing whatever to it; yet are they *necessary* as the means by which it enters.

Another word here which precludes all ground of human attainment and completely excludes the idea of earning salvation by anything of ours, is the verb used. The apostle does *not* say "purchase" or "merit", but *"inherit"*. And how come we to "inherit"? By the same way as any come to an inheritance, namely, by being the true heirs to it. And *how* do we become "heirs" of this inheritance? By God's gratuitous adoption. "Ye have received the Spirit of adoption, whereby we cry, Abba, Father. The Spirit Himself beareth witness with our spirit, that we are the children of God: and if children, then heirs" (Rom. 8:15-17). God, by an act of His sovereign will, made us His children (Eph. 1:4, 5). This Divine grace, this free assignment, is the foundation of all; and God's faithfulness is pledged to preserve us unto our inheritance (v. 10). Yet, we are *such* heirs as have *means* assigned to us for obtaining our inheritance, and we are required to apply ourselves thereunto.

"For when God made promise to Abraham, because he could sware by no greater, He sware by Himself" (v. 13). The opening "For" denotes that the apostle is here giving a reason why he had appealed to the example of the patriarchs, as those who "through faith and patience inherit the promises": that they really did so, he now proves by a most illustrious instance. Paul here cites the case of one whom he knew would be most notable and forcible. God made promise to Abraham, but he did not obtain the fulfillment thereof until after he had "patiently endured" (v. 15).

The one to whom God made promise was Abraham. He was originally called "Abram", which signifies "an exalted father". Upon Jehovah's renewal of the covenant to him, his name was changed to Abraham, God giving as the reason "for a father of many nations have I made thee" (Gen. 17:5). The reference was not only to those nations which should proceed naturally from him—the descendants of Ishmael (Gen. 17:20) and of Keturah's sons (Gen. 25:1-4)—but to the elect of God scattered throughout the world, who should be brought to embrace his faith and emulate his works. Therefore is he designated "the father of all them that believe", and "the father of us all" (Rom. 4:11, 16).

"Because he could sware by no greater, He sware by Himself". The assurance which was given to Abraham was the greatest that Heaven itself could afford: a promise and an oath. We say the greatest, for in v. 16 the apostle declares that amongst men an "oath" is an end of strife; how much more when the great God Himself takes one! Moreover, observe He swear "by Himself": He staked Himself; it was as though He had said, I will cease to be God if I do not perform this. The Lord pledged His veracity, declared the event should be as certain as His existence, and that it should be secured by all the perfections of His nature. Dr. J. Brown has rightly pointed out, "The declaration was not in reality made more certain by the addition of an oath, but so solemn a form of asseveration was calculated to give a deeper impression of its certainty".

"Saying, Surely blessing I will bless thee, and multiplying I will multiply thee" (v. 14). It seems strange that almost all of the commentators have quite missed the reference in the preceding verse. There we read, "God made promise to Abraham". Some have regarded this as pointing back to the first promise Jehovah made to the patriarch in Gen. 12:2, renewed in 15:5; others have cited Gen. 17:2, 6; still others, the promise recorded in Gen. 17:15, 16; and thus they limit the "patiently endured" (Heb. 6:15) to a space of twenty-five years, and regard the "he obtained the promise" as finding its fulfillment at the birth of Isaac. But these conjectures are completely set aside by the words of our present verse, which are a direct quotation from Gen. 22:17, and that was uttered *after* Isaac was born.

That which God swore to was to bless Abraham with all blessings, and that unto the end: "Surely, blessing I will bless thee". The phrase is a Hebrew mode of expression, denoting emphasis and certainty. Such reduplication is a vehement affirmation, partaking of the nature of an oath: where such is used, it was that men might know God is in earnest in that which He expressed. It also respects and *extends* the thing promised or threatened: I will do without fail, without measure, and eternally without end. It is indeed solemn to note the first occurrence in Scripture of this mode of expression. We find it in the awful threat which the Lord God made unto Adam: "But of the tree of the knowledge of good and evil, thou shalt not eat of it: for in the day that thou eatest thereof dying thou shalt die" (Gen. 2:17).

It is Gen. 2:17 which supplies the first key that unlocks the meaning of Gen 22:17. These are the first two occurrences in Holy

Writ of this unusual form of speech. They stand in direct antithesis the one to the other. The first concerned the curse, the second respected the blessing. The one was the sentence of irrevocable doom, the other was the promise of irreversible bliss. Each was uttered to an individual who stood as the head and representative of a family, upon whose members the curse and the blessing fell. Each head sustained a *double* relationship. Adam was the head of the entire human family, and the condemnation for his sin has been imputed to all his descendants (Rom. 5:12, 18, 19). But in a narrower sense Adam was the head of the non-elect, who not only share his condemnation, partake of his sinful nature, but also suffer his eternal doom. In like manner, Abraham was the head of a natural family, that is, all who have descended from him; and they share in the temporal blessings which God promised their father. But in a narrower sense Abraham (type of Christ as the "everlasting Father" Isa. 9:6 and cf. Isa. 53:10 "His seed", and His "children" in Heb. 2:13) was the head of God's elect, who are made partakers of his faith, performers of his works, and participants of his spiritual and eternal blessings.

It was through their failing to look upon Abraham as the type of Christ as the Head and Father of God's elect, which caused the commentators to miss the deeper and spiritual significance of God's promise and oath to him in Gen. 22. In the closing verses of Heb. 6 the Holy Spirit has Himself expounded the type for us, and in our next article (D. V.) we shall seek to set before the reader some of the supporting proofs of what we have here little more than barely asserted. The temporal blessings wherewith God blessed Abraham—"God hath blessed Abraham in all things" (Gen. 24:1 and cf. v. 35)—were typical of the spiritual blessings wherewith God has blessed Christ. So too the earthly inheritance guaranteed unto Abraham's seed, was a figure and pledge of the Heavenly inheritance which pertains to Christ's seed. Let the reader ponder carefully Luke 1:70-75 where we find the type merging into the antitype.

"Surely, blessing I will bless thee" is further interpreted for us in Gal. 3:14, where we read, "That the blessing of Abraham might come on the Gentiles through Jesus Christ". Thus, in blessing Abraham, God blessed all the heirs of promise, and pledges Himself to bestow on them what He had sworn to give unto him: "If ye be Christ's then are ye Abraham's seed, and heirs according to the promise" (Gal. 3:29). That the deeper and ultimate signification of Gen. 22:17 had reference to spiritual and future "blessing" is not only established, unequivocally, by Rom. 9:7, 8, but also by the fact that otherwise there had been *no relevancy* in Paul's setting before the Hebrews, and us, the example of Abraham.

That with which God promised to bless Abraham and his seed was faith, holiness, perseverance, and at the end, salvation (Gal. 3:14). That which God pledged Himself unto with an oath was that His power, His long-suffering, should be engaged to the uttermost to work upon the hearts of Abraham and his spiritual children, so that they would effectually attain unto salvation. Abraham was to live on the earth for many long years after God appeared unto him in Gen. 22. He was to live in an adverse world where he would meet with various temptations, much opposition, many discouragements; but God undertook to deliver, support, succor, sustain him unto the end, so that His oath should be accomplished. Proof of this is given in our next verse.

"And so after he had patiently endured, he obtained the promise" (v. 15). This means that, amid all the temptations and trials to which he was exposed, Abraham studiously persevered in believing and expecting God to make good His word. The emphatic and all-important word here is "And *so*" which joins together what was said in vv. 13, 14 and what follows here in v. 15. It was in *this* way and manner of God's dealing with him; it was in *this* way of conducting himself. He "patiently endured", which covers the whole space from the time that God appeared to him in Gen. 22 until he died, at the age of one hundred and seventy-five years (Gen. 25:7). It is this exercise of hope unto the end which Paul was pressing upon the Hebrews. They professed to be Abraham's children, let them, then, manifest Abraham's spirit.

"He obtained the promise": by installments. First, an earnest of it in this life, having the blessing of God in his own soul; enjoying communion with Him and all that that included—peace, joy, strength, victory. By faith in the promise, he saw Christ's day, and was glad (John 8:56). Second, a more complete entering into the blessing of God when he left this world of sin and sorrow, and departed to be with Christ, which is "far better" (Phil. 1:23) than the most intimate fellowship which may be had with Him down here. Abraham had now entered on the peace and joy of Paradise, obtaining the Heavenly Country (Heb. 11:16), of which Canaan was but the type. Third, following the resurrection, when the purpose of God shall be fully realized in perfect and unending blessing and glory.

CHAPTER TWENTY-NINE

The Anchor of the Soul

(Heb. 6:16-20)

In our last article we saw that the Holy Spirit through Paul exhorted the people of God to "be not slothful, but followers of them who through faith and patience inherit the promises" (v. 12). This declaration was illustrated and exemplified from the history of one who has been highly venerated both by Jews and believing Gentiles, namely, Abraham, of whom it is here declared, "after he had patiently endured, he received the promise" (v. 16). We cannot but admire again the heavenly wisdom given to the apostle, inspiring him to bring in Abraham at this particular point of his epistle. In chapter 3 we saw how that, before he set forth the superiority of Christ over Moses, he first made specific mention of the typical mediator's *faithfulness* (v. 5); so here, ere setting forth the superiority of Christ over Abraham (which *is* done in 7:4), he first records his triumphant *endurance*. How this shows that we ought to use every lawful means possible in seeking to remove the prejudices of people against God's truth!

The mention of Abraham in Heb. 6 should occasion real searchings of heart before God on the part of all who claim to be Christians. Abraham is "the father of all them that believe" (Rom. 4:11), but as Christ so emphatically declared to those in His day who boasted that Abraham was their father, "If ye were Abraham's children, ye *would do* (not merely "ye ought to do"!) the *works* of Abraham" (John 8:39), and as Rom. 4:12 tells us, Abraham is "the father of circumcision (i.e. spiritual circumcision: Col. 2:11) to those who are not of the (natural) circumcision only, but who also *walk* in the steps of that faith of their father Abraham". In his day (1680) J. Owen said, "It is a sad consideration which way and by what means some men think to come to Heaven, or carry themselves as if they think so. There are *but few* who deem more than a naked profession to be necessary thereunto, but living in all sorts of sins, they yet suppose they shall inherit the promises of God.

This was not the way of the holy men of old, whose example is proposed to us. True, some think that faith at least be necessary hereunto, but by faith they understand little more than a mere profession of true religion".

It behooves us, if we value our souls, to examine closely the Scriptural account of the nature and character of Abraham's faith. It was far more than a bare assenting to the veracity of God's Word. It was an operative faith, which caused him to separate himself from the world (Heb. 11:8, 9), which led him to take the place of a stranger and pilgrim down here (Heb. 11:13), which enabled him to patiently endure under severe trials and testings. In the light of other scriptures, the words, "patiently endured" (Heb. 6:15) enable us to fill in many a blank in the Genesis history. Patiently "endured" what? Mysterious providences, the seeming slowness of God to make good His promises, that which to sight and sense appeared to repudiate His very love (Gen. 22:2). Patiently "endured" what? The attacks of Satan upon his faith, the insinuations of the Serpent that God had ceased to be gracious, the temptation of the Devil to be enriched by the king of Sodom (Gen. 14:21). Patiently "endured" what? The cruel sneers, the biting taunts, the persecution of his fellow-men, who hated him because his godly walk condemned their ungodly ways. Yes, like his Redeemer afterwards, and like each one of his believing children today, "he endured the contradiction of sinners against himself".

But the Holy Spirit had another design here in referring to the case of Abraham. Having so faithfully warned us of the danger of apostasy, having so earnestly set before us the imperative need of faithful perseverance, He now closes this lengthy parenthesis with a most glorious message of *comfort,* which is designed to set the hearts of God's children at perfect rest, allay their fears of uncertainty as to their ultimate issue, strengthen their faith, deepen their assurance, and cause them to look forward to the future with the most implicit confidence. It is ever God's way to wound before He heals, to alarm the conscience before He speaks peace to it, to press upon us our responsibility ere He assures of His preserving power. "For it is God which worketh in you both to will and to do of His good pleasure", is preceded by "work out your own salvation with fear and trembling" (Phil. 2:12, 13).

And *what* is it that the Holy Spirit here uses *to comfort* the hearts of God's tried and troubled and trembling people? Why, the wondrous and glorious Gospel of His grace. This He does by now making known the deeper design and significance of His reference to Abraham. He shows that the promise which God made to "the father of all that believe", to which promise He designed to add His oath, concerned not Abraham alone, but is, without fail, to be made good to all his spiritual seed. Yea, He shows how God's dealings with Abraham in time, were but a shadowing-forth on this earth-plane of His covenant-transactions with Christ and His seed in Heaven ere time began. May the Lord grant the much-needed wisdom, guidance and grace, that both the writer and reader may be led to a right and clear apprehension of this most blessed subject.

Ere turning to v. 16 let us attempt to show the connection of our present passage with its context, by giving a brief analysis of the verses which were before us in the preceding article. 1. Abraham is set before us as an example: v. 12 and the opening "For" of v. 13. 2. God made promise to Abraham: v. 13. 3. That promise had immediate reference to Christ and the benefits of His mediation: Gal. 3:16. 4. In addition to His promise, God placed Himself on oath to Abraham: v. 13. 5. The peculiar nature of that oath: God sware by Himself: v. 13. 6. God sware by Himself because there was none greater to whom He might appeal: v. 13. 7. Abraham's faith, resting on the ground of God's promise and oath, patiently endured and obtained the promise: v. 15.

The emphatic and important words of v. 15 are its opening "And *so*", or "And *thus*", the reference being to the absolute faithfulness of the divine promise, followed by the divine oath, namely "Surely, blessing I will bless thee" (v. 14). In other words, God's oath to Abraham was the guarantee that He would continue to effectively work in him and invincibly preserve him to the end of his earthly course, so that he should infallibly enter into the promised blessing. Though Abraham was to be left in the place of trial and testing for another seventy-five years, his entrance was not left contingent upon his own mutable will. Though it is only through "faith and patience" any inherit the promises (v. 12), yet God has solemnly pledged Himself to sustain these graces in His own unto the end of their wilderness journey and right across Jordan itself, until entrance into Canaan is secured: "These *all* died in faith" (Heb. 11:13).

"For men verily sware by the greater: and an oath for confirmation is to them an end of all strife" (v. 16). The design of this verse is to give us an explanation of *why* it is that the great God has placed Himself on oath. When we consider who He is and what He is, we may well be amazed at His action. When we remember His exalted majesty, that he "humbles" Himself to so much as "behold" the things that are in heaven (Psa. 113:6), there is surely cause for wonderment to find Him "swearing" by Himself. When we remember that He is the God of Truth, who cannot lie, there is reason for us to enquire why He deemed not His bare word sufficient.

"For men verily sware by the greater: and an oath for confirmation is to them an end of all strife". The opening "for" looks back to God "sware by Himself" of v. 13. The apostle here appeals to a custom which has obtained among men in all ages. When one party avers one thing, and another, another, and each stands firmly by what he says, there is not only mutual contradiction, but endless strife. Where matters of interest and importance are concerned between two or more men, the difference between them can only be settled by them being placed on oath. In such cases an oath is necessary for the governing and peace of mankind, for without it strife must be perpetual, or else ended by violence. Thus, the purpose or design of oaths among men is to place bounds upon their contradictions and make an end of their contentions.

Strikingly has Dr. J. Owen pointed out in his remarks upon v. 16: "As these words are applied to or are used to illustrate the state of things between God and our souls, we may observe from them: First, that there is, as we are in a state of nature (looking at the elect as the descendants of fallen Adam—A. W. P.), a difference and strife between God and us. Second, the promises of God are gracious proposals of the only way and means for the ending of that strife. Third, the oath of God interposed for the confirmation of these promises (better, "in addition to" the promises—A. W. P.) is every way sufficient to secure believers against all objections and temptations in all straits and trials, about peace with God through Jesus Christ".

"Wherein God, willing more abundantly to show unto the heirs of promise the immutability of His counsel, confirmed it by oath" (v. 17). The relative "wherein" or "wherefore" has, we believe, both an immediate connection with v. 16, and a more remote one to what has been declared in v. 13. Regarding it, first, as a conclusion drawn from the general principle enunciated in the preceding verse, its force is this: since an oath serves to establish man's words among his fellows, the great God has condescended to employ this means and method to confirm the faith of His people. Because an oath gives certainty among men unto the point sworn to, God has graciously deigned that the heirs of promise shall have the comfort of a Divine dual certainty. The more remote connections with v. 13 will appear in the course of our exposition: it is to here give assurance that what God so solemnly pledged Himself to do for and give unto Abraham, is equally sure and certain to and for all his children—the "wherein" signifies "in which" *oath.*

God's design in swearing by Himself was not only that Abraham might be fully persuaded of the absolute certainty of His blessing, but that the "heirs of promise" should also have pledge and proof of the immutability of His counsel concerning them; for the mind and will of God was the same toward all of the elect as it was toward the patriarch himself. Though we are lifted to a much greater height in these closing verses of Heb. 6, yet the application which the apostle is here led to make of God's dealings with Abraham, is identical in principle with what we find in Rom. 4. There we read of Abraham believing God and that it was counted unto him for (better "unto") righteousness, and in v. 16 the conclusion is drawn: "Therefore it is of faith, that it might be by grace; to the end the promise might be sure to *all* the seed"; while in vv. 23, 24 we are told, "Now it was not written for his sake alone, that it was reckoned to him, but for *us also,* to whom it shall be reckoned, if we believe on Him that raised up Jesus our Lord from the dead"—cf. Gal. 3:29.

We come now to enquire, What is the "immutability of His counsel" which God determined to show the more abundantly unto the heirs of promise? To ascertain this, we need first to consider God's "counsel". Like the expression the "will of God", His "counsel" has a *double* reference and usage in the N. T. There is the revealed "will" of God, set forth in the Scriptures, which defines and measures human responsibility (1 Thess. 4:3, e. g.), but which "will" is perfectly done by none of us; there is also the secret and invincible will of God (Rom. 9:19 etc.), which is wrought out through each of us. So we read, on the one hand, that "the Pharisees and lawyers *rejected* the counsel of God against themselves" (Luke 7:30); while on the other hand, it is said of the crucifiers of Christ, they "were gathered together *for to do* whatsoever Thy hand and Thy counsel determined before *to be done*" (Acts 4:27, 28). The "*immutability* of His counsel" declares plainly in which of the two senses the term is to be taken in Heb. 6.

The "counsel" of God in Heb. 6:17 signifies His everlasting decree or eternal purpose. It is employed thus of Christ's death in Acts 2:23, "Him, being delivered by the determinate counsel, and foreknowledge of God". It bears the same meaning in Eph. 1, as is abundantly clear if v. 9 be compared with v. 11: in the former we read, "Having made known unto us the mystery of His will, according to His good pleasure which He hath *purposed* in Himself"; in the latter it is said, "being predestinated according to the purpose of Him who worketh all things after *the counsel* of His own will". Both of those verses take us back to the Divine determination before this world was created; equally plain is it that both of them are treating of the eternal resolutions of God concerning the *salvation* of His people: cf. 1 Thess. 2:13.

Still more specially the "counsel" of God in Heb. 6:17 concerns the holy and wise purpose of His will to give His Son Jesus Christ to be of the seed of Abraham for the salvation of all the elect, and that, in such a way, and accompanied by such blessings, as would infallibly secure their faith, perseverance, and entrance into Glory. In other words, the "counsel" of God respects the agreement which He entered into with Christ in the Everlasting Covenant, that upon His fulfillment of the stipulated conditions, the promises made to Him concerning His seed should most certainly be fulfilled. Proof of this is found in comparing Luke 1:72, 73, with Gal. 3:16, 17. In the former we read of Zacharias prophesying that God was "to remember His holy *covenant,* the *oath* which He sware to our father Abraham". In the latter, the Holy Spirit brings out the hidden meaning of God's dealings with the patriarch: "Now to Abraham and his seed were the *promises* made. He saith not, And to seeds, as of many; but as of one, And to thy seed, which is Christ. And this I say, the covenant, that was confirmed before of God *in Christ*".

Referring to the covenants made by Jehovah with the patriarchs, as affording so many types of that Everlasting Covenant (Heb. 13:20) made with Christ, Mr. Hervey (1756) when refuting the terrible heresies of John Wesley, wrote: "True, it is recorded that God made a covenant with Abraham, with Isaac, with Jacob, and with David: but were they in a capacity to enter into a covenant with their Maker? to stand for themselves or be surety for others? I think not. The passages mean no more than the Lord's *manifesting,* in an especial manner, the grand Covenant to them, ratifying and confirming their personal interest in it, and further assuring them that *Christ,* the great Covenant-Head, should spring from their seed. This accounts for that remarkable and singular mode of expression which often occurs in Scripture: 'I will make a covenant with them'. Yet there follows no mention of any conditions but only a promise of unconditional blessings".

Now what is particularly important to note here is, that God was "willing more abundantly to *show* unto the heirs of promise, the *immutability* of His counsel", and therefore, "confirmed it by (or as the margin much more accurately renders it "interposed Himself by") an oath". This leads us to call attention to the distinction between God's "counsel" and His "promise". His "counsel" is that which, originally, was a profound and an impenetrable secret in Himself; His "promise" is an open and declared revelation of His will. It is most blessed to perceive that God's promises are but the transcripts of His eternal decrees; His promises now make known to us in words the hitherto secret counsels of His heart. Thus, "the immutability of His counsel" is that from which His sure promises proceed and by which it is expressed.

But in addition to His promise, God was willing "more abundantly" to "show", or reveal, or make known to His people, the unchangeableness of His counsel. All proceeds from the *will* of God. He freely purposed to give unto the elect, while they are in this world, not only abundant, but "more abundant" proofs of His everlasting love (Jer. 31:3), His gracious concern for their assurance, peace and joy. This He did by "interposing Himself by an oath". The Greek word which the A. V. has rendered in the text "confirmed", has for its prime meaning "to mediate" or "intervene". This at once directs our thoughts to the Mediator, of whom Abraham was the type. It was *to Christ* that the original Promise and Oath were made. Hence, in Titus 1:2 we read, "In hope of eternal life, which God, that cannot lie, promised before the world began": as the elect were not then in existence, the promise must have been made to their Head. Concerning God's oath to Christ we read, "The Lord hath sworn, and will not repent, Thou art a priest forever after the order of Melchizedek" (Psa. 110:4).

Now it is not unto all mankind, but only unto a certain number of persons to whom God designs to manifest the immutability of His counsel, and to communicate the effects thereof. These are here denominated "the heirs of promise" which includes all the saints of God both under the Old and N. T. They are called "heirs of promise" on a double account: with respect unto the promise itself, and the thing promised. They are not yet the actual possessors, but waiting in expectation (cf. 1:14): proof of this is obtained by comparing Heb. 11:13, 17, 19. In this the members are conformed to their Head, for though Christ is the "Heir of all things" (1:2), yet He, too, is "expecting" (see 10:13). The "heirs of promise" here are the same as "the children of promise" in Rom. 9:8.

"That by two immutable things in which it was impossible for God to lie, we might have a strong consolation, who have fled for refuge to lay hold upon the hope set before us" (v. 18). In order to simplify our exposition of this verse, we propose taking up its contents in their inverse order, and doing so under a series of questions. First, what is "the hope set before us?" Where is it thus "set before us", What is meant by "fled for refuge *to* lay hold upon the hope"? What is the "strong consolation"? How do the "two immutable things" supply this strong consolation?

In seeking to ascertain the character of "the hope" of v. 18 it needs to be carefully distinguished from the "strong consolation", which at once intimates that it is not the grace of hope within the heart of the believer. Further corroboration of this is found in the words, "set before us", which clearly speaks of what is objective rather than subjective; and too, it is to be "laid hold of". Moreover, what is said of this "hope" in v. 19 excludes the idea of an internal expectation. The needed help is found in 7-19 where of the "better hope" it is said, "by the which we draw nigh unto God": John 14:6, Eph. 2:18 etc. In 1 Tim. 1:1 the Lord Jesus Christ is distinctly designated "our Hope", and is He not the One whom God hath "set before" His people? Is not "that blessed Hope" for which we are to be "looking" (Titus 2:13), Christ Himself?

Where is it that Christ is "set before us" as "the hope"? Surely, in the Gospel of God's grace. It is there that the *only* hope for lost sinners is made known. The Gospel of God is "the Gospel of Christ" (Rom. 1:16), for it exhibits the excellencies of His glorious person and proclaims the efficacy of His finished work. Therefore in Rom. 3:25 it is said of Christ Jesus, "Whom God hath *set forth* a propitiation through faith in His blood"; while to the Galatians Paul affirmed, "before whose eyes Jesus Christ hath been evidently (openly) *set forth* among you—crucified". In the Gospel, Christ is presented both as an Object of Faith and an Object of Hope. As an Object of Faith it is what He has done for the elect, providing for them a perfect legal standing before God: this is mainly developed in Romans. As an Object of Hope it is what Christ will yet do for His people, bring them out of this wilderness into the Promised Land. In Hebrews we are seen as yet in the place of trial, moving toward the Inheritance.

What is meant by "fled for refuge to lay hold upon the hope set before us"? It expresses that which the Gospel requires from those who hear it—appropriating it unto one's self. Saving faith is explained under various figures. Sometimes as "believing", which means the heart resting upon Christ and His finished work. Sometimes as "Coming to Christ", which means a turning from every other refuge and closing with Him as He is set forth in the Gospel. Sometimes as a "setting to our seal that God is true" (John 3:33 cf. Isa. 44:5), which means ratifying His testimony by our receiving it. Sometimes as the committal of our soul and its eternal interests into the hands of the Lord (2 Tim. 1:12). Sometimes as a "submitting ourselves unto the righteousness of God" (Rom. 10:3), which means repudiating our own works and resting upon the vicarious obedience and sacrifice of Christ. Here, it is pictured as a "fleeing for refuge", the figure being taken from an O. T. type.

Under the Law, God made merciful provision for the man who had unintentionally slain another: that provision was certain cities appointed for refuge for such. Those cities are spoken of in Num. 35, Deut. 19, Josh. 20. Those cities were built on high hills or mountains (Josh. 20:7), that those seeking asylum there, might have no difficulty in keeping them in sight. So the servants of Christ who hold Him up, are likened unto "a city which is set upon a hill" (Matt. 5:14). They were a refuge from "the avenger of blood" (Josh. 20:3): cf. "flee from the wrath to come" (Matt. 3:7). They had a causeway of stones approaching them as a path to guide thereto (Deut. 19:3): so in the Gospel a way of approach is revealed unto Christ. Those who succeeded in entering these cities secured protection and safety (Num. 35:15): so Christ has declared "him that cometh to Me I will in no wise cast out" (John 6:37).

Now the particular point to be noted in the above type is that the one who desired shelter from the avenger of blood had to personally *flee to* the city of refuge. The figure is very impressive. Here was a man living in peace and comfort, fearing none; but having now slain another at unawares, everything is suddenly changed. Fear within, and danger without, beset on either hand. The avenger of blood threatens, and nothing is left but to flee to the appointed place of refuge, for there alone is peace and safety to be found. Thus it is with the sinner. In his natural condition, a false serenity and comfort are his. Then, unawares to him, the Holy Spirit convicts him of sin, and he is filled with distress and alarm, till he cries, "What must I do to be saved"? The Divine answer is, "Flee for refuge and *lay hold of* the hope set before us".

But let us not fail to note here the immeasurable superiority of Christianity over Judaism as seen in the vast difference between the "refuge" under the Law, and that made known in the Gospel. The cities of refuge were available only for those who had unintentionally killed a person. But we have been conscious, deliberate, lifelong rebels against God; nevertheless Christ says, "Come unto Me *all* ye that labour and are heavy-laden, and I will give you rest". Again, the manslayer in the city was safe, yet his very refuge was a *prison*: it is the very opposite with the believer—Christ opened for him the prison-door and set him at liberty (Isa. 61:2), Christ "makes free" (John 8:36). Again, in entering the city of refuge he turned away from his inheritance, his land and cattle; but the one who lays hold of Christ obtains an inheritance (1 Peter 1:4). For the manslayer to return to his inheritance meant death; for the Christian, death means going to his inheritance.

Those who have fled to Christ to "lay hold on eternal life" (1 Tim. 6:12), are entitled to enjoy "strong consolation". On this the Puritan Manton said, "There are three words by which the fruits and effects of certainty and assurance is expressed, which imply so many degrees of it: peace, comfort, and joy. Peace, denotes rest from accusations of conscience. Comfort, a temperate and habitual confidence. Joy, an actual feeling, or hightide of comfort, an elevation of the saints". Strong consolation is a firm and fixed persuasion of the love of God toward us, and the assurance that "our light affliction, which is but for a moment, worketh for us a far more exceeding eternal weight of glory" (2 Cor. 4:17). "David encouraged himself in the Lord *his* God" (1 Sam. 30:6).

It remains for us now to consider what it is which supplies and supports the "strong consolation" in the believer. This is stated at the beginning of our verse: "That by two immutable things in which it is impossible for God to lie". These are, His promise and His oath. The assurance of the believer rests upon the unchanging veracity of God. Were He influenced by His creatures, God would be constantly changing His plans (as we do), willing one thing today and another to-morrow; in such case who could confide in Him? None, for no one would know what to expect; thus, all certainty would be at an end. But, blessed be His name, our God is "without variableness or shadow of turning" (James 1:17), and therefore the immutability of His counsel is the very life of our assurance.

For the stay of our hearts and the full assurance of our faith, God has graciously given to us an irrevocable deed of settlement, namely, His promise, followed by His oath, whereby the whole inheritance is infallibly secured unto every heir of promise. Heaven and earth shall pass away, but God's words never shall (Luke 21:33). All the promises recorded in Scripture are but copies of God's assurances made *to Christ* for us from everlasting, so that the Divine oaths and covenants mentioned in Holy Writ are but transcripts of the original Covenant and Oath between God and Christ before the foundation of the world. Note how the words "impossible for God to lie", link up with "in hope of eternal life, which God, that cannot lie, promised before the world began" (Titus 1:2)!

Near the close of the previous article we pointed out how that the deeper and spiritual significance of God's promise and oath to Abraham in Gen. 22 has been missed by most of the commentators, through their failure to see in him a type of Christ as the Head and Father of God's elect. There we find God swearing to the patriarch, "Blessing I will bless thee." The application of these words to Christ as the Representative of His people is clearly seen in Psa. 45:2, where God says to Him who is Fairer than the children of men, "God hath *blessed* Thee *forever*". Let it also be pointed out that God's promise and oath to David in Psa. 89 also gives an adumbration of

His transactions with the Mediator before the world began: "My Covenant will I not break . . . His seed shall endure forever" (vv. 34-36). Thus, our "strong consolation" issues from the implicit assurance that God has bound Himself in Christ *to* "bless" His people. "For all the promises of God *in Him* (Christ) are Yea, and in Him Amen" (2 Cor. 1:20)!

"Which (hope) we have as an anchor of the soul, both sure and steadfast, and which entereth into that within the veil" (v. 19). We deeply regret that we feel obligated to part company with every commentator that we have consulted on this verse. Owing to the general mistake of making the "hope" of v. 18 a subjective one, hardly any two are agreed upon the meaning of the "anchor" here. Some regard it as God's promise; others, His oath; others, Christ's priesthood; others, the believer's assurance; and so on. The only point upon which there is common consent is, that the figure is *dropped* in the very next clause!—"entereth into that within the veil". Below we give the literal rendering of Bagster's Interlinear.

"Which as an anchor we have of the soul both certain and firm, and entering into that within the veil". Now an anchor is used for securing a ship, particularly in times of storm, to prevent it from *drifting*. It is an *invisible* thing, sinking down beneath the waters and gripping firmly the ground beneath. The winds may roar and the waves lash the ship, but it rides them steadily, being held fast by something outside itself. Surely the figure is plain. The "anchor" is *Christ Himself,* sustaining His people down here in this world, in the midst of the wicked, who are likened unto "the troubled sea, when it cannot rest" (Isa. 57:20). Did He not declare, "Neither shall any pluck them out of My hand" (John 10:28)? Certainly there is nothing in us "both sure and steadfast": it is the love (John 13:1), power (Matt. 28:18, 20), and faithfulness (Heb. 7:25) of Christ which is in view.

"Whither the Forerunner is for us entered, Jesus, made an High Priest forever, after the order of Melchizedek" (v. 20). Surely this explains for us the previous verse: it was the entrance of Christ into Heaven which settles fast the "Anchor" within the veil! It was *for us* Christ has gone on High! A "forerunner" is one who has already traversed every step of the race which is set before us (12:1, 2), and who has entered into possession of that toward which he ran. Because Christ has been where we now are, we shall soon be where He now is. Thus, the force of this figurative title of our Redeemer is not only designed to give assurance of our security, but to show us *where* that security lies—entirely outside of ourselves: held fast by a triumphant and ascended Christ. Hence the force of His name here: "Jesus", who "*shall* save His people from their sins" (Matt. 1:21).

Condensing from Dr. Owen's excellent remarks:—Christ is a "Forerunner" *for us,* first, by way of *declaration.* It belongs unto a forerunner to carry tidings and declare what success has been obtained in the affair of which he is to render account. So when the Lord Christ entered Heaven, He made an open declaration of His victory by spoiling principalities and leading captivity captive: see Psa. 45:4-6, 68:18, 24-26. Second, by way of *preparation.* This He did by opening the way for our prayers and worship: 10:19-22 and making ready a place for us, John 14:2, 3. Third, by way of *occupation.* He has gone into Heaven, in our name, to take possession and reserve it for us: Acts 26:18, 1 Peter 1:4.

"Made an high priest forever, after the order of Melchizedek". Having warned us of our danger (5:11 to 6:8), having exhorted us to continue pressing forward (6:11-15), having assured our hearts of infallible preservation (6:16-19), the apostle now returns to the very point he had dropped at 5:10. This final clause of Heb. 6 forms a pertinent and perfect transition between the apostle's digression at 5:11 and onwards, and the description of Christ's priesthood which follows in chapter 7, etc. He now declares who and what that "Forerunner" was, who *for us has* gone on High, even Jesus, our great High Priest. The apostle *has* led us on to the "perfection" which he mentioned at the beginning of this chapter (6:1, 3)—Christ within the veil!

CHAPTER THIRTY

Melchizedek

(Heb. 7:1-3)

In 2:17 the apostle announced that the Lord Jesus is "a merciful and faithful High Priest in things pertaining to God", while in 3:1 he calls on those who are partakers of the heavenly calling to "Consider the Apostle and High Priest of our profession". Having shown in chapters 3 and 4 the superiority of Christianity's Apostle over Judaism's, viz, Moses, whose work was completed by Joshua, Paul then declared that "We have a great High Priest, that is passed through the heavens, Jesus the Son of God", an High Priest who can be touched with the feeling of our infirmities, seeing that He also was tempted in all points like us (in His spirit, His soul, and His body), sin excepted; for which reason we are bidden to "Come boldly unto the throne of grace, that we may obtain mercy, and find grace to help in time of need" (4:14-16).

In the opening verses of Heb. 5 we are shown how Christ fulfilled the Aaronic type, and how that He possessed every necessary perfection to qualify Him for filling the sacerdotal office, see articles 19 to 21. But while the Holy Spirit there shows how Christ provided the substance of what was foreshadowed by the Levitical priests, He is also particular to exhibit how that Christ excelled them at every point. Finally, he declares that the Lord Jesus was, "Called of God an High Priest after the order of Melchizedek" (v. 10). We have previously called attention to it, but as this detail is so important and so little understood, we repeat: it is highly essential to observe that Christ is *not* there said to be "High Priest *of* the order of Melchizedek", but "*after* the order of", etc. The difference between the two expressions is real and radical: "of" would have *limited* His priesthood to that particular order; "after" simply shows that there is a *resemblance* between them, as there also was between Aaron's and Christ's.

At 5:11 the apostle declared, "Of whom we have many things to say and hard to be uttered, seeing ye are dull of hearing". The *difficulty* lay in the strong disinclination of man to relinquish that which has long been cherished, which nowhere appears more evident than in connection with religious things. To say that Christ was a High Priest "after the order *of Melchizedek*" was tantamount to affirming that the *Aaronic* order was Divinely set aside, and with it, all the ordinances and ceremonies of the Mosaic law. "This", as we said in an earlier article, "was the hardest thing of all for a Hebrew, even a converted one, to bow to, for it meant repudiating everything that was seen, and cleaving to that which was altogether invisible. It meant forsaking that which their fathers had honoured for fifteen hundred years, and espousing that which the great majority of their brethren according to the flesh denounced as Satanic.

The Hebrews had become "dull of hearing". They were too slothful to make the effort needed for a proper understanding of the nature of Christ's priestly office and work. In 3:1 the apostle had called on them to, "*Consider* the Apostle and High Priest of our profession", and in 7:4 he again says, "Now *consider*". The Greek word means to "ponder intensely" to "behold diligently", to "*weigh* thoroughly" the things proposed unto us. It is at this point so many fail: they imagine all that is required of them is to *hear* the Word of God expounded, and if anything appears to them hard to understand, they conclude it is not for them; hence, they make little progress in Divine things and fail to "increase in the knowledge of God" (Col. 1:10). And this is not simply an "infirmity", it reveals a sad state of soul; it shows a lack of *interest* in spiritual things. This was the state of the Hebrews: they had gone back.

The condition of soul in which a Christian is has very much to do with his spiritual receptivity. He may hear the best of preaching and read the soundest of books, yet if his heart be not right with God, he will not be profited. His head knowledge of Truth may be increased and his pride puffed up, but his soul is not fed, nor is his walk influenced Godwards. It was thus with the Corinthians, therefore we find the apostle writing to them, "And I, brethren, could not speak unto you as unto spiritual, but as unto carnal, as babes in Christ" (1 Cor. 3:1). It was thus with the Hebrews: the spirit of the apostle was straitened. He longed to expound to them the excellency of the glories of Christ's priesthood, but he had to pause and address himself to their sorrowful state of heart. In this he has left an example which all teachers do well to weigh and imitate.

As we have seen, at 5:11 the apostle makes a digression, which is continued to the end of the 6th chapter. It is most instructive to observe the *order* he followed. The better to appreciate it, let us review the contents of this parenthetical section in their inverse order. In chapter 7, he sets forth the official glories of Christ. But what immediately precedes? This: at the close of 6 (vv. 16-20) he presents the sure ground which true Christians occupy for having a "strong consolation". Thus, it is only as the heart is set at perfect rest before God, fully assured of His favour, of His unchanging grace, that the soul is in any condition to ponder, to appreciate, to revel in the glories of Christ. It is faith's realization of the unceasing and effectual intercession of our great High Priest within the veil, which keeps the heart in peace. The contemplation of the essential Holiness of God would fill the soul with despair, but it is turned into hope and joy by seeing *Jesus* at His right hand "for us". The secret of victory is to be, in spirit, where our Forerunner is.

And what precedes the blessed assurance which the closing verses of 6 are designed to convey to the believer? This: a call to faithful perseverance in running the race set before us; a bidding of us "be not slothful, but followers of them who through faith and patience inherit the promises" (vv. 9-15). We are not entitled to the comfort which comes from resting upon the immutability of the Divine counsels while we are following a course of self-will and self-pleasing. Only those who are really walking with God have any right to the *joy* of His salvation. To talk of our certainty of reaching Heaven while out of the path of obedience, is nothing but a carnal presumption.

And what, in turn, precedes the call to a steady continuation in welldoing, to the exercise of faith and love? This: a solemn warning against the danger of apostasy (vv. 4-7). The sluggards of 5:11-14 must be aroused, the careless plainly told of what the final outcome would be were indifference to the righteous claims of God persisted in. There are some who refuse to allow that vv. 4-7 contain a warning given to real Christians against the danger of apostasy. They say it would be quite inconsistent for the Holy Spirit to so warn them, while in vv. 16-20 He gives the most absolute assurance of their security. Ah, but mark it well, the assurance in vv. 16-20 is for "the heirs of promise", and not for all professing believers. The warning is to make us examine ourselves and make sure that we *are* "heirs". This, the truly regenerate *will* do; whereas the self-complacent and presumptuous will ignore it, to their own eternal undoing.

In confirmation of what has been pointed out above, we quote the following from J. Owen: "As the minds of men are to be greatly prepared for the communication of spiritual mysteries unto them, so the best preparation is by the cure of their sinful and corrupt affections, with the removal of their barrenness under what they have already heard and been instructed in. It is to no purpose, yea, it is but the putting of new wine into old bottles to the loss of all, to be daily leading men into the knowledge of higher mysteries, whilst they live in a neglect of the practice of what they have been taught already".

At the close of his hortatory digression, the apostle returns to the precise point at which his orderly argument had been interrupted, as will immediately appear by comparing 5:10 and 6:20. Jesus was, and is for ever, High Priest. This was an entirely new doctrine for the Hebrews. Our Lord Himself had made no specific reference to it during the days of His earthly ministry, nor is there any record of it in the preaching of the apostles. Yet the teaching of both One and the others was based upon and assumed this fundamental fact. But now the Holy Spirit was pleased to give a clear unfolding of this precious truth. It was "hard" for even converted Jews to receive. Their chief objection would be that, to assert Christ was High Priest, yea, the *only* High Priest of His Church, was affirming something inconsistent with and contrary to the Law, for He did not (according to the flesh) belong to the Levitical tribe, He was not in the line of the priests.

It is most important for us to take account of this difficulty which presented itself to the minds of the Hebrews, for unless we recognize that one of the chief objects before the apostle in chapter 7 was to *remove* this very difficulty, we are certain to err in our understanding of the details of his argument. It was not the design of the apostle to teach that the nature and functions of Christ's priesthood had no resemblance to that of the Aaronic. Far from it. He could not now contradict all that he has so explicitly set forth in 5:1-9. There he had plainly shown that the Lord Jesus *had* fulfilled the Aaronic type by Himself offering to God a perfect and final Sacrifice for the sins of His people. To this he again returns in chapter 9, where he declares that Christ had (as Aaron foreshadowed) "by His own blood entered into the Holy Place, having obtained eternal redemption" (v. 12). Let it not be forgotten that the atoning ministry of Israel's high priest was consummated *within* the veil, Lev. 16:12-14.

In Heb. 7 the apostle proves that so far from the priestly office and work of the Lord Jesus conflicting with what God had instituted through Moses, it was the fulfilment of His own counsels as made known in the O.T. Scriptures. At the same time he takes occasion to submit the proof that the priesthood of Christ was far more glorious than that of Aaron's. This he does by an appeal to an ancient oracle, the mystical meaning of which had been hidden from the Jews, yea, the very letter of which appears to have been quite forgotten by them. We refer to the 110th Psalm, which will come before us in the course of examining our present chapter.

"For this Melchizedek, king of Salem, priest of the most high God" (v. 1). At the close of chapter 6 the Holy Spirit directs our gaze into the Holiest, whither for us the Forerunner hath entered, even Jesus our great High Priest. He now proceeds to emphasise the *dignity* of His priesthood, showing that it is accompanied by royal majesty, that it is intransmissible, and that it abideth forever. Thus our confidence in Him should be complete and entire, unwavering and unceasing. Thus too we may perceive again the immeasurable superiority of Christianity over Judaism by the super-excellency of its Priest.

"For this Melchizedek, king of Salem, priest of the most high God". The opening "For" has, we believe, a double connection. More immediately, it forms the closest possible link between what is declared in 6:20, and what is to immediately follow. There it was affirmed that "Jesus is made an High Priest *forever,* after the order of Melchizedek"; here it will be shown that thus it was, *mystically,* with Melchizedek himself. This will be the more apparent if the second half of v. 2 and the whole of v. 3, saving its final clause, be placed in a parenthesis, reading it thus: "For this Melchizedek, king of Salem, priest of the most high God, abideth a priest continually". More remotely the opening "For" of the verse, looks back to 5:10, 11: he now brings forth the "many things" he had to say to him.

"For this Melchizedek, king of Salem, priest of the most high God". Two things are here affirmed of Melchizedek: he was king, and he was priest. Almost endless conjectures have been made as to the *identity* of Melchizedek. Questions have been raised as to what order of beings he belonged to. Some have insisted that he was a Divine person, others that he was an angel, still others that he was Christ Himself in theophanic manifestation—as when He appeared to Joshua (Josh. 5:14), or in Babylon's furnace (Dan. 3:25), etc. Others, allowing that he was only a man, have speculated as to his nationality, family connections, and so on. But as the Holy Spirit has not seen fit to give us any information on these points, we deem it irreverence (Deut. 29:29) to indulge in any surmises thereon.

The first time Melchizedek is brought before us on the pages of Holy Writ is in Gen. 14. There he confronted Abraham, without introduction, in the land of Canaan. At that time all the world had fallen into the grossest of idolatry and the most awful immorality: Rom. 1:19-31. Even the progenitors of Abraham worshipped false gods: Josh. 24:2. At that time Canaan was inhabited chiefly by the Sodomites on the one hand (Gen. 13), and by the Amorites (Gen. 15:16) on the other. Yet, in the very midst of these people who were sinners above others, God was pleased to raise up a man who was an illustrious type of Christ! A signal instance was this of the absolute sovereignty of God. He can raise up instruments for His service and unto His glory, when, where, and as it pleases Him. He can raise up the greatest light in the midst of the greatest darkness: Matt. 4:16.

Melchizedek was "king of Salem": in the light of Psa. 76:2 there can be no doubt but what this was the earlier or original name for Jerusalem: "In Salem also is His tabernacle, and His dwelling-place in Zion". Only *Jerusalem* can there be intended. Further, Melchizedek was "priest of the most high God", and this in the days of Abraham! Thus, Jerusalem had a king many centuries before David, and God had a priest which He owned long ere Aaron was called! It has been rightly pointed out that, "The argument of the apostle, deducing and illustrating the superiority of Christ's priesthood over the Aaronic, from and by the relation of Melchizedek to the Levitical priesthood, is in some respects analogous to the argument of the apostle with regard to the law, and its parenthetical and inferior position, as compared with the Gospel . . . the Jews were shocked when the apostle Paul taught that it was not necessary for the Gentiles to observe the law; that for the new covenant church the law of Moses was no longer the rule and form of life. And therefore the apostle in his epistle to the Galatians, tells them that the law was given four hundred years after the promise had been made unto Abraham, and that therefore there was no injustice, and no inconsistency, in the bringing in of a new dispensation, which was in fact only a return in a fuller and more perfect manner to that which was from the beginning in the mind of God" (A. Saphir).

There is, indeed, a still closer analogy than has been pointed out by Mr. Saphir between Paul's argument in Heb. 7 and that which he used to the Galatians. Melchizedek was the king-priest of Jerusalem. Now in Gal. 4:26 we are told that, "Jerusalem which is above, is free, which is the mother of us all". The word "above" there has misled almost all of the commentators. The primary reference is not to location, but to *time,* it is antithetical from "now is", *not,* from "below"! In the immediate context the apostle contrasts two covenants, each of which was associated with a city. Paul there calls attention to the fact that the "promise" which God made to Abraham both preceded and outlasted the law! so too does the "Jerusalem" of the promise. Melchizedek was connected with Jerusalem before the Law was first given, and it was a type of Heaven: Heb. 11:10, etc.

It is indeed striking to discover that God's first priest was this king of Salem—which signifies "peace", Jerusalem meaning "the foundation of peace". Jerusalem was to be the place where the incarnate Son of God was to begin the exercise of His sacerdotal office; moreover, it was to be the seat of His local church (Acts 1 to 15) until the significance of the type had been effected. In the history of that unique city we see the sovereign pleasure of God again exercised and exemplified, for He appoints various intervals of blessing unto places. Jerusalem was first privileged with the presence of this priest of the most high God. Afterwards, for a long season, it was given over to the idolatrous Jebusites: see Josh. 15:63, 2. Sam. 5:6,etc. Then, in process of time, it was again visited with Divine favour and made the headquarters of the solemn worship of Jehovah. Now, as for centuries past, it is "trodden down of the Gentiles" (Luke 21:24). But in the future it will again be the centre of Divine blessing on earth: Isa. 2:1-4. In like manner God hath dealt with many another place and city.

"Who met Abraham returning from the slaughter of the kings, and blessed him" (v. 1). The historical reference is to Gen. 14:18, 19. "Whether any intercourse had previously taken place between these two venerable men, or whether they afterwards continued to have occasional intercourse, we cannot tell; though the probability seems to be, that Melchizedek was not a stranger to Abraham when he came forth to meet him, and that, in an age when the worshippers of the true God were comparatively few, two such men as Abraham and Melchizedek did not live in the same district and country without forming a close intimacy" (Dr. J. Brown).

"And blessed him". This was a part of the priestly office as we learn from Deut. 21:5: "And the priests the sons of Levi shall come near for the Lord thy God hath chosen to minister unto Him, and *to bless* in the name of the Lord". The "blessing" Abraham received, is recorded in Gen. 14:19: "Blessed be Abraham of the most high God, Possessor of heaven and earth". Absolutely, only God can either bless or curse, for He only has sovereign power over all good and evil. This power He exercises directly (Gen. 12:3): yet by a gracious concession and by His institution, God also allows men to invoke blessings on others. In the O.T. we find parents blessing their children (Gen. 9:26, 27:27, 48:20, etc.), and the priests blessing the people (Num. 6:24-26).

In both instances it was *Christ* that was typically in view. "In the blessing of Abraham by Melchizedek, all believers are virtually blessed by Jesus Christ,—Melchizedek was a type of Christ, and represented Him in what He was and did, as our apostle declares. And Abraham in all these things, bare the person of, or represented, all his posterity according to the faith. Therefore doth our apostle in the foregoing chapter entitle all believers, unto the promises made unto him, and the inheritance of them. There is, therefore, more than a bare story in this matter. A blessing is in it conveyed unto all believers in the way of an ordinance forever" (J. Owen). It deserves to be noticed that the final act of Christ ere leaving this earth was that "He led them out as far as to Bethany, and He lifted up His hands, and *blessed* them" (Luke 24:50).

"To whom also Abraham gave a tenth part of all" (v. 2). Melchizedek's "blessing" of Abraham was the *exercise* of his priesthood; Abraham's paying him tithes was the *recognition* of it. Abraham had just obtained a most memorable victory over the kings of Canaan, and now in his making an offering to Melchizedek, he acknowledged that it was God who had given him the victory and owned that Melchizedek was His servant. Under the Mosaic dispensation we find the Levitical priests were supported by the tithes of the people: Num. 18:24. In like manner, God's servants today ought to be so maintained: 1 Cor. 9:9, 10. Melchizedek's receiving of Abraham's tithe was a sacerdotal act: it was given as *to God,* and received by *His* officer in this world. This comes out plainly in the apostle's reasoning thereon in the later verses.

"First being by interpretation King of righteousness, and after that also King of Salem, which is King of peace" (v. 2). The Holy Spirit now gives us the mystical signification of the proper names used in the previous verse, which conveys more than a hint to us that there is nothing meaningless or superfluous in the perfect Word of God. Everything has an "interpretation". "In the Scripture everything is of importance; we cannot read and interpret the Scripture as any other book, since Scripture is not like any other book, even as no other book is like the Scripture. The Scripture is among books what the man Christ Jesus is among men . . . These quotations and expositions of Scripture in Scripture are 'grapes of Eshcol', examples of, not exceptions to, the fruitful Carmel, whence they come. Thus who can fail to see the significance of the name Seth , who was given instead of Abel, one who was 'firm and enduring' in the place of him who 'vanished'? or of the name of Joshua (God's Saviour), who brought Israel into the promised land"? (A. Saphir).

This 2nd verse of Heb. 7 furnishes a clear and decisive proof of the *verbal* inspiration of the Scriptures. The revelation which God has given to us was not communicated in the rough, and then left to men to express it in their own words. No; so far from that being the case, every "jot and tittle" of the originals were given under the immediate superintendence of the Holy Spirit. "Hence the names of persons and places, the omissions of circumstances, the use of the singular or plural number, the application of a title—all things are under the control of the all-wise and gracious Spirit of God. Compare Paul's commentary on the word 'all' in Psa. 8:7, and the important deductions from it in Heb. 2:8 and 1 Cor. 15:27; on the word 'new' Jer. 31, Heb. 8:13; the singular 'seed' Gal. 3:16. What a wonderful superstructure is built on Psa. 110:4! Each word is full of most important and blessed meaning. In Psa. 32:1, 2 no mention is made of works, hence Rom. 4:6" (A. Saphir).

Let us consider now the "interpretation" which is here given us. Melchizedek means "king of righteousness" and Salem "king of peace". But observe it well that the Holy Spirit has also emphasized the *order* of these two: "first" king of righteousness, "after that also" king of peace. This calls attention to another important and blessed detail in our type. Doubtless, the historical Melchizedek was both a righteous and peaceable king, but what the apostle here takes up is not the personal characteristics of this man, but how he represented Christ in His mediatorial office and work. Now the "*King* of righteousness" and "of peace" is the Author, Cause, and Dispenser of righteousness and peace. Christ is the Maker and Giver of peace because He is "the Lord our righteousness" (Jer. 23:6). Righteousness must go first, and then peace will follow after. This is the uniform order of Scripture wherever the two are mentioned together: peace never precedes righteousness. Mark well the following passages:

"Surely His salvation is nigh them that fear Him; that glory may dwell in our land. Mercy and truth are met together: righteousness and peace have kissed" (Psa. 85:9, 10). "And the work of righteousness shall be peace; and the effect of righteousness quietness and assurance forever" (Isa. 32:17). "In His days shall the righteous flourish; and abundance of peace so long as the moon endureth" (Psa. 72:7). Jesus Christ is "the Righteous" One (1 John 2:1). He came here to "fulfill all righteousness" (Matt. 3:15), to "magnify the law and make it honourable" (Isa. 42:21). He came here as the vicarious Representative of His people, being made under the law for them (Gal. 4:4), obeying the law for them (Matt. 5:17), and thus wrought out a perfect obedience for them (Rom 5:19). Therefore are they made "the righteousness of God in Him" (2 Cor. 5:21). He also came here to pacify the wrath of God against His people's sins (Eph. 2:3) to be a propitiation (Rom. 3:25), to "make peace through the blood of His cross" (Col. 1:20). Hence we are told, "Therefore being justified by faith we have peace with God through our Lord Jesus Christ" (Rom. 5:1).

How minutely accurate, then, how Divinely perfect was the type! The very word Melchizedek means "King of righteousness", while the name of his capitol signifies "peace". Well did J. Owen remark: "I am persuaded that God Himself, by some providence of His, or other intimation of His mind, gave that name of 'peace' first unto that city, because there He designed not only to rest in His typical worship for a season, but also in the fulness of time, there to accomplish the great work of peace-making between Himself and mankind . . . Wherefore our apostle doth justly argue from the signification of those names which were given, both to the person and place, by divine authority and guidance, that they might teach and fore-signify the things whereunto by him they are applied".

Christ is not only the Producer of righteousness and the Maker and Giver of peace, but He is also the *King* of both. All authority has been given to Him in heaven and in earth (Matt. 28:18). He is, even now, upholding all things by the word of His power (Heb. 1:3). He is expressly declared to be "the blessed and only Potentate, the King of kings and the Lord of lords" (1 Tim. 6:15). In the Millennium this will be openly demonstrated here upon earth. Then it will appear to all that He is a *righteous* Branch, for as King He shall "reign and prosper, and shall execute judgment and justice in the earth" (Jer. 23:5), and, as Isa. 9:7 tells us, "Of the increase of His government *and peace* there shall be no end". Meanwhile, faith views Him today as King, King of righteousness and King of peace.

"Without father, without mother, without pedigree, having neither beginning of days, nor end of life; but made like unto the Son of God" (v. 3). Up to this point everything has been plain and simple, but here, judging from the labourious strugglings of most expositors, we enter deep water. Yet, in reality, it is not so. Men, as usual, have created their own difficulty; and, as is generally the case, they have done so through ignoring the immediate context. Had these statements in v. 3 referred to him as a *man,* it would surely be quite impossible to understand them. But it is not as man he is referred to, but as *priest.* Once this is clearly seen and firmly grasped little or no difficulty remains.

That Melchizedek was not a superhuman creature, a divine or angelic being, is unequivocally established by Heb. 5:1, where we are expressly told, "For *every* high priest taken *from among men* is ordained for men in things pertaining to God". To be possessed of human nature is an essential prerequisite in order for one to occupy and exercise the sacerdotal office. The Son of God could not serve as Priest till He became incarnate. Observe carefully how that in v. 4 Melchizedek is expressly declared to be a "man". What, then, it may be asked, is the meaning of the strange statements about him in v. 3? We answer, their meaning is to be explained on the principle of the apostle's subject in this passage.

"Without father, without mother, without descent". Now in connection with the Aaronic priesthood, personal genealogy was a vital prerequisite, hence the great care with which they preserved their pedigree: see Ezra 2:61, 62. But, in contradistinction from them, Melchizedek was priest of an order where natural descent was not regarded, an order free from the restrictions of the Levitical, Num. 3:10, etc; therefore was he an accurate type of Christ, who belonged not to the tribe of Levi. Neither the book of Genesis, nor any of the later scriptures, say a word about Melchizedek's parentage, and this *silence* was a part of the type.

"Having neither beginning of days nor end of life" is to be explained on the same principle. The Jewish priests "began" their "days" *as priests* at the age of twenty-five, when they were permitted to wait upon their brethren: Num. 8:24 and cf. 1 Chron. 23:27, 28. At the age of thirty they began their regular priestly duties: Num. 4:3. At the age of fifty their *priestly* "life" ended: "from the age of fifty years they shall *cease* waiting upon the service, and shall serve no more" (Num. 8:25). But no such restriction was placed upon the sacerdotal ministry of Melchizedek: so, in this too, he was an eminent type of Christ.

"But made like unto the Son of God", or, more literally "but assimilated to the Son of God". It is very striking to note that it is not the Son of God who was "assimilated to Melchizedek", but vice versa. In the order of *time* Christ subsisted before Melchizedek; in the order of *nature,* Melchizedek was a priest before Christ was. The priesthood of the Son of God, ordained and appointed by the Eternal Three, was the *original,* and Melchizedek's priesthood furnished the *copy,* and a copy *given in advance* is the same thing as the type. Melchizedek was "assimilated to the Son of God" as a type. First, as priest of the most high God. Second, as being a royal priest, possessing personal majesty and authority. Third, as being the king of righteousness. Fourth, as king of peace. Fifth, as the one who "blessed Abraham". Sixth, as the one who received the grateful gifts of God's people represented by Abraham. Seventh, as not owing his priesthood to natural genealogy. Eighth, as abiding a priest beyond the bounds of the Levitical limitations.

"Abideth a priest continually" (v. 3). Note carefully it is not that the *natural* life of Melchizedek had no end, but that his *priestly* life did not cease at the age of fifty; in other words, he continued a priest to the very end of his earthly existence, which shows he had no vicar or successor, deriving a priesthood from his. "The expression 'abideth a priest *continually*', therefore, is the equivalent to saying that he had a *perpetual priesthood* in contradistinction from those whose office terminated at a definite period, or whose office passed over into the hands of others" (A. Barnes). In the verses that follow, the apostle reasons from these facts and shows the superiority of Melchizedek as a priest to Aaron and his sons. This, D. V. will come before us in our next article.

CHAPTER THIRTY-ONE

Melchizedek, Continued

(Heb. 7:4-10)

The chief design of the apostle in this chapter was not to declare the *nature* of Christ's priesthood, nor to describe the exercise thereof; instead, he dwells upon the *excellency* of it. The nature of Christ's sacerdotal office had been treated of in the first half of chap. 5 and is dealt with again, at length, in chap. 9. But here he occupies us with the great *dignity* of it. His reason for so doing was to display the immeasurable superiority of Christianity's High Priest over that of Judaism's, and that, that the faith of the Hebrews might be established and their hearts drawn out in love and worship to Him. Unless the scope of the apostle's theme in this chapter be clearly apprehended, it is well-nigh impossible to appreciate and understand the details of his argument.

The proof for the *excellency* of Christ's priesthood is drawn from the O.T. In His written Word God had given hints of an alteration from the Levitical priesthood, and the introduction of another more efficacious and glorious. It is true that those hints were of such a character that their signification could not be perceived at the time, for it is "the glory of God to *conceal* a thing" (Prov. 25:2), and this (in part) that His creatures may be taught their complete dependency upon Him, and that He may have the honour of *revealing* what they by mere searching cannot find out. He has chosen to make known His counsels gradually, so that "the path of the just is as the shining light, that shineth *more and more* unto the perfect day" (Prov. 4:18).

As "life and immortality", so all spiritual truth, was brought to light by the Gospel (2 Tim. 1:10). Much truth was enfolded in the prophecies, promises, and institutions of the O.T., yet in such a way as that it was in a great measure incomprehensible until God's time came to unfold them (1 Peter 1:10, 11). The great secret of the manifold wisdom of God was hidden in Himself from the beginning of the world (Eph. 3:9, 10), yet not so absolutely so, that no intimation of it had been given. But it had been given in *such* a way in the Scriptures that much was obscure to the understanding of the saints in all generations till it was interpreted and displayed by the Gospel. More than once we read of Israel's chief seer and singer speaking of inclining his ear unto a "parable" and opening his "*dark* saying" upon the harp (Psa. 49:4, 78:2). In sharp contrast therefrom, in the N.T. dispensation, "the darkness is past, and the true light *now* shineth" (1 John 2:8).

In consequence of the fuller revelation which God has made to us through the Gospel, all the glorious evidences of His grace which now appear unto us in the O.T. Scriptures, is in consequence of a *reflection* of light upon them from the N.T. This it is which supplies the key to our present Epistle. In Luke 24:27 we read of how Christ began at Moses and the prophets, expounding unto the two disciples who were journeying to Emmaus, "the things concerning Himself", while in v. 45 we are told that He "opened the understanding" of the eleven "that they might understand the Scriptures". It has been thought by some (and we deem it quite probable) that in this very Hebrews' Epistle the Holy Spirit has recorded for *our* instruction and joy the very things which the risen Saviour communicated to those two favoured disciples. Whether this be the case or no, certain it is that the leading design of the Spirit in this Epistle is to give us light on many O. T. mysteries by means of the fuller revelation which God has now made by and through Jesus Christ.

A notable illustration and example of this principle appears in the case of Melchizedek, the priest-king. That strange and striking individual is first introduced to us in the sacred narrative in Gen. 14. Then a single verbal reference is made to him again in the 110th Psalm, and nothing more is said of him in the O. T. Therefore we need not be surprised that the Jews appear to have given little or no consideration to him. It is not until he is contemplated in the light of the N. T. that we are able to discern in him an eminent type of Christ. This we sought to examine in our last article, all that we now emphasise is that the chief points which the apostle dwells upon are that Melchizedek had neither predecessor nor successor in his sacred office. Melchizedek did not belong to a *line* of priests as did Eleazar, Eli, etc. It was in *this* respect, more especially, that he was "made like unto the Son of God", our great High Priest.

The various appellations under which our Lord is referred to in this Epistle call for due attention. They are not used at haphazard, but with precision and design. In 2:9 it is "Jesus" that faith beholds—the humiliated but now glorified Saviour. In 3:6 it is "Christ", the Anointed One, who is over God's house. But in 7:3

it is "the Son of God", as High Priest, unto whom Melchizedek was made a similitude. The Spirit here jealously guards the honour of Him whom it is His office and delight to glorify. He hereby intimates to the Hebrews that though Melchizedek were such an excellent person, yet he was infinitely beneath Him whom he represented. The typical person was but man; the antitype, Divine! Furthermore, one who was more than mortal was required in order to fulfil that which Melchizedek foreshadowed: he who should be capable of discharging an always-living, constant-abiding, uninterrupted priesthood, *must* be "the Son of God"!

In the first three verses of Heb. 7 the apostle mentions those details in which Melchizedek resembled the great and glorious Priest of Christianity; in vv. 4 to 10 he *applies* the type unto his immediate purpose and design. Having affirmed that Christ, the promised Messiah, was a Priest after the order of Melchizedek (6:20), and having given a description of the person and office of that typical character from the inspired narrative of Moses (Gen. 14:), he now dwells upon various details in the type in order to establish the argument which he has in hand. That which the apostle particularly designed to prove, was that a more excellent priesthood than that of Aaron's, having been introduced according to the purpose and promise of God, it necessarily followed that the ceremonies and institutions connected with it had now been abolished.

"Now consider how great this man was, unto whom even the patriarch Abraham gave the tenth of the spoils" (v. 4). The apostle here calls upon the Hebrews to attentively mark and seriously ponder the official dignity of this ancient servant of God. The word "man" has been supplied by the translators, and should have been placed in italics. In the Greek it is simply "now consider how great this", i.e. royal priest. Think of how great he "must have been", seems preferable to "was". His exalted rank appears from the fact that none other than Abraham, the father and head of Israel, had shown him deference.

The force of the apostle's reasoning here is easily perceived. To give tithes to another who is the servant of God is a token of official respect, it is the recognition and acknowledgement of his superior status. The value of such official tokens is measured by the dignity and rank of the person making them. Now Abraham was a person of very high dignity, both naturally and spiritually. Naturally he was the founder of the Jewish nation; spiritually he was the "father" of all believers (Rom. 4). In his person was concentrated all the sacred dignity belonging to the people of God. How "great" then must be Melchizedek, seeing that Abraham himself owned his official superiority! And therefore how "great" must be that *order* of priesthood to which he belonged!

That upon which the Jews insisted as their chief and fundamental privilege, and which they were unwilling to forego, was the greatness of their ancestors, considered as the high favorites of God. They so gloried in Abraham and their being *his* children, that they opposed this to the person and doctrine of Christ Himself (John 8:33, 53). With regard to official dignity, they looked upon Aaron and his successors as to be preferred above all the world. Whilst they clung to such fleshly honours, the Gospel of Christ, which addressed them as lost sinners, could not be but distasteful to them. To disabuse their minds, to demonstrate that those in whom they trusted came far short in dignity, honour, and greatness, of the true High Priest, the apostle presses upon them the eminence of him who was a type of Christ, and shows that the greatest of all their ancestors paid obeisance to him.

Three proofs of the eminence of Melchizedek are found in the verse before us. First, in the nomination of the person that was subject unto him: "*even* Abraham". Second, in the dignity of Abraham; "the patriarch". Third, in that Abraham gave him a tenth of the spoils. Abraham was not only the root and stock of the Israelitish people, but he was the one who first received the promise of the covenant (Gen. 15:18); therefore they esteemed him next unto God Himself. A "patriarch" is a father, prince or ruler of a family. The sons of Jacob are thus denominated (Acts 7:8, 9), for the twelve tribes descended from them. None else is termed a "patriarch" except David (Acts 2:29), and he, because the royal family came from his loins. But David and Jacob's sons, all sprang from Abraham, thus was he, pre-eminently, "*the* patriarch". Yet great as Abraham was, Melchizedek was still greater, for he was "priest of the most high God", and as such the father of the faithful owned him.

Let us not miss the *practical* lesson which the above facts teach us. Therein we learn of what *true* "greatness" consists. The Christian is to measure things by a different standard from that which worldlings employ. They look upon those who occupy prominent social and political positions as being the eminent of the earth. The vulgar mind esteems the wealthy and opulent as those who are most to be envied. But the anointed eye sees things in another light: the fashion of this world passeth away. Death levels all distinctions. Presidents and millionaires, kings and queens, are no more than the poorest beggar when their bodies are reduced to lifeless clay. And what of their souls? Ah, what concern have such after *eternal* interests? Learn, my reader, that true "greatness" consists in the favour of God and our nearness to Him. The meanest of His saints have been made "kings and priests unto God" (Rev. 1:6).

Ere leaving this verse, a few words need to be said upon the subject of *tithing*. There are few things on which many of the Lord's people are more astray than the matter of giving to His cause and work. Are our offerings to be regulated by sentiment and impulse, or by principle and conscience? That is only another way of asking, Does God leave us to the promptings of gratitude and generosity, or has He definitely specified His mind and stated *what* portion of His gifts to us are due Him in return? Surely He has not left this important point undefined. He has given us His Word to be a lamp unto our feet, and therefore He cannot have left us in darkness concerning any obligation or privilege that pertains to our dealings with Him.

At a very early date the Lord made it known that a definite portion of the saints' income should be devoted to Him who is the Giver of all. There was a period of twenty-five centuries from Adam until the time that God gave the law to Israel at Sinai, but it is a great mistake to suppose that His people were, at that time, without a definite communication from Him upon their several duties. A careful study of the book of Genesis reveals clear traces of a primitive revelation, which seems to have centered about these things: the offering of sacrifices to God, the observance of the Sabbath, and the giving of tithes. While we cannot today place our finger upon any positive enactment or command of God for any of those three things in those early days, nevertheless, from what *is* recorded we are *compelled* to assume that such must have been given.

No one can point to a "thus saith the Lord" requiring Noah to offer a sacrifice to Him, nor can we assign chapter and verse giving a command for the saints to tithe ere the law was given; yet is it impossible to account for either without presupposing a revelation of God's mind on those points. The fact that Abraham *did* give a tithe or tenth to Melchizedek, intimates that he acted in accordance with God's will. So too the words of Jacob in Gen. 28:22 suggests the same thing. This principle of recognizing God's ownership and owning His goodness, was later incorporated into the Mosaic law: Lev. 27:30. Finally, it is taken note of here in Heb. 7, and in the humble judgment of the writer the passage which is before us presents an argument which admits of no refutation. Abraham paid tithes to Melchizedek, and Abraham is the father of all that believe (Rom. 4; Gal. 3). He is the pattern man of faith. He is the outstanding exemplar of the stranger and pilgrim on earth whose Home is in Heaven. Melchizedek is the type of Christ. If then Abraham gave the tithe to Melchizedek, most assuredly every Christian should give tithes to Christ, our great High Priest.

"And verily they that are of the sons of Levi, who receive the office of the priesthood, have a commandment to take tithes of the people according to the law, that is, of their brethren, though they come out of the loins of Abraham; But he whose descent is not counted from them received tithes of Abraham, and blessed him that had the promises" (vv. 5, 6). In these verses the apostle strengthens the argument drawn from the important facts presented in v. 4, while at the same time he anticipates and obviates any counter argument which might be advanced against him. His argument consists of two parts: Abraham gave tithes to Melchizedek, Abraham was blest by him. In response, the Jews might reply, *That* does not establish the superiority of Melchizedek over the Levitical order, for the Aaronic priesthood also received tithes. To this the apostle answers by pointing out that Aaron's sons were all descended from Abraham, and therefore they, in their progenitor, paid tithes to the royal priest of Jerusalem, and by so doing owned his pre-eminence. Let us amplify this analysis.

In v. 5 the apostle acknowledges that God had granted the Levitical priests the right to receive tithes from His people (Num. 18:21-24), and thus they were set above all other Israelites; nevertheless, they too had "come out of the loins of Abraham", and inasmuch as *he* had given a tenth to a priest of another order, his descendants were therefore inferior to *that* priest. Moreover, the Levites had "received" the priestly office, and accepted tithes by command "according to the law". Thus, the Aaronic priesthood was wholly *derived* in its functions and privileges. But not so Melchizedek's. *He* was under no law. He was "king", as well as priest, and therefore belonged to a superior order. In this also he was a type of Christ, who, by virtue of His Divine nature, has authority *in Himself,* to receive and to bless. The words "take tithes . . . of their brethren" finds its counterpart in 1 Cor. 9:11-14. The Aaronic priesthood was not supported by a tax levied on the idolatrous Canaanites, but by the gifts of the Lord's people!

The manner in which the apostle expresses himself in v. 5 deserves our closest notice, his language plainly intimating that his eye was on the high sovereignty of God. Observe that he did not simply say, "the priests have a commandment to take tithes", but "they that are *of* the sons of Levi". God distributed dignity and bestowed office in His Church (Acts 7:38) as it pleased Him. Not all the posterity of Abraham were set apart to receive tithes, and not all who belonged to the tribe of Levi; but only the family of Aaron was called to the priesthood. This appointment of His imperial will God required all to submit to: Num. 16:9, 10. It was something new to Israel to see the whole tribe of Levi taken into peculiar (official) nearness to Jehovah; yet to it they submitted. But when the "priests" were taken *out of* the tribe of Levi and exalted above all, some rebelled: Num. 16:1-3, etc.

The same principle holds good today. It is true, blessedly true, and God forbid that we should say a word to weaken it, that all believers enjoy equal nearness to God, that every one of them belongs to that "holy priesthood" who are to "offer up spiritual sacrifices acceptable to God by Jesus Christ" (1 Peter 2:5). Nevertheless, all believers are *not* called by God to occupy the same position of ministerial honour, all are not called to be preachers of His Gospel or teachers of His Word (James 3:1). God calls and equips whom He pleases to engage in His public service, and bids the rank and file of His people "obey them that have the rule over you, and submit yourselves" (Heb. 13:17). Yet, sad to say, in some circles the sin of Korah is repeated. They demand an ecclesiastical socialism, where any and all are allowed to speak. They "*heap* to themselves teachers" (2 Tim. 4:3). This ought not to be.

In v. 6 the apostle repeats the same thing he had said in v. 2. The Levitical priesthood received tithes from those descended from Abraham, and that was an evidence of official dignity conferred upon them by God's appointment. But Melchizedek received tithes of Abraham himself, which not only manifested his superiority to Aaron but to him from whom Aaron sprang. The apostle's insisting on this so particularly shows how difficult a matter it is to dispossess the minds of men of things which they have long held and in which they boast. The Jews clung tenaciously to their descent from Abraham, in fact rested upon it for salvation. Much patience is required in order to deal faithfully but lovingly with those in error. "In *meekness* instructing those that oppose themselves" (2 Tim. 2:25) is a needed word for every teacher.

Melchizedek not only received tithes from Abraham, but he actually pronounced blessing upon him, which was a further evidence of his official superiority to the patriarch. To make this detail the more emphatic, the apostle stresses the dignity of Abraham, for the more glorious he was, the more illustrious the dignity of the one qualified to pronounce a benediction upon him. Thus Abraham is here referred to as he who "had the promises". He was the first of the Israelitish race with whom God made the covenant of life. It was no ordinary honour which Jehovah conferred upon the father of the faithful. As the immediate result of his receiving the promises, Abraham "saw" the Day of Christ (John 8:56). Yet great as was the privilege and honour bestowed upon Abraham it did not hinder him from showing subjection to Melchizedek, God's vicegerent.

There is an important practical lesson for us in v. 6. The one who had received the "promises" of God was now blest! Ah, we may have the promises of God stored in our minds and at our tongue's end, but unless we also have the blessing of God, what do they avail us? Moreover, it is particularly, the blessing *of Christ* (typified by Melchizedek) which makes the promises of God effectual to us. Christ is Himself the great subject of the promises (2 Cor. 1:20), and the whole blessing of them comes forth from Him alone (Eph. 1:3). In Him, from Him, and by Him, are all blessings to be obtained. Apart from Christ all are under the curse.

"And without all contradiction the less is blessed of the better" (v. 7). This verse summarises the argument contained in vv. 4-6. "These words are plainly to be understood with limitations. It does not follow that, because a priest under the law blessed the king, he was in a civil capacity the king's superior, any more than that a Christian minister instructing or even reproving a man of high civil rank who is a member of the church of which he is pastor, is civilly his superior. The apostle's argument is: The person who accepts of priestly benediction from an individual acknowledges his spiritual superiority, just as the highest authority in the land, if he were becoming a member of a voluntary Christian society, would acknowledge that its pastor was 'over him in the Lord' " (John Brown).

"Let us first know what the word *blessed* means here. It means indeed a solemn praying, by which he who is invested with some high and public honour, recommends to God men in private stations and under his ministry. Another way of blessing is when we pray for one another, which is commonly done by all the godly. But this blessing mentioned by the apostle was a symbol of greater authority. Thus Isaac blessed his son Jacob, and Jacob himself blessed his grandsons (Gen. 27:30, 48:15). This was not done mutually, for the son could not do like the father; but a higher authority was required for such a blessing as this. And this appears more evident still from Num. 6:23, where a command is given to the priest to bless the people, and then a promise is immediately added, that they would be blessed whom they blessed. It hence appears that the blessing of the priest depended on this,—that it was not so much man's blessing as that of God. For as the priest in offering sacrifices represented Christ, so in blessing the people he was nothing more than a minister and legate of the supreme God" (John Calvin).

The application of the principles expressed by the above writers to the case in hand is apparent. The blessing of the priest in O. T.

times (type of Christ's blessing His people now), though pronounced as the minister of God, was an evidence of high honour of the one uttering it. Though Abraham was more eminent than any of his descendants, yet he himself was indebted to the royal priest of Jerusalem.

"And here men that die receive tithes; but there he of whom it is witnessed that he liveth" (v. 8). Here the apostle advances a further argument to support his demonstration of the inferiority of the Aaronic order of priesthood to the Melchizedekean: the "here" referring to the former, the "there" to the latter as stated in Gen. 14. The point singled out for notice is that, the Levitical order of office was but temporary, not so of that priest who blest Abraham. "The type is described as having no end; the order of priesthood which it represents is therefore eternal" (Calvin). The Scripture makes no mention of the death of Melchizedek when it relates that tithes were paid to him; so the authority of his priesthood is limited to no time, but on the contrary there is given an intimation of perpetuity.

Some have stumbled over the statement here made about Melchizedek: "it is witnessed that he liveth". These words have been appealed to in proof that he was a superhuman being. But if this statement be interpreted in the light of its context, there is no difficulty. It was not absolutely and personally that Melchizedek still lived, but typically and as a representation of Christ. Scripture frequently attributes to the type what is found alone in the antitype. Thus, the paschal lamb was expressly called *God's* passover (Ex. 12:11), when in reality it was only a pledge and token thereof. So the emblems on the Lord's table are denominated the body and blood of Christ, because they *represent* such. The blessedness of this detail will come before us, D. V., in the later verses.

"And as I may so say, Levi also, who receiveth tithes, paid tithes in Abraham. For he was yet in the loins of his father, when Melchizedek met him" (vv. 9, 10). In these verses the apostle meets the last objection which a carping Jew could make upon the subject. Against what the apostle had been saying, it might be advanced: Granting that Abraham himself paid tithes to Melchizedek, it does not follow that Melchizedek was superior to all Abraham's descendants. Abraham was, in some sense, a priest (Gen. 12:7), yet he was not so by virtue of any office which God had instituted in His Church. But in the days of Moses, Jehovah did institute an order and office of priesthood in the family of Aaron, and were not they, by Divine appointment, superior, because superceding the earlier order of Melchizedek? This the apostle makes reply to.

Many find it difficult to follow his line of thought, and that, because they are so ill-acquainted with the most important truth of headship and representation. Let us quote here from F. S. Sampson, "Abraham was truly the covenant-head of his posterity in the line of Isaac and Jacob, in whose descendants the promises made to him were fulfilled. It was in virtue of this covenant with Abraham, that the Jews inherited their distinguished privileges as a nation. It was the transaction with Abraham which brought them into the relation of a 'peculiar people' to Jehovah; and hence, in his patriarchal character and acts, he stood forth as the representative or federal head of the nation, so far as all the promises, privileges, and institutions of the Judaical were concerned. He was both their natural progenitor and their covenant-head, by the appointment of God. We must remember that He was concerned, through His providence and promises, in all this business. Therefore, when Abraham paid tithes to Melchizedek as a priest of the most High God, and received a blessing from him, it was a historical fact intentionally introduced by God's providence, with a view to its becoming a feature of the type (so to speak) which Melchizedek, in his history and functions, was foreordained to present, of the supreme and eternal High Priest. This providential incident prefigured and represented, by the Divine intention, the supremacy of the antitype; and in it Abraham acknowledged the official superiority of the type, not only over himself, but over his posterity then in his loins, represented by and acting in him".

The principle of federal representation lies at the very base of all God's dealings with men, as a careful study of Rom. 5:12-19 and 1 Cor. 15:45-47 reveals. Adam stood for and transacted on the behalf of the whole human race, so that what he did, they *legally* did; hence his sin, guilt and death, are imputed to all his posterity, and God deals with them accordingly. So too Christ stood for and transacted on the behalf of all His seed, so that what He did, they *legally* did; hence, His meeting the demands of the law, His death and resurrection-life, are imputed to all who believe on Him. In like manner, Abraham stood for and transacted on the behalf of all his posterity, so that God's covenanting with him, is to be regarded as His covenanting with them also. Proof of this is found in the title *here* (and nowhere else) given to Abraham, viz., "the patriarch" (v. 4), which means, head or father of a people.

Thus the apostle here brings to a head his argument by pointing out that, virtually and representatively (not personally and actually), Levi himself had paid tithes to Melchizedek. We repeat, that Abraham in Genesis is not to be considered only as a private individual, but also as the head and representative of all his children.

When Abraham gave tithes he did so not only in his own name, but also in that of all his descendants. Abraham had been called of God and separated to His service as the head of His elect people. There was more than a natural relation between him and his descendants. Jehovah promised to be a God unto him *and* to his seed after him, and therefore Abraham covenanted with God in the name of and as the representative of his seed. What God gave unto Abraham He gave unto his children, but he received the grant of it as the representative of his children, who, four hundred years later, took possession of it.

The typical teaching of Gen. 14 is exceedingly rich, but difficult to apprehend through lack of familiarity with the leading principles which interpret it. In Melchizedek's blessing of Abraham, we have a foreshadowing of Christ, as our great High Priest, blessing the whole election of grace (Luke 24:50). In Abraham's owning Melchizedek as priest of the most high God by giving him tithes, we have prefigured the subjection to Christ of all His believing people. It lay outside the apostle's scope to fully expound this type in Heb. 7 (cf. 9:5). Here he practically confines himself to a single point, viz., showing that the High Priest of Christianity far exceeded in honour and glory that of Judaism's. His argument in vv. 9, 10 is to the effect that Melchizedek had been as much and as truly honoured by Abraham as though the whole Levitical priesthood had personally done him homage.

The all-important and inexpressibly blessed truth for us to lay hold of is that in vv. 9, 10 we have an *illustration* of the most soul-satisfying truth revealed in Holy Writ. Just as Levi was "*in* Abraham", not only seminally but representatively, so every one of God's children was "*in* Christ" when He wrought out that glorious work which has honoured and pleased God high above everything else. When the death-sentence of the law fell upon Christ, it fell upon the believer, so that he can unhesitatingly say, "I was crucified with Christ" (Gal. 2:20). So too when Christ arose in triumph from the tomb, all His people shared His victory (Eph. 2:5, 6). When He ascended on high, they ascended too. Let all Christian readers pray earnestly that God may be pleased to reveal to them the meaning, blessedness, and fulness of those words "In Christ".

CHAPTER THIRTY-TWO

The Priesthood Changed

(Heb. 7:11-16)

In 5:1-9 the apostle has shown (in part, for he returns to the same theme again in chap. 9) how Christ fulfilled that which Aaron had foreshadowed of Him as the High Priest of His people. Then, in 5:11 he declares Christ had been hailed by God as High Priest "after the order of Melchizedek". Immediately following, the apostle adds that, though he had "many things" to say of him, he was restrained through the Hebrews' dullness. After a lengthy parenthesis in which he corrects their faulty condition, return is made to the subject of Christ's priesthood in 6:20, which is amplified in chap. 7. The main object now before him was to show that Christ is superior to the Jewish high priest, and, in proof, he appeals to the striking type of Melchizedek. Concerning that type he pointed out that not only was Melchizedek greater in his own person than Aaron, but that his superiority had been *owned* by the whole Levitical stock, inasmuch as they, represented by Abraham, had done homage to him.

In the second section of chap 7 which begins at v. 11, the apostle points out the inevitable inferences which must be drawn from and the certain corollaries which are involved in what had just been shown. The fact that the Messiah was Priest after the order of Melchizedek, necessarily set aside the Levitical order. The fact that God had sent His Son to perform a sacerdotal work, plainly signified that the ministry of Aaron and his successors was inadequate. The fact that "perfection" was not brought in till Christ offered Himself as a sacrifice to God, clearly showed that imperfection attached to those who preceded Him. To bring this out the more clearly was the great design of the apostle in the verses which are to be before us. He had now reached that which was the most difficult for the Jews to receive, viz., that what had been so long venerated by their fathers had now been set aside by God.

To announce that the Mosaic economy was temporary, inadequate, defective, was unbelievable to a pious but unregenerate Israelite, and it was something which was far from easy to prove to a regenerated Jew. They believed that the Levitical system of priesthood *was* "perfect". It had been instituted by Jehovah Himself, so surely it must be sufficient and permanent! If the whole Aaronic system was of Divine appointment how could it possibly be, *in itself,* so unsatisfactory that it must now be discarded? The apostle might have reasoned from the analogies supplied by Nature. Many things made by God— such as chrysalis for the butterfly—serve a temporary purpose and then become useless when a more perfect stage of development is reached. But the apostle takes much higher ground and proves by invincible logic that the Levitical system *was* imperfect, and therefore had been superceded by something else.

God had raised up a Priest who belonged not to the Levitical tribe. This the believing Hebrews freely granted: that Jesus Christ had by His sacrifice put away their sins and brought them nigh unto God, was the glorious truth they espoused when they received the Gospel. But they were slow to perceive and acknowledge the necessary *implications* of it. That the Lord Jesus was Priest "after the order of Melchizedek", intimated unequivocally that the priesthood which preceded His was incapable of producing "perfection", for there was no need of introducing something new if the old met all the requirements of God. But more: not only did Christ's bringing in "perfection" presuppose the imperfection of the old order, but it necessarily involved a *change of economy,* i.e. all that was distinctly associated with the Levitical system was now effete, out of date. It is *this* which the apostle proceeds to show.

It was never the intention of God that the Levitical priesthood should remain forever, for in the *Old* Testament Scriptures He gave intimation of *another* Priest, of another order, rising to supercede the former. That intimation was to be found, first, in Gen. 14, where the head and representative of the whole Jewish race had owned Melchizedek as the priest of the most High God. Still plainer was the prophecy which God gave to David. In the 110th Psalm He had greeted the Messiah with these words, "Sit Thou at My right hand" (v. 1), and then He had declared, "The Lord hath sworn, and will not repent, Thou art a priest forever after the order of Melchizedek" (v. 4). This the apostle here cites, and by so doing bases his argument on a ground which no pious Jew could gainsay: the inspired and infallible testimony of Holy Scripture. Therefore if Christ was Priest "after the order of Melchizedek", the Aaronic *must be* imperfect, or there had been no need for introducing this change.

"If therefore perfection were by the Levitical priesthood (for under it the people received the law), what further need that another priest should rise after the order of Melchizedek, and not be called after the order of Aaron?" (v. 11). The apostle now points out some of the *consequences* of Christ's being a Priest "after the order of Melchizedek". The first he mentions is that the Levitical was unable to bring in "perfection". This was evident. Had it done so there was no need for introducing another. But wherein was it that the Levitical system fell short? What was it that it failed to procure? To answer these questions we need to carefully weigh the expression "perfection".

The term "perfection" is one of the characteristic and key-words of this Epistle. It has a different shade of meaning than it has in the other Pauline Epistles. Unless careful attention be paid to its immediate connections, we are almost certain to fall into an erroneous conception of its force. It has to do more with *relationship* than experience, though as the relationship is spiritually apprehended a corresponding experience follows. It concerns the *objective* side of things rather than the subjective. It looks to the judicial and vital aspect rather than to the experimental and practical. Its first occurrences are in 2:10 and 5:9, used of Christ Himself, where the obvious reference is what pertained to Him officially rather than personally. Then it is found in 6:1—compare our comments thereon. In 9:9 we are told that in O.T. times the gifts and sacrifices offered "could not make him that did the service perfect as pertaining to the conscience". The same thing is affirmed in 10:1. But in blessed contrast therefrom we read, "For by one offering He hath perfected forever them that are sanctified" (10:14).

"Perfection" means the bringing of a thing to that completeness of condition designed for it. Doctrinally it refers to the producing of a satisfactory and final relation between God and men. It speaks of that unchangable standing in the favour and blessing of God which Christ has secured for His people. In 12:23 we read of "the spirits of just men *made perfect*", which does not mean that the O.T. saints had been perfected in holiness and happiness (though that, of course, was true of them), but that they had been "made perfect" as their *title* to heavenly glory. This did not take place till the sacrifice of Christ had been offered, though, in the certain prospect of its accomplishment, they had received the blessings which flow from it long before: cf. 11:40.

In our present section the apostle insists that "perfection" could not be produced by the Levites, and that a priesthood which *did* bring in perfection must be superior. It therefore remains for us to enquire next, What are the great *ends* of priesthood? What is it that the priest should effect? The priest was the mediator who drew near unto God on behalf of others. His work was to present to Him a sacrifice for the satisfying of Divine justice. It was to effect such a procuring of His favour and such a securing of a standing-ground before Him for those whom he represented, that their conscience might be at peace. It was to come forth from His presence that he might pronounce blessing. *Had* the Levitical priesthood been able to obtain these things? Had Aaron and his successors obtained God's remission from all the consequences of sin and brought in a complete and abiding redemption? No, indeed.

The office and work of a priesthood may be considered two ways: first, as it respects *God,* who is the prime and immediate object of all the proper acts of that office; second, as it respects *His people,* who are the subject of its blessings and the beneficiaries of its administration. As priesthood respects God, its chief design was to make expiation of sin by means of an atoning sacrifice. But this the Levitical priesthood was unable to do. A typical, ceremonial, and temporary value attached to their sacerdotal ministrations; but an effectual, vital, and permanent did not. This is positively stated in 10:4, "For it is not possible that the blood of bulls and of goats should take away sins". Why, then, were such appointed? To exhibit the holy claims of God and the requirements of His justice; to prefigure the great Sacrifice yet to come.

Let us next inquire, *What* was the "perfection" which *Christ* hath brought in? And here we cannot do better than give a summary of the most helpful exposition of J. Owen. That which Christ hath produced to the glory of God and the blessing of His people is, first, *righteousness.* The introduction of all imperfection was by sin. This made the law weak (Rom. 8:3) and sinners to be "without strength" (Rom. 5:6). Therefore perfection must be introduced by righteousness. *That* was the fundamental of the new covenant: see Isa. 60:21, Psa. 72:7, etc. Therefore do the saints speak of Christ as "The Lord our righteousness" (Jer. 23:6). Christ has brought in an "everlasting righteousness" (Dan. 9:24), and therefore are believers "made the righteousness of God in Him" (2 Cor. 5:21).

Second, *peace* is the next thing which belongs to the evangelical "perfection" of Christianity. As the High Priest of the covenant it pertained to the Lord Jesus to make peace between God and sinners. "When we were enemies, we were reconciled to God by the death of His Son" (Rom. 5:10). Therefore is He denominated "The Prince of peace" (Isa. 9:6): He is such because He has "made peace through the blood of His cross" (Col. 1:20). The result of this is that believers have "peace with God through our Lord Jesus Christ" (Rom. 5:1). Thus the evangel we proclaim is "The Gospel of peace" (Eph. 6:15).

Third, *light.* God designed for Christians a greater measure of spiritual light and knowledge of the mysteries of His wisdom and grace than were attainable under the law. God reserved for His Son the honour of making known the *fulness* of His counsels (John 1:18, Heb. 1:1, 2). There was under the Levitical priesthood but a "*shadow* of good things to come" (Heb. 10:1), but the mystery of them remained hid in God (Eph. 3:9). The prophets themselves perceived not the depths of their own predictions (1 Peter 1:11, 12). Hence, the attitude of the O.T. Church was a looking forward unto a fuller revelation: "till the day break, and the shadows flee away" (Song of Sol. 2:17, 4:6). The contrast between the two economies is seen in 1 John 2:8, "The darkness is past, and the true light *now* shineth".

Fourth, *access to God.* There belongs to the "perfection" which Christ hath brought in, a liberty and boldness of approach unto the throne of grace that was not only unknown but expressly forbidden under the law. At Sinai the people were fenced off at the foot of the mount, when Jehovah appeared to Moses on its summit. In the tabernacle, none save the priests were suffered to go beyond the outer court, and they not at all into the holy of holies where God dwelt. How blessed is the contrast today. "For through Him we both *have access* by one Spirit unto the Father" (Eph. 2:18). To us the word is, "Having therefore, brethren, boldness to enter into the holiest by the blood of Jesus, let us draw near with a true heart in full assurance of faith" (Heb. 10:19, 22).

Fifth, the *unveiling of the future state.* Christ hath "brought life and immortality to light through the Gospel" (2 Tim. 1:10). Whatever knowledge of resurrection and eternal blessedness individual saints enjoyed in O.T. times, it was *not* conveyed to them by the ministrations of the Levitical priesthood. That which characterized the people under the Mosaic law was that they "through fear of death were all their lifetime subject to bondage" (Heb. 2:15). Nor could it be otherwise while the curse of the law hung over them. But now our great High Priest has endured the curse for us. He entered the devouring jaws of death. But He did not remain there. He triumphed over the grave, and in the resurrection of Christ His people have the evidence, guarantee, and pattern, of their own victory too. He has gone on High, and that as *our* "Forerunner" (6:20). And His request is, "Father, I will that they also, whom Thou hast given Me, be with Me where I am" (John 17:24).

Sixth, *joy.* "The kingdom of God is . . . righteousness and peace and joy in the Holy Spirit" (Rom. 14:17). True it is that many of the O.T. saints rejoiced greatly in the Lord, yet it was not by virtue of the Levitical priesthood. The ground of their joy was that death would be swallowed up in victory (Isa. 25:8), and that awaited the death and resurrection of Christ. Therefore did Abraham rejoice to see *His* day (John 8:56). But ordinarily their joy was mixed and allayed with a respect unto temporal things: see Lev. 23:39-41, Deut. 12:11, 12, 18, etc. But the Christian has a joy "unspeakable, and full of glory" (1 Peter 1:8). It is that inexpressible satisfaction which is wrought in the love of God by Jesus Christ. This gives the soul a repose in all trials, refreshment when it is weary, peace in trouble, delight in tribulations: Rom. 5:1-5.

Seventh, *glorying in the Lord.* This is the fruit of joy. One chief design of the Gospel is to exclude all human boasting, to empty us of glorying in self (Rom. 3:27, Eph. 2:9). God has so ordered things that no flesh should now glory in His presence, so that he that glorieth must glory in the Lord (1 Cor. 1:29, 31). Thus it was promised of old: see Isa. 45:25. Glorying in the Lord is that high exultation of spirit which causes believers to esteem their interest in heavenly things high above things present, to despise and condemn all that is contrary thereto, to say with the apostle, "God forbid that I should glory save in the cross of our Lord Jesus Christ". If the reader desires to follow up more fully the contrast between the glory and excellency of the two economies, the Mosaic and the Christian, let him study 2 Cor. 3.

Ere leaving this blessed subject, let us make a brief practical application of what has been before us. To be a real Christian is to have a personal and vital interest in and be an actual participant of those blessings which the "perfection" of Christ has brought in. Multitudes make an outward profession of the same; few have an experimental acquaintance with them. Again; the pre-eminence of Christianity over Judaism is entirely spiritual and cannot be discerned by the carnal eye: wherein it excels has been pointed out above—it consists of a clearer knowledge of God, a freer approach to Him, a fuller enjoyment of Him. Finally, let it be said that the attempts to find glory and satisfaction in outward forms and ceremonies is to prefer the Levitical priesthood before that of Christ's. *That* is the outstanding sin of all ritualists.

A brief word needs to be added upon the parenthetic clause of v. 11: "For under it the people received the law". Its evident design was to strengthen the apostle's argument. It is brought in as a subsidiary proof that "perfection" could not be by the Levitical priesthood. We are therefore disposed to regard "the law" here as referring to the whole system of the Mosaic economy. The passive "received the law" is a single word in the Greek, and really means "were legalized". The reference is not to bring to the actual giving of the law, but to the state of the people under it, their being brought beneath its power. The law demanded perfect righteousness, but fallen man was incapable of producing it (Rom. 3:19,20;8:3); nor could the Levitical priesthood effect it. Thus the only hope lay outside of themselves. "*Christ* is the end of the law for righteousness to every one that believeth" (Rom. 10:4).

"For the priesthood being changed, there is made of necessity a change also of the law" (v. 12). Here the apostle names the second *consequence* which must be drawn from the facts stated in vv. 1-10. First, the Levitical priesthood was inadequate, incapable of producing "perfection". Second, therefore it was but a temporary institution, and the whole economy connected with it must be set aside. In other words, Judaism as such, was now defunct. Thus "a change of the law" means a change of dispensation, a change of Divine administration. This at once fixes the meaning of "law" in the parenthetic clause of the previous verse. The reference is not to the ten commandments, but to the Mosaic system.

The "change also of the law" or setting aside of the Mosaic system was that to which the Jews were so strenuously opposed. They stoned Stephen (Acts 7:58, 59), and vented their rage upon Paul, on this very charge (Acts 21:28). Yea, many who professed the faith of the Gospel continued to obstinately contend that the Mosaic law remained in force (Acts 21:20). It was this same contention which caused so much trouble in the early churches, the Judaisers harassing the Gentile converts with their insistence upon circumcision and subjection to the ceremonial law. Difficult as it was for a pious Jew to believe that God should have set aside as dead and useless the whole solemn system of worship, which He had appointed in so glorious a manner and accepted for so many centuries, yet the proof that He *had* done so was abundant and clear. The law and the Gospel could not mix. Works and grace are antithetical. Moses must disappear when Christ was revealed: carefully compare Mark 9:5-8! So far from God's people being the losers they are immeasurably the gainers by His bringing in the "better hope" (7:19).

"For He of whom these things are spoken pertaineth to another tribe, of which no man gave attendance at the altar" (v. 13). The argument of this verse, introduced by the "for" makes it plain that it is *not* the moral law which the apostle had reference to at the close of the preceding verse: the closing words of the next verse make this still more evident. We mention this because certain "Dispensationalists" have appealed to Heb. 7:12 in their misguided efforts to show that Christians are, in no sense, under the ten commandments. The moral law is not at all under discussion in this passage. 1 Cor. 9:21, Matt. 5:18, etc. are quite sufficient to prove that the moral law has not been (and never will be) repealed.

"For He of whom these things are spoken pertaineth to another tribe, of which no man gave attendance at the altar". The apostle's object here is to give further proof that the Levitical priesthood, and the entire ceremonial law, has been set aside by God. He appeals to the fact that our Lord, according to the flesh, belonged not to the tribe of Levi, and therefore His sacerdotal office was not according to the Aaronic order. The expression "attendance at the altar" signifies, "exercising priestly functions". The "these things" looks back to what is said at the end of v. 11, which receives amplification in vv. 17, 21.

The honour of the Aaronic order of priesthood continued, by Divine appointment and privilege, within the bounds of the Levitical tribe: Ex. 40:12-16. None belonging to any other tribe in Israel was suffered to officiate at the altar or minister in the holy place. So strictly was this institution observed, that when one of Israel's kings dared to violate it, the judgment of God fell immediately upon him (2 Chron. 26:18-21). In smiting Uzziah with leprosy God maintained the sanctity of His law, and gave a most solemn warning against any obtruding into holy office who have received no Divine call to it. Furthermore, this exercise of God's severity should have been more than a hint to Israelites that when *He* did introduce a priest of another tribe then the priesthood of the old order *must* have been Divinely set aside.

"For it is evident that our Lord sprang out of Judah; of which tribe Moses spake nothing concerning priesthood" (v. 14). The opening "for" at once denotes the apostle is here continuing his proof that the Levitical priesthood and economy was now a thing of the past so far as God's recognition of it was concerned. His words here contain a double assertion: our Lord, according to His humanity, belonged to the tribe of Judah; of that tribe Moses revealed nothing concerning priesthood. All that was needed to complete the proof of his argument was that Christ *was* a Priest: this he shows in the ensuing verses. The appeal made to this verse by those who deny that the Lord Jesus entered upon His priestly office till after His ascension, proceeds from such gross ignorance or malice that it deserves no direct refutation.

First, it was "evident" that our Lord "sprang"—as the "Rod" out of Jesse's stem—from Judah. This was included in the faith of believers that the Messiah was to come out of the royal tribe. Such prophecies as Gen. 49:8-10, 2 Sam. 7:12, Isa. 11:1-5, Micah 5:2 had made that very plain. The genealogy recorded in Matt. 1 established the same fact. Whoever therefore acknowledge the Lord

Jesus to be the true Messiah, as all to whom the apostle was directly writing did, (though most of them still clung to the ceremonial law), granted that He was of the tribe of Judah. Nor did the unbelieving Jews deny it. In passing, we have noted that Judah signifies "praise": Christ still dwells in the midst of His people's praises!

Second, about Judah Moses spake nothing concerning priesthood. The apostle's object is to render it conclusive that God's raising up of a Priest out of the royal tribe, must necessarily exclude all the house of Aaron from sharing His office. Moses did specify that the priesthood should be exercised by those belonging to the tribe of Levi, but he nowhere intimated that a time would come when it should be transferred to the royal family. Again we may take note of the significance of the *silences* of Scripture, and the justification of arguing therefrom. As, for example, no mention is made of the month in which the Saviour was born, intimating that God did not intend us to celebrate the anniversary of His birth: cf. Jer. 7:31. Paul here reasons from the silence of Moses as being quite sufficient to show that the legal or Aaronic priesthood could not be transferred to the tribe of Judah.

"And it is yet far more evident: for that after the similitude of Melchizedek there ariseth another priest" (v. 15). In this and the next verse the apostle presents the third *consequence* which follows from the facts set forth in vv. 1-10. First, he had pointed out from those facts that, it necessarily followed the Levitical priesthood was inadequate, for it was unable to bring in "perfection". Second, therefore it was evident that the Levitical priesthood could only be a temporary institution, and that the whole economy connected with and based upon it must be set aside. Third, he now insists that the priesthood of Christ must be radically different from and be immeasurably superior to the Levitical order. So much for the general scope of these two verses. Let us now attend to their details.

"And it is yet far more evident". *What* is it that was "far more evident"? What was the particular point to which the apostle was here calling the Hebrews' attention? Not that Christ had sprung from the tribe of Judah, nor that He fulfilled the Melchizedek type, but that the Levitical priesthood and economy was now obsolete. The proof that this *was* so obvious is presented in what immediately follows. That proof may be expressed thus: the priesthood of Christ was no temporary expedient, brought in only to supply the deficiency of the Levitical order. No; it was a permanent office and abiding ministry. Therefore as God would not own two separate and different priesthoods, the former and inferior must give place to the latter. The second, "consequence" had been drawn from the tribal humanity of Christ; this third "consequence", from the character of His priesthood.

"And it is yet far more evident". It is to be carefully noted that the apostle did not say "it is far more *certain*". No, he was not absolutely comparing one thing with another, but comparing them only with respect to their evidential significance, the relative force of those facts to all who were capable of weighing them. The fact that God had caused our great "High Priest" to spring from the tribe of Judah rather than from that of Levi, made it obvious that the Aaronic order could no longer continue. But the further fact that He had been made "after the similitude of Melchizedek", rendered this still more obvious. The apostle is but adding argument to argument, in order to show how wrong it was for the Hebrews to still cling to Judaism.

"For that after the similitude of Melchizedek there ariseth another priest". The Greek word for "similitude" means "likeness" and occurs elsewhere only in 4:15. The emphatic here is "*another* priest". It is not "allos" which means another of the same species, but "heteros", another of a totally different order: one who was a stranger to the house of Aaron. Let the reader consult Ex. 29:33, Lev. 22:10, Num. 16:40, and he will see how impossible it was for one from the tribe of Judah to perpetuate the Levitical priesthood. The word "ariseth" is also very emphatic. It means to be brought forth after an extraordinary manner: cf. Judges 5:7, Deut. 18:18, Luke 1:69. The arising of Christ in His priestly office put an end to the Aaronic, just as His arising in the hearts of His people (2 Peter 1:19) puts an end to their looking to anything or anyone else for salvation.

"Who is made, not after the law of a carnal commandment, but after the power of an endless life" (v. 16). This completes the sentence begun in v. 15. The apostle is still showing how manifest it was that the Levitical priesthood had been set aside, for one infinitely superior had now been set up by God. The contrast here made between the two is very striking. The Aaronic was constituted "according to the law of commandment fleshly". The same expression is used in Eph. 2:15 to designate the whole system of worship under Judaism. This emphatic denomination may be accounted for by the fact that under it commandments were so multiplied, and because of the severity wherewith obedience was exacted. The Levitical priesthood was "carnal", first, inasmuch as the sacrifices offered at their consecration were the bodies of beasts. Second, inasmuch as the priesthood was by fleshly propagation, from father to son. Third, inasmuch as their ministration availed *only* to the "purifying of the flesh" (9:13). In sharp contrast, Christ was not dedicated to His office by the sacrifice of beasts, nor did He claim any right to it by His natural descent.

"Who is made . . . after the power of an endless life". Let the reader compare our remarks on 5:5. The Lord Christ did not merely on His own authority and power take the priestly office upon Himself, but by the appointment of His Father. The way or manner in which He *was* "made priest" is here stated: according to "the power of an indissoluable life". These words have been grossly wrested by those who seek to prove by them that Christ never entered upon the priestly office until after His resurrection. It is truly pitiable to find those who ought to know better echoing the errors of "annihilationists". Christ officiated as priest before His resurrection, or He could not have offered Himself as a sacrifice to God. As this will, D. V., come before us again in the 9th chapter we will say no more thereon at the present juncture.

Christ's "indissoluable life" here has unquestionable reference to His life as *the Son of God*. Upon *that* depends His own mediatorial life forever, and His conferring eternal life upon His people: John 5:26, 27. It was only by the Mediator being made priest "after *the power of* an indissoluable life" that He was qualified to discharge that office, whereby *God* was to redeem His church with His own blood (Acts 20:28)—i.e. here called "His blood" because the humanity had been taken up into union with the second person in the Godhead. Should it be objected, But Christ died! True, yet his *person* still lived: though actually dead in His human nature, He was still alive in His indissoluable person, and therefore there was *no* interruption whatever to the discharge of His sacerdotal office; no, not for a moment. Thus the contrast between Aaron and Christ is that of a mortal man and "The King eternal, immortal, invisible" (1 Tim. 1:17).

How deeply thankful should every Christian be for *such* a Priest. The eternal Word became flesh. The Lord of glory stooped to become man. As the God-man He mediates between the ineffably holy God and sinful creatures. The Saviour is none other than Immanuel (Matt. 1:21, 23). In His humanity, He suffered, bled and died. But in His Divine-human person He Himself quickened that humanity (John 2:19, 10:18). We profess not to understand the mystery, but by grace, we believe what the Scriptures record concerning Him. The "life" that was given to Christ as the Mediator (unlike that of His humanity) was an indestructible one. Therefore He is "a Priest *forever*", and therefore "He ever liveth to make intercession" (7:25). Hallelujah!

CHAPTER THIRTY-THREE

Judaism Set Aside

(Heb. 7:17-19)

As stated in the opening paragraphs of the preceding article, the apostle had now reached (in the second section of Heb.7) the most difficult and delicate part of his task, namely, to satisfy believing Jews that God had set aside the entire system which He had Himself instituted in the days of Moses. It is exceedingly difficult for us to form any adequate estimate of what that meant to them; in truth, it was the severest test to which the faith of God's people has ever been put. To be assured that God had discarded as dead and useless the entire order of solemn worship which He had appointed in so glorious a manner and which He had accepted for so many generations, was indeed a sore trial of faith. To acquiesce in His sovereign pleasure in this momentous matter called for no ordinary measure of grace. To establish the truth thereof Paul was led of the Spirit to enter into such detail that every valid objection was fairly met and clearly refuted.

There are many today who quite fail to appreciate the reason why the apostle should here pursue his argument so laboriously and enter into so many minute details. That these should strike anyone as "dry", uninteresting and unprofitable, is because he is insensible of the vast importance of what the apostle had before him. Rightly did John Owen affirm that "he hath the greatest argument in hand that was ever controverted in the church of God, and upon the determination whereof the salvation or ruin of the church did depend. The worship he treated of was immediately instituted by God Himself, and had now continued near fifteen hundred years in the church. All that while it had been the certain rule of God's acceptance of the people, or of His anger toward them; for whilst they complied with it, His blessing was continually upon them, and the neglect of it was still punished with severity".

The final exhortation which God had given to Israel through the last of His prophets was, "Remember ye the law of Moses My servant . . . lest I come and smite the earth with a curse" (Mal.

4:4-6). *Those* are the closing words of the Old Testament! So highly did the Jews esteem their great and singular privileges above all other nations, that they would rather die than part with them. So high ran their feelings against those who pressed upon them the claims of Christ that, the charge preferred against the first Christian martyr was, "We have heard him speak blasphemous words *against Moses* and God . . . This man ceaseth not to speak blasphemous words against the holy place *and the law*" (Acts 6:11, 13): and though he remonstrated so faithfully, earnestly, and tenderly with them, they "gnashed on him with their teeth" and "stoned" him (Acts 7:54, 59). It was therefore most necessary that Paul should proceed cautiously, carefully and slowly, omitting nothing that was of any force in favour of the cause he was pleading.

The truth of God requires no vindication from us, nor are we called upon to attempt any justification for what may strike some as being unnecessarily tedious. Yet, in addition to intimating the needs be for Paul to enter so microscopically into the signification and application of the details of the Melchizedek type, we may profitably observe how that he has left an example which servants of God today need to take to heart. The course here followed by this beloved teacher supplies a most helpful illustration of what is meant by believers being "established in the *present* truth" (2 Peter 1:12). All truth is eternal, and in itself is equally valuable and applicable to each age and generation. Yet portions of it are especially so from their timely pertinency to particular seasons, and that because of the opposition made against them. Thus Paul's teaching here about the abolishing of the Mosaic ceremonies with the introduction of a new priesthood and new ordinances of worship was *then* the "*present* truth" in the knowledge and confirmation of which the people of God were vitally concerned. The same principle holds good continuously. Each portion of God's truth may become of peculiar urgency by virtue of some special opposition thereto.

In His sovereign wisdom God is pleased to exercise and try the faith of His saints by various heresies which are fierce, persistent, and subtle oppositions to His Truth. None of the Devil's agents, while posing as the champions of the Cause of Christ or as revealing new and fuller "light" from Heaven, reject *all* the Gospel or repudiate *all* the fundamentals of the faith. No, Satan is far too clever to show *his* hand so openly. Rather do his wolves, who aim at robbing God's children of their inheritance, appear in sheep's clothing, and pretend to great reverence for the Scriptures. Instead of repudiating the entire faith delivered to the saints, they insidiously direct their attack upon some single portion thereof; and thus a defense of what is directly opposed becomes the "present truth" for that day in which the saints need establishing, because of the Enemy's attempt to overthrow them.

Though Satan hates all Truth, yet he is far too wary to send his satellites among the people of God and openly deny *all* that they hold dear. Nor can he gain *any* advantage over them while they are really walking *with* God, in humble, dependent, obedient submission to Him. No, he has to watch and wait until he discovers what professing Christians, because of their lust and prejudices, are most inclined to receive. As the spirit of worldliness increases among them, then he presses that which is most calculated to hide from their view the *heavenly* calling of God's people and its inseparable consequence of walking down here as *"strangers and pilgrims"*. As the spirit of egotism and pride is allowed a large place, then that which humbles and abases the flesh is withheld and a species of intellectualism which puffs up, is substituted.

It is indeed solemn and saddening to review the course which Christendom has followed during the last two or three generations in the light of the above principle. As the denying of self and the daily taking up of the cross declined, the heart was prepared for the Satanic delusion that because salvation is by grace alone, that therefore obedience to God, submission to His law, and the actual *doing* of His Word, are quite unnecessary; and thus Paul has been pitted against James, and the teaching of the latter ignored. That there is a Strait gate to be entered and a Narrow way to be traversed, before "life" is actually reached, is almost universally denied by those who pose as the servants of God; yet that only solemnly confirms our Lord's words, "Few there be that find it" (Matt. 7:14).

Again; as the "professing Church" became more infected with the *lawlessness* abounding in the world, the teaching that the Sabbath is "Jewish" and that the Law of God has been totally abolished, became very acceptable to those intent on pleasing themselves. As the exalted standard of holiness which God has set before His people became lowered by those professing to speak in His name, the monstrous idea that *repentance* belongs only to the "Kingdom age" was readily espoused. As the masses of those who bore the name of Christ refused to take upon them His *yoke* and learn of Him who was "meek and lowly in heart", the horrible heresy that the searching precepts of the Sermon on the Mount (found in Matt. 5-7) are not addressed to Christians living today, was greedily devoured. Ah, it is just these things which are now being opposed that have become the "present truth", in which numbers of God's people most need to be "established". It is at these very points that God is now causing the faith of His people to be tested, and the true servants of the Lord will seek grace, wisdom and courage, to emulate the example here left by Paul, and spare no pains to root and ground the saints in what is most needful for them. Such is the *practical application* we need to make of the principle exemplified by the apostle in Heb. 7.

In the verses immediately preceding our present passage, the apostle had shown that the abolition of the Levitical order was inevitable. First, he pointed out that *before* Aaron had been called, God Himself had owned another priesthood which was far more excellent, namely, that of Melchizedek's. Second, the introduction of that more excellent priesthood for a season, was designed to prefigure what was afterwards to be established, therefore another priesthood had to arise and be given unto the Church in answer to that ancient type. Third, the new priest after the order of Melchizedek could not consist side by side with that of Levi's, for He belonged to another tribe, and His sacrifice was of another kind. Hence, inasmuch as the Aaronic priesthood could not take away sins nor make the worshipper perfect before God, and because Christ's sacerdotal work effected these, therefore the former must give place to the latter. Still further reasons for the necessity of this the apostle continues to advance.

"For He testified, Thou art a priest forever after the order of Melchizedek" (v. 17). This verse completes the sentence begun at v. 15, the design of the whole being to afford a demonstration of what had been said in v. 11. In v. 11 a deduction is drawn from the signification of the Melchizedek type. That type announced the rising of a Priest distinct from and superior to the order of Aaron. From that fact the apostle points out, first, that the Levitical order must be inadequate, imperfect, and therefore must give way before that which was more excellent; and second, that the revocation of the Aaronic order necessarily involved the setting aside of the whole dispensation or economy connected therewith.

Though the "logic" of his argument was perfect and could not be gainsaid, the apostle does not ask the Hebrews to rest their faith on mere reasoning, but proceeds to *prove* what he has said by an appeal to those Scriptures which they owned as the inspired and authoritative Word of God. He reminds them that not only had the Lord given them more than a hint in the historical narrative of Genesis, that One should arise and fulfill the priestly type recorded therein, but he points out that in one of the great Messianic Psalms Jehovah Himself addresses the Messiah as "A Priest forever after the order of Melchizedek". We cannot but marvel at the wondrous and perfect ways of our God. At the very time when the church of Israel was in the highest enjoyment of the Levitical priesthood, whose office depended wholly on their genealogy, the Holy Spirit deemed it well to inform them through David that a Priest was to come and be independent of any line of fleshly descent, namely, after the order of Melchizedek, who had none, Psa. 110:4.

Well may we reverently ponder and admire the sovereign wisdom of the Holy Spirit in bringing forth truth unto light according as the state of God's people require. Here again we see exemplified that basic principle in all God's dealings with men: "first the blade, then the ear, after that the full corn in the ear" (Mark 4:28). First, He inserted in Genesis a very brief account of a person who was a type of Christ. Second, almost a thousand years afterwards, when, it *may* be all understanding of the Genesis type had been lost, and the people of God were fully satisfied in a priesthood of quite another nature, the Holy Spirit in one word of prophecy intimated that, what Moses had recorded of him to whom Abraham paid tithes, was a foreshadowing of another Priest who was afterwards to arise. Thus God not only gave Israel light upon an important piece of ancient history, but also signified to them that the priesthood which they then enjoyed was not always to continue, but would be superceded by one of another and better nature.

But notwithstanding the plain prophecy recorded in the 110th Psalm, it is evident that at the coming of the Saviour and the fulfilment of both type and prophecy, the Jews had lost all knowledge and understanding of the mystery of Gen. 14 and the promises renewed through David. They thought it strange that there should be a Priest that had no genealogy, no solemn consecration at the hands of man, and no formal investiture with His office. Therefore does the apostle proceed so slowly and carefully in the opening of this mystery, prefacing the same not only by the assertion of how hard it was to understand it aright(5:10), but also with a lengthy discourse (5:11 to 6:20) to prepare their hearts for a diligent attention thereto. The difficulty before him was not only because the true understanding of Gen. 14 and Psalm 110 had been lost, but because the carnality of those to whom he wrote made them reluctant to admit that the raising up of Christ as Priest after the order of Melchizedek necessarily involved the termination of the Levitical priesthood and the whole system of worship connected therewith.

Difficult as it was for the Jew to be weaned from that system in which he had been brought up and to which he was so deeply attached, nevertheless, his very salvation turned thereon. Therefore we are not to wonder at the apostle's insisting so much on the setting aside of Judaism, for that was the very hinge on which the eternal salvation or destruction of the whole Nation did turn. If they would not forego their old priesthood and worship, their ruin was unavoidable. Christ would either be received by them, or "profit them nothing" (Gal. 5:2). Thus it was that it fell out with the great majority of them! turning away from the Lord Jesus, they clung tenaciously to their ancient institutions and perished in their unbelief.

Nor should we lose sight of the analogy and parallel furnished by the Jews in connection with salvation today. While it be true that salvation is wholly of grace, and in nowise obtained by any efforts or works of the creature, nevertheless, it is equally true that none can obtain that salvation until there be a complete break from the world and their old manner of life in it. Conversion is a turning *to* God, and to turn to God there must be a turning *from* all that is opposed to Him. None are saved till they "come" to Christ, and the very term "coming to Christ" implies a *leaving* of what is contrary to Him. The Lord Jesus does not save men *in* their sins, but *from* their sins, and before He saves them from their sins, there must be a *repenting* of sin (Luke 13:3), and no man savingly repents of his sins while he lives in and loves them. The wicked have to *forsake* their "way" *before* God will "pardon" (Isa. 55:7). The sinner has to turn his back on the far country, yea, leave it behind him, before he can approach the Father and receive the "best robe" (Luke 15)!

Should any object to what has just been said, But *that* is to make man, in part, his own saviour! We reply, Not at all. There is nothing whatever meritorious about repentance, any more than there is about faith. Neither of them are virtues entitling a sinner to salvation, yet they *are* required qualifications, in the same way that an empty-handed beggar is qualified for my charity or a sick person is fit to receive the attention of a physician. Scripture does not teach that a man must reform his life in order to win God's approval, but it does affirm "he that covereth his sins shall not prosper; but whoso confesseth and forsaketh them shall have mercy" (Prov. 28:13).

"For He testifieth, Thou art a priest forever after the order of Melchizedek." Note "He testifieth", not simply "He said". The words of the Holy Spirit through David are here appealed to by the apostle in support of what he had said. Brief as is that citation, it nevertheless substantiates all the principle points Paul had made: first, here was proof that there *should be* another priest not of the tribe of Levi, for Jehovah here affirms of Christ, who sprang from Judah. "Thou art a priest". Second, He was a priest "after the order of Melchizedek". Third, God Himself owned Him as such.

Fourth, He was so "after the power of an endless life" (v. 16), for He is priest "forever".

Perhaps one more word needs to be added upon Christ's being "a priest forever after the order of Melchizedek". The priesthood of Christ was, in the mind of God, the eternal idea and original exemplar. Accordingly, God called forth Melchizedek, and invested him with his office in such a manner that he might fitly foreshadow Christ. Hence he and his priesthood became an external adumbration of the priesthood of Christ, and therefore is He said to remain a priest "after" his "order", that is suitably unto the representation made thereof in him.

"For there is verily a disannulling of the commandment going before the weakness and unprofitableness thereof" (v. 18). In v. 12 the apostle had affirmed that the priesthood being changed, there was of necessity a change made of the law also. Having, in vv. 15-17, proved the former, he now proceeds to confirm the unescapable inference from it, and this he does by showing that the Priesthood promised and now given, was in all things inconsistent with the Levitical. In v. 12 he had used the milder term "change"; now he insists that the old regime could not be altered and adjusted to the new order of things, but had been altogether "disannulled".

"For there is verily a disannulling of the commandment going before". The reference here is to the entire system of the Mosaic institutions. That system is here spoken of as "the commandment going before". It was of Divine appointment and authority, yet was it only designed "until the time of reformation" (9:10). The "going before" signifies the introduction of the new Priest in fulfilment of the promise in Psalm 110. The commandment going before was that which regulated the worship of God and obedience to Him prior to the Christian dispensation; but this had now been cancelled and a new law of worship given.

It is indeed striking to note the *warnings* which God gave to Israel of the disannulling of the law. First, at the very beginning He gave a clear intimation that it *had not* a perpetuity annexed to it. Immediately after the giving of the law *as a covenant* to Israel, they broke the covenant by setting up the golden calf at Horeb; whereupon Moses breaks the tables of stone, whereon the law was given. Had God intended that that covenant should be perpetuated, He would not have suffered its first constitution to have been accompanied with an express emblem of its abolition. Second, Moses implicitly declared after the giving of the law that God would provoke Israel to jealousy by a foolish people (*see* Deut. 33:21), which was by calling of the Gentiles (Rom. 10:19); whereupon the law of commandments contained in ordinances, was of necessity to be taken out of the way! Third, through Jeremiah (chap. 31, etc.) Jehovah made known that, following the revocation of the old, a "*new* covenant" should be established with the Church! In these and other ways was Israel forewarned that the time would come when the whole Mosaic law, as to its covenant efficacy, would be repealed, unto the unspeakable advantage of God's people.

If it be asked how and when the commandment respecting Judaism was "disannulled", the answer is, First, virtually and really by Christ Himself. He had fulfilled and accomplished it in His own person, and by so doing took away its obligatory power. Second, formerly, by the new ordinances which Christ instituted. The Lord's supper (Matt. 26:26-29) and Christian baptism (Matt. 28:19) were altogether inconsistent with the ordinances of the law, for these declared that was passed and done, which they directed unto as future and yet to come. Third, declaratively by the revealed will of God: in Acts 15 we learn how the Holy Spirit through the apostles (v. 28) expressly declared that the Gentile converts were *not* under obligation to heed the Mosaic law (v. 24). Fourth, providentially, in A. D. 70, when God caused Jerusalem and the temple to be destroyed.

"For the weakness and unprofitableness thereof". Here the apostle assigns the reason why God had annulled the Mosaic law. In v. 11 the apostle had asked, If "perfection were obtainable by the Levitical priesthood what need was there for another priesthood to arise? Here he plainly declares that the whole system was, relatively speaking, worthless. This raises a difficulty of no small dimension, namely, in assigning such imperfections to a system which had been given by God Himself. How can it be supposed that the good and holy Jehovah should prescribe such a law unto His people as was always weak and unprofitable?

Absolutely considered no reflection can be made upon the Mosaic law, for it was the product of Divine wisdom, holiness and truth. But with respect unto the *people* to whom it was given, and the *end* for which it was given, imperfection *did* attach to it. It was given to *sinners* who were defiled and guilty, and therefore was the law "weak through the flesh" (Rom. 8:3), its subject having no power to meet its high demands. Moreover, it was (in itself) incapable of meeting their deep needs; taking away their sins, bestowing life on them, conforming them to God's holiness. Why, then, was it given? It was "added because of transgression, till the Seed should come to whom the promise was made" (Gal. 3:19). It discovered the nature of sin, so that the conscience of man might be sensible thereof. It restrained sin by prohibitions and threatenings, so that it did not run out to an excess of riot. It represented, though obscurely, the ways and means by which sin could be expiated. Finally, it made known the imperative need for the coming of Christ to do for men what they could not do of and for themselves.

"For the law made nothing perfect, but the bringing in of a better hope did; by the which we draw nigh unto God" (v 19). There are three things for us to note in this verse. First, the apostle names a particular instance in which the law was "weak and unprofitable". Second, he specifies what had been introduced in the room of that which had been disannulled. Third, he mentions the design of the law was that it "made nothing perfect". "It did not make the church-state perfect, it did not make the worship of God perfect, it did not perfect the promises given to Abraham in their accomplishment, it did not make a perfect covenant between God and man; it had a shadow, an obscure representation, of all these things, but it made nothing perfect" (John Owen).

Above, we sought to answer to the question, Why should God have given His people a law which made nothing perfect? It may further be pointed out that in all things the sovereignty of God is to be submitted unto; and for humble souls there is beauty and blessedness in Divine sovereignty. When the Lord Jesus rejoiced in spirit and returned thanks because heavenly mysteries had been hid from the wise and prudent and revealed unto babes, He assigned no other reason than, "Even so Father, for so it seemed good in Thy sight" (Luke 10:21). And until we recognize an excellency in *all* God's dispensations, simply because they are *His*, who giveth no account of His matters, we shall never admire His ways.

Again, men have sinned, and apostatised from God, and therefore it was but just and equal that they should not be re-instated in their reparation at once. "As God left the generality of the world without the knowledge of what He intended, so He saw good to keep the Church in a state of expectancy, as to the condition of liberty and deliverance intended. He could have created the world in an hour or moment; but He chose to do so in the space of six days, that the glory of His works might be distinctly represented unto angels and men. And He could, immediately after the fall, have introduced the promised Seed, in whose advent the Church must of necessity enjoy all the perfection which it is capable of in this world. But to teach the Church the greatness of their sin and misery, and to work in them an acknowledgement of His unspeakable grace, God proceeded gradually in the very revelation of Him, and caused them to wait under earnest desires and expectations many ages for Christ's coming" (John Owen).

Finally and primarily, God designed that the Lord Jesus should in *all* things have the pre-eminence. This was due Him because of the glory of His person and the transcendent excellency of His work. But if the law could have made anything perfect, it is evident that this could not have been. Christ is the centre of all God's counsels, the key to every problem. All things are being directed to His ultimate honour and praise. The system of Judaism, with its mysteries and shadows, served as a suitable background, from which might shine forth the more gloriously the full blaze of God's perfections made manifest by His incarnate Son. "The darkness is past, and the true light now shineth" (1 John 2:8).

"But the bringing in of a better hope did". When a sufficient discovery had been made of the insufficiency of the law to make things "perfect", God introduced that which did. A parallel passage is found in Rom. 8:3, 4. There too we read of the law being "weak", and, that, through the faultiness of those to whom it was addressed. There too we read of the law being followed by God's sending something "better", namely, His own Son. There too we read of the "perfection" which Christ has brought in for His people. The same thing will come before us again, D. V., when we arrive at Heb. 10:1-10.

"Hope" is used metonymically, that is to say, for the object itself, the thing hoped for. From the giving of the first promise in Gen. 3:15, renewed in Gen. 12:3 and 17:8, the coming of Christ unto this world was the great thing which believers longed for. Abraham rejoiced to see His day (John 8:56), as did the prophets search diligently concerning it (1 Peter 1:11, 12). Hence, we read of Simeon "waiting for the Consolation of Israel" (Luke 2:25) and of aged Anna speaking of the newly-born Saviour to "all them that *looked for* redemption in Jerusalem" (Luke 2:38). In like manner, the "blessed hope" set before God's saints throughout this dispensation is the "appearing of the glory of the great God and our Saviour Jesus Christ" (Titus 2:13).

By the introduction of the "better hope" believers now "draw nigh unto God". The verb here is a sacerdotal term, denoting the approach of priests to God in His worship. By nature we were unable so to do, for we were "alienated from the life of God" (Eph. 4:18). Sin separated between us and the thrice Holy One. But now we who once were far off "are made nigh by the blood of Christ" (Eph. 2:13), in consequence whereof both believing Jews and Gentiles "have access by one Spirit unto the Father" (Eph. 2:18), for the whole election of grace have been made "a holy priesthood, to offer up spiritual sacrifices, acceptable to God by Jesus Christ" (1 Peter 2:5). The right and privilege of believers drawing nigh unto God Himself and the throne of His grace, is further opened in Heb. 10, particularly vv. 19-22. Everything which kept us at a distance from God has been removed by the bringing in of the Better Hope.

In its complete realization and ultimate fulfillment, it is still the "better *hope*". Believers are yet here on earth; there is much within and without which mars and interrupts their communion with God. Their being "made perfect" in their state and experience (Heb. 11:40), and their being actually conducted into the Father's presence (John 14:1-3) is yet future. But blessed be God, our sins have been put away, we already have "*access* by faith into this grace wherein we stand" (Rom. 5:2). The Forerunner has "*for us* entered" within the veil (Heb. 10:19, 20). Then, in the meantime, "Let us therefore come boldly unto the throne of grace, that we may obtain mercy, and find grace to help in time of need" (Heb. 4:16). The Lord grant it for His name's sake.

CHAPTER THIRTY-FOUR

Judaism Set Aside

(Heb. 7:20-24)

It may be well for us to recall the principal design of the apostle in this section of his epistle. This was twofold; first, to demonstrate that the great High Priest of Christianity is far more excellent than was the typical high priest of Judaism, and that, that the faith of the Hebrews might be established and their hearts drawn out in love and worship to Him. Second, to show that it necessarily followed God's bringing in of the new order of priesthood, the old order was completely set aside. The method of proof which the Spirit moved the apostle to pursue was, an appeal to a notable O. T. type, confirmed by the citation of a Messianic prophecy. From this there was no possible appeal by any who really bowed to the Divine authority of Holy Writ. Blessed it is to see how graciously God has always provided a sure foundation for the faith of His people to rest upon. Yet it is only as His Word is diligently searched that this foundation is fully discovered, and even that, by the directing and illuminating guidance of the Holy Spirit.

An analysis of our chapter reveals that Christ's superiority over Aaron appears in the following points. First, Aaron was but a man; Christ was "the Son of God" (v.3—and note the repetition of this item at the close of the argument in v. 28!). Second, Aaron belonged to the tribe of Levi; Christ, according to the flesh, sprang from the royal tribe (v. 14), and is the Priest-King. Third, Aaron was made "after the law of a carnal commandment"; Christ, "after the power of an endless life" (v. 16). Fourth, Aaron "made nothing perfect"; Christ did (v. 19). Fifth, Aaron was unable to bring the sinner, "nigh unto God" (v. 19); Christ has (v. 25). Sixth, Aaron was not inducted into his priestly office by a Divine oath; Christ was (v. 21). Seventh, Aaron had many successors (v. 23); Christ had none. Eighth, Aaron died (v. 23); Christ "ever liveth" (v. 25). Ninth, Aaron was a sinner (v. 27); Christ was "separate from sinners" (v. 26). Tenth, Aaron was only the priestly head of an earthly people; Christ has been "made higher than the heavens"

(v. 26). Eleventh, Aaron had to offer sacrifice "daily" (v. 27); Christ's sacrifice is "once for all". Twelfth, Aaron was filled with "infirmity" (v. 28); Christ is "perfected forevermore". Well may we praise God for "*such* a High Priest" (v. 26).

In view of the introduction of this Priest par excellent, what room was there for another? No longer was there any need of the type, for the Antitype had appeared. Symbols and shadows have served their purpose when the substance itself is manifested. The things of childhood are put away when manhood is reached. A crutch is dispensed with when the limb is restored. When that which is perfect is come, then that which is in part is done away with. This is the unescapable inference which the apostle dwells upon here. "For there is *verily*—of a truth which cannot be gainsaid, as a fact which cannot be controverted—a disannulling of the commandment going before". And why? Because "the priesthood being changed, there is made of necessity a change also of the law." The whole system of Judaism had been set aside by God.

One cannot read through the O. T. without marvelling at the long-suffering of the Lord. Notwithstanding the many and great provocations of Israel, He did not set Judaism aside until the end for which He had appointed it had actually been reached. When the promised Messiah appeared, the temple still stood in Jerusalem, its priesthood still functioned, the sacrifices were still offered. But now its purpose had been served, its mission accomplished. The antitype of the temple was seen in the person of God incarnate (John 2:21); that which Aaron foreshadowed was fulfilled in the great High Priest of Christianity; and all the sacrifices found their perfected sequel in the final offering of the Lord Jesus. Therefore did God take "the law of commandments contained in ordinances" and nailed it to the cross (Col. 2:14), where He left it completely accomplished.

In the verses which are to be before us the apostle dwells upon two things. First, he calls attention to a most significant and deeply important item in the prophecy given through David, and this, that Christ was constituted Priest by Divine oath, which exalts Him high above priesthood under the law. The profound meaning and inestimable value of this fact will come before us in what follows. Second, he affirms that Christ is Priest forever, and this in order to show that there should never more be any need of another priest, nor any possibility of a return of the Levitical priesthood. Marvelously full and comprehensive was that brief word in Psa. 110, supplying for us an example of what unsearchable stores of wisdom and truth are laid up in every verse of Scripture, if we are given spiritual sight in their investigation. Signal proof also is this of the *verbal* inspiration of Scripture: every phrase, every word, was indited by Divine wisdom and has its own value and meaning.

"And inasmuch as not without an oath He was made priest" (v. 20). The opening word has the force of "Moreover": it is not that the apostle is here drawing a conclusion from a promise previously laid down; instead he moves forward in the argument before him. He here introduces a new consideration for the confirmation of the leading design before him. That the contents of the verse depend upon what follows was the conviction of the translators, as may be seen from the fact that they supply the ellipsis (the words in italics) from v. 21. That which the apostle now insisted upon was, that the dignity of Christ's sacerdotal office was commensurate with the solemnity of His appointment to it.

Nothing was lacking on the part of God to give eminency and stability unto the priesthood of Christ: "Not without an oath". This was due unto the glory of His person. The Son of God, in infinite grace, condescending to take upon Him the priestly office and discharge all the duties of it, it was meet that any thing which would contribute unto the glory or efficacy of it, should accompany His undertakings. In this God showed how jealous He is for the honour of His Beloved; in all things He must have the pre-eminence. In everything that He undertook, He was preferred above all others who were ever employed in the service of God, or who ever shall be; and therefore was He made a Priest "not without an oath".

Moreover, God deemed it needful to encourage and secure the faith of His people. There were many things defective in the priesthood under the law, and it suited the design of God that it should be so. He never intended that the faith of the church should terminate in those priests. But upon the introduction of the priesthood of Christ God has exhibited all that faith is to look unto and lean upon, and therefore did He, in infinite wisdom and grace, grant the highest and most specific evidence of the everlasting continuation of His priesthood. In this manner has He shown that this appointment of His will and mercy is absolutely unchanging, so that if we comply not therewith we must perish forever. (Condensed from John Owen).

The priesthood of Aaron was not instituted with an oath; Christ's was. Now that which is connected with an oath can never be changed, for God is immutable. "In the same way as He sware unto Abraham, 'Surely blessing I will bless thee', in order that by two immutable things in which it is impossible for God to lie, we might have abundant assurance of hope; even thus is it that because the High Priesthood of Jesus can never be altered, because it is based upon the eternal decree and counsel of God, and because it is essentially connected with the very nature and purpose of God Himself, it is introduced with an oath. The Lord hath sworn, and will not repent" (A. Saphir).

"For those priests were made without an oath; but this with an oath, by Him that said unto Him, the Lord sware and will not repent, Thou art a priest forever after the order of Melchizedek" (v. 21). It should be particularly noted that God never solemnly interposed Himself with an oath with respect unto privilege or mercy but that in each instance it had *Christ* in view. Thus, He sware by Himself unto Abraham that in his seed all the nations of the earth should be blessed, whereby He announced the immutability of His counsel to send His Son to take His seed upon Him. So also He sware unto David by His holiness that his seed, Christ, should sit on his throne forever".

"For those priests were made without an oath, but this with an oath". Although there is never the slightest alteration in the internal acting of God's will nor the least changing of His purpose, for with Him there is *no* "variableness or shadow of turning", yet, He frequently alters His works, His providences, and even some of the things which He appoints unto men at different times, unless they be confirmed with an oath. The Levitical priests were by Divine appointment, and therefore the people of Israel were obligated to obey them. But they did not enter their office by Divine oath, the absence of this intimating that God reserved to Himself the liberty to make an alteration when He saw good.

"But this with an oath, by Him that said unto Him, The Lord sware and will not repent, Thou art a Priest forever after the order of Melchizedek". The person swearing is God the Father, the One unto whom He speaks is God the Son: "The Lord said unto my Lord" (Psa. 110:1). The oath of God is the open declaration of His eternal purpose and unchanging decree. Thus is the same act and counsel of God's will spoken of in Psa. 2:7. "I will *declare* the *decree*". Therefore when God is pleased to unveil His decree or reveal His purpose, testifying it to be absolute and unchanging, He does it by way of oath: see 6:13, 14, 17 and our comments thereon.

Should it be asked, *When* did God thus sware unto Christ? We must distinguish between two things, or more accurately, two aspects of the same thing, namely: the Divine decree or purpose itself, and the revelation or declaration of it, for the "oath" includes both. As to the decree itself, that takes us back to those eternal federal transactions between the Father and the Son, when the "Everlasting Covenant" was entered into. As to the revelation of it, that was through David. Thus, the many modern commentators who regard this oath as being made with Christ upon His ascension into heaven are seriously mistaken, for that would completely invalidate the apostle's argument here. Had Christ offered His sacrifice *before* God sware unto Him, He had no pre-eminence herein over the Aaronical priests. The oath must precede His entrance upon and discharge of His priestly office, or otherwise the force of the apostle's reasoning here would utterly break down.

Not only did God's oath to Christ make manifest the exalted dignity of Christianity's High Priest, but it also denoted the great importance of the economy which He introduced and now administers. "No wise or good man interposes his oath in a matter of trivial consequence. If he voluntarily gives his oath, it is a plain proof that he considers that matter as one of importance. That economy must then be a high and holy one indeed with regard to which Jehovah swares; and this circumstance must elevate it far above every other economy, though Divine in its origin, that is not distinguished by this highest conceivable mark of its importance in the estimation of Him who alone hath wisdom. But the oath of God marks not only the importance, but the *stability* of the economy in reference to which it is made. God is never represented in Scripture as swaring to everything but what was fixed and immutable" (John Brown).

"By Him that said unto Him, The Lord sware and will not repent, Thou art a Priest forever after the order of Melchizedek". As this is the final reference in Scripture to Melchizedek perhaps we had better summarise the cardinal features in which he foreshadowed Christ. First, Melchizedek was the only priest of his class or order, and thus pointed to the solitariness of Christ's priesthood—He shares it with none. Second, Melchizedek had no predecessor, and therefore his right to office depended not on fleshly descent; foreshadowing the fact that Christ's priesthood was quite distinct from the Aaronic. Third, Melchizedek had no successor: typifying the fact that Christ's priesthood is final and eternal. Once again we would stress the fact that it is not said Christ is priest *of* the order of Melchizedek, had He been so, the resemblance between them had been destroyed in a vital particular. Christ did not succeed Melchizedek, but was his Antitype. Unto those who object that nothing is said in the O. T. about Melchizedek's offering sacrifice to God, we would reply, Neither is there anything said of his *making intercession!* It was not in *those* things that God designed him to prefigure Christ, but in the particulars pointed out above.

"By so much was Jesus made a surety of a better testament" (v. 22). The "by so much" answers to the "in as much" of v. 20, hence our present verse is in immediate connection with v. 20, thus:

"And inasmuch as He was not made a priest without an oath, He is by so much made the surety of a better testament". V. 21, though containing the confirmation or proof of the principal assertion, is rightly placed in a parenthesis. On the close connection between vv. 20 and 22, J. Owen said:

"There may be a twofold design in the words. 1. That His being made a priest by an oath, made Him meet to be the surety of a better testament; or, 2. That the testament whereof He was the surety, must needs be better than the other; because He who was the surety of it was made a priest by an oath." In the one way, he proved the dignity of the priesthood of Christ from the new testament; and in the other, the dignity of the new testament from the priesthood of Christ. And we may reconcile both these verses by affirming that really and efficiently the priesthood gives dignity unto the new testament, and declaratively the new testament sets forth the dignity of the priesthood of Christ.

"By so much was Jesus made a surety of a better testament". These words clearly presuppose three things. First, that another covenant had existed between God and His people prior to the appearing of Christ. This is dealt with more expressly in Heb. 8, where the old and the new covenants are compared and contrasted. Second, that in some respect or respects the old covenant was good —implied by the contrastive "better". The old covenant *was* good in itself, as the product of God's wisdom and righteousness; it served a good purpose, for its statutes restrained sin and promoted godliness; its design was good, for it pointed forward to Christ. Third, that the old covenant had a "surety". Many have erred at this point through failing to distinguish between a "mediator" and a "surety". Moses was the typical mediator; Aaron, the typical surety, for he it was who offered solemn sacrifices in the name and on behalf of the people, making atonement for them according to the terms of the covenant.

"By so much was Jesus made a surety of a better covenant." Here for the first time in this chapter the apostle expressly names the person who had been referred to and described. Declaration had been made of the nature of the priesthood of Him who was to fill the office according to the Melchizedek type, but now definite application of the whole is made unto the Saviour. Two questions had long engaged the attention of the Jews: the nature of the Messiah's office, and who that person should be. The apostle had demonstrated from their own Scriptures that the Messiah was to be a Priest, yet not of the Levitical stock; as he had also shown the necessary consequences of this. Now he asserts that it was *Jesus* who is this Priest, for He alone has fulfilled the type and discharged the principal duty of that office. Concerning "Jesus" it is here affirmed that He was "made a Surety". He was "made so" or appointed so by the will and act of God the Father: compare 1:4, 3:2, 5:5 and our comments thereon for the force of this term "made". The whole undertaking of Christ, and the efficacy for the discharge of His office, depended entirely upon the appointment of God the Father.

"The Greek word for 'surety' properly means a bondsman: one who pledges his name, property or influence, that a certain thing shall be done. When a contract is made, a debt contracted, or a note given, a friend often becomes the *surety* in the case, and is himself responsible if the terms of the contract are not complied with" (A. Barnes). A "surety" is one who agrees to undertake for another who is lacking in ability to discharge his own obligations. Whatever undertaking the surety makes, whether in words of promise, or in the depositing of real security in the hands of the arbitrator, or by any other personal engagement of life of body, it implies the *defect* of the person for whom any one becomes surety. The surety is *sponsor for* another, standing in the room of and acting for one who is incompetent to act for himself: he represents that other person, and pledges to make good his engagements. Thus, Christ was not a Surety for God, for *He* needed none; but for His own poor, failing and deficient people, who were unable to meet their obligations, incapable of discharging their liabilities. In view of this, Christ agreed to undertake for them, fully pay all their debts, and completely satisfied every demand which God had against them.

A beautiful illustration of the "surety" is found in Gen. 43:8, 9, "And Judah said unto Israel his father, send the lad with me, and we will arise and go; that we may live, and not die, both me and thou, and also our little ones. I will be *surety* for him; of *my* hand shalt thou require him: if I bring him not unto thee, and set him before thee, then let *me* bear the blame forever". Blessed is it to find how faithful Judah was to his agreement. Later, Joseph's cup was found in Benjamin's sack (44:12), and on their return into Egypt and re-appearance before Joseph the governor, we hear him saying, "For thy servant became surety for the lad unto my father, saying, If I bring him not unto thee, then I shall bear the blame, to my father forever. Now therefore, I pray thee, let thy servant abide *instead of* the lad, *a bondman* to my lord; and let the lad go with his brethren" (44:32, 33).

A blessed N.T. example is found in the case of Paul who volunteered to be surety for Onesimus: "If he hath wronged thee, or oweth thee ought, *put that on mine account;* I Paul have written it with mine own hand, *I will repay*" (Philemon 18, 19). In like manner Christ engaged Himself unto the Father for His elect, saying, Charge to My account whatsoever My people owe Thee, and I will fully discharge their debts. This is an office in which Christ sustains a *representative character* in relation to those sinners for whom He interposed. It was Christ pledging Himself, or making Himself responsible, for the fulfilment of all that the Everlasting Covenant required on the part of those who are to share its provisions. It is as the Surety of the Covenant that Christ is called the "Second Man", the "Last Adam" (1 Cor. 15:47). This title, then, views Christ as *identifying Himself* with those whom the Father gave to Him, and on whose behalf He accomplished the great work assigned Him (see John 6:38, 39, etc.) in their room and stead, making full satisfaction to God.

Let us now observe that Jesus was made "a Surety of a better testament", or "covenant", as the term should be rendered, for the word denotes an arrangement or constitution, a dispensation or economy. It signifies that order of things introduced by Christ, in contrast from the order of things which obtained under the Mosaic regime. The Mosaic covenant was administered by the instrumentality of the Levitical priesthood, but the better covenant by Jesus, the Son of God: that was transitory and changing; this is permanent and eternal. It is so because those who enjoy its blessings receive an enablement to comply with its terms, fulfill its conditions, and yield the obedience which God requires therein. For by the ordination of God, our Surety merited and procured for them the Holy Spirit, and all the needed supplies of grace to make them new creatures, and empower to yield obedience to God from a new principle of spiritual life, and that, faithfully to the end.

It is the *Surety* by the Divine oath which gives stability unto the covenant. God entered into a covenant with the first Adam (see Hos. 6:6 margin), but it had no "surety"! And therefore though our first parent had all the tremendous advantages of a sinless nature filled with holy inclinations, and free from all evil imaginations, desires and habits, yet he broke the covenant and forfeited all the benefits thereof. God made a covenant with Israel at Sinai (Ex. 19 and 24), and appointed the high priest to act as the typical surety of it; yet, as we have seen, that covenant and that surety, made nothing perfect. The purpose of that covenant was to demonstrate the need of another and better one. In contradistinction from these God has made with His elect, in Christ, a covenant "ordered in all things and sure", "for He laid help upon One that is mighty" (Psa. 89:19).

And what is the practical application to God's children today of what has been before us? Surely this, that just so far as the new covenant surpasses the old, are we under greater obligations unto God, "for unto whomsoever much is given, of him shall be much required" (Luke 12:48). That just so far as the Surety of the better covenant exceeds in dignity and glory the surety under the old regime, are we under higher obligation of rendering to Him more complete submission, deeper devotion, fuller obedience. O my brethren, *what is due* unto that blessed One who left heaven's glory and came here to this sincurst world to discharge our obligations, pay our debts, suffer and die in our room and stead! May His love truly "constrain" us to gladsome and whole-hearted surrender to Him, no longer seeking to please ourselves, but living to and for *His* honour and praise. If we do not, that is certain proof that we are yet in our sins, strangers to the Surety of the better covenant.

"And they truly were many priests, because they were not suffered to continue by reason of death" (v. 23). In this and the following verse the apostle advances his last argument from the consideration of Christ's priesthood as represented by that of Melchizedek. His design is to present further proof of the excellency of it above the Levitical, and of His person above theirs. That Paul is still looking back to Melchizedek as a type of Christ, is evident from the description which he had given of him in the earlier verses, namely, that he "abideth a priest continually" (v. 3), and that "it is witnessed that he liveth" (v. 8), for his priesthood did not terminate at the age of fifty as did that of the Levitical. This is the particular detail of the type which is here seized and improved upon, for it was that which gives virtue and efficacy to everything else he had insisted upon. Set *this* aside and all the other advantages and excellencies he had named would be quite ineffectual to secure "perfection". What lasting profit could it be to the Church to have so glorious a Priest for a season, and then be deprived of Him by the expiration of His office?

Just as what the apostle declares of Christ in v. 24 hath respect to what he had before observed concerning Melchizedek, so what he affirms in v. 23 of the Levitical priests looks back to what he had before declared about them, namely, that they were all mortal men, and nothing more, for they actually died in their successive generations: see v. 8. The apostle expresses himself very emphatically "and truly". It was not a dubious point he was now handling, but one which was well known and could not be controverted. "They truly were *many* priests". It is of the *high* priest's only, Aaron and his successors, of whom he speaks. Jewish records inform us that there were no fewer than eighty-three high priests from Aaron, the first, to Phinehas, who perished with the temple. Thirteen lived under the tabernacle prior to Solomon, eighteen under the first temple before its destruction by the Babylonians, the remainder under the second temple till A. D. 70.

The reason for this multiplication of priests was "because they were not suffered to continue by reason of death". Notwithstanding the great dignity of their office, and the solemnities with which they were installed in it, they were but men, subject to infirmity and dissolution, like those for whom they ministered. Mortality suffered them not to continue in the execution of their office. It forbade them so to do in the name of the great sovereign Lord of life and death. A signal instance of this was given in Aaron himself, the first of them. God, to show the nature of that priesthood unto the people, and to manifest that the everlasting Priest was yet to come, commanded Aaron to die *in the sight of* all the congregation: Num: 20:25-29! In like manner, death seized upon each of his successors. Thereby did God intimate unto Israel that *imperfection* attached to that office which was so frequently interrupted in its administration.

"But this man, because He continueth ever, hath an unchangeable priesthood" (v. 24). This is the final proof in our present passage for the immeasurable superiority of our great High Priest over the Levitical priests. The Surety of the better covenant has an unchanging priesthood. The reason for and the ground on which this rests is here stated: "because He continueth ever". The apostle is not here proving the absolute perpetuity of Christ's sacerdotal office, but the continuous and uninterrupted administration of it. This was the faith of the Jews concerning the Messiah and His office: "We have heard out of the law that Christ abideth forever" (John 12:34), which was interposed as a difficulty and said by them in reply to our Lord's declaration that He was to be lifted up in death. It was this perpetuity of office that was principally typed out in Melchizedek.

Against this it might be replied, But Jesus Christ died also, no less truly and really than did Aaron and his successors, and thus it would follow that He had no more an uninterrupted priesthood than they. To obviate this difficulty, many of our moderns have fallen back on the error of the Socinians, that Christ did not become a Priest at all until after His resurrection. But such a reply cuts the knot, instead of untieing it. This figment we have already confuted in previous articles. Nor is there anything here in Heb. 7 which warrants the idea that the administration of Christ's priesthood is in heaven only. The whole context here shows plainly to all who are not blinded by prejudice that the apostle is treating of the *whole* of Christ's sacerdotal office.

The death of Christ was a vastly different thing from the death of the Levitical priests, for His death did not prevent Him abiding a priest, as theirs did. First, He died *as* a Priest; they died *from* being priests; He died in His office, they died out of office. Second, personal death was no part of their *work,* whereas to die was the chief priestly duty incumbent upon the Lord Jesus. Third, when they fell under the power of death, they could not extricate themselves from it and return to life and the service of the sanctuary, but the Son of God had power to lay down His life and take it again. So far from death putting an end to His priesthood, it did not even interrupt the exercise of it. Christ died as a priest, because He was also the Sacrifice for sins, yet through the indissoluableness of His person, His soul and body still subsisting in the person of the Son of God. He abode active in His office without any break: "He *continueth forever*".

It necessarily follows from what has been pointed out above that Christ hath "an unchangeable priesthood", subject to no alteration, that cannot pass away. The entire office of the priesthood pertaining and belonging to the new covenant, with its administration, are strictly confirmed unto the person of Jesus, the Son of God. There are none that succeed, any more than any (except typically) preceded Him. This at once exposes and gives the lie to the abominable blasphemy of the Papists who call their ministers "priests", affirming that they perform the proper work of such by offering sacrifice. It is highly derogatory to the honour of Christ, and subversive of the whole teaching of Scripture, to maintain that any person is now invested with priestly office and performs its proper work. They who wickedly assume this character encroach upon Christ's lone prerogative, and to suppose them to be what they pretend, would be to regard our Redeemer as a priest, not after the order of Melchizedek, but after the order of Aaron, which admitted of successors.

The abiding of Christ as Priest manifests the continuance of His care for His people. The same love which caused Him, as Priest, to lay down His life for them, remains unchanged within Him. Therefore each one may, with the same confidence, go unto Him with all their concerns, as poor and afflicted people went to Him while He was here upon earth. Again: it is upon the perpetuity of Christ's priesthood that the *security* of His Church rests. "Do we meet with troubles, trials, difficulties, temptations, and distresses? Hath not the church done so in former ages? But was any one true believer ever lost forever? Did not Satan rage, and the world gnash their teeth, to see their power broken by the faith, patience, and suffering of them whom they hated? And was it from their own wisdom and courage that they were so preserved? Did they overcome the enemy by their own blood, or were they delivered by their own power? No; instead, all their preservation and success, their deliverance and eternal Salvation, depended solely on the care and power of their merciful High Priest". Blessed be His name, He is "the same yesterday, and today, and forever". Hallelujah, what a Saviour! what a Surety! what a Priest!

CHAPTER THIRTY-FIVE

The Perfect Priest

(Heb. 7:25-28)

The principal subject in the verses which are to be before us is the same as that which has engaged the apostle throughout this 7th chapter, namely, the pre-eminent excellency of the great High Priest of Christianity. That which he is setting forth is the superiority of our Lord's High Priesthood over that of the Levitical. The various proofs may be expressed thus. First, because Christ is called of God after the order of Melchizedek, 5:10. In enlarging upon the fact, here in chapter 7, the apostle did three things: evidenced the superiority of Melchizedek over the order of Aaron, 7:1-10; appealed to the Messianic prediction of Psa. 110:4 in proof that Christ *had been* called after the order of Melchizedek; shows that the fulfilment of this prophecy necessarily involved the setting aside of the Levitical order.

The second proof of the superiority of Christ's Priesthood over the Aaronic order was, the distinguishing solemnity of its institution, namely, by the Divine oath, 7:20-22. Third, it was proved by the perpetual permanency of His Priesthood, 7:23, 24. Fourth, it is proved by the saving efficacy of His priestly work, 7:25. Fifth, it is proved by the personal qualifications which He possesses to serve as Priest, 7:26-28. Sixth, it is proved by the Heavenly Sanctuary in which He now ministers, 8:1-5. Seventh, it is proved by the New Covenant with which it is connected, 8:6-13.

Or again, we may view the contents of Heb. 7 as a setting forth of the *results* from God's having brought in Christ as Priest after the order of Melchizedek. First, it necessarily follows that the Levitical order of priesthood has been abrogated, for that order could not possibly consist side by side with His, v. 11. Second, in consequence of this change of priesthood, the whole Mosaic ritual has been repealed, v. 12. The reason of this is obvious, the entire ceremonial law pre-supposed the Aaronic priesthood, to which it was adapted and on which it was based — remove the foundation and the whole structure falls. Third, the introduction of of Christ as Priest ushered in an entirely new and immeasurably better economy, vv. 19-24. Finally, the providing of such a great High Priest infallibly secures the salvation of all God's people vv. 25-28.

In the closing verses of our chapter the apostle brings the whole preceding discourse unto an issue, by making application of it unto the faith and comfort of the Church. His object was not only to open up mysterious Old Testament scriptures, nor only to demonstrate the glory and pre-eminence of Christianity over Judaism, by virtue of the priesthood of Christ; but his chief design was to make evident the efficacy and eternal advantages of all true believers by these things. The climax to which he had been leading up is before us in v. 25, which he enlarges upon in the end of the chapter. That which Christians ought to seek and what they should expect from the blessed and glorious priesthood of Christ is what he now undertakes to make known. In like manner, in all his epistles the apostle makes it clear that the purpose of God in the whole mystery of redemption by Jesus Christ and the institutions of the Gospel, is the salvation of His elect unto the praise of the glory. of His grace.

"Wherefore He is able also to save them to the uttermost that come unto God by Him, seeing He ever liveth to make intercession for them" (v. 25). First, let us endeavour to ponder this inexpressibly precious word in the light of its context. The opening "Wherefore" denotes that an inference is here drawn from that which had previously been said. What then is the premise, or what are the premises, on which this conclusion rests? Or, in plainer language, *Why* is it that Christ is here said to be able to "save unto the uttermost"? "Wherefore"—because of the oath of His consecration (v. 20), because of the immutability of the Father's purpose (He "will not repent") v. 21, because of the better covenant of which He is "Surety" (v. 22), and because He "continueth ever" an unchanging Priest (v. 24)—"He is able also to save them unto the uttermost". This we take it, is the connection between v. 25 and its context.

From the consideration of the glorious truth and office of Christ as Priest, the apostle, to strengthen the faith and increase the consolation of God's people, points out the infallible corollary: "He is able". All power is His, abundant sufficiency of ability to accomplish His design of grace. This is the second time we are reminded of the capability of our High Priest. First, in 2:18 it was said, "For in that He Himself hath suffered being tempted, He is able to succor them that are tempted", and see our comments thereon. That which is particularly in view is not the ability of His nature, but of His *office*. It is still the pre-eminency of Christ above the legal high priests which is chiefly intended. By reason of their personal infirmities and the limited tenure of their office, they were unable to effect that which those desiring to approach unto God most stood in need of. But our great High Priest, being free from all such imperfections, "*is* able". Because His priesthood is indissoluable and perpetual, His office is all-sufficient to meet every need of God's people.

"Wherefore He is able to save them to the uttermost". It is no mere temporal or transcient deliverance which Christ effects for His people, but a supernatural, spiritual and eternal one. The word "save" denotes some evil and danger from which deliverance is secured. This is *sin,* with all its terrible consequences—pollution, guilt, the curse of the law, the captivity of Satan, the wrath to come. Wherefore it is written of Christ that He saves His people "from their sins" (Matt. 1:21), "from the curse" (Gal. 3:13), "from the wrath to come" (1 Thess. 1:10). "He is *able* also to save". It was no easy matter to subdue Satan, fulfill the law, take away sin, placate God, procure pardon, purchase grace and glory, with all that belongs unto God's great salvation. But God "laid help upon One that is mighty" (Psa. 89:19), and He who hath undertaken this work is able to accomplish it, and that by the means He hath designed to use and the way wherein He will proceed.

Now the way in which He has designed to save His people, is by the discharge of Christ's priestly office. God has appointed no other means to that end. We must look for it therein, or go without it. Alas, multitudes are like those sons of Belial who said of Saul when God had anointed him king, "How shall this man save us? and despised him" (1 Sam. 10:27). They understand not (nor do they desire to know) *how* Christ is able to save sinners by His priestly work, and therefore, under various pretences, they trust to themselves, and despise Him. "All false religion is but a choice of other things for men to place their trust in with a neglect of Christ. And all superstition, instances of it, be they great or small" (John Owen).

"Wherefore He is able also to save unto the uttermost." The last word here may have a double sense: it may respect either the perfection of the work, or its duration, so it is variously rendered, completely and entirely or forevermore and forever. Take its first meaning: Christ will not effect part of our salvation and then leave what remains to ourselves or to others. "He does not relinquish it by reason of death, but He lives on as long as it is necessary that anything should be done for the salvation of His people (A. Barnes). Consider its second meaning: whatever hindrances and difficulties lie in the way of the salvation of believers, the Lord Jesus is fully competent, by virtue of the exercise of His priestly office, to carry out the work for them unto eternal perfection. No matter what oppositions may arise, He is more than sufficient to cope with and overcome them all. Combining the two meanings: a complete salvation is a never-ending one.

"Them that come unto God by Him". This clause defines who are the partakers of His salvation. Christ is able to save unto the uttermost, yet all are not saved by Him, yea, they are few indeed that are saved. Multitudes hear of Him, but, loving more the things of time and sense, refusing to forsake all and follow Him, they "will not come" to Him that they "might have life" (John 5:40). Only those who come unto God by Him, does He save. To come to God means, first, to believe on Him (Heb. 11:6); second, to draw nigh to Him in worship (10:1, 22). It is the latter sense which is here principally in view, for the apostle is speaking of the state of the Church under the new covenant, and its advantage over that of Judaism, by virtue of its relation unto the priesthood of Christ. "They that come unto God by Christ are such, as believing in Him, do give up themselves in holy obedience to worship God in and by Him" (John Owen).

To come unto God by Jesus Christ is holy worship. So as to be therein interested in His saving power as the High Priest of His people is to come, first, in *obedience* unto His authority, as to the way or manner of it. There must be a bowing to His sceptre and a practical owning of His lordship, otherwise we are rebels and idolators, not worshippers. Second, with *reliance* upon His mediation as to the acceptance of it, counting on the sufficiency of His sacrifice to atone for our sins and His intercession to procure the acceptance of our persons and offerings. Third, with *faith* in His person as the foundation of it; so to believe in Him as vested with His holy office that the discharge of it *will* save even to the uttermost them that come unto God by Him. Unless we are true believers, our worship will not be accepted.

First, the quickened sinner comes to Christ, is *drawn* to Him by the Father (John 6:44), and through Christ he comes unto God: cf. 1 Peter 3:18. In His priestly office Christ saves from sin unto God. His righteousness carries them beyond Himself as Mediator unto God Himself: cf. Heb. 10:22. Thus "coming to God' is the fruit and consequence of "coming to Christ". God is a just and holy God, yet may the believing sinner, in and through Christ, have communication with Him. Suppose I am under an awakening sense of the terrible majesty and consuming holiness of God: I tremble, and dare not approach unto Him—alas, where are they these days who ever have such an experience? But, later, the Holy Spirit takes of the things of Christ and shows them unto me—His compassion for sinners, His mediatory office, His all-sufficient love: then my fears are silenced, and I draw near unto God praising Him for His unspeakable gift. Nor does Christ's "ability" to save depend upon my coming to Him, rather does it lie in His power to overcome the reluctance of "His own" and incline them *to* come: see John 17:20.

"Seeing that He ever liveth to make intercession for them." These words express the reason why Christ is able to effectually save His people: that which secures them is His perpetual life—"He ever liveth"; His perpetual work—"to make intercession". This is what gives efficacy to the priesthood of Christ. The Lord Jesus lives a mediatorial life in Heaven for His people: as He died for them, so He lives *for them*, and therefore does He assure them "because I live, ye shall live also" (John 14:19). Comparatively few today either understand or appreciate this blessed fact. That Christ died for them, all who assent to the Gospel profess to believe; but that there is an equally vital necessity for Him to now live for and make intercession for them, is something which they perceive not. Nevertheless, Scripture is clear on this point: "If Christ be not raised, your faith is vain; ye are yet in your sins" (1 Cor. 15:17).

"There are many Christians who dwell on the crucifixion of Jesus in a one-sided way. We cannot dwell too much on the glorious truth that Jesus Christ was crucified for our sins. Yet it is not on the crucifixion, but on Christ the Lord, that our faith rests; and not on Christ as He was on the cross do we dwell, but on Christ who was dead and is risen again, and liveth at the right hand of God, making intercession for us . . . When Jesus died upon the cross He put away our sins, but this was only removing an obstacle. The ultimate object of His death upon the cross was His resurrection and ascension, that through suffering He should enter into glory, that He should be the perfect Mediator between God and man, presenting us unto God and bestowing upon us all the blessings which He has purchased for us with His precious blood. He has obtained eternal redemption on the cross, He *applies* the blessings of eternal redemption from the holy of holies. If Christ was not risen we should still be in our sins; and if such a thing were possible, though we might be forgiven, we should be dead and without the Spirit" (A. Saphir).

So stupendous is the work of saving believers unto the uttermost, it is necessary for the Lord Jesus to live a mediatory life in heaven for the perfecting and accomplishing thereof. It is indeed generally acknowledged by professing Christians that sinners could not be saved without the death of Christ, but that believers could not be saved without the resurrection-ministry of Christ is not so freely owned or considered. Yet, Rom. 5:10 is very explicit on the point: "For if, when we were enemies we were reconciled to God by the death of His Son, *much more,* being reconciled, we shall be saved by His life". Let Rom. 8:33-35 also be duly weighed. It is one thing to recognize that, by the once offering of Himself, Christ has "obtained eternal redemption for us" (9:12), it is quite another to perceive that His intercession is required in order to the *fruits* of His oblation *being applied* to those for whom it was made.

It appears to many that, seeing Christ fulfilled all righteousness for His people, redeemed them by His blood, made full atonement for their sins, nothing more was needed. But had Christ left us to build our eternal safety on the foundation which He laid, had He ascended on High to enjoy His reward *without* continuing to exercise His priestly office on our behalf, had He merely secured our right and title unto the heavenly inheritance and left us to press forward to it unaided by Him, everyone of us would quickly fall a prey to the powerful adversaries which constantly seek our destruction. When God "laid the *foundations* of the earth", the "morning stars sang together, and all the sons of God (angels) shouted for joy" (Job 38:4, 7), yet were the *continued* actings of God's creative power required unto the perfection of the earth. So the foundation of the new creation was laid gloriously in the death and resurrection of Christ, causing triumphant praise unto God (Col. 2:15, 1 Tim. 3:16), yet that praise is founded upon the guarantee of Christ's unchanging love, care, and power, to complete the work He has undertaken.

Those for whom Christ died are not taken to Heaven the moment they believe, but are still left here in the Enemy's country; nor are they yet glorified, instead, the "flesh", with all its defiling influences, is still left within them. Therefore do they stand in urgent need of the priestly care of Christ, that, in answer to His intercession, God might send them His Spirit, grant them renewed supplies of grace, deliver them from their foes, keep them in communication with the Father, answer the accusations of Satan, preserve them unto the end of their earthly course, and, then receive them unto Himself and "present them faultless before the presence of His glory" (Jude 24). "Who can express the opposition that continues to be made unto this work of completing the salvation of believers? What power is able to conflict and conquer the remaining strength of sin, the opposition of Satan and the world? How innumerable are the temptations which every individual believer is exposed unto, each of them in its own nature pernicious and ruinous" (John Owen).

"The most glorious prospect that we can take into the things that are within the veil, into the remaining transactions of the work of our salvation in the most holy place, is in the representation that is made unto us of the intercession of Christ. Our High Priest has entered within the veil where no eye can pierce unto Him, yet is He there as High Priest, which makes Heaven itself to be a glorious temple. Herein we see Him by faith still vested with the office of the priesthood and continuing with the discharge of it. Hence, in His appearance to John, He was clothed with a garment down to the foot and girded about the paps with a golden girdle: both of which were sacerdotal vestments, Rev. 1:13" (Condensed from John Owen).

"The intercession of Christ is the great evidence of the continuance of His love and care, His pity and compassion towards His Church.... But how shall we know that the Lord Christ is thus tender, loving, compassionate, that He continueth so to be; what evidence or testimony have we of it? It is true, He was eminently so when He was upon the earth in the days of His flesh, and when He laid down His life for us. We know not what changes may be wrought in nature itself, by its investiture with glory; nor how inconsistent those affections which in us cannot be separated from some weakness and sorrow, are with His present state and dignity. But herein we have an infallible demonstration of it, that He yet continueth in the exercise of that office, with respect thereunto all those affections of love, pity and compassion are ascribed unto Him" (John Owen).

"For such an High Priest became us, holy, harmless, undefiled, separate from sinners, and made higher than the heavens" (v. 26). In this verse the apostle shows that in order for sinners to come unto God, they have need of an High Priest to encourage and enable them so to do. Not only is a high priest necessary, but there must be one possessed of certain qualifications of excellencies, if ever we are to obtain access to the thrice Holy One. Such a Priest is here described; such a Priest "became us", was requisite for and suited to poor sinners. None other could expiate our sins, purge our conscience from dead works, procure acceptance with God for us, purchase eternal redemption, administer supplies of grace enabling us to live unto God in all the duties of faith, obedience and worship, comforting us in trials, delivering from temptations, preserving us unto eternal glory.

The only high priest fitted to officiate before God on the behalf of desperately-wicked sinners was one who was "holy". That which is here in view is the absolute purity of Christ's *nature.* He was entirely free from the slightest spot or taint of our original defilement. Instead of being, as we were, "conceived in sin and shapen in iniquity", His humanity was "that *holy* thing" (Luke 1:35). His conception being miraculous, by the immediate operation of the Holy Spirit, and not derived to Him by natural generation, He was completely exempt from the pollutions which corrupts every one of Adam's descendants. He could say, "the prince of this world cometh, and hath nothing in Me" (John 14:30): there was nothing within Him to which the Evil one could make a successful appeal. And *such* an High Priest "became us". Had His nature been defiled, He had been disqualified either to be Priest or Sacrifice. This holiness of His nature was imperative in order to answer for the unholiness of our nature.

Second, He was "harmless". "Holy" tells of what Christ was Godwards: perfectly conformed to the Divine will inwardly, evidenced by His perfect outward conduct. "Harmless" tells of what He was manwards. He is the only one who has ever walked this earth who never contaminated, tempted, injured, those with whom He came into contact. As "holy", He loved the Lord His God with all His heart; as "harmless" He loved His neighbour as Himself. He lived not for self, but was ever at the disposal of others. He went about doing good. When reviled, He reviled not again. When ill-treated, He never retaliated. He was the Lamb in the midst of wolves. He was the Sun of righteousness with healing in His wings. How perfectly adapted was He, then, to serve as Priest and meet the exigencies of His people!

Third, "undefiled". He not only entered this world "holy" and "harmless", but He was so when He left it. Tabernacling for thirty-three years in a world under the curse, mingling daily with sinners, He contracted no defilement. Just as the rays of the sun may shine into the foulest stream without losing any of their purity, so Christ moved in and out amongst the vilest without the glory of His holiness being sullied in the slightest degree. Christ was "undefiled" morally, as the priests under the law were required to be ceremonially. He was never infected by the evils around Him. He touched the leper, and the leper was cleansed. He came into contact with death, and death was conquered. He was in the presence of the Devil for forty days, and was as spotless at the close as He was at the beginning of them.

Fourth, "separate from sinners". The position of this clause in our verse must govern its interpretation. It has a double force. It is intimately related to what precedes, as it is closely connected with the words immediately following. As it comes after the "holy, harmless, undefiled", it gives a summary of what Christ was in Himself, emphasising His uniqueness and demonstrating His fitness to officiate as Priest. *He* was the "Blessed" Man of the first Psalm: He walked not in the counsel of the ungodly, stood not in the way of sinners, sat not in the seat of scorners. He was the true Nazarite of Numbers 6. Though He lived amongst sinners, He was infinitely apart from them, in nature and character, motive and conduct. He was in the world, but *not* "of" it. Thus was He qualified to act as Mediator between God and sinners.

"Separate from sinners". As this clause prepares the way for "made higher than the heavens", it stands in sharp antithesis from "He was numbered with transgressors". On the cross, we behold Him in the place of sinners, but He occupies that place no longer. Death is for ever behind Him. He is now, in the absolute sense, "separate from sinners", that is, distinguished from those for whom He is interceding. He has been removed from their society unto another sphere. Thus, this clause points another contrast from the high priest under the law. Aaron offered atonement for sinners, and continued amongst them afterwards. Not so Christ.

"Made higher than the heavens". "This refers to the present place and state of our great High Priest. He was for a season made lower than the angels, and descended into the lower parts of the earth, and that, for the discharge of the principle part of His priestly office, namely, the offering of Himself for a sacrifice unto God. But He abode not in that state, nor would He discharge His whole office, and all the duties of it, therein. And therefore He was made higher than the heavens. He was not made higher than the heavens, that He might be a Priest; but *being* our High Priest, and *as* our High Priest, He was so made, for the discharge of that part of His office which yet remained to be perfected: for He was to live forever to make intercession for us" (John Owen).

"Absolute perfection of character is not the only requisite in a high priest suited to our circumstances; he must be possessed also of dignified station, or high authority, of unlimited power. He must be one 'made higher than the heavens'. The phrase is peculiar. It nowhere else occurs in Scripture; but its meaning is obvious enough. He must occupy a place of the highest honour and power. And He must be '*made* higher than the heavens'. Those words plainly imply that His elevation above the heavens is something conferred on Him. It must be beneath the heavens in order to the discharge of some of the functions of His office, and that in consequence of the successful discharge of them, He must be exalted far above all heavens, for the discharge of other functions, and for gaining the grand object, the ultimate end, of His office" (John Brown).

"Jesus went into the holy of holies which was typified in the tabernacle. Above all created heavens, above angels and principalities, Jesus is now in the true Sanctuary, in the presence of God, and there He is enthroned as our perfect High Priest. His position in Heaven demonstrates that when He offered up Himself He put away sin forever, even as it sets forth His divine glory. For who but the Son of God can sit at the right hand of the Majesty on High? As it is written, 'Be Thou exalted, O God, above the heavens' (Psa. 57:5)" (A. Saphir). "*Made* higher than the heavens" by God: this proves that complete expiation has already been made. It emphasises the fact that Christ has entered the Heavenly Sanctuary on our behalf: see 4:14, 8:1, 2, 9:24 and Eph. 1:20-23. It announces that He has been exalted above every order of created things. It makes known how immeasurably superior is our High Priest over Aaron.

Ere passing from this verse let us take to heart its searching practical application. The perfections of our High Priest are what we ought to be conformable to. "If we give up ourselves to the conduct of this High Priest, if by Him alone we design to approach unto God, then conformity unto Him in holiness of nature and life, according to our measure, is indispensably required of us. None can more dishonour the Lord Christ, no more perniciously deceive and betray their own souls, than by professing Him to be *their* Priest, with their trust thereby to be saved by Him, and yet *not endeavour to be* holy, harmless, undefiled, separate from sinners, like unto Him" (John Owen).

"Who needeth not daily, as those high priests, to offer up sacrifice (first for his own sins, and then for the people's:) for this He did once, when He offered Himself" (v. 27). Let the reader note carefully our punctuation of this verse: by placing the central clause in a parenthesis (as it obviously should be) we are relieved of a difficulty which has baffled most of the commentators. In this and the next verse the apostle names other instances in which our High Priest is pre-eminent over those of the order of Aaron. His perfections, described in v. 26, exempted Him from all the infirmities of the Levitical priests, which disqualified them from making personal atonement. The design of the apostle is to show that Christ was infinitely well-pleasing unto God, and because He was under no necessity to sacrifice for Himself, the offering which He made for His people is of eternal validity. "This he did *once*" announces there is no need of any further repetition.

The apostle is still contrasting Christ from the Levitical high priests. How could they pacify the declarative holiness of God which had been outraged by others, when God was justly displeased with them for their own sins? They were obliged to offer "daily" from time to time, "day by day" or again and again, by periodical repetition, for their own sins—cf. "from year to year" (10:1), and note that the Heb. of Ex. 13:10 "from year to year" is, literally, "days to days". Not only did the legal high priest have to sacrifice for his own sins, the offering which he presented on behalf of the people had no abiding efficacy, but had to be repeated annually. Whereas Christ, being perfect, needed no sacrifice for Himself; and His offering being perfect, there is no need for any further one. Christ's sacrifice abides "a new and living one" (10:20).

"For the law maketh men high priests which have infirmity; but the word of the oath which was since the law, maketh the Son, who is perfected forevermore" (v.28). In this verse the apostle sums up the whole of His preceding discourse, evidencing the true foundation on which he had built. Those who still adhered to the Mosaic institutions allowed that there must be a priest over God's people, for without such there could be no approach unto Him. So it was under the law, and if the same order be not continued, then the Church must needs be under a great disadvantage. As Owen rightly said, "To lose the high priest of our religion, is to lose the Sun out of the firmament of the Church."

Now the apostle has granted that the high priests who officiated in the tabernacle and temple were appointed by God to that office. His opponents were persuaded that these priests would continue in the church without change or alteration. God has designed a time when they were to be removed, and a Priest of another order introduced in their room. This change so far from being regrettable, was to the great advantage, safety, blessedness, glory of the Church. First, the Levitical priests were appointed under, by "the law"; but the new and perfect Priest "*since* the law" (i.e. in Psa. 110:4), showing Christ had superceded them. Second, they were but "men"; Christ was the "Son of God." Third, they were "made" by "the law"; Christ by "the word of the oath". Fourth, they had "infirmity"; the Son had none. Fifth, they served only in their day and generation; He "for evermore".

"But the word of the oath, which was since the law, maketh the Son, who is perfected for evermore". "The apostle turns again, in a most emphatic and conclusive manner, unto the key-note which he had struck at the beginning of the epistle. The law of Moses constitutes priests that were changing continually. But the Word which came with the oath after the law, consecrated forevermore as High Priest Him who is the *Son*: compare the same emphasis on 'Son' in 1:1, 2. Only the Son could be the High Priest, and He *became* the High Priest. Through His incarnation, through all the experiences of His life of sorrow and of faith, through His death on the cross, through His resurrection and ascension, Jesus is perfected forevermore" (A. Saphir). Christ abides perpetually in His priestly office because of the validity of His perfect Sacrifice. Hallelujah.

CHAPTER THIRTY-SIX

The Perfect Priest

(Heb. 8:1-5)

"This chapter is a continuation of the argument which has been prosecuted in the previous chapters respecting the priesthood of Christ. The apostle had demonstrated that He was to be a priest, and that he was to be, not of the Levitical order, but of the order of Melchizedek. As a consequence, he had proved that this involved a change of the law, appointing the priesthood, and that in respect to permanency and happy moral influence, the priesthood of Christ far surpassed the Jewish. This thought he pursues in the chapter, and shows particularly that it involved a change in the nature of the covenant between God and His people. In the prosecution of this, he (1) states the sum or principal point of the whole matter under discussion—that the priesthood of Christ was real and permanent, while that of the Hebrew economy was typical, and was destined in its own nature to be temporary: vv. 1-3. (2) There was a fitness and propriety of His being removed to heaven to perform the functions of His office there—since if He had remained on earth, He could not have officiated as priest, that duty being by the law of Moses entrusted to others pertaining to another tribe: vv. 4, 5. (3). Christ had obtained a more exalted ministry than the Jewish priests held, because He was the Mediator in a better covenant—a covenant that related rather to the heart than to external observances: vv. 6-13" (Albert Barnes).

The above is perhaps about as good an analysis of Heb. 8 as can be supplied. We too are satisfied that the passage which is before us is both a continuation and a summarization of the whole preceding discussion of the apostle. In the previous chapters he has produced indubitable proof that Jesus of Nazareth, the Son of God, is the great High Priest of God's people, infinitely superior to all the priests who went before Him. The closing verses of chapter 7 especially, supply a conclusive demonstration that He was priest and exercised the priestly office, while He was here on earth, and which He is now continuing to do in heaven. First, The description given of Him *as* "High Priest" in 7:26 has no pertinency whatever if it treats of what He was here upon earth. Take the expression, "undefiled"—what is there *in heaven* to defile? Nothing whatever. But understanding it to describe one of Christ's perfections while He was here in the world, it is full of significance.

Rightly did Geo. Smeaton declare, "Heb. 7:26, 27 show Christ on earth, as both Priest and Sacrifice. The 'such' of v. 26 refers not back to vv. 1-25, but to v. 27, cf. 8:1. The qualifications described, 'holy, harmless, undefiled, separate from sinners,' are descriptive of what He was here on earth when brought into contact with sin and sinners". Again; mark well the expression, "made higher than the heavens" in 7:26. *Who* was? The first part of the verse tells us: our "High Priest"! Note also that the last clause of v. 27, "this He did once, when He *offered* up Himself". Who did "this"? Who is the "He"? The Lord Jesus, of course. And in *what* specific character is He there viewed? Why, as "High Priest". As we are told in 2:17, "He was a merciful and faithful High Priest in things pertaining to God, *to make* propitiation (Gk.) for the sins of the people", and as Rom. 3:25 plainly declares, He made propitiation at the cross. So again, in 4:14 we read, "Seeing then that we *have* a great High Priest that is passed into the heavens". He did not enter heaven to become a priest, He *was* "Priest" when He "passed into the heavens". Language could not be plainer.

There is no excuse whatever for a mistake at this point, and our only reason for labouring it is that many who have boasted so loudly of their orthodoxy have systematically denied it. That Christ's sacrifice was a *priestly* one is clear from Eph. 5:2, "Christ . . . hath given Himself for us an offering and a sacrifice to God": not only as a "sacrifice" but as "an offering", and none *offered* to God the sacrifices of Israel save the priests. That Christ did not become Priest *after* He entered into heaven is also unequivocally established by Heb. 9:11, 12, "But Christ being come *an High Priest* of good things to come, by a greater and more perfect tabernacle, not made with hands . . . by His own blood He entered in once into the holy place, having obtained eternal redemption for us". He passed into heaven *in the capacity* of High Priest. Therefore we say that they who teach Christ became priest after His ascension are unconsciously or consciously, ignorantly or maliciously, corrupting the Truth of God and denying one of the most cardinal articles of our holy faith.

The line of argument followed by the apostle in the opening verses of Heb. 8 is not easily perceived. So far as the Lord has deigned to open their meaning to us, we understand it to be thus: Since Christ has ascended to the right hand of God, and now sits there as a Priest upon His throne, proof has been given that He is not a Minister of the earthly and Jewish sanctuary, but of the antitypical and heavenly one. Having set forth in chapter 7 the pre-eminence of Christ's priesthood over the Aaronic order and His all-sufficient qualifications for the office, the apostle now proceeds to evince His faithful execution of the same, and this, to the end of 10:19. In chapter 7 it is the excellency of our High Priest's *person* which is demonstrated; here in 8 it is His *ministry* which is contemplated. Note how in v. 2 He is spoken of as "a Minister of the sanctuary", that in v. 3 He has "somewhat also to offer", and observe the word "serve" in v. 5 and "ministry" in v. 6. In chapter 8 we are further shown the excellency of our Redeemer's sacerdotal office, first, from the high Sanctuary in which it is now exercised (vv. 1-5); second, from its functions corresponding with the better Covenant with which it is connected (vv. 6-13).

"Now of the things which we have spoken this is the sum: We have such an High Priest who is set on the right hand of the throne of the majesty in the heavens" (v. 1). The participle is in the present tense and should be rendered "of the things of which we are speaking" (cf. R. V.), the general reference being to the entire contents of the epistle, the specific to what is found in 4:14 to 10:18. "This is the sum" or crowning point: it is here that all the previous teaching of the epistle culminates, for the priesthood of Christ is, really, its distinguishing theme.

"We have *such* an High Priest", looks back, particularly, to 7:26. John Brown pointed out the very close connection which exists between the closing verses of 7 and the opening ones of 8, thus, "It is to be borne in mind that the high-priesthood of Jesus Christ is the great subject of discussion in the section of the epistle of which these words form a part; and that, after having shown the reality of our Lord's high priesthood by two arguments (chap. 5)—the one derived from His legitimate investiture with this office, the other from His successful discharge of its functions—the apostle proceeds to show the pre-eminent excellence and dignity of our Lord's high-priesthood. He, with much ingenuity, deduces four arguments for the superiority of our Lord's priesthood to that of Aaron and his sons from the ancient oracle recorded in Psa. 110:4: 'The Lord hath sworn and will not repent, Thou art a priest forever after the order of Melchizedek'. A fifth argument suggested by, though not so wholly grounded on, this ancient oracle, is entered on in 7:26, and is prosecuted, if we mistake not, down to the middle of the 6th verse of chapter 8, where a new argument for the superiority of our Lord to the Aaronical priests obviously commences, the substance of which is this:—The superiority of our

Lord's priesthood above that of Aaron and his sons is evident from the superior excellence of the covenant with which His priesthood is connected.

"The substance of the argument contained at the middle of v. 6 of chapter 8, may be thus expressed:—To fit a person for the successful discharge of the priesthood in reference to man, certain qualifications are necessary. These qualifications are wanting in the Aaronical priesthood: they are to be found in the highest perfection in Christ Jesus. We, that is, *men,* need a high priest 'holy, harmless, undefiled, made higher than the heavens'. Jewish priests do not answer to this description: Jesus Christ does. In Him we, *Christians,* have such a High Priest; and the conclusion is, He has received 'a more excellent ministry'. In this way, I apprehend, everything hangs well together, and the apostle's argumentative illustration appears complete and satisfactory. Indeed, the recurrence of the phrase '*such* a high priest' (7:26), and 'we have *such* a high priest' (8:1), seems intended for the express purpose of showing that the train of thought is continuous."

"We have such an high priest, who is set on the right hand of the throne of the Majesty in the heavens". These words point another contrast between Christ and the Levitical priests. It is true that our Lord Jesus entered for a season, a condition of deep humiliation, taking upon Him the form of a servant, being made in the likeness of sin's flesh; and this was necessary unto the sacrifice which He was to offer. But as to His *durable* and abiding state, wherein He continues to discharge His priestly office, He is incomparably exalted above Aaron and his successors. After the Jewish high priest had offered the annual sacrifice of expiation unto God, he passed within the veil with the blood, presenting it before Him. But he stood before the typical mercy seat with holy awe, and upon the fulfillment of his duty immediately withdrew. But Christ, after He had offered His sacrifice unto God, entered heaven itself, not to stand in humble reverence before the throne, but to sit at God's right hand; and that, not for a season, but forevermore.

The immediate design of the Holy Spirit was to comfort the hearts and establish the faith of the sorely-tried Hebrews, who were constantly represented by their unbelieving fellows for no longer having fellowship with the sacred rites of Judaism, and thus, in their esteem, being without any temple, priest or sacrifice. The apostle therefore reminds them again that "We *have* such an High Priest", who, though invisible, has been exalted in dignity and glory far above those who serve under the law of a carnal commandment. For Christians today the "*We* have such an High Priest" defines the relation of Christ to God's elect: fallen angels and reprobate sinners have no High Priest, that is one reason why their punishment shall be *eternal* — there will never be a Mediator to plead their cause.

The great object before the apostle in this epistle was to present that which was calculated to draw the hearts of the Hebrews away from the temple at Jerusalem, to the true Sanctuary of Christian worship on High. It is for that reason that the *ascension* of Christ occupies so prominent a place in it. One of the objections which carnal critics have advanced against the Pauline authorship of Hebrews is the fact that only once (13:20) is the *resurrection* of Christ directly referred to, whereas in all the other epistles of Paul it is given a place of great prominence. But the reason for this is easily accounted for. The emphasis in Hebrews is placed upon Christ's being at God's right hand (1:3, 1:13, 8:1, 8:9, 10:12, 12:2) for the purpose of assuring those who were deprived of the temple-services in Jerusalem, that they *had* the reality and substance of those things which were merely typical and temporary, and that the real Sanctuary was not on earth, but in heaven, and there Christ Himself is now officiating.

"Who is set on the right hand of the throne of the Majesty in the heavens". The exalted position which our great High Priest now occupies should commend both His person and His office in our esteem and assure us what abundant cause we have for expecting the successful discharge of its functions. Who is "set" or "seated": Acts 7:55 warns us against interpreting this in a carnal or literal manner. With 8:1 should be compared 1:3 (see our comments thereon) and 12:2. There are some verbal variations to be noted. In 1:3, where Christ's personal glory as "Son" is in view, there was no need to mention "the throne". In 12:2, where it is the reward of the man Christ Jesus, the "throne" is seen, but the "Majesty in the heavens" is not added. Here, in 8:1, where the dignity and glory of His priestly office is affirmed, we have mentioned both "the throne" and the "Majesty" of God.

"A Minister of the sanctuary" (v. 2). This is exceedingly blessed. "Having declared the glory and dignity which He is exalted unto, as sitting down at the right hand of the throne of the Majesty in heaven, what can be farther expected from Him? There He lives, eternally happy in the enjoyment of His own blessedness and glory. Is it not reasonable it should be so, after all the hardships and miseries which He, being the Son of God, underwent in this world? Who can expect that He should any longer condescend unto office and duty? Neither generally have men any other thoughts concerning Him. But where then would lie the advantage of the

Church in His exaltation which the apostle designs in an especial manner to demonstrate"? (John Owen).

Our blessed Redeemer, in His exalted glory, still condescends to exercise the office of a public minister in the behalf of His Church. It is required that our faith should not only apprehend what Christ did for us while He was here on earth, but also appropriate what He is now doing for His people in heaven. Indeed, the very life and efficacy of the whole of His mediation depends upon His *present* work on our behalf. Nowhere does the marvelous grace and the wondrous love of the Saviour more gloriously appear than in the ministry in which He is now constantly engaged. As all the shame, suffering, and pains of death deterred Him not from making an oblation for His people, so all the honour and glory, dignity and dominion with which He is now invested, diverts Him not from presenting its virtues before God and pressing for its blessings to be bestowed upon those for whom it was offered. His attention is still concentrated on His poor people in this wilderness world.

The "Sanctuary" in which our great High Priest ministers is Heaven itself: cf. 9:24, 10:19. It is the place where the majesty and glory of God are most fully displayed. "He looked down from the height of His sanctuary, from heaven did the Lord behold the earth" (Psa. 102:19). Heaven is here called "the Sanctuary" because it is *there* really dwells and actually abides all that was typically prefigured in the holy places of Israel's tabernacle. In the heavenly Sanctuary does Christ now discharge His priestly office for the good of His Church. It was a joyful time for Israel when Aaron entered the holy of holies, for he carried with him the blood which made atonement for all their sins. So the presence of Christ in heaven, pleading the efficacy of His meritorious blood, should fill the hearts of His people with joy unspeakable: cf. John 14:28.

"And of the true tabernacle, which the Lord pitched, and not man" (v. 2). This is not, as so many have supposed, an amplification of the preceding clause, but instead, a quite distinct thing. The word "true" is not here used in opposition to what is false (the temples of the heathen), but in contrast from the tabernacle of Israel, which was typical, shadowy, temporary. It has the force of that which is real, solid, and abiding. Israel's tabernacle was but an effigy of the antitypical one. "Moses gave you not that bread from heaven, but My Father giveth you the *true* Bread from heaven" (John 6:32), gives the force of the term. But what is the "true *tabernacle*" here referred to? We answer, the Redeemer's humanity, in which He ministers before God on high. In proof of this note, first, the metaphor of a "tabernacle" is used for the body of man in 2 Cor. 5:1 and 2 Peter 1:13. Second, the Holy Spirit has expressly used this term (in the Greek) in John 1:14, "The Word became flesh and *tabernacled* among us". Third, in Heb. 9:11 "tabernacle" manifestly refers to Christ's humanity—observe it is there distinguished from "the holy place" (sanctuary) in 9:12!

In addition to what has been said above, it should be pointed out that the tabernacle of Israel was the outstanding O. T. type of the incarnate Redeemer. We have more fully developed this wondrous and beautiful truth in our exposition of John 1:14, to which we would refer the interested reader. Here we must confine ourselves to only two or three details. God sanctified Israel's tabernacle as a place to dwell in (Ex. 29:44, 45); so in Christ "dwelleth all the fulness of the Godhead bodily" (Col. 2:9). God's glory was most conspicuously manifested in the tabernacle—"The glory of the Lord filled the tabernacle" (Ex. 40:34); so of Christ the apostle declared "we beheld His glory, the glory as of the only begotten of the Father" (John 1:14). In the tabernacle, sacrifices and incense were offered to God, and all holy services were performed; so Christ in His body offered up His own sacrifice, prayers, and all holy services (Heb. 5:7, 10:5). To the tabernacle the people brought all their offerings (Lev. 1:3), so must we bring all ours to Christ (Heb. 13:15).

"The true tabernacle, which the Lord pitched, and not man". Here there is a manifest reference to the virgin-birth, the supernatural character of our Lord's humanity, being parallel with "A body hast *Thou* prepared Me" (10:5). The verb, "pitched" is a word proper unto the erection and establishment of a tabernacle—the fixing of stakes and pillars, with the fastening of cords thereto, was the principal means of setting up one (Isa. 54:2). It is the *preparation* of Christ's humanity which is signified: a body which was to be taken down, folded up for a season, and afterwards to be erected again, without the breaking or loss of any part of it. "Which the Lord pitched" shows the Divine origin of Christ's humanity: cf. Matt. 1:20. The words "and not man" declare that no human father was concerned with His generation: cf. Luke 1:34, 35.

"For every high priest is ordained to offer gifts and sacrifices: wherefore it is of necessity that this man have somewhat also to offer" (v. 3). The opening word of this verse intimates that the apostle is here supplying a confirmation of what he had declared in vv. 1, 2. He argues from a general to a particular: "*every* high priest is ordained *to offer*" (that being the specific purpose for which God calls him to this office) therefore, Christ, the great High Priest, must also have been ordained for that end. Thus, the Lord

Jesus has done and is still doing that which appertains to the antitypical Sanctuary.

In the opening verses of our chapter we behold the Redeemer in the heavenly sanctuary, ministering there before God on the behalf of His people. "But *how* did He enter into this sanctuary? The high priests under the law entered into their sanctuary after having offered a sacrifice; and *so also* did the great High Priest of our profession. 'For every high priest is ordained to offer gifts and sacrifices: wherefore it is of necessity that this man have somewhat also to offer'. No attentive reader can help being sensible that these words, taken by themselves, do not convey a distinct, complete, satisfactory meaning. The statement is obviously elliptical; and the following seems to be the most probable way of supplying the ellipsis: We have a High Priest which has entered into the heavenly sanctuary, the true holy of holies. Every high priest is appointed to offer up sacrificial gifts in order to his entrance into the earthly sanctuary: it was necessary, as the antitype must correspond to the type, that this illustrious Priest should have somewhat also to offer, for the purpose of opening His way into the true sanctuary.

"Christ's being there, in the heavenly sanctuary, is the proof at once that an expiatory sacrifice has been offered, and that that sacrifice has been effectual. And what was this 'somewhat' which it was necessary that He should offer in order to His entering into the true sanctuary? We have but to look back to find the answer. It was 'Himself', 'holy, harmless, undefiled, separate from sinners'. His perfect, cheerful obedience to the preceptive part of the Divine law, and His perfect, cheerful obedience to the sanctioning part of it, opened for Him, as a High Priest, His way into that true holy place, where in the presence of God He acts as a public functionary in the name of His redeemed ones.

"It is plain that He could not have the sacrifices prescribed by the law to offer, for He did not belong to that class of persons to whom the offering of those was by law restricted; but He had a better sacrifice: read Heb. 10:5-13" (John Brown). "The apostle intends to show (v. 3) that Christ's priesthood cannot co-exist with the Levitical priesthood. He proves it in this way:—The law appointed priests to offer sacrifices to God; it hence appears that the priesthood is an empty name without a sacrifice. But Christ had no sacrifice such as was offered under the law; it hence follows that His priesthood is not earthly or carnal, but one of a more excellent character" (John Calvin).

Thus far the Holy Spirit has affirmed that the great High Priest of Christians is enthroned in heaven (v. 1); that He is there a

"Minister", serving in the antitypical Sanctuary, and that, in the "true tabernacle", His own humanity (v. 2); and that His right to entrance there was His own perfect sacrifice (v. 3). He now declares, "For if He were on earth, He should not be a priest, seeing that there are priests that offer gifts according to the law" (v. 4). The opening "For" looks back to what had been declared in vv. 1, 2, and introduces a further proof that the *continuation* of Christ's priestly ministry *must be* in the heavenly sanctuary. The earthly system, Judaism, had its own priests who offered gifts "according to the law." "This mere earthly, typical, inferior priesthood has been already provided for, its rules are fixed, and the order of men defined who fill its functions; and according to those rules, Christ Jesus could not be one of them, not being of the right tribe. The fact, therefore, that He has priestly functions, a fact before proved, shows that His priesthood is in a different sanctuary" (F. S. Sampson).

This 4th verse is the one that is most appealed to by those who deny that Christ entered the priestly office before His ascension. But if it be examined carefully in the light of its setting, nothing whatever is to be found in it which favours the Socinian view. That which the apostle is treating of here in chapter 8 is the *full* execution of the *whole* of Christ's priesthood: thereunto belonged not only the once oblation of Himself, but His continual intercession as well. Now that intercession must be made in heaven, at God's right hand. We say "must" for the O. T. types require it. Aaron had to carry incense, as well as blood, into the holy of holies (Lev. 16). Had Christ remained on earth after His resurrection, only half of His priestly work had been performed. His ascension was necessary for the maintenance of God's governmental rights, for the vindication of the Redeemer Himself, and for the wellbeing of His people; that what He had begun on earth might be continued, consummated and fully accomplished in heaven. The expiatory sacrifice of Christ had been offered once for all, but He must take His place as an Intercessor at God's right hand, if His Church should enjoy the benefits of it.

In this 4th verse the apostle is not only confirming his statement in vv. 1, 2, but he is also anticipating the objecting Jews: But you Christians have no high priest on earth! True, says the apostle, and well it is that we do not. It is to be carefully noted that the Spirit does not here say that when Christ *was* on earth He was *not* a Priest — no, He would not flatly contradict what he had plainly affirmed in 2:17, 5:7-9, 7:26, 27. Instead, He says "If He *were* on earth," that is, had He remained here, He would not have completely discharged His sacerdotal functions. Had Christ stayed on earth, He had left His office imperfect, seeing that His people needed One to "appear in the presence of God" (9:24) for them. If Aaron had only offered sacrifice at the brazen altar, and had not carried the blood within the veil, he had left his work only half done.

"Seeing that there are priests that offer gifts according to the law" (v. 4). This states the reason *why* Christ had not been a perfect priest if He had not gone to heaven: there were already priests, and that, of a tribe which He was not of, that offered gifts on earth, yea, had done so long before He became incarnate. Therefore if the entire design of Christ's priesthood had been merely to be a priest on earth, they would plead possession before Him. But, as v. 5 immediately proceeds to tell us, those priests only served "unto the example and shadow of heavenly things." Nothing but a real priesthood in heaven could supercede and abolish theirs. This is brought out plainly in 9:8: the "first tabernacle" was to stand until a Priest went into heaven and executed that office there: so that if Christ is to be Priest alone, He must become a Priest interceding in heaven, or otherwise, the Levitical priests would share that office with Him.

To sum up. The first clause of v. 4 is not an absolute, but a relative statement: "For if He were on earth, He would not be a priest". And why? "Seeing that there are priests that offer gifts according to the law", that is, the place is already occupied. Yes, but *what* place? Why that of offering gifts *according to the law.* Since Christ was above the law, the ideal and perfect Priest, He could not officiate in the temple at Jerusalem, for not only did His fleshly descent from Judah hinder this, but the sanctuary in which He now presents His sacrifice must correspond in dignity to the supreme excellency of His office. Thus, so far from His absence from the earth casting any suspicion on Him it is the necessary consequence of His being who He is and of having done what He has done.

"Who serve unto the example and shadow of heavenly things, as Moses was admonished of God when he was about to make the tabernacle: for, See, saith He, thou make all things according to the pattern showed to thee in the mount" (v. 5). Here the apostle furnishes further proof of what he had said at the beginning of v. 4. The presence of the type necessarily implies the absence of the Antitype (cf. 9:8-10), because the very nature of a type is to symbolise visibly an absent and unseen reality. From the Divine viewpoint, Judaism was set aside, ended, when God rent the veil of the temple (Matt. 27:51); but from the human, it was not abolished till Titus destroyed Jerusalem in A. D. 70. Israel's priests still served, but the only significance of their ministry was a typical one.

The design of the Spirit in v. 5 is obvious. There was something above and beyond the material tabernacle which God prescribed to Moses: that which he built, only furnished a faint foreshadowing of spiritual and heavenly realities, which are now actualised by Christ on High. The entire ministry of Israel's priests had to do with earthly and carnal things, which provided but a dim outline of things above. The word "example" signifies type, and is rendered "figures" in 9:24. The term "shadow" means an adumbration, and is opposed to the substance or reality; see Col. 2:17, Heb. 10:1. "Shadows" are but fading and transitory, have no substance of themselves, and but darkly represent.

"See, saith He, thou make all things according to the pattern showed to thee in the mount." "This passage is found in Ex. 25:40, and the apostle adduces it here on purpose, so that he might prove that the whole service according to the Law was nothing more than a picture, as it were, designed to shadow forth what is found spiritually in Christ" (John Calvin).

The practical application to us of the teaching of v. 5 is: Christians ought to exercise the utmost care and diligence to ascertain the revealed mind of God in what *He* requires from us in our worship of Him. Though Moses was learned in all the wisdom of Egypt, that was of no value or avail when it came to spiritual acts. He must do *all* things precisely as Jehovah ordered. In connection with what is styled "Divine worship" today, the great majority of professing Christians follow the dictates of their own wisdom, or inclination of their fleshly lusts, rather than Holy Scripture. Others mechanically follow the traditions of their fathers, or the requirements of popular custom. The result is that the Holy Spirit is grieved and quenched by the worldly inventions of carnal men, and Christ is *outside* the whole thing. Far better not to worship God at all, than to mock Him with human "will worship" (Col. 2:23). Far better to worship Him scripturally in the seclusion of our homes, than fellowship the abominable mockery that is now going on in almost all of the so-called "churches".

CHAPTER THIRTY-SEVEN

The Two Covenants

(Heb. 8:6-9)

In the 7th chapter the apostle has demonstrated by irrefutable logic and upon the authority of Holy Scripture that the priesthood of Christ has superceded the Aaronic order. Here in chapter 8 he makes manifest the superior *ministry* of our great High Priest. First, He is "seated" (v. 1). Second, He is seated on the throne of Deity (v. 1). Third, He is a Minister of the heavenly sanctuary (v. 2). Fourth, His own person provides the antitype of the tabernacle (v. 2). Fifth, He is presenting before God a more excellent sacrifice (vv. 3-6). Sixth, He is Mediator of a superior covenant (v. 6). Seventh, that covenant has to do with "better promises" (v. 6). That upon which the Holy Spirit would here have us focalize our attention is the *place* where our High Priest ministers, and the immeasurable superiority of the *economy* which He is now administering.

This 8th chapter of Hebrews treats of two things: the sphere of our High Priest's ministry and the better covenant with which it is connected: the one being in suited accord with the other. The 6th verse gives the connecting link between them. The apostle's object in introducing the "new covenant" at this stage of his argument is obvious. It was to the old covenant that the whole administration of the Levitical priesthood was confined. The entire church-state of the Jews, with all the ordinances and worship of it, and all the privileges connected with it, depended wholly on the covenant which God made with them at Sinai. But the introduction of the new Priesthood necessarily abolished that covenant, and put an end to all the sacred ministrations which belong to it. This it is which the apostle here undertakes to prove.

"The question which troubled the minds and hearts of the Hebrews was their relation to the Levitical priesthood, and to the old dispensation. The temple was still in Jerusalem, and the Levitical ordinances appointed by Moses were still being observed. Although the Sun had risen, the moon had not yet disappeared. It was waning; it was ready to vanish away. Now it became an urgent necessity for the Hebrew Christians to understand that Christ was the true and eternal High Priest in the heavenly sanctuary, and that the new and everlasting covenant with Judah and Israel was connected with the gospel promise, and not with the law. God Himself had made the first covenant old by promising the new. And now that Christ had entered into the holy of holies by His own blood, the old covenant had passed away; and yet the promises of God to His chosen people remained firm and unchanged" (A. Saphir).

That God *had* "changed" the order of priesthood (7:12) was, as we have seen, clearly evidenced by His causing Christ to spring from the tribe of Judah (7:14). God's raising up of a Priest from *that* tribe necessarily excluded those belonging to the house of Aaron from the sacerdotal office, just as God's raising up David to sit upon the throne, forever set aside the descendants of Saul from the regal office. Herein we may discern one reason why Jehovah ordained and gave such strict regulations for the distribution of Israel into their tribes, namely, that He might provide for their instruction as to the continuance of the legal worship among them, which could no longer be continued than while the priesthood was reserved unto the tribe of Levi.

This Divine change in the order of priesthood necessarily entailed a change of covenant or economy, as a change of the royal family denotes a new dynasty, or as a new president involves a change of government. The economy with which Christ is connected as far excels the old order of things as His sacerdotal office exceeded that of Aaron's. Thus the apostle is here really advancing one more argument or proof for the pre-eminence of our Lord's priesthood. As a Minister or public functionary Jesus Christ is as far superior in dignity to the Levites as the dispensation over which He presides is of a far superior order than the dispensation in which they served.

In approaching the subject of the two covenants, the old and the new, it should be pointed out that it is not always an easy matter to determine whether the "old covenant" designates the Mosaic economy or the covenant of works which God made with Adam (Hos. 6:7 margin); nor to decide whether the "new covenant" refers to the Gospel dispensation introduced by Christ, or to the covenant of grace which was inaugurated by the first promise made to Adam (Gen. 3:15) and confirmed to Abraham (Gen. 17). In each case the context must decide. We may add that the principal passages where the two covenants are described and contrasted are found in 2 Cor. 3, Gal. 3 and 4, Heb. 8, 9 and 12.

"But now hath He obtained a more excellent ministry, by how much also He is the Mediator of a better covenant, which was established upon better promises" (v. 6). "This verse is a transition from one subject to another; namely, from the excellency of the priesthood of Christ above that of the law, to the excellency of the new covenant above the old. And herein also the apostle artificially compriseth and confirmeth his last argument, of the pre-eminence of Christ, His priesthood and ministry, above that of the law. And this He doth from the nature and excellency of that covenant whereof He was the Mediator in the discharge of His office" (John Owen).

"But now hath He obtained a more excellent ministry." The apostle here introduces his important assertion by a time-mark, the "But now" signifying at this season. It points a contrast from the period of the Mosaic dispensation, when Israel's priests served "unto the example and shadow of heavenly things" (v. 5). A close parallel is found in Rom. 3:21, "but now the righteousness of God without the law is manifested," which is defined in v. 26 as "to declare *at this time* His righteousness: that He might be just, and the Justifier of him which believeth in Jesus" (v. 26). God in His infinite wisdom gives proper times and seasons to all His dispensations toward His Church. The Lord hastens or consummates all His works of grace in their own appointed time: see Isa. 60:22. Our duty is to leave the ordering of all the concerns of His people, in the accomplishment of His promises, to God in His own good time: Acts 1:7.

That which is here ascribed unto Christ is "a more excellent ministry." The priests of old had a ministry, and an excellent one, for it was by Divine appointment they served at the altar (v. 5). So Christ has a ministry, and "a more excellent" one. In v. 2 He is designated "a Minister of the sanctuary." He is called such not with respect unto one particular act of administration, but because a standing office has been committed to Him. The service to which Christ has been called is of a higher order and more excellent nature than any which Aaron ever discharged. It is a "more excellent ministry" because it is the real and substantial one, of which the Levitical was but the emblem; it pertains to things in heaven, while theirs was restricted to the earthly tabernacle; it is enduring while theirs was but temporary.

This more excellent ministry Christ is here said to have "obtained." The way whereby the Lord Jesus entered on the whole office and work of His mediation has been expressed in 1:4 as by "inheritance": that is, by free grant and perpetual donation, made unto Him as the Son—compare our comments on that verse. There were two things which concurred unto His obtaining this ministry: first, the eternal purpose and counsel of God, decreeing Him thereunto (1 Peter 1:20, Rev. 13:8). Second, the actual call of God (Heb. 5:4, 5), which carried with it His unction of the Spirit above measure (Psa. 45:7), for the holy discharge of His whole office. Thus, Christ obtained this ministry not by any legal constitution, fleshly succession, or carnal ordination, as did the Levitical priests. The exaltation of the human nature of Christ into union with His Deity, for the office of this glorious ministry, depended solely upon the sovereign wisdom, grace, and love of God.

"But now hath He obtained a more excellent ministry, by how much also He is the Mediator of a better covenant." The particular point which the apostle here makes, or rather the conclusion which he here draws from the premises laid down, had been anticipated and intimated in what he said in 7:20, 22. There he had declared that the excellency of the covenant of which Christ has been made Surety and Mediator has a proportion with the pre-eminence of His priesthood above that of Aaron's. His being made a Priest by Divine oath (which the Levites were not) fitted Him to be the Surety of a better economy. Conversely, the covenant of which He is Surety must needs be better than the old regime because He who was the Surety of it had been made so by Divine oath. Thus, the dignity of Christ's priesthood is demonstrated by the excellency of the new covenant, and declaratively the new covenant sets forth the dignity of Christ's priesthood.

"He is the Mediator of a better covenant." It is most important to recognize that Christ is a *sacerdotal* Mediator. This is made clear by 1 Tim. 2:5, 6, "For there is one God, and one Mediator between God and men, the man Christ Jesus; Who gave Himself *a ransom* for all, to be testified in due time." The mediating Priest intervenes with sacrifice and intercession for the reconciling of God and sinners. As we shall (D. V.) yet see, Heb. 9:15 expressly declares that Christ's priestly work was the very purpose of His being appointed Mediator. So in 12:24 His sacrifice is again made prominent in connection with His mediation. Thus the *sacerdotal* character of His mediation cannot be scripturally gainsaid.

Christ has obtained a more excellent priestly ministry corresponding to the superior dispensation of which He is the Mediator. "But now (in this Christian dispensation) hath He (as 'Priest') obtained (from God) a more excellent ministry (than Aaron's) by how much *also* He is the Mediator of a better covenant." He is not only Priest, but Mediator; Priest because He is Mediator, Mediator because He is Priest. It is *by* His priestly office and work that He exercises His mediatorship, standing between two parties and reconciling them. He thus combines in His own person what was divided between two under the old economy, Moses being the typical mediator, Aaron the typical surety. As "Surety" Christ *pledged* Himself to see that the terms of the covenant were faithfully carried out; as "Mediator," He is *negotiating* for His people's blessing. The word "covenant" in this chapter signifies an arrangement or constitution of things, an economy or dispensation. The "old covenant" was that peculiar order of things under which the Jewish people were placed in consequence of the transactions at Sinai. The "new" or "better covenant" is that order of things which has been introduced by Jesus Christ, namely, the Christian dispensation.

"He is the Mediator of a better covenant." A mediator is a middle person between two parties entering into covenant, and if they be of different natures, a perfect mediator would have to partake of each of their natures in his own person. This Christ has done. Such mediation presupposes that the two parties are at such variance they cannot treat directly with the other; unless this were so, a go-between would be needless. See this fact illustrated in Deut. 5:23-27. In voluntarily undertaking to serve as Mediator, two things were required of Christ: first, that He should remove whatever kept the covenantors at a distance, taking away the cause of enmity between them. Second, that He should purchase and procure, in a way suited to the glory of God, the actual communication of all the good things prepared and proposed in this covenant (grace and glory) unto those on whose behalf He acts as Surety. Finally, He who is this Mediator must be accepted, trusted, and rested in by both parties entering into covenant. On God's part, He has openly declared that He is "well pleased" with Christ (Matt. 3:17); on the part of His elect, they are made willing "in the day of His power" (Psa. 110:3).

"Which was established upon better promises." Every covenant between God and man, must be founded on and resolved into promises. Hence, essentially, a promise and a covenant are all one, and God calls an absolute promise founded on an absolute decree, His covenant, Gen. 9:11. And His purpose for the continuation of the course of nature to the end of the world, He calls His covenant with day and night, Jer. 33:20. The being and essence of a Divine covenant lies in the promise. Hence are they called 'the covenants of promise,' Eph. 2:12. Such as are founded on and consist in promises. And it is necessary that so it should be" (John Owen).

"Which was established upon better promises." The word "established" here is important to note, for it plainly intimates to us that the apostle is *not* here treating of the Everlasting Covenant *absolutely,* and as it had been virtually administered from the foundation of the world in the way of a promise; but relatively, as it had been *formally* introduced on earth *as* a new dispensation or economy. In the Divine administration of the Everlasting Covenant it has now been reduced to a fixed statute or ordinance. The term "established" signifies *legally established,* formally established as by a law. All is now fixed in the Church by Divine arrangement and secured by inviolable sanctions. In 7:11 the Greek verb here rendered "established" is translated "received the law"—compare our comments thereon. "The covenant to which the priesthood of Christ refers has been also established by law. It has been promulgated by Divine authority. The truth with regard to it has been 'spoken by the Son of God, and confirmed to us by those who heard Him; and God has borne witness with signs and miracles, and gifts of the Holy Spirit,' according to His own will" (John Brown).

"Established upon better promises." Caution requires to be exercised and great care taken at this point lest we err in our understanding of the particular contrast which is here pointed by the word "better." "The promises in the first covenant pertained *mainly* to the present life. They were promises of length of days; of increase of numbers; of seed time and harvest; of national privileges, and of extraordinary peace, abundance and prosperity. That there was also the promise of eternal life, it would be wrong to doubt; but this was not the main thing. In the new covenant, however, the promise of spiritual blessings become the *principal* thing. The mind is directed to heaven; the heart is cheered with the hopes of immortal life; the favour of God and the anticipation of heaven are secured in the most ample and solemn manner" (A. Barnes). Observe well the two words which are emphasized in the above quotation. In O.T. times God "commanded *the* blessing, life *forever more*" (Psa. 133:3), not only temporal life in Canaan; while His people in N.T. times have "promise of the life that *now is,*" as well as "of that which is to come" (1 Tim. 4:8)!

Rightly did A. Saphir point out, "The contrast between the old and the new would be viewed in a false light, if we forgot that in the old dispensation spiritual reality and blessings were presented, and were actually embraced in faith by the people of God. The law had a positive or evangelical aspect, although herein also it was elementary and transitory, it acted as a guardian and a tutor; as the snow is not merely an indication of winter, and a contrast to the bright and genial sunshine, and the refreshing verdure of summer, but is also a beneficent protection, cherishing and preparing the soil for the approaching blessings from above. But now the winter is passed, the fullness has come."

The "better promises" are described in vv. 10-13: they are summed up in justification and sanctification, or more briefly still, in *redemption.* "But what he adds is not without some difficulty,—that the covenant of the Gospel was proclaimed on better promises; for it is certain that the fathers who lived under the Law had the same hope of eternal life set before them as we have, as they had the grace of adoption in common with us, then faith must have rested on the same promises. But the comparison made by the apostle refers to the *form* rather than to the substance; for though God promised to them the same salvation which He at this day promises to us, yet neither the manner nor the character of the revelation is the same or equal to what we enjoy" (John Calvin). Thus, the "promises" with which the new covenant is concerned are "better" in that they *mainly* respect spiritual and eternal blessings, rather than earthly and temporal ones; in that they have been ratified by the bloodshedding of Christ; in that they are now openly proclaimed to God's elect among the Gentiles as well as the Jews.

"For if that first covenant had been faultless then should no place have been sought for the second" (v. 7). The covenant which is here referred to is that into which Jehovah entered with Israel at Sinai: see Ex. 19:5; 34:27, 28; Deut. 4:13. Israel's response is recorded in Ex. 19:8, 24:3. It was ratified by blood:Ex. 24:4-8. *This* was not the "first" covenant absolutely, but the first made with Israel *nationally.* Previously, God had made a covenant with Adam (Hos.6:7), and in some respects the Covenant at Sinai adumbrated it, for it was chiefly one of *works.* So too He had made a covenant with Abraham, which in some respects adumbrated the Everlasting Covenant, inasmuch as it was one purely of *grace.* Prior to Sinai, God dealt with Israel on the basis of the Abrahamic covenant, as is clear from Ex. 2:24; 6:3, 4. But it was on the ground of the Sinaitic covenant that Israel entered Canaan: see Josh. 7:11, 15; Judges 2:19-21; 1 Kings 11:11; Jer. 34:18, 19.

"For if that first covenant had been faultless then should no place have been sought for the second." The connection between this and the preceding verse, intimated by the opening "For" is as follows: there the apostle had affirmed that the Christian covenant is superior to the Judaic; here, he demonstrates the same thing by arguing from the fact that the old covenant must have been defective, otherwise the new had been superfluous. It is an inference drawn from the facts of the situation. If there was need for a second, the first could not have been perfect, failing to secure that which was most desirable. A parallel is found in Gal. 3:21.

"For if that first covenant had been faultless, then should no place have been sought for the second." Wherein lay its "faultiness?" It was wholly external, accompanied by no internal efficacy. It set before Israel an objective standard but supplied no power to measure up to it. It treated with men in the flesh, and therefore the law was impotent through the weakness of the flesh (Rom. 8:3). It provided a sacrifice for sin, but the value thereof was only ceremonial and transient, failing to actually put away sin. It was unable to secure actual redemption. Hence because of its inadequacy, a new and better covenant was needed.

"Every work of God is perfect, viewed in connection with the purpose which He means it to serve. In this point of view, the 'first covenant' was faultless. But when viewed in the light in which the Jews generally considered it, as a saving economy, in all the extent of that word, it was not 'faultless.' It could not expiate moral guilt; it could not wash away moral pollution; it could not justify, it could not sanctify, it could not save. Its priesthood were not perfected—they were weak and inefficient; its sacrifices 'could not take away sin,' make perfect as concerning the conscience, or procure 'access with freedom into the holiest of all.' In one word, 'it made nothing perfect' " (John Brown).

"For finding fault with them, He saith, Behold, the days come, saith the Lord, when I will make a new covenant with the house of Israel and with the house of Judah" (v. 8). The opening "For" denotes that the apostle now confirms what he had just affirmed in vv. 6, 7: the proof is found in what immediately follows. The "finding fault" may refer either to the old covenant, or to the people themselves who were under it: finding fault "with it" or "with them." In view of what is added in v. 9 the translation of the A. V. is to be preferred. It was against the people that God complained for their having broken His covenant.

"He saith, Behold, the days come," etc. The word "Behold" announces the importance of what follows, and calls to a diligent and admiring attention of the same. "Behold" bids us be filled with wonderment at this marvel of grace. It is indeed striking to observe that the apostle did not rely upon logical deductions and inferences, conclusive though they were. A change of priesthood necessarily involved a change of covenant, or dispensational administration. Nevertheless, obvious as this was, Paul rested not until he *proved* his assertions with a definite and pertinent "thus saith the Lord." He would not have the faith of the Hebrews stand in the wisdom of man, but in the power of God. Blessed example for God's servants today to follow. Alas that so many people are contented with the dogmatic assertions of some man who "ought to know what he is saying," instead of demanding clear proof from the Scriptures.

The text which the apostle here quotes in proof of his assertion is taken from Jer. 31:31. It is most blessed to note the time when God gave this precious promise to His people. Beautifully has A. Saphir pointed out, "It is in the night of adversity that the Lord sends forth bright stars of consoling hope. When the darkest clouds of woe were gathering above Jerusalem, and the prophet himself was in the lowest depths of sorrow, God gave to him the most glorious prophecies of Judah's great redemption and future blessedness. The advent and reign of Messiah, the Lord our righteousness the royal dominion and priesthood of Israel's Redeemer, the gift of the Holy Spirit, the renewal and restoration of God's chosen people, the days of unbroken prosperity and blessedness—all the golden Messianic future was predicted in the last days of Jerusalem, when the magnificent fabric of its temple was about to sink into the dust, and its walls and palaces were about to be thrown prostrate on the ground."

This new covenant God promised to make with "the house of Israel and with the house of Judah." The word, "Israel" is used in the Scriptures in no less than four distinct senses. First, it is the name which God gave to Jacob when he wrestled with the angel and prevailed as a prince (Gen. 32:28). Second, it denotes his fleshly descendants called "the children of Israel," that is, the Jewish nation. Third, it is employed of the ten tribes, the kingdom of Samaria or Ephraim, in contradistinction from the kingdom of Judah, and this, after the Nation was rent asunder in the days of Jeroboam. Fourth, it is applied spiritually to the whole of God's people (Gal. 6:16). To which we may add, fifth, in Isa. 49:3 (note the verses which follow) it appears to be applied to Christ Himself, as identified with His people. Personally, we believe that it is the second and the fourth of these usages that obtain in our present passage.

The law of *first mention* helps us here. The initial occurrence of any expression or word in Scripture defines its scope and fixes, very largely, its consequent significance. So it is in this case. The name "Israel" was first given to Jacob: from that point onwards he is the man with a double name, sometimes being referred to as Jacob, sometimes as Israel, according as the "old man" or "new man" was uppermost within him. This more than hints at the *double* application of this name; oftentimes it is applied to Jacob's *natural* descendants, at other times to his *spiritual* brethren. When Christ affirmed of Nathanael "Behold an Israelite indeed, in whom is no guile" (John 1:47), it was the same as though He had said, "Behold a true

Israelite, a spiritual prince with God." To insist that "Israel" *always* signifies the fleshly descendants of Jacob betrays excuseless ignorance: why does the Holy Spirit speak of "Israel *after the flesh*" in 1 Cor. 10:18 if there be no Israel *after the spirit!*

The writer has no doubt whatever in his mind that the time is not far distant when God is going to resume His dealings with the Jewish people, restore them unto their own land, send back their Messiah and Redeemer, save them from their sins, and fulfill to them His ancient promise through Jeremiah. Nevertheless, we are fully assured that it is a serious mistake to *limit* the prophecy of Jeremiah (or any other prediction) to a *single* fulfillment. It is abundantly clear from 2 Cor. 3 that Christians in this dispensation are already enjoying the good of the new covenant which God has made with them. Moreover, are we not reminded at the Lord's table of our Saviour's words, "This cup is the new testament," or "covenant in My blood" (1 Cor. 11:25)?

It should be pointed out that O.T. Israel were typical and mystically significant of the whole Church of God. For that reason were the promises of grace under the old economy given unto the saints of God under the name of "Israel," "Judah," etc. (carefully compare Rom. 2:28, 29), because they were types of those who should really and effectually be made partakers of them. Hence it is that in 2 Cor. 1:20 we are told that "*All* the promises of God in Him (Christ) are Yea, and in Him Amen, unto the glory of God *by us.*" Hence it is we read that "Jesus Christ was a Minister of the circumcision for the truth of God, to confirm the promises unto the fathers, *and* that the *Gentiles* might glorify God for His mercy" (Rom. 15:8, 9). And hence it is that the apostle Paul writing to Christians says, "*Having* therefore these promises"—the preceding verses quoting from Lev. 26:12, etc! For the same reason in Heb. 13:6 the Christian is assured that the promise which the Lord made to Joshua belongs to him too.

Thus, by "the house of Israel" and the "house of Judah" in Heb. 8:8 we understand, first, the mystical and spiritual Israel and Judah; second, the application of this covenant to the literal and fleshly Israel and Judah in the day to come. In other words, we regard those expressions as denominating the whole Church of elect believers, typified of old, by the fleshly descendants of Abraham. Nor is it without reason that the Holy Spirit has here used *both* these names: we believe His (veiled) design was to take in God's elect among the Jews *and* the Gentiles. Our reason for believing this is because that in the very first inspired sermon preached after the new covenant had been established, Peter said to the *convicted* Jews, "the promise is unto you, and to your children (descendants) and to all that are afar off, as many as the Lord our God shall call" (Acts 2:39). It is indeed remarkable that the two emphasized words have a *double* reference. First, they applied to the literal house of Israel, who were then *outside* the land, in the dispersion (Dan. 9:7); second, to elect Gentiles, away from God: see Eph. 2:13!

At the time God announced His purpose and promise through Jeremiah, the fleshly descendants of Abraham were divided in *two* hostile groups. They had separate kings and separate centers of worship. They were at enmity with one another. As such they fitly adumbrated the great division between God's elect among the Jews and the Gentiles in their natural and dispensational state. There was a middle wall or partition between them (Eph. 2:14). There was "enmity" between them (Eph. 2:16). But just as God announced through Ezekiel (37:16, 17) that the diversified houses of Judah and Israel should "become one," so His elect among the Jews and the Gentiles are now one in Christ (Eph. 2:14-18)! Therefore are all born-again believers designated the "children" and "seed" of *Abraham* (Gal. 3:7, 29), and thus are they "blessed *with* faithful Abraham" (Gal. 3:9).

"Not according to the covenant that I made with their fathers in the day when I took them by the hand to lead them out of the land of Egypt; because they continued not in My covenant, and I regarded them not, saith the Lord" (v.9). The contrast between the two covenants is first expressed negatively: "not according." The differences between them are many and great. The former was mainly typical, the latter has the substance. The one was administered under an imperfect priesthood, the latter under a perfect one. The one had to do, primarily, with that which was external; the other is, mainly, internal. The Mosaic covenant was restricted to one nation, the Christian is international in its scope.

The old covenant is spoken of as dating from the day when the Lord took Israel, "by the hand to lead them out of the land of Egypt." This language emphasizes the woeful and helpless condition that Israel was then in: unable to deliver themselves out of their bondage, like children incapable of walking unless supported and led. As Deut. 1:31 says, "The Lord thy God bare thee, as a man doth bear his son, in all the way that ye went." So in Hos. 11:3 God says, "I taught them to go, taking them by the arms." Such expressions also accentuate the infinite condescension of God toward His people: that He should (so to speak) bow down Himself to reach them in their lowly estate.

"But they continued not in My covenant, and I regarded them not, saith the Lord." "They soon forgat God's works, they waited not for His counsel" (Psa. 106:13). The principal reference is to Israel's conduct at Sinai, when during the absence of Moses in the mount, they "thrust Him from them" (Acts 7:39), and made and worshipped the golden calf. That was but prophetic or indicative of their whole history. Their shameful conduct is mentioned here for the purpose of magnifying that marvellous grace that shall yet make the new covenant with such a people. "I regarded them not" refers to God's governmental dealings with Israel: the severity He exercised, consuming them in the wilderness. In view of which we may well heed that searching word, "Wherefore let him that thinketh he standeth take heed lest *he* fall" (1 Cor. 10:12).

CHAPTER THIRTY-EIGHT

The Two Covenants

(Heb. 8:10-13)

The subject of the two covenants supplies the principal key which unlocks for us the meaning of God's dispensational dealings with His people here on earth. Its importance and blessedness is not surpassed by anything within the entire range of Divine revelation. Yet, sad to say, it is something which is scarcely known at all today by the majority of professing Christians. Covenant-relationship has always been the basis on which God has dealt with His people. The foundation of all is the Everlasting Covenant, a compact or agreement which God made with Christ as the Head and Representative of the whole election of grace. We would refer the interested reader unto two articles upon it, which appeared in the Jan. and Feb. 1930 issues of this magazine. What we shall here endeavour to treat of is the *administration* of that covenant, as it was made known by God, and the various *forms* in which it was established among His saints.

There was an original covenant made with Adam and all mankind in him: see Hos. 6:7 margin. This consisted of an agreement between God and man concerning obedience and disobedience, reward and punishment. To that covenant were annexed promises and threatenings, which were expressed in visible signs or symbols; the first, in the tree of life; the latter in the tree of the knowledge of good and evil. By these did God *establish* the original law of creation as a covenant. On the part of man, it was required that he should accept of this law. It was a covenant of works, and had no mediator. That arrangement or constitution formed the basis on which God dealt with Adam, but it ceased as soon as sin entered the world. God had provided a way of salvation for His own elect apart from their personal obligation to sinless obedience *as the condition of life,* and that through their Surety discharging all their responsibilities in His own person. This was made known in the first promise God proclaimed: Gen. 3:15. All who receive the grace which is tendered through the promises of the Gospel, are delivered from the curse of that covenant which Adam, their legal representative, broke.

But though this first earthly covenant is no longer administered *as a "covenant,"* nevertheless, all those of Adam's descendants who receive not the grace of God as it is tendered to them in the promises of the Gospel, *are* under the law and curse of the Adamic covenant, because the obedience which it requires of the creature unto the Creator, and the penalty which it threatens and the curse it pronounces upon the disobedient, has never been met for them by a substitute. Therefore, if any man believe not, the wrath of God (not "cometh," but) *abideth* on him (John 3:36), and this, because the command and curse, which result from the relation between man and his Maker, and the inflexible righteousness of God as the supreme Governor and Judge of all mankind, must be fulfilled.

Now the children of Israel were not formally placed under the Adamic covenant absolutely, as a *covenant of life,* for, from the days of Abraham the *promise* (a renewal of Gen. 3:15; see Gen. 12: 1-3, 17:6-8, etc.) was given unto him and his seed. Let it be carefully noted that in Gal. 3:17 the apostle proves that *no* "law" would afterwards be given, nor covenant made, that should or could disannul that promise. Had Israel been brought under the Adamic covenant of works it *would* have disannulled the promise, for that covenant and the promise of Grace are diametrically opposed. Moreover, had Israel come formally under the Adamic covenant of works they were all under the curse, and so had all perished eternally.

That there were other *federal* transactions between God and His Church *before* the giving of the law at Sinai, is abundantly clear from the book of Genesis. God entered into covenant with Abraham, making him promises on behalf of his descendants, and appointing a solemn outward seal for its confirmation and establishment. *That* covenant contained the very nature and essence of what is termed the "new covenant." Proof of this is found in the fact that the Lord Jesus is said to be "a Mediator of the circumcision, for the truth of God to *confirm* the promises made to the fathers" (Rom. 15:8). As He was the Mediator of the new covenant, so far was He from rescinding the promises which God made to Abraham, Isaac, and Jacob, that it belonged to His office to ratify and establish them. But it was at Sinai that the Lord entered formally into covenant with Israel as a nation (Heb. 8:9), a covenant which had all the institutions of Divine worship annexed to it (Heb. 9:1-6).

In contrast from the covenant which God made with Israel at Sinai, Christ is made "the Mediator of a better covenant" (Heb. 8:6). This is the covenant of grace, being so called in contrast from that of works, which was made with us in Adam. For these two, grace and works, do divide the ways of our relation to God, being opposite the one to the other (Rom. 11:6). Of this covenant of grace Christ was its Mediator from the beginning of the world, namely, from the giving of the first promise in Gen. 3:15, for that promise was given in view of His incarnation and all that He should accomplish by His future and actual mediation. Christ was as truly the Surety of Abel as He was of the apostle Paul, and God had "respect unto" (was favourable toward and accepted) the one on the ground of Christ's suretyship as much as He did the other. To this it may be replied, If such be the case, then wherein lies the superior privilege of the Gospel-dispensation over that of the Mosaic?

In seeking an answer to the above question, it is needful to recognize (as was pointed out in our last article) that the "new covenant" referred to in Heb. 8 is not the new covenant *absolutely* considered, and as it had been *virtually* administered from the days of Gen. 3:15 in a way of *promise.* For considered thus it was quite consistent with the covenant that God made with Israel at Sinai: in Gal. 3:17 the apostle proves that the renewal of the covenant (as a promise) to Abraham, was in no way abrogated by the giving of the law. Instead, in Heb. 8 the apostle is treating of such *an establishment of* the new covenant as demanded the revocation of the Sinaitic constitution. What this "establishment" was, is made clear in Heb. 9 and 10: it was the *ordinances of worship* connected with it.

When Christianity had been formally established by God, not only was the old covenant annulled, but the entire system of sacred worship whereby it was administered, was set aside. When the "new covenant" was first given in the way of a *promise* (Gen. 3:15, renewed Gen. 12,17, etc.), it did not introduce a system of worship and privileges expressive of the same. But the *promise* of the new covenant *was* included in the Mosaic covenant, nor was it inconsistent with its rights and ceremonies, nay not even with them composed into a yoke of bondage. And why? Because all those rites and ceremonies were added *after* the making of the covenant in Ex. 19 and 24; nevertheless what was added did not and could not overthrow the promise. As the Mosaic system was completed, then all the worship of the Church was to proceed from it and to be conformed to it.

No sinner was ever saved but by virtue of the new covenant and the mediation of Christ therein. The new covenant of grace (in contrast from the old covenant of works made with the human race in Adam) was extant and effectual throughout the O. T. era. Then what is the "better covenant" with its "better promises" which the death of Christ has inaugurated? We say again, it is not a new covenant *absolutely* considered. There are many plain passages in the Psalms and the Prophets which show that the Church of old knew and believed the blessed truth of justification and salvation by Christ, and walked with God in the faith thereof: compare Rom. 4:3-9. Let those who have access to the incomparable and immortal "Institutes" of Calvin read carefully chapters nine to eleven in book 2.

"The Church under the Old Testament, had the same promise of Christ, the same interest in Him by faith, remission of sins, reconciliation with God, justification and salvation by the same way and means that believers have under the New. And whereas the essence and substance of the covenant consists in these things, they are not said to be under another covenant, but only a different *administration* of it. But this was so different from that which is established in the Gospel after the coming of Christ, that it hath the appearance and name of another covenant" (John Owen).

The leading differences between the two *administrations* of the covenant of grace may be reduced to the following heads. First, the *manner* in which the love of God in Christ is made known. The miracle recorded in Mark 8:23, 24 illustrates and adumbrates the two states. The O. T. saints had sight, but the Object set before their faith was seen at a distance, and through clouds and shadows. The N. T. saints "with open face behold the glory of God in a mirror" (2 Cor. 3:18). Second, in its *more plentiful* communication of grace unto the Church: John 1:16. O. T. believers had grace given to them (Gen. 6:8, etc.), but we an "abundance of grace" (Rom. 5:17). Third, in our *access* to God. The revelation of God at Sinai filled the people with terror; His revelation of Himself in Christ, fills us with joy. They were shut out from the holy place; we have freedom to approach His throne (Heb. 4:16). Fourth, the *extent* of the dispensation of Divine grace. Under the O. T. it was restricted to one nation; now it extends to all nations.

The covenant of grace was the same, as to its *substance,* from the beginning. It passed through the whole dispensation of times before the law, and under the law, of the same nature and efficacy, unalterable, everlasting, "ordered in all things and sure." The covenant of grace considered absolutely was the promise of grace in and by Christ Jesus (2 Tim. 1:9, Titus 1:2), and that was the *only* way and means of salvation unto the elect from the entrance of sin. Absolutely, in O. T. times, the covenant consisted only in *promise,* and as such is referred to in Acts 2:39, Heb. 6:14-16. The full and lawful "establishment" of it (Heb. 8:6), whence it became *formally* a "covenant" unto the whole Church, was future only. Two things were needed to change the "promise" into a "new covenant": the shedding of the blood of the only Sacrifice which belonged to it, and the institution of that worship in keeping therewith.

Whilst the O. T. Church enjoyed all the *spiritual* benefits of the promise, wherein the *substance* of the covenant is contained, before it was confirmed and made the sole rule of worship unto the Church, it was not inconsistent with the holiness and wisdom of God to bring His people under any other covenant, or prescribe unto them what forms of worship He pleased, for they did not render ineffectual the promise before given. Nor did the institutions of the Mosaic covenant divert from, but rather led to, the future establishment of the promise. Yea, the laws and worship of the Mosaic economy were of present use and advantage to the Church while it remained in its state of minority (Gal. 4). For much of the above we are indebted, under God, to the writings of John Owen (1670 A. D.). We now turn again to our passage.

"For this is the covenant that I will make with the house of Israel after those days, saith the Lord; I will put My laws into their minds, and write them in their hearts: and I will be to them a God, and they shall be to Me a people" (v. 10). "The design of the apostle, or what is the general argument which he is in pursuit of, must still be borne in mind, while considering the testimonies which he produceth in the confirmation of it. His design is to prove that the Lord Christ is the Mediator and Surety of a *better* covenant, than that wherein the service of God was managed by the high priests according to the law. For hence it follows, that His priesthood is greater and far more excellent than theirs. To this end he doth not only prove that God promised to make such a covenant, but also declares the nature and properties of it, in the words of the prophets. And so, by comparing it with the former covenant, he manifests its excellency above it. In particular, in this testimony, the imperfection of that covenant is demonstrated from its issue. For it did not effectually maintain peace and mutual love between God and the people; but being broken by them, they were thereon rejected of God. This rendered all the other benefits and advantages of it, useless. Wherefore, the apostle insists from the prophet, on those promises of this other covenant, which infallibly prevent the like issue, securing the people's obedience forever, and so the love and relation of God unto them as their God" (John Owen).

The apostle is here contrasting the Christian dispensation from the Mosaic. Having in the previous verse declared in general the abrogation of the old covenant, because of its inadequacy through the weakness of the flesh, he here describes the new covenant which has supplanted it. He shows it to be so excellent in its constitution that none should object against its substitution in place of the old: such is the force of the opening "For." The formal "this is the covenant" announces that it is the duty of Christians to make themselves distinctly and fully informed in the privileges belonging unto them. It was for this very end that the writings of the evangelists and apostles were added to those of the prophets. This new covenant is made with "the house of Israel," which we understand mystically, comprising under it *all* the people of God. It is taken spiritually for the whole Church, the "Israel of God" (Gal. 6:16).

"After those days" is in antithesis from "in the day" of v. 9, which was an indefinite expression covering the interval between God's sending Moses into Egypt and the arrival of Israel before Sinai. "After those days" means, following the O. T. era. The dispensation which succeeds that is called "the time of reformation" in 9:10. Now just as God's making of the first covenant with Israel was preceded by many things that were preparatory to the solemn establishment of the same—such as His sending of Moses to announce unto them His designs of grace, His delivering them out of the house of bondage, His miraculous conducting of them through the Red Sea, His making known His law at Sinai—so the new covenant was *gradually* made and established, and that by sundry acts preparatory for it or confirmatory of it. As this is so little understood we must enter into details.

First, the introduction of the new covenant was made by the ministry of John the Baptist (Luke 16:16). He was sent to prepare the way of the Lord. Until his appearing the Jews were bound absolutely unto the covenant at Sinai, without any alteration or addition to any ordinance of worship. But John's ministry was "the beginning of the Gospel" (Mark 1:1, 2). He called the people off from resting in the privileges of the old covenant (Matt. 3:8-10), and instituted a new ordinance of worship, baptism. He pointed away from Moses to the Lamb of God. Thus, his ministry was the beginning of the accomplishment of God's promise through Jeremiah. Second, the incarnation and ministry of the Lord Jesus was a further advance unto the same. His appearing in the flesh laid an axe to the root of the whole Mosaic dispensation (Matt. 3:10), though the tree was not immediately cut down. By His miracles and teaching Christ furnished abundant proof that He was the Mediator of the new covenant.

Third, the way for the introduction of the new covenant having been prepared, it was solemnly enacted and confirmed in and by

Christ's *death:* thereby the "promise" became a "testament" (Heb. 9:14-16). From that time onwards, the old covenant and its administration had received its full accomplishment (Eph. 2:14-16, Col. 2:14, 15), and it continued to abide only in the longsuffering of God, to be taken out of the way in His own time and manner. Fourth, the new covenant was further established in the *resurrection* of Christ. The old covenant could not be abrogated till its curse had been borne, and that was discharged absolutely when Christ was "loosed from the pains of death" and delivered from the grave. Fifth, the new covenant was promulgated and confirmed on the day of Pentecost, answering to the promulgation of the law at Sinai, some weeks after Israel had been delivered out of Egypt. From Pentecost onwards the whole Church of God was absolved from any duty with respect unto the old covenant and the worship of it (although it was not manifest as yet unto their consciences), and the ordinances of worship and all the institutions of the new covenant now became obligatory upon them. Sixth, the question was formally and officially raised as to the continuance of the obligatory form of the old covenant, and the contrary was expressly affirmed by the apostles under the infallible superintendence of the Holy Spirit: Acts 15:1-29.

But at this point a difficulty, already noticed, may recur to our minds: Were not the things mentioned in Heb. 8:10-13, the grace and mercy therein expressed, actually communicated to God's elect both before Sinai and afterwards? Did not all who truly believed and feared God enjoy these same identical blessings? Unquestionably. What then is the solution? This: the apostle is not here contrasting the internal operations of Divine grace in the Old and N.T. saints, but as Calvin rightly taught, the "reference is to the economical condition of the Church." The contrast is between that which *characterized* the Judaic and the Christian dispensations in the *outward* confirmation of the covenant. While there were individuals like David and Daniel, perhaps many such, in whom the Spirit wrought effectually, yet it is evident that the great majority of Abraham's natural descendants had no experimental acquaintance with the external revelation God had given.

"I will put My laws into their minds, and write them in their hearts." That this is *not* an experience peculiar to Christians or restored Christians is clear from Psa. 37:30, 31, "The mouth of the righteous speaketh wisdom, and his tongue talketh of judgment. The law of His God is *in his heart*." So, too in Psa. 19:7, 8, we read, "The law of the Lord is perfect converting the soul . . . the statutes of the Lord are right, rejoicing the heart." But that the major portion of Israel, or even a considerable number of them, were regenerated, at any period in the lengthy history of that nation, there is nothing whatever to show: instead, there is very much to the contrary. *This* experience is enjoyed by none save God's elect, and in every age they have been but a "little flock."

"I will put My laws into their minds." These words have reference to the effectual operations of the Spirit in His supernatural and saving illumination of our understandings, whereby they are made habitually conformable unto the whole law of God, which is our rule of obedience in the new covenant. The carnal mind is enmity against God, and is not subject to His law, neither indeed can be (Rom. 8:7). But when we are renewed by the Spirit, He works in us a submission to the authority and revealed will of God. As the Lord opened the heart of Lydia "that she *attended unto* the things which were spoken of Paul" (Acts 16:14), so in the miracle of the new birth, the Christian is given an ear to heed and a mind to perceive the holiness, justice, and goodness of God's law. Yea, that law is effectually *applied* to him, so that it becomes the former of his thoughts, the subject of his meditation, and the regulater of his ways.

The preacher may announce the law of God to the outward ear, but only the Spirit can engrave it on the mind. The realization of this fact ought to drive every minister to his knees. No matter how diligently he has prepared his sermon, no matter how clearly and faithfully he expounds God's truth, no matter how solemnly and searchingly he endeavors to press it on the individual's conscience, unless God Himself gives His Word an entrance into the soul, nothing spiritual and eternal is accomplished. Nowhere is the deadness of the "churches" more plainly evidenced today than by the *absence* of concerted and definite prayer immediately before and immediately after the Word is preached: the "song service" has been substituted for the prayer service. O that God's own people might be aroused to the need of their coming together and crying, "Lord, open the eyes of these men" (2 Kings 6:20).

"And write them in their hearts." It is this which renders the former part actually effectual. The "heart" as distinguished from the "mind" comprises the affections and the will. First, the understanding is informed, and then the heart is reformed. An active principle of obedience is imparted, and this is nothing else than a *love* for God Himself. Where there is a real love for God, there is a genuine desire and determination to *please* Him. The heart of the natural man is "alienated" from God and opposed to His authority. That is why, at Sinai, God wrote the commandments upon stones — not so much to secure the outward letter of them, as to represent the *hardness of the hearts* of the people unto whom they were given. But at regeneration God takes away the heart of stone, and gives a heart of flesh (Ezek. 36:26)—pliable, living, responsive.

Let each reader pause here and lift up his or her heart to God, asking for grace and wisdom to honestly examine themselves in the light of this verse. You may sit under a sound and scriptural ministry every Sabbath, but *what effect* has it upon your inner man? You may be well acquainted with the letter of the Word, but how far is it *directing* the details of your daily walk? Does your mind dwell most on temporal or eternal things, material or spiritual? What engages your thoughts in your seasons of recreation? Is your heart fixed upon God or upon the world? There are thousands of professing Christians who can *talk* glibly of the Scriptures, but whose lives give no evidence that *God* has written His laws in their hearts. Are *you* one of this class?

"And I will be to them a God, and they shall be to Me a people." This expresses covenant-relationship. It is placed in the center of these promises because it is the spring from which the grace of the other blessings doth proceed. The wicked are living in this world "without God, and without hope" (Eph. 2:12), but unto the righteous He says, "I am thy Shield, thy exceeding great Reward" (Gen. 15:1). "Happy is that people, that is in such a case, happy is that people, whose God is the Lord" (Psa. 144:15). When He says "I will be to them a God" it means that He will act toward His people according to all that is implied in the name of *God*. He will be their Lawgiver, their Counselor, their Protector, their Guide. He will supply all their needs, deliver from all dangers, and bring them unto everlasting felicity. He will be faithful and longsuffering, bearing with their frailties, never leaving nor forsaking them. "And they shall be My people" expresses both a dignity and a duty. Their dignity is set forth in 1 Peter 2:9; their duty in the verses which follow.

"And they shall not teach every man his neighbor, and every man his brother, saying, Know the Lord: for all shall know Me, from the least to the greatest" (v. 11). These words point a contrast from the general spiritual ignorance which obtained among the Jews: cf. Isa. 1:3, etc. "The words in the 11th verse are not to be understood absolutely, but comparatively. They intimate, that under that covenant there shall be a striking contrast to the ignorance which characterized the great body of those who were under the Old Covenant; that the revelation of the Divine will shall be far more extensive and clear under the new than under the old economy; and that there shall be a correspondingly enlarged communication of the enlightened influences of the Holy Spirit. They probably also are intended to suggest the idea, that that kind of knowledge which is the peculiar glory of the New Covenant is a kind of knowledge which cannot be communicated by brother teaching brother, but comes directly from Him — the great Teacher, whose grand characteristic is this, that whom He teaches, He makes apt to learn" (John Brown).

"And they shall not teach every man his neighbor, and every man his brother, saying, Know the Lord." During the Mosaic economy, and particularly in the last century before Christ, there was an external teaching of the Law, which the people trusted and rested in without any regard for God's teaching by the inward circumcision of the heart. Such teaching had degenerated into rival schools and sects, such as the Pharisees, Sadducees, Herodians, Essenes, etc., and they made void the Word of God through their traditions (Mark 7:13). It was against such the last of Israel's prophets had announced. "The Lord will cut off . . . the master and the scholar out of the tabernacles of **Jacob"** (Mal. 2:12). Or, our verse probably has more direct reference to the general knowledge of God which obtained during the Mosaic economy, when He revealed Himself under types and shadows, and was known through "parables and dark sayings." These were now supplanted by the full blaze of the Gospel's light.

"For all shall know Me, from the least to the greatest." God is now known in the full revelation which He has made of Himself in the person of His incarnate Son: John 1:18. As we are told in 1 John 5:20, "And we know that the Son of God is come, and hath given us an understanding, that we may *know* Him that is true": "know Him" in the sense that we recognize, own, and practically obey Him as *God*. This spiritual, experimental, vital, saving knowledge of God is now communicated unto all of His elect. As the Saviour announced, "They shall be all taught of God" (John 6:45): taught His will and all the mysteries of godliness, which by the Word are revealed. *This* "knowledge" of God cannot be imparted by any external teaching alone, but is the result of the Spirit's operations, though He frequently, yea generally, uses the oral and written ministry of God's servants as His instruments therein.

"For I will be merciful to their unrighteousness, and their sins and their iniquities will I remember no more" (v. 12). "This is the great foundational promise and grace of the new covenant. For though it be last expressed, yet, in order of nature, it precedeth the other mercies and privileges mentioned, and is the foundation of the communication of them unto us. This the casual 'for' at the beginning of the verse doth demonstrate. What I have spoken, saith the Lord, shall be accomplished, '*For* I will be merciful,' etc., without which there could be no participation of the other things mentioned. Wherefore, not only an addition of new grace and mercy is expressed in these words, but a reason also is rendered why, or on what grounds, He would bestow on them those other mercies" (John Owen).

In v. 12 a reason is given why God bestows the wondrous blessings enumerated in vv. 10, 11. The word here rendered "merciful" is *propitious,* for it is not absolute mercy without any satisfaction having been taken by justice, but grace shown on the ground of a propitiation: cf. Rom. 3:24, 25. Christ died to render God propitious toward sinners (Heb. 2:17), and in and through Him alone is God merciful toward the sins of His people. Just so long as Christ is rejected, the sinner is under the curse. But as soon as He is received, the blessings described in vv. 10-12 become his. Note there are just seven blessings named, which exemplifies the perfection of the new covenant.

It is to be noted that no less than three terms are used in v. 12 to describe the fearful evils of which the sinner is guilty, thus emphasizing his obnoxiousness to the holy God, and magnifying the grace which saves him. "Unrighteousness" signifies a wrong done unto God, against man's sovereign Ruler and Benefactor. "Sin" is a missing of the mark, the glorifying of God, which is what ought ever to be aimed at. "Iniquity" has the force of lawlessness, a setting up of my will against God's, a living to please self rather than for His glory. How marvelous is the propitious favour of God toward those who are guilty of such multiplied enormities! The apostle's object was to point another contrast between the covenants. That which *characterized* Judaism was a reign of law and justice: that which distinguishes Christianity is the "Throne of Grace." Note that no "conditions" are here stipulated. But does not the new covenant require repentance and faith? Assuredly: Mark 1:15. But He who requires these has promised also to work them in His people: Acts 5:31.

"In that He saith, A new, He hath made the first old. Now that which decayeth and waxeth old is ready to vanish away" (v. 13). That the translators failed to perceive the drift of the apostle's reasoning here is evident from their adding the word "covenant" in italics. This was not only unnecessary, but its introduction serves to hide the force of the first half of this verse. In it the apostle draws an inference from what God had said through Jeremiah. He singles out one word, "new," and on it bases an argument: because Christianity is the "establishment" of the *new* covenant, then the preceding economy must have grown "old," and "old" is significative of that which draws near its end! How this shows us, once more, that every jot and tittle of Scripture is authoritative, full of meaning, and of sufficient evidence for what may be deduced from it!

"Now that which decayeth and waxeth old is ready to vanish away." Here is the conclusion of the apostle's argument. If the first covenant had been adequate no place had been sought for a second (v. 7). But place *was* sought for the second (v. 8), therefore the first covenant was not faultless. The old covenant had continued for fifteen hundred years, from Moses to Christ; but its purpose had now been served. God gave Israel more than a hint that the Mosaic economy would not last forever, when his providence permitted the nation to be carried down into Babylon. Upon their return from captivity, neither the temple nor its priesthood were ever restored to their pristine glory. And now, as the apostle wrote, in less than ten years Jerusalem and the temple were completely destroyed. If then the Jewish covenant was abolished because it was "old," how much more ought the "old man" to be put off (Eph. 4:24), and the "old leaven" purged out (1 Cor. 5:7)!

CHAPTER THIRTY-NINE

The Typical Tabernacle

(Heb. 9:1-5)

The principal design of the apostle in this epistle was to prove and make manifest that the "old covenant" which Jehovah made with Israel at Sinai, with all the ordinances of worship and the privileges connected therewith, had been Divinely annulled. This involved a complete change in the church-state of the Hebrews, but so far from this being a thing to deplore, it was to their unspeakable advantage. A "new covenant" had been inaugurated, and the blessings connected with it so far excelled those which had belonged to the old dispensation, that nothing but blind prejudice and perverse unbelief could refuse the true light which now shone, and prefer in its stead the dark shadows of a previous night. God never asks anybody to give up any thing without proffering something far better in return; and they who despise His offer are the losers. But prejudice is strong, and never harder to overcome than in connection with religious customs. Therefore does the Spirit labour so patiently in His argument throughout these chapters.

The chief obstacle in the way of the Hebrews' faith was their failure to perceive that every thing connected with the ceremonial law — the tabernacle, priesthood, sacrifices — was *typical* in its significance and value. Because it was typical, it was only preparatory and transient, for once the Antitype materialized its purpose was served. The shadows were no longer needed when the Substance was manifested. The scaffolding is dispensed with, taken away, as soon as the finished building appears. The toys of the nursery become obsolete when manhood is reached. Everything is beautiful in its proper season. Heavy garments are needed when the cold of winter is upon us, but they would be troublesome in summer's sunshine. Once we recognize that God Himself has acted on this principle in His dispensational dealings with His people, much becomes plain which otherwise would be quite obscure.

The apostle had closed the 8th chapter by pointing out, "Now that which decayeth and waxeth old is ready to vanish away." In those words the Spirit had intimated the unescapable inference which must be drawn from the oracle given through Jeremiah. He had predicted a "*new* covenant," which received its fulfillment in the establishing of Christianity. The ushering in of the new order of Divine worship necessarily denoted that the previous economy was "old," and if so, its end must be nigh. The force of 8:13 is as follows: "In that *He* says a 'new' ": God would not have done so unless *He* had made the first "old." The "He hath made the first old" has an active significance and denotes an authoritative act of God upon the old economy, whereby the calling of the other "new" was the sign and evidence. God did not call the Christian dispensation "*another* covenant," or a "*second* covenant," but a "new" one, thereby declaring that the Judaic covenant was obsolete.

The connecting link between the closing verses of chapter 8 and the opening verses of 9 may perhaps be set forth thus: although the old covenant or Mosaic economy was "ready to vanish away," nevertheless, it yields, even for Christians, important and valuable teachings. It is full of most blessed *typical* import, the record of which has been preserved both for the glory of its Author and the edification and joy of His saints. Wonderful indeed were the pictorial fore-shadowings which the Lord gave in the days of Israel's kindergarten. The importance of them was more than hinted at by God when, though He took but six days to make heaven and earth, He spent no less than forty days when instructing Moses concerning the making of the tabernacle. That clearly denoted that the work of redemptive grace, which was prefigured in Jehovah's earthly dwelling place, was far more glorious than the work of creation. Thereby are we taught to look away from the things which are seen, and fix our minds and affections upon that sphere where the Son of God reigns in light and love.

"The general design of this chapter is the same as the two preceding, to show that Christ as High Priest is superior to the Jewish high priest. This the apostle had already shown to be true in regard to His *rank,* and to the *dispensation* of which He was the Mediator. He proceeds now to show that this was also true in reference to *the efficacy of the sacrifice* which He made: and in order to do this, he gives an account of the ancient Jewish sacrifices, and compares them with that made by the Redeemer. The essential point is, that the former dispensation was mere shadow, type, or figure, and that the latter was real and efficacious." — (A. Barnes).

"Then verily the first had also ordinances of the Divine service, and a worldly sanctuary" (v. 1). Having in the former chapter given further proof of the excellency of Christ's sacerdotal office, by describing the superior covenant that was ratified thereby, the apostle now prepares the way to set forth the *execution* of that office, following the same method of procedure in so doing. Just as he had drawn a comparison between Aaron and Christ, so he now sets the ministrations of the one over against the Other, and this in order to prove that that of Christ's was most certainly to be preferred. He first approaches the execution of the Levitical priests' office by mentioning several rites and types which appertained thereto.

"Then verily the first had also ordinances of Divine service, and a worldly sanctuary." The apostle here begins the comparison which he draws between the old covenant and the new with respect to the services and sacrifices whereby the one and the other was established and confirmed. In so doing he is still dealing with what was to all pious Israelites a most tender consideration. It was in the services and sacrifices which belonged to the priestly office in the tabernacle that they had been taught to place all their confidence for reconciliation with God. If the apostle's previous contention respecting the abolition of the legal priesthood was granted, then it necessarily followed that the sanctuary in which they served and all the offerings which Moses had so solemnly appointed, became useless too. It calls for our closest attention and deepest admiration to observe how the Spirit led the apostle to approach an issue so startling and momentous.

First, he is so far from denying that the ritual of Judaism was of human invention, that he declares, "verily (of truth) the first covenant had also ordinances of *Divine* service." Thus he follows the same method employed in the preceding chapters. In drawing his comparisons between Israel's prophets and Christ, the angels and Christ, Moses and Christ, Joshua and Christ, Aaron and Christ, he had said nothing whatever in disparagement of the inferior. So far from reviling the first member in each comparison, he had dwelt upon that which was in its favour: the more they could be legitimately magnified, the greater the glory accruing to Christ when it was proved how far He excelled them. So here: the apostle granted the principal point which an objector would make—why should the first covenant be annulled if God Himself had made it? Before giving answer to this (seemingly) most difficult question, he allows and affirms that the service of Judaism *was* of Divine institution. Thus, in the earliest ages of human history God had graciously appointed means for His people to use.

The expression "ordinances of divine service" calls for a word or two by way of explanation. The word which is here rendered "ordinances" (margin "ceremonies") signifies rites, statutes, institutions. They were the appointments of God, which He alone had the right to prescribe, and which His people were under solemn bonds of observing, and that without any alteration or deviation. These "ordinances" were of "divine service" which is a single word in the original. In its verbal form it is found in 8:5, "to serve unto the example and shadow of heavenly things." In the N.T. it is always found in connection with religious or divine service: in Acts 24:14, Phil. 3:3 it is translated "worship." It signifies to serve in godly fear or trembling, thus implying an holy awe and reverence for the One served — cf. Heb. 12:28. Thus, the complete clause means that under the Mosaic economy God gave His people authoritative enactments to direct their worship of Him. This law of worship was a hedge which Jehovah placed around Israel to keep them from the abominations of the heathen. It was concerning this very thing that God had so many controversies with His people under the old covenant.

Care needs to be duly paid to the tense which the apostle here used: he said not "verily the first covenant *has* also ordinances, of divine service," but "*had*". He is obviously referring to the past. The Mosaic economy had those ordinances from the time God covenanted with Israel at Sinai. But *that* covenant was no longer in force; it had been Divinely annulled. The "verily the first covenant had *also* ordinances of Divine worship," clearly intimates that the new covenant too has Divine "ordinances." We press this because there are some who now affirm that even Christian baptism and the Lord's supper are "Jewish" ceremonies, which belong not to this present dispensation. But this error is sufficiently refuted by this word "also" — found in the very epistle which was written to prove that Judaism has given place to Christianity!

"And a worldly sanctuary." The reference is (as the next verse plainly shows) to the Tabernacle, which Moses made in all things according to the pattern shown him in the mount. Many have been sorely puzzled as to why the Holy Spirit should designate the holy sanctuary of Jehovah a "worldly" one. Yet this adjective should not present any difficulty. It is not used invidiously, still less as denoting anything which is evil. "Worldly" is not here opposed to "spiritual," but as that which belongs to the earth rather than to the heavens. Thus the force of "worldly" here emphasises the fact that the Mosaic economy was but a transient one, and not eternal. The tabernacle was made here in this world, out of perishing materials found in the world, and was but a portable tent, which might at pleasure be taken down and set up again; while the efficacy of its services extended only unto worldly things, and procured not that which was vital and eternal. Note how in 9:24

the "holy places made with hands" are set in antithesis from "heaven itself."

We cannot but admire the wisdom given to the apostle in handling a matter so delicate and difficult. While his object was to show the immeasurable superiority of that which has been brought in by Christ over that which Judaism had enjoyed, at the same time he would own that which was of God in it. Thus, on the one hand, he acknowledges the service of the Levitical priests as "divine," yet, to pave the way for his further proof that Christ is a Minister of the heavenly sanctuary (8:1, 2), he points out that the tabernacle of Judaism was but a "worldly" one. "The antithesis to worldly is heavenly, uncreated, eternal. Thus in the epistle to the Galatians, the apostle, speaking of the legal parenthetical dispensation, says we were then in bondage under the 'elements of the world' (4:3); and in the epistle to the Colossians he contrasts with the 'rudiments of the world' (2:20) the heavenly position of the believer who has died with Christ, and 'is no longer living in the world,' but seeking the things above" (A. Saphir).

"For there was a tabernacle made; the first, wherein was the candlestick, and the table, and the shewbread; which is called the sanctuary" (v. 2). "The subject spoken of is the tabernacle: that which is in general affirmed of it is that it was 'made.' There is a distribution of it into two parts in this and the following verse. These parts are described and distinguished by, first, their names; second, their situation with respect unto one another; third, their contents or sacred utensils. The one is described in this verse, by its situation: it was the 'first,' that which was first entered into; then by its utensils, which were three; then by its name; it was called the sanctuary" (J. Owen).

"For there was a tabernacle made." A full description of it is to be found in the book of Exodus. The "tent" proper was thirty cubits, or forty-five feet in length, ten cubits, or fifteen feet in breadth, and the same in height. In shape it formed an oblong square. It was divided by a veil into two parts of unequal size. This continued to form God's house of worship until the days of Solomon, when it was replaced by the more permanent and magnificent temple. It is pertinent to ask at this point, Why should the Holy Spirit here refer to the "tabernacle" rather than to the temple, which was still standing at the time the apostle was writing? The word "tabernacle" is found ten times in this epistle, but the "temple" is not mentioned once. This is the more remarkable because Paul, more than any of the apostles, emphasized the resurrection of Christ, and the temple particularly foreshadowed Him in His resurrection and eternal glory; whereas the tabernacle principally prefigured

Christ in His humiliation and lowliness. Yet the difficulty is easily solved: the temple was not erected till after Israel were thoroughly settled in their inheritance, and the Holy Spirit is here addressing a people who were yet in the wilderness!

The Holy Spirit now makes a bare allusion to the holy vessels which occupied the two compartments of the tabernacle. But what *rule* has been given us to guide in and fix with certainty the interpretation of the mystical signification of these things? Certainly God has not left His people to the worthless devisings of their own imaginations. No, in this very epistle, He has graciously informed us that the tabernacle, and all contained in it, were typical of Christ, yet not as He may be considered absolutely, but as the Church is in mystical union with Him, for throughout Hebrews He is viewed in the discharge of His *mediatory* office. Thus the tabernacle, its holy vessels and services, supplied a representation of the person, work, offices and glories of Christ as the Head of His people. That it did so is clear from 8:2—see our comments thereon. The "*true* tabernacle" there mentioned (our Lord's humanity) is not opposed to what is false and erroneous (the shrines of the heathen), but to the tabernacle of Moses, which was but figurative and transitory. In the Lord Jesus we have the substance of what Israel had only the shadow.

"For there was a tabernacle made: the first (compartment) wherein was the candlestick." It is to be noted that no mention is here made of the outer court. In this omission, as in so many others, the anointed eye may clearly discern the absolute control of the Spirit over the sacred writers, moving and guiding them in every detail. In our articles upon Exodus (1926 etc.) we have attempted a much fuller exposition than can here be given. Suffice it now to say that everything connected with the outer court was fulfilled by Christ in the days of His flesh. The very fact that it *was* the "outer" court, accessible to all the people and unroofed, at once denotes to us Christ here in the world, openly manifested before men. Its brazen altar spoke of the cross, where God publicly dealt with the sins of His people. Its fine-linen hangings spoke of Christ meeting the claims of God's righteousness and holiness. Its sixty pillars tell of the strength and power of Christ, "mighty to save." Its laver foreshadowed Christ cleansing His Church with the washing of water by the Word (John 13).

Now as the outer court viewed Christ on earth, so the holy places pointed to Him in heaven. The holy place was a chamber which was entered by none save the priestly family, where those favoured servants of Jehovah ministered before Him. It was therefore the place of *communion*. In perfect keeping with this, each of the three vessels that stood therein spoke of *fellowship.* The lampstand foreshadowed Christ as the *power* for fellowship, as supplying the light necessary to it. The table with its twelve loaves, prefigured Christ as the *substance* of our fellowship, the One on whom we feast. The incense altar typified Christ as the *maintainer* of fellowship, by His intercession securing our continued acceptance before the Father. The reason why the "incense altar" is not mentioned here in Heb. 9 will be taken up when we come to v. 4.

"For there was a tabernacle made: the first (compartment) wherein was the candlestick," or better, "lampstand." There was no window in the tabernacle, for the light of nature cannot reveal spiritual things. It was therefore illuminated from this holy vessel, which was placed on the south side, near the veil which concealed the holy of holies. A full description of it is given in Ex. 25:31-36. It was made of beaten gold, all of one piece, with all its lamps and ornamentations, so that it was without either joints or screws. Pure olive oil was provided for it.

The very fact that the lampstand stood in the holy place, at once shows that it is *not* Christ as "the Light of the world" which is typified. It is strange that many of the commentators have erred here. The words of Christ on this point are clear enough: "as long as I am in the world, I am the light of the world" (John 9:5 and cf. 12:35, 36): only then was He manifested here as such. But men loved darkness rather than light. They rejected the Light, and so far as they were concerned, extinguished it. Since Christ was put to death by wicked hands, the world has never again gazed on the Light. He is now hidden from their eyes. But He who was slain by the world, rose again, and then ascended on high; it is there in the Holy Place in God's presence, that the Light now dwells. And while there—O marvelous privilege—the saints have access to Him.

Black shadows rest upon the world which has cast out the Light of Life: "the way of the wicked is as darkness" (Prov. 4:19). It is now night-time, for the "Dayspring from on high" is absent. The lampstand tells of the gracious provision which God has made for His own beloved people during the interval of darkness, ere the Sun of righteousness shall rise once more, and usher in for this earth that morning without clouds. Its seven branches and lamps constantly fed by oil, represented the fullness of light that is in Christ Jesus, and which by Him is communicated to His whole Church. The "oil" was poured *into* its lamps and then shed forth light *from* them. Such was and is the economical relation of the Spirit unto the Mediator. First, Christ was "anointed" with the Spirit "above His fellows" (Psa. 45:7 and cf. John 3:34), and then

He sent forth the Spirit (Acts 2:33). Objectively the Spirit conveys light to us through the Word; subjectively, by inward and supernatural illumination.

"And the table and shewbread" (v. 2). Though intimately connected, yet these two objects may be distinguished in their typical significance. The natural relation of the one to the other, helps us to perceive their spiritual meaning: the bread was placed upon and thus was supported by the table. The "table" speaks of *communion.* A beautiful picture of this is found in 2 Sam. 9. There David asks, "Is there yet any that is left of the house of Saul, that I may show him kindness for Jonathan's sake?" (v. 1). A lovely illustration was this of the wondrous grace of God, showing kindness to those who belong to the house of His enemy, and that for the sake of His Beloved. There *was* one, even Mephibosheth, lame on his feet; him David "sent and fetched" unto himself. And then, to show he is fully reconciled to this grandson of his foe, David said, "but Mephibosheth thy master's son shall eat bread always at my table" (v. 10)—evidencing that he had been brought into the place of most intimate fellowship. 1 Cor. 10:20, 21 also shows the spiritual significance of the "table."

The "shewbread," or twelve loaves on the table, also spoke of Christ. "My Father giveth you the true bread from heaven" (John 6:32). The word "shewbread" is literally "bread of faces," faces being put by a figure for *presence*—pointing to the Divine presence in which the bread stood; "shewbread *before Me* always" (Ex. 25:30). The twelve loaves, like the twelve precious stones in the high priest's breastplate, pictured the twelve tribes of Israel being represented before God. Thus, in type, it was the Lord Jesus identifying Himself with His covenant people.

"And after the second veil, the tabernacle which is called the holiest of all" (v. 3). The first veil was the "hanging" over the entrance into the tabernacle, shutting off from view what was inside from those who were in the outer court. It is described in Ex. 26:36, 37. The second veil, described in Ex. 26:31-33 and explained in Heb. 10:20, was a heavy curtain which concealed the contents of the holy of holies from those in the holy place. The Levitical family ministered in the holy place, but none save the holiest of all, and he only one day in the year. Three things have been mentioned as occupying a place in the first tabernacle; seven objects are now mentioned in connection with the holiest of all.

"Which had the golden censer" (v. 4). First, we would note the minute accuracy of the wording here. In v. 2 it was said *"Wherein was* the candlestick," etc., for the objects there mentioned belonged properly to the first compartment. But here it is, "*which had* the golden censer." Why? Because this utensil did not form part of the furniture of the holy of holies. To what then is the reference? Plainly to what is recorded in Lev. 16:12, 13, "And he shall take a censer full of burning coals of fire from off the (brazen) altar before the Lord, and his hands full of sweet incense beaten small, and bring *within the veil*: And he shall put the incense upon the fire before the Lord, that the cloud of the incense may cover the mercyseat that is upon the testimony, that he die not."

For three hundred and fifty-nine days in the year Aaron ministered at the golden or incense altar, which stood in the holy place; but on the remaining day, the annual "Day of Atonement," he did not. Instead, he used the "golden censer" of incense, passing with it within the veil. It is *this* which explains why there is no mention of the "golden altar" in v. 2, for the Holy Spirit is here treating (see the later verses) of the Judaic ritual on the Day of Atonement, and the fulfillment of the type by the Lord Jesus. That which was represented by the "golden censer" was the acceptability of Christ's person to God and the efficacy of His intercession. The beautiful type of Lev. 16:12, 13 denotes that, in consequence of the satisfaction which Christ made unto God, completed at the cross, His mediatory intercession is a sweet savour unto the Father, and effective unto the salvation of His Church. The fact that the smoke of this perfume covered the ark and the mercyseat, wherein was the law, and over which the symbol of the Divine presence abode, denoted that Christ has magnified the law, met its every requirement, and is the end of the law for righteousness unto everybody that believeth.

"And the ark of the covenant overlaid round about with gold, wherein was the golden pot that had manna, and Aaron's rod that budded, and the tables of the covenant" (v. 4). The ark, with the mercyseat which formed its lid or cover, was the most glorious and mysterious vessel of the tabernacle. It was the first thing made (Ex. 25:10, 11), yea, the whole sanctuary was built for no other end but to be, as it were, a house and habitation for the ark (Ex. 26:33). The ark was the outstanding symbol that God Himself was present among His people and that His covenant-blessing was resting upon them. It was the coffer in which the tables of the law were preserved. Its pre-eminence above all the other vessels was shown in the days of Solomon, for the ark alone was transferred from the tabernacle to the temple.

The ark was an outstanding figure of the incarnate Son of God. The wood of which it was made, typified His sinless humanity. "Shittim" wood never rotted, and the Septuagint translation of the O.T. renders it "incorruptible wood." The wood was overlaid, within and without, with gold, prefiguring Christ's Divine glory. The two materials of which the ark was made symbolised the *union* of the two natures in the Godman—"God manifest in flesh" (1 Tim. 3:16). The ark formed God's throne in Israel: "Thou that dwellest between the cherubim" (Psa. 80:1). Christ is the only One who perfectly enthroned God, honouring His government in all things. Each of the seven names given to the ark in the O.T. sets forth some excellency in the person of Christ. Everything connected with its most remarkable history, as in Num. 10:33, 14:44, Josh. 3:5-17, 6:4-20, etc., received its antitypical fulfillment in the Godman.

"Wherein was the golden pot that had manna." Some have imagined a contradiction between this statement and what is said in 1 Kings 8:9, "There was nothing in the ark save the two tables of stone." But there is no conflict between the two passages, for they are not treating of the same point in time. Heb. 9:4 is speaking of what was in the ark during the days when it was lodged in the tabernacle, whereas I Kings 8:9 tells of what comprised its contents after it came to rest in the temple. It is important to note this distinction, for it supplies the key to the spiritual interpretation of our verse: Heb. 9:4 makes known God's provisions in Christ for His people while they are journeying through the wilderness. Thus the "manna" was Israel's food from Egypt to Canaan: type of Christ as the heavenly sustenance for our souls. The preservation of the manna in the golden pot, speaks of Christ in glory at God's right hand.

"And Aaron's rod that budded." The reference is to what is recorded in Num. 17. In the preceding chapter we read of a revolt against Moses and Aaron, occasioned by jealousy at the authority which God had delegated to His two servants. The revolt of Korah and his company was visited by summary judgment from on high, and was followed by a manifest vindication of Aaron. The form that vindication took is most instructive. The Lord bade Moses take the twelve tribal rods, writing the name of Aaron on Levi's, laying them up before the ark, and affirming that the one which should be made to blossom would indicate which had been chosen of God to the priestly tribe. Next morning it was found that Aaron's rod had "brought forth buds, and blossomed blossoms, and yielded almonds." Afterwards God ordered Moses to place Aaron's rod before the ark "to be kept for a token against the rebels." The lifeless rod being made to blossom was a figure of God's vindication of

His rejected Son by raising Him from the dead. Thus it speaks of the resurrection-power of our great High Priest.

"And the tables of the covenant." The reference is to Deut. 10:1-5. The preservation of the two tables of stone (on which were inscribed the ten commandments) in the ark, foreshadowed Christ magnifying the law and making it honourable (Isa. 42:21). The fulfillment of this type is stated in Psa. 40:7, 8, where we hear the Mediator saying, "Lo, I come: in the volume of the book it is written of Me; I delight to do Thy will, O My God; Yea, *Thy law is within My heart.*" The Representative of God's people was "made under the law" (Gal. 4:4), and perfectly did He "fulfill" it (Matt. 5:17). Therefore is it written, "by the obedience of One shall many be made righteous" (Rom. 5:19). Thus may each believer exclaim, "In the Lord have I righteousness and strength" (Isa. 45:24).

"And over it the cherubims of glory shadowing the mercyseat; of which we cannot now speak particularly" (v. 5). At either end of the mercyseat was the form of a cherub with outstretched wings, meeting in the center, thus overshadowing and as it were protecting God's throne. That there is some profound significance connected with their figures is clear from the prominent place which they occupy in connection with the description of the mercyseat given in Ex. 25:17-22: mention is there made of the cherubim, in either the singular or plural number, no less than seven times. The mention of them in Gen. 3:24 suggests that they are associated with the administration of God's judicial authority. In Rev. 4:6-8 (cf. Ezek. 1:5-10) they are related to God's throne. Here in Heb. 9 they are called the "cherubim of glory" because the Skekinah abode between them.

The mercyseat, or better, "propitiatory," was the throne upon which the high priest placed the expiatory blood. It was *not* the place where propitiation was made—that was at the brazen altar—but where its abiding value was borne witness to before God. Rom. 3:25 gives us the antitype: by the Gospel God now "sets forth" (Gal. 3:1) Christ as the One by whom He has been placated, as the One by whom His holy wrath against the sins of His people has been pacified, as the One by whom the righteous demands of His law were satisfied, as the One by whom every attribute of Deity was glorified. Christ Himself is God's restingplace in whom He now meets poor sinners in all the fulness of His grace because of the propitiation made by Him on the cross.

The last clause of the verse is translated more literally in Bagster's Interlinear thus: "concerning which it is not now (the time) to speak in detail"—the "concerning which" is not to be restricted to that which is found here in v. 5, but takes in all that has been mentioned in vv. 2-5. It would have led the apostle too far away from his subject of the high priest's service, to give an interpretation of the spiritual meaning of the tabernacle and everything in it. Nevertheless, he plainly intimates that every part of it had a specific significance as typical of the Lord Jesus and His ministry.

CHAPTER FORTY

The Contrasted Priests

(Heb. 9:6-10)

At the commencement of our last article we stated that, the principal design of the apostle in this epistle was to prove and make manifest that the "old covenant" which Jehovah made with Israel at Sinai, with all the ordinances of worship and privileges connected therewith had been Divinely annulled. This involved a complete change in the church-state of the Hebrews, but so far from this being a thing to be deplored, it was to their unspeakable advantage. In prosecuting this design, the Holy Spirit through Paul does, as it were, remove the veil from off the face of Moses. In 2 Cor. 3:13 we read, "And not as Moses, which put a veil over his face, that the children of Israel could not steadfastly look to the end of that which is abolished." These words direct attention to a profound spiritual truth which God (in keeping with His dispensational ways) caused to be mystically adumbrated or shadowed forth by a material and visible object.

In 2 Cor. 3:7 the apostle had spoken of the brightness of Moses' face as a symbol of his ministry: the revelation which he received was a divine and glorious one. But because the truth communicated through Moses was in an *obscure* form (by types and emblems) he veiled himself. Paul, as a minister of the "new covenant" used "great plainness of speech" (2 Cor. 3:12) i.e. employing no "dark parables" or enigmatic prophecies, still less mysterious ceremonies. Moses wore a veil "that the children of Israel could not steadfastly look to the end of that which is abolished" (3:7) i.e. to prevent their seeing the termination or fading away of the celestial brightness of his countenance. The mystical meaning of this was, God would not allow Israel to know at that time that the dispensation of the Levitical or legal ministry would ultimately cease. The publication of that fact was reserved for a much later date.

"But their minds were blinded: for until this day remaineth the same veil untaken away in the reading of the old covenant; which veil is done away in Christ" (2 Cor. 3:14). Yes, that "veil" which lay so heavily over the Mosaic types is now "done away in Christ," for He is that Antitype, the key which unlocks them, the sun which illuminates them. This, it is the great purpose of the Hebrews' epistle to demonstrate. Here is *doctrinally* removed the "veil" from off the Mosaic institutions. Here the Spirit makes known the nature and purpose of the "old covenant." Here He declares the significance and temporal efficacy of all institutions and ordinances of Israel's worship. Here He announces that the Levitical rites and ceremonies made a representation of heavenly things, but insists that those heavenly things could not themselves be introduced and established without the removal of what had adumbrated them. Here He shows that the glory of God shines in the face of Jesus Christ.

Three things there were which constituted the glory of the old covenant, and which the Jews so rested in they refused the Gospel out of an adherence unto them: the priestly office; the tabernacle with all its furniture, wherein that office was exercised; the duties and worship of the priests in that tabernacle by sacrifices, especially those wherein there was a solemn expiation of the sins of the whole congregation. In reference to them, the apostle proves: first, that none of them could make perfect the state of the Church, nor really effect assured peace and confidence between God and the worshippers. Second, that they were but typical, ordained to represent that which was far more sublime and excellent than themselves. Third, that the Lord Jesus Christ, in His person and mediation, was really and substantially, all that they did but prefigure, and that He was and did what they could only direct unto an expectation of.

In Heb. 7 the apostle has fully evidenced this in connection with the priestly office. In the 8th chapter he has done the same in general unto the tabernacle, confirming this by that great collateral argument taken from the nature and excellency of that covenant whereby the incarnate Son was the Surety and Mediator. Here in the 9th, he takes up the services and sacrifices which belonged unto the priestly office in the tabernacle. It was in them that the Jews placed their greatest confidence for reconciliation with God, and concerning which they boasted of the excellency of their Church-state and worship. Because this was the chief point of difference between the Gospel-proclamation and those who repudiated it, and because it was that whereon the whole doctrine of the justification of sinners before God did depend, the apostle enters into minute detail, declaring the nature, use and efficacy of the sacrifices of the law, and manifesting the nature, glory and efficacy of the sacrifice of Christ, whereby those others had been put an end to (condensed from John Owen).

"Now when these things were thus ordained, the priests went always into the first tabernacle, accomplishing the service of God" (v. 6). Having made a brief reference to the structure of the tabernacle in its two compartments, and the furniture belonging to each of them respectively, the apostle now turns to consider the uses for which they were designed unto in the service of God. First, he says "these things were thus ordained," or as the R. V. more correctly renders it, "thus prepared," for the Greek word (translated "made" in v. 2), signifies to dispose and arrange. When the things mentioned in vv. 2-5 had been made and duly ordered, they stood not for a magnificent show, but were designed for constant use in the service of God. Hereby we are taught that, for any service to be acceptable to God, it must be in strict accord with the pattern He has given us in His Word: carefully ponder (1 Chron. 15:12, 13). Everything was duly prepared for Divine service *before* that service was performed. So in public service or Divine worship today there must be fit persons who, under the Spirit, are to lead it—"*able* ministers of the new testament" (2 Cor. 3:6); fit arrangements and order (1 Cor. 14:40), not mere human tradition (Matt. 15:9); a fit message unto edification (1 Cor. 14:26).

"The priests went always into the first tabernacle." They only were allowed in the holy place that were the sons of Aaron; but even these were suffered to penetrate no farther, being barred from entrance into the holy of holies. This was in contrast from the high priest who entered the inner sanctuary, yet only on one day in the year. The word "always" is translated "continually" in 13:15. It signifies constantly, at all times as occasion did require. Christians have been made "kings and priests unto God" (Rev. 1:6), and they are bidden to "give thanks *always* for all things unto God and the Father in the name of our Lord Jesus Christ" (Eph. 5:20); to "rejoice *evermore*" and "pray *without ceasing*" (1 Thess. 5:16, 17).

"Accomplishing the service of God." The translators have rightly added the last two words, for the "service" here is a Divine one. "Accomplishing the service of God" means that they officiated in the ministry of the sacred ceremonies. The *daily* services of the priests were two: the dressing of the lamps of the candlestick: supplying them with the holy oil, trimming their wicks, etc.; this was done every evening and morning. Second, the service of the golden altar, whereon they burned incense every day, with fire taken from off the brazen altar, and this immediately after the offering of the evening and morning sacrifices. Whilst this service was being performed, the people without gave themselves unto prayer (Luke 1:10). Their *weekly* service was to change the shewbread on the table, which was done every Sabbath, in the morning. All of this was typical of the *continual application* of the benefits of the sacrifice and mediation of Christ unto His people here in the world.

The *practical* application to Christians now of what has just been before us, should be obvious. There ought to be family worship, both in the morning and in the evening. The replenishing of the oil in the lamps for continuous light, should find its counterpart in the daily looking to God for needed light from His Word, to direct our steps in the ordering of home and business life to *His* acceptance and praise. God has declared, "Them that honour Me I will honour, and they that despise Me shall be lightly esteemed" (1 Sam. 2:30). If God be not honoured in the home by the family "altar," then we cannot count upon Him blessing our homes! The burning of the incense should receive its antitype in morning and evening praise and prayer unto God: owning Him as the Giver of every good and every perfect gift, thanking Him for spiritual and temporal mercies, casting all our care upon Him, pleading His promises, and trusting Him for a continuance of His favours. The Greek word here for "accomplishing" is a compound, which signifies to "completely finish"— rendered "perfecting" in 2 Cor. 7:1— denoting their service was not done by halves. May we too serve God wholeheartedly.

"But into the second went the high priest alone once every year, not without blood, which he offered for himself, and the errors of the people" (v. 7). That to which the apostle here refers is the great anniversary - sacrifice of expiation, whose institution and solemnities are described at length in Lev. 16. On the tenth day of the seventh month (which corresponds to our September) Israel's high priest, unattended and unassisted by his subordinates, entered within the holy of holies, there to present propitiating sacrifices before Jehovah. Divested of his garments of "glory and beauty" (Ex. 28:2 etc.) and clad only in "the holy linen" (Lev. 16:4), he first entered the sacred precincts bearing a censer full of burning coals and his hands full of incense, which was to be placed upon the coals, so that a cloud of incense should cover the mercyseat (Lev. 16:12, 13); which spoke of the fragrant excellency of Christ's person unto God, when He offered Himself an atoning sacrifice. Second, he took of the blood of the bullock, which had been killed for a sin-offering for himself and his house (Lev. 16:11), and sprinkled its blood upon and before the mercyseat (16:14). Third, he went out and killed the goat which was a sin-offering for the people, and did with its blood as he had with that of the bullocks (16:15).

When the high priest's work within the veil had been completed, he came forth and laid both his hands on the head of the live goat, and confessed over him "all of the iniquities of the children of Israel and all their transgressions in all their sins, putting them upon the head of the goat," which was then sent away "unto a land not inhabited" (Lev. 16:21, 22); all of which was typical of the Atonement made by the Lord Jesus, and of the plenary remission of sins through His blood. In the shedding of the victims' blood and offering it by fire on the altar, there was a representation made of the vicarious imputation of guilt to the sacrifice, and the expiation of it through death. In the carrying of the blood into the presence of Jehovah and the sprinkling of it upon His throne, witness was borne to His *acceptance* of the atonement which had been made. In the placing of the sins of Israel upon the live goat and its carrying of them away into a land uninhabited, there was a foreshadowing of the blessed truth that, as far as the east is from the west so far hath God removed the transgressions of His people from before Him.

"Into the second veil went the high priest *alone*:" "There shall be no man in the tabernacle of the congregation when he goeth in to make an atonement" (Lev. 16:17). This denoted that Christ alone was qualified to appear before God on behalf of His people: none other was fit to mediate for them. "*Once* every year," to foreshadow the fact that Christ entered heaven for His people once for all: Heb. 9:12. "Which he offered for himself," for he too was a sinner, and therefore incompetent to make real, efficacious and acceptable atonement for others; thereby intimating that he must yet give place to Another. "And for the errors of the people," which is to be interpreted in the light of the O. T. expression "sins of ignorance" (Lev. 4:2; 5:15; Num. 15:22-29), which are contrasted from deliberate or presumptuous sins (see Num. 15:30, 31). Under the dispensation of law God graciously made provision for the infirmities of His people, granting them sacrifices for sins committed unwillingly and unwittingly. But for determined and open rebellion against His laws, no atoning sacrifice was available: *see* Heb. 10:26.

The distinction pointed out above is the key to Psa. 51:16, "For Thou desirest not sacrifice, else would I give it." There is no room for doubt that David knew full well the terrible character of the sins which he committed against Uriah and his wife. Later, when he was convicted of this, he realized that *the law* made no provision for forgiveness. What, then, did he do? Psa. 51:1-3 tells us: he laid hold on God Himself and said, "The sacrifices of God are a broken spirit: a broken and a contrite heart, O God, Thou wilt not despise" (v. 17). It was faith, penitently, appropriating the mercy of God in Christ.

"The Holy Spirit this signifying, that the way into the holiest of all was not yet made manifest, while as the first tabernacle was yet standing" (v. 8). The apostle now makes known the use which he intended to make of the description which had been given of the tabernacle and its furniture in vv. 2-5: from the structure and order of its services he would prove the pre-eminency of the priesthood and sacrifice of Christ above those which had belonged to the tabernacle. He points out that the Holy Spirit had provided instruction for Israel in the very disposal of their ancient institutions. Inasmuch as none but the high priest was permitted to pass within the veil, it was plainly intimated that under the Mosaic dispensation the people were *barred* from the very presence of God. Such a state of affairs could not be the ultimate and ideal, and therefore must be set aside before that which was perfect could be introduced.

"The Holy Spirit this signifying:" the reference is to the arrangements which obtained in the tabernacle, as specified in the preceding verses. Here we learn that the third person of the blessed Trinity was immediately concerned in the original instructions given to Israel. This intimates in a most striking way the perfect union, unison and co-operation of the persons of the Godhead in all that They do. 2 Peter 1:21 declares that, "holy men of old spake, moved by the Holy Spirit," prominent among whom was Moses. In Ex. 35:1 we read, "Moses gathered all the congregation of the children of Israel together, and said unto them, These are the words which the Lord hath commanded"—the Holy Spirit moving Him to give an accurate record of all that he had heard from the Lord.

"The Holy Spirit this signifying," or making evident, that "the way into the holiest of all was not yet made manifest." *How* did He thus "signify" this fact? By the very framework of the tabernacle: that is, by allowing the people to go no farther than the outer court, and the priests themselves only into the first compartment. "For things in His wisdom were thus disposed, that there should be the first tabernacle whereinto the priests did enter every day, accomplishing the Divine services that God required. Howbeit in that tabernacle there were not the pledges of the gracious presence of God. It was not the especial residence of His glory. But the peculiar habitation of God was separated from it by a veil, and no person living might so much as look into it on pain of death. But yet, lest the church should apprehend, that indeed there was no approach, here, nor hereafter, for any person into the gracious presence of God; He ordained that once a year the high priest, and he alone, should enter into that holy place with blood. Hereby he plainly signified, that an entrance *there was to be,* and that with boldness, thereinto. For unto what end else did He allow and appoint, that once a year there should be an entrance into it by the high priest, in the name of and for the service of the church? But this entrance being *only* once a year, by the high priest only, and that with the blood of the covenant, which was always to be observed whilst that tabernacle continued, he did manifest that the access represented was not to be obtained during that season; for all believers in their own persons were utterly excluded from it" (J. Owen).

"The way into the holiest of all was not yet made manifest." The apostle is not now speaking of the second compartment in the tabernacle (as in v. 3), but of that which was typified by it. "Now, in that most holy place, were all the signs and pledges of the gracious presence of God; the testimonies of our reconciliation by the blood of the atonement, and of our peace with Him thereby. Wherefore, to enter into these holies is nothing but to have an access with liberty, freedom and boldness, into the gracious presence of God on the account of reconciliation and peace made with Him. This the apostle doth so plainly and positively declare in 10:19-22 that I somewhat wonder so many learned expositors could utterly miss of his meaning in this place. The holies then is the gracious presence of God, whereunto believers draw nigh, in the confidence of the atonement made for them, and acceptance thereon: see Rom. 5:1-3, Eph. 2:14-18, Heb. 4:14, 15" (J. Owen).

But let us observe more closely this expression "the *way* into the holiest of all." This way is no other but the sacrifice of Christ, the true High Priest of the Church: as He Himself declared, "I am the Way, the Truth and the Life, no man cometh unto the Father but by Me" (John 14:6). Thus the ultimate reference here in "the holiest of all" is to Heaven itself, yet having a present and spiritual application unto access to and communion with God. The "way" into this is through faith in the sacrifice of Christ. Marvelously was this adumbrated here on earth at the moment of His death, for then the veil of the temple was rent in twain from the top to the bottom (Matt. 27:51), thereby opening a way into the holy of holies.

But this access to God, or way into the holiest of all, "was not yet made manifest, while as the first tabernacle was yet standing." It is to be very carefully noted that the apostle did *not* say that there was then no way "provided" or "made use of," but only that it was not, during O. T. times, "made manifest." There *was* an entrance into the presence of God, both unto grace and glory, for His elect, from the days of Abel and onwards, but that "way" was not openly and publicly displayed. By virtue of the everlasting covenant (the agreement between the Father and the Son), and in view of Christ's satisfaction in the fulness of time, salvation was applied to saints then, and they were saved by faith as we are now, for the Lamb was slain from the foundation of the world. But the open manifestation of these things waited for the actual exhibition of Christ in the flesh, the full declaration of His person and mediation by the Gospel, and the introduction and establishment of all the privileges of Gospel worship.

"While as the first tabernacle was yet standing." The reference here is *not* to the first compartment or holy place, into which the priests entered and where they served, but is used synecdochially (a part put for the whole) for the entire legal system, which included the temples of Solomon and Zerubbabel. The "first tabernacle" is here spoken of in contrast from the "true tabernacle" of 8:2, namely, the humanity of Christ, which was the antitype and succeeded in the room of the type—cf. Rev. 13:6! The apostle is here treating of what had its standing before God whilst the "first covenant" and Aaronic priesthood remained valid. He cannot be here referring to the "first tabernacle" as a building, for *that* had become a thing of the past, long centuries before he wrote this epistle. Yet the temples that succeeded it had their standing on the basis of the old covenant. This had now been annulled, and with it the whole system of worship which had so long obtained in Judaism.

"Which was a figure for the time then present, in which were offered both gifts and sacrifices, that could not make him that did the service perfect as pertaining to the conscience" (v. 9). Having briefly pointed out the emblematic significance of the *two* compartments of the tabernacle, the apostle now approaches his leading object in this paragraph, namely, to demonstrate that Christ had "obtained a more excellent ministry" than that which had belonged to the Levitical priesthood. This he does by giving a brief summary of the imperfections of the tabernacle and all its services, wherein the *administration* of the old covenant did consist. By calling attention to the defects of inadequacy of the Judaic system, the apostle adopted the most effective method of exposing the unreasonableness of the rejection of the more glorious Gospel by the majority of the Jews, and at the same time showed what folly and wickedness it would be for the believing Hebrews to return to that system.

The apostle's design in vv. 9, 10 is to show that, notwithstanding the outward excellency and glory of the tabernacle-system (through Divine appointment), yet, in the will and wisdom of God, that system was only designed to continue for a season, and that the time of its expiation had now arrived. That the Levitical priesthood and their services were never intended by God to occupy a *perpetual* place in the worship of His church, was evident from the fact that they were utterly unable to effect for His saints that which He had purposed and promised. Not only did the presence of the veil, which excluded all save Aaron from the presence-chamber of Jehovah, intimate that the ideal state had not yet come; not only did the annual *repetition* of the great atoning-sacrifice indicate that, as yet, the all-efficacious Sacrifice had not yet been offered; but all the gifts and sacrifices combined failed to "perfect as pertaining to the conscience." They were only "a figure for the time then present," an institution and provision of God "until the time of reformation."

"Which was a figure for the time then present." The "which was" includes the tabernacle in both its parts, with all its vessels and services. The Greek word for "figure" here is not the same as the one rendered "type" in Rom. 5:14 and "examples" in 1 Cor. 10:6, 11, but is the term commonly translated "parable," as in Matt. 13:3, 10 etc. It is used here for one thing representing another. It signifies "figurative instruction." By means of obscure mystical signs and symbols God taught the ancient church. The great mystery of our redemption by Christ was principally made known by a parable, which was addressed to the eyes rather than to the ears. That was the method which God was pleased to employ, the means He used under the law, of making known things to come. "Which was a figure," is the Holy Spirit's affirmation that the structure, fabric, furniture and rites of the tabernacle were all vested with a Divine and spiritual significance. That the truly regenerate among Israel were acquainted with this fact is illustrated by the prayer of David, "Open Thou mine eyes, that I may behold wondrous things out of Thy law" (Psa. 119:18).

"Which was a figure for the time then present." The verb here is of the preter-imperfect tense, signifying a time that *was* then present, but is *now* past. The reference is to what had preceded the establishment of the new covenant, before the full Gospel revelation had been made. The figurative instruction which God gave to the early Church was not designed to be of permanent duration. Nevertheless, a sovereign God saw fit to continue that obscure and figurative representation of spiritual mysteries for no less than fifteen hundred years. His ways are ever the opposite of man's. "It is the glory of God to *conceal* a thing" (Prov. 25:2)! But how thankful we should be that "the darkness is past, and the true light now shineth" (I John 2:8). Still, let it not be overlooked that the revelation God made through the tabernacle was sufficient for the faith and obedience of Israel had it been diligently attended unto.

"In which were offered both gifts and sacrifices." The Greek word for "sacrifices" is derived from a verb which means to kill, thus the reference here is to those oblations which were slaughtered. As distinguished from these, "gifts" were without life and sense, such as the meal-offering, oil, frankincense and salt which were mingled therewith (Lev. 2), the first-fruits, tithes, and all free-will offerings, which were presented by the priests. These were "offered" unto

God, and that in the tabernacle, for there alone was it meet to offer them. So also was the "tabernacle" (8:2) of Christ alone suited for its designed end. And what is the particular message this should have for the Christian heart? Surely to remind him of that word, "I beseech you therefore, brethren, by the mercies of God that ye present your bodies a living sacrifice, holy acceptable unto God, which is your reasonable service" (Rom. 12:1).

"That could not make him perfect as pertaining to the conscience." These words are not to be understood as restricted to the officiating priest, rather do they look more directly to the person in whose stead he presented the offering to God. Here the apostle points out the imperfection of the whole tabernacle-order of things, and its impotency unto the great end that might be expected from it. To "perfect" a worshipper is to fit him, legally and experimentally, for communion with God, and for this there must be both justification and sanctification, and neither of these could the Levitical priests procure. They could neither remit guilt from before God, nor remove the stains of it from the soul. Where those are lacking, there can be no peace or assurance in the heart, and then the real spirit of worship is absent. As this (D. V.) comes before us again in 10:2, we will not here further enlarge.

Ere passing on to the next verse, it may be enquired, If then the Levitical sacrifices failed at this vital point, why were they ever appointed by God at all? To this question two answers may be returned. First, those sacrifices availed to remove the temporal governmental consequence of Israel's sins; when rightly offered, they freed from political and external punishment, so that continuance in the land of Canaan was preserved; but they cancelled not the wages of sin, removed not the eternal punishment which was due unto every sin by the law. Second, they directed the faith of the regenerate forward to the perfect sacrifice of Christ (which the Levitical offerings typically represented), the virtue and value of which was available to faith's appropriation from the beginning.

"Which stood only in meats and drinks, and divers washings, and carnal ordinances, imposed until the time of reformation" (v. 10). To convince those to whom he was writing that the Levitical ceremonies were incapable of perfecting the conscience, the apostle here demonstrates the truth of this by pointing out their inadequate nature and character. The ordinances of Judaism corresponded closely with the old covenant, which was made with man in the flesh: its sanctuary and furniture were material—things of sight and sense; its ministry was not spiritual, but had to do only with external rites; its ablutions effected nothing more than a ceremonial cleansing, and entirely failed to purify the heart, as faith does (Acts 15:9).

The "service" of the tabernacle-system "stood only in meats and drinks." This expression refers to the sacrifices and libations, which consisted of flesh and bread, oil and wine. "And divers washings": first, that of the priests themselves (Ex. 29:4 etc.), for whose use the "laver" was chiefly intended (Ex. 30:18, 31:9 etc.); second, of the various parts of the burnt-offering sacrifice (Lev. 1:9, 13); third, of the people themselves when they had contracted defilement (Lev. 15:8,16 etc.). "And carnal ordinances" which refers, most probably, to the whole system of laws pertaining to diet and manner of life. "Which stood *only* in," this is emphatic; the rites of Judaism were *solely* external and fleshly, there being nothing spiritual joined with them. Thus their insufficiency to procure spiritual and eternal blessings was evident: legal meats and drinks could not nourish the soul; ceremonial washings could not purify the heart.

"Imposed until the time of reformation." "The word for 'imposed' is properly 'lying on them,' that is, as a burden. There was a weight in all these legal rites and ceremonies, which is called a yoke, and too heavy for the people to bear (Acts 15:10). And if the imposition of them be principally intended, as we render the word 'impose,' it respects the bondage they were brought into by them. Men may have a weight lying on them, and yet not be brought into bondage thereby. But these things were so 'imposed' on them, as that they might feel their weight and groan under the burden of it. Of this bondage the apostle treats at large in the epistle to the Galatians. And it was impossible that those things should perfect a church-state, which in themselves were such a burden, and effective of such a bondage" (John Owen).

The institutions of the Levitical service possessed a general character of externality and materialty: as v. 13 of our chapter says, they sanctified "to the purifying of the *flesh,*" but they reached not the dire needs of the soul. Therefore they were not designed to continue forever, but for a determined and limited season, namely, "unto the time of reformation," which expression respected the appearing of the promised Messiah to inaugurate the new and better covenant: see Luke 1:68-74. "But when the fullness of the time was come, God sent forth His Son, made of a woman, made under the law; to redeem them that were under the law, that we might receive the adoption of sons" (Gal. 4:4, 5).

CHAPTER FORTY-ONE

Eternal Redemption

(Heb. 9:11-14)

In 8:6 the apostle had affirmed, "He is the Mediator of a better covenant." Such a declaration would raise a number of important issues which are here anticipated and settled. Who is the High Priest of the new covenant? What is the tabernacle wherein He administered His office? What are the particular services He performed, answering to those which God appointed unto Aaron and His successors? Wherein do the services of the new High Priest excel those of the Levitical? These were pressing questions, and it was necessary for them to be Divinely answered, not only for the silencing of objectors, but that the faith of believing Jews might be established. Thus, in 9:11, 12 we have the actual ministry of Christ declared, in vv. 13, 14 the proofs that it was "more excellent."

The 9th chapter of Hebrews contains a particular exemplification of this general proposition: Christ is the substance of the Levitical shadows. The general proposition was stated in 8:1, 2: Christians have an High Priest who is a Minister of the true tabernacle. Here in chapter 9 confirmation is given of what was pointed out at the close of 8, namely, that Christ's bringing in of the new covenant did abrogate the old. In exemplifying this fact mention is made in 9:1-10 of sundry shadows of the law, in v. 11 and onwards it is shown that the antitypical accomplishment of them was in and by Jesus Christ. The contents of vv. 1-10 may be reduced to two heads: ordinances of Divine service, and a worldly sanctuary in which they were observed. In vv. 11 to 28 the Spirit magnifies the excellency of Christ's priesthood by showing that He brought in what the Aaronic rites were unable to secure (condensed from W. Gouge, 1650).

The contents of these verses which are now to be before us set forth the ministry of Christ as "the Mediator of the new covenant." They describe His initial work as the High Priest of His people. They set forth the inestimable value of His sacrifice, and what it procured. They magnify His precious blood and the character of that redemption which was purchased thereby. Each verse calls for a separate article, and every clause in them demands our closest and most reverent attention. May the Spirit of God deign to open unto us something of their blessed contents, and apply them in power to our hearts. We purposely cut down our introductory comments that more space may be reserved for the exposition.

"But Christ being come an high priest of goods things to come, by a greater and more perfect tabernacle, not made with hands, that is to say, not of this building; Neither by the blood of goats and calves, but by His own blood, He entered in once into the holy place, having obtained eternal redemption for us" (vv. 11, 12). "These words naturally call attention to two things: The official character with which our Lord is invested, and the ministry which He has performed in that official character. His official character: He is 'come an high priest of good things to come.' His ministry in that official character: 'He has obtained eternal redemption for His people,' " (John Brown).

"But Christ being come an High Priest." The opening word emphasises a contrast: the legal high priest "could not make him that did the service perfect, as pertaining to the conscience" (v. 9): "*But* Christ"—could. The title here given the Saviour deserves particular notice. He is referred to in a considerable variety of ways in this epistle, and many different designations are there accorded Him. Each one is used with fine discrimination, and the reader loses much by failing to distinguish the force of "Jesus," "Christ," "Jesus Christ," "our Lord," "The Son," etc. Here (and also in 3:6, 14; 5:5; 6:1; 9:14, 24, 28; 11:26) it is "Christ," the Messiah (John 1:41), His official designation, a term that means "The Anointed," see Psa. 2:2 and cf. Acts 4:26. Great emphasis is placed by the Holy Spirit upon this title: "the Christ" (John 20:31), "that Christ" (John 6:69), "very Christ" (Acts 9:22), "The Lord's Christ" (Luke 2:26), "The Christ of God" (Luke 9:20).

"But Christ being come an High Priest." Under the name of the Messiah or Anointed One, He had been promised unto Israel for many centuries, and now the accomplishment had arrived. In a moment of doubt, His forerunner, in prison, sent unto Him asking, "Art Thou He that should come?" (Matt. 11:3). Upon the fulfillment of God's promise that He would send the Messiah, give a perfect revelation of His will, and bring in "perfection," the faith of the Jewish church was built. And now God's Word was verified, the true Light shone. The awaited One had come: "in the character in which He was promised, having done all that it was promised He should do" (John Brown). Therefore does the Holy Spirit here give the Redeemer His official, and distinctively Hebrew, title. "But Christ being come" no doubt looks back, especially to Psa. 40:7.

"But Christ being come an High Priest." True, He came also as Prophet (Deut. 18:15, 18), and as King (Matt. 2:2), but here the Holy Spirit especially emphasises the sacerdotal office of Christ, because it was in the exercise of *that* He offered Himself as a sacrifice unto God. The words which we are now considering begin a new division of this Epistle, though it is intimately related to what has gone before. In 9:11 to 10:22 the Holy Spirit sets before us the antitype of Lev. 16, which records the work of Israel's high priest on the annual day of atonement. There we behold Aaron officiating both outside the veil and within it. So the priestly functions of Christ fall into two great divisions, as they were performed on earth and as they are now continued in heaven. Before our great High Priest could enter the Holiest on high and there make intercession before God, He had first to make an atonement for the sins of those He represented, which was accomplished in His state of abjection here below, being consummated by His offering Himself a sacrifice unto God: 7:27, 8:3, 9:26.

A priest is one who officiates in the name of others, who approaches to God in order to make atonement for them by sacrifice. The design of his ministry is to render the Object of their worship propitious, to avert His wrath from men, to procure their restoration to His favour: see Lev. 16. Thus, the work of the priest is mediatory. Since the fact of sin is a cardinal one in the case of man, the function of a mediating priest for man must be mainly expiatory and reconciling: Heb. 8:3. It should serve as a most solemn warning unto all today that, while the Jews believed their Messiah would be both a prophet and king, they had no expectation of His also being priest, who should redeem sinners unto God. One who should go forth in the terror of His power, subjugating the nations and restoring the kingdom to Israel, appealed to their carnality; but for One to minister at the altar, employ His interest with God on behalf of transgressors, draw near to the Divine Majesty in their name, and mediate peace between them and an offended Creator, seems to have had *no* place in their thoughts. Hence it is that the *priesthood* of Christ is given such a prominent place in this epistle to the *Hebrews*.

"But Christ being come an High Priest." As to the *time* of His investiture with this office, it was clearly co-incident to the general office of *Mediator*. At the same moment that God appointed His Son "Mediator," He was constituted the Prophet, the Priest, and the Potentate of His Church. Prospectively, that took place in the eternal councils of the blessed Trinity, when in the "everlasting covenant" the Father appointed the Son and the Son agreed to be the Mediator between Him and His people. Historically, the Son became the Mediator at the moment of His incarnation: there is "one Mediator betwen God and men, the *Man* Christ Jesus" (1 Tim. 2:5); as soon as He was born, He was hailed as "*Christ,* the Lord" (Luke 2:11). Formally, He was officially consecrated to this office at His baptism, when He was "*anointed* (Christed) with the Holy Spirit and with power" (Acts. 10:38).

"But Christ being come an High Priest," and this according to the eternal oath of the Father, which "oath" was afterwards made known to the sons of men in time. This was before us when we considered 7:20-25. It was "by the word of the oath" that the Son is consecrated to His priestly office (7:28), the "oath" denoting God's eternal purpose and unchanging decree. In Psa. 2:7 we read that God said, "I *will declare* the decree," and accordingly in Psa. 110:4 we are told, "The Lord hath sworn, and will not repent, Thou art a priest forever after the order of Melchizedek"—there it was openly published. That God's "oath" *preceded* Christ's entrance upon and discharge of His sacerdotal office is clear from Heb. 7:20-25, otherwise the force of the apostle's reasoning there would be completely overthrown.

"But Christ *being come* an High Priest," otherwise He *could not* have "offered" Himself a sacrifice to God. As we saw when pondering 5:6, 7, Christ was exercising His sacerdotal functions in "the days of His flesh," i.e., the time of His humiliation. So too it was as "a merciful and faithful High Priest" that Christ "made propitiation for the sins of the people" (2:17). The types foreshadowed the same thing, especially Lev. 16. Aaron was not constituted a priest by entering the holy of holies; he was such before, or otherwise he could not have passed within the veil. Every passage which speaks of Christ's *one* oblation or His "offering" Himself *once* are conclusive as His being a priest on earth, for that word "once" cannot possibly be understood of what He is now doing in heaven; it must refer to His death as an historical fact, completed and finished here below: it is in designed contrast from His *continuous* intercession which is based upon it. The priestly sacrifice which He offered is emphatically described as co-incident with His death: 9:26. Any one of the common people could slay the sin-offering (Lev. 4:27-29), but none save the priest could *offer* it to God (Lev. 4:30)! Thus, every verse which speaks of Christ "offering" Himself to God emphasises the *priestly* character of His sacrifice.

"An high priest of good things to come." The reference here is to that more excellent dispensation which the Messiah was to inaugurate. Old Testament prophecy had announced many blessings and privileges which He would bring in, and accordingly the Jews had looked forward to better things than they had enjoyed under the old economy. The apostle here announces that this time had actually arrived, that the promised blessings had been procured by the High Priest of Christianity. As the result of Christ's advent, life and death, righteousness had been established, peace had been made, and a new and living way opened, which gave access to the very presence of God. Different far were *these* blessings from what the carnal Jews of Christ's day desired. Of course the "good things to come" are not to be restricted to those blessings which God's people already enjoy, but include as well those which yet await them. The "good things" are summed up in "grace and glory," and are in contrast from "the wrath to come" (Matt. 3:7).

"By a greater and more perfect tabernacle." This repeats what was said in 8:2. The reference is to the human nature which the Son of God took unto Himself. "The Word became flesh and (Greek) *tabernacled* among us " (John 1:14). Christ officiated in a much more glorious habitation than any in which Aaron and his successors served. Most appropriately was the humanity of the Saviour called a "tabernacle" for "in Him dwelleth all the fulness of the Godhead bodily" (Col. 2:9). Additional confirmation that the "greater and more perfect tabernacle" here referred to Christ's body, is supplied by Heb. 10:20, where the Holy Spirit again applies to Him the language of the Mosaic tabernacle and shows that in the Lord Jesus is found the antitype—"through the *veil*, that is to say His *flesh*."

"By a greater and more perfect tabernacle." There is both a comparison and a contrast between the tent which Moses pitched and the human habitat in which the Son of God abides: for the comparison we refer the reader to our comments upon 8:2. The contrast is first pointed by the word "greater," the Antitype far surpassing the type both in dignity and worth. The humanity of Christ, in its conception, its framing, its gracious endowments by the Holy Spirit, and particularly because of its union to and subsistence in the divine person of the Son, was far more excellent and glorious than any earthly fabric could be. "The human nature of Christ doth thus more excel the old tabernacle, than the sun does the meanest star" (John Owen). Of old God declared, "I will make a man more precious than fine gold; even a man than the golden wedge of Ophir" (Isa. 13:12)—a prophecy which obviously had its fulfillment in the Man Christ Jesus.

"And more perfect tabernacle": this points the second contrast between the type and the Antitype. As the word "greater" refers to the superior dignity and excellency of the humanity of Christ over the materials which comprised the tabernacle of Moses, so the "more perfect" respects its sacred use. The body of Christ was "more perfectly fitted and suited unto the end of a tabernacle, both for the inhabitation of the divine nature, and the means of exercising the sacerdotal office in making atonement for sin, than the other was. So it is expressed in 10:5, 'Sacrifice and burnt-offering Thou wouldst not, but a body hast Thou prepared Me.' This was that which God accepted, wherewith He was well pleased, when He rejected the other to that end" (John Owen). Probably the Holy Spirit has used this expression "more perfect" here because it was also through Christ's service in this "tabernacle" that His people had been "perfected forever."

"Not made with hands, that is to say, not of this building." Further reference is here made to the humanity of Christ by a double negation: "Not made with hands" is set in opposition to the Jewish tabernacle, which was made by the hands of men (Ex. 36:1-8). The humanity of Christ was the product of Him that hath no hands, even God Himself. Thus the expression here is the same as "which the Lord pitched, and not man" in 8:2. Then how much "greater" was the "more perfect Tabernacle"! The temple of Solomon was a most sumptuous and costly building, yet was it erected by human workmen, and therefore was it an act of infinite condescension for the great God to dwell therein: "But will God indeed dwell on the earth? behold, the heaven and heaven of heavens cannot contain Thee; how much less this house that I have builded?" (1 Kings 8:27). Reference to the supernatural humanity of Christ was made in Dan. 2:45: He was to be a "Stone," cut out of the same quarry with us, yet "without hands," i. e., without the help of nature, begotten by a man.

"That is to say, not of this building," words added to further define the preceding clause—the term rendered "building" is translated "creature" in 4:13. The humanity of Christ belonged to a totally different order of things than ours: there is no parallel in the whole range of creation. "Although the substance of His human nature was of the same kind with ours, yet the *production* of it in the world, was such an act of Divine power, as excels all other Divine operations whatever. Wherefore, God speaking of it, saith 'The Lord hath created a new thing in the earth, A woman shall compass a Man' (Jer. 31:22) or conceive Him without natural generation" (John Owen). How blessed to see that God is so far from being confined to natural means for the effecting of His holy counsels, that He can, when He pleases, dispense with all the ordinary methods and "laws" by which He works, and act contrary to them.

"Neither by the blood of goats and calves, but by His own blood He entered in once into the holy place, having obtained eternal redemption for us" (v. 12). Having shown that in Christ's person we have the antitype of the tabernacle, the apostle now proceeds to set forth that which was foreshadowed by the entrance of Israel's high priest into the holy of holies on the day of atonement: this he does both negatively and positively, that the difference between the shadow and the substance might more evidently appear. The design of this verse is to display the pre-eminence of Christ in the discharge of His priestly office above the legal high priest. This is seen, first, in the excellency of His sacrifice, which was His own blood; second, in the holy place whereinto He entered by virtue of it, which was Heaven itself; third in the effect of it, in that by it He procured "eternal redemption."

"Neither by the blood of goats and calves": it was by means of these that Aaron entered the holy of holies on the day of atonement (Lev. 16:14, 15)—the apostle here uses the plural number because of the annual repetition of the same sacrifice. In Lev. 16, the "calf" or young bullock (of one year old) is mentioned first; perhaps the order is here reversed because the "goat" was specifically for the people, and it is Christ redeeming His people which is the dominant thought. It was by virtue of the blood of these animals that Aaron entered so as to be accepted with God. The reference here is *not* directly to what the high priest brought with him into the holiest—or the "incense" too had been mentioned—but to the *title* which the sacrifices gave him to approach unto the Holy One of Israel.

"But by His own blood He entered in once into the holy place." Here we are brought directly unto the great mystery of the priestly work of Christ, especially as to the sacrifice which He offered unto God to make an atonement for the sins of His people. The "holy place"—called in 9:8 "the Holiest of all"—signifying Heaven itself, the dwelling-place of God. This is unequivocally established by 9:24 "into heaven itself." There never was any place to which this title of "holy place" so suitably belonged: thus it is designated in Psa. 20:6 "His holy heaven." And *when* was it that Christ entered Heaven by virtue of the merits of His own blood? Almost all of the commentators take the reference here as being to His ascension. But this we deem to be a mistake, and one from which erroneous conclusions of a most serious nature have been drawn. The writer is fully satisfied that what is affirmed in this verse took place immediately after Christ, on the cross, triumphantly cried "It is finished." Some of our reasons for believing this we give below.

First, the typical priest's entrance within the veil took place immediately after the victim's death: its body being carried without the camp to be burned in a public place, its blood being taken into the holiest, to be sprinkled on the propitiatory, covering the ark. Those closely-connected acts in the ritual were so related that, the burning followed last in order. Now Heb. 13:11 clearly establishes the fact that that typical action coincided with Christ's sacrifice outside Jerusalem: therefore, to make Christ's entrance into heaven occur forty days after His death, destroys the type. In pouring out His blood on the cross and surrendering His spirit into the hands of the Father, Christ expiated sin, and at that very moment the veil of the temple was rent, to denote His entrance into the presence of God. No sooner had He expired, than He entered Heaven, claiming it for Himself and His seed. His resurrection testified to the fact that God *had* accepted His sacrifice, that justice had been fully satisfied, and that He was now entitled to the reward of His obedience. His resurrection was the antitype of Aaron's *return* from the holy of holies unto the people, which was designed as a proof that Divine wrath had been averted and forgiveness secured.

Second, Aaron began by laying aside his robes of glory (Lev. 16:4), putting on only linen garments: *that* was far more in keeping with Christ's abasement at the cross, than His triumph and glory at His ascension. Third, when Aaron entered the holy of holies, atonement was not yet completed: that awaited his sprinkling of the blood upon the propitiatory. Therefore, if the antitype of this occurred not until the ascension of Christ, His sacrifice waited forty days for God's acceptance of it. Fourth, while Aaron was within the veil, the people without were full of fear for the high priest, lest he fail to appease God. Similar was the state of Christ's disciples during the interval between His death and resurrection: they remained in a state of suspense and doubt, dejection and dread. But far different were they immediately after His ascension: contrast Luke 24:21 and 24:52, 53! Fifth, God's rending of the veil at the moment of Christ's death was deeply significant: it was the Divine imprimature upon the Son's "It is finished." It was the outward adumbration in the visible realm to image forth what had taken place in the spiritual —Christ's entrance into heaven. In like manner, Christ's appearance to the disciples after His death, and His "peace be unto you," evidenced that peace *had* been made, that the atonement was completed.

"By His own blood He entered in," entered heaven as the Surety of His people, as their "Forerunner" (6:20). That which gave Him the right to do so was the perfect satisfaction which He had made, a satisfaction which honoured God more than all our sins dishonoured Him, which magnified the law and made it honourable. It was *not* the shedding of His blood alone which constituted His satisfaction or atonement, any more than a heart-belief in His resurrection (Rom. 10:9) without "faith in His blood" (Rom. 3:25) would save a sinner. He "became obedient *unto* death, even the death of the cross" (Phil 2:8), and what He there voluntarily endured was the climax and consummation of His redemptive work. "His *own* blood" emphasises its inestimable value. It was the blood of the "Son" (Heb. 1:2, 3). It was the blood of "God" incarnate (Acts 20:28). Well might the Holy Spirit call it "precious" (1 Pet. 1:19). No greater price could have been paid for our redemption. How vile and accursed, then, must *sin* be, seeing it can only be expiated by so costly a sacrifice! What *claims* Christ has upon His own! Well might He say, "Whosoever he be of you that forsaketh not all that he hath, he cannot be My disciple" (Luke 14:33).

"He entered in once into the holy place." The word "once" is that which has led so many to conclude that the reference was to the Saviour's ascension. But this, we have endeavored to show above, is a mistake. As we shall (D.V.) yet see, Heb. 9 and 10 contemplate a *double* entrance of Christ into heaven in fulfillment of the *double* type—Aaron and Melchizedek. That Christ *did* enter heaven at death is clear from His words to the thief (Luke 23:43); 2 Cor. 12:2, 4 places "paradise" in the third heaven. In every other passage where the term "once" occurs concerning the atoning work of Christ, it is always used contrastively with the *frequent* repetitions of the O. T. sacrifices: see 7:27; 9:7, 25, 26; 10:11, 12. That which is contemplated is Christ's *presenting* His satisfaction unto God. His ascension was for the purpose of intercession, which is *continuous*, and not completed.

"Having obtained eternal redemption," and this before He entered Heaven. To "redeem" is to deliver a person from a state of bondage, and that by the payment of an adequate ransom-price. Four things were required unto our redemption. It must be effected by the expiating of our sins. It must be by such an expiation that God, as the supreme Ruler and Judge should accept. It must be by rendering such a satisfaction to the Law, that its precepts are fulfilled and its penalty endured, so that its curse is removed. It must annul the power of Satan over us. How all of this was accomplished by the Redeemer, we have shown in our articles upon His "Satisfaction." This "redemption" is *eternal*, which is in contrast from Israel's of old —after their deliverance from Egypt they became in bondage to the Philistines and others. As the blood of Christ can never lose its efficacy, so none redeemed by Him can ever again be brought under sin's dominion.

"For if the blood of bulls and of goats, and the ashes of an heifer sprinkling the unclean, sanctifieth to the purifying of the flesh: How much more shall the blood of Christ" (vv. 13, 14). Having again demonstrated the pre-eminency of our Priest in vv. 11, 12, the apostle now exhibits the superior efficacy of His sacrifice. By a synedoche all sacrifices of expiation and all ordinances of purification appointed under the law are here summarized: the blood of lambs, etc., being included. The particular reference in the "ashes of an heifer" being to Num. 19:2-17, with which should be carefully compared John 13:1-15. It is principally the *use* of the ordinance of Num. 19 which is here in view. An heifer having been burned, its ashes were preserved, that, being mixed with pure water, they might be sprinkled on persons who had become legally unclean. When an Israelite, through contact with death, became ceremonially defiled, he was cut off from all the public worship of Jehovah; but when he carried out the instructions of Num. 19 he was restored.

Those "ashes," then, were a most merciful provision of God; without them, all acceptable worship had soon ceased. They had *an* efficacy, for they availed to the purifying of the flesh, which was a temporary, external and ceremonial cleansing. Typically, they pointed to that spiritual, inward and eternal cleansing which the blood of Christ provides. "The defilements which befall believers are many, and some of them unavoidable whilst they live in this world; yea, the best of their services have defilements adhering to them. Were it not that the blood of Christ, in its purifying virtue, is in a continual readiness unto faith, that God therein had opened a fountain for sin and uncleanness, the worship of the church would not be acceptable unto Him. In a constant application thereunto, doth the exercise of faith much consist" (John Owen).

"How much more shall the blood of Christ," etc. If the blood and ashes of beasts, under the appointment of God, were efficacious unto an external and temporary justification and sanctification—that is, the removal of both guilt and ceremonial pollution—how much more shall the sacrifice of Him who was promised of old, was the Anointed and therefore the One ordained and accepted of God, effectually and eternally cleanse those to whom it is applied. "The blood of Christ is comprehensive of *all* that He did and suffered in order unto our redemption, inasmuch as the shedding of it was the way and means whereby He offered Himself (in and by it) unto God" (John Owen).

"Who through the eternal Spirit offered Himself." There has been considerable difference of opinion as to whether the "eternal Spirit" has reference to the Divine nature of Christ animating and sustaining His humanity, or to the third Person of the Trinity. That which settles the point for us is this: Christ "offered *Himself*" to God: that is, in His entire person, while acting in His mediatorial office. As the

Mediator, He took upon Him the "form of a servant," and therefore was He filled and energised by the Spirit in all that He did. Christ was "*obedient* unto death:" as He was subject to the Spirit in going into the wilderness (Matt. 4:1), so the Spirit led Him a willing victim to the cross. This wondrous statement shows us the perfect co-operation of the Eternal Three, concurring in the great work of redemption.

Christ offered Himself "without spot," to God. There is a double reference in these words: unto the purity of His person, and to the holiness of His life. There is both a moral and a legal sense to the expression. It speaks of Christ's fitness and meetness *to be* a sacrifice for our sins. Not only was there no blemish in His nature and no defect in His character, but there was every moral excellence. He had *fulfilled* the law in thought, word and deed, having loved the Lord His God with all His heart and His neighbour as Himself. Therefore was He fully qualified to act for His people.

"Purge your conscience from dead works." This is one of the effects produced by Christ's sacrifice, an effect which the legal ordinances were incapable of securing. Because Christ's sacrifice has expiated our sins, when the Spirit applies its virtues to the heart, that is, when He gives faith to appropriate them, our sense of guilt is removed, peace is communicated, and we are enabled to approach God not only without dread, but as joyous worshippers. The "conscience" is here specially singled out (cf. 10:22 for the larger meaning) because it is the proper seat of the *guilt* of sin, charging it on the soul, and hindering an approach unto God. By "dead works" are meant our sins as unto their guilt and defilement —cf. our comments on 6:1. True believers are delivered from the curse of the law, which is *death*.

"To serve the living God," not simply in outward form but in sincerity and in truth. This is the advantage and blessing which we receive from our conscience being purged. Christians have both the right and the liberty to "serve God." The "living God" cannot be served by those who are dead in sins, and therefore alienated from Him. But the sacrifice of Christ has purchased the gift of the Spirit unto all for whom He died, and the Spirit renews and equips the saint for acceptable worship. "This is the end of our purgation: for we are not washed by Christ that we may plunge ourselves again into new filth, but that our purity may serve to glorify God" (John Calvin). Under the word "serve" is comprised all the duties which we owe unto God, not only as His creatures, but as His children. Then let us earnestly seek grace to put Rom. 12:1 into daily practise.

CHAPTER FORTY-TWO

The Mediator

(9:15)

The proposition which the apostle is occupied with proving and illustrating in this section of the epistle is that which was laid down in 8:6, "But now hath He obtained a more excellent ministry, by how much also He is the Mediator of a better covenant, which was established upon better promises." In the verses which were before us in the last article, the superiority of Christ over Aaron was brought out in the following respects. First, in that He officiated in a more excellent tabernacle (v. 11). Second, in that He offered to God a superior sacrifice (vv. 11, 14). Third, in that He has entered a more glorious sanctuary (v. 12). Fourth, in that He secured a more efficacious redemption (v. 12). Fifth, in that He was moved by a more excellent Spirit (v. 14). Sixth, in that He obtained for His people a better cleansing (v. 14). Seventh, in that He made possible for them a nobler service (v. 14).

Christ has "obtained eternal redemption" for His people. As we pointed out in our last article, to "redeem" signifies to liberate by the paying of a ransom-price: "If the Son shall make you free, ye shall be free indeed" (John 8:36). The freedom which the Christian has is, first, a *legal* one: he has been "redeemed from the curse of the law" (Gal. 3:13). Because of this, second, he enjoys an *experimental* freedom from the power of sin: "sin shall not have dominion over you" (Rom. 6:14). Justification and sanctification are never separated: where God imputes the righteousness of Christ, He also imparts a principle of holiness, the latter being the fruit or consequence of the former; both being necessary before we can be admitted into heaven. Because the blood of Christ has fully met every claim of God upon and against His people, its virtues and purifying effects are applied to them by the Spirit. Both of these were foreshadowed under the Levitical types of the old economy, and are seen in 9:13.

"The blood of bulls and of goats and the ashes of an heifer sprinkling the unclean" sanctified "to the purifying of the flesh."

There is here both a comparison and a contrast. The comparison is between the type and the Antitype; the contrast, between what the one and what the other effected. Those typical rites procured only a temporary "redemption" from the governmental consequences of sin; Christ's sacrifice has secured an "eternal redemption" from all the consequences of sin. A double type is referred to in 9:13. No single sacrifice could adequately represent the power and efficacy of the blood of Christ. By the "*blood* of bulls and goats" the *guilt* of Israel's sins were temporarily removed; by the sprinkling of the "*ashes* of an heifer" they were ceremonially purified from the defilements of the wilderness. We quote below a valuable footnote from A. Saphir:

"The ashes of an heifer. It was to take away the defilement of death. The institution is recorded in the book of Numbers as relating to the provision God makes for His people in their wilderness journey. As no blood of the slain victim was 'incorruptible,' it was necessary, in order to show the cleansing by blood from defilement through contact with death to have as it were the essential principle of blood, presented in a permanent and available form. The red heifer, which had never been under the yoke, symbolizes life in its most vigorous, perfect, and fruitful form. She was slain without the camp (Heb. 13:11, Num. 19:3, 4). She was *wholly* burnt, flesh, skin, and blood, the priest casting cedar-wood, hyssop, and scarlet into the fire. The ashes of the burnt heifer, put into flowing water, were then sprinkled with hyssop for ceremonial purification. . . . Christ is the fulfillment. For the blood of Christ is not merely, so to speak, the key unlocking the holy of holies to Him as our High Priest and Redeemer, it is not merely our ransom by which we are delivered out of bondage, and, freed from the curse, are brought nigh unto God; but it also separates us from death and sin. It is incorruptible, always cleansing and vivifying; through this blood we are separated from this evil world, and overcome; by this blood we keep our garments white (John 6:53, Rev. 7:14).

"What had necessarily to be separated in the types, is here in unity and perfection. Likewise, what *really* and *potentially* is given to us when we are first brought into the state of reconciliation and access, of justification and sanctification, is in our actual experience continually repeated. We have been cleansed and sanctified once and forever; the same blood, remembered and believed in, cleanseth us continually. The difference between this continual cleansing and the first (according to John 13:10) must never be forgotten, or we fall into a legal condition, going back from the holy of holies into the holy place. But, on the other hand we must not forget the *living* character of the blood, which by the Spirit is continually applied to us, and by which we have peace, renewal of the sense of pardon, and strength for service (1 Pet. 1:2)."

Having pointed out what God's people are redeemed *from*, the Holy Spirit next makes a brief notice of what Christ has redeemed *unto*. He has delivered us from the curse of the law and the bondage of sin; He has also procured for us an "eternal inheritance": His satisfaction has merited for us the favour and image of God and everlasting bliss in His presence. In referring to this, the Spirit also takes occasion to bring out the fact that the sacrifice of Christ was necessary in order for God to make good His promises of old. Herein too He once more meets the Jewish prejudice — why must this great High Priest *die?* The death of Christ was requisite in order to the accomplishing of God's engagements to Abraham and his (spiritual) seed, to confirm His covenant-pledges, which, once more, brings into view the relation which Christ sustains to the everlasting covenant.

"And for this cause He is the Mediator of the new testament, that by means of death, for the redemption of the transgressions under the first testament, they which are called might receive the promise of eternal inheritance" (v. 15). Each word in this verse requires to be duly weighed and carefully considered both in the light of what immediately precedes and follows, otherwise we are certain to err. The opening "And" is plain intimation that no new subject begins here, which at once disposes of the figment that this and the next verses require to be placed in a parenthesis. The apostle continues to treat of what was before him in the verses which we considered in the last article. He is still showing the excellency of our High Priest and the superior efficacy of His sacrifice. That the contents of this verse are by no means free from difficulty is readily allowed, yet its leading thoughts are plain enough.

"And for this cause He is the Mediator of the new testament." The Greek words for "for this cause" are rendered "therefore" in 1:9 and other places. They signify, because of this, or for this reason. There has been a great deal of discussion as to precisely what is referred to in "for *this* cause": some insisting that it looks back to what has been affirmed in the previous verses, others contending that it points forward to that which is declared in the second half of this verse. Personally, we believe that *both* are included. There is a fulness to God's words which is not to be found in man's, and whenever an expression is capable of two or more meanings, warranted by the context and the analogy of faith, both should be retained. Let us then look at the two thoughts here brought together.

"For this cause": because of the superior nature and efficacy of the sacrifice which Christ was to offer, God appointed Him to be the Mediator of the new covenant. It was out of (prospective) regard unto the fitness of Christ's person and the excellency of His offering, that God ordained Him to make mediation between Himself and His fallen people. Because He should make an effectual atonement for their sins and provide a way whereby their troubled consciences might have peace, God decreed that His Son, becoming incarnate, should interpose between poor sinners and the awful Majesty they have offended. "For this cause": and also, because it was only by means of death that the transgressions under the first testament could be redeemed and the called receive the promise of eternal inheritance, Christ was appointed Mediator of the new covenant.

With his usual sagacity John Owen combined both ideas: "It is evident there is a reason rendered in these words, of the necessity of the death and sacrifice of Christ, by which alone our consciences may be purged from dead works. And this reason is intended in these words, 'For this cause.' And this necessity of the death of Christ, the apostle proves both from the nature of His office, namely, that He was to be the Mediator of the new covenant, which, being a testament, required the death of the testator; *and* from what was to be effected thereby, namely, the redemption of transgressions, and the purchase of an eternal inheritance. Wherefore, *these* are the things which he hath respect unto in these words."

"He is the Mediator of the new testament." It seems strange that some of the best of the expositors understand this to mean that *after* Christ had "offered Himself without spot to God" he became "the Mediator," which is indeed a turning of things upside down and a putting an effect for a cause. A mediator is one who stands between two parties, and two parties at variance, and that with the object of settling the difference between them, that is, of effecting a reconciliation. Hence we read, "For there is one God, and one Mediator between God and men, the man Christ Jesus; Who gave Himself a ransom for all, to be testified in due time" (1 Tim. 2:5, 6). The second half of our verse ought to have prevented such a blunder: "He is the Mediator of the new testament, that *by means of death*. . . . they which are called might receive the promise of eternal inheritance."

As we pointed out in our comments upon 8:6, it is most important to recognise that Christ is a *sacerdotal* Mediator, that is, one who has interposed His sacrifice and intercession between God and His people in order to their reconciliation. In voluntarily undertaking to serve as Mediator between God and His people considered as fallen creatures, two things were required from Christ. First, that He should completely remove that which kept the covenanters at a distance, that is, take away the cause of enmity between them. Second, that He should purchase and procure, in a way suited unto the glory of God, the actual communication of all the good things — summed up in "grace and glory" (Psa. 84:11) — which belong to those whose Surety He was. *This* is the foundation of the "merits" of Christ and of the grant of all blessings unto us for His sake.

In what has just been pointed out, we may perceive an additional signification to the opening "And" of our verse. Christ is not only "High Priest" (vv. 11 to 14), but "Mediator" too. He undertook office upon office in order to our greater good. Christ is, in the "new covenant" or "testament," the Mediator, Surety, Priest and Sacrifice, all in His own person. In order that we may have something like a definite conception of these, let us consider, separately, the various relations which our blessed Redeemer sustains to the everlasting covenant. First, He is the *Surety* of it: Heb. 7:22. As such He engaged to render full satisfaction to God on behalf of His people, to do and suffer for them all that the law required. He transferred to Himself all their obligations, undertaking to pay all their debts. In other words, He substituted Himself in their place and stead, in consequence of which there was a double imputation: God reckoning to Christ all their liabilities, God imputing to them His perfect righteousness (2 Cor. 5:21).

As the "Surety" Christ most blessedly fulfilled the type of Gen. 43:9, being Sponsor to His Father for all His beloved Benjamins, Heb. 2:13, Isa. 49:5, 6, John 10:16. Second, as the *Mediator* of the covenant (Heb. 12:24), He took His place between God and His people, undertaking to maintain the interests and secure the honour of both parties, by perfectly reconciling the one to the other. As the "Mediator" Christ has blessedly fulfilled the type of Jacob's "ladder," uniting heaven and earth. Third, as the *Messenger* (Mal. 3:1) or "Angel" of the covenant (Rev. 8:3-5) He makes known God's purpose and will to His people, and presents their requests and worship to Him. Fourth, as the *Testator* of the covenant (Heb. 9:16) He has ratified it and made bequests and gifts to His people. Finally, and really first, as the *Head* of the whole election of grace, the covenant was made with Him by God: Psa. 89:3, etc.

"For this cause He is the Mediator of the new testament." Here again there has been an almost endless controversy as to whether this last word should be rendered "covenant" or "testament," that is, "will." The same Greek word has been translated by both these

English terms, some think wrongly so, for a "covenant" is, strictly speaking, an agreement or contract between two parties: the one promising to do certain things upon the fulfilment of certain conditions by the other; whereas a "testament" or "will" is where one bequeaths certain things as gifts. Thus there seems to be little or nothing in common between the two concepts, in fact, that which is quite contrary. Nevertheless, our English translators have rendered the Greek word *both* ways, and we believe, rightly so. Nevertheless it remains for us to enquire, *why* should the same term be rendered "covenant" in 8:6 and "testament" in 9:15? Briefly, the facts are as follows.

First, the word "diatheke" occurs in the Greek N. T. thirty-three times, having been translated (in the A. V.) "covenant" twenty times (twice in the plural number) and "testament" thirteen times, four of the latter being used in connection with the Lord's supper. Second, in the Sept. version (the translation of the Heb. O. T. into Greek) this word "diatheke" occurs just over two hundred and fifty times, where, in the great majority of instances, it is used to translate "berith." Third, the Greek word "diatheke" is not that which properly denotes a covenant, compact, or agreement; instead, the technical terms for *that* is "syntheke," but the Spirit never once uses this word in the N. T. Fourth, on the other hand, it should be noted that the Hebrew language has no distinctive word which means a will or testament. Fifth, the most common use of the term "diatheke" in the N. T., particularly in 2 Cor. 3 and in Hebrews, neither denotes a "covenant" proper (a stipulated agreement) nor a "will," but instead, an economy, a dispensational arrangement or ordering of things.

Now it needs to be very carefully noted that from Heb. 9:15 to the end of the chapter, the apostle argues from the nature of a will or "testament" among men, as he distinctly affirms in v. 16. His manifest object in so doing was to confirm the Christian's faith in the expectation of the benefits of this "covenant" or "testament." Nor did he violate the rules of language in this, straining neither the meaning of the Heb. "berith" nor the Greek "diatheke," for there is, actually, a close affinity between the two things. There are "covenants" which have in them free grants or donations, which is of the nature of a "testament"; and there are "testaments" whose force is resolved into conditions and agreements—as when a man wills an estate to his wife on the stipulation that she remains a widow—which is borrowed from the nature of a "covenant."

If we go back to the O. T. and study the various "covenants" which God made with men, it will be found again and again that they were merely declarations whereby He would communicate good things unto them, which has more of the nature of a "testament" in it. Sometimes the word "covenant" was used simply to express a free promise, with an effectual donation and communication of the thing promised, which also has more of the nature of a "testament" than of a "covenant." Thus, once more, we perceive a fulness in the words of the Holy Spirit which definitions from human dictionaries do not include. That which *was* a "covenant," has become *to us* a "testament." The "covenant" was made by God with Christ. By His death that which God pledged Himself to do unto the heirs of promise in return for the work which Christ was to perform, is now *bequeathed* to us as a free gift: what was a legal stipulation between the Father and the Mediator, comes to us purely as a matter of grace.

Some have insisted that "the Mediator of the new covenant" is understandable, but that "Mediator of the new testament" is no more intelligible than the "testator of a covenant" would be. Our answer is that, the Spirit of God is not tied by the artificial rules which bind human grammarians. Rom. 8:17 tells us that Christians are "heirs of God," that is of the Father, yet He has not *died!* No figure must be pressed too far. Some have argued that because the Church is the Body of Christ, it cannot also be His "Bride," but such carnal reasoning is altogether inadmissible upon spiritual and Divine things; as well might we argue that because Christ calls us "brethren" (Heb. 2:12), therefore we cannot be His "children" (Heb. 2:13); or that because Christ is the "everlasting Father" of Israel (Isa. 9:6), He cannot also be their "Husband" (Isa. 54:5). The truth is, that Christ is both the Mediator of the new covenant, and the Mediator of the new testament, looking at the same office from two different angles. God has so confirmed the promises in Christ (2 Cor. 1:20), that at His death He made a legacy of them and bequeathed them to His people in a testamentary form.

To sum up what has been said on this difficult but important subject: throughout the N. T. the Holy Spirit has intentionally used only the one word "diatheke"—though there was another in the Greek language ("syntheke") which more exactly expressed a "covenant"—because it was capable of a double application, and that, because the Son of God is not only the Mediator of a new covenant, but also the Testator of His own gifts. Thereby God would fix our gaze on the *cross* of Christ and see there that what had up to that day existed as a "covenant," then became for the first time, a "testament"; and that while the covenant between the Father and the Son is from everlasting, the "new *testament*" dates only from Calvary.

"For the redemption of the transgressions under the first testament." This states one of the principal ends which God had in view when appointing Christ to be the "Mediator," namely, to deliver His people from all the bondage they were subject to as the result of their violations of His law, and that by the payment of a satisfactory price. But, it may be asked, why not "the redemption of the transgressors" rather than "transgressions"? Did Christ purchase sins? The reference is to His expiation of His people's iniquities, and they were "debts," and Christ's death was a *discharge* of that debt. "The discharge of a debt is a buying it out. Thus to redeem sins is no more harsh a phrase than to be 'delivered for our offences' (Rom. 4:25), or 'who gave Himself for our sins' (Gal. 1:4), or to be 'merciful to their unrighteousness,' Heb. 8:12" (Wm. Gouge).

"For the redemption of the transgressions under the first testament." In these words the Spirit makes a further exhibition of the virtue and efficacy of Christ's death, by affirming that it paid the price of remitting the sins of the O. T. saints. Here again the apostle is countering the Jewish prejudice. The death of Christ was necessary not only if sinners of N. T. times should be fitted to serve the living God (v. 14), but also to meet the claims which God had against the O. T. saints. The efficacy of Christ's atonement was retrospective as well as prospective: cf. Rom. 3:25. The true (in contrast from the typical), spiritual (in contrast from the ceremonial), and eternal (in contrast from the temporal), "redemption" of the O. T. saints was effected by the sacrifice of Christ. The same thing is clearly implied in Heb. 9:26: had not the one offering of Christ — as the Lamb "foreordained before the foundation of the world" (1 Pet. 1:19, 20) — been of perpetual efficacy from the days of Abel onwards, then it had been necessary to *repeat* it constantly in order to redeem believers of each generation. It was God's eternal purpose that Christ's atonement, settled in the "everlasting covenant," should be available to faith from the beginning. Hence, the apostle said, "Through this Man is preached unto you the forgiveness of sins (cf. Gal. 3:8, Heb. 4:2), and by Him *all* that believe—O. T. saints as truly as the N. T.—are justified from all things" (Acts 13:38, 39).

"Now, if any one asks, whether sins under the Law were remitted to the fathers, we must bear in mind the solution already stated,—that they *were* remitted; but remitted *through Christ*. Then notwithstanding their external expiations, they were always held guilty. For this reason Paul says that the law was a handwriting against us (Col. 2:14). For when the sinner came forward and openly confessed that he was guilty before God, and acknowledged by sacrificing an innocent animal that he was worthy of eternal death, what did he obtain by his victim, except that he sealed his own death as it were by this handwriting? In short, even then they only reposed in the remission of sins, when they looked to Christ. But if only a regard to Christ took away sins, they could never have been freed from them, had they continued to rest in the law" (J. Calvin).

"For the redemption of the transgressions under the first testament." It remains for us to ask, Why *this* limitation? for Christ atoned for the sins of those who were to believe as much as for those who had, before He became incarnate, looked in faith to Him. First, because a measure of doubt or uncertainty could exist only concerning them. Some have taught, and possibly some in the apostle's day thought, that nought but earthly blessings would be the portion of those who died before the present dispensation. Therefore to remove such a doubt, it is affirmed that O. T. believers too were redeemed by Christ's blood. Second, because the apostle had pressed so hard the fact that the Levitical sacrifices could not remove moral guilt from those who lived under the Mosaic economy, he shows Christ's sacrifice had. Third, because by just consequence it follows that, if those who trusted Christ of old had redemption of *their* transgressions through Him, much more they who are under the new testament. "The blood of Jesus Christ His Son cleanseth us from all sin" (1 John 1:7): it was just as efficacious in taking away the transgressions of believers before it was actually shed, as it is of cleansing believers today, nineteen centuries after it was shed.

"They which are called might receive the promise of eternal inheritance." Here the "heirs" are designated by character rather than by name, by this qualification (Greek) "they which have been called," that is, effectually so, or truly converted to God. In John 1:12 this privilege of heirship is settled upon "believers," such as do heartily accept of Christ and His grace. In Acts 26:18 and Col. 1:12 the heirs are described as "sanctified," that is, as personally dedicated to God and set apart to live unto Him. This expression "the called" is a descriptive appellation of the true spiritual people of God, and looks back to the "call" of Abraham (Heb. 11:8), who, in consequence of the mighty workings of divine grace in his heart, turned his back upon the world and the things of the flesh (Gen. 12:1), and entered the path of faith's obedience to God. Only those possessing these marks are the spiritual "children" of Abraham, such as have been "called with a *holy* calling" (2 Tim. 1:9).

"Might receive the promise of eternal inheritance." This is the goal toward which the apostle has been steadily moving, as he has passed from clause to clause in this verse. That the called of God might receive the promise of eternal inheritance was the grand ultimate object of the "everlasting covenant" so far as men are concerned, and the chief design of the new testament. But an obstacle stood in the way, namely, the transgressions or sins of those who should be "called." In order to the removal of that obstacle, Christ must die that death which was due unto those transgressions. For the Son of God to die, He must be appointed unto a mediatorial position and become incarnate. Because He was so appointed, because He did so die, because He has redeemed from all transgressions, the "eternal inheritance" is sure unto all His people, His heirs, the "called" of God.

"Might receive the promise of eternal inheritance." The children of Israel received from God an external call which separated them from the heathen, and when they were redeemed from Egypt they received promise of a temporal or earthly inheritance. But inside that Nation was "a remnant according to the election of *grace*," and they, individually, received from God an inward call, which made them the heirs of an eternal inheritance. It is of these latter that our verse speaks, yet as including also the saints of the present dispensation. Promise of an "eternal inheritance" had the O. T. saints. They had the Gospel preached unto them (Heb. 4:2). They were saved through "the grace of the Lord Jesus Christ" (Acts 15:11) as well as we. They "did all eat the *same* spiritual meat and did all drink the same spiritual drink," even Christ (1 Cor. 10:3, 4). And therefore did they "desire a better country, that is, an *heavenly*" (Heb. 11:16). How all of this sets aside the preposterous figment of the modern "dispensationalists," who relegate "Israel" to an inferior inheritance from that which belongs to "the Church"!

"Might receive the promise of eternal inheritance." What is meant by the first four words here? First, let us very briefly define the "eternal inheritance." By it we understand God's "great salvation" (Heb. 2:3), considering it in its most comprehensive sense, as including justification, sanctification and glorification. It is that blessed estate which Christ has purchased for "His own," here called an "inheritance" to remind us that the way whereby we come unto it is by a gratuitous adoption, and not by any merits of our own. Now as the state of those who are to receive it is twofold, namely, in this life and in that which is to come, so there are two parts of this inheritance: "grace and glory." Even now "eternal life" is communicated to those who are called according to God's purpose.

But "grace" is only "glory" begun: the best "wine" is reserved for the time to come. For the future aspect of the "eternal inheritance" see 1 Peter 1:3-5.

The way whereby God conveys this "eternal inheritance" is by "promise": *see* Gal. 3:18 and Heb. 6:15-18. And this for a threefold reason at least. First, to manifest the absolute *freeness* of the grant of it: the "promise" is everywhere opposed unto everything of "works" or desert in ourselves: Rom. 4:14, etc. Second, to give *security* unto all the heirs of it, for the very veracity and faithfulness of God is behind the promise: Titus 1:1, etc. Since God has "promised" *to* bestow the "inheritance," nothing in, of, or from the heirs can possibly be an occasion of their forefeiting it: 1 Thess. 5:24. Third, that it might be *by faith,* for what God promises necessarily requires faith, and faith only, unto its reception: Rom. 4:16. The *"receive* the promise" has a double force. First, it is to "mix faith" with it (Heb. 4:2), to *appropriate* it (Heb. 11:13, 17), so as not to stagger at it in unbelief (Rom. 4:20, 21). Second, it is to receive the *fulfilment* of it. As unto the *foundation* of the whole inheritance, in the sacrifice of Christ, and all the grace, mercy and love, with the fruits thereof, these are communicated to believers in this life: Gal. 3:14. As unto the *consummation,* the future state in glory, we "receive the promise" by faith, rest thereon, and live in the joyous expectation of it: Heb. 11:13.

In conclusion, let us sum up the contents of this remarkable verse, adopting the analysis of John Owen. 1. God has designed an "eternal inheritance" unto certain persons. 2. The way in which a right or title is conveyed thereunto is by "promise." 3. The persons unto whom this inheritance is designed, are the "called." 4. The obstacle which stood in the way of their enjoyment of this inheritance was their "transgressions." 5. That this obstacle might be removed, and the inheritance enjoyed, God made a "new covenant," because none of the sacrifices under the first covenant, could expiate sins. 6. The ground of the efficacy of the "new covenant" unto this end was, that it had a Mediator, a great High Priest. 7. The means whereby the Mediator of the new covenant did expiate the sins against the first testament was by "death," and this of necessity, seeing that this new covenant, being also a "testament," required the death of the Testator. 8. The death of this Mediator has taken away sins by "the redemption of transgressions." Thus, the promise is sure unto all the seed.

CHAPTER FORTY-THREE

The New Testament

(Heb. 9:16-22)

Having affirmed (9:12, 14) that the blood of Christ is the means of the believer's redemption, in v. 15, the apostle proceeds to make further proof of this basic and vital truth. His argument here is taken from the design and object of Christ's priesthood, which was to *confirm* the covenant God had made with His people, and which could only be done by blood. First, he affirms that the Saviour was "the Mediator of the new testament." Many functions were undertaken by Him. Just as one type could not set forth all that the Lord Jesus did and suffered, so no single office could display all the relations which He sustained and all the benefits He procured for us. That which is done by a prophet, by a priest, by a king, by a surety, by a mediator, by a husband, by a father, that and more has been done by Christ. And the more clearly we observe in Scripture the many undertakings of Christ for us, as seen in His *varied relations,* the more will He be endeared to our hearts, and the more will faith be strengthened.

Christ's undertaking to be a "Mediator" both procured a covenant to pass between God and men, and also engaged Himself for the performance thereof on both parts. This could only be by a full satisfaction being rendered to Divine justice, by the shedding of blood infinitely valuable as His was. To assure His people of their partaking of the benefits of God's covenant, the cross of Christ has turned that covenant into a *testament,* so that the conditions of the covenant on God's part (its requirements: namely, perfect obedience rendered to His law, and thus "everlasting righteousness" being brought in: Dan. 9:24; and full satisfaction being taken by the law for the sins of His people) might be so many *legacies,* which being ratified by the death of the Testator, none might disannul.

Unspeakably blessed as are the truths expressed (so freely) above, there is another which is still more precious for faith to apprehend and rest on, and that is, that behind all offices (so to speak), lying at the foundation of the whole dispensation of God's grace toward His people, is the *mystical oneness* of Christ and His Church: a legal oneness, which ultimates by the Spirit's work in a *vital* union, so that Christ is the Head and believers are the members of one Person (1 Cor. 12:12, 13). *This,* and this alone, constituted the just ground for God to impute to Christ all the sins of His people, and to impute to them the righteousness of Christ for their justification of life. What Christ did in obeying the law is reckoned to them as though that obedience had been performed by them; and in like manner, what they deserved on account of their sins was charged to and endured by Him, as though they themselves had suffered it: see 2 Cor. 5:21.

The first spring of the *union* between Christ and His Church lay in that eternal compact between the Father and the Son respecting the salvation of His people contemplated as fallen in Adam. In view of the human nature which He was to assume, the Lord Christ was "predestinated" or "foreordained" (1 Pet. 1:20) unto grace and glory, and that by virtue of the *union* of flesh unto His Godhead. This grace and glory of the God-man was the exemplary cause and *pattern* of *our* predestination: Rom. 8:29, Phil. 3:21. It was also the cause and means of the communicating of all grace and glory unto us, for we were "chosen in Him before the foundation of the world" (Eph. 1:4). Christ was thus elected (Isa. 42:1) as Head of the Church, His mystical body. All the elect of God were then committed unto Him, to be delivered from sin and death, and brought unto the enjoyment of God: John 17:6, Rev. 1:5, 6.

In the prosecution of this design of God, and to effect the accomplishment of the "everlasting covenant" (Heb. 13:20), Christ undertook to be the "Surety" of that covenant (Heb. 7:22), engaging to answer for all the liabilities of His people and to discharge all their legal responsibilities. Yet was it as Priest that Christ acted as Surety: *God's* "Priest," *our* "Surety." That is to say, all the activities of Christ were of a sacerdotal character, having God for their immediate object; but as these activities were all performed on our behalf, He was a Surety or Sponsor for us also. As the "Surety" of the covenant, Christ undertook to discharge all the debts of those who are made partakers of its benefits. As our Surety He also merited and procured from God the Holy Spirit, to communicate to His people all needful supplies of grace to make them new creatures, which enables them to yield obedience to God from a new principle of spiritual life, and that faithfully unto the end.

When considering the *administration* of the "everlasting covenant" in time, we contemplate the *actual application* of the grace, benefits and privileges of it unto those for whose sakes it was devised and drawn up. For this the *death* of the Mediator was required, for only through His blood-shedding is the whole grace of the covenant made effectual unto us. This it is which is affirmed in 9:15, and which we considered at length in our last article. In the passage which is now to be before us, the apostle does two things: first, he refers to a well known fact which is everywhere recognised among men, namely, that a will or testament requires the death of the testator to give it validity. Second, he refers to an O. T. type which exemplifies the principle which he is here setting before us.

"For where a testament is, there must also of necessity be the death of the testator. For a testament is of force after men are dead: otherwise it is of no strength at all while the testator liveth" (vv. 16, 17). That which is found in vv. 16-23 is really of the nature of a parenthesis, brought in for the purpose of showing *why* it was necessary for the incarnate Son to die. In v. 24 the apostle returns to his proofs for the superiority of the ministry of Christ over Aaron's. What we have in vv. 16, 17, is brought in to show both the need for and the purpose of the death of Christ, the argument being drawn from the character and design of that covenant of which He is the Mediator. Because that covenant was also to be a "testament" it was confirmed by the death of the Testator. Appeal is made to the only use of a will or testament among men.

The method by which the apostle here demonstrates the necessity of Christ's death as He was "the mediator of the new testament" is not merely from the signification of the word "diatheke" (though we must not lose sight of its force), but as he is speaking principally of the two "covenants" (i. e. the two forms under which the "everlasting covenant" has been *administered*), it is the *affinity* which there is between a solemn covenant, and a testament, that he has respect unto. For it is to be carefully noted that the apostle speaks not of the death of Christ merely as it was a *death,* which is all that is required of a "testament" as such, without any consideration of the *nature* of the testator's death; but he speaks of it also (and primarily) as it was a *sacrifice* by the shedding of His blood (vv. 12, 14, 18-23), which belongs to a Divine *covenant,* and is in no way required by a "testament." Thus, we see again the needs-be for retaining the *double* meaning and force of the Greek word here.

There has been much needless wrangling over the Divine person alluded to under the word "Testator," some insisting it is Christ, some the Father, others arguing the impossibility of the latter because the Father has never died. We believe that, in this case, Saphir was right when he said, "The testator is, properly speaking, God; for we are God's heirs; but it is God in Christ." Had he referred the reader to 2 Cor. 5:19 his statement had been given scriptural confirmation. The "everlasting covenant" or Covenant of Grace has the nature of a "testament" from these four considerations or facts. First, it proceeded from the *will* of God: He freely made it (Heb. 6:17). Second, it contained various legacies or gifts: to Christ, God bequeathed the elect as His inheritance (Deut. 32:9, Psa. 16:6, Luke 22:29); to the elect themselves, that they should be joint-heirs with Him (Rom. 8:17, Rev. 3:21). Third, it is unalterable (Gal. 3:15), "ordered in all things and sure" (2 Sam. 23:5); having been duly witnessed to (1 John 5:7), hence, being of the nature of a "testament" there are *no* stipulations for men to fulfil (Gal. 3:18). Fourth, the death of Christ has secured the administration of it.

A deed is not valid without a seal; a will cannot be probated until the legatee dies, nor were God's covenants with men (the historical adumbrations of the "everlasting covenant") ratified except by blood-shedding. Thus it was with His covenant with Abraham (Gen. 15:9, 18); thus it was with His covenant with Israel at Sinai (Ex. 24:6). Thus, unto the confirmation of a "testament" there must be the *death* of the testator; unto the ratification of a "covenant" the *blood* of a sacrifice was required. Thereby does the apostle prove conclusively the necessity for the sacrificial death of Christ as the Mediator, both as the Mediator of a "covenant" and as the Mediator of a "testament": for through His sacrificial death, both the *promises* contained in the "covenant" and the *bequeathments* of the "testament," are made irrevocably sure to all His seed. We trust, then that we have been enabled to clear up the great difficulty which the word "diatheke" has caused so many, and shown that it has a *double* meaning and force in *this* passage.

It remains for us to point out that the O. T. supplies us with a most striking type which blessedly illustrates the principle enunciated in this 16th verse. But note first of all that v. 15 opens with "For" and that this comes right after the mention of "the Mediator of the new testament," and the promise of "eternal inheritance" in v. 15. Now the "mediator" of the "old testament" was Moses, and it was not until his *death,* though immediately after it, that Israel entered their inheritance, the land of Canaan! Looked at from the standpoint of God's government, the death of Moses was because of his sin (Numb. 20:10-12); but considered in relation to his *official* position, as "the servant over the house of God," it had another and deeper meaning as Deut. 3:26 shows, "the Lord was wroth with me *for your sakes*"—how blessedly did this foreshadow the reason why God's wrath was visited upon Christ: Christ, as Moses, must die before the inheritance could be ours.

In v. 17 it is not of the making of a testament which is referred to, but its execution: its efficacy depends solely on the testator's death. The words "is of force" mean, is firm and cannot be annulled; it must be executed according to the mind of the one who devised it. The reason why it is of "no strength" during his lifetime, is because it is then subject to alteration, according to the pleasure of him who made it. All the blessings of "grace and glory" were the property of Christ, for He was "appointed Heir of all things" (Heb. 1:2): but in His death, He made a bequeathment of them unto all the elect. Another analogy between a human testament and the testamentary character of Christ's death is that, an absolute grant is made without any conditions. So is the kingdom of heaven bequeathed to all the elect, so that nothing can defeat His will. Whatever there is in the Gospel which prescribes conditions, that belongs to it as it is a "covenant" and not as a "testament." Finally, the testator assigns the time when his heirs shall be admitted into the actual possession of his goods; so too has Christ determined the season when each shall enter both into grace and glory.

Perhaps a brief word should be added by way of amplification to the bare statement made above respecting the conditions which the Gospel prescribes unto those who are the beneficiaries of Christ's "testament." Repentance and faith are required by the Gospel; yet, strictly speaking they are *not* "conditions" of our entering into the enjoyment of Christ's gifts. Faith is a *means* to receive and partake of the things promised, repentance is a *qualification* whereby we may know that *we* are the persons to whom such promises belong. Nevertheless, it is to be remembered that He who has made the promises works in His elect these graces of repentance and faith: Acts 5:31, Phil. 1:29.

"It is a great and gracious condescension in the Holy Spirit to give encouragement and confirmation unto our faith, by a representation of the truth and reality of spiritual things, in those which are temporal and agreeing with them in their general nature, whereby they are presented unto the common understandings of men. This way of proceding the apostle calls, a speaking 'after the manner of men' (Gal. 3:15). Of the same kind were all the parables used by our Saviour; for it is all one whether these representations be taken from things real, or from those which, according unto the same rule of reason and right, are framed on purpose for that end" (John Owen).

"Whereupon neither the first was dedicated without blood. For when Moses had spoken every precept to all the people according to the law, he took the blood of calves and of goats, with water, and scarlet wool, and hyssop, and sprinkled both the book, and all the people, saying, This is the blood of the testament which God hath enjoined unto you. Moreover he sprinkled with blood both the tabernacle, and all the vessels of the ministry. And almost all things are by the law purged with blood; and without shedding of blood is no remission" (vv. 18-22). In these verses the apostle is still pressing upon the Hebrews the necessity for the blood-shedding of Christ. Their national history witnessed to the fact that when God entered into covenant with their fathers, that covenant was confirmed by solemn sacrifice.

In the verses upon which we are now to comment, the apostle is not merely proving that the old covenant or testament was confirmed with blood, for had that been his only object, he could have dispatched it in very few words; rather does he also declare what was the *use* of blood in sacrifices on all occasions under the law, and thereby he demonstrates the use and efficacy of Christ's blood as unto the ends of the new covenant. The ends of the blood under the old covenant were two, namely, purification and pardon, both of which were confirmed in the expiation of sin. Unless the main design of the Spirit in these verses be steadily kept in view, we miss the deeper meaning of many of their details.

What has just been said above, supplies the explanation of what has seemed a problem to some, namely that in these verses the apostle mentions five or six details which are not found in the historical narrative of Ex. 24. But the Holy Spirit is not here limiting our view to Ex. 24, but gathers up what is found in various places of the law; and that, because He not only designed to prove the dedication of the covenant by blood, but also to show the whole use of the blood under the law, as unto purification and remission of sin. And He does this with the purpose of declaring the virtue and efficacy of the blood of Christ under the new testament, whereunto He makes an application of all the things in the verses which follow. The "Moreover" at the beginning of v. 21 is plain intimation that the Spirit is here contemplating something *in addition to* that which is found in Ex. 24.

V. 18. The opening word is usually rendered "therefore" or "wherefore": it denotes the drawing of an inference; it confirms a general rule by a special instance. In v. 16 the general rule is stated; now, says the apostle, think it not strange that the new testament was confirmed by the death of the Testator, for this is so necessary that, the first one also was confirmed in the same manner; and that, not only by death, but not "without *blood,*" which was required for the ratification of a solemn covenant. That to which reference is made is the "first" testament or covenant. Here the apostle makes clear what he intended by the first or old covenant, on which he had discoursed at large in chapter 8: it was the covenant made with Israel at Horeb. Just a few words on the character of it.

Its terms had all the nature of a formal covenant. These were the things written in the book (Ex. 24:4, 7) which were an epitome of the whole law, as contained in Ex. 20-23. The revelation of its terms were made by Jehovah Himself, speaking with awful voice from the summit of Sinai: Ex. 19, 20. Following the fundamental rule of the covenant, as contained in the Ten Commandments, were other statutes and rites, given for the directing of their walking with God. The same was solemnly delivered to Israel by Moses, and proposed unto them for their acceptation. Upon their approbation of it, the book was read in the hearing of all the people after it had been duly sprinkled with the blood of the covenant (Ex. 24:7). Thereupon, for the first time, Jehovah was called "The God of Israel" (Ex. 24:10), and that by virtue of the covenant. This formed the foundation of His consequent dealings with them: all His chastening judgments upon Israel were due to their breaking of His covenant.

While there is a contrast, sharp and clear, between the old testament and the new, yet it should not be overlooked that there was also that which bound them together. This was ably expressed by A. Saphir: "The promise given to Abraham, and not to Moses, was not superseded or forgotten in the giving of the law. When God dealt with Israel in the wilderness, He gave them the promise that they should be a peculiar treasure unto Him above all people: 'for all the earth is Mine'; and that they should possess the land as an inheritance (Ex. 19:5, 6; 23:30; Deut. 15:4). Based upon this promise, and corresponding with the Divine election and favour, is the law which God gave to His people. As He had chosen and redeemed them so that they were to be a holy people, and to walk before Him, even as in the Ten Commandments the gospel of election and redemption came first: 'I am the Lord thy God, which brought thee out of Egypt.' Hence this covenant or dispensation, although it was a covenant, not of grace and Divine gifts and enablings, but of works, was connected with and based upon redemption, and it was dedicated, as the apostle emphatically says, not without blood.

"Both the book, or record of the covenant, and all the people, were sprinkled with the blood of typical sacrifices. For without blood is no remission of sins, and the promises of God can only be obtained through atonement. But we know that this is a figure of the one great Sacrifice, and that therefore all the promises and blessings under the old dispensation, underlying and sustaining it, were through the prospective death of the true Mediator. When therefore the spiritual Israelite was convinced by the law of sin, both as guilt and as a condition of impurity and strengthlessness, he was confronted by the promise of the inheritance, which *always* was of grace, unconditional and sure, and in a righteous and holy manner through expiation."

V. 19. The one made use of for the dedication of the covenant was Moses. On God's part he was immediately called unto this employment: Ex. 3. On the part of the people, he was desired and chosen to transact all things between God and them, because they were not able to bear the effects of His immediate presence: Ex. 19:19, Deut. 5:22-27; and this choice of a spokesman on their part, God approved (v. 27). Thus Moses became in a general way a "mediator" between God and men in the giving of the law (Gal. 3:19). Thereby we are shown that there can be no covenant between God and sinful men, but in the hands of a Mediator, for man has neither meetness, merits, nor ability to be an undertaker of the terms of God's covenant in his own person.

Moses spake "every precept unto the people." This intimates the particular character of the old testament. It consisted primarily of commandments of obedience (Eph. 2:15), promising no assistance for the performance of them. The "new testament" is of another nature: it is one of *promises,* and although it also has precepts requiring obedience, yet is it (as a covenant) wholly founded in the promise, whereby strength and assistance for the performance of that obedience are given to us. Moses' reading "*every* precept unto the people" emphasizes the fact that all the good things they were to receive by virtue of the covenant, depended on their observance of all that was commanded them; for a curse was denounced against every one that "continued not in all things written in the law to do them" (Deut. 27:26). Obviously, *such* a "covenant" was never ordained for the saving of sinners: its insufficiency for that end is what the apostle demonstrates in the sequel.

We are again indebted to the exposition of J. Owen for much of the above, and now give in condensed form some of his observations on the contents of v. 19. Here, for the first time, was any part of God's Word committed to writing. This book of the law was written that it might be read to *all* the people: it was not to be restricted to the priests, as containing mysteries unlawful to be divulged. It was written and read in the language which the people understood and spake, which condemns Rome's use of the Latin in her public services. Again; God never required the observance of any rites or duties of worship, without a previous warrant from His Word. How thankful should we be for the *written* Word!

That which Moses performed on this occasion was to sprinkle the blood. Ex. 24:6 informs us that he took "half of the blood" and sprinkled it "on the altar" (on which was the book); the other half on the people. The one was *God's* part; the other *theirs*. Thereby the *mutual* agreement of Jehovah and the people was indicated. Typically, this foreshadowed the twofold efficacy of Christ's blood, to make salvation Godwards and to save manwards; or, to the remission of our sins unto justification, and the purification of our persons unto sanctification. The "scarlet wool," probably bound around the "hyssop" (which was a common weed), was employed as a sprinkler, as that which served to *apply* the blood in the basons upon the people; "water" being mixed with the blood to keep it fluid and aspersible. In like manner, the communication of the benefits of Christ's death unto sanctification, is called the "sprinkling of the blood of Jesus Christ" (1 Pet. 1:2). To avail us, the blood must not only be "shed," but "sprinkled."

The mingling of the "water" with the "blood" was to represent the "blood *and* water" which flowed from the pierced side of the Saviour (John 19:34, 35), the spiritual "mystery" and meaning of which is profound and blessed. In 1 John 5:6 the Holy Spirit has particularly emphasized the fact that the Christ came "by water and blood." He came not only to make atonement for our sins by His blood that we might be justified, but also to sprinkle us with the efficacy of His blood in the communication of the Spirit unto sanctification, which is compared unto "water": see John 7:38, 39, Titus 3:5. The application of the blood to the "book" of the covenant was an intimation that atonement could be made by blood for the sins against its precepts, and the application of the "water" to it told of its purity. The sprinkler pointed to the humanity of Christ, through which all grace is communicated to us: the "scarlet wool" speaking of His personal glory (Dan. 5:7 etc.), and the "hyssop," the meanest of plant-life (1 Kings 4:33), being a figure of His lowly outward appearance.

V. 20. In these words Moses reminded Israel of the foundation of their acceptance of the covenant, which foundation was the authority of God requiring them so to do; the word "enjoined" also emphasised the nature of the covenant itself: it consisted principally not of promises which had been given to them, but of "precepts" which called for hearty obedience. By quoting here these words of Moses "this is the blood of the testament," the apostle proves that not only death, but a sacrificial death, was required in order to the consecration and establishment of the first covenant. The blood was the confirmatory sign, the token between God and the people of their mutual engagements in that covenant. Thus did God from earliest times teach His people, by type and shadow, the supreme value of the blood of His Son. These words of Moses were plainly alluded to by the Saviour in the institution of His "supper": "This is My blood of the new testament" (Matt. 26:28) i. e., this represents My blood, by the shedding of which the new testament is confirmed.

V. 21. The apostle now reminds the Hebrews that, not only was the old testament itself dedicated with blood, but that also all the ways and means of solemn worship were purified by the same. His purpose in bringing in this additional fact was to prove that not only was the blood of Christ in sacrifice *necessary*, but also to demonstrate its *efficacy* in the removing of sins and thereby qualifying sinners to be worshippers of the most holy God. The historical reference here is to what is found in Lev. 16:14, 16, 18. The spiritual meaning of the tabernacle's furniture being sprinkled with blood was at least twofold: first, in themselves those vessels were holy by God's institution, yet in the use of them by polluted men, they became defiled, and needed purging. Second, to teach the Israelites and us that, the very means of grace which we use, are only made acceptable to God through the merits of Christ's sacrifice.

What we have just sought to point out above, brings before us a most important and humbling truth. In all those things wherein we have to do with God, and whereby we approach unto Him, nothing but the blood of Christ and the Spirit's application of it unto our consciences, gives us a gracious acceptance with Him. The best of our performances are defiled by the flesh; our very prayers and repentances are unclean, and cannot be received by God except as we plead before Him the precious blood of Christ. "The people were hereby taught that, God could not be looked to for salvation, nor rightly worshipped, except faith in every case looked to an intervening blood. For the majesty of God is justly to be dreaded by us, and the way to His presence is nothing to us but a dangerous labyrinth, until we know that He is pacified towards us through the blood of Christ, and that this blood affords to us a free access. All kinds of worship are then faulty and impure until, Christ cleanses them by the sprinkling of His blood. . . If this thought only came to our mind, that what we read is not written so much with ink as with the blood of Christ, that when the Gospel is preached, His sacred blood distils together with the voice, there would be far greater attention as well as reverence on our part" (John Calvin).

V. 22. "By the law" signifies "according unto the law," that is, according to its institution and rule, in that way of faith and obedience which the people were obligated unto. This has been shown by the apostle in the verses preceding. His design being to prove both the necessity for the death of Christ and the efficacy of His blood unto the purging of sins, whereof the legal institutions were types. The qualifying "almost" takes into consideration the exceptions of "fire" (Num. 31:23) and "water" (Lev. 22:6, 7 etc.): but let it be carefully noted that these exceptions were of such things as wherein the worship of God was *not* immediately concerned, nor where the conscience was defiled; they were only of external pollutions, by things in their own nature indifferent, having nothing of *sin* in them; yet were they designed as *warnings* against things which *did* defile. The "almost" also takes note of the exception in Lev. 5:11.

The last clause of v. 22 enunciates an axiom universally true, and in every age. The curse of the law was, and still is, "the soul that sinneth it shall die" (Ezek. 18:20). But whereas there is no man "that sinneth not" (Eccl. 7:20), God, in His grace, provided that there should be a testification of the remission of sins, and that the curse of the law should not be immediately executed on them that sinned. This He did by allowing the people to make atonement for those sins by the blood of sacrifices: Lev. 17:11. Thereby God made known two things. First, to the Israelites that, by the blood of animals there should be a *political* or temporal remission of their sins granted, so that they should not die under the sentence of that law which was the rule of government over their nation. Second, that a real spiritual and eternal forgiveness should be granted unto faith in the sacrifice of Christ, which was represented by the slain animals. The present application of this verse is that, no salvation is possible for any soul that rejects the sacrifice of Christ.

CHAPTER FORTY-FOUR

The Great Sacrifice

(Heb. 9:23-28)

Our present passage is so exceeding full that it is expedient we should reduce our introductory remarks. Perhaps about all it is necessary to say is, that here in Hebrews the apostle is treating of the priestly ministry of Christ, and demonstrating the immeasurable superiority of His sacerdotal functions over those of the legal priests. In the verses which are now to be before us, the apostle makes a definite application of that which has been treated of in the preceding section. A contrast is now drawn between the types and their Antitype. Therein we are shown that inasmuch as the Great Sacrifice which Christ offered unto God was the substance of all the O. T. shadows, it was efficacious, all-sufficient, final.

In 9:1-10 a declaration is made of sundry types and shadows of the law. In 9:11-28 a manifestation of the accomplishment of them is seen in the person and work of the Lord Jesus. In this second section we are shown the excellency of Christ's priesthood in the effecting of those things and the securing of those blessings which Aaron and his sacrificing of animals could not effect and secure. First, the affirmation is made that Christ has entered into the true tabernacle, Heaven itself; that He did so on the ground of His own infinitely meritorious blood, the value of which is evidenced by the fact that it has "obtained eternal redemption" (vv. 11, 12). Second, confirmation of this is then made: inasmuch as the blood of beasts purified the flesh, much more can the blood of Christ purge the conscience (vv. 13, 14). Moreover the Mediatorial office which Christ undertook guaranteed our salvation (v. 15). So too the validity of the covenant-testament insured the same (vv. 16, 17); as also the types pledged it (vv. 19-22).

In 9:23 (which properly belonged to our last section) the apostle concludes the main point he has been discussing, namely, that the typical things being purged with animal's blood, there must needs be a more excellent way of purifying and consecrating heavenly things, and that was by the precious blood of the incarnate Son of God Himself. Having established this fact, he now returns to the other points of difference between the legal priests and Christ. Those priests entered only an earthly tabernacle, but Christ has gone into Heaven itself (vv. 24, 25). The entrance of Israel's high priest into the holy of holies was repeated year by year, but Christ entered once for all (vv. 25, 26). This is confirmed by the fact that men die but once, still less could the God-man suffer death repeatedly (vv. 27, 28). Hence the blessed issue to all who rest upon the Great Sacrifice is, that He shall appear unto them "without sin unto salvation" (v. 28).

"Therefore (it was) necessary that the patterns of things in the heavens should be purified with these; but the heavenly things themselves with better sacrifices than these" (v. 23). The opening word denotes that a conclusion is now drawn from the premises just established, a conclusion which has respect unto *both* parts of the assertion made. In this verse the apostle brings to a head, or sums up, his previous argument concerning the typical purification of all things under the law, and the spiritual purification which has been effected by the sacrifice of Christ. "The general principle involved in these words is, plainly, that in expiation the victim must correspond in dignity to the nature of the offences expiated, and the value of the blessings secured. Animal blood might expiate ceremonial guilt and secure temporary blessings, but in order to secure the expiation of moral guilt and the attainment of eternal blessings, a nobler victim must bleed" (John Brown).

"Therefore necessary (it was)": the reference is both to the type and the Antitype. It was so from God's institution and appointment. There was nothing in the nature of the typical objects themselves which demanded a purgation by sacrifice, but, inasmuch as God designed to foreshadow heavenly things by them, it was requisite that they should be purged with blood. Likewise, inasmuch as God ordained that the heavenly things should be purified, it was necessary that a superior sacrifice should be made, for the typical offerings were altogether inadequate to such an end. Such "necessity" was relative, and not absolute, for God was never under any compulsion. His infinite wisdom deemed such a method fitting and suited to His glory and the good of His elect.

The "patterns" or "figures" (v. 23) were the things which the apostle had been treating of, namely, the covenant, the book, the people, the tabernacle and all its vessels of ministry. The "things in the heavens" were the everlasting covenant, the Church, and its redemption by Jesus Christ. The "heavenly things" had been designed in the mind of God in all their order, causes, beauty, and tendency unto His own glory, from all eternity; but they were "hid" in Himself (Eph. 3:8-10). Of these was God pleased to grant a typical resemblance, a shadowy similitude, an earthly adumbration, in the calling of Israel, His covenant with them, and the appointing of the tabernacle with its priesthood. By this means He deigned to instruct the early Church, and in their conformity to that typical order of things did their faith and obedience consist; the spiritual meaning of which the O. T. saints did, in measure, understand (Psa. 119:18).

"The heavenly things." "By heavenly things, I understand all the effects of the counsel of God in Christ, in the redemption, salvation, worship, and eternal glory of the Church; that is, Christ Himself in all His offices, with all the spiritual and eternal effects of them on the souls and consciences of men, with all the worship of God by Him according unto the Gospel. For of all these things, those of the law were the patterns. God did in and by them give a representation of all these things" (John Owen). More specifically Christ Himself and His sacrifice were typified by the legal rites. So also all the spiritual blessings which His mediation has secured are "heavenly things": see John 3:12, Eph. 1:3, Heb. 3:1. The Church too (Phil. 3:20) and Heaven itself as the abode of Christ and His redeemed are included (John 14:1-3). But here a difficulty presents itself: how could such objects as those be said to be "purified"?

Of all the things mentioned above not one of them is capable of real purification from uncleanness excepting the Church, that is, the souls and consciences of its members. Yet the difficulty is more seeming than real. The term "purification" has a twofold sense, namely, of external dedication unto God and internal purification, both of which are, generally included in the term "sanctification" as it is used in Scripture. Thus, the covenant, the book of the covenant, the tabernacle, and all its vessels were "purified" in the first sense, that is, solemnly dedicated unto God and His service. In like manner were all the "heavenly things" themselves "purified." Christ was consecrated, dedicated unto God in His own blood: John 17:19, Heb. 2:10 etc. Heaven itself was dedicated to be an habitation forever unto the mystical body of Christ, in perfect peace with the angels who never sinned: Eph. 1:10, Heb. 12:22-24.

Yet there was also an internal "purification" of most of these "heavenly things." The souls and consciences of the members of the Church were *really* cleansed, purified and sanctified with an inward and spiritual purification: Eph. 5:25, 26, Titus 2:14. It has been "washed" in the blood of Christ (Rev. 1:5) and is thereby cleansed from all sin (1 John 1:7). And Heaven itself, was in some sense purified—as the tabernacle was, because of the sins of the people in whose midst it stood (Lev. 16:16). When the angels apostatised, sin entered Heaven itself, and therefore was not pure in the sight of God (*see* Job 15:15). And upon the sin of man, a breach was made, enmity ensued, between the holy angels above and fallen men below; so that Heaven was no meet place for an habitation unto them both, until they were reconciled, which was only accomplished in the sacrifice of Christ (Eph. 1:10, Col. 1:20).

One other detail needs to be considered: "But the heavenly things with better sacrifices." It is the use of the plural number here in connection with the sacrifice of Christ which has occasioned difficulty to some. It is a figure of speech known as an "enallage," the plural being put for the singular by way of *emphasis*. It is so expressed because the great sacrifice not only confirmed the signification, virtue, and benefits of all others, but exceeded in dignity, design and efficacy all others. Again; under the law there were five chief offerings appointed unto Israel: the burnt, the meal, the peace, the sin, the trespass (see Lev. 1-5), and in Christ's great Sacrifice we have the antitype of all five, and hence His has superseded theirs. Thus, the plural, "sacrifices" here emphasises the one offering of Christ, expresses its superlative excellency, and denotes that it provides the substance of the many shadows under the law.

If the reader will read straight on through Heb. 9:18-23 he will then be in a position to appreciate the lovely sequel which is recorded in Ex. 24:8-11. A most glorious type was that. There we have a scene for which there is nothing approaching a parallel on all the pages of inspiration until the incarnation of the Son of God be reached. What we have there in Ex. 24 might well be termed the O. T. Mount of Transfiguration. There we see not only Moses and Aaron, Nadab and Abihu, but also seventy "elders" (representatives of the people) in the very *presence of God*, perfectly at ease, eating and drinking there. The key-word to that marvelous incident is the "Then" at the beginning of v. 9, which brings out the inestimable value of the *blood* which had been sprinkled, and shows the grand privilege which it had procured, even making possible *communion* with God. The antitype of this is presented in Heb. 10:22.

"For Christ is not entered into the holy places made with hands, the figures of the true; but into heaven itself, now to appear in the presence of God for us" (v. 24). The opening "For" denotes that a further reason is being advanced to demonstrate the superiority of Christ's sacrifice over those which were offered under the law. In v. 23 this was shown by its power to "purify" *better objects* than the typical offerings could dedicate or cleanse. Here the proof is drawn from the *place* which Christ entered after He had offered Himself a sacrifice unto God, namely, into Heaven itself. That which was the peculiar dignity of the high priest of Israel, and wherein the principal discharge of his duty did consist, was that he entered that sacred abode where the typical and visible representation of the presence of God was made. The antitype of this is what is here before us.

"For Christ." The Mediator is again denominated by His official title. In addition to our notes thereon under v. 14, we may point out that this title "The Anointed" imports three things. First, the *offices* or functions which the Son of God undertook for the salvation of His people. These were three in number and each was foreshadowed of old: the prophetic (1 Kings 19:16, Psa. 105:15), the priestly (Lev. 8:12, 30; Psa. 133:2), the kingly (1 Sam. 10:1, 16:13). Second, the *right* which He has to undertake those functions: He who "anointed" Christ was the Father (Acts 10:38), thereby appointing and authorising Him (Heb. 5:5). Third, His *ability* to perform those functions whereunto He was anointed: therefore did He declare "the Spirit of the Lord is upon Me, *because* He hath *anointed* Me to preach" etc. (Luke 4:18). That expression "the Spirit of the Lord is upon Me" referred to that Divine enduement which had been conferred upon Him: cf. John 3:34.

"For Christ is not entered into the holy places made with hands, the figures of the true." The negative is first expressed in order to emphasise the contrast which follows. Three things are here said of respect to its institution, it was the "holy of holies," and that, because it had been dedicated as the chamber where the special pledges of God's presence were given. Second, as to its fabric, though framed by Divine command, it was but of human workmanship, "made with hands." Third, as to its principal end or design, it was a resemblance or figure of heavenly things. From the Sept. translation of "holy of holies" by "the holy places," it seems that they used the plural number to supply the lack in the Greek language of a suitable superlative.

"But into Heaven itself." This entrance of Christ into the celestial Sanctuary is to be distinguished from His entering "once into the holy place" of v. 12. In our exposition of that verse we sought to show at some length that the reference there is to what took place immediately after the Saviour expired upon the cross, when, in fulfillment of the type of Lev. 16:14, He appeared before the Father to present to Him the memorial of His completed satisfaction. Aaron's entrance into the holy of holies was not for the purpose of making atonement—*that* was effected outside (Lev. 16:11)—but to *present* to God an atonement already accomplished. Nor could Aaron's passing within the veil, clad only in his "linen" garments

(Lev. 16:4 and contrast Ex. 28:2—etc.), possibly be a figure of Christ's triumphant admission into heaven with all the jubilation belonging to a coronation day. We must constantly distinguish between Christ as the antitype of Aaron, and Christ as the antitype of Melchizedek. Aaron pointed to nothing after Christ's *resurrection*; Melchizedek did. The "once" of 9:12 emphasises the finality of Christ's sacrifice. His "entrance" here in 9:24 was for the purpose of intercession, which is *continuous*: 7:25.

The entrance of our royal High Priest into heaven was necessary for rendering His sacrifice effective in the *application* of the benefits of it to the Church. As J. Owen pointed out, the entrance of Christ into heaven on His ascension, may be considered two ways. "1. As it was *regal,* glorious and triumphant; so it belonged to His kingly office, as that wherein He triumphed over all the enemies of the Church: see it described in Eph. 4:8-10 from Psa. 68:18. Satan, the world, death and hell being conquered, and all power committed to Him, He entered triumphantly into heaven. So it was regal. 2. As it was *sacerdotal.* Peace and reconciliation being made by the blood of the cross, the covenant being confirmed, eternal redemption obtained, He entered as our High Priest into the holy place, the temple of God above, to make His sacrifice effectual to His Church, and to apply the benefits of it thereunto."

Christ entered Heaven as the great High Priest of His Church, as the Mediator of the new covenant, as the "Forerunner" of His people (6:20), as their "Advocate" (1 John 2:1), and the "First-born of many brethren." His design in so doing was "to appear in the presence of God for us." This He does "now," at the present season, and always. What the typical priest did was of no continuance. But this "now" is expressive of the whole season and duration of time from the entrance of Christ into heaven to the consummation of all things. Absolutely, His entrance into Heaven had other ends in view (John 17:5, Heb. 1:3—"upholding" etc.), but to appear before God for His people as their High Priest, was the only end or object of His entering Heaven, considered *as* God's "Temple," where is the "throne of grace." How this manifests Christ's full assurance of the success of His undertaking, His complete discharge from all that guilt which had been imputed to Him. Had He not made a full end of our sins, He could not have appeared with confidence as our Surety in the presence of God!

"To appear in the presence of God for us." This is an act of His sacerdotal office. Not only *is* it our Hight Priest who does so "appear," but He doth so *as* the High Priest of His Church. Nevertheless, it is such an act as necessarily implies the offering of Himself as a sacrifice for sin antecedent thereto, for it was *with* the blood of the atoning sacrifice that Aaron entered into the holy place (Lev. 16) as the head and representative of the people. In this appearance Christ presents Himself to God "as a lamb that had been slain" (Rev. 5:6)! It is *that* which gives validity and efficacy to His "appearing." The word "appear" is a forensic one, as of an Attorney before the Judge. He has gone there to seek from God and dispense to His people those blessings which He purchased for them. He has gone there to plead the infinite merits of His sacrifice, as a permanent reason why they should be saved: Rom. 8:34, Heb. 7:25. This supplies the great testimony to the continuance of Christ's love, care and compassion toward the Church: it is their interests which He promotes.

"Nor yet that He should offer Himself often, as the high priest entereth into the holy place every year with blood of others" (v. 25). In this verse the apostle does two things: meets an objection which might be made, and continues to demonstrate the superior excellency of the Great Sacrifice. The objection could be framed thus: If Aaron's entrance into the holy of holies was a type of Christ's entering heaven, then must He, like the legal high priest, enter oft. This the apostle here denies. Such a conclusion by no means follows, in fact, is utterly erroneous. God did not require this from Christ, there was no need of it, and, as he shows in the next verse, it was impossible that He should.

Such is the absolute perfection of the one offering of Christ, that it stands in need of, that it will admit of, *no* repetition in any kind. Therefore does the apostle declare that if *it* be despised or neglected, "there remaineth no more sacrifice for sins" (10:26). This absolute perfection of the one offering of Christ arises from, first, the dignity of His person: Acts 20:28. It was the God-man who obeyed, suffered and died: nothing superior, nothing equal, could again be offered. Second, from the nature of the sacrifice itself. In the internal gracious workings of Christ, grace and obedience could never be more glorified than they had been by Immanuel Himself. So too, in the punishment He underwent: He suffered to the full, the whole curse of the law; hence, any further offering or atonement would be highly blasphemous. Third, from the love of the Father unto Him and delight in Him. In His one offering God was well pleased, and in it *He* rests. Hence the impossibility of any repetition—condensed from J. Owen.

"Nor yet that He should offer Himself often." In these positive and pointed words the Holy Spirit has plainly anticipated and repudiated the blasphemous practice of the Papists, who in their daily "mass" pretend to sacrifice Christ afresh, and by their "priests" present Him as an offering to God, claiming that the bread and wine are transubstantiated into the real flesh and blood of Christ. Therefore are they guilty of the unspeakably dreadful sin of crucifying *to themselves* the Son of God afresh, and putting Him to an open shame (Heb. 6:6), for by their pretended "real sacrifice of Christ" they, through their daily repetition of it, deny its sufficiency and finality (Heb. 10:2), degrading it below that of the annual atonement of Israel, which was made by the blood of beasts.

"As the high priest entereth into the holy place every year with blood of others." On these words W. Gouge beautifully pointed out that, "Herein we have an evidence of God's tender respect to man in sparing his blood. Though man were ordained a priest to typify Christ's priesthood, though man in that function were to appear before God, though he were to bear their names, yea, and their sins (Ex. 28:38), all of which Christ did, yet when it came to the shedding of his blood, as Christ did His, God spared him, and accepted the blood of beasts, as He accepted the ram for Isaac (Gen. 22:13). How this magnifies God's love to us, who was so tender of *man,* and yet spared not His own Son (Rom. 8:32)!"

"For then must He often have suffered since the foundation of the world: but now once in the end of the world hath He appeared to put away sin by the sacrifice of Himself" (v. 26). This verse consists of two parts. First, a reason is given confirming the assertion made in v. 25: had Christ been obliged to "offer Himself often" to God, then must He have "suffered" afresh "from the foundation of the world," that is, died afresh in each generation of human history. Second, a confirmation of that reason taken from the appointment of God: only once, and that in the fulness of time, did Christ come to earth to be a sacrifice for the sins of His people. Thus the apostle exposes the gross absurdity of the objection he met in v. 25: to admit that, would be to say Christ's blood had no more efficacy than that which the Jewish high priest offered.

The force of the apostle's argument rests upon two evident suppositions. First, that the "offering" (v. 25) and "suffering" (v. 26) of Christ are inseparable. It was in and by His suffering that the Lord Jesus offered Himself unto God, and that because He was Himself both the Priest and the Sacrifice. Aaron "offered" repeatedly, yet he never once "suffered," for *he* was not the sacrifice itself. It was the bullock which was slain, that suffered. But Christ being both Priest and Sacrifice could not "offer" without "suffering," and herein does the force of the argument principally consist. The very especial nature of Christ's offering or sacrifice, which was by the shedding of His blood in death, precluded a repetition thereof.

Second, the apostle's argument here is also built on the fact that there *was* a necessity for the expiation of the sin of all that were to be saved from the foundation of the world. Sin entered the world immediately after it was founded, by the apostasy of our first parents. Notwithstanding, numbers of sinners, as Abel, Enoch, Noah, Abraham and the spiritual remnant in Israel had their sins pardoned and were eternally saved; yet no sacrifice which they offered could remit moral guilt or redeem their souls. No; *their* salvation was also effected by virtue of the sacrifice of Christ. Hence it follows unavoidably that unless the merits of His own one offering extended unto the taking away of all their sins, then either He must have suffered often, or they perish. Contrariwise, seeing that elect sinners *were* saved through Christ "from the foundation of the world," much more will the virtues of the Great Sacrifice extend unto the end of the world.

"But now," not at the beginning of human history; "once," that is, once for all, never to be repeated; "in the end of the world," or in "the fullness of time" (Gal. 4:4). This expression "end of the world" or more literally, "consummation of the ages" is here used antithetically from "since the foundation of the world" which usually has reference to the first entrance of sin into the world, and God's dispensation of grace in Christ thereon; as "before the foundation of the world" (Eph. 1:4 etc.) expresses eternity and God's counsels therein. The Divine distinctions of time with respect to God's grace toward His Church, may be referred to three general heads: that before the law, during the law, and since the incarnation of Christ unto the end of the world. This last season, absolutely considered, is called the "fulness of times" (Eph. 1:10), when all that God had designed in the dispensation of His grace was come to a head, and wherein no alteration should be made till the earth was no more.

"Hath He appeared to put away sin by the sacrifice of Himself." He "appeared" here on earth (the Greek word is quite different from the one used in v. 24): of old He had been obscurely shadowed forth in types, but now He was "*manifest* in flesh" (1 Tim. 3:16). The end or purpose of this appearing of Christ was to "put away sin"—the Greek word is a very strong one, and is rendered "disannuling" in 7:18. Let it be carefully noted that this declaration is made only as it respects the Church of Christ. He made a complete atonement for all the sin of all His people, receiving its wages, expiating its guilt, destroying its dominion. The results are that, when God *applies* to the penitent believer the virtues of Christ's sacrifice, all condemnation is removed (Rom. 8:1), and its reigning power is destroyed (Rom. 6:14).

"And as it is appointed unto men once to die, but after this the judgment: so Christ was once offered to bear the sins of many; and unto them that look for Him shall He appear the second time without sin unto salvation" (v. 27, 28). In these verses the apostle concludes his exposition of the causes, nature, designs and efficacy of the sacrifice of Christ, wherewith the new covenant was dedicated and confirmed. In them a three-fold confirmation is made of the uniqueness and sufficiency of the Saviour's atonement. First a comparison is drawn: pointed by the "as" and "so". Second a declaration is made as to why Christ died: it was to "bear the sins of many." Third, the resultant consequence of this is stated at the end of v. 28.

First, the comparison. This is between the death of men by the decretory sentence of God, and the offering of Christ by God's appointment. "It is appointed unto men once to die." That "appointment" was a *penal* one, being the sentence and curse of the broken law (Gen. 2:17), consisting of two parts: temporal death and eternal judgment. Death is not the result of chance, nor is it a "debt of nature," a condition to which man was made subject by the law of his creation. Death is something more than the result of physiological law: the same God who sustained Methusalah for well nigh a thousand years, would have sustained Adam's body for all eternity had he never fallen. Sinless angels are immortal. Death is the wages of *sin* (Rom. 6:23). The case of Enoch and Elijah, Lazarus and that generation of believers alive on earth at the return of Christ (1 Cor. 15:51), are only exceptions to the common rule, by mere acts of Divine sovereignty.

"After this the judgment." This, by the same Divine, unalterable constitution, is also "appointed" unto all: Acts 17:31. Death does not make an end of man, but is subservient to something else, which is equally certain and inevitable in its own season. As death leaves men, so shall judgment find them. This "judgment" is here opposed to the "salvation" of believers at the second appearing of Christ. It is the judgment of the wicked at the last great day: Rom. 2:5. It will be the executing upon them of the condemnatory sentence of the law, the irrevocable curse of God—eternal banishment from Him, for indescribable and eternal torments to be inflicted upon them.

"So Christ was once offered." As the death-sentence, as a penal infliction, was passed upon all of Adam's descendants (Rom. 5:12) viewed as criminals, as having broken the law in the person of their federal head, *so* Christ was "appointed" or sentenced by God, the Judge of all, to undergo the curse of the law, on the behalf and in the stead of those whom He represented. "So Christ was once offered to bear the sin of many." Here we see that deliverance from the curse which the wisdom and grace of God provided for

His elect. The Anointed One, *as* the High Priest of His people, presented to God an all-sufficient and final satisfaction for all the sins of all who have been, from eternity, given to Him by the Father. Thus vv. 27, 28 present the antithesis of the Law and the Gospel, as it relates to "men" indefinitely, and to the "many" specifically. The sins of many He "bare"—had imputed to Him, received the punishment of, and fully expiated—in His own body on the tree (1 Pet. 2:24).

"And unto them that look for Him shall He appear the second time without sin unto salvation." This needs to be interpreted in harmony with its context, and as furnishing the antitype of what is found in Lev. 16. The word for "appear" here is not the one commonly used for the return of Christ—it means "to be seen." When Aaron disappeared within the veil, the people waited with eager expectation until he came out again to bless them. So Christ, having made atonement, and gone into heaven, shall yet re-appear and be seen by those who wait for Him. As men after death, must yet appear the "second time" in their body, to undergo condemnation therein; so Christ shall appear the second time, to bestow on God's elect eternal salvation.

"Unto them that look for Him:" that is, all the redeemed, the "many" whose sins He bore. Though the vision tarry, they wait for it (Hab. 2:3). Five things are included in this word "look for." First, the steadfast faith *of* His appearing, resting with implicit confidence on His promise in John 14:2, 3. Second, a real love unto it: 2 Tim. 4:8. Third, an ardent longing after it, so that they cry, "Even so, come, Lord Jesus" (Rev. 22:20). Fourth, a patient waiting for it, in the midst of many discouragements: James 5:7, 8. Fifth, a personal preparation for it: Matt: 25:10, Luke 12:35-37.

"Without (imputed) sin, unto salvation." Hereby Christ's second advent is contrasted from His first. When he appeared the first time, it was *with* "sin" upon Him (John 1:29) as the Surety of sinners. Therefore was He the Man of sorrows, and afflicted from His youth up (Psa. 88:15). But He will re-appear in a very different state: as the Conqueror of sin and Satan, the Saviour of His people, the King of kings and Lord of lords. At His return, the efficacy of His once-for-all offering will be openly manifested. The question of His peoples' sins having been finally settled at the cross, He will then *glorify* His redeemed. "For our conversation is in heaven: from whence also we look for the Saviour, the Lord Jesus Christ: Who shall change our vile body, that it may be fashioned like unto His glorious body, according to the working whereby He is able even to subdue all things unto Himself" (Phil. 3:20, 21).

CHAPTER FORTY-FIVE

The Typical Sacrifice

(Heb. 10:1-4)

The 10th chapter of our epistle has two main divisions: the first is occupied with a setting forth of the sufficiency of Christ's sacrifice unto those who believe, vv. 1-20; the second is devoted to the making of a practical application of the doctrine of the first section unto faith, obedience, and perseverance, vv. 21-39. The principal design of the Spirit therein is to exhibit the excellency and efficacy of Christ's satisfaction, and this, not so much Godwards, as saintwards, showing the inestimable blessings which it has procured for the favoured members of the household of faith. The method which the apostle was inspired to follow in carrying out this design, was to, once more, set in antithesis the typical sacrifices of the Mosaic dispensation with the one Sacrifice of Christianity, contrasting the shadow with the Substance, and this, in order to bring out the inadequacy of the one and the sufficiency of the other to provide a perfect standing before God, with the resultant privilege of drawing near to Him as accepted worshippers.

Because the sacrifices under the old covenant were incapable, in and of themselves, to satisfy the claims of a holy God, they were also unable to meet the needs of those who brought them. Because that, of themselves, they could not make peace with God, neither could they give peace to the conscience of the offerer. Because they failed to make real atonement for sin, they could not cleanse the sinner. Therefore does the apostle point out that the Aaronic offerings were but "shadows," that the repetition of them intimated their insufficiency, that the fact of unexpiated sin was recalled to memory each time a victim was slain, and that inasmuch as it was merely the blood of *beasts* which was shed, it was impossible that such a medium or offering could either placate the wrath of God or procure His blessing upon those who presented such sacrifices.

The connection between Heb. 10 and what immediately precedes is very blessed. In the closing verse of chapter 9 two things are joined together: the cross of Christ and His second coming. And *what* intervenes between Calvary and the actual entrance into Glory of those who were there redeemed and reconciled to God? This: the Christian-life on earth, and it is *this* which is mainly in view in the closing chapters of our epistle. It is the *present* status, privileges, walk, discipline and responsibilities of the saints which are therein set forth. That which is exhibited in the first twenty verses of Heb. 10 is the *perfect standing* before God which the regenerated believer now has, and his blessed privilege as a worshipper of entering in spirit within the Heavenly courts while waiting down here for the promised return of his Saviour. Having shown in chapter 9 that atonement has been accomplished, that the heavenly places were purified when the Redeemer entered the Holiest, the Spirit now emphasises the fact that the believer has been fitted to draw nigh unto God Himself as a purged and accepted worshipper.

In previous sections the apostle has contrasted the priests of the Levitical dispensation with our great High Priest, he has opposed the vastly different covenants or economies to which each belonged, he has shown the immeasurable superiority of Christ's one offering of Himself over the many sacrifices of old, he has placed in antithesis the respective "tabernacles" in which Aaron and Christ officiated. Each and all of these was designed to press upon the wavering Hebrews the deficiency of Judaism and the excellency of Christianity. Now he shows that not only are the two systems with all that pertains to them as different as a flickering candle and the shining of the sun, but that the *privileges enjoyed* by the individuals belonging to the one and the other are as widely separated as is light from darkness. The Mosaic system, as such, was neither able to impart permanent peace to the conscience nor give access into the presence of God, but the Satisfaction of Christ *has* procured these precious blessings unto those who flee to Him for refuge.

The order of thought which is followed in the first main division of our present chapter ought not to be difficult to grasp. First, we have an affirmation and demonstration of the deficiency of the legal sacrifices to "perfect" the worshipper: vv. 1-4. Second, we have a manifestation and exemplification of the sufficiency of Christ's sacrifice to "perfect forever" (v. 14) those for whom He made satisfaction unto God: vv. 5-20. Thus the apostle proves again the imperative need for the supplanting of all the unefficacious offerings of Judaism by the all-sufficient offering of Christ. In the developing of the first point, an assertion is made of the inadequacy of the Levitical sacrifices to expiate sin and meet the dire needs of the offerer (v. 1). A confirmation of the truth of this assertion is drawn from the frequency of their repetition (v. 2). It is shown that the annual typical propitiation was only a constant re-opening of the question of sin (v. 3). From these facts the inevitable conclusion is drawn that it was impossible for such sacrifices to remove sins.

"For the law having a shadow of good things to come, not the very image of the things, can never with those sacrifices which they offered year by year continually make the comers thereunto perfect" (v. 1). Three questions are suggested to the thoughtful reader of this verse. First, exactly what is the contrast pointed by "shadow" and "image"? Second, what is meant by the comers being made "perfect"? Third, why did God appoint sacrifices that were so unefficacious? These shall be our points of focus as we endeavour to expound this verse.

"For the law having a shadow of good things to come." The opening "For" intimates that what is introduced thereby is an inference drawn from what had previously been stated. Having shown that the sacrifice of Christ had met all the demands of God and had confirmed the new covenant, the apostle concludes from thence that, inasmuch as the Levitical sacrifices could not effect those ends which had been accomplished by Christ's, they must be taken out of the way. The "law" here is not to be restricted to the ceremonial, as the words "*having* a shadow" warn us; still less is it the *moral* law, which, absolutely considered, had no sacrifices belonging to it. No, the reference is to the whole of the Mosaic economy, or more specifically, to the covenant which God made with Israel at Sinai, with all the institutions of worship belonging thereto.

"Shadow is put first emphatically; only a shadow or outline of the substantial and eternal blessings promised. A shadow has no substance; but brings before the mind the form of the body from which it is projected! The 'image' itself is given to us in Christ, a full and permanent embodiment of the good things to come" (A. Saphir). We believe this presents the correct idea: it is clearly borne out by Col. 2:17, "which are a shadow of things to come, but the body is of Christ." The apostle is there speaking of the same things as he treats of here in 10:1: the Mosaic economy, with all its ordinances and institutions of worship, gave only an earthly adumbration or representation, and did not possess the substance, reality, or "body": *that* is found only in Christ Himself, to whom the O. T. shadows pointed. A "shadow" gives a representation of a body, a more or less just one of its form and size, yet only an obscure and imperfect one—compare our remarks on 8:5.

The "good things to come" (future, not when this epistle was written, but at the time that the Mosaic economy was instituted) has reference to all those blessings and privileges which have come to the church in consequence of the incarnation of Christ and the discharge of His office. Well might they be designated "*good* things," for there is no alloy or mixture of evil with them; other things are "good" relatively, but these things absolutely. The "image" or substance of them is found in Christ, and set forth in His Gospel: for a similar use of the term "image" cf. Rom. 8:29. "This therefore is that which the apostle denies concerning the law. It had not the actual accomplishment of the promise of good things; it had not Christ exhibited in the flesh; it had not the true real sacrifice of perfect expiation: it represented these things; it had a shadow of them, but enjoyed not, exhibited not the things themselves. Herein was its imperfection and weakness, so that by none of its sacrifices could it make the Church perfect" (J. Owen).

"Can never with those sacrifices which they offered year by year continually make the comers thereunto perfect." In these words we have the inference or conclusion for which the "For" at the beginning of the verse prepares us: if the law contained in it nothing better than a "shadow," it is obvious that its sacrifices could not possibly make perfect those who offered them. J. Owen has most helpfully pointed out that the Greek word here rendered "continually" signifies "forever," occurring elsewhere in this epistle only in 7:3, 10:12, 14 (Bagster's Interlinear gives "in perpetuity") and that it should be connected not with the clause preceding, but with the one following, thus: "the law by its sacrifices could not perfect forever, or unto the uttermost, the comers thereto."

Three things are affirmed in the second half of our verse. First, the impotency of the "law" or old covenant, or Mosaic economy. It could *never* "make perfect." It could by no means, in no way do so; it was impossible that it should. This is stated so emphatically in order to remove from the minds of the Hebrews *all* expectations of perfection with Judaism. Second, that with respect unto which this impotency of the law is here ascribed was its "sacrifices," which was the very thing in which most of the Jews had chiefly placed their hopes. But not only is that affirmed of the sacrifices in general, but also in particular of the great sacrifice on the day of atonement, which was offered "year by year": if *that* was ineffectual, how much more so the minor offerings! Third, that wherein its impotency lay was its inability to "perfect" the "comers."

Concerning the meaning of "perfect" here, we would refer back to our exposition of 7:11. For the benefit of those who do not have access to the Aug. 1930 issue, we would point out that the term "perfect" is one of the key-words of this epistle, close attention needing to be paid to its contexts. It has to do more with *relationship* than experience. It concerns the *objective* side of things rather than the subjective. It looks to the judicial and vital aspect, more than to the practical. "Perfection" means the bringing of a thing to that completeness of condition designed for it. Doctrinally it refers to the producing of a satisfactory and final relationship between God and His people. It speaks of that unchanging standing in the favour and blessing of God which Christ has secured for His saints. See also our notes on 2:10; 5:9; 6:1.

That "perfection" which God requires is absolute conformity to His moral law, so that not only is there no guilt of transgression resting upon us, but a full, flawless, and rewardable obedience to our account. How impossible it was for the slaying of beasts to secure *this* is self-evident. The "comers thereunto" are defined in v. 2 as "the worshippers": it was those who made use of the Levitical sacrifices in the worship of God. This term "come" in the Hebrews' epistle has its root in the "bring" of Lev. 1:2, the Hebrew word there signifying those who "draw nigh" with an oblation, coming thus to the altar. Though the slaying of beasts procured a temporary expiation, it did not secure an eternal forgiveness, it did not perfect "continually" or "for ever." Hence, the effect produced on the conscience of the offerer was only a transient one, for a sense of sin returned upon him, forcing him unto a repetition of the same sacrifices, as the apostle declares in the next verse. This brings us to our third question: Why did God appoint unto Israel sacrifices so ineffectual?

Many answers might be returned to this question. Though the Levitical offerings failed to procure an eternal redemption, yet were they by no means useless and without value. First of all, they served to keep in the minds of Israel the fact that God is ineffably holy and will not tolerate evil. They were constantly reminded that the wages of sin is death. They were taught thereby that a constant *acknowledgement* of their sins was imperative if communion with the Lord was to be maintained. In the second place, by means of these types and shadows God was pointing out to them the direction from which true salvation must come, namely, in a sinless Victim enduring in their stead the righteous penalty which their sins called for. Thereby God instructed them to look forward in faith to the time when the Redeemer should appear, and the great Sacrifice be offered for the sins of His people. Third, there was an efficacy in the O. T. sacrifices to remove temporal judgment, to give ceremonial ablution, and to maintain external fellowship with Jehovah. They who despised the sacrifices were "cut off" or excommunicated; but those who offered them maintained their place in the congregation of the Lord.

Ere passing on to the next verse let us seek to make practical application unto ourselves of what has been before us. In coming to God, that is, drawing nigh unto Him as worshippers, the first qualification in us is that we are legitimately assured of the perfect expiation (cancellation) of our sins. When this foundation is not laid in the soul and conscience, all attempts to approach God as worshippers are highly presumptuous, for no guilty person can stand before Him. To offer thanksgiving and praise to him *before* we know we have been forgiven and accepted by Him, is to repeat the high-handed sin of Cain. The very first things proposed to us in the Gospel are that we own our undone condition, judge ourselves unsparingly, turn from our sins, and appropriate to our deep need the grace of God as it is tendered to us in Jesus Christ. Only as the heart is truly contrite and faith lays hold of the atoning blood of the Lamb, is any sinner entitled to draw nigh unto the Holy One.

"For then would they not have ceased to be offered? because that the worshippers once purged should have had no more conscience of sins" (v. 2). The contents of this verse enable us to grasp more clearly the particular aspects of Truth which our present chapter is dealing with. It is not so much what the sacrifices effected Godwards, as manwards: it is their purifying effects upon the worshipper which is mainly in view. This is quite evident from the expressions "once purged" and "no more conscience of sins." In like manner, the principal thing in the verses which follow is the setting forth of what Christ's atonement has secured for *His people*: see vv. 10, 14, 19.

"For then would they not have ceased to be offered? "This verse is added as a proof of the reason concerning the impotency of the foresaid legal sacrifices. The reason was taken from the *reiteration* of those sacrifices, whereby it was made manifest that they could not make perfect. The argument may be framed thus: That which makes perfect ceaseth when it hath made perfect; but the sacrifices which were offered year by year, ceased not; therefore they could not have made perfect" (W. Gouge). In reply it might be opposed: The repetition of the sacrifice was not through any inherent defect in it, but because the offerer had acquired fresh guilt; the offering expiated all sin up to the time it was offered, but new sins being committed, another sacrifice became necessary. Let us face this difficulty.

There *was* a defect in the sacrifices themselves, as will be seen more plainly when we reach v. 4; *they* were altogether inadequate for meeting the *infinite* demands of God, they were altogether insufficient to compensate for the wrong done to God's manifestative glory and could not repair the loss of His honour. None save a sacrifice which possessed intrinsic merits, having an *infinite* value, could make real and final satisfaction. That Sacrifice has been offered, and so perfect is it that it stands in no need of addition. The Atonement of Christ is of perpetual efficacy unto God, and is ever available to faith. No matter how often application be made unto it, its power never wanes and its preciousness never diminishes.

"Because that the worshippers once purged should have had no more conscience of sins." The final words fix for us the meaning, or rather scope, of the "once purged" here. That sacrificial term may denote either (or both) the removal of the guilt of sin or the pollution thereof: the one is taken away by justification, the other by sanctification. The one is the effect of the sacerdotal actings of Christ toward God, in making atonement for sin; the other is by the Spirit's application of the virtues of that Sacrifice to our souls and consciences, whereby they are cleansed, renewed, and changed. It is the former *only* which is before us here, namely, such a purging of sin as takes away its condemning power from the conscience on account of the *guilt* of it. But this the Levitical sacrifices failed to do, as the next verse shows.

"No more conscience of sins." This does *not* mean that the one who has been "purged" or justified has no further *consciousness* of sins, for no one is more painfully aware of them and of the indwelling "flesh" than is a regenerated soul. *That* is his great burden and sorrow. No, the one who is insensible to the evil and demerit of indwelling sin is a deluded soul: "If we say we have no sin, we deceive ourselves, and the truth is not in us" (1 John 1:8). Nor do the last words of Heb. 10:2 in anywise intimate that there is no need for a Christian's being deeply exercised over his sins and that God does not require him to repent of and confess them, and make repeated application to the Throne of Grace for "mercy" through the sacrifice of Christ. "He that covereth his sins shall not prosper: but whoso confesseth and forsaketh them shall have mercy" (Prov. 28:13): this holds good in *every* dispensation.

"No more conscience of sins" signifies freedom from an apprehensive or terrifying sense of what they deserved. It means complete deliverance from the fear of God's ever imputing them to us. It is the blessed recognition that "there is therefore now no condemnation to them which are in Christ Jesus" (Rom. 8:1). Faith has laid hold of the precious testimony of God unto the efficacy of the blood of Christ as having satisfied His every demand. If we really believe that the wages of sin were paid to our sinless Substitute, how can we be fearful that they will yet be paid to us! The word "conscience" is compounded from two words meaning "with knowledge," that is, a *joint*-knowledge of good and evil. Conscience is the eye of the soul, discerning right from wrong, yet is it dependent—as the eye is—on light. To and through the conscience God speaks as Light (1 John 1:5). When His light first breaks in and shows me what I am, I get a bad conscience; when it is purged by blood (through faith laying hold of its efficacy) I obtain a cleansed one.

It is important to observe that our verse does not say the worshipper should have "no conscience of sins," but "no *more* conscience" of them. This confirms the idea that the "continually" ("for ever") of the previous verse is to be connected not with the "sacrifices," but with "perfect." It would be a great mistake to suppose that the Levitical sacrifices altogether failed to remove sins from before God: Lev. 4:2, 31; 16:11, 22 show otherwise. Nor was it that those sacrifices failed to remove the load of conscious guilt from those who offered them: in such case we should never have read of them *rejoicing* before God. No, what the apostle is here insisting upon is that those sacrifices only gave peace of conscience *pro tem*: they were unable to lay a foundation for permanent rest and abiding peace.

But what of the sins of the Christian *after* he has been "purged" or justified? John 13:10 makes answer: "he that is washed (Greek, "has been bathed") needeth not save to wash his feet, but is clean every whit." By the blood of Christ the Christian has been completely cleansed once for all, so far as the judicial and eternal consequences of sin are concerned: "By one offering He hath perfected *forever* them that are sanctified" (Heb. 10:14), thereby providing for them such stable peace and consolation as that they need not a fresh sacrifice to be made for them day by day. The Gospel makes known how those who sin every day may enjoy peace with God all their days, and that is by a daily confession of sins to God (judging themselves for them and truly repenting of them) and a daily appropriation to themselves of the cleansing power of Christ's precious blood for the defilements of their daily walk.

"But in those sacrifices there is a remembrance again of sins every year" (v. 3). The first word of this verse denotes the nature of the argument insisted upon. In the second verse it had been pointed out that, had the worshippers been legally perfected they would have had no more conscience of sins; *but,* says the apostle, it was *not* so with them: God appointed nothing in vain, and He had not only prescribed the repetition of those sacrifices, but also that in each offering there should be a "remembrance" made of sin, as of that which was to be expiated. It was by God's own institution (Lev. 16:21, 22) that there should be an "express remembrance," or a remembrance expressed by acknowledgement: See

Gen. 41:9; 42:21. By an appeal to this patent fact did the apostle confirm what had been declared in vv. 1, 2.

But at this point a real difficulty confronts us: the first four verses of this chapter are designed as a background to bring out more plainly the glorious truth presented in what follows: in other words, a contrast is pointed by showing what the Levitical sacrifices could not procure, Christ's *has*—"By one offering He hath perfected forever them that are sanctified" (v. 14). Yet, notwithstanding, the fact remains that Christians ought not only once a year, but every day, call to remembrance and penitently confess the same, yea, our Lord Himself has taught us to pray every day for the pardon of our sins: Luke 11:3, 4. Wherein, then, lies the *difference* between the Levitical sacrifices and Christ's, seeing that after *both* of them there is equally a remembrance of sin again to be made? Though the problem seems intricate, yet is its solution simple.

Those under the Mosaic economy confessed their sins preparatory for and in order to a *new atonement* of them; not so the Christian. Our "remembrance" and confession respects only the *application* of the efficacy and virtue of that perfect Atonement which has been made once for all. With them, their remembrance looked to the curse of the law which was to be answered, and the wrath of God which was to be appeased; with us, that which is involved is the *imparting* of the benefits of Christ's sacrifice unto our conscience, whereby we have assured peace with God. Confession of sin is as necessary under the new covenant as under the old, but with an entirely different *end in view*: it is not as a part of the compensation for the guilt of it, nor as a means of pacifying the conscience so that we may still go on in sin; but to fill us with self-abasement, to induce greater watchfulness against sin, to glorify God for the mercy available, and to obtain a *sense of* His pardon in our own souls.

"For it is not possible that the blood of bulls and of goats should take away sins" (v. 4). Here the apostle brings to a head that which has been set forth in the preceding verses: seeing that the law contained only a "shadow" of real redemption and could not perfect unto perpetuity the worshippers (v. 1), and seeing that "conscience of sins" remained (v. 2) as was evidenced by the very design of the annual and typical propitiation (v. 3), it therefore inevitably followed that it was "impossible" such sacrifices should "take away" or properly expiate sins. Such, we take it, is the force of the opening "For" here.

There is a necessity of sin being "taken away," both from before the Governor of the world and from the conscience of His people. But this, the blood of beasts could not effect. Why not? First and foremost because God had not instituted animal sacrifices for *that* purpose. All the virtues and efficacy of the ordinances of Divine worship depend upon the end unto which *God* has instituted them. The blood of animals offered in sacrifice was designed of God to *represent* the way in which sin was to be removed, but not by itself to *effect* it. Nor did it comport with the Divine will and wisdom that it should. God had declared His severity against sin, with the necessity of its punishment to the glory of His righteousness and sovereign rule over His creatures. A most solemn demonstration of this was made at Sinai, in the giving of the fiery law: Ex. 19:16-24: but what consistency had there been between that and the satisfying of God's awful justice, and the removal of sin by such beggarly means as that of the blood of bulls and goats? In such case there had been no manner of proportion manifested between the infinite demerits of sin and the feeble instruments of its expiation.

It was impossible for any mere creature to satisfy the demands of the all-mighty Governor of the universe. The highest angel could never have adequately made compensation for the tremendous wrong which sin had done God, nor repair the loss of His manifestative glory; yea, had not Christ's sinless and holy humanity — in which He performed the stupendous work of redemption — been united in His deity, *that* could not have met the claims of God nor merited eternal salvation for His people. Far less could the blood of beasts vindicate the honour of an infinite Majesty, pacify His righteous wrath, meet the requirements of His holy law, nor even cleanse the conscience and heart of man. "The blood of bulls and goats were external, earthly, and carnal things; but to take away sin was an internal, Divine, and spiritual matter" (W. Gouge). Though the Levitical sacrifices possessed, by God's institution, an efficacy to remove an outward and ceremonial defilement, they could not take away an inward and moral pollution.

This 4th verse enunciates and illustrates a deeply important principle which exposes the great error of Ritualists. As we have pointed out above, all ordinances of Divine worship derive their value from God's institution: they can only effect that which He has appointed, they have in them no inherent efficacy. While they may usefully *represent* spiritual truths, they have no spiritual virtue of their own, and cannot of and by themselves secure spiritual results. The offerings of Judaism had a Divinely appointed meaning and value, but they could not take away sins. The same holds good of the two ordinances of Christianity. Baptism and the Lord's Supper have been ordained of God. They have a symbolical significance. They represent blessed realities. But they have no inherent power either to remove sin, regenerate souls, or impart spiritual blessing. It is only as faith looks beyond the symbol to Him who is symbolized that the soul receives blessing.

Ere closing, perhaps we ought to anticipate a question which is likely to have arisen in the minds of the readers. In view of what is affirmed in the verses which have been before us, are we to conclude that *none* of the Old Testament saints had a perfect and permanent standing before God? No, indeed, for such an inference would manifestly clash with many plain O. T. passages and with the promises which the Church had under the old covenant. The apostle is not here denying absolutely that no one had spiritual access to God and real peace of conscience before Him, but is merely affirming that *such* blessings could not be secured *by means* of the Levitical sacrifices. But those who belonged to the "remnant according to the election of grace" (Rom. 11:5) had faith given them to look beyond the shadow to the Substance: see Job 19:25; Psa. 23:6; Song of Sol. 2:16; Isa. 12:2; Dan. 12:2, etc.

CHAPTER FORTY-SIX

The Divine Incarnation

(Heb. 10:5-7)

In the first four verses of our present chapter the apostle was moved to press upon the Hebrews the insufficiency of the Levitical sacrifices to bring about those spiritual and eternal effects that were needed in order for poor sinners being fitted to stand before God as accepted worshippers. His design in so doing was to pave the way for setting before them the dire need for and the absolute sufficiency of Christ's sacrifice. First, he affirmed that the old covenant provided a "shadow" of the future "good things," but not the substance itself (v. 1). Under the Mosaic economy men were taught that ceremonial guilt, acquired through breaking the ceremonial law, severed from ceremonial fellowship with God, and that the offering of the prescribed sacrifices procured ceremonial forgiveness (Lev. 4:20) and restored to external fellowship, and thereby temporal punishment was averted. In this way there was adumbrated in a lower sphere what Christ's sacrifice was to accomplish in a higher.

That there was an insufficiency to the typical sacrifices was plainly intimated by their frequent repetition (v. 2). Had the offerer been *so* "purged" as to have "no more conscience of sins," that is, had his moral guilt been fully and finally expiated, then no further offering had been needed. Even though God's people continually commit fresh sins a new sacrifice is not required. Why? Because the one perfect Sacrifice *has made* complete satisfaction unto God, and is of perpetual efficacy before Him: therefore is it ever available to penitence and faith, for application unto fresh pardons. But no such sufficiency pertained to the typical sacrifices: a temporary and outward cleansing they could effect, but nothing more. "For though thou wash thee with nitre, and take thee much soap, thine iniquity is marked before Me, saith the Lord God" (Jer. 2:22).

There was no proportion between the infinite demerits of sin, the demands of God's justice, and the slaying of *beasts*. Whether the matter be viewed in the light of God's nature, of man's soul, or of the exceeding sinfulness of sin, it was obvious that the blood of bulls and goats could not possibly make atonement (v. 4). Nor was this fact altogether unknown in Old Testament times: did not one of Jehovah's prophets declare, "Wherewith shall I come before the Lord, and bow myself before the high God? shall I come before Him with burnt offerings, with calves that are a year old? Will the Lord be pleased with thousands of rams, with ten thousands of rivers of oil? shall I give my firstborn for my transgression, the fruit of my body for the sin of my soul?" (Micah 6:6, 7)! But later this light was lost to the carnal Jews, who, like the darkened Gentiles, came to believe that a real and efficacious atonement *was* made by the offering of animal blood unto God.

"It was therefore necessary that the patterns of things in the heavens should be purified with these; but the heavenly things themselves with *better* sacrifices" (Heb. 9:23). Yet patent as this now is to any renewed mind, it was an exceedingly difficult matter to convince the Jews of it. The Levitical sacrifices were of Divine institution and not of human invention. Their fathers had offered them for fifteen centuries; thus, to affirm at this late date that they were set aside by God made a big demand upon their faith, their prejudices, their affections. Nevertheless, the logic of the apostle was invincible, the force of his arguments unanswerable. But it is blessed to observe that he did not rest his case here; instead, he referred once more to an authority against which no appeal could be allowed.

As we have passed from chapter to chapter, and followed the inspired unfolding of the pre-eminency of Christianity over Judaism, we have been deeply impressed by the fact that, at *every* crucial point, *proof* has been furnished from the Old Testament Scriptures. When affirming the excellency of the Son over angels (1:4), appeal was made to Psa. 97:7 (1:6). When insisting on the exaltation of the humbled Messiah over all the works of God's hands (2:6-9), Psa. 8:4-6 was cited. When declaring the superiority of Christ's priesthood over Aaron's, Psa. 110:4 was given in substantiation of it (6:20). When pointing out the superseding of the old covenant by the new, Jer. 31:31 was shown to have taught that very thing (8:8). And now that the all-important point has been reached for showing the imperative necessity of the abolition of the Levitical offerings, another of their own Scriptures is referred to as announcing to the Hebrews this identical fact. How all this demonstrates the inestimable worth and the final authority of Holy Writ!

"Wherefore when He cometh into the world, He saith, Sacrifice and offering Thou wouldst not, but a body hast Thou prepared Me: In burnt offerings and sacrifices for sin Thou hast had no pleasure. Then said I, Lo, I come (in the volume of the book it is written of Me), to do Thy will, O God" (vv. 5-7). These verses contain a direct quotation from the 40th Psalm, which, equally with the 2nd, 16th, 22nd, 10th, etc., was a Messianic one. In it the Lord Jesus is heard speaking, speaking to His Father; and well does it behoove us to give our utmost attention to every syllable that He here utters.

The citation which is here made from the O. T. Scriptures is introduced with, "Wherefore when He cometh into the world, He saith." The precise force of the opening "Wherefore" is not easily determined: it seems to signify, In accord with the facts pointed out in the first four verses; or, in proof thereof, listen to the prophetic language of Christ Himself. J. Owen suggested: "It doth not give an account why the words following were spoken, but why the things themselves were so ordered and disposed." The "Wherefore" is a logical particle intimating that by virtue of the impotency of the O. T. sacrifices, Christ came not to offer those fruitless sacrifices, but to do the will of God in their room. The Mosaic worship, with all its complicated ritual, was superseded by something better coming in its stead. Christ took away the first, that He might establish the second.

The passage which is here before us calls for a whole book to be written thereon, rather than a single article: so blessed, so wondrous, so important are its contents. In it we behold the amazing grace and wisdom of the Father, the matchless love and obedience of the Son, and the federal agreement which was between the Father and the Son with reference to the work of redemption and the salvation of the Church. In it too we see demonstrated again the perfect harmony which exists between the old and the New Testament and the declaration of these things. In it we are taken back to a point before the foundation of the world, and are permitted to learn something of the august counsels of the Eternal Three. In it we are shown the means which the Divine wisdom appointed for the carrying out of those counsels. It is both our duty and privilege to prayerfully inquire and diligently search into the mind of the Holy Spirit therein.

"Wherefore when He cometh into the world." The One who is here before us is the second person in the Holy Trinity. It is He who had been in the Father's delight from all eternity. It is none other than the One by whom and *for* whom all things were created "that are in heaven, and that are in earth, visible and invisible" (Col. 1:16); who is "over all, God blessed forever" (Rom. 9:5). This ineffably blessed and glorious One condescended not merely to behold, or even to send an ambassador, but to personally come into this world. And, wonder of wonders, He came here not "in the form of God," bearing all the manifested insignia of Deity, nor even in the appearance of an angel, as occasionally He did in O. T. times; but instead, He came in "the form of a *servant*," and was actually "made under the law." May our hearts be truly bowed in wonderment and worship at this amazing and unparalleled marvel.

"When the fulness of the time was come" (Gal. 4:4), when the sinfulness of man and his utter helplessness to extricate himself from his dreadful misery had been completely demonstrated; when the insufficiency of Judaism and the powerlessness of the Levitical sacrifices had been made manifest; then it pleased the Son to become incarnate, execute the eternal purpose of the Godhead, fulfill the terms of the everlasting covenant, make good the prophecies and promises of the O. T. Scriptures, and perform that stupendous work which would bring an incalculable revenue of praise to the Triune God, glorify Him above all His other works, put away the sins of His people, and provide for them a perfect and everlasting righteousness which would entitle and fit them to dwell forever in the Father's House. So transcendent are these things that only those whom the Spirit of Truth deigns to illuminate and instruct are capable, in any measure, of apprehending and entering into their ineffable meaning and preciousness. May it please Him, in His sovereign grace, to shine now upon the hearts and understandings of both writer and reader.

"Wherefore when He cometh into the world, He saith, Sacrifice and offering Thou wouldest not, but a body hast Thou prepared Me." Here we behold the perfect intelligence of the Son concerning the mind and will of the Father. In the eternal purpose of the Triune God, Christ, *as* Mediator had been "set up from everlasting" (Prov. 8:23). The Lord had "possessed Him," He was "by Him, as One brought up with Him" (Prov. 8:22, 30). As such, nothing was concealed from Him; all the counsels of Deity were made known to Him. Therefore did He declare, after His incarnation, "The Father loveth the Son, and showeth Him all things" (John 5:20). An illustration of this fact is before us in our present passage.

"He saith, Sacrifice and offering Thou wouldst not, but a body hast Thou prepared Me." But here a difficulty presents itself: the Levitical sacrifices had been instituted by God Himself, how then could it be said that He willed them not? The solution is simple: the language here (as is not infrequently the case in Scripture) is to be taken relatively, and not absolutely. There was one real sense in which the O. T. sacrifices were acceptable to God, and another in which they were not so. The reference here is not to the actual appointment of the sacrifices, for Heb. 10:8 tells us they were "offered according to the law" which God had given to Israel. Nor is the reference to the obedience of the people concerning them during the Mosaic economy, for God both required and approved them at their hands. Nor is it that the apostle is merely speaking from the *present* viewpoint (as some have superficially supposed), i. e., that the sacrifices were *no longer* pleasing to Him. No, our text strikes much deeper: God willed not those sacrifices for the *ends* which He ordained the Sacrifice of Christ to effect.

"*But* a body hast Thou prepared Me." The first word of this clause serves to define the preceding one: the body of Christ is placed over against, substituted in the stead of, replaces, the Levitical offerings. Let the reader recall the whole context: there the Holy Spirit has shown the utter inadequacy of the blood of bulls and goats, the impossibility of its meeting the highest claims of God and the deepest need of sinners. God had not appointed animal sacrifices for *those* ends: He *never* took pleasure in them with reference thereto; according to the will of God they were altogether insufficient for any such purpose. From all eternity it was Christ, the "Lamb," who had been "foreordained" to make satisfaction unto God for His people (1 Peter 1:20). The Levitical sacrifices were never designed by God as anything more than a temporary means to shadow forth the great Sacrifice. This, the Mediator Himself was fully cognizant of from before the foundation of the world.

"But a body hast Thou prepared Me." The term "a body" is a synedochial expression (a part put for the whole, as when we say a farmer has so many "head" of cattle, or a manufacturer employs so many "hands") of the whole human nature of Christ, consisting of spirit and soul and body. As to some of the reasons why the Holy Spirit here threw the emphasis on Christ's "body" rather than on His "soul" (as in Isa. 53:10) we would humbly suggest the following. First, to emphasise the fact that the offering of Christ was to be by *death,* and this the body alone was subject to. Second, because the new covenant was to be *confirmed* by the offering of Christ, and this was to be by blood, which is contained in the body alone. Third, to make more evident the conformity of the Head to His members who were "partakers of flesh and blood." Fourth, to remind us that Christ's whole human *nature* (that "holy *thing*," Luke 1:35) was not a distinct *person.*

"But a body hast Thou prepared Me." The verb has a double force: the humanity of Christ was both foreordained and created by the Father. The first reference in the "prepared" here is the same as in Isa. 30:33. "Tophet is *ordained* of old, for the king it is *prepared";* "the things which God hath *prepared* for them that love Him" (1 Cor. 2:9); "the vessels of mercy, which He hath afore *prepared* unto glory" (Rom. 9:23). In His eternal counsels, God has resolved that the Son should become incarnate; in the everlasting covenant the Father had proposed and the Son had agreed that, at the appointed time, Christ should be made in the likeness of men. The second reference in the word "prepared" is to the actual creating of Christ's humanity, that it might be fitted for the work unto which it was designed.

"But a body hast Thou prepared Me." Commentators have needlessly perplexed themselves and their readers by discovering a discrepancy between these words and Psa. 40:6 which reads, "Mine ears hast Thou opened" or "digged" (margin). Really, there is no discord whatever between the two expressions: one is figurative, the other literal; both having the same sense. They refer to an act of the Father towards the Son, the purpose of the action being designed to make Him meet to do the will of God in a way of obedience. The metaphor used by the Psalmist possessed a double significance. First, the "ear" is that member of the body whereby we hear the commands we are to obey, hence nothing is more frequent in Scripture than to express obedience by hearing and hearkening. Here too the part is put for the whole. In His Divine nature alone, it was impossible for the Son, who was co-equal with the Father, to come under the law; therefore did He prepare for Him another nature, in which He *could* render submission to Him.

It is impossible that anyone should have ears of any use but by having a body, and it is through the ears that instruction unto obedience is received. It is to this the incarnate Son made reference when, in the language of prophecy, He declared, "He wakeneth morning by morning, He wakeneth Mine ear to hear as the learned. The Lord God hath opened Mine ear, and I was not rebellious, neither turned away back" (Isa. 50:4, 5). Thus the figure used in Psa. 40:6 intimated that the Father did so order things toward the Messiah that He should have a nature wherein He might be free and able to be in subjection to the will of God; intimating, moreover, the quality of it, namely, in having ears to hear, which belong only to a "body."

The second significance of the figure used in Psa. 40:6 may be discovered by a comparison with Ex. 21:6, where we learn of the provision made by the law to meet the case of a Hebrew servant, who chose to remain in voluntary servitude rather than accept his freedom, as he might do, at the seventh year of release. "Mine ears hast Thou digged" announced the Saviour's readiness to act as God's "Servant:" Isa. 42:1, 53:11. Only it is to be duly noted that in Ex. 21:6 it is "ear," whereas in Psa. 40:6 it is "ears"—in *all* things Christ has the "pre-eminence!" There was never any devotion either to Master or Spouse which could be compared with His: there was (so to speak) an over-plus of willingness in Him. "A body hast Thou prepared Me" presents the same idea, only in another form: His human nature was assumed for the very purpose of being the vehicle of service. Christ came here to be the substance of all the O. T. shadows, Ex. 21:1-6 not excepted. In becoming Man, the Son took upon Him "the form of a servant" (Phil. 2:7).

"A body hast Thou prepared Me." "The origin of the salvation of the Church is in a peculiar manner ascribed unto the Father—*His* will, His grace, His wisdom, His good pleasure, His love, His sending of the Son, are everywhere proposed as the *eternal springs* of all acts of power, grace and goodness, tending unto the salvation of the Church. And therefore doth the Lord Christ on all occasions declare that He came to do the Father's will, seek His glory, make known His name, that the praise of *His* grace might be exalted" (J. Owen). It was by the Holy Spirit that the human nature of the Redeemer was created. His body was "prepared" not by the ordinary laws of procreation, but by the supernatural power of the third person of the Trinity working upon and within Mary. There is thus a clear allusion here to the Virgin-birth of the Lord Jesus.

"He prepared Him such a body, such a human nature, as might be of the same nature with ours, for whom He was to accomplish His work therein. For it was necessary that it should be cognate and allied unto ours, that He might be meet to act on our behalf, and to suffer in our stead. He did not form Him a body out of the dust of the earth, as He did that of Adam, whereby He could not have been of the same race of mankind with us; nor merely out of nothing, as He created the angels whom He was not to save (2:14-16). He took our flesh and blood proceeding from the loins of Abraham. He so prepared it, as that it should be no way subject unto that depravation and pollution, that came on our whole nature by sin. This could not have been done, had His body been prepared by carnal generation—the way and means of conveying the taint of original sin, which befell our nature, unto all individual persons—for this would have rendered Him every way unmeet for His whole work of mediation (7:26) . . . This body or human nature, thus prepared for Christ, was exposed unto all sorts of temptations from outward causes. But yet was it so sanctified by the perfection of grace, and fortified by the fullness of the Spirit dwelling therein, that it was not possible it should be touched with the least taint or guilt of sin" (J. Owen).

Summing up this important point: though the actual operation in the production of our Saviour's humanity was the immediate work of the Holy Spirit (Luke 1:35), nevertheless, the preparation thereof was also the work of the Father in a real and peculiar manner, namely, in the infinitely wise and authoritative contrivance of it, and so ordering of it by His counsel and will. The Father originated it in the decreetive disposition of all things, the Holy Spirit actually wrought it, and the Son Himself assumed it. Not that there was any distinction of time in these separate actings of the Holy Three in this matter, but only a disposition of *order* in Their operation. In the *same* instant of time the Father authoritatively willed that holy humanity into existence, the Holy Spirit efficiently created it, and the Son personally took it upon Him as His own.

"In burnt offerings and sacrifices for sin Thou hast had no pleasure" (v. 6). These words amplify and define the central portion of the preceding verse. There we hear the Son, just prior to His incarnation saying to the Father, "Sacrifice and offering Thou wouldest not." Against this a carping objector might reply, True, God never willed those sacrifices and offerings which our idolatrous fathers presented to Baal, nor those which the heathen gave to their gods; but that is a very different thing from saying that no animal sacrifice satisfied Jehovah. Such an objection is here set aside by the plain declaration that even the Levitical offerings contented God not.

"In burnt offerings and sacrifices for sin Thou hast had no pleasure." In these words Christ comprehended *all* the sacrifice under the Mosaic economy which had respect to the expiation of sin and also the worship of God. In v. 5 the term "sacrifice" includes all those offerings which the Israelites brought to the Lord for the purpose of obtaining His pardon; under the word "offering" was embraced all the gifts which they brought with the object of expressing thanksgiving for blessings received at His hands. Here in v. 6 the latter are, by a synedoche, referred to by "burnt offerings," and the former by sacrifices "for sin." Concerning both of them Christ said to the Father "Thou wouldest not" (v. 5) and "Thou hast had no pleasure."

The difference between "Thou wouldest not" and "Thou hast had no pleasure" is, the former declares that God had never *designed* the Levitical offerings should make a perfect satisfaction unto Himself; the latter, that He *delighted not* in them. Such language is to be understood relatively and not absolutely. God *had* required sacrifices at the hands of Israel: He had "imposed" them "until the time of reformation" (Heb. 9:10). Absolutely they could neither be said to be wholly nugatory in themselves nor displeasing to God, but as they could not produce any real atonement for sin, they did not correspond in the proper sense of the term either to the Divine pleasure nor to the law of God, but only foreshadowed what was to come. God had ordained a satisfaction possessing such moral obedience and personal excellency that there would need no more repetition thereof. These words "in burnt offerings and sacrifices for sin Thou hast had no pleasure" serve as a background to bring out in more vivid relief the blessedness of "This is My beloved Son in whom I *am* well pleased" (Matt. 3:17)!

Once more we would point out how that the teaching of these verses supply a timely warning against our making a wrong use of symbolic ordinances. "Whatever may be the use or efficacy of any ordinances of worship, yet if they are employed or trusted unto for *such* ends as God hath *not* designed them unto, He accepts not of our persons in them, nor approves of the things themselves. Thus He declares Himself concerning the most solemn institutions of the old Testament. And those under the New have been no less abused in this way, than those of old" (J. Owen).

"Then said I, Lo, I come (in the volume of the book it is written of Me), to do Thy will, O God" (v. 7). Those words express the readiness and willingness of the Son to do all that had been ordained unto the making of a full satisfaction to God and the salvation of His people. They contain the second branch of the antithesis pointed in the quotation which is here made from the Messianic Psalm. They record the response of the Son's mind and will to the design and purpose of the Father. They conduct us back to the eternal counsels of the Godhead, in which the Father had expressed His determination to have an adequate compensation for the insult to His honour which sin should give, His disapproval of animal sacrifices as the names thereof, His decision that the Son should become incarnate and in human form magnify the law and make it honourable; with the Son's free and perfect acquiescence therein.

"Lo, I come to do Thy will, O God." That "will" was not only to "take away sins" (v. 4), which the Levitical offerings had not effected, but was also to make His people "perfect" (v. 1 and cf. v. 14). It was the gracious design of God not only to remove all the effects of sin, original and personal, which provoked His judicial hatred of us (Eph. 2:3), but also to provide for and give to them such a righteousness as would occasion Him more cause to love us than ever, and loving to delight in us. His "will" meant not only peace and pardon to us, but grace and favour: as the angels announced to the Bethlehem shepherds, the coming of Christ meant not only "glory to God in the highest, and on earth peace," but also "good will toward men." He had predestinated not only to forgive us, but to have us adopted and graciously "accepted," and that "to the praise of the glory of His grace" (Eph. 1:5, 6).

The "will" of God which the Son came here to execute was that "eternal purpose which He had purposed in Christ Jesus our Lord" (Eph. 3:11). Had He so pleased, God could have "taken away sin" by taking away sinners, and so made a short work of it, by removing them both at one stroke—as Ezekiel speaks (12:3-4). But instead, He purposed to take away sins in such a way that favoured sinners should stand justified before Him. Again, had He so pleased, God could have taken off the sins of His people by a sole and sovereign act of pardon. To *hate* sin is an act of His *nature,* but to *express* His hatred *by punishing* sin is an act of His *will,* and therefore might be wholly suspended. Were it an act of the Divine nature to punish sin, then whosoever sinned would die for it immediately; but being an act of His will, He oftentimes suspends the punishment. Seeing He is prepared to forebear for a while, He *could* have foreborne forever. But His wisdom—the "*counsel* of His own will" (Eph. 1:11) deemed it best to require an adequate satisfaction.

What has just been said receives plain confirmation in the words used by the suffering Saviour in Gethsemane: "And He said, Abba, Father *all* things *are possible* unto Thee: take away this cup from Me; nevertheless, not what I will, but what Thou wilt." Here the incarnate Son lets us know that the reason why it was not possible for the awful cup of wrath to pass from Him was because God had *ordained* that He *should* drink it, and *not* because there was *no* other alternative. We indeed can perceive none other, and *relatively* speaking there was none other *after* the everlasting covenant had been sealed; yet *absolutely* considered, speaking from the viewpoint both of God's infinite wisdom and sovereign pleasure, He *could,* had He so pleased, have saved us in another way. Never allow the thought that sin has produced a situation which in anywise limits or restrains the *Almighty.* It was *by* His will that sin entered!

Had God so pleased, He *could* have accepted the blood of beasts as a full and final atonement for our sins. The *only* reason why He did not was because He had decreed that *Christ* should make atonement. He determined in Himself that if He had satisfaction it should be a full and perfect one. *Everything* must be resolved into and traced up to the *sovereign* pleasure of Him who "worketh *all* things after the counsel of His own *will*" (Eph. 1:11). It is in the light of what has just been said that we must interpret Heb. 10:4: it was "not possible" because of the eternal purpose of the Triune Jehovah. God would have satisfaction to the full, or none at all. This the Son knew, and to it He fully consented.

The Son was in perfect accord with the will of the Father from before the foundation of the world. As Zech. 6:13 tells us "and the covenant of peace shall be between Them *Both*": the reference being to the "everlasting covenant" (Heb. 13:20). The "counsel of peace" signifies the compact or agreement which was between the Father and the Son. It was, then, by His own voluntary consent that the Son was made "Surety of a better covenant" (Heb. 7:22), a title which necessarily imports a definite undertaking on His part, namely, His agreeing to yield that obedience to the law which His people owed, to make reparation to Divine justice on behalf of their sins, and thus discharge the whole of their debt. By a free act of His own will, the Son consented to execute that stupendous work which the Father had proposed unto Him.

This consent of the Son to His Father's proposal to Him before the foundation of the world, was, *renewed* by Him at the moment of His incarnation: "Wherefore *when He cometh into the world,* He saith . . . a body hast Thou prepared Me . . . Then said I, Lo, I come . . . to do Thy will O God." He freely acquiesced in assuming to Himself a human nature, to take on Himself the "form of a servant," to be "made under the law," to become "obedient unto death." He told the Father so in the above words, which are recorded for His glory and for our instruction, wonderment and joy. The further consideration of them, as well as the meaning of "in the volume of the book it is written of Me" we must defer (D. V.) till our next article.

CHAPTER FORTY-SEVEN

Christ's Dedication

(Heb. 10:7-10)

"As in all our obedience there are two principal ingredients to the true and right constitution of it, namely, the *matter* of the obedience itself, and the *principle* and fountain of it in us: whereof the one, the apostle calls the 'deed,' the other 'the will' (2 Cor. 8:11)—which latter God accepts in us, oftentimes without, always more than, the deed or matter of obedience itself—even so in Christ's obedience, which is the pattern and measure of ours, there are those two eminent parts which complete it. First, the obedience itself, and the worth and value of it in that it is *His*—so great a person's. Second, the willingness, the readiness to undertake and the heartiness to perform it. The dignity of His person gave the value and merit to the obedience performed by Him. But the will, the zeal in His performance gives the acceptance, and hath besides a necessary influence into the worth of it, and the virtue and efficacy of it to sanctify us. All of which you have in Heb. 10:7-10.

"The 'offering of the body of Jesus Christ:' there is the matter, His becoming 'obedient unto death' (Phil. 2:8). Then there is the readiness by which He did so, 'Lo, I come to do thy will, O God,' This calls for not only a distinct but a more eminent consideration, both necessarily concurring to our sanctification and salvation. Now the story of His willingness to redeem and save is of four parts. 1. His actual consent and undertaking to the work, made and given to the Father from everlasting. 2. The continuance of His will to stand to it from everlasting unto the time of His incarnation. 3. The renewal of this consent when He came into the world. 4. The steadfast continuance of that will all along in the performance, from the cradle to the cross.

"It was necessary that Christ's *consent* should be then given, even from everlasting, and that as God made a promise to Him for us, so also that He should give consent unto God. Yea; and indeed it was one reason why it was necessary that our Mediator should be God, and existent from eternity, not only to the end that

He might be privy to the first design and contrivement of our salvation, and know the bottom of God's mind and heart in it, and receive all the promises of God from God for us, but also in this respect, that His own very consent should go to it from the first, even as soon as His Father should design it. And it was most meet it should be so; for the performance and all the working part of it was to be His, to be laid upon His shoulders to execute, and it was a hard task, and therefore reasonable He should both know it from the first, seeing He was extant together with His Father. It was fit that both His heart and head should be in it from the first. And you have all in one Scripture, Isa. 9:6, where, when Christ is promised, 'Unto us a Child is born, unto us a Son is given,' observe under *what* titles He is set for unto us:

" 'Wonderful Counsellor, the mighty God, the everlasting Father,' where everlastingness, which is affixed to one, is yet common to those other two. The 'everlasting Counsellor,' as well as 'everlasting Father,' for He was both *Counsellor* and *Father*, in that He was the *Mighty God,* and all alike from everlasting. For, being God, and with His Father as a Son from everlasting, He must needs be a *Counsellor* with Him, and so privy unto all God meant to do, especially in that very business, for the performance of which He is there said to be *given* as a Son, and born as a Child, and the effecting of which is also said to be laid wholly on His shoulder. Certainly in this case, if God could hide nothing from Abraham He was to do, much less God from Christ, who was God with Him from everlasting. And as He was for this cause to be privy to it for the cognisance of the matter, so to have given His actual *consent* likewise thereunto; for He was to be the Father and Founder of all that was to be done in it. And in that very respect and in relation to that act of will, then passed, whereby He became a 'Father' of that business for us, it is He is styled the 'everlasting Father.' For it is in respect of that everlastingness He is God, and so 'Father' from everlasting, as well as God from everlasting; a 'Counsellor' for us with God, a 'Father' of us in our salvation. God's 'Counsellor,' because His wisdom was jointly in that plot and the contrivement of it; and 'Father' both of us and this design, because of *His* will in it, and undertaking to effect it. In that His heart and will were in it as well as the Father's He was therefore the 'Father' of it as well as God, and brought it to perfection" (Adopted, with slight variations, from T. Goodwin, 1600-1680).

Concerning the *continuance* of the Son's willingness to the Father's purpose, from everlasting to the time when His humanity was conceived in the Virgin's womb, we have more than a hint in that remarkable passage found in Prov. 8. There (by the Spirit of prophecy) we are permitted to hear Him say of the Father, "Then I was by Him, as One brought up with him." But not only so, He added, "And I was daily His delight, *rejoicing always* before Him; rejoicing in the habitable part (that portion where His tabernacle was to be placed) of His earth; and My delights were *with* the sons of men" (vv. 30, 31). Thus we see how His heart was more set upon the redeeming of His people than all other works. The theophanic manifestations which He made of Himself from time to time during the O. T. period, illustrated the same fact: see Gen. 12:7, Ex. 3:2-9, Dan. 3:25 etc.

But it is the *renewing* of His consent when Christ came into the world which we would particularly contemplate. This may well be called the will of *consecration* of Himself by a vow to this great work, then solemnly made and given. This was the *dedication* of His holy "Temple" (John 2:19), foreshadowed of old by Solomon in the dedication of the temple which he erected unto God. This took place at the moment that His humanity was conceived by the Virgin: "*When* He cometh into the world, He saith . . . a body (a vehicle of service) hast Thou prepared Me. . . . Lo, I come, to do Thy will, O God." How truly marvellous and blessed that it pleased the Holy Spirit (the Divine Secretary of Heaven, and Recorder of the everlasting covenant) to write down for our learning the very words which the Son uttered to His Father at the moment when He condescended to take our nature and become incarnate! Equally wonderful is it that we are permitted to hear the very words which the Father addressed to the Son on His return to Heaven: "The Lord said to My Lord, Sit Thou at My right hand, till I make Thine enemies Thy footstool" (Psa. 110:1).

"When He cometh into the world, He saith." The Speaker is none other than the second person in the Divine Trinity. *He* was the One who took that "body" into everlasting union with Himself —an infinitely greater condescension than for the noblest king to marry the meanest servant-girl. The ineffably glorious Son of God was personally humbled far more and gave much more away than did that humanity when it was humiliated by being nailed to the cross. Therefore was His willingness to this tremendous stoop eminently requisite and recorded for our comfort and praise. Thus, at the very moment that the human nature was amaking, and not yet capable of giving its *own* consent, He who was the Brightness of the Father's glory and the express Image of His person, announced *His* readiness. Inexpressibly blessed is this; may the contemplation thereof bow us in worship before Him. "Worthy is the Lamb!"

"Then said I, Lo, I come (in the volume of the book it is written of Me), to do Thy will, O God" (v. 7). There is a *double reference* (as is so often the case with the words of God) in the parenthetical clause. The "book" He mentioned *primarily* regarded the archives of God's eternal counsels, the scroll of His decrees Secondarily, it concerned the Holy Scriptures, which are a partial transcript of that record of the Divine will which is preserved on High (Psa. 119:89). In that "book," drawn up by the Holy Spirit, it is written of Christ, the God-man Mediator for *He* is the Sum and Substance of all the Divine counsels (Eph. 3:11), as well as the Depository of all the Divine promises (2 Cor. 1:20). The Son was perfectly cognisant of all that was written in that book, for He had been "Counsellor" with the Father. The term "volume" is the right translation of the Hebrew word "magillah" in Psa. 40:7, but the Greek word "kephalis" ought most certainly to be rendered "head" —"kephale" occurs seventy-six times in the N. T., and is *always* rendered "head" elsewhere.

A most wondrous and blessed revelation is here made known to us: "in the head of the book" of God's decrees, at *the beginning* thereof, it is "written of" Christ! In that book is recorded the names of all God's favoured children: Luke 10:20, Heb. 12:23; but at the *head* of them is *Christ's,* for "in *all* things" *He must* have the "pre-eminence" (Col. 1:18). Thus, the first name on that heavenly scroll of the Divine decrees is that of the Mediator Himself! So too in the Holy Scriptures, which give us a copy, in part, the *first* name in the O. T. is that of Christ as Creator (Gen. 1:1 cf. John 1:1-3), and the *first* name in the N.T. is "Jesus Christ" (Matt. 1:1)! Yes, "in the *head* of the Book" it is written of *Him.*

The Man Christ Jesus was the *first* one chosen of God; chosen to be taken into everlasting union with the second person of the Trinity. Therefore does the Father say to us, "Behold My Servant, whom I uphold, Mine *Elect* in whom My soul delighteth" (Isa. 42:1). The Church was chosen in Christ (Eph. 1:4) and then given to Christ (Heb. 2:13). The Man Christ Jesus, taken into union with God the Son, was appointed to be the Head of the whole election of grace, and they to be members of His mystical Body (Eph. 1:22, 23; 5:30). "Christ be My first elect He said; Then chose our souls in Christ our Head."

Precious too is it to discover that the *human* nature of Christ *also* consented to the terms of the everlasting covenant, for it was something distinct from the Divine nature of God the Son, and so had a distinct will, and was directly concerned in the Great Transaction, for *it* was to be made the subject of all the sufferings and was to be the sacrifice offered up. The fundamental consent was the Divine Person's, and this He gave when assuming our nature; but there was also an accessory consent of the human nature, now married into one person with the Divine. How soon then, *when* was it that the human nature gave *its* consent? No doubt many will deem this a question which it is impossible for us to answer, and that any effort so to do would be a prying into "secret things." Not so: it belongs to those things which *are* revealed.

Ere turning to the consideration of this marvelous detail, we must not overlook the *willingness* of the virgin Mary to be—in such an unprecedented manner, and in a way which (humanly speaking) seriously endangered her own moral reputation—the mother of our Lord's sacred humanity. This is most blessedly shown us in the inspired record of Luke's Gospel. There we learn that this amazing honour, yet sore trial, was proposed to her (*not* forced upon her, for God never violates human accountability!) by the angel: "Behold, thou shalt conceive in thy womb, and bring forth a Son, and shalt call His name Jesus" (1:31). Mark now her meek response: "Behold the handmaid of *the Lord*"—I give myself up to Him—"*be it* unto me *according to* thy word" (1:38). Not until *after* she had herself acquiesced, did she "conceive"— note the word "before" in Luke 2:21 and compare with Luke 1:31-38. Thus does God make His people "willing" in the day of His power (Psa. 110:3).

Returning now to the willingness of our Lord's *humanity* in consenting to God's eternal purpose: "This may safely be affirmed, that as soon as, or when first He began to put forth any *acts of reason,* that then His will was guided to direct its aim and intentions to God as His Father, from Himself as the Mediator. And look, as in infant's hearts, *if they had been born in innocency,* there would have been sown the notion of God, whom they should *first* have known, whatever else they knew; and the moral law being written in their hearts, they should have directed their actions to God and His glory, through a natural instinct and tendency of spirit. Thus it was in Christ when an infant, and such holy principles guided Him to that, which was that will of God for Him, and to be performed by Him; and which was to sway and direct all His actions and thoughts, that were to be the matter of our justification, which were to be exerted more and more according to the capacity of reason as it should grow" (T. Goodwin).

There was a meetness, yea a needs-be for this. For what Christ did as a Child had a meritoriousness in it, as much as what He did when a full-grown Man. So too what He suffered, even in His very circumcision, is made influential unto the sanctification of His people through the virtue of it, equally with what He suffered on the cross. *His* coat was "*without* seam" (John 19:23): the righteousness He wrought out for His Church was a *unit*—beginning at Bethlehem's manger, consummated at Calvary. It is the 22nd Psalm which furnishes a definite answer to our question, and reveals *how* early the Saviour was dedicated to God. Hear His gracious and unique words: "Thou art He that took Me out of the womb: Thou didst make Me hope upon My mother's breasts. I was cast upon Thee *from the womb*: Thou art My *God* from My mother's belly" (vv. 9, 10). O my brethren and sisters, prostrate your souls in adoration before this Holy One, who from the very first instant after He entered this world was unreservedly dedicated and consecrated to God, owning Him, relying wholly upon Him.

In this we may behold the fulfilment of a lovely and striking type, namely, that of the Nazarite, to which Matt. 2:23 directly, though not exclusively, refers. The "Nazarite" was one who, voluntarily, separated and devoted himself entirely unto the Lord (Num. 6:12). Samson is the outstanding illustration of this in the O. T.: the parallels between him and Christ are remarkable. 1. An angel announced to his mother her conception (Judges 13:2-3). 2. The prophecy of the angel is recorded. 3. He was sent to a woman utterly barren, to show her conception was extraordinary. 4. Her son was to be a Nazarite, that is, "holy to the Lord" (Num. 6:8). 5. He was to be "a Nazarite unto God *from the womb*" (Judges 13:5). 6. It was declared that her son should be a deliverer of Israel (v. 5). 7. Israel was then subject to the Gentiles (the Philistines), as the Jews were to the Romans when Christ was born. 8. It was in his *death* that he wrought his mightiest victory!

Equally striking, equally blessed, are the first words which the N. T. records as being uttered by our Saviour: "know ye not that in the (affairs) of My Father it behoves to be Me" (Bagster Interlinear). The Greek is very emphatic, the last word before "Me" signifying to be completely and continuously given up to it, and is rendered "wholly" in 1 Tim. 4:15. The reader is familiar with the context of Luke 2:49. The Saviour's mother appears to have chided Him, and, in substance, He said: True you are My earthly parent, and I have been subject to you hitherto in your particular province, but do you not know that I have another Father, far higher than you, who hath commanded Me, by virtue of My office of Mediator, other manner of business? I am the Christ, devoted to the Father's interests; His will and law is written in My heart; I am not Mine own!

Let us revert for a moment to the 40th Psalm. There we hear the Saviour saying, "Mine ears hast Thou digged" (v. 6): that figurative language applied only to His humanity. The metaphor employed is taken from Ex. 21:1-6. The Hebrew servant was entitled to, "go out free" at the end of the sixth year, but an exception was allowed for: "If the servant shall plainly say, I love my master, my wife, and my children; I will not go out free: then . . . his master shall bore his ear through with an aul, and he shall serve him for ever" (vv. 5, 6). The antitype of this is seen in Christ. As creatures, *we* are *necessarily* born "under the law," subjects of the government of God. With the Man Christ Jesus, it was otherwise. His humanity, having been taken into union with the second person in the Trinity, was altogether exempt from any servile subjection, just as a woman ceases to be a *subject* when married to a king. It was an act of unparalleled condescension, by His own voluntary will, that the God-man entered the place of service; and *love,* love to His God, to His Church, His people, was the moving-cause.

Observe another thing in the prophetic language of the Mediator in Psa. 40: "Then said I, Lo, I come: in the volume of the book it is written of Me; I delight to do Thy will, O My God: yea, Thy law is within My heart" (vv. 7, 8). When the appointed hour arrived the Son volunteered to fulfill every jot and tittle which had been recorded of Him in the Book of God's decrees—transcribed (in part) on the pages of Holy Writ. He carried all of it written in His heart. This was even more than to have His ear "bored"—to give free consent to the Father's purpose; it was, as it *would* have been *if* infants had been born in innocency, to have God's law (the *expression* of His *will!*) as the moulding principle and controlling factor of His human nature, dwelling in the very centre of His affections. Thus could He say, "My *meat* (My very sustenance and substance) is to do the will of Him that sent Me, and to finish His work" (John 4:34) i.e. *actualize* what the Father had *ordained.*

Our theme is exhaustless; eternity will be too short to contemplate it. Bear with the writer, dear reader, as he endeavours to follow it a step further. "But I have a baptism to be baptised with; and how am I straitened till it be accomplished!" (Luke 12:50). What words were those! The Lord Jesus knew the unspeakable *bitterness* of that baptism, a baptism such as no mere creature could have endured; nevertheless, He panted after it. His very heart was contracted by the delay. Never woman desired more to be delivered than did He to finish His travail, to pass over that "brook" (Psa. 110:7), that sea of wrath into which He should be immersed. Note His remarkable word to Judas: "that thou doest do *quickly*" (John 13:27).

Again, mark how when He first announced to His disciples His forthcoming sufferings and death (Matt. 16:21), and Peter "took Him (aside as a friend out of natural affection) and began to rebuke Him, saying, Pity thyself, Lord"—Thou who art going about doing good, ministering to the needy, allow not Thyself to suffer such indignities, such an ignominious end. And how did Christ receive this word? Did He appreciate it? No, never did He take any word so ill; never did His holy zeal flash forth more vividly than then. He turned and said unto Peter, "Get thee behind Me, Satan; thou art an offense unto Me." Never such word was spoken unto saint, before or since. The word "offense" means an occasion of stumbling; Peter's counsel had that tendency in it—to turn Him aside from that great work upon which His heart was so fully set.

There is a remarkable word in the "Pascal Discourse" which it is impossible to explain or account for except on the ground of that holy impatience or zeal which consumed the Saviour to make an end of the work the Father had assigned Him. After Judas had gone out to betray Him, the Saviour redeemed the time by speaking at length to the Eleven, and in the midst of so doing He said, "But that the world may know that I love the Father; and as the Father gave Me commandment, even so I do. Arise, let us go hence" (John 14:31). He was in haste to be gone, lest the band headed by the betrayer should miss Him in the garden. Then He looked (as it were) at the hour-glass of His life, and seeing that the sands of time had not yet completely run out, He resumed and completed His address.

The closer he drew to the final conflict, the more blessedly did appear the perfectness of His consecration to God. When the moment of arrest arrived, and Peter drew his sword and attempted resistance, the Saviour exclaimed, "The cup which My Father hath given Me, shall I not drink it?" (John 18:11). When conducted to the hall of judgment, He was *not dragged,* as an unwilling victim, but was "*led* as a sheep to the slaughter" (Acts 8:32). Hear His own words— spoken centuries before by the Spirit of prophecy—"The Lord God hath opened Mine ear, and I was *not* rebellious, neither turned away back. I *gave* My back to the smiters, and My cheeks to them that plucked off the hair: I *hid not* My face from shame and spitting" (Isa. 50:5, 6). *That* (excepting the cross itself) was the hardest part of what had been assigned Him, yet He rebelled not. O blessed Saviour grant us more of Thy spirit.

He never showed the slightest sign of reluctancy till Gethsemane was reached, when He took (as it were) a more immediate look into the awful cup which He was to drink, and saw in it the wrath of God and His being made a "curse." Then, to exhibit the *holiness* of His nature, shrinking from being "made sin" (2 Cor. 5:21), to demonstrate the *reality* of His humanity—trembling, horrified, in anguish at what awaited Him; and to *manifest* His unquenchable love to us, by making known more clearly *what* He suffered on our behalf, He cried, "If it be possible, let this cup pass from Me." Yet instantly He was quieted: "Nevertheless, *not* My will be done, but

Thine." Thus we are shown again His full and perfect acquiesence to the Father's purpose, and that the *one* and *only* object before Him was the doing of *the Father's* will.

Yet one more thought on this precious subject: "Lo, I come to *do* Thy will, O God." Weigh well the verb. It was not merely that the Son consented to passively endure whatever the Father was pleased to lay upon Him, but also that He desired to actively perform the work which had been alloted to Him. Though that work involved immeasurable humiliation, untold anguish. though it entailed not only Bethlehem's manger but Calvary's cross, He hesitated not. As a child, as a Man, in life and in death, He was "obedient" to His God. *Our* disobedience was voluntary, so the satisfaction which He made for us was voluntary. Though what He did was done out of love for us, *yet chiefly* in subjection to God's will and out of love to Him. "I love the Father; and as the Father gave Me commandment, even so I do" (John 14:31)!

Let us pause long enough to make one word of application. In view of all that has been before us, of what surpassing *value* must be *such* obedience! When we remember that the One we have been contemplating is none other than the Almighty, who, "hath measured the waters in the hollow of His hand and meted heaven with a span" (Isa. 40:12), then is it not obvious that *this* humiliation and consecration must possess a dignity and efficacy which has more than compensated God for all the dreadful disobedience of His people! It was the Divine excellency of Christ's person which gave infinite worth to all that He did as the God-man-Mediator; therefore is He able to "save unto the uttermost them that come unto God by Him." O Christian reader look away from self with its ten thousand failures, to Him who is "Altogether Lovely." No matter how black and foul thy sins, the precious blood of *such* an One cleanseth from them all. And what wholehearted devotion is due unto Him from us! O may His love truly constrain us to obey and please Him.

"Above when He said, Sacrifice and offering and burnt offerings and offering for sin Thou wouldest not, neither hast pleasure therein, which are offered by the law; Then said He, Lo, I come to do Thy will, O God. He taketh away the first, that He may establish the second" (vv. 8, 9). In these words we have the apostle's inspired comment upon the remarkable quotation given from Psa. 40. Repetition is here made that the conclusion drawn might the more plainly appear. That to which attention is now directed is to the *order* of statement, and what that order necessarily intimated. The first word of v. 8 ("Above") and the first of v. 9 ("Then") are placed in opposition and it is to them that the "first" and the "second" at the end of v. 9 looks.

Granting that the Levitical sacrifices were "offered by the law," nevertheless, God rejected them as the means of making real expiation of sin and the saving of His church. This He had made known as far back as the days of David; nor was it a new decision that God formed then, for what He spoke through His prophets in time was but the revelation of what He had decreed in eternity. This the Son, the Mediator, was cognizant of, therefore did He say, "Lo I come to do Thy will, O God." "Lo" Behold! a word signalizing what a glorious spectacle was then presented to God, to angels, and to men. "I come" from Heaven to earth, from the "form of God" to the "form of a servant;" come forth like the rising of the sun, with light and healing in his wings, or as a giant rejoicing to run his race. To "do Thy will," to perform Thy counsels, to execute what Thou requirest, to render that entire service of love which Thy people owed unto the law, to perform the great work of redemption. Thus, the perfect obedience of Christ is placed in direct contrast from the whole of the Levitical offerings: His accomplishing what theirs could not.

"He taketh away the first, that He may establish the second." This inference is patent; no other conclusion could be drawn. The Levitical offerings were unefficacious to accomplish the purpose of God; the satisfaction of the incarnate Son had. The Greek word for "taketh away" is even stronger than the term applied to the old covenant—"made old" and "vanish away" (8:13). It is usually applied to the taking away of life (Acts 16:27). Dead things are not only useless, but prove harmful carrion, fit only to be *buried!* Thus it was with the Mosaic shadows. So also an equally emphatic and final word is used in connection with the one offering of our Lord's: it has "established" the will of God concerning the Church. That is, it has placed it on such an immutable foundation that it shall never be moved or altered.

"By the which will we are sanctified through the offering of the body of Jesus Christ once for all" (v. 10). This is a commentary upon the whole passage. "By," or better "*in* which will" refers not to Christ's, for the preceding verse speaks of the will of the Father, purposing that Christ should offer the perfect and acceptable sacrifice. Moreover, the "will" is *distinguished from* the "offering" of the Redeemer. The "Thy will" of v. 9 refers to the eternal agreement between the Father and the Son in connection with the covenant of redemption, the performing of His "commandment" (John 10:18). "*In* which will" gives the sphere or element in which the great sacrifice was offered and in which the elect are "sanctified."

"In the which will we are sanctified through the offering of the body of Jesus Christ once for all." "Sanctified" positionally, restored to God's favour, standing accepted before Him. The death of Christ was a "sacrifice" (7:27, 9:23), by which He put away sin (9:26) and provided for the purging of our conscience (9:14) and the setting apart of our persons unto God (10:14). All these passages affirm that the death of Christ was a sacrifice by which the elect are separated as a peculiar people unto the worship of the living God. It is important to see the type realized in the Antitype. "As the ancient sacrifices, as symbols in the lower sphere, freed the worshipper from merited (temporal) punishment, because the guilt passed over to the victim, so the death of Christ, in a higher sphere, not only *displayed* the punishment due to us for sin, but the actual *removal* of that punishment. It puts us in the position of a people near to God, a holy people, as Israel were in a typical (or ceremonial) sense" (G. Smeaton).

"In the which will we are sanctified through the offering of the body of Jesus Christ once for all." "Sanctified is here to be taken in its widest latitude, as including a full expiation of sin, a complete dedication to God, a real purification of our natures, a permanent peace of conscience unto which belongs the privilege of immediate access to God. Faith is the instrumental cause, whereby we enter into the good of it. The Spirit's work within is the efficient cause, whereby we are enabled to believe and lay hold of it. The redemptive work of Christ is the meritorious cause, whereby He earned for us the gift of His Spirit to renew us. But the sovereign and eternal will of the Father is the supreme and originating cause. All that the will of God ordained for the good of His Church is communicated to us through the satisfaction or offering of Christ, but this is only apprehended by an understanding enlightened and a heart opened by the Holy Spirit.

CHAPTER FORTY-EIGHT

The Perfecting of the Church

(Heb. 10: 11-14)

The connection between our present passage and the verses preceding is so close, the relation between them so intimate, that what is now to be before us cannot be understood, and appreciated apart from the other. The design of the whole is to show the superlative excellency of the sacrifice of Christ and what it has procured for His people, with the inevitable setting aside of all the typical offerings. This great change in the outward worship of God's saints on earth was no temporary expediency in view of the failures of fleshly Israel, but was ordained by the Divine counsels before the foundation of the world, recorded in the Book of God's decrees, and, in due time, transcribed upon the pages of Holy Scripture; the 40th Psalm having announced the alteration which was to be brought about by the incarnation and advent to this earth of the Son of God.

Most blessedly does that Messianic Psalm acquaint us with what passed between the Father and the Son and of the covenant agreed upon by Them. Most blessedly are we there shown not only the Son's acquiescence to the Father's purpose, but also His readiness and joy to execute the same. The strenuous undertaking was to rest upon *His* shoulder, the burden and heat of the day was to be borne by Him, the humiliation and pains of death were to be His portion; yet so far from rebelling against this frightful ordeal, He exclaimed "I *delight* to do Thy will, O My God" (Psa. 40:8). So dear to Him was the Father's glory, so filled with zeal was He to accomplish His counsels, so deep was His longing to magnify His law and make it honourable, that His very "meat" was to do and accomplish His will. Never did famished mortal so crave food to satisfy hunger, as did the God-man Mediator to perform the Father's pleasure.

He too knew full well that the blood of bulls and goats could never repair the damage which sin had wrought. He too had heartily concurred in the august Council of the Trinity that, if satisfaction were to be made unto Divine justice, then an *adequate* one should be given, one which should be suited in every way to meet *all* the aspects of the case. Inasmuch as it was man who had revolted against the Divine government and broken the Divine law, He was willing to become Man, and in the same nature which had apostatized from God render perfect obedience to Him. Inasmuch as "the Law" was the rule of obedience (Jer. 31:33), comprehending all God's demands, the entire service of love which creatures owe unto their Maker, the Son consented to be "made under the law" (Gal. 4:4) and "fulfil" its precepts (Matt. 5:17). Inasmuch as the penalty of that law was death unto the transgressor, He agreed to be "made a curse for us."

It was *not* that all of this was *forced on* the Son, but that He freely agreed thereto. If there are verses which tell us the Father "sent" the Son, there are other passages which declare that the Son "came." Blessedly was this foreshadowed in Gen. 22, where we behold an earthly adumbration of that "counsel of peace" which was between "Both" the Father and the son (Zech. 6:13). There we are shown a human father willing to sacrifice his beloved son upon the altar, and there too we see a human son (then fully grown) willing to be slain! Marvelously did that set forth the *mutual* consent of the Divine persons with regard to the Great Transaction. Mark attentively, those precious words, "So they went *both* of them *together*" (Gen. 22:8)! As we follow Isaac upon mount Moriah, his actions said, "Lo, I come to do *Thy* will, O my God."

In man three things combine to the doing of a thing. First, there is the exercise of *will,* which is the *prime* mover and spring of all the rest. Second, there is the exercise of *wisdom,* by which he plans and arranges. Third, the putting forth of *strength* to accomplish the same. So it is in the Divine Trinity in connection with the salvation of the Church and all that that entails. "Will" is more generally ascribed to the Father: Matt. 11:26, Eph. 1:11, etc. "Wisdom" is more eminently attributed to the Son, the "Wonderful Counsellor," called so often "Wisdom" in the book of Proverbs, Luke 7:35, 11:49 etc. "Might" to the Holy Spirit—Luke 1:35, where He is designated "the Power of the Highest." The Father contrived the great work of redemption, the Son transacted it, and the Holy Spirit applies the same. Here in Heb. 10 things are traced back to the first great cause of our salvation, namely, the sovereign will of the Father.

The closer the whole passage be read, the more will it appear that the apostle was moved to ascend in thought to the originating source of redemption. In v. 5 we hear the Lord Jesus saying to the Father concerning the legal sacrifices, "Thou wouldest not," i.e. they were not what Thou didst eternally purpose should take away sins. To this He adds, "But a body hast Thou *prepared* Me," which (as we have shown) in its deepest meaning signifies: a human nature hast Thou *ordained* for Me, to be the meet vehicle of service in which I should render an adequate satisfaction. Next, He makes reference to the Book of God's eternal decrees, in view of which He declares, "I come to do Thy *will,* O God." Finally, the Holy Spirit sums up the whole by affirming "in the which will we are sanctified through the offering of the body of Jesus Christ once."

We feel it a bounden duty to enlarge upon this fundamental truth, the more so in view of the present almost universal denial of the absolute sovereignty of God. The Holy Spirit has Himself here emphasised the fact that God's imperial pleasure was the sole moving-cause even in that greatest of all the Divine works, through which is communicated the chiefest glory to God and highest good to His people. God was under *no* necessity to save any. He "spared not the angels that sinned, but cast them down to hell" (2 Peter 2:4); and had it so pleased Him, He had done the same with the whole human race. There was *no* necessity in His *nature* which compelled or even required Him to show mercy; had there been, mercy had been bestowed on the fallen angels! The Almighty is under *no* restraint either from anything outside or anything inside Himself; to affirm the contrary, would be to repudiate the absolute freedom of His will.

Still less was God under any necessity of giving His own beloved Son if He chose to redeem a part of Adam's race. He who declares, "All nations before Him are as nothing: and they are *counted to Him* less than nothing, and vanity. To whom then will ye liken God?" (Isa. 40:17, 18) is not to be measured by human reason nor limited by our unbelief. Had God so pleased He had made this earth a thousand times bigger than it is; and had He so pleased, He had created it a thousand times smaller. In like manner, He was absolutely free to use whatsoever means *He* determined in order to save His people from their sins. The sending forth of His Son to be made of a woman and to die upon the cross, was *not* a work of His *nature,* but of His *will;* as He now begets us "of His own will" (James 1:18). True it "became" Him so to do (Heb. 2:10), and He is infinitely honoured thereby, yet He could have refused had He so pleased.

Thus, the "will" of God referred to throughout Heb. 10 is that eternal, gracious, free purpose, by which God determined in Himself to recover His elect out of lost mankind, to remove their sins, sanctify their persons, and bring them nigh unto the everlasting enjoyment of Himself. This act of the will of God was without any meritorious cause foreseen in them, and altogether apart from anything outside Himself to dispose Him thereto. It was His own free and uncaused act by which God purposed so to do. Nor have we the smallest occasion to regard this supremacy of the Most High with any aversion. God is no Tyrant, nor does He act capriciously, *His* will is a wise and holy one, therefore do we read of Him working "all things after the *counsel* of His own will" (Eph. 1:11), and therefore did He devise a plan whereby His *grace* might be most magnified.

It was for this reason He determined that His people should be saved in such a way as to remove *all* ground for boasting in themselves, and to glory only in God Himself. Therefore did He appoint His own Son to be their Saviour, and that by rendering to Him such a satisfaction as would meet every requirement of justice and every demand of the most enlightened conscience. God's end and aim in giving Christ to die was to advance the glory of His *grace,* which consists in having the monarchy and *sole* prerogative in saving sinners attributed unto it; the highest of whose honour and eminency is this, that *it* alone "reigns" (Rom. 5:21), and hath not and could not have any competitor therein. As it is the excellency of God that He is God alone, and there is none beside Him, so it is of His Son that He is Saviour alone and there is none beside Him (Acts 4:12).

Unto God the Son, made Man, has been assigned an office which no creature in earth or heaven could possibly fill. The fullest trial and manifestation of this is made in a case of less difficulty (than that of making satisfaction to Divine justice for sin) in Rev. 5. There we read of a challenge given, "Who is worthy to open the book"—which was sealed and held in the hand of God seated on His throne—"and to loose the seals thereof?" Waiving the question as to *what* "book" this was, we note the response: "And no one in heaven, nor in earth, neither under the earth, was able to open the book, neither to look thereon" (v. 3). Even the beloved John was discouraged, and "wept much because no one was found worthy to open and to read the book" (v. 4). Mark the unspeakably blessed sequel: "One of the elders saith unto me, Weep not; behold, the Lion of the tribe of Judah, the Root of David, *hath* prevailed to open the book and to loose the seals thereof. And I beheld, and, Lo, in the midst of the throne . . . stood a Lamb as it had been slain . . . and He came and took the book out of the right hand of Him that sat upon the throne" (vv. 5-7). If then no mere creature was fit to *reveal* redemption, how much less to *effect* it!

Thus, the *origin* of our salvation is found in the sovereign will of God; the *means,* in the satisfaction made by His incarnate Son.

The two things are brought together in v. 10, "In the which will we are sanctified through the offering of the body of Jesus Christ once." "In the which will" has reference to what is recorded in the Book of God's decrees. That "will" was that His people should be "sanctified" unto Him, set apart with acceptance to Him. This was to be effected through "the offering" of Christ, which began at the first moment of His birth and ended when on the cross He cried, "It is finished." This was "once for all."

It was an absolute necessity that there should be these two things: the originating will of God the Father, the consenting will of the Mediator to make full satisfaction for sin. Necessary it was that the Father should be willing and call His Son to this work, for *He* was the person unto whom the satisfaction was to be made. Had Christ performed all that He did, freely and gladly, yet, unless the Father had first decreed that He *should* and had "called" Him unto it, then had He rejected the whole, asking "who hath required this at Thy hand?" Therefore has the Spirit insisted upon this foundational fact again and again in the course of this epistle: see 2:10; 3:4, 5; 6:17 etc. Thus does 10:10 ascribe as much, yea more, to God's appointing and accepting of Christ's sacrifice, as to the merits of Christ unto the sanctification of His people.

"And every priest standeth daily ministering and offering oftentimes the same sacrifices, which can never take away sins: But this Man, after He had offered one sacrifice for sins, for ever sat down on the right hand of God; from henceforth expecting, till His enemies be made His footstool. For by one offering He hath perfected forever them that are sanctified" (vv. 11-14). "These words are an entrance into the close of that long blessed discourse of the apostle, concerning the priesthood and sacrifice of Christ, their dignity and efficacy; which he shuts up and finisheth in the following verses, confirming the whole with the testimony of the Holy Spirit before producing by Him.

"Four things doth he here instruct us in, by way of recapitulation of what he had declared and proved before. 1. The state of the legal priests and sacrifices, as unto the recognition of them, by which he had proved before their utter insufficiency to take away sin (v. 11). 2. In that one offering of Christ, and that once offered, in opposition thereunto (v. 12). 3. The consequence thereof on the part of Christ; whereof there are two parts. First, His state and condition immediately ensuing thereon (v. 12), manifesting the dignity, efficacy and absolute perfection of His offering. Secondly, as unto the continuance of His state and condition afterwards (v. 13). 4. The absolute effect of his sacrifice, which was the sanctification of the Church (v. 14)" (J. Owen).

"And every priest standeth daily ministering and offering oftentimes the same sacrifices, which can never take away sins" (v. 11). The opening "And" links this verse with the 10th, for the purpose of accentuating the blessedness of what is there declared. Once more the Holy Spirit emphasises the contrast between the all-sufficient offering of Christ and the unefficacious offerings under the law. This is brought out under five details, upon which there is little need for us to enlarge at length.

First, under the law the sacerdotal office was filled by *many*: attention is called to this by the "*every* priest," which is set over against the "this Man" of v. 12, who was competent by Himself to do all God required. Second, the Levitical priests *stood*. This was true both of the high priests and of all under him. No chair or seat was provided for them in either the tabernacle or temple, for their work was never ended. Third, they were employed *daily*, which showed they were unable to do immediately and once for all that which would satisfy God. Fourth, they oftentimes presented "the *same* sacrifices": true, they varied in detail and design, nevertheless they had this in common, that, they were irrational creatures, incapable of offering intelligent and acceptable obedience to God. Fifth, they could not meet the infinite demands of justice, expiate sins, nor provide a permanent resting-place for an exercised conscience.

An improvement should be made of what has just been before us, by pointing out the utter worthlessness of all human devices for appeasing God and comforting the conscience. If the Levitical offerings, which were of Divine appointment, were unable to really meet either the full requirements of God or the deepest need of sinners, how much less can the contrivances of man do so! How vain are the Romish inventions of confession, absolution, indulgencies, masses, penances, purgatory, and the like tom-fooleries! Equally vain are the austerities of some Protestants: the signing of a temperance-pledge, giving up of tobacco, and other reformations, with tears, fastings, and religious performances designed to make peace with God. The salvation of the Lord does not come to a soul via any such things. "Not by works of righteousness which we have done, but according to His mercy He saved us, *by* the washing of regeneration and renewing of the Holy Spirit; which He shed on us abundantly *through* Jesus Christ our Saviour" (Titus 3:5, 6).

"But this man, after He had offered one sacrifice for sins for ever sat down on the right hand of God" (v. 12). The opening word denotes that a contrast is here presented from what was before us in v. 11: it is the Holy Spirit placing in antithesis the one perfect and efficacious offering of Christ from the unavailing sacrifices of the law. The word "Man" ought to be in italics: if any word is to be supplied it should be that of "Priest." The Greek simply reads, "But He," the pronoun being emphatic. It is the sacerdotal work of the Mediator which is in view. He came and once for all laid Himself on the Divine altar as an atonement to God—the entire course of His obedience terminating and being consummated at the cross.

There is both a comparison and a contrast here between Christ and Aaron and his successors. Both were priests; both offered a sacrifice for sins; but there the analogy between them ends. They were many; He alone. They offered numerous sacrifices; He, but one. They continued to offer sacrifices; His is complete and final. Their offerings were unefficacious; His, has actually removed sins. They stood; He has sat down. They ministered *unto* God; He is seated at the right hand of God. The typical high priest entered the holiest only for a brief season, one day in the year; Christ has gone on High "forever." He has not ceased to be a Priest, nor to exercise that office; but He is now "a Priest upon His *throne*" (Zech. 6:13). The position He occupies witnesses to the supreme excellency of His work, and attests the acceptance of His sacrifice by God.

The glorious place which our once humiliated Saviour has been accorded, supplies conclusive evidence of the value and finality of His redemptive work. "The very fact that Christ is in heaven, accepted by His Father, proves that His work must be done. Why, beloved, as long as an ambassador from our country is at a foreign court, there must be peace; and as long as Jesus Christ our Saviour is at His Father's court, it shows that there is real peace between His people and His Father. Well, as He will be there for ever, that shows our peace must be continued and shall never cease. But that peace could not have been continual, unless the atonement had been wholly made, unless justice had been entirely satisfied" (C. H. Spurgeon).

Commentators have been divided as to whether the "for ever" is to be connected with the Saviour's one sacrifice or to His sitting down at God's right hand. The Greek, while hardly conclusive, decidedly favours the latter. Perhaps the double thought is designed. They who insist that the "for ever" *must* be joined to the first clause, argue that it cannot be so with the second because 1 Thess. 4:16, Rev. 19:11 etc. show that the Saviour will yet leave Heaven. As well might appeal be made to Christ's "standing" to receive Stephen (Acts 7:55). But the difficulty is self-created through *carnalizing* the metaphor used. "For ever sat down" is in designed contrast from the "standeth daily" of v. 11. Christ has ceased for ever from the priestly work of making oblation: He will never again be engaged in such a task; but He has *other* characters to fill beside that of Maker of atonement.

"For ever sat down on the right hand of God." Four times in this epistle is reference made to Christ's being seated on High, yet is there no repetition. On each occasion the reference is found connected with an entirely different line of thought. First, in 1:3 it is His seat of personal glory which is in view: the whole context before and after showing that. Second, in 8:1 it is the seat of priestly pre-eminence which He occupies, namely, His superiority over all others who filled the sacerdotal office. Third, here in 10:12 it is the seat of sacrificial acceptance, God's witness to the value of His satisfaction. Fourth, in 12:2 it is the seat of the Victor, the prize given for having successfully run His race.

The One born in Bethlehem's manger, who on earth had not where to lay His head, who died upon the cross, and whose body was laid in a borrowed grave, is now in Heaven. He has been given a place higher than that of the arch-angel, He has been exalted above all created things. There is a *glorified Man* at God's right hand! Christ is the *only one* among all the hosts above who *deserves* to be there! It is naught but Divine *favour* which gives holy angels and redeemed sinners a place in the Father's House; but the Man Christ Jesus has *merited* that high honour!

"The highest place that Heaven affords,
Is His by sovereign *right,*
King of kings and Lord of lords,
He reigns there in the Light."

Unspeakably blessed is this; the more so when it be realized that Christ has entered heaven *for His people.* He has gone there in his *official* character. He has gone there as our Representative; to appear before God "for us" (Heb. 9:24). He is there as our great High Priest, bearing our names on His breastplate. Wondrous and precious are those words, "Whither the *fore*-runner is *for us* entered, even Jesus" (Heb. 6:20). There the mighty Victor sits "crowned with glory and honour." He occupies the Throne of universal dominion, of all-mighty power, of sovereign and illimitable grace. He is making all grace. He is making all things work together for the good of His own. The kingly scepter shall He wield until all His redeemed are with Him in glory.

"From henceforth expecting till His enemies be made His footstool" (v. 13). In these words we have the seventh and last N. T. reference made to the 110th Psalm. There we read, "The Lord said unto my Lord, Sit Thou at My right hand, until I make Thine enemies Thy footstool" (v. 1). Allusion is here made to that promise of the Father to the Son for the purpose of supplying additional confirmation of what had just been declared. In vv. 10, 12 (also in 14), the utter *needlessness* for any repetition of Christ's sacrifice is shown, here the *impossibility* of it. From the beginning, a state of glory and position of honour had been appointed the Mediator following on the presentation of His offering to God. He was to take His place on the throne of heaven, till His foes were completely subjugated: therefore to enter the place of service and die again He was no longer capable!

The suffering Saviour has been invested with unlimited power and dominion, and nothing now remains but the accomplishing of all those effects which His sacrifice was designed to procure. These are twofold; the saving of His elect, the subjugating of all revolters against God, for "He hath appointed a day in the which He will judge the world in righteousness by that Man whom He hath ordained" (Acts 17:31). The Redeemer having perfected His great work, now calmly awaits the fulfilment of the Father's promise: cf. 1 Cor. 15:25-27. Christ will yet put forth His mighty power and overthrow every proud rebel against Him. He will yet say, "I will tread them in Mine anger, and trample them in My fury, and their blood shall be sprinkled upon My garments . . . for the day of vengeance is in Mine heart" (Isa. 63:3, 4): cf. Rev. 14:20. Then will men experience the terribleness of "the wrath of the Lamb" (Rev. 6:16).

The "*wrath* of the Lamb" is as much a perfection as is the "*love* of Christ." In His overthrow of God's adversaries, His glory shines as truly as when He conducts the redeemed into the Father's House. He is equally to be adored when we behold His vesture stained with the blood of His enemies, as when we see His life ebbing from His side pierced for us. Each was an intrinsic part of that work assigned Him of the Father. Though in our present state we are apt to shrink-back with horror, as we contemplate Him saying to those who despised and rejected Him. "Depart from Me, ye cursed," yet in that day we shall praise Him for it. "Oh! what a triumph that will be, when men, wicked men, persecutors, and those who opposed Christ, are all cast into the lake that burneth" (C. H. Spurgeon).

A remarkable adumbration (shadowing forth) of what has just been before us was made by God in A. D. 70. During the days of His flesh, the enemies of Christ pursued Him with relentless hatred. Nor was their enmity appeased when they had hounded Him to death: their rage continued to vent itself upon His followers. No one can read through the book of Acts without discovering many an evidence of the rancour of apostate Judaism against the early Christians. Loudly did the Jews boast of their triumph against Jesus of Nazareth, and for a time it looked as though they would prevail against His church. Though the issue hung in suspense for some years, God made a complete end to the same by utterly destroying them as a nation, and thereby gave a pledge of the eternal destruction of those who obey not the Gospel. In sending the Romans to burn their city and raze their temple, we discover a solemn foreshadowing of that which shall yet take place when Christ says, "But those Mine enemies, which would not that I should reign over them, bring hither and slay before Me" (Luke 19:27).

But let our final thought of this 13th verse be one of a different tenor. In the word "expecting" we have manifested again the lovely moral perfections of the Mediator. Christ is able to destroy all His enemies in a moment, yet for nineteen centuries He has bided His time. Why? Because, even in Heaven, He meekly and gladly bows to the Father's pleasure. His final triumph is still postponed, because He calmly *waits* that day which God has "appointed" (Acts 17:31). Therefore do we read of "the kingdom and *patience* of Jesus Christ" (Rev. 1:9). In this too He sets us an example. Whatever be our lot and condition, however the forces of evil rage against us, we are to possess our souls in patience (Luke 21:19), knowing that there is a *"set time"* to favour Zion (Psa. 102:13). Ere long, every enemy of Christ and of His church shall be overthrown — overthrown, *not* "reconciled": "His enemies be made His footstool" plainly gives the lie to the dreams of Universalists!

"For by one offering He hath perfected for ever them that are sanctified" (v. 14). Three things claim our attention here: first, the relation of this view to the context; second, what is meant by "perfected for ever"?; third, who are the "sanctified"? The link between our verse and what precedes is contained in the opening "For," which has a double force. First, it intimates that what is now said furnishes additional proof for the thesis of the whole passage: the very fact that the one offering of Christ has "perfected for ever" (contrast 7:**17**!) those sanctified by God, gives further demonstration of the efficacy and sufficiency of it, and the needlessness of any repetition. Second, the same fact manifests the meetness of the Mediator's sitting at God's right hand until His enemies are made His footstool—His work having accomplished such a blessed result, He is entitled both to rest and reward.

"For by one offering He hath perfected for ever them that are sanctified." The word for "perfected" literally means "completed" or "consummated." It is more of an objective than a subjective perfection which is here in view, as the immediate context and the whole epistle shows. This verse is not speaking of the Church's eternal state in Glory, but of its present standing before God. By His sacrifice Christ has procured for His people the full pardon of sin and peace before God thereon. The "one offering" of the Lord Jesus possesses such infinite merits (being that of an infinite or Divine person in a holy humanity), that it has wrought out a complete expiation and secured for "His own" personal acceptance with and access to God, a priestly standing and covenant nearness before Him.

Because their salvation has been accomplished by the vicarious obedience and vicarious suffering, in life and in death, by no less a person than Immanuel, because He glorified God's law by keeping it fully and enduring its curse, His people are both perfectly justified and perfectly sanctified, that is, a complete righteousness and complete fitness to worship in the Temple of God is theirs, not in themselves, but through Christ their Head. Their *title* to heaven is founded alone on the righteousness of Christ imputed to them. Their *fitness* is given when the Holy Spirit regenerates them. Their present *enjoyment* of the same is determined by the maintenance of communion with God day by day. Their perfect and eternal enjoyment thereof will issue from their *glorification* at the return of the Saviour.

The word "perfected" here is to be understood in a sacrificial rather than in an experimental sense. It has reference to the Christian's *right* to stand in the holy presence of God in unclouded peace. Our title so to do is as valid now as it will be when we are glorified, for that title rests alone on the sacrificial work of our Substitute, finished on the cross. It rests on something altogether external to ourselves, altogether apart from what God's sovereign grace works in us or through us, either when we first believe or afterwards. We are precious in the sight of God according to the preciousness of Christ: see Eph. 1:6, John 17:22, 23. Yet, let it be added that, this perfect objective sanctification (our consecration to God by *Christ*) in no wise renders the less requisite our need of being constantly cleansed, experimentally, by the Spirit's use of the Word: John 13:10, 1 Pet. 1:2 etc.

Those perfected by the "one offering" of Christ are "them that are sanctified," or more literally, simply "the sanctified," the reference being to those who were *eternally set apart* by the Father

(Jude 1). The persons of the elect are variously designated in this epistle. They are referred to as "heirs of salvation" (1:14), "sons" (2:10), "brethren" of Christ, (2:12), "partakers of the heavenly calling" (3:1), "heirs of promise" (6:17), "the house of Israel" and "of Judah" (8:8); but here "the sanctified," because the Spirit's object in the whole of this passage is to trace everything to its originating source, namely, the imperial will of a sovereign God.

CHAPTER FORTY-NINE

Sanctification

(Heb. 10:15-18)

The verses which are now to be before us bring to a close the principal argument which the apostle was setting before the Hebrews; that which follows, partakes more of the nature of a series of exhortations, drawn from the thesis which had previously been established. The immeasurable superiority of Christianity over Judaism, seen in the glorious person of our great High Priest and the perfect efficacy of His sacrifice, had been fully demonstrated. "Here we are come unto a full end of the dogmatical part of this epistle, a portion of Scripture filled with heavenly and glorious mysteries, the light of the church of the Gentiles, the glory of the people Israel, the foundation and bulwark of faith evangelical" (J. Owen). Immediately afterward that eminent expositor added, (words which most suitably express the writer's own sentiments) the following:—

"I do therefore here, with all humility, and sense of my own weakness and utter inability for so great a work, thankfully own the guidance and assistance which hath been given to me in the interpretation of it, so far as it is, or may be of use unto the church, as a mere effect of sovereign and undeserved grace. From that alone it is, that having many and many a time been at an utter loss as to the mind of the Holy Spirit, and finding no relief in the worthy labours of others, He hath graciously answered my poor, weak supplications, in supplies of the light and evidence of truth."

The relation of our present passage to what has been before us in the last article is this: in vv. 11-14 the perfection of Christ's sacrifice is declared: first, comparatively in 11-14, and then singly in 14; while in vv. 15-17 a further proof or confirmation of this is given from the Old Testament Scriptures. So efficacious was the mediatorial work of Christ that, "by one offering He hath perfected forever them that are sanctified." Said the Puritan Charnock, "That one offering was of such infinite value that it perfectly purchased the taking away of sin, both in the guilt, filth, and power, and was a sufficient price for all the grace believers should need for their perfect sanctification to the end of the world. There was the satisfaction of His blood for the removal of our guilt, and a treasure of merit for the supply of our grace" (Vol. 5, p. 231).

There is a further link between our preceding portion and the present one. In v. 14 the apostle had declared "For by one offering He hath perfected forever them that are sanctified," now he describes those marks by which the "sanctified" are to be *identified.* Unto those who really value their souls and are deeply concerned about their eternal destiny, this is a vitally important consideration. How may I know that I am one of that favoured company for whom the incarnate Son of God offered Himself a sacrifice for sin? What clear and conclusive evidence do I possess that I am among the "sanctified?" Answer to these weighty questions is furnished in the verses which we are now to ponder. May each reader join with the writer in begging God to grant him an honest heart and a discerning eye to see whether or no they describe what has been actually made good in his own experience.

"Whereof the Holy Spirit also is a witness to us: for after that He had said before, This is the covenant that I will make with them after those days, saith the Lord, I will put My laws into their hearts, and in their minds will I write them; and their sins and iniquities will I remember no more. Now where remission of these is, there is no more offering for sin" (vv. 15-18). There are two parts to the assertion made in v. 14: first, "them that are sanctified"; second, such are "perfected forever." In the proof-text which the apostle here gives, both of these are found, though in the inverse order: the "sanctified" are they in whose hearts God puts His laws; those who are "perfected forever" are they whose sins God remembers no more.

"Whereof the Holy Spirit also is a witness to us" (v. 15). "The foundation of the whole preceding discourse of the apostle, concerning the glory of the priesthood of Christ, and the efficacy of His sacrifice, was laid in the description of the new covenant, whereof He was the Mediator, which was confirmed and ratified by His sacrifice, as the old covenant was by the blood of bulls and goats (9:10-13). Having now abundantly proved and demonstrated what he designed concerning them both, His priesthood and His sacrifice, He gives us a confirmation of the whole, from the testimony of the Holy Spirit, in the description of that covenant which he had given before. And because the crisis to which he had brought his argument and disputation, was, that the Lord Christ, by reason of the dignity of His person and office, with the everlasting efficacy of His sacrifice, was to offer Himself but once, which virtually includes all that he had before taught and declared, including in it an immediate demonstration of the insufficiency of all those sacrifices which were often repeated, and consequently their removal out of the church; he returns unto those words of the Holy Spirit for the proof of this particular also" (J. Owen).

"Whereof the Holy Spirit also is a witness to us" (v. 15). Three questions are suggested by these words. First, *unto what* is the Holy Spirit a "Witness?" Second, what is the "also" to be connected with — *who else* has witnessed to the same thing? Third, *how* does the Holy Spirit "witness?" Let us, then, seek answers to these queries.

Unto what is it that the Holy Spirit is here said to be a "Witness?" If we go back no farther than the preceding verse, the answer would be, unto the fact that the one satisfaction which has been made by the Redeemer secures the eternal perfection of all who are sanctified; what follows in vv. 16-18 bears this out. Nevertheless, we are persuaded that it is necessary to look farther afield if we are to obtain the deeper and fuller answer. The satisfaction made by the Redeemer was the fulfilling of the Divine "will," the performing of that which had been stipulated in the everlasting covenant; and it is of *that* the whole context is speaking. The Holy Spirit was present when that wondrous compact was made between the Father and the Mediator, and through Jeremiah He made known a part of its glorious promises. The proof of this will become clearer as we advance.

Second, "whereof the Holy Spirit *also* is a witness to us" looks back to v. 9. There we have the testimony of the Son unto the eternal decree which God had made, and which He had come to execute; here (in vv. 17, 18) that of the Spirit to what the Father had promised the Mediator He would do unto His covenant people. Thus, we may here behold the three persons of the Godhead concurring. Yet there is such a fullness to the words of Scripture that we do not think what has just been pointed out exhausts the scope of this word "also." The leading thought of the context (and of the epistle) is the sufficiency, finality, and efficacy of the one sacrifice of Christ. *That* was "witnessed" to when the Mediator "*sat down* on the right hand of God" (v. 12); and the Holy Spirit is *also* a witness to us of the same blessed fact by means of His work of sanctification in the hearts and minds of those for whom Christ died.

As to *how* the Spirit witnesses to us, the first method is by means of the written Word; specifically, by what He gave out by the prophet Jeremiah. The apostle had argued the *sufficiency* of Christ's sacrifice from its singularity (v. 12), in contrast from the many sacrifices of Judaism (v. 11); and the *finality* of it from the fact that He was now "sat down," indicating that His work of oblation was finished. To this the Hebrews might object that what the apostle had pointed out were but plausible reasonings, to which they could not acquiesce unless they were confirmed by the clear testimony of Scripture; and therefore did he now quote once more from the memorable prophecy of Jeremiah 31, which clearly established the conclusions he had drawn. *How* the terms of that prophecy ratified his deductions will appear in the sequel.

"Whereof the Holy Spirit also is a witness to us." As we have seen, the first reference here is to what is recorded in Jer. 31:31-34. The Holy Spirit is the Author of the Scriptures, for "The prophecy came not at any time by the will of man, but holy men of God spake *moved by the Holy Spirit*" (2 Pet. 1:21). But more, the Holy Scriptures are also the testimony of the Holy Spirit because of His presence and authority in them continually. As we read the written Word, we are to recognize the voice of the Spirit of truth speaking to us immediately out of them. As we do this, we shall recognize that Word as the final court of appeal in *all* matters of conduct. That Word alone is that whereunto our faith is to be resolved.

"Whereof the Holy Spirit is also a witness *to us*." The last two words need to be carefully observed in these days, when there are so many who (under the guise of "rightly dividing the Word") would rob the children of God of a part of their needed bread—let the reader be much on his guard against such men. What the prophet Jeremiah gave out was for the people of God in *his* day. True, and hundreds of years later the apostle did not hesitate to say that what Jeremiah wrote was equally *"to us"*; note particularly, not only "for" us, but "*to* us"! The whole of God's Word, beginning to end, was written for the good of His people until the end of the world.

But further, the Holy Spirit is not only a Witness unto us of the everlasting covenant and of the efficacy of Christ's offering through the written Word objectively, but also by His application of that Word to us subjectively. As said the apostle unto the Corinthians, "Forasmuch as ye are manifestly declared to be the epistle of Christ ministered by us, written not with ink, but with the Spirit of the living God; not in tables of stone, but in **fleshy** tables *of the heart*" (2 Cor. 3:3). A cause is known by its effects, a tree by its fruits; so the value and virtue of Christ's sacrifice are witnessed to us by the Spirit through the powerful workings of His grace on our hearts. Every grace implanted by the Spirit in the Christian's soul was purchased by the obedience and blood of Christ, and are living evidences of the worth of them.

"For after that He had said before" (v. 15). The particular proof-text from Jeremiah which the apostle was about to quote is prefaced by these words of his own, as also is the clause "saith the Lord" in the next verse the apostle's language. If it be asked, *what* was it that was said "before?" the answer is, "This is the covenant that I will make with them." If it be inquired, what is that which is said *after?* even this: "I will put My laws into their hearts" etc. The particular point to be observed is, that these Divine mercies of God's putting His laws into our hearts and forgiving our sins, are the immediate fruits of Christ's sacrifice, but more remotely, are the fulfillment of God's covenant-promises unto the Mediator.

The everlasting covenant which God made with Christ is *the ground* of all the good which He does to His people. Proof of this statement is supplied in many a scripture, which is little pondered in these days. For example, in Ex. 6:5 we find Jehovah saying to Moses, "I have remembered My covenant," which is rendered as the reason for His bringing of Israel out of Egypt. Again, in Psa. 105:8 we are told, "He hath remembered His covenant forever." So in Ezek. 16:60 God declares, "Nevertheless I will remember My covenant with thee in the days of thy youth, and I will establish unto thee an everlasting covenant." While in Luke 1, we read in the prophecy of Zacharias, "Blessed be the Lord God of Israel; for He hath visited and redeemed His people, and hath raised up an horn of salvation for us in the house of His servant David; as He spake by the mouth of His holy prophets, which have been since the world began: that we should be saved from our enemies, and from the hand of all that hate us; To perform the mercy to our fathers, and *to remember His holy covenant*" (vv. 68-72).

"This is the covenant that I will make with them after those days, saith the Lord" (v. 16). The reference is to the "new covenant" of Jer. 31:31, so called not because it was new *made,* for with respect to its original constitution it was made with the elect in Christ their Head from all eternity (Titus 1:1,2); nor as newly *revealed,* for it was made known in measure to the O.T. saints; but it is so referred to in distinction from the former *administration* of it, which had waxen old and vanished away. It is also called "new" because of the "new heart," "new spirit," "new song" which it bestows, and because of new ordinances (baptism and the Lord's supper) which have displaced the old ones of circumcision and the passover-supper. Further, it may suitably be designated as "new" because its vigour and efficacy are perpetual; it will never be antiquated or give place to another.

"I will put My law into their hearts, and in their minds will I write them" (v. 16). And who are the favoured ones in whom God works thus? Those whom He eternally set apart (Eph. 1:4), those whom He gave to the Mediator (John 17:6), those for whom Christ died: "whom He did predestinate, those He also called" (Rom. 8:30). These, and these only, are the ones with whom God deals so graciously. Others may, through religious instruction or personal effort, acquire a theoretical acquaintance with the laws of God, but only His elect have a vital knowledge of Him.

"I will put My laws into their hearts." As we deem this expression of tremendous importance, we will endeavor to explain it according to the measure of light which God has granted us thereon. First, it will aid us to an understanding thereof if we consider the case of Adam. When he left the Creator's hands the law of God was in his heart, or, in other words, he was endowed with all sorts of holy properties, instincts and inclinations unto whatsoever God did command, and an antipathy against all He forbade. That was the "law" of the nature of his heart. The laws of God in Adam were Adam's original *nature,* or constitution of His spirit and soul, as it is the law of nature in beasts to love their young, and of birds to build their nests.

"When God created man at first, He gave him not an outward law written in letters or delivered in words, but an inward law put into his heart, and concreated with him, and wrought in the frame of his soul. And the whole substance of this law of God, the mass of it, was not merely dictates or beams of light in his understanding, directing what to do; but also real, lively, and spiritual dispositions, and inclinations in his will and affections, carrying him on to what was so directed, as to pray, love God, and fear Him; to seek His glory in a spiritual and holy manner. They were inward abilities suited to every duty" (T. Goodwin, Vol. 6, p. 402). The external command of Gen. 2:17 was designed as the *test* of his responsibility; what God had graciously placed within him, was the equipment for the discharging of his responsibility.

Should it be inquired, where is the scripture which teaches that God placed His laws in the heart of unfallen Adam? it is sufficient to reply that Psa. 40:8 presents *Christ* as saying, "Thy law is within My heart," and Rom. 5:14 declares that Adam was "*the figure* of Him that was to come." But more, just as we may discover what grain the earth bears by the stubble which is found in the field, so we may ascertain what was in unfallen man by the ruins of what is yet to be seen in fallen and corrupt humanity. Rom. 2:14 says the Gentiles "do *by nature* the things contained in the law": their very conscience tells them that immorality and murder are crimes. Thus, as an evidence that the law of God was originally the very "nature" of Adam, we have the shadow of it in the hearts of all men.

Alas, Adam did not continue as God created him: he fell, and the consequence was that his heart was corrupted, his very "nature" vitiated, so that the things he once loved he now hated, and what he should have hated, he now served. Thus it is with all of his fallen descendants: being "alienated from the life of God through the ignorance that is in them, because of the blindness of their heart" (Eph. 4:18) their carnal mind "is not subject to the law of God, neither indeed can be" (Rom. 8:7). Instead of that holy "nature" or spiritual propensities and properties, man is now indwelt and dominated by *sin;* hence, Rom. 7:23 teaches us that sin is a "law" in our members, namely, "the law of sin and death" (Rom. 8:2). And thus it is that in Jer. 17:1 (as the opposite of Heb. 10:16) sin and corruption in the heart is said to be *"written* with a pen of iron, with the point of a diamond."

Now in regeneration and sanctification the "image" of God, after which Adam was originally created, is again stamped upon the soul: see Col. 3:10; the laws of God are written on the Christian's heart, so that it becomes his very "nature" to serve, obey, please, honour, and glorify God. Because the law of God is renewed again in the soul, it is termed the "law of the mind" (Rom. 7:23), for the mind is now regulated by the authority of God and turns as instinctively to Him as does the sunflower to the sun, and as the needle answers to the loadstone. Thus, the renewed heart *"delights* in the law of God" (Rom. 7:22), and "serves the law of God" (Rom. 7:25), it being its very "nature" so to do.

This wondrous change which takes place in each of those for whom Christ died is here attributed directly and absolutely to God: "*I will* put My laws into their hearts, and in their minds *will I* write them." This is much more than a bare offer being made unto men, far beyond an ineffectual invitation which is to be received. It is an invincible and miraculous operation of the Holy Spirit, which thoroughly transforms the favoured subjects to it. Only He who first made man, can remake him. None but the Almighty can repair the awful damage which the Fall wrought, counteract the dreadful power of sin, deliver the heart from the lusts of the flesh, the thraldom of the world, the bondage of Satan, and re-write upon it His holy law, so that He will be loved supremely and served sincerely and gladly.

"I will put My laws into their hearts." This is in contrast from those who were under the old, or Sinaitic covenant. There the "ten words" were engraven upon tables of stone, not only to intimate thereby their fixed and permanent authority, but also to figure forth the *hardness* of the hearts of the unregenerate people to whom they were given. But under the new covenant — that is, the *administration* of the everlasting covenant and the *application* of its grace to God's elect in this Gospel dispensation — God gives efficacy to His holy law in the souls of His people. First, by subduing and largely removing the enmity of the natural heart against Him and his law, which subduing is figuratively spoken of as a circumcising of the heart (Deut. 30:6) and a "taking away the stony heart" (Ezek. 36:26). Second, by implanting the principle of obedience to His law, which is figuratively referred to as the giving of "an heart of flesh" and the "writing of His laws upon the heart."

Observe very particularly, dear reader, that God here says *not* "I will put My promises" but "My *laws* in their hearts." He will not relinquish His claims: unreserved subjection to His will is what His justice requires and what His power secures. The grand triumph of grace is, that "enmity" against the law (Rom. 8:7) is displaced by "love" for the law (Psa. 119:97). This is it which explains that word in Psa. 19:7, "The *law* of the Lord is perfect *converting* the soul." It will probably surprise most of our readers (alas that it should do so) to be told that the Gospel never yet "converted" anybody. No, it is the law which the Spirit uses to convict of rebellion against God, and not until the soul penitently repudiates and forsakes his rebellion, is it ready for the message of peace which the Gospel brings.

The careful reader will notice there is a slight difference between the wording of Heb. 8:10 and 10:16. In the former it is "I will put My laws into their minds, and write them in their hearts," but in the passage now before us the two clauses are reversed. One reason for this is as follows: Heb. 8:10 give the Divine *order of operation*: the mind is first informed, and then the heart is reformed. Moreover, in Heb. 8:10 it is a question of *knowing God,* and for that, the understanding must be enlightened before the affections can be drawn out of Him — none will love an unknown God. The Spirit begins by conveying to the regenerate an efficacious knowledge of the authority and excellency of God's laws, giving them a powerful realization both of their binding force and spirituality; and then He communicates a love for them, so that their hearts are heartily inclined toward them.

When the apostle defines the seat of the corruption of our nature, he places it in the "mind" and "heart": "Walk not as other Gentiles walk, in the vanity of their *mind;* having the understanding darkened, being alienated from the life of God through the ignorance that is in them, because of the blindness of their *heart.*" Therefore does the Divine work of sanctification, or the renovating of our natures, consist of the rectifying both of the mind and heart, and this, by furnishing them with the principles of faith, love, and adherence to God. Thus, *the grace of* the new covenant (purchased for His people by Christ) is as extensive to repair our "nature" as sin is (in its residence and power) to deprave us. God desireth truth "in the inward parts" (Psa. 51:6) — not that outward conformity to His law may be dispensed with, for that is required too, but unless it proceed from an inward love for His law, the external actions cannot be accepted by Him.

"From these things we may easily discern the nature of that grace which is contained in this first branch of the first promise of the covenant. And this is the effectual operation of His Spirit, in the renovation and saving illumination of our minds, whereby they are habitually made conformable unto the whole law of God, that is, the rule and the law of our obedience in the new covenant, and enabled unto all acts and duties that are required of us. And this is the first grace promised and communicated unto us by virtue of this covenant, as it was necessary that so it should be. For, 1. the mind is the principal seat of all spiritual obedience. 2. The proper and peculiar actings of the mind in discerning, knowing, judging, must go before the actings of the will and affections, much more before all outward practices. 3. The depravation of the mind is such by blindness, darkness, vanity and enmity, that nothing can inflame our souls, or make an entrance towards the reparation of our natures, but an internal, spiritual, saving operation of grace upon the mind" (J. Owen).

In Heb. 10:16 the heart is mentioned before the mind because the Spirit is here giving the Divine standard for us to measure ourselves by: it is the test whereby we may ascertain whether or no we are among the "sanctified," who have been perfected forever by the one offering of Christ. An intellectual knowledge of God's laws is no proof of regeneration, but a genuine heart-acquaintance with them is. The questions I need to honestly face are such as these: Is there within me that which answers to the Law without me? That is, is it actually and truly my desire and determination to be regulated and controlled by the revealed will of God? Is it the deepest longing of my soul, and the chief business of my life, to please and serve God? Is it the great burden of my prayers that He will work in me "both to will and to do of *His* good pleasure?" Is my deepest grief occasioned by my failure to be altogether holy in my wishes and words and ways? Experimentally, the more we love God, the more shall we discern the excellency of His law.

"And their sins and iniquities will I remember no more" (v. 17). Notice again the *order* of our passage: what is found here comes *after* v. 16, and not before. In the order of grace, justification (of which forgiveness is the negative side) precedes sanctification, but in the believer's apprehension it is otherwise: I can only ascertain God's justifying of me, by making sure I have within the fruits of His sanctifying me. I must study the effects to discover the cause. In like manner, God elects before He calls, or regenerates, but I have to make my *calling* "sure" in order to obtain evidence of my election: see 2 Pet. 1:10. There are many who give no sign of God's law being written in their hearts, who nevertheless claim to have had their sins forgiven by Him; but such are sadly deceived. Scripture entitles none to regard themselves as Divinely pardoned save those who have been saved from self-will and self-pleasing.

"And their sins and iniquities will I remember no more." These words must not be understood to signify that the sins of God's people have vanished from His *essential* mind, but rather that they will never be recalled by Him as He exercises His office as *Judge*. Our Substitute having already discharged our liabilities and Justice having been fully satisfied, payment cannot be demanded twice over. "There is therefore now no condemnation to them which are in Christ Jesus" (Rom. 8:1). This is the negative side of the believer's justification, that his sins are *not* reckoned to his account; the positive aspect is that the perfect law-righteousness of Christ *is* imputed to him.

"Now where remission of these is, there is no more offering for sin" (v. 18). Here the apostle draws the irrefutable conclusion from the premises he had so fully established. Before pondering it, let us give a brief summary of these wonderful verses. First, the everlasting covenant is the foundation of all God's gracious dealings with His elect. Second, that eternal compact between the Father and the Mediator is now being administered under the "new covenant." Third, the design of this covenant is not to set apart a people unto external holiness only, but to so sanctify them that they should be holy in heart and life. Fourth, this sanctification of the elect is effected by the communication of effectual grace unto them for their conversion and obedience, which is here (under a figure) spoken of as God's putting His laws into their hearts and writing them in their minds. Fifth, this practical sanctification is God's *continuation* of that work of grace which He begins in us at regeneration — our glorification is the *completing* of the same, for then the last remains of sin will be removed from us, and we shall be perfectly conformed to the image of His Son.

"Now where remission of these is, there is no more offering for sin." These words give the apostle's application of the Scripture quoted from Jeremiah, which was made for the express purpose of demonstrating the perfection of Christ's sacrifice. The conclusion is irresistible: the one offering of Christ has secured that the grace of the everlasting covenant *shall be* communicated unto all of those for whom He died, both in the sanctifying and justifying of their persons. Since then their sins are all gone from before the face of God, *no* further sacrifice is needed.

CHAPTER FIFTY

Access to God

(Heb. 10:19-23)

The verses which are now to engage our attention contain the apostle's transition from the doctrinal to the practical part of the epistle, for privileges and duties are never to be separated. Having at great length discoursed upon the priestly office of Christ in the foregoing part of the epistle, he now sums up in a few words the scope and substance of all he had been saying (vv. 19-21), and then draws the plain inference from the whole (v. 22). Like a wise masterbuilder, he first digs till he comes to the foundation, and then calls himself and others to build upon it with confidence. Having demonstrated the vast superiority of Christianity over Judaism, the apostle now exhorts his Christian readers to avail themselves of all their blessed advantages and enjoy the great privileges which have been conferred upon them.

"The apostle's great argument is concluded, and the result is placed before us in a very short summary. We have boldness to enter into the holiest by the blood of Jesus, by a new and living way; and we have in the heavenly sanctuary a great Priest over the house of God. All difficulties have been removed, perfectly and forever. We have access; and He who is the way is also the end of the way; He is even now our great Priest, interceding for us, and our all-sufficient Mediator, providing us with every needful help.

"On this foundation rests a threefold exhortation. 1. Let us draw near with a true heart, in the full assurance of faith. 2. Let us hold fast the profession of hope without wavering. 3. Let us consider one another to provoke unto love and to good works, labouring and waiting together, and helping one another in the unity of brethren. Faith, hope, and love — this is the threefold result of Christ's entrance into heaven, spiritually discerned. A believing, hoping, and loving attitude of heart corresponds to the new covenant revelation of Divine grace" (A. Saphir).

"In these words the apostle enters on the last part of the epistle, which is wholly hortatory. For though there be some occasional intermixtures of doctrine consonant to those which are insisted on before, yet the professed design of the whole remainder of the epistle is to propose to, and press on the Hebrews such duties of various sorts, as the truths he had insisted on, do direct unto, and make necessary to all that believe. And in all his exhortations there is a mixture of the *ground* of the duties exhorted to, of their *necessity,* and of the *privilege* which we have in being admitted to them, and accepted with them, all taken from the priesthood and sacrifice of Christ, with the effects of them, and the benefits which we receive thereby" (J. Owen).

The same order of Truth may be clearly seen in other epistles of the apostle Paul. In Romans, the first eleven chapters are devoted to doctrinal exposition, the next four being practical, setting forth the Christian's duties: see Rom. 12:1. Likewise in Ephesians: the first three chapters set forth the sovereign grace of God, the last three the Christian's responsibilities: see 4:1. From this the teacher and preacher may gather important instruction, showing him *how* to handle the Word, so that the whole man may be edified. The understanding needs to be enlightened, the conscience searched and comforted, the heart inflamed, the will moved, the affections well ordered. Nothing but doctrine, will produce a cold and conceited people; nothing but exhortation, a discouraged and ill-instructed people.

"Having therefore, brethren, boldness to enter into the holiest by the blood of Jesus" (v. 19). "The preceding part of this epistle has been chiefly occupied with stating, proving, and illustrating some of the grand peculiarities of Christian doctrine; and the remaining part of it is entirely devoted to an injunction and enforcement of those duties which naturally result from the foregoing statements. The paragraph vv. 19-23, obviously consists of two parts: — a statement of principles, which are taken for granted as having been fully proved; and an injunction of duties grounded on the admission of these principles" (J. Brown).

The great privilege which is here announced unto Christians is that they may draw near unto God as accepted worshippers. This privilege is presented under a recapitulation of the principal points which the apostle had been treating of, namely, first, Christians have liberty to enter the presence of God (v. 19). Second, a way has been prepared for them so to do (v. 20). Third, a Guide is provided to direct them in that way (v. 21). These three points are here amplified by showing the nature of this "liberty": it is with "boldness," to enter the presence of God, and that by virtue of Christ's blood. The "way" is described as a "new" and "living" one, and it is ready for our use because Christ has "consecrated" it. The "Guide" is presented by His function, "priest"; His dignity, "great"; His authority, "over the house of God."

"Having therefore, brethren, boldness to enter into the holiest by the blood of Jesus." To "enter into the holiest" is, as v. 22 shows, to "draw near" unto God in Christ, for "no one cometh unto the Father but by Him" (John 14:6). The "Holiest" here is only another name for Heaven, the dwellingplace of God, being designated so in this instance because the holy of holies in the tabernacle and the temple was the type thereof. This is established by what was before us in 9:24, "For Christ is not entered into the holy places made with hands, the figures of the true; but into heaven itself." It is most blessed to link with 10:19 what is said in 9:12: "by His own blood *He* entered in once into the holy place"; the title of the members of His body for entering in the Sanctuary on high, is the same as that of their Head's!

The boldness to "enter into the holiest" which is spoken of in our text is not to be limited to the Christian's going to heaven at death or at the return of the Saviour, but is to be understood as referring to that access unto God in spirit, and by faith, which he now has. Here again we see the tremendous contrast from the conditions obtaining under the old and the new covenants. Under Judaism as such, the Israelites were rigidly excluded from drawing nigh unto Jehovah; His dwellingplace was sealed against them. Nay, even the Levites, privileged as they were to minister in the tabernacle, were barred from the holy of holies. But now the right has been accorded unto all who partake of the blessings of the new covenant, to enjoy free access unto God, to draw near unto His throne as supplicants, to enter His temple as worshippers, to sit at His table as happy children.

Most blessedly was this set forth by Christ in the close of that remarkable parable in Luke 15. There we find the prodigal — having "come to himself"—saying, "I will arise and *go to* my Father." He arose and went, and *where* do we find him? Outside the door, or looking in at the window? No, but *inside* the House. Sovereign grace had given him boldness to "enter." And why not? Having confessed his sins, he had received the "kiss" of reconciliation, and the "best robe" had been placed upon him, and thus he was *fitted* to enjoy the Father's house. In perfect accord with our Lord's teaching in that parable, we have been told here in Heb. 10 that "by one offering He hath perfected forever them that are sanctified," and because of this, God has put His laws into their hearts, written them upon their minds, and avowed that their sins and iniquities He would "remember no more."

Here, then, is the force of the "therefore" in our present verse. Inasmuch as Christ's satisfaction has removed every legal obstacle, and inasmuch as the work of the Spirit in the Christian has made him "*meet to be* partaker of the inheritance of the saints in light" (Col. 1:12), there is not only nothing to hinder, but every reason and motive to induce us *to* draw near unto God and pour out our hearts before Him in thanksgiving, praise, and worship. In 4:16 we are invited to "come boldly unto the throne of grace, that we may *obtain mercy,* and find grace to help in time of need"; but here in 10:19-22 it is *worship* which is more specifically in view — entrance into "the holiest," which was the place of worship and communion, see Num. 7:89.

A further word of explanation needs to be given on the term "boldness." Saphir rightly pointed out that this expression "must be understood here objectively, not subjectively, else the subsequent exhortation would be meaningless"; in other words, the reference is to something outside ourselves and not to a condition of heart. Literally, the Greek signifies "Having therefore, brethren, boldness for entrance into the holiest," and hence, some have rendered it "the *right* of entrance." Most probably the word is designed to point a double contrast from conditions under the old covenant. Those under it had a legal prohibition against entering the sacred abode of Jehovah, but Christians have a perfect title to do so. Again, those under Judaism were *afraid* to do so, whereas faith now perceives that we may come to God with the fullest assurance, because He has accepted us "in the Beloved" (Eph. 1:6). There is no valid reason why we should hesitate to draw near unto our Father in perfect freedom of spirit.

"By the blood of Jesus." This is the meritorious cause which procures the Christian's right of entrance into the "Holiest" — the place where all the tokens of God's grace and glory are displayed (9:3, 4). The blood of the Jewish sacrifices did not and could not obtain such liberty of access into the immediate presence of God. The blood of Jesus *has* done so, both in respect unto God as an oblation, and in respect unto the consciences of believers by its application. As an oblation or sacrifice, the atonement of Christ has removed every legal obstacle between God and believers. It fulfilled the demands of His law, removed its curse, and broke down the "middle wall of partition"; in token whereof, the veil of the temple was rent in twain from the top to the bottom, when the Saviour expired. So too the Holy Spirit has so applied the efficacy of the blood to the consciences of Christians that they are delivered from a sense of guilt, freed from their dread of God, and enabled to approach Him in a spirit of liberty.

"By a new and living way, which He hath consecrated for us, through the veil, that is to say, His flesh" (v. 20). This presents to us the second inducement and encouragement for Christians to avail themselves and make use of the unspeakable privilege which Christ has secured for them. In order to understand these verses, it is necessary to bear in mind that N. T. privileges are here expressed in the O.T. dialect. The highest privilege of fallen man is to have access unto the presence of God, his offended Lord and Sovereign: the only way of approach is through Christ, of whom the tabernacle (and the temple) was an illustrious type. In allusion to those figures Christ is here presented to our faith in a threefold view.

First, as a *gate* or door, by which we enter into the Holiest. No sooner had Adam sinned, than the door of access to the majesty of God was bolted against him, and all his posterity, the cherubim with the flaming sword standing in his way (Gen. 3:24). But now the flaming sword of justice being quenched in the blood of the Surety (Zech. 13:7), the door of access is again wide open. The infinite wisdom of God has devised a way how His "banished" may be brought home again to His presence. (2 Sam. 14:14), namely, through the satisfaction of Christ.

Second, to encourage us in our approaches to God in Christ. He is also presented to us under the figure of "a new and living *way,* which He hath consecrated *for us.*" "Having told us that we have 'an entrance into the holiest,' he now declares what the way is whereby we may do so. The only way into the holiest under the tabernacle was a passage with blood through the sanctuary, and then a turning aside of the veil. But the whole church was forbidden the use of this way, and it was appointed for no other end but typically, that in due time there should be a way opened unto believers into the presence of God, which was not yet prepared. And this the apostle describes. 1. From the preparation of it: 'which He hath consecrated.' 2. From the properties of it: it was a 'new and living way.' 3. From the tendency of it, which he expresseth, first, typically, or with respect unto the old way under the tabernacle: it was 'through the veil.' Secondly, in an exposition of that type: 'that is, His flesh.' In the whole, there is a description of the exercise of faith in our access unto God by Christ Jesus" (J. Owen).

In the previous verse it was declared that heaven has been opened unto the people of God. But here Christ is set forth more as the antitype of that "ladder" (Gen. 28:12, John 1:51), which, being set up on earth, reaches to heaven. In this respect Christ is styled "the Way, the Truth and the Life" (John 14:6), for He is the only true "way" which conducts unto God. That "way" is variously referred to in Scripture as the "way of life" (Prov. 10:17), the "way of holiness" (Isa. 35:8), the "good way" (Jer. 6:16), the "way of peace" (Luke 1:79), the "way of salvation" (Acts 16:17). All of these refer to the same thing, namely, the only path unto heaven. Christ Himself is that "way" in a twofold sense: first, when the heart turns away from every other object which competes for the first place in its affections, abandons all confidence in its own righteousness, and lays hold of the Saviour. Second, when grace is diligently sought to take Christ as our Exemplar, following "*His* steps" in the path of unreserved and joyful obedience to God.

The "way" to God is here said to be "a new and living" one. The word for "new" is really "newly slain," for the simple verb "occido" from which it is compounded signifies "to slay." The avenue of approach to God has been opened unto us because Christ was put to death in this way. But this word "new" is *not* to be taken absolutely, as though this "way" had no existence previously to the death of Christ, for all the O. T. saints had passed along it too. No, it was neither completely "new" as to its contrivance, revelation, or use. Why then is it called "new"? In distinction from the old way of life under the covenant of works, in keeping with the new covenant, because it was now only made fully manifest (Eph. 3:5), and because of its perennial vigour—it will never grow old.

This "way" unto God is also said to be a "living" one, and this for at least three reasons. First, in opposition unto the way to God under Judaism, which was by the *death* of an animal, and was the cause of death unto any who used it, excepting the high priest. Second, because of its perpetual efficacy: it is not a lifeless thing, but has a spiritual and vital power in our access to God. Third, because of its effects: it leads to life, and effectually brings us thereunto. "It is called a living way, because all that symbolizes Christ must be represented as possessing vitality. Thus we read of Him as the living stone, the living bread, etc." (A. Saphir). Probably this epithet also looks to Christ's resurrection: though slain, the grave could not hold Him; He is now "alive for evermore," and by working in His people repentance, faith, and obedience, conducts them safely through unto life everlasting.

This new and living way unto God has been "consecrated for us" by Christ. It is a path consecrated by Him for the service and salvation of man; a way of access to the eternal sanctuary for the sinner which has been set apart by the Redeemer for this service of men" (A. Barnes). As Christ Himself is the "way," the meaning would be, that He has dedicated Himself for the use of sinners in their dealings with God — "for their sakes I sanctify Myself" (John 17:19). As the "way" is also to be regarded as the path which we are called upon to follow through this world as we journey to heaven, Christ has "consecrated" or fitted it for our use by leaving us an example that we should follow His steps — "when He putteth forth His own sheep, He goeth *before* them" (John 10:4).

"The phrase 'consecrated for us' giveth us to understand that Christ hath made the way to heaven fit for us, and this by His three offices. First, as a Priest, He hath truly dedicated it, and that by His own blood, as by the blood of sacrifices things were consecrated under the law. Christ by His blood has taken away our sins, which made the way to heaven impassible. Second, as a Prophet, He hath revealed and made known this way to us. This He did while He was on earth, by Himself; and since His taking into heaven, He hath done it by His ministers (Eph. 4:11). Third, as a King, He causes the way to be laid out, fenced in, and made common for all His people; so as it may well be styled the King's highway" (Wm. Gouge).

"Through the veil, that is to say, His flesh." It is through the humanity of Christ that the way to heaven has been opened, renewed and consecrated. But prior to His death, the very life which was lived by the man Christ Jesus only served to emphasize the awful distance which sinners were from God, just as the beautiful veil in the tabernacle shut out the Israelite from His presence. Moreover, the humanity of Christ was a sin-bearing one, for the iniquities of His people had all been imputed to Him. While, then, the flesh of Christ was uncrucified, proof was before the eyes of men that the curse was not abolished. As long as He tabernacled in this world, it was evident that sin was not yet put away. The veil must be rent, Christ must die, before access to God was possible. When God rent the veil of the temple, clear intimation was given that every hindrance had been removed, and that the way was opened into His presence.

"And having an High Priest over the house of God" (v. 21). Here is the third great privilege of the Christian, the third inducement which is presented to him for approaching unto God, the third character in which Christ is presented unto faith. Whereas it might be objected that though the door be opened and a new and living way consecrated, yet we are too impotent to walk therein, or too sinful to enter into the holiest; therefore, to obviate this, Christ is now set forth as Priest over the house of God. O what encouragement is here! As Priest Christ is "ordained *for* men in things pertaining to God" (5:1). He is a living Saviour within the veil, interceding for His people, maintaining their interests before the Father.

"And having an High Priest over the house of God." The opening "And" shows that the contents of this verse form a link in the chain begun in v. 19, so that they furnish a further ground to help us in approaching unto God. The next word "having," while not in the Greek, is obviously understood, and as the principal verb (needed to complete the sentence) is fetched from v. 19. The adjective should be rendered "great" and not "high": it is not a relative term, in comparison with other priests; but an absolute one, denoting Christ's dignity and excellency: He is "great" in His person, in His worthiness, in His position, in His power, in His compassion.

To show for whom in particular Christ *is* the great Priest, it is here added "over the house of God." "The apostle doth not here consider the sacrifice of Christ, but what He is and doth after His sacrifice, now that He is exalted in heaven; for this was the second part of the office of the high priest. The first was to offer sacrifice for the people, the other was to take the oversight of the house of God: see Zech. 3:6, 7 — Joshua being an eminent type of Christ" (J. Owen). The "house of God" represents the whole family of God both of heaven and earth: compare 3:6. The church here below is what is first comprised in this expression for it is unto it that this encouragement is given, and unto whom this motive of drawing nigh is proposed. But as it is in the heavenly sanctuary that Christ now ministers, and into which we enter by our prayers and spiritual worship, so the "house of God" includes both the church militant and the church triumphant.

When it is said that Christ is "*over* the house of God," it is His headship, lordship, authority, which is in view. The Lord Christ presides over the persons, duties, and worship of believers. In that all their acceptable worship is of His appointment; in that He assists the worshippers by His Spirit for the performance of every duty; in that He directs the government of the church, ordains its officers, and administers its laws; in that He makes their service acceptable with God. He is King in Zion, wielding the scepter, protecting the interests of His church, and, according to His pleasure, overthrowing its enemies. It is the Lord who adds to the church those who are to be saved. He is the alone Head, and as the wife is to be subject to her husband in all things, so the members of Christ's mystical body are to own no other Lord. From Him we are to take our orders; unto Him we must yet render an account.

"Let us draw near with a true heart in full assurance of faith, having our hearts sprinkled from an evil conscience, and our bodies washed with pure water" (v. 22). Having described the threefold privilege which Christians have been granted, the apostle now points out the threefold duty which is entailed; the first of which is here in view, namely, to enter the Holiest, to draw near unto God, as joyful worshippers. To "draw near" unto God is a sacerdotal act, common to all the saints, who are made priests unto God" (Rev. 1:6): the Greek word expressing the whole performance of all Divine worship, approaching unto the Most High to present their praises and petitions, both publicly and privately.

"To draw near to God is an act of the heart or mind, whereby the soul, under the influence of the Spirit, sweetly, and irresistibly returns to God in Christ as its only center of rest. There is a constant improvement of the merit and mediation of Christ in every address made to the Majesty on high. The believer, as it were, fixes himself in the cleft of the Rock of ages; he gets into the secret place of the blessed stair, by which we ascend unto heaven; and then he lifts up his voice in drawing near to God, by the new and living way. He says with David 'I will go unto the altar of God, unto God my exceeding joy.' And if God hides His face, the soul will wait, and bode good at His hand, saying, 'hope thou in God, for I shall yet praise Him: He will command His loving kindness in the daytime, and in the night His song shall be with me.' And if the Lord smiles and grants an answer of peace, he will not ascribe his success to his own faith or fervour, but unto Christ alone" (Condensed from Eben. Erskine, 1733).

"Let us draw near with a true heart in full assurance of faith." This is the requisite manner in which we must approach unto God. It is not sufficient to assume a reverent posture of body, or worship with our lips only; nor is God honoured when we give way to unbelief. A "true heart" is opposed to a double, doubting, distrustful, and hypocritical heart. All dissimilation is to be avoided in our dealings with Him who "trieth the hearts and the reins" and "whose eyes are like a flame of fire."

God desireth truth in the inward parts, and therefore, "Son, give Me thine heart" (Prov. 23:26) is His first demand upon us. Nothing short of this will ever satisfy Him. But more; there must be "a true heart": a sincere, genuine, honest desire and determination to render unto Him that which is His due. We cannot impose upon Him. Beautiful language designed for the ears of men, or emotional earnestness which is only for effect, does not deceive God. "God is spirit; and they that worship Him, *must* worship in spirit and in truth" (John 4:24). How this condemns those who rest satisfied with the mere outward performance of duty, and those who are content to substitute an imposing ritual for real heart dealings with God! O to be able to say with David, "with my whole heart have I sought Thee."

"In full assurance of faith": which means, negatively, without doubting or wavering; positively, with unshaken confidence — not in myself, nor in my faith, but in the merits of Christ, as giving the unquestionable title to draw near unto the thrice holy God. "Full assurance of faith" points to the heart resting and relying upon the absolute sufficiency of the blood of Christ which was shed for my sins, and the efficacy of His present intercession to maintain my standing before God. Faith looks away from self, and eyes the great Priest, who takes my feeble praise or petitions, and, purifying and perfuming them with His own sweet incense (Rev. 8:3, 4), renders them acceptable to God. But let not Satan deter any timid child of God from drawing near unto Him because fearful that he neither possesses a "true heart" or "full assurance of faith." No, if he cannot consciously come *with* them, then let him earnestly come unto the throne of grace *for* them.

"Having our hearts sprinkled from an evil conscience, and our bodies washed with pure water." Here we have a description of the characters of those who are qualified or fitted to enter the Holiest. A twofold preparation is required in order to draw near unto God: the individual must have been both justified and sanctified. Here those two Divine blessings are referred to under the typical terms which obtained during the old covenant.

"Having your hearts sprinkled from an evil conscience." The Jewish cleansing or "sprinkling" with blood related only to that which was eternal, and could not make the conscience perfect (9:9); but the sacrifice of Christ was designed to give peace to the troubled mind and confidence before God. An "evil conscience" is one that accuses of guilt and oppresses because of unpardoned sin. It is by the exercise of faith in the sufficiency of the atoning blood of Christ — the Spirit applying experimentally its efficacious virtue — the conscience is purged. "Being justified by faith, we have peace with God" (Rom. 5:1): we are freed from a sense of condemnation, and the troubled heart rests in Christ.

"And our bodies washed with pure water." This figurative language is an allusion to the cleansing of the priests when they were consecrated to the service of God (Ex. 29:4). The antitypical fulfillment of this is defined in Titus 3:5 as "the washing of regeneration and renewing of the Holy Spirit." But here the emphasis is thrown on the *outward* effects of regeneration upon the daily life of the believer. We need both an internal and an external purification; therefore are we exhorted, "let us cleanse ourselves from all filthiness of the flesh and spirit, perfecting holiness in the fear of God" (2 Cor. 7:1). The sanctity of the body is emphatically enjoined in Scripture: see Rom. 12:1; 1 Cor. 6:16, 20.

The whole of this 22nd verse contains most important teaching on the practical side of communion with God. While the first reference in the cleansing of the conscience and the washing of the body be to the initial experience of the Christian at his new birth, yet they are by no means to be limited thereto. There is a constant cleansing needed, if we are to consciously draw near to the holy God. Daily do we need to confess our sins, that we may be daily pardoned and "cleansed from all unrighteousness" (1 John 1:9). An uneasy conscience is as real a barrier to fellowship with Jehovah, as ceremonial defilement was to a Jew. So too our walk needs to be incessantly washed with the water of the Word (John 13). The Levitical priests were not only washed at the time of induction into their holy office, but were required to wash their hands and feet *every time* they entered the sacred sanctuary (Ex. 30:19, 20).

It is just at this very point that there is so much sad failure today. There is so little exercise of heart before God; so feeble a realization of His high and holy requirements; so much attempting to rush into His presence without any previous preparation. "Due preparation, by *fresh* applications of our souls unto the efficacy of the blood of Christ for the purification of our hearts, that we may be meet to draw nigh to God, is required of us. This the apostle hath special respect to, and the want of it is the bane of public worship. Where this is not, there is no due reverence of God, no sanctification of His name, nor any benefit to be expected unto our own souls" (John Owen).

CHAPTER FIFTY-ONE

Christian Perseverance

(Heb. 10:23, 24)

The verses which are now to be before us are a continuation of those which we pondered in our last article, the whole forming a practical application to the doctrine which the apostle had been expounding in the body of this Epistle. In vv. 17-21 a summary is given of the inestimable blessings and privileges which Christ has secured for His people, namely, their sins and iniquities being blotted out from before the face of the Judge of all (vv. 17, 18), the title to approach unto God as acceptable worshippers (vv. 19-21), the Divine provision for their spiritual maintenance: a great Priest over the house of God (v. 21). Then, in vv. 22-24 the duties and responsibilities of Christians are briefly epitomized, and that, in such terms as we may the better perceive the intimate connection between the results secured by the great Oblation and the corresponding obligations on its beneficiaries.

The passage we are now engaged with is a hortatory one. As we pointed out in our last, the method which is generally followed by the Holy Spirit is to first display the riches of Divine grace, and then to set forth the response which becomes its objects. So it is here. All that is found in vv. 22-24 looks back to and derives its force from the "therefore" at the beginning of v. 19. There is a threefold privilege named: Divine grace has given freedom unto all Christians to approach the heavenly mercy-seat (v. 19); it has bestowed this title through Christ's having "consecrated" for them the way into God's presence (v. 20); and this blessing is permanent, because there abides a great Priest to mediate for them (v. 21). Agreeing thereto, there is a threefold responsibility resting upon the saint, set forth thus: "let us draw near" (v. 22), "let us hold fast the profession of our faith" (v. 23), "let us consider one another to provoke unto love" (v. 24).

The first part of this threefold exhortation matches the first blessing named in the preceding verses: because the all-sufficient sacrifice of Christ has made a perfect and effectual atonement for all the sins of His people, (thereby removing the one great legal barrier which excluded them from the presence of the thrice Holy One), let them freely draw near unto their reconciled God, without fear or doubting. The second part of this exhortation agrees with the second great blessing specified: since Christ has "consecrated for us" a new and living way in which to walk, having left us an example that we should follow His steps, "let us hold fast the profession of our faith without wavering." The third member of the composite exhortation corresponds to the third privilege enumerated: since we have a great Priest over the house of God, "let us consider one another to provoke unto love and good works," and thus conduct ourselves becomingly as in His house.

The order in the three parts of this exhortation calls for our closest attention. The first, treats of our relation to God: the worshipping of Him in spirit and in truth, and in order to do this, the maintaining of a good conscience and the separating of ourselves from all that pollutes. The second, deals with our conduct before men in the world: the refusal to be poisoned by their unbelief and lawlessness, and this by a steady perseverance in the path of duty. The third, defines our responsibility toward fellow-Christians: the mortifying of a selfish spirit, by keeping steadily in view the highest welfare of our brethren and sisters, seeking to encourage them by a godly example, and thus stirring them up unto holy diligence and zeal both Godward and manward. Thus we may see how very comprehensive is the scope of this exhortation, and admire its beautiful arrangement. How much we often miss through failing to carefully note the *connection* of Scripture!

"Let us hold fast the profession of our faith without wavering: For He is faithful that promised" (v. 23). There is some uncertainty as to the Greek here: some manuscripts having "faith" others "hope"; both the R. V. and Bag. Inter. have "the confession of our (the) hope." It seems to us that the A. V. is to be preferred, for while it is true that if we adopt the alternative, we then have "faith" v. 22, "hope" in v. 23, and "love" in v. 24, yet this is more than offset by the weighty fact that *perseverance in the faith* is the theme which is steadily followed by the apostle not only throughout the remainder of this 10th chapter, but also throughout the 11th. We shall therefore adhere to our present version, excepting that "confession" is preferable to "profession."

"Let us hold fast the profession of faith without wavering." The duty here pressed is the same as that which the apostle has spoken of in each parenthesis in his argument (compare 2:13; 3:6 to 4:12; 5:11 to 6:20): the doctrinal section giving force and power unto it. "Faith is here taken in both the principal acceptations of it, namely, that faith whereby we believe, and the faith or doctrine which we do believe. Of both which we make the same profession: of one, as the inward principle; of the other, as the outward rule. This solemn profession of our faith is two-fold: initial, and by the way of continuation in all the acts and duties required thereunto. The first is a solemn giving up of ourselves unto Christ, in a professed subjection unto the Gospel, *and* the ordinances of Divine worship therein contained" (J. Owen).

"Let us hold fast the profession of faith without wavering." Three questions here call for consideration, namely: first, what is meant by "the confession of our faith?" Second, what is signified by "holding it fast?" Third, what is denoted by holding it fast "without wavering?" As the theme here treated of is of such vital importance, and as it is dealt with so very unsatisfactorily by many present-day preachers, we will endeavor to exercise double care as the Spirit is pleased to enable us.

The "confession of our faith" is that solemn acknowledgment which is made by a person when he publicly claims to be a Christian. It is the avowal that he has renounced the world, the flesh, and the devil, for Christ. It is the declaration that he disowns his own wisdom, righteousness and will, and receives the Lord Jesus as his Prophet, Priest and King: his Prophet to instruct him in the will of God, his Priest to meet for him the claims of God, his King to administer in and over him the government of God. It is the owning that he hates sin and desires to be delivered from its power and penalty; that he loves holiness and longs to be conformed to the image of God's Son. It is the claiming that he has thrown down the weapons of his warfare against God, and has now completely surrendered to His just demands upon him. It is the testification that he is prepared to deny self, take up his cross daily, and follow that example which Christ has left him as to how to *live for God* in this world. In a word, it is the publishing abroad that he has from his very heart "received Christ Jesus *the Lord*" (Col. 2:6). And let it be said plainly and emphatically, that no one acknowledging *less* than this is *scripturally* entitled to be regarded as a Christian.

"The apostle spends the whole remainder of the Epistle in the pressing and confirming of *this* exhortation, on a compliance wherewith the *eternal* condition of our souls *doth depend*. And this he doth, partly by declaring the means whereby we may be helped in the discharge of this duty; partly by denouncing the eternal ruin and sure destruction that will follow the neglect of it; and partly by encouragements from their own former experiences, and the strength of our faith; and partly by evidencing unto us, in a multitude of examples, how we may overcome the difficulty that would occur unto us in this way, with other various cogent reasonings; as we shall see, if God pleaseth, in our progress" (J. Owen).

To "*hold fast* the confession of our faith" means to continue in and press forward along the path we profess to have entered; and that, notwithstanding all the threats of persecutors, sophistical reasonings of false teachers, and allurements of the world. Your very safety depends upon this, for if you deny the faith you are "worse than an infidel" who has never professed it. God plainly warns us that if after we have escaped the pollutions of the world through the knowledge of the Lord and Saviour Jesus Christ, we are again entangled therein and overcome, then, "the latter end is worse with them than the beginning: For it had been better for them not to have known the way of righteousness, than, after they have known it to turn from the holy commandment delivered unto them" (2 Pet. 2:20, 21). It is one thing to *make* "confession of faith," it is quite another to "hold fast" the same; mulitudes do the former, exceedingly few the latter. It is easy to avow myself a Christian, but it is most difficult indeed to *live* the life of one.

Concerning the force of the Greek word rendered "hold fast," J. Owen stated that there is included in the sense of it, "First, a supposition of great difficulty, with danger and opposition against this holding the profession of our faith. Second, the putting forth of the utmost of our strength and endeavors in the defence of it. Third, a constant perseverance in it, denoted by its being termed 'keep' in 1 Cor. 15:2: possess it with constancy." If our readers could only realize the mighty power and inveterate enmity of those enemies who are seeking to destroy them, none would deem such language too strong. Sin within is ever seeking to vanquish the Christian. The world without is constantly endeavoring to draw him away from the path of godliness. Our adversary the Devil is going about as a roaring lion, seeking whom he may devour. That wonderful allegory of Bunyan's, by no means overdrew the picture when he represented the pilgrim as being menaced by mighty giants and a dreadful apollyon, which must either be slain by him, or himself be destroyed by them.

Sad indeed is it to witness so many young professing Christians just starting out on their arduous journey to Heaven, being told that the words "He that endureth to the end shall be saved" apply not to them, but only to the Jews; and that while unfaithfulness on their part will forfeit some "millennial" crown, yet so long as they have accepted Christ as their personal Saviour, no matter how they must indulge the flesh or fraternize with the world, Heaven itself cannot be missed. Little wonder that there is now such a deplorably low standard of Christian living among those who listen to such soul-ruinous error. Not so did teachers of the past, who firmly held the eternal security of Christ's redeemed, pervert that blessed truth. No, they preserved the balance, by insisting that God only preserved His people *in the path of obedience* to Him, and that they who *forsake* that path make it evident that *they* are *not* His people, no matter what their profession, and no matter what past "experience" they had.

To illustrate what we have in mind, an article appearing in a recent issue of a periodical, on the subject of the security of a Christian, begins thus: "The person who believes in the Lord Jesus Christ as the one who died for all sin on the cross, and has accepted Him as his own personal Saviour, is saved. And more, can never again, under any circumstances or conditions whatsoever, no matter what he may do or not do, be lost." Such an unqualified, unguarded, unbalanced statement as that is misleading, and dangerous to the highest degree; the more so, as nothing that follows in the article in any wise modifies it. But more: stated thus, it is *un*scriptural. God's Word says, "Whose house are we, *if* we hold fast the confidence and the rejoicing of the hope firm unto the *end*" (Heb. 3:6). And again, "if ye live after the flesh, ye shall die" (Rom. 8:13); that is, die eternally, suffer the "second death," for "life" and "death" throughout the epistle of the Romans is *eternal.*

Such a statement as the above (made thoroughly in good faith, we doubt not; yet by one who is the unwitting victim of a school of extremists) leaves completely out of sight the Christian's *responsibility,* yea, altogether repudiates it. Side by side with the blessed truth of Divine preservation, the Scriptures uniformly put the solemn truth of Christian perseverance. Are the Lord's people told that they are "*Kept* by the power of God through faith" (1 Pet. 1:5)? So are they also exhorted to "*keep thy heart* with all diligence, for out of it are the issues of life" (Prov. 4:23); "*Keep himself* unspotted from the world" (James 1:27); "*keep yourselves* from idols" (1 John 5:21); "*keep yourselves* in the love of God" (Jude 21). And it is not honest to quote one class of these texts and *not* quote, with *equal* diligence and emphasis, the other.

"Let us hold fast the profession of our faith without wavering." The one-sided teaching of a certain school today renders such an exhortation as this, as not only superfluous, but meaningless. If my *only* concern (as so many are now affirming) is to trust in the finished work of Christ, and rely upon the promise of God to take me to Heaven; if I have committed my soul and its eternal interests into the hands of God, so that it is now only *His* responsibility to guard and preserve me; then it is quite unnecessary to bid me guard myself. How absurd are the reasonings of men, once they depart from the Truth! As well might I argue that because I have committed my body into the hands of God, and am counting upon Him to keep me in health, that therefore no matter how I neglect the laws of health, no matter what I eat or do not eat, He will infallibly preserve me from sickness and death. Not so; if I drink poison, I shall come to an untimely grave. Likewise, if I live after the flesh, I shall die.

The apostles believed in no *mechanical* salvation. They busied themselves in "confirming the souls of the disciples and exhorting them to *continue* in the faith" (Acts 14:22). According to the lop-sided logic of many teachers today, it is quite *un*-necessary to exhort Christians *to* "continue in the faith"; they *will* do so. But be not wise above what is written, and deem not yourselves to be more consistent than the apostles. They "*exhorted* them all that with purpose of heart they would *cleave unto* the Lord" (Acts 11:23), yea, "persuaded them to *continue* in the grace of God" (Acts 13:43). The beloved Paul held no such views that, because his converts had been genuinely saved there was therefore no need for him to be any further concerned about their *eternal* welfare: rather did he send Timothy "to know your faith, *lest* by some means the Tempter have tempted you, and our labour be *in vain*" (1 Thess. 3:5). So Peter warned the saints, "Beware lest ye also, being led away with the error of the wicked fall from your own steadfastness" (2 Pet. 3:17).

Should we be asked, Then do you no longer believe in the absolute and eternal security of the saints? Our answer is, We do, as it is set forth in Holy Writ; but we most certainly do not believe in that wretched perversion of it which has now become so current and popular. The Christian preservation set forth in God's Word is not merely a remaining on earth for some time after faith and regeneration have been produced, and then being admitted, *as a matter of course,* to Heaven, *without a regard* to the moral history of the intervening period. No, Christian perseverance is a continuing in faith and holiness, a remaining steadfast in believing and in bringing forth all the fruits of righteousness. It is persisting in that course which the *converted* one has entered: a perseverance unto the end in the exercise of faith and in the practice of godliness. Men who are influenced more by selfish considerations of their own safety and security, than they are with God's commands and precepts, His honour and glory, are not Christians at all.

The *balance* between Divine preservation and human perseverance was well presented by John Owen when he wrote, "It is true our persistency in Christ doth not, as to the issue and event, depend absolutely on our own diligence. The unalterableness of our union with Christ, on the account of the faithfulness of the covenant of grace, is that which doth and shall eventually secure it. But yet *our own* diligent endeavour is such an *indispensable means* for that end, as that without it, it will *not* be brought about. Diligence and endeavor in this matter are like Paul's mariners, when he was ship-wrecked at Melita. God had before given him the lives of all that sailed with him in the ship (Acts 27:24), and he 'believed that it should be even as God had told him.' So now the preservation of their lives depended absolutely on the faithfulness and power of God. *But yet,* when the mariners began to fly out of the ship, Paul tells the centurion that, unless the men stayed, they *could not* be saved (v. 31). But what need he think of ship-men, when God had promised and taken upon Himself the preservation of them all? He knew full well that *He* would preserve them; but *yet* that He would do so *by* the use of means.

"If we are in Christ, God hath given us the lives of our souls, and hath taken upon Himself, in His covenant, the preservation of them. But *yet* we may say, with reference unto the *means* that He hath appointed, when storms and trials arise, *unless we use our* diligent endeavors, *we* cannot be saved. Hence are the many cautions which are given, not only in this epistle, wherein they abound, but in other places of scripture also, that we should take heed of apostasy and falling away; as 'let him that thinketh he standeth, take heed lest he fall' (1 Cor. 10:12), 'Hold that fast which thou hast, that no man take thy crown' (Rev. 3:11) . . . consider what it is *to* 'abide in Christ': what watchfulness, what diligence, what endeavor, are required thereunto. Men would have it to be a plant that needs neither watering, manuring, nor pruning, but one which will thrive alone of itself. Is it any wonder if we see so many either decaying or unthrifty professors? and so many that are utterly turned off from their first engagements!" (Vol. 25, pages 171-173).

From the last two sentences quoted above, we may perceive that the same evil against which we are here contending—a *carnal* security, which Scripture nowhere warrants—had an existence in the palmy days of the Puritans. Verily there is *no* new thing under the sun! Nearly three hundred years ago that faithful teacher and prince of expositors had to protest against the one-sided perversion of the precious truth of the Divine preservation of the saints. But no wonder: the devil plainly revealed his methods when he pressed upon Christ the Divine promise that God had given His angels charge to "bear Thee up," but the Saviour refused to recklessly ignore the requirements of self-preservation! From John Calvin's comments upon John 8:31 we extract the following: "If, therefore, we wish that Christ should reckon us to be His disciples, we must endeavour to persevere."

Scripture, not logic, is our rule of faith; and not one or two statements taken out of their contexts, but the whole analogy of faith. Error is truth perverted, truth distorted, truth out of proportion. To short-sighted human reason there appears to be a clash between Divine justice and Divine mercy, between God's sovereignty and man's responsibility, between law and grace, between faith and good works; but he who is really taught of the Spirit, is enabled to discern their perfect consistency. "As *sorrowful,* yet always *rejoicing*" (2 Cor. 6:10) is a puzzling paradox to the carnal mind. To read that the Son makes His people "free," and yet that He requires them to "take His *yoke*" upon them, is an enigma unto many. To *"rejoice* with *trembling*" (Psa. 2:11) seems a contradiction in terms to some carping minds. No less contradictory appears God's promise to *keep* His people, and His requiring to *keep themselves* under pain of eternal damnation. Yet the last mentioned are just as *consistent* as are the other things referred to throughout this paragraph.

"For He is faithful that promised." At first glance it is not very easy perhaps to perceive the precise relation of these words to the preceding exhortation: that they are added by way of encouragement seems fairly obvious, for the more that we spiritually ponder the veracity of the Promiser, the more will our faith be strengthened; the more we realize that we have to do with One who cannot lie, the greater confidence shall we have in His Word. Instead of being unduly occupied with the difficulties of the way, we need to look off unto Him who has so graciously given us His "exceeding great and precious promises" (2 Pet. 1:4) to cheer and gladden us. Yet this hardly explains the immediate connection between the two parts of this verse, nor does it answer the question as to whether or not any *particular* promise is here in view.

"For He is faithful that promised." Perhaps the bearing which these words have upon the preceding injunction has been brought out as well by A. Barnes as any. "To induce them to hold fast their profession, the apostle adds this additional consideration. God, who had promised eternal life to them, was faithful to all that He had said. The argument here is, (1) That since *God* is so faithful to us, we ought to be faithful to Him. (2) The fact that *He* is faithful is an *encouragement* to us. We are dependent on Him for grace to hold fast our profession. If He were to prove unfaithful, we should have no strength to do it. But this He never does; and we may be assured that *all* that He has promised He will perform. To the service of *such* a God, therefore, we should adhere without wavering."

If we compare 4:1 and 6:15 light is cast upon *what* specific "promise" is here contemplated. In the former we read, "Let us therefore fear, lest a promise being left of entering into His rest, any of you should seem to come short of it"; in the latter we are told, "And so, after he (Abraham) had patiently endured (persevered) he obtained the promise." It is to be most particularly noted that all through this epistle "salvation" is viewed as a *future* thing. *This* is an aspect of salvation (a vitally important one too) which is mostly omitted from present-day preaching and teaching. In the Hebrews (as likewise in the epistles of Peter) the saints are contemplated as being yet in the wilderness, which is the place of testing and of danger. It is only those who diligently heed the solemn warning of 3:12 who win through, "Take heed brethren, lest there be in any of you an evil heart of unbelief, in departing from the living God."

"And let us consider one another to provoke unto love and to good works" (v. 24). The opening "And" serves two purposes: it is a plain indication that the contents of this verse are closely related to what has just been before us; it is a pointed intimation that we ought to be as considerate and careful about the spiritual edification of other saints as we are of our own. Thus there are two things here which claim our consideration: the precise nature of the duty enjoined, and the connection between it and the exhortation of v. 23.

"And let us consider one another." There are no fewer than eleven Greek words used in the N.T. which are all rendered by our one English term "consider": four of them being simple verbs, and seven of them compounds for the purpose of particular emphasis. The first signifies the serious observing of a matter: Acts 15:6; the second a careful deliberation: Heb. 7:4; the third, to narrowly spy or investigate as a watchman: Gal. 6:1; the fourth, to turn a matter over in the mind: 2 Tim. 2:7. The first simple verb is compounded in Acts 12:12 and means to seriously consult with one's self about a matter. The second simple verb is compounded in Heb. 13:7, and means to diligently review a thing. The fourth simple verb is compounded in Acts 11:6, and means to thoroughly weigh a matter so as to come to a full knowledge of it: this is the one used in our present text. In Mark 6:52 is a different compound: the disciples failed to compare things together. In Heb. 12:3 another compound signifies to reckon up—*all* that Christ suffered. In John 11:50 is a similar compound: to reckon thoroughly. In Matt. 6:28 "consider the lilies" means to learn thoroughly so as to be instructed thereby. The practical lesson to be learned from all this is, that the things of God call for our utmost attention.

"And let us consider one another:" let us diligently bear in mind and continually have in view the good of our fellow-pilgrims. The term "consider" is very emphatic, being the same as in 3:1, where we are bidden to "Consider the Apostle and High Priest of our profession Christ Jesus." Here it signifies a conscientious care and circumspection over the spiritual estate and welfare of other Christians. They are brethren and sisters in Christ, members of the same family: a tie far nearer and dearer than any earthly one unites you to them and them to you. "Consider" not only their blessed relation to you, but also their circumstances, their trials, their temptations, their infirmities, their needs. Seek grace to be of service, of help, of blessing to them. Remember that they have their conflicts too, their discouragements, their falls: "Wherefore lift up the hands which hang down and the feeble knees" (Heb. 12:12).

"And let us consider one another to provoke unto love and to good works." Here is expressed the chief design or end of our consideration for one another: it is to provoke or stir up unto the performance of duties; to strengthen zeal, to inflame affections, to excite unto godly living. We are to provoke one another by means of a godly example, by suitable exhortations, by unselfish acts of kindness. We are to fire one another "unto love," which is not a mere sentiment or natural affability, but a holy principle of action, which seeks the highest good of its object. Christian love is righteous, and never winks at sin; it is faithful, which shrinks not from warning or rebuking where such is necessary. "And good works" is to be the issue, the fruit, of godly love. "And this is love, that we walk after His commandments" (2 John 6).

The relation between this exhortation in v. 24 and the one in v. 23 is very intimate. Love and good works are both the effects and evidences of the sincere confession of saving faith, and therefore a diligent attendance unto them is an essential means of constancy in our confession. Christian perseverance is nothing less than a continuance in practical godliness, in the path of obedience to Christ and love unto His brethren. Therefore are we called upon to watch over one another with a view to steadfastness in the faith and fruitfulness in our lives. No Christian liveth unto himself (Rom. 14:7): each one of us is either a help or a hindrance, a blessing or a curse unto those we associate with. *Which* is it? The Lord stir up both writer and reader to a more unselfish and loving concern for the spiritual good of those who are fellow-members of the same Body.

CHAPTER FIFTY-TWO

Apostasy

(Heb. 10:25-27)

We have now reached one of the most solemn and fear-inspiring passages to be found not only in this epistle, but in all the Word of God. May the Holy Spirit fit each of our hearts to approach it in that godly trembling which becomes those who have within their own hearts the seeds of apostasy. Let it be duly considered at the outset that the verses which are now to be before us were addressed not to those who made no profession of being genuine Christians, but instead, unto them whom the Spirit of truth owned as "holy brethren, partakers of the heavenly calling" (3:1). Nevertheless, *He* now dehorts them from stepping over the brink of that awful precipice which was before them, and faithfully warns of the certain destruction which would follow did they do so. Instead of replying to this with arguments drawn from the eternal security of God's saints, let us seek grace to honestly face the terrible danger which menaces each of us while we remain in this world of sin, and to use all necessary means to avoid so fearful and fatal a calamity.

In the past, dear reader, there have been thousands who were just as confident that *they* had been genuinely saved and were truly trusting in the merits of the finished work of Christ to take them safely through to Heaven, as *you* may be; nevertheless, they are now in the torments of Hell. Their confidence was a carnal one; their "faith," no better than that which the demons have. Their faith was but a natural one which rested on the bare letter of Scripture. It was not a supernatural one, wrought in the heart by God. They were too confident that their faith *was* a saving one, to thoroughly, searchingly, frequently, *test* it by the Scriptures, to discover whether or no it was bringing forth those *fruits* which are inseparable from the faith of God's elect. If they read an article like this, they proudly concluded that it belonged to some one else. So cocksure were they that *they* were born again so many years ago, they refused to heed the command of 2 Cor. 13:5 "*Prove* your own selves." And now it is too late. They wasted their day of opportunity, and the "blackness of darkness" is their portion forever.

In view of this solemn and awful fact, the writer earnestly calls upon himself and each reader to get down before God and sincerely cry, "Search me, O God: reveal me to myself. If I am deceived, undeceive me ere it be eternally too late. Enable me to measure myself faithfully by Thy Word, so that I may discover whether or no my heart has been renewed, whether I have abandoned every course of self-will and truly surrendered to Thee; whether I have so repented that I hate all sin, and fervently long to be free from its power, loathe myself and seek diligently to deny myself; whether my faith is that which overcomes the world (1 John 5:4), or whether it be only a mere notional thing which produces no godly living; whether I am a fruitful branch of the vine, or only a cumberer of the ground; in short, whether I be a *new* creature in Christ, or only a painted hypocrite." If I have an honest heart, then I am willing, yea anxious to face and know the *real* truth about myself.

Perhaps some readers are ready to say, I already know the truth about myself: I believe what God's Word tells me: I am a sinner, with no good thing dwelling in me; my only hope is in Christ. Yes, dear friend, but Christ *saves* His people *from* their sins. Christ sends His Holy Spirit into their hearts, so that they are radically changed from what they were previously. The Holy Spirit sheds abroad the love of God in the hearts of those He regenerates, and *that* love is manifested by a deep desire and sincere determination to *please Him* who loves me. When Christ saves a soul, He saves not only from Hell, but from the power of sin; He delivers him from the dominion of Satan, and from the love of the world; He delivers him from the fear of man, the lusts of the flesh, the love of self. True He has not yet *completed* this blessed work. True, the sinful nature is not yet eradicated, but one who is saved has been delivered from the dominion of sin (Rom. 6:14). Salvation is a supernatural thing, which changes the heart, renews the will, transforms the life, so that it is evident to all around that a *miracle* of grace has been wrought.

Thus, it is not sufficient for me to ask have I repudiated my own righteousness, have I renounced all my good works to fit me for heaven, am I trusting alone to Christ? Many will earnestly and sincerely affirm these things, who yet give no evidence that they have passed from death unto life. Then what more is necessary for me to ascertain whether or no *my* faith be a truly saving one? This, there are certain things which "*accompany* salvation" (Heb. 6:9), things which are inseparable from it; and for *these* I must look, and be sure I have them. A bundle of wood that sends forth neither heat nor smoke, has no fire under it. A tree, which in summer, bears neither fruit nor leaves, is dead. So a faith which does not issue in godly living, in an obedient walk, in spiritual fruit, is not the faith of God's elect. O my reader, I beg you to diligently and faithfully examine yourself by the light of God's unerring Word. Claim not to be a child of Abraham, unless you do the *works* of Abraham (John 8:39).

What is apostasy? It is a making shipwreck of the faith (1 Tim. 1:19). It is the heart's departure from the living God (Heb. 3:12). It is a returning to and being overcome by the world, after a previous escape from its pollutions through the knowledge of the Lord and Saviour Jesus Christ (2 Pet. 2:20). There are various steps which precede it. First, there is a *looking back* (Luke 9:62), like Lot's wife, who though she had outwardly left Sodom, yet her heart was still there. Second, there is a *drawing back* (Heb. 10:38): the requirements of Christ are too exacting to any longer appeal to the heart. Third, there is a *turning back* (John 6:66): the path of godliness is too narrow to suit the lustings of the flesh. Fourth, there is a *falling back,* which is fatal: "that they might go and fall backward, and be broken" (Isa. 28:13).

"Not forsaking the assembling of ourselves together, as the manner of some, but exhorting; and so much the more, as ye see the day approaching" (v. 25). This verse forms the transition between the subject of Christian perseverance, treated of in vv. 23, 24, and that of apostasy, which is developed in v. 26 and onwards, though it is much more closely related to the latter than to the former. Most of the commentators are astray on this point, through failing to observe the absence of the word "And" at the beginning of it, and because they perceive not the significance of the word "forsake." In reality, the contents of this verse form a faithful warning against apostasy. First, the Hebrews are cautioned against forsaking public worship. Second, it is pointed out that "some" had already done so. Third, they are bidden to exhort one another with increased diligence.

"Not forsaking the assembling of ourselves together." Before attempting exposition of these words, let us first relieve them of a false application which some seek to make of them today. Just as of old Satan made a wrong use of Psa. 91:11, 12 in his tempting of the Saviour (Matt. 4:6), so he does with the verse before us. Few are aware of how often the Devil brings a Scripture before our minds. When a Christian is seeking to be out and out for Christ, the Devil will quote to him "Be not righteous overmuch" (Eccl. 7:16); likewise when a child of God resolves to obey 2 Tim. 3:5 and Heb. 13:13 and separate from all who do not *live* godly, the Enemy reminds him of "not forsaking the assembling of ourselves together." Romanists used the same text in the early days of the Reformation, and charged Luther and his friends with disobeying this Divine command. But God's Word does not contradict itself:

it does not tell us in one place "Be ye not unequally yoked together with unbelievers" (2 Cor. 6:14), and here bid the "sheep" to fraternise with "goats." When rightly understood, this verse affords no handle to those who seek to discourage faithfulness to Christ.

"Not forsaking the assembling of ourselves together." J. Owen rightly pointed out that, "There is a synecdoche (a part put for the whole) in the word 'assembling,' and it is put for the whole worship of Christ, because worship was performed in their assemblies; and he that forsakes the assemblies, forsakes the worship of Christ, as some of them did when exposed to danger." What is here dehorted is the total relinquishment of Christianity. It is not "Cease not to *attend* the assembly," but "forsake not," *abandon* not the assembling of yourselves together. It is not the sin of sloth or of schism which is here considered, but that of apostasy. If a professing Christian forsook the Christian churches and became a Mohammedan he would disobey this verse; but for one who puts the honour of Christ before everything else, to turn his back upon the so-called churches where He is now so grievously dishonoured, is *not* a failure to comply with its terms.

The Greek word for "Forsake not" is a *very* strong and emphatic one, being a double compound, and signifies "to abandon in time of danger." It is the word used by the agonizing Redeemer on the Cross, when He cried, "My God, My God, why hast Thou *forsaken* Me?" It was used by Him again when He declared, "Thou wilt not *leave* My soul in hell, neither wilt Thou suffer Thine Holy One to see corruption" (Acts 2:27). It is the word employed by Paul in 2 Tim. 4:10, "Demas hath *forsaken* me, having loved this present world." It is found in only one other place in this epistle, where it is in obvious antithesis from the verse now before us: "He hath said, I will never leave thee, nor *forsake* thee" (13:5). Thus it will appear that a total and final abandonment of the public profession of Christianity is what is here warned against.

One may therefore discern how that v. 25 supplies a most appropriate link between vv. 23, 24 and v. 26. Verse 25 prescribes another means to enable the wavering Hebrews to remain constant in the Christian faith. If they were to "hold fast the confession of faith without wavering," and if they were to "consider one another to provoke unto love and to good works," then they must not "forsake the assembling" of themselves together. The word for "assembling together" is a double compound, and occurs elsewhere in the New Testament only in 2 Thess. 2:1: "our gathering together unto Him," that is unto Christ; this also shows that the "assembling together" here is under one Head, and that the "forsaking" is because *He* has been turned away from.

To enforce the above caution, the apostle adds, "as the manner of some is." The Greek word for "manner" signifies "custom," and is so translated in Luke 2:42. This supplies additional confirmation that the evil against which the Hebrews were dehorted was no mere occasionally absenting themselves from the Christian churches, but a deliberate, fixed and final departure from them. In John 6:66 we read that "From that time many of His disciples went back, and walked *no more* with Him"; John also wrote of those who "went out from us, but they were not of us" (1 John 2:19); whilst at the close of his labours Paul had to say "All they which are in Asia be turned away from me" (2 Tim. 1:15). So here, some who had made a profession of the Christian faith had now abandoned the same and gone back to Judaism. It was to warn the others against this fatal step that the apostle now wrote as he did—compare 1 Cor. 10:12, Rom. 11:20.

"But exhorting one another: and so much the more, as ye see the day approaching." Here is the positive side of our verse. This is another of the means appointed by God to confirm Christians in their holy confession. To "exhort one another" is a duty to which all Christians are called; alas, how rarely is it performed these evil days. Yet, from the human side, such failure is hardly to be wondered at. The vast majority of professing Christians wish to be petted and flattered, rather than exhorted and cautioned. Most of them are so hypersensitive that the slightest criticism offends them. One who seeks grace to be faithful and to act in *true* "love" to those whom he supposes are his brethren and sisters in Christ, has a thankless task before him, so far as man is concerned— he will soon lose nearly all his "friends" (?) and sever the "fellowship" (?) which exists between him and them. But this will only give a little taste of "the fellowship of *His* sufferings." Heb. 3:13 is still God's command!

"And so much the more, as ye see the day approaching." There seems little room for doubt that the first reference here is to the destruction of the Jewish commonwealth, which was now very nigh, for this epistle was written within less than eight years before Jerusalem was captured by Titus. That terrible catastrophe had been foretold, again and again, by Israel's prophets, and was plainly announced by the Lord Jesus in Luke 21. The approach of that dreadful "day" could be plainly *seen* or perceived by those possessing spiritual discernment: the continued refusal of the Nation to repent of their murder of Christ, and the abandoning of Christianity for an apostate Judaism by such large numbers, clearly presaged the bursting of the storm of God's judgment. This very fact supplied an additional motive for genuine Christians to remain faithful. The Lord Jesus promised that His followers should be preserved from the destruction of Jerusalem, but *only* as they attended to His cautions in Luke 21:8, 19, 34, etc., only as they persevered in faith and holiness, Matt. 24:13. The particular motive unto diligence here set before the Hebrews is applicable to other Christians just to the extent that they find themselves in similar circumstances.

"For if we sin wilfully after that we have received the knowledge of the truth, there remaineth no more sacrifice for sins" (v. 26). The general truth here set forth is that, Should those who have been converted and become Christians apostatise from Christ their state would be hopeless. This is presented under the following details. First, because of the nature of this sin, namely, a deliberate and final abandonment of the Christian faith. Second, the ones warned against the committal of it. Third, the terrible aggravation of it did such commit it. Fourth, the unpardonableness of it.

"For if we sin wilfully." The causal particle whereby this verse is premised has at least a threefold force. First and more immediately, it points the plain and inevitable conclusion from what has just been said in v. 25: they who "forsake" and abandon the Christian assemblies with all that they stand for, commit a sin for which the sacrifice of Christ avails not. Should it be said that Scripture declares "the blood of Christ cleanseth from *all* sin," the reply is, that it only says "the blood of Jesus Christ His Son cleanseth *us* from all sin," and none of those spoken of throughout that verse (1 John 1:7) ever commit *this* sin! Moreover, that very same epistle plainly teaches there is a sin for which the blood of Christ does not avail: see 1 John 5:16. Second, and more generally, a reason is here adduced as to why Christians need to heed the exhortations given in vv. 22-25: the duties therein prescribed are the means which God has appointed for preserving His people against this unpardonable crime. Third and more remotely, a solemn warning is here given against a wrong use being made of the precious promise recorded in 10:17—that blessed declaration is not designed to encourage a course of carelessness and recklessness.

"For if we sin wilfully." "The word *sin* here is plainly used in a somewhat peculiar sense. It is descriptive not of sin generally, but of a particular kind of sin,—apostasy from the faith and profession of the truth, once known and professed. 'The angels that sinned' are the apostate angels. The apostasy described is not so much an act of apostasy as a state of apostasy. It is not, 'If we have sinned, if we have apostatized'; but 'If we *sin,* if we apostatize, if we continue in apostasy' " (John Brown). English translators prior to the

A. V. read "If we sin *willingly,*" the change being made in 1611, to *avoid* giving countenance to the supposition that there is no recovery after *any* voluntary sin. The Greek word will not permit of this change: the only other occurrence of it in 1 Pet. 5:2, clearly gives its scope: "Taking the oversight not by constraint, but willingly."

"For if we sin willingly," that is voluntarily, of our own accord, where no constraint is used. The reference is to a definite decision, where an individual deliberately determines to abandon Christ and turn away from God. "In the Jewish law, as is indeed the case everywhere, a distinction is made between sins of oversight, inadvertence, or ignorance (Lev. 4:2, 13, 22; 5:15; Num. 15:24, 27-29: compare Acts 3:17, 17:30), and sins of presumption, sins that are deliberately and intentionally committed: see Ex. 21:14, Num. 15:30, Deut. 17:12, Psa. 19:13. The apostle here has reference, evidently, to such a distinction, and means to speak of a decided and deliberate purpose to break away from the restraints and obligations of the Christian religion" (A. Barnes).

"For if we sin willingly," etc. Who are the ones that are here warned against this terrible sin? Who are they that are in danger of committing it? The answer is, *all* who make a profession of faith in the Lord Jesus. But are genuine Christians in any such danger? Looked at from the standpoint of God's everlasting covenant, which He made with them in the person of their Sponsor, which covenant is "ordered in all things and sure;" — no. Looked at according to their standing and state in Christ, as those who have been "perfected forever" (10:14); — no. But considered as they are in themselves, mutable creatures (as was *un*-fallen Adam), without any strength of their own; — yes. Viewed as those who still have the sinful nature within them, — yes. Contemplated as those who are yet the objects of Satan's relentless attacks, — yes. But it may be said, "God sees His people *only* in Christ." Not so, is the reply. Were that the case, He would never chasten (Heb. 12:5-10) us! God views the Christian both in Christ legally *and* in this world actually. He addresses us as responsible beings (2 Pet. 1:10) and regulates the manifestations of His love for us according to our conduct (John 14:23).

It is to be carefully noted that the apostle Paul did not say, "If *ye* sin willingly," but "if *we,*" thus including himself. Two reasons may be suggested for this. First, to soften a little the severity of this terrible warning. He shows there is no respect of persons in this matter: were he to commit this dreadful sin himself, he too would suffer the same unmitigable doom. Hereby he sets all preachers and teachers a godly example. Such was his general custom: compare the "we" in 2:3; 3:6, 14; 12:25; and the "us" in 4:1, 11! Second, to emphasize the unvarying outworking of this law: no exceptions are made. The apostle includes himself to show that even he himself could not look to escape the Divine vengeance here denounced, if he fell into the sin here described.

"After that we have received the knowledge of the truth." These words not only serve to identify the ones who are cautioned against apostasy, but are added to emphasize the enormity of the sin. It would not be through ignorance or lack of knowledge, but after being enlightened, they abandoned Christianity. The "Truth" rather than the "Gospel" is here specifically mentioned, so as to heighten the contrast—it is for a *lie* that Christ is rejected. The word "knowledge" here is a compound and signifies "acknowledgement," and is so rendered in Titus 1:1, Phile. 6. Owen says, "the word is not used any where to express the mere conceptions or notions of the mind about this, but such acknowledgement of it as arises from some sense of its power and excellency." To "receive" this acknowledgement of the truth includes an act of the mind in understanding it, an act of the will in consenting, and an act of the heart in embracing it.

"Wherefore the sin here intended, is plainly a relinquishment and renunciation of the truth of the gospel, and the promises thereof, with all duty thereunto belonging, after we have been convinced of its truth, and avowed its power and excellency. There is no more required but that this be 'willingly': not upon a sudden surprizal and temptation, as Peter denied Christ; not on those compulsions and fears which may work a present dissimulation, without an internal rejection of the Gospel; not through darkness, ignorance making an impression for a season on the minds and reasonings of men: which things, though exceedingly evil and dangerous, may befall them who yet contract not the guilt of this crime. But it is required thereunto, that men who thus sin, do it by choice, and of their own accord, from the internal depravity of their own mind, and an evil heart of unbelief to depart from the living God; that they do it by, and with the preference of another way of religion, and a resting therein before or above the Gospel" (John Owen).

The unpardonableness of this sin is affirmed in the words "there remaineth no more sacrifice for sins." A similar passage, which throws light on our present verse, is found in 1 Sam. 3:14, "And therefore I have sworn unto the house of Eli, that the iniquity of Eli's house shall not be purged with sacrifice or offering forever." As there were certain sins which, in O. T. times, from their heinousness and the high-handed rebellion of their perpetrators, had no sacrifice allowed them, but "died without mercy" (v. 29); so it is now with those who apostatise from Christ: there is no relief appointed for them, no means for the expiation of their sin. They voluntarily and finally reject the Gospel, forfeit all interest in the sacrifice of Christ.

Ere leaving this verse, let it be said emphatically that there is nothing in it which in anywise conflicts with the blessed truth of the eternal security of God's *saints.* The apostle did not here say the Hebrews *had* apostatised, nor did he affirm they *would* do so. No, instead, he faithfully points out the sure, dreadful, and eternal consequences *did* they do so. "For IF we sin willingly." It was to keep them from it that he here sets it down by way of supposition, just as in Rom. 8:13 he says, "For *if* ye live after the flesh, ye shall die." As to how far a person *may* go in the taking up of Christianity, and as to what the Spirit may work in him *short* of actual regeneration, and then that one apostatise, only God knows. And, as to how close a real Christian may come to *presumptuous* (Psa. 19:13) sinning, and yet remain innocent of "the great transgression," only God can decide. We are only in the place of safety while we maintain the attitude of complete dependency upon the Lord and of unreserved subjection to Him. To indulge the flesh is *dangerous;* to persist in the course of self-gratification is *highly* dangerous; and to remain therein unto the end, would be *fatal.*

"But a certain fearful looking for of judgment and fiery indignation, which shall devour the adversaries" (v. 27). The positive punishment of apostates is here announced. "When a man under the law had contracted the guilt of any such sin, as was indispensably capital in its punishment, for the legal expiation thereof no sacrifice was appointed or allowed, such as murder, adultery, blasphemy, he had nothing remaining but a fearful expectation of the execution of the sentence of the law against him. And it is evident that in this context, the apostle argues from the less unto the greater; if it was so, that this was the case of him who so sinned against Moses' law, how much more must it be so with them that sin against the gospel, whose sin is incomparably greater, and the punishment more severe?" (J. Owen.)

The Divine punishment which shall be visited upon apostates is first spoken of under the general term "judgment," as in 9:27. This signifies that it will be a righteous sentence proportioned unto their awful crime: there will be a full and open trial, with an impartial judicial condemnation of them. The term is also used to express the punishment itself (James 2:13, 2 Pet. 2:3): both meanings are probably included here. There is no mean between pardon and damnation. The sure approach of this judgment is referred to as "a certain fearful looking-for of" it. The word "certain" here signifies something which is not fully defined, as in "a certain woman" (Mark 5:25), "a certain nobleman" (John 4:46): it therefore denotes the "judgment" is inexpressible, such as no human heart can conceive or tongue portray. "Fearful" intimates the punishment will be so dreadful that when men come to apprehend it they are filled with horror and dismay. "Looking-for" shows that the apostates already have an earnest of God's wrath in their consciences even now.

"And fiery indignation," or "fierceness of fire" as in the Amer. R. V., or more literally, "of fire fervor" (Bag. Inter.). This describes more closely the *nature* of the "judgment" awaiting them. The terms used denote the resistless, tormenting, destroying efficacy of God's terrible wrath, and emphasizes its dreadful fierceness. God is highly incensed against the apostates, and inconceivably and indescribably dreadful will be His dealings with them: it will express and answer to His *infinite* justice, holiness, and power. "For, behold, the Lord will come with fire and with His chariots, like a whirlwind, to render His anger against the earth, and His rebuke with flames of fire" (Isa. 66:15). No doubt the reference in our verse is to the final judgment at the last day, and the eternal destruction of God's enemies. A solemn and graphic shadowing forth of this was given by God when His sword and fiery judgment fell upon the Jews in A. D. 70, destroying their church-state by fire and sword.

"Which shall devour the adversaries." There is probably an allusion here to the dreadful fate which overtook Nadab and Abihu, concerning whom it is written "there went out fire from the Lord, and *devoured* them (Lev. 10:2), and also the judgment visited upon Korah, Dathan and Abiram, when "the ground clave asunder that was under them, and the earth opened her mouth, and swallowed them up," so that they went down "alive into the Pit" (Num. 16:30-33). The "adversaries" are those who are actuated by a principle of hostile opposition to Christ and Christianity. They are enemies of God, and God will show Himself to be their Enemy. God's wrath shall "devour them as to all happiness, all blessedness, all hopes, comfort and relief at once; but it shall not consume their being. This is that which this fire shall ever prey upon them, and never utterly consume them" (J. Owen). From such a doom may Divine grace deliver both writer and reader.

CHAPTER FIFTY-THREE

The Apostates' Doom

(Heb. 10:28-31)

The verses which are now to be before us complete the section begun at v. 26, the sum of which is the apostates' doom. They fall naturally into two parts, the one containing a description of their sin; the other, a declaration of their punishment. For the purpose of solemn emphasis, each of these is repeated. In v. 26 the sin itself is mentioned; in the last clause of v. 26 and in v. 27 the punishment of it is affirmed. In vv. 28, 29 the apostle confirms the equity of the fore-named judgment by an argument drawn from the Mosaic law, under which he shows the terrible character of the sin which is here in view. In vv. 30, 31 he establishes the certainty of the punishment by an appeal to the character of God as revealed in His Word. This repetition in a subject so solemn, is well calculated to awe every thoughtful reader, and ought to produce the most searching effect upon his conscience and heart.

As we have pointed out in preceding articles, this section (vv. 26-31) was introduced by the apostle for the purpose of enforcing the exhortation found in vv. 22-24, the sum of which is, a call unto Christians to persevere in a state and practice of godliness. Grossly has this passage been perverted by theological factions belonging to two extremes. The one has misused it in the endeavour to bolster up their false doctrine of regenerated people falling from grace and being eternally lost. Without now going into that subject, it is sufficient to say that Heb. 10:26-31 contains not a word which *directly* supports the chief contention of the Arminians. What we have in this passage is only hypothetical, "For *if* we sin willingly," i.e. deliberately, fully, and finally abandon the profession of Christianity — *not* that the Holy Spirit here says any of the regenerate Hebrews *had,* or *would* do so. A similar and still more pointed case is found in those words of Christ's. "Yet ye have not known Him: but I know Him: and *if* I should say, I know Him not, I shall be a liar like unto you" (John 8:55).

The second party of those who have misunderstood this passage, are Calvinists possessing more zeal than wisdom. Anxious to maintain their ground against the Arminians, most of them have devoted their energies to show that regenerated Christians do not come within the scope of v. 26 at all; that instead, it treats only of nominal professors, of those having nothing more than a head-knowledge of the Truth, and making merely a lip-profession of the same. And thus has the great Enemy of souls succeeded in getting some of the true servants of God to blunt the sharp edge of this solemn verse, and nullify its searching power over the conscience of the saints. It is sufficient refutation of this theory to point out that the apostle is here addressing those who were "partakers of the heavenly calling" (3:1), and in the "we" of 10:26 included *himself!* We will not take any notice of a third theory, of modern "dispensationalists," who affirm that none but *Jews* could commit the sin here mentioned, beyond saying that our space is too valuable to waste in exposing such trifling with Holy Scripture.

But what has been pointed out above presents a serious difficulty to many. We may state it thus: If it be impossible for truly regenerated people to ever perish, then why should the Holy Spirit move the apostle to so much in hypothetically describing the irremediable doom *if* they should apostatise? Such a difficulty is occasioned, in the first place, through a *one-sided* conception of the Christian, through considering him only as he exists in the purpose of God, and not also remembering what he still is in himself: unless the latter be steadily held in mind, we are in grave danger of denying, or at least ignoring, the Christian's *responsibility.* That the Christian *is* to be viewed in this twofold way is abundantly clear from many Scriptures. For example, in the purpose of God, the Christian is already "glorified" (Rom. 8:30), yet he certainly is not so in himself! Here in Heb. 10:26 etc. (as in many other passages) the Christian is *not* addressed from the viewpoint of God's eternal purpose, but as he yet is in himself — in need of solemn warnings, as well as exhortations.

Again; the difficulty which so many one-sided thinkers find in this subject is to be attributed to their failure in duly recognizing the *relation* which God has appointed between His own eternal counsels and the accomplishment of the same through wisely ordained *means.* There are some who reason (most superficially) that if God has ordained a certain soul to be saved, he *will* be, whether he exercised faith in Christ or no. Not so: 2 Thess. 2:13 clearly proves the contrary — the "end" and the "means" are there inseparably joined together. It is quite true that where God has appointed a certain individual "unto salvation," He will infallibly give him a saving faith; but that does not mean that the Holy Spirit will believe *for* him; no, the individual will, must, *exercise* the faith which has been given him. In like manner, God has eternally decreed that every regenerated soul shall get safely through to Heaven, yet He certainly has not ordained that any shall do so whether or not they use the means which He has appointed for their preservation. Christians are "kept by the power of God *through faith*" (1 Pet. 1:5) — *there* is the human responsibility side.

Looked at as he still is in himself, the Christian is eminently liable to "make shipwreck of the faith" (1 Tim. 1:19). He still has within him a nature which craves the vanities of the world, and that craving has to be denied, or he will never reach Heaven. He is yet in the place of terrible danger, menaced by deadly temptations, and it is only as he constantly watches and prays against the same that he is preserved from them. He is the immediate and incessant object of the Devil's malice, for he is ever going about as a roaring lion seeking whom he may devour; and it is only as the Christian takes unto himself (appropriates and uses) the armour of God's providing, that he can withstand the great Enemy of souls. It is because of these things that he urgently needs the exhortations and warnings of Holy Writ. God has faithfully pointed out to us what lies at the end of every path of self-will and self-indulgence. God has mercifully placed a hedge across each precipice which confronts the professing Christian, and woe be to him if he disregards those warnings and pushes through that hedge.

In this solemn passage of Heb. 10, the apostle is pointing out the sure and certain connection there is between apostasy and irrevocable damnation, thereby warning all who bear the name of Christ to take the most careful and constant pains in *avoiding* that unpardonable sin. To say that real Christians need no such warning because they *cannot* possibly commit *that* sin, is, we repeat, to lose sight of the connection which God himself has established between His predestined *ends* and the *means* whereby they are reached. The end unto which God has predestined His people is their eternal bliss in Heaven, and one of the means by which that end is reached, is through their taking heed to the solemn warning He has given against that which would prevent their reaching Heaven. It is not wisdom, but madness, to scoff at those warnings. As well might Joseph have objected that there was no need for him and his family to flee into Egypt (Matt. 2), seeing that it was *impossible* for the Christ-Child to be slain by Herod!

What each of us needs to watch against is the first buddings of apostasy, the first steps which lead to that sin of sins. It is not reached at a single bound, but is the fatal culmination of a diseased heart. Thus, while the writer and the reader, may be in no immediate danger of apostasy itself, we *are* of that which, if allowed and continued in, would certainly lead to it. A man who is now enjoying good health is in no immediate danger of dying from tuberculosis; yet if he recklessly exposed himself to the wet and cold, if he refrained from taking that nourishing food which supplies strength to resist disease, or had he a heavy cough on the chest and made no effort to break it up, then would he very likely fall a victim to consumption. So it is spiritually. Nay, in the case of the Christian, the *seed* of eternal death is already in him. That seed is *sin,* and it is only as grace is daily and diligently sought, for the thwarting of its inclinations and suppressing of its activities, that it is hindered from fully developing to a fatal end.

A small leak neglected will sink a ship just as effectually as the most boisterous sea. So one sin indulged in and not repented of, will terminate in eternal punishment. Well did J. Owen say, "We ought to take heed of every neglect of the person of Christ and of His authority, lest we enter into some degree or other of the guilt of this great offense." Or, still better, well may both writer and reader earnestly cry unto God, "Keep back Thy servant also from presumptuous sins; let them not have dominion over me: then shall I be upright, and I shall be innocent from the great transgression" (Psa. 19:13). Rightly did Spurgeon say on this verse, "Secret sin is a stepping-stone to presumptuous sin, and *that* is the vestibule of 'the sin which is unto death' " (Treasury of David.) To sin "presumptuously" is to knowingly and deliberately ignore God's commandments, defying His authority and recklessly going on in a course of self-pleasing regardless of consequences. When one has reached that terrible stage, he is but a short step indeed from committing the sin for which there is no forgiveness, and then to be abandoned by God both in this world and in that which is to come.

As this solemn subject is so vitally related to our eternal welfare, and as the pulpit and religious press of today maintain a guilty silence thereon, let us briefly point out some of the steps which inevitably lead to "presumptuous" sinning. When a professing Christian ceases to maintain a daily repentance and confession to God of all known sins, his conscience is already asleep and no longer responsive to the voice of the Holy Spirit. If over and above this, he comes before God as a worshipper, to praise and thank Him for mercies received, he is but dissembling, and mocking Him. If he continues in a state of impenitence, thus allowing and siding with the sin into which at first, he was unwittingly and unwillingly betrayed, his heart will be so hardened that he will commit new sins deliberately, against light and knowledge, and that with a high hand, and thus be guilty of *presumptuous* sins, of openly defying God.

The terrible thing is that in these degenerate times the consciences of thousands have been drugged by preachers (whom it is greatly to be feared are themselves spiritually dead, and helping forward the work of Satan) that have presented "the eternal security of the saints" in such an unscriptural way, as to convey to their poor hearers the impression that, provided they once "accepted Christ as their personal Saviour" Heaven is now their certain portion, that guilt can nevermore rest upon them, and that no matter what sins they may commit nothing can possibly jeopardize their eternal interests. The consequence has been — and this is no imaginary fear of ours, but a patent fact of observation on every side — that a carnal security has been imparted, so that in the midst of fleshly gratification and worldly living it is, humanly speaking, quite impossible to disturb their false peace or terrify their conscience.

All around us are professing Christians sinning with a high hand against God, and yet suffering from no qualms of conscience. And why? Because while they believe that some "millennial crown" or "reward" may be forfeited should they fail to deny self and daily take up their cross and follow Christ, yet they have not the slightest realization or fear that *they* are hastening to Hell as swiftly as time wings its flight. They fondly imagine that the blood of Christ covers all their sins. Horrible blasphemy! Dear reader, make no mistake upon this point, and suffer no false prophet to cause you to believe the contrary, the blood of Christ covers *no sins that have not been truly repented of and confessed to God with a broken heart.* But presumptuous sins are not easily repented of, for they *harden* the heart and make it steel itself against God. In proof note, "But they refused to hearken, and pulled away the shoulder, and stopped their ears that they should not hear. Yea, they made their hearts as an adamant stone, lest they should hear the law, and the words which the Lord of hosts hath sent" (Zech. 7:11, 12).

Rightly then does Thomas Scott say on Heb. 10:26, "We cannot too awfully alarm the secure, self-confident, and presumptuous, as every deliberate sin against light and conscience, is a step towards the tremendous precipice described by the apostle." Alas, alas, Satan has, through the "Bible teachers" done his work so well that, unless the Holy Spirit performs a miracle, it is impossible *to* "alarm" such. The great masses of professing Christians of our day regard God Himself much as they would an indulgent old man in his dotage, who so loves his grandchildren as to be blind to all their faults. The ineffably holy God of Scripture is no longer believed in: but multitudes will yet find, to their eternal sorrow, that it is " a *fearful* thing" to fall into *His* hands. We make no apology for this lengthy introduction, for our aim is not so much to write a commentary on this Epistle, as it is to reach the consciences and hearts of poor, misguided, and deluded souls, who have been fearfully deceived by the very men whom they have regarded as the champions of orthodoxy.

"He that despised Moses' law died without mercy under two or three witnesses: of how much sorer punishment, suppose ye, shall he be thought worthy who hath trodden under foot the Son of God, and hath counted the blood of the covenant wherewith He was sanctified, an unholy thing, and hath done despite unto the Spirit of grace?" (vv. 28, 29). Having named the principal means for the Christian's maintenance of constancy in the faith (vv. 22-25), the apostle proceeded to enforce his exhortations to perseverance, and against backsliding and apostasy, by some weighty considerations. First, from the terrible character of the sin of apostasy: it is a sinning willingly after a knowledge of the Truth has been received and assented to, v. 26. Second, from the dreadful state of such: no sacrifice avails for them, naught but judgment awaits them, vv. 26, 27. Third, from the analogy of God's severity in the past vv. 28, 29. Fourth, from what Scripture affirms of God's vindicative justice, vv. 30, 31.

"He that despised Moses' law died without mercy under two or three witnesses." The apostle proceeds to confirm the sentence passed upon the apostate Christian in vv. 26, 27, by an appeal to God's awful but righteous justice in the past. If the despiser of the Mosaic law was dealt with so unsparingly, how much more severe must be the punishment meted out to those who scorn the authority of the Gospel! The Greek word for "despise" means to utterly reject a thing, to set aside or cast it off, to treat it with contempt. The one who thus flouted the Divine legislation through Moses, was he who renounced its authority, and determinately and obstinately refused to comply with its requirements. Such an one suffered the capital punishment. Probably such passages as Deut. 13:6-9; 17:2-7 were before the apostle's mind.

"Of how much sorer punishment suppose ye, shall he be thought worthy who hath trodden under foot the Son of God?" The apostle's inspired logic here is the very reverse of that which obtains in the corrupt theology of present-day Christendom. The popular idea in these degenerate times is that, under the Gospel regime (or "dispensation of grace") God has acted, is acting, and will act much more mildly with transgressors, than He did under the Mosaic economy. The very opposite is the truth. No judgment from Heaven one-half as severe as that which overtook Jerusalem in *A. D.* 70, is recorded in Scripture from Exodus 19 to Malachi 4! Nor is there anything in God's dealings with Israel during O. T. times which can begin to compare with the awful severity of His "wrath" as depicted in the book of Revelation! Every despiser of the *Lordship* of Christ shall yet discover that a far hotter place has been reserved for him in Hell, than what will be the portion of lawless rebels who lived under the old covenant.

"Of how much sorer punishment, suppose ye, shall he be thought worthy, who hath trodden under foot the Son of God?" There are degrees of heinousness in sinning (John 19:11), and so there are degrees in the punishment of their perpetrators (Luke 12:47, 48). Here, this solemn truth is presented in the interrogative form (cf. 2:3) so as to search the conscience of each reader. If I have been favoured with a knowledge of the Gospel (denied to half the human race), if I have been enlightened by the Holy Spirit (which is more than multitudes of Romanists are), if I profess to have received Christ as my Saviour and have praised Him for His redeeming grace, — what punishment can fitly meet my crimes if I now despise His lordship, flout His authority, break His commandments, walk with His enemies, and go on sinning presumptuously, till I end by committing the "great transgression?"

"Of how much sorer punishment, suppose ye, shall he be thought worthy, who hath trodden under foot the Son of God, and hath counted the blood of the covenant, wherewith He was sanctified, an unholy thing, and hath done despite unto the Spirit of grace?" Instead of contenting himself with a general declaration of the equity of God's dealings with apostates, the apostle here adduces additional particulars of the crime before him. In this verse we have brought before us the awful aggravations of the sin of apostacy, showing what is implied and involved in this unpardoned transgression. Three things are specified, at each of which we shall briefly glance.

First, "who hath trodden under foot the Son of God." Once more we would call attention to the varied manner in which the Holy Spirit refers to the Saviour in this epistle. Here, it is not "Jesus," or "Christ," but the "Son of God," and that, because His purpose is to emphasize the infinite dignity of the One slighted. It is not a mere man, nor even an angel, but none less than the second person of the Holy Trinity who is so grievously insulted! Backsliding and apostasy is a treating of the Lord of glory with the utmost contempt. What could be worse? The figure here employed is very expressive and solemn: to "tread under foot" is the basest use to which a thing can be put. It signifies a scornful spurning of an object as a thing that is worthless, and is applied to swine trampling pearls under their feet (Matt. 7:6). O my reader, when we deliberately ignore the claims of God's Son and despise His commandments, we are treading His authority beneath our feet!

Second, "and hath counted the blood of the covenant, wherewith He was sanctified, an unholy thing." Here, as J. Owen rightly pointed out, "The second aggravation of the sin spoken of, is its opposition to the *office* of Christ, especially His priestly office, and the sacrifice He offered thereby, called here 'the blood of the covenant'." In our exposition of chap 9, we sought to show in what sense the blood of Christ was "the blood of the covenant." It was that whereby the new covenant and testament was confirmed and made effectual unto all its grace, to those who believe; being the foundation of all God's actings toward Christ in His resurrection, exaltation and intercession — cf. 13:20. Now the backslider and apostate does, by his conduct, treat that precious blood as though it were a worthless thing. There are many degrees of this frightful sin. But O my reader, whenever we give rein to our lusts and are not constrained by the love of Christ to render Him that devotion and obedience which are His due, we are, in fact, despising the blood of the covenant.

Third, "and hath done despite unto the Spirit of grace." This is the greatest aggravation of all: "whosoever shall speak a word against the Son of man, it shall be forgiven him: but unto him that blasphemeth against the Holy Spirit it shall not be forgiven him" (Luke 12:10). It is by the Spirit the Christian was regenerated, enlightened, convicted, and brought to Christ. It is by the Spirit the Christian is led and fed, taught and sanctified. What reverence is due Him as a Divine person! What gratitude as a Divine benefactor! How dreadful the sin then which treats Him with insolence, which scorns to attend unto His winsome voice, which despises His gracious entreaties! While the grossest form of the sin here referred to is, malignantly imputing unto Satan the works of the Spirit, yet there are milder degrees of it. O my reader, let us earnestly endeavor to keep from grieving Him (Eph. 4:30), and more completely yield ourselves to be "led" (Rom. 8:14) by Him along the highway of practical holiness.

Saith the Lord Almighty, "To this man will I look, even to him that is poor (in spirit), and of a contrite heart, and *trembleth* at My Word" (Isa. 66:2). Surely if there is a passage any where in Holy Writ which should cause each of us to "tremble," it is the one now before us! Not tremble lest we *have* already committed this unpardonable sin, for they who have done so are beyond all exercise of conscience, being given up by God to hardness of heart; no, but tremble *lest* we should begin a course of backsliding, which, if unarrested, would certainly lead thereto. "Wherefore let him that thinketh he standeth, take heed lest he fall" (I Cor. 10:12). O my reader, make this your daily prayer, "Hold up my goings in *Thy* paths, that my footsteps slip not" (Psa. 17:5).

"For we know Him that hath said, Vengeance belongeth unto Me, I will recompense, saith the Lord. And again, The Lord shall judge His people" (v. 30). In this verse further confirmation is supplied of the awful severity and the absolute certainty of the punishment of apostates. Once more we have an example of a most important principle which regulated the apostle in his ministry, both oral and written. In vv. 28, 29 he had given a specimen of spiritual reasoning, drawing a clear and logical inference from the less to the greater; yet decisive and unanswerable as this was, he rested not his case upon it, but instead, established it by quoting from Holy Scriptures. Let servants of God today act upon the same principle, and give a definite "Thus saith the Lord" for all they advance.

"For we know Him that hath said." Here our attention is directed unto the Divine character, what God is in Himself. Nothing behoves us more than to frequently and fully consider *who it is* with whom we have to do. Our conception of the Divine character plays an important part in moulding our hearts and regulating our conduct, therefore it is that we find the apostle, in another place, praying that the saints may be "increasing in the knowledge of God" (Col. 1:10). It is a most profitable exercise for the soul to be often engaged in contemplating the Divine attributes, pondering God's all-mighty power, ineffable holiness, unimpeachable veracity, exact justice, absolute faithfulness and terrible severity. Christ Himself has bidden us "Fear Him which is able to destroy both soul and body in hell" (Matt. 10:28). The better God's character be known, the more we heed that exhortation of Christ's, the clearer shall we perceive that there is nothing unsuited to the holiness of God in what Scripture affirms concerning His dealings with the wicked. It is because the true nature of sin is so little viewed in the light of God's awful holiness, that so many fail to recognize its *infinite* demerits.

"For we know Him that hath said, Vengeance belongeth unto Me, I will recompense saith the Lord." The reference is to Deut. 32:35, though the apostle does not quote word for word as we now have that text. Moses was there reminding of the office which God holds as the Judge of all the earth: as such, He enforces His righteous law, and inflicts its just punishment on wilful and impenitent sinners. Though, in His unsearchable wisdom, He is often pleased to forbear for a while — for He "bears with much longsuffering the vessels of wrath fitted to destruction" (Rom. 9:22) — nevertheless, God will yet pay to every transgressor the full wages to which their sins have earned. God bore long with the Antediluvians, but at the end He destroyed them by the flood. Wondrous was His patience toward the Sodomites, but at His appointed season, He rained down fire and brimstone upon them. With amazing forbearance He tolerates the immeasurable wickedness of the world, but the Day is swiftly approaching when He will avenge Himself upon all who now so stoutly oppose Him.

"And again, The Lord shall judge His people." A most important example is here given as a guide to teach us how scripture is to be *applied*. The reference is to what is recorded in Deut. 32:36, but there it is God's care exercised on behalf of His people, while here it is His vengeance upon their enemies. Some have cavilled at the appositeness of the apostle's quotation. Yet they should not. Each *particular* scripture has a *general* application, and is *not* to be limited unto those first addressed. If God undertakes to protect His people, He will certainly exercise judgement on those who apostatise. He did so in the past (see 1 Cor. 10:5); He will do so in the future: 2 Thess. 1:7, 8. The rule which is established by this quotation from Deut. is, that all Scripture is equally applicable unto all cases of the like nature. What God says concerning those who are the enemies of His people, becomes applicable to His people *should* they break and reject His covenant.

"It is a fearful thing to fall into the hands of the living God" (v. 31). Here is the unescapable conclusion which must be drawn from all that has been before us. This word "fearful" ought to make every trifler with sin tremble as did Belshazzar when he saw the Hand writing upon the wall. To "fall into the hands of" is a metaphor, denoting the utter helplessness of the victim when captured by his enemy. The One into whose hands the apostate falls is "the living God." "A mortal man, however incensed he may be, cannot carry his vengeance beyond death; but God's power is not bounded by so narrow limits" (J. Calvin). No, forever and ever will God's wrath burn against the objects of His judgment. Nor will the supplications of sinners prevail upon Him: see Prov. 1:28, Ezek. 8:18.

By the penitent and obedient, God is loved and adored; but by the impenitent and defiant, He is to be dreaded. The wicked may now pride themselves that in the day of judgment they will placate God by their tears, but they will then find that not only His justice, but His outraged mercy also calls aloud for His vengeance upon them. Men may now be beguiled by visions of a "larger hope," but in that Day they shall discover it is only another of Satan's lies.

O how the "terror of the Lord" (2 Cor. 5:11) ought to stir up God's servants to warn and persuade men before the day of grace is finally closed. And how it should make each one of us walk softly before God, sparing no pains to make our calling and election "sure." It is only as we *"add"* to our faith, virtue, knowledge, self-control, perseverance, godliness, brotherly-kindness, and love, that we have scriptural assurance that *we* shall "never fall" (2 Pet. 1:5-10).

CHAPTER FIFTY-FOUR

The Path of Tribulation

(Heb. 10:32-34)

God has not promised His people a smooth path through this world; instead, He has ordained that "we must through much tribulation" enter His kingdom (Acts 14:22). Why should it be otherwise, seeing we are now in a territory which is under His curse. And what has brought down that curse, but *sin.* Seeing then that there still is a world of sin both without and within each one of us, why should it be thought strange if we are made to taste the bitterness of its products! Suppose it were otherwise, what would be the effect? Suppose this present life were free from sorrows, sufferings, separations; ah, would we not be content with our present portion? Wisely then has God ordered it that we should be constantly reminded of the fact "*this* is *not* your rest, because it is polluted" (Micah 2:10). Trials and tribulations are needful if there is to be wrought in us "a desire to depart and to be with Christ, which is far better" (Phil. 1:23).

The word "tribulation" is derived from the Latin "tribulum," which was a flail used by the Romans to separate the wheat from the chaff. How much "chaff" remains even in the one who has been genuinely converted! How much of the "flesh" mingles with and mars his spiritual exercises! How much which is merely "natural" is mixed with his youthful zeal and energetic activities! How much of carnal wisdom and leaning unto our own understanding there is, till God is pleased to deepen His work of grace in the soul! And one of the principal instruments which He employs in that blessed work is the "tribulum" or flail. By means of sore disappointments, thwarted plans, inward fightings, painful afflictions, does He "take forth the precious from the vile" (Jer. 15:19), and remove the dross from the pure gold. It is by weaning us from the things of earth that He fits us for setting our affections on things above. It is by drying up creature-streams of satisfaction that He makes His children thirst for the Fountain of living water.

"Tribulation worketh patience" (Rom. 5:3). Patience is a grace which has both a passive and an active side. Passively, it is a meekly bowing to the sovereign pleasure of God, a saying, "The cup which my Father hath given me, shall I not drink it"? (John 18:11). Actively, it is a steady perseverance in the path of duty. This is one of the great ends which God has in view in the afflicting of His children: to effect in them "a meek and quiet spirit." "Tribulation worketh patience; and patience, experience." It is one thing to obtain a theoretical knowledge of a truth by means of reading, it is quite another to have a real and inward acquaintance with the same. As the tried and tempest-tossed soul bows meekly to the providential dealings of God, he experimentally learns what is "that good, and acceptable, and perfect will of God" (Rom. 12:2). "And experience, hope," which is a firm expectation of a continuance of sustaining grace and final glory. Since then our sufferings are one of the means which God has appointed for the Christian's sanctification, preparing us for usefulness here, and for Heaven hereafter, let us glory in them.

But let us lift our thoughts still higher. "Consider Him that endured such contradiction of sinners against Himself, lest ye be wearied and faint in your minds" (Heb. 12:3). Ah, it is unto *His* image which the saint is predestined to be conformed (Rom. 8:29), first in suffering, and then in glory. Let each troubled and groaning child of God call to remembrance the afflictions through which the Man of sorrows passed! Is it not fitting that the servant should drink of the cup which his Master drank? O my brethren, the highest honour God confers upon any of us in this life, is when He permits us to suffer a little for Christ's sake. O for grace to say with the beloved apostle, "Most gladly therefore will I rather glory in my infirmities that the power of Christ may rest upon me" (2 Cor. 12:9). "If ye be reproached for the name of Christ, happy are ye" (1 Pet. 4:14).

"No man should be moved by these afflictions: for yourselves know that we are appointed thereunto" (1 Thess. 3:3). Yet afflictions do not come upon all saints in the same form, nor to the same degree. God is sovereign in this, as in everything else. He knows what will best promote the spiritual good of His people. All is ordered by Him in infinite wisdom and infinite love. As has been well said, "God had one Son without sin, but none without sorrow." Yet the sorrow is not unmixed: God tempers His winds unto the lambs. With every temptation or trial He provides a way to escape. In the midst of sorest trouble His all-suffering grace is available. The promise is sure, "Cast thy burden upon the Lord, and He shall sustain thee" (Psa. 55:22), and where faith is enabled to rest in the Lord, His sustaining power is realized in the soul.

Afflictions are not all that the Lord sends His people: He daily loadeth them with His benefits (Psa. 68:19). The smilings of His face greatly outnumber the frowns of His providence. There are far more sunny days than cloudy ones. But our memories are fickle: when we enter the Wilderness, we so quickly forget our exodus from Egypt, and deliverance at the Red Sea. When water gives out (Ex. 17), we fail to call to remembrance the miraculous supply of manna (Ex. 16). It was thus with the apostles. When they had forgotten to take bread, the Lord Jesus tenderly remonstrated with them, saying, "O ye of little faith . . . Do ye not understand, neither remember the five loaves of the five thousand and how many baskets ye took up? Neither the seven loaves of the four thousand, and how many baskets ye took up?" (Matt. 16:5-10). O how much peace and joy we lose in the present through our sinful failure in not calling to remembrance the Lord's past deliverances and mercies.

"Thou shalt remember *all* the way which the Lord thy God led thee" (Deut. 8:2). Sit down and *review* God's previous dealings with thee: bring before your hearts His tender patience, His unchanging faithfulness, His powerful interpositions, His gracious gifts. There have been times in the past when your own folly brought you into deep waters of trouble, but God did not cast you off. You fretted and murmured, but God did not abandon you. You were full of fears and unbelief, yet God suffered you not to starve. He neither dealt with you after your sins, nor rewarded you according to your iniquities. Instead, He proved Himself to be *unto you* the "God of *all* grace" (1 Pet. 5:10). There were times in the past when every door of hope seemed fast closed, when every man's hand and heart appeared to be against you, when the Enemy came in like a flood, and it looked very much as though you would be drowned. But help *was* at hand. In the *fourth* watch of the night the Lord Jesus appeared on the waters, and you were delivered. Then *remember* this, and let the realization of past deliverances comfort and stay your heart in the midst of the present emergency.

Many are the appeals made unto us in the Word of God to do this very thing. Varied and numerous are the motives employed by the Holy Spirit in the Scripture of Truth to stir up God's children unto constancy of heart and the performance of duty when "circumstances" seem to be all against them. Every attribute of God is made a distinct ground for urging us to run with perseverance the race that is set before us. The promises of God are given to cheer, and His warnings stir up our hearts unto a fuller compliance with His revealed will. Rewards are promised to those who overcome the flesh, the world, and the Devil, while eternal woes are threatened unto those failing to do so. Faith is to be stimulated by the record given of God's grace which sustained fellow-pilgrims in by-gone days; hope is to be stirred into action by the glorious Goal which the Word holds up to view. And, as we have said, fresh courage for the present is to be drawn by us from calling to mind God's goodness in the past. It is *this* particular motive which the apostle pressed on the Hebrews in the passage which is now before us.

"But call to remembrance the former days, in which, after ye were illuminated, ye endured a great fight of afflictions" (v. 32). In vv. 16-21 the apostle had given a brief summary of the inestimable privileges which are the present portion of the regenerated people of God. In vv. 22-24 he had exhorted them to make a suitable response to such blessings. In vv. 25-31 he had fortified their minds against temptations to apostasy, or to wilful and presumptuous sins. He now bids them to recall the earlier days of their profession, and to consider what they had already ventured, suffered and renounced for Christ, and how they had been supernaturally sustained under their trials: the force of this was, disgrace not your former conduct by now casting away your confidence which hath great recompense of reward.

"But call to remembrance the former days, in which, after ye were illuminated." The beginnings of God's work of grace in their souls is here spoken of as being "illuminated." The Holy Spirit had revealed to them their depravity and impotency, their lost and miserable state by nature. He had brought before them the unchanging demands of God's righteous law, and their utter failure to meet those claims. He had pointed them to the Lord Jesus, who, as the Sponsor and Surety of His people, had assumed all their liabilities, kept the law in their stead, and died for their sins. For God who commanded the light to shine out of darkness, had "shined into their hearts, to give the light of the knowledge of the glory of God in the face of Jesus Christ" (2 Cor. 4:6). Thus He had granted unto them an experimental acquaintance with the Gospel, so that they had felt in their own consciences and hearts the power of its truth. How unspeakably solemn is it to note that this too had been the experience of the apostates in Heb. 6:4-6, for the very word here rendered "illuminated" is there translated, "enlightened."

Right after their illumination by God, they were called upon to feel something of the rage of His enemies. At the beginning of this dispensation those who made profession of Christianity were hotly persecuted, and the believing Hebrews had not escaped. This the apostle would remind them of: "After ye were illuminated, ye endured a great fight of afflictions." As soon as God had quickened their hearts and shone upon their understandings so that they embraced His incarnate Son as their Lord and Saviour, earth and hell combined against them. By nature we are in the dark, and while in it we meet with no opposition from Satan or the world; but when, by grace we determined to follow the example which Christ has left us, we were soon brought into the fellowship of His sufferings. By such experiences we are reminded that God has called us to the combat, that as good soldiers of Jesus Christ we are to "endure hardness" (2 Tim. 2:3), and need to take unto ourselves the armour which God has provided (Eph. 6:10-18) — not to speculate about, but to *use* it.

The attitude toward and the conduct of the Hebrew Christians under this "great fight of afflictions" during the days of their "first love," is here summed up, first, in the one word "endured." They had not fainted or given way to despondency, nor had they renounced their profession. They failed in no part of the conflict, but came off conquerors. This they had been enabled unto by the efficacious grace of God. They had been wondrously and blessedly supported under their sufferings. From Acts 8 we learn that when the church at Jerusalem was sorely persecuted, its members so far from abandoning Christianity, were scattered abroad, and "went everywhere preaching the Word" (v. 4). How greatly was the Captain of their salvation honoured by this valour of His soldiers. It is a noticeable fact of history that *babes* in Christ have often been the bravest of all in facing suffering and death: perhaps because the great and glorious change involved in the passing from death unto life is *fresher* in their minds than in that of older Christians. Now it was to the recollection of these things unto which the apostles here called the flagging and tempted Hebrews.

"But call to remembrance." "It is not the bare remembrance he intends, for it is impossible men should absolutely forget such a season. Men are apt enough to remember the times of their sufferings, especially such as are here mentioned, accompanied with all sorts of injurious treatments from men. But the apostle would have them *so* call to mind, as to consider withal, what support they had under their sufferings, what satisfaction in them, what deliverance from them, that they might not despond upon the approach of the like trials and evils on the same account. If we remember our sufferings only as unto what is evil and afflictive in them, what we lose, what we endure, and undergo; such a remembrance will weaken and dispirit us, as unto our future trials. Hereon many cast about to deliver themselves for the future, by undue means and sinful compliances, in a desertion of their profession; the thing the apostle was jealous of concerning these Hebrews. But if, withal, we call to mind what was the Cause for which we suffered; the honour that is in such sufferings, outbalancing all the contempt and reproaches of the world; the presence of God enjoyed in them; and the reward proposed unto us; the calling these things to mind, will greatly strengthen us against future trials; provided we retain the same love unto, and valuation of the things for which we suffered, as we had in those former days" (John Owen).

"The remembrance then of past warfare, if it had been carried on faithfully and diligently under the banner of Christ, is at length useful to us, not as a pretext for sloth, as though we had already served our time, but to render us more active in finishing the remaining part of our course. For Christ has not enlisted us on this condition, that we should after a few years ask for a discharge, like soldiers who have served their time, but that we should pursue our warfare even unto the end" (John Calvin). It therefore becomes a solemn and searching question for each of us to face: to what extent am I *now* being antagonized by the world? Something must be seriously wrong with me if I have the good-will of everybody. God's Word emphatically declares, "All that will live godly in Christ Jesus *shall* suffer persecution" (2 Tim. 3:12).

"Partly, whilst ye were made a gazing-stock, both by reproaches and afflictions; and partly, whilst ye became companions of them that were so used" (v. 33). In this verse the apostle mentions one or two features of what their "great fight of affliction" had consisted. Some of them were made a public spectacle to their neighbors, by the malicious accusations brought against them, and by the derision and punishment laid upon them; while others were the "partners" of those who were also cruelly treated. The principal reference here is to the loss which they had sustained in their characters and reputations, and unto many people (especially those of a sensitive temperament) this is a sore trial; almost anything is easier to bear than obloquy and disgrace. But sufficient for the disciple to be as his Master: they slandered Him, and said He had a demon.

Reproach and slander are exceedingly trying, and if we are not upon our guard, if we fail to gird up the loins of our minds (1 Pet. 1:13), we are likely to be so cast down by them as to be incapacitated for duty. Despondency and despair are never excusable in the Christian, and must be steadily resisted. We need to make up our minds that if, by grace, we are determined to follow the example which Christ has left us we shall have many enemies — especially in the religious world — who will scruple at no misrepresentations of our motives and actions. We must learn to undervalue our reputations, and be content to be regarded as "the offscouring of all things"; we must seek grace to emulate Him who "set His face like a flint" (Isa. 50:7), who "endured the cross, *despising* the shame" (Heb. 12:2). Unless we cultivate His spirit we shall be at a great disadvantage when sufferings come upon us.

Not only had the Hebrew Christians suffered personally, but they had fellowship also in the sufferings of others. This is a Christian duty, and, we may add, a privilege. As members of the same Family, as fellow-pilgrims toward the better Country, as called to serve together under the same Banner, it is only meet that we should bear "one another's burdens," and "weep with them that weep." Of Moses it is recorded that "He refused to be called the son of Pharaoh's daughter, choosing rather to suffer affliction with the people of God, than to enjoy the pleasure of sin for a season" (Heb. 11:24, 25). To be a companion of those who suffer for Christ, is an evidence of our love for His brethren, of courage in suffering, and of readiness to succour those who are persecuted because of the Gospel. We do well to frequently ponder Matt. 25:42-45.

"For ye had compassion of me in my bonds" (v. 34). The apostle here makes grateful acknowledgment of the sympathy which the Hebrews had shown him in an hour of need. The historical reference may be to the time when he lay bound in chains at Jerusalem (Acts 21:33), when their love for him was shown by their prayers, and perhaps letters and gifts. It is the bounden duty for Christians to express in a practical way their compassion for any of Christ's suffering servants, doing everything in their power to succour, support and relieve them. Equally so is it the duty of God's ministers to thankfully own the kindness shown them: Christ himself will yet publicly bear witness unto the services of love which have been shown unto His brethren (Matt. 25:34-40).

"For ye had compassion of me in my bonds." These words supply one of the many proofs that the apostle Paul was the author of this Epistle, for of the other persons whom some have fancied wrote it, such as Luke, Barnabas, Clement etc., there is no hint anywhere in Scripture, nor we believe in ecclesiastical history, of any of them suffering bonds in Judea. But the lying of Paul in bonds and imprisonments, was renowned above all others. Hence he styled himself in particular "Paul, prisoner of Jesus Christ" (Phile. 1), and gloried in this peculiar honour as "an ambassador in bonds" (Eph. 6:20), and as such, desired the saints at Colosse to remember him at the throne of grace (4:3). Thus, his "bonds" being above all others so familiar, such a subject of the churches' prayers, this reference here in Heb. 10:34 at once identifies the writer.

"And took joyfully the spoiling of your goods" (v. 34). This supplies further information upon the deportment of the Hebrews under their trials: they had not only patiently "endured" the great fight of affliction, but were happy in being counted worthy to suffer for

Christ — a blessed triumph was that of the mighty grace of God over the weakness of the flesh. God is able to strengthen in the inner man "with all might, according to His glorious power, unto all patience and longsuffering, with joyfulness" (Col. 1:11). Ordinarily, few things are more calculated to distress the minds of men than their being cruelly plundered of those things for which they have laboured hard, and which they and their families still need: wailing and lamentations commonly accompany them. Blessed is it when the heart is brought to hold lightly all earthly comforts and conveniences, for it is easier then to part with them should we be called upon to do so.

"Knowing in yourselves that we have in heaven a better and enduring substance" (v. 34). This clause supplies the key to the previous one, showing the ground of their joy. Faith looked away from things seen to those unseen, reckoning that "the sufferings of this present time are not worthy to be compared with the glory which shall be revealed in us" (Rom. 8:18); "For our light affliction, which is but for a moment, worketh for us a far more exceeding and eternal weight of glory" (2 Cor. 4:17). Where the heart's affections are truly set upon things above (Col. 3:2), few tears will be shed over the loss of any earthly baubles. True, it is *natural* to mourn when rudely deprived of material possessions, but it is *supernatural* to rise above such grieving.

The true riches of the Christian are not accessible to human or Satanic plunderers. Men may strip us of all our worldly possessions, but they cannot take from us the love of God, the salvation of Christ, the comforts of the Holy Spirit, the hope of eternal glory. Said one who was waylaid by a bandit, who demanded his money or his life: "Money, I have none on me; my *life* is hid with Christ in God." The poor worldling may give way to despair when business is bad, bonds deteriorate, and banks smash, but no child of God ought ever to do so: he has been begotten unto an inheritance which is "incorruptible, and undefiled, and that fadeth not away, reserved in heaven" (1 Pet. 1:4). Yet it is only as faith is in exercise, as the heart is really occupied with our heavenly portion, that we *enjoy* them, and regard all else as but "vanity and vexation of spirit."

"What was it that enabled them thus to bear up under their sufferings? They knew in themselves that they had in heaven a better and a more enduring substance. Observe, first; the happiness of the saints in heaven is 'substance,' something of real weight and worth — all things here are but shadows. Secondly, it is a better substance than anything they can have or lose here. Thirdly, it is an enduring substance; it will outlive time, and run parallel with eternity. They can never spend it; their enemies can never take it from them as they did their earthly goods. Fourthly, this will make a rich amends for all they can lose and suffer here. In heaven they shall have a better life, a better estate, better liberty, better society, better hearts, better work, everything better" (Matt. Henry).

"Knowing in yourselves that we have in heaven a better and an enduring substance." Let us now weigh carefully the first three words of this clause: these Hebrew saints had a firm conviction of heart concerning their heavenly portion. It does not say, "knowing from God's promises," but "knowing *in yourselves*." This presents a side of the Truth, an aspect of Christian assurance, which is rarely dwelt upon in these days; instead, it is widely ridiculed and denied, many insisting that the only basis of assurance is the bare letter of Scripture. It is quite true that the foundation of our confidence is the written Word, but that is *not* the *only* ground, any more than a marriage-certificate is the sole proof which a woman has that the man who loves, cherishes, and lives with her, is her husband. No, one has only to read impartially through the first Epistle of John in order to discover that he who is walking with God and enjoying the light of His countenance, has many evidences that he is a new creature in Christ Jesus.

"Knowing in yourselves." The one who is following on to know the Lord (Hos. 6:3), not only has the testimony of God's Word without, but he has also the witness of the Spirit within him, that he is a child and heir of God (Rom. 8:16, 17). In his regeneration and begun-experimental sanctification, he has received "the first-fruits of the Spirit (Rom. 8:23). In consequence, he now has new desires, new conflicts, new joys, new sorrows. Faith purifies his heart (Acts 15:9). He has received the Spirit of adoption, whereby he cries "Abba Father." From what he finds in his own heart, he *knows* that he is heaven-born and heaven-bound. Let those who are strangers to a supernatural work of grace in their own hearts mock and scoff all they please, let them sneer at introspection, call it mysticism, or any thing else they wish, but one who is scripturally assured of the Spirit's work within him, refuses to be laughed-out of his surest proof that *he* is a child of God.

Granted that many have been and are deluded: acknowledging that the unregenerate heart is "deceitful above all things"; admitting that the Devil has lulled thousands into hell by means of happy feelings within them; yet none of these things alter or affect to the slightest degree the fact that it is both the duty and privilege of every genuine Christian to know *in himself* that he has passed from death unto life. Provided he be denying self, taking up his cross, and following Christ in the path of obedience, he will have cause for rejoicing in the testimony of a good conscience (2 Cor. 1:12). But if he yields to lusts of the flesh, fellowships with an ungodly world, and gets into a backslidden state, then the joy of his salvation will be lost. Nothing then is of greater practical importance than that the Christian should keep clean and unstained his inward evidences that he is journeying toward heaven.

"Such, then, are the things which the apostle wishes the Hebrew Christians to 'call to remembrance.' It is easy to see how the calling of these things to remembrance was calculated to serve his purpose — to guard them from apostasy, and establish them in the faith and profession of the Gospel. It is as if he had said, 'Why shrink from suffering for Christianity now? Were you not exposed to suffering from the beginning? When you first became Christians, did you not willingly undergo sufferings on account of it? And is not Christianity as worthy of being suffered for as ever? Is not Jesus the same yesterday, and today, and forever? Did not the faith and hope of Christianity formerly support you under your sufferings, and make you feel that they were but the light afflictions of a moment? and are they not as able to support you now as then? Has the substance in heaven become less real, or less enduring? and have you not as good evidence now as you had then that to the persevering Christian such treasure is laid up? Are you willing to lose all the benefit of the sacrifices you have made, and the sufferings you have sustained? and they will all go for nothing if you endure not unto the end!' These are considerations all naturally suggested by the words of the apostle, and all well calculated to induce them 'to hold fast the profession of their faith without wavering'." (John Brown).

CHAPTER FIFTY-FIVE

The Saving of the Soul

(Heb. 10:35-39)

As there is so much ground covered by the verses which are now to be before us, we shall dispense with our usual introductory paragraphs. In lieu of them, we present a brief analysis of the present passage. V. 35 really belongs to the section which we took up in our last article. In vv. 32-35 the apostle gives a persuasion unto perseverance in the Christian life. First, he bids the Hebrews call to remembrance what they had suffered for Christ's sake in days gone by: then let them not now renounce their faith and thereby render void their early witness — vv. 32, 33. Second, he reminded them of the ground on which they had willingly suffered hardships and losses, namely, because they had the inward assurance and evidence that in Heaven they had a better and enduring substance: then, inasmuch as it changed not, why should they? — v. 34. From these facts, the conclusion is drawn that a duty is rightly required from them, upon the performance of which the reward should be given them — v. 35.

In the last section of Heb. 10 the apostle first confirms the exhortation he had just insisted on, and points to the chief aids to perseverance, namely, patience and faith — v. 36. Second, he encourages the Lord's people by the prospect of the sure and speedy coming of the Redeemer who would then reward them — v. 37. Third, he warns again of the fearful state of the apostate — v. 38. Fourth, he affirms that they who persevered to the end, believe to the saving of the soul — v. 39. The obvious design of these verses is to stir up Christians unto utmost earnestness in making their calling and election sure, to guard them against the danger of backsliding, and to bear their trials with submission to the will of God. May it please the Holy Spirit to apply this passage in power to the heart of both writer and reader, that our meditation may issue in fruit to the glory of our blessed Lord.

"Cast not away therefore your confidence, which hath great recompense of reward" (v. 35). Let us notice first the force of the "therefore." This is an inference drawn from the foregoing: since you have already suffered so many things in your persons and goods, and inasmuch as Divine grace supported and carried you through with constancy and joy, do not be discouraged and give way to despair at the approach of similar trials. Further, this "therefore" is drawn from the blissful prospect which the sure promise of God holds before His faithful people, and gives point to the admonition: inasmuch as confidence persisted in is going to be richly repaid, cast it not away.

"Cast not away therefore your confidence." The word "confidence" here has respect unto an attitude or state of heart Godwards. It is the same term (in the Greek) as is translated "boldness" in 10:19. It is found again in 1 John 3:21, "then have we confidence toward God"; and 5:14, "this is the confidence that we have in Him." It is not so much faith itself, as one of the products or fruits thereof. It is closer akin to hope. It is that effect of faith which fits the Christian for freedom and readiness unto all his spiritual duties, notwithstanding difficulties and discouragements. It is that frame of spirit which carries us cheerfully through all those sufferings which a real profession of the Gospel entails. More specifically, this "confidence" may be defined as fortitude of mind, courage of heart, and constancy of will.

From what has just been said, it will be seen that we do not agree with those commentators who understand v. 35 as dehorting against the abandonment of Christianity. The apostle's admonition here strikes deeper than a warning against forsaking the outward profession of the Gospel. It is addressed against that state of heart, which, if it became chronic, would likely lead to the external forsaking of Christ. What is needed in the face of trials and persecution is boldness of mind, the heart being freed from bondage and fear, through a prevailing persuasion of our acceptance with God in the performance of those duties which He has appointed us. It was this particular grace which was admired in Peter and John in Acts 4:13. It is only as the mind remains convinced of the righteousness of our cause, and as the heart is assured we are doing that which is well-pleasing to God, that, when we are criticised and condemned by men, and are menaced by their frowns and threats, we shall be "steadfast, unmoveable, always abounding in the work of the Lord" (1 Cor. 15:58), in nothing moved by our adversaries.

This confidence in and toward God, which had hitherto sustained the persecuted Hebrews, they are here bidden to "cast not away." Here again the responsibility of the Christian is addressed. There are those who insist we can no more control our "confidence" — weaken or strengthen it — than we can control the wind. But this is to lose sight of the fact that we are moral creatures and accountable for the use or misuse of all our faculties. If I allow my mind to dwell upon the difficulties before me, the disadvantages I may suffer through faithfulness to Christ, or listen to the whisperings of Satan as to how I can avoid trouble by little compromises, then my courage will soon wane, and *I* shall be to blame. On the other hand, if I seek grace to dwell upon God's promises, realize it is an honour to suffer for Christ's sake, and remind myself that whatever I lose here is not worthy to be compared with what I shall gain hereafter, then, assured that God is for me, I shall care not who be against me.

To encourage the tempted Hebrews the apostle at once added, "which hath great recompense of reward." From these words it is very evident that the true Christian may, and should, have his eye upon the reward that is promised those who suffer for the Gospel's sake. Nor does this verse by any means stand alone: "Blessed are ye, when men shall revile you, and persecute you, and shall say all manner of evil against you falsely, for My sake: Rejoice, and be exceeding glad, for great is your reward in Heaven" (Matt. 5:11, 12)—notice carefully the words "in Heaven," which at once exposes the error of those who declare that the "Sermon on the Mount" belongs not to and is not about those who are members of the Body of Christ, but is "Jewish" and "Millennial." Christians are not sufficiently occupied with their reward in Heaven.

The subject of "Rewards" is too large a one for us to now canvass in detail, yet in view of present-day errors something needs to be said thereon. Not a few suppose that the concepts presented by "grace" and "reward" are irreconcilably at variance. The trouble with such people is that, instead of searching the Scriptures to discover how the Holy Spirit has *used* the term, they turn to a human dictionary. In human affairs a "reward" commonly (though not always) denotes the recognition and recompensing of a *meritorious* performance; but not so is its general usage in Scripture. Take the first occurrence of the word: in Gen. 15:1 we find Jehovah saying unto Abraham, "Fear not, Abram: I am thy shield, and thy exceeding great reward": how utterly impossible for the patriarch to have done anything to *deserve* this! Once it is plainly perceived that *in Scripture* the term "reward" has in it *no* thought of a meet return for a *meritorious* performance, much of the fog with which modern "dispensationalists" have surrounded the subject will be cleared away.

"Which hath great recompense of reward." Rightly did John Calvin point out in his comments on this verse: "By mentioning 'reward,' he diminishes nothing from the gratuitous promise of salvation, for the faithful know that their labour is not in vain in the Lord in such a way that they still rest on God's mercy alone. But it has been often stated elsewhere how 'reward' is *not* incompatible with the *gratuitous* imputation of righteousness." If those who suppose that Christians living since the days of J. N. Darby and "Dr." Scofield appeared on the scene have "much more light" than they who preceded them, would only *read* the Reformers and the Puritans with an unprejudiced mind, they would soon be obliged to revise their ideas. In many respects we have gone backwards instead of forwards, and only too often the "light" which is in men, is but *darkness,* and "how great is that darkness" (Matt. 6:23)! — so great that it closes their eyes against all true light.

"For ye have need of patience, that, after ye have done the will of God, ye might receive the promise" (v. 36). The opening "for" intimates that the apostle is here confirming the exhortation which he had just insisted upon. "The reward can be obtained only by holding fast this confidence — by adhering steadily and perseveringly to Christ and His cause" (John Brown). Patience, or endurance in the path of obedience, fidelity and suffering, is indispensably necessary if we are to be preserved unto salvation. Let those who will, call this teaching *legalistic;* the only other alternative is lawlessness and licentiousness. Though it is *not* "for," yet it is "*through* faith and patience" or "perseverance," that we "inherit the promises" (Heb. 6:12).

No one who is familiar with the writings of John Owen the Puritan, who proclaimed the free grace of God and the gratuitousness of His salvation in such certain terms, will accuse him of legality or of inculcating creature-merits; yet he, in his comments in Heb. 10:35, 36 wrote, "Wherefore, 'the recompense of the reward' here intended, is the glory of Heaven, proposed as a crown unto them that overcome in their sufferings for the Gospel. And the future glory, which, as unto its original cause, is the fruit of the good pleasure and sovereign grace of God, whose pleasure it is to give us the kingdom; and as unto its procuring cause is the sole purchase of the blood of Christ, who obtained for us eternal redemption; and it is, on both accounts, a free gift of God, for 'the wages of sin is death, but the gift of God through Christ is life eternal' (so as it can be no way merited nor procured by ourselves, by virtue of any proportion by the rules of justice between what we do or suffer, and what is promised), is yet constantly promised to suffering believers, under the name of a recompense or a reward. For it doth not become the greatness and goodness of God to call His own people unto sufferings for His name, and unto His glory, and therein to the loss of their lives many times, with all enjoyments here below, and not propose unto them, nor provide for them, that which shall be infinitely better than all that they so undergo. This confidence '*hath*' this recompense of reward; that is, it gives a right and title unto the future reward of glory: it hath in it the promise and constitution of God; whoever abides in its exercise, shall be no longer in the issue."

"For ye have need of patience." The apostle did not charge them with being destitute of this grace, for all who are born of the Spirit bear, in some measure, the fruit of the Spirit, and this among the rest (Gal. 5:22); those who are brought into the kingdom of Jesus Christ, are into His patience also (Rev. 1:9). No, the apostle signified that they needed the exercise, continuance, and increase of this grace: compare Zeph. 2:3 where the "meek" are exhorted to *seek* "meekness." That unto which the apostle would bestir these saints was, that they receive afflictions as from the hand of God, to bear reproaches and persecutions from men as that unto which He had "appointed" them (1 Thess. 3:3), to commit their cause unto the Lord and rest in Him (Psa. 37:5, 6); to bear up, and not sink under trials, and to live in the constant expectation of Heaven.

The Hebrew Christians (like we sometimes are) were tempted to become weary of well doing. Numbers of their fellows who had once appeared to be zealous believers, had apostatized, and the rest would soon be sorely tried. It was necessary then that they should arm their minds with the spirit of resignation and persevering constancy, that having done the will of God, by steadfastly cleaving to Christ, and obeying Him through all temptations and sufferings, they might afterwards receive the promised gift of eternal life. The principle of this verse remains unchanged. Satan is the same, and so also is the world, and they who will live godly cannot escape trials and tribulations. Nor is it desirable that we should: some of the finer and more delicate of the Christian graces can only be developed under stress and suffering. Then how much we need to pray for God to sanctify to our good each affliction which comes upon us, so that fruit may issue to His praise and that we may so conduct ourselves as to be encouragements to fellow-pilgrims.

The exercise of this grace of patience is to be continued until "after ye have done the will of God." There is no dismission from the discharge of this duty while we are left here upon earth. While the more immediate reference is unto *meekly bearing* whatever the sovereign will of our all-wise and infinitely loving God has ordained for us, yet the *active walking* in the way of God's commandments is also included, as is evident from the word "done." The will of God, as it is made known in His Word, is the alone rule by which we are to live and all our ways are to be conformed. That revealed will of God is not only to be believed and revered by us, but *prac-*

ticed as well. No situation in which we can be placed, no threatenings of men however terrible, can ever justify us for disobeying God. True, there will be seasons of sore testing, times when it seems that our trials are more than flesh and blood can endure, and then it is that we most have "need of patience"; nor will Divine succour and supernatural grace be withheld if we humbly and trustfully seek it.

"That, after ye have done the will of God, ye might receive the promise." Here the "great recompense of reward" of the previous verse is designated "the promise," partly to guard against the error that eternal life can be earned, or that Heaven can be merited by creature performances; and partly to emphasize the *certainty* of that which is promised unto all who endure unto the end. The "promise" is here put for the things promised, as in 6:12, 17; 11:13, 39. It is called "*the* promise" as in 1 John 2:25 etc., because it is the grand comprehensive promise, including all others, being the glorious consummation to which they point. Nor should any stumble because they cannot perceive the consistency of a thing being *both* a "reward" and a "promise." We find the same conjunction of concepts in Col. 3:24, "Ye shall receive the *reward* of the inheritance; *for* ye *serve* the Lord Christ": it is so denominated to show that it is *not* merited by works, but is bestowed by free grace, and will certainly be enjoyed by all the elect; and yet, it will only be obtained by them as they persevere in the path of duty.

"For yet a little while, and He that shall come will come, and will not tarry" (v. 37). The causal "For" denotes that the apostle was about to confirm what he had just said: he both adds a word to strengthen their "confidence" and "patience," and also points them to the near approach of the time when they should receive their "reward." The Greek is very expressive and emphatic. The apostle used a word which signifies "a little while," and then for further emphasis added a particle meaning "very," and this he still further intensified by repeating it; thus, literally rendered this clause reads, "For yet a very, very little while, and He that shall come will come."

"There is indeed nothing that avails more to sustain our minds, should they at any time become faint, than the hope of a speedy and near termination. As a general holds forth to his soldiers the prospect that the war will soon end, provided they hold out a little longer; so the apostle reminds us that the Lord will shortly come to deliver us from all evils, provided our minds faint not through want of firmness. And in order that this consolation might have more assurance and authority, he adduces the testimony of Habakkuk. But as he follows the Greek version, he departs somewhat from the words of the prophet" (John Calvin). Frequently does the Holy Spirit emphasize the exceeding (comparative) brevity of the saints' sufferings in this world; "Weeping may endure for a night, but joy cometh in the morning" (Psa. 30:5); "And the God of peace shall bruise Satan under your feet *shortly*" (Rom. 16:20); "For our light affliction, which is but for a moment" (2 Cor. 4:17).

"For yet a little while, and He that shall come will come, and will not tarry." The reference here is to the person of the Lord Jesus, as is evident from Hab. 2:3, to which the apostle here alludes. Like so many prophecies, that word of Habakkuk's was to receive a threefold fulfillment: a literal and initial one, a spiritual and continuous one, a final and complete one. The literal was the Divine incarnation, when the Son of God came here in flesh. The final will be His return in visible glory and power. The spiritual has reference to the destruction of Jerusalem in A. D. 70 when that which most obstructed the manifestation of Christ's kingdom on earth was destroyed — with the overthrow of the Temple and its worship, official Judaism came to an end. The Christians in Palestine were being constantly persecuted by the Jews, but their conquest by Titus and their consequent dispersion put an end to this. That event was less than ten years distant when Paul wrote: compare our remarks on "see the day approaching" (10:25).

We trust that none will conclude from what has been said above that we regard v. 37 as containing *no* reference to the final coming of Christ. What we have sought to point out was the *immediate* purport of its contents unto the Hebrews. But it also contains a message for us, a message of hope and comfort. It is *our* privilege too to be waiting for God's Son from Heaven. Let us add that it is a big mistake to regard *every* mention of the "coming" of Christ in the N. T. Scriptures as referring to His "appearing the second time" (Heb. 9:28). In John 14:18, 28, the reference was to Christ's "coming" by His Spirit; in John 14:23 to His "coming" in loving manifestation to the individual soul; in Eph. 2:17 He "came" by the Gospel; in Rev. 2:5 His "coming" is in chastisement. Careful study of each verse is required in order to distinguish between these several aspects.

"Now the just shall live by faith: but if any man draw back, My soul shall have no pleasure in him" (v. 38). The first half of this verse is a quotation from Hab. 2:4, and its pertinency to the admonition which the apostle was pressing upon the Hebrews is not difficult to perceive. The prophet is cited in proof that perseverance is one of the distinguishing characteristics of a child of God. He who has been justified by God, through the imputation of Christ's righteousness to his account, lives by faith as the influencing principle of his life. Thus the apostle declared, "The life which I now live in the flesh I live by the faith of the Son of God" (Gal. 2:20). The one whom God has exonerated from the curse and condemnation of the law, is not him who has merely "believed," but is the man who *continues* "believing," with all that that word includes, and involves. Let the reader fully note the force of the present perfect "believ*eth*" in John 3:15, 16, 18; 5:24 etc., and contrast the "for a while believed" of Luke 8:13!

The use of the future tense "shall live" announces and enforces the necessity for the continued exercise of faith. It is true that one who has been justified by God was previously quickened, for we are "justified by faith" (Acts 13:39, Rom. 5:1 etc.), and one who is dead in trespasses and sins cannot savingly believe — note the "called" *before* "justified" in Rom. 8:30. It is also true that the real Christian *lives* by faith, for that is the very nature of indwelling grace. But it is equally true that the "just *shall live* by faith." The constant exercise of faith by the saint is as essential to his final salvation as it was to his initial salvation. Just as the soul can only be delivered from the wrath to come by repentance (self-judgment) and personal faith in the Lord Jesus, so we can only be delivered from the power of indwelling sin, from the temptations of Satan, from an enticing world which seeks to destroy us, by a steady and persistent *walking* by faith.

Patient endurance is a fruit of faith, yet it is only as that vital and root grace is in daily exercise, that the Christian is enabled to stand firm amid the storms of life. Those whom God declares righteous in Christ are to pass their lives here, not in doubt and fear, but in the maintenance of a calm trust in and a joyful obedience to Him. Only as the heart is engaged with God and feeds upon His Word, will the soul be invigorated and fitted to press onwards when everything outward seems to be against him. It is by our faith being drawn out unto things above that we receive the needed strength which causes us to look away from the discouraging and distracting scene around us. As faith lives upon Christ (John 6:56, 57), it draws virtue from Him, as the branch derives sap from the root of the vine. Faith makes us resign ourselves and our affairs to Christ's disposing, cheerfully treading the path of duty and patiently waiting that issue which He will give. Faith is assured that our Head knows far better than we do what is good and best.

"But if any man draw back, My soul shall have no pleasure in him." It seems to the writer that the translators of the A. V. took an unwarranted liberty with the Word of God when they inserted (in italics) the words "any man" and changed "and" (kai) into "but": the Holy Scripture should never be altered to suit our ideas of evangelical truth—the R. V. correctly gives "if he shrink back," and Bag. Int. "and if he draw back." Yes, *if* the "just" man himself were to draw back and continue in apostasy, he would finally perish. "By this solemn consideration, therefore, the apostle urges on them the importance of perseverance, and the guilt and danger of apostasy from the Christian faith. *If* such a case should occur, no matter what might have been the former condition, and no matter what love or zeal might have been evinced, yet such an apostasy would expose the individual to the certain wrath of God. His former love could not save him, any more than the former obedience of the angels saved them from the horrors of eternal chains and darkness" (A. Barnes).

"And if he drew back, My soul shall have no pleasure in him." Once more the apostle faithfully warns the Hebrew Christians (and us) of the dreadful consequence which would attend the continuance in a course of backsliding. He who thinks that by refusing to take up his cross daily and follow the example left by Christ, can escape the world's reproach and persecution and yet go to Heaven, is fatally deluding himself. Said the Lord Jesus, "For whosoever will save his life shall lose it" (Matt. 16:25): that is, he who is so diligent in looking after his temporal prospects, worldly reputation and personal comforts, shall eternally lose his soul.

It was to stir up the Hebrews unto the more diligent labouring after living the life of faith that the apostle here pointed out the terrible alternative: unless they maintained a steady trust in God and an obedient submission unto His revealed will, they were in grave danger of backsliding and apostatising. If any should "draw back" then God would have "*no* pleasure in him," which is but the negative way of saying that he would be an object of abhorrence. But observe closely, it does not say God would have "no *more* pleasure in him," which would conflict with the uniform teaching of the Word concerning the *unchanging* love of God (Mal. 3:6, John 13:1, Rom. 8:35-39) toward His own. O the minute accuracy of Holy Writ! The practical application of this solemn word to us is, that in order to have a scripturally-grounded assurance of God's taking pleasure in *us,* we must continue cleaving closely unto Him.

"But we are not of them who draw back unto perdition; but of them that believe to the saving of the soul" (v. 39). The word "perdition" shows plainly that the "drawing back" of the previous verse is a fatal and final one. Nevertheless, so far is v. 38 from establishing the doom of any child of God, the apostle assures the

Hebrews that no such fate would overtake them. What is added here in this verse, was to prevent their being unduly affrighted with the solemn warnings previously given, and lest they should conclude that Paul thought evilly of them: though he had warned, he did not regard them as treading the broad road to destruction, instead he was "persuaded better things of them" (6:9). "Let it be noticed that this truth belongs also to us, for we, whom God has favoured with the light of the Gospel, ought to acknowledge that we have been called in order that we may advance more and more in our obedience to God, and strive constantly to draw nearer to Him. This is the real preservation of the soul, for by so doing we shall escape eternal perdition" (J. Calvin).

"In this the apostle expresses the fullest conviction that none of those to whom he wrote would apostatise. The case which he had been describing was only a supposable case, not one which he believed would occur. He had only been stating what *must* happen if a sincere Christian should apostatise. But he did not mean to say that this *would* occur in regard to them. He made a statement of a general principle under the Divine administration, and he designed that this should be a means of keeping them in the path of life" (A. Barnes). Christians may grow cold, neglect the means of grace, backslide, fall into grievous sins as did David and Peter; but they shall not "draw back *unto perdition*." No, they have been predestinated "to be conformed unto" the image of Christ (Rom. 8:29), and God's purpose cannot fail. They are the objects of Christ's intercession (John 17:15, 24), and that is efficacious (John 11:42). They are *restored* by the good Shepherd when they go astray (Psa. 23:3).

As the term "perdition" denoted that eternal damnation is the doom of apostates, so the word "salvation" here has reference to that ultimate consummation of the portion of all true believers. It is to be carefully noted that the apostle did not say, "them that have believed to the salvation of the soul," but "them that believe to the saving of the soul." The difference is real and radical. There is a blessed sense in which every regenerated believer *has been* saved by Christ, yet there is also another and most important sense in which his salvation is *yet future*: see Rom. 13:11, 1 Pet. 1:5, 9. The complete and final salvation of the Christian is dependent upon his *continued* trust in and obedience to God in Christ, *not* as the *cause* thereof, yet as the indispensable *means* thereto.

It is gloriously true that Christians are "kept by the power of God." He who prepares Heaven for them preserves them unto it. But by what instrument or means? The same verse tells us:

"through faith" (1 Pet. 1:5). To depend upon an invisible God for a happiness that awaits us in an invisible world, when in the meantime He permits us to be harassed with all sorts of temptations, trials and troubles, requires faith — real faith, supernatural faith. Through faith alone can the heart be sustained till we obtain salvation. Nothing but a God-given and God-maintained faith can enable us to row against the stream of flesh and blood, and so deny its cravings that we shall win through to Heaven at last. The "flesh" is for sparing and pampering the body; but "faith" is for the "saving of the soul."

CHAPTER FIFTY-SIX

The Excellency of Faith

(Heb. 11:1-3)

Ere we take up the contents of the 11th chapter let us briefly review the ground already covered. Chapters 1 and 2 are more or less introductory in their character. In them the wondrous *person* of the God-man Mediator is presented to our view, as superior to the O. T. prophets and as excelling the angels. The first main division of the Epistle commences at 3:1 and runs to the end of 4:15, and treats of the *mission* of Christ: this is seen to surpass that of either Moses or Joshua, for neither of them led the people into the real rest of God; the section is followed by a practical application in 4:16. The second principal division begins with 5:1 and extends to 10:18, and deals with the *priesthood* of Christ: this is shown to transcend the Aaronic in dignity, efficacy and permanency; the section is followed by a practical application, contained in 10:19 to 12:29. The closing chapter forms a conclusion to the Epistle.

"The general nature of this Epistle, as unto the kind of writing, is paranetical or hortatory, which is taken from its end and design. The exhortation proposed is to constancy and perseverance in the faith of the Lord Jesus Christ, and in the profession of the Gospel, against temptations and persecutions. Both these the Hebrews had to conflict with in their profession; the one from the Judaical church-state itself, the other from the members of it. Their temptations to draw back and forsake their profession, arose from the consideration of the Judaical church-state and Mosaic ordinances of worship, which they were called by the Gospel to relinquish. The Divine institution of that state, with its worship, the solemnity of the covenant whereon it was established, the glory of its priesthood, sacrifices and other Divine ordinances (Rom. 9:4), with their efficacy for acceptance with God, were continually proposed unto them, and pressed on them, to allure and draw them off from the Gospel. And the trial was very great, after the inconsistency of the two states was made manifest. This gave occasion to the whole *doctrinal* part of the Epistle, the exposition of which, by Divine grace and assistance, we have passed through. For therein declaring the nature, use, end, and signification of all Divine institutions under the O. T.; and allowing unto them all the glory and efficacy which they could pretend unto, the writer of this Epistle declares from the Scripture itself that the state of the Gospel church, in its high-priest, sacrifice, covenant, worship, privileges and efficacy, is incomparably to be preferred above that of the O. T.; yea, that all the excellency and glory of that state, and all that belonged unto it, consisted only in the representation that was made thereby, of the greater glory of Christ and the Gospel, without which they were of no use, and therefore ruinous or pernicious to be persisted in.

"After he had fixed their minds in the truth, and armed them against the temptations which they were continually exposed to; the apostle proceeds to the second means, whereby their steadiness and constancy in the profession of the Gospel, which he exhorted them unto, was already assaulted, and was yet like to be assaulted with greater force and fury. This arose from the opposition which befell them, and from the persecutions of all sorts that they had endured, and were still like to undergo, for their faith in Christ Jesus with the profession thereof, and observance of the holy worship ordained in the Gospel. This they suffered from the obstinate *members* of the Jewish church, as they did the other (temptation) from the *state* of that church itself. An account hereof the apostle enters upon in the close of the foregoing chapter; and withal declares unto them the only way and means on their part, whereby they may be preserved, and kept constant in their profession notwithstanding all the evils that might befall them therein, and this is by faith alone. From their *temptations* they were delivered by the *doctrine* of the truth, and from the *opposition* made unto them, by *faith* in exercise" (J. Owen).

The particular character of the section begun at 10:19 is not difficult to ascertain: it is addressed to our responsibility. This is at once evident in the "Let us" of 10:22, 23, 24. In 10:32-36 there is a call to patient waiting for the fulfillment of God's promises. Nothing but real faith in the veracity of the Promiser can sustain the heart and prompt to steady endurance during a protracted season of trial and suffering. Hence in 10:38 the apostle quotes that striking word from Habakkuk, "The just shall live *by faith.*" That sentence really forms the text of which Heb. 11 is the sermon. The central design of this chapter is to evidence the *patience* of those who, in former ages, endured by faith before they received the fulfillment of God's promises: note particularly vv. 13, 39.

"Whoever made this (v. 1) the beginning of the eleventh chapter, has unwisely disjointed the context; for the object of the apostle was to prove what he had already said — that there is need of patience. He had quoted the testimony of Habakkuk, who says that the just lives by faith; he now shows what remained to be proved — that faith can be no more separated from patience than from itself. The order then of what he says is this: 'We shall not reach the goal of salvation except we have patience, for the prophet declares that the just lives by faith; but faith directs us to things afar off which we do not as yet enjoy; it then necessarily includes patience.' Therefore the minor proposition in the argument is this, 'Faith is the substance of things hoped for' " (J. Calvin).

"The apostle now, for the illustration and enforcement of his exhortation, brings forward a great variety of instances, from the history of former ages, in which *faith* had enabled individuals to perform very difficult duties, endure very severe trials, and obtain very important blessings. The principles of the apostle's exhortation are plainly these: 'They who turn back, turn back unto perdition. It is only they who persevere in believing that obtain the salvation of the soul. Nothing but a persevering faith can enable a person, through a constant continuance in well-doing, and a patient, humble submission to the will of God, to obtain that glory, honour, and immortality which the Gospel promises. Nothing but a persevering faith can do this; and a persevering faith can do it, as is plain from what it has done in former ages" (John Brown).

The order of thought followed by the apostle in Heb. 11 was ably and helpfully set forth by an early Puritan: "The parts of this whole chapter are two: 1. a general *description* of faith: vv. 1 to 4. 2. An *illustration* or declaration of that description, by a large rehearsal of manifold *examples* of ancient and worthy men in the Old Testament: vv. 4 to 40. The description of faith consists of three actions or effects of faith, set down in three several verses. The first effect is that faith makes things which are not (but only are hoped for), after a sort, to subsist and to be present with the believer: v. 1. The second effect is that faith makes a believer approved of God: v. 2. The third effect is that faith makes a man understand and believe things incredible to sense and reason" (Wm. Perkins, 1595).

"Now faith is the substance of things hoped for, the evidence of things not seen" (v. 1). The opening "Now" has almost the force of "for," denoting a farther confirmation of what had just been declared. At the close of chapter 10 the apostle had just affirmed that the saving of the soul is obtained through believing, whereupon he now takes occasion to show what faith is and does. That faith can, and does, preserve the soul, prompting to steadfastness under all sorts of trials and issuing in salvation, may not only be argued from the effects which is its very nature to produce, but is illustrated and demonstrated by one example after another, cited in the verses which follow. It is important to bear in mind at the outset that Heb. 11 is an amplification and exemplification of 10:38, 39: the "faith" which the apostle is describing and illustrating is that which has the *saving of the soul* annexed to it.

"In v. 1 there is the thing described, and the description itself. The thing described is Faith; the description is this: 'It is the substance of things hoped for' etc. The description is proper, according to the rules of art: habits (or graces) are described by their formal acts, and acts restrained to their proper objects; so faith is here described by its primary and formal acts, which are referred to their distinct objects. The acts of faith are two: it is the substance, it is the evidence. Think it not strange that I call them *acts,* for that is it the apostle intends; therefore Beza says, in rendering this place, he had rather paraphrase the text than obscure the scope, and he interpreteth it thus — Faith substantiates or gives a subsistence to our hopes, and demonstrates things not seen. There is a great deal of difference between the acts of faith and the effects of faith. The effects of faith are reckoned up throughout this chapter; the formal acts of faith are in this verse. These acts are suited with their objects. As the matters of belief are yet to come, faith gives them a substance, a being, as they are hidden from the eyes of sense and carnal reason; faith also gives them an evidence, and doth convince men of the worth of them; so that one of these acts belongs to the *understanding,* the other to the *will*" (Thos. Manton, 1670).

The contents of v. 1 do not furnish so much a formal definition of faith, as they supply a terse description of how it operates and what it produces. Faith, whether natural or spiritual, is the belief of a testimony. Here, faith is believing the testimony of God. How it operates in reference to the subjects of this testimony, whether they be considered simply as future, or as both invisible and future, and the effects produced in and on the soul, the Holy Spirit here explains. First, He tells us that "faith is the substance of things hoped for." The Greek word rendered "substance" has been variously translated. The margin of the A. V. gives "ground or confidence." The R. V. has "assurance" in the text, and "giving substance to" in the margin. The Greek word is "hypostasis" and is rendered "confident" (should be "this *confidence* of boasting," as in Bag. Int.) in both 2 Cor. 9:4 and 11:17; "person" (should be "subsistence" or "essential being") in Heb. 1:3; and "confidence" in 3:14. Personally, the writer believes it has a double force, so will seek to expound it accordingly.

"Faith is the *confidence* of things hoped for." In this chapter (and in general throughout the N.T.) "faith" is far more than a bare assent to any thing revealed and declared by God: it is a firm persuasion of that which is hoped for, because it assures its possessor not only that there *are* such things, but that through the power and faithfulness of God he shall yet *possess* them. Thus it becomes the ground of expectation. The Word of God is the *objective* foundation on which my hopes rest, but faith provides a *subjective* foundation, for it convinces me of the certainty of them. Faith and confidence are inseparable: just so far as I am counting upon the ability and fidelity of the Promiser, shall I be confident of receiving the things promised and which I am expecting. "We *believe* and are *sure*" (John 6:69).

From what has just been said, the reader will perhaps perceive better the force of the rather peculiar word "substance" in the text of the A. V. It comes from two Latin words, sub stans meaning "standing under." Faith provides a firm standing-ground while I await the fulfillment of God's promises. Faith furnishes my heart with a sure support during the interval. Faith believes God and relies upon His veracity: as it does so, the heart is anchored and remains steady, no matter how fierce the storm nor how protracted the season of waiting. "These all died in faith, *not* having received the (fulfillment of the) promises; *but* having seen them afar off, and were persuaded of them, and embraced them" (Heb. 11:13). Real faith issues in a confident and standing expectation of future things.

"Faith is the *substance* of things hoped for": as the marginal reading of the R. V. suggests, "giving substance to." Crediting the sure testimony of God, resting on His promises, and expecting the accomplishment of them, faith gives the object hoped for at a *future* period, a *present* reality and power in the soul, as if already possessed; for the believer is satisfied with the security afforded, and *acts* under the full persuasion that God will not fail of His engagement. Faith gives the soul an *appropriating hold* of them. "Faith is a firm persuasion and expectation that God will perform all that He has promised to us in Christ; and this persuasion is so strong that it gives the soul a kind of possession and present fruition of those things, gives them a subsistence in the soul by the firstfruits and foretastes of them; so that believers in the exercise of faith are filled with joy unspeakable and full of glory" (Matt. Henry).

The confident expectation which faith inspires, gives the objects of the Christian's hope a present and actual being in his heart. Faith does not look out with cold thoughts about things to come, but imparts life and reality to them. Faith does for us spiritually what fancy does for us naturally. There is a faculty of the understanding which enables us to *picture* to the mind's eye things which are yet future. But faith does more: it gives not an imaginary appearance to things, but a real subsistence. Faith is a grace which unites subject and object: there is no need to ascend to Heaven, for faith makes distant things nigh (see Rom. 10:6, 7). Faith, then, is the bond of union between the soul and the things God has promised. By believing we "receive"; by believing in Christ, He becomes *ours* (John 1:12). Therefore does faith enable the Christian to praise the Lord for future blessings as though he were already in the full possession of them.

But *how* does faith bring to the heart a present subsistence of future things? First, by drawing from the promises that which, by Divine institution, is stored up in them: hence they are called the "*breasts* of consolation" (Isa. 66:11). Second, by making the promises the food of the soul (Jer. 15:16), which cannot be unless they are really *present* unto it. Third, by conveying an experience of their power, as unto all the ends of which they are purposed: it is as Divine truth is appropriated and assimilated that it becomes powerfully operative in the soul. Fourth, by communicating unto us the firstfruits of the promises: faith gives a living reality to what it absorbs, and so real and potent is the impression made, that the heart is changed into the same image (2 Cor. 3:18).

Ere passing on, let us pause for a word of application. Many profess to "believe," but *what influence* have their hopes upon them? How are they affected by the things which their faith claims to have laid hold of? I profess to believe that sin is a most heinous thing—do I fear, hate, shun it? I believe that ere long I shall stand before the judgment-seat of Christ—does my conduct evince that I am living in the light of that solemn day? I believe that the world is an empty bauble—do I despise its painted tinsel? I believe that God will supply all my need—am I fearful about the morrow? I believe that prayer is an essential means unto growth in grace—do I spend much time in the secret place? I believe that Christ is coming back again—am I diligent in seeking to have my lamp trimmed and burning? Faith is evident by its fruits, works, effects.

Faith is "the evidence of things not seen." The Greek noun here rendered "evidence" ("proving" in the R. V., with "test" in the margin) is derived from a verb which signifies to *convince*, and that by demonstration. It was used by the Lord Jesus when He uttered that challenge, "which of you convicteth Me of sin?" (John 8:46). The noun occurs in only one other place, namely, 2 Tim. 3:16, "All scripture is . . . profitable for doctrine, for *reproof*," or "conviction"—to give assurance and certainty of what is true. Thus, the word "evidence" in our text denotes that which furnishes proof, so that one is assured of the reality and certainty of things Divine. "Faith," then, is first the *hand* of the soul which "lays hold of" the contents of God's promises; second, it is the *eye* of the soul which looks out toward and represents them clearly and convincingly to us.

To unbelievers the invisible, spiritual, and future things revealed in God's Word seem dubious and unreal, for they have no medium to perceive them: "the natural man receiveth not the things of the Spirit of God; for they are foolishness unto him; neither can he know them, because they are spiritually discerned" (1 Cor. 2:14). But the child of God *sees* "Him who is invisible" (Heb. 11:27). Perhaps we might illustrate it thus: two men stand on the deck of a ship gazing toward the far horizon; the one sees nothing, the other describes the details of a distant steamer. The former has only his unaided eyesight, the latter is using a telescope! Now just as a powerful glass brings home to the eye an object beyond the range of natural vision, so faith gives reality to the heart of things outside the range of our physical senses. Faith sets Divine things before the soul in all the light and power of demonstration, and thus provides inward conviction of their existence. "Faith demonstrates to the eye of the mind the reality of those things which cannot be discerned by the eye of the body" (Matt. Henry).

The natural man prefers a life of sense, and to believe nothing more than that which is capable of scientifical demonstration. When eternal things, yet invisible, are pressed upon him, he is full of objections against them. Those are the objections of unbelief, stirred into activity by the "fiery darts" of Satan, and nought but the shield of faith can quench them. But when the Holy Spirit renews the heart, the prevailing power of unbelief is broken; faith argues "*God* has said it, so it *must* be true." Faith so convinces the understanding that it is compelled, by force of arguments unanswerable, to believe the certainty of all God has spoken. The conviction is so powerful that the heart is influenced thereby, and the will moved to conform thereto. This it is which causes the Christian to *forsake* the "pleasures of sin" which are only "for a season" (Heb. 11:25), because by faith he has *laid hold of* those satisfying "pleasures at God's right hand" which are "for evermore" (Psa. 16:11).

To sum up the contents of v. 1. To unbelief, the objects which God sets before us in His Word seem unreal and unlikely, nebulous and vague. But faith visualizes the unseen, giving substantiality to the things hoped for and reality to things invisible. Faith shuts its eyes to all that is seen, and opens its ears to all God has said. Faith is a convictive power which overcomes carnal reasonings, carnal prejudices, and carnal excuses. It enlightens the judgment, moulds the heart, moves the will, and reforms the life. It takes us off earthly things and worldly vanities, and occupies us with spiritual and Divine realities. It emboldens against discouragements, laughs at difficulties, resists the Devil, and triumphs over temptations. It does so because it unites the soul to God and draws strength from Him. Thus faith is altogether a supernatural thing.

"For by it the elders obtained a good report" (v. 2). Having described the principal qualities of faith, the apostle now proceeds to give further proof of its excellency, as is evident from the opening "For." It is by faith we are approved of God. By the "elders" is signified those who lived in former times, namely, the O.T. saints—included among the "fathers" or 1:1. It was not by their amiability, sincerity, earnestness, or any other natural virtue, but by *faith* that the ancients "obtained a good report." This declaration was made by the apostle with the purpose of reminding the Hebrews that their pious progenitors were justified by faith, and to the end of the chapter he shows that *faith* was the principle of all their holy obedience, eminent services, and patient sufferings in the cause of God. Therefore those who were *spiritually* united to them must have something more than physical descent from them.

"For by it the elders obtained a good report." Observe the beautiful accuracy of Scripture: it was not *for* their faith (nor could it be without it!), but "by" their faith: it was not a cause, yet it was a condition; there was nothing meritorious in it, yet it was a necessary means. Let us also observe that faith is no new thing, but a grace planted in the hearts of God's elect from the beginning. Then, as now, faith was the substance of things hoped for—promises to be accomplished in the future. The faith of Abel laid hold of Christ as truly as does ours. God has had but one way of salvation since sin entered the world: "by grace, through faith, not of works." They are grossly mistaken who suppose that under the old covenant people were saved by keeping the law. The "fathers" had the same promises we have: not merely of Canaan, but of heaven—see 11:16.

The Greek for "obtained a good report" is not in the active voice, but the passive: literally, "were witnessed of," an honourable testimony being borne to them—cf. vv. 4, 5. God took care that a record should be kept (complete in Heaven, in part transcribed in the Scriptures) of all the actings of their faith. God has borne witness to the fact that Enoch "walked with Him" (Gen. 5:24), that David was "a man after His own heart" (1 Sam. 13:14), that Abraham was His "friend" (2 Chron. 20:7). This testimony of His acceptance of them because of their faith was borne by God. Not only externally in His Word, but in their consciences. He gave them His Spirit who assured them of their acceptance: Psa. 51:12, Acts 15:8. Let writer and reader learn to esteem what God does: let us value a Christian not for his intellect, natural charms, or social position, but for his *faith,* evidenced by an obedient walk and godly life.

We cannot do better in closing our comments upon v. 2 than by giving the "practical observations" on it of John Owen: "1. Instances or examples are the most powerful confirmations of practical truths. 2. They who have a good testimony from God shall never want reproaches from the world. 3. It is faith alone, which, from the beginning of the world (or from the giving of the first promise), was the means and way of obtaining acceptance with God. 4. The faith of true believers, from the beginning of the world, was fixed on things future, hoped for, invisible. 5. That faith whereby men please God acts itself in a fixed contemplation on things future and invisible, from whence it derived an encouragement and strength to endure and abide firm in profession, against all opposition and persecutions. 6. Men may be despised, vilified, and reproached in the world, yet if they have faith, if they are true believers, they are accepted with God, and He will give them a good report."

"Through faith we understand that the worlds were framed by the word of God, so that things which are seen were not made of things which do appear" (v. 3). There is a much closer connection between this verse and the two preceding ones than most of the commentators have perceived. The apostle is still setting forth the importance and excellency of faith: here he affirms that through it its favoured possessors are enabled to apprehend things which are high above the reach of human reason. The origin of the universe presents a problem which neither science nor philosophy can solve, as is evident from their conflicting and ridiculous attempts; but that difficulty vanishes entirely before *faith.*

"Through faith we *understand.*" Faith is the vehicle or medium of spiritual perception: "if thou wouldest believe, thou shouldest *see* the glory of God" (John 11:40); "which God hath created to be received with thanksgiving of them which believe *and know* the truth" (1 Tim. 4:3). Faith is not a *blind* reliance on the Word of God, but an intelligent persuasion of its veracity, wisdom, beauty. So far from Christians being the credulous fools the world deems them, they are the wisest of earth's inhabitants. The "fools" are they who are "slow of heart to believe" (Luke 24:25). Through faith in what has been revealed in the Scriptures we *know* that the universe is created and fashioned by God. "What does faith give us to understand concerning the worlds, that is, the upper, middle, lower regions of the universe? 1. That they were not eternal, nor did they produce themselves, but they were made by another. 2. That the Maker of the world is God; He is the Maker of all things; and whosoever is so must be God. 3. That He made the world with great exactness; it was a framed work, in every thing duly adapted and disposed to answer its end, and to express the perfections of the Creator. 4. That God made the world by His word; that is, by His essential wisdom and eternal Son, *and* by His active will, saying, Let it be done, and it was done. 5. That the world was thus framed out of nothing, out of no pre-existent matter, contrary to the received maxim, that out of nothing nothing can be made, which, though true of created power, can have no place with God, who can call things that are not as if they were, and command them into being. These things we understand by faith" (Matt. Henry).

"That the worlds were framed by the word of God." The word for "worlds" *in the Greek* signifies "ages," but by a metonymy it is here used of the universe. "The celestial world, with its inhabitants, the angels; the starry and ethereal worlds, with all that is in them, the sun, moon, stars, and fowls of the air; the terrestrial world, with all upon it, man, beasts etc.; and the watery world, the sea, and all that is therein" (John Gill). These "worlds were made at the beginning of mundane time and have continued throughout all ages. "The apostle accommodated his expression to the received opinion *of the Jews,* and their way of expressing themselves about the world. 'Olam' denotes the world as to the subsistence of it, and as to its duration" (J. Owen). We do not, then, espouse Bullinger's strange view of this verse.

The "worlds," or universe, were "framed," that is, were adjusted and disposed into a wise and beautiful order, by "the word of God." That expression is used in a threefold sense. First, there is the essential and personal Word, the eternal Son of God (John 1:1). Second, there is the written, ever-living Word, the Holy Scriptures (John 10:35). Third, there is the Word of Power or manifestation of the invincible will of God. It is the last-mentioned that is in view in Heb. 11:3. The Greek for "word" is *not* "logos" (as in John 1:1), but "rhema" (as in Heb. 1:3); "rhema" signifies a word *spoken.* The reference is to God's imperial fiat. His effectual command, as throughout Gen. 1: "God *said* (the manifestation of His invincible will) let light be, and light was." "For He spake, and it was done; He commanded and it stood fast" (Psa. 33:9). An illustration of the Word of His Power (see Heb. 1:3) is found in John 5:28, 29.

"So that things which are seen, were not made of things which do appear." There is some difficulty (in the Greek) in ascertaining the precise meaning of this phrase. Personally, we are inclined to regard it as referring back to Gen. 1:2. The verse before us concerns more directly the *fashioning* of the present heavens and earth, though that necessarily presupposes their original creation. The elements were submerged and darkness enshrouded them. The *practical* force of this verse to us is: our "faith" does not rest upon what "appears" outwardly, but is satisfied with the bare Word of God. Since God created the universe out of nothing, how easily can He preserve and sustain us when there is not anything (to our view) in sight! He who can call worlds into existence by the Word of His Power, can command supplies for the neediest of His creatures.

CHAPTER FIFTY-SEVEN

The Faith of Abel

(Heb. 11:4)

The 11th chapter of Hebrews has three divisions. The first, which comprises vv. 1 to 3, is introductory, setting forth the *excellency* of faith. The second, which is covered by vv. 4 to 7, outlines the *life* of faith. The third, which begins at v. 8 and runs to the end of the chapter, fills in that outline, and, as well, describes the *achievements* of faith. The first division we went over in our last article. There we saw the excellency of faith proved by four facts. Faith gives a reality and substantiality unto those things which the Word of God warrants us to hope for (v. 1). Faith furnishes proof to the heart of those spiritual things which cannot be discovered by our natural senses (v. 1). Faith secured to the O.T. saints a good report (v. 2). Faith enables its favoured possessor to understand that which is incomprehensible to mere reason, imparting a knowledge to which philosophers and scientists are strangers (v. 3). Thus, the tremendous importance and inestimable value of faith is at once apparent.

The second division of our chapter may be outlined thus. First, the beginning of the life of faith (v. 4). Second, the character of the life of faith, showing of what it consists (v. 5). Third, a warning and an encouragement is given (v. 6). Fourth, the end of the life of faith, or the goal to which it conducts (v. 7). That which the Holy Spirit now sets before us, is far more than a list of O.T. worthies, or a miniature picture-gallery of the saints of bygone days. To those whom God grants a receptive heart and anointed eye, there is here deep and important doctrinal instruction, as well as most blessed practical teaching. The contents of Heb. 11 concern our eternal peace, and it behooves us to give them our most prayerful and diligent attention. May it please the Spirit of Truth to act as our Guide, as we seek to pass from verse to verse.

"By faith Abel offered unto God a more excellent sacrifice than Cain, by which he obtained witness that he was righteous, God testifying of his gifts; and by it he being dead yet speaketh" (v. 4). Rightly understood, this verse describes *the beginning* of the life of faith. Let us seek to weigh attentively each separate expression in it.

First, it was "by faith" that Abel offered unto God his sacrifice. He is the first man, according to the sacred record, who ever did so. He had no established precedent to follow, no example to emulate, no outward encouragement to stimulate. Thus, his conduct was not suggested by popular custom, nor was his action regulated by "common sense." Neither carnal reason nor personal inclinations could have moved Abel to present a bleeding lamb for God's acceptance. How, then, is his strange procedure to be accounted for? Our text answers: it was "by faith" he acted, and not by fancy or by feelings. But what is signified by this expression? Ah, the mere words "by faith" are far more familiar unto many, than their real import is understood. Vague and visionary indeed are the conceptions which multitudes now entertain thereon. We must not, then, take anything for granted; but rather proceed slowly, and seek to make quite sure of our ground.

The one scripture which, perhaps, more than any other unlocks for us the meaning of the "by faith" which is found so frequently in Heb. 11 is Rom. 10:17. There we read, "Faith cometh by hearing and hearing by the Word of God." Faith must have a foundation to rest upon, and that foundation must be the Word of Him that cannot lie. God speaks, and the heart receives and acts upon what He says. True, there are two kinds of "hearing," just as there are two kinds of "faith." There is an outward "hearing," and there is an inward "hearing": the one merely informs, the other influences; the one simply instructs the mind, the other moulds the heart and moves the will. So there is a twofold meaning to the term "The Word of God" (see our remarks on 11:3), namely, the Word as written, and the Word as operative, when God speaks in living power to the soul. Hence, there is a twofold "faith": the one which is merely an intellectual assenting to what God has revealed, and that which is a vital and supernatural principle of action, which "worketh by love" (Gal. 5:6).

Now we need hardly say that it is the *second* of these which is in view here in Heb. 11:4, and throughout the chapter. But let us move carefully, step by step. It was "by faith" that Abel offered unto God his acceptable sacrifice, and as Rom. 10:17 declares, "faith cometh by hearing and hearing by the Word of God." It therefore follows that God had definitely revealed His will, that Abel believed that revelation, and that he acted accordingly. Now in O.T. times, God spake to men sometimes directly, sometimes through others. In this instance, we believe the reference is to what God had said to Adam and Eve, and which they had communicated to Cain and Abel. By turning back to Gen. 3 we discover *what* the Lord said to their parents.

"Unto the woman He said, I will greatly multiply thy sorrow and thy conception; in sorrow thou shalt bring forth children; and thy desire shall be to thy husband, and he shall rule over thee. And unto Adam He said, Because thou hast hearkened unto the voice of thy wife, and hast eaten of the tree, of which I commanded thee, saying, Thou shalt not eat of it; cursed is the ground for thy sake; in sorrow shalt thou eat of it all the days of thy life; Thorns also and thistles shall it bring forth to thee; and thou shalt eat the herb of the field; In the sweat of thy face shalt thou eat bread, till thou return unto the ground; for out of it wast thou taken; for dust thou art, and unto dust shalt thou return" (Gen. 3:16-19). But further: "Unto Adam also and to his wife did the Lord God make coats of skins, and clothed them" (v. 21). Here the Lord spoke to Adam and Eve by action: four things were clearly intimated. First, that in order for a sinner to stand before the thrice holy God, he needed *a covering*. Second, that that which was of human manufacture (3:7), was worthless. Third, that God Himself must *provide* the requisite covering. Fourth, that the necessary covering could only be obtained *by death*, by blood-shedding.

In Gen. 3:15 and 21 we have the first Gospel-sermon which was ever preached on this earth, and that, by the Lord Himself. Life must come out of death. Cain and Abel, and the whole human race, sinned in Adam (Rom. 5:12, 18, 19), and the wages of sin is *death*, penal death. Either I must be paid those wages and suffer that death, or another—an innocent one, on whom death has no claim—must be paid those wages in my stead. And in order to my receiving the benefit of that substitute's compassion, there must be a link of contact between me and him. *Faith* it is which unites to Christ. Saving faith, then, in its simplest form, is the placing of a Substitute between my guilty self and a sin-hating God.

Now what we have just gone over above, was made known (probably through Adam) to Cain and Abel. How do we know this? Because, as we have seen, Abel brought his offerings to God "by faith," and Rom. 10:17 makes it clear that "faith" presupposes a Divine revelation. Further confirmation of this is found in Gen. 4:7: when Cain's countenance fell at the rejection of his offering, the Lord said unto him, "If thou doest well, shalt thou not be accepted? and if thou doest not well, sin lieth at the door." Thus a Divine institution of sacrifice, clearly defined and made known, is here plainly implied. It was as though God had said to Cain, "Did I promise to accept any other offering than which conformed to My prescription?"

"By faith Abel offered unto God a more excellent sacrifice than Cain." Three things here claim our attention: the spring of Abel's action (faith), the nature of his offering, wherein it was more excellent than Cain's. The first of these we have already considered, the second we will now examine. The language of our present verse refers us back to Gen. 4; there we read, "And Abel, he also brought of the firstlings of his flock and of the fat thereof" (v. 4). His action here ("brought") is in sharp contrast from his parents in Gen. 3:8, who "hid themselves *from* the presence of the Lord God." The contrast is most significant: a consciousness of guilt caused Adam and Eve to flee; a sense of need moved Abel to seek the Lord. The difference between them is to be attributed unto the respective workings of conscience and faith. An uneasy conscience never of itself, leads to Christ—"And they which heard, being convicted by their own conscience, *went out* one by one . . . and Jesus was left alone" (John 8:9).

"And Abel, he also brought of the firstlings of his flock and of the fat thereof" (Gen. 4:4). The separate mention of the "fat" tells us that the lamb had been slain. By killing the lamb and offering it to God, Abel acknowledged at least five things. First, he owned that God was righteous in driving fallen man out of Eden (Gen. 3:24). Second, he owned that he was a guilty sinner, and that death was his just due. Third, he owned that God was holy, and must punish sin. Fourth, he owned that God was merciful, and willing to accept the death of an innocent substitute in his place. Fifth, he owned that he looked for acceptance with God in Christ the Lamb. Therefore did he, *by faith,* place the blood of his firstlings of his flock (type of Him who is "the Firstborn" or Head "of every creature"—Col. 1:15) between his sins and the avenging justice of God.

Here, then, is where the life of faith begins. There must first be a bowing unto the righteous verdict of the Divine Judge that I am a sinner, a transgressor, of His holy law, and therefore justly under its "curse" or death-sentence. No excuses have I to offer, no merits have I to plead, no mitigation of the sentence can I fairly ask for. My best performances are only filthy rags in the sight of Him who knows that they were wrought out of self-love and to promote self's interests, rather than for His glory. I can but plead guilty, and hide my face for very shame. But as the Gospel of His grace is applied to my stricken conscience by the power of the Spirit, hope revives. As He makes known to me the amazing fact that the Lamb of God died so that all who bow to God's verdict, own themselves as lost, and hate themselves for their sins, might live; and then faith stretches forth a trembling hand and lays hold of the Redeemer, and the criminal is pardoned, and accepted by God.

Having pondered the character of Abel's sacrifice, let us now consider wherein it was "more excellent" than Cain's. In Gen. 4:3 we read, "Cain brought of the fruit of the ground an offering unto the Lord." Cain was no infidel, for he owned the existence of God; nor was he irreligious, for he came before Him as a worshipper; but he refused to conform to the Divine appointment. By carefully noting the nature of his offering, we may observe four things. First, it was a bloodless one, and "without shedding of blood is no remission" (Heb. 9:22). Second, it was merely the fruit of his toils, the product of his labours. Third, he deliberately ignored the sentence of God in Gen. 3:17: "Cursed is the ground." Fourth, he despised the grace made known in Gen. 3:21.

Thus, in Cain we behold the first *hypocrite.* He refused to comply with the revealed will of God, yet cloaked his rebellion by coming before Him as a worshipper. He would not obey the Divine appointment, yet brought an offering to the Lord. He believed not that his case was so desperate that death was his due, and could only be escaped by another suffering it in his stead; yet he sought to approach unto the Lord, and patronize Him. This is the "way of Cain" spoken of by Jude (v. 11). It is the way of self-will, of unbelief, of disobedience, and of religious hypocrisy. What a contrast from Abel! Thus we see how there was a striking foreshadowment from the beginning of human history that the church on earth is a *mixed* assembly, made up of wheat and tares.

Cain and Abel stand before us as two representative men. They head the two, and the only two classes, which are to be found in the religious world. They typified, respectively, the two sections of Christendom. Cain, the elder, who is mentioned *first* in Gen. 4 and therefore represents the prominent section, sets forth that vast company who honour God with their lips, but whose hearts are far from Him; who think to pay God a compliment, but who refuse to meet His requirements; who pose as worshippers, but live to please themselves. Abel, on the other hand, *hated by* Cain, foreshadowed that "little flock," the members of which are brought to feel their sinnerhood, bow to God's will, comply with His commandments, fly to Christ for refuge, and are accepted by God.

Most solemnly too do Cain and Abel furnish us with a striking example of the *sovereignty* of Divine grace. Both of them were "shapen in iniquity and conceived in sin," for both were the fallen sons of fallen parents, and both of them were born outside of Eden; yet one was "of that Wicked one" (1 John 3:12), while the other was one of God's elect. Marvelously and most blessedly may we here behold the fact that sovereign grace is "no respecter of persons," but passes by (to human ideas) the most likely, and pitches upon the unlikely. Being the younger of the two, Abel was inferior in dignity; God Himself said to Cain, "Thou shalt rule over him" (Gen 4:7). But spiritual blessings do not follow the order of external privileges: Shem is preferred before Japheth (Gen. 5:32, 10:2, 21); Isaac before Ishmael, Jacob before Esau.

"By (a Divinely-given and Divinely-wrought) faith, Abel offered unto God a more excellent sacrifice than Cain." The superiority of Abel's worship may, perhaps, be set forth thus. First, it was offered *in obedience to* God's revealed will. This lies at the very foundation of all actions which are acceptable unto God: nothing can be pleasing unto Him except that which *He* has stipulated: every thing else is "will worship" (Col. 2:23). Second, it was offered "by faith": this tells us that there was something more than the mere performance of an outward duty; only that is approved of God which proceeds from the living principle of faith, kindled in the heart by the Holy Spirit. True obedience and faith are never apart: therefore we read of "the obedience of faith" (Rom. 1:5). Yet though inseparable, they are distinguishable in thought: faith respects the word of *promise;* obedience the word of *command,* for promises and precepts go hand in hand. We act in obedience, when the commandment is uppermost in our minds and hearts, which puts us to the performing of duties; we act in faith, when the promise is looked to and the reward is counted upon.

Third, Abel had a "willing mind" (2 Cor. 8:12). Faith works by "love" (Gal. 5:6). This is seen in the fact that he brought *of his best*: it was "of the firstlings of his flock," which God afterwards took as His portion (Ex. 13:12); when slain, it was the "fat" which he presented which later God also claimed as His own (Lev. 3:16; 7:25). Thus, it was of the most precious and valuable things on earth which Abel brought to God. So it is our best which He requires of us: "Son, give Me thine heart" (Prov. 23:26): it is "with the *heart* man believeth unto righteousness" (Rom. 10:10). Fourth, his sacrificial offering looked forward to and adumbrated the great sacrifice, the Lamb of God which taketh away the sin of the world. In all these four things Abel excelled Cain. Cain did not act in obedience, for he disregarded the Divine appointment. He did not offer in faith. Nothing is said of any choice of excellent fruit: it was as though he brought the first which came to hand. His offering contained no foreshadowment of Christ.

Ere passing on, let us seek to gather up the *practical* teaching of what has been before us. 1. To serve God acceptably we must disregard all human inventions, lean not unto our own understandings or inclinations, and adhere strictly to the revelation which He made of His will. 2. All obedience, service, and worship, must proceed from faith, for "without faith it is impossible to please Him" (Heb. 11:6): where this be lacking, no matter how exact the performance of our duty, it is unacceptable to God. 3. We are to serve God with the best that we have: with the best of our abilities, and with the best of our substance; only as *love* constrains us will there be a doing it "heartily as unto the Lord." 4. In all our religious exercises Christ must be before us, for only as they are perfumed with His merits can they meet with God's acceptance.

"By which he obtained witness that he was righteous." There is a little uncertainty as to whether the "by which" refers to Abel's 'faith" or to the "more excellent sacrifice" which he offered. Though the latter be the nearest antecedent, yet, with Owen, Gouge, and Manton, we believe the reference is to his faith. First, because it is not the apostle's design in this chapter to specify the kind of sacrifices which were acceptable unto God. Second, because his obvious purpose was to illustrate and demonstrate the efficacy of faith. Third, because the apostle here exemplifies what he had just said of the O.T. saints, namely, that by faith "they obtained a good report" (v. 2). Fourth, because this agrees much more closely with the Analogy of Faith: by the one perfect offering of Christ is the Christian *constituted* "righteous" before God; but it is through faith that he obtains *witness* of the same to his heart.

"By which he obtained witness that he was righteous." Herein we are supplied with an illustration of "For them that honour Me, I will honour" (1 Sam. 2:30). In keeping God's precepts there is "great reward" (Psa. 19:11). God will be no man's debtor: he who obediently, humbly, trustfully, lovingly, respects His appointments and obeys His commandments, shall be recompensed—not as a recognition of merit, but as what is Divinely meet and gracious. God did not leave Abel in a state of uncertainty, ignorant as to whether or not his offering was approved. The Lord was pleased to assure Abel that the sacrifice had been accepted, and that he was accounted just before Him. The Greek word for "he obtained witness" is the same as is rendered "obtained a good report" in v. 2.

"By which he obtained witness that he was righteous." This too is recorded for our instruction and comfort. From these words we learn it is the good pleasure of God that His obedient and believing children should *know* His mind concerning them. Where there is a justifying faith in Christ which moves the Christian to walk according to the Divine precepts, God honours that faith by granting assurance to its possessor. When we are enabled by faith to plead the most excellent Sacrifice and to present acceptable worship unto God, then we obtain testimony from Him through His Word and by His Spirit that our persons and services are accepted by Him. In Abel's case, He received from God an outward attestation; in the case of the Christian today it is the inward authentication of his conscience (2 Cor. 1:12), to which the Holy Spirit also adds His confirmation (Rom. 8:15).

"God testifying of his gifts." We are not told in Gen. 4 in so many words *how* He did so, but the Analogy of Faith leaves little room for doubt. By comparing other Scriptures, it may be that the Lord evidenced His acceptance of Abel's offering (and thereby testified that he was "righteous") by causing fire to descend from heaven and consume the sacrifice, which, in turn, ascended to Him as a sweet-smelling savour. In Lev. 9:24 we read, "And there came a fire out from before the Lord, and consumed upon the altar the burnt offering and the fat." So too, we are told, "Then the fire of the Lord fell, and consumed the burnt sacrifice" (1 Kings 18:38). Compare also Judges 6:21; 13:19, 20; 1 Chron. 21:26; Psa. 20:3 margin. There is, however, no certainty on this point.

"By which (faith) he obtained witness that he was righteous, God testifying of his gifts." The second clause is explanatory of the former: the parallel is found in Gen. 4:4, where we read, "and the Lord had respect unto Abel *and* to his offering." He testified in the approbation of his offering, that He had respect unto his person; that is, that He judged, esteemed, and accounted him righteous, for otherwise God is no respecter of persons. Whosoever God accepts or respects, He testifieth him to be righteous, that is, to be justified, and freely accepted with Him. This Abel was by faith, antecedently unto his offering. He was not made righteous, he was not justified by his sacrifice, but therein show his faith by his works; and God, by acceptance of his works of obedience, justified him, as Abraham was justified by works, namely, *declaratively,* He declared him so to be. Our persons must be first justified, before our works of obedience can be accepted with God; for by that acceptance He testifies that we are righteous (John Owen).

"And by it he being dead yet speaketh." Marvellously full are the words of God. His commandment is "exceeding broad" (Psa. 119:96). In every sentence of Holy Writ there is both a depth and breadth which our unaided minds are incapable of perceiving and appreciating. Only as the Holy Spirit, the Inspirer and Giver of the Word, deigns to "guide" us (John 16:13), only as He teaches us to compare passage with passage, so that in His light we "see light" (Psa. 36:9), are we enabled to discern, in fuller measure, the beauty, meaning, and many-sidedness of any verse or clause. Such is the case in the sentence now before us. We are convinced that there is at least a threefold meaning and reference in it. Briefly, we will consider these in turn.

"And by it he being dead yet speaketh." The first and most obvious signification of these words is that, by his faith's obedience, as recorded in Gen. 4 and Heb. 11, Abel preaches to us a most important sermon. His worship and the fruits thereof are registered in the everlasting records of Holy Scripture, and thereby he speaketh as evidently as though we heard him audibly. There comes to us a voice from the far distant past, from the other side of the flood, saying, "Fallen man can only approach unto God through the death of an innocent Substitute: yet none save God's elect will ever feel their need of such, set aside their own inclinations, bow to God's revealed will, and submit to His appointment; but they who do so, obtain witness that they are 'righteous' (cf. Matt. 13:43), and receive Divine assurance that they are accepted in the Beloved and that their obedience (imperfect in itself, yet proceeding from a heart which desires and seeks to *fully* please Him) is approved for His sake."

"And by it he being dead yet speaketh." And *how* did he die? By the murderous hand of a religious hypocrite who hated him. Then began that which the apostle affirms still to continue: "he that was born after the flesh, persecuted him that was born after the Spirit" (Gal. 4:29). Here was the first public and visible display of that enmity between the (mystical) seed of the woman and the (mystical) seed of the Serpent. Abel's death was therefore also a pledge and representation of the death of Christ Himself — murdered by the religious world. Those whom God approves must expect to be disproved of men, more particularly by those professing to be Christian. But the time is coming when the present situation shall be reversed. In Gen. 4:10 God said to Cain "the voice of thy brother's blood *crieth* unto Me from the ground." Abel's own blood "speaketh," crying to God for vengeance.

"And by it he being dead yet speaketh." Though ruthlessly slain by his brother, the soul of Abel exists in a separate state, alive, conscious, and vocal. He is among that company of whom the apostle said, "I saw under the altar the souls of them that were slain for the Word of God, and for the testimony which they held, and they *cried* with a loud voice, saying, How long, O Lord, holy and true, dost Thou not judge and avenge our blood on them that dwell on the earth?" (Rev. 6:9, 10). Thus, Abel is not only a type of the persecution and suffering of the godly, but gives a pledge of the certain vengeance which God will take in due time upon their oppressors. God shall yet avenge His own elect (those in heaven as well as those on earth) who cry unto Him day and night for Him *to* avenge them (Luke 18:7, 8). Let us then seek grace to possess our souls in patience, knowing that ere long God will reward the righteous and punish the wicked.

CHAPTER FIFTY-EIGHT

The Faith of Enoch

(Heb. 11:5, 6)

The apostle makes it his principal design in this chapter to convince the Hebrews of the nature, importance and efficacy of saving faith. In the execution of his design, he first described the essential actings of faith (v. 1), and then in all that follows he treats of the effects, fruits, and achievements of faith. It is blessed to behold how that once more his appeal was to the Holy Scriptures. Not by abstract arguments, still less by bare assertions, would he persuade them; but instead, by setting forth some of the many examples and proofs which the sacred records furnished. Having reminded them of what the faith-obedience of Abel procured, namely, the obtaining of a witness from God that he was righteous, the apostle cites the case of Enoch who exemplifies another aspect and consequent of faith.

The *order* observed by the Holy Spirit in Heb. 11 is not the historical one. A careful reading of its contents will make this clear. For example, reference is made in v. 9 to Isaac and Jacob before attention is directed to Sarah in v. 11; the falling down of Jericho's walls (v. 30), is mentioned before the faith of Rahab (v. 31); in v. 32 Gideon is mentioned before Barak, Samson before Jephtha, and David before Samuel. Thus it is evident that we are to "search" for something deeper. Since the chronological order is departed from again and again, must there not be a spiritual significance to the way in which the O. T. saints are here referred to? Without a doubt such must be the case. The reason for this is not far to seek: it is the *experimental* order which is followed in this chapter. If the Lord permits, this will become plainer and plainer as we proceed from verse to verse.

That which the three examples supplied in vv. 4 to 7 set before us is an outline of the life of faith. Abel is mentioned first not because he was born before Enoch and Noah, but because what is recorded of him in Gen. 4 illustrated and demonstrated where the life of faith begins. In like manner, Enoch is referred to next not because he is mentioned before Noah in the book of Genesis, but because what was found in him (or rather, what Divine grace had wrought in him), must precede that which was typified by the builder of the ark. Each of these three men adumbrated a distinct feature or aspect of the life of faith, and the order concerning them is inviolable. Another before us, has characterized them thus: in Abel we see faith's worship, in Enoch faith's walk, in Noah faith's witness. This, we believe, is an accurate and helpful way of stating it, and the more it be pondered, the more its beauty and blessedness should be perceived.

But man ever reverses God's order, and never was this fact more plainly evident to the anointed eye than in these degenerate times in which our lot is cast. Witnessing and working ("service") is what are so much emphasized today. Yet dear reader, Heb. 11 does not begin with the example of Noah. No indeed. Noah was preceded by Enoch, and for this reason: there can be no Divinely-acceptable witness or work unless and until there is a walking with God! Enoch's walk with God must come before any service which is pleasing *to Him.* Alas that this is so much lost sight of now. Alas that, so generally, as soon as a young person makes profession of being a Christian, he or she is pushed into some form of "Christian activity" — open-air speaking, personal work, teaching a Sunday school class — when God's word so plainly says, *"Not a novice* (margin, "one newly come to the faith") lest being lifted up with pride (which almost always proves to be the case) he fall into the condemnation of the Devil" (1 Tim. 3:6).

O how much we miss and lose through failing to give close heed to the *order* of God's words. Frequently have we emphasized this fact in these pages, yet not too frequently. God is a God of order, and the moment we depart from His arrangements, confusion, with all its attendant evils, at once ensues. We cannot pay too strict attention to the order in which things are presented to us in Holy Writ, for only as we do so, are we in the position to learn some of its most salutary lessons and admire its heavenly wisdom. Such is the case here. Enoch's walk of faith must precede Noah's witnessing by faith; and this, in turn, must be preceded by Abel's worship of faith. There must be that setting aside of our own preferences and ways, that bowing to God's will, that submitting to His appointments, that obedience to His requirements, before there can be any real walking with Him. Obedience *to* Him, then walking *with* Him, then witnessing *for* Him, is Heaven's unchanging order.

"By faith Enoch was translated that he should not see death; and was not found, because God had translated him: for before his translation he had this testimony, that he pleased God" (v. 5). The case of Abel shows us *where* the life of faith begins; the example of Enoch teaches us *of what* the life of faith consists. Now just as we had to refer to Gen. 4 to understand Heb. 11:4, so we have to turn back to Gen. 5 for its light to be thrown upon our present verse.

"And Enoch walked with God: and he was not; for God took him" (Gen. 5:24). Here we have set forth, in the form of a brief summary, the new life of the believer: to "walk with God." Previously, Enoch had "walked according to the course of this world" (Eph. 2:2), had gone his "own way" (Isa. 53:6) of self-pleasing, and unconcerned about the future, had thought only of the present. But now he had been "reconciled to God" (2 Cor. 5:20), for "Can two walk together, except they be *agreed?*" (Amos 3:3). The term "walk" signifies a voluntary act, a steady advance, a progress in spiritual things. To "walk with God" imports a life surrendered to God, a life controlled by God, a life lived for God. It is to that our present verse has reference.

"By faith Enoch was translated that he should not see death; and was not found, because God had translated him: for before his translation he had this testimony, that he pleased God." It should be obvious to any Spirit-taught heart that we need to look beneath the surface here if we are to discover the *spiritual principle* of the verse, and seek grace to apply it to ourselves. As a mere historical statement it is doubtless a very interesting one, yet as such it imparts no strength to my needy soul. The bare fact that a man who walked this earth thousands of years ago escaped death may astonish, but it supplies no practical help. What we wish to press upon the reader is, the need for asking each portion of Scripture he reads, the question, What is there here, what practical lesson, *to help me* while I am left on earth? Nor is this always discovered in a moment: prayer, patience, meditation are required.

As we endeavor to *study* our verse with the object of ascertaining its practical meaning and message for us today, the first thing the thoughtful ponderer will notice is the repetition of the word "translated": this occurring no less than three times in one verse, is evidently the keyword. According to its etymology, "translated" signifies to carry across, to bear up, to remove, to change from one place to another. This at once brings to mind (if the Word of Christ be dwelling in us richly) that verse, "Who hath delivered us from the power of darkness and *hath translated us* into the kingdom of His dear Son" (Col. 1:13). This refers to the grand fact of the Christian's present standing and state before God: he has "passed from death unto life" (John 5:24). Now it is the Christian's privilege and duty to live in the power of this fact, and have it made good in his actual case and experience; and this *will be* so, just in proportion as he is enabled to live and walk *by faith.*

"By faith Enoch was translated that he should not see death": the word "see" here has the force of taste or experience. Enoch was not to be overcome by death: but let us not limit our thoughts unto physical death. Just as Enoch's "translation" from earth to heaven has a deeper meaning than the natural, so "that he should not see death" signifies more than an escape from the grave. "Death" is the wages of sin, the curse of the broken law. We are living in a world which is under God's righteous curse and death is plainly stamped across everything in it. But when faith is in exercise, the soul is lifted above this scene, and its favoured possessor is enabled to "walk in newness of life." As we saw when pondering the opening verse, it is the nature of faith to bring near things future, and to obtain proof and enjoyment of what is invisible to natural sight. Just so far as we walk by faith, is the heart "translated," raised above this poor world; and then it is we experience the "*power* of His (Christ's) resurrection" (Phil. 3:10).

Let us now link vv. 4 and 5 together, observing their *doctrinal* force. When a sinner, by surrender to God and faith in the sacrifice of Christ, is pronounced righteous by the Judge of all, he is made an heir of eternal life, and sin and death can no more have dominion over him: that is, no longer have any legal claim upon him. It is *this* which is illustrated here: the very next saint who is mentioned after Abel, was taken to Heaven *without* dying, thereby demonstrating that the power of "death" over the Christian has been annulled. First a sinner saved through the blood of the Lamb (Abel), then a saved sinner removed from earth to Heaven, and nothing between. How inexpressibly blessed! Words fail us, and we can but bow in silent wonderment, and worship. How "great" is God's salvation!

Now that which is a fact of Christian doctrine needs to become a fact of Christian experience: we need to enjoy the good, the power, the blessedness of it in our souls day by day. And this can only be as a supernatural faith is in exercise. A bare knowledge of doctrine is practically worthless, unless the heart earnestly seeks from God a practical out-working of it. It is one thing to believe that I have judicially passed from death unto life, it is quite another to live practically in the realm of LIFE. But that is exactly what a *life of faith* is: it is a being lifted above the things which are seen, and a being occupied with those things which are unseen. It is for the affections to be no longer set on things on the earth, but to have them fixed on things in Heaven.

Perhaps the reader is inclined to say, The ideal you set before us is indeed beautiful, but it is impossible for flesh and blood to attain unto it. Quite true, dear friend; we fully grant it. Of himself the Christian can no more live practically upon resurrection-ground than Enoch could transport himself to Heaven. But observe carefully the very next words in our wonderful text: "because *God* had translated him." Again we beg you not to carnalize these words, and see in them *only* a reference to his bodily removal to Heaven; or to see in them nothing more than a type and pledge of the Rapture — the fulfillment of 1 Thess. 4:16, 17: that is the prophetical significance; but there is a spiritual meaning and practical application also, and this is what we so much desire to make clear unto each spiritual reader.

Enoch's translation to heaven was a miracle, and that which is spiritually symbolized is a supernatural experience. The whole Christian life, from start to finish, is a *supernatural* thing. The new birth is a miracle of grace, for one who is dead in trespasses and sins can no more regenerate himself than he can create a world. A spiritual repentance and spiritual faith are imparted by "the operation of God" (Col. 2:12), for a fallen creature can no more originate them than he could give himself being. To have the heart divorced from the world, to be brought to hate the things we once loved and to now love the things we once hated, is the alone fruitage of the almighty work of the Holy Spirit. And for the heart to function in the realm of resurrection-life, while its possessor is left in a scene of death, can only be made possible and become actual as the supernatural grace of God sustains and calls into exercise a supernatural faith. Only God can daily wean our hearts from the things of this world of death and bring us into real communion with the Prince of Life.

A word of caution here. Let us be on our guard against fatalistically folding our arms and saying, God has not ordained that I should live the *translated* life. True, God is sovereign and distributes His favors as He pleases. True, He grants more grace to some of His own people than to others of them. Yet it is also written that, "Ye have not, because ye ask not" (James 4:2). Moreover, observe well the next words in our text: "before his translation he had this testimony, that he pleased God." Ah, does not *that* explain why *our* faith is so feeble, and why the things of earth forge such heavy chains about our hearts? God is not likely to strengthen and increase our faith while we are so largely indifferent to *His* pleasure. There must first be the daily, diligent, prayerful striving to please Him in all things; this is absolutely essential if we are to enter into the experience of the *translated* life.

Let us seek to anticipate a possible objection. Some may be saying, The *translated life* — the continuous exercise of faith which frees the heart from the graveclothes of this world — is so exceedingly *difficult* these days. Then let us remind you of the times in which Enoch lived. It was just before the Flood, and probably conditions then were far worse than they are now. "And Enoch also, the seventh from Adam, prophesied of these, saying, Behold, the Lord cometh with ten thousands of His saints: To execute judgment upon all, and to convince all that are ungodly among them of all their ungodly deeds which they have ungodly committed, and of all their hard speeches which ungodly sinners have spoken against Him" (Jude 14, 15). It must be remembered that those words had an historical force, as well as a prophetical. Thus, a life of pleasing God, of walking with Him, of the heart being lifted above the world, was no easier then than now. Yet Divine grace made this actual in Enoch; and that grace is as potent today as it was then.

Oftentimes it is helpful to reverse the clauses of a verse so as to perceive more clearly their relation. In order to illustrate this, and because we are so anxious for the reader to lay hold of the vitally-important teaching of Heb. 11:5, we will treat it accordingly. "Before his translation he had this testimony, that he pleased God." Do I? Do you? That is a most timely inquiry. If we are *not* "pleasing God," then the more knowledge we have of His truth, the worse for us. "That servant which *knew* his Lord's will, and prepared not himself, neither *did* according to His will, shall be beaten with many stripes" (Luke 12:47). God will not be mocked. Fair words and reverent postures cannot deceive Him. It is not how much light do I have, but how far am I in complete subjection to the Lord?

"God had translated him." Of course He did. God always honours those who honour Him; but let us remember that same verse adds, "And they that despise Me shall be lightly esteemed" (1 Sam. 2:30). God is too holy to encourage self-pleasing and put a premium upon self-indulgence. While we gratify the flesh, the blessing of the Spirit will be withheld. While our hearts are so much occupied with the concerns of earth, He will not make the things of Heaven real and efficacious to us. O my reader, if God be not working mightily in your life and mine, showing Himself strong on our behalf (2 Chron. 16:9), then something is seriously wrong with us.

"By faith Enoch was translated that he should not see death." Remember what was before us in the preceding article: "Faith cometh by hearing, and hearing by the Word of God" (Rom. 10:17). Faith always presupposes a Divine revelation. Faith must have a foundation to rest upon, and that foundation must be the word of Him that cannot lie. God had spoken, and Enoch believed. But what a testing of faith! God declared that Enoch should be removed from earth to Heaven, without passing through the portals of the grave. One, two, three hundred years passed; but Enoch *believed God,* and before the fourth century was completed His promise was fulfilled. "That he should not see death" was the reward of his pleasing God. And He does not change: where there is a genuine "pleasing" of Him, a real walking with Him, He elevates the heart above this scene into the realm of life, light and liberty.

Ere passing on to the next verse, let us enumerate other points of interest and value contained in this one, though we can do no more than barely mention them. 1. God is not tied to the order of nature: Gen. 3:19 was set aside in the cases of Enoch and Elijah. 2. God puts great outward (providential) differences between those equally accepted by Him: He did so between Abel and Enoch. 3. To exhibit the world's enmity God suffered Abel to be martyred, to comfort His people God preserved Enoch. 4. What God did for Enoch He can and will yet do for a whole generation of His saints (1 Cor. 15:51). 5. There is a future life for believers: the removal of Enoch to Heaven plainly intimated this. 6. The body is partaker with the soul in life eternal: the corporeal translation of Enoch showed this. 7. The godliest do not always live the longest: all mentioned in Gen. 5 stayed on earth a much greater time than did Enoch. 8. They who live with God hereafter must learn to please God ere they depart hence. 9. They who walk with God please Him. 10. They who please God shall not lack testimony thereof.

"But without faith it is impossible to please Him: for he that cometh to God must believe that He is, and that He is a rewarder of them that diligently seek Him" (v. 6). The apostle had just spoken of Enoch's translation as a consequent of his pleasing God, and now from the fact of his pleasing God, proves his faith. The adversative particle "But" is used to introduce a syllogism. The argument is framed thus: God Himself had translated Enoch, who before his translation had pleased Him (as his translation evidenced); but without faith it is impossible to please God: — therefore Enoch was by faith translated. Thus, this declaration in v. 6 has special reference to the last clause in the verse preceding. The argument is drawn from the impossibility of the contrary: as it is impossible to please God without faith, and as Enoch received testimony that he *did* please God, then he must have had faith — a justifying and sanctifying faith.

While there is an intimate relation between our present verse and the one immediately preceding, and while as we shall yet see (the Lord willing) that it is closely connected with the case of Noah in v. 7, yet it also makes its own particular contribution unto the theme which the apostle is here developing, supplying both a solemn warning and a blessed encouragement. The Holy Spirit still had before Him the special need of the wavering Hebrews, and would press upon them the fact that the great thing God required was not attendance on outward ordinances, but the diligent seeking unto Him by a whole-hearted trust. Where faith was missing, nothing could meet with His approval; but where faith really existed and was exercised, it would be richly rewarded. This principle is unchanging, so that the central message of our verse speaks loudly to us today, and should search the heart of each one of us.

"But without faith it is impossible to please Him." Most solemnly do these words attest the total depravity of man. So corrupt is the fallen creature, both in soul and body, in every power and part thereof, and so polluted is everything that issues from him, that he cannot of and by himself do anything that is acceptable to the Holy One. "So then they that are in the flesh *cannot* please God" (Rom. 8:8): "they that are in the flesh" means, they that are still in their natural or unregenerate state. A bitter fountain cannot send forth sweet waters. But faith looks out of self to Christ, applies unto His righteousness, pleads *His* worth and worthiness, and does all things Godward in the name and through the mediation of the Lord Jesus. Thus, by faith we *may* please God.

"But without faith it is impossible to please Him." Yet in all ages there have been many who attempted to please God without faith. Cain began it, but failed woefully. All in their Divine worship profess a desire to please God, and hope that they do so; why otherwise should they make the attempt? But, as the apostle declares in another place, many seek unto God "but not by faith, but as it were by the works of the law" (Rom. 9:32). But where faith be lacking, let men desire, design, and do what they will, they can never attain unto Divine acceptance. "But to Him that worketh not, but believeth on Him that justifieth the ungodly, his *faith* is counted for ("unto") righteousness" (Rom. 4:5). Whatever be the necessity of other graces, faith is that which alone obtains acceptance with God.

In order to please God four things must concur, all of which are accomplished by faith. First, the person of him that pleaseth God must be accepted of Him (Gen. 4:4). Second, the thing done that pleaseth God must be in accord with His will (Heb. 13:21). Third, the manner of doing it must be pleasing to God: it must be performed in humility (1 Cor. 15:10), in sincerity (Isa. 38:3), in cheerfulness (2 Cor. 8:12; 9:7). Fourth, the end in view must be God's glory (1 Cor. 10:31). Now faith is the only means whereby these four requirements are met. By faith in Christ the person is accepted of God. Faith makes us submit ourselves to God's will. Faith causes us to examine the manner of what we do Godwards. Faith aims at God's glory: of Abraham it is recorded that he "was strong in faith, giving glory to God" (Rom. 4:20).

How essential it is then that each of us examine himself diligently and make sure that he has *faith.* It is by faith the convicted and repentant sinner is saved (Acts 16:31). It is by faith that Christ dwells in the heart (Eph. 3:17). It is by faith that we live (Gal. 2:20). It is by faith that we stand (Rom. 11:20; 2 Cor. 1:24). It is by faith we walk (2 Cor. 5:7). It is by faith the Devil is successfully resisted (1 Pet. 5:8, 9). It is by faith we are experimentally sanctified (Acts 26:18). It is by faith we have access to God (Eph. 3:12, Heb. 10:22). It is by faith that we fight the good fight (1 Tim. 6:12). It is by faith that the world is overcome (1 John 5:4). Reader, are you certain that *you* have the "faith of God's elect" (Titus 1:1)? If not, it is high time you make sure, for "without faith it is *impossible* to please God."

CHAPTER FIFTY-NINE

The Faith of Noah

(Heb. 11:6, 7)

The verses which are now to engage our attention are by no means free of difficulty, especially unto those who have sat under a ministry which has failed to preserve the balance between Divine grace and Divine righteousness. Where the free favour of God has been strongly emphasized and His *claims* largely ignored, where privileges have been stressed and duties almost neglected, it is far from easy to view many Scriptures in their true perspective. When those who have heard little more than the decrying of creature-abilities and the denunciation of creature-merits are asked to honestly and seriously face the terms of Heb. 11:6, 7, they are quite unable to fit them into their system of theology. Where such be the case, it is proof positive that something is wrong with our theology. Often those who are least cramped by sectarian bias find that the truth of God is too large, too many-sided, to be squeezed into human definitions and creeds.

Others of our readers are probably wondering what it is we have reference to above when we say that our present portion of Heb. 11 is by no means free of difficulty. Then let us raise a few questions upon these verses. If the exercise of faith be pleasing to God, does this signify that it is a thing meritorious? How is this concept to be avoided in the light of the statement that God is a Rewarder of them that diligently seek Him? How does a "reward" consist with pure grace? And what is the doctrinal force of the next verse? Does the case of Noah teach salvation by works? If he had not gone to so much expense and labour in building the ark, would he and his house have escaped the flood? Was his becoming "heir of righteousness" something that he earned by his obedient toil? How can this conclusion be fairly avoided? We shall endeavour to keep these questions before us in the course of our exposition.

"But without faith it is impossible to please Him: for he that cometh to God must believe that He is, and that He is a rewarder of them that diligently seek Him" (v. 6). There is a threefold "coming to God": an initial, a continuous, and a final. The first takes place at conversion, the second is repeated throughout the Christian's life, the third occurs at death or the second coming of Christ. To come to God signifies to seek and have fellowship with Him. It denotes a desire to enter into His favour and become a partaker of His blessings in this life and of His salvation in the life to come. It is the heart's approach unto Him in and through Christ: John 14:6, Heb. 7:25. But before there is a conscious access to Him, God has to be diligently sought.

None come to God, none truly seek Him, until they are made conscious of their lost condition. The Spirit must first work in the soul a realization that sin has alienated us "from the life of God" (Eph. 4:18). We have to be made to feel that we are *away from* God, out of His favour, under His righteous condemnation, before we shall really do as the prodigal did, and say "I will arise and go to My Father, and will say unto Him, Father, I have sinned against heaven, and before Thee" (Luke 15:18). The same principle holds good in connection with the repeated "coming" of the Christian (1 Pet. 2:4); it is a sense of need which causes us to seek Him who is the Giver of every good and every perfect gift. There is also a maintained communion with God in the performance of holy duties: in all the exercises of godliness we renew our access to God in Christ: in reading of or hearing His Word, we come to Him as Teacher, in prayer we come to Him as Benefactor.

But to seek God aright, He has to be sought in faith, for "without faith it is impossible to please Him," therefore, "he that cometh to God *must* believe that He is, and that He is a rewarder of them that diligently seek Him." There has to be first a firm persuasion of His being, and second of His bounty. To believe that "He is" means much more than assenting to the fact of a "First Cause" or to allow that there is a "Supreme Being"; it means to believe in the character of God *as* He has revealed Himself in His works, in His Word, and in Christ. He must be conceived of aright, or otherwise we are only pursuing a phantom of our own imagination. Thus, to believe that "God is" is to exercise faith upon Him as *such* a Being as His Word declares Him to be: supreme sovereign, ineffably holy, almighty, inflexibly just, yet abounding in mercy and grace toward poor sinners through Christ.

Not only is the heart to go out unto God as His being and character is revealed in Scripture, but particularly, faith is to lay hold of His graciousness: that He is "a *Rewarder*" etc. The acting of faith toward God as a "Rewarder" is the heart's apprehension and anticipation of the fact that He is ready and willing to conduct Himself to needy sinners in a way of bounty, that He will act in all things toward them in a manner suitable unto the proposal of which He makes of Himself through the Gospel. It was the realization of this (in addition to his felt need) which stirred the prodigal to act. Just as it would be useless to pray unless there were an hope that God hears and that He will answer prayer, so no sinner will really seek unto God until there is born in his heart an expectation of mercy from Him, that He will receive him graciously. This is a laying hold of His promise.

In Scripture, privileges are propounded with their necessary limitations, and we disjoint the whole system of Truth if we separate the recompence from the duty. There is something to be done on our part: God is a "Rewarder," but *of whom?* Of those who "diligently seek Him." "The wicked shall be turned into Hell, all the nations that forget God" (Psa. 9:17): not only "deny," but "forget" Him; as they cast God out of their thoughts and affections, so He will cast them out of His presence. What is meant by "diligently seek Him"? To "seek" God is to forsake, deny, go out of self, and take Him alone for our Ruler and satisfying Portion. To seek Him "diligently" is to seek Him early (Prov. 8:17), wholeheartedly (Psa. 119:10), earnestly (Psa. 27:4), unweariedly (Luke 11:8). How does a thirsty man seek water? The promise is, "And ye shall seek Me and find Me, when ye shall search for Me with all your heart" (Jer. 29:13 and cf. 2 Chron. 15:15).

And *how* does God "reward" the diligent seeker? By offering Himself graciously to be found of them who penitently, earnestly, trustfully approach Him through the appointed Mediator. By granting them access into His favour: this He did not unto Cain, who sought Him in a wrong manner. By actually bestowing His favour upon them, as He did upon the prodigal. By forgiving their sins and blotting out their iniquities (Isa. 55:7). By writing His laws in their hearts, so that they now desire and determine to forsake all idols and serve Him only. By giving them assurance of their acceptance in the Beloved, and granting them sweet foretastes of the rest and bliss which awaits them on High. By ministering to their every need, both spiritual and temporal. Finally, by taking them to heaven, where they shall spend eternity in the unclouded enjoyment of the wondrous riches of His grace.

But does this word "Rewarder" have a legalistic ring to it? Not if it be understood rightly. Does it signify that our "diligent seeking" is a meritorious performance which is entitled to recognition? Of course it does not. What, then, is meant? First, let us quote from the helpful comments of John Owen: "That which these words of the apostle hath respect to, and which is the ground of the faith here required, is contained in the revelation that God made of Himself unto Abraham, 'Fear not: Abram: I am thy shield, and they exceeding great reward' (Gen. 15:1). God is so a rewarder unto them that seek Him, as that He is Himself their reward, which eternally excludes all thoughts of merit in them that are so rewarded. Who can merit God to be his reward? Rewarding in God, especially where He Himself is the reward, is an act of infinite grace and bounty. And this gives us full direction unto the object of faith here intended, namely, God in Christ, as revealed in the promise of Him, giving Himself unto believers as a reward, (to be their God) in a way of infinite goodness and bounty. The proposal hereof, is that alone which gives encouragement to come unto Him, which the apostle designs to declare."

"Now to him that worketh is the reward not reckoned of grace, but of debt" (Rom. 4:4): is not the implication clear that *grace* itself also "rewards"? Grace and reward are no more inconsistent than the high sovereignty of God and the real responsibility of man, or between the fact that Christ is and was both "Servant" (Isa. 42:1) and "Lord" (John 13:13). The language of Col. 3:24 makes this clear as a sunbeam: "Knowing that of the Lord ye shall receive the reward of the inheritance: for ye serve the Lord Christ." The "inheritance" is Heaven itself, salvation in its consummation. But is not salvation a free gift? Yes, indeed; nevertheless it has to be "bought" by its recipients (Isa. 55:1), yet "without money and without price." Salvation is both a "gift" and a "reward."

While it be true that Heaven cannot be earned by the sinner, it is equally true that Heaven is not for idlers and loiterers. God has to be "diligently sought." To enter the strait gate the soul has to agonize (Luke 13:24). We are called upon to "labour" for that meat which endureth unto eternal life (John 6:27) and to enter into the heavenly rest (Heb. 4:11). Such efforts God "rewards," not because they are meritorious, but because He deems it meet to recognize and recompense them. There are those who teach that in serving God we ought to have no "respect unto the recompense of the reward" (Heb. 11:26), but this verse refutes them, for the apostle explicitly declares that this forms a necessary part of that truth which is to be believed in order to our pleasing God.

Heaven, or completed salvation, is spoken of as a "reward" to intimate the character of those to whom it is given, namely, the diligent labourer. Second, because it is not bestowed until our work is completed: 2 Tim. 4:7, 8. Third, to intimate the sureness of it: we may as confidently expect it as does the labourer who has been hired by an honest master: James 1:12. This "reward" is principally in the next life: Heb. 11:16, 2 Cor. 4:17 — it is then that all true godliness shall be richly recompensed: Mark 10:29, 30. It only remains for us now to add that the *ground* on which God bestows the "reward" is the infinite merits of Christ, and out of respect unto His own promise. *That which* He "rewards" is the work of His own Spirit within us, so that we have no ground for boasting.

"By faith Noah, being warned of God of things not seen as yet, moved with fear, prepared an ark to the saving of his house; by the which he condemned the world, and became heir of the righteousness which is by faith" (v. 7). The apostle now presents a concrete example which illustrates what he had said in v. 6. God's dealings with Noah and the world in his time were plainly a sample and pledge of His dealing with the world in all ages, particularly so when its history is finally wound up. Inasmuch as God is the Rewarder of those who diligently seek Him, it necessarily follows that He is also the Revenger of all who despise Him. In the destruction of the old world, God showed His displeasure against sin (Job 22:15, 16); in the preservation of Noah, He made manifest the privileges of His own people (2 Pet. 2:9). That the whole was a *pledge* and type is clear from 2 Pet. 3:6, 7.

In the verse which is now before us three things claim attention. First, Noah's faith and its ground, namely the warning he had received from God. Second, the effects of his faith, namely, internally, the impulse of "fear"; externally, his obedience in making the ark under God's orders. Third, the consequences of his faith, namely, the saving of his house, the condemning of the world, his becoming heir of the righteousness which is by faith. But ere taking up these points, let us face and endeavour to remove a difficulty which some feel this verse raises. Let us put it this way: was Noah saved by his own works? We believe the answer is both Yes, and No. We beg the reader to exercise patience and prayerfully ponder what follows, and not cry out rank heresy and refuse to read further.

If Noah had not "prepared an ark" in obedience to God's command, would he not have perished in the flood? Then was it his own efforts which preserved him from death in the great deluge? No indeed; it was the preserving power of God. That ark had neither mast, sail, nor steering-wheel: only the gracious hand of the Lord kept that frail barque from being splintered to atoms on the rocks and the mountains. Then what is the relation between these two things? This: Noah made use of the *means* which God had prescribed, and by His grace and power those means were made effectual unto his preservation. Must not the farmer toil in his fields? yet it is God alone who gives him the increase. Must I not observe the laws of hygiene and eat wholesome food? yet only as God blesses them to me am I kept in health. So it is in spiritual things:

salvation by grace alone *does not exclude* the imperative necessity of our using the means which God has appointed and prescribed.

The temporal deliverance of Noah from the flood is undoubtedly an adumbration of the eternal deliverance of God's elect from the wrath to come: and here, as everywhere, the type is accurate and perfect. Nor can any sophistical quibbling honestly get rid of the fact that Noah's building of the Ark — a most costly and arduous work!—was a means towards his preservation. Then does the case of Noah supply a clear example of salvation by works? Again we answer boldly, Yes and No. But the difficulty is greatly relieved if we bear in mind that Noah was *already a saved man* before God bade him build the Ark! A reference to Gen. 6:8, 9 and a comparison with 6:14, 22 makes this unmistakably plain. But does not this fact overthrow all that has been said in the previous paragraphs? Not at all. The Christian's salvation is not only a past thing (2 Tim. 1:9), but a present (Phil. 2:12) and future (Rom. 13:11) thing too! We trust that the solution of the difficulty will be more evident as we proceed with our exposition of the verse.

As we have before pointed out, the first three verses of Heb. 11 are introductory, their design being to set forth the importance and excellency of faith. Then, in vv. 4-7, we have an outline of the life of faith: the beginning of it is seen in v. 4, the nature of what it consists in v. 5, a warning and encouragement is supplied in v. 6, and the end of it is shown in v. 7. Before bringing before us the glorious goal which the life of faith reaches, v. 7 gives us the other side of what was before us in v. 5: there we saw faith elevating above a world of death, carrying the heart of its favoured possessor into Heaven. But we are still in the world, and that is the place of opposition, of danger, and hence, of testing. Thus in v. 7 we are not only shown what faith obtains, but *how* it obtains, it.

Now as we found it necessary to go back to Gen. 3 and 4 to interpret Heb. 11:4, and to Gen. 5:24 to get the meaning of 11:5, so now we have to consult Gen. 6 in order to discover what is here adumbrated. Let the reader turn back to Gen. 6:5-22. There we find unsparing Divine judgment announced (v. 13), a way of deliverance presented to one who had "found grace" in the Lord's eyes (v. 14), faith's obedience called for if escape was to be had from judgment (v. 14), the Divinely prescribed means to be used (v. 15); by employing those means deliverance was obtained. Now in like manner, a most solemn warning has been given us, an announcement of coming judgment: see 2 Thess. 1:7, 8; 2 Pet. 3:10-17—let the reader duly observe that both of these passages are found in epistles addressed to God's children.

In saying above that Heb. 11:7 gives us the other side of what is spiritually set forth in v. 5, we mean that it gives us the *balancing* truth. It is most important to observe this, for otherwise we are very liable to entertain a mystical concept of v. 5 and become lopsided. Satan is ready to tell us that v. 5 presents to us a beautiful ideal, but one which is altogether impracticable for ordinary people—alright for preachers, but impossible for others. After reading our article on v. 5, many are likely to exclaim: We cannot be thinking of heavenly things all the time, we have our daily duties to attend to here on earth: the only way we could reach the standard of v. 5 would be by entering a monastery or convent, entirely secluding ourselves from the world; and surely God does not require this of us. No, indeed; that was the great mistake of the "Dark Ages."

"By faith Noah being warned of God of things not seen as yet, moved with fear, prepared an ark to the saving of his house." This gives us the other side of v. 5. It shows that we *have* duties to perform on earth, and intimates *how* they are to be discharged — by faith, in the fear of God, implicitly obeying His commands. And more: our present verse insists on the fact (now so little apprehended) that, the performing these duties, the rendering of faith's obedience to God, is indispensably necessary to our very salvation. The "salvation" of the soul is yet future: note "saving" and *not* "salvation" in Heb. 10:39, and also compare 1 Pet. 1:5. In order to be saved from the destructive power of sin, the ruinous allurements of the world, and the devouring assaults of Satan, we *must* tread the path of obedience to Christ (Heb. 5:9), for only there do we escape these fatal foes. Let the reader prayerfully ponder Mark 9:43-50; Luke 14:26, 27, 33; Rom. 8:13; 1 Cor. 9:27; Col. 3:5; Heb. 3:12, 14.

Heb. 11:5 and 7 supplement each other. Verse 5 shows us that by the exercise of faith our affections are elevated above the earth and set upon things above. Verse 7 teaches us that our lives on earth are to be regulated by heavenly principles. The real Christian is a heavenly man living on earth *as* a heavenly man; that is to say, he is governed by spiritual and Divine principles, and not by fleshly motives and worldly interests. The Christian performs many of the same deeds as the non-Christian does, yet with a far different object and aim. All that I do should be done in obedience to God, in joyous response to His revealed will. Let us be specific and come to details. Let the Christian wife read Eph. 5:22-24 and the husband 5:25-31, and let each recognize that in obeying the husband and loving the wife, they are *obeying God*. Let Christian employees ponder Eph. 6:5-7, and recognize that in obeying their masters they are obeying the Lord; contrariwise, in sulking or speaking against them, they murmur against the Lord!

Now such obedience to God's commandments in the ordinary relationships of life are necessary unto salvation. If this staggers the reader, let him contemplate the opposite. Those precepts and commands have been given us by God, and to disregard them is rebellion, and to refuse compliance is defiance; and no rebel against God can enter Heaven. Unless our wills have been broken, unless our hearts have been brought into subjection to God, we have no scriptural warrant for concluding that He has *begun* a good work in us (Phil. 1:6). "He that saith I know Him, and keepeth not His commandments, is a liar, and the truth is not in him" (1 John 2:4). The only path which leads to heaven is that of walking in obedience to God's commands.

Now the salvation of the soul lies at the *end* of that path. Does the reader exclaim, I thought it was at the beginning of it, and that none but a regenerate person could or would walk therein. From one standpoint that is quite true. When genuinely converted a sinner *is* saved from the eternal penalty of his sins, and *is* "delivered from the wrath to come." But is he there and then removed to Heaven? With very rare exceptions he is not. Instead, God leaves him here in this world. And this world is the place of danger, for temptations to return unto its ways and pleasures abound on every side. Moreover, the judgment of God hangs over it, and one day will burst upon and consume it. And who will escape that destruction? Only those who, like Noah, have a faith which is moved with fear and produces obedience. But it is now high time that we considered more closely the details of v. 7.

"By faith Noah, being warned of God of things not seen as yet, moved with fear, prepared an ark to the saving of his house." Ah, here is the key to our verse, hung right upon the very door of it. Like every other one of God's elect, Noah was saved by grace through faith; and yet not by a faith that was inactive—Eph. 2:10 follows v. 9! *Faith* was the spring of all his works: a faith which was far more than an intellectual assent, one which was a supernatural principle that sovereign grace had wrought in him. God had determined to send a flood and destroy the wicked world, but ere doing so, He acquainted Noah with His purpose. He has done the same with us: see Rom. 1:18. That Divine warning was the ground of Noah's faith. He argued not, nor reasoned about its incredibility; instead, he believed God. The *threatening,* as well as the promise of God, is the object of faith; the justice of God is to be eyed, as well as His mercy!

Human reason was altogether opposed unto what God had made known to Noah. Hitherto there had been no rain (Gen. 2:6), then why expect an overwhelming deluge? It seemed utterly unlikely God would destroy the whole human race, and His mercy be thus utterly swallowed up by His avenging justice. The threatening judgment was a long way off (120 years: Gen. 6:3), and during that time the world might well repent and reform. When he preached to men (2 Pet. 2:5) none believed his message: why then should he be so fearful, when every one else was at ease? To build an ark of such huge dimensions was an enormous undertaking, and, as well, would involve the scoffs of all his fellows. And even if the flood came, how could the ark float with such an immensely heavy burden— it had no anchor to stay her, no mast and sail to steady her, no steering-wheel to direct. Was it not quite inpracticable, for Noah was quite inexperienced nautically. Moreover, for him and his family to dwell for an indefinite period in a sealed ark was far from a pleasant prospect unto the flesh and blood. But against all these carnal objections faith offered a steady resistance, and *believed God!*

"Moved with fear." This evidenced the reality and power of his faith, for saving faith not only "worketh by love" (Gal. 5:6), but in "fear and trembling" (Phil. 2:12). A reverential awe of God is a sure fruit of saving faith. That "fear" acted as a salutary impetus in Noah and operated as a powerful motive in his building of the ark. "His believing the word of God, had this effect on him . . . a reverential fear it is of God's threatenings, and not an anxious solicitous fear of the evil threatened. In the warning given him, he considered the greatness, the holiness, and the power of God, with the vengeance becoming those holy properties of His nature, which He threatened to bring on the world. Seeing God by faith under this representation of Him, he was filled with a reverential fear of Him. See Habak. 3:16, Psa. 119:120, Mal. 2:5" (J. Owen).

"Prepared an ark to the saving of his house." As Matthew Henry says, "Faith first influences our affections and then our actions." "Faith without works is dead" (James 2:20), particularly works of obedience. "Thus did Noah: according to all that God commanded him, so did he" (Gen. 6:22). Privilege and duty are inseparably connected, yet duty will never be performed where faith is absent. Faith in Noah caused him to persevere in his arduous labours amid many difficulties and discouragements. Thus his building of the ark was the work of faith and patience, a labour of Godly fear, an act of obedience, a means to his preservation— for God's covenant with him (Gen. 6:18) did not preclude his diligent use of means; and a type of Christ. As it was by faith-obedience he prepared the ark, so by faith's obedience came the "saving of his house." God always honours those who honour Him. This temporal salvation was a figure of the eternal salvation unto which we are pressing forward for note that the destruction of the anti-deluvians was an *eternal* one—for their spirits are now "in prison" (1 Pet. 3:19)! Observe it is *our* responsibility to seek after our own salvation and those committed to us: see Acts 2:40, 2 Tim 4:16.

"By the which he condemned the world." The reference is to all that precedes. By his own example, by his faith in God's warning, his reverential awe of God's holiness and justice, his implicit and unflagging obedience in preparing the ark, Noah "condemned" the unbelieving, unconcerned, godless people all around him. One man is said to "condemn," another when, by his godly actions, he shows what the other should do, and which by doing not, his guilt is aggravated; see Matt. 12:41, 42. The Sabbath-keeper "condemns" the Sabbath-breaker. He who abandons a worldly church and goes forth unto Christ outside the camp, "condemns" the compromiser. Noah's diligent and costly labours increased the guilt of the careless, who rested in a false security. Though we cannot convert the wicked, yet we must be careful to set before them such an example of personal piety that they are left "without excuse."

"And became heir of the righteousness which is by faith." The "righteousness" here referred to is that perfect obedience of Christ which God imputes unto all who savingly believe on His Son: Jer. 23:6, Rom. 5:19, 2 Cor. 5:21. This righteousness is sometimes called, absolutely, the "righteousness of God" (Rom. 1:17, etc.), sometimes the "gift of righteousness . . . by one, Jesus Christ" (Rom. 5:17), sometimes "the righteousness which is of God by faith" (Phil. 3:9); in all of which our free and gratuitous justification by the righteousness of Christ reckoned to our account through faith, is intended. In saying that Noah "became heir" of this righteousness, there may be a double significance. First, by faith's obedience he *evidenced* himself *to be* a justified man (Gen. 6:9), as Abraham did when he offered up Isaac (James 2:21). Second, he *established his title* to that righteousness which is here spoken of as an "inheritance": this is in contrast from Esau who despised his. That righteousness which Christ purchased for His people is here denominated an "inheritance," to emphasize the dignity and excellency of it, to magnify the freeness of its tenure, to declare the certainty and inviolability of it.

The actual entrance upon our Inheritance is yet future. "That being justified by His grace, we should be made heirs according to the *hope of* eternal life" (Titus 3:7). The great question for each of us to settle is, Am I an "heir"? To help us do so, let me inquire,

Have I the *spirit* of one? Is my main care to make sure that I have the *birthright?* Am I putting the claims of God and His righteousness (Matt. 6:33) above everything else? Have I such thoughts of the blessedness of my portion in Christ that nothing can induce me to sell or part with it (Heb. 12:16)? Is my heart wrapped up in that inheritance so that I am groaning within myself, "waiting for the adoption" (Rom. 8:23)? Am I walking by faith, with the fear of God upon me, diligently attending to His commandments, thereby condemning the world? If so, thrice blessed am I: and soon shall I be saved "to sin no more."

CHAPTER SIXTY

The Call of Abraham

(Heb. 11:8)

"The scope of the apostle in this chapter is to prove that the doctrine of faith is an ancient doctrine and that faith hath been always exercised about things not seen, not liable to the judgment of sense and reason. He had proved both points by instances of the fathers before the flood, and now he comes to prove them by the examples of those that were eminent for faith after the flood. And in the first place he pitcheth upon Abraham—a fit instance; he was the father of the faithful, and a person of whom the Hebrews boasted; his life was nothing else but a continual practice of faith, and therefore he insisteth upon Abraham longer than upon any other of the patriarchs. The first thing for which Abraham is commended in Scripture is his obedience to God, when He called him out of his country; now the apostle shows this was an effect of faith" (T. Manton, 1660).

The second division of Heb. 11 begins with the verse which is now to be before us. As pointed out in previous articles, vv. 4-7 present an outline of the life of faith. In v. 4 we are shown where the life of faith *begins,* namely, at that point where the conscience is awakened to our lost condition, where the soul makes a complete surrender to God, and where the heart rests upon the perfect satisfaction made by Christ our Surety. In v. 5 we are shown the *character* of the life of faith: a pleasing of God, a walking with Him, the heart elevated above this world of death. In vv. 6, 7 we are shown the *end* of the life of faith: a diligent seeking of God, a heart which is moved by His fear to use those means which He appointed and prescribed, issuing in the saving of the soul and establishing its title to be an heir of the righteousness which is by faith. Wonderfully comprehensive are the contents of these opening verses, and well repaid will be the prayerful student who ponders them again and again.

From v. 8 to the end of the chapter, the Holy Spirit gives us fuller details concerning the life of faith, viewing it from different angles, contemplating varied aspects, and exhibiting the different trials to which it is subject and the blessed triumphs which Divine grace enables it to achieve. Fitly does this new section of our chapter open by presenting to us the case of Abraham. In his days a new and important era of human history commenced. Hitherto God had maintained a general relation to the whole human race, but at the Tower of Babel that relation was broken. It was there that mankind, as a whole, consummated their revolt against their Maker, in consequence of which He abandoned them. To that point is to be traced the origin of "Heathendom": Rom. 1:18-30 should be read in this connection. From this point onwards God's dealings with men were virtually confined to Abraham and his posterity.

That a new division of our chapter commences at v. 8 is further evident from the fact that Abraham is designated "the *father* of all them that believe" (Rom. 4:11), which means not only that he is (as it were) the earthly head of the whole election of grace, but the one after whose likeness his spiritual children are conformed. There is a family likeness between Abraham and the true Christian, for if we are Christ's then are we "Abraham's seed and heirs according to promise" (Gal. 3:29), for "they which are of faith, the same are the children of Abraham" (Gal. 3:7), which is evidenced by them doing "the works of Abraham" (John 8:39), for these are the marks of identification. In like manner, Christ declared of the Pharisees, "Ye are of your father the Devil, and the lusts (desires and behests) of your father, ye will (are determined) to do" (John 8:44). The wicked bear the family likeness of the Wicked one. The "fatherhood of Abraham" is twofold: natural, as the progenitor of a physical seed; spiritual, as the pattern to which his children are morally conformed.

"By faith Abraham, when he was called to go out into a place which he should after receive for an inheritance, obeyed; and he went out, not knowing whither he went" (v. 8). In taking up the study of this verse our first concern should be to ascertain its meaning and message *for us today*. In order to discover this, we must begin by seeking to know what was shadowed forth in the great incident here recorded. A little meditation should make it obvious that the central thing referred to is the Divine call of which Abraham was made the recipient. This is confirmed by a reference to Gen. 12:1, where we have the historical account of that to which the Spirit by the apostle here alludes. Further proof is furnished by Act 7:2, 3. This, then must be our startingpoint.

"And we know that all things work together for good to them that love God, to them who are *the called* according to His purpose" (Rom. 8:28). There are two distinct kinds of "calls" from God mentioned in Scripture: a general and a particular, an outward and an inward, an inoperative and an effectual. The general, external, and inefficacious "call" is given to all who hear the Gospel, or come under the sound of the Word. *This* call is *refused* by all. It is found in such passages as the following: "Unto you, O men, I call; My voice is to the sons of man" (Prov. 8:4); "For many be called, but few chosen" (Matt. 20:16); "And sent His servant at supper-time to say to them that were bidden, Come; for all things are now ready. And they all with one consent began to make excuse" (Luke 14:17, 18); "Because I have called, and ye refuse; I have stretched out My hand, and no man regarded" etc. (Prov. 1:24-28).

The special, inward, and efficacious "call' of God comes only to His elect. It is responded to by each favoured one who receives it. It is referred to in such passages as the following: "The dead shall hear the voice of the Son of God, and they that hear shall live" (John 5:25); "He calleth His own sheep by name, and leadeth them out. And when He putteth forth His sheep, He goeth before them, and the sheep follow Him: for they know His voice . . . and other sheep I have, which are not of this fold: them also I must bring, and they shall hear My voice" (John 10:3, 4, 16); "Whom He called, them He also justified" (Rom. 8:30); "Not many wise men after the flesh, not many mighty, not many noble, are called: but God hath chosen the foolish things of the world to confound the wise" (1 Cor. 1:26-27). This call is illustrated and exemplified in such cases as Matthew (Luke 5:27, 28), Zacchaeus (Luke 19:5, 6), Saul of Tarsus (Acts 9:4, 5).

The individual, internal, and invincible call of God is an act of sovereign grace, accompanied by all-mighty power, quickening those who are dead in trespasses and sins, imparting to them spiritual life. This Divine call is regeneration, or the new birth, when its favoured recipient is brought "out of darkness into His marvelous light" (1 Pet. 2:9). Now *this* is what is before us in Heb. 11:8, which gives additional proof that this verse commences a new section of the chapter. The wondrous call which Abraham received from God is necessarily placed at the head of the Spirit's detailed description of the life of faith; necessarily, we say, for faith itself is utterly impossible until the soul has been Divinely quickened.

Let us first contemplate the state that Abraham was in until and at the time God called him. To view him in his unregenerate condition is a duty which the Holy Spirit pressed upon Israel of old: "Look unto the rock whence ye are hewn, and to the *hole of the pit* whence ye are digged: look unto Abraham your father, and unto Sarah that bare you" (Isa. 51:1, 2). Help is afforded if we turn to Josh. 24:2, "Thus saith the Lord God of Israel, your fathers dwelt on the other side of the flood in old time, Terah, the father of Abraham, and the father of Nachor: and they *served other gods.*" Abraham, then, belonged to a heathen family, and dwelt in a great city, until he was seventy. No doubt he lived his life after the same manner as his fellows—content with the "husks" which the swine feed upon, with little or no serious thoughts of the Hereafter. Thus it is with each of God's elect till the Divine call comes to them and arrests them in their self-will, mad, and destructive course.

"The God of glory appeared unto our father Abraham, when he was in Mesopotamia, before he dwelt in Charran" (Acts 7:2). What marvelous grace! The God of glory condescended to draw near and reveal Himself unto one that was sunk in sin, immersed in idolatry, having no concern for the Divine honour. There was nothing in Abraham to deserve God's notice, still less to merit His esteem. But more: not only was the *grace* of God here signally evident, but the *sovereignty* of His grace was displayed in thus singling him out from the midst of all his fellows. As He says in Isa. 51:2, "I called him *alone,* and blessed him." "Why God should not call his father and kindred, there can be no answer but this: God hath mercy on whom He will (Rom. 9:18). He calleth Isaac and refuseth Ishmael; loveth Jacob, and hateth Esau; taketh Abel, and leaveth Cain: even because He will, and for no cause that we know" (W. Perkins, 1595).

"The God of glory appeared unto our father Abraham" (Acts 7:2). All that is included in these words, we know not; as to how God "appeared" unto him, we cannot say. But of two things we may be certain: for the first time in Abraham's life God became a *living Reality* to him; further, he perceived that He was an all-glorious Being. Thus it is, sooner or later, in the personal experience of each of God's elect. In the midst of their worldliness, self-seeking and self-pleasing, one day He of whom they had but the vaguest notions, and whom they sought to dismiss from their thoughts, appears before their hearts—terrifying, awakening, and then attracting. Now it is they can say, "I have heard of Thee by the hearing of the ear, but now mine eye seeth Thee" (Job 42:5).

O dear reader, our desire here is not simply to write an article, but to be used of God in addressing a definite message from Him straight to your inmost heart. Suffer us then to inquire, Do you know anything about what has been said in the above paragraph? Has God become a living Reality to your soul? Has He really drawn near to you, manifested Himself in His awe-inspiring Majesty, and had direct and personal dealings with your soul? Or do you know no more about Him than what *others* write and say of Him?

This is a question of vital moment, for if He does not have personal dealings with you here in a way of grace, He will have personal dealings with you hereafter, in a way of justice and judgment. Then "Seek ye the Lord while He may be found, call ye upon Him while he is near" (Isa. 55:6).

This, then, is one important aspect of regeneration: God graciously makes a personal revelation of Himself to the soul. The result is that He "who commanded the light to shine out of darkness, hath shined in our hearts, to give the light of the knowledge of the glory of God in the face of Jesus Christ" (2 Cor. 4:6). The favoured individual in whom this miracle of grace is wrought, is now brought out of that dreadful state in which he lay by nature, whereby "the natural man receiveth not the things of the Spirit of God, for they are foolishness unto him; neither can he know them, because they are spiritually discerned" (1 Cor. 2:14). So fearful is that state in which all the unregenerate lie, it is described as "having the understanding darkened, being alienated from the life of God through the ignorance that is in them, because of the blindness of their heart" (Eph. 4:18). But at the new birth the soul is delivered from the terrible darkness of sin and depravity into which the fall of Adam has brought all his descendants, and is ushered into the marvelous and glorious light of God.

Let us next consider the accompaniment or *terms* of the call which Abraham now received from God. A record of this is found in Gen. 12:1, "Get thee out of thy country, and from thy kindred, and from thy father's house, unto a land that I will show thee." What a testing of faith was this! What a trial to flesh and blood! Abraham was already seventy years of age, and long journeys and the break-up of old associations do not commend themselves to elderly people. To leave the land of his birth, to forsake home and estate, to sever family ties and leave loved ones behind, to abandon present certainty for (what seemed to human wisdom) a future uncertainty, and go forth not knowing whither, must have seemed hard and harsh unto natural sentiment. Why, then, should God make such a demand? To prove Abraham, to give the death-blow to his natural corruptions, to demonstrate the might of His grace. Yet we must look for something deeper, and that which applies directly to us.

As we have pointed out above, God's appearing to Abraham and his call of him, speaks to us of that miracle of grace which takes place in the soul at regeneration. Now the evidence of regeneration is found in a genuine *conversion*: it is that complete break from the old life, both inner and outer, which furnishes proof of the new birth. It is plain to any renewed mind that when a soul has been favoured with a real and personal manifestation of God, that a move or response is called for from him. It is simply impossible that he should continue his old manner of life. A new Object is before him, a new relationship has been established, new desires now fill his heart, and new responsibilities claim him. The moment a man truly realizes that he has to do with God, there must be a radical change: "Therefore if any man be in Christ, he is a new creature; old things are passed away, behold, all things are become new" (2 Cor. 5:17).

The call which Abraham received from God required a double response from him: he was to leave the land of his birth, and forsake his own kindred. What, then is the *spiritual* significance of these things? Remember that Abraham was a *pattern* case, for he is the "father" of all Christians, and the children must be conformed to the family likeness. Abraham is the prototype of those who are "holy brethren, partakers of the heavenly calling" (Heb. 3:1). Now the spiritual application to us of what was adumbrated by the terms of Abraham's call is twofold: doctrinal and practical, legal and experimental. Let us, briefly, consider them separately.

"Get thee out of thy country" finds its counterpart in the fact that the Christian is one who has been, by grace, the redemptive work of Christ, and the miraculous operation of the Spirit, delivered from his *old position*. By nature, the Christian was a member of "the world," the whole of which "lieth in the Wicked one" (1 John 5:19), and so is headed for destruction. But God's elect have been delivered from this: Christ "gave Himself for our sins, that He might deliver us from this present evil world, according to the will of God our Father" (Gal. 1:4); therefore does He say unto His own, "because ye are *not of* the world, but I have chosen you out of the world, therefore the world hateth you" (John 15:19).

"Get thee out of thy country" finding its fulfillment, first, in the Christian's being delivered from his *old condition,* namely, "in the flesh": "Knowing this, that our old man is crucified with Him, that the body of sin might be destroyed, that henceforth we should not serve sin" (Rom. 6:6). He has now been made a member of a new family. "Behold, what manner of love the Father hath bestowed upon us, that we should be called the sons of God" (1 John 3:1). He is now brought into union with a new "kindred," for all born-again souls are his brethren and sisters in Christ: "They that are in the flesh cannot please God; but ye are *not in* the flesh, but in the Spirit, if so be that the Spirit of God dwell in you" (Rom. 8:8, 9). Thus, the call of God is a separating one — from our old standing and state, into a new one.

Now what has just been pointed out above is already, from the Divine side, an accomplished fact. Legally, the Christian no longer belongs to "the world" nor is he "in the flesh." But this has to be entered into practically from the human side, and made good in our actual experience. Because our "citizenship is in heaven" (Phil. 3:20), we are to live here as "strangers and pilgrims." A practical separation from the world is demanded of us, for "the friendship of the world is enmity with God" (James 4:4); therefore does God say, "Be ye not unequally yoked together with unbelievers . . . come out from among them, and be ye separate" (2 Cor. 6:14, 17). So too the "flesh," still in us, is to be allowed no rein. "I beseech you therefore brethren, by the mercies of God, that ye present your bodies a living sacrifice, holy, acceptable unto God, which is your reasonable service" (Rom. 12:1); "Make not provision for the flesh to fulfill the lusts thereof" (Rom. 13:14); "Mortify therefore your members which are upon the earth" (Col. 3:5).

The claims of Christ upon His people are paramount. He reminds them that, "ye are not your own, for ye are bought with a price" (1 Cor. 6:19, 20). Therefore does He say, "If any man come to Me, and hate not his father, and mother, and wife, and children, and brethren, and sisters, yea, and his own life also, he cannot be My disciple" (Luke 14:26). Their response is declared in, "They that are Christ's *have* crucified the flesh with the affections and lusts" (Gal. 5:24). Thus, the terms of the call which Abraham received from God are addressed to *our* hearts. A complete break from the old life is required of us.

Practical *separation from the world* is imperative. This was typed out of old in the history of Abraham's descendants. They had settled down in Egypt—figure of the world—and after they had come under the blood of the lamb, and before they entered Canaan (type of Heaven), they *must* leave the land of Pharaoh. Hence too God says of our Surety "Out of Egypt have I called My Son" (Matt. 2:15): the Head must be conformed to the members, and the members to their Head. Practical mortification of *the flesh* is equally imperative, "For if ye live after the flesh, ye shall die (eternally): but if ye through the Spirit do mortify the deeds of the body, ye shall live" (eternally): (Rom. 8:13); "but he that soweth to his flesh, shall of the flesh reap corruption; but he that soweth to the Spirit, shall of the Spirit reap life everlasting" (Gal. 6:8).

"By faith Abraham, when he was called to go out into a place which he should after receive for an inheritance, obeyed; and he went out, not knowing whither he went." This verse, read in the light of Gen. 12:1, clearly signifies that God demanded the supreme place in Abraham's affections. His life was no longer to be regulated by self-will, self-love, self-pleasing; self was to be entirely set aside, "crucified." Henceforth, the will and word of God was to govern and direct him in all things. Henceforth he was to be a man without a *home* on earth, but seeking one in Heaven, and treading that path which alone leads thither.

Now it should be very evident from what has been said above that, regeneration or an effectual call from God is a *miraculous* thing, as far above the reach of nature as the heavens are above the earth. When God makes a personal revelation of Himself to the soul, this is accompanied by the communication of supernatural grace, which produces supernatural fruit. It was contrary to nature for Abraham to leave home and country, and go forth "not knowing whither he went." Equally it is contrary to nature for the Christian to separate from the world and crucify the flesh. A miracle of Divine grace has to be wrought within him, before any man will really deny self and live in complete subjection to God. And this leads us to say that, genuine cases of regeneration are much rarer than many suppose. The spiritual children of Abraham are very far from being a numerous company, as is abundantly evident from the fact that few indeed bear his likeness. Out of all the thousands of professing Christians around us, how many manifest Abraham's faith or do Abraham's works?

"By faith Abraham, when he was called to go out into a place which he should after receive for an inheritance, obeyed; and he went out, not knowing whither he went." This verse, read in the light upon which we would fix our attention is Abraham's *obedience*. A saving faith is one which heeds the Divine commands, as well as relies upon the Divine promises. Make no mistake upon this point, dear reader: Christ is "the Author of eternal salvation unto all them that *obey* Him" (Heb. 5:9). Abraham placed himself unreservedly in the hands of God, surrendered to His lordship, and subscribed to His wisdom as best fitted to direct him. And so must we, or we shall never be "carried into Abraham's bosom" (Luke 16:22).

Abraham "obeyed, and he went out." There are two things there: "obeyed" signifies the consent of his mind, "and went out" tells of his actual performance. He obeyed not only in word, but in deed. In this, he was in marked contrast from the rebellious one mentioned in Matt. 21:30, "I go, sir, and went not." "The first act of saving faith consists in a discovery and sight of the infinite greatness, goodness, and other excellencies of the nature of God, so as to judge it our duty upon His call, His command, and promise, to deny ourselves, to relinquish all things, and to do so accordingly" (John Owen). Such ought our obedience to be unto God's call, and to every manifestation of His will. It must be a simple obedience in subjection to His authority, without inquiring after the reason thereof, and without objecting any scruples or difficulties against it.

"Observe that faith, wherever it is, bringeth forth obedience: by faith Abraham, being called, obeyed God. Faith and obedience can never be severed; as the sun and the light, fire and heat. Therefore we read of the 'obedience of faith' (Rom. 1:5). Obedience is faith's daughter. Faith hath not only to do with the grace of God, but with the duty of the creature. By apprehending grace, it works upon duty: 'faith worketh by love' (Gal. 5:6); it fills the soul with the apprehensions of God's love, and then makes use of the sweetness of love to urge us to more work or obedience. All our obedience to God comes from love of God, and our love comes from the persuasion of God's love to us. The argument and discourse that is in a sanctified soul is set down thus: 'I live by the faith of the Son of God, who loved me and gave Himself for me' (Gal. 2:20). Wilt thou not do this for God, that loved thee? for Jesus Christ, that gave Himself for thee? Faith works towards obedience by commanding the affections" (Thos. Manton, 1680).

"He went forth *not* knowing whither he went." How this demonstrates the reality and power of his faith—to leave a present possession for a future one. Abraham's obedience is the more conspicuous because at the time God called him, He did not specify which land he was to journey to, nor where it was located. Thus, it was by faith and not by sight, that he moved forward. Implicit confidence in the One who had called him was needed on the part of Abraham. Imagine a total stranger coming and bidding you follow him, without telling you where! To undertake a journey of unknown length, one of difficulty and danger, towards a land of which he knew nothing, called for real faith in the living God. See here the power of faith to triumph over fleshly disinclinations, to surmount obstacles, to perform difficult duties. Reader, is *this* the nature of *your* faith? Is your faith producing works which are not only *above* the power of mere nature to perform, but also directly *contrary* thereto?

Abraham's faith is hard to find these days. There is much talk and boasting, but most of it is empty words—the *works* of Abraham are conspicuous by their absence, in the vast majority of those who claim to be his children. The Christian is required to set his affections on things above, and not on things below (Col. 3:2). He is required to walk by faith, and not by sight; to tread the path of obedience to God's commands, and not please himself; to go and do whatever the Lord bids him. Even if God's commands appear severe or unreasonable, we must obey them: "Let no man deceive himself: if any man among you seemeth to be wise in this world, let him become a fool, that he may be wise" (1 Cor. 3:18); "And He said to them all, if any man will come after Me, let him deny himself, and take up his cross daily, and follow Me" (Luke 9:23).

But such an obedience as God requires can only proceed from a *supernatural* faith. An unshakable confidence in the living God, and unreserved surrender to His holy will, each step of our lives being ordered by His word (Psa. 119:105), can only issue from a miraculous work of grace which He has Himself wrought in the heart. How many there are who profess to be God's people yet only obey Him so long as they consider that their *own* interests are being served! How many are unwilling to quit trading on the Sabbath because they fear a few dollars will be lost! Now just as a traveller on foot, who takes a long journey through an unknown country, seeks a reliable guide, commits himself to his leading, trusts to his knowledge, and follows him implicitly o'er hill and dale, so God requires us to commit ourselves fully unto Him, trusting His faithfulness, wisdom and power, and yielding to every demand which He makes upon us.

"He went forth not knowing whither he went." Most probably many of his neighbours and acquaintances in Chaldea would inquire why he was leaving them, and where he was bound for. Imagine their surprise when Abraham had to say, I know not. Could *they* appreciate the fact that he was walking by faith and not by sight? Would they commend him for following Divine orders? Would they not rather deem him crazy? And, dear reader, the Godless will no more understand the motives which prompt the real children of God today, than could the Chaldeans understand Abraham; the unregenerate professing Christians all around us, will no more approve of our strict compliance with God's commands, than did Abraham's heathen neighbours. The world is governed by the senses, not faith; lives to please self, not God. And if the world does not deem you and me crazy, then there is something radically wrong with our hearts and lives.

One other point remains to be considered, and we must reluctantly conclude this article. The obedience of Abraham's faith was *unto* "a land which he should afterward receive for an inheritance" (v. 8). Literally, that "inheritance" was Canaan; spiritually, it foreshadowed Heaven. Now had Abraham refused to make the radical break which he did from his old life, crucify the affections of the flesh, and leave Chaldea, he had never reached the promised land. The Christian's "Inheritance" is purely of *grace,* for what can any man do in time to earn something which is eternal? Utterly impossible is it for any finite creature to perform anything which deserves an infinite reward. Nevertheless, God has marked out a certain path which conducts to the promised Inheritance: the path of obedience, the "Narrow Way" which "leadeth *unto* Life" (Matt. 7:14), and only those ever reach Heaven who tread *that* path to the end.

As the utmost confusion now reigns upon this subject, and as many are, through an unwarranted reserve, afraid to speak out plainly thereon, we feel obliged to add a little more. Unqualified obedience is required from us: *not* to furnish title to Heaven—that is found alone in the merits of Christ; not to fit us for Heaven—that is supplied alone by the supernatural work of the Spirit in the heart; but that God may be owned and honoured by us as we journey thither, that we may prove and manifest the sufficiency of His grace, that we may furnish evidences we *are* HIS children, that we may be preserved from those things which would otherwise destroy us—only in the path of obedience can we avoid those foes which are seeking to slay us.

O dear reader, as you value your soul we intreat you not to spurn this article, and particularly its closing paragraphs, because its teaching differs radically from what you are accustomed to hear or read. The path of obedience *must* be trod if ever you are to reach Heaven. Many are acquainted with that path or "way," but they walk not therein: *see* 2 Pet. 2:20. Many, like Lot's wife, make a start along it, and then turn from it: see Luke 9:62. Many follow it for quite a while, but fail to persevere; and, like Israel of old, perish in the wilderness. No rebel can enter Heaven; one who is wrapt up in self cannot; no disobedient soul will. Only those will partake of the heavenly "inheritance" who are "children of Abraham," who have his faith, follow his examples, perform his works. May the Lord deign to add His blessing to the above, and to Him shall be all the praise.

CHAPTER SIXTY-ONE

The Life of Abraham

(Heb. 11:9, 10)

In the preceding article we considered the appearing of the Lord unto idolatrous Abraham in Chaldea, the call which he then received to make a complete break from his old life, and to go forward in faith in complete subjection to the revealed will of God. This we contemplated as a figure and type, an illustration and example of one essential feature of regeneration, namely, God's effectually calling His elect from death unto life, out of darkness into His marvelous light, with the blessed fruits this produces. As we saw on the last occasion, a mighty change was wrought in Abraham, so that his manner of life was completely altered: "By faith Abraham, when he was called to go out into a place which he should after receive for an inheritance, obeyed; and he went out, not knowing whither he went."

Ere turning unto the verses which are to form our present portion, let us first ask and seek to answer the following question: Was Abraham's response to God's call a perfect one? Was his obedience flawless? Ah, dear reader, is it difficult to anticipate the answer? There has been only one perfect life lived on this earth. Moreover, had there been no failure in Abraham's walk, would not the type have been faulty? But God's types are accurate at every point, and in His Word the Spirit has portrayed the characters of His people in the colours of truth and reality: He has faithfully described them as they actually were. True, a supernatural work of grace had been wrought in Abraham, but the "flesh" had not been removed from him. True, a supernatural faith had been communicated to him, but the root of unbelief had not been taken out of him. Two contrary principles were at work within Abraham (as they are in us), and *both* of these were evidenced.

God's requirements from Abraham were clearly made known: "Get thee out of thy country and from thy kindred, and from thy father's house, unto a land that I will show thee" (Gen. 12:1). The first response which he made to this is recorded in Gen. 11:31, "And

Terah took Abram his son, and Lot the son of Haran his son's son, and Sarai his daughter-in-law, his son Abram's wife; and they went forth with them from Ur of the Chaldees, to go into the land of Canaan; and they came unto Haran, and dwelt there." He left Chaldea, but instead of separating from his "kindred," he suffered his nephew Lot to accompany him; instead of forsaking his father's house, Terah was permitted to take the lead; and instead of entering Canaan, Abraham stopped short and settled in Haran. Abraham temporized: his obedience was partial, faltering, tardy. He yielded to the affections of the flesh. Alas, cannot both writer and reader see here a plain reflection of himself, a portrayal of his own sad failures! Yes, "As in water face answereth to face, so the heart of man to man" (Prov. 27:19).

But let us earnestly seek grace at this point to be much upon our guard lest we "wrest" (2 Pet. 3:16) to our own hurt what has just been before us. If the thought arises "O well, Abraham was not perfect, *he* did not always do as God commanded him, so it cannot be expected that *I* should do any better than he did," then recognize that this is a temptation from the Devil. Abraham's failures are not recorded for us to shelter behind, for us to make them so many palliations for our own sinful falls; no, rather are they to be regarded as so many warnings for us to take to heart and prayerfully heed. Such warnings only leave us the more without excuse. And when we discover that we have sadly repeated the backslidings of the O. T. saints, that very discovery should but humble us the more before God, move to a deeper repentance, lead to increasing self-distrust, and issue in a more earnest and constant seeking of Divine Grace to uphold and maintain us in the paths of righteousness.

Though Abraham failed, there was no failure in God. Blessed indeed is it to behold His long-suffering, His super-abounding grace, His unchanging faithfulness, and the eventual fulfilling of His own purpose. This reveals to us, for the joy of our hearts and the worshipping praise of our souls, another reason why the Holy Spirit has so faithfully placed on record the shadows as well as the lights in the lives of the O. T. saints: they are to serve not only as solemn warnings for us to heed, but also as so many examples of that marvelous patience of God that bears so long and so tenderly with the dullness and waywardness of His children; examples too of that infinite mercy which deals with His people not after their sins, nor rewards them according to their iniquities. O how the realization of this should melt our hearts, and evoke true worship and thanksgiving unto "the God of *all* grace" (1 Pet. 5:10). It will be so, it must be so, in every truly regenerate soul; though the unregenerate will only turn the very grace of God "into lasciviousness" (Jude 4) unto their eternal undoing.

The sequel to Gen. 11:31 is found in 12:5, "And Abram took Sarai his wife, and Lot his brother's son, and all their substance that they had gathered, and the souls that they had gotten in Haran; and they went forth to go into the land of Canaan, and into the land of Canaan they came." Though Abraham had settled down in Haran, God would not allow him to continue there indefinitely. The Lord had purposed that he should enter Canaan, and no purpose of His can fail. God therefore tumbled him out of the nest which he had made for himself (Deut. 32:11), and very solemn is it to observe the means which he used: "And Terah died in Haran (Gen. 11:32 and cf. Acts 7:4) — death had to come in before Abraham left Halfway House! He never started across the wilderness until death severed that tie of the flesh which had held him back. But that with which we desire to be specially occupied at this point is the wondrous love of God toward His erring child.

"I am the Lord, I change not; therefore ye sons of Jacob are not consumed" (Mal. 3:6). Blessed, thrice blessed, is this. Though the dogs are likely to consume it unto their own ruin, yet that must not make us withhold this sweet portion of "the children's bread." The immutability of the Divine nature is the saints' indemnity; God's unchangeableness affords the fullest assurance of His faithfulness in the promises. No change in us can alter His mind, no unfaithfulness on our part will cause Him to revoke His word. Unstable though we be, sorely tempted as we often are, tripped up as may frequently be our case, yet God "*shall* also confirm us unto the end . . . God is faithful" (1 Cor. 1:8, 9). The powers of Satan and the world are against us, suffering and death before us, a treacherous and fearful heart within us; yet God *will* "confirm us unto the end." He did Abraham; He will us. Hallelujah.

"By faith he sojourned in the land of promise, as in a strange country, dwelling in tabernacles with Isaac and Jacob, the heirs with him of the same promise" (v. 9). This verse brings before us the second effect or proof of Abraham's faith. In the previous verse the apostle had spoken of the place from whence Abraham was called, here of the place to which he was called. There he had shown the power of faith in self-denial in obedience to God's command, here we behold the patience and constancy of faith in waiting for the fulfillment of the promise. But the mere reading of this verse by itself is not likely to make much impression upon us: we need to diligently consult and carefully ponder other passages, in order to be in a position to appreciate its real force.

First of all we are told, "And Abram passed through the land unto the place of Sichem, unto the plain of Moreh. And the Canaanite was then in the land." Unless a supernatural work of grace had been wrought in Abraham's heart, subduing (though not eradicating) his natural desires and reasonings, he certainly would not have remained in Canaan. An idolatrous people were already occupying the land. Again, we are told that "He (God) gave him none inheritance in it, no, not so much as to set his foot on" (Acts 7:5). Only the unclaimed tracts, which were commonly utilized by those having flocks and herds, were available for his use. Not an acre did he own, for he had to "purchase" a plot of ground as a burying place for his dead (Gen. 23). What a trial of faith was this, for Heb. 11:8 expressly declares that he was afterward to "receive" that land "for an inheritance." Yet instead of this presenting a difficulty, it only enhances the beauty and accuracy of the type.

The Christian has also been begotten "to an inheritance" (1 Pet. 1:4), but he does not fully enter into it the moment he is called from death unto life. No, instead, he is left here (very often) for many years to fight his way through an hostile world and against an opposing Devil. During that fight he meets with many discouragements and receives numerous wounds. Hard duties have to be performed, difficulties overcome, and trials endured, before the Christian enters fully into that inheritance unto which Divine grace has appointed him. And nought but a Divinely bestowed and Divinely maintained faith is sufficient for these things: that alone will sustain the heart in the face of losses, reproaches, painful delays. It was thus with Abraham: it was "by faith" he left the land of his birth, started out on a journey he knew not whither, crossed a dreary wilderness, and then sojourned in tents for more than half a century in a strange land. Rightly did the Puritan Manton say:

"From God's training up Abraham in a course of difficulties, we see it is no easy matter to go to Heaven; there is a great deal of ado to unsettle a believer from the world, and there is a great deal of ado to fix the heart in the expectation of Heaven. First there must be self-denial in coming out of the world, and divorcing ourselves from our bosom sins and dearest interests; and then there must be patience shown in waiting for God's mercy to eternal life, waiting His leisure as well as performing His will. Here is the time of our exercise, and we must expect it, since the father of the faithful was thus trained up ere he could inherit the promises."

"By faith he sojourned in the land of promise, as in a strange country." The force of this will be more apparent if we link together two statements in Genesis: "And the Canaanite was then in the land" (12:6) "And the Lord said, unto Abram . . . all the land which thou seest to thee will I give it and to thy seed forever" (13:14, 15). Here was the ground which Abraham's faith rested upon, the plain word of Him that cannot lie. Upon that promise his heart reposed, and therefore he was occupied not with the Canaanites who were then in the land, but with the invisible Jehovah who had pledged it unto him. How different was the case of the spies, who, in a later day, went up into this very land, with the assurance of the Lord that it was a "good land." Their report was "the land through which we have gone to search it, is a land that eateth up the inhabitants thereof; and all the people that we *saw* in it are men of a great stature. And there we *saw* the giants, the sons of Anak, which come of the giants: and we were in our own sight as grasshoppers, and so we were in their sight" (Num. 13:32, 33).

"By faith he sojourned in the land of promise, as in a strange country." As it was by faith that Abraham went out of Chaldea, so it was by faith he remained out of the country of which he was originally a native. This illustrates the fact that not only do we become Christians by an act of faith (the yielding up of the whole man unto God), but that as Christians we are called upon to *live* by faith (Gal. 2:20), to walk by faith and not by sight (2 Cor. 5:7). The place where Abraham now abode is here styled "the land of promise," rather than Canaan, to teach us that it is God's promise which puts vigour into faith. Note how both Moses and Joshua, at a later day, sought to quicken the faith of the Israelites by this means: "Hear therefore, O Israel, and observe to do, that it may be well with thee, and that ye may increase mightily, as the Lord God of thy fathers *hath promised* thee" (Deut. 6:3). "And the Lord your God, He shall expel them from before you, and drive them from out of your sight; and ye shall possess their land, as the Lord your God *hath promised* you" (Josh. 23:5).

"As in a strange country." This tells us how Abraham regarded that land which was then occupied by the Canaanites, and how he conducted himself in it. He purchased no farm, built no house, and entered into no alliance with its people. True, he entered into a league of peace and amity with Aner, Eshcol, and Mamre (Gen. 14:13), but it was as a stranger, and not as one who had any thing of his own in the land. He reckoned that country no more his own, than any other land in the world. He took no part in its politics, had nothing to do with its religion, had very little social intercourse with its people, but lived by faith and found his joy and satisfaction in communion with the Lord. This teaches us that though the Christian is still in the world, he is not of it, nor must he cultivate its friendship (James 4:4). He may use it as necessity requires, but he must ever be on his prayerful guard against abusing it (1 Cor. 7:31).

"Dwelling in tents." These words inform us both of Abraham's manner of life and disposition of heart during his sojourning in Canaan. Let us consider them from this twofold viewpoint. Abraham did not conduct himself as the possessor of Canaan, but as a foreigner and pilgrim in it. To Heth he confessed, "I am a stranger and sojourner with you" (Gen. 23:4). As the father of the faithful he set an example of self-denial and patience. It was not that he was unable to purchase an estate, build an elaborate mansion, and settle down in some attractive spot, for Gen. 13:2 tells us that "Abraham was very rich in cattle, in silver, and in gold"; but God had not called him unto this. Ah, my reader, a palace without the enjoyed presence of the Lord, is but an empty bauble; whereas a prison-dungeon occupied by one in real communion with Him, may be the very vestibule of Heaven.

Living in a strange country, surrounded by wicked heathen, had it not been wiser for Abraham to erect a strongly fortified castle? A "tent" offers little or no defense against attack. Ah, but "the angel of the Lord encampeth round about them that fear Him, and delivereth them." And Abraham both feared and trusted God. "Where faith enables men to live unto God, as unto their eternal concerns, it will enable them to trust unto Him in all the difficulties, dangers, and hazards of this life. To pretend a trust in God as unto our souls and invisible things, and not resign our temporal concerns with patience and quietness unto His disposal, is a vain pretense. And we may take hence an eminent trial of our faith. Too many deceive themselves with a presumption of faith in the promises of God, as unto things future and eternal. They suppose that they do so believe, as that they shall be eternally saved, but if they are brought into any trial, as unto things temporal, wherein they are concerned, they know not what belongs unto the life of faith, nor how to trust God in a due manner. It was not so with Abraham: his faith acted itself uniformly with respect to the providences, as well as the promises of God" (J. Owen).

Abram's "dwelling in tents" also denoted the disposition of his heart. A life of faith is one which has respect unto things spiritual and eternal, and therefore one of its fruits is to be contented with a very small portion of earthly things. Faith not only begets a confidence and joy in the things promised, but it also works a composure of spirit and submission to the Lord's will. A little would serve Abraham on earth because he expected so much in Heaven. Nothing is more calculated to deliver the heart from covetousness, from lusting after the perishing things of time and sense, from envying the poor rich, than to heed that exhortation, "Set your affection on things above, not on things on the earth" (Col. 3:2).

But it is one thing to quote that verse, and another to put it into practice. If we are the children of Abraham, we must emulate the example of Abraham. Are *our* carnal affections mortified? Can we submit to a pilgrim's fare without murmuring? Are we enduring hardness as good soldiers of Jesus Christ (2 Tim. 2:3)?

The tent-life of the patriarchs demonstrated their pilgrim character: it made manifest their contentment to live upon the *surface* of the earth, for a tent has no foundation, and can be pitched or struck at short notice. They were sojourners here and just passing through this wilderness-scene without striking their roots into it. Their tent life spoke of their separation from the world's allurements, politics, friendships, religion. It is deeply significant to note that when reference is made to Abraham's "tent," there is mention also of his "altar": "and pitched his tent, having Bethel on the west and Hai on the east, and there he builded an altar unto the Lord" (Gen. 12:8); "and he went on his journeys . . . unto the place where his tent had been at the beginning, unto the place of the altar" (13:3, 4); "Then Abram removed his tent, and came and dwelt in the plain of Mamre, which is in Hebron, and built there an altar unto the Lord" (13:18). Observe carefully the *order* in each of these passages: there must be heart *separation* from the world before a thrice holy God can be *worshipped* in spirit and in truth.

"Dwelling in tents with Isaac and Jacob, the heirs with him of the same promise." The Greek here is more expressive than our translation: "in tents dwelling": the Holy Spirit emphasized first not the act of dwelling, but the fact that this dwelling was in *tents*. The mention of Isaac and Jacob in this verse is for the purpose of calling our attention unto the further fact that Abraham continued thus for the space of almost a century, Jacob not being born until he had sojourned in Canaan for eighty-five years! Herein we are taught that "when we are once engaged and have given up ourselves to God in a way of believing, there must be no choice, no dividing or halting, no halving; but we must follow Him fully, wholly, living by faith in all things" (J. Owen), and that unto the very end of our earthly course.

There does not seem to be anything requiring us to believe that Isaac and Jacob shared Abraham's tent, rather is the thought that they also lived the same pilgrim's life in Canaan: as Abraham was a sojourner in that land, without any possession there, so were they. The "with" may be extended to cover all that is said in the previous part of the verse, indicating it was "by faith" that both Abraham's son and grandson followed the example set them. The words which follow confirm this: they were "the heirs with him of the same promise." That is indeed a striking expression, for ordinarily sons are merely "heirs" and not joint-heirs with their parents. This is to show us that Isaac was not indebted to Abraham for the promise, nor Jacob to Isaac, each receiving the same promise direct from God. This is clear from a comparison of Gen. 13:15 and 17:8 with 26:3 and 28:13, 35:12. It also tells us that if we are to have an interest in the blessings of Abraham, we must walk in the steps of his faith.

Very blessed and yet very searching is the principle exemplified in the last clause of v. 9. God's saints are all of the same spiritual disposition. They are members of the same family, united to the same Christ, indwelt by the same Spirit. "And the multitude of them that believed were of one heart and of one soul" (Acts 4:32). They are governed by the same laws: "I will put My laws into their mind and write them in their hearts" (Heb. 8:10). They all have one aim, to please God and glorify Him on earth. They are called to the same privileges: "to them that have obtained like precious faith with us" etc. (2 Pet. 1:1).

"For he looked for a city which hath foundations, whose Builder and Maker is God" (v. 10). Ah, here is the explanation of what has been before us in the previous verse, as the opening "for" intimates; Abraham was walking by faith, and not by sight, and therefore his heart was set upon things above and not upon things below. It is the exercise of faith and hope upon heavenly objects which makes us carry ourselves with a loose heart toward worldly comforts. Abraham realized that his portion and possession was not on earth, but in Heaven. It was this which made him content to dwell in tents. He did not build a city, as Cain did (Gen. 4:17), but "looked for" one of which God Himself is the Maker. What an illustration and exemplification was this of the opening verse of our chapter: "Now faith is the substance of things hoped for, the evidence of things not seen."

That for which Abraham looked was Heaven itself, here likened unto a city with foundations, in manifest antithesis from the "tents" which have no foundations. Various figures are used to express the saints' everlasting portion. It is called an "inheritance" (1 Pet. 1:4), to signify the freeness of its tenure. It is denominated "many mansions" in the Father's House. It is styled an "heavenly country" (Heb. 11:16) to signify its spaciousness. There are various resemblances between Heaven and a "city." A city is a civil society that is under government: so in Heaven there is a society of angels and saints ruled by God: Heb. 12:22-24. In Bible days a city was a place of safety, being surrounded by strong and high walls: so in Heaven we shall be eternally secure from sin and Satan, death and every enemy. A city is well stocked with provisions: so in Heaven nothing will be lacking which is good and blessed. The "foundations" of the Heavenly City are the eternal decree and love of God, the unalterable covenant of grace, Christ Jesus the Rock of Ages, on which it stands firm and immovable.

It is the power of a faith which is active and operative that will sustain the heart under hardships and sufferings as nothing else will. "For which cause we faint not: but though our outward man perish, yet the inward is renewed day by day. For our light affliction, which is but for a moment, worketh for us a far more exceeding and eternal weight of glory; while we look not at the things which are seen, but at the things which are not seen: for the things which are seen are temporal, but the things which are not seen are eternal" (2 Cor. 4:16-18). As J. Owen well said, "This is a full description of Abraham's faith, in the operation and effect here ascribed to it by the apostle. And herein it is exemplary and encouraging to all believers under their present trials and sufferings."

Ah, my brethren and sisters, do we not see from that which has been before us *why* the attractions of the world or the depressing effects of suffering, have such a power upon us? Is it not because we are negligent in the stirring up of our faith to "lay hold of the hope which is set before us"? If we meditated more frequently upon the glory and bliss of Heaven, and were favoured with foretastes of it in our souls, would we not sigh after it more ardently and press forward unto it more earnestly? "Abraham rejoiced to see Christ's day, and he saw it, and was glad" (John 8:56); and if we had more serious and spiritual thoughts of the Day to come, we would not be so sad as we often are. "He that hath this hope in Him, purifieth himself, even as He is pure" (1 John 3:3), for it lifts the heart above this scene and carries us in spirit within the veil. The more our hearts are attracted to Heaven, the less will the poor things of this world appeal to us.

CHAPTER SIXTY-TWO

The Faith of Sarah

(Heb. 11:11, 12)

In the verses which are now to be before us the apostle calls attention to the marvelous power of a God-given faith to exercise itself in the presence of most discouraging circumstances, persevere in the face of the most formidable obstacles, and trust God to do that which unto human reason seemed utterly impossible. They show us that this faith was exercised by a frail and aged woman, who at first was hindered and opposed by the workings of unbelief, but who in the end relied upon the veracity of God and rested upon His promise. They show what an intensely practical thing faith is: that it not only lifts up the soul to Heaven, but is able to draw down strength for the body on earth. They demonstrate what great endings sometimes issue from small beginnings, and that like a stone thrown into a lake produces ever-enlarging circles on the rippling waters, so faith issues in fruit which increases from generation to generation.

The more the 11th verse of our present chapter be pondered, the more evident will it appear the faith there spoken of is of a radically different order from that mental and theoretical faith of cozy-chair dreamers. The "faith" of the vast majority of professing Christians is as different from that described in Heb. 11 as darkness is from light. The one ends in talk, the other was expressed in deeds. The one breaks down when put to the test, the other survived every trial to which it was exposed. The one is inoperative and ineffectual, the other was active and powerful. The one is unproductive, the other issued in fruits to the glory of God. Ah, is it not evident that the great difference between them is, that one is merely human, the other Divine; one merely natural, the other altogether supernatural? This it is which our hearts and consciences need to lay hold of and turn into earnest prayer.

That which has just been pointed out ought to deeply exercise both writer and reader. It ought to search us through and through, causing us to seriously and diligently weigh the character of our "faith." It is of little use to be entertained by interesting articles, unless they lead to careful self-examination. It is of little profit to be made to wonder at the achievements of the faith of those O. T. saints, unless we are shamed by them, and made to cry mightily unto God for Him to work in us a "like precious faith." Unless our faith issues in works which mere nature cannot produce, unless it is enabling us to "overcome the world" (1 John 5:4) and triumph over the lusts of the flesh, then we have grave cause to fear that our faith is not "the faith of God's elect" (Titus 1:1). Cry with David, "Examine me, O Lord, and prove me; try my reins and my heart" (Psa. 26:2).

It is not that any Christian lives a life of perfect faith — only the Lord Jesus ever did that. No, for in the first place, like all the other spiritual graces, it is subject to growth (2 Thess. 1:3), and full maturity is not reached in this life. In the second place, faith is not always in exercise, nor can we command its activities: He who bestowed it, must also renew it. In the third place, the faith of every saint falters at times: it did in Abraham, in Moses, in Elijah, in the apostles. The flesh is still in us, and therefore the reasonings of unbelief are ever ready (unless Divine grace subdue them) to oppose the actings of faith. We are not then urging the reader to search in himself for a faith that is perfect, either in its growth, its constancy or its achievements. Rather are we to seek Divine aid and make sure whether we have *any* faith which is superior to what has been acquired through religious education; whether we have a faith which, despite the strugglings of unbelief, *does* trust the living God; whether we have a faith which produces any fruit which manifestly issues from a spiritual root.

Having spoken of Abraham's faith, the apostle now makes mention of Sarah's. "Observe what a blessing it is when a husband and wife are both partners of faith, when both in the same yoke draw one way. Abraham is the father of the faithful, and Sarah is recommended among believers as having a fellowship in the same promises, and in the same troubles and trials. So it is said of Zachariah and Elizabeth, 'And they were both righteous before God, walking in all the commandments and ordinances of the Lord blameless' (Luke 1:6). It is a mighty encouragement when the constant companion of our lives is also a fellow in the same faith. This should direct us in the matter of choice: she cannot be a meet help that goeth a contrary way in religion. Religion decayeth in families by nothing so much as by want of care in matches" (T. Manton).

"Through faith also Sarah herself received strength to conceive seed, and was delivered of a child when she was past age, because she judged Him faithful who had promised" (v. 11). There are five things upon which our attention needs to be focused. First, the impediments of her faith: these were, her barrenness, old age, and unbelief. Second, the effect of her faith: she "received strength to conceive." Third, the constancy of her faith: she trusted God unto an actual deliverance or birth of the child. Fourth, the foundation of her faith: she rested upon the veracity of the Divine Promiser. Fifth, the fruit of her faith: the numerous posterity which issued from her son Isaac. Let us consider each of these separately.

"Through faith also Sarah herself." The Greek is just the same here as in all the other verses, and should have been rendered uniformly "By faith" etc. The word "also" seems to be added for a double purpose. First to counteract and correct any error which might suppose that women were debarred the blessings and privileges of grace. It is true that in the official sphere God has prohibited them from occupying the place of rule or usurping authority over the men, so that they are commanded to be silent in the churches (1 Cor. 14:34), are not permitted to teach (1 Tim. 2:12), and are bidden to be in subjection to their husbands (Eph. 5:22). But in the spiritual sphere all inequalities disappear, for "there is neither Jew nor Greek, there is neither bond nor free, there is neither male nor female: for ye are all one in Christ Jesus" (Gal. 3:28), and therefore the believing husband and the believing wife are "heirs together of the grace of life."

In the second place, this added "also" informs us that, though a woman, Sarah exercised the same faith as had Abraham. She had left Chaldea when he did, accompanied him to Canaan, dwelt with him in tents. Not only so, but she personally acted faith upon the living God. Necessarily so, for she was equally concerned in the Divine revelation with Abraham, and was as much a party to the great difficulties of its accomplishment. The blessing of the promised seed was assigned to and appropriated by her, as much as to and by him; and therefore is she proposed unto the Church as an example (1 Pet. 3:5, 6). "As Abraham was the father of the faithful, or of the church, so she was the mother of it, so as that the distinct mention of her faith was necessary. She was the free woman from whence the Church sprang: Gal. 4:22, 23. And all believing women are her daughters: 1 Pet. 3:6" (J. Owen).

"By faith also Sarah herself received strength." The word "herself" is emphatic: it was not her husband only, by whose faith she might receive the blessing, but by her own faith that she received strength, and this, notwithstanding the very real and formidable obstacles which stood in the way of her exercising it. These, as we have pointed out, were three in number. First, she had not borne any children during the customary years of pregnancy: as

Gen. 11:30 informs us, "Sarah was barren"; "Sarah, Abram's wife, bare him no children" (Gen. 16:1). Second, she was long past the age of childbearing, for she was now "ninety years old" (Gen. 17:17). Third, the workings of unbelief interposed, persuading her that it was altogether against nature and reason for a woman, under such circumstances, to give birth unto a child. This comes out in Gen. 18. There we read of three men appearing unto Abraham, one of whom was the Lord in theophanic manifestation. Unto him He said, "Sarah thy wife shall have a son." Upon hearing this "Sarah laughed within herself."

Sarah's laughter was that of doubting and distrust, for she said, "I am waxed old." At once the Lord rebukes her unbelief, asking "Is there anything too hard for the Lord! At the time appointed I will return unto thee, according to the time of life, and Sarah shall have a son." Solemn indeed is the sequel. "Then Sarah denied, saying, I laughed not; for she was afraid. And He said, Nay; but thou didst laugh" (v. 15). It is always a shame to do amiss, but a greater shame to deny it. It was a sin to give way to unbelief, but it was adding iniquity unto iniquity to cover it with a lie. But we deceive ourselves if we think to impose upon God, for nothing can be concealed from His all-seeing eye. By comparing Heb. 11:11 with what is recorded in Gen. 18, we learn that after the Lord had reproved Sarah's unbelief, and she began to realize that the promise came from God, her faith was called into exercise. Because her laughter came from weakness and not from scorn, God smote her not, as He did Zacharias for his unbelief (Luke 1:20).

Varied are the lessons which may be learned from the above incident. Many times the Word does not take effect immediately. It did not in Sarah's case: though afterward she believed, at first she laughed. It was only when the Divine promise was *repeated* that her faith began to act. Let preachers and Christian parents, who are discouraged by lack of success, lay this to heart. Again; see here that before faith is established often there is a conflict: "shall I have a child who am old?" — reason opposed the promise. Just as when a fire is kindled the smoke is seen before the flame, so ere the heart rests upon the Word there is generally doubting and fear. Once more; observe how graciously God hides the defects of His children: nothing is said of Rahab's lie (Heb. 11:31), of Job's impatience (James 5:11), nor here of Sarah's laughing, "Be ye therefore followers of God, as dear children; and walk in love" (Eph. 5:1, 2)!

Let us next consider what is here ascribed unto the faith of Sarah: "she received strength to conceive seed." She obtained that which previously was not in her: there was now a restoration of her nature to perform its normal functions. Her dead womb was supernaturally vivified. In response to her faith, the Omnipotent One did for Sarah what He had done to Abraham in response to his trusting of Him: "I have made thee a father of many nations, before Him, whom he believed, even God, who *quickeneth* the dead" (Rom. 4:17). "All things are possible with God"; yes, and it is also true that "All things are possible to him that believeth" (Mark 9:23): how blessedly and strikingly does the incident now before us illustrate this! O that it may speak unto each of our hearts and cause us to long after and pray for an increase of our faith. What is more glorifying to God than a confident looking unto Him to work in and through us that which mere nature cannot produce.

"By faith also Sarah herself received strength." Christian reader, this is recorded both for thine instruction and encouragement. Faith worked a vigour in Sarah's body where it was not before. Is it not written "But they that wait upon the Lord shall *renew their strength*" (Isa. 40:31)? Do we really believe this? Do we act as though we did? The writer can bear witness to the veracity of that promise. When he was in Australia, editing this Magazine, keeping up with a heavy correspondence, and preaching five and six times each week, when it was over one hundred in the shade, many a time has he dragged his weary body into the pulpit, and then looked unto the Lord for a definite reinvigoration of body. Never did He fail us. After speaking for two hours we generally felt fresher than we did when we arose at the beginning of the day. And why not? Has not God promised to "supply *all* our need"? Of how many is it true that "they have not, because they (in faith) ask not" (James 4:2).

Ah, dear reader, "Bodily exercise profiteth little: but godliness is profitable unto all things, having promise of the life that *now* is, and of that which is to come" (1 Tim. 4:8): "profitable" for the body, as well as for the soul. While we strongly reprobate much that is now going on under the name of "Faith-Healing," yet we have as little patience with the pretended hyper-sanctity which disdains any looking unto God for the supply of our bodily needs. In this same chapter which we are now commenting upon, we read of others who "out of weakness were made strong" (v. 34). Sad it is to see so many of God's dear children living far beneath their privileges. True, many are under the chastening hand of God. But this should not be so: the cause should be sought, the wrong righted, the sin confessed, restoration both spiritual and temporal diligently sought.

We do not wish to convey the impression that the only application unto us of these words, "By faith also Sarah herself received strength," has reference to the reviving of the physical body: not so, though that is, undoubtedly, the first lesson to be learned. But there is a higher signification too. Many a Christian feels his spiritual weakness: that is well, yet instead of this hindering, it should bestir to lay hold of the Lord's strength (Isa. 27:5). In the final analysis, it is nothing but lack of faith which so often allows the "flesh" to hinder us from bringing forth the Gospel-fruits of holiness. Despair not of personal frailty, but go forward in the strength of God: "Be strong in the Lord, and in the power of His might" (Eph. 6:10): turn this into believing prayer for Divine enablement. "Though thy beginning was small, yet thy latter end should greatly increase" (Job. 8:7).

Does the reader still say, "Ah, but such an experience is not for me; alas, I am so unworthy, so helpless; I feel so lifeless and listless." So was Sarah! Yet, "by faith" she "received strength." And, dear friend, faith is not occupied with self, but with God. "Abraham considered not his own body" (Rom. 4:19), nor did Sarah. Each of them looked away from self, and counted upon God to work a miracle. And God did not fail them: He is pledged to honour those who honour Him, and nothing honours Him more than a trustful expectation. He always responds to faith. There is no reason why you should remain weak and listless. True, without Christ you can do nothing; but there is an infinite fulness in Him (John 1:16) for you to draw from. Then from this day onwards, let your attitude be "I can do all things through Christ which strengtheneth me" (Phil. 4:13). Apply to Him, count upon Him: "my son, be strong in the grace that is in Christ Jesus" (2 Tim. 2:1).

"And was delivered of a child." The "and" here connects what follows with each of the preceding verbs. It was "by faith" that Sarah "received strength," and it was also "by faith" that she was now "delivered of a child." It is the constancy and perseverance of her faith which is here intimated. There was no abortion, no miscarriage; she trusted God right through unto the end. This brings before us a subject upon which very little is written these days: the duty and privilege of Christian women counting upon God for a safe issue in the most trying and critical season in their lives. Faith is to be exercised not only in acts of worship, but in the ordinary offices of our daily affairs. We are to eat and drink in faith, work and sleep in faith; and the Christian wife should be delivered of her child by faith. The danger is great, and if in any extremity there is need of faith, much more so where life itself is involved. Let us seek to condense from the helpful comments of the Puritan Manton.

First, we must be sensible what *need* we have to exercise faith in this case, that we may not run upon danger blindfold; and if we escape, then to think our deliverance a mere chance. Rachel died in this case; so also did the wife of Phineas (1 Sam. 4:19, 20): a great hazard is run, and therefore you must be sensible of it. The more difficulty and danger be apprehended, the better the opportunity for the exercise of faith: 2 Chron. 20:12, 2 Cor. 1:9. Second, because the sorrows of travail are a monument of God's displeasure against sin (Gen. 3:16), therefore this must put you the more earnestly to seek an interest in Christ, that you may have remedy against sin. Third, meditate upon the promise of 1 Tim. 2:15, which is made good eternally or temporally as God sees fit. Fourth, the faith you exercise must be the glorifying of His power and submitting to His will. This expresses the kind of faith which is proper to all temporal mercies: Lord, if Thou wilt, Thou canst save me — it is sufficient to ease the heart of a great deal of trouble and perplexing fear.

"And was delivered of a child." As we have pointed out in the last paragraph, this clause is added to show the continuance of Sarah's faith and the blessing of God upon her. True faith not only appropriates His promise, but continues resting on the same till that which is believed be actually accomplished. The principle of this is enunciated in Heb. 3:14 and 10:36. "For we are made partakers of Christ, if we hold the beginning of our confidence steadfast *unto the end*"; "Cast not away therefore your confidence." It is at this point so many fail. They endeavour to lay hold of a Divine promise, but in the interval of testing let go of it. This is why Christ said, "If ye have faith *and doubt not,* ye shall not only do this" etc. Matt. 21:21 — "doubt not," not only at the moment of pleading the promise, but during the time you are awaiting its fulfillment. Hence also, unto "Trust in the Lord with all thine heart" is added "and lean not unto thine own understanding" (Prov. 3:5).

"When she was past age." This clause is added so as to heighten the miracle which God so graciously wrought in response to Sarah's faith. It magnifies the glory of His power. It is recorded for our encouragement. It shows us that no difficulty or hindrance should cause a disbelief of the promise. God is not tied down to the order of nature, nor limited by any secondary causes. He will turn nature upside down rather than not be as good as His word. He has brought water out of a rock, made iron to float (2 Kings 6:6), sustained two million people in a howling wilderness. These things should arouse the Christian to wait upon God with full confidence in the face of the utmost emergency. Yea, the greater the impediments which confront us, faith should be increased. The trustful heart says, Here is a fit occasion for faith; now that all creature-streams have run dry is a grand opportunity for counting on God to show Himself strong on my behalf. What cannot He do! He made a woman of ninety to bear a child — a thing quite contrary to nature — so I may surely expect Him to work wonders for me too.

"Because she judged Him faithful who had promised." Here is the secret of the whole thing. Here was the ground of Sarah's confidence, the foundation on which faith rested. She did not look at God's promises through the mist of interposing obstacles, but she viewed the difficulties and hindrances through the clear light of God's promises. The act which is here ascribed unto Sarah is, that she "judged" or reckoned, reputed and esteemed, God to be faithful: she was assured that He would make good His word, on which He had caused her to hope. God had spoken: Sarah had heard; in spite of all that seemed to make it impossible that the promise should be fulfilled in her case, she steadfastly believed. Rightly did Luther say, "If you would trust God, you must learn to crucify the question How." "Faithful is He that calleth you, who also will do" (1 Thess. 5:24): this is sufficient for the heart to rest upon; faith will cheerfully leave it with Omniscience as to *how* the promise will be made good to us.

"Because she judged Him faithful who had promised." Let it be carefully noted that Sarah's faith went beyond the promise. While her mind dwelt upon *the thing* promised, it seemed unto her altogether incredible, but when she took her thoughts off all secondary causes and fixed them on God Himself, then the difficulties no longer disturbed her: her heart was at rest in God. She knew that God could be depended upon: He is "faithful" — able, willing, sure to perform His word. Sarah looked beyond the promise to the Promiser, and as she did so all doubting was stilled. She rested with full confidence on the immutability of Him that cannot lie, knowing that where Divine veracity is engaged, omnipotence will make it good. It is by believing meditations upon the character of God that faith is fed and strengthened to expect the blessing, despite all apparent difficulties and supposed impossibilities. It is the heart's contemplation of the perfections of God which causes faith to prevail. As this is of such vital practical importance, let us devote another paragraph to enlarging thereon.

To fix our minds on the *things* promised, to have an assured expectation of the enjoyment of them, without the heart first resting upon the veracity, immutability, and omnipotency of God, is but a deceiving imagination. Rightly did J. Owen point out that, "The formal object of faith in the Divine promises, is not the things promised in the first place, *but God Himself* in His essential excellencies, of truth, or faithfulness and power." Nevertheless, the Divine perfections do not, of themselves, work faith in us: it is only as the heart believingly ponders the Divine attributes that we shall "judge" or conclude Him faithful that has promised. It is the man whose mind is stayed upon God Himself, who is kept in "perfect peace" (Isa. 26:3): that is, he who joyfully contemplates who and what God is that will be preserved from doubting and wavering while waiting the fulfillment of the promise. As it was with Sarah, so it is with us: every promise of God has tacitly annexed to it this consideration, "Is any thing too hard for the Lord!"

"Wherefore also from one were born, and that too of (one) having become dead, even as the stars of the heaven in multitude, and as the sand which (is) by the shore of the sea the countless" (v. 12). We have quoted the rendering given in the Bagster Interlinear because it is more literal and accurate than our A. V. The "him" in the English translation is misleading, for in this verse there is no masculine pronoun: at the most the "one" must refer to one couple, but personally we believe it points to one woman, Sarah, as the "born" (rather than "begotten") intimates. We regard this 12th verse as setting forth the fruit of her faith, namely the numerous posterity which issued from her son, Isaac. The double reference to the "sand" and the "stars" calls attention to the twofold seed: the earthly and the heavenly, the natural and the spiritual Israel.

Like the "great multitude which no man could number" of Rev. 7:9, so "as the stars of the sky for multitude and as the sand which is by the seashore innumerable" of our present verse, is obviously an hyperbole: it is figurative language, and not to be understood literally. This may seem a bold and unwarrantable statement to some of our readers, yet if scripture be compared with scripture, no other conclusion is possible. The following passages make this clear: Deut. 1:10, Josh. 11:4, Judges 7:12, 1 Sam. 13:5, 2 Sam. 17:11, 1 Kings 4:20. For other examples of this figure of speech see Deut. 9:1, Psa. 78:27, Isa. 60:22, John 21:25. Hyperboles are employed not to move us to believe untruths, but, by emphasis, arrest our attention and cause us to heed weighty matters. The following rules are to be observed in the employment of them. First, they are to be used only of such things as are indeed true in the substance of them. Second, only of things which are worthy of more than ordinary consideration. Third, set out, as nearly as possible, in proverbial language. Fourth, expressed in words of similarity and dissimilarity, rather than by words of equality and inequality (W. Gouge).

But let our final thought be upon the rich recompense whereby God rewarded the faith of Sarah. The opening "Therefore" of

v. 12 points the blessed consequence of her relying upon the faithfulness of God in the face of the utmost natural discouragements. From her faith there issued Isaac, and from him, ultimately, Christ Himself. And this is recorded for our instruction. Who can estimate the fruits of faith? Who can tell how many lives may be affected for good, even in generations yet to come, through your faith and my faith today! Oh how the thought of this should stir us up to cry more earnestly "Lord, increase our faith" to the praise of the glory of Thy grace: Amen.

CHAPTER SIXTY-THREE

The Perseverance of Faith

(Heb. 11:13, 14)

Having described some of the eminent acts of faith put forth by the earliest members of God's family, the apostle now pauses to insert a general commendation of the faith of those he had already named, and (as is clear from vv. 39, 40) of others yet to follow. This commendation is set forth in v. 13 and is amplified in the next three verses. The evident design of the Holy Spirit in this was to press upon the Hebrews, and upon us, the imperative need of such a faith as would last, wear, overcome obstacles, and endure unto the end. Even the natural man is capable of "making good resolutions" and has flashes of endeavour to please God, but he is entirely lacking in that principle which "beareth all things, believeth all things, hopeth all things, endureth all things" (1 Cor. 13:7).

The faith of God's elect is like unto its Divine Author in these respects: it is living, incorruptible, and cannot be conquered by the Devil. Being implanted by God, the gift and grace of faith can never be lost. Strikingly was this illustrated in the history of the patriarchs. Called upon to leave the land of their birth, to sojourn in a country filled with idolaters, owning no portion of it, dwelling in tents, suffering many hardships and trials, and living without any such peculiar temporal advantages as might answer to the singular favour which the Lord declared He bore to them; nevertheless they all *died in faith.* The eye of their hearts saw clearly the blessings God had promised, and persuaded that they would be theirs in due season, they joyfully anticipated their future portion and gave up present advantages for the sake thereof.

In the verses which are to be before us the apostle, then, stresses the great importance of seeking and possessing a persevering faith, therefore does he make mention of the fact that as long as they remained in this world, the O. T. saints were believers in the promises of God. It is the durability and constancy of their faith which is commended. Despite all the workings of unbelief within (records of which are found in Genesis in the cases of Abraham, Isaac, and

Jacob) and all the assaults of temptation from without, they persisted in clinging to God and His Word. They lived by faith, and they died in faith: therefore have they left us an example that we should follow their steps. Beautifully did John Calvin point out:

"There is expressed here a difference between us and the fathers: though God gave to the fathers only a taste of that grace which is largely poured on us, though He showed to them at a distance only an obscure representation of Christ, who is now set forth to us clearly before our eyes, yet they were satisfied and never fell away from their faith: how much greater reason then have we at this day to persevere! If we grow faint, we are doubly inexcusable. It is then an enhancing circumstance, that the fathers had a distant view of the spiritual kingdom of Christ, while we at this day have so near view of it, and that they hailed the promises afar off, while we have them as it were quite near us, for if they nevertheless persevered even unto death, what sloth will it be to become wearied in faith, when the Lord sustains us by so many helps. Were any one to object and say, that they could not have believed without receiving the promises on which faith is necessarily founded: to this the answer is, that the expression is to be understood comparatively; for they were far from that high position to which God has raised us. Hence it is that though they had the same salvation promised them, yet they had not the promises so clearly revealed to them as they are to us under the kingdom of Christ: but they were content to behold them afar off."

"These all died in faith" (v. 13), or, more literally, "In (or "according to") faith died these all." Differing from most of the commentators, we believe those words take in the persons mentioned previously, from Abel onwards: "these all" grammatically include those who precede as well as those which follow — the relative pronoun embracing all those set forth in the catalogue, namely, young and old, male and female, great and small. "The same Spirit works in all, and shows forth His power in all, 2 Cor. 4:13" (W. Gouge). Against this it may be objected that Enoch died not. True but the apostle is referring only to those that died, just as Gen. 46:7 must be understood as excepting Joseph who was already in Egypt. Moreover, though Enoch died not as the others, he was removed from earth to heaven, and before his translation he continued living by faith unto the very end, which is the main thing here intended.

"In (or "according to") faith died all these." The faith in which they died is the same as that described in the first verse of our chapter, namely, a justifying and sanctifying faith. That they "died in faith" does not necessarily mean that their faith was actually in exercise during the hour of death, but more strictly, that they never apostatised from the faith: though they actually obtained or possessed not that which was the object of their faith, nevertheless, unto the end of their earthly pilgrimage they confidently looked forward unto the same. Five effects or workings of their faith are here mentioned, each of which we must carefully ponder. First, they "received not the promises." Second, but they saw them "afar off." Third, they were "persuaded of them." Fourth, they "embraced" them. Fifth, in consequence thereof they "confessed that they were strangers and pilgrims on the earth."

As we shall see (D. V.) when taking up later verses, some of the O. T. saints died in the actual exercise of faith. To die in faith is to have an assured confidence in an estate of glory and bliss. "And hereunto is required: 1. The firm belief of a substantial existence after this life; without this, all faith and hope must perish in death. 2. A resignation and trust of their departing souls into the care and power of God. 3. The belief in a future state of blessedness and rest, here called an heavenly country, a city prepared for them by God. 4. Faith of the resurrection of their bodies after death, and that their entire persons, which had undergone the pilgrimage of this life, might be instated in eternal rest" (J. Owen).

Thousands who are now in their graves were taught that it was wrong to expect death and make suitable preparation for it. They were told that the return of Christ was so near, He would certainly come during their lifetime. Alas, the writer has, in measure, been guilty of the same thing. True, it is both the Christian's happy privilege and bounden duty to be "looking for that blessed hope, and the glorious appearing of the great God and our Saviour Jesus Christ" (Titus 2:13), for this is the grand prospect which God hath set before His people in all ages; but He has nowhere told us *when* His Son shall descend; He *may* do so today, He may not for hundreds of years. But to say that "looking for that blessed hope" makes it wrong to anticipate death is manifestly absurd: the O. T. saints had just as definite promises for the first advent of Christ as the N. T. saints have for His second, and they thought frequently of death!

It is greatly to be feared that much of the popularity with which the "premillennial and imminent coming of Christ" has been received, may be attributed to a carnal dread of death: a strong appeal is made to the flesh when people can be persuaded that they are likely to escape the grave. That one generation of Christians will do so is clear from 1 Cor. 15:51, 1 Thess 4:17, but how many generations have already supposed that *theirs* was the one which would be raptured to heaven, and how many of them were quite unprepared when death overtook them, only that Day will show. We are well aware that these lines are not likely to meet with a favourable reception from some of our readers, but we are not seeking to please them, but God. Any man who is ready to die is prepared for the Lord's return: as you may very likely die before the second advent, it is only the part of wisdom to make sure you are prepared for death.

And who are they whose souls are prepared for the dissolution of the body? Those who have disarmed death beforehand by plucking out its sting, and this by seeking reconciliation with God through Jesus Christ. The hornet is harmless when its sting is extracted; a snake need not be dreaded if its fang and poison have been removed. So it is with death. "The sting of death is *sin*" (1 Cor. 15:56), and if we have repented of our sins, turned from them with full purpose of heart to serve God, and have sought and obtained forgiveness and healing in the atoning and cleansing blood of Christ, then death cannot harm us—it will but conduct us into the presence of God and everlasting felicity. Who are ready to die? Those who evidence and establish their title to Eternal Life by personal holiness, which is the "firstfruits" of heavenly glory. It is by *walking in* the light of God's Word that we make it manifest that we are meet for the Inheritance of the saints in Light.

"In (or "according to") faith died all these." To die in faith we must live by faith. And for this there must be, first, diligent labour to obtain a knowledge of Divine things. The understanding must be instructed before the path of duty can be known. "Teach me Thy way," "Order my steps in Thy Word," must be our daily prayer. Second, the hiding of God's Word in our hearts. Its precepts must be meditated upon, memorized, and made conscious of: only then will our affections and lives be conformed to them. God's Word is designed to be not only a light to our understanding, but also a lamp upon our path: our walk is to be guided by it. Third, the regular contemplation of Christ by the soul: a worshipful and adoring consideration of His fathomless love, His marvelous grace, His infinite compassion, His present intercession. This will deliver from a legal spirit, warm the heart, supply strength for duty, and make us *want to* please Him.

"In faith died all these, not having received the promises." The word "promises" is a metonymy, for the things promised. Literally they *had* "received the promises," for that which they had heard from God was the basis of their faith: this is clear from vv. 10, 14, 16. The things promised concerned the spiritual blessings of the Gospel dispensation and the future heavenly inheritance. The promises made to the fathers and "elders" had respect unto Christ the blessed "Seed" and to Heaven of which Canaan was the type. Observe that this first clause of v. 13 plainly intimates that *the same* promises were given—though the outer shell of them varied—to Abel, Enoch, and Noah, as were afterwards repeated to Abraham, Isaac and Jacob. Each one died in the firm expectation of the promised Messiah, and in believing views of the heavenly glory. *So* to die, was comfortable to themselves, and confirming to others the reality of what they professed.

"Not having received the promises." The Greek word for "received" signifies the actual participation in and possession of: faith, then, relies upon and rests in that which is not yet ours. A large part of the life of faith consists in laying hold of and enjoying the things promised, before the actual possession of them is obtained. It is by meditating upon and extracting their sweetness that the soul is fed and strengthened. The present spiritual happiness of the Christian consists more in promises and expectant anticipation than an actual possession, for "faith is the substance of things hoped for, the evidence of things not seen." It is this which enables us to say, "For I reckon that the sufferings of this present time are not worthy to be compared with the glory which *shall be* revealed in us" (Rom. 8:18).

"But having seen them afar off." This, because the eyes of their understanding had been Divinely enlightened (Eph. 1:18), and thus they were able to perceive in the promises the wisdom, goodness, and love of God. True, the fulfillment of those promises would be in the remote future, but the eye of faith is strong and endowed with long-distant vision. Thus it was with Abraham: he "rejoiced to see My day," said Christ, "and he saw it and was glad" (John 8:56). Thus it was with Moses, who "had respect unto the recompense of the reward" and "endured as seeing Him who is invisible" (Heb. 11:26, 27). Solemn indeed is the contrast presented in 2 Pet. 1:9, where we read of those who failed to add to their faith virtue, knowledge, self-control, patience, godliness, brotherly-kindness, love, and in consequence of an undeveloped Christian character "cannot see afar off."

"And were persuaded of them." This announces the soul's satisfactory acquiescence in the veracity of God as to the making good of His Word. It was the setting to of their seal that He is true (John 3:33), which is done when the heart truly receives His testimony. The word "persuaded" means an assured confidence, which is what faith works in the mind. A blessed example of this is seen in the case of Abraham, who, though about an hundred years old and his wife's womb dead, yet when God declared they should have a son, he was "fully persuaded that what He has promised,

He was able also to perform" (Rom. 4:21). Ah, my reader, is it not because we are so dilatory in meditating upon the "exceeding great and precious promises" of God, that our hearts are so little persuaded of the verity and value of them!

"And embrace them," not with a cold and formal reception of them, but with a warm and hearty welcome: such is the nature of true faith when it lays hold of the promises of salvation. This is ever the effect of assurance: a thankful and joyful appropriation of the things of God. Faith not only discerns the value of spiritual things, is fully persuaded of their reality, but also loves them. Faith adheres as well as assents: in Scripture faith is expressed by taste as well as sight. Faith "sees" with the understanding, is "persuaded" in the heart, and "embraces" by the will. Thus the *order* of the verbs in this verse teaches us an important practical lesson. The promises of God are first viewed or contemplated, then rested upon as reliable, and then delighted in. If then we would have livelier affections we must meditate more upon the promises of God: it is the mind which affects the heart.

Ere passing on, let us enquire, Are God's promises really precious unto us? Perhaps we are ready to answer at once, Yes: but let us test ourselves. Do our hearts cling to them with love and delight? Can we truly say, "I have rejoiced in the way of Thy testimonies, as much as in all riches" (Psa. 119:14)? What influence do God's promises have upon us in seasons of trial and grief? Do they supply us with more comfort than the dearest things of this world? In the midst of distress and sorrow, do we realize that "our light affliction, which is but for a moment, worketh for us a far more exceeding and eternal weight of glory" (2 Cor. 4:17)? What effect do God's promises have upon our praying? Do we plead them before the Throne of Grace? Do we say with David "Remember the word unto Thy servant, upon which Thou hast caused me to hope" (Psa. 119:49)?

"And confessed that they were strangers and pilgrims on the earth." They who really embrace the promises of God are suitably affected and influenced by them: their delight in heavenly things is manifested by a weanedness from earthly things—as the woman at the well forgot her bucket when Christ was revealed to her soul (John 4:28). When a man truly becomes a Christian he at once begins to view time, and all the objects of time, in a very different light from what he did before. So it was with the patriarchs: their faith had a powerful and transforming effect upon their lives. They made profession of their faith and hope: they made it manifest that their chief interest was neither in nor of the world. They had such a satisfying portion in the promises of God that they publicly renounced such a concern in the world as other men take whose portion is only in this life.

The patriarchs made no secret of the fact that their citizenship and inheritance was elsewhere. Unto the sons of Heth, Abraham confessed "I am a stranger and a sojourner with you" (Gen. 23:4). Unto Pharaoh Jacob said, "The days of the years of my *pilgrimage* are an hundred and thirty" (Gen. 47:9). Nor is this to be explained on the ground that other nations were then in occupation of Canaan: long after Israel entered into possession of that land David cried, "Hear my prayer, O Lord, and give ear unto my cry; hold not Thy peace at my tears: for I am a stranger with Thee, and a sojourner as all my fathers were" (Psa. 39:12); and again, "I am a stranger in the earth: hide not Thy commandments from me" (Psa. 119:19). So too before all the congregation he owned unto God, "For we are strangers before Thee, and sojourners, as were all our fathers" (1 Chron. 29:15). Clear proof do these verses furnish that the O.T. saints equally with the New, apprehended their *heavenly* calling and glory.

"And confessed that they were strangers and pilgrims on the earth." The two terms, though very similar in thought, are not identical. The one refers more to the position, the place taken; the other to condition, how one conducts himself in that place. They were "strangers" because their home was in heaven; "pilgrims," because journeying thither. As another has said, "It is possible to be a 'pilgrim' without being a 'stranger.' But once we realize our true strangership we are perforce compelled to be 'pilgrims.' We may be 'pilgrims', and yet, in our pilgrimage, may visit all the cities and churches in the world, and include them all in our embrace; but if we are true 'sojourners' we shall be 'strangers' to them all, and shall be compelled, as Abraham was, to erect our own solitary altar to Jehovah in the midst of them all. How could Abraham be a worshipper with the Canaanites? Impossible! This is why the 'altar' is so closely connected with the 'tent' in Gen. 12:8 and in Abraham's sojourney" (E. W. B.).

That which was spiritually typified by the outward life of the patriarchs as "strangers and pilgrims" was the Christian's renunciation of the world. As those whose citizenship is in heaven, (Phil. 3:20), we are bidden to be "not conformed to this world" (Rom. 12:2). The patriarchs demonstrated that they were "strangers" by taking no part in the apostate religion, politics, or social life of the Canaanites; and evidenced that they were "pilgrims" by dwelling in tents, moving about from place to place. How far are *we* making manifest our crucifixion to the world (Gal. 6:14)? Does our daily walk show we are "partakers of the heavenly calling"?

Have we ceased looking on this world as our home, and its people as our people? Are we seeking to lay up treasure in heaven, or do we still hanker after the fleshpots of Egypt? When we pray "Lord, conform me to Thine image," do we mean "strip me of all which hinders"!

The figure of the "stranger" applied to the child of God here on earth, is very pertinent and full. The analogies between one who is in a foreign country and the Christian in this world, are marked and numerous. In a strange land one is not appreciated for his birth, but is avoided: John 15:19. The habits, ways, language are strange to him: 1 Pet. 4:4. He has to be content with a stranger's fare: 1 Tim. 6:8. He needs to be careful not to give offense to the government: Col. 4:5. He has to continually enquire his way: Psa. 5:8. Unless he conforms to the ways of that foreign country, he is easily identified: Matt. 26:73. He is often assailed with home-sickness, for his heart is not where his body is: Phil 1:23.

The figure of the "pilgrim" as it applies to the Christian is equally suggestive. Moving on from place to place, he never feels at home. He finds himself very much alone, for he meets with few who are traveling his way. Those he does encounter afford him very little encouragement, for they think him queer. He is very grateful for any kindness shown him: sensible of his dependence on Providence, he is thankful whenever God grants him favour in the eyes of the wicked. He carries nothing with him but what he deems useful for his journey: all superfluities are regarded as incumbrances. He tarries not to gaze upon the various vanities around him. He never thinks of turning back because of the difficulties of the way: he has a definite goal in view, and toward it he steadily presses.

We ought to evidence that we are "strangers and pilgrims" by using the things of this world (when *necessity* requires), but not abusing them (1 Cor. 7:31). By being contented with that portion of this world's goods which God has assigned us (Phil. 4:11). By conscientiously seeking to discharge our own responsibility, and not being "a busybody in other men's matters" (1 Pet. 4:15). By being moderate and temperate in all things, and thus "abstaining from fleshly lusts which war against the soul" (1 Pet. 2:11). By laying aside every hindering weight and mortifying our members which are upon the earth, so that we may run with patience the race that is set before us (Heb. 12:1). By daily keeping in mind the brevity and uncertainty of this life (Prov. 27:1). By constantly keeping before the heart our future inheritance, knowing that we shall only be satisfied when we awake in our Lord's likeness.

"If they in spirit amid dark clouds, took a flight into the celestial country, what ought we to do at this day? for Christ stretches forth His hand to us as it were openly, from Heaven, to raise us up to Himself. If the land of Canaan did not engross their attention, how more weaned from things below ought we to be, who have no promised habitation in this world?" (John Calvin). When Basil (a devoted servant of Christ, at the beginning of the "Dark Ages") was threatened with exile by Modestus, he said, "I know no banishment, who have no abiding-place here in the world. I do not count this place mine, nor can I say the other is not mine; rather all is God's whose stranger and pilgrim I am."

"For they that say such things declare plainly that they seek a country" (v. 14). In these words a logical inference is drawn from the last clause of the preceding verse, which supplies a valuable hint on how the Scriptures are to be expounded. The apostle here makes known unto us what was signified by the confession of the patriarchs. Just as the negative implies the positive—"thou shalt not covet" meaning also, "thou shalt be content with what God has given"—so for saints to conduct themselves as strangers and pilgrims, and that unto the end of their sojourning in this world, makes manifest the fact that they are journeying heavenwards. "This is the genuine and proper way of interpreting Scripture: when from the words themselves, considered with relation to the persons speaking them, and to all their circumstances we declare what was their determinate mind and sense" (J. Owen).

"For they that say such things declare plainly that they seek a country." Their confession of strangership implied more than that they had not yet entered their promised Inheritance: it likewise showed they were earnestly pressing toward it. They had every reason so to do: it was their own "Country," for it was there God had blest them with all spiritual blessings before the foundation of the world (Eph. 1:3, 4), it was from there they had been born again (John 3:3, margin), it was there that their Father, Saviour and fellow-saints dwell. To "seek" the promised Inheritance denotes that earnest quest of the believer after that which he supremely desires. It is this which distinguishes him from the empty professor: the latter desires that which is good for himself, as Balaam said, "Let me die the death of the righteous" (Num. 23:10); but only the regenerate can truly say, "One thing have I desired of the Lord, that will I *seek after;* that I may dwell in the house of the Lord all the days of my life" (Psa. 27:4).

To "seek" after Heaven must be the chief aim and supreme task which the Christian sets before him: laying aside all that would hinder, and using every means which God has appointed. The world must be held loosely, the affections be set upon things above, and the heart constantly exercised about treading the Narrow Way, which alone leads thither. "Seek a Country": "Their designs are for it, their desires are after it, their discourses about it; they diligently endeavour to clear up their title to it, to have their temper suited to it, and have their conversation in it, and come to the enjoyment of it" (Matt. Henry). Heaven is here called a "Country" because of its largeness; it is a pleasant Country, the Land of uprightness, rest and joy. May Divine grace conduct both writer and reader into it.

CHAPTER SIXTY-FOUR

The Reward of Faith

(Heb. 11:15, 16)

Once more we would remind ourselves of the particular circumstances those saints were in to whom our Epistle was first addressed. Only as we do so are we in the best position to discern the meaning of its contents, and best fitted to make a right application of the same unto ourselves. It is not that the Hebrews were Jews according to the flesh and we Gentiles, for they, equally with us, were "holy brethren, partakers of the heavenly calling" (3:1). No, it is the peculiar position which they occupied, with the pressing temptations that solicited them, which we need to carefully ponder. Divine grace had called them out of Judaism (John 10:3) but Divine judgment had not yet fallen upon Judaism. The temple was still intact, and its services continued, and as long as they did so, an appeal was made to the Hebrews to return thereunto.

Now that historical situation adumbrated a moral one. The Christian has been called out from the world to follow Christ, but the judgment of God has not yet fallen upon the world and burned it up. No, it still stands, and we are yet in it, and as long as this is the case, Satan seeks to get us to return thereunto. It is this which enables us to see the force of those verses which are now engaging our attention. Keeping in mind what has just been said, the reader should have no difficulty in discerning why the apostle reminds us, first, that the patriarchs lived on earth as strangers and pilgrims; and secondly, that they went not back again to the land of their birth. As we saw in our last article, that which was typified by the patriarchs living in separation from the Canaanites and their "dwelling in tents," was the Christian's renunciation of this world; that which was foreshadowed by their refusal to return unto Chaldea was the Christian's *continued* renunciation of the world, and his actual winning through to Heaven.

In the verses which are now to be before us clear light is thrown upon an essential element in the Christian life. They present to us an aspect of Truth which, in some circles, is largely ignored or denied today. There are those who have pressed the blessed truth of the eternal Security of the Saints with a zeal that was not always according to knowledge: they have presented it in a way that suggests God preserves His people altogether apart from their use of means. They have stated it in a manner as to virtually deny the Christian's responsibility. They have implied that, having committed my soul unto the keeping of the Lord, I have no more to do with its safety, than I have with money which I have entrusted to the custody of a bank or the government. The result has been that, many who have accepted this false presentation of the truth have felt quite at ease in a course of careless and reckless living.

So one-sided is the teaching we refer to, that its advocates will not allow for a moment that there is the slightest danger of a real Christian apostatizing. If a servant of God insists that there is, and yet he also affirms that no real saint of God has perished or ever will, they consider him inconsistent and illogical. They seem unable to recognize the fact that while it be perfectly true from the side of God's eternal counsels, the value of Christ's redemption, the efficacy of the Spirit's work, that none of the elect can be finally lost; yet it is equally true from the side of the Christian's frailty, the existence of the flesh still within, his being subject unto the assaults of Satan, and his living in a wicked world, that real (not theoretical or imaginary) danger menaces him from every side. No, they fondly imagine that there is only one side to the subject, the Divine side.

But the verses we are now to ponder show the fallacy of this. So far from affirming that there was no possibility of the patriarchs going back again to that country which they had left — which, in type, would mean a returning to the world — the apostle boldly affirms (caring not who might charge him with being inconsistent with himself) that if their hearts had been set upon Chaldea, they "might have had opportunity to have returned." Had they grown weary of dwelling in tents and moving about from place to place in a strange land, and purposed to retrace their steps to Mesopotamia, what was there to hinder them so doing? True, *that* would have been an act of unbelief and disobedience, a despising and relinquishing of the promises; yet, from the human side, the way for them so to act was always open. Let us now weigh the details of our passage.

"And truly, if they had been mindful of that country from whence they came out, they might have had opportunity to have returned" (v. 15). There is a threefold connection between these words and that which immediately precedes. First, at the beginning of v. 13 the apostle had affirmed that all those to whom he was referring (and to whom he was directing the special attention of the Hebrews) had "in faith died"; in all that follows to the end of v. 16 he furnishes proof of his assertion. Second, in v. 15 the apostle continues the inference he had drawn in v. 14 from the last clause of v. 13: the confession made by the patriarchs manifested that their hearts were set upon Heaven, which was further evidenced by their refusal to return to Chaldea. Third, he anticipates and removes an objection: seeing that God had commanded them to take up their residence in another land (Canaan), they were "strangers" there by necessity. No, says the apostle; they were "strangers and pilgrims" by their own consent too: their hearts as well as their bodies were separated from Chaldea.

The patriarch's remaining in a strange land was quite a voluntary thing on their part. And this brings us unto the very heart of what is a real difficulty for many: they do not see that when God "draws" a person (John 6:44), He does no violence to his will, that though exercising His sovereignty man also retains his freedom. Both are true, and hold good of the Christian life at every stage of it. Conversion itself is wholly brought about by the mighty operations of Divine grace, nevertheless it is also a free act on the part of the creature. Those who are effectually called by God out of darkness into His marvelous light, do, at conversion, surrender their whole being to Him, renouncing the flesh, the world, and the Devil, and vow to wage (by His grace) a ceaseless warfare against them. The Christian life is the habitual continuance of what took place at conversion, the carrying out of the vows then made, the putting of it into practice.

Immediately before conversion a fierce conflict takes place in the soul. On the one side is the Devil, seeking to retain his captive by presenting to it the pleasures of sin and the allurements of the world, telling the soul that there will be no more happiness if these be relinquished and the rigid requirements of Christ's commandments be heeded. On the other side is the Holy Spirit, declaring that the wages of sin is death, that the world is doomed to destruction, and that unless we renounce sin and forsake the world, we must eternally perish. Furthermore, the Holy Spirit presses upon us that nothing short of a whole-hearted surrender to the Lordship of Christ can bring us into "*the way of* salvation." Torn between these conflicting impressions upon his mind, the soul is bidden to sit down and "count the cost" (Luke 14:28); to deliberately weigh the offers of Satan and the terms of Christian discipleship, and to definitely make his choice between them.

It is not that man has the power within himself to refuse the evil and choose the good; it is not that God has left it for the creature to determine his own destiny; it is not that the temptations of Satan are equally powerful with the convictions of the Holy Spirit, and that *our* decision turns the scale between them. No indeed: not so do the Scriptures teach, and not so does this writer believe. Sin has robbed fallen man of all *Power* to do good, yet not his *obligation* to perform it. The destiny of all creatures has been unalterably fixed by the eternal decrees of God, yet not in such a way as to reduce them to irresponsible automatons. The operations of the Holy Spirit in God's elect are invincible, yet they do no violence to the human will. But while salvation, from beginning to end, is to be wholly ascribed to the free and sovereign grace of God, it nevertheless remains that conversion itself is the voluntary act of man, his own conscious and free surrendering of himself to God in Christ.

Now the same diverse factors enter into the Christian life itself. Necessarily so, for, as said above, the Christian life is but a progressive continuance of how we begin. Repentance is not once and for all, but as often as we are conscious of having displeased God. Believing in Christ is not a single act which needs no repeating, but a constant requirement, as the "believeth" of John 3:16, and the "coming" of 1 Pet. 2:4 plainly shows. So too our renunciation of the world is to be a daily process. The same objects which enthralled us before conversion are still to hand, and unless we are much upon our guard, unless our hearts are warmed and charmed by the loveliness of Christ, through maintaining a close fellowship with Him, they will soon gain power over us. Satan is ever ready to tempt, and unless we diligently seek grace to resist him, will trip us up.

"And truly, if they had been mindful of that country from whence they came out, they might have had opportunity to have returned," but as the next verse shows, they did not do so. In this they were in striking and blessed contrast from Esau, who sold his birthright, valuing temporal things more highly than spiritual. In contrast from the Children of Israel who said one to another, "Let us make a captain, and let us return to Egypt" (Num. 14:4). In contrast from the Gadarenes, who preferred their hogs to Christ and His salvation (Mark 5). In contrast from the stony-ground hearers who "have no root, which for a while believed, and in time of temptation fall away" (Luke 8:13). In contrast from the apostates of 2 Pet. 2:20-22, the latter end of whom is "worse with them than the beginning." Solemn warnings are these which each professing Christian needs to take to heart.

Note how positively the apostle expressed it: "And truly" or "verily." "If they had been mindful," which means, had their minds frequently dwelt upon Chaldea, had their hearts desired it. How this shows the great importance of "girding up the loins of our minds" (1 Pet. 1:13), of disciplining our thoughts, for as a man "thinketh in his heart, so is he" (Prov. 23:7). "It is in the nature of faith to mortify, not only corrupt and sinful lusts, but our natural affections, and their most vehement inclinations, though in themselves innocent, if they are any way uncompliant with duties of obedience to the commands of God — yea herein lies the principal trial of the sincerity and power of faith. Our lives, parents, wives, children, houses, possessions, our country, are the principal, proper, lawful objects of our natural affections. But when they, or any of them, stand in the way of God's commands, if they are hindrances to the doing or suffering any thing according to His will, faith doth not only mortify, weaken and take off that love, but gives us a comparative hatred of them" (J. Owen).

"They might have had opportunity to have returned." They knew the way, were well furnished with funds, had plenty of time at their disposal, and health and strength for the journey. The Canaanites would not have grieved at their departure (Gen. 26:18-21), and undoubtedly their old friends would have heartily welcomed them back again. In like manner (as we have said before), the way back was wide open for the Hebrews to return unto Judaism: it was their special snare, and a constant and habitual renunciation of it was required of them. So too if *we* choose to return unto the world and engage again in all its vain pursuits, there are "opportunities" enough: enticements abound on every hand, and worldly friends would heartily welcome us to their society if we would but lower our colours, drop our godliness, and follow their course.

But the patriarchs did not go back again to that country from whence they came out: instead, they persevered in the path of duty, and despite all discouragements followed that course which the Divine commandments marked out for them. In this they have left us an example. They hankered not after the wealth, honours, pleasures, or society of Chaldea: their hearts were engaged with something vastly superior. They knew that in Heaven they had "a better and enduring substance," and therefore they disdained the baubles which once had satisfied them. Divine grace had taught them that those sources of joy which they had once so eagerly sought, were "cisterns that can hold no water" (Jer. 2:13); but that in Christ they had an ever-flowing well, that springeth up unto everlasting life. Grace had taught them that it is sinful to make material things the chief objects of this life: they sought first the kingdom of God and His righteousness.

So little did Abraham esteem Chaldea that he would not go thither in person to obtain a wife for his son, nor suffer Isaac to go, but sent his servant and made him swear that he would not bring her thither, if she were unwilling to come—another illustration that nothing is more voluntary than godliness. So it is with the Christian when he is first converted: the world has lost all its attractions for him, nor can it regain its hold upon his heart so long as he walks with God. The acutest test comes in seasons of prosperity. "David professeth himself to be a stranger and a pilgrim, not only when he was hunted like a partridge upon the mountains, but when he was in his palace, and in his best estate. We are not to renounce our comforts, and throw away God's blessings; but we are to renounce our carnal affections. We cannot get out of the world when we please, but we must get the world out of us. It is a great trial of grace to refuse the opportunity; it is the most difficult lesson to learn how to abound, more difficult than to learn how to want, and to be abased; to have comforts, and yet to have the heart weaned from comforts; not to be necessarily mortified, but to be voluntarily mortified" (T. Manton).

It is not the absence of temptation, but the resisting of and prevailing over them which evidences the efficacy of indwelling grace. The power of voluntary godliness is manifested in the conflict, when we have the "opportunity" to go wrong, but decline it. Joseph had not only a temptation, but the "occasion" for yielding to it, yet grace forbade (Gen. 39:9). It was the command of God which held back the patriarchs from returning to Chaldea, and the same controls the hearts of all the regenerate. "It is easy to be good when we cannot be otherwise, or when all temptations to the contrary are out of the way. All the seeming goodness there is in so many, they owe it to the want of a temptation and to the want of an opportunity of doing otherwise" (T. Manton). Not so with the real Christians.

"But now they desire a better country, that is, an heavenly; wherefore God is not ashamed to be called their God: for He hath prepared for them a city" (v. 16). The first half of this verse gives the positive side of what has been before us, and amplified what was said in v. 14. It is not enough to renounce the world, but we must also have our hearts carried forth unto better things: we must believe in and seek Heaven itself. There are some disdain worldly profits, but instead of seeking the true riches, are immersed in worldly pleasures. Others while despising fleshly recreations and dissipations, devote themselves to more serious occupations, yet "labour for that which satisfieth not" (Isa. 55:2). But the Christian, while passing through it, makes a sanctified use of the world, and has his affections set upon things above.

"But now they desire a better country, that is an heavenly." It helps us to link together the four statements made concerning this. First, Abraham *"looked for* a **city**" (v. 10), which denotes faith's expectations of blessedness to come: it was not a mere passing glance of the mind, but a serious and constant anticipation of Celestial Bliss. Second, "They *seek* a Country" (v. 14): they make it the great aim and business of their lives to avoid every hindrance, overcome every obstacle, and steadfastly press forward along the Narrow Way that leads thither: "Laying up in store for themselves a good foundation against the time to come, that they may lay hold on eternal life" (1 Tim. 6:19). Third, "they *desire* a better Country" (v. 16): they long to be relieved from the body of this death, removed from this scene of sin, and be taken to be forever with the Lord: "We ourselves groan within ourselves, waiting for the adoption, the redemption of our body" (Rom. 8:23): he that has had a taste of Heaven in the joy of the spirit, his heart cries "when shall I come to the full enjoyment of my Inheritance!" Fourth, "they *declare plainly* that they seek a country" (v. 14): their daily walk makes it manifest that they belong not to this world, but are citizens of Heaven.

One of the best evidences that we are truly seeking Heaven, is the possession of hearts that are weaned from this world. None will ever enter the Father's House on high in whose soul the first fruits of heavenly peace and joy does not grow now. He who finds his satisfaction in temporal things is woefully deceived if he imagines he can enjoy eternal things. He whose joy is all gone when earthly possessions are snatched from him, knows nothing of that peace which "passeth all understanding." And yet, if the auto, radio, newspaper, money to go to the movies, were taken away from the average "church-member," what would he then have left to make life worth living? O how few can really say, "Although the figtree shall not blossom, neither shall fruit be in the vines; the labour of the olive shall fail, and the fields shall yield no meat; the flock shall be cut off from the fold, and there shall be no herd in the stalls: Yet I will rejoice in the Lord, I will joy in the God of my salvation" (Hab. 3:17, 18).

"Wherefore God is not ashamed to be called their God." "The word 'wherefore' denotes not the procuring or meritorious cause of the thing itself, but the consequent or what ensued thereon" (J. Owen). God will be no man's Debtor: "them that honour Me, I will honour" (1 Sam. 2:30 and cf. 2 Tim. 2:21) is His sure promise. By confessing they were strangers and pilgrims, the patriarchs had avowed their supreme desire for and hope of a portion superior to any that could be found on earth. Hence, because they were willing to renounce all worldly prospects so as to follow God in an obedient faith, for the sake of an invisible but eternal inheritance, He did not disdain to be known as their Friend and Portion. "We are hence to conclude that there is no place for us among God's children except we renounce the world, and that there will be for us no inheritance in Heaven except we become pilgrims on earth" (J. Calvin).

"God is not ashamed to be called their God." Here was the grand reward of their faith. So well did God approve of their desire and design, He was pleased to give evidence of His special regard unto them. "Not ashamed" literally signifies that He had no cause to "blush" because He had been disgraced by them — it is God speaking after the manner of men; it is the negative way of saying that He made a joyous acknowledgement of them, as a father does of dutiful children. When we think not only of the personal unworthiness of the patriarchs (fallen, sinful creatures), but also of their contemptible situation — "dwelling in tents" in a strange land — we may well marvel at the infinite condescension of the Maker of the universe identifying Himself with them. What incredible grace for the Divine Majesty to avow Himself the God of worms of the earth!

Ah, those who renounce the world for God's sake shall not be the losers. But observe it was not simply, "God is not ashamed *to be* their God," but "to be *called* their God." He took this very title in a peculiar manner: unto Moses he said, "I am the God of thy father, the God of Abraham, the God of Isaac, and the God of Jacob" (Ex. 3:6). Thus, to be "called their God" means that He was their covenant God and Father. Not only is He the God of His children by creation and providence, but He is also unto them "the God of all grace" (1 Pet. 5:10), as He is the God of Christ and all the elect in Him. This He manifests by quickening, enlightening, guiding, protecting and making all things work together for their good. He continues to be such a God unto them through life and in death, so that they may depend upon His love, be assured of His faithfulness, count upon His power, and be safely carried through every trial, till they are landed on the shores of Eternal Bliss.

"God is not ashamed to be called their God." The wider reference is to all the elect, who have a special interest in Him. These are known, first, by the manner of their coming into this relation. God brings His people into this special relation by effectually calling them and then when He has taken possession of their hearts, they choose Him for their all-sufficient portion, and completely give up themselves to Him. Their language is, "whom have I in heaven but Thee? and there is none upon earth that I desire beside Thee" (Psa.

73:25). Their surrender to Him is evidenced by, "Lord, what wilt Thou have me to do"? (Acts 9:6). Second, by their manner of living in this relation. They glorify God by their subjection to Him, love for Him, trust in Him. Unto those who have renounced all idols, God is not ashamed to be known as their God.

Now if God be our "God" how *contented* we should be! "The Lord is the portion of mine inheritance and of my cup: Thou maintainest my lot. The lines are fallen unto me in pleasant places; yea, I have a goodly heritage" (Psa. 16:5, 6): this should ever be our language. How *confident* we should be! "The Lord is my Shepherd: I shall not want" (Psa. 23:1): this should ever be our boast. How *joyful* we should be! "Because Thy loving kindness is better than life, my lips shall praise Thee" (Psa. 63:3): this should ever be our confession. "Thou wilt show me the path of life: in Thy presence is fulness of joy; at Thy right hand there are pleasures forevermore" (Psa. 16:11): when brought Home to glory we shall better understand what this connotes — "*their* God."

How may I know that God is *my* "God"? Did you ever enter into covenant with Him? "Was your spirit ever subdued to yield to Him? Do you remember when you were bond-slaves of Satan, that God broke in upon you with a mighty and powerful work of grace, subduing your heart, and causing you to yield, to give the hand to Him, to come and lie at his feet, and lay down the weapons of defiance? Didst thou ever come as a guilty creature, willing to take laws from God? Though it be God's condescension to capitulate with us, yet we do not capitulate with Him as equals, but as a subdued creature, who is taken captive and ready to be destroyed every moment, and is therefore willing to yield and cry quarter. How do you behave yourselves in the covenant? Do you love God as the chiefest good? Do you seek His glory as the utmost end? Do you obey Him as the highest Lord? Do you depend on Him as your only Paymaster? This is to give God the glory of a God" (T. Manton).

"For He hath prepared for them a City." Here is the crowning evidence that He *is* their "God." The "City" is Heaven itself. It is spoken of as "prepared" because God did, in His eternal counsels, appoint it: see Matt. 20:23, 1 Cor. 2:9. But sin entered? True, and Christ has put away the sins of His people, and has entered Heaven as their Representative and Forerunner: therefore has He gone there to "prepare" a place for us, having laid the foundation for this in His own merits; and hence we read of "the purchased possession" (Eph. 1:14). He is now in Heaven possessing it in our name. O what cause have we to bow in wonderment and worship.

CHAPTER SIXTY-FIVE

The Faith of Abraham

(Heb. 11:17-19)

This chapter is the chronology of faith, or a record of some of the outstanding acts which that grace has produced in all ages. The apostle having mentioned the works wrought by the faith of those who lived before the Flood (vv. 4-7), and having spoken of the patriarchs in general (vv. 8-16), now mentions them in detail. He begins again with that of Abraham, who in this glorious constellation shines forth as a star of the first magnitude, and therefore is fittingly styled the father of the faithful. Three principal products of his faith are here singled out: his leaving the land of his birth, upon the call of God (v. 8); the manner of his life in Canaan, sojourning in tents (v. 9); and his offering up of Isaac. The first pictures conversion, the second the Christian's life in this world, the third the triumphant consummation of faith.

Among all the actings of Abraham's faith nothing was more remarkable and noteworthy than the offering up of his son Isaac. Not only was it the most wonderful work of faith ever wrought, and therefore is the most illustrious of all examples for us to follow (the life and death of Christ alone excepted), but it also supplies the most blessed shadowing out of the love of God the Father in the gift of His dear Son. The resemblances pointed by the type are numerous and striking. Abraham offered up a son, his only begotten son. Abraham delivered up his son to a sacrificial death, and, in purpose, smote him. But observe too how the antitype excelled the type. Abraham's son was only a man. Abraham offered up Isaac under Divine command: God was under no constraint, but gave Christ freely. Abraham's son suffered not; Christ did.

Let it not be forgotten that the chief design before the apostle throughout this chapter, was to demonstrate unto his tried brethren the great efficacy of faith: its power to sustain a very great trial, to perform a very difficult duty, and to obtain a very important blessing. Unmistakably were these three things illustrated in the case we are now to consider. As we have already seen, it was not without good reason that Abraham is designated the father of all who believe. But among all the actings of his faith none was more memorable than its exercise upon Mount Moriah. If we consider the object of it, the occasion of it, the hindrances which stood in his way, and his blessed victory, we cannot but admire and wonder at the power of Divine grace triumphing over the weakness of the flesh.

"By faith Abraham, when he was tried, offered up Isaac: and he that had received the promises offered up his only begotten son" (v. 17). For a clearer understanding of this verse we need to consult Gen. 22: there we read, "And it came to pass after these things, that God did tempt Abraham, and said unto him, Abraham: and he said, Behold, here I am. And He said, Take now thy son, thine only son Isaac, whom thou lovest, and get thee into the land of Moriah; and offer him there for a burnt offering upon one of the mountains which I will tell thee of" (vv. 1, 2). The whole of what follows in Gen. 22, to the end of v. 19, should be carefully read. Before attempting to expound our present verse and make application to ourselves of its practical teachings, let us seek to remove one or two difficulties which may stand in the way of the thoughtful reader.

First, "By faith Abraham, when he was tried, offered up Isaac." The word "offered up" is the same that is used for slaying and offering up sacrifices. Here then is the problem: how could Abraham "offer up" his son *by faith,* seeing that it was against both the law of nature and the law of God for a man to slay his own son? Gen. 22:2, however, shows that his faith had a sure foundation to rest upon,for the Lord Himself had commanded him so to do. But this only appears to remove the difficulty one stage farther back: God Himself had laid it down as a law that "whoso sheddeth man's blood, by man shall his blood be shed" (Gen. 9:6). True, but though His creatures are bound by the laws He has prescribed them, God Himself is not.

God is under no law, but is absolute Sovereign. Moreover, He is the Lord of life, both Giver and Preserver of it, and therefore has He an indisputable right to dispose of it, to take it away when He pleases, by what means or instruments He sees fit. God possesses supreme authority, and when He pleases sets aside His own laws, or issues new ones contrary to those given previously. By His own imperial fiat, Jehovah now, by special and extraordinary command, constituted it a duty for Abraham to do what before had been a sin. In similar manner, He who gave commandment "thou shalt not make unto thee any graven image or any likeness" (Ex. 20:4), ordered Moses *to make* a brazen serpent (Num. 21:8)! Learn, then, that God is bound by no law, being above all law.

Second, but how could it be truly said that Abraham "offered up Isaac," seeing that he did not actually slay him? In regard to his willingness, in regard to his set purpose, and in regard to God's acceptance of the will for the deed, he *did* do so. There was no reserve in his heart, and there was no failure in his honest endeavours. He took the three days' journey to the appointed place of sacrifice; he bound Isaac unto the altar, and took the knife into his hand to slay him. And God accepted the will for the deed. This exemplifies a most important principle in connection with God's acceptance of the Christian's obedience. The terms of His law have not been lowered: God still requires of us personal, perpetual, and perfect obedience. But this we are unable to render to Him while in our present state. And so, for Christ's sake, where the heart (at which God ever looks) *truly desires* to fully please Him in all things, and makes an honest and *sincere effort* to do so, God graciously accepts the will for the deed. Carefully ponder 2 Cor. 8:12 which illustrates the same blessed fact, and note the word "willing" in Heb. 13:18!

Third, the statement made in Gen. 22:1, "God did tempt Abraham," or as our text says, "when he was tried," for that is exactly what both the original Heb. and Greek word signifies: to make trial of. "It is an act of God whereby He proveth and makes experience of the loyalty and obedience of His servants" (W. Perkins). And this *not* for His own information (for He "knoweth our thoughts afar off"), but for their own knowledge and that of their fellows. Christ put the rich young ruler to the proof when He said, "Go, sell that thou hast, and give to the poor" (Matt. 19:21). So too He made trial of the Canaanitish woman when He said, "It is not meet to take the children's bread and to cast it to the dogs" (Matt. 15:26).

"By faith Abraham, when he was tried, offered up Isaac." In order to understand and appreciate the fact that it was "by *faith*" Abraham offered up Isaac, we must examine more closely the nature of that test to which the Lord submitted the one whom He condescended to call his "friend." In bidding him to sacrifice his beloved son, that ordeal combined in it various and distinct features: it was a testing of his submission or loyalty to God; it was a testing of his affections, as to whom he really loved the more: God or Isaac; it was a testing of which was the stronger within him: grace or sin; but supremely, it was a testing of his *faith*.

Carnal writers see in this incident little more than a severe trial of Abraham's natural affections. It cannot be otherwise, for water never rises above its own level; and carnal men are incapable of discerning spiritual things. But it is to be carefully noted that

Heb. 11:17 does not say, "In submission to God's holy will, Abraham offered up Isaac," though that was true; nor "out of supreme love for God he offered his son," though that was also the case. Instead, the Holy Spirit declares that it was *"by faith"* that the patriarch acted, declaring that "he that had *received the promises* offered up his only begotten son." Most of the modern commentators, filled with fleshly sentiment rather than with the Holy Spirit, completely miss this point, which is the central beauty of our verse. Let us seek then to attend unto it the more particularly.

In calling upon Abraham to sacrifice his son as a burnt offering, the Lord submitted his faith to a fiery ordeal. How so? Because God's promises to Abraham concerning his "seed" centered in Isaac, and in bidding him slay his only son, He appeared to contradict Himself. Ishmael had been cast out, and Isaac's posterity alone was to be reckoned to Abraham as the blessed seed among whom God would have His church. Isaac had been given to Abraham after he had long gone childless and when Sarah's womb was dead, therefore there was no likelihood of his having any more sons by her. At the time, Isaac himself was childless, and to kill him looked like cutting off all his hopes. How then could Abraham reconcile the Divine command with the Divine promise? To sacrifice his son and heir was not only contrary to his natural affections, but opposed to carnal reason as well.

In like manner God tests the faith of His people today. He calls upon them to perform the acts of obedience which are contrary to their natural affections and which are opposed to carnal reason. "If any man will come after Me, let him deny himself, and take up his cross, and follow Me" (Matt. 16:24). How many a Christian has had his or her affections drawn out toward a non-Christian, and then has come to them that piercing word, "Be ye not unequally yoked together with unbelievers" (2 Cor. 6:14)! How many a child of God has had his membership in a "church" where he saw that Christ was dishonoured; to heed that Divine command, "Wherefore come out from among them, and be ye separate, saith the Lord" (2 Cor. 6:17) entailed leaving behind those near and dear in the flesh; but the call of God could not be disregarded, no matter how painful obedience to it might be.

But when are we put to such a trial as to offer up our Isaac? To this question the Puritan Manton returned a threefold answer. First, in the case of *submission to* the strokes of providence, when near relations are taken away from us. God knows how to strike us in the right vein; there will be the greatest trial where our love is set. Second, in case of *self-denial,* forsaking our choicest interests for a good conscience. We must not only part with mean things, but such as we prize above anything in the world. When God requires it (as He did with the writer) that we should forsake father and mother, we must not demur; nay, our lives should not be dear unto us (Acts 20:24). Third, in *mortifying* our bosom lust: this is what is signified by cutting off a "right hand" or plucking out a "right eye" (Matt. 5:29, 30).

Let us notice the *time* when Abraham was thus tested. The Holy Spirit has emphasized this in Gen. 22:1 by saying, "And it came to pass after these things, that God did tempt Abraham." A double reference seems to be made in these words. First, a general one to all the preceding trials which Abraham had endured — his journey to Canaan, his sojourning there in tents, the long, long wait for the promised heir. Now that he had passed through a great fight of afflictions, he is called upon to suffer a yet severer test. Ah, God educates His children little by little: as they grow in grace harder tasks are assigned them, and deeper waters are called upon to be passed through, that enlarged opportunities may be afforded for manifesting their increased faith in God. It is not the raw recruit, but the scarred veteran, who is assigned a place in the front ranks in the battle. Think it not strange then, fellow-Christian, if thy God is now appointing thee severer tests than He did some years ago.

Second, a more specific reference is made in Gen. 22:1 to what is recorded in the previous chapter: the miraculous birth of Isaac, the great feast that Abraham made, when he was weaned (v. 8), and the casting out of Ishmael (v. 14). The cup of the patriarch's joy was now full. His outlook seemed most promising: not a cloud appeared on the horizon. Yet it was then, like a heavy clap of thunder out of a clear sky, that the most trying test of all came upon him! Yes, and so it was just after God had pronounced Job "a perfect man and an upright" that He delivered all that he had into Satan's hands (Job. 1:8, 12). So too it was when Paul had been rapt to the third heaven, when he received such "abundance of revelations," that there was given him "a thorn in the flesh, the messenger of Satan to buffet him" (2 Cor. 12:1-7).

How we need to seek grace that we may be enabled to hold every thing down here with a light hand. Rightly did an old writer say, "Build not thy nest on any earthly tree, for the whole forest is doomed to be cut down." It is not only for God's glory, but for our own good, that we set our affections upon "things above." And in view of what has just been before us, how necessary it is that we should *expect* and seek in advance to be prepared for severe trials. Are we not bidden to "hear for the time to come" (Isa. 42:23)? The more we calmly anticipate future trials, the less likely are we to be staggered and overcome by them when they arrive: "Beloved, think it not strange concerning the fiery trial which is to try you, as though some strange thing happened unto you" (1 Pet. 4:12).

Having observed the time when Abraham was tested, let us now consider the *severity* of his trial. And first *the act* itself. Abraham was ordered to slay, not all his bullocks and herds, but a human being; and that not one of his faithful servants, but his beloved son. Abraham was bidden, not to banish from home or send him out of Canaan, but to cut him off out of the land of the living. He was commanded to do a thing for which no reason could be assigned save the authority of Him who gave the command. He was bidden to do that which was most abhorrent to natural feeling. He must not only consent unto the death of his dear Isaac, but himself be his executioner. He was to slay one who was guilty of no crime, but who (according to the Divine record) was an unusually dutiful, loving, and obedient child. Was ever such a demand made upon a human creature before or since!

Second, consider *the offerer*. In our text he is presented in a particular character: "he that had received the promises," which is the key clause to the verse. God had declared unto Abraham that He would establish an everlasting covenant with Isaac and with his seed after him (Gen. 17:9). Isaac, and none other, was the "seed" by whose posterity Canaan should be possessed (Gen. 12:7). It was through him that all nations should be blessed (Gen. 17:7), and therefore it must be through him that Christ, according to the flesh, would proceed. These promises Abraham had "received": he had given credit for them, firmly believed them, fully expected their performance. Now the accomplishment of those promises depended upon the preservation of Isaac's life — at least until he had a son; and to sacrifice him now, appeared to render them all null and void, making their fulfillment impossible.

"He that had received the promises"— "which noteth not only the revelation of the promises, concerning a numerous issue, and the Messiah to come of his loins, but the entertaining of them and cordial assent to them. He received them not only a private believer, but as a feoffee in trust for the use of the church. In the first ages of the world God had some eminent persons who received a revelation of His will in the name of the rest. This was Abraham's case, and he is here viewed not only as a father, a loving father, but as one who had received the promises as a public person, and father of the faithful—the person whom God had chosen in whom to deposit the promises" (T. Manton). Herein lay the *spiritual* acuteness of the trial: would he not in slaying Isaac be faithless to his trust? would he not by his own act place the gravestone on all hope for the fulfillment of such promises?

Forcibly did Matt. Henry, when commenting upon the time at which Abraham received this trying command from God, say, "After he had received the promises that this Isaac should build up his family, and that 'in him his seed should be called' (Heb. 11:18), and that he should be one of the progenitors of the Messiah, and all nations blessed in Him; so that in being called to offer up his Isaac, he seemed to be called to destroy and cut off his own family, to cancel the promises of God, to prevent the coming of Christ, to destroy the whole truth, to sacrifice his own soul and his hope of salvation, to cut off the church of God at one blow; a most terrible trial!" If Isaac were slain, then *all* seemed to be lost.

It may be asked, But *why* should God thus try the faith of the patriarch? For Abraham's own sake that he might the better know the efficacy of that grace which God had bestowed upon him. As the suspending of a heavy weight upon a chain reveals either its weakness or its strength, so God places His people in varied circumstances which manifest that state of their hearts—whether or no their trust be really in Him. The Lord tried Hezekiah to show unto him his frailty (2 Chron. 32:31); he tried Job to show that though He slew him yet would he trust in God. Second, for the sake of others, that Abraham might be an example to them. God had called him to be the father of the faithful, and therefore would He show unto all generations of his children what grace He had conferred upon him—what a worthy "father" or pattern he was (condensed from W. Gouge).

In like manner, God tries His people today and puts to the proof the grace which He has communicated to their hearts: this, both for His own glory, and for their own comfort. The Lord is determined to make it manifest that He has on earth a people who will forsake any comfort and endure any misery rather than forego their plain duty; who love Him better than their own lives, and who are prepared to trust Him in the dark. So too we are the gainers, for we never have clearer proof of the reality of grace than when we are under sore trials. "Knowing that tribulation worketh patience, and patience experience, and experience hope" (Rom. 5:3, 4). As another has said, "By knocking upon the vessel we see whether it is full or empty, cracked or sound, so by these knocks of providence we are discovered."

Rightly did John Owen point out, "Trials are the only touchstone of faith, without which men must want (lack) the best evidence of its sincerity and efficacy, and the best way of testifying it unto others. Wherefore we ought not to be afraid of trials, because of the admirable advantages of faith, in and by them." Yea, the Word of God goes farther, and bids us, "Count it all joy when ye fall into divers temptations" or "trials," declaring "that the trying of your faith worketh patience; but let patience have her perfect work, that ye may be perfect and entire, wanting nothing" (James 1:2-4). So too, "Though now for a season, if need be, ye are in heaviness through manifold temptations (or "trials") that the trial of your faith, being much more precious than of gold that perisheth, though it be tried with fire, might be found unto praise and honour, and glory at the appearing of Jesus Christ" (1 Pet. 1:6, 7).

In conclusion, let us observe how Abraham conducted himself under this sore trial: "he that had received the promises offered up his only begotten son." Many instructive details concerning this are recorded in Gen. 22. There it will be found that Abraham consulted not with Sarah—why should he, when he already *knew* God's will on the matter! Nor was there any disputing with God, as to the apparently flagrant disprepancy between His present command and His previous promises. Nor was there any delay: "And Abraham rose up early in the morning, and saddled his ass, and took two of his young men with him, and Isaac his son, and clave the wood for the burnt offering, and rose up, and went unto the place of which God had told him" (Gen. 22:3). And how is his unparalleled action to be accounted for? From what super-fleshly principle did it spring? A single word gives the answer: FAITH. Not a theoretical faith, not a mere head-knowledge of God, but a real, living, spiritual, triumphant, *faith.*

"*By faith* Abraham, when he was tried, offered up Isaac." By faith in the Divine justice and wisdom behind the command so to act. By faith in the veracity and faithfulness of God to make good His own promises. Fully assured that God was able to fulfil His word, Abraham closed his eyes to all difficulties, and steadfastly counted upon the power of Him that cannot lie. This is the very nature or character of a *spiritual* faith: it persuades the soul of God's absolute supremacy, unerring wisdom, unchanging righteousness, infinite love, almighty power. In other words, it rests upon the *character* of the living God, and trusts Him in the face of every obstacle. Spiritual faith makes its favoured possessor judge that the greatest suffering is better than the least sin; yea, it unhesitatingly avows "Thy loving kindness is better than life" (Psa. 63:3).

We must leave for our next article the consideration of the remainder of our passage. But in view of what has already been before us, is not both writer and reader constrained to cry unto God, "Lord, have mercy upon me! Pardon my vile unbelief, and graciously subdue its awful power. Be pleased, for Christ's sake, to work in me that spiritual and supernatural faith which will honour Thee and bear fruits to Thy glory. And if Thou hast, in Thy discriminating grace, already communicated to me this precious, precious gift, then graciously deign to strengthen it by the power of Thy Holy Spirit; call it forth into more frequent exercise and action. Amen."

CHAPTER SIXTY-SIX

The Faith of Abraham

(Heb. 11:17-19)

"Yield yourselves unto God, as those that are alive from the dead, and your members as instruments of righteousness unto God" (Rom. 6:13). The Lord has an absolute claim upon us, upon all that we have. As our Maker and Sovereign He has the right to demand from us anything He pleases, and whatsoever He requires we must yield (1 Chron. 29:11). All that we have comes from Him, and must be held for Him, and at His disposal (1 Chron. 29:14). The Christain is under yet deeper obligations to part with anything God may ask from him: loving gratitude for Christ and His so great salvation, must loosen our hold on every cherished temporal thing. The bounty of God should encourage us to surrender freely whatever He calls for, for none ever lose by giving up anything to God. Yet powerful as are these considerations to any renewed mind, the fact remains that they move us not until *faith* is in exercise. Faith it is which causes us to yield to God, respond to His claims, and answer His calls.

"By faith Abraham, when he was tried, offered up Isaac; and he that had received the promises offered up his only begotten son. Of whom it was said, That in Isaac shall thy Seed be called: Accounting that God was able to raise him up, even from the dead; from whence also he received him in a figure" (Heb. 11:17-19). The apostle's purpose in citing this remarkable incident, was to show that it is the property of faith to carry its possessor through the greatest trials, with a cheerful submission and acceptable obedience to the will of God. In order to make this clearer unto the reader, let us endeavour to exhibit the powerful influence which faith has to support the soul under and carry it through testings and trials.

First, faith judgeth of all things aright: it impresses us with a sense of the uncertainty and fleetingness of earthly things, and causes us to highly esteem invisible and heavenly things. Faith is a spiritual prudence opposed not only to ignorance, but also to folly: so much unbelief as we have, so much folly is ours—"O fools and slow of heart to believe" (Luke 24:25). Faith is a spiritual wisdom, teaching us to value the favour of God, the smiles of His countenance, the comforts of Heaven; it shows us that all outward things are nothing in comparison with inward peace and joy. Carnal reason prizes the concernments of the present life and grasps at its riches and honors; sense is occupied with fleshly pleasures; but faith knows "Thy loving kindness is better than life" (Psa. 63:3).

Second, faith solves all riddles and doubts when we are in a dilemma: what a problem confronted Abraham; what! shall I offer Isaac and bring to nought God's promises, or must I disobey Him on the other side? Faith removed the difficulty: "accounting that God was able to raise him up even from the dead." Faith believes the accomplishment of the promise, whatever reason and sense may say to the contrary; it cuts the knot by a resolute dependence upon the power and fidelity of God. Faith casts down carnal imaginations and every high thing that exalteth itself against God, and brings into captivity every thought to the obedience of Christ.

Third, faith is a grace which looks to future things, and in the light of their reality the hardest trials seem nothing. Sense is occupied only with things present, and thus to nature it appears troublesome and bitter to deny ourselves. But the language of faith is, "For our light affliction, which is but for a moment, worketh for us a far more exceeding and eternal weight of glory; *while* we look not at the things which are seen, but at the things which are not seen" (2 Cor. 4:17, 18). Faith looks within the veil, and so has a mighty influence to support the soul in time of trial. He who walks in the light of Eternity goes calmly and happily along through the mists and fogs of time; neither the frowns of men nor the blandishments of the world affect him, for he has a ravishing and affecting sight of the glorious Inheritance to which he is journeying.

Fourth, "faith worketh by love" (Gal. 5:6), and then nothing is too near and dear to us if the relinquishing of them will glorify God. Faith not only looks forward, but backward; it reminds the soul of what great things God has done for us in Christ. He has given us His beloved Son, and *He* is worth infinitely more than all we can give to Him. Yes, faith apprehends the wondrous love of God in Christ, and says, If He gave the Darling of His bosom to die for me, shall I stick at any little sacrifice? If God gave me Christ shall I deny Him my Isaac: I love him well, but I love God better. Thus faith works, urging the soul with the love of God, that we may out of thankfulness to Him part with those comforts which He requires of us.

"Of whom it was said, That in Isaac shall thy Seed be called" (v. 18). This was brought in by the apostle to show wherein lay the greatest obstacle before Abraham's faith. First, he was called on to "offer up" his son and heir. Second, and this after he had "received the promises." Third, not Ishmael, but his "only begotten" or well-beloved Isaac—this is the force of the expression: it is a term of endearment as John 1:18, 3:16 shows. Fourth, he must slay the one from whom the Messiah Himself was to issue, for this is clearly the meaning of the Divine promise recorded in v. 18.

Long ago John Owen called attention to the fact that the Socinians (Unitarians) reduced God's promise to Abraham unto two heads: first that of a numerous posterity, and second that this posterity should inhabit and enjoy the land of Canaan as an inheritance. But this, as he pointed out, directly contradicts the apostle, who in Heb. 11:39 affirms that, when they had possessed the land of Canaan almost unto the utmost period of its grant unto them, had *not* received the accomplishment of the promise—we wish our modern "dispensationalists" would ponder that verse. While it is true that the numerous posterity of Abraham and their occupancy of Canaan were both means and pledges of the fulfillment of the promise, yet Acts 2:38, 39 and Gal. 3:16 make it unmistakably plain that the subject-matter of the promise was Christ Himself, with the whole work of His meditation for the redemption and salvation of His Church.

"Of whom it was said, That in Isaac shall thy Seed be called." This Divine promise is first found in Gen. 21:12, and the occasion of God's giving it unto Abraham supplies us with another help towards determining its significance. In the context there, we find that the Lord had given orders for the casting out of Hagar and her son, and we read, "And the thing was very grievous in Abraham's sight because of his son" (Gen. 21:11). Then it was, to console his stricken heart, that Jehovah said unto His "friend": grieve not over Hagar's son, for I will give thee One who is better than a million Ishmaels; I will give thee a son from whom shall descend none other than the promised Saviour and Redeemer. And now Abraham was called upon to slay him who was the marked-out progenitor of the Messiah! No ordinary faith was called for here!

Who can doubt but that now Abraham was sorely pressed by Satan! Would he not point out how "inconsistent" God was?—as he frequently will to us, if we are foolish enough to listen to his vile accusations. Would he not appeal to his sentiments and say, How will Sarah regard you when she learns that you have killed and reduced to ashes the child of her old age? Would he not seek to persuade Abraham that God was playing with him, that He did not really mean to be taken seriously, that he could not be so cruel as to require a righteous father to be the executioner of his own dutiful son? In the light of all that is revealed of our great Enemy in Holy Writ, and in view of our own experience of his fiendish assaults, who can doubt but what Abraham now became the immediate object of the Devil's attack.

Ah, nothing but a mind that was stayed upon the Lord could have then resisted the Devil, and performed a task which was so difficult and painful. "Had he been weak in faith, he would have doubted whether two revelations, apparently inconsistent, could come from the same God, or, if they did, whether such a God ought to be trusted and obeyed. But being strong in faith, he reasoned in this way: This is plainly God's command, I have satisfactory evidence of that; and therefore it ought to be immediately and implicitly obeyed. I know Him to be perfectly wise and righteous, and what He commands must be right. Obedience to this command does indeed seem to throw obstacles in the way of the fulfillment of a number of promises which God has made to me. I am quite sure that God has made those promises; I am quite sure that He will perform them. How He is to perform them, I cannot tell. That is His province, not mine. It is His to promise, and mine to believe; His to command, and mine to obey" (John Brown).

The incident we are now considering shows us again that faith has to do not only with the promises of God, but with His precepts as well. Yea, this is the central thing which is here set before us. Abraham had been "strong in faith" when God had declared he should have a son by his aged wife (Rom. 4:19), not being staggered by the seemingly insurmountable difficulty that stood in the way; and now he was strong in faith when God bade him slay his son, refusing to be deterred by the apparently immovable obstacle which his act would interpose before his receiving the Seed through Isaac. Ah, dear reader, make no mistake upon this point: a faith which is not as much and as truly engaged with the precepts as it is with the promises of God, is not the faith of Abraham, and therefore is not the faith of God's elect. Spiritual faith does not pick and choose: it fears God as well as loves Him.

As the promises are not believed with a lively faith unless they draw off our hearts from the carnal vanities to seek that happiness which they offer us, so the commandments are not believed rightly unless we be fully resolved to acquiesce in them as the only rule to guide us in the obtaining that happiness, and to adhere to and obey them. The Psalmist declared, "I have *believed* Thy *commandments*" (119:66); he recognized God's authority behind them, there was a readiness of heart to hear His voice in them, there was a determination of will for his actions to be regulated by them. So it was with Abraham, and so it must be with us if we would furnish proof that *he* is *our* "father." "If ye were Abraham's children, ye would do the works of Abraham" (John 8:39).

God's Word is not to be taken piece-meal by us, but received into our hearts as a whole: every part must affect us, and stir up dispositions in us which each several part is suited to produce. If the promises stir up comfort and joy, the commandments must stir up love, fear, and obedience. The precepts are a part of Divine revelation. The same Word which calls upon us to believe in Christ as an all-sufficient Saviour, also bids us to believe the commandments of God, for the moulding of our hearts and the guiding of our ways. There is a necessary connection between the precepts and the promises, for the latter cannot do us good until the former be heeded: our consent to the Law precedes our faith in the Gospel. God's commands "are not grievous" (1John 5:3). Christ must be accepted as Lawgiver before He becomes our Redeemer: Isa. 33:22.

How the readiness of Abraham to sacrifice his son condemns those who oppose God's commands, and will not sacrifice their wicked and filthy lusts! "Whosoever he be of you," says Christ, "that *forsaketh not* all that he hath, he *cannot* by My disciple" (Luke 14:33): by which He meant, until he does in heart sincerity and resolute endeavor turn away from all that stands in competition (for our affections) with the Lord Jesus, he cannot become a Christian: see Isa. 55:7. In vain do we claim to be saved if the world still rules our hearts. Divine grace not only delivers from the wrath to come, but even now it effectually "teaches" its recipients to *deny* "all ungodliness and worldly lusts, that we should live soberly, righteously, and godly in this present world" (Titus 2:12).

"Accounting that God was able to raise him up, even from the dead" (v. 19). Here we learn what was the immediate object of Abraham's faith on this occasion, namely, the mighty power of God. He was fully assured that the Lord would work a miracle rather than fail of His promise. Ah, my brethren, it is by meditating upon God's sufficiency that the heart is quietened and faith is established. In times of temptation when the soul is heavy with doubts and fears, great relief may be obtained by pondering the Divine attributes, particularly, God's omnipotency. His all-mighty power is a special prop to faith. The faith of saints has in all ages been much strengthened hereby. Thus it was with the three Hebrews: "our God whom we serve *is able* to deliver us from the burning fiery furnace" (Dan. 3:17)! "With God *all* things are possible" (Mark 10:27): He is able to make good His word, though all earth and hell seem to make against it.

Here too we see exhibited another of faith's attributes, namely, the committal of events unto God. Carnal reason is unable to rest until a solution is in sight, until it can see a way out of its difficulties. But faith spreads the need before God, rolls the burden upon Him, and calmly leaves the solution to Him. "Commit thy works unto the Lord, and thy thoughts shall be established" (Prov. 16:3): when this is truly done by faith we are eased of many tossings of mind and agitations of soul that would otherwise distress us. So here, Abraham committed the event unto God, reckoning on His power to raise Isaac again, though he should be killed. This is the very nature of spiritual faith: to refer our case unto Him, and wait calmly and expectantly for the promised deliverance, though we can neither perceive nor imagine the manner in which it shall be brought about. "Commit thy way unto the Lord: trust also in Him; and He *shall* bring to pass" (Psa. 37:5).

O how little faith is in exercise among the professing people of God today. Occupied almost wholly with the rising tide of evil in the world, with the rapid spread of Romanism, with the apostasy of Protestantism, the vast majority of those now bearing the name of Christ conclude that we are facing a hopeless situation. Such people seem to be ignorant of the history of the past. Both in O.T. times and at different periods of this dispensation, things have been far worse than they now are. Moreover, such trembling pessimists *leave out God*: is not HE "able" to cope with the present situation? A hesitating "Yes" may be given, at once nullified by the query, "But where is the promise that He *will* do so?" Where? Why in Isa. 59:19, "When the enemy shall come in like a flood (has he not already done so!), the Spirit of the Lord *shall* lift up a standard against him"—but who *believes* it!

Ah, my Christian reader, ponder thoughtfully that blessed affirmation of Him that cannot lie, and then bow the head in shame for thine *unbelief*. Every thing in the world may seem to lie dead against the fulfillment of many a Divine promise, yet no matter how dark and dreadful the outlook appears, the Church of God on earth today is not facing nearly so critical and desperate a situation as did the father of the faithful when he had his knife at the breast of him on whose one life the accomplishment of *all* the promises did depend. Yet he rested in the faithfulness and power of God to secure His own veracity: and so may we do also at this present juncture. He who responded to the faith of sorely-tried

Abraham, to the faith of Moses when Israel stood before the Red Sea, to the three Hebrews when cast in Babylon's furnace, *will* to ours, if we *really* trust Him. Forsake then your newspapers, brethren, get ye to your knees, and pray expectantly for a fresh outpouring of the Holy Spirit. Man's extremity is always God's opportunity.

"Accounting that God was able to raise him up, even from the dead." This supplies an interesting sidelight on the spiritual intelligence of the patriarchs. The O.T. saints were very far from being as ignorant as some of our superficial moderns suppose. Erroneous conclusions have often been drawn from the silence of Genesis on various matters: the later books of Scripture frequently supplement the concise accounts supplied in the earlier ones. Rightly did J. Owen point out, "Abraham firmly believed, not only in the immortality of the souls of men, but also the resurrection from the dead. Had he not done so, he could not have betaken himself unto this relief in his distress. Other things he might have thought of, wherein God might have exercised His power; but he could not believe that He would do it, in that which itself was not believed by him."

Some, perhaps, think that Owen drew too much on his imagination, that he read into Heb 11:19 what is not really there. If so, they are mistaken. There is one clear statement in Gen. 22, which, though not quoted by the eminent Puritan, fully establishes his assertion: there we are told that the patriarch said unto his young men, "I and the lad will go yonder and worship, *and come again to you*" (v. 5). This is exceedingly blessed. It shows us that Abraham was not occupied with his faith, his obedience, or with anything in himself, but solely with the living God: the "worship" of Him filled his heart and engaged all his thoughts. The added words "and come again to you" make it unmistakably plain that Abraham confidently expected Jehovah to raise again from the dead the one he was about to sacrifice unto Him as a burnt offering. A wonderful triumph of faith was this: recorded for the praise of the glory of God's grace, and for our instruction.

O my dear brethren and sisters in Christ, we want you to do something more than read through this article: we long for you to *meditate* upon this blessed sequel to Abraham's sore trial. He was tested as none other ever was, and grand was the outcome; but between that testing and its happy issue there was the exercise of faith, the counting upon God to interpose on his behalf, the trusting in His all-sufficient power. And God did not fail him: though He tried his faith to the limit, yet in the nick of time the Lord intervened. This is recorded for our encouragement, especially for those who are now passing through a fiery furnace. He who can *deliver from death,* what cannot He do! Say then with one of old, "Neither is there any Rock (to stay ourselves upon) like our God" (1 Sam. 2:2): Hannah had found a mighty support to her faith in the power of God.

"By faith Abraham . . . offered up Isaac . . . accounting that God was able to raise him up." Faith, then, *expects* a recompense from God. Faith knows that it is a saving bargain to lose things for Christ's sake. Faith looks for a restitution of comforts again, either in kind or in value: "There is no man that hath left house, or brethren, . . . for My sake and the Gospel's, but he shall receive an hundredfold now in this time, houses and brethren. . . and in the world to come eternal life" (Mark 10:29, 30)—that is, either actually so, or an abundant equivalent. When one of the kings of Israel was bidden by the Lord to dismiss the army he had hired, he was troubled, and asked, "What shall we do for the hundred talents which I have given to the army of Israel" (2 Chron 25:9); whereupon the prophet replied, "The Lord is able to give thee much more than this"! When a man, through faithfulness to Christ, is exposed unto the frowns of the world, and his family faces starvation, let him know that God *will* undertake for him. The Lord will be no man's Debtor.

"From whence also he received him in a figure" (v. 19). Abraham had, as to his purpose, sacrificed Isaac, so that he considered him as dead; and he (thus) received him back from the dead — not really, but in a manner bearing likeness to such a miracle. This illustrates and demonstrates the truth of what has just been said above. God returns again to us what we offer to Him: "whatsoever a man soweth that shall he also reap" (Gal. 6:7). "That which he hath given will He pay him again" (Prov. 19:17), for He will not be beholden to any of His creatures. Hannah gave up Samuel to the Lord, and she had many more children in return (1 Sam. 2:20, 21). How great, then, is the folly of those who withhold from God anything which He asks of them: how they forsake their own mercies, stand in their own light, and hinder their own good.

"From whence also he received him in a figure." Here is the grand outcome of the patriarch's faith. First, the trial was withdrawn, Isaac was spared: the speediest way to end a trial is to be completely resigned to it; if we would save our life, we must lose it. Second, he had the expressed approval of the Lord, "now I know that thou fearest God" (Gen. 22:12): he whose conscience is clear before God enjoys great peace. Third, he had a clearer view of Christ than he had before: "Abraham saw My day" said the Saviour—the closer we keep to the path of obedience the more real and precious will Christ be unto us. Fourth, he obtained a fuller revelation of God's name: he called Him "Jehovah-Jireh" (Gen. 22:14): the more we stand the test of trial the better instructed shall we be in the things of God. Fifth, the covenant was confirmed to him (Gen. 22:16, 17): the quickest road to full assurance is full obedience.

CHAPTER SIXTY-SEVEN

The Faith of Isaac

(Heb. 11:20)

Though Isaac lived the longest of the four great patriarchs, yet less is recorded about him than any of the others: some twelve chapters are devoted to the biography of Abraham, and a similar number each to Jacob and Joseph, but excepting for one or two brief mentionings before and after, the history of Isaac is condensed into two chapters, Gen. 26, 27. Contrasting his character with those of his father, and of his son, we may remark that there is noted less of Abraham's triumphs of faith, and less of Jacob's failures. Taking it on the whole, the life of Isaac is a disappointing one: it begins brightly, but ends amid the shadows — like that of so many, it failed to fulfil its early promise.

The one act in Isaac's life which the Holy Spirit selected for mention in the Scroll of Faith takes us back to Gen. 27, where, as the Puritan Owen well said, "There is none (other story) in the scripture filled with more intricacies and difficulties as unto a right judgment of the things related, though the matter of fact be clearly and distinctly set down. The whole represents unto us Divine sovereignty, wisdom and faithfulness, working effectually through the frailties, infirmities, and sins of all the persons concerned in the matter."

Gen. 27 opens by presenting unto us Isaac in his old age, and declares that "his eyes were dim, so that he could not see" (v. 1). It ought not to need saying that we have there something more than a mere reference to the state of his physical eyes, yet in these days when so many glory in their understanding the Word "literally," God's servants need to dwell upon the most elementary spiritual truths. Everything in Holy Writ has a deeper significance than the "literal," and we are greatly the losers when we limit ourselves to the "letter" of any verse. Let us contrast this statement concerning Isaac's defective vision with what is recorded of another servant of God at the same advanced age: "And Moses was an hundred and twenty years old when he died: *his* eye was not dim" (Deut. 34:7).

Gen. 27 shows us the low state into which a child of God may get. Isaac presents unto us a solemn warning of the evil consequences which follow failure to judge and refuse our natural appetites. If we do not mortify our members which are upon the earth, if we do not abstain from fleshly lusts that war against the soul, then the fine edge of our spiritual life will be blunted, and the fine gold will become dim. If we live to eat, instead of eating to live, our spiritual vision is bound to be defective. Discernment is a by-product, the fruit and result of the denying of self, and following of Christ (John 8:12). It was this self-abnegation which was so conspicuous in Moses: he learned to refuse that which appealed to the flesh — a position of honour as the son of Pharaoh's daughter; that is why *his* "eye was not dim." He saw that the brick-making Hebrews were the people of God, the objects of His sovereign favour, and following his spiritual promptings, threw in his lot with them.

How different was the case with poor Isaac! Instead of keeping his body in subjection, he indulged it. More than a hint of this is given in Gen. 25:28, "And Isaac loved Esau because he did eat of his venison": this brought him under the influence of one who could be of no help to him spiritually, and he loved him because he ministered unto his fleshly appetites. And now in Gen. 27, when he thought that the end of his days was near, and he desired to bestow the patriarchal blessing upon his son, instead of giving himself to fasting and prayer, and then acting in accord with the revealed will of God, we are told that he called for Esau and said, "Now therefore take, I pray thee, thy weapons, thy quiver and thy bow, and go out to the field, and hunt me some venison; and make me some savoury meat, such as I love, and bring it to me, that I may eat; that my soul may bless thee before I die" (Gen. 27:3, 4). This is what furnishes the key to the immediate sequel.

"And the Lord said unto her (viz., Rebekah), Two nations are in thy womb, and two manner of people shall be separated from thy bowels; and the one people shall be stronger than the other people; and the elder shall serve the younger" (Gen. 25:23). This is the scripture which supplies the second key to the whole incident recorded in Gen. 27 and opens for us Heb. 11:20. Here we find God making known the destiny of Jacob and Esau: observe that this revelation was made unto the mother (who had "inquired of the Lord": v. 22), and not to their father. That, later on, Isaac himself became acquainted with its terms, is clear, but as to how far he really apprehended their meaning, is not easy to say.

The word that the Lord had spoken unto her, Rebekah believed; yet she failed to exercise full confidence in Him. When she saw Isaac's marked partiality for Esau, and learned that her husband was about to perform the last religious act of a patriarchal priest and pronounce blessing on his sons, she became fearful. When she heard Isaac bid Esau make him some "savoury meat" — evidently desiring to enkindle or intensify his affections for Esau, so that he might bless him with all his heart — she imagined that the purpose of God was about to be thwarted, and resorted unto measures which ill become a daughter of Jehovah, and which can by no means be justified. We will not dwell upon the deception which she prompted Jacob to adopt, but would point out that it supplies a solemn example of a real faith being resolutely fixed on the Divine promises, but employing irregular ways and wrong means for the obtaining of them.

In what follows we see how Isaac was deceived by Jacob posing as Esau. Though uneasy and suspicious at first, his fears were largely allayed by Jacob's lies: though perceiving the voice was that of the younger son, yet his hands appeared to be those of the elder. Pathetic indeed is it to see the aged patriarch reduced unto the sense of touch in his efforts to identify the one who had now brought him the longed-for venison. It is *this* which should speak loudly to our hearts: he who yields to the lusts of the flesh injures his spiritual instincts, and opens wide the door for the Devil to impose upon him and deceive him with his lies! He who allows natural sentiments and affections to override the requirements of God's revealed will, is reduced to a humiliated state in the end. How often it proves that a man's spiritual foes are they of his own household! Isaac loved Esau unwisely.

But now we must face a difficult question: Did Isaac deliberately pit himself against the known counsel of God? Did he defiantly purpose to bestow upon Esau what he was assured the Lord had appointed for Jacob? "Whatever may be spoken in excuse of Isaac, it is certain he failed greatly in two things. First, in his inordinate love to Esau (whom he could not but know to be a profane person), and that on so slight an account as eating of his venison: Gen. 25:28. Second, in that he had not sufficiently enquired into the mind of God, in the oracle that his wife received concerning their sons. There is not question on the one hand, but that he knew of it; nor on the other, that he did not understand it. For if the holy man had known that it was the determinate will of God, he would not have contradicted it. But this arose from want of diligent enquiry by prayer, into the mind of God" (John Owen)).

We heartily agree with these remarks of the eminent Puritan. While the conduct of Isaac on this occasion was far from becoming a child of God who concluded his earthly pilgrimage was now nearly complete, yet charity forbids us to put the worst possible construction upon his action. While his affection for Esau was misplaced, yet, in the absence of any clear scriptural proof, we are not warranted in thinking that he sinned presumptuously, by deliberately resisting the revealed will of God; rather must we conclude that he had no clear understanding of the Divine oracle given to Rebekah — his spiritual discernment was dim, as well as his physical vision! As to the unworthy part played by Rebekah and Jacob, their efforts are to be regarded not so much as the feverish energies of the flesh, seeking to force the fulfilment of God's promise, but as well-meant but misguided intentions to *prevent* the thwarting of God's purpose. Their fears remind us of Uzzah's in 2 Sam. 6:6.

The one bright spot in the sombre picture which the Holy Spirit has so faithfully painted for us in Gen. 27, found in v. 33. Right after Isaac had pronounced the major blessing on Jacob, Esau entered the tent, bringing with him the savoury meat which he had prepared for his father. Isaac now realized the deception which had been played upon him, and we are told that he "trembled very exceedingly." Was he shaking with rage at Jacob's treachery? No indeed. Was he, as one commentator has suggested, fearful that he might suffer injury at the hands of the hot-headed Esau? No, his next words explode such a theory. Rather was it he now realized that he had been out of harmony with the Divine will, and that God had providentially intervened to effect His own counsels. He was awed to the very depths of his soul.

Blessed indeed is it to behold how the spirit triumphed over the flesh. Instead of bursting out with an angry curse upon the head of Jacob, Isaac said, "I have blessed him, yea, and he *shall be* blessed." That was the language of faith overcoming his natural partiality for Esau. It was the recognizing and acknowledging of the immutability and invincibility of the Divine decrees. He realized that God is in one mind, and none can turn Him: that though there are many devices in a man's heart, nevertheless the counsel of the Lord that shall stand (Prov. 19:21). Nor could the tears of Esau move the patriarch. Now that the entrance of God's words had given him light, now that the over-ruling hand of God had secured His own appointment, Isaac was firm as a rock. The righteous may fall, but they cannot be utterly cast down.

"By faith Isaac blessed Jacob and Esau concerning things to come" (Heb. 11:20). Jacob, the younger, had the precedency and principal blessing. Strikingly did this exemplify the high sovereignty of God. To take the younger, and leave the elder to perish in their ways, is a course the Lord has often followed, from the beginning of the world. Abel, the junior, was preferred before Cain. Shem was given the precedency over Japheth the elder (Gen. 10:21). Afterwards, Abraham, the younger, was taken to be God's favourite. Of

Abraham's two sons, the older one, Ishmael, was passed by, and in Isaac was the Seed called. Later, David, who was the youngest of Jesse's eight sons, was selected to be the man after God's own heart. And God still writes, as with a sunbeam in the course of His providence, that He will have mercy on whom He will have mercy.

The "blessing" which Isaac pronounced upon Jacob was vastly superior to the portion allotted Esau, though if we look no deeper than the letter of the words which their father used, there appears to be very little difference between them. Unto Jacob Isaac said, "God give thee of the dew of heaven, and the fatness of the earth; and plenty of corn and wine" (Gen. 27:28); what follows in v. 29 chiefly concerned his posterity. Unto Esau Isaac said, "Behold, thy dwelling shall be the fatness of the earth, and of the dew of heaven from above: and by thy sword shalt thou live, and shalt serve thy brother" (Gen. 27:39, 40). Apart from the younger son having the pre-eminence over the elder, wherein lay the peculiar excellence of his portion? If there had been nothing *spiritual* in the promise, it would have been no comfort to Jacob at all, for the temporal things mentioned were not his portion: as he acknowledged to Pharaoh, "few and evil have the days of the years of my life been" (Gen. 47:9).

What has just been before us supplies a notable example of how the O. T. promises and prophecies are to be interpreted; not carnally, but mystically. That Jacob's portion far excelled Esau's is clear from Heb. 12:17, where it is denominated, "*the* blessing." What that is was made clearer when Isaac *repeated* his benediction upon Jacob, saying, "And give the blessing of Abraham to thee and to thy seed" (Gen. 28:4). Here is the key which we need to unlock its meaning; as Gal. 3:9, 14, 29 clearly enough shows, the "blessing of Abraham" (into which elect Gentiles enter, through Christ) is purely a spiritual thing. Further proof that the same spiritual blessing which God promised to Abraham was also made over by Isaac to Jacob, is found in his words, "I have blessed him, and yea, and he shall be blessed" (Gen. 27:33), for Jehovah had employed the same language when blessing the father of all believers: "in blessing I will bless thee" (Gen. 22:17). To this may be added Isaac's "Cursed be every one that curseth thee, and blessed be he that blesseth thee" (Gen. 27:29), being part of the very words God used to Abraham, see Gen. 12:2, 3.

Now in seeking to rightly understand the language of Isaac's prophecy, it must be recognized that (oftentimes) in the O. T. heavenly things were referred to in earthly terms, that spiritual blessings were set forth under the figure of material things. Due attention to this fact will render luminous many a passage. Such is the case here: under the emblems of the "dew of heaven and the fatness of the earth," three great spiritual blessings were intended. First, that he was to have a real relation to Christ, that he should be one of the progenitors of the Messiah—this was the chief favour and dignity bestowed upon "Abraham." It is in the light of this that we are to understand Gen. 27:29 as ultimately referring: "let the people serve thee, and nations bow down to thee," that is, to the top branch which should proceed from him — unto Christ, unto whom all men are commanded to render allegiance (Psa. 2:10-12).

Second, the next great blessing of "Abraham" was that he should be the priest that should continue the worship of God and teach the laws of God (Gen. 26:5). The bowing down of his brethren to Jacob (Gen. 27:29), was the owning of his priestly dignity. Herein also lay Jacob's blessing: to be in the church, and to have the church continued in his line. This was symbolically pointed to in "that thou mayest inherit the land" (Gen. 28:4). "The church is the ark of Noah, which is only preserved in the midst of floods and deep waters. The church is the land of Goshen, which only enjoys the benefits of light, when there is nothing but darkness round about elsewhere. It is the fleece of Gideon, being wet with the dews of heaven, moistened with the influences of grace, when all the ground round about is dry" (T. Manton). As to how high is the honour of having the church continued in our line, the Spirit intimates in Gen. 10:21—Eber being the father of the Hebrews, who worshipped God.

Third, another privilege of Jacob above Esau was this, that he was taken into covenant with God: "the blessing of Abraham shall come upon thee." And what was that? This, "I will be *thy God,* and the God of thy seed" (Gen. 17:7). This is the greatest happiness of any people, to have God for *their* God — to be in covenant with Him. Thus when Noah came to pronounce blessings and curses on his children, by the spirit of prophecy, he said, "Blessed be the Lord God of Shem" (Gen. 9:26). Afterward the same promise was made unto all Israel: "I am the Lord thy God, which have brought thee out of the land of Egypt, out of the house of bondage" (Ex 20:2). So under the new covenant (the present administration of the everlasting covenant), he says, "I will be to them a God, and they shall be to Me a people" (Heb. 8:10). To be a "God" to any, is to supply them with all good things, necessary for temporal or spiritual life.

The fulfilment of Isaac's prophetic blessing upon his sons was mainly in their descendants, rather than in their own persons: Jacob's spiritual children, Esau's natural. Concerning the latter, we would note two details. First, Isaac said to him "thou shalt serve thy brother"; second, "and it shall come to pass when thou shalt have the dominion, that thou shalt break his yoke from off thy neck" (Gen. 27:40). For long centuries there seemed no likelihood of the first part of this prediction being fulfilled, but eight hundred years later, David said, "over Edom will I cast out my shoe" (Psa. 60:8), which meant, he would bring the haughty descendants of Esau into a low and base state of subjection to him; which was duly acomplished—"all they of Edom become David's *servants*" (2 Sam. 8:14)! Though their subjugation continued for a lengthy period, yet, in the days of Jehoshaphat, we read, "In his days Edom revolted from under the hand of Judah, and made a king over themselves" (2 Kings 8:20)!

"By faith Isaac blessed Jacob and Esau concerning things to come." This "blessing" was more than a dying father expressing good-will unto his sons: it was extraordinary: Isaac spoke as a prophet to God, announcing the future of his posterity, and the varied portions each should receive. As the mouthpiece of Jehovah, he did, by the spirit of prophecy, announce beforehand what should be the particular estate of each of his two sons; and so his words have been fulfilled. Though parents today are not thus supernaturally endowed to foretell the future of their children, nevertheless, it is their duty and privilege to search the Scriptures and ascertain what promises God has left to the righteous *and to their seed,* and plead them before Him.

But seeing Isaac thus spake by the immediate impulse of the Spirit, how can it be said that "by faith" he blessed his sons? This brings in the human side, and shows how he discharged his responsibility. He gathered together and rested upon the promises which God had made to him, both directly, and through Abraham and Rebekah. The principal ones we have already considered. He had been present when the Lord said unto his father what is found in Gen. 22:16-18, and he had himself been made the recipient of the Divine promises recorded in Gen. 26:2-4. And now, many years later, we find his heart resting upon what he had heard from God, firmly embracing His promises, and with unshaken confidence announcing the future estates of his distant posterity.

That Isaac blessed Jacob and Esau "concerning things to come," gives us a striking example of what is said in the opening verse of our chapter. "Now faith is the substance of things hoped for, the evidence of things not seen." "Abraham was now dead, and Isaac was expecting soon to be buried in the grave he had purchased in the Land given to him and his seed. There was nothing to be seen for faith to rest on; nothing that gave the smallest ground for hope; nothing to make it even probable (apart from what he had heard and believed) that his descendants, either Jacob or Esau, would ever possess the land which had been promised to them" (E. W. B.) There was no human probability at the time Isaac spake which could have been the basis of his calculations: all that he said issued from implicit faith in the bare Word of God.

This is the great practical lesson for us to learn here: the strength of Isaac's faith should stir us up to cry unto God for an increased measure thereof. With most precious confidence Isaac disposed of Canaan as if he already had the peaceable possession of it. Yet, in fact, he owned not an acre of that Land, and had no human right to anything there save a burying-place. Moreover, at the time he prophesied there was a famine in Canaan, and he was an exile in Gerah. "Let people serve thee, and let nations bow down to thee" (Gen. 27:29), would, to one that viewed only the outward case of Isaac, seem like empty words. Ah, my brethren, we too ought to be as certain of the blessings to come, which God has promised, as if they were present, even though we see no apparent likelihood of them.

It may be objected against what has been said above, that, from the account which is supplied in Gen. 27, Isaac "blessed" Jacob in ignorance rather than "by faith." To this it may be replied, first, the object of faith is always God Himself, and the ground on which it rests is His revealed will. So in Isaac's case, his faith was fixed upon the covenant God and was exercised upon His sure Word, and this was by no means negatived by his mistaking Jacob for Esau. Second, it illustrates the fact that the faith of God's people is usually accompanied by some infirmity: in Isaac's case, his partiality for Esau. Third, after he discovered the deception which had been played upon him, he made no effort to recall the blessing pronounced upon the disguised Jacob — sweetly acquiescing unto the Divine Sovereignty — but confirming it; and though with tears Esau sought to change his mind, he could not.

Here too we behold the strength of Isaac's faith: as soon as he perceived the providential hand of God crossing his natural affections, instead of murmuring and rebelling, he yielded and submitted to the Lord. This is ever the work of true faith: it makes the soul yield to God's will against our fleshly inclinations, as also against the bent of our own reason. Faith knows that God is so great, so powerful, so glorious, that His commands must be obeyed. As it was with Abraham, so in the case of Isaac: faith viewed the precepts as well as the promise; it moves us to tread the path of obedience. May our faith be more and more evidenced by walking in those good works which God hath before ordained that we should walk in them.

CHAPTER SIXTY-EIGHT

The Faith of Jacob

(Heb. 11:21)

It has been well said that "Though the grace of faith is of universal use throughout our whole lives, yet it is especially so when we come to die. Faith has its great work to do at the last, to help believers to finish well, to die to the Lord, so as to honour Him, by patience, hope, and joy, so as to leave a witness behind them of the truth of God's Word and the excellency of His ways, for the conviction and establishment of all that attend them in their dying moments" (Matt. Henry). God is greatly glorified when His people leave this world with their flag flying at full mast: when the spirit triumphs over the flesh, when the world is consciously and gladly left behind for Heaven. For this *faith* must be in exercise.

It is not without good reason, we may be sure, that in the description which the Holy Spirit has given us of the life of faith in Heb. 11, He has furnished us with no less than three examples—and these in successive verses—of the actings of faith in the final crisis and conflict. We believe that, among other reasons, God would hereby assure His trembling and doubting children, that He who has begun a good work in them, will most certainly sustain and complete the same; that He who has in His sovereignty committed this precious grace to their hearts, will not suffer it to languish when its support is most sorely needed; that He who has enabled His people to exercise faith during the vigour of life, will not withdraw His quickening power during the weakness of death.

As the writer grows older, he is saddened by discovering how very little is now being given out, either orally or in written ministry, for the instruction and comfort of God's people concerning the dying of Christians. The devil is not inactive in seeking to strike terror into the hearts of God's people, and knowing this, it is the bounden duty of Christ's servants to expose the groundlessness and hollowness of Satan's lies. Not a few have been deterred from so doing by heeding the mistaken notion that, for a Christian to think of and prepare for death is dishonouring to Christ, and inconsistent with the "imminency" of His coming. But such a notion is refuted in our present passage. Let it be carefully considered that, when in

Heb. 12:1 the Holy Spirit bids *us* "run with patience the race that is set before us," He bases that exhortation on the fact that we are "compassed about with so great a cloud of witnesses," the reference being unto the men of God who are before in Heb. 11, who all *"died in faith"* (v. 13).

A God-given and a God-sustained faith is not only sufficient to enable the feeblest saint to overcome the solicitations of the flesh, the attractions of the world, and the temptations of Satan, but it is also able to give him a triumphant passage through death. This is one of the prominent things set forth in this wondrous and blessed chapter. In Heb. 11 the Holy Spirit has set out at length the works, the achievements, the fruits, the glories, of faith, and not the least of them is its power to support the soul, comfort the heart, illumine the understanding, and direct the will, in the last earthly struggle. While Heb. 11:20, 21 and 22 have this in common, yet each contributes its own distinctive feature. In the case of Isaac, we see a dying faith triumphing over the affections of the flesh; in the case of Jacob, dying faith overcoming the interference of man; and in Joseph, scorning the worthless pageantry of the world.

Of old Balaam said, "Let me die the death of the righteous, and let my last end be like his" (Num. 23:10): well might he wish to do so. The writer has not a shadow of doubt that every Christian who has, in the main current of his life, walked with God, his last hours on earth (normally speaking, for we consider not here the exceptional cases of those taken Home suddenly) are the brightest and most blissful of all. Prov. 4:18, of itself, it fully sufficient to warrant this thought. The Christian is not always permitted to bear testimony of this so as to be intelligent unto those surrounding him, but even though his poor body be convulsed with pain, and physical unconsciousness set in, yet the soul cutting adrift from its earthly moorings, is then blest with a sight and sense of his precious Redeemer such as he never had before (Acts 7:55).

"Mark the perfect man, and behold the upright; for the end of that man is peace" (Psa. 37:37). A peaceful death has concluded the troublous life of many a good man. As the late C. H. Spurgeon said on this verse, "With believers it may rain in the morning, thunder at midday, and pour torrents in the afternoon, but it must clear up ere the sun go down." Most aptly do his words apply to the case of Jacob. A stormy passage indeed was his, but the waters were smooth as he entered the port. Cloudy and dark were many of the hours of his life, but the sunset bathed it with radiant splendour at its close.

"By faith Jacob when he was a dying" (Heb. 11:21). Ah, but to "die" by faith, we must needs live by faith. And a life of faith is not like the shining of the sun on a calm and clear day, its rays meeting with no resistance from the atmosphere; rather is it more like the sun rising upon a foggy morning, its rays struggling to pierce through and dispel the opposing mists. Jacob walked by faith, but the exercise thereof encountered many a struggle, and had to fight hard for each victory. In spite of all his faults and failings (and each of us is just as full of the same), Jacob dearly prized his interest in the everlasting covenant, trusted in God, and highly esteemed His promises. It is a very faulty and one-sided estimate of his character which fails to take these things into account. The old nature was strong within him; yes, and so too was the new.

Though his infirmities led Jacob to employ unlawful means for the procuring of it, yet his heart *valued* the "birthright," which profane Esau despised (Gen. 25). Though he yielded unto the foolish suggestions of his mother to deceive Isaac, yet his faith covetly eyed the promises of God. Though there may have been a measure of fleshly bargaining in his vow, yet Jacob was anxious for the Lord to be his God (Gen. 28:21). Though he stole away from Laban in fear, when his father-in-law overtook him, he glorified God in the tribute he paid Him (Gen. 31:53). Though he was terrified at Esau, nevertheless he sought unto the Lord, pleaded His promises (Gen.32:12), and obtained an answer of peace. Though later he grovelled at the feet of his brother, in the sequel we find him prevailing with God (Gen. 32:28). Equally with Abraham and Isaac, "by faith he sojourned in the land of promise, as in a strange country, dwelling in tents" (Heb. 11:9).

But it was during the closing days of his life that Jacob's faith shone most brightly. When giving permission for Benjamin to accompany his other sons on their second trip to Egypt, he said "God Almighty (or "God the Sufficient One") give you mercy before the man" (Gen. 43:14). This was the title under which the Lord had blessed Abraham (Gen. 17:1), as it was also the one Isaac employed when he blessed Jacob (Gen. 28:3): thus in using it here, we see how Jacob rested on the covenant promise. Arriving in Egypt, the aged patriarch was presented unto its mighty monarch. Blessed is it to see how he conducted himself: instead of cringing before the ruler of the greatest empire of the old world, we are told that "Jacob blessed Pharaoh" (Gen. 47:7); with becoming dignity he conducted himself as a child of the King of kings (Heb. 7:7), and carried himself as became an ambassador of the Most High.

"By faith Jacob when he was a dying, blessed both the sons of Joseph." This takes us back to what is recorded in Gen. 48. What is found there is quite distinct from what is said in the next chapter, where Jacob is seen as God's prophet announcing the future of all his twelve sons. But here he is concerned only with Joseph and his two sons. Before considering the particular detail which our text treats of, let us note the sentence which immediately precedes it. "And he blessed Joseph" (48:15): in this we may admire the overruling hand of God, and also find here the key to what follows.

In Deut. 21:17 we read, "But he shall acknowledge the son of the hated for the first-born, by giving him a double portion of all that he hath: for he is the beginning of his strength; the right of the firstborn is his." It was the right of the firstborn to have a double portion, and this is exactly what we find Jacob bestowing upon Joseph, for both Ephraim and Manasseh were allotted a distinct tribal part and place in the promised inheritance. This, by right, belonged unto Joseph, though the Devil had tried to cheat him out of it, using Laban to deceive Jacob by substituting Leah in Rebekah's place, and Joseph was *her* firstborn; and now by the providence of God the primogeniture is restored to him. So too God permitted Reuben to sin so that the way might be open for this: "Now the sons of Reuben, the firstborn of Israel, (for he was the firstborn) but, forasmuch as he defiled his father's bed, his birthright was given unto the sons of Joseph" (1 Chron. 5:1).

Earlier in this interview, Jacob had said, "And now thy two sons, Ephraim and Manasseh, which were born unto thee in the land of Egypt, before I came unto thee into Egypt, *are mine*" (Gen. 48:5). Those two sons of Joseph had been borne to him by an Egyptian wife, and in a foreign land, but now they were to be adopted and incorporated into the body of the holy seed. For note, when Jacob blessed them he said, "The Angel which redeemed me from all evil, bless the lads; and let my name be named on them, and the name of my fathers, Abraham and Isaac" (v. 16). By that blessing he sought to draw their hearts away from Egypt and their kinsfolk there, that they might be annexed to the church and share with the people of God.

"By faith Jacob when he was a dying, blessed both the sons of Joseph." In this case the R. V. is more accurate: "blessed *each* of the sons of Joseph," for their blessing was not collective, but a distinctive and discriminating one. In fact the leading feature of the dying Jacob's faith is most particularly to be seen at this very point. When Joseph brought his two sons before their grandfather to receive his patriarchal blessing, he placed Manasseh the elder, to his right hand, and Ephraim the younger to his left. His object in this was that Manasseh might receive the first and superior portion. Right there it was that the faith of Jacob was most tested. At this time Joseph was governor over all Egypt, and second only to Pharaoh himself in authority and power; moreover he was Jacob's favorite son, yet the dying patriarch had now to withstand him.

"And Israel stretched out his right hand, and laid it upon Ephraim's head, who was the younger, and his left hand upon Manasseh's head, guiding his hands wittingly; for Manasseh was the firstborn" (Gen. 48:14). Herein we behold *the manner* in which the blessing was bestowed. Once more the younger, by the appointment of God, was perferred before the elder, for the Lord distributes His favours as He pleases, saying "Is it not lawful for Me to do what I will with Mine own?" (Matt. 20:15). Unto the high sovereignty of God Jacob here submissively bowed. It was not a thing of chance that he crossed his hands, for the Hebrew of "guiding his hands wittingly" is "made his hands to understand." It was the understanding of faith, for his physical eyes were too dim to see what he was doing—true faith is ever opposed to sight! Note how the Holy Spirit emphasizes the fact that it was "Isaac" (and not "Jacob") who did this.

"And he blessed Joseph, and said, God, before whom my fathers Abraham and Isaac did walk" (Gen. 48:15). Very blessed is this. Despite his physical decay, there was no abatement of his spiritual strength: notwithstanding the weakness of old age, he abode firm in faith and in the vigorous exercise of it. Here in the verse before us, we behold Jacob recognizing and asserting the covenant which Jehovah had made with his fathers. This is the very life of faith: to lay hold of, draw strength from, and walk in the light of the everlasting covenant, for it is the foundation of all our blessings, the charter of our inheritance, the guaranty of our eternal glory and bliss. He who keeps it in view will have a happy deathbed, a peaceful end, (and a God-honouring exit from this world of sin and suffering.

"The God which fed me all my life long unto this day" (Gen. 48:15). As Jacob had made a solemn acknowledgment of the spiritual blessing which he had received by virtue of the everlasting covenant, so he also owned the temporal mercies of which he had been the favoured recipient. "It was a work of faith to retain a precious thankful remembrance of Divine providence in a constant provision of all needful temporal supplies, from first to last, during the whole course of his life" (John Owen). As it is an act of faith to cordially consent unto the dealings of God with us in a providential way, so it is a fruit of faith to make a confession by the mouth concerning Him. Note: God is honoured before those attending Him when a dying saint bears testimony unto His faithfulness in having supplied all his need.

"The Angel which redeemed me from all evil, bless the lads" (Gen. 48:16). "He reflects on all the hazards, trials and evils that befell him, and the exercise of his faith in them all. Now all his dangers were past, all his evils conquered, all his fears removed, he retains by faith a sense of the goodness and kindness of God in rescuing him out of them all" (J. Owen). "Thou shalt remember all the way which the Lord thy God led thee" (Deut. 8:2): as the children of Israel were called upon to do this at the close of their wilderness journey, so we cannot be more profitably employed in the closing hours of our earthly pilgrimage than by recalling and reviewing that grace which delivered us from so many dangers known and unknown.

"And let my name be named on them, and the name of my fathers Abraham and Isaac; and let them grow into a multitude in the midst of the earth" (Gen. 48:16). Jacob was not ambitious for a continuance of their present greatness in Egypt, but desired for them the blessings of the covenant. Joseph could have left to his sons a rich patrimony in Egypt, but he brought them to Jacob to receive his benediction. Ah, the baubles of this world are nothing in comparison with the blessings of Zion: see Psa. 128:5; 134:3; 133:3. The spiritual blessings of the Redeemer far exceed in value the temporal mercies of the Creator: it was the former which Joseph coveted for his sons, and which Jacob now prophetically bestowed.

"And when Joseph saw that his father laid his right hand upon the head of Ephraim, it displeased him; and he held up his father's hand to remove it from Ephraim's head unto Manasseh's head. And Joseph said unto his father, not so, my father; for this is the firstborn; put thy right hand upon *his* head" (Gen. 48:17, 18). Here we see the will of man asserting itself, which, when left to itself, is ever opposed to God. Joseph had *his* wishes concerning the matter, and did not hesitate to express them; though, be it noted unto his credit, he meekly acquiesced at the finish.

"And his father refused, and said, I know it, my son, I know it" (Gen. 48:19). It was at *this* point that Jacob's faith shone most brightly; the repeated "I *know* it" marks the great strength of his faith. He had "heard" from God (Rom. 10:17), he believed God, he submitted to God. Jacob was no more to be influenced by "the will of man" here, than in the preceding verse Isaac was by "the will of the flesh"; faith overcame both. Learn, my reader, that sometimes faith has to cross the wish and will of a loved one!

Plainly it was "by faith" that the dying Israel blessed each of the sons of Joseph. Certainly it was not by sight. "To 'sight' what could be more unlikely than that these two young Egyptian princes, for such they were, should ever forsake Egypt, the land of their birth, and migrate into Canaan? What more improbable than that they should 'each' become a separate tribe? What more unlooked for, than that, of these two, the younger should be exalted above the elder, both in importance and number?" (E. W. B.)

"He also shall become a people, and he also shall be great; but truly his younger brother shall be greater than he, and his seed shall become a multitude of nations" (Gen. 48:19). Not only does God make a great difference between the elect and the reprobate, but He does not deal alike with His own children, neither in temporals nor spirituals. There are some of His favoured people to whom God manifests Himself more familiarly, grants them more liberal supplies of His grace, and more plentiful comforts — there was a specially favoured three among the twelve apostles. Some Christians have more opportunities to glorify God than others, higher privileges of service, greater abilities and gifts — the "talents" were not distributed equally: one had five, another three, another one. But let us not murmur: all have more than they can improve.

"And worshipped, leaning upon the top of his staff" (Heb. 11:21). There is some room for question as to what incident the apostle is here referring to. Some think that (like Moses did "exceeding fear and quake": Heb. 12:21) it is entirely a N. T. revelation; others (the writer included) regard it as alluding to what is recorded in Gen. 47:31. The only difficulty in connection with this view is, that here we read Jacob "worshipped upon the top of his staff," there that "he bowed himself upon the bed's head." Concerning this variation we agree with Owen that "he did *both,* namely, bow towards the head of the bed, and at the same time lean on his staff, as we are assured by comparing the Divine writers together."

The occasion of Jacob's "worship" was as follows: "And the time drew nigh that Israel must die: And he called his son Joseph, and said unto him, If now I have found grace in thy sight, put, I pray thee, thy hand under my thigh, and deal kindly and truly with me; bury me not, I pray thee, in Egypt: But I will lie with my fathers, and thou shalt carry me out of Egypt, and bury me in their buryingplace. And he said, I will do as thou hast said" (Gen. 47:29, 30). It was far more than a sentimental whim which moved the patriarch to desire that his body be interred in the holy land: it was the working of faith, a blessed exhibition of his confidence in God.

It was not the pomp and pageantry of his burial which concerned Jacob, but *the place* of it which he was so solicitous about. Not in Egypt among idolators, must his bones be laid to rest, for with them he cared not to have any fellowship in life; and now he desired no proximity unto them in death — he would show that God's people are a *separated* people. No, it was in the buryingplace of his fathers he wished to be laid. First, to show forth his union with Abraham and Isaac in the covenant. Second, to express his faith in the promises of God, which concerned Canaan, and not Egypt. Third, to draw off the minds of his descendants from a continuance in Egypt: setting before them an example that *they* should think of returning to the promised land at the proper time, and thereby confirming them in the belief of possessing it. Fourth, to signify he would go before them, and, as it were, take possession of the land on their behalf. Fifth, to intimate that Canaan was a type of Heaven, the "Better Country" (Heb. 11:16), the eternal Resting-place of all the people of God.

The asking of Joseph to place his hand under his thigh, was a gesture in swearing (Gen. 24:2, 3), as the raising of the hand now is with us. It was not that Jacob doubted his son's veracity, but it signified the eagerness of his entreaty, and the intensity of his mind about the matter: what an important thing it was to him. No doubt it was also designed to forestall any objection which Pharaoh might make after his death: see Gen. 50:5, 6. Jacob was in bed at the time, but gathering together his little remaining strength, he raised himself to sit upright, and then bowing his body, and so that it might be supported, he leaned upon his staff, worshipping God.

The Holy Spirit's mention here of Jacob's reverent gesture in worshipping God, intimates to us that it well becomes a worshipper of the Most High to manifest the inward devotion of the soul by a fitting posture of the body. God has redeemed both, and He is to be honoured by both: 1 Cor. 6:20. Shall we serve God with that which costs us nothing? Sitting or lying at prayer savours more of sloth and carelessness, than of reverence and zeal. Carnal men, in pursuit of their fleshly lusts, can weary and waste the body; shall Christians shelter behind every inconvenience and excuse? Christ exposed His body to the utmost suffering, shall not His love constrain us to deny selfish ease and sloth!

Having secured the promise from Joseph that his will should be carried out, Jacob bowed before God in worship, for now he realized the Lord was making good the promise recorded in Gen. 46:4. In his great weakness he had bowed toward his bed's head so as to adore God, completing now his representation of reverence and faith by leaning upon the top of his staff. In that emblematic action he signified his complete dependence upon God, testified to his condition as a pilgrim in the earth, and emphasized his weariness of the world and his readiness to part from it. He praised God for all He had done for him, and for the approaching prospect of everlasting bliss. Blessed is it to find that the Holy Spirit's final word about Jacob in Scripture (Heb. 11:21) depicts him in the act of ***worship!***

CHAPTER SIXTY-NINE

The Faith of Joseph

(Heb. 11:22)

At the early age of seventeen Joseph was carried away into a foreign country, into a heathen land. There he remained for many years surrounded by idolaters, and during all that time he, probably, never came into contact with a single child of God. Moreover, in those days there was no Bible to read, for none of God's Word had then been committed to writing. Yet amid all sorts of temptations and trials, he remained true unto the Lord. Thirteen years in prison did not embitter him; being made lord over Egypt did not spoil him; evil examples all around, did not corrupt him. O the mighty power of Divine grace to *preserve* its favoured objects. But let the reader carefully bear in mind that, in his earliest years, Joseph had received a godly training! O how this ought to encourage Christian parents: do your part in faithfully teaching the children, and with God's blessing, it will abide with them, even though they move into a foreign land.

It may strike some of our readers that the apostle made a strange selection here from the remarkable history of Joseph. No reference is given unto his faithfulness to God in declaring what He had made known to him (Gen. 37:5), his chastity (Gen. 39:10), his patience under affliction (Psa. 105:18, 19), his wisdom and prudence (Gen. 39:22; 47:14), his fear of God (Gen. 42:18); his compassion (Gen. 42:24), his overcoming evil with good (Gen. 45:10), his reverence to his father, and that when he was advanced unto outward dignity above him (Gen. 48:12), his obedience to his father (Gen. 47:31); instead, the whole of his memorable life is passed over, and we are introduced to the final scene. But this seeming difficulty is at once removed if we bear in mind the Spirit's scope in this chapter, namely, to encourage the fearful and wavering Hebrews, by bringing before them striking examples of the efficacy and sufficiency of faith to carry its favoured possessor safely through every difficulty, and utimately conduct him into the promised inheritance.

Not only was there a particular reason in the case of those who first received this Epistle, why the Holy Spirit should conduct them unto the expiring moments of Joseph, but there is also a wider purpose why (in this description of the whole Life of Faith) He should do so. Faith is a grace which honours God and stands its possessor in good stead, in death as well as life. The worldling may appear to prosper, and his journey through life seem to be smooth and easy, but how does he fare in the supreme crisis? what support is there for his heart when God calls him to pass out of time into eternity? "For what is the hope of the hypocrite, though he hath gained, when God taketh away his soul?" Ignorance may exclude terror, and sottishness may still the conscience; but there can be no true peace, no firm confidence, no triumphant joy for those out of Christ. Only he can die worshipping and glorifying God for His promises who possesses genuine faith.

If the kind providence of God preserves his faculties unto the end, a Christian ought not to be passive in death, and die like a beast. No, this is the last time he can do any thing for God on earth, and therefore he should take a fresh and firm hold of His everlasting covenant, "ordered in all things and sure," going over in his mind the amazing grace of the Triune God toward him; the Father, in having from the beginning, chosen him unto salvation; the Son for having obeyed, suffered and died in his room and stead; the Holy Spirit for having sought him out when dead in sins, quickened him into newness of life, shed abroad the love of God in his heart, and put a new song in his mouth. He should review the faithfulness and goodness of God toward him all through his pilgrimage. He should rest on the promises, and view the glorious future awaiting him. Thereby, praise and thanksgiving will fill his soul and mouth, and God will be greatly honoured before the onlookers.

When faith is active during the dying hours of a saint, not only is his own heart spiritually upheld and comforted, but God is honoured and others are confirmed. A carnal man cannot speak well of the world when he comes to pass through the dark valley; no, he dares not commend his wordly life to others. But a godly man can speak well of God, and commend His covenant to others. So it was with Jacob (Gen. 48:15, 16). So it was with Joshua: "Behold, this day I am going the way of all the earth: and ye know in all your hearts and in all your souls, that not one thing hath failed of all the good things which the Lord your God spake concerning you; all are come to pass unto you, and not one thing hath failed thereof" (Josh. 23:14).

So was it also with Joseph. He could have left to his sons nobility of blood, a rich patrimony in Egypt, but he brought them to his father to receive *his* blessing (Gen. 48:12). And what was that? To invest them with the right of entering into the visible privileges of the covenant. Ah, to Joseph, the riches of Egypt were nothing in comparison with the blessings of Zion. And so again now: when his hours on earth were numbered, Joseph thinks not of the temporal position of honour which he had occupied so long, but was engaged only with the things of God and the promised inheritance. See here the power of a godly example: Joseph had witnessed the last acts of his father, and now he follows in his steps. The good examples of superiors and seniors are of great force unto those who look up to them—how careful they should be, then, of their conduct! Let us seek to emulate that which is praiseworthy in our betters: Phil. 3:17; Heb. 13:7.

"By faith Joseph, when he died, made mention of the departing of the children of Israel; and gave commandment concerning his bones" (v. 22). First, let us observe *the time* when Joseph's faith was here exercised. It was during his closing hours upon earth. Most of his long life had been spent in Egypt, and during its later stages, had been elevated unto a dizzy height; for as Acts 7:10 tells us, he was made "governor" or lord over Egypt, and over all Pharaoh's house. But neither the honours nor the luxuries which Joseph received while in the land of exile, made that holy man forget the promises of God, nor bound his soul to the earth. His mind was engaged in higher things than the perishing baubles of this world. Learn them, my reader, it is only as our hearts ascend to heaven that we are able to look down with contempt upon that which this world prizes so much.

From the case of Joseph we may see that earthly honour and wealth do not *in themselves* injure: where there is a gracious heart to manage them, they can be employed with advantage and used to God's glory. Many examples may be cited in proof of this. God has ever had a few of His saints even in Caesar's "household" (Phil. 4:22). Material things are God's gifts, and so must be improved unto His praise. There is as much faith, yea more, in moderating the affections under a full estate, as there is in depending upon God for supplies when we have nothing. Nevertheless, to learn "*how* to abound" (Phil. 4:12) is a hard lesson. To keep the mind stayed upon God and the heart from settling down here, calls for much exercise of soul; therefore are we exhorted "if riches increase, set not your hearts upon them" (Psa. 62:10)—but be thankful for them, and seek to use them unto God's honour.

No, the poor do not have such temptations to overcome as do the rich. The poor are driven to depend upon God: they have no other alternative save abject despair. But there is more choice to those who have plenty: *their* great danger is to lose sight of the Giver and become immersed in His gifts. Not so with Joseph: to him Egypt was nothing in comparison with Canaan. Then let us seek grace to be of his spirit: true greatness of mind is to count the highest things of earth as nothing when weighed against the things of Heaven. It is a great mercy when the affluence of temporal things does not take the heart off the promises, but for this there has to be a constant crying unto Him to quicken our spiritual sensibilities, keep us in close communication with Himself, wean us from things below.

But neither the riches nor the honours of Egypt could secure Joseph from death, nor did they make him unmindful or afraid of it. The time had arrived when he saw that his end was at hand, and he met it with a confident spirit. And thus it should be with us. But in order to do this we must be all our lifetime preparing for *that* hour. Reader, there can be no dissembling then. Allow me to ask: Is your soul truly yielded up to God? Do you hold this world with a light hand? Are God's promises your daily food? Life is held by a very uncertain tenure. Unless the Lord returns first, death will be the last great enemy with which you have to contend, and you will need to have on all your armour. If you have not on the breastplate of righteousness and the helmet of salvation, what will you do in the swellings of Jordan, when Satan is often permitted to make his fiercest attack?

"By faith Joseph, when he died, made mention of the departing of the children of Israel." Let us consider next *the strength* of his faith. It will be noted by the careful reader that the margin gives an alternative rendering, namely, "By faith Joseph, when he died, *remembered* the departing of the children of Israel": the Greek will allow of either translation, and personally we believe that the *fulness* of the Spirit's words requires that both meanings be kept before us. That which is in view here is very striking and blessed. The word "remembered" shows that Joseph's mind was now engaged with the promise which the Lord had made to Abraham, recorded in Gen. 15:14-16. The alternative translation "he *made mention of* the departing of the children of Israel," signifies that Joseph testifies his own faith and hope in the sure words of the living God.

At the end of Joseph's long and memorable career his thoughts were occupied not so much with what God had wrought for him, but with what He had promised unto His people: in other words, he was dwelling not upon the past, but with that which was yet future. In his heart were the "things hoped for" (Heb. 11:1)! More than two hundred years had passed since Jehovah had spoken what is recorded in Gen. 15. Part of the prediction which He there made, had been fulfilled; but to carnal reason there seemed very little prospect that the remainder of it would come to pass. First, God had announced that the seed of Abraham should be "a stranger in the land that is not theirs" (Gen. 15:13), which had been confirmed when Jacob carried all his household down into Egypt. Second, God had declared the descendants of Abraham should "serve" the Egyptians and "they shall afflict them four hundred years" (15:13): but to outward sight, *that* now appeared most unlikely. The posterity of the patriarchs had been given favour in Pharaoh's eyes (Gen. 45:16-18), the "best" of the land was set apart for their use (Gen. 47:6), there they "multiplied exceedingly (Gen. 47:27), and so great was the respect of the Egyptians that they "mourned" for Jacob seventy days (Gen. 50:3). Joseph himself was their great benefactor and deliverer from the famine: why, then, should his descendants be hated and oppressed by them? Ah, faith does not reason, but *believes*.

Third, God had declared that He would judge the Egyptians for their afflicting of His people (15:14), which was fulfilled in the awful plagues recorded in the early chapters of Exodus. Finally, God had promised "and afterward shall they come out with great substance . . . in the fourth generation they shall come hither (into Canaan) again" (15:14, 16). It was unto this that the heart of Joseph was now looking forward, and nothing but *real* spiritual faith could have counted upon the same. If, after his death, the Hebrews (without a leader) were to be sorely afflicted, and that for a *lengthy* season; if they were to be reduced unto helpless slaves, who could reasonably hope that all this should be followed by their leaving the land of Egypt with "great substance," and returning to the land of Canaan? Ah, FAITH is fully assured that God's promises *will be* fulfilled, no matter how long they may be delayed.

Faith is gifted with long-distant sight, and therefore is it able to look beyond all the hills and mountains of difficulty unto the shining horizon of the Divine promises. Consequently, faith is blessed with patience, and calmly awaits the destined hour for God to intervene and act: therefore does it heed that word, "For the vision is yet for an appointed time; but at the end it shall speak, and not lie; though it tarry, wait for it; because it will *surely* come" (Habak. 2:3). Though the Hebrews were to lie under Egyptian bondage for a long season, Joseph had not a doubt but that the Lord would, in His appointed time, bring them forth with a high hand. God's *delays,* dear reader, are not to deny our prayers and mock our hopes, but are for the disciplining of our hearts—to subdue our impatience, which wants things in our *own* way and time; to quicken us to call more earnestly upon Him, and to fit us for receiving His mercies when they are given.

God often defers His help till the very last moment. It was so with Abraham offering up Isaac; only when his son had been bound to the altar, and he had taken the knife into his hand to slay him, did God intervene. It was so with Israel at the Red Sea (Ex. 14:13). It was so with the disciples in the storm: "the ship was covered with the waves," before Christ calmed the sea (Matt. 8:24-26). It was so with Peter in prison; only a very few hours before his execution did God free him (Acts 12:6-8). So, too, God works in mysterious ways *His* wonders to perform, and often in a manner quite contrary to outward likelihood. The history of Joseph affords a striking example. He was first made a slave in Egypt, and this in order to his being made ruler over it—who would have thought that the prison was the way to the court! So it was with his descendants: when their tale of bricks was doubled and the straw withheld, who would have looked for deliverance! Yes, *God's* ways are strange to flesh and blood: often He allows error to arise to clear the Truth; bondage often makes way for liberty; persecution and affliction have often proved blessings in disguise.

"And Joseph said unto his brethren, I die; and God will surely visit you, and bring you out of this land unto the land which He sware to Abraham, to Isaac, and to Jacob" (Gen. 50:24). How plainly and how blessedly does this bring out the *strength* of Joseph's faith; There was no hesitancy or doubt: he was fully assured that God cannot lie, and that He would, *"surely"* make good His word. Equally certain is it that God's promises unto us will be fulfilled: "I will never leave thee, nor forsake thee" (Heb. 13:5). Therefore may the dying saint exclaim "Though I walk through the valley of the shadow of death, I will fear no evil; for Thou art with me" (Psa. 23:4). So too our faith may look beyond the grave unto the glorious resurrection, and say with David, "my flesh also shall rest *in hope*" (Psa. 16:9).

"By faith Joseph, when he died, made mention of the departing of the children of Israel." Let us now take note of *the breadth* of his faith. A true Christian is known by his affection for Zion. The cause of Christ upon earth is *dearer* to him than the prosperity or disposition of his personal estate. "We know that we have passed from death unto life, because we love the brethren" (1 John 3:14). Thus it was with Joseph; before he gave commandment concerning his bones, he was first concerned with the future exodus of Israel and their settlement in Canaan! How different with the empty professor, who is ruled by self-love, and has no heart for the people of God. He may be interested in the progress of *his own* denomination, but he has no concern for the Church at large. Far otherwise is it with the genuine saint: "If I forget thee, O Jerusalem, let my right hand forget her cunning. If I do not remember thee, let my tongue cleave to the roof of my mouth. if I prefer not Jerusalem above my chief joy" (Psa. 137:5, 6). So Joseph, at the very time of his death, was engaged with the future happiness of God's people.

Beautiful indeed is it to see the dying Joseph unselfishly thinking about the welfare of others. O may God deliver the writer and the reader from a narrow heart and a contracted spirit. True faith not only desires that it shall be well with our own soul, but with the Church at large. Behold another lovely example of this in the case of the dying daughter-in-law of Eli, the high priest: "And she said, The glory of God is departed from Israel; for the ark of God is taken" (1 Sam. 4:22)—not my father-in-law is dead, not my husband has been slain, but "the glory is departed." But most blessed of all is the case of Him of whom Joseph was here a type. As our precious Saviour drew near the Cross, yea, on the very night of His betrayal, it is recorded that "having loved His own which were in the world, He loved them to the end" (John 13:1). The interests of God's people were ever upon His heart.

Let us note how another aspect of the *breadth* of true faith was illustrated by Joseph. Faith not only believes the promises which God has given to His saints individually, but also lays hold of those given to the Church collectively. There have been many seasons when the cause of Christ on earth has languished sorely; when it has been in a low state spiritually; when eminent leaders had been all called home, and when fierce persecution broke out against the little flock which they had left behind. Even so, they still had that sure word, "Upon this Rock I will build My Church, and the gates of hades shall not prevail against it" (Matt. 16:18). In all ages the enemy has sought to destroy the people of God, but the Lord has defeated his designs and rendered his opposition ineffectual. O for a faith to *now* lay hold of this promise, "When the Enemy shall come in like a flood the Spirit of the Lord shall lift up a standard against him" (Isa. 59:19).

"And gave commandment concerning his bones." The reference here is to what is recorded in Gen. 50:25, "And Joseph took an oath saying God will surely visit you, and ye will carry up my bones from hence." This brings out another characteristic of his faith: the *public avowal* of it. Joseph's faith was no secret thing, hidden in his own heart, about which others knew nothing. No, though he had occupied for so long an eminent situation, he was not ashamed to now let others know that he found his support and confidence in the promises of God. He had been of great dignity and authority among the Egyptians, and his fame for wisdom and prudence was great among the nations. It was therefore the more necessary for him to *openly renounce* all alliance with them, lest posterity think he had become an Egyptian. Had he liked and loved the Egyptians, he had wanted his tomb among them; but his heart was elsewhere.

"And gave commandment concerning his bones." This was not a superstitious request, as though it made any difference whether our bodies be deposited in "consecrated" ground or no. Rather it was first, to exhibit his belief in the promises of Jehovah; though he could not go in person into the land of Canaan, yet he would have his bones carried thither, and thus symbolically (as it were) take possession of it. Second, to confirm the hope of his brethren, and thus draw their hearts from the goodly portion in Goshen. He would sharpen the desire of the Nation to earnestly aspire after the promised redemption when he was dead. Third, to establish a public memorial, by which on all occasions, his posterity might call to mind the truth of the promise.

Proof that this dying request of Joseph's was designed as a *public memorial* is found in noting a significant change between the wording of Gen. 50:24 and 50:25. In the former, Joseph "said unto his brethren"; in the latter, he "took an oath of the children of Israel" (cf. Ex. 13:19): by the heads of their tribes, he brought the whole people into this engagement—binding on after generations. Thus Joseph established this monument of his being of the favoured seed of Abraham. Joseph's requesting his brethren to "take an oath" illustrates the power of example: cf. Gen. 47:31! He made reference to his "bones" rather than to his "body," because he knew another two centuries must yet run their course. The whole transaction was an emblematic pledge of *the communion of saints.* Though the Christian at death be cut off from his loved ones on earth, he is introduced unto the spirits of the just in Heaven.

CHAPTER SEVENTY

The Faith of Moses' Parents

(Heb. 11:23)

"By faith Moses when he was born, was hid three months of his parents." A considerable length of time elapsed between what is recorded in the preceding verse and what is here before us. That interval is bridged by what is found in Exodus 1. There we see a marked revolution taking place in the lot of the Hebrews. In the days of Joseph, the Egyptians had been kind, giving them the land of Goshen to dwell in. Then followed another dynasty, and a king arose who "knew not Joseph"—probably a foreigner who had conquered Egypt. This new monarch was a tyrant of the worst kind, who sorely oppressed the descendants of Abraham. So subject to drastic changes are the fortunes both of individuals and nations: hence the force of those words, "In the days of prosperity be joyful, in the day of adversity consider: God also hath set one over against the other, to the end that man should find nothing after him" (Eccl. 7:14).

The policy of the new ruler of Egypt quickly became apparent: "And he said unto his people, Behold, the people of the children of Israel are more and mightier than we: come on, let us deal wisely with them, lest they multiply, and it come to pass, that when there falleth out any war, they join also unto our enemies" (Ex. 1:9, 10). Ah, but though "there are many devices in a man's heart, nevertheless the counsel of the Lord that shall stand" (Prov. 19:21). So it proved here, for "the more they afflicted them, the more they multiplied and grew" (Ex. 1:12). Yes, "the Lord bringeth the counsel of the heathen to naught: He maketh the devices of the people of none effect. The counsel of the Lord standeth forever, the thoughts of His heart to all generations" (Psa. 33:10, 11).

Next, the king of Egypt gave orders to the midwives that every male child of the Hebrews should be slain at birth (Ex. 1:15, 16). But all the laws which men may make against the promises that God has given to His church, are doomed to certain failure. God had promised unto Abraham a numerous "seed" (Gen. 13:15), and had declared to Jacob, "fear not to go down into Egypt, for I will there make of thee a great nation" (Gen. 46:3); as well, then, might Pharaoh attempt to stop the sun from shining as prevent the growth of the children of Israel. Therefore do we read, "But the midwives feared God, and did not as the king of Egypt commanded them, but saved the men children alive" (Ex. 1:17).

Refusing to accept defeat, "Pharaoh charged all his people, saying, Every son that is born ye shall cast into the river" (Ex. 1:22). Now that the execution of this barbarous edict had been entrusted unto his own people, no doubt Pharaoh imagined that success was fully assured for his evil design: yet it was at this very season that God brought to the birth the one who was to emancipate his suffering nation. "How blind are poor sinful mortals, in all their contrivances against the church of God. When they think all things secure, and that they shall not fail of their end, that their counsels are laid so deep as not to be blown upon, their power so uncontrollable and the way in which they are engaged so effectual, that God Himself can hardly deliver it out of their hands; He that sits on high laughs them to scorn, and with an Almighty facility lays provisions for the deliverance of His church, and for *their* ultimate ruin" (John Owen).

"And Pharaoh charged all his people, saying, Every son that is born ye shall cast into the river, and every daughter ye shall save alive. And there went a man of the house of Levi, and took to wife a daughter of Levi, and the woman conceived, and bare a son" (Ex. 1:22 and 2:1, 2). Amram and Jochebed refused to be intimidated by the cruel commandment of the king, and acted as though no injunction had been issued by him. Were they reckless and foolish? No indeed, they took their orders from a far higher authority than any earthly potentate. The fear of the Lord was upon them, and therefore were they delivered from that fear of man which bringeth a snare. In covenant relationship with the God of Abraham, Isaac and Jacob, this godly couple from the tribe of Levi allowed not the wrath of man to disrupt their domestic happiness.

"By faith Moses, when he was born, was hid three months of his parents." "It is the faith of Moses' parents that is here celebrated. But because it is mentioned principally to introduce the discourse of himself and his faith, and also that which is spoken belongs unto *his honour;* it is thus peculiarly expressed. He saith not 'By faith the parents of Moses when he was born, hid him,' but 'By faith Moses, when he was born,was hid three months of his parents'; that is, by the faith of the parents who hid him" (John Owen). Ah, here is the explanation of the conduct of Amram and Jochebed: it was "by faith" they acted: it was a living, supernatural, spiritual faith which sustained their hearts in this crisis, and kept them "in perfect peace" (Isa. 26:3). Nothing will so quieten the mind and still its fears as a real trusting in the Lord of hosts.

The birth of Moses occurred during the very height and fury of the attack that was being made upon the infant males of the Hebrews. Herein we may discover a striking foreshadowment of the attempt which was made upon the life of the Christ-child, when, in his efforts to slay Him, Herod gave orders that all the children in Bethlehem and in all the coasts thereof from two years old and under, should be slain (Matt. 2:16). Many a typical representation of the principal events in the life of the Redeemer is to be found in the Old Testament, and at scores of points did Moses in particular prefigure the great Deliverer of His people. It is a deeply interesting line of study, which we commend to our readers, to go over the history of Moses and note down the many details in which he pictured the Lord Jesus.

"By faith Moses, when he was born, was hid three months of his parents, because they saw he was a proper child; and they were not afraid of the king's commandment." It seems clear from the final clause that Pharaoh had either given orders that the Hebrews should notify his officers whenever a male child was born unto them, or that they themselves should throw him into the river. Instead of complying with this atrocious enactment, the parents of Moses concealed their infant for three months, which supplies us with a clear example of "We ought to obey God rather than men" (Acts 5:29). It is true that the Lord requires His people to "be in subjection unto the higher powers" (Rom. 13:1), but this holds good *only so long as* the "higher powers" (human governors) require the Christian to do nothing which God has forbidden, or prohibit nothing which God has commanded. The inferior authority must always give place before the superior. As this is a principle of great importance practically, and one concerning which confusion exists in some quarters, let us amplify a little.

Holy Scripture must never be made to contradict itself: one of its precepts must never be pressed so far as to nullify another; each one is to be interpreted and applied in harmony with the general analogy of faith, and in the light of the modifications which the Spirit Himself has given. For example; children are required to honour their parents, yet Eph. 6:1 shows that their obedience is to be "in the Lord"; if a parent required something directly opposed unto Holy Writ, then he is not to be obeyed. Christian wives are required by God to submit themselves unto their husbands, and that, "in everything" (Eph. 5:24), obeying them (1 Pet.

3:6); nevertheless, their subjection is to be of the same character as that of the Church unto Christ (Eph. 5:24); and inasmuch as He never demands anything from the Church which is evil, so He does not require the wife to obey injunctions which are positively harmful — if a thoughtless husband should insist on that which would be highly injurious to his wife's health, she is to refuse him. Submission does not mean slavery!

Now the same modification we have pointed out above obtains in connection with the exhortations of Rom. 13:1-7. In proof, let us cite a clear example to the point from either Testament. In Dan. 3 we find that the king of Babylon— the head of the "powers that be"— erected an image unto himself, and demanded that on a given signal, all must "fall down and worship" the same (v. 5). But the three Hebrew captives declared, "Be it known unto thee O king, that we will not serve thy gods, nor worship the golden image which thou hast set up" (v. 18); and the Lord vindicated their non-compliance. In Acts 4 we see Peter and John arrested by the Jewish "powers," who, "Commanded them not to speak at all nor teach in the name of Jesus" (v. 18). Did the apostles submit to this ordinance? No, instead they said, "Whether it be right in the sight of God to hearken unto you more than unto God, judge ye" (v. 19). As Rom. 13:4 declares, the magistrate is "the minister of God to thee *for good*": should he require that which the Word condemns as evil, he is not to be obeyed.

And what was it that enabled the parents of Moses to act so boldly and set at nought the royal edict? Our text furnishes clear answer: it was "by faith" they acted. Had they been destitute of faith, most probably the "king's commandment" would have filled them with dismay, and in order that their own lives should be spared, would have promptly informed his officers of the birth of Moses. But instead of so notifying the Egyptians, they concealed the fact, and though by preserving the child they followed a course which was highly hazardous to sense, yet under God it became the path of security. Thus, the particular aspect of our theme which here receives illustration is *the courage and boldness of faith*: faith overcoming the fear of man. That brings before us another characteristic of this heavenly grace, one which evidences its excellency, and one which should move us to pray daily for an increase of the same.

Faith is a spiritual grace which enables its possessor to look away from human terrors, and to confide in an unseen God. It declares, "The Lord is my light and my salvation; whom shall I fear? the Lord is the strength of my life; of whom shall I be afraid?" (Psa. 27:1). True it is that *this* faith is not always in exercise, yea, more often is its bright shining overcast by the clouds of unbelief, and eclipsed by the murky dust which Satan raises in the soul. We say, "this faith," for there are thousands of professing Christians all around us who boast that *their* faith is constantly in exercise, and that they are rarely if ever tormented by doubts or filled with alarms. Ah, reader, the "faith" of such people is not "the faith of God's elect" (Titus 1:1), entirely dependent upon the renewing power of the Holy Spirit; no, it is but a natural faith in the bare letter of Scripture, which by an act of their own will they can call into exercise whenever they please. But unto such the many "Fear not's" of God's Word have no application! But when the dew of Heaven falls upon the regenerated heart, its language is, "What time I am afraid, I will trust in Thee" (Psa. 56:3).

Great indeed is the power of a God-given and God-sustained faith: not only to produce outward works, but to affect the workings of the soul within. This is something which is not sufficiently considered these days, when attention is confined almost exclusively to "visible results." Faith regulates the affections: it curbs impetuosity and works patience, it chases away gloom and brings peace and joy, it subdues carnal fears and produces courage. Moreover, faith not only sustains the hearts under severe trials, performs difficult duties, but (as the sequel here shows) obtains important benefits. How pertinent, then, was this particular case unto those to whom this Epistle was first sent! How well was it calculated to encourage the sorely-tried and wavering Hebrews to remain faithful to Christ and to trust God with the issue and outcome!

"By faith Moses, when he was born, was hid three months of his parents." Probably two things are included in these words: first, that they concealed all tidings of his birth; second, that they hid him in some part of the house. No doubt their diligence was accomplished by fervent cries to God, and the putting forth of a daily trust in Him. The fact that it was "by faith" that they "*hid*" him, shows that real spiritual faith is cautious and wary, and not reckless and presumptuous. Though faith overcomes carnal fear, yet it does not disdain the use of lawful means for overcoming danger. It is fanaticism, and not faith, which tempts God. To needlessly expose ourselves unto danger is sinful. Faith is no enemy unto lawful means as Acts 27:31 plainly enough shows.

It is to be observed that the words of our text go beyond Ex. 2:2, where the preserving of Moses is attributed unto his mother. As both the parents were engaged in the hazard, both had a hand in the work; no doubt Amram took the lead in advice and contriving, and Jochebed in the actual execution. As the parents have a joint interest in their children, both should share in the care and training of them, each seeking to help the other. Where there is an agreement between husband and wife in faith and in the fear of God, it makes way for a blessed success in their duties. When difficult tasks confront husbands and wives, it is their wisdom to apply themselves unto that part and phase of it which each is best suited for. "It is a happy thing where yoke-fellows draw together in the yoke of faith, as the heirs of the grace of God; and where they do this in a religious concern for the good of their children, to preserve them not only from those who would destroy their lives, but corrupt their minds" (M. Henry).

The "three months" teaches us that the parents of Moses *persevered* in that which they began well. They were prudent from the hour of his birth, and they maintained their vigilance. It is no use to shut the stable-door when the horse is gone. Care in preventing danger is to be continued as long as the danger is threatened. Some, perhaps, may ask, Would it be right for the people of God today to give shelter to one of His saints or servants who was being unjustly hounded by "the power that be"? Surely; it is always the duty of love to shield others from harm. But suppose the hidden one is being inquired-after by the authorities, may they still be concealed? Yes, if it is done without the impeachment of the truth, for it is never permissible to lie — to do so shows a distrust of the sufficiency of God. Should the officers ask whether you are sheltering one they seek, either remain silent, or so prudently word your answer as will neither betray the party nor be guilty of falsehood.

Others may ask, Since God purposed to make Moses the leader of His people and accomplish such a memorable work through him, why did He not by some wonderful and powerful miracle preserve him from the rage of Pharaoh? Answer: God was able to send a legion of angels for his protection, or to have visibly displayed His might by other means; but He did not. It is generally God's pleasure to show His power through weak and despised means. Thus it was during the infancy of His own incarnate Son: God warned Joseph by a dream, and he took the young child and His mother into Egypt, remaining there till Herod was dead. Frequently it pleases the Most High to magnify His providence by things which men despise, by feeble instruments, and this, that it may the more plainly appear the excellency of the power is *of Him*.

In the preservation of the infant Moses, we may see a blessed illustration of how God preserves His elect through infancy and childhood, and from all that threatens their existence prior to the time when He regenerates them. This is expressed in Jude 1: "Preserved in Jesus Christ and called." How blessed is it for the Christian to look back behind the time when God called him out of the darkness into His marvelous light, and discern His guarding hand upon him when he was dead in trespasses and sins. There are few if any of the Lord's people who cannot recall more than one incident in early life when there was "but a step" betwixt them and death; yet even then, as in the case of the infant Moses, a kind Providence was watching over them. Then let us return thanks for the same.

"By faith Moses, when he was born, was hid three months of his parents, *because they saw he was a proper child*: and they were not afraid of the king's commandment." It is really surprising how many of the commentators, led by sentiment, have quite missed the meaning of this verse. Ex. 2:2 states that his mother saw "that he was a goodly child": the Hebrew word ("tob") being the same term whereby God approved of His works of creation and declared them perfect (Gen. 1), from which the conclusion has been drawn that, it was the exceeding fairness or beauty of the babe which so endeared him to his parents they were moved to disregard the king's edict, and take special pains to preserve him. But this is only carnalizing Scripture, in fact, contradicting what the Holy Spirit has here said.

Heb. 11:23 distinctly affirms that it was "by faith" the parents of Moses acted, and *this* it is which explains their conduct. Now Rom. 10:17 tells us, "faith cometh by hearing, and hearing by the word of God": thus Amram and Jochebed must have received a Divine revelation (not recorded in the O.T.), and this word from God formed the foundation of their confidence, and supplied the motive-power of what they did. It is true they knew from the prophecy given to Abram (Gen. 15) that the time for the deliverance of Israel from Egypt was drawing near, as they also knew from the prediction of Joseph (Gen. 50:24) that God was going to undertake for His people. Yet we are persuaded that Heb. 11:23 refers to something more definite and specific. Most probably the Lord made known to these parents that *their* child was to be the promised deliverer, and furnished them beforehand with a description of him.

This revelation which Amram and Jochebed "heard" from God they *believed,* and that, before Moses was born. When, in due time, he was given to them, they "saw he was a proper child"—it was *the discernment of faith,* and not the mere admiration of nature. As Acts 7:20 declares "in which time was born Moses, and was beautiful to God" (Bagster Inter.), which indicates an appearance of something Divine or supernatural. They recognized he was peculiarly grateful and acceptable to God: they perceived something remarkable in him, which was the Divine token to them that he would be the deliverer of Israel. "Probably there was some mark of future excellency impressed on the child, which gave promise of something extraordinary" (J. Calvin). "The beauty of the Lord set upon him as a presage that he was born to great things, and that by conversing with God his face would shine (Ex. 34:29), and what bright and illustrious actions he should do for the deliverance of Israel, and how his name should shine in the sacred record" (Matt. Henry).

Resting with implicit confidence upon the revelation which they had received from Jehovah, their faith now confirmed by God's mark of identification upon the babe, the parents of Moses preferred its safety before their own. It was not simply they trusted God for the outcome, but in their souls was that faith which is "the substance of things hoped for" (11:1), and in consequence "they were *not afraid* of the king's commandments." Had it been only a natural or human admiration which they had for a signally beautiful child, then it had been "by affection" or "by infatuation" they hid the infant; and that would only have intensified their "fear," for the more they admired the infant, the more afraid would they have been of harm befalling it.

Mere beauty is by no means a sure sign of excellency, as 1 Sam. 16:7, 2 Sam. 14:25, Prov. 31:30 plainly enough show. No, the infant Moses was "beautiful *to God*" (Acts 7:20), and perceiving this, Amram and Jochebed acted accordingly. First, they "hid" him for three months, "and when she could no longer hide him, she took for him an ark of bull-rushes" etc. (Ex. 2:3): it may be that the Egyptians searched the houses of the Hebrews every three months. No doubt it was under the Divine direction that the parents of Moses now acted, for surely the placing of this precious child by the brink of the fatal "river" (Ex. 1:22) was the last thing that carnal reason had suggested! We do not at all agree with those who think the faith of Moses' parents wavered when they placed him in the ark: when one lawful means of preservation from persecution will no longer secure, it is a duty to betake ourselves unto some other which is more likely to do so —Matt. 10:23.

In the kind providence of God, His interests and ours are often twined together, and then nature is allowed to work; though even then, grace must bear sway. So it was here: the parents of Moses had received a direct commandment from God how to act and what to do (as the "by faith" clearly denotes), and in their case, what He prescribed harmonized with their own feelings. But sometimes

God's requirements and our natural affections clash, as was the case when He required Abraham to offer up Isaac, and then the claims of the lower must yield to the Higher. When the current of human affection clashes not with God's express precepts we may follow it, for He allows us to take in the help of nature: "a brother beloved . . . *both in the flesh* and in the Lord" (Philemon 16).

CHAPTER SEVENTY-ONE

The Faith of Moses

(Heb. 11:24-25)

"The apostle, as we showed before, takes his instances from the three states of the church under the O.T. The first was that which was constituted in the giving of the first promise, continuing to the call of Abraham. Herein his first instance is that of Abel, in whose sacrifice the faith of that state of the church was first publicly confessed, and by whose martyrdom it was confirmed. The next state had its beginning and confirmation in the call of Abraham, with the covenant made with him and the token thereof. He therefore is the second great instance on the roll of testimonies. The constitution and consecration of the third state of the church was in giving of the law; and herein an instance is given in the law-giver himself. All to manifest, that whatever outward variations the church was liable to, and pass under, yet faith and the promises were the same, of the same efficacy and power under them all" (John Owen).

In approaching the careful study of our present verses it is of great importance to observe that they begin *a new section* of Heb. 11: if this be not seen, they cannot be interpreted aright. The opening verse of each section of this chapter takes us back to *the beginning of* the life of Faith, and each one presents a different aspect of the nature or character of saving faith. The first three verses of Heb. 11 are introductory, the fourth beginning the first division. There, in the example of Abel, we see where the life of faith begins (at conversion), namely with the conscience being awakened to a consciousness of our lost condition, with the soul making a complete surrender to God, and with the heart resting upon the perfect satisfaction made by Christ our Surety. That which is chiefly emphasized there is *faith in the blood.* But placing his faith in the blood of Christ *is not all* that is done by a sinner when he passes from death unto life.

The second section of Heb. 11 commences at v. 8 where we have set before us another aspect of conversion, or the starting-point of the Life of Faith. Conversion is the reflex action or effect from a soul which has received an effectual call from God. This is illustrated by the case of Abraham, who was, originally, an idolater, as we all were in our unregenerate state. The Lord of glory appeared unto him, quickened him into newness of life, delivered him from his former manner of existence, and gave him the promise of a future inheritance. The response of Abraham was radical and revolutionary: he set aside his natural inclinations, crucified his fleshly affections, and entered upon an entirely new path. That which is central in *his* case was, *implicit obedience*, the setting aside of his own will, and the becoming completely subject to the will of God. But even that *is not all* that is done by the sinner when he passes from death unto life.

The case of Moses brings before us yet another side of conversion, or the beginning of the Life of Faith, a side which is sadly ignored in most of the "evangelism" of our day. It describes a leading characteristic of *saving* faith, which few professing Christians now hear (still less know) anything about. It shows us that saving faith does something more than "believe" or "accept Christ as a personal Saviour." It exhibits faith as a definite decision of the mind, as an act of the will, as a personal and studied *choice*. It reveals the fundamental fact that saving faith includes, yea, begins with, a deliberate renunciation or turning away from all that is opposed to God, a determination to utterly *deny self* and an electing to submit unto whatever trials may be incident to a life of piety. It shows us that a saving faith causes its possessor to turn away from godless companions, and henceforth seek fellowship with the despised saints of God.

There is much more involved in the act of saving faith than is generally supposed. "We mistake it if we think it *only to be* a strong confidence. It is so indeed; but there are other things also. It is such an appreciative esteem of our Christ and His benefits, that all other things are lessened in our opinion, estimation, and affection. The nature of faith is set forth by the apostle when he saith, 'What things were gain to me, those I counted loss for Christ; yet, doubtless, and I count all things but loss for the excellency of the knowledge of Christ Jesus my Lord, for whom I have suffered the loss of all things, and do count them but dung that I may win Christ; and be found in Him, not having mine own righteousness which is of the law, but that which is through the faith of Christ, the righteousness which is of God by faith; that I may know Him, and the power of His resurrection, and the fellowship of His sufferings, being made conformable unto His death' (Phil. 3:7-10). And therefore true faith makes us dead to the world, and all the interests and honours thereof: and is to be known not so much by our confidence, as *by our mortification and weanedness;* when we carry all our comforts in our hands, as ready to part with them, if the Lord called us to leave them" (Thos. Manton, 1660).

"By faith Moses, when he was come to years, refused to be called the son of Pharaoh's daughter; Choosing rather to suffer affliction with the people of God, than to enjoy the pleasures of sin for a season" (vv. 24, 25). Here we see the nature and influence of a saving faith. Two things are to be particularly noted: in it there is an act of relinquishment, and an act of embracing. In conversion, there is a turning from, and also a turning unto. Hence, before the sinner is invited to "return unto the Lord," he is first bidden to "*forsake* his way," yes, *his* way—having "his *own* way." So too we are called on to "repent" first, and then "be converted," that our sins may be "blotted out" (Acts. 3:19).

"If any man will come after Me, let him deny himself" (Matt. 16:24). What is meant by the *denying* of "self"? This, the abridging ourselves of those things which are pleasing to the flesh. There are three things which are chiefly prized by the natural man—life, wealth, and honour; and so in the verses which immediately follow, Christ propounded three maxims to counter them. First, he says, "For whosoever will save his life shall lose it; and whosoever will lose his life for My sake shall find it" (v. 25): that is, he who thinks first and foremost of his own life, whose great aim is to minister unto "number one," shall perish. Second, "For what is a man profited, if he shall gain the whole world, and lose his own soul?" (v. 26): showing us the comparative worthlessness of earthly riches. Third, "For the Son of man shall come in the glory of His Father with His angels; and then shall He reward every man according to his works" (v. 27): *that* is the honour we should seek.

"By faith Moses, when he was come to years, refused to be called the son of Pharaoh's daughter." Here was a notable case of self-denial: Moses deliberately renounced the privileges and pleasures of a royal palace. It was not that he was now disowned and cast out by the woman who had adopted him; but that he voluntarily relinquished a position of affluence and ease, disdaining both its wealth and dignities. Nor was this the rash impulse of an inexperienced youth, but the studied decision of one who had now reached the age of forty (Acts 7:23). The disciples said, "We have forsaken all, and followed Thee" (Matt. 19:27): their "all" was a net and fishing-smack; but Moses abandoned a principality!

The denying of self is absolutely essential; and where it exists not, grace is absent. The first article in the covenant is, "thou shalt have no other gods before Me": *He* must have the pre-eminence in our hearts and lives. God has not the glory of *God* unless we honour

Him thus. Now God does not have the uppermost place in our hearts until *His* favour be esteemed above all things, and until we dread above everything the offending *of Him.* As long as we can break with God in order to preserve any worldly interest of ours, we prefer that interest above God. If we are content to offend God rather than displease our friends or relatives, then we are greatly deceived if we regard ourselves as genuine Christians. "He that loveth father or mother more than Me is not worthy of Me; and he that loveth son or daughter more than Me is not worthy of Me" (Matt 10:37).

"Faith is a grace that will teach a man to openly renounce all worldly honours, advantages, and preferments, with the advantage annexed thereto. When God calls us from them, we cannot enjoy them with a good conscience" (Thos. Manton). We are often put to the test of having to choose between God and things, duty and pleasure, heeding our conscience or gratifying the flesh. The presence and vigour of faith is to be proved by our *self-denial!* It is easy to speak contemptuously of the world and earthly things, but what is my *first care?* Is it to *seek* God or temporal prosperity? To *please* Him or self? If I am hankering after an increase in wages, or a better position, and am fretful because of disappointment, it is a sure proof that a worldly spirit governs me. What is my *chief delight?* earthly riches, honours, comforts, or communion with God? Can I truly say, "For a day in Thy courts is better than a thousand" (Psa. 84:10)?

"All believers are not called to make the same sacrifices, or to endure the same trials for righteousness' sake, nor have all the same measure of faith; yet, without some experience and consciousness of *this* kind, we are not warranted to conclude that we are of Moses' religion; for a common walking-stick more resembles Aaron's fruitful rod, than the faith of many modern professors of evangelical truth does the self-denying faith of Moses or Abraham" (Thos. Scott). The faith of God's elect is a faith which "overcomes the world" (1 John 5:4), and not one which suffers its possessor to be overcome! "They that are Christ's have crucified the flesh with the affections and lusts" (Gal. 5:24); not ought to, but *have* done so —in some real measure at least!

The great *refusal* of Moses consisted in a firm resolution of mind not to remain in that state wherein he had been brought up. This was not attained, we may be sure, without a hard fight, without the exercise of faith in prayer and trust in God. He knew full well all that his decision involved, yet, by grace, made it unhesitatingly. His resolution was made known not by a formal avowal, but by deeds, for actions ever speak louder than words. There is no hint in the sacred record that Moses verbally acquainted his foster-mother with his decision, but his converse with his brethren (Ex. 2:11 etc.) revealed where his heart was, and identified him with their religion and covenant. Ah, dear reader, it is one thing to *talk* well about the things of God, but it is quite another to *walk* accordingly; as it is one thing to pen articles and deliver sermons, and quite another to *practice* what we preach!

Not only was Moses' renunciation of his favoured position a grand triumph over the lusts of the flesh, but it was also a notable victory over carnal reason. First of all, his action would seem to indicate the height of *ingratitude* against his foster-mother. Pharaoh's daughter had spared his life as an infant, brought him into her own home, reared him as her son, and had him educated in all the wisdom of the Egyptians. For him to turn his back upon her now would appear as though he was devoid of appreciation—so little is the natural man able to understand the motives which regulate the workings of faith. The truth is that, the commandments of the second table are binding upon us no further than our compliance with them is agreeable to our obedience unto the commandments of the first table. The saint is neither to accept favours from the world, nor to express gratitude for the same, if such be contrary to the fear of God, and the maintenance of a good conscience.

We are never to be dutiful to man at the expense of being undutiful to God. All relations must give way before preserving a clear conscience toward Him. His rights are paramount, and must be recognized and responded to, no matter how much the doing so may clash with our seeming obligations unto our fellows. A friend or kinsman may be entertaining me in his home, and show me much kindness through the week, but that will not justify or require me to join him on a picnic or frolic on the Sabbath day. "If any man come to Me, and hate not his father, and mother, and wife, and children, and brethren, and sisters, yea, and his own life also, he *cannot* be My disciple" (Luke 14:26). The language of the Christian ought ever to be, "wist ye not that I must be about *my Father's* business?" (Luke 2:49).

To enjoy worldly honours is not evil in itself, for good men have lived in bad courts. Daniel is a clear case in point: most of his life was spent in high civic office. When Divine providence has given worldly riches or worldly prestige to us, they are to be entertained and enjoyed, yet with a holy jealousy and prayerful watchfulness that we be not puffed up by them, remembering that, "Better it is to be of an humble spirit with the lowly, than to divide the spoil with the proud" (Prov. 16:19). But such things are to be renounced when they are sinful in themselves, or when they cannot be retained with a clear conscience. Against his conscience, Pilate preferred to condemn Christ than lose Caesar's friendship, and stands before us in Holy Writ as a lasting warning. "Watch and pray, that *ye* enter not into temptation: the spirit indeed is willing, but the flesh is weak" (Matt. 26:41).

Again; not only did Moses' great refusal seem like gross ingratitude unto her who had adopted him, but it also looked like flying in the face of Providence. It was God who had placed him where he was; why, then, should he forsake such an advantageous position? Had Moses leaned unto his own understanding and listened to the dictates of carnal reason, he had found many pretexts for remaining where he then was. Why not stay there and seek to reform Egypt? Why not use his great influence with the king on behalf of the oppressed Hebrews? Had he remained in the court of Pharaoh, he would escape much affliction; yes, and miss too the "recompense of the reward." Ah, my reader, unbelief is very fertile, argues very plausibly, and can suggest many logical reasons why we *should not* practice self-denial!

What was it, then, which prompted Moses to make this noble sacrifice? A patriotic impulse? a fanatical love for his brethren? No, he was guided neither by reason nor sentiment: it was "by *faith*" that Moses refused to be called the son of Pharaoh's daughter. It was the clinging of his heart to the Divine promise, the apprehension of things not seen by the outward eye, the confident expectation of future reward. Ah, it is faith which imparts to the heart a true estimate of things, which views objects in their real light, and which discerns the comparative worthlessness of what the poor worldling prizes so highly, and through his mad quest after which he loses his soul. Faith views the eternity to come, and when faith is in healthy exercise, its possessor finds it easy to relinquish the baubles of time and sense. Then it is the saint exclaims. "Surely every man walketh in a vain show: surely they are disquieted in vain: he heapeth up riches and knoweth not who shall gather them" (Psa. 39:6).

What a truly remarkable thing that one in Egypt's court *should have* such a "faith"! Moses had been brought up in a heathen palace, where there was no knowledge of the true God; yea, nothing but idolatry, wantonness, and profanity. Yes, some of Christ's sheep are situated in queer and unexpected places, nevertheless the Shepherd seeks them out, and either delivers them from or sustains them in it: the wife of "Herod's steward" (Luke 8:3), the saints in Nero's "household" (Phil. 4:22) are notable examples. What illustrations are these of "The Lord shall send the rod of Thy strength out of Zion: rule Thou in the midst of Thine enemies" (Psa. 110:2)! However His enemies may rage, seek to blot out His name and root out His kingdom, Chirst shall preserve a remnant according to the election of grace "even where Satan's throne is" (Rev. 2:13).

Some one may object, "But Joseph had faith as well as Moses, yet he did not leave the court, but continued there till his death." Circumstances alter cases! Their occasions and conditions were not alike. "God raised up Joseph to feed His people in Egypt, therefore his abode in the court was necessary under kings that favoured them; but Moses was called not to feed His people in Egypt, but to lead them out of Egypt; and the king of Egypt was now become their enemy, and kept them under bitter bondage. To remain in an idolatrous court of a pagan prince is one thing; but to remain in a persecuting court, where he must be accessary to their persecutions, is another thing" (T. Manton).

"Choosing rather to suffer affliction with the people of God, than to enjoy the pleasures of sin for a season" (v. 25). This gives us the positive side of Moses's glorious decision. There is both a negative and a positive side to faith. First, a *refusing,* and then a *choosing,* and that order is unchanging. There must be a "ceasing to do evil" before there can be a "learning to do well" (Isa. 1:16, 17); there must be a "hating the evil" before there is a "loving the good" (Amos 5:15); there must be a "confessing *and forsaking*" of sin, before there is "mercy" (Prov. 28:13). The prodigal must *leave* the far country, before he can go to the Father (Luke 15). The sinner must abandon his idols, before he can take up the Cross and follow Christ (Mark 10:21). There must be a turning to God, "*from* idols," before there can be a "serving the living and true God" (1 Thess. 1:9). The heart must turn its back upon the world, before it can receive Christ as Lord and Saviour.

"Moses gave up the *world;* and ambition had the prospect of honour and greatness; the culture of the most civilized state was fascinating to the mind; treasure and wealth held out potent allurement. And all this—and does it not comprise 'all that is in the world,' and in its most attractive and elevated manner?—Moses gave up. And, on the other side, what awaited him? To join a down-trodden nation of slaves, whose only riches was the promise of the invisible God" (A. Saphir). A man is known by his *choice.* Do you do evil for a little profit? Do you avoid duty because of some trifling inconvenience? Are you turned out of the way because of reproach?

Moses preferred to *suffer* affliction with the people of God than to *enjoy* the pleasures of sin for a brief season. Do you? He judged it the greatest misery of all to live in sin. Do you? Here is an important test: which gives you greater grief, sin or bodily affliction? Which troubles you the more: suffering loss in the world, or displeasing God? There are thousands of professing Christians who complain of their physical aches and pains, but how rarely do we hear any groaning over the body of sin and death! When you are afflicted in the body, which is your dominant desire: to be freed from the suffering, or for God to *sanctify* the suffering unto the good of your soul? Ah, my reader, what *real and supernatural* difference is there between you and the moral worldling? Is it only in your creed, what you believe with the intellect? "The demons believe."

Yes, it is our *refusal* and our *choice* which identifies us, which makes it manifest whether we are children of the devil or children of God. It is the property of a gracious heart to prefer the greatest suffering—physical, mental, or social—to the least sin; and when sin is committed, it is repudiated, sorrowed over, confessed, and forsaken. When "suffering" is inflicted upon saints by persecutors, the offense is done unto us; but "sin" is committed against God! "Sin" separates from God (Isa. 59:2), "suffering" drives the Christians nearer to God. "Affliction" only affects the body, "sin" injures the soul. "Affliction" is from God (Heb. 12:5-11), but "sin" is from the devil. But naught save a real, spiritual, supernatural faith will prefer suffering affliction with the people of God, than to enjoy the pleasures of sin for a season.

"None of the exemplifications of the importance of believing, brought forth by the apostle, is better fitted to serve his purpose than that which we have been considering. The Hebrew Christians were called on to part with an honour which they were accustomed to value above all other dignities. They were excommunicated by their unbelieving brethren, and denied the name of true children of Abraham. Their unbelieving countrymen were enjoying wealth and honour. The little flock they were called on to join were suffering affliction and reproach. Now, how is this to be done? Look at Moses. Believe as Moses believed, and you will find it easy to judge, choose, and act as Moses did. If you believe what Christ has plainly revealed, that 'it is His Father's good pleasure to give' His little flock, after passing through much tribulation, 'the kingdom'; if you are persuaded that, according to His declaration, 'wrath is coming to the uttermost' on their oppressors, you will not hesitate to separate yourselves completely from your unbelieving country-men.

"The practical bearing of the passage is not confined to the Hebrew converts, or to the Christians of the primitive age. In every country, and in every age, Jesus proclaims 'If any man would be My disciple he must deny himself, he must take up the cross, and follow Me.' The power of the present world can only be put down by 'the power of the world to come'; and as it is through *sense* that the first power operates on our minds, it is through *faith* alone that the second power can operate on our minds. Some find it impossible to make the sacrifices Christianity requires, because they have no faith. They must be made; otherwise our Christianity is but a name, our faith is but a pretense, and our hope a delusion" (John Brown).

CHAPTER SEVENTY-TWO

The Faith of Moses

(Heb. 11:25-26)

"The person here instanced as one that lived by faith, is Moses. And an eminent instance it is to his purpose, especially in his dealings with the Hebrews, and that on sundry accounts. 1. Of his person. None was ever in the old world more signalized by Providence in his birth, education, and actions, than he was. Hence his renown was both then, and in all ages after, very great in the world. The report and estimation of his acts and wisdom, were famous among all the nations of the earth. Yet this person lived and acted, and did all his works *by faith*. 2. Of his great work, which was the typical redemption of the church. A work it was great in itself; so God expresseth it to be, and such as was never wrought in the earth before (Deut. 4:32-34). Yet greater in the typical respect which it had to His eternal redemption of the Church by Jesus Christ. 3. On the account of his office. He was the lawgiver, whence it is manifest, that *the law is not opposite to faith*, seeing the lawgiver himself lived thereby" (John Owen).

Each example of faith supplied by the Holy Spirit in Heb. 11 presents a distinctive feature or fruit of that spiritual grace. The faith which is here described is *saving* faith, without which no man is accepted by God (see v. 6). It is true that all Christians are not given the same measure of faith, nor do all of them manifest it in the same manner. All flowers are not of the same hue, nor are they equally fragrant; yet every variety differs radically from weeds! Not every saint is called upon to build an ark, offer up his son in sacrifice, or forsake a palace; nevertheless, there is that in the heart and life of *every* regenerate soul which plainly distinguishes him from those who are dead in trespasses and sins, and which clearly bears the mark of the *supernatural*—there is that in him which mere nature does not and cannot bring forth.

While it be true that very few Christians are called upon to leave a palace, yet every one who would become a Christian *is required* to forsake the world: not physically, but morally. God does not bid us become hermits, or enter a convent or monastery — that is only the Devil's perversion of the truth of separation; but He *does* insist that the sinner must cast away the idols of the world, turn from its vain pleasures, cease walking in its evil ways, and set his affections upon things above. Scripture is unmistakably plain upon this point, declaring, "Know ye not that the friendship of the world is enmity with God? whosoever therefore will be a friend of the world, is the enemy of God" (James 4:4). That which was adumbrated by Moses in our present passage was, the heart's renunciation of a vain and perishing world, and giving God His true place in the affections.

In our last article we saw how Moses voluntarily relinquished his position of a nobleman in Pharaoh's court, and preferred to have fellowship with the despised and suffering people of God. In this he was a blessed type of Him who was rich, yet for our sakes became poor, who descended from the glory of Heaven, and was born in a manger; who laid aside His robes of majesty, and took upon Him the form of a servant. And my reader, His people are predestinated "to be conformed to" *His* image (Rom. 8:29). He has left them an example, and there is no other route to Heaven, but by "following His steps": see John 10:4! There is a real and practical oneness between the Head and the members of His mystical body, and that practical oneness consists in *self-sacrifice*. Unless the spirit of self-sacrifice rules my heart, I am no *Christian!*

The way to Heaven is a "narrow" one and the entrance to it is "strait," and few there be that find it (Matt. 7:13, 14). Because that way *is* "narrow," opposed to all the inclinations of flesh and blood, Christ bids us to "sit down and count the cost" (Luke 14:31) before we start out. The "cost" is far too high for all who have never had a miracle of grace wrought within them, for it includes the cutting off of a right hand and the plucking out of a right eye (Matt. 5:29, 30)—*that* is why 1 Pet. 4:18 asks, "If the righteous *scarcely* be saved (or "*with difficulty* be saved") where shall the ungodly and the sinner appear"! Few indeed are, like Moses, willing to pay the "cost." Alas, the vast majority, even in Christendom, are like Esau (Heb. 12:16) or the Gadarenes (Mark 5:14, 15)—they prefer to indulge the flesh rather than deny it.

The *difficulty* of salvation, or the "straitness" of the gate and the "narrowness" of the way which leadeth into Life, was strikingly prefigured by the alluring temptations and carnal obstacles which had to be overcome by Moses. As we pointed out in our last article, his noble decision not only involved the leaving of Pharaoh's palace, the apparent ingratitude toward his foster-mother, the ignoring of the precedent set up by Joseph; but, it also meant the throwing in his lot with a despised people, enduring all the discomforts and hardships of their wilderness wanderings, and the bringing down upon his head not only the contempt of his former associates, but having to endure the murmurings and criticisms of the Hebrews themselves. Ah, my reader, *such a choice* as Moses made was altogether contrary to flesh and blood, and can be accounted for only on the ground that a miracle of Divine grace had been wrought within him. As our Lord declared, "With men *this is impossible,* but with God all things are possible" (Matt. 19:26).

From what has been said above, is it not unmistakably evident that as great a distance as that which separates heaven from earth divides *Scriptural* "Conversion" from that which goes under the name of "conversion" in the vast majority of the so-called "churches" today! A genuine and saving Conversion is a radical and revolutionary experience. It is vastly more than the taking up of a sound creed, believing what the Bible says about Christ, or joining some religious assembly. It is something which strikes down to the very roots of a man's being, causing him to make an unreserved surrender of himself to the claims of God, henceforth seeking to please and glorify Him. This issues, necessarily, in a complete break from the world, and the former manner of life; in other words, "if any man be in Christ, he is *new* creature: old things are passed away; behold all things are become new" (2 Cor. 5:17).

"By faith Moses, when he was come to years, refused to be called the son of Pharaoh's daughter" (v. 24). It is the first two words of this verse which supply an adequate explanation of the noble conduct of Moses here. A God-given faith is occupied with something better than the things of sight and sense, and therefore does it discern clearly the utter vanity of worldly greatness and honour. Faith has to do *with God,* and when the mind be truly stayed upon Him, neither the riches nor the pleasures of earth can attract, still less enthrawl. Faith relies upon and is obedient unto a personal revelation from on High, for "faith cometh by hearing, and hearing by the word of God" (Rom. 10:17). Moses had "heard," Moses "believed," Moses *acted on* what he had heard from God.

"Choosing rather to suffer affliction with the people of God, than to enjoy the pleasures of sin for a season" (v. 25). Yes, each of us *has to choose* between life and death (Deut. 30:15), between sin and holiness, between the world and Christ, between fellowship with the children of God and friendship with the children of the Devil. When Moses took the part of an Israelite against an Egyptian (Ex. 2), he declared plainly that he preferred the former to the latter, that the promises of God meant far more to him than the fame or luxury of an earthly court. Yet at that time the seed of Abraham were in an exceedingly low state, nevertheless Moses knew that the promises which God had made unto the patriarchs could not fail.

That was *faith* indeed: to willingly forego the attractive prospects which lay before him in the land of the Nile, and deliberately prefer a path of hardship. What he had "heard" from God was to him so grand, so great, so glorious, that, after thoughtfully balancing the one over against the other, Moses rejected material aggrandisement for spiritual riches: he considered it to be a far higher honour to be a child of Abraham than to be called the son of Pharaoh's daughter. He might have *reasoned* that "a bird in the hand is worth two in the bush," and have "made the most of his (present) opportunity," rather than have set his heart on an unseen future; but the spirit triumphed over the flesh. O how we need to pray for grace to enable us to "approve things that are excellent," that we may be "sincere and without offence till the day of Christ" (Phil. 1:10).

It is to be duly noted that Moses elected to suffer affliction with the Hebrews not because they were his people, but because they were *God's* people. "The object of his choice was God; the One who chose his fathers, who revealed to them His truth and grace, and commanded them to walk before Him without fear; the God who was not ashamed to be called their God, and to whom he had been dedicated in his infancy" (A. Saphir). Observe that fellowship with "the people of God" necessarily involves, in some form or other, "affliction." Yes, God has ordained that "we must through much tribulation enter into His kingdom" (Acts 14:22), and declares, "all that will live godly in Christ Jesus shall suffer persecution" (2 Tim. 3:12). But *why* should this be so? Why has not God appointed a smoother path and a pleasanter lot for His high favourites while they pass through this world? We subjoin one or two of the many answers which may be returned to this question.

God has decreed that the general state of His people on earth shall be one of hardship, opposition, persecution. First, to arouse them to spiritual diligence. He has told them in His Word "This is not your rest" (Micah 2:10), nevertheless there is a tendency in us to settle down here. Again and again God bids us to watch and pray, to be sober and vigilant, alert and active; but only too often His exhortations fall on deaf ears. The "wise virgins" slumbered and slept as well as the "foolish" ones, and need *awakening;* because they will not heed such calls as are found in Rom. 13:11, Eph. 5:14 etc. He uses the Enemy to arouse us. Second, to wean us from the world: because there is that in us which still loves the world, God, in His mercy, often stirs them up to hate us. Third, to conform us more fully unto the image of Christ: the Head endured the contradiction of sinners *against* Himself, and His body is called to have "fellowship in His sufferings."

The "pleasures of sin" in v. 25 has immediate reference to the riches and dignities of Pharaoh's court, which Moses could no longer enjoy without being unfaithful to God and His people. To have gone on living in the palace, would be despising Jehovah and His covenant with Abraham's seed. It would have been preferring his own advancement and ease rather than the deliverance of his people; he would have been conducting himself as a worldling, rather than as a stranger and pilgrim in this scene; and worse, he would have been conniving at Pharaoh's cruel treatment of the Hebrews. Moreover, to have resisted the impulse of the Spirit on his heart would have been *sin.* This shows us that things which are not sinful in themselves, become so when used or enjoyed at the wrong time. Every thing is beautiful in its season: "There is a time to weep, and a time to laugh" (Eccl. 3:4).

The principle we have just enunciated above is of great practical importance. Material things become snares if employed intemperately. God has granted us permission to "use" the things of this world, but has forbidden the "abuse" of them (1 Cor. 7:31). Temporal blessings become a curse if they are allowed to hinder us from the discharge of duty. All associations must be severed which deter us from having fellowship with the saints. Personal ease and comfort is to be set aside when our brethren are "suffering afflictions" and need a helping hand. Alas, only God knows how many professing Christians have continued to enjoy the *luxuries* of life, while thousands were without some of the bare *necessities* of life.

Everything which is severed from true Godliness is included in this expression "the pleasures of sin." Temporal mercies are to be enjoyed with thankfulness to God, but only so far and so long as they help to promise a true following of the example which Christ has left us. Alas, how many are seeking their happiness in the things of the flesh, rather than in the things of the Spirit. Scripture says, "Better is little with the fear of the Lord, than great treasure and trouble therewith" (Prov. 15:16)—but how few believe it! Mark it well, dear reader, the "pleasures of sin" are only for "a season," and a solemnly brief season at that: they must end either in speedy repentance or speedy ruin. How blessed is the contrast presented in Psa. 16:11, "At Thy right hand there are pleasures *for evermore*"! Is my heart set upon *them?* If so, I am making it my chief concern, every day, to walk along *the only path* which leads to them.

"Esteeming the reproach of Christ greater riches than the treasures in Egypt" (v. 26). Here the Holy Spirit mentions a third instance of Moses' contempt of the world: first, of its honours (v.

24), then of its pleasures (v. 25), now, of its wealth. Note the emphatic graduation in the decision of Moses as intimated in the three verbs: first, he "refused" to be any longer acknowledged as the adopted son of Egypt's princess. Second, he "chose" or deliberately elected to become identified with and throw in his lot among the despised and suffering people of God. Third, he "esteemed" the reproach this involved, as high above that which he relinquished and renounced. The same Greek word is rendered "judged" in v. 11, showing that it was no rash conclusion which he jumped to hastily, but that it was the mature consideration of his mind and heart. Another has compared the three verbs here with Mark 4:28: "First the blade, then the ear, after that the full corn in the ear."

This 26th verse is an amplification of what is found in the 24th and 25th, and announces both the intelligence of Moses' choice and the fervour of spiritual affection which prompted it. The decision that he made was not a reluctant and forced one, but ready and joyous. It was not merely he perceived that identifying himself with the Hebrews was a bounden duty, and therefore he must "make the best of a bad job" and put up with the hardships such a course entailed, but that he gladly preferred the same — *Christ* meaning infinitely more to him than everything which was to be found in Egypt. Reader, is the denying of self and taking up of the cross something which you grudgingly perform, or does the "love of Christ constrain" (2 Cor. 5:14) you thereto? Can you, in your measure, say with the apostle, "Therefore I take pleasure in infirmities, in reproaches, in necessities, in persecutions, in distresses for Christ's sake" (2 Cor. 12:10)?

What is meant here by "the reproach of Christ"? The Saviour was not born till many centuries later; true, but those whom the Father gave to Him before the foundation of the world, were, from Abel onwards, well acquainted with Him: see John 8:56. Christ had a being before He was born of the virgin: we read of Israel "tempting Christ" in the wilderness (1 Cor. 10:9). From the beginning, Christ was Head of the Church, and in His own person led His own people, and was present in their midst, under the name of "the Angel of the Covenant." Let the interested reader carefully ponder the terms of Ex. 23:20-22, and it should be plain that no *created* "angel" is there in view. Thus, whatever that people suffered, it was the reproach "of Christ," who had taken them under His protection. There was a communion between Christ and His people, as real and as intimate as that union and communion which exists between Him and His people now: weigh well Isa. 63:9, Zech. 2:8, and compare with Acts 9:4, Matt. 25:34 and clear proof of this will be obtained.

The "reproach of Christ," then, signifies first, Christ *personally* as identified with His people. Second, it has reference to Christ *mystically,* His redeemed as one with Him in humiliation and persecution. "Christ and the church were considered from the beginning, as one mystical body; so as that what the one underwent, the other is esteemed to undergo the same" (John Owen). In marriage the wife takes the name and status of her husband, because they have become "one flesh": in like manner, the Church is called "Christ" in 1 Cor. 12:12, Gal. 3:16 because of its union and communion with Him, because of the likeness and sympathy between them. Nor was this blessed mystery kept concealed—as modern "dispensationalists" wrongly declare—from the O.T. saints, as a careful comparison of Jer. 23:6 with 33:16 makes very evident. Moses had "heard" from God that the Hebrews were His people, and the remnant among them "according to the election of grace" were ordained to be "joint heirs with Christ," and believing what he heard, he voluntarily and gladly decided to throw in his lot with them.

That the mystical body of Christ, the Church, is in view here in Heb. 11:26—for the Head and His members can never be separated, though they may be viewed distinctly—is abundantly clear by a careful comparison of the preceding clauses. Verses 25 and 26 are obviously parallel, and explain one another. In the former we are told that, Moses "chose rather to suffer affliction with the people of God, than to enjoy the pleasures of sin for a season." Thus, there is a threefold parallelism: the "reproach of v. 26 agrees with and is interpreted by the "suffering affliction" of v. 25, "the Christ" of v. 26 corresponds with and is defined by "the people of God" in v. 25; and the "treasures of Egypt" balances with and explains the "pleasures of sin for a season."

"For he had respect unto the recompence of the reward." This was what strengthened and supported the faith of Moses. He had never forsaken the honours and comforts of the palace unless his heart had been fixed upon the eternal recompence. Faith realizes that peace of conscience is better than a big bank-balance, that communion with God is infinitely to be preferred above the favours of an earthly court. Moses knew that he would be no loser by such a choice: faith sees that nothing is lost which is quitted for Christ's sake — though the name of Moses was removed from Egypt's records, it has been accorded a prominent place upon the imperishable pages of Holy Writ. See here the vast difference between worldlings and saints; the former estimate things by sight, the latter by faith; the former through the coloured glass of corrupt reason and carnal sense, the latter by the light of God's Word. Thus they wonder at each other: the worldling *thinks* the real Christian is crazy, the Christian *knows* the poor worldling is spiritually insane.

The heart of Moses was set upon something more blessed than the perishing things he was relinquishing. The "he had respect" is a compound in the Greek, and properly signifies to look from one thing to another: he looked from the things of time to those of eternity, for "faith is the substance of those things hoped for, the evidence of things not seen": cf. 2 Cor. 4:17. This is one of the great properties of faith: to frequently and trustfully ponder the promise of Eternal Life, which we are to dwell in forever after this scene of sin is left behind. Faith perceives that the way to "save" is to "lose" (Matt. 16:25), that present self-denial will yet be honoured by enrichment, knowing that if now we suffer with Christ we shall be "also glorified together" (Rom. 8:17). How this condemns the practice of many who spend their lives in the greedy pursuit of the world, with no regard to God or their eternal interests, but think that if they call on Him for mercy with their last gasp, all will be well. Such people terribly deceive themselves by failing to see that Eternal Life is a "reward"—see Luke 1:74, 75: we must labour in the works of godliness in *this* life.

That which Moses had "respect unto" is here called "the recompence of the reward." This is the all-sufficient presence of God with His people now (Gen. 15:1), and the great and final reward of Eternal Glory which is given by God, and received by His people as a compensation for all their sufferings. This is one of the N.T. passages which proves the O.T. saints had a much clearer understanding of the future state of the redeemed than is now commonly supposed. For the reward of good works see Heb. 6:9, of patience 6:12, of suffering 10:34. The calling of Heaven a "reward" in nowise imports any desert on man's part, but abundant kindness in God, who will not suffer anything to be done or endured for Christ's sake without recompence. It is called a "reward" to encourage obedience (Psa. 19:11) and allure our hearts (Matt. 5:12). That a *gift* may be a "reward" is clear from Col. 3:24. It is also called a "reward" because it is God's *owning of* the Spirit's work in and through His people. Since eternal glory is a "reward" let us be patient under present suffering: Rom. 8:18. It is legitimate to view the reward of Heaven while serving here—not that this is to be the chief or only motive (for that would be a religion of selfishness), but as faith's anticipation: cf. Phil. 3:8-14. The reward is "gratuitous that God hath annexed to faith and obedience, not merited or deserved by them, *but infallibly annexed* unto them in a way of sovereign bounty" (John Owen).

CHAPTER SEVENTY-THREE

The Faith of Moses

(Heb. 11: 26-27)

In our last two articles (upon 11:24-26) we had before us the striking example of the power of faith to rise above the honours, riches, and pleasures of the world; now we are to behold it triumphing over *its terrors.* Faith not only elevates the heart above the delights of sense, but it also delivers it from the fear of man. Faith and fear are opposites, and yet, strange to say, they are often found dwelling within the same breast; but where one is dominant the other is dormant. The constant attitude of the Christian should be, "Behold, God is my salvation: I will trust, *and not be afraid*" (Isa. 12:2). But alas, what ought to be, and what is, are two vastly different things. Nevertheless, when the grace of faith *is* in exercise, its language is, "What time I am afraid, I will trust in Thee" (Psa. 56:3). So it was with Moses: he is here commended for his courage.

The leading feature of that particular working of Moses' faith which we are now to consider was its *durability.* That which engaged our attention on the last two occasions occurred when our hero had "come to years." Forty years had elapsed since then, during which he passed through varied experiences and sore trials. But now that he is eighty years of age, faith is still active within him. That spiritual grace moved him to withstand the attractions of Egypt's court, had led him to relinquish a position of high honour and wealth, had caused him to throw in his lot with the despised people of God; and now we behold faith enabling him to endure the wrath of the King. A God-given faith not only resists temptations, but it also endures trials, and refuses to be daunted by the gravest dangers. Faith not only flourishes under the dews of the Spirit, but it survives the fires of Satanic assault.

True faith neither courts the smiles of men nor shuns their frowns. Herein it differs radically from that natural faith, which is all that is possessed by thousands who think they are children of God. Only yesterday we received a letter in which a friend wrote,

"I know some professing Christians who boasted that the prospect of being out of work did not trouble them at all: for they knew every need would be supplied. Now that they have no work, they are not nearly so confident, but are wondering how in the world they are going to get along." So too we read of the stony ground hearer, "The same is he that heareth the Word, and anon with joy receiveth it; Yet hath he not root in himself, but dureth for awhile: *for when tribulation or persecution* ariseth because of the Word, by and by he is offended" (Matt. 13:20, 21). Far otherwise was it with Moses.

"By faith he forsook Egypt, not fearing the wrath of the king; for he endured, as seeing Him who is invisible." Moses left Egypt on two different occasions, and there is some diversity of opinion among the commentators as to which of them is here in view. Personally, we think there is little or no room for doubt that the Holy Spirit *did not* have reference unto the first, for we are told, "And Moses *feared*, and said, Surely this thing is known. Now when Pharaoh heard this thing, he sought to slay Moses. But Moses fled from the face of Pharaoh, and dwelt in the land of Midian" (Ex. 2:14, 15). There he fled as the criminal, here he went forth as the commander of God's people! then he left Egypt in terror, but now "by faith."

There are some, however, who find difficulty in the fact that Moses' leaving of Egypt is here mentioned *before* his keeping of the passover and sprinkling of the blood in v. 28. But this difficulty is self-created, by confining our present text unto a single event, instead of understanding it to refer unto *the whole conduct* of Moses: his forsaking of Egypt is a general expression, which includes all *his* renouncing a continuance therein and his steady determination to depart therefrom. So too his "not fearing the wrath of the king" must not be restricted unto the state of his heart immediately following the Exodus, but also takes in his resolution and courage during the whole of his dealings with Pharaoh. And herein we may perceive again the *stability* of his faith, which withstood the most fiery ordeals, and which remained steadfast to the end. Thus did he supply a blessed illustration of "Who are kept by the power of God through faith unto salvation, ready to be revealed in the last time" (1 Pet. 1:5).

The experiences through which Moses passed and the testings to which his faith was subjected, were no ordinary ones. First, he was bidden to enter the presence of Pharaoh and say, "Thus saith the Lord God of Israel, Let My people go, that they may hold a feast unto Me in the wilderness" (Ex. 5:1). Let it be duly considered that for forty years Moses had lived the life of a shepherd in

Midian, and now, with no army behind him, with none in Egypt's court ready to second his request, he has to make this demand of the haughty monarch who reigned over the greatest empire then on earth. Such a task called for no ordinary faith. Nor did he meet with a favourable reception; instead, we are told "And Pharaoh said, Who is the Lord, that I should obey His voice to let Israel go? I know not the Lord, neither will I let Israel go" (Ex. 5:2).

Not only did the idolatrous king refuse point-blank to grant Moses' request, but he said, "Wherefore do ye, Moses and Aaron, hinder the people from their work? get you unto your burdens... Ye shall no more give the people straw to make brick, as heretofore: let them go and gather straw for themselves" (Ex. 5:4, 7). Well might the heart of the stoutest quake under such circumstances as these. To add to his troubles the heads of the Israelites came unto Moses and said, "The Lord look upon you, and judge; because ye have made our savor to be abhorred in the eyes of Pharaoh, and in the eyes of his servants, to put a sword in their hand to slay us" (Ex. 5:21). Ah, faith must be tested; nor must it expect to receive any encouragement or assistance from men, no, not even from our own brethren—it must stand alone in the power of God.

Later, Moses was required to interview Pharaoh again, *after* Jehovah had informed him He had "hardened" his heart, and say, "The Lord God of the Hebrews hath sent me unto thee, saying, Let My people go, that they may serve Me in the wilderness: and, behold, hitherto thou wouldest not hear. Thus saith the Lord, In this thou shalt know that I am the Lord: behold, I will smite with the rod that is in mine hand upon the waters which are in the river, and they shall be turned to blood. And the fish that is in the river shall die, and the river shall stink; and the Egyptians shall loathe to drink of the water of the river" (Ex. 7:16-18). It is easy for us now, knowing all about the happy sequel, to entirely *under-estimate* the severity of this trial. Seek to visualize the whole scene. Here was an insignificant Hebrew, belonging to a company of *slaves*, with no powerful "union" to press their claims. There was the powerful monarch of Egypt, who, humanly speaking had only to give the word to his officers, and Moses had been seized, beaten, tortured, murdered. Yet, notwithstanding, he "feared not the wrath of the king."

We cannot now follow Moses through all the stages of his great contest with Pharaoh, but would pass on to the closing scene. After the tenth plague, Pharaoh called for Moses and proposed a compromise, which, upon Moses refusing, he said, "Get thee from me, take heed to thyself, see my face no more; for in that day thou seest my face thou shalt die" (10:28). But Moses "feared not the wrath of the king," and boldly announced the final plague. Not only so, he declared that his servants should yet pay him homage (Ex. 11:4-8). "He had before him a bloody tyrant, armed with all the power of Egypt, threatening him with present death if he persisted in the work and duty which God had committed to him; but he was so far from being terrified, or declining his duty in the least, that he professeth his resolution to proceed, and denounceth destruction to the tyrant himself" (John Owen).

After the tenth plague had been executed, Moses led the children of Israel out of the land in which they had long groaned in bondage. "By faith he forsook Egypt, not fearing the wrath of the king." Even now he was not terrified by thoughts of what the enraged monarch might do, nor at the powerful forces which he most probably would send in pursuit; but staying his mind upon God, he was assured of the Divine protection. He allowed not gloomy forebodings to discourage him. Yet once more we would say, it is easy for us (in the light of our knowledge of the sequel) to under-estimate this marvel. Visualize the scene again. On the one hand was a powerful nation, who had long held the Hebrews in serfdom, and would therefore be extremely loath to let them altogether escape; on the other hand, here was a vast concourse of people, including many thousands of women and children, unorganized, unarmed, unaccustomed to travel, with a howling wilderness before them.

Ah, my reader, does not such a situation as we have hastily sketched above, seem utterly hopeless? There did not seem one chance in a thousand of succeeding. Yet the spirit of Moses was undaunted, and he is here commended to us for his courage and resolution. But more; Pharaoh, accompanied by six hundred chariots and a great armed force, pursued them, and "when Pharaoh drew nigh, the children of Israel lifted up their eyes, and, behold, the Egyptians marched after them: and they were sore afraid; and the children of Israel cried out unto the Lord. And they said unto Moses, Because there were no graves in Egypt, hast thou taken us away to die in the wilderness? Wherefore hast thou dealt thus with us to carry us forth out of Egypt?" (Ex. 14:10, 11). Here was the crucial moment, the supreme test. Did Moses' heart fail him, was he now terrified by "the wrath of the king"? No indeed; so far from it, he calmly and confidently said unto the people, "*Fear ye not*, stand still and see the salvation of the Lord, which He will show you today: for the Egyptians whom ye have seen today, ye shall see them again no more forever. The Lord shall fight for you, and ye shall hold your peace" (Ex. 14:13, 14).

O how the undaunted courage of Moses shames *our* petty fears! What cause have we to blush, and hang our heads in shame. Many are there who fear very much less than the wrath of a "king": such things as darkness and solitude, or even the rustling of a leaf, will frighten them. No doubt such fear is constitutional with some, but with the great majority it is a guilty conscience which makes them alarmed at a shadow. The best way for weak ones to overcome their timidity is to cultivate the sense of God's presence; and for the guilty, to confess and forsake their sins. "The wicked flee when no man pursueth; but the righteous are bold as a lion" (Prov. 28:1). Fear is the result of distrust, of taking the eye off God, of being unduly occupied with difficulties and troubles.

And what was it that enabled Moses to conduct himself with such firmness and boldness? What was it that delivered his heart from fearing the wrath of the king? FAITH, a spiritual, supernatural, God-given, God-energized faith. Reader, do you know anything, experimentally, of *such* a faith? Again we would be reminded that "Faith cometh by hearing, and hearing by the Word of God" (Rom. 10:17). Moses had heard, he had heard something from God, and his faith laid hold of and rested upon the same. What was it that he had heard? This, "Certainly I will be with thee; and this shall be a token unto thee, that I have sent you: when thou hast brought forth the people out of Egypt, ye *shall* serve God upon this mountain" (Ex. 3:12). So, too, if we are Christians, God has said to us, "I will never leave thee, nor forsake thee." Therefore "we may boldly say, The Lord is my Helper, and I will not fear what man shall do unto me" (Heb. 13:5,6).

Perhaps some one may ask, But was there *no wavering* in Moses' faith? Yes, dear reader, for he was a man of like passions with us. They who have a faith which never varies, which remains the same whether it be cloudy and stormy, or fair and sun-shiny, have nothing but a natural and letter faith. A spiritual and supernatural faith is one which *we* did not originate and is one which we cannot call into exercise whenever we please: God imparted it, and He alone can renew and call it into action. When the leaders of Israel murmured against Moses, and charged him with endangering their lives (Ex. 5:21), we are told that, Moses returned unto the Lord, and said, Lord, wherefore hast Thou so *evil* entreated this people? why is it that Thou hast sent me? For since I came to Pharaoh to speak in Thy name, he hath done evil to this people; *neither hast Thou delivered Thy people at all*" (Ex. 5:22, 25). Blessed is it to behold the patience of God with His failing servant, and to see how He comforted and strengthened him: Ex. 6:1-8.

"By faith he forsook Egypt." Faith assures the heart of a *better portion* in return for any thing God calls us to relinquish. No matter how attractive to the senses, no matter how popular with our fellows, no matter how necessary it may seem for the interests of our family, faith is convinced that God will not suffer us to be the losers: 1 Sam. 2:30. So Abraham left Chaldea, so Ruth forsook Moab (1:16). Here is one way in which a true faith may be discerned and known: if we were born and brought up in an idolatrous place, where honors, pleasures and treasures might be enjoyed, and we, for conscience sake, have forsaken that place, then surely we have a *spiritual* faith. Few are now required to do as Abraham did, but all *are* commanded to obey 2 Cor. 6:14, 17.

Ah, there are many who forsake Egypt's (the world's) vices and pleasures, who do not separate from *its religion,* and *that* was the central thing in the final test which Moses' faith had to overcome. Again and again Pharaoh sought a compromise, but with inflexible firmness Moses stood his ground. The demand of God was, "Let My people go, that they may hold a feast unto Me *in the wilderness*" (Ex. 5:1): there must be a complete separation from the religion of the world. But that is something which the world cannot brook, for the withdrawal of God's people condemns them; hence we find Pharaoh saying, "Go ye, sacrifice to your God *in the land*" (Ex. 8:25). But Moses was not to be moved, "We will go three days' journey into the wilderness, and sacrifice to the Lord our God *as* He shall command us" (8:27).

Next we are told Pharaoh said, "I will let you go, that ye may sacrifice to the Lord your God in the wilderness, only *ye shall not go very far away*" (8:28): this was tantamount to saying, "If you are determined to adopt this holier than thou attitude, there is no reason why there should be a complete break between us." After the Lord had further plagued Egypt, the king again sent for Moses and Aaron and asked, "*Who* are they that shall go?" Moses answered, "We will go with our young and with our old, with our sons, and with our daughters, with our flocks and with our herds" (10:9). But that was too much for Pharaoh, who replied, "Not so: go now *ye that are men*, and serve the Lord" (10:11). See here in Pharaoh, my reader, our great Adversary, striving to get us to temporize: "If you are determined to forsake the church, at least leave your children in the Sunday School!" How subtle the Devil is! What a *living* book is the Word! How thoroughly suited to our present lot and needs!

One more effort was made by Pharaoh to induce Moses to render only a partial obedience unto God's demands: "Go ye, serve the Lord,*only let your flocks and your herds be stayed*" (10:24)—If you must be so unsociable, if you will be so mulish and not allow your children to remain in Sunday School, at least retain your *membership* with us and *pay* into the "church-treasury" as hitherto! Ah, had Moses feared the wrath of the king, he had yielded this point. Instead, he remained firm, and said, "Thou must give us *also* sacrifices and burnt offerings, that we may sacrifice unto the Lord our God. Our cattle also *shall go* with us; there shall *not an hoof* be left behind: for thereof must we take to serve the Lord our God" (10:25, 26). Well might the apostle write, "Lest Satan should get an advantage of us: *for we are not ignorant of his devices*" (2 Cor. 2:11)—no, for they have been fully exposed to us in Holy writ.

All of what has been before us above is included in these words "By faith he *forsook Egypt,*" and all of it is "written for *our* learning" (Rom. 15:4). The offers made by Pharaoh to Moses to prevent Israel from completely forsaking Egypt in their worship of the Lord, are, in essence, the very temptations which His people now have to overcome, if they are to fully heed and obey 2 Cor. 6:14, 17, "Be ye not unequally yoked together with unbelievers: for what fellowship hath righteousness with unrighteousness? . . . Wherefore come out from among them, and be ye separate, saith the Lord, *and touch not* the unclean thing." O my Christian reader, seek grace to obtain the uncompromising spirit of Moses. When urged to worship God in "Egypt" (i. e. the white-washed "churches" *of the world*), say it is impossible, for "what communion hath light with darkness!" When pressed to leave your children in a worldly Sunday School, to be instructed by those who have not the fear of God upon them, refuse. When invited to at least retain your membership in the Holy Spirit-deserted "churches" and contribute of your means to their upkeep, decline to do so.

"Not fearing the wrath of the king." The courage of Moses is here set forth in three degrees: he feared not *man*; he feared not the greatest of men, a *king;* he feared not that which most affrights people, the *wrath of a king*—"The king's wrath is as the roaring of a lion" (Prov. 19:12). It was his faith in God which expelled this fear. When faith is exercised the greatest terrors cannot alarm saints. And, my reader, those who "forsake Egypt," especially *religions* of Egypt, must expect to encounter the "wrath" of man: none hates so bitterly, none acts so cruelly, none comes out more in his true colors, than the worldly religionist when the veneer of hypocritical piety has been seen through by a child of God. Yet *his* "wrath" is less to be feared than was Pharaoh's: "If God be for us, who can be against us!"

"For he endured, as seeing Him who is invisible." Ah, here is the key to all that has been before us, Moses "endured," which tells us of the state of his heart. He "endured" the attractive honors and alluring pleasures of Egypt's court; he "endured" the repeated compromises of Pharaoh; he "endured" the terrors which his conduct might inspire. His courage was no mere flash in the pan, or momentary bravado; but was steady and real. O how little of *this* faith and its blessed fruit of holy boldness, is now to be seen in poor, degenerate Christendom. Yet how could it be otherwise, when worldliness has "quenched" the Spirit on every hand? May we who have, by sovereign grace, been drawn to Christ outside the camp, be very jealous and watchful against grieving the Spirit.

The precise word which is here rendered "endured" is not employed elsewhere in the N.T. Scholars tell us that it is derived from a root meaning strength or fortitude, to bear evils, undergo dangers with resolution and courage, so as not to faint beneath them, but hold on our way to the end. It was a word most appropriate to express the firmness of Moses' mind in this work of faith in "forsaking Egypt." He met with a long course of difficulties, and was repeatedly threatened by the king; and, in addition, he had to endure a great conflict with his own unbelieving brethren. But he strengthened himself with spiritual courage and resolution to abide in his duty to the finish. *How*? Whereby was his strength renewed?

"For he endured, as seeing Him who is invisible." Ah, it was no mulish stupidity nor obstinate imprudence that wrought such a resolution in Moses, but the constant occupation of his heart with the Divine perfections. We say "the *constant* occupation," for note carefully our text does not say "he endured because he *saw* Him who is invisible," but "as *seeing* Him who is invisible"—it was a continuous act! O to be able to say in our measure, "I have *set the Lord always before me*" (Psa. 16:8). This is absolutely essential if faith and courage are to be kept healthy. Nothing else will enable *us* to "endure" the frictions and trials of life, the attractions and distractions of the world, the assaults of Satan.

"He endured as seeing Him who is invisible." "God is said to be invisible (as He *is* absolutely) in respect of His essence, and is often so called in the Scripture: Rom. 1:20, Col. 1:15, 1 Tim. 1:17. But there is a peculiar reason for this description of Him here. Moses was in that state and condition, and had those things to do, wherein he stood in need continually of Divine power and assistance. Whence this should proceed, he could not discern by his senses, his bodily eyes could behold no present assistant, for God is 'invisible'.

And it requires an especial act of the mind in expecting help from Him who cannot be seen. Wherefore this is here ascribed to him. He saw Him who was in Himself invisible; that is, he saw by faith, whom he could not see with his eyes" (John Owen). This word "invisible" shows the uselessness (as well as sin) of making images to represent God, and warns against our forming any apprehensions in our mind patterned after the likeness of any visible object. Though God be invisible, yet He sees us!

"He endured as seeing Him who is invisible." "A double act of the faith of Moses is intended herein. 1. A clear, distinct view and apprehension of God in His omnipresence, power and faithfulness. 2. A fixed trust in Him on their account, at all times and on all occasions. This he rested on, this he trusted to, that God was everywhere present with him, able to protect him, and faithful in the discharge of His promise" (John Owen). God is the proper object of faith: on which it rests, from which it expects every good and to which it returns the glory for all.

O the surpassing excellency of faith. It takes in eternal, invisible, infinite objects. By His providences God often appears to be against His people, but faith knows He is for them. In this world we are subject to many trials and miseries, but faith knows that "all things work together for good to them that love God." The bodies of God's children die, are buried, and return to dust; but faith beholds a glorious resurrection for them. O the wondrous power of faith to rise above the things of sight and sense. It is true that neither the impartation of faith, nor its growth and exercise, lie within *our* power; nevertheless, we *are* responsible to avoid those things which becloud and weaken faith, and we are responsible to nourish faith. How very few make serious efforts *to see* "Him who is invisible!"

CHAPTER SEVENTY-FOUR

The Faith of Moses

(Heb. 11:28)

There is more about Moses than any other individual in this 11th chapter of Hebrews. No less than five definite actings of his faith are there recorded. The reason for this is not far to seek. He was the law-giver, and the boast of the Jews of Christ's day was, "We are Moses' disciples" (John 9:28). They were seeking acceptance with God on the ground of their own doings. They supposed that their outward conformity to the ordinances of Moses would secure the approbation of Heaven, and therefore, "They being ignorant of God's righteousness, and going about to establish their own righteousness, have not submitted themselves unto the righteousness of God" (Rom. 10:3). It was under this influence that these converted Hebrews had been brought up, and therefore did the Holy Spirit press upon them the fact that it was *by faith*, and not by a legal spirit, their renowned ancestor had lived and acted.

The particular acting of Moses' faith which we are now to consider was one which would be singularly pertinent to the Spirit's design here: it manifested his trust in the Lamb and testified to the value which he placed upon the sprinkled blood. Instituting and observing the feast of the passover, the leader of the Israelites set an example that could not be ignored without fatal consequences. It completely repudiated the awful error of thinking to escape from the wrath of God in consequence of any performances on the part of the creature. It effectively shuts up the sinner to Christ as his *only* hope. Let it be duly considered that the "passover" was the *first* ordinance given to Israel.

How striking it is to see the law-giver himself preaching, by those actings of his recorded in our text, "*By grace* are ye saved through faith; and that not of yourselves: it is the gift of God: not of works, lest any man should boast" (Eph. 2:8, 9). How great is the ignorance, then, which supposes that salvation by grace is peculiar to this Christian dispensation—as though God has several ways of redeeming sinners. No, my reader, from the beginning to the end of human history every fallen descendant of Adam which enters Heaven will owe it to sovereign grace, flowing to him through the appointed channel of faith, entirely irrespective of all his works, religious or irreligious, before he first trusts in Christ. Abel was saved thus: Heb. 11:4. Noah "found grace in the eyes of the Lord: Gen. 6:8. Abraham "believed God, and it was counted unto him for ("unto") righteousness": Rom. 4:3. And the children of Israel were delivered from the Angel of Death because they were sheltered beneath the blood of the lamb.

That which is now before our consideration formed an appropriate and blessed climax to the actings of Moses' faith recorded here in Heb. 11: all the others led up to one. His *refusing* to be called the son of Pharaoh's daughter, his *choosing* rather to suffer affliction with the people of God than to enjoy the pleasures of sin for a season, his *esteeming* the reproach of Christ greater riches than the treasures of Egypt, and his *forsaking* of Egypt would all have been in vain spiritually, that is, so far as his salvation was concerned, unless those had been followed by *faith in the lamb* and the efficacy of *its blood*. Turning away from the world is not sufficient: there must also be a turning unto God. The forsaking of sin is not enough: there must also be the laying hold of Christ. *This* is what is typically in view in our present text.

It is highly important that the closest attention be paid to *the order of truth* set forth in Heb. 11:24-28. If this be done, the defectiveness of much modern "evangelism" will at once be apparent. The keeping of the passover and the sprinkling of the blood *is not the first thing* recorded of Moses! No man can rightly value the blood of Christ while his heart is still wrapped up in the world, and to invite and exhort him to put his trust in the same, is being guilty of casting pearls before swine. No man can savingly believe in Christ while he is determined to "enjoy the pleasures of sin for a season." *Repentance precedes faith* (Mark 1:15; Acts 20:21): and repentance is a sorrowing over sin, a hatred of sin, and a turning from sin; and where there is no genuine repentance, there can be no "remission of sins": Mark 1:4. Let every preacher who reads this article carefully weigh *all* that is here recorded of Moses, and faithfully instruct his congregation that the different exercises of heart recorded in Heb. 11:24-27 *must* precede that which is stated in v. 28.

It is really deplorable that such elementary aspects of Truth as we have just pointed out above need to be stressed at this late date. Yet such is the tragic case. Laodicean Christendom is boasting of its riches, and knows not that it is poor and wretched and naked. Part of those "riches" which she boasts so loudly of today, is the "great increase of light" which it is supposed that the study of prophetic" and "dispensational" truth has brought to us. Yet not only is that a subtle device of Satan's coming as "an angel of *light*" (2 Cor. 11:14), to *darken* men's understandings, and make them believe that his lies are "wonderful discoveries" and openings up of the Scriptures, but the present generation *has far less* real Light than Christendom enjoyed a century ago. By which we mean, there is far less faithful and fearless preaching of those things which make for practical godliness and holy living. But that is not the worst: Scriptural evangelism has well-nigh disappeared from the earth.

The "Gospel" which is being preached today is only calculated to deceive souls and bolster them up in a false hope. To make men believe that God loves them, while they are under His wrath (see John 3:36), is worse than a physician telling a diabetic subject that he may safely eat all he wishes. To withhold the preaching of *the Law* —its Divine authority, its inexorable demands, its spirituality (in requiring *inward* conformity to it: Matt. 5:22, 28), its awful curse —is to omit that which alone conveys a true knowledge of sin: *see* Rom. 3:20, 7:7. To cry "Believe, believe," and say nothing about *repentance*, is to falsify the terms of salvation: Luke 24:47; Acts 17:30. To invite sinners to receive Christ as their "Saviour" *before* they surrender to Him as their Lord, is to present a *false* "way of salvation." To bid the lost "come to Christ" without telling them they must first "forsake the world," is to fill the "churches" with unconverted souls. To tell sinners they may find rest unto their souls *without* taking Christ's YOKE upon them, is to give the lie unto the Master's own teaching: Matt. 11:29.

We offer no apology for this seeming digression from our present subject. Once again we would point out that it is our earnest desire in this series of articles to write something more than a "commentary" on Hebrews, or give a bare "exposition" of its text: rather do we seek (as the Holy Spirit is pleased to enable) to address ourselves directly to the hearts of our readers, and press upon them *the personal and present* application of each verse to their own souls. In all probability a large proportion of the readers of this magazine are *deceived* souls, and we do not want to have to answer for their blood in the Day to come. Many of them have been lulled to sleep by the chloroforming "evangelism" of the day. Therefore we earnestly beg each one who scans these paragraphs to seriously and solemnly ask, Is there anything in my own heart's history which answers to that which is said of Moses in Heb. 11:24-27? If there is not, if you are not "*crucified to the world*" (Gal. 6:14), then Satan is fatally deluding you if you imagine that you are under the blood of Christ.

Suffer us then, dear reader, to continue addressing you directly, for a moment longer. We do not ask, first, Are you "resting on the finished work of Christ?" There are thousands who imagine they are so doing, who have never been converted. No, rather would we inquire, Have you *made your peace with God?* We are well aware *that* expression is ridiculed and denounced by a certain class who pose as being ultra-spiritual and exceptionally well-taught in the Scriptures, but they only betray their ignorance of the Word: see Isa. 27:5, Luke 14:32. By asking whether you have "made your peace with God," we mean, Have you ceased fighting against Him, and have you yielded to His demands? Have you thrown down the weapons of your rebellion, and expressed an honest desire and determination to be in subjection to Him? Have you realized that living to please yourself and have your own way, is a species of defiance, and have you truly surrendered yourself unto His claims?

"Through faith he kept the passover, and the sprinkling of blood, lest He that destroyed the firstborn, should touch them" (v. 28). Let it be pointed out again that *this* was the point unto which all the previous actings of Moses' faith led. While it is true that no sinner can "keep the Passover" or find protection under "the sprinkling of blood," while his heart still loves the world, and is filled with its idols, nevertheless, his separation from and relinquishing of all which is opposed to God, obtains not salvation for him. The blotting out of sins does not become ours until the atonement of Christ is received into our hearts by faith. Thus, by taking Heb. 11:24-28 *as a whole*, we see how both the righteousness and the grace of God were honoured and magnified.

Our present verse looks back to and gives an abridgement of that which is recorded in Ex. 12. It tells us of a further fruit of a supernatural faith. At first sight it may appear unto many that *this* particular work of faith is far less remarkable than some of those which have engaged our attention in previous articles. Yet when it be duly considered, when all the attendant circumstances are properly weighed, it will be seen that the conduct of Moses on this occasion was as much opposed to human reason and carnal wisdom, and issued from a Divine work of grace in his heart, as did Abraham's leaving of Chaldea for an unknown country, his offering up of Isaac, or Joseph's "making mention of the departing of the children of Israel." We quote now from another who has brought out this point most forcibly and helpfully.

"The institution of the Passover was an act of faith, similar to that of Noah's preparation of the ark (v. 7). To realize what this faith must have been, we have to go back to 'that night,' and note the special circumstances, which can alone explain the meaning of the words 'by faith.' God's judgments had been poured out on Egypt and its king, and its people. A crisis had arrived, for, after nine plagues had been sent, Pharaoh and the Egyptians still remained obdurate. Indeed, Moses had been threatened with death if he ever came into Pharaoh's presence again (Ex. 10, 28, 29). On the other hand, the Hebrews were in more evil case than ever; and Moses, who was to have delivered them, had not made good his promises.

"It was at such a moment that Moses *heard* from God what he was to do. To sight and to sense it must have seemed most inadequate, and quite unlikely to accomplish the desired result. Why should this last plague be expected to accomplish what the nine had failed to do, with all their cumulative terrors? Why should the mere sprinkling of the blood have such a remarkable effect? And if they were indeed to leave Egypt 'that same night' why should the people be burdened with all those minute ceremonial observances at the very moment when they ought to be making preparation for their departure!

"Nothing but *faith* could be of any avail here. Everything was opposed to human understanding, and human reasoning. With all the consciousness of ill-success upon him, nothing but unfeigned faith in the living God, and what he had heard from Him, could have enabled Moses to go to the people and rehearse all the intricacies of the Paschal observances, and tell them to exercise the greatest care in the selection of a lamb on the tenth day of the month, to be slain on the fourteenth day, and eaten with (to them) an unmeaning ceremonial.

"It called for no ordinary confidence in what Moses had *heard* from God to enable him to go to his brethren who, in their deep distress, must have been ill-disposed to listen; for, hitherto, his efforts had only increased the hatred of their oppressors and their own miseries as bondmen. It would, to human sight, be a difficult if not impossible task to persuade the people, and convince them of the absolute necessity of complying with all the minute details of the observance of the Paschal ordinance. But this is just where *faith* came in. This was just the field on which it could obtain its greatest victory. Hence we read that 'by faith' every difficulty was overcome; the Feast was observed, and the Exodus accomplished. All was based on 'the hearing of faith.' The words of Jehovah produced the faith, and were at once the cause and effect of all the blessings" (E.W.B.).

It should be evident, then, from what has been pointed out above that the actions of Moses recorded in Ex. 11 and 12 proceeded from no mere natural faith, but were the supernatural fruit issuing from a supernatural root. His conduct must have exposed him unto the ridicule of the Egyptians, but with implicit confidence in the wisdom, distinguishing mercy, and faithfulness of Jehovah, he acted. See here, again, how inseparable are faith and obedience: the very "faith" of Moses which is mentioned in our present text, *consisted in* an implicit compliance with all the regulations specified by the Lord. He observed the passover in his own person, and he ordered the people to do likewise, though it involved their procuring many thousands of lambs. He observed the passover in fullest assurance that thereby all the firstborn of the Hebrews would be delivered. Though all Israel kept the passover, it was by Moses that God delivered the institution of it.

The passover was one of the most solemn institutions of the O. T., and one of the most eminent types of Christ. "1. It was a lamb that was the matter of his ordinance (Ex. 12:3). And in allusion hereunto, as also to other sacrifices that were instituted afterwards, Christ is called 'The Lamb of God' (John 1:29). 2. This lamb was to be taken out from the flock of the sheep (v. 5). So was the Lord Christ to be taken out of the flock of the church of mankind, in His participation of our nature, that He might be a meet sacrifice for us (Heb. 2:14-17). 3. This lamb being taken from the flock was to be shut up separate from it (Ex. 12:6). So although the Lord Christ was taken from amongst men, yet He was separate from sinners (Heb. 7:26), that is, absolutely free from all that contagion of sin which others are infected withal. 4. This lamb was to be without blemish (Ex. 12:5), which is applied unto the Lord Christ: 'a Lamb without blemish and without spot' (1 Pet. 1:19). 5. This lamb was to be slain, and was slain accordingly (v. 6). So was Christ slain for us; a Lamb, in the efficacy of His death, slain, from the foundation of the world (Rev. 13:8). 6. This lamb was so slain, as that it was a sacrifice (v. 27); it was the sacrifice of the Lord's passover. And Christ our passover was sacrificed for us (1 Cor. 5:7). 7. The lamb being slain, was to be roasted (vv. 8, 9), which signified the fiery wrath that Christ was to undergo for our deliverance. 8. That 'not a bone of him shall be broken' (v. 46), was expressly to declare the manner of the death of Christ (John 19:33-36). 9. The eating of him, which was also enjoined, and that wholly and entirely (vv. 8, 9), was to instruct the church in the spiritual food of the flesh and blood of Christ, in the communication of the fruits of His mediation unto us by faith" (John Owen).

By faith he kept the passover, and the sprinkling of blood, lest He that destroyed the firstborn should touch them." Two things are here noted separately, the lamb and its blood. In type they spoke, distinctively, of the person and work of Christ, for it was *the person* of Christ which gave value to His work—His Divine person being the "altar" which "sanctified" the offering of His humanity (Matt. 23:

19). This is ever the *order* of Scripture: "Behold (1) the Lamb of God, which (2) taketh away the sin of the world" (John 1:29); "I determined not to know anything among you save (1) Jesus Christ and (2) Him crucified" (1 Cor. 2:2); "in the midst of the elders stood (1) a Lamb (2) as it had been slain" (Rev. 5:6). Here is the Analogy of Faith for the preacher to follow today: It is not the blood which is first to be proclaimed to the sinner, but the wondrous and glorious God-man Mediator who shed His blood for His people.

The Hebrews, equally with the Egyptians, were exposed unto the Divine vengeance, when the Angel of Death went forth on his dread work that memorable night, for "*all* have sinned and come short of the glory of God." And naught but their placing the substitutionary death of an innocent victim between their guilty selves and an holy God, could protect from the judgment announced against them. Trusting in their descent from Abraham would avail them not. Appeal to their good works and religious performances would have sufficed not. They might have spent the entire night in fasting and prayer, in penitently confessing their sins and crying unto God for mercy, but none of those exercises would have stood them in any good stead. "When I *see the blood,* I will pass over you" (Ex. 12:13) made known the all-essential requirement. So it is now; nothing but *the blood of Christ* can cleanse from sin and deliver from the death-penalty of God's broken law.

"Through faith" or better "By faith," for the Greek here is the same as in the previous verse. "He kept the passover," that is, both instituted and observed it, as the Redeemer did His own "supper." "And the sprinkling of blood": this emphasizes an important distinction. "Without *shedding* of blood is no remission" (Heb. 9:22), and without *sprinkling* of blood (cf. 1 Pet. 1:2) the virtues of Christ's atonement are not brought unto the soul. The "sprinkling" of the blood has reference to *the application* to one's own self. The shedding of Christ's blood is the *ground* on which atonement was made for the sins of His people; the sprinkling of it is the *means* of reaping benefit thereby. The sprinkling of the blood on the door of the house in Ex. 12:13 was both a sign to the Destroyer that He should not enter, and an assurance to the household that they were safe.

It is by a spiritual "sprinkling" or applying of Christ's blood that all the benefit thereof redounds to us. It corresponds to the laying of a plaster on a sore, to the drinking of a wholesome potion, to the eating of food, to the putting on of a garment: the *benefit* of all these ariseth from a *fit application* of them. The blood of Christ is "sprinkled" on the soul in two ways. First, by the Spirit of God (1 Cor. 6:11), who inwardly persuades the soul of a *right* that *it* hath to Christ and to all that He did and suffered for our redemption. Second, by faith (Acts 15:9), for faith is the hand of the soul which *receives* all spiritual benefits. Faith moves the regenerated soul to rest upon Christ for a personal benefit of His obedience unto death. On this ground the apostle exhorts, "Let us draw near with a true heart in a full assurance of faith, having our hearts *sprinkled from* an evil (guilty) conscience" (Heb. 10:22).

"Lest He that destroyed the firstborn should touch them." Primarily, the Destroyer was the Lord Himself (Ex. 12:12, 23); secondarily, and instrumentally, the reference is to an angel: compare 2 Sam. 24:16, 2 Kings 19:35. Whoever is not "sprinkled" with the blood of Christ is exposed to the anger of God. But so secure are those who are under the same, that the Destroyer shall not so much as "touch" them—He shall do them *no harm*: cf. 1 John 5:18. God proportioned His judgment upon Egypt according to their sin: Pharaoh had ordered his people to cast every son born unto the Hebrews into the river (Ex. 1:22), and now *their* firstborn were to be slain. Thus God manifested the equity of His proceedings against them. "Be not deceived, God is not mocked: for whatsoever a man soweth, *that* shall he also reap" (Gal. 6:7).

Our verse as a whole teaches Christians that there must be *the exercise of faith* in order to a right use of the means and institutions which God has appointed: whether in reading the Word, in prayer, in baptism, or the Lord's supper: "*without* faith it is impossible to please Him." It also shows us that real faith will not use that for which it has no Divine warrant. An active obedience unto the authority of Christ in His commands is exactly required in all that we do in Divine worship. Well suited to the case of the Hebrews was the example of Moses: to exercise faith in the Lamb and persevere in the duties which God has appointed. No matter how unreasonable it might seem to carnal wisdom, no matter what inconvenience and persecution it might entail, trust in and obedience to the Lord was their duty and blessedness.

CHAPTER SEVENTY-FIVE

The Faith of Israel

(Heb. 11:29)

The apostle's object in this 11th chapter of Hebrews is to show the power of real faith in God to produce supernatural acts, to overcome difficulties which are insuperable to mere nature, and to endure trials which are too much for flesh blood to bear up under. Various examples have been adduced in illustration. A further notable one is now before us. In it we see how faith enabled Israel to fearlessly venture themselves to enter a strangely formed valley between two mountainous ridges of water, and to reach in safety the opposite shore. In like manner, a real faith in God will enable the Christian to pass through trials and troubles which destroy multitudes of his fellow-creatures, and which will in due time conduct him unto the enjoyment of perfect bliss.

The force of the above example is greatly heightened by a striking and most solemn contrast. The power of faith in enabling Israel to safely cross the Red Sea is demonstrated by the helpless and hopeless destruction of the Egyptians, who sought to follow them. "The Egyptians pursued, and went in after them to the midst of the sea, even all Pharaoh's horses, his chariots and his horsemen" (Ex. 14:23). But they had no faith. They were moved by passion, by hatred of the Hebrews. It was night when the army of God undertook their strange journey, yet though dark, the hosts of Pharaoh presumptuously and blindly followed. But now had arrived the hour when the long-insulted Divine forbearance was to be avenged.

"And it came to pass, that in the morning watch the Lord looked unto the host of the Egyptians through the pillar of fire and of the cloud, and troubled the hosts of the Egyptians; and took off their chariot wheels, that they drave them heavily; so that the Egyptians said, Let us flee from the face of Israel, for the Lord fighteth for them against the Egyptians" (Ex. 14:24, 25). But it was too late. The haughty monarch of Egypt and his powerful retinue now discovered how vain it was to fling themselves against the bosses of Jehovah's buckler: that which had been a channel of deliverance to the believing Israelites, became the grave of their enemies. Thereby are we shown that all attempts of unbelievers to obtain what faith secures is utterly futile, and doomed to certain disappointment.

But here a difficulty presents itself, and a formidable one it has proved unto most of those who sought to grapple with it. In our text we are told that, "By faith they passed through the Red Sea," whereas in Heb. 3:18, 19 it is said, "To whom sware He that they should not enter into His rest, but to them that believed not? So we see that they could not enter in because of unbelief." Was, then, their faith only a temporary one, like that of the stony-ground hearers? No, for the "faith" mentioned in every other verse in Heb. 11 was a saving one, and we dare not arbitrarily assume this in v. 29 was an altogether different one.

The solution of our present difficulty lies in attentively noting the pronoun which the Holy Spirit has here employed: "By faith *they* passed through the Red Sea." It is not there said "By faith the children of Israel" did so, for it is very evident from their later history that the vast majority of them were "a very froward generation, children in whom was *no* faith" (Deut. 32:20). The reference, then, in our text is unto Moses and Aaron, Caleb and Joshua, and the believing remnant among the Hebrews. But, it may be asked, Did not the unbelieving portion of the Nation also pass safely through the Red Sea? Truly, and herein we have illustration of the fact that unbelievers are frequently made partakers of temporal blessings as the result of their association with people of God. Another example of this same principle is found in Acts 27:24 where we see that an entire ship's company were spared for Paul's sake.

"By faith they passed through the Red Sea, as by dry land; which the Egyptians assaying to do were drowned" (11:29). In seeking to expound this verse we cannot do better than adopt the division of the Puritan Manton thereon, considering it three ways: historically, sacramentally, and applicatively. First, then, historically.

Our text takes us back to what is recorded in Ex. 14. There we learn that when at last Pharaoh consented to let the Hebrews go, he soon repented of his grant, and being informed by his spies that the Israelites were entangled in the straits of Pihahiroth, he determined to pursue, and either recover or destroy them. At the head of a great military force he swiftly went after them. The consequence was that "When Pharaoh drew nigh, the children of Israel lifted up their eyes, and, behold the Egyptians marched after them: and they were sore afraid; and the children of Israel cried out unto the Lord. And they said unto Moses, Because there were no graves in Egypt, hast thou taken us away to die in the the wilderness? wherefore hast thou dealt thus with us, to carry us forth out of Egypt? Is not this the word that we did tell thee in Egypt, saying Let us alone, that we may serve the Egyptians? For it had been better for us to serve the Egyptians, than that we should die in the wilderness" (Ex. 14:10-12).

A truly desperate situation now faced Moses and the company he was leading. "Shut in between the great fortress 'Migdol,' which was on the 'Shur' or wall (built to protect Egypt from Asia), and the sea, with Pharaoh's host behind, and shut in on the other side by the wilderness: Ex. 14:2,3. It was indeed a crisis" (E. W. B.). What could the poor Israelites do? Fight they dare not, being a multitude of undisciplined people, of all sexes and ages, and pursued by a regular and powerful army of enemies. Fly they could not, for they were completely hemmed in on every side. To all outward appearance their case seemed hopeless; and to human reason, nothing but sore destruction might be expected.

The situation which confronted Israel *was* a hopeless one so far as *they* were concerned, and had not the Lord shown Himself strong on their behalf, they had undoubtedly perished. But, "if God be *for* us, who can be against us"? Ah, my reader, that is the great thing for each of us to make sure of, and when we have done so, to seek grace to rest with unshaken confidence upon it. Has not God promised, "When thou passest through the waters I will be with thee; and through the rivers, they shall not overthrow thee" (Isa. 43:2)! What better assurance than that can the believing heart ask for? No matter how deep and wide stretching, no matter how dark and foreboding the "waters" of adverse circumstances may be unto sight and sense, has not He who cannot lie declared, "They *shall not* overflow thee"!

"And Moses said unto the people, Fear ye not, stand still, and see the salvation of the Lord, which He will show to you today: for the Egyptians whom ye have seen today, ye shall see them again no more for ever" (Ex. 14:13). Undeterred by the chiding of the people, and wisely making no reply thereto, Moses turned their minds away from the outward danger and directed their thoughts unto Jehovah. They had "lifted up their eyes and beheld the Egyptians" (v. 10), and in consequence they were sore afraid; but there was something else for *faith* to "see," namely, "the salvation (or deliverance) of Jehovah," which was not yet visible to natural sight. If they were steadfastly occupied with *that* their trembling hearts would be stilled.

Admire, dear reader, the confident assurance which Divine grace wrought in the heart of Moses, for by nature he was a frail man of like passions and infirmities as us. But there was no wavering or doubting on his part: "see the salvation of the Lord, which He *will* show you today": that was the language of faith—of a supernatural, God-given faith. Moses was not engaged with the difficulties and dangers of the trying situation which confronted them; instead, he was occupied with One before whom all difficulties disappear like mists before the rising sun. "The Lord shall fight for you, and ye shall hold your peace" (v. 14). Once the soul is able to rest on that fact, doubtings end and alarms are silenced.

"Faith cometh by hearing, and hearing by the word of God" (Rom. 10:17). Faith must have a foundation to stand upon, and the only firm and sure one is the promise of the living God. "Fear ye not, stand still, and see the salvation of the Lord, which He will show you today ... The Lord shall fight for you, and ye shall hold your peace" afforded the necessary ground for the faith of each believing Hebrew to rest upon. The eye of faith must see that Divine "salvation" or deliverance, before the eye of sense beheld it: only the sure word of God could give strength to their hearts to advance into the ocean before them. When the promise had been "heard," and not before, then came the order "Go forward."

"And the Lord said unto Moses, Wherefore criest thou unto Me? speak unto the children of Israel, that they go forward: But lift thou up thy rod, and stretch out thine hand over the sea, and divide it: and the children of Israel shall go on dry ground through the midst of the sea" (Ex. 14:15, 16). Thus we learn that the heart of Moses was engaged in silent supplication at this time. The Lord's statement here is not to be understood as a rebuke. No, Moses was waiting the word of command, and until it was given, he stayed himself upon the Lord. "And the children of Israel went into the midst of the sea upon the dry ground: and the waters were a wall unto them on their right hand, and on their left" (v. 22).

"When Moses gave the signal by his rod, the sea miraculously retreated, standing up like heaps of congealed ice on either side while they passed through. This is done, and they go on safely; the sea flanked them on both sides; the rear was secured by the cloudy and fiery pillar interposing between them and Pharaoh's army, till such a time as all were out of danger, and safely arrived at the further shore; and so neither man nor child was hurt. The Egyptians followed the chase, as malice is perverse and blind, and those whom God designeth to destruction take the ready course to bring it upon their own heads; for at the signal again of Moses stretching forth his rod, the returning waters swallowed them all up in a moment" (T. Manton).

"A greater instance, with respect unto the work of Divine providence, of the power of faith on the one hand, and of unbelief with obdurate presumption on the other, there is not on record in the whole book of God. Here we have the end and issue of the long controversy that was between these two people, the Egyptians and the Israelites; a certain type and evidence of what will be the last end of the contest between the world and the church. Their long conflict shall end in the complete salvation of the one, and the utter destruction of the other" (John Owen).

Though it was night, the Divine pillar of cloud "gave light" unto Israel (Ex. 14:19). Dreadful indeed must have appeared those walls of water, for the sea would be raised unto a very great height on either side of them. It called for no ordinary faith to put themselves between such walls, as were ready in their own nature to fall on them unto their destruction any moment, abiding upright only under an invisible restraint. But they had the command of God for their warrant and the promise of God for their security, and these, when laid hold of, are sufficient to overcome all fears and dangers. That Moses himself, to guide and encourage them (and as the type of Christ) took the lead, is clear from Isa. 63:11-13, "God led them through the sea by the right hand of Moses."

Let us now briefly consider the remarkable incident related in our text from a *sacramental* viewpoint. In 1 Cor.10:1,2 we are told, "Moreover, brethren, I would not that ye should be ignorant, how that all our fathers were under the cloud, and all passed through the sea, and were all baptised unto Moses in the cloud and in the sea." From this scripture we learn that Israel's passage through the Red Sea had the same signification that Christian baptism now hath. The points of resemblance are many, and were developed at length by Manton, and more so by Gouge, from whom we here give a digest.

1. The ministry of Moses was confirmed by this miracle, so that the Israelites were obliged to take him for their leader and lawgiver: so the miracles wrought by Christ assure us that He was sent by God as our lawgiver, which we must hear and obey. 2. Israel's experience is (figuratively) denominated a "baptism" because it signified the difference which God puts between His people and His enemies: the deliverance of Israel from the Egyptians was sealed by their passage through the Sea. Similarly baptism is said to be an answering figure to the ark of Noah (1 Pet. 3:20, 21): as those on the ark were exempted from the deluge, so those in Christ are exempted from the deluge of wrath which will yet overwhelm the world.

3. They were baptised "in the cloud and in the sea," because by submitting to God's command they gave up themselves to His direction: so in baptism we dedicate ourselves unto Christ, avowing Him to be our Lord and Master. 4. The passing through the Red Sea and baptism had both the same outward sign, which is water (Matt. 3:6). 5. They had like rites, which were entering into the water and coming out of it (Acts 8:38, 39). 6. They had both the same ground,

which was God's command and promise (Ex. 14:13, 16 and Matt. 28:19, Mark 16:16). 7. They were both for the same people, namely, the children of God (Matt. 28:19). 8. They were but once administered (Eph. 4:5).

Let us now consider some of the *practical* lessons which this marvelous incident is designed to teach us. 1. The children of God are sometimes called on *to face great trials*: a Red Sea of difficulty and trouble confronts them. Let it be duly observed that it was not an enemy who put the sea there, but God Himself! This tells us that the Red Sea represents some great and trying providence which the Lord places in the path of each new-born Christian: it is in order to try his faith and test the sincerity of his trust in God. Often this trial is encountered soon after conversion. Sometimes it arises from opposition of ungodly members of our own family. Or, you are engaged in some business—perhaps requiring you to work on the Sabbath day—in which you cannot now conscientiously continue. It means renouncing your means of livelihood, and you cannot see how it can be done and provide things honest in the sight of all men. As you emerged from the bondage of Egypt you thought it would be easy to surrender everything to God, but now a Red Sea of testing is before you, and it appears unfordable.

2. The children of God are sometimes *terrified by powerful enemies*. The Egyptian who pursued Israel up to the Red Sea may be spiritualised to represent those sins of the Christians from which he expected to be completely delivered. For a little while after conversion sin does not much trouble the newly-regenerated saint: he is filled with joy and praise at the great things which the Lord has done for him. But it is not long before he discovers with the apostle "I see another law in my members, warring against the law of my mind, and bringing me into captivity to the law of sin which is in my members" (Rom. 7:23). Satan now pursues the young saint, and often it seems as though all the powers of hell were let loose against him. At such a time our sins appear more formidable to us than before they were forgiven: in Egypt our taskmasters only appeared with their whips, but now they are mounted and in chariots! Ah, after conversion sin looks far more frightful to the saint than ever it did before, and we feel the plague of our heart much more acutely.

3. The people of God are often *troubled with faint hearts*. When the children of Israel saw the Egyptians they were sore afraid, and when they beheld the Red Sea they murmured against their deliverer. A faint heart is the worst foe a Christian has here: when the anchor of faith is fixed deep in the Rock, he need never fear the storm; but when the hand of faith be palsied, or the eye of faith be

dim, it will go hard with us. When faith is dormant the most insignificant stream will make us quiver and cry: I shall be drowned in the flood; but when faith is dominant it fears not an ocean of difficulty or danger. The babe in Christ has but little faith, for he has but little experience: he has not yet proved God's promises and knows not His faithfulness. But as he grows in grace and in the knowledge of the Lord, and becomes established in the faith, he will not despair before Red Seas and Egyptians; but meanwhile, he often trembles and asks, "How shall I ever find deliverance?"

4. The people of God are here instucted *how to act under great trials*. The first word the Israelites received in the hour of their great emergency was, "Fear ye not, stand still"; the second was "And see the salvation (deliverance) of the Lord, which He will show you today"; the third was, "Go forward" (Ex. 14:13, 15). It is of first importance that we should diligently attend to the Divine order of those three things: we are not equipped and ready to "Go forward" until we have "seen" (by faith) the "salvation of the Lord," and that cannot be properly seen until our fears are calmed and we stand still; or, in other words, till we turn from all self-help and cease from all the feverish activites of the flesh.

The continuous call of God to the Christian is "Go forward": persevering steadfastly along the path of duty, walking in that narrow way which the Divine commands and precepts have laid down for us. No matter what obstacles may confront you, no matter what your circumstances may be, no matter what Red Sea of difficulty or danger be before you, "Go forward" is God's authoritative word to you. "Ah, but often that is far from being an easy thing to do!" Quite true, dear friend; yea, we will state it still more strongly: it is often *impossible* to mere nature. What, then, is to be done when the heart faints, when the soul is well-nigh overwhelmed by the greatness of the difficulty or danger, standing right in your path? Two things; first "Stand still." Your own efforts to better matters have brought no relief, your own wisdom can devise no solution; very well, then "stand still": cease from all attempts at self-help.

"But," you answer, "I have my responsibilities to discharge, my duties to perform." Quite true: but admittedly you have now reached the place where a Red Sea is before you; you are dismayed and know not which way to turn. Here, then, is God's word to you in this dire emergency: "Stand still." This means, Get down on your knees, and cry unto the Lord: tell Him all about your trouble, unburden yourself freely and fully unto Him; spread your urgent need before Him. Probably, you answer, "I have done so, and thus far no way through my Red Sea has appeared before me." Then, you are now ready for His next word.

"And see the salvation (deliverance) of the Lord, which He *will* show you." And what does that mean? This, *the exercise of faith* in the living God, the trusting in Him to *undertake* for you, the confident expectation He *will do so.* Cry unto the Holy Spirit to work this faith in you: remain on your knees until He has given you real assurance that your Father *will* show Himself strong on your behalf; wait before Him till one of His promises is applied to your heart in power. *Then,* you are ready to "Go forward," to resume your duties and discharge your responsibilities: to look for work, to go on with renewed strength. The Christian is only ready to "Go forward" when faith has *seen* that which is invisible to sight and sense, namely, the "salvation (deliverance) of the Lord" *before* it is actually wrought for us!

The way in which the Christian is required to walk as he journeys through this world on his way to Heaven is *the path of obedience* to God's commands. Naught but a spiritual faith inclines the heart to comply with God's demands, and upon compliance to expect the mercy promised: "Lord, I have hoped for Thy salvation, and done Thy commandments" (Psa. 119:166). This is the great business of faith: as the Israelites were to obey God, and to wait for His deliverance out of their imminent danger. Naught but a God-given faith imparts courage to obey God in the most difficult crisis. If we be bidden to go into the Red Sea we must not forbear, for none of God's commands are to be disputed, however contrary they be to flesh and blood. Faith teaches us to depend upon God in greatest extremities. Faith receives the promise of God upon the conditions or terms which He has specified. If Israel were to receive the "salvation" of the Lord," they *must* do what He bade. Faith and obedience can no more be separated than can light and heat in the sun.

As Abraham, at the call of God, went out of Chaldea, "not knowing whither he went," so Israel were required to "Go forward" though the Sea stretched before them. Probably it was not until their feet touched the brink that the waters divided. Nature might have gone over it, but *faith* passed safely "through" it! They feared they would be destroyed by Pharaoh's hosts. The very last thing that they would have looked to as a means of escape would be the Sea! Yet, in obedience to the Divine command, "The children of Israel went into the midst of the Sea upon the dry ground: and the waters were a wall unto them on their right hand, and on their left" (Ex. 14:22). Learn, then, dear reader, we never lose by obeying God.

"By faith they passed through the Red Sea." True faith lifts a man above himself, puts into him a spirit which is more than human, and enables him to rise above the obstacles of reason and sense.

Faith emboldened the hitherto trembling Israelites to venture through that strange chasm between the watery walls. "As by dry land" is added to magnify the Divine providence in making a path in the ocean's bottom fit for women and children to tread upon—like a plain and beaten highway. By faith they "passed through": they took not only a few steps, but continued to perseveringly march mile after mile and hour after hour. Hesitate not, my brother, to venture upon anything which God calleth you unto; be assured that He will safely carry you through all difficulties and dangers. "Which the Egyptians assaying to do, were drowned": the very means of Israel's deliverance was their destruction: *see* 2 Cor. 2:16! It was a just retribution for the slaying of the male Hebrew children in the waters (Ex. 1).

5. The people of God may *be assured of the Divine providence.* When Israel "by faith," obeyed the Divine command to "Go forward," God wrought a miracle and delivered them from their dire situation. This is recorded for the encouragement of *our* hearts. It was God who had placed the Red Sea where it was, and it was God who opened the way for Israel through it. So, Christian reader, it is God (and *not* the Devil) who has brought about the problem, the emergency, the danger which now confronts you; for "*of Him* .... are all things" (Rom. 11:36). As He has made thy Red Sea, only He can cleave a way through it for you. Trust, then, in His unerring wisdom. Count upon His mighty power working on your behalf. "Stand still" and rest yourself upon God. View "by faith" anticipatively, expectantly, His "salvation" or deliverance. "Go forward" in obedience to His commands, and He will show Himself strong on thy behalf. *He* never fails those who fully trust and unreservedly obey Him.

CHAPTER SEVENTY-SIX

The Faith of Israel

(Heb. 11:30)

In the preceding verse we had the faith of the believing remnant of Israel under the command and example of Moses, in our present text we have an exhibition and triumph of their faith under the leadership of Joshua. There we beheld what faith accomplished under their exodus from Egypt, here we see what it achieved upon their entering the promised land. As the yoke of bondage was by faith broken asunder, so by the same faith the people of God were to obtain possession of Canaan. Thereby we are taught that the true life of the saint is, from beginning to end, one of faith. Without faith no progress can be made, no victories be obtained, no fruit be brought forth unto God's glory. It is solemn to note that an interval of forty years' duration comes in between Heb. 11:29 and 30. Those years were occupied in the wilderness. They were a judgment from God because of unbelief (Heb. 3). Reader, how many years of your life record no actings of faith to the praise of Divine grace?

The remarkable incident referred to in our text is related at length in the 6th chapter of Joshua, which opens by telling us, "Now Jericho was straitly shut up, because of the children of Israel: none went out, and none came in." Israel had reached the borders of Canaan. They had safely crossed the Jordan, but could not enter the land because of Jericho, which was a powerful fortress barring their ingress. This was one of the cities which had affrighted the spies, causing them to say, "The people is greater and taller than we: the cities are great and walled up to heaven" (Deut. 1:28): to their eyes the cities appeared impregnable, and far too secure for them to take.

Jericho was a frontier town. It was the key-city at the entrance to Canaan. Its capture was absolutely necessary before any progress could be made by Israel in their conquering and occupying of their promised inheritance. Failure to capture it would not only discourage the children of Israel, but would greatly strengthen the morale of the

Canaanites. It was the enemy's leading stronghold, which doubtless, they considered to be quite invulnerable. Yet it fell to a people who possessed no artillery, and without them fighting any battle. All they did, in response to Jehovah's order, was to march by faith around the city once each day for six days, and then seven times on the seventh day, when they gave a great shout, and the walls fell down flat before them. Many important lessons are taught us therein, a few of which we will briefly mention, before dwelling at greater length upon the outstanding one.

First, God's ways are often entirely different from ours. Who ever heard of a powerful fortress being completely demolished in response to a company of people walking around it? Ah, God delights in staining the pride of man. The leader and lawgiver of Israel was preserved in an ark of bulrushes. The mighty giant of the Philistines was overcome by a sling and a stone. The prophet Elijah was sustained by a widow's handful of meal. The forerunner of Christ dwelt in a wilderness and fed upon locusts and wild honey. The Saviour Himself was born in a stable and laid in a manger. His selected ambassadors were, for the most part, unlettered fishermen. Striking illustrations are these of the sentence beginning this paragraph. The things which are highly esteemed among men are abomination in the sight of God. It is well for us to remember this.

Second, God is independent of all natural means and superior to all the "laws of nature." It is true that, as a general rule, God is pleased to bless the use of natural means, and that He frequently accomplishes His ends by the operations of those laws of nature which He has set in motion; but it is a great mistake to imagine that He is tied down either by the one or the other. What natural "means" were employed in Israel's crossing of the Jordan or their capturing of Jericho? What natural "means" were used in the preserving of Daniel in the lion's den or Jonah in the whale's belly? And what "laws of nature" were observed in connection with the birth of Isaac, the feeding of Elijah by the ravens, or the preserving whole the three Hebrews in Babylon's fiery furnace? Yes, God *is* superior to all means and laws. It is well for us to remember this too.

Third, formidable difficulties and powerful oppositions are encountered in the Warfare of Faith. One will not follow the path of faith very far before he comes face to face with that which challenges all his courage and defies all his natural resources and powers. Jordan rivers and Jericho fortresses still exist. But though the one may be unfordable and the other appear impregnable, yet they are the veriest trifles to the Almighty. The dimensions which they assume unto our vision, are largely determined by the measure in which our hearts are engaged with the omnipotent One. Those formidable difficulties and powerful obstacles are placed in our path *by God,* for the purpose of testing us, for the training of faith, as opportunities to trust in and glorify the Lord.

Fourth, Satan's strongholds cannot stand before a people who are obedient to and who rely fully upon the living God. This fact is surely written in large letters across Joshua 6. The Canaanites were completely under the dominion of the Evil one, yet here we see one of their principal fortresses tumbling down like a frail booth when a powerful wind strikes it. To unbelief these cities might appear "walled up to heaven" and seem impregnable, but faith laughs at such things, knowing that God has only to breathe upon them and they will collapse at once. Thus it was in the early days of Christianity, when the imposing citadels of Paganism crumbled away before the faithful ministry of the apostles. Thus it was at the time of the great Reformation in the sixteenth century, when the kingdom of the Papacy was shaken to its very foundations by the courageous preaching of Luther and his contemporaries. Thus it was, in many parts, some fifty years ago, when the high places of heathendom fell down before onslaughts of the missionaries.

And why is it we are not witnessing the same Gospel triumphs in our generation? Why is it that Romanism has now regained so much of its lost ground, and is forging ahead in so many directions? Why is it that on the "foreign field" the forces of Satan are advancing instead of retreating? And why is it that in the so-called Christian lands a growing number of Jerichos defy the prayers and efforts of the saints? Is it because God's arm is now waxed short? Perish the thought. Is it because the Scriptures are obsolete and unfitted to the needs of this twentieth century? Far far from it. What, then, is the matter? This: *there is a grieved Spirit in our midst,* and in consequence *His power is withheld.* The Holy Spirit of God has been "quenched" (1 Thess. 5:19), and therefore the feverish and frenzied efforts of present-day Christendom avail not.

And *why* is the Spirit of God "grieved"? *What is it* that has "quenched" His power in our midst? This, we have departed from *God's way,* we have ignored His orders, we have substituted human devices, we have put our confidence in carnal weapons. Instead of encompassing the walls of Jericho after the Divine order, we have resorted to worldly allurements, seeking to win over the Canaanites by fleshly attractions. My brethren, we cannot hope to have Israel's victories until we emulate Israel's example. We will never again witness a return to apostolic progress until we get back to apostolic methods. There can be no improvement until we truly recognize that it is "Not by might, nor by power, but by My Spirit, saith the Lord of hosts" (Zech. 4:6). And the power of the Spirit will not be manifested in our midst until we once more enter the path of obedience, *doing God's work in God's prescribed way,* and confidently counting upon Him to honour and bless such efforts.

Fifth, but the outstanding lesson to be learned from this incident is that which is stated in our text, where the fall of Jericho is attributed to *the faith* of the believing Israelites. "Do we think enough of faith, choosen by Divine omnipotent love, to be its channel? God alone doeth great marvels, but it is through the faith of His saints. All the victories of Israel were wrought by faith. Divine power and grace redeemed them on that memorable night; but it was the faith of Moses which kept the passover and the sprinkling of blood. It was God who divided the Red Sea, but in answer to the silent prayer of faith which ascended from the heart of His servant. All miracles of healing recorded in the Gospels were wrought by faith. Jesus prayed to His Father, and then fed the multitude with five loaves and two fishes. Jesus lifted up His eyes to heaven, and then said 'Ephphatha, Be thou loosed.' Jesus by faith thanked God that He heard Him always, and then uttered His mighty 'Lazarus, come forth.'

"And faith was wrought also in the recipient of Divine favour: 'Thy faith hath healed thee'; 'Be it unto thee as thou hast believed.' Such were frequently Christ's words. The people who perished in the wilderness entered not into God's rest because of unbelief; and because of their unbelief, Jesus could not show many miracles in some places: 'Believe only, and thou shalt see the glory of God.'

"Israel's history is the history of God's omnipotent saving grace and of man's faith. From heaven descend miracles; from earth ascends faith. From the election of Abraham to the birth of Moses, from the passover and the Red Sea to the dividing of the river Jordan, all is miracle, and all has to go through the faith of some chosen saint. Israel is before Jericho, a walled and fenced city; it is not by power and might, but by faith, that they are to take it" (A. Saphir).

Let us consider the *various aspects of faith* which were manifested by the believing Israelites on this memorable occasion. 1. the *daring* of their faith. When Israel crossed the Jordan, they, as it were, burned all their bridges and boats behind them. They were cut off from flight; they had no houses to which they could retire, and no fortress to which they could retreat. They were now in the enemy's territory, and victory or death were the only alternatives. To march peacefully and quietly around those walls of Jericho seemed a perilous undertaking: what was to hinder the Canaanites from shooting at or casting down rocks upon them. It was truly an adventure of faith, and it is venturesome faith which God delights to honour. Unbelief is hestitant and timorous, but bold faith is confident and courageous. O to be "strong in the Lord, and in the power of His might."

There are three degrees of faith. There is a faith which *receives,* when as empty-handed beggars we come to Christ and accept Him as our Lord and Saviour: John 1:12. There is also a faith which *reckons,* which counts upon God to fulfill His promises and undertake for us: 2 Tim. 1:12. There is also a faith which *risks,* which dares something for the Lord. This aspect of faith was exemplified by Moses when he ventured to confront the king of Egypt and make known Jehovah's demands. This daring of faith was manifested by David when he went forth to engage the mighty Goliath. We see it again in Elijah, when, single-handed, he encountered the host of Jezebel's false prophets on Carmel. We see it again when Daniel dared to be cast into the lion's den rather than comply with the idolatrous edict of Babylon's king. We see it again and again in the journeys and ministry of the apostle Paul, who flinched not before dangers of every imaginable order, that he might make known the unsearchable riches of Christ.

And in each of the instances mentioned above we behold in the sequel how God *honoured* those trusting and daring hearts. It is venturesome faith which He ever delights to reward. He Himself bids us come to the throne of grace with holy "boldness," that we may find grace to help in time of need. O how this rebukes *our* timidity and reserve. How few today are prepared to *risk anything* in the service of our Lord. How little of the courage and daring of our fathers is now in evidence. What a lot of trembling and fearful soldiers are found today in the army of Christ. O how urgent is the need for some Spirit-filled man of faith to go forth and cry in the language of Carey, "Ask great things of God; expect great things from God; *undertake great things for God.*" It is well to look before we leap, but many look so long that they never leap at all!

2. The *obedience* of their faith. This appears from a reading of Josh. 6:3, 4 and 6-8: all concerned carried out the Lord's instructions to the letter. To do nothing more than walk and walk and walk around the walls of Jericho must have appeared a childish and ridiculous thing; yet the believing remnant complied with the Lord's command. God promised to deliver Jericho into their hands: Joshua and his believing fellows rested on His word and carried out His orders. The Lord requires us to use whatever means He prescribes, no matter how unlikely and inadequate they may seem to us. It is true that Divine power overthrew Jericho's walls, yet it was also by faith's obedience they fell. God had made it known that the manifestation of His power should be via a particular way;

it was inseparably connected with certain actions which were to be performed by His people.

How was Israel to capture that mighty fortress of the Canaanites? Consider their condition! For centuries they had been a nation of slaves. For the last forty years they had been weary wanderers in the wilderness. And now their great leader, Moses, was dead! They were without any military experience, devoid of artillery, and had no trained army. All true; but they were not left to themselves: the living God was for them; and so long as they responded to His revealed will, all went well with them. In like manner God has not left us to our own devisings, but has given us plain and full directions, and He requires us to do the work which He has appointed us in the way He has commanded. Implicit obedience to His orders is absolutely essential if we are to have *His* blessing.

Implicit obedience unto the known will of God marked all Israel's arrangements for the siege of Jericho. Minute intructions were given them for their strange campaign. They were to march in a certain order, each being required to take the place assigned him. They were to march at a specified hour, and encompass the city a given number of times. At the command of the Lord they were to be silent, and at the command of the Lord they were to shout. There was no room for human scheming, no place for carnal planning, no need for human reasoning as to what should be done. Everything was prescribed for them, and faith's obedience was all that was required from them. The orders which God gave to Joshua might have seemed unreasonable and absurd to his men, yet they *must* be faithfully executed if victory was to be theirs. And as it was then, so it is still. But O how slow we are to learn this lesson.

Reader, the commands and precepts of God *often* appear strange unto carnal wisdom. How absurd did God's orders appear to the great Naaman, when he was bidden to bathe his leprous body in the Jordan. How contrary to all human ideas was it for God to send the prophet Elijah to be fed for many months by a widow who had naught but a handful of meal and a little oil. How unreasonable it must have seemed to the twelve apostles when Christ bade them tell the great multitude to sit down, and only five small loaves and two little fishes were in sight. And how unreasonable does it appear unto multitudes of professing Christians today when they are told to cast away all the worldly devices which have been brought into the "churches" and substitute fasting and prayer. How slow we are to recognize that it is the *obedience of faith* which God requires.

3. The *discipline* of their faith. "And Joshua had commanded the people, saying, Ye shall not shout, nor make any noise with your voice, neither shall any word proceed out of your mouth, until the

day I bid you shout; then shall ye shout" (Josh. 6:10). Their silence at the beginning was as necessary as their shouting at the finish. Why? These men were the immediate descendants of the greatest grumblers who ever lived. Their fathers complained and murmured until God swore in His wrath they should not enter into His rest.

How much mischief had been caused if every man had been left free to express *his* "opinion"! How many would have been ready to advise Joshua what method of strategy to employ. One would have reasoned that the only way to capture Jericho was by starving out its inhabitants through a protracted siege. Another would have suggested the use of ladders to scale its walls. Another would have advocated heavy battering-rams to force a way in. Another would have suggested tunneling under the walls. One and all would have ridiculed the plan which Joshua adopted. Ah, my readers, if the Jerichos which now confront the people of God are to be captured, then not only must the mouths of murmurers be stopped, but all leaning unto our own understanding must be abandoned.

O how often are the sinews of faith cut by the injudicious and unfriendly criticisms of those who pose as our Christian friends. How often is the man of God hindered by the Christ-dishonouring doubts and carnal suggestion of his fellows. A brother in the Lord, who had been without employment, recently wrote us that he had been rebuked for not making known his needs to his friends. Ah, let us not forget that the very first line which the Holy Spirit gives us in His picture of the "blessed" man is, that he "walketh not in the counsel of the ungodly" (Psa. 1:1). How much mischief is wrought by people perpetually talking of the *difficulties* in the task confronting us. All real Christian work is beset with difficulties—Satan sees to that!

The soldiers of Christ must be trained: faith must be disciplined: each one in the ranks of the Lord's hosts must learn there is "a time to keep silence and a time to speak" (Eccl. 3:7). The children of Israel were not ordered to go forth in battle array and make any sally upon this garrison of the Canaanites. Instead, in solemn silence, in sacred procession, they were to encompass the city. This was a great trial of faith for such a procedure seemed very unlikely to accomplish the desired end. Not only so, but it would expose them to the contempt of their enemies, who must have sneered at their harmless procession. Yet this was the way which *God* had ordered: He loves to do great things by contemptible means, that the glory may be His.

4. The *patience* of their faith: "By faith the walls of Jericho fell down, *after they were compassed about seven days*." They did not

fall the first day that Israel marched around them, nor the second, nor the third. No, it was not until they had journeyed about them thirteen times, that the power of God was displayed. And why? To test their patience, as well as their faith and obedience; to prove whether they really believed the Lord's promise or no, when He enjoined the use of such weak and unlikely means; and to give them a more distinct apprehension that the conquest of Canaan was the Lord's, and not theirs. When nothing happened the first twelve times Israel encompassed Jericho, it became the more evident that their enemies would not be overcome by the power of man, but by God.

Not only the mercy, but the *timing* of it, is in the hands of God, and therefore are we bidden, "Rest in the Lord, and *wait patiently for Him*" (Psa. 37:7). Alas, how sadly do we fail at this point. How easily we become discouraged if our Jericho does not fall the first or second time we encompass it: "the vision is yet for an appointed time . . . though it tarry, *wait for it*, because it will surely come" (Hab. 2:3). But O how impatient is the flesh. It was at this point that Abraham failed: when Sarah bare not the promised son, he determined to have one by Hagar. It was at this point Moses first failed—taking things into his own hands (Ex. 2:11, 12), instead of waiting God's time. "*Tarry ye* at Jerusalem" was the last word which the Redeemer gave unto the apostles before He ascended.

"Men ought always to pray, *and not to faint*" (Luke 18:1). How much we need to take this word to heart: how often we have "fainted" when victory was almost in sight! Ah, we thought that the walls of our Jericho would never fall; but they *did*, at the appointed time. God is in no hurry, and it is required of us that "he that believeth shall not make haste" (Isa. 28:16). But we find it much harder to *wait* than we do to believe: that is, probably, the weakest spot in our armour, and the point at which we fail most frequently. Then let us be more definite and earnest in begging the Holy Spirit to work in us the spiritual grace of patience. Let us seek grace to lay hold of that word, "Let us not be weary in well doing: for in due season we shall reap, if we faint not" (Gal. 6:9).

5. The *anticipation* of their faith: "So the people shouted when the priests blew with the trumpets: and it came to pass, when the people heard the sound of the trumpet, and people shouted with a great shout, that the wall fell down flat, so that the people went up into the city, every man straight before him, and they took the city" (Josh. 6:20). Our space is nearly exhausted, so we must condense. What we would now particularly observe is that the people shouted *before* the walls fell down—it was faith *expecting* the victory. "What things so-ever ye desire, when ye pray, *believe that ye receive*, and ye shall have" (Mark. 11:24). It reminds us

of the missionary Moffatt, who laboured for years among the Bechuanas and saw not a single seal to his ministry. Some of his far-distant friends in England wrote him saying they wished to make a present, and asked him to specify what it should be. He answered "a communion set." Months after, when it arrived, more than a dozen converted natives sat down with him to remember the Lord's death!

How the whole of Josh. 6 has been recorded for our learning. "The walls of unbelief, superstition, and ungodliness, yield to no earthly armour and power. It is not by compulsion, nor by reasoning; it is not by weapons which this world supplies, that these walls can be destroyed. It is by the Word of God, and by the Word declared in faith. Ministers and people, they who blow the trumpet, and also the people who are with them, are to be united together in the power of God" (A. Saphir). Each of us is confronted with a Jericho: whether it be the preacher in the field of service where God calls him to labour, the Sunday-school teacher in the call before her, or the individual Christian who is seeking to overcome some habit or disposition. Remember Joshua, and take courage! If there be the daring, the discipline, the obedience, the patience, and the expectation of faith, the victory is sure in God's appointed time.

Once more we have been shown the wondrous power of real faith to bring to pass that which is beyond mere nature: compare Matt. 17:20, 1 John 5:4; persevering trust and obedience enabled Israel to accomplish what had otherwise been impossible. Again, we have seen that faith in God's promise of protection and the use of His appointed means, far surpasses all worldly methods of defense: compare 2 Chron. 20:20. Contrariwise, we behold what a worthless thing it is to trust in outward and material things: the walls of Jericho were both strong and high, yet they afforded no security against God's power—"vain is the help of man." Though God required Israel to use the utmost of their courage, submission, and patience, yet He took it upon Himself to bless their efforts and effect the work of power. Barriers more difficult than the walls of Jericho stand between the Christian and holiness: how are they to be removed? By faith's obedience; *compare* 2 Cor. 10:4, 5.

CHAPTER SEVENTY-SEVEN

The Faith of Rahab

(Heb. 11:31)

The inestimable value of spiritual faith is strikingly demonstrated in the case we are about to consider. The apostle had cited the faith of such illustrious characters as Enoch and Noah, Abraham and Moses; he had mentioned that of a believing company as they had passed through the Red Sea and had marched around Jericho; now he gives an instance of one who had been a notorious sinner, as though to shame us if *our* faith falls short of her's who had formerly been an harlot. Having shown that the patriarchs, who were so highly venerated by the Jews, were honored by God solely on account of their faith and its fruits, we next behold how an alien woman, belonging to an accursed race, was, because of her faith, adopted into the O.T. Church. "It hence follows that, those who are most exalted are of no account before God, unless they have faith; and that, on the other hand, those who are hardly allowed a place among the profane and the reprobate, are by faith introduced into the company of angels" (John Calvin).

Rahab was a Canaanite, and therefore by nature "an alien from the commonwealth of Israel" and "a stranger from the covenants of promise." In her conversion and admission into the O. T. Church, she was, in a peculiar manner, both a type and a pledge of the calling of *the Gentiles* and their reception into the Church of Christ in N.T. times. Thus did coming events cast their shadows before them. In such cases as Rahab and Ruth God gave early intimations that His redemptive purpose was not confined to a single people, but that it would reach out unto individuals among all nations. Their incorporation among the Hebrews was a plain foreshadowment of the "wild olive tree" being grafted in and being made a partaker of "the root and fatness of the (good) olive tree" (Rom. 11:17).

The salvation of Rahab was a signal instance of *the sovereignty* of God. "She was not only a Gentile, but an Amoritess, of that race and seed which in general was devoted unto utter destruction. She was therefore an instance of God's sovereignty in dispensing with His positive laws, as it seemed good unto Him; for of His own mere pleasure He exempted her from the doom announced against all those of her origin and tradition" (John Owen). Being the supreme Potentate, God is not bound by any law or consideration other than His own imperial will; and therefore does He have mercy on whom He will have mercy, and whom He will He hardens (Rom. 9:18).

Most blessedly do we also behold here the amazing *grace* of God. Not only did Rahab belong to a heathen race, but she was an abandoned profligate, a "harlot." In singling her out to be the recipient of His saving favours, God indeed made it evident that He is no respecter of persons. By her own choice she was given up to the vilest of sins, but by the Divine choice she was predestinated to be delivered from that lust which is the most effective in detaining persons under its power, washing her whiter than snow by the precious blood of Christ, and giving her a place in His own family. It is in just such cases that the unmerited favour of God shines forth the more illustriously. There was nothing whatever in this poor fallen woman to commend her unto the favour of God, but where sin abounded grace did much more abound.

Not only may we behold in Rahab's case the exercise of Divine sovereignty and the manifestation of Divine grace, but we may also pause and admire the wondrous working of God's *power*. This is best perceived as we take into careful consideration the almost unparalleled element which enters into her case. Here the Holy Spirit wrought entirely apart from the ordinary means of grace. There were no Sabbaths observed in Jericho, there were no Scriptures available for reading, there were no prophets sounding forth messages from Heaven; nevertheless, Rahab was quickened into newness of life and brought into a saving knowledge of the true God. Let it be duly noted that this woman, who had previously wallowed in open sin, was regenerated and converted *before* the spies came to her house: their visit simply afforded an opportunity for the avowal and public manifestation of her faith.

Let us also contemplate the marvelous workings of Divine *providence* on this occasion. As the two spies, sent forth by Joshua to reconnoiter Jericho, drew near that heathen stronghold, they had no idea that one of God's elect sojourned there; and had they been aware of the fact, they had no means of knowing how to locate her in a city of such size. Admire and adore, then, the secret hand of God which directed them to the very house in which His child abode. "The Lord knoweth them that are His," and in the cloudy and dark day He searches them out. The same God who sent Annanias to the street called "Straight" to deliver Saul from blindness, guided the two spies unto the house of Rahab to deliver her from death.

In like manner, wherever there is one or more of His elect amid the darkness of heathendom, He sends His Word or His servants to enlighten and edify the same.

But it is with *the faith of Rahab* we must be chiefly engaged on this occasion. It will be observed that she is mentioned in Heb. 11 *after* the destruction of Jericho, though she "received the spies in peace" before that city was destroyed. The reason for this is because her preservation—which was the fruit of her faith—was after the hosts of Israel had encompassed that city seven days. In seeking to ponder what is recorded in Scripture concerning the faith of Rahab we propose to look separately at the ground, the effect, the nature, the confession, the breadth, the imperfection, and the reward of the same.

1. *The ground of her faith.* "Faith cometh by hearing, and hearing by the Word of God" (Rom. 10:17). This does not mean that faith is *originated* by hearing the Word of God, any more than the shining of the sun imparts light unto the eye; no, faith is imparted by a sovereign act of the Spirit, and then it is instructed and nourished by the Word. In the prophetic song of Moses at the Red Sea it was declared, "The people shall *hear and be afraid*: sorrow shall take hold on the inhabitants of Palestina. Then the dukes of Edom shall be amazed; the mighty men of Moab, trembling shall take hold upon them; all the inhabitants of Canaan shall melt away. Fear and dread shall fall upon them; by the greatness of Thine arm they shall be as still as a stone; till Thy people pass over, O Lord, till the people pass over, which Thou hast purchased" (Ex. 15:14-16).

A striking fulfillment of the above prediction is found in the words of Rahab to the two spies: "I know that the Lord hath given you the land, and that your terror is fallen upon us, and that all the inhabitants of the land faint because of you. For we have *heard* how the Lord dried up the water of the Red Sea for you, when ye came out of Egypt; and what ye did unto the two kings of the Amorites, that were on the other side Jordan, Sihon and Og, whom ye utterly destroyed. And as soon as we had *heard* these things, our hearts *did melt*, neither did there remain any more courage in any man, because of you; for the Lord your God, He is God in heaven above, and in earth beneath" (Josh. 2:9-11). This it is which explains the reference in Heb. 11:31 unto the other inhabitants of Jericho, who perished because they "believed not." The knowledge which they had of God and His wondrous works, through the reports which had reached their ears, rendered them without excuse.

What has just been before us affords an example of a most solemn fact which is oft repeated: how souls are affected by the Truth, and how quickly the impressions made wear off. The inhabitants of

Jericho were deeply stirred by the reports of God's judgments upon the wicked; they feared it was their turn next, and their hearts melted within them. How, then, are we to explain the fact that they did not all of them immediately and earnestly cry unto God for mercy? We believe the answer is found in Eccl. 8:11, "Because sentence against an evil work is not executed speedily, therefore the heart of the sons of men is fully set in them to do evil." As the hosts of Israel encompassed Jericho each day and then returned quietly to their camp, space for repentance was granted its inhabitants; but when six days had passed, and the walls of the city remained as strong as ever, they felt quite secure, and hardened their hearts.

How, then, are we to account for the difference in Rahab? In this way: with them it was simply the stirrings of conscience and the workings of their natural fears, which soon subsided; but in her case the power of the Holy Spirit had wrought within her : God had "opened her heart," and consequently she "attended unto the things which were spoken" (Acts 16:14). In other words, Rahab had been sovereignly quickened into newness of life, by which she was capacitated unto a saving knowledge of God Himself and the receiving His word with meekness. Thus it was with the Thessalonian saints, whom the apostle reminded, "For our Gospel came not unto you in word only, but also *in power* and in the Holy Spirit" (1 Thess 1:5). It is only in *such* cases that a radical and lasting effect is produced.

We must learn, then, to distinguish between three things: the Divine gift of faith, the foundation provided for its support, and the assurance that issues for its resting upon that foundation. The gift of faith is imparted at regeneration, being one of the attributes of the new nature: "all men have not faith" (2 Thess. 3:2) because all are not born again. The firm foundation which is provided for faith to rest upon is the sure Word of God: by it alone is faith supported—instructed and fed. The assurance which issues from faith's resting upon this foundation is that confidence and certainty which fills the heart when God's Word is received implicitly into it. Thus it was with Rahab. Quickened by the Spirit, faith was planted within her soul, hence when the report reached her of God's wondrous works, she received it "not as the word of men, but as it is in truth, the Word of God" (1 Thess. 2:13), and therefore did she say, "*I know* that the Lord hath given you the land."

2. *The effect of her faith.* The faith of God's elect is a living, energetic principle, which "worketh by love" (Gal. 5:6) and produces fruit to the glory of God. Herein it differs radically from that notional and inoperative faith of frothy professors, which goes no deeper than an intellectual assenting to certain doctrinal propositions, and ends in fair but empty words. That faith which is unaccom-

panied by an obedient walk and abounds not in good works, is "dead, being alone" (James 2:17). Different far was the faith of Rahab. Of her we read, "Likewise also was not Rahab the harlot justified by works, when she had received the messengers, and had sent them out another way?" (James 2:25). This does not mean that her good works were the meritorious ground of her acceptance with God, but that they were the evidence before men that a spiritual principle had been communicated to her, the fruits of which justified or vindicated her profession, demonstrating that she was a member of "the Household of Faith."

In "receiving the spies with peace" she made it manifest that she had a heart for the people of God, and was ready to do all in her power to help them. That clause of our text which we are now considering summarizes all that is recorded of her kindly conduct unto those two men in Josh. 2. She welcomed them into her home, engaged them in spiritual conversation, made provision for their safety, hid them from danger, and refused to betray them. We believe there is a latent reference to her kindness (as well as to Abraham's) in Heb. 13:1-3, for the word translated "messengers" in James 2:25 is the same as is rendered "angels" in Heb. 13:2: "Let brotherly love continue, Be not forgetful to entertain strangers: for thereby some have entertained angels unawares. Remember them that are in bonds, as bound with them; and them which suffer adversity as being yourselves also in the body." Alas, that so many professing Christians today, instead of heeding this exhortation, are almost ready to rend each other to pieces over every difference of opinion.

3. *The nature of her faith.* It was a *singular* faith. "The city of Jericho was about to be attacked: within its walls there were hosts of people of all classes and characters, and they knew right well that if their city should be set upon and stormed they would all be put to death. But yet strange to say, there was not one of them who repented of sin or who even asked for mercy, except this woman who had been a harlot. She and she alone was delivered, a solitary one amongst a multitude. Now, have you ever felt that it is a very hard thing to have a singular faith? It is the easiest thing in the world to believe as everybody else believes, but the difficulty is to believe a thing alone, when no one else thinks as you think; to be the solitary champion of a righteous cause, when the enemy mustereth his thousands to the battle. Now this was the faith of Rahab. She had not one who felt as she did, who could enter into her feelings and realize the value of her faith. She stood alone. O it is a noble thing to be the lonely follower of despised Truth.

"Rahab's faith was a *sanctifying* one. Did Rahab continue a harlot after she had faith? No, she did not. I do not believe she was a harlot at the time the men went to her house, though the name still stuck to her, as such ill names will; but I am sure she was not afterwards, for Salmon the prince of Judah married her . . . . You cannot have faith, and yet live in sin. To believe is to be holy. The two things must go together. That faith is a dead faith, a corrupt faith, a rotten faith, which lives in sin that grace may abound. Rahab was a sanctified woman. O that God might sanctify some that are here" (C. H. Spurgeon).

Her's was a *self-denying faith.* This is seen in her preferring the will of God before the safety of her country, and sheltering these men who were strangers before the pleasing of her fellow-citizens. But it appeared most conspicuously in the venturing of her own life rather than to betray the messengers of Joshua, who were worshippers of the true God. Her action was fraught with the most dangerous consequences to her; but her fidelity to God made her scorn the threatenings of her citizens, the promiscuous events of war, and the burning of her city. Thus, by faith she, in effect, renounced all for God. When He calls us to do so, we must part with all that we hold near and dear in this world. Spiritual faith is best evidenced by acts of self-denying obedience (condensed from T. Manton).

4. *The confession of her faith.* This is recorded in Josh. 2:9-11, which shows it was made at the first opening she had. It was quite a comprehensive one: she owned the wondrous works of the Lord, was assured He had given Canaan unto His people, and acknowledged Him as the God of heaven and earth. Thereby she renounced all the idols of the heathen, glorified God with her lips, and illustrated the rule we have in Rom. 10:10, "For with the heart man believeth unto righteousness, and with the mouth confession is made unto salvation." Moreover, by placing the scarlet cord in her window, she, as it were, publicly displayed her colors and made it known under whose banner she had enlisted. How her conduct puts to shame those who after a long profession of the truth are ready to tremble at the first approach of danger, and deem it prudence to keep at a safe distance from those who are exposed to persecution.

"It is in the nature of true, real, saving faith, immediately, or at its first opportunity, to declare and protest itself in confession before men. Our confession is absolutely inseparable from faith. Where men, on some light and convictions, do suppose themselves to have faith, yet, through fear or shame, do not come up to the ways of expressing it in confession prescribed in the scripture, their religion is in vain. And therefore our Lord Jesus Christ, in the Gospel, doth constantly lay the same weight on confession as on believing itself: Matt. 10:33, Luke 9:26. And the fearful, that is, those who fly from public profession in times of danger and persecution, shall be no less assuredly excluded from the heavenly Jerusalem, than unbelievers themselves: Rev. 21:8." (J. Owen).

5. *The breadth of her faith.* Very blessed is it to note her further word to the spies: "Now therefore, I pray you, swear unto me by the Lord, since I have showed you kindness, that ye will also shew kindness unto my father's house, and give me a true token: And that ye will save alive my father, and my mother, and my brethren, and my sisters, and all that they have, and deliver our lives from death" (Josh. 2:12, 13). Some contracted hearts, in which the very milk of human kindness seems to have congealed, would deem Rahab's request highly presumptuous. Personally, we believe that her soul was so overflowing with gratitude unto the Lord for His saving such an abandoned wretch, that her faith now perceived something of the infinitude of the Divine mercy, and believed that such a God would be willing to show grace unto the whole of her family. Nor was she disappointed.

O that the breadth of Rahab's faith may speak unto our hearts. O that the blessed Holy Spirit may fill us with compassion for our unsaved relatives and friends, and stir us up to wrestle with God in prayer on their behalf. It is right that we *should* desire God to show mercy unto those who are near and dear to us: not to do so, would show we were lacking in natural affection; it only becomes wrong when we ignore God's sovereignty and dictate instead of supplicate. It is blessed to observe that He who hath said "according unto your faith be it unto you" and "all things are possible unto him that believeth," *responded* to Rahab's faith, and saved her entire household: though they, of course, only found deliverance by sheltering in the same house with her in which hung the scarlet cord—only under the blood is there safety.

6. *The imperfection of her faith.* This appears in the reply which she returned to the king of Jericho (recorded in Josh. 2:3-5) when he sent unto Rahab requesting her to deliver up the two spies. Fearful of their lives, she told lies, pretending she knew not whence men had come, and affirming they were no longer in her house. Such a procedure on her part can by no means be justified, for her answer was contrary unto the known truth. The course she followed resembled the direction which Rebekah gave to her son Jacob: in the general her intent was the fruit of great faith, for it had respect unto the promise of God (Gen. 25:33), but in various details (Gen. 27:6, 7, etc.) it can in no wise be approved. The Lord, in His tender mercy, is pleased to pass by many of the infirmities of His children, when He sees an upright heart and a desire to accomplish His promises. "If Thou, Lord, shouldest mark iniquities, O Lord, who shall stand?" (Psa. 130:3) God bears with much weakness, especially in the lambs of His flock.

"I observe there was a mixture of infirmity in this act, an officious lie, which cannot be excused, though God in mercy pardoned it. This is not for our imitation, yet it is for our instruction; and it shows us this, that faith in the beginning hath many weaknesses. Those that have faith do not altogether act out of faith, but there is somewhat of the flesh mingled with that of the spirit. But this is passed by out of God's indulgence; He accepteth us notwithstanding our sins before faith, and notwithstanding our weaknesses in believing. Before faith she was a harlot; in believing she makes a lie. God doth reward the good of our actions and pardon the evil of them, not to encourage us in sinning, but to raise our love to Him who forgives us so great a debt, receives us graciously, and pardons our manifold weaknesses" (T. Manton).

It is blessed to see that neither in our text nor in James 2:25 does the Holy Spirit make any reference unto Rahab's failure; instead, in both places, He mentions that which was praiseworthy, and to her credit. It is the very opposite with the malevolent world, which is ever ready to overlook the good and reflect only upon the evil of an action performed by a child of God. It is a gracious spirit which throws the mantle of charity over the deformities and defects in a brother or sister in Christ, as it is honouring to God to dwell upon that which His Holy Spirit has wrought in them. If we were quicker to judge ourselves for *our own* sad failures, we would not be so ready to blaze abroad the faults of our fellows. Let each of us seek grace to heed that exhortation, "Whatsoever things are true, whatsoever things are honest, whatsoever things are just, whatsoever things are pure, whatsoever things are lovely, whatsoever things are of good report; if there be any virtue, and if there be any praise, *think* on these things" (Phil. 4:8).

7. *The reward of her faith.* "By faith the harlot Rahab *perished not* with them that believed not." The historical account of this is found in Josh. 6:22, 23, "But Joshua had said unto the two men that had spied out the country, Go into the harlot's house, and bring out thence the woman, and all that she hath, as ye sware unto her. And the young men that were spies went in, and brought out Rahab, and her father, and her mother, and her brethren, and all that she had; and they brought out all her kindred, and left them without the camp of Israel."

But not only was Rahab, and the whole of her family, preserved from the burning of Jericho which immediately followed, but as Josh. 6:25 tells us, she "dwelt in Israel." Thus, from being the slave of Satan she was adopted into the family of God; from being a citizen of heathen Jericho she was given a place in the congregation of the Lord. Nor was that all; later, she became the honored wife of a prince in Judah, the mother of Boaz, and one of the grandmothers of David. Her name is inscribed upon the imperishable scroll of sacred history; it is recorded in Matt. 1 among the ancestresses of the Saviour—she was one of the mothers of Jesus! From what depths of sin and shame did sovereign grace deliver this poor woman; to what a height of honor and dignity did sovereign grace elevate her. Truly, the rewards of faith are most excellent and glorious.

CHAPTER SEVENTY-EIGHT

The Faith of the Judges

(Heb. 11:32)

In some respects the verse we have now arrived at is the most difficult one in our chapter. It commences the last division of the same. Therein the apostle changes his method of treatment, and instead of particularizing individual examples of faith, he groups together a number of men and summarizes the actings of their faith. The selection made, out of many others who could have been given, is most startling: those whose names we might have expected had been registered on this honour roll are omitted, while others we have never thought of are given a place. The order in which they are recorded seems strange, for it is not that of the chronological. This has puzzled some: one eminent commentator stating "The apostle does not observe strict order, reciting them in haste": which is not to be allowed for a moment, for it ignores the superintending guidance of the Holy Spirit. Again; "the prodigies performed by these men cannot be presented for *our* emulation": why, then, are they referred to?

The principle of guidance in the selection of some of the men here mentioned is obviously that of *sovereign grace*: no otherwise can we account for the passing over of such illustrious characters as Caleb and Deborah, Hannah and Asaph, and the inclusion of Jephthah and Samson—in the latter the free favour of God was more conspicuously displayed. The order in which they are mentioned is not that of time, but *of dignity,* for Barak lived before Gideon, Jephthah before Samson, and Samuel before David: God reckons those most excellent who bring forth the best fruits of faith —the more we excell in faith, the more God will honour us. Where faith shines the brightest the least are accounted the greatest, and the last become first; then how *we* should labour daily for an increase of faith.

Five of the six men named in our text were judges who ruled over Israel, though they came from very humble callings. From this we may learn that faith is a spiritual grace suited not only unto the temple, but also to the judicial bench and throne; that it is needed not only by those who occupy positions in the private walks of life, but also by those who fill public office. Governors equally with the governed require to have a true faith in the living God: instead of disqualifying them for the discharge of their important duties, it would be of inestimable value to them—enabling them to face difficulties and dangers with calmness, inspiring with courage, endowing with wisdom, and preserving from many temptations which confront those in high places. He who is blest with a spiritual faith will have lowly thoughts of himself, as had Barak, Gideon, and David.

Remarkable achievements are credited to the men whose names are now before us. As we read the historical account of them in the book of Judges we may well marvel at them, but it is only as we view them in the light of what is said here in Heb. 11 that we shall understand them aright. Other men besides these have vanquished lions, put armies to flight, and subdued kingdoms; yet *their* deeds proceeded from a very different principle. The mighty works of men chronicled in the Old Testament are given for a higher purpose than the indulging of our love of the sensational. The exploits of Gideon and Barak, Samson and David, are only recorded in Holy writ as they were wrought *by faith*: thus the Holy Spirit honours *His own* work.

One prominent feature which distinguishes many of the extraordinary performances of men of God set down in Scripture from the prodigies done by men of the world is, that the Holy Spirit moved the sacred historians to faithfully register the infirmities under which faith so often wrought and the weakness which preceded it. The faith of these men was very far from being perfect, either in degree, stability, or unmixed purity. Like ours so often is, their faith was mingled with fear, oppressed by unbelief, hard beset by carnal reasonings. We have only to read through the 6th of Judges to see that the faith of the first one named in our text was painfully slow in exercise, though by grace, it was afterward mighty in execution. They were men of like passions with us, and from that fact we may take comfort—not in sheltering behind the same, but by refusing to despair when our faith is at a low ebb.

One thing which is common to all the individuals mentioned in our text is that the history of each of them was cast in a day of great spiritual declension. The time in which they lived is described at length in the book of Judges. Following the deaths of Moses and Joshua, Israel grievously departed from the Lord: cast off His law, worshipped the idols of the heathen, and "every man did that which was right in his own eyes" (21:25); darkness covered the earth, and gross darkness the people. Yet even in those days God left not Himself without witness: inexpressibly blessed is it to behold the faith of individuals shining in the midst of a failed testimony; that here and there was a lamp maintained, illuminating the surrounding darkness. Nor is the number here specified without significance for to the six individuals mentioned are linked the "prophets" (who also ministered in seasons of apostasy), making *seven* in all—telling of the completeness of the provision made by the grace of God.

Thus we may see how that Heb. 11, which describes at length the Life of Faith, would have been incomplete had no notice been taken of those times when Israel so grievously departed from God. It was during seasons of great spiritual darkness and gloom that faith wrought many of its mightiest works and achieved some of its most noteable victories. For faith is not dependent on favourable outward conditions; it is sustained and energized by One who is infinitely superior to all cirumstances. What is mentioned in our text and the verses which immediately follow, is recorded *for our encouragement.* We too are living in a day when Christendom is in a sad state, when there is widespread departure from God and His Word, when vital and practical holiness is at a low ebb. But the arm of the Lord is not waxed short, and they who lean hard upon it shall be sustained and enabled to do exploits in His name.

"And what shall I more say? for the time would fail me to tell of Gideon, and of Barak, and of Samson, and of Jephthath, of David also, and Samuel and of the prophets" (v. 32). The apostle had already given abundant proof that "faith is the substance of things hoped for, the evidence of things not seen" (v. 1), and had shown that "by it the elders obtained a good report" (v. 2); yet he had by no means said all which might be given on the subject. Numerous and noteable examples of the power and fruits of faith had been advanced, and many others might still be cited; but it would not be convenient to enumerate each instance of faith recorded in the O. T. To have done so, would extend the epistle beyond due limits: so we now have a bare mention of the names of others, followed by a description in general terms of the effects of their faith.

The characters which we are now to contemplate, like the apostles of Christ, and in smaller measure the reformers at the close of the "Dark Ages," were extraordinary men, specially raised up by God in times of crisis, for the good of His Church and the benefit of the commonwealth. This needs to be carefully borne in mind, or otherwise we shall view them in a false perspective. Their calling was extraordinary, and so were their performances. They were endowed with uncommon powers, and supernaturally energized for their particular tasks. That which distinguished them from men like Caesar, Charlemagne and Napoleon, was that they were *men of faith.* It is not that the apostle by any means commends *all* that they did, or that he excuses their manifold imperfections, which cannot be vindicated; he makes mention here only of their faith.

Gideon was raised up by God at a time when Israel's fortunes were sunk to a low ebb. Three judges had preceded him, delivering the people of God from the hand of their enemies; but a fourth time they had apostatized, and now they were groaning under the servitude of the Midianites. So great was the number of those who had invaded their territory, that they "left no sustenance for Israel" and "Israel was greatly impoverished because of the Midianites" (Judges 6:4, 6). But that was not the worst: the worship of Baal prevailed to such an extent among the favoured covenant people of God, that to oppose it was considered a criminal act, deserving of death (Judges 6:28-30). Nevertheless God had promised "the Lord shall judge His people, and repent Himself for His servants, when He seeth that their power is gone" (Deut. 32:36), and now, once again, He was about to make good this word.

To be delivered from the dire situation which now faced Israel, called for a "mighty man of valor," and such was Gideon, as we learn from the language in which the angel of the Lord first addressed him (Judges 6:12). But something more than natural courage and daring was required in the one whom the Lord would employ—he must be an *humble* man of God, that the glory might rebound unto Him alone. In order to that, the instrument had first to be prepared for the tasks to be performed—the servant fitted for the service he must do. "God must first do His work with Gideon, before Gideon could do his work for God. To accomplish this, God makes the wine-press of Joash to be to Gideon what He made the backside of the desert to be to Moses" (E. W. B.). The servant of God must first be made to feel his weakness, before he is taught that all-sufficient strength is available for him in the Lord. Thus it was with Gideon; thus it is still.

It is blessed to observe the Lord's dealings with Gideon: He now said "Jehovah is with thee" (Judges 6:12). This was to exercise his heart, which is ever the prime requisite. Aroused, Gideon enquired, "Oh my Lord, if the Lord be with us, why then is all this befallen us? and where be all His miracles which our fathers told us of?" etc. (v. 13). Second "the Lord looked upon him, and said, Go in this thy might, and thou shalt save Israel from the hand of the Midianites: have not I sent thee!" (v. 14). It is at this point so many interpreters go astray in their understanding of this incident. The *saint's* "might" is in realized helplessness: "For when I am weak, then am I strong" (2 Cor. 12:10). That word of Jehovah's was designed to bring Gideon to the consciousness of *his own* utter inability to deliver Israel from the yoke of the Midianites.

The instrument must be experimentally fitted ere the Lord will employ it in His service; and the first part of this fitting process is to empty it of self-sufficiency that it may then be thoroughly dependent upon Himself. Gideon's "might" consisted in conscious weakness, and as soon as that was realized he would be forced to believe the Lord's declaration "Thou shalt save Israel." That was the word addressed to his heart, and was the foundation on which his faith was to rest. Gideon now asked, "Oh my Lord, wherewith shall I save Israel? behold, my family is *poor* in Manasseh, and *I am the least* in my father's house" (v. 15): the Divine arrow had hit its mark, as Gideon's humble confession attests.

The Lord has only one response unto acknowledged helplessness: "*Surely I will be with thee,* and thou shalt smite the Midianites as one man" (v. 16). How blessed! When faith truly realizes this, it exclaims, "I can do all things through Christ which strengtheneth me" (Phil. 4:13). From that assuring word of the Almighty Gideon knew that he had "found grace" in His sight, and asked for a sign: "Not because he doubted, but because he believed; not to prove the truth of Jehovah's word, but because he would prove the truth of Jehovah's grace, in the acceptance of his offerings which he proposed to go and fetch: vv. 17,18" (E. W. B.).

Next, Gideon prepared and presented his offering (v. 19), and was bidden to place the same upon a rock (v. 20). This was followed by a miracle, fire issuing from the rock and consuming the offering, by which he "obtained witness" that he had found grace in Jehovah's sight—the supernatural fire denoting his acceptance with God, filling him with awe and terror. Immediately the Lord quieted his heart with, "*Peace* be unto thee; fear not: thou shalt not die" (v. 23): thus did he receive Jehovah's blessing: that Gideon's faith laid hold of that benediction is very evident from the next verse, "Then Gideon built an altar there unto the Lord, and called it Jehovah-shalom"—"The Lord send *peace*."

The heart of Gideon being now fitted and established, God gave him his first commission: "Take thy father's young bullock, even the second bullock of seven years old, and throw down the altar of Baal that thy father hath, and cut down the grove that is by it: And build an altar unto the Lord thy God upon the top of this rock, in the ordered place; and take the second bullock and offer a burnt sacrifice with the wood of the grove which thou shalt cut down" (vv. 25, 26). Such definiteness of language at once evidenced to Gideon that he had to do with One who knew everything—the bullocks his father had, and their very ages. Like his father Abraham, Gideon believed God and obeyed His command, for we read that, "It came to pass *the same night* . . . Gideon took ten men of his servants and did as the Lord commanded." At this distant date, his action may seem to us trivial, but the sequel shows that Gideon acted at the imminent peril of his life: "Then the men of the city said unto Joash, Bring out thy son, that he may die: because he hath cut down the altar of Baal, and because he hath cut down the grove that was by it" (v. 30).

The immediate sequel supplied a much more severe testing of Gideon: "Then all the Midianites and the Amalekites and the children of the East were gathered together, and went over, and pitched in the valley of Jezreel" (v. 33). Enraged at the overthrow of the altar of Baal, the Midianites gathered their forces together and with their allies came up against Israel for battle. It is to be expected that Satan will wax furious when his territory is invaded and the Lord is magnified in the place where he has reigned supreme: that is why it so often follows that when a Christian has done his duty, it *seems* as though he has only made bad matters worse, by increasing his troubles. Then it is that he is sorely tempted to regret he has been so 'radical' in his conduct and to effect a compromise. Such a temptation is to be steadfastly resisted. More; the increasing troubles which faithfulness brings upon him, are to be regarded as a golden opportunity for further exercises and acts of *faith*. Thus Gideon acted, and so should we.

We cannot now enter into a detailed comment upon the response made by Gideon to the open menace of the Midianities, and all that is recorded of him in Judges 6-8, but we commend those chapters unto the careful pondering of the reader. Let him carefully note, first, that "the Spirit of the Lord came upon Gideon" (6:34), which supplies the key to all that follows: safeguarding the glory of God (preventing us from ascribing the honor to Gideon), and furnishing the vital word of instruction for our own hearts. We cannot overcome Satan nor refuse his temptation in our own strength. We cannot increase faith, or even maintain it in exercise, by any resolution of mind or act of our own will. We cannot achieve victories to the praise of our God by our own faithfulness. It is only as we are strengthened with might by the Holy Spirit in the inner man, that we are furnished for the battle against the forces of evil; and that strength is to be definitely, diligently, and trustfully sought.

The infirmities of Gideon appear in that he imagined he must head a large army if the Midianites were to be vanquished: it was only little by little that his heart was instructed, and the lesson was learned that God is not dependent upon *numbers*. His repeated request for confirmatory signs (6:36-40) also shows us that it is not all at once the saint learns to walk by faith and not by sight. But the Lord is long-suffering to usward, and bears with our infirmities when the heart is truly upright before Him. He granted Gideon the signs requested, though that is no guarantee He will do so for us;

and He corrected his notion that a large force was needed: only a small fragment was employed—"by the three hundred men that lapped will I save you" (7:7). Then, when Gideon *believed* the Lord and *obeyed* His orders, this word was given, "Arise get thee down unto the host, for I have delivered it into thine hand" (7:9), which was completely verified in the sequel. Thus did the Lord use and work mightily by one who was poor and little in his own eyes (6:15), and who "did as the Lord had said unto him" (6:27).

Barak. Time (or space) fails us to enter into a full consideration of his history and exploits, so we must condense. Barak was raised up by God near the close of the twenty years when Jabin the king of Canaan "mightily oppressed the children of Israel" (Judges 4:3). Deborah was acting as judge at that time—proof of the terribly low state into which the covenant people had fallen (cf. Isa. 3:12); though she was not a "judge" in the proper sense of the term (see 4:3 and carefully compare 2:18), but a "prophetess," and therefore a mouthpiece of God. It was through her that the Lord spake to Barak, saying "Hath not the Lord God of Israel commanded, Go and draw toward mount Tabor, and take with thee ten thousand men of the children of Napthali and of the children of Zebulun? And I will draw unto thee to the river Kishon Sisera, the captain of Jabin's army, with his chariots and his multitude; and I will deliver him into thine hand" (Judges 4:6, 7): *that* was to be the ground of Barak's faith, *that* was the sure promise which described the thing to be "hoped for." The infirmity of Barak is seen in 4:8, but the obedience of his faith appears in 4:10. A further word was given to him, "Up, for this is the day in which the Lord hath delivered Sisera into thine hand: is not the Lord gone out before thee!" (4:14): he "heard," "believed," and obeyed, and a great victory was secured. It was *by faith* in God's promise that Barak went forth against the enormous army of Sisera and vanquished the same.

Samson. Many mighty deeds are recorded of him in the book of Judges, such as his rending to pieces a lion, as though it had been a kid; his slaying of a thousand Philistines, single-handed, with the jawbone of an ass; his carrying of the gates of Gaza and their posts on his shoulders up a steep hill; his bursting asunder the strongest cords when bound by his enemies; his overturning the pillars on which stood the great temple of Dagon. How, then, did Samson perform these prodigies? *By faith.* In the O.T. it is said, "the Spirit of the Lord came upon him," but that does not mean he was involuntarily impelled by a Divine power, like a hurricane carries things through the air blindly and unwittingly. No, the Spirit deals with men not as stocks and stones, but as moral agents; enlightening their minds, controlling their hearts, inclining their wills, and supplying physical strength for whatever tasks God allots.

"Faith cometh by hearing," and in Samson's case he "heard" through his parents the promise which God had made concerning him: "he shall begin to deliver Israel out of the hand of the Philistines" (Judges 13:5). The strength of his mother's faith comes out beautifully in 13:23, where, quieting the fear of her husband, she said, "If the Lord were pleased to kill us, He would not have received a burnt offering and a meat offering at our hands, neither would He have showed us all these things, nor would as at this time have told us such things as these." Brought up in the strong faith of his parents, Samson *believed* what he "heard" from God through them, grew up in the confidence of the same and conducted himself accordingly. His last act was his greatest and best, furnishing the strongest evidence of his faith in God and being of most profit to His church. After being so sorely chastened for his sins, and considering the situation he was then in, it called for no ordinary confidence in the Lord to do what is recorded in Judges 16:28-30.

Jephthah. By calling, Gideon was a farmer, Barak a soldier, Samson a religious Nazarite, while David was the youngest of his family and despised by his brethren; Samuel was first used by God while still a child; thus we may see how God delights to use lowly and weak instruments. But more striking still is the case now before us: Jephthah was one of dishonorable birth, a bastard (11:1, 2) which the law excluded from the congregation of the Lord (Deut. 23:2). Yet God, in an especial and extraordinary manner conferred His Spirit upon Jephthah and advanced him to the highest dignity and function amongst His people and prospered him exceedingly. From this we may learn that no outward condition, be it ever so base, can serve as a hindrance to God's grace. That he was a man who feared the Lord is clear from Judges 11:9, 10. His message to the king of Ammon (11:14-27) shows that he *believed* what was recorded in the Scripture of Truth: he ascribed Israel's victories to the Lord (vv. 21, 23) and called on Him to judge between Israel and Ammon (v. 27); and Jehovah rewarded his faith by delivering the Ammonites into his hand. His fidelity and perseverance in the faith is seen in the keeping of his vow of banning his daughter to continual virginity.

David. There is little need for us to attempt here an enumeration of the many works and fruits of his faith, nor to point out how often unbelief wrought within and through him. We agree with John Brown that it is likely the Holy Spirit has particular reference in our text unto David's victorious combat with Goliath, when, quite a youth, and totally inexperienced in the arts and guiles of warfare, armed only with a sling and a few pebbles, he engaged in open fight the mighty giant of the Philistines, who was a veteran in the field and heavily armed for the duel. How are we to explain David's temerity and success? In this way: he had received a revelation from God (as 1 Sam. 17:46, 47 plainly intimates), he rested on the same with implicit confidence, and acted accordingly. By faith he ventured; by faith he overcame.

Samuel. "The event to which we are disposed to think it most probable, from its miraculous character, that the apostle refers, is that recorded in 1 Sam. 12:16-18: 'Now therefore stand and see this great thing, which the Lord will do before your eyes. Is it not wheat-harvest today, I will call unto the Lord, and He shall send thunder and rain; that ye may perceive and see that your wickedness is great, which ye have done in the sight of the Lord, in asking you a king. So Samuel called unto the Lord; and the Lord sent thunder and rain that day: and all the people greatly feared the Lord and Samuel.' A revelation was made to Samuel that the Divine power was to be put forth in connection with certain words which he spoke. He believed that revelation; he spoke the words, and the event followed" (John Brown).

The Prophets. They too exemplified the power of faith, both in what they did and in what they suffered. By faith they were enabled to achieve and to endure what otherwise they could not have achieved or endured. They delivered nothing but what they received: hence the frequency of their announcement, "Thus saith the Lord." They concealed nothing they had received: though it was a "burden" to them (Mal. 1:1, etc.), and though they knew full well their message would be most unpalatable, they faithfully delivered the Word of God. They were undaunted by the people's opposition, setting their face as a flint (Ezek. 3:8, 9). They humbly submitted to God's requirements: Isa. 20:3, Jer. 27:2, Ezek. 4:11, 12. They wrought mighty works, especially Elijah and Elisha. All these things manifested the efficacy and might of a real faith in the living God. "Lord, increase our faith."

CHAPTER SEVENTY-NINE

The Achievements of Faith

(Heb. 11:33, 34)

True faith performs a prominent part in all experimental godliness. Where there is a total absence of the grace of faith, a man is without God and without hope in this world; but where that spiritual principle exists, if only in the very small degree, there has taken place a wondrous and miraculous change. The one who is the subject of it may not, for a time, understand its nature; but instead, make the greatest mistakes about it; nevertheless, that change is no less than one passing from death unto life. "If ye have faith as a grain of mustard-seed" (Matt. 17:20): that little grain has a principle of *life* in it, and contains in embryo the future plant; so with the implanting of the principle of grace in the heart—it will yet develop into, or rather be consummated in, Glory.

It behooves each one of us to take diligent pains in ascertaining the *origin* of our faith. There are various kinds of faith spoken of in the Scriptures: there is a dead faith, a demon's faith, a fancied and forced faith, a creature and presumptuous faith—all of which are to be dreaded, for they come not from above. But spiritual faith is *Divine* in its origin: "it is the gift of God" (Eph. 2:8). True faith is no offspring of nature, but has a celestial birth: "every good and every perfect gift *is from above,* and cometh down from the Father of lights" (James 1:17). Spiritual faith is the heart's persuasion of the Truth of God, and is produced in us by the almighty creative power of the Holy Spirit, when He applies the Word in life-giving energy to the soul.

Now this faith is not only Divinely-communicated, but it is Divinely-*sustained.* Spiritual faith is neither self-sustained nor man-sustained. It does not support itself, nor does its possessor support it. It depends entirely upon God. Alas, alas the "faith" of the vast majority of professing Christians, instead of being of this *self-helpless* nature, fills them with a deceiving self-ability. Nothing is so dependent upon God in Christ; nothing so utterly unable to live without the Spirit's supporting power, as that faith which He Himself produces in the heart. But the "faith" of multitudes today is of a totally different nature, and we might accommodate and apply to them those words of Paul's, "Now ye are full, now ye are rich, ye have reigned as kings"—but *without* the Spirit.

This faith is not only Divinely-given and Divinely-sustained, but it is also Divinely-*energized*: it acts only by the quickening power of God. "Without Me," said Christ, "ye can do *nothing*" (John 15:5); then, certainly, without *His* enablement we cannot act faith upon Himself or His promises. But a spurious faith, springing up out of mere nature, self-made and self-supporting, is also a self-acting one. The possessors of it can believe when they like, as they like, and what they like. There is Christ, *they* can lay hold of Him. There are His promises: *they* can appropriate them. There are His offices: *they* can act faith upon them. Alas, such ability savours nothing of the faith which God gives to His people, and which causes them to lie at the footstool of His mercy as humble supplicants.

This faith is also *Divinely*-increased: "*Lord*, increase our faith" (Luke 17:5). But let it be pointed out that such an "increase" does not render the Christian less dependent upon the Spirit of God — that would be a miserable increase: like the prodigal son getting his portion of goods and setting up for himself. Nor is it such an increase that now remains at one level, always acting with a certain power, always in the same lively exercise. Far from it; real Christians know from painful experience how often *their* faith is at a low ebb, and when apparently the most needed, is the worst crippled in its actings. Nor is it such an increase that its possessors should necessarily be conscious of it. Moses knew not that his face shone. Most probably the centurion and the Canaanitish woman little thought that they had "great faith." Sometimes those who have the most faith feel they have very little, if any at all; while sometimes those who have little, say they are rich and increased with goods.

In what, then, does an increase of faith consist? Is not the Christian's growth, *as a believer,* a growth in a true, living, spiritual, experimental knowledge of himself as a sinner, and of God in Christ as the Father of mercies? Faith is fed by knowledge: not by mere notions in the brain, for those only feed a false and presumptuous confidence; but by a spiritual and Divine knowledge. As *this* knowledge increases, faith increases; as this knoweldge is confirmed in the soul, faith is confirmed and strengthened. "Blessed is the man whom Thou *chastenest,* O Lord, *and teachest* him out of Thy law" (Psa. 94:12). Again; "He *led* him about, He *instructed* him" (Deut. 32:10): God leads into a great variety of circumstances, and in these circumstances He causes His people to receive instruction. In that way they learn the truth in an *experimental* manner, and what they receive from the Word is confirmed more and more unto them. In that way they learn the vanity of the world, the fickleness of the creature, the depravity of their own hearts.

Now this Divinely-given and Divinely-supported faith is renewed or stirred into exercise by the operations of the Holy Spirit, and brings forth fruit "after its own kind"; that is, fruit which is spiritual in its nature and supernatural in its character. In other words, faith is an active principle: it "*worketh* by love" (Gal. 5:6). As it is energized by its Giver, it produces that which mere human nature is utterly incapable of producing. An unmistakable proof of this is seen in our present verses, where we read, "Who through faith subdued kingdoms, wrought righteousness, obtained promises, stopped the mouths of lions, quenched the violence of fire, escaped the edge of the sword, out of weakness were made strong, waxed valiant in fight, turned to flight the armies of the aliens" (Heb. 11:33, 34).

There are two ways in which the remarkable contents of these verses may be considered: according as we look at their letter in a natural way, or according as we ponder them with an anointed eye. Water will not rise above its own level: the heart of the natural man being a stranger to spiritual things, cannot discern them when they are spread before him — that is why the majority of the commentaries are so largely devoted to the historical, grammatical, and geographical details of Scripture. There *is* an historical allusion in each clause of our text, but what the true Christian desires, is to know the spiritual purport and the practical application of them unto himself. Only thus do the Scriptures become a *living* Word unto him. This is what we have sought to keep steadily in mind as we have passed from verse to verse of Heb. 11, and which we will endeavor to be occupied with now.

"Who through faith subdued kingdoms." The opening word takes us back to the list of worthies mentioned in the preceding verse, and here we are supplied with an enumeration of some of the wonderful works performed by them: nine fruits of their faith are mentioned — compare the ninefold "fruit of the Spirit" in Gal. 5: 22, 23. Therein we behold once more the marvelous and miraculous efficacy of a spiritual faith. "These instances are taken from things of all sorts to show that there is nothing of any kind whatever wherein we may be concerned but that faith will be useful and helpful" (J. Owen). No matter what our lot may be — "pleasing or painful"; no matter what station we are called to fill — high or low; no matter how formidable or difficult the obstacles which confront us, "*All* things are possible to him that believeth" (Mark 9:23).

"Through faith subdued kingdoms." The word here used for "subdue" means "to fight or contend, to enter into a trial of strength, of courage on the field, to prevail in battle." The historical allusion is to the exploits of Joshua and David: "Joshua subdued the kingdoms in Canaan, and David subdued those which were around that country, such as Moab, Ammon and Syria; and they both subdued these kingdoms through believing" (J. Brown). The important point to recognize is that the "kingdoms" here "subdued" were those which sought to prevent the people of God (Israel) from entering into and enjoying their rightful inheritance. Now let us spiritualize that fact. The Christian has been begotten "unto an inheritance" (1 Pet. 1:3, 4): that "inheritance" is to be enjoyed *now,* by faith, for "faith is the substance of things hoped for, the evidence of things not seen." But there are powerful enemies seeking to harass and hinder us, and they must be "subdued."

There are two principal "kingdoms" which the Christian is called upon to "subdue": one is within himself, the other without him — the "flesh" and the "world." It was to the former of these that the apostle had reference when he said, "But I keep under my body, and bring it into subjection" (1 Cor. 9:27). The same task is set before the Christian: "For as ye have yielded your members servants to uncleanness and to iniquity, unto iniquity, even so now yield your members servants to righteousness unto holiness" (Rom. 6:19). The "flesh" or sinful nature within us *must be* "subdued," or it will certainly slay us—bring about our eternal undoing: "For if ye live after the flesh, ye shall die; but if ye through the Spirit do mortify the deeds of the body, ye shall live" (Rom. 8:13).

"He that is slow to anger is better than the mighty, and he that *ruleth his spirit* than he that taketh a city" (Prov. 16:32). Does the reader exclaim, Such a task is a hopeless one! Joshua might have said the same when he first set foot in Canaan, and found it occupied with a powerful and hostile people. And, my reader, Joshua did not "subdue" them in a day, nor in a year! No, it was accomplished little by little. It meant fierce fighting, it meant the exercise of much courage and patience, it meant surmounting varied discouragements; but at the end God crowned his labors with success. And remember that it was *by faith* he "subdued kingdoms." Ah, faith looks to God and draws vigor and strength from Him. True, I *am* weak and impatient in myself, yet "I can do all things through Christ which strengtheneth me" (Phil. 4:13).

There is also a "kingdom" without, which the Christian must "subdue," or else he will be destroyed by it: "Know ye not that the friendship of the world is enmity with God" (James 4:4). And *how* is the "world" to be "subdued?" 1 John 5:4 gives us the answer: "This is the victory that overcometh the world, *our faith.*" Sweetly is this signified in the Song of Sol.: "Who is this that *com-*

eth up from the wilderness?" (8:5). Here the child of God, though toiling and struggling, worn and weary, is represented as rising above the world. And *how* is this accomplished? How is it that the spouse of Christ is enabled to rise above the immense hindrance of "the lust of the flesh, the lust of the eyes, and the pride of life" — those things which are "in the world" (1 John 2:16)? She is seen *"leaning upon* her Beloved" (Song. of Sol. 8:5). As He is our object, the world loses its power over us; as He is our strength, we get the victory over it.

"Wrought righteousness." In their narrower sense, these words signify "to execute judgment, to enforce the laws of justice:" the historical reference would then be to such passages as Josh. 11: 10-15, 1 Sam. 24:10, 2 Sam. 8:15. But in its wider scope "wrought righteousness" means the living of a holy life: "Lord, who shall abide in Thy tabernacle? who shall dwell in Thy holy hill? He that walketh uprightly, and worketh righteousness, and speaketh the truth in his heart" (Psa. 15: 1, 2). "In every nation he that feareth Him, and worketh righteousness, is accepted with Him" (Acts 10:35). "Righteousness" signifies up to the required standard; and to work righteousness means, walking according to the rule of God's Word: "Therefore all things whatsoever ye would that men should do to you, do ye even so to them: for this is the law and the prophets" (Matt. 7:12).

Now right actions must spring from right principles and must be performed with right ends, if they are to be acceptable to God. In other words, they must issue from a living faith and have in view the glory of God. It is the absence of *faith* and the substituting of *self-interest* for the honor of the Lord, which is the cause of all the injustice and oppression in the world today. But let it now be carefully noted that "subdued kingdoms" *precedes* "wrought righteousness." This order is unchanging: evil must be hated before good can be loved (Amos. 5:15), self must be denied before Christ can be followed (Matt. 16:24), the old man must be put off before the new man can be put on (Eph. 4:22-24). In other words, the "flesh" must be mortified before the "spirit" can be manifested.

"Obtained promises," or secured the blessings promised. God assured Joshua that he should conquer Canaan, Gideon that he should defeat the Midianites, David that he should be king over all Israel. But outwardly, tremendous difficulties stood in the way of the accomplishment of those things, yea, apparent impossibilities prevented them. Gideon was put upon a great improbability when he was commanded to take but three hundred men, fall upon and destroy an immense host. David and his little company seemed to be no match for the armed forces of Saul, and after his death, for years the throne seemed as far away as ever. But where there is a real trust in the living God the most formidable difficulties may be overcome.

"Obtained promises." Ah, it is one thing to hear and read about the wonderful things which the faith of *others* secures, but what about your *own* experience, dear reader? You may sincerely think that you believe in and are resting upon the sure promises of God, but are you obtaining a *fulfillment* of them in your own daily life? Are the blessings set forth in the promises actually in your possession? Are you securing the things promised? If not, is the reason to be found in your failure to heed what here precedes? *Before* "obtained promises" comes "subdued kingdoms" and then "wrought righteousness." We must not expect to "obtain" the precious things set before us in the promises until we definitely and diligently set about the subjugation of the flesh, and *walk* according to the rules of God's Word — regulating our conduct by its precepts and commands.

"Stopped the mouths of lions." The historical reference is, of course, to Daniel in the den. It shows again the marvelous power of faith. This comes out clearly in Dan. 6:23: "So Daniel was taken up out of the den, and no manner of hurt was found upon him, *because he believed* in his God." But how far may this be of help to us? Is the answer far to seek? There are ferocious people, as well as fierce animals! There are savage oppressors and persecutors who seek to intimidate, if not destroy, the mild and harmless Christian. True, yet they should not terrify us, still less spoil our testimony, by causing us to hide our light under a bushel. Daniel would not be forced into compromising by the threat of the lions of Babylon, nor should we be by the menacing looks, words, and actions of the world's lions today. Say with one of old, "I will trust and not be afraid."

"Stopped the mouths of lions." Why it almost looks as though faith were omnipotent! What cannot real faith do! We dare not set any limitations to it, for faith has to do with the living God, and nothing is too hard for Him. Ah, dear reader, faith lays hold of *the Almighty,* and not until your faith learns to do that, is it of much worth. Is the Lord God a living reality to you, or do you have but a theoretical knowledge of Him? The ultimate reference in our text is to him of whom it is said, "The devil, as a roaring lion, walketh about, seeking whom he may devour" (I Pet. 5:8). His mouth is opened against many a child of God, uttering lies, telling him that his profession is an empty one. Have you learned to "stop his mouth?" Do his false accusations no longer terrify you? Does he now find it useless to thus harass you any longer? It all depends: "stopped the mouths of lions" is preceded by *"obtained promises"!*

"Quenched the violence of fire." The reference is to the three Hebrews in Babylon's furnace. It shows the efficacy of faith to rest upon the power of God in the face of great danger, yea, before what seemed to be certain death. Those three Hebrews resolved to perform their duty, no matter what the event, committing themselves unto the disposition of a sovereign God, with full persuasion of His power to do whatever He pleased, and which would be most for His glory. Such an exercise of faith appears very, very marvelous to us. Ah, let it be fully borne in mind that Daniel and his fellows trusted God in times of peace and prosperity, as well as in seasons of peril and adversity. If we live by faith, it will not be difficult to die by faith.

"Quenched the violence of fire." A twofold spiritual application may be made of these words. First, we read of "the fiery darts of the wicked" (Eph. 6:16), and these are to be "quenched" by "taking the shield of faith." If we are subduing kingdoms, working righteousness, and obtaining promises, neither the mouth of the lion will be able to intimidate us, nor *the temptations* of the devil overcome us. Second, we read of faith which is "tried with fire" (1 Pet. 1:7) or fierce afflictions: this fire (like Babylon's) is *not* "put out," but its "violence" or *power to injure,* is "quenched." If the soul cleaves to God naught can harm it. It is faith, and not water, which quenches the fire: behold the martyrs *singing* amid the flames!

"Escaped the edge of the sword." The historical reference is to such passages as 1 Sam. 18:4, 1 Kings 18:10, 19:1-3, Jer. 39:15-18: in several of which it seems as though those eminent servants of God escaped from danger more by fear than by faith — by *fleeing* from those who threatened their lives. The life of faith is many-sided, and care needs to be taken to preserve the balance: to keep from mere passivity on the one hand, and from fanatical presumption on the other. While the Christian is to walk by faith, yet there is wrestling (Eph. 6:12) and fighting to be done (1 Tim. 6:12); we are to seek grace and develop all heroic virtues, such as courage, valor, hardness (2 Tim. 2:3), and endeavor by Divine aid to overcome everything which hinders us entering into God's best. On the other side, the Christian must not refuse the use and aid of all lawful means in times of danger: "when they persecute you in this city *flee ye* into another" (Matt. 10:23) — to refuse to do so, is not faith, but presumption.

"Escaped the edge of the sword." What is the deeper meaning of this? Our minds at once turn to Heb. 4:12, "The Word of God is quick and powerful, and sharper than any twoedged sword": confirmation of this is found in the fact that the Greek of our text reads "Escaped the *edges* of the sword." But *how* is the Christian to "escape" the edges of the Spirit's Sword? By being in practical subjection to the precepts of Scripture, walking in communion with God. It is when we get into a backslidden state and give way to the lusts of the flesh, that the Word condemns our ways, pierces our conscience, and strikes terror to our hearts. God does not wound or afflict "willingly" (Lam. 3:33), but only when our conduct is displeasing to Him. If our hearts be right with God, His Word will strengthen and comfort, rather than cut and wound us. If we *judge* ourselves for all that is wrong, the Sword will not smite us; when we fail to, the Word searches and convicts us. Note Rev. 19:15, where the same figure of the "sharp sword" is seen in Christ's mouth as he comes forth to destroy His enemies!

"Out of weakness were made strong." In those words there may be a latent reference to Samson in the closing scene of his life, but most probably the historical allusion is unto Hezekiah. In 2 Kings 20:1 we are told that Hezekiah was "sick unto death," and then that he prayed unto the Lord, which was in marked contrast from Ahaziah (2 Kings 1:2) and Asa (2 Chron. 16:12). 2 Kings 20:3 is much misunderstood: the key to it is found in 1 Kings 2:4. Hezekiah was conscious of his integrity, and sincere desire to please God, but he had no son to succeed him to the throne, and therefore did he here call to mind His promise. The Lord responded to his faith, restored him to health, added fifteen years to his life, and gave him a son.

"Out of weakness were made strong." It is not simply that "the weak were strengthened," but "out of *weakness* were made strong," the emphasis being upon an extremity of feebleness. It shows us that the vigor of faith is not dependent upon health of the body! It is written "The prayer of faith (not the "anointing" of the "elders") shall save the sick" (James 5:15 and cf. Phil. 2:27). But our text is not to be restricted to physical "weakness;" God is able to make the doctrinally and spiritually weak to stand: Rom. 14:4. The secret of the Christian's strength lies in maintaining a consciousness of his weakness (2 Cor. 12:10). The trouble is that as we grow older, most of us grow more independent and self-sufficient. The fact is that the oldest Christian has no more strength *in himself* than he had when he was but a "babe in Christ." Just so soon as we fail to feel and acknowledge before God our personal weakness, do we fail to prove the sufficiency of God's grace! Seek strength from Him daily.

"Waxed valiant in fight." Probably the reference is to Samson (Judges 15:15) and David. The phrase signifies that these heroes of faith refused to be intimidated by the might and number of their enemies; undaunted by the great odds against them, they refused to give way to a spirit of cowardice, and entered into a pitched battle against their foes: compare Deut. 31:23, Josh. 1:7, Psa. 3:6, Acts 4:29. Once again we would stress the importance of the *order* here: "waxed valiant in fight" is preceded by "out of weakness were made strong!" and that in turn by "escaped the *edge* of the Sword"! May we not easily perceive here why it is that we are so quickly and so frequently overcome by our spiritual foes?

"Turned to flight the armies of the aliens." Such passages as Josh. 10:1-10 and 2 Sam. 5:17-25 may be consulted for typical illustrations of what is here in view, carefully bearing in mind that while the power of God, giving success to the efforts of Joshua and David, was the efficient cause of their victories, yet instrumentally, it was "through faith" they were wrought. The path of faith is one of conflict because the Adversary contests every step of the way. The chief reason why the individual Christian experiences so little victory in his spiritual warfare, is because his *faith* is so little in exercise. And we may add, the chief reason why the Church collectively is failing so lamentably to "turn to flight the armies of the aliens" is because there is so much jealousy and strife among its own members!

CHAPTER EIGHTY

The Pinnacle of Faith

(Heb. 11:35, 36)

In His lengthy but most blessed description of the Life of Faith the Spirit of God has, in Heb. 11, passed from one phase of it to another, exhibiting to our view its many-sidedness. But there was one other aspect thereof which required to be delineated in order to give completeness to the whole, and that we have designated the "pinnacle" of faith, for to *suffer* for God, to meekly endure whatever affliction He is pleased to put upon us, to lay down our lives for the sake of His Truth if called upon to do so, is the highest point which faith can reach. Therefore, in the text which is now to engage our attention, He moved the apostle to pass on to an entirely different sort of the fruits of faith from those mentioned in the preceding verses, and shows us the power of faith to support the soul under sufferings, even the acutest afflictions to which the human mind and body can be subjected.

"For hearing of these great and glorious things, they might be apt to think that they were not so immediately concerned in them. For *their* condition was poor, persecuted, exposed to all evils, and death itself, for the profession of the Gospel. Their interest, therefore, was to inquire, what help in, what relief from faith they might expect in that condition? What will faith do where men are to be oppressed, persecuted and slain? Wherefore, the apostle, applying himself directly unto their condition, with what they suffered, and further feared on the account of their profession of the Gospel; he produceth a multitude of examples, as so many testimonies unto the power of faith in safe-guarding and preserving the souls of believers under the greatest sufferings that human nature can be exposed unto" (John Owen).

Not only were these instances of the sufferings of the O. T. saints pertinent to the circumstances the Hebrew Christians of Paul's time were in, but *we* too need to be informed of what faith in God and fidelity to His Truth, may entail. At the outset of the Christian life, we are bidden to first sit down and "count the cost" (Luke 14:28), which means that we are required to contemplate those sufferings which the following of Christ is likely to involve, and it is well that we should frequently remind ourselves that "we must through much tribulation enter into the kingdom of God" (Acts 14:22). It is criminal silence on the part of any servant of God *to conceal from his hearers* that a true profession of the name of Christ will necessarily bring down upon us not only the scorn and opposition of the outside world, but also the hatred and persecution of the false religious world. "Beloved, think it not strange concerning the fiery trial which is to try you, as though some strange thing happened unto you" (1 Pet. 4:12).

The Lord Jesus Christ dealt openly in this matter, and plainly made known what was likely to befall those whom He called to follow Him, and expressly affirmed that He would admit none into the ranks of *His* disciples save those who denied themselves, took up their *cross,* and engaged to undergo all sorts of sufferings for His sake and the Gospel's. He deceived none with fair promises of a smooth and easy passage through this world. So too does His faithful apostle, in the verses which are to be before us, after setting before the Hebrews some of the grand and glorious achievements which the faith of their predecessors had wrought, now remind them of *others* who were called upon to exercise *their* faith in the greatest miseries that could be undergone. Great trials and sore afflictions are to be expected in the path of faith. The Saviour Himself encountered them, and sufficient for the disciple to be as his Master.

"All the evils here enumerated, did befall the persons intended, on the account of their *faith*, and the profession thereof. The apostle does not present unto the Hebrews a company of miserable, distressed creatures, that fell into that state through their own default, or merely on the account of a common providence, disposing their lot in this world into such a state of misery, as it is with many; but all the things mentioned, they underwent merely and solely on the account of their faith in God, and the profession of true religion. So as that their case differed in nothing from that which they might be called unto" (J. Owen).

But not only were these sufferings encountered in the path of fidelity to God, but it was the exercise of *faith* which enabled those O. T. worthies to patiently and spiritually endure them. Faith is a grace which draws down from Heaven whatever blessing of God is most needful to the saint, and therefore does it stand him in as good stead in the night of adversity as in the day of prosperity. Faith is a new-creation principle in the soul, which not only energises its possessor to perform exploits, but it also enables him to hold his head above the dark waters when floods threaten to drown him. Faith suffices the Christian to face danger calmly, to continue steadfast in duty when menaced by the most foreboding outlook, to stand his ground when threatened with sorest sufferings. Faith imparts a steadfastness of purpose, a noble courage, a tranquillity of mind, which no human education or fleshly efforts can supply. Faith makes the righteous as bold as a lion, refusing to recant though horrible tortures and a martyr's death be the only alternative.

Faith gives its possessor patience under adversities, for by faith he sees them in a scriptural light and bears them by the enabling strength of Christ. How good and profitable is a sanctified affliction, but then only is it sanctified to us when faith is "mixed with" it. When faith is not in exercise, the heart is occupied with the things which are seen and temporal: only the creature's hand or the creature's treachery is viewed, and peevishness and resentment prevail; or worse still, we are tempted to entertain hard thoughts against God, and to say "the Lord has forsaken me, the Lord has forgotten me." But when the Spirit renews us in the inner man, and faith becomes active again, how differently do things then appear! Then we take ourselves to task and say, "Why art thou cast down O my soul, hope thou in God."

It belongs entirely unto the sovereign pleasure of God to order and dispose the outward conditions through which His Church passes upon earth; seasons of prosperity and times of adversity are regulated by Him as He deems best. Eras of peace and security and eras of persecution and peril are interchangeable, like day and night, summer and winter. Yet God does not act arbitrarily. It was not until after Abraham left Bethel and its altar, and journeyed southward (Egyptwards) that there arose a famine in the land (Gen. 12:8-10). It was only when Israel "forsook the Lord God of their father . . . and followed other gods," that His anger was kindled against them, and "He delivered them into the hands of spoilers that spoiled them, and He sold them into the hands of their enemies round about" (Judges 2:11-14). It was only when men "slept" that He suffered the Enemy to sow "tares" among the wheat (Matt. 13:25). It was after Ephesus *left* her "first love" that the Smyrnean era of persecution was experienced (Rev. 2:4 and 9, 10). And it is because so many of the professing servants of God repudiated His law during the previous generation, that we are now plagued with a reign of lawlessness in the church, home, and state.

God will not be mocked, and in His righteous government He visits the iniquities of the fathers upon their children, and hence it is that seasons of prosperity are followed by seasons of adversity. Yet during these seasons of adversity, whether they take the form of spiritual dearth or of physical peril, the godly remnant who sigh and cry because of the abominations which are found in what are termed the public "places of worship," or who meekly endure the persecutions of hypocritical professors or of the openly ungodly world, are no less acceptable with God, and are *as precious in His sight* as those whose lot was previously cast in times of the greatest earthly felicity.

The darker the night, the more evident the few stars twinkling between the clouds. The more awful be the state of professing Christendom as a whole, the more suitable is the background for the children of God to display their colours. The fiercer be the opposition made against a spiritual faith, the grander the opportunity for bringing forth its choicest fruit. There is no higher aspect of faith than that which brings the heart to patiently submit unto whatever God sends us, to meekly acquiesce unto His sovereign will, to say "the cup which my Father hath given me, shall I not drink it?" (John 18:11). Oftentimes the faith which *suffers* is greater than the faith that can boast an open triumph. "Love beareth all things" (1 Cor. 13:7), and faith when it reaches the pinnacle of attainment declares, "though He slay me, yet will I trust in Him."

"There is as much glory unto a spiritual eye, in the catalogue of the effects of faith that follow, as in that which went before. The church is no less beautiful and glorious when encompassed, and seemingly overwhelmed with all the evils and dreadful miseries here recounted, than when it is in the greatest peace and prosperity. To look, indeed, only on the outside of them, gives a terrible undesirable prospect. But to see faith and love to God, working effectually under them all, to see comforts retained, yea, consolations abounding, holiness prompted, God glorified, the world condemned, the souls of men profited, and at length triumphant over all; this is beautiful and glorious . . . .

"It may also be observed that the apostle takes most of these instances, if not all of them, from the time of the persecution of the church under Antiochus, the king of Syria, in the days of the Maccabees. And we may consider concerning this reason: 1. That it was after the closing of the canon of the Scripture, or putting of the last hand unto writings by Divine inspiration under the O. T. Wherefore, as the apostle represented these things from the notoriety of fact then fresh in memory, and it may be, some books then written of those things, like the books of the Maccabees, yet remaining: yet as they are delivered out unto the church *by him*, they proceeded from Divine inspiration. 2. That in those days wherein these things fell out, there was no extraordinary prophet in the church. Prophecy, as the Jews confess, ceased under the second temple. And this makes it evident that the rule of the Word, and the ordinary ministry of the church, *is sufficient* to maintain believers in their duty against all oppositions whatever. 3. That this last persecution of the church under the O. T. by Antiochus, was typical of the last persecution of the Christian church under antichrist; as is evident to all that compare Dan. 8:10-14, 23-25; 11:36-39 with that of the Revelation in sundry places. And indeed the martyrologies of those who have suffered under the Roman antichrist, are a better exposition of this context than any that can be given in words" (J. Owen).

"Women received their dead raised to life again" (v. 35). Some have complained because this clause is not placed at the end of v. 34, urging that it belongs there much more appropriately than it does at the beginning of v. 35, being a fitting climax to the miraculous achievements of faith enumerated in vv. 33, 34. While it be true that the particular item here before us belongs to the same class of miracles found in the preceding verse, yet personally we regard it as suitable for placing at the head of what follows in vv. 35-38, for it forms a suitable *transition* from the one to the other. And in this respect: those women passed through the sufferings of a sore bereavement before they had their beloved children restored to them—a reward for their kindness unto God's servants.

"Women received their dead raised to life again." The historical reference is to what is recorded in 1 Kings 17:22-24 and 2 Kings 4:35-37. How those remarkable cases show us once more that there is nothing too hard or difficult for *faith* to effect when it works according to the revealed will of God! But what is the *spiritual* application of this unto us today? Is it not faith's seeking the Spirit's renewal of languishing graces? the practical heeding of that word "Strengthen the things that remain, that are ready to die" (Rev. 3:2)! Or, to take a more extreme case, is it not a word of hope to the backslidden Christian, who has to all appearances lapsed back into a state of unregeneracy? Is it not faith's response to that word (addressed to Christians) "Awake thou that sleepest, and arise from the dead, and Christ shall give thee light" (Eph. 5:14)!

"And others were tortured, not accepting deliverance" (v. 35). It is very touching to remember that the hand which first penned those words had taken a prominent part in inflicting torture upon the saints of God (Acts 8:3, 9:1), but, by grace, he was now a *sharer* of them (2 Cor. 11:24-27). The word "torture" here signifies "were racked": those O. T. saints were fastened to a device and then a wrench was turned which caused their joints to be pulled out of their sockets— a method of torture frequently resorted to by fiendish Romanists when seeking to force Protestants to recant. By this fearful form of suffering the graces of God's people were tested and tried.

"Not accepting deliverance." It was offered to them, but at the price of apostasy. Two alternatives were set before them: disloyalty to the Lord, or enduring the most excruciating suffering; surrender of the Truth, or being tortured by devils in human form. Freedom from this torture was offered to them in return for forsaking their profession. This is expressly affirmed of Eliezer and his seven brethren in 2 Maccabees. Yea, they were not only offered freedom from tortures and death, but promised great rewards and promotions, which they steadfastly refused. The *principal* design of Satan in setting torture before God's saints is not to slay their bodies, but is to *destroy their souls*. Space has always been given to the victim for consideration and recantation: entreaties have been mingled with threats to induce a renouncing of their profession.

Thus, the real test presented was, which did these saints of God esteem more highly: the present comfort of their bodies or the eternal interests of their souls? Let it be remembered that they were men and women of like passion with us: their bodies were made of the same tender and sensitive flesh as ours are, but such was the care they had for their souls, so genuine was their faith and hope in a better resurrection, that they listened not to the appeals and whinings of the outward man. The *same* issue is drawn, though in another form, today: alas, what countless millions of people lose their souls eternally for the temporary gratification of their vile bodies. Reader, which do you esteem the more highly: your body or your soul? Your *actions* supply the answer: which receives the more thought, care and attention; *which* is "denied," and *which* is catered unto?

"Not accepting deliverance." The word for "deliverance" here is commonly translated "redemption" in the N. T.: its usage in this verse helps to a clearer understanding of that important term, and emphasizes the difference between it and "ransom." "Ransom" is the paying of the price which justice requires, but "redemption" is the actual emancipation of the one for whom the price was paid. These saints refused to accept a temporal "redemption" or "deliverance," because to have done so on the terms it was proffered to them would have meant the renunciation of their profession, apostasy from God. It was "through *faith*" they made this noble decision; it was love for the truth, which caused them to hold fast that which was infinitely dearer to them than an escape from bodily suffering. They had "bought the Truth," at the price of turning their backs on the world and their former religious friends, and bringing down upon themselves the scorn and hatred of them. And now they refused to "sell the Truth" (Prov. 23:23) out of a mere regard to bodily ease.

"Not accepting deliverance, that they might obtain a better resurrection": that last clause shows the *ground* of their steadfastness. The primary force of the expression *here* is a figurative one, as the verse as a whole clearly shows: they were offered *a* "resurrection" on the condition of their recantation, namely a "resurrection" from reproach to honour, from poverty to riches, from pain to ease and pleasure—it was a "resurrection" from the physical torture which threatened them: compare Heb. 11:19. But their hearts were occupied with something far, far better than being raised up to earthly comforts and honours; their faith anticipated that morning without clouds, when their bodies would be raised in glory,made like Christ's, and taken to be with Him forever. It was the hope of *that* which supported their souls in the face of extreme peril and sustained them under acutest sufferings.

"That they might obtain a better resurrection." In passing, let it be noted that God had set before the *Old* Testament saints the hope of resurrection—they were not nearly so ignorant as the dispensationalists make them out to be, in fact were far wiser than most of our moderns. Resurrection has always been the topstone in the building of faith (Job 19:25, 26), that which promised eternal reward, and that which gave life unto their obedience. A further proof of this fact is found in Acts 24:14-16: the faith of the "fathers" embraced "a resurrection of the dead, both of the just and of the unjust." That glorious resurrection will more than compensate for any bodily denials or bodily sufferings which the Christian makes or experiences for Christ's sake.

"And others had trial of mockings, and scourgings, yea, moreover of bonds and imprisonments" (v. 36). This verse supplies further details of what some of the O. T. saints were called upon to suffer for their fidelity to the Truth, sufferings which have been frequently duplicated during this Christian era. We are here informed of the various methods which the enemies of God employed in the afflicting of His people; no stone was left unturned in their persevering and merciless efforts to produce a denial of the Faith. While these things are harrowing to our feelings, yet they also serve to make manifest the sufficiency of Divine grace to support its recipients under most painful trials, and should evoke thanksgiving and praise unto Him that is able to make the weak stand up under the fiercest assaults of the Enemy.

"And others had trial of mockings." Let us, when we are reproached for Christ's sake and ridiculed because of our adherence to God's truth, call to mind that *this* was the *mildest* form of suffering which many who went before us on the pilgrim path were called upon to endure! The sneers and unkind words of our foes are not worthy of a pang in comparison with the far sorer pains which other believers have had to bear. It has ever been the portion of God's servants and people to be derided, reproached, and insulted: see Gal. 4:29, 2 Chron. 36:16, Jer. 20:7, Lam. 3:14; and my reader, if *we* are not being "mocked"—sneered at, scoffed at—it is because we are too lax in our ways and too worldly in our walk. Human nature has not changed; Satan has not changed; the world has not changed; and the more Christlike is our life the more shall we drink—in our measure—of the cup He drank from.

"And scourgings." The reference is to the lashings of their backs with whipcords of wire, which were most painful to experience, for they lacerated the flesh, drew blood, and macerated the body. It was not only a painful form of suffering, but a most humiliating one as well, for "scourgings" were reserved for the basest and most degenerate of men. The Lord Jesus was subjected to this form of ignominy and suffering from His enemies (Matt. 27:26), and so also were His apostles (Acts 5:40, 16:23). It is true that *we* are now (for the immediate present) spared these corporeal "scourgings," but there is such a thing as being lashed by the tongue and harrowed in our minds; nevertheless, happy are we (Matt. 5:10-12) if we are so honoured as to experience a little fellowship with the sufferings of Christ. But let us see well to it that we do not retaliate: ponder carefully and turn into earnest prayer Psa. 38:12-14; 1 Pet. 2:21-23.

"Yea, moreover of bonds." The reference is to cords, chains, manacles and fetters, binding them fast, so that they could not run away. In this item we see how "the excellent" of the earth (Psa. 16:3) were basely dealt with as though they had been the vilest of malefactors. Does your heart go out in pity to them, dear reader? Ah, what if *you* are "bound" even now with something far, far worse than outer and material ropes and chains! Multitudes are held fast by habits they cannot break; their souls are fettered by iniquities from which they cannot free themselves. Sin has taken them captive, and has full dominion over them. Has it over you? Or, has Christ set you free—not from the hateful presence of indwelling sin, but from its reigning power. Daily ought we to pray and strive against everything which limits us spiritually.

"And imprisonments," which was the lot commonly apportioned to robbers and murderers. Here again we see the saints of God treated as the offscouring of the earth, and let it be remembered that the prisons of those days were of a far different order from the comfortable buildings in which criminals are now incarcerated. One has only to read the experience of Jeremiah 38:11-13 to get some idea of the meaning of this word in our text: God's children were thrown into dark and damp dungeons, far below the level of the earth, unheated, unpaved, unilluminated. One cannot read this clause in our text without thinking of dear Bunyan. Ah, my reader, nothing but a *real* faith in the living God could have enabled those believers to have remained faithful unto death. The whole of the verses which have been before us, exhibit the efficacy and *sufficiency* of a spiritual faith to endure the worst that men and devils could inflict upon its favoured possessors. Is *yours* only an easy-chair "faith"?

CHAPTER EIGHTY-ONE

The Pinnacle of Faith

(Heb. 11:37, 38)

There has been no greater instance of the degeneracy of human nature and its likeness to the Devil than in the fearful fact that so many who have occupied prominent positions—magistrates, ecclesiastical dignitaries, kings and emperors—were not content to take the bare lives of true worshippers of God by the sword, but invented the most fiendish methods of torture to destroy them. That educated men and women in high places, that those professing the name of Christ, should conduct themselves like savages, that their rage against the "excellent of the earth" should express itself in such villainy and inhumanity, is a most dreadful demonstration of human depravity when the hand of God is withdrawn. With what infinite patience does the Most High bear with the vessels of wrath fitted to destruction!

But why should God allow many of His dear children to encounter such terrible experiences? Among other answers, the following may be suggested. First, for the more thorough trial of His champions, that their faith, courage, patience, and other graces, might be more manifest. Second, to seal or ratify more plainly the Truth which they profess. Third, to encourage and strengthen the faith of their weaker brethren. Fourth, to give them more sensible evidence of what Christ endured for them. Fifth, to cause them to perceive the better the torments of Hell: if those whom God loves are permitted to endure such grievous and painful trials, what must we understand of those torments which the wrath of God inflicts upon those whom He hates!

The teaching of Scripture upon the various reasons why God calls upon His children to suffer at the hands of the openly wicked, or, as is more often the case, from those professing to be His people, is full of valuable instruction, and calls for prayerful pondering. One of the advantages gained from such an exercise is the plainer perception of the very real and radical difference there is between that spiritual and supernatural faith which is possessed by God's elect, and that notional and natural faith which is all that millions of empty professors have. Should it please God to remove His restraining hand and permit open and fierce persecution to once more break forth upon the true followers of the Lamb, the difference just mentioned would be made apparent, for "When tribulation ariseth because of the Word," the stony-ground hearer is soon "offended" (Matt. 13:21), or, as Luke 8:13 expresses it "fall away." But different far is it with the good-ground hearer.

"The trial of your faith, being much more precious than of gold that perisheth, though it be tried with fire, might be found unto praise and honour and glory at the appearing of Jesus Christ" (1 Pet. 1:7). That faith which is "the gift of God" *endures to the end.* The testing of that faith, the fiery trial thereof serves the better to make manifest the Divine origin of it: only that faith which has come from God is able to endure the testing of God. Just as it is in *the furnace* that genuine gold is most quickly distinguished from tinsel, so it is under sore trials that the difference between spiritual and natural faith becomes the more appearent. Like much of the *imitation* jewelry of the day, the creatures-faith of empty professors, may look more glittering, be more bulky, and have more attraction for the outward eye, and be better calculated to adorn its possessor, than does the genuine faith of God's elect, which is often small in size, dull in appearance and lacking in attractiveness to the human beholder.

Yes, dear reader, it is *the fiery* trial which puts to the proof the kind of faith we really possess. Let the two faiths—that natural faith which man originates, and exercises by an act of his own will, and that spiritual faith which is the gift of God and which man can no more exercise of himself than he can create a world—be placed side by side in the crucible; let the burning flame try which is the genuine metal; let the hot fire play around them both, and the false faith (like imitation gold) will soon melt away into a shapeless mass of base metal; but the true faith will come forth uninjured by the fire, having lost nothing but what it could well spare—the dross with which it has been mixed. See that fact strikingly and solemnly adumbrated in Dan. 3: the furnace of Babylon harmed not the three Hebrews who were cast into it—it merely destroyed their bonds; but it *consumed* the Babylonians (v. 22)!

Let it be duly noted that in 1 Pet. 1:7 the apostle, when comparing faith with gold, accredits to the former a higher value: it is "much more precious than of gold that perisheth." Gold, though its genuineness may be proved by enduring the test of fire, is yet a perishing thing—a thing of the earth, a thing of time. That gold for which men toil so labouriously and sell their souls to acquire, is of no avail on a deathbed, still less will it stand any in good stead in the Day of Judgment! At death it has to be left behind, for none can take it with him into the next life. Then how much more precious is that *faith* which, instead of, like gold, leaving its possessor under the wrath of God, will be "found unto praise and honour and glory at the appearing of Jesus Christ!"

But the point to which we would now direct special attention is that it is not so much the faith itself as "the *trial* of faith" which is more precious than of gold which perisheth. This is clear to the spiritual mind: trials and temptations are the means which God employs to make manifest to the soul the reality and strength of that faith which He bestows, for there is in every trial and temptation an opposition made to the faith which is in the heart, and trial and temptation, so to speak, threatens the life of faith. How so? Because under the trial, God, for the most part, *hides* Himself: the light of His countenance is no longer visible, His smile is overcast by a dark providence. Nevertheless, He puts forth a secret power which upholds the soul, otherwise it would sink into utter despair, be swallowed up by the power of unbelief. Here, then, is the conflict: the trial fighting against faith, and that faith against the trial.

Now then in this trial, under this sharp conflict, in this hot furnace, the spiritual and supernatural faith is not burned or destroyed, but instead, grips firmly the promise, and the faithfulness of Him who has given it. And thus trial of faith becomes exceedingly *precious*. It is "precious" to its possessor when its genuineness is made the more manifest to him. It is "precious" in the sight of God's people, who discern it, and derive strength and comfort from what they witness in the experience of a fellow-saint who is thus tried and blessed. It is "precious" in the sight of God Himself, who crowns it with His own manifest approbation and puts upon it the seal of His approving smile. But above all things it will be found "precious" at the final appearing of the Lord Jesus in glory, for then He "will be admired in all them that believe" (2 Thess. 1:10).

To suffer the hardest things as well as to do the greatest, is all one to faith. It is equally ready for both when God shall require; and it is equally effectual in both, as God shall strengthen. The performing of spectacular exploits and the enduring of terrible affliction, differ almost as much to the flesh as do Heaven and Hell, but they are one to faith when duty calls. This is very evident from the section of Heb. 11 which is now before us (vv. 33-38), the closing portion of which is about to engage our attention. At the beginning of this section we are furnished with a list of the marvels which were wrought by a God-given faith: at the close thereof we are given a list of fearful sufferings and privations which were patiently and courageously borne by a God-sustained faith.

The latter, as much as the former, demonstrates the supernatural character of that faith which is in view throughout our chapter; yea, forms a most glorious climax thereto.

We say that the fearful sufferings experienced by God's people form a blessed climax in the Spirit's unfolding of the Life of Faith: those sufferings mark, in fact, the pinnacle of its attainments. Why so? Because they make manifest a heart that is completely subject to God, that bows submissively to whatever He is pleased to send, which has been so completely won to Him that torture and death are deliberately chosen and gladly preferred to apostasy from Him. A "Meek and quiet spirit" is of "great price" in the sight of God (1 Pet. 3:4), and nothing more plainly evidences the *meekness* of the Christian — his lying passive as clay in the hands of the Potter — as faith's willing acceptance of whatever lot our Father sees fit to appoint us. To be faithful unto death, to have unshakable confidence in the Lord, though He suffers us to be slain, to trust Him when to sight and sense it seems He has deserted us, is the highest exercise of all of faith.

Ere closing these introductory paraghaphs, let us seek to point out the various *actings of faith* in times of danger, trial, and persecution. First, faith recognizes that "the Lord God omnipotent reigneth" (Rev. 19:6), that He is on the throne of the universe, and "doeth according to His will in the army of Heaven, and among the inhabitants of the earth: and none can stay His hand" (Dan. 4: 35). Yes, dear reader, a spiritual faith perceives that things do not happen by chance, but that everything is regulated by the Lord God. Second, faith recognizes that everything which enters our lives is ordered by Him who is our Father, and that our enemies can do nothing whatever against us without His direct permission— the Devil could not touch Job nor sift Peter until he first obtained leave from the Lord! Oh what a sure resting-place is there here for the troubled and trembling heart. Third, faith recognizes that, no matter how fiercely Satan may be permitted to rage against us, or how sorely men persecute, their malicious efforts will be made to work together for *our good* (Rom. 8:28).

Fourth, by mixing itself with God's promises, faith obtains present help, strength and consolation from God. It derives peace and comfort from that sure word, "When thou passeth through the waters, I will be with thee; and through the rivers, they shall not overflow thee: when thou walkest through the fire, thou shalt not be burned, neither shall the flame kindle upon thee" (Isa. 43:2). It counts upon the assurance "God is faithful, who will not suffer you to be tempted above that ye are able, but will with the temptation also make a way to escape, that ye may be able to bear it"

(1 Cor. 10:13). Finally, faith looks away from the present conflict, and views the promised rest. It anticipates the future reward, and as it does so, is assured that "the sufferings of this present time are not worthy to be compared with the glory which shall be revealed in us" (Rom. 8:18). Such are some of the workings of faith when God's children are called upon to pass through the furnace.

"They were stoned, they were sawn asunder, were tempted, were slain with the sword: they wandered about in sheepskins and goatskins; being destitute, afflicted, tormented; Of whom the world was not worthy: they wandered in deserts, and in mountains, and in dens and caves of the earth" (vv. 37, 38). These verses continue the list of sufferings begun in v. 35. They enumerate the various kinds of persecution to which many of the O. T. saints were subjected. They are of two types: first, such as fell under the utmost rage of their enemies, enduring a martyr's death; second, such as to escape death, exposed themselves to great miseries which were undergone in this life.

It may be helpful at this point for us to raise the question, How are such dreadful sufferings to be harmonized with the Divine promises of *temporal* blessings on those whose ways please the Lord? Dispensationalists are very fond of emphasizing the *temporal* character of the O. T. promises, imagining that the promises of the N. T. are of a greatly superior character. In this they err seriously. On the one hand, the verses which are now under consideration describe the temporal experiences of some of the most eminent of the *Old* T. saints; on the other hand, the *New* T. expressly affirms godliness has "promise of the life *that now is,* and of that which is to come" (1 Tim. 4:8). The answer to our opening query is very simple: such promises as those in Deut. 28:1-6 (which still hold good to *faith!*) are to be understood with two exceptions: unless our sins call down Divine chastisements, or unless God is pleased to make trial of our graces by afflictions.

"They were stoned." This form of death was appointed by God Himself to be inflicted upon notorious malefactors: Lev. 20:2, Josh. 7:24, 25. But our text has reference to the Satanic perversion of this Divine institution, for here it is the enemies of God inflicting this punishment upon His beloved and faithful people. "The devil is never more a devil nor more outrageous, than when he gets a pretense of God's weapons into his own hands" (Owen). Stephen, the first Christian martyr, suffered death in this form. It is touching to remember that the one who first penned our text, himself "consented" to the stoning of Stephen (Acts 8:1): later he himself was stoned at Lystra.

"They were sawn asunder." This was a barbarous method of execution which the later Jews seemed to have learned from the heathen. There is no record in Scripture of anyone being put to death in this way, though tradition says Isaiah ended his earthly career in this manner. That some of the heroes of faith perished in this way is clear from our text, evidencing the malice of the Devil and the brutal rage of persecution. Their endurance of such torture demonstrates the reality and power of the Spirit's support, enabling them to remain true to God, and in the midst of their agonies sweetly commit their spirits into His hands, to the astonishment of their murderers. How this should stir us up to bear patiently the far smaller trials we may be called upon to encounter.

"Were tempted." This may be considered two ways, as pointing to an *aggravation* of their sufferings, or as referring to a *separate* trial of faith; we will take it in both respects. First, as signifying an intensification of their other trials, the reference would be to their persecutors setting before them the promise of relief upon their repudiation of the Truth — liberty at the price of perfidy. The baits of immunity and advancement were offered to them on the condition that they would abandon their strictness and join the ranks of the loose livers of that day. We believe that our text also includes *the temptings of Satan,* seeking to fill their minds with doubts as to God's goodness and power, urging them to recede from the stand they have taken. Because they remained resolute, refusing to yield to the insidious demands of their persecutors, they were cruelly butchered.

"Were tempted" may in the second place, be contemplated as referring to that life of ease and pleasure which worldly advancement and riches might provide. History solemnly records that numbers of those who courageously endured long and cruel imprisonment (and other sore trials) for the Truth's sake during the reign of the papist and bloody queen Mary of England, yet upon the accession of Queen Elizabeth were freed, elevated to high places, and obtaining much wealth and power, denied the power of godliness and made shipwreck of faith and a good conscience. But those in our text were possessed of a faith like unto that of Moses (11:24-26), and therefore were enabled to withstand the powerful temptations of the world. Poverty, dear reader, is often sent by God upon His people as a merciful means of delivering them from the dangerous snares which wealth entails.

"Were slain with the sword": there is probably a double reference here. First, to the sword of *violence,* when persecutors in their fury fell upon the servants and people of God, butchering them for their fidelity: see 1 Sam. 22:18, 21, 1 Kings 19:10. Second, the sword of *justice,* or rather injustice, the law being enforced against the saints. Probably this form of death is mentioned last to signify the *multitude* of martyrs who by their blood sealed up the Truth: literally rendered our text reads, "they died in the slaughter of the sword," which denotes the insatiable thirst of the persecutors and the large number which they felled. Papists have exceeded pagans herein: witness their cruel massacres in France and other places: well may the Holy Spirit represent the whore Babylon as being "drunk with the blood of the saints" (Rev. 17:6).

"They wandered about in sheepskins and goatskins," which means they were hounded out of their homes, and forced to go forth and exist as they might, without any settled habitation. "They were driven out to share the lot of wild animals, and were reduced to wear their skins, instead of clothes woven by man. This form of suffering is mentioned here, to show, on the one hand, the cruelty of religious persecution; and, on the other hand, the mighty sustaining power of faith. What power indeed is this! It was not merely the compulsion such as that which enforced the wandering of society's outlaws. It was rather the deliberate choice like that of Moses (vv. 24-26). Any day, any one of these wanderers could have rejoined their fellowmen, enjoyed their society, and shared their comforts; but they preferred this lot to apostasy" (E. W. B.)

"Being destitute, afflicted, tormented." These terms set forth the variety and intensity of the sufferings experienced by the homeless saints. "Destitute" means they were deprived of the ordinary necessities of life, and further signifies they were denied the kind assistance of relatives and friends: they were driven forth without the means of subsistence and were beyond the reach of succour from all who cared for them. "Afflicted" probably has reference to their state of mind: they were not emotionless stoics, but felt acutely their sad condition. No doubt the Enemy took full advantage of their state and injected many unbelieving and harassing thoughts into their minds. "Tormented" is rather too strong a word here: we understand the reference to be unto the ill-treatment they met with from the unfriendly strangers encountered in their wanderings, who regarded them without any pity and evilly treated them.

"Of whom the world was not worthy." This parenthetic clause is brought in here for the purpose of removing an objection: many might suppose that these despised wanderers were only receiving their just due, as not being fit to live in decent society. To remove this scandal the apostle put the blame where it rightly belonged, affirming that it was society which was unworthy of having the saints of God in their midst. In its wider aspect, the "world" here takes in the whole company of the ungodly; but in its narrower sense (that of the context), it has reference to the apostate "world" — all history, sacred and secular — is harmonious on this point: the most merciless, conscienceless, cruel, and inveterate persecutors of God's elect have been *religious* people!

"Of whom the world was not worthy." Here we see the difference between *God's* estimate and that of unregenerate religionists concerning the Children of Faith. God regards them as "the excellent" of the earth in whom is His "delight" (Psa. 16:3). "A true believer by reason of his union with Christ, and of the abode of the Spirit of sanctification in him, is worth more than a million of worlds; as a rich and precious jewel is more worth than many loads of filthy mud" (W. Gouge). The excellency of saints appears also in the benefit and blessings which they bring to the places where they reside: they are the "salt of the earth," though the corrupt multitude around them realizes it not. Their presence stays the hand of Divine judgment (Gen. 19:22), brings down blessing (Gen. 30:27), and their prayers secure Divine healing (Gen. 20:17). How little does the world realize how much it owes to those whom they hate so bitterly!

"They wandered in deserts, and in mountains, in dens and caves of the earth." Not only were they without a settled habitation, but they were compelled to resort to desolate places and the dens of wild beasts, in order to escape the fury of their foes. The word for "wandering" here is different from the one used in the previous verse: there it signifies to go up and down from house to house, or town to town, in hope of finding succour; but in which they were disappointed. Here the term denotes a wandering in unknown territory, going (like a blind man) they knew not whither: it is the term used of Abraham in v. 8, and of Hagar in Gen. 21:14, and of wandering sheep in Matt. 18:12. What a commentary upon fallen human nature: these saints of God were safer among the beasts of the field than in the religious world inflamed by the Devil! While these lines are being read, there are probably some of God's children in foreign lands suffering these very experiences.

Seeing that faith in the living God will alone support the soul under manifold trials, how necessary it is that we labour in the fear of the Lord to get our hearts rooted and grounded in the

Truth, so that when afflictions or persecutions come we may be enabled to show forth the power and fruits of this spiritual grace. Faith has to overcome the fear of man as well as the love of the world! Whatever sufferings God may appoint in the path of duty, they are to be patiently borne as seeing Him who is invisible. Their enemies clothed in death in the most hideous and horrible forms that hatred could devise, yet the faith of those saints boldly met and endured it. How thankful *we* should be that God's restraining hand is still upon the reprobate, for human nature has not improved any.

CHAPTER EIGHTY-TWO

The Family of Faith

(Heb. 11:39, 40)

"And these all, having obtained a good report through faith, received not the promise: God having provided some better thing for us, that they without us should not be made perfect" (vv. 39, 40). Several details in these verses call for careful consideration. First, to what does "the promise" here refer to? Second, in what sense had the O. T. saints "not received" the promise? Third, what is the "better thing" which God provided for us? Fourth, what is here meant by "be made perfect"? Widely different answers have been returned to these questions, and even the most reliable of the commentators are by no means agreed; therefore it would ill-become us to speak dogmatically, where men of God differ. Instead of wearying the reader with their diversive views, we will expound our text according to what measure of light God has granted us upon it.

As we approach our task there are several considerations which need to be borne in mind, the observing of which should aid us not a little. First, ascertaining the relation of our text to that which precedes. Second, discovering the exact relation of its several clauses. Third, studying it in the light of the distinctive and dominant theme of the particular epistle in which it occurs. Fourth, weighing its leading terms in connection with their usage in parallel passages. If these four things be duly attended to we ought not to go far wrong in our interpretation. Our purpose in enumerating them is principally to indicate to your preach-ears the methods which should be followed in the critical examination of any difficult passage.

As to the connection between our present verses and those which precede, there is no difficulty. The apostle, having so forcibly and largely, set out the virtue and vigour of faith, by the admirable workings and fruits thereof, both in doing and in suffering, now gives a general summary: they all "obtained a good report." The relations of the several clauses of our text to each other, may be set out thus: "and these all" refer to the entire company which has been before us in the previous verses; a "good report" is asscribed to them; yet they had not "received the promise"; because God had provided something "better" for the N. T. saints. The dominant theme of Hebrews is, The immeasurable superiority of Christianity over Judaism. The leading terms in our text will be pondered in what follows.

"And these all, having obtained a good report through faith." Two things are here in view: the persons spoken of, and that which is predicated of them. The reference is to all spoken of in the previous parts of the chapter, and by necessary inference, to all believers before the incarnation of Christ who exhibited a true faith. The words "*these* all" is restrictive, excluding others who had not the faith here mentioned. "Many more than these lived before Christ was exhibited, yea, lived in the time and place that some of these did, yet received no good report. Cain lived and offered a sacrifice with Abel, yet was none of these. Ham was in the ark with Shem; Ishmael in Abraham's family with Isaac; Esau in the same womb with Jacob; Dathan and Abiram came through the Red Sea with Caleb and Joshua: many other wicked unbelievers were mixed with believers, yet they obtained not any such good report. Though their outward condition was alike, yet their inward disposition was much different" (W. Gouge).

Thus it is today. There are two widely different classes of people who come under the sound of the Word: those who believe it, and those who believe it not. And those of the former class have also to be divided, for while there are a few in whom that Word works effectually in a spiritual way, many have nothing more than a natural faith in its letter. This latter faith — which so many today mistake for a saving one — is merely an intellectual assent to the Divine authority of the Bible and to the verities of its contents — like that possessed by most of the Jews of Christ's day, and which though good so far as it goes, changes not the heart nor issues in a godly life. A supernatural faith, which is wrought in the soul by the operations of the Holy Spirit, issues in supernatural works, such as those attributed unto the men and women mentioned in our chapter. It is a Divine principle which enables its possessor to overcome the world, patiently endure the sorest afflictions, and love God and His truth more than life itself.

"Having obtained a good report through faith." Because of their trusting in Christ alone for salvation, and because of their walking in subjection to His revealed will, they received approbation. There is probably a threefold reference in the words now before us. First, unto God's own testimony which He bore to them: this is found in

His Word, where their names receive honourable mention, and where the fruits of their faith are imperishably preserved. Second, to the Spirit's bearing witness with their spirit that they were the children of God (Rom. 8:16), the rejoicing which they had from the testimony of a good conscience (2 Cor. 1:12): this in blessed contrast from the world's estimate of them, who regarded and treated them as the offscouring of all things. Third, to the esteem in which they were held by the Church, their fellow-saints testifying to the unworldliness of their lives: this shows our faith should be evidenced by such good works that it is justified before men.

"Received not the promise." The singular number here implies some pre-eminent excellent thing promised, and this is Jesus Christ, the Divine Saviour. He is said to be given according to "the promise" (Acts 13:23). God's "promise" was declared to be fulfilled when He brought Christ forth (Acts 13:32, 33). In Acts 2:39 and 26:6 Christ is set forth under this term "promise." Christ Himself is the prime promise, not only because He was the substance of the first promise given after the fall (Gen. 3:15), but also because He is the complement or accomplishment of all the promises (2 Cor. 1:20). The great promise of God to send His Son, born of a woman, to save His people from their sins, was the Object of Faith of the Church throughout all the generations of the O. T. era. Therein we may discern the rich grace of God in providing for the spiritual needs of His saints from earliest times.

"Received not the promise." As several times before in this epistle, "promise" is here used metonymically for the thing promised, and this it is which explains the "received not." As Owen expressed it, "The promise as a faithful engagement pledge of future good, they received, but the good thing itself was not in their days exhibited." They did not live to see historically accomplished that which their faith specifically embraced. As the Lord Jesus declared to His disciples, "Many prophets and righteous men have desired to see those things which ye see, and have not seen them, and to hear those things which ye hear, and have not heard them" (Matt. 13:17). Herein we behold the strength and perseverance of faith, that they continued to look, unwaveringly, for so many centuries for Him that should come, and came not in their lifetime.

"God having provided some better thing for us." The verb here looks back to the eternal counsels of Divine grace, to the Everlasting Covenant; it is a word which denotes God's determination, designation and appointment of Christ to be the propitiatory sacrifice, and the exact season for His advent. "When the fulness of time was come (the season ordained by Heaven), God sent forth His Son"

(Gal. 4:4). Thus it should be clear that the contrast which is pointed in the sentence before us, is that between "the promise" *given* and "the promise" *performed*. It is at that point, and no other, we find the essential difference between the faith of the O. T. saints and the faith of the N. T. saints: the one looked forward to a Saviour that *was* to come, the other looks back to a Saviour who *has* come.

It seems strange that what is really so obvious and simple should have been regarded by many as obscure and difficult. In His "Great Cloud of Witnesses" E. W. Bullinger began comments on this passage by saying, "These verses must be among those to which Peter referred when he said, speaking of Paul's epistles, there are 'some things hard to be understood.' For they confessedly present no small difficulty." But what is there here which is "hard to be understood"? The very epistle in which this verse occurs supplies a sure key to its correct interpretation. As we have said above, the great theme of it is, The immeasurable superiority of Christianity over Judaism, and those of our readers who have followed us through this series of expositions, will recall how many illustrations of this have been before us. Another one is present in 11:39, 40: "*they* received not the (fulfillment of) the promise," *we* have—"God having provided some better thing for us": cf. 7:19, 22; 8:6; 9:23; 10:34 for the word "better."

It is really pathetic and deplorable to see what most of the moderns make of our present verse. In their anxiety to magnify the contrast between the Mosaic and Christian economies, and in their ignorance of much of the contents of the O.T. scriptures, they have seized upon these words "God having provided some better thing for us" to bolster up one of their chief errors, and have read into them that which any one having even a superficial acquaintaince with the Psalms and Prophets should have no difficulty in perceiving to be utterly untenable. Some have said that the "better thing" which we Christians have is eternal life, others that it is regeneration and the indwelling of the Spirit, others that it is membership in the Body of Christ with the heavenly calling that entails—denying that these blessings were enjoyed by any of the O. T. saints. Such is a fair sample of the rubbish which is now to be found in most of the "ministry," oral and written, of this degenerate age.

In their crude and arbitrary attempts to rightly divide the word of truth, those calling themselves "dispensationalists" have wrongly divided the family of God. The entire Election of Grace have God for their Father, Christ for their Saviour, the Holy Spirit for their Comforter. All who are saved, from the beginning to the end of earth's history, are the objects of God's everlasting love, share alike in the benefits of Christ's atonement, and are begotten by the Spirit unto the same inheritance. God communicated to Abel the same kind of faith as He does to His children today. Abraham was justified in precisely the same manner as Christians are now (Rom. 4:2). Moses bore the "reproach of Christ," and had respect unto the identical "recompense of the reward" (Heb. 11:26) as is set before us. David was as truly a stranger and pilgrim on earth as we are (Psa. 119:19), and looked unto the same eternal pleasures at God's right hand as we do (Psa. 16:11; 23:6).

The worst mistakes made by the "dispensationalists" grow out of their failures at the following points: first, to see the organic union between the Mosaic and Christian economies; second, to perceive that the "old covenant" and the "new covenant" were but two different administrations under which the blessings of the "everlasting covenant" are imparted; third, to distinguish between the spiritual remnant and the nation itself. The relation between the patriarchal and the Mosaic dispensations and this Christian era may be stated thus: they stood to each other, partly as the beginning does to the end, and partly as the shell does to the kernel. The former were preparatory, the latter is the full development—first the blade (in the patriarchal dispensation), then the ear (the Mosaic), and now the full corn in the ear, in this Christian era. In the former we have the type and shadow; in the latter, the antitype and substance. Christianity is but the full development of what existed in former ages, or a grander exemplification of the truths and principles which were then revealed.

The great fact that the Everlasting Covenant which God made with Christ as the Head of His Church formed the basis of all His dealings with His people, and that the terms and blessings of that Eternal Chapter were being administered by Him under the "old" and "new" covenants, may be illustrated from secular history. In practically every country there are two chief political parties. The policy, and particularly the methods followed, by these rival factions, differ radically, yet though the one may succeed the other in power, and though great changes mark their alternative regimes, and though many diverse laws may be enacted or cancelled from time to time, yet *the fundamental constitution* of the country remains unchanged. Thus it is under the Mosaic and Christian economies: widely different as they are in many incidental details, nevertheless God's moral government is always according to the same fundamental principles of grace and righteousness, mercy and justice, truth and faithfulness, in the one era equally as much as in the other.

The distinction between the regenerated remnant and the unregenerate nation during O. T. times, is as real and radical as that which now exists between real Christians and the mulitude of empty professors with which Christendom abounds; yea, one is the type of the other. Just as empty professors now possess a "form of godliness" but are destitute of its "power," so the great bulk of the lineal descendants of Abraham were occupied only with the externals of Judaism—witness the scribes and pharisees of Christ's day; and just as the lifeless religionists of our time are taken up with the "letter" of the Word and have no experimental acquaintance with its spiritual realities, so the unquickened Israelites of old were engaged with the outward shell of their ritual, but never penetrated to its kernel. There was an election within an election, a remnant who were Jews "inwardly" (Rom. 2:29), among the great company surrounding them who were Jews only in name, outwardly.

The spiritual portion of that O. T. remnant of God's saints was identically the same as that of the Christian's now. They were the recipients of the free gift of grace in Christ (Gen. 6:8) as we are. They possessed eternal life (Psa. 133:3) as truly as we do. They rejoiced in the knowledge of sins forgiven (Psa. 32:1, 2) as heartily as we do. They were as really instructed by the Spirit (Neh. 9:20) as we are. Nor were they left in total ignorance of the glorious future awaiting them: "These all died in faith, not having received the promises, but having seen them afar off, and were persuaded of them, and embraced them, and confessed that they were strangers and pilgrims on the earth. For they that say such things declare plainly that they seek a country" (vv. 13, 14). The word for "Country" there is not the ordinary one "chora," but "patris," which signifies Homeland, or Fatherland—*such* a "country" as one's father dwells in.

The question, then, returns upon us: Seeing the O. T. saints enjoyed all the essential spiritual blessings of which Christians now partake, *exactly what is* the "better thing" which God "provides for us"? The answer is a *superior administration* of the Everlasting Covenant: 13:20. In what particular respects? Chiefly in these. First, we now have a better view of Christ than the O. T. saints had: they saw Him, chiefly through types and promises, whereas we view Him in the accomplishment and fulfilment of them. Second, there is now a broader foundation for faith to rest upon: they looked for a Christ who was to come and who would put away their sins; we look at a Christ who has come and who has put away our sins. Third, they were as minors, under teachers and governors; whereas we are in the position, dispensationally, of those who have attained their majority: Gal. 4:1-7. Fourth, there is now a wider outpouring of God's grace: it is no longer confined to an elect remnant in one nation, but reaches out to His favoured people scattered among all nations.

"That they without us should not be made perfect." "The law (or Mosaic economy) made nothing perfect but the bringing in of a better hope did" (7:19). The "perfecting" of a thing consists in the well-finishing of it, and a full accomplishment of all things appertaining thereto. There is no doubt that the ultimate reference of our text is to the eternal glory of the whole Family of Faith in heaven; yet we believe it also includes the various *degrees* by which that perfection is attained, and the *means* thereunto. They are, first, the taking away of sin—which makes man most imperfect—and the clothing him with the robe of righteousness, in which he may appear perfect before God. These were secured by the life and death of Jesus Christ. In that, the O. T. saints were not "made perfect *without us,*" for their sins and our sins were expiated by the *same* Sacrifice, and their persons and our persons are justified by the *same* Righteousness.

Second, the subduing of the power of indwelling sin, enabling those justified to walk in the paths of righteousness, which is through the enabling of the Spirit. In this too the O. T. saints were not (relatively) "made perfect *without us,*" as is clear from Psa. 23:4; 51:11 etc. Third, the Spirit enabling those who are united to Christ to stand up against all assaults, and to persevere in a spiritual growth; in this also the O. T. saints were not "made perfect *without us,*" as is evident by a comparison of Psa. 97:10 with 1 Pet. 1:15. Fourth, the receiving of the soul to Glory when it leaves the body: this also was common to Old and N. T. saints alike—we are not unmindful of the carnal theory held by some who imagine that prior to the death of Christ, the souls of saints went only to some imaginary Paradise "in the heart of the earth"; but this is much too near akin to the subterranean *limbus* of Romanism to merit any refutation.

Fifth, the resurrection of the body. In this the whole Family of Faith shall share alike, and at the same time: "In Christ shall all be made alive; but every man in his own order: Christ the first-fruits, afterwards *they that are Christ's* at His coming" (1 Cor. 15:22, 23). And *who are* "Christ's"? why, *all* that the Father gave to Him, *all* that He purchased with His blood. God's Word knows nothing of His people being raised in sections, at intervals. Sixth, the re-union between the soul and body, which takes place at Christ's appearing. In Heb. 12:23 the O. T. saints are referred to as "the *spirits* of just men made perfect, but they are still "waiting for the adoption, to wit, the redemption of the body" (Rom. 8:23). In this too all the redeemed shall share alike, being "caught up *together* to meet the Lord in the air" (1 Thess. 4:17).

Seventh, the entrance into eternal glory, when Old and N. T. saints alike shall, all together, be "forever with the Lord." Then shall be completely realized that ancient oracle concerning Shiloh "unto Him shall the gathering of the people be" (Gen. 49:10. Then shall be fulfilled that mystical word, "I say unto you, that many shall come from the east and west, and shall sit down with Abraham, and Isaac, and Jacob, in the Kingdom of heaven" (Matt. 8:11). As the Lord Jesus declared, "I lay down My life for the (O. T.) sheep; And other (N. T.) sheep I have which are not of this fold: them also I must bring, and they shall hear My voice; and there shall be *one flock* (Greek and R. V.), one Shepherd" (John 10:15, 16). Then it shall be that Christ will "gather *together in one* the children of God that are scattered abroad" (John 11:52)—not only among all nations, but through all dispensations.

In all of these seven degrees mentioned above are the elect of God "made perfect"; in all of them shall the O. T. and N. T. saints share alike: all shall come "in the unity of the faith, and of the knowledge of the Son of God, unto a perfect man, unto the measure of the stature of the fulness of Christ" (Eph. 4:13). God deferred the resurrection and final glorification of the O. T. saints until the saints of this N. T. era should be called out and gathered into the one Body: "God has so arranged matters, that the complete accomplishment of the promise, both to the Old and New Testament believers, shall *take place together*; 'they' shall be made perfect, but not without 'us'; we and they shall attain perfection together" (John Brown). Thus to "be made perfect" is here the equivalent of *receiving* (the full accomplishment of) the promise, or enjoying together the complete realization of the "better thing." Verses 39 and 40 are inseparably linked together, and the language used in the one serves to interpret that employed in the other, both being coloured by the dominant theme of this epistle.

Thus our understanding of these two verses which have occasioned so much trouble to many of the commentators, is as follows. First, though the O. T. saints lived under an inferior administration of the Everlasting Covenant than we do, nevertheless, they "obtained a good report" and went to Heaven at death. Second, the "better thing" which God has provided for the N. T. saints is a superior administration of the Everlasting Covenant, that is, we enjoy superior *means* of grace to what they had. Spiritual and heavenly blessings were presented unto the Church in the patriarchal and Mosaic dispensations under temporal and earthly images: Canaan being a figure of Heaven; Christ and His atonement being set forth under symbolic ceremonies and obscure ordinances. As the substance exceeds the shadows so is the state of the Church under the "new" covenant superior to its state under the "old." Third, God has ordered that the entire Family of Faith shall be "perfected" by the same Sacrifice, and shall together enjoy its purchased blessings throughout an endless eternity.

The *practical application* of the whole of the above unto our hearts, was well put by John Calvin: "If they on whom the light of grace had not as yet so brightly shone, displayed so great a constancy in and during evils, what ought the full brightness of the Gospel to produce in us! A small spark of light led them to heaven; when the sun of righteousness shines over us, with what pretence can we excuse ourselves if we still cleave to the earth?"

CHAPTER EIGHTY-THREE

The Demands of Faith

(Heb. 12:1)

Our present verse is a call to constancy in the Christian profession; it is an exhortation unto steadfastness in the Christian life; it is a pressing appeal for making personal holiness our supreme business and quest. In substance our text is parallel with such verses as Matt. 16:24, Rom. 6:13, 2 Cor. 7:1, Phil. 3:12-14, Titus 2:12, 1 Pet. 2:9-12. This summarization of the Christian's twofold duty is given again and again in the Scriptures: the duty of mortification and of vivification, the putting off of the "old man" and the putting on of the "new man" (Eph. 4:22-24). Analyzing the particular terms of our text, we find there is, first, the duty enjoined: to "run the race that is set before us." Second, the obstacles to be overcome: "lay aside every weight" etc. Third, the essential grace which is requisite thereto: "patience." Fourth, the encouragement given: the "great cloud of witnesses."

The opening "Wherefore" in our text looks back to 10:35, 36, where the apostle had urged, "Cast not away therefore your confidence, which hath great recompense of reward. For ye have need of patience, that, after ye have done the will of God, ye might receive the promise." That exhortation had been followed by a lengthy proof of the efficacy of persevering faith to enable its possessors to do whatever God commands, however difficult; to endure whatever God appoints, however severe; to obtain what He promises, however seemingly unattainable. All of this had been copiously illustrated in chapter 11, by a review of the history of God's people in the past, who had exemplified so strikingly and so blessedly the nature, the trails, and the triumphs of a spiritual faith. Having affirmed the *unity* of the family of God, the oneness of the Old and New T. saints, assuring the latter that God has provided some better thing for us, the apostle now repeats the exhortation unto steadfast perseverance in the path of faith and obedience.

"*Wherefore* seeing we also are compassed about with so great a cloud of witnesses, *let us*." Here the apostle applies the various illustrations given in the preceding chapter, making use of them as a grand motive to perseverance in the Christian faith and state. "If all the saints of God lived, suffered, endured, and conquered by faith, shall not we also? If the saints who lived before the Incarnation, before the redemption was accomplished, before the High Priest entered the heavenly sanctuary, trusted in the midst of discouragements and trials, how much more aught we who know the name of Jesus, who have received the beginning, the installment of the great Messianic promise?" (A. Saphir). Herein we are shown that only then do we read the O. T. narratives unto profit when we draw from them incentives to practical godliness.

In Hebrews 11 we have had described at length many aspects and characteristics of *the life of faith.* There we saw that a life of faith is an intensely practical thing, consisting of very much more than day-dreaming, or being regaled with joyous emotions, or even resting in orthodox views of the truth. By faith Noah built an ark, Abraham separated from his idolatrous neighbors and gained a rich inheritance, Moses forsook Egypt and became leader of Israel's hosts. By faith the Red Sea was crossed, Jericho captured, Goliath slain, the mouths of lions were closed, the violence of fire was quenched. A spiritual faith, then, is not a passive thing, but an active, energetic, vigorous, and fruitful one. The *same* line of thought is continued in the passage which is now before us, the *same* branch of truth is there in view again, only under a figure—a figure very emphatic and graphic.

"Let us *run* with patience the race that is set before us." Here the Christian is likened unto an athlete, and his life unto the running of a race. This is one of a number of figures used in the N. T. to describe the Christian life. Believers are likened to shining lights, branches of the vine, soldiers, strangers and pilgrims: the last-mentioned more closely resembling the figure employed in our text, but with this difference: travellers may rest for awhile, and refresh themselves, but the racer must *continue* running or he ceases to be a "racer." The figure of the race occurs frequently, both in the Old and N. T.: Psa. 119:32, Song of S. 1:4, 1 Cor. 9:24, Phil. 3:14, 2 Tim. 4:7. Very solemn is that word in Gal. 5:7, "ye *did* run well": the Lord, in His mercy, grant that *that* may never be said of writer or reader.

The principal thoughts suggested by the figure of the "race" are rigorous self-denial and discipline, vigorous exertion, persevering endurance. The Christian life is not a thing of passive luxuriation, but of active "*fighting* the good fight of faith!" The Christian is not called to lie down on flowery beds of ease, but to run a race, and athletics are strenuous, demanding self-sacrifice, hard training, the putting forth of every ounce of energy possessed. I am afraid that in this work-hating and pleasure-loving age, we do not keep this aspect of the truth sufficiently before us: we take things too placidly and lazily. The charge which God brought against Israel of old applies very largely to Christendom today: "Woe to them that are *at ease* in Zion" (Amos. 6:1): to be "at ease" is the very opposite of "running the race."

The "race" is that life of faith and obedience, that pursuit of personal holiness, to which the Christian is called by God. Turning from sin and the world in penitence and trust to Christ is not the finishing-post, but only the starting-point. The Christian race begins at the new birth, and ends not till we are summoned to leave this world. The prize to be run for is heavenly glory. The ground to be covered is our journey through this life. The track itself is "set before us": marked out in the Word. The rules to be observed, the path which is to be traversed, the difficulties to be overcome, the dangers to be avoided, the source and secret of the needed strength, are all plainly revealed in the holy Scriptures. If we lose, the blame is entirely ours; if we succeed, the glory belongs to God alone.

The prime thought suggested in the figure of running the race set before us is not that of speed, but of self-discipline, whole-hearted endeavour, the calling into action of every spiritual faculty possessed by the new man. In his helpful commentary, J. Brown pointed out that a race is *vigorous* exercise. Christianity consists not in abstract speculations, enthusiastic feelings, or specious talk, but in directing all our energies into holy actions. It is a *laborious* exertion: the flesh, the world, the devil are like a fierce gale blowing against us, and only intense effort can overcome them. It is a *regulated* exertion: to run around in a circle is strenuous activity, but it will not bring us to the goal; we must follow strictly the prescribed course. It is *progressive* exertion: there is to be a growth in grace, an adding to faith of virtue, etc. (2 Pet. 1:5-7), a reaching forth unto those things which are before.

"Let us *run* with patience the race that is set before us." We only "run" when we are very anxious to get to a certain place, when there is some attraction stimulating us. That word "run" then presupposes the heart eagerly set upon the goal. That "goal" is complete deliverance from the power of indwelling sin, perfect conformity to the lovely image of Christ, entrance into the promised rest and bliss on High. It is only as *that* is kept steadily in view, only as faith and hope are in real and daily exercise, that we shall progress along the path of obedience. To look back will cause us to halt or stumble; to look down at the roughness and difficulties of the way will discourage and produce slackening, but to keep the prize in view will nerve to steady endeavour. It was thus our great Exemplar ran: "Who for the JOY *that was set before Him*" (v. 2).

But let us now consider, secondly, the means prescribed: "let us lay aside every weight, and the sin which doth so easily beset us." That might be tersely expressed in several different forms: let us relinquish those things which would impede our spiritual progress; let us endeavour with might and main to overcome every hindering obstacle; let us attend diligently unto the way or method which will enable us to make the best speed. While sitting at our ease we are hardly conscious of the weight of our clothes, the articles held in our hands, or the cumbersome objects we may have in our pockets. But let us be aroused by the howlings of fierce animals, let us be pursued by hungry wolves, and methinks that none of us would have much difficulty in understanding the meaning of those words "let us lay aside every *weight!*"

"Let us lay aside every weight, and the sin which doth so easily beset us." While no doubt each of these expressions has a definite and separate force, yet we are satisfied that a certain school of writers err in drawing too sharp and broad a line of distinction between them, for a careful examination of their contentions will show that the very things they consider to be merely "weights," are, in reality, *sins*. The fact is that in most quarters there has been, for many years past, a deplorable lowering of the standard of Divine holiness, and numerous infractions of God's righteous law have been wrongly termed "failures," "mistakes," and "minor blemishes," etc. Anything which minimizes the reality and enormity of sin is to be steadfastly resisted; anything which tends to excuse human "weaknesses" is to be rejected; anything which reduces that standard of absolute perfection which God requires us to constantly aim at—*every* missing of which is a *sin*—is to be shunned.

"Let us lay aside every weight, and the sin which doth so easily beset us" is parallel with, "If any man will come after Me, let him deny himself, and take up his cross" (Matt. 16:24), and "let us cleanse ourselves from all filthiness of the flesh and of the spirit" (2 Cor. 7:1). In other words, this dehortation is a calling upon the Christian to "mortify the deeds of the body" (Rom. 8:13), to "abstain from fleshly lusts which war against the soul" (1 Pet. 2:11). There are two things which racers discard: all unnecessary burdens, and long flowing garments which would entangle them. Probably there is a reference to both of these in our text: the former being considered under "weights," or those things we voluntarily encumber ourselves with, but which should be dropped; the latter, "the sin which doth so easily beset us" referring to inward depravity.

"Let us lay aside every weight" is a call to the sedulous and daily mortification of our hearts to all that would mar communion with Christ: it is parallel with "*denying* ungodliness and worldly lusts" (Titus 2:12). Everything which requires us to take time and strength away from God-appointed duties, everything which tends to bind the mind to earthly things and hinders our affections from being set upon things above, is to be cheerfully relinquished for Christ's sake. Everything which impedes my progress in running the race which God has set before me is to be dropped. But let it be carefully recognized that our text makes *no* reference to the dropping of *duties* which we have no right to lay aside. The performing of real and legitimate duty is never a hindrance to the spiritual life, though from a wrong attitude of mind and the allowance of the spirit of *discontent*, they often become so.

Many make a great mistake in entertaining the thought that their spiritual life is being much hindered by the very things which should, by Divine grace, be a real help to them. Opposition in the home from ungodly relatives, trials in connection with their daily work, the immediate presence of the wicked in the shop or office, *are* a real trial (and God intends they *should* be—to remind us we are still in a world which lieth in the Wicked one, to exercise our graces, to prove the sufficiency of His strength), but they need not be hindrances or "weights." Many erroneously suppose they would make much more progress spiritually if only their "circumstances" were altered. This is a serious mistake, and a murmuring against God's providential dealings with us. *He* shapes our "circumstances" as a helpful discipline to the soul, and only as we learn to rise above "circumstances," and walk with God in them, are we "running the race that is set before *us*." The *person* is the same no matter what "circumstances" he may be in!

While the "weights" in our text have no reference to those duties which God requires us to discharge—for *He* never calls us to any thing which would draw us away from communion with Himself; yet they *do* apply in a very real sense unto a multitude of cares which many of God's people *impose upon themselves*—cares which are a grievous drag upon the soul. The artificial state in which many people now live, which custom, society, the world, imposes, *does* indeed bind many heavy burdens on the backs of their silly victims. If we accept that scale of "duties" which the fashion of this world imposes, we *shall* find them "weights" which seriously impede our spiritual progress: spending valuable time in reading newspapers and other secular litearature in order to "keep up with the times," exchanging "social calls" with worldlings, spending money on all sorts of unnecessary things so as to be abreast of our neighbors, are "weights" burdening many, and those "weights" are *sins*.

By "weights," then, may be understood every form of intemperance or the immoderate and hurtful use made of any of those things which God has given us "richly to *enjoy*" (1 Tim. 6:17). Yes, to "enjoy" be it noted, and not only to *use*. The Creator has placed many things in this world — like the beautiful flowers and the singing birds — for our pleasure, as well as for the bare supply of our bodily needs. This should be borne in mind, for there is a danger here, as every where, of lopsidedness. We are well aware that in this age of fleshly indulgence the majority are greatly in danger of erring on the side of laxity, yet in avoiding this sin, others are in danger of swinging to the other extreme and being "righteous over much" (Eccl. 7:16), adopting a form of monastic austerity, totally abstaining from things which Scripture in nowise prohibits.

Each Christian has to decide for himself, by an honest searching of Scripture and an earnest seeking of wisdom from God, *what* are "weights" which hinder *him*. While on the one hand it is wrong to assume an haughty and independent attitude, refusing to weigh in the balances of the sanctuary the conscientious scruples and prejudices of fellow-Christians; on the other hand it is equally wrong to suffer any to lord it over our consciences, and deprive us of our Christian liberty. "Let every man be fully persuaded in his own mind." It is not the lawful use of God's creatures, but the intemperate abuse of them which Scripture condemns. More die from over eating than over drinking. Some constitutions are injured as much by coffee as by whiskey. Some are undermining their health by a constant round of exertions; others enervate themselves by spending too much time in bed.

The Greek word for "weights" is "tumor or swelling," so that an excresence, a superfluity, is what is in view. A "weight" is something which we are at liberty to cast aside, but which instead we choose to retain. It is anything which retards our progress, anything which unfits us for the discharge of our God-assigned duties, anything which dulls the conscience, blunts the edge of our spiritual appetite, or chokes the spirit of prayer. The "cares of this world" weigh down the soul just as effectually as does a greedy grasping after the things of earth. The allowance of the spirit of envy will be as injurious spiritually as would an attendance at the movies. Fellowshipping at a Christ-dishonouring "church" quenches that Spirit as quickly as would seeking diversion at the dance hall. The habit of gossiping may do more damage to the Spiritual life than the excessive smoking of tobacco.

One of the best indications that I *have* entered the race is the discovery that certain things, which previously never exercised my conscience, are a hindrance to me; and the further I "run," the more conscious shall I be of the "weights"; and the more determined I am, by God's grace, to reach the winning post, the more readily shall I drop them. So many professing Christians never seem to have any "weights," and we never see them *drop* anything. Ah, the fact is, they have never entered the race. O to be able to say with Paul, "I count all things but loss for the excellency of the knowledge of Christ Jesus my Lord" (Phil. 3:8). When this is true of us, we shall not find it difficult, but rather easy to obey that injunction, "Go from the presence of a foolish man (or woman) when thou perceivest not in him the *lips* of knowledge" (Prov. 14:7); and so with many other scriptural exhortations.

"And the sin which doth so easily beset (Greek "encompass") us." As we have already pointed out, the writer regards the "weights" as external temptations which have to be resisted, evil habits which are to be dropped; and "the sin" as referring to indwelling corruption, with a special reference (as the whole context suggests) to the workings of *unbelief*: compare Heb. 3:13. It is true that each of us has some special form of sin to which we are most prone, and that he is more sorely tempted from one direction than another; but we think it is very clear from all which precedes our text that what the apostle has particularly in mind here is that which most seeks to hinder the exercise of *faith*. Let the reader ponder John 16:8, 9.

"This is confirmed by the experience of all who have been exercised in this case, who have met with great difficulties in, and have been called to suffer for, the profession of the Gospel. Ask of them what they have found in such cases to be their most dangerous enemy; what hath had the most easy and frequent access unto their minds, to disturb and dishearten them, of the power thereof they have been most afraid; they will all answer with one voice, it is the evil of their own unbelieving hearts. This hath continually attempted to entangle them, to betray them, in taking part with all outward temptations. When this is conquered, all things are plain and easy unto them. It may be some of them have had their particular temptations which they may reflect upon; but any other evil by sin, which is *common unto them all,* as this *is,* they can fix on none" (John Owen).

But *how* is the Christian to "lay aside" indwelling sin and its particular workings of unbelief? This injunction is parallel with Eph. 4:22, "That ye put off concerning the former conversation the old man, which is corrupt according to the deceitful lusts." And how is *that* to be done? By heeding the exhortation of Rom. 6:11, 12, "Reckon ye also yourselves to be dead indeed unto sin, but alive unto God through Jesus Christ our Lord. Let not sin therefore reign in your mortal body, that ye should obey it in the lusts thereof." In other words, by faith's recognition of my legal oneness with Christ, and by drawing from His fulness. Indwelling sin is to be "laid aside" by daily mortification (Rom. 8:13), by seeking grace to resist its solicitations (Titus 2:11, 12), by repenting, confessing, and forsaking the effects of its activities (Prov. 28:13), by diligently using the means which God has provided for holy living (Gal. 5:16).

"Run *with patience* the race that is set before us." Perseverance or endurance is the prime prerequisite for the discharge of this duty. The good-ground hearer brought forth fruit "with patience" (Luke 8:15). We are bidden to be "followers of those who through faith *and patience* inherit the promises" (Heb. 6:12). The "race" appointed is a lengthy one, for it extends throughout the whole of our earthly pilgrimage. The course is narrow, and to the flesh, rough. The racer often becomes disheartened by the difficulties encountered. But "Let us not be weary in well doing, for in due season we shall reap, if we faint not" (Gal. 6:9).

But how is this needed "patience" to be acquired? A twofold answer is given, the second part of which will be before us in the next article. First, by heeding the encouragement which is here set before us: "*Wherefore* seeing we also are compassed about with so great a cloud of witnesses *let us* lay aside . . . *let us* run." The reference is to the heroes of faith mentioned in the previous chapter: they compose a testimony for God, and speak unto future generations to be constant as they were. They witness to how noble a thing life may be when it is lived by faith. They witness to the faithfulness of God who sustained them, and enabled them to triumph over their foes, and overcome their difficulties. In likening these numerous witnesses unto a "cloud" there is no doubt a reference unto the Cloud which guided Israel in the wilderness: they *followed* it all the way to Canaan! So must we follow the noble example of the O. T. saints in their faith, obedience, and perseverance.

"Wherefore seeing we also are compassed about with so great a clould of witnesses, *let us*." This is mentioned as an incentive, to console and assure us we are not alone. As we look around at the empty profession on every side, and behold the looseness and laxity of so many who bear the name of Christ, Satan seeks to make us believe that we are wrong, too "strict," and rebukes us for our "singularity." No doubt he employed the same tactics with Noah, with Abraham, with Moses; but they heeded him not. Nor should we. We are *not* "singular": if faithful to Christ we are following "the footsteps of the flock" (Song of Sol. 1:8). Others before us have trod the same path, met with the same hindrances, fought the same fight. *They* persevered, conquered, and won the crown:

then "*let us* run." That is the thought and force of the opening words of our text.

"We who have still to walk in the narrow path which alone leads to glory are encouraged and instructed by the cloud of witnesses, the innumerable company of saints, who testified amid the most varied circumstances of suffering and temptation, that the just live by *faith,* and that faith is the victory which overcometh the world. The memory of those children of God, whose lives are recorded for our learning and consolation, animates us, and we feel upheld as it were by their sympathy and by the consciousness, that although few and weak, strangers and pilgrims on earth, we belong to a great and mighty, nay, a victorious army, part of which has already entered into the land of peace" (A. Saphir).

CHAPTER EIGHTY-FOUR

The Object of Faith

(Heb. 12:2)

The verse which is now to engage our attention continues and completes the important exhortation found in the one which was before us in the last article. The two verses are so closely related that only the requirements of space obliged us to separate them. The latter supplies such a blessed sequel to the former that it will be necessary to present a summary of our comments thereon. We saw that the Christian life, the life of faith and obedience, is presented under the figure of a "race," which denotes that so far from its being a thing of dreamy contemplation or abstract speculation, it is one of activity, exertion, and progressive motion, for faith without works is dead. But the "race" speaks not only of activity, but of *regulated* activity, following the course which is "set before us." Many professing Christians are engaged in multitudinous efforts which God has never bidden them undertake: that is like running round and round in a circle. To follow the appointed track means that our energies be directed by the precepts of Holy Writ.

The order presented in Heb. 12:1 is the negative before the positive: there must be the "laying aside" of hindering weights, before we can "run" the race set before us. This order is fundamental, and is emphasized all through Scripture. There must be a turning from the world, before there can be a real turning unto the Lord (Isa. 55:7); self must be denied before Christ can be followed (Matt. 16:24). There must be a putting off the old man, before there can be any true putting on of the new man (Eph. 4:22-24). There has to be a "denying ungodliness and worldly lusts," before we can "live soberly, righteously and godly in this present world" (Titus 3:12). There has to be a "cleansing of ourselves from all filthiness of the flesh and spirit," before there can be any "perfecting holiness in the fear of God" (2 Cor. 7:1). We must "be not conformed to this world," before we can be "transformed by the renewing of our mind," so that we may "*prove* what is that good and acceptable and perfect will of God" (Rom. 12:2, 3).

Before the plants and flowers will flourish in the garden weeds must be rooted up, otherwise all the labours of the gardener will come to naught. As the Lord Jesus taught so plainly in the Parable of the Sower, where the "thorns" are permitted to thrive, the good Seed, the Word, is "choked" (Matt. 13:22); and it is very searching and solemn to note, by a careful comparison of the three records of it, that Christ interpreted this figure of the "thorns" more fully than any other single detail. He defined those choking "thorns" as "the *cares* of this life and the *deceitfulness* of riches," "the lust of *other* things and *pleasures* of this life." If those things fill and rule our hearts, our relish for spiritual things will be quenched, our strength to perform Christian duties will be sapped, our lives will be fruitless, and we shall be merely cumberers of the ground—the garden of our souls being filled with briars and weeds.

Hence it is that the *first* call in Heb. 12:1 is "let us lay aside every weight." "Inordinate care for the present life, and fondness for it, is a dead weight for the soul, that pulls it down when it should ascend upwards and pulls it back when it should press forwards" (Matt. Henry). It is the practical duty of *mortification* which is here inculcated, the abstaining from those fleshly lusts "which war against the soul" (1 Pet. 2:11). The racer must be as lightly clad as possible if he is to run swiftly: all that would cumber and impede him must be relinquished. Undue concern over temporal affairs, inordinate affection for the things of this life, the intemperate use of any material blessings, undue familiarity with the ungodly, are "weights" which prevent progress in godliness. A bag of gold would be as great a handicap to a runner as a bag of lead!

It is to be carefully noted that the laying aside of "every weight" *precedes* "and the sin which does so easily beset us", which has reference to indwelling corruption. Each Christian imagines that he is very anxious to be completely delivered from the power of indwelling sin: ah, but our hearts are very deceitful, and ever causing us to think more highly of ourselves than we ought to think. A criterion is given in this passage by which we may gauge the sincerity of our desires: our longing to be delivered from indwelling evil is to be measured by our willingness and readiness to *lay aside the "weights."* I may think I am earnestly desirous of having a beautiful garden, and may go to much expense and trouble in purchasing and planting some lovely flowers; but if I am too careless and lazy to diligently fight the weeds, what is my desire worth? So, if I disregard that word "make not provision for the flesh unto the lusts thereof" (Rom. 13:14), how sincere is my desire to be delivered from "the flesh!"

"And let us run with patience the race that is set before us." For this two things are needed: speed and strength—"rejoiceth as a *strong* man to run a race" (Psa. 19:5): the one being opposed to sloth and negligence, the other to weakness. These are the prime requisites: strength in grace, diligence in exercise. Speed is included in the word "run", but how is the strength to be obtained? This "race" calls for both the doing and suffering for Christ, the pressing forward toward the mark set before us, the progressing from one degree of strength to another, the putting forth of our utmost efforts, the enduring unto the end. Ah, who is sufficient for such a task? First, we are reminded of those who have preceded us, many, a "great cloud": and *their* faith is recorded for our instruction, their victory for our encouragement. Yet that is not sufficient: their cases afford us a motive, but they do not supply the needed power. Hence, we are next told:

"Looking unto Jesus the Author and Finisher of our faith; who for the joy that was set before Him endured the cross, despising the shame, and is set down at the right hand of the throne of God" (v. 2). "The cloud of witnesses is not the object on which our heart is fixed. They testify of faith, and we cherish their memory with gratitude, and walk with a firmer step because of the music of their lives. Our eye, however, is fixed, not on many, but on One; not on the army, but the Leader; not on the servants, but the Lord. We see Jesus only, and from Him we derive our true strength, even as He is our light of life" (A. Saphir). In all things Christ has the pre-eminence: He is placed here not among the other "racers," but as One who, instead of exemplifying certain characteristics of faith, as they did, is the "Author and Finisher" of faith in His own person.

Our text presents the Lord as the supreme Example for racers, as well as the great Object of their faith, though this is somewhat obscured by the rendering of the A. V. Our text is *not* referring to Christ begetting faith in His people and sustaining it to the end, though that is a truth plainly enough taught elsewhere. Instead, He is here viewed as the One, who Himself began and completed the whole course of faith, so as to be Himself the one perfect example and witness of what faith is. It was because of "the joy set before Him"—steadily and trustfully held in view—that *He* ran His race. *His* "enduring of the cross" was the completest trial and most perfect exemplification of faith. In consequence, He is now seated at the right hand of God, as both the Pattern and Object of faith, and His promise is "to him that overcometh will I grant to sit with Me in My throne, even as I also overcame, and am set down with My Father in His throne" (Rev. 3:21).

It is to be duly noted that the little word "our" is a supplement, being supplied by the translators: it may without detriment, and with some advantage, be omitted. The Greek word for "Author" does not mean so much one who "causes" or "originates," as one who "takes the lead." The same word is rendered "*Captain* of our salvation" in 2:10, and in Acts 3:15, the "*Prince* of life." There its obvious meaning is Leader or Chief, one going in advance of those who follow. The Saviour is here represented as the Leader of all the long procession of those who had lived by faith, as the great Pattern for us to imitate. Confirmation of this is found in the Spirit's use of the personal name "Jesus" here, rather than His title of office—"Christ." Stress is thereby laid upon His humanity. The Man Jesus was so truly made like unto His brethren in all things that the life which He lived was the life of faith.

Yes, the life which Jesus lived here upon earth was a life of faith. This has not been given sufficient prominence. In this, as in all things, He is our perfect Model. "By faith He walked, looking always unto the Father, speaking and acting in filial dependence on the Father, and in filial reception out of the Father's fullness. By faith He looked away from all discouragements, difficulties, and oppositions, committing His cause to the Lord, who had sent Him, to the Father, whose will He had come to fulfil. By faith He resisted and overcame all temptation, whether it came from Satan, or from the false Messianic expectations of Israel, or from His own disciples. By faith He performed the signs and wonders, in which the power and love of God's salvation were symbolized. Before He raised Lazarus from the grave, He, in the energy of faith, thanked God, who heard Him alway. And here we are taught the nature of all His miracles: He trusted in God. He gave the command, 'Have faith in God', out of the fullness of His own experience" (A. Saphir).

But let us enter into some detail. *What is* a life of faith? First, it is a life *lived in complete dependence upon God*. "Trust in the Lord with all thine heart, and lean not unto thine own understanding . . . in all thy ways acknowledge Him" (Prov. 3:5, 6.) Never did any so entirely, so unreservedly, so perfectly cast himself upon God as did the Man Christ Jesus; never was another so completely yielded to God's will. "I live by the Father" (John 6:57) was His own avowal. When tempted to turn stones into bread to satisfy His hunger, He replied "man shall not live by bread alone." So sure was He of God's love and care for Him that He held fast to His trust and waited for Him. So patent to all was His absolute dependence upon God, that the very scorners around the cross turned it into a bitter taunt.—"He trusted in the Lord that He would deliver Him, let Him deliver Him, seeing He delighted in Him" (Psa. 22:8).

Second, a life of faith is a life *lived in communion with God*. And never did another live in such a deep and constant realization of the Divine presence as did the Man Christ Jesus. "I have set the Lord *always* before Me" (Psa. 16:8) was His own avowal. "He that sent

Me is *with* Me" (John 8:29) was ever a present fact to His consciousness. He could say, "I was cast upon Thee from the womb: Thou art My God from My mother's belly" (Psa. 22:10). "And in the morning, rising a great while before day, He went out, and departed into a solitary place, and there *prayed*" (Mark 1:35). From Bethlehem to Calvary He enjoyed unbroken and unclouded fellowship with the Father; and after the three hours of awful darkness was over, He cried "Father, into Thy hands I commit My spirit."

Third, a life of faith is a life lived *in obedience to God.* Faith worketh by love (Gal. 5:6), and love delights to please its object. Faith has respect not only to the promises of God, but to His precepts as well. Faith not only trusts God for the future, but it also produces present subjection to His will. Supremely was this fact exemplified by the Man Christ Jesus. "I do always those things which please Him" (John 8:29) He declared. "I must be about My Father's business" (Luke 2:49) characterized the whole of His earthly course. Ever and anon we find Him conducting Himself. "that the Scriptures might be fulfilled." He lived by *every* word of God. At the close He said, "I have kept My Father's commandments, and abide in His love" (John 15:10).

Fourth, a life of faith is a life *of assured confidence in the unseen future.* It is a looking away from the things of time and sense, a rising above the shows and delusions of this world, and having the affections set upon things above. "Faith is the substance of things hoped for, the evidence of things not seen" (11:1), enabling its possessor to live now in the power and enjoyment of that which is to come. That which enthralls and enchains the ungodly had no power over the perfect Man: "I have *overcome* the world" (John 16:31), He declared. When the Devil offered Him all its kingdoms, He promptly answered, "Get thee hence, Satan." So vivid was Jesus' realization of the unseen, that, in the midst of earth's engagements, He called Himself "the Son of man which *is* in heaven" (John 3:13).

"And so, dear brethren, this Jesus, in the absoluteness of His dependence upon the Father, in the completeness of His trust in Him, in the submission of His will to that Supreme command, in the unbroken communion which He held with God, in the vividness with which the Unseen ever burned before Him, and dwarfed and extinguished all the lights of the present, and in the respect which He had 'unto the recompense of the reward'; nerving Him for all pain and shame, has set before us all the example of a life of faith, and is our Pattern as in everything, in this too.

"How blessed it is to feel, when we reach out our hands and grope in the darkness for the unseen hand, when we try to bow our wills to that Divine will; when we seek to look beyond the mists of 'that dim spot which men call earth,' and to discern the land that is very far off; and when we endeavour to nerve ourselves for duty and sacrifice by bright visions of a future hope, that on this path of faith too, when He 'putteth forth His sheep, He goeth before them,' and has bade us do nothing which He Himself has not done! 'I will put My trust in Him,' He says first, and then He turns to us and commands, 'Believe in God, believe also in Me' " (A. Maclaren, to whom we are indebted for much in this article).

Alas, how very little real Christianity there is in the world today! Christianity consists in being conformed unto the image of God's Son. "Looking unto Jesus" constantly, trustfully, submissively, lovingly; the heart occupied with, the mind stayed upon Him—*that* is the whole secret of practical Christianity. Just in proportion as I am occupied with the example which Christ has left me, just in proportion as I am living upon Him and drawing from His fulness, am I realizing the ideal He has set before me. In Him is the power, from Him must be received the strength for running "with patience" or steadfast perseverance, the race. Genuine Christianity is a life lived in communion with Christ: a life lived by faith, as His was. "For to me to live is Christ" (Phil. 1:21); "Christ liveth in me; and the life which I now live in the flesh, I live by the faith of the Son of God" (Gal. 2:20)—Christ living in me and through me.

There are four things said in our text about the Saviour's life, each of which we need to ponder carefully. First, *the motive or reason which prompted Jesus to do and suffer*, wherein He is presented as our example and encouragement: "who for the joy that was set before Him." Here is made known to us what was the final moving cause in His mind which sustained the Saviour to a persevering performance of duty, and of the endurance of all sufferings that duty entailed. Various definitions have been given of that "joy," and probably all of them are included within its scope. The glory of God was what the Redeemer preferred above all things: Heb. 10:5-9, but that glory was inseparably bound up with the personal exaltation of the Redeemer and the salvation of His Church following the accomplishment of the work given Him to do. This was "set before Him" in the everlasting covenant.

Thus the "joy" that was set before Jesus was the doing of God's will, and His anticipation of the glorious reward which should be given Him in return. Heb. 12:2 sustains the figure used in the previous verse: it is as the model Racer our Saviour is here viewed. At the winning-post hung a crown, in full view of the racers, and this was ever before the eye of the Captain of our salvation, as He pursued the course appointed Him by the Father. He steadily kept before Him the cheering and blissful reward: His heart laid hold of the Messianic promises and prophecies recorded in Holy Writ: He had in steady prospect that satisfaction with which the travail of His soul would be fully compensated. By faith Abraham looked forward to a "City" (11:10); by faith Isaac anticipated "things to come" (11:20); by faith Moses "had respect unto the recompense of the reward" (11:26); and by faith, Jesus lived and died in the enjoyment of that which was "set before Him."

Second, He "endured the cross." Therein we have *the Commander's example to His soldiers* of heroic fortitude. Those words signify far more than that He experienced the shame and pain of crucifixion: they tell us that He stood steadfast under it all. He endured the cross not sullenly or even stoically, but in the highest and noblest sense of the term—with holy composure of soul. He never wavered or faltered, murmured or complained: "The cup which My Father hath given Me, shall I not drink it" (John 18:11)! And He has left us an example that we should "follow His steps" (1 Pet. 2:21), and therefore does He declare, "If any man will come after *Me*, let him deny himself, and take up *his* cross" (Matt. 16:24). Strength for this task is to be found by "looking unto Jesus," by keeping steadily before faith's eye the crown, the *joy* awaiting us.

Third, "despising the shame." Therein we see *the Captain's contempt of whatever sought to bar His progress.* We scarcely think of associating this word "despising" with the meek and lowly Jesus. It is an ugly term, yet there are things which deserve it. The Saviour viewed things in their true perspective; He estimated them at their proper worth: in the light of the joy set before Him, He regarded hardship, ignominy, persecution, sufferings from men, as trifles. Here, too, He has left us "an example." But alas, instead of scorning it, *we* magnify and are intimidated by "the shame." How many are ashamed to be scripturally baptized and wear His uniform. How many are ashamed to openly confess Christ before the world. Meditate more upon the reward, the crown, the eternal joy—*that* outweighs all the little sacrifices we are now called upon to make.

Fourth, "and is set down at the right hand of the throne of God." Here we witness *the Captain's triumph,* His actual entrance into the joy anticipated, His being crowned with glory and honour. His "sitting down" denoted three things. First, *rest* after finished work, the race run. Second, being invested with *dominion*: He now occupies the place of supreme sovereignty: Matt. 28:18, Phil. 2:10. Third, being intrusted with the prerogative of *judgment*: John 17:2, Acts 17:30. And what have these three things to do with us, His unworthy followers? Much indeed: eternal rest is assured the successful racer: Rev. 13:14. A place on Christ's throne is promised the overcomer: Rev. 3:21. Dominion too is the future portion of him who vanquishes this world: Rev. 2:26, 27. Finally, it is written "Do ye not know that the saints shall *judge* the world? "Do ye not know we shall judge angels?" (1 Cor. 6:2, 3). "Joint heirs with Christ: *if so be* that we *suffer with Him*, that we may be also glorified together" (Rom. 8:17).

One other word in our text yet remains to be considered: "looking unto Jesus the Author (Captain) and *Finisher* (Perfecter) of our faith." We have already seen from the other occurrences of this term (in its various forms) in our Epistle, that it is a very full one. Here, we believe, it has at least a twofold force. First, Completer: Jesus is the *first* and the *last* as an example of confidence in and submission unto God: He is the most complete model of faith and obedience that can be brought before us. Instead of including Him with the heroes of faith in chapter 11, He is here distinguished from them, as being above them. He is the Alpha and Omega, the Beginning and the Ending: as there was none hitherto who could be compared with Him, so there will be none hereafter. "Author and Finisher" or "Captain and Completer" means Jesus is beyond all comparison.

The fact that we are bidden to be looking unto Jesus *as* "the Leader and Finisher of faith" also denotes that He perfects our faith. How? First, by His grace flowing into us. We need something more than a flawless Model set before us: who can in his own strength imitate the perfect Man? But Christ has not only gone before His own, He also dwells in their hearts by faith, and as they yield themselves to His control (and only so) does He live *through* them. Second, by *leading us* (Psa. 23:3) along the path of discipline and trial, drawing our hearts away from the things of earth, and fixing them upon Himself. He often makes us lonesome here that we may seek *His* companionship. Finally, by actually conducting us to glory: He will "come again" (John 14:2) and conform us to His image.

"Looking unto Jesus." The person of the Saviour is to be the "mark" on which the eyes of those who are pressing forward for the prize of the high calling of God, are to be fixed. Be constantly "looking" to Him, trustfully, submissively, hopefully, expectantly. He is the Fountain of all grace (John 1:16): our every need is supplied by God "according to His riches in glory *by Christ Jesus*" (Phil. 4:19). Then seek the help of the Holy Spirit that the eye of faith be steadfastly fixed on Christ. He has declared "I will never leave thee, nor forsake thee," then let us add, "The Lord is my Helper, I will not fear what man shall do unto me" (Heb. 13:5, 6). Salvation is by grace, *through faith*: it is through "faith" we are saved, not only from Hell, but also from this world (1 John 5:4), from temptation, from the power of indwelling sin—by coming to Christ, *trusting* in Him, drawing from *Him*.

What are the things which *hinder* us running? An active Devil, an evil world, indwelling sin, mysterious trials, fierce opposition, afflictions which almost make us doubt the love of the Father. Then call to mind the "great cloud of witnesses": they were men of like passions with us, they encountered the same difficulties and discouragements, they met with the same hindrances and obstacles. But they ran "with patience," they overcame, they won the victor's crown. How? By "looking unto Jesus": see Heb. 11:26. But more: look away from difficulties (Rom. 4:19), from self, from fellow-racers, unto Him who has left us an example to follow, in whom dwelleth all the fulness of the Godhead bodily, so that *He is able* to succour the tempted, strengthen the weak, guide the perplexed, supply our every need. Let the heart be centered in and the mind stayed upon HIM.

The more we are "looking unto Jesus" the easier will it be to "lay aside every weight." It is at this point so many fail. If the Christian denies self of different things *without an adequate motive* (*for Christ's sake*), he will still secretly hanker after the things relinquished, or ere long return to them, or become proud of his little sacrifices and become self-righteous. The most effective way of getting a child to drop any dirty or injurious object, is to proffer him something better. The best way to make a tired horse move more quickly, is not to use the whip, but to turn his head toward *home*! So, if our hearts be occupied with the sacrificial love of Christ for us, we shall be "constrained" thereby to drop all that which displeases Him; and the more we dwell upon the Joy set before us, the more strength shall we have to run "with patience the race that is set before us."

CHAPTER EIGHTY-FIVE

A Call to Steadfastness

(Heb. 12:3, 4)

At first sight it is not easy to trace the thread which unites the passage that was last before us and the verses which are now to engage our attention: there appears to be no direct connection between the opening verses of Heb. 12 and those which follow. But a closer examination of them shows they are intimately related: in vv. 3, 4 the apostle completes the exhortation with which the chapter opens. In v. 1 the apostle borrowed a figure from the Grecian Games, namely, the marathon race, and now in v. 4 he refers to another part of those games—the contest between the gladiators in the arena. Second, he had specified the principal grace required for the Christian race, namely, "Patience" or perseverance; so now in v. 3 he is urging them against faintness of mind or impatience. Third, he had enforced his exhortation by bidding the saints to "look unto Jesus" their great Exemplar; so here he calls on them to "consider Him" and emulate His steadfastness.

Yet, the verses which are now before us are not a mere repetition of those immediately preceding: rather do they present another, though closely related aspect of the Christian life or "race." In v. 1 the racers are bidden to "lay aside every weight," and in v. 3 it is the "contradiction of sinners" which has to be endured: the former, are hindrances which proceed more from *within*; the latter, are obstacles which are encountered from *without*. In the former case, it is the evil solicitations of the flesh which would have to be resisted; in the other, it is the persecutions of the world which have to be endured. In v. 1 it is "the sin which doth so easily beset" or "encircle us"—inward depravity—which must be "laid aside"; in v. 4 it is martyrdom which must be prepared for, lest we yield to the "sin" of apostasy.

Now the secret of success, the way to victory, is the same in either case. To enable us to "lay aside" all that hinders from within, there has to be a trustful "looking unto Jesus," and to enable us to "endure" the oppositions encountered from without and to "strive" against inconstancy and wavering in our profession, we must thoughtfully "consider Him" who was hounded and persecuted as none other ever was. As the incentive to self-denial we are to be occupied with our great Leader, and remember how much *He* "laid aside" for us—He who was rich for our sakes became poor; He who was "in the form of God" divested Himself of His robes of glory and took upon Him "the form of a servant." *We* are not called on to do something which He did not—*He* vacated the throne and took up His cross! Likewise, the chief source of comfort and encouragement when we are called upon to suffer for His sake, is to call to mind the infinitely greater sufferings which He endured for our sakes.

The more we endeavour to emulate the example which the Lord Jesus has left us, the more shall we be opposed from without; the more closely we follow Him, the greater will be the enmity of our fellow-men against us. Our lives will condemn theirs, our ways will be a perpetual rebuke to them, and they will do all they can to discourage and hinder, provoke and oppose. And the tendency of such persecution is to dishearten us, to tempt us to compromise, to ask "What is the use?" Because of this, the blessed Spirit bids us, "Consider Him that endured such contradiction of sinners against Himself, lest ye be wearied and faint in your minds." Let the experiences through which *Christ* passed be the subject of daily contemplation. The record of His unparalleled temptations and trials, His endurance, and His victory, is to be the grand source of our instruction, comfort and encouragement. If we have grown "faint and weary" in our minds, it is because we have failed to properly and profitably "consider Him."

Supremely important is a knowledge of the Scriptures concerning the Lord Jesus: there can be no experimental holiness, no growth in grace apart from the same. Vital godliness consists in a practical conformity to the image of God's Son: it is to follow the example which He has left us, to take His yoke upon us and learn of Him. For this, there must needs be an intimate knowledge of His ways, a prayerful and believing study of the record of His life, a daily reading of and meditating thereon. That is why the four Gospels are placed at the *beginning* of the N.T.—they are of first importance. What we have in the Epistles is principally an interpretation and application of the four Gospels to the details of our walk. O that we may say with ever-deepening purpose of heart, "I count all things but loss for the excellency of the knowledge of Christ Jesus my Lord" (Phil. 3:8). O that we may "follow on to *know* the Lord" (Hos. 6:3).

"For consider Him that endured such contradiction of sinners against Himself, lest ye be wearied and faint in your minds. Ye have not yet resisted unto blood, striving against sin" (Heb. 12:3,

4). The whole of this is a dehortation or caution against an evil, which if yielded to will prevent our discharge of the duty inculcated in vv. 1, 2. That which is dehorted against is "be not wearied" — give not up the race, abandon not your Christian profession. The way whereby we may fall into that evil is by becoming "faint" in our minds. The means to prevent this is the diligent contemplation of our great Exemplar.

In vv. 1, 2 the apostle had exhorted unto a patient or persevering pressing forward in the path of faith and obedience. In vv. 3-11 he presents a number of considerations or motives to hearten us in our course, seeking particularly to counteract the enervating influence which difficulties are apt to exert upon the minds of God's tried people. The tendency of strong and lasting opposition and persecution is to discourage, which if yielded unto leads to despair. To strengthen the hearts of those tried Hebrews, the apostle bade them consider the case of Christ Himself: *He* encountered far worse sufferings than we do, yet He patiently "endured" them (v. 3). Then they were reminded that their case was by no means desperate and extreme — they had not yet been called to suffer a death of martyrdom. Finally, their very difficulties were the loving chastisement of their Father, designed for their profit (vv. 5-11). By what a variety of means does the blessed Spirit strengthen, stablish, and comfort tried believers!

Are you, dear reader, disheartened by the hard usage you are receiving from men, yea, from the religious world; are you fearful as you anticipate the persecutions which may yet attend your Christian profession; or, are you too ready to show resentment against those who oppose you? Then *"consider Him* that endured such contradiction of sinners against Himself." The connecting "For" has the force here of "moreover:" in addition to "looking unto Jesus" as your Leader and Perfecter, consider Him in His steadfastness under relentless persecution. Faith has many actings or forms of exercise: it is to reflect, contemplate, call to mind — God's past ways with us, His dealings with His people of old, and particularly the recorded history of His beloved and incarnate Son. We are greatly the losers if we fail to cultivate the habit of devout consideration and holy meditation. The Greek word for "consider" is not the same as the one used in 3:1 and 10:24; in fact it is a term which occurs, in this form, nowhere else in the N. T.

The Greek word for "consider" in our text is derived from the one rendered "proportion" in Rom. 12:6. It is a mathematical term, signifying *to compute* by comparing things together in their due proportions. It means: form a just and accurate estimate. "For consider Him that endured such contradiction of sinners against

Himself:" draw an analogy between *His* sufferings and *yours,* and what proportion is there between them! Weigh well *who* He was, the place He took, the infinite perfection of His character and deeds; and then the base ingratitude, the gross injustice, the cruel persecution He met with. Calculate and estimate the constancy of the opposition He encountered, the type of men who maligned Him, the variety and intensity of His sore trials, and the spirit of meekness and patience with which He bore them. And what are *our* trifling trials when compared with *His* agonies, or even to our *deserts*! O my soul blush with shame because of thy murmurings.

"Consider Him" in the ineffable excellency of His person. He was none other than the Lord of glory, the Beloved of the Father, the second person in the sacred Trinity, the Creator of heaven and earth. Now, since *He* suffered here on earth, why should you, having enlisted under His banner, think it strange that you should be called on to endure a little hardness in His service! Consider his *relationship* to you: He is your Redeemer and Proprietor: is it not sufficient for the disciple to be as his Master, the servant as his Lord? If the Head was spared not trial and shame, shall the members of His body complain if they be called on to have some fellowship with Him in this? When you are tempted to throw down your colours and capitulate to the Enemy, or even to murmur at your hard lot, "Consider Him" who when here "had not where to lay His head."

The particular sufferings of Christ which are here singled out for our consideration are, the "contradiction of sinners" which He encountered. He was opposed constantly, by word and action; He was opposed by His own people according to the flesh; He was opposed by the very ones to whom He ministered in infinite grace and loving-kindness. That opposition began at His birth, when there was no room in the inn — *He* was not wanted. It was seen again in His infancy, when Herod sought to slay Him, and His parents were forced to flee with Him into Egypt. Little else is told us in the N.T., about His early years, but there is a Messianic prophecy in Psa. 88:15 where we hear Him pathetically saying, "I am afflicted and ready to die from My youth up!" As soon as His public ministry commenced, and during the whole of its three years' course, He endured one unbroken, relentless, "contradiction of sinners against Himself."

The Lord Jesus was derided as the Prophet, mocked as the King, and treated with the utmost contempt as the Priest and Saviour. He was accused of deceiving (John 7:12) and perverting the people (Luke 23:14). His teaching was opposed, and His person was insulted. Because He conversed with and befriended publicans and sinners, He was "murmured" at (Luke 15:2). Because He performed works of mercy on the sabbath day, He was charged with breaking the law (Mark 3:2). The gracious miracles which He wrought upon the sick and demon-possessed, were attributed to His being in league with the Devil (Matt. 12:24). He was regarded as a low-born fanatic. He was branded as a "glutton and winebibber." He was accused of speaking against Caesar (John 19:12), whereas He had expressly bidden men to render unto Caesar what rightly belonged to him (Matt. 22:21). Though He was the Holy One of God, there was scarcely anything about Him that was not opposed.

"For consider Him who endured *such* contradiction" Here is emphasised the greatness of Christ's sufferings: "*such* contradiction" — so bitter, so severe, so malicious, so protracted; everything which the evil wits of men and Satan could invent. That word "such" is also added to awaken our wonderment and worship. Though the incarnate Son of God, He was spat upon, contemptuously arrayed in a purple robe and His enemies bowed the knee before Him in mockery. They buffeted Him and smote Him on the face. They tore His back with scourgings, as was foretold by the Psalmist (129:3). They condemned Him to a criminal's death, and nailed Him to the Cross, and that, between two thieves, to add to His shame. And this, at the hands of men who, though they made a great show of sanctity, were "sinners."

Christ *felt keenly* that "contradiction," for He was the Man of sorrows and acquainted with grief. At the end, He exclaimed "reproach hath broken My heart" (Psa. 69:20). Nevertheless, He turned not aside from the path of duty, still less did He abandon His mission. He fled not from His enemies, and fainted not under their merciless persecution: instead, He *"endured"* it. As we pointed out in our exposition of the previous verse, that word is used of Christ in its highest and noblest sense. He bore patiently every ignominy that was heaped upon Him. He never retaliated or reviled His traducers. He remained steadfast unto the end, and finished the work which had been given Him to do. When the supreme crises arrived, He faltered not, but "set His face as a flint to go up to Jerusalem" (Isa. 50:7, Luke 9:51).

Do you, tried reader, feel that your cup of opposition is a little fuller than that of some of your fellow Christians? Then look away to the cup which Christ drank! Here is the Divine antidote against weariness: Christ meekly and triumphantly "endured" far, far worse than anything you are called on to suffer for His sake; yet He fainted not. When you are weary in your mind because of trials and injuries from the enemies of God, "consider" Christ, and this will quieten and suppress thy corrupt propensities to murmuring and impatience. Set *Him* before thy heart as the grand example and encouragement — example in patience, encouragement in the blessed issue: "If we suffer, we shall also reign with Him" (2 Tim. 2:12). Faith's consideration of Him will work a conformity unto Him in our souls which will preserve from fainting.

"Lest ye be wearied and faint in your minds." There is no connecting "and" in the Greek: two distinct thoughts are presented: "lest ye be wearied," that is, so discouraged as to quit; "faint in your mind," states the cause thereof. The word for "weary" here is a strong one: it signifies exhausted, being so despondent as to break one's resolution. In its ultimate meaning, it refers to such a state of despondency as an utter sinking of spirit, through the difficulties, trials, opposition and persecution encountered as to "look back" (Luke 9:62), and either partially or wholly abandon one's profession of the Gospel. In other words, it is another warning against apostasy. What we are cautioned against here is the opposite of that which the Lord commended in the Ephesian Church, "And for My name's sake hast laboured, and hast not fainted" (Rev. 2:3) — here there *is* perseverance in the Christian profession despite all opposition.

At different periods of history God has permitted fierce opposition to break out against His people, to test the reality and strength of their attachment to Christ. This was the case with those to whom our Epistle was first addressed: they were being exposed to great trials and sufferings, temptations and privations; hence the timeliness of this exhortation, and its accompanying warning. Reproaches, losses, imprisonments, scourgings, being threatened with death, have a strong tendency to produce dejection and despair; they present a powerful temptation to give up the fight. And nought but the vigorous activity of faith will fortify the mind under religious persecution. Only as the heart is encouragingly occupied with *Christ's endurance* of the "contradiction of sinners against Himself," will our resolution be strong to endure unto the end: "In the world ye shall have tribulations: but be of good cheer: *I* have overcome the world" (John 16:33).

"Faint in your minds." This it is which, if not resisted and corrected, leads to the "weariness" or utter exhaustion of the previous clause. This faintness of mind is the reverse of vigour and cheerfulness. If, under the strong opposition and fierce persecution, we are to "endure unto the end," then we must watch diligently against the allowance of such faintness of mind. There is a spiritual vigour required in order to perseverence in the Christian profession during times of persecution. Hence it is that we are exhorted, "Forasmuch then as Christ hath suffered for us in the flesh, *arm yourselves* likewise with the same mind" (1 Pet. 4:1); "For we wrestle not against flesh and blood, but against principalities, against powers, against the rulers of the darkness of this world, against wicked spirits in the heavenlies. *Wherefore take unto you* the whole armour of God, that ye may be able to withstand in the evil day, and having done all to stand" (Eph. 6:12, 13); "Watch ye, stand fast in the faith, *quit you like men,* be strong" (1 Cor. 16:13).

Any degree of faintness of mind in the Christian results from and consists in a remitting of the cheerful actions of faith in the various duties which God has called us to discharge. Nothing but the regular exercise of *faith* keeps the soul calm and restful, patient and prayerful. If faith ceases to be operative, and our mind be left to cope with difficulties and trials in our own natural strength, then we shall soon grow weary of a *persecuted* Christian profession. Herein lies the beginning of all spiritual declension — a lack of the due exercise of faith, and that in turn, is the result of the heart growing cold toward Christ! If faith be in healthy exercise, we shall say, "For I reckon that the sufferings of this present time are not worthy to be compared with the glory which shall be revealed in us" (Rom. 8:18), realizing that "our light affliction, which is but for a moment, worketh for us a far more exceeding and eternal weight of glory" (2 Cor. 4:17); ah, but *that* consciousness is only *"while we look not* at the things which are seen, but at the things which are not seen" (v. 18).

"Consider *Him:*" there is the remedy against faintness of mind; there is the preservative from such "weariness" of dejection of spirits that we are ready to throw down our weapons and throw up our hands in utter despair. It is the diligent consideration of the person of Christ, the *Object* of faith, the *Food* of faith, the *Supporter* of faith. It is by drawing an analogy between His infinitely sorer sufferings and our present hardships. It is by making application unto ourselves of what is to be found in Him suitable to our own case. Are we called on to suffer a little for Him, then let our eye be turned on Him who went before us in the same path of trial. Make a comparison between what *He* "endured" and what *you* are called to struggle with, and surely you will be ashamed to complain! "Let this mind be in you, which was also in Christ Jesus" (Phil. 2:5). Admire and imitate His meekness — weeping over His enemies, and praying for His murderers!

"Ye have not yet resisted unto blood, striving against sin" (v. 4). The persons here immediately addressed — the "ye" — were the Hebrews themselves. Because of their profession of Christianity, because of their loyalty to Christ, they had suffered severely in various ways. Plain reference to something of what they had already been called on to endure is made in 10:32-34, "But call to remembrance the former days, in which, after ye were illuminated, ye endured a great fight of afflictions; partly whilst ye were made a gazing-stock both by reproaches and afflictions; and partly whilst ye became companions of them that were so used. For ye had compassion of me in my bonds, and took joyfully the spoiling of your goods." Thus, the Hebrew saints had been sorely oppressed by their unbelieving brethren among the Jews; it is that which gave such point to the exhortation and warning in the previous verse.

"Ye have not yet resisted unto blood, striving against sin." Here is the second consideration which the apostle pressed upon his afflicted brethren: not only to ponder the far greater opposition which their Saviour encountered, but also to bear in mind that their own sufferings were not so severe as they might have been, or as possibly they would yet be. It is an argument made by reasoning from the greater to the less, and from comparing their present state with that which might await them: what could be expected to sustain their hearts and deliver from apostasy when under the supreme test of death by violence, if they fainted beneath lesser afflictions? We, too, should honestly face the same alternative: if unkind words and sneers make us waver now, how would we acquit ourselves if called on to face a martyr's death!

The present state of the oppressed Hebrews is here expressed negatively: "ye have not yet resisted unto blood." True, they had already met with various forms of suffering, but not yet had they been called upon to lay down their lives. As Heb. 10:32-34 clearly intimates, they had well acquitted themselves during the first stages of their trials, but their warfare was not yet ended. They had need to bear in mind that word of Christ, "Men ought always to pray, *and not to faint*" (Luke 18:1); and that exhortation of the Holy Spirit, "let us not be weary in well doing: for in due season we shall reap, *if we faint not*" (Gal. 6:9).

"Ye have not yet resisted unto blood." The apostle here hinted to the Hebrews what might yet have to be endured by them, namely a bloody and violent death—by stoning, or the sword, or fire. *That* is the utmost which fiendish persecutors can afflict. Men may kill the body, but when they have done that, they can do no more. God has set bounds to their rage: none will hound or harm His people in the next world! Those who engage in the Christian profession, who serve under the banner of Christ, have no guarantee that they may not be called unto the utmost suffering of blood on account of their allegiance to him; for *that* is what His adversaries have always desired. Hence, Christ bids us to "sit down and count the cost" (Luke 14:28), of being His disciples. God has decreed that many, in different ages should be martyred for His own praise, the glory of Christ and the honour of the Gospel.

"Ye have not yet resisted unto blood, striving against sin." "Sin" is here personified, regarded as a combatant which has to be overcome. The various persecutions, hardships, afflictions, difficulties of the way, in consequence of our attachment to Christ, become so many occasions and means which sin seeks to employ in order to hinder and oppose us. The Christian is called to a contest with sin. The apostle continues his allusion to the Grecian Games, changing from the racer to the combatant. The great contest is in the believer's heart between grace and sin, the flesh and the spirit (Gal. 5:17). Sin seeks to quench faith and kill obedience: therefore sin is to be "striven against" for our very souls are at stake. There is no place for sloth in this deadly contest; no furloughs are granted!

"Striving against sin." That which the Hebrews were striving against was apostasy, going to the full lengths of sin — abandoning their Christian profession. Persecution was the means which indwelling depravity sought to use, to employ in slaying faith and fidelity to Christ. That terrible wickedness was to be steadfastly resisted, by fighting against weariness in the conflict. O to say with the apostle, "I am ready not to be bound only, but also *to die* at Jerusalem for the name of the Lord Jesus" (Acts 21:13): but in order to reach *that* state of soul, there has to be a close walking with Him day by day, and a patient bearing of the minor trials. "If thou hast run with the footmen and they have wearied thee, then how canst thou contend with horses? and if in the land of peace, wherein thou trustedst, they wearied thee, then how wilt thou do in the swelling of Jordan?" (Jer. 12:5).

CHAPTER EIGHTY-SIX

Divine Chastisement

(Heb. 12:5)

The grand truth of Divine Chastisement is inexpressibly blessed, and one which we can neglect only to our great loss. It is of deep importance, for when Scripturally apprehended it preserves from some serious errors by which Satan has succeeded (as "an angel of light") in deceiving and destroying not a few. For example, it sounds the death-knell to that wide-spread delusion of "sinless perfectionism." The passage which is to be before us unmistakably exposes the wild fanaticism of those who imagine that, as the result of some "second work of grace," the carnal nature has been eradicated from their beings, so that, while perhaps not so wise, they are as pure as the angels which never sinned, and lead lives which are blameless in the sight of the thrice holy God. Poor blinded souls: such have not even experienced a *first* "work of Divine grace" in their souls: "If we say we have no sin, we deceive ourselves, and the truth is not in us" (1 John 1:8).

"My son despise not thou the chastening of the Lord, nor faint when thou art rebuked of Him; for whom the Lord loveth He chasteneth, and scourgeth every son whom He receiveth" (Heb. 12:5, 6). How plain and emphatic is that! God *does* find something to "rebuke" in us, and uses the rod upon *every one* of His children. Chastisement for sin is a family mark, a sign of sonship, a proof of God's love, a token of His Fatherly kindness and care; it is an inestimable mercy, a choice new-covenant blessing. Woe to the man whom God chastens not, whom He suffers to go recklessly on in the boastful and presumptuous security which so many now mistake for faith. There is a reckoning to come of which he little dreams. Were he a *son,* he would be chastened for his sin; he would be brought to repentance and godly sorrow, he would with grief of heart confess his backslidings, and then be blest with pardon and peace.

The truth of Divine chastisement corrects another serious error, which has become quite common in certain quarters, namely, that

God views His people so completely in Christ that He sees no sin in them. It is true, blessedly true, that of His elect it is stated, "He hath not beheld iniquity in Jacob, neither hath He seen perverseness in Israel" (Num. 23:21), and that Christ declares of His spouse "Thou art all fair, My love; there is no spot in thee" (Song of S. 4:7). The testimony of Scripture is most express that in regard to the justification or acceptance of the *persons* of the elect, they are "complete in Him" — Christ (Col. 2:10); "accepted in the Beloved" (Eph. 1:6) — washed in Christ's blood, clothed with His righteousness. In *that* sense, God sees no sin in them; none to punish. But we must not use that precious truth to set aside another, revealed with equal clearness, and thus fall into serious error.

God *does* see sin in His children and chastises them for it. Even though the non-imputation of sin to the believer (Rom. 4:8) and the chastisement of sin in believers (1 Cor. 11:30-32) were irreconcilable to human reason, we are bound to receive *both* on the authority of Holy Writ. Let us beware lest we fall under the solemn charge of Mal. 2:9, "Ye have not kept My ways, but have been *partial* in the law." What could be plainer than this, "I will make Him my Firstborn, higher than the kings of the earth. My mercy will I keep for Him for evermore, and My covenant shall stand fast with Him. His seed also will I make to endure forever and His throne as the days of heaven. If His children forsake My law, and walk not in My judgments; if they break My statutes, and keep not My commandments; then will I visit their transgression with the rod, and their iniquity with stripes. Nevertheless My loving kindness will I not utterly take from Him, nor suffer My faithfulness to fail" (Psa. 89:27-33). Five things are clearly revealed there. Christ Himself is addressed under the name of "David." Second, His children *break* God's statutes. Third, in *them* there is "iniquity" and "transgression." Fourth, God *will* "visit" their transgression "with the rod!" Fifth, yet will He not cast them off.

What could express more clearly the fact that God *does* see sin in believers, and that He *does* chastise them for it? For, be it noted, the whole of the above passage speaks of believers. It is the language, not of the Law, but of the Gospel. Blessed promises are there made to believers in Christ: the unchanging loving-kindness of God, His covenant-faithfulness toward them, His spiritual blessing of them. But "stripes" and the "rod" are there promised too! Then let us not dare to separate what God has joined together. How do we know anything concerning the acceptance of the elect in Christ? The answer must be, Only on the testimony of Holy

Writ. Very well; from *the same* unerring Testimony we also know that God chastises His people for their sins. It is at our imminent peril that we reject either of these complementary truths.

The same fact is plainly presented again in Heb. 12:7-10, "If ye endure chastening, God dealeth with you as with sons: for what son is he whom the Father chasteneth not? But if ye be without chastisement, whereof all are partakers, then are ye bastards, and not sons. Furthermore we have had fathers of our flesh which corrected us, and we gave them reverence: shall we not much rather be in subjection unto the Father of spirits, and live? For they verily, for a few days chastened us after their own pleasure; but He for our profit, that we might be partakers of His holiness." The apostle there draws an analogy from the natural relationship of father and child. Why do earthly parents chastise their children? Is it not for their *faults?* Can we justify a parent for chastening a child where there was no fault, nothing in him which called for the rod? In that case, it would be positive tyranny, actual cruelty. If the same be not true *spiritually,* then the comparison must fall to the ground. Heb. 12 proves conclusively that, if God does not chastise me then I am an unbeliever, and I sign my own condemnation as a bastard.

Yet it is very necessary for us to point out, at this stage, that *all* the sufferings of believers in this world are *not* Divine rebukes for personal transgressions. Here too we need to be on our guard against lopsidedness. After we have apprehended the fact that God *does* take notice of the iniquities of His people and use the rod upon them, it is so easy to jump to the conclusion that when we see an afflicted Christian, God must be visiting His displeasure upon him. That is a sad and serious error. Some of the very choicest of God's saints have been called on to endure the most painful and protracted sufferings; some of the most faithful and eminent servants of Christ have encountered the most relentless and extreme persecution. Not only is this a fact of observation, but it is plainly revealed in Holy Writ.

As we turn to God's Word for light on the subject of suffering among the saints, we find it affirmed, "Many are the afflictions of the righteous, but the Lord delivereth him out of them all" (Psa. 34:19). Those "afflictions" are sent by God upon different ones for various reasons. Sometimes for the *prevention* of sin: the experience of the beloved apostle was a case in point, "And *lest* I should be exalted above measure through the abundance of the revelations, there was given to me a thorn in the flesh, the messenger of Satan to buffet me, *lest* I should be exalted above measure" (2 Cor. 12:7). Sometimes sore trials are sent for the testing and strengthening of our *graces*: "My brethren, count it all joy when ye fall into divers temptations; knowing this, that the trying of your faith worketh patience" (James 1:2, 3). Sometimes God's servants and people are called on to endure fierce persecution for a confirmatory testimony to the Truth: "And they departed from the presence of the council, rejoicing that they were counted worthy to suffer shame for His name" (Acts 5:41).

Yet here again we need to be much on our guard, for the flesh is ever ready to *pervert* even the holy things of God, and make an evil use of that which is good. When God is chastising a Christian for his sins, it is so easy for him to suppose such is *not* the case, and falsely comfort himself with the thought that God is only developing his graces, or permitting him to have closer fellowship with the sufferings of Christ. Where we are visited with afflictions *personally,* it is always the safest policy to assume that God has a controversy with us; humble ourselves beneath His mighty hand, and say with Job, "Show me *wherefore* Thou contendest with me" (10:2); and when He *has* convicted me of my fault, to penitently confess and forsake it. But where *others* are concerned, it is not for us to judge—though sometimes God reveals the cause to His *servants* (Amos 3:7).

In the passage which is to be before us, the apostle presents a third consideration why heed should be given unto the exhortation at the beginning of Heb. 12, which calls to patient perseverance in the path of faith and obedience, notwithstanding all the obstacles, difficulties, and dangers which may be encountered therein. He now draws a motive from the nature of those sufferings considered in the light of *God's end in them*: all the trials and persecutions which He may call on His people to endure are *necessary,* not only as testimonies to the truth, to the reality of His grace in them, but also as chastisements which are required by us, wherein God has a blessed design toward us. This argument is enforced by several considerations to the end of v. 13. How we should admire and adore the consummate wisdom of God which has so marvellously ordered all, that the very things which manifest the *hatred* of men against us, are evidences of *His love* toward us! How the realization of this should strengthen patience!

O how many of God's dear children have found, in every age, that the afflictions which have come upon them from a hostile world, were soul-purging medicines from the Lord. By them they have been bestirred, revived, and mortified to things down here; and made partakers of God's holiness, to their own unspeakable advantage and comfort. Truly wondrous are the ways of our great God.

Hereby doth He defeat the counsels and expectations of the wicked, having a design to accomplish by their agency something which they know not of. These very reproaches, imprisonments, stripes, with the loss of goods and danger of their lives, with which the world opposed them for their ruin; *God* makes use of for their refining, consolation and joy. Truly He "maketh the wrath of man to praise Him" (Psa. 76:10). O that our hearts and minds may be duly impressed with the wisdom, power and grace of Him who bringeth a clean thing out of an unclean.

"In all these things is the wisdom and goodness of God, in contriving and effecting these things, to the glory of His grace, and the salvation of His Church, to be admired" (John Owen). But herein we may see, once more, the imperative need for *faith* — a God-given, God-sustained, spiritual, supernatural FAITH. Carnal reason can see no more in our persecutions than the malice and rage of evil men. Our senses perceive nothing beyond material losses and painful physical discomforts. But faith discovers *the Father's* hand directing all things: faith is assured that all proceeds from His boundless *love*: faith realizes that He has in view *the good of our souls*. The more this is apprehended by the exercise of faith, not only the better for our peace of mind, but the readier shall we be to diligently apply ourselves in seeking to learn God's lessons for us in every chastisement He lays upon us.

The opening "And" of v. 5 shows the apostle is continuing to present motives to stir unto a perseverance in the faith, notwithstanding sufferings for the same. The first motive was taken from the example of the O. T. worthies (v. 1). The second, from the illustrious pattern of Jesus (vv. 2-4). This is the third: the Author of these sufferings—our Father—and His loving design in them. There is also a more immediate connection with v. 4 pointed by the "And:" it presents a tacit rebuke for being ready to faint under the lesser trials, wherewith they were exercised. Here He gives a reason how and why it was they were thus making that reason the means of introducing a new argument. The reason why they were ready to faint was their inattention to the direction and encouragement which God has supplied for them—our failure to appropriate God's gracious provisions for us is the rise of all our spiritual miscarriages.

The Hebrew Christians to whom this epistle was first addressed were passing through a great fight of afflictions, and miserably were they acquitting themselves. They were the little remnant out of the Jewish nation who had believed on their Messiah during the days of His public ministry, plus those Jews who had been converted under the preaching of the apostles. It is highly probable that they had expected the Messianic kingdom would at once be set up on earth, and that they would be allotted the chief places of honour in it. But the millennium had not begun, and their own lot became increasingly bitter. They were not only hated by the Gentiles, but ostracised by their unbelieving brethren, and it became a hard matter for them to make even a bare living. Providence held a frowning face. Many who had made a profession of Christianity had gone back to Judaism and were prospering temporally. As the afflictions of the believing Jews increased they too were sorely tempted to turn their back upon the new Faith. Had they been wrong in embracing Christianity? Was high heaven displeased because they had identified themselves with Jesus of Nazareth? Did not their sufferings go to show that God no longer regarded them with favour?

Now it is most blessed and instructive to see how the apostle met the unbelieving reasoning of their hearts. He appealed to *their own scriptures*, reminding them of an exhortation found in Prov. 3:11, 12: "And ye have forgotten the exhortation which speaketh unto you as unto children, My son, despise not thou the chastenings of the Lord, nor faint when thou art rebuked of Him" (Heb. 12:5). As we pointed out so often in our exposition of the earlier chapters of this Epistle, at every critical point in his argument the apostle's appeal was to the written Word of God—an example which is binding on every servant of Christ to follow. That Word is the final court of appeal for every controversial matter, and the more its authority is respected, the more is its Author honoured. Not only so, but the more God's children are brought to turn to its instruction, the more will they be built up and established in the true faith. Moreover, "Whatsoever things were written aforetime were written for *our* learning, that we through patience and comfort of the Scriptures might have hope" (Rom. 15:4): it is to them alone we must turn for solid comfort. Great will be our loss if we fail to do so.

"And ye have forgotten the exhortation which speaketh *unto you.*" Note well the words we have placed in italics. The exhortation to which the apostle referred was uttered over a thousand years previously, under the Mosaic dispensation; nevertheless the apostle insists that it was addressed equally unto the *New T.* saints! How this exposes the cardinal error of modern "dispensationalists," who seek to rob Christians of the greater part of God's precious Word. Under the pretense of "rightly dividing" the Word, they would filch from *them* all that God gave to His people prior to the beginning of the present era. Such a devilish device is to be steadfastly resisted by us. All that is found in the book of Proverbs is as much God the Father's instruction to *us* as are the contents of the Pauline epistles! Throughout that book God addresses us individually as "My *son:*" see 1:8, 3:1, 4:1, 5:1, etc. Surely that is quite sufficient for every spiritual mind—no laboured argument is needed.

The appositeness of Prov. 3:11, 12 to the case of the afflicted Hebrews gave great force to the apostle's citing of it here. That passage would enable them to perceive that *their* case was by no means unprecedented or peculiar, that it was in fact no otherwise with them than it had been with others of God's children in former ages and that long before the Lord had graciously laid in provision for their encouragement: "My son, despise not the chastening of the Lord; neither be weary of His correction: For whom the Lord loveth He correcteth, even as a Father the son in whom He delighteth" (Prov. 3:11, 12). It has ever been God's way to correct those in whom He delights, to chastise His children; but so far from that salutary discipline causing us to faint, it should strengthen and comfort our hearts, being assured that such chastening proceeds from His *love,* and that the exhortation to perseverance in the path of duty is issued *by Him.* It is the height of pride and ingratitude not to comply with *His* tender entreaties.

But the apostle had to say to the suffering Hebrews, "Ye have *forgotten* the exhortation." To forget God's gracious instruction is at least an infirmity, and with it they are here taxed. To forget the encouragements which the Father has given us is a serious fault: it is expressly forbidden: "Beware lest thou forget the Lord" (Deut. 6:12). It was taxed upon the Jews of old, "They soon forgat His works . . . . They forgat God their Saviour, which had done great things in Egypt" (Psa. 106:13, 21). Forgetfulness is a part of that corruption which has seized man by his fall: all the faculties of his soul have been seriously injured—the memory, which was placed in man to be a treasury, in which to lay up the directions and consolations of God's Word, has not escaped the universal wreckage. But that by no means excuses us: it is a *fault,* to be striven and prayed against. As ministers see occasion, they are to stir up God's people to use means for the strengthening of the memory—especially by the formation of the habit of holy *meditation* in Divine things.

Thus it was with the Hebrews, in some measure at least: they had "forgotten" that which should have stood in good stead in the hour of their need. Under their trials and persecution, they ought, in an especial manner, to have called to mind that Divine exhortation of Prov. 3:11, 12 for their encouragement: had they believingly appropriated it, they had been kept from fainting. Alas, how often we are like them! "The want of a diligent consideration of the provision that God hath made in the Scripture for our encouragement to duty and comfort under difficulties, is a sinful forgetfulness, and is of dangerous consequence to our souls" (John Owen).

"Which speaketh unto you as unto children." It is very striking indeed to observe the tense of the verb here: the apostle was quoting a sentence of Scripture which had been written a thousand years previously, yet he does not say "which *hath* spoken," but "which *speaketh* unto you!" The same may be seen again in that sevenfold exhortation of Rev. 2 and 3, "He that hath an ear let him hear what the Spirit *saith* (not "said") unto the churches." The Holy Scriptures are a living Word, in which God speaks to men in every generation. Holy Writ is not a dumb or dead letter: it has a voice in it, ever speaking of God Himself. "The Holy Spirit is always present in the Word, and speaks in it equally and alike to the church in all ages. He doth in it speak as immediately to us, as if we were the first and only persons to whom He spake. And this should teach us, with what *reverence* we ought to attend to the Scriptures, namely, as to the way and means whereby *God Himself* speaks directly to us" (John Owen.)

"Which speaketh unto you as unto *children*." The apostle emphasises the fact that God addresses an exhortation in Prov. 3:11. to "My son," which shows plainly that His relation to the *Old T.* saints was that of a Father to His children. This at once refutes a glaring error made by some who pose as being ultra-orthodox, more deeply taught in the Word than others. They have insisted that the Fatherhood of God was never revealed until the Son became incarnate; but every verse in the Proverbs where God says "My son" reveals their mistake. That the O.T. saints were instructed in this blessed relationship is clear from other passages: "Like as a father pitieth his children, *so the Lord* pitieth them that fear Him" (Psa. 103:13). This relation unto God is by virtue of their (and our) union with Christ: *He* is "the Son." and being one with Him, members of His body, they were "sons" too.

This precious relationship is the ground of the soul's confidence in God. "If God speaks to them as to *children*, they have good ground to fly to God as to a Father, and in all time of need to ask and seek of Him all needful blessings (Matt. 7:11), yea, and in faith to depend on Him for the same (Matt. 6:31, 32). What useful things shall they want? What hurtful thing need such to fear? If God deal with us as with *children*, He *will* provide for them every good thing, He will protect them from every hurtful thing, He will hear their prayers, He will accept their services, He will bear with their infirmities, He will support them under all their burdens, and assist them against all their assaults; though through their own weakness, or the violence of some temptation, they should be drawn from Him, yet will He be ready to meet them in the mid-way, turning to Him — instance the mind of the father of the prodigal towards him" (W. Gouge).

CHAPTER EIGHTY-SEVEN

Divine Chastisement

(Heb. 12:5)

It is of first importance that we learn to draw a sharp distinction between Divine punishment and Divine chastisement—important for maintaining the honour and glory of God, and for the peace of mind of the Christian. The distinction is very simple, yet is it often lost sight of. God's people can never by any possibility be *punished* for their sins, for God has already punished them at the Cross. The Lord Jesus, our blessed Substitute, suffered the full penalty of all our guilt, hence it is written, "the blood of Jesus Christ His Son cleanseth us from all sin" (I John 1:7). Neither the justice nor the love of God will permit Him to again exact payment of what Christ discharged to the full. The difference between punishment and chastisement lies not in *the nature of* the sufferings of the afflicted: it is most important to bear this in mind. There is a threefold distinction between the two.

First, *the character* in which God acts. In the former God acts as *Judge*, in the latter as *Father*. Sentence of punishment is the act of a judge, a penal sentence passed on those who are charged with guilt. Punishment can never fall upon a child of God in this judicial sense, because his guilt was all transferred to Christ: "Who His own self bare our sins in His own body on the tree." But while the believer's sins cannot be punished, while the Christian cannot be condemned (Rom. 8:33), yet he may be *chastised*. The Christian occupies an entirely different position from the non-Christian: he is a member of the family of God. The relationship which now exists between him and God is that of Parent and child; and as a son he must be disciplined for wrong-doing. Folly is bound up in the hearts of all God's children, and the rod is necessary to rebuke, to subdue, to humble.

The second distinction between Divine punishment and Divine chastisement lies in *the recipients* of each. The objects of the former are His enemies; the subjects of the latter, His children. As the Judge of all the earth God will yet take vengeance on all His foes; as the Father of His family God maintains discipline over all His children. The one is judicial, the other parental. A third distinction is seen in *the design* of each: the one is retributive, the other remedial. The one flows from His anger, the other from His love. Divine punishment is never sent for the good of sinners, but for the honouring of God's law and the maintenance of His government. Divine chastisement is sent for the *well-being* of His children: "We have had fathers of our flesh which corrected us and we gave them reverence: shall we not much rather be in subjection unto the Father of spirits, and live? For they verily for a few days chastened us after their own pleasure; but He *for our profit*, that we might be partakers of His holiness" (Heb. 12:9, 10).

The above distinctions should at once rebuke the thoughts which are so generally entertained among Christians. When the believer is smarting under the rod, let him not say, God is now punishing me for my sins. *That* can never be; *that* is most dishonouring to the blood of Christ. God is *correcting* thee in love, not smiting in wrath. Nor should the Christian regard the chastening of the Lord as a sort of necessary evil to which he must bow as submissively as possible. No, it proceeds from God's goodness and faithfulness and is one of the greatest blessings for which we have to thank Him. Chastisement evidences our Divine sonship; the father of a family does not concern himself with those on the outside: but those within he guides and disciplines to make them conform to his will. Chastisement is designed for our good, to promote our highest interests. Look beyond the rod to the All-wise hand that wields it!

Unhappily there is no word in the English language which is capable of doing justice to the Greek term here. "Paideia" which is rendered "chastening" is only another form of "paidion" which signifies "young children," being the tender word that was employed by the Saviour in John 21:5 and Heb. 2:13. One can see at a glance the direct connection which exists between the words "disciple" and "discipline:" equally close in the Greek is the relation between "children" and "chastening"—*son training* would be better. It has reference to God's education, nurture and discipline of His children. It is the Father's wise and loving correction which is in view.

It is true that much chastisement is the rod in the hand of the Father correcting His erring child, but it is a serious mistake to confine our thoughts to this one aspect of the subject. Chastisement is by no means always God's scourging of His refractory sons. Some of the saintliest of God's people, some of the most obedient of His children, have been and are the greatest sufferers. Oft times God's chastenings instead of being retributive are corrective. They are sent to empty us of self-sufficiency and self-righteousness; they are given to discover to us hidden transgressions, to teach us the plague of our own hearts. Or again; chastisements are sent to strengthen our faith, to raise us to higher levels of experience, to bring us into a condition of greater usefulness. Still again; Divine chastisement is sent as a preventative, to keep under pride, to save us from being unduly elated over success in God's service. Let us consider, briefly, four entirely different examples.

David. In his case the rod was laid upon him for grievous sins, for open wickedness. His fall was occasioned by self-confidence and self-righteousness. If the reader will diligently compare the two songs of David recorded in 2 Samuel 22 and 23, the one written near the beginning of his life, the other near the end, he will be struck by the great difference of spirit manifested by the writer in each. Read 2 Samuel 22:22-25, and you will not be surprised that God suffered him to have a fall. Then turn to chapter 23, and mark the blessed change. At the beginning of v. 5 there is a heart-broken confession of failure. In vv. 10-12, there is a God-glorifying profession, attributing victory unto the Lord. The severe scourging of David was not in vain.

Job. Probably he tasted of every kind of suffering which falls to man's lot: family bereavements, loss of property, grievous bodily afflictions, came fast, one on top of another. But God's end in them all was that Job should benefit therefrom and be a greater partaker of His holiness. There was not a little of self-satisfaction and self-righteousness in Job at the beginning; but at the end, when he was brought face to face with the thrice Holy One, he "abhorred *himself*" (42:6). In David's case the chastisement was retributive; in Job's corrective.

Abraham. In him we see an illustration of an entirely different aspect of chastening. Most of the trials to which he was subject were neither because of open sins nor for the correction of inward faults. Rather were they sent for the development of spiritual graces. Abraham was sorely tried in various ways, but it was in order that faith might be strengthened, and that patience might have its perfect work in him. Abraham was weaned from the things of this world, that he might enjoy closer fellowship with Jehovah and become "the friend" of God.

Paul. "And *lest* I should be exalted above measure through the abundance of the revelations, there was given to me a thorn in the flesh, the messenger of Satan to buffet me, lest I should be exalted above measure" (2 Cor. 12:7). This "thorn" was sent not because of failure and sin, but as a preventative against pride. Note the "lest" both at the beginning and end of the verse. The result of this "thorn" was that the beloved apostle was made more conscious of his weakness. Thus chastisement has for one of its main objects the breaking down of self-sufficiency, the bringing us to the end of ourselves.

Now in view of these widely different aspects—chastisements which are retributive, corrective, educative, and preventative—how incompetent are we to *diagnose*, and how great is the folly of pronouncing a judgment concerning others! Let us not conclude when we see a fellow-Christian under the rod of God that he is necessarily being taken to task for his sins. Let us now consider *the spirit* in which Divine chastisements are to be received. "My son, despise not thou the chastening of the Lord, nor faint when thou art rebuked of Him" (v. 5).

Not all chastisement is sanctified to the recipient of it. Some are hardened thereby; others are crushed beneath it. Much depends on the spirit in which afflictions are received. There is no virtue in trials and troubles in themselves: it is only as they are blest by God that the Christian is profited thereby. As Heb. 12:11 informs us, it is those who are "*exercised*" under God's rod that bring forth "the peaceable fruit of righteousness." A sensitive conscience and a tender heart are the needed adjuncts.

In our text the Christian is warned against two entirely different dangers: despise not, despair not. These are two extremes against which it is ever necessary to keep a sharp look-out. Just as every truth of Scripture has its balancing counterpart, so has every evil its opposite. On the one hand there is a haughty spirit which laughs at the rod, a stubborn will which refuses to be humbled thereby. On the other hand there is a fainting which utterly sinks beneath it and gives way to despondency. Spurgeon said, "The way of righteousness is a difficult pass between two mountains of error, and the great secret of the Christian's life is to wend his way along the narrow valley." Let us then ponder separately the two things which the Christian is here warned against: "My son, despise not thou the chastening of the Lord, nor faint when thou are rebuked of Him."

"The Greek word for 'despise' is nowhere used in the Scripture, but in this place. It signifies to 'set lightly by,' to have little esteem of, not to value any thing according to its worth and use. The Hebrew word means 'to reprobate, to reject, to despise.' We render the apostle's word by 'despise,' which yet doth not intend a despising that is so formally, but only interpretatively. Directly to despise and condemn or reject the chastisements of the Lord is a sin that perhaps none of His sons or children do fall into. But not to esteem of them as we ought, not to improve them unto their proper end, not to comply with the will of God in them, is interpretatively to despise them" (John Owen). As the point now before us is one which is of great practical importance to afflicted Christians, we will describe a number of ways in which God's chastisement may be "despised."

First, *by callousness*. There is a general lack of regard unto *God's* admonitions and instructions when troubles and sufferings come upon Christians. Too often they view them as the common and inevitable ills which man is heir unto, and perceive not that *their Father* hath any special hand or design in them. Hence they are stoically accepted in a fatalistic attitude. To be stoical under adversity is the policy of carnal wisdom: make the best of a bad job is the sum of its philosophy. The man of the world knows no better than to grit his teeth and brave things out: having no Divine Comforter, Counsellor, or Physician, he has to fall back upon his own poor resources. But it is inexpressibly sad when we find the child of God conducting himself as does a child of the Devil.

This is what is dehorted against in our present text: "despise not thou the chastening of the Lord." Observe well the personal emphasis —"*thou*:" no matter how thy fellow-creatures act when the clouds of providence frown upon them, see well to it that *thou* comportest thyself as becometh a son of God. Take to heart the caution here given. Stout-heartedness and stiff-neckedness is to be expected from a rebel, but one who has found grace in the eyes of the Lord should humble himself beneath His mighty hand the moment He gives any intimation of His displeasure. Scorn not the least trials: each has instruction wrapped up in it. Many a child would be spared the rod if he heeded the parent's *frown*! So it is spiritually. Instead of hardening ourselves to endure stoically, there should be a melting of heart.

Second, *by complaining*. This is what the Hebrews did in the wilderness; and there are still many murmurers in Israel's camp to-day. A little sickness, and we become so cross that our friends are afraid to come near us. A few days in bed, and we fret and fume like a bullock unaccustomed to the yoke. We peevishly ask, Why this affliction? what have I done to deserve it? We look around with envious eyes, and are discontented because others are carrying a lighter load. Beware, my reader: it goes hard with murmurers. God always chastises twice if we are not humbled by the first. Remind yourself of how much dross there yet is among the gold. View the corruptions of your own heart, and marvel that God has not smitten you far more severely.

This is what is dehorted against here: "despise not thou the chastening of the Lord." Instead of complaining, there should be a holy submitting unto the good will of God. There is a dreadful amount of complaining among Christians to-day, due to failure to nip this evil weed in the bud. Grumbling at the weather, being cross when things are lost or mislaid, murmuring because some one has failed to show us the respect which we consider ourselves entitled unto. *God's hand* in these things—for nothing happens by chance under

His government: everything has a meaning and message if our hearts are open to receive it—is lost sight of. That is to "despise" His rod when it is laid but gently upon us, and this it is which necessitates heavier blows. Form the habit of heeding His *taps*, and you will be less likely to receive His *raps*.

Third, *by criticisms.* How often we question the usefulness of chastisement. As Christians we seem to have little more spiritual good sense than we had natural wisdom as children. As boys we thought that the *rod* was the least necessary thing in the home. It is so with the children of God. When things go as we like them, when some unexpected temporal blessing is bestowed, we have no difficulty in ascribing all to a kind Providence; but when our plans are thwarted, when losses are ours, it is very different. Yet, is it not written, "I form the light *and* create darkness, I make peace, *and* create evil: I the Lord do all these things" (Isa. 45:7).

How often is the thing formed ready to complain "Why hast Thou made me *thus*?" We say, I cannot see how *this* can possibly profit my soul: if I had better health, I could attend the house of prayer more frequently; if I had been spared those losses in business, I would have more money for the Lord's work! What good can possibly come out of this calamity? Like Jacob we exclaim, "All these things are against me." What is this but to "despise" the rod? Shall thy ignorance challenge God's wisdom? Shall thy shortsightedness arraign omniscience? O for grace to be as a "weaned child" (Psa. 131:2).

Fourth, *by carelessness.* So many fail to mend their ways. The exhortation of our text is much needed by all of us. There are many who *have* "despised" the rod, and in consequence they have *not* profited thereby. Many a Christian has been corrected by God, but in vain. Sickness, reverses, bereavements have come, but they have not been sanctified by prayerful self-examination. O brethren and sisters, take heed. If God be chastening "consider your ways" (Hag. 1:5), "ponder the path of thy feet" (Prov. 4:26). Be assured that there is some reason for the chastening. Many a Christian would not have been chastised half so severely had he diligently inquired as to the cause of it.

"Cause me to understand wherein I have erred" (Job 6:24); "show me wherefore Thou contendest with me" (10:2), expresses the attitude we should take whenever God's hand is laid upon us. We are bidden "*hear ye* the rod" (Micah 6:9), that is, to pay a due regard to God's voice in our trials and afflictions, and to correct that in our lives with which He is displeased. In chastisement God is to be viewed not only as a Father but also as a Teacher: valuable lessons are to be learned therefrom if we cultivate a teachable spirit. Not so to do, failure to improve them unto their proper design and to comply with the will of God in them, is to "despise" His loving reproofs. But we must turn now to the second half of our verse.

"Nor faint when thou art rebuked of Him." This word presupposes that we have not "despised" God's chastening, but *have heeded it*—inquired as to the cause and reason of it, and have discovered He is evidencing that He is displeased with us. The learned tell us that the word for "rebuked," both in the Hebrew and in the Greek, signifies "a reproof by rational conviction:" the conscience has been pricked, and God has discovered unto the heart that there is something in our ways—which before we took no notice of—which has convinced us of the needs-be for our present afflictions. He makes us to understand *what it is* that is wrong in our lives: we are "rebuked" in our conscience. Our response should be to humble ourselves before Him, confess the fault, and seek grace to right it; and in order to this we are cautioned against "fainting" in our minds. Let us mention several forms of this particular evil of "fainting."

First, *when we give up all exertion.* This is done when we sink down in despondency. The smitten one concludes that it is more than he can possibly endure. His heart fails him; darkness swallows him up; the sun of hope is eclipsed, and the voice of thanksgiving is silent. To "faint" means rendering ourselves unfit for the discharge of our duties. When a person faints, he is rendered motionless. How many Christians are ready to completely give up the fight when adversity enters their lives. How many are rendered quite inert when trouble comes their way. How many by their attitude say, God's hand is heavy upon me: I can do nothing. Ah, beloved, "sorrow not, even as others which have no hope" (1 Thess. 4:13). "Faint not when thou art rebuked of Him:" go to the Lord about it; recognise *His* hand in it. Remember thine afflictions are among the "all things" which work together for good.

Second, *when we question our sonship.* There are not a few Christians who, when the rod descends upon them, conclude that they are not sons of God after all. They forget that it is written "Many are the afflictions of the righteous (Psa. 34:19), and that we must "through *much* tribulation enter into the kingdom of God" (Acts 14:22). One says, "But if I were His child, I should not be in this poverty, misery, shame." Listen to v.8. "But if ye be without chastisement, whereof all are partakers, then are ye bastards and not sons." Learn, then, to look upon trials as proofs of God's love—purging, pruning, purifying thee. The father of a family does not concern himself much about those on the outside of his household: it is they who are within whom he guards and guides, nurtures and conforms to his will. So it is with God.

Third, *when we give way to unbelief.* This is occasioned by our failure to seek God's support under trials, and lay hold of His promises—"weeping may endure for a night, but joy cometh in the morning" (Psa. 30:5). Sure are we to "faint" if we lose sight of the Lord, and cherish not His words of consolation. David was encouraging himself against unbelief when he took himself to task and said, "Why art thou cast down O my soul? and why art thou disquieted in me? hope thou in God: for I shall yet praise Him for the help of His countenance" (Psa. 42:5): if only *that* attitude be maintained by us, we shall be preserved from sinking when troubles come upon us.

Fourth, *when we despair.* When unbelief dominates the heart, despondency soon becomes our portion. Some indulge the gloomy fancy that they will never again get from under the rod in this life; ah, it is a long lane that has no turning! Perhaps a reader says, "But I have prayed and prayed, and yet the dark clouds have not lifted." Then comfort yourself with the reflection: it is always the darkest hour which precedes the dawn. Perhaps another says, "I have pleaded His promises, but things are no better with me: I thought God delivered those who called upon Him; I *have* called, but He has not delivered, and I fear He never will." What! child of God, speak of thy Father thus? You say, He will never leave off smiting because He has smitten so long; rather conclude, He has now smitten so long, I must soon be delivered. Fight hard, my brother, against this attitude of despair, lest your complaining cause others to stumble. Despise not; faint not. May Divine grace preserve both writer and reader from either of these sinful extremes.

N.B. For several of the leading thoughts in the above article, we are indebted to a sermon by the late C. H. Spurgeon.

CHAPTER EIGHTY-EIGHT

Divine Chastisement

(Heb. 12:6)

The problem of suffering is a very real one in this world, and to not a few of our readers a personal and acute one. While some of us are freely supplied with comforts, others are constantly exercised over procuring the bare necessities of life. While some of us have long been favoured with good health, others know not what it is to go through a day without sickness and pain. While some homes have not been visited by death for many years, others are called upon again and again to pass through the deep waters of family bereavement. Yes, dear friend; the problem of suffering, the encountering of severe trials, is a very personal thing for not a few of the members of the household of faith. Nor is it the *external* afflictions which occasion the most anguish: it is the questionings they raise, the doubts they stimulate, the dark clouds of unbelief which they so often bring over the heart.

Very often it is in seasons of trial and trouble that Satan is most successful in getting in his evil work. When he perceives the uselessness of attempting to bring believers under the bondage in which he keeps unbelievers, he bides his time for the shooting at them of other arrows which he has in his quiver. Though he is unable to drag them down to the commission of the grosser outward forms of sin, he waits his opportunity for tempting them to be guilty of inward sins. Though he cannot infect them with the poison of evolutionism and higher criticism, he despairs not of seducing them with questions of God's goodness. It is when adversity comes the Christian's way, when sore trials multiply, when the soul is oppressed and the mind distressed, that the Devil seeks to instill and strengthen doubtings of God's love, and to call into question the faithfulness of His promises.

Moreover, there come seasons in the lives of many saints when to sight and sense it *seems* as though God Himself had ceased to care for His needy and afflicted child. Earnest prayer is made for the mitigation of the sufferings, but relief is not granted. Grace is sought to meekly bear the burden which has been laid upon the suffering one; yet, so far from any sensible answer being received, self-will, impatience, unbelief, are more active than ever. Instead of the peace of God ruling the heart, unrest and enmity occupy its throne. Instead of quietness within, there is turmoil and resentment. Instead of "giving thanks always for all things unto God" (Eph. 5:20), the soul is filled with unkind thoughts and feelings against Him. This is cause for anguish unto the renewed heart; yet, at times, struggle against the evil as the Christian may, he is overcome by it.

Then it is that the afflicted one cries out, "Why standest Thou *afar off,* O Lord, why *hidest* Thou Thyself in times of trouble?" (Psa. 10:1). To the distressed saint, the Lord seems to *stand* still, as if He coldly looked on from a distance, and did not sympathize with the afflicted one. Nay, worse, the Lord appears to be *afar off,* and no longer "a very present help in trouble," but rather an inaccessible mountain, which it is impossible to reach. The felt presence of the Lord is the stay, the strength, the consolation of the believer; the lifting up of the light of His countenance upon us, is what sustains and cheers us in this dark world. But when *that* is withheld, when we no longer have the joy of His presence with us, drab indeed is the prospect, sad the heart. It is the *hiding* of our Father's face which cuts to the quick. When trouble *and desertion* come together, it is unbearable.

Then it is that the word comes to us, "My son, despise not thou the chastening of the Lord, nor faint when thou art rebuked of Him" (Heb. 12:5). Ah, it is easy for us to perceive the meetness of such an admonition as this while things are going smoothly and pleasantly for us. While our lot is congenial, or at least bearable, we have little difficulty in discerning what a sin it is for any Christian to either "despise" God's chastenings or to "faint" beneath them. But when tribulation comes upon us, when distress and anguish fill our hearts, it is quite another matter. Not only do we become guilty of one of the very evils here dehorted from, but we are very apt to excuse and extenuate our peevishness or faintness. There is a tendency in all of us to pity ourselves, to take sides with ourselves against God, and even to justify the uprisings of our hearts against Him.

Have we never, in self-vindication, said, "Well, after all we are *human;* it is *natural* that we should chafe against the rod or give way to despondency when we are afflicted. It is all very well to tell us that we *should not,* but how can we help ourselves? we cannot change our natures; we are frail men and women, and not angels." And what has been the issue from the fruit of this self-pity and self-vindication? Review the past, dear friend, and recall how you felt and acted inwardly when God was tearing up your cozy nest, overturning your cherished plans, dashing to pieces your fondest hopes, afflicting you painfully in your affairs, your body, or your family circle. Did it not issue in calling into question the wisdom of God's ways, the justice of His dealings with you, His kindness towards you? Did it not result in your having still stronger doubts of His very goodness?

In Heb. 12:5 the Christian is cautioned against either despising the Lord's chastenings or fainting beneath them. Yet, notwithstanding this plain warning, there remains a tendency in all of us not only to disregard the same, but to act contrary thereto. The apostle anticipates this evil, and points out the remedy. The mind of the Christian must be fortified against it. But how? By calling to remembrance *the source* from which all his testings, trials, tribulations and troubles proceed, namely, the blessed, wondrous, unchanging love of God. "My son, despise not thou the chastenings of the Lord, nor faint when thou art rebuked of Him. FOR whom the Lord *loveth,* He chasteneth." Here a reason is advanced why we *should not* despise God's chastening nor faint beneath it—all proceeds from His *love.* Yes, even the bitter disappointments, the sore trials, the things which occasion an aching heart, are not only appointed by unerring wisdom, but are sent by infinite Love! It is the apprehension and appropriation of this glorious fact, and that alone, which will preserve us from both the evils forbidden in v. 5.

The way to victory over suffering is to keep sorrow from filling the soul: "Let not your *heart* be troubled" (John 14:1). So long as the waves wash only the deck of the ship, there is no danger of its foundering; but when the tempest breaks through the hatches and submerges the hold, then disaster is nigh. No matter what floods of tribulation break over us, it is our duty and our privilege to have peace within: "keep thy *heart* with all diligence" (Prov. 4:23): suffer no doubtings of God's wisdom, faithfulness, goodness, to take root there. But how am I to prevent their so doing? *"Keep yourselves in the love of God"* (Jude 21), is the inspired answer, the sure remedy, the way to victory. There, in one word, we have made known to us the secret of how to overcome all questionings of God's providential ways, all murmurings against His dealings with us.

"Keep yourselves in the love of God." It is as though a parent said to his child, "Keep yourself in the sunshine:" the sun shines whether he enjoys it or not, but he is responsible not to walk in the shade and thus lose its genial glow. So God's love for His people abides unchanging, but how few of them keep themselves in the warmth of it. The saint is to be "rooted and grounded in love" (Eph. 3:17); "rooted" like a tree in rich and fertile soil; "grounded" like a house built upon a rock. Observe that both of these figures speak of *hidden* processes: the root-life of a tree is concealed from human eyes, and the foundations of a house are laid deep in the ground. Thus it should be with each child of God: the heart is to be fixed, nourished by the love of God.

It is one thing to believe intellectually that "God is love" and that He loves His people, but it is quite another to enjoy and live in that love in the soul. To be "rooted and grounded in love" means to have a settled assurance of God's love for us, such an assurance as nothing can shake. This is the deep need of every Christian, and no pains are to be spared in the obtaining thereof. Those passages in Scripture which speak of the wondrous love of God, should be read frequently and meditated upon daily. There should be a diligent striving to apprehend God's love more fully and richly. Dwell upon the many unmistakable proofs which God has made of His love to you: the gift of His Word, the gift of His Son, the gift of His Spirit. What greater, what clearer proofs do we require! Steadfastly resist every temptation to question His love: "keep yourselves *in* the love of God." Let *that* be the realm in which you live, the atmosphere you breathe, the warmth in which you thrive.

This life is but a schooling. In saying this we are uttering a platitude, yet it is a truth of which all Christians need to be constantly reminded. This is the period of our childhood and minority. Now in childhood everything has, or should have, the character of education and discipline. Dear parents and teachers are constantly directing, warning, rebuking; the whole of the child-life is under rule, restraint and guidance. But the only object is the child himself—his good, his character, his future; and the only motive is love. Now as childhood is to the rest of our life, so is the whole of our earthly sojourn to our future and heavenly life. Therefore let us seek to cultivate the spirit of childhood. Let us regard it as natural that we *should be* daily rebuked and corrected. Let us behave with the docility and meekness of children, with their trustful and sweet assurance that *love* is behind all our chastenings, that we are in the tender hands of our Father.

But if this attitude is to be maintained, *faith* must be kept in steady exercise: only thus shall we judge aright of afflictions. Sense is ever ready to slander and belie the Divine perfections. Sense beclouds the understanding and causes us to wrongly interpret God's dispensations with us. Why so? Because sense estimates things from their outside and by their present feeling. "No chastening *for the present* seemeth to be joyous, but grievous" (Heb. 12:11), and therefore if when under the rod we judge of God's love and care for us by our *sense of* His present dealings, we are likely to conclude that He has but little regard for us. Herein lies the urgent need for the putting forth of faith, for "faith is the evidence of things not seen." *Faith* is the only remedy for this double evil. Faith interprets things not according to the outside or visible, but according to the promise. Faith looks upon providences not as a present disconnected piece, but in its entirety to the end of things.

Sense perceives in our trials naught but expressions of God's disregard or anger, but faith can discern Divine wisdom and love in the sorest troubles. Faith is able to unfold the riddles and solve the mysteries of providence. Faith can extract honey and sweetness out of gall and wormwood. Faith discerns that God's heart is filled with love toward us, even when His hand is heavy and smarts upon us. The bucket goes down into the well the deeper, that it may come up the fuller. Faith perceives God's design in the chastening is our good. It is through faith "that He would show thee the secrets of wisdom, that they are double to that which is" (Job 11:6). By the "secrets of wisdom" is meant the *hidden* ways of God's providence. Divine providence has two faces: the one of rigor, the other of clemency; sense looks upon the former only, faith enjoys the latter.

Faith not only looks beneath the surface of things and sees the sweet orange beneath the bitter rind, but it looks beyond the present and anticipates the blessed sequel. Of the Psalmist it is recorded, "I said *in my haste,* I am cut off from before Thine eyes" (31:22). The fumes of passion dim our vision when we look only at what is present. Asaph declared, "My feet were almost gone, my steps had well-nigh slipped; for I was envious at the foolish, when I saw the prosperity of the wicked" (Psa. 73:2, 3); but when he went into the sanctuary of God he said, "Then understood I *their end*" (v. 17), and that quieted him. Faith is occupied not with the scaffolding, but with the completed building; not with the medicine, but with the healthful effects it produces; not with the painful rod, but with the peaceable fruit of righteousness in which it issues.

Suffering, then, is a test of the heart; chastisement is a challenge to faith—our faith in His wisdom, His faithfulness, His love. As we have sought to show above the great need of the Christian is to keep himself in the love of God, for the soul to have an unshaken assurance of His tender care for us: "casting all your care upon Him, for He careth for you" (1 Pet. 5:7). But the knowledge of that "care" can only be experimentally maintained by the exercise of faith—especially is this the case in times of trouble. A preacher once asked a despondent friend, "Why is that cow looking over the wall?" And the answer was, "Because she cannot look through it." The illustration may be crude, yet it gives point to an important truth. Discouraged reader, look over the things which so much distress you, and behold the Father's smiling face; look above the frowning clouds of His providence, and see the sunshine of His never changing love.

"For whom the Lord loveth He chasteneth, and scourgeth every son whom He receiveth" (v.6). There is something very striking and unusual about this verse, for it is found, in slightly varied form, in no less than five different books of the Bible:—"Happy is the man whom God correcteth: therefore despise not thou the chastening of the Almighty" (Job 5:17); "Blessed is the man whom Thou chastenest, O Lord, and teachest him out of Thy law" (Psa. 94:12); "Whom the Lord loveth He correcteth, even as a father the son in whom he delighteth" (Prov. 3:12); "As many as I love, I rebuke and chasten" (Rev. 3:19). Probably there is a twofold reason for this reiteration. First, it hints at the importance and blessedness of this truth. God repeats it so frequently lest we should forget, and thus lose the comfort and cheer of realising that Divine chastisement proceeds from *love.* This must be a precious word if God thought it well to say it five times over! Second, such repetition also implies our slowness to believe it; by nature our evil hearts are inclined in the opposite direction. Though our text affirms so emphatically that the Christian's chastisements proceed from God's love, we are ever ready to attribute them to His harshness. It is really very humbling that the Holy Spirit should deem it necessary to repeat this statement so often.

"For whom the Lord loveth He chasteneth, and scourgeth every son whom He receiveth." Four things are to be noted. First, the best of God's children *need* chastisement—"every son." There is no Christian but what has faults and follies which require correcting: "in many things we all offend" (James 3:2). Second, God *will correct* all whom He adopts into His family. However He may now let the reprobate alone in their sins, He will not ignore the failings of His people—to be suffered to go on unrebuked in wickedness is a sure sign of alienation from God. Third, in this God acts as a *Father*: no wise and good parent will wink at the faults of his own children: his very relation and affection to them oblige him to take notice of the same. Fourth, God's disciplinary dealings with His sons proceed from and make manifest His *love* to them: it is this fact we would now particularly concentrate upon.

1. The Christian's chastisements *flow from* God's love. Not from His anger or hardness, nor from arbitrary dealings, but from God's heart do our afflictions proceed. It is love which regulates all the ways of God in dealing with His own. It was love which *elected* them. The heart is not warmed when our election is traced back

merely to God's sovereign will, but our affections are stirred when we read "in *love* having predestinated us" (Eph. 1:4, 5). It was love which *redeemed* us. We do not reach the centre of the atonement when we see nothing more in the Cross than a vindication of the law and a satisfaction of justice: "God so *loved* the world that He gave His only begotten Son" (John 3:16). It is love which regenerates or *effectually calls* us: "with loving kindness have I drawn thee" (Jer. 31:3). The new birth is not only a marvel of Divine wisdom and a miracle of Divine power, but it is also and superlatively a product of God's affection.

In like manner it is *love* which ordained our trials and orders our chastisements. O Christian, never doubt the love of God. A quaint old Quaker, who was a farmer, had a weather-vane on the roof of his barn, from which stood out in clear-cut letters "God is love." One day a preacher was being driven to the Quaker's home; his host called attention to the vane and its text. The preacher turned and said, "I don't like that at all: it misrepresents the Divine character—God's love is not variable like the weather." Said the Quaker, "Friend you have misinterpreted its significance; that text on the weather-vane is to remind me that, no matter which way the wind is blowing, no matter from which direction the storm may come, still, "God is love."

2. The Christian's chastisements *express* God's love. Oftentimes we do not think so. As God's children we think and act very much as we did when children naturally. When we were little and our parents insisted that we should perform a certain duty we failed to appreciate the love which had respect unto our future well-being. Or, when our parents denied us something on which we had set our hearts, we felt we were very hardly dealt with. Yet was it *love* which said "No" to us. So it is spiritually. The love of God not only gives, but also *withholds*. No doubt this is the explanation for some of our unanswered prayers: God loves us too much to give what would not really be for our profit. The duties insisted upon, the rebukes given, the things withheld, are all *expressions of* His faithful love.

Chastisements manifest God's care of us. He does not regard us with unconcern and neglect, as men usually do their illegitimate children, but He has a true parent's solicitation for us: "Like as a father pitieth his children so the Lord pitieth them that fear Him" (Psa. 103:13). "And He humbled thee, and suffered thee to hunger, and fed thee with manna, which thou knewest not, neither did thy fathers know; that He might make thee know that man doth not live by bread only, but by every word that proceedeth out of the mouth of the Lord doth man live" (Deut. 8:3). There are several important sermons wrapped up in that verse, but we have not the space here to even outline them. God brings into the wilderness that we may be drawn nearer Himself. He dries up cisterns that we may seek and enjoy the Fountain. He destroys our nest down here that our affection may be set upon things above.

3. The Christian's chastisements *magnify* God's love. Our very trials make manifest the fulness and reveal the perfections of God's love. What a word is that in Lam. 3:33; "He doth not afflict willingly"! If God consulted only His own pleasure, He would not afflict us at all: it is for our profit that He "scourges." Ever remember that the great High Priest Himself is "*touched* with the feeling of our infirmities"; yet, notwithstanding, He employs the rod! God is love, and nothing is so sensitive as love. Concerning the trials and tribulations of Israel of old, it is written, "In all their affliction *He* was afflicted" (Isa. 63:9); yet out of love He chastens. How this manifests and magnifies the unselfishness of God's love!

Here, then is the Christian supplied with an effectual shield to turn aside the fiery darts of the wicked one. As we said at the beginning, Satan ever seeks to take advantage of our trials: like the fiend that he is, he makes his fiercest assaults when we are most cast down. Thus it was that he attacked Job—"Curse God and die." And thus some of us have found it. Did he not, in the hour of suffering and sorrow, seek to remind you that when you had become increasingly diligent in seeking to please and glorify God, the darkest clouds of adversity followed; and say, How unjust God is; what a miserable reward for your devotion and zeal! Here is your recourse, fellow-Christian: say to the Devil, "It is written, 'Whom the Lord loveth He chasteneth.' "

Again; if Satan cannot succeed in traducing the character of God and cause us to doubt His goodness and question His love, then he will assail our assurance. The Devil is most persevering: if a frontal attack fails, then he will make one from the rear. He will assault your assurance of sonship: he will whisper "*You* are no child of His: look at your condition, consider your circumstances, contrast those of other Christians. *You* cannot be an object of God's favour; you are deceiving yourself; your profession is an empty one. If you *were* God's child, He would treat you very differently. Such privations, such losses, such pains, show that you cannot be one of His." But say to him, "It is written, 'Whom the Lord loveth He chasteneth.' "

Let our final thought be upon the last word of our text: "For whom the Lord loveth He chasteneth, and scourgeth every son whom He *receiveth*." The one whom God scourges is not rejected, but "received"—received up into glory, welcomed in His House above. First the cross, then the crown, is God's unchanging order. This was vividly illustrated in the history of the children of Israel: God "chose them in the furnace of affliction," and many and bitter were their trials ere they reached the promised land. So it is with us. First the wilderness, then Canaan; first the scourging, and then the "receiving." May we keep ourselves more and more in the love of God.

CHAPTER EIGHTY-NINE

Divine Chastisement

(Heb. 12:7, 8)

The all-important matter in connection with Divine chastenings, so far as the Christian is concerned, is the spirit in which he *receives* them. Whether or not we "profit" from them, turns entirely on the exercises of our minds and hearts under them. The advantages or disadvantages which outward things bring to us, is to be measured by the effects they produce in us. Material blessings become curses if our souls are not the gainers thereby, while material losses prove benedictions if our spiritual graces are enriched therefrom. The difference between our spiritual impoverishment or our spiritual enrichment from the varied experiences of this life, will very largely be determined by our heart-attitude toward them, the spirit in which they are encountered, and our subsequent conduct under them. It is all summed up in that word "For as he thinketh in his heart, so is he" (Prov. 23:7).

As the careful reader passes from verse to verse of Hebrews 12: 3-11, he will observe how the Holy Spirit has repeatedly stressed this particular point, namely, *the spirit in which* God's chastisements are to be received. First, the tried and troubled saint is bidden to consider Him who was called upon to pass through a far rougher and deeper sea of suffering than any which His followers encounter, and this contemplation of Him is urged "lest we be wearied and faint in our minds" (v.3.). Second, we are bidden to "despise not" the chastenings of the Lord, "nor faint" when we are rebuked of Him (v. 5). Third, our Christian duty is to "endure" chastening as becometh the sons of God (v. 7). Fourth, it is pointed out that since we gave reverence to our earthly fathers when they corrected us, much more should we "rather be in subjection" unto our heavenly Father (v. 9). Finally, we learn there will only be the "peaceable fruit of righteousness" issuing from our afflictions, if we are duly "exercised thereby" (v. 11).

In the previous articles we have sought to point out some of the principal considerations which should help the believer to receive God's chastisements in a meet and becoming spirit. We have considered the blessed example left us by our Captain: may we who have enlisted under His banner diligently follow the same. We have seen that, however severe may be our trials, they are by no means extreme: we have not yet "resisted unto blood"—martyrdom has not overtaken *us,* as it did many who preceded us: shall we succumb to the showers, when they defied the fiercest storms! We have dwelt upon the needs-be for Divine reproof and correction. We have pointed out the blessed distinction there is between Divine punishment and Divine chastisement. We have contemplated the source from which all proceeds, namely, the *love* of our Father. We have shown the imperative necessity for the exercise of faith, if the heart is to be kept in peace while the rod is upon us.

"If ye endure chastening, God dealeth with you as with sons; for what son is he whom the father chasteneth not? But if ye be without chastisement, whereof all are partakers, then are ye bastards, and not sons" (vv. 7, 8). In these verses another consideration is presented for the comfort of those whom God is chastening. That of which we are here reminded is, that, when the Christian comports himself properly under Divine correction, he gives proof of his Divine sonship. If he endure them in a manner becoming to his profession, he supplies evidence of his Divine adoption. Blessed indeed is this, an unanswerable reply to Satan's evil insinuation: so far from the disciplinary afflictions which the believer encounters showing that God loves him not, they afford a golden opportunity for him to exercise and display *his* unquestioning love of the Father. If we undergo chastisements with patience and perseverance, then do we make manifest, both to ourselves and to others, the genuineness of our profession.

In the verses which are now before us the apostle draws an inference from and makes a particular application of what had been previously affirmed, thereby confirming the exhortation. There are three things therein to be particularly noted. First, the duty which has been enjoined: Divine chastisements are to be "endured" by us: that which is included and involved by that term we shall seek to show in what follows. Second, the great benefit which is gained by a proper endurance of those chastisements: evidence is thereby obtained that God is dealing with us as "sons:" not as enemies whom He hates, but as dear children whom He loves. Third, a solemn contrast is then drawn, calculated to unmask hypocrites and expose empty professors: those who are without Divine chastisement are not sons at all, but "bastards"— claiming the Church for their mother, yet having not God for their Father: what is signified thereby will appear in the sequel.

"If ye endure chastening, God dealeth with you as with sons." This statement supplements what was before us in v. 5. Both of them speak of the spirit in which chastisements are to be received by the Christian, only with this difference: v. 5 gives the negative side, v. 7 the positive. On the one hand, we are not to "despise" or "faint" under them; on the other hand, they are to be "endured." It has become an English proverb that "what cannot be cured must be endured," which is but another way of saying that we must grit our teeth and make the best of a bad job. It scarcely needs pointing out that the Holy Spirit has not used the term here in its lowest and carnal sense, but rather in its noblest and spiritual signification.

In order to ascertain the force and scope of any word which is used in Holy Scripture neither its acceptation in ordinary speech nor its dictionary etymology is to be consulted; instead, a concordance must be used, so as to find out how it is actually employed on the sacred page. In the case now before us, we do not have far to seek, for in the immediate context it is found in a connection where it cannot be misunderstood. In v. 2 we read that the Saviour "endured the cross," and in v. 3 that He "endured such contradiction of sinners against Himself." It was in the highest and noblest sense that Christ "endured" His sufferings: He remained steadfast under the sorest trials, forsaking not the path of duty. He meekly and heroically bore the acutest afflictions without murmuring against or fainting under them. How, then, is the Christian to conduct himself in the fires? We subjoin a sevenfold answer.

First, the Christian is to "endure" chastisement *inquiringly*. While it be true that all chastisement is not the consequence of personal disobedience or sinful conduct, yet much of it is so, and therefore it is always the part of wisdom for us to seek for the *why* of it. There is a cause for every effect, and a reason for all God's dealings. The Lord does not act capriciously, nor does He afflict willingly (Lam. 3:33). Every time the Father's rod falls upon us it is a call to self-examination, for pondering the path of our feet, for heeding that repeated word in Haggai "Consider your ways." It is our bounden duty to search ourselves and seek to discover the reason of God's displeasure. This may not be a pleasant exercise, and if we are honest with ourselves it is likely to occasion us much concern and sorrow; nevertheless, a broken and contrite heart is never despised by the One with whom we have to do.

Alas, only too often this self-examination and inquiring into the cause of our affliction is quite neglected, *relief* therefrom being the uppermost thought in the sufferer's mind. There is a most solemn warning upon this point in 2 Chron 16:12, 13, "And Asa in the thirty and ninth year of his reign was diseased in his feet, until his disease was exceeding great; yet in his disease *he sought not to the Lord,* but the physicians. And Asa slept with his fathers." How many professing Christians do likewise to-day. As soon as sickness strikes them, their first thought and desire is not that the affliction may be sanctified unto their souls, but how quickly their bodies may be relieved. We do not fully agree with some brethren who affirm that the Christian ought never to call in a doctor, and that the whole medical fraternity is of the Devil—in such case the Holy Spirit had never denominated Luke "the beloved physician," nor had Christ said the sick "need" a physician. On the other hand, it is unmistakably evident that physical healing is not the first need of an ailing saint.

Second, the Christian is to "endure" chastisement *prayerfully*. If our inquiry is to be prosecuted successfully, then we are in urgent need of Divine assistance. Those who rely upon their own judgment are certain to err. As our hearts are exercised as to the *cause* of the chastening, we need to seek earnestly unto God, for it is only in *His* light that we "see light" (Psa. 36:9). It is not sufficient to examine ourselves: we must request the Divine physician to diagnose our case, saying "Search me, O God, and know my heart: try me, and know my thoughts and see if there be any wicked way in me, and lead me in the way everlasting" (Psa. 139:23, 24). Nevertheless, let it be pointed out that such a request cannot be presented sincerely unless we have personally endeavoured to thoroughly search ourselves and purpose to continue so doing.

Prayer was never designed to be a substitute for the personal discharge of duty: rather is it appointed as a means for procuring help therein. While it remains our duty to honestly scrutinise our hearts and inspect our ways, measuring them by the holy requirements of Scripture, yet only the immediate assistance of the Spirit will enable us to prosecute our quest with any real profit and success. Therefore we need to enter the secret place and inquire of the Lord "show me *wherefore* Thou contendest with me" (Job 10:2). If we sincerely ask Him to make known unto us what it is in our ways He is displeased with, and for which He is now rebuking us, He will not mock us. Request of Him the hearing ear, and He will tell what is wrong. Let there be no reserve, but an honest desire to know what needs correcting, and He will show you.

Third, the Christian is to "endure" chastisement *humbly*. When the Lord has responded to your request and has made known the cause of His chastening, see to it that you quarrel not with Him. If there be any feeling that the scourging is heavier than you deserve, the thought must be promptly rejected. "Wherefore doth a living man complain, a man for the punishment (or chastisement) of his sins?" (Lam. 3:39). If we take issue with the Most High, we shall only be made to smart the more for our pains. Rather must we seek grace to heed that word, "Humble yourselves therefore under the mighty hand of God" (1 Pet. 5:6). Ask Him to quicken conscience, shine into your heart, and bring to light the hidden things of darkness, so that you may perceive your inward sins as well as your outward. And then will you exclaim, "I know, O Lord, that Thy judgments are right, and that Thou in faithfulness hast afflicted me" (Psa. 119:75).

Fourth, the Christian is to "endure" chastisement *patiently*. Probably that is the prime thought in our text: steadfastness, a resolute continuance in the path of duty, an abiding service of God with all our hearts, notwithstanding the present trial, is what we are called unto. But Satan whispers, "What is the use? you *have* endeavoured, earnestly, to please the Lord, and how is He rewarding you? You cannot satisfy Him: the more you give, the more He demands; He is a hard and tyrannical Master." Such vile suggestions must be put from us as the malicious lies of him who hates God and seeks to encompass our destruction. God has only your good in view when the rod is laid upon you. Just as the grass needs to be mown to preserve its freshness, as the vine has to be pruned to ensure its fruitfulness, as friction is necessary to produce electric power, as fire alone will consume the dross, even so the discipline of trial is indispensable for the education of the Christian.

"Let us not be weary in well doing: for in due season we shall reap, if we faint not" (Gal. 6:9). Keep before you the example of Christ: He was led as a lamb to the slaughter, yet before His shearers He was "dumb." He never fretted or murmured, and we are to "follow His steps." "Let patience have her perfect work" (James 1:4). For this we have to be much in prayer; for this we need the strengthening help of the Holy Spirit. God tells us that chastisement is not "joyous" but "grievous": if it were not, it would not be "chastening." But He also assures us that "*afterwards* it yieldeth the peaceable fruit of righteousness unto them which are exercised thereby" (Heb. 12:11). Lay hold of that word "afterward": anticipate the happy sequel, and in the comfort thereof continue pressing forward along the path of duty. "Better is *the end* of a thing than the beginning thereof: and the patient in spirit is better than the proud in spirit" (Eccl. 7:8).

Fifth, the Christian is to "endure" chastisement *believingly*. This was how Job endured his: "The Lord gave, and the Lord hath taken away; blessed be the name of the Lord" (1:21). Ah, he looked behind all secondary causes, and perceived that above the Sabeans and Chaldeans was Jehovah Himself. But is it not at *this* point we most often fail? Only too frequently we see only the injustice of men, the malice of the world, the enmity of Satan, in our trials: that is walking by sight. Faith brings God into the scene. "I had fainted, unless I had believed to see the goodness of the Lord in the land of the living" (Psa. 27:13). It is an adage of the world that

"Seeing is believing:" but in the spiritual realm, the order is reversed: there we must "believe" in order to "see." And *what is it* which the saint most desires *to* "see"? Why, "the goodness of the Lord," for unless he sees *that,* he "faints." And *how* does faith see "the goodness of the Lord" in chastisements? By viewing them as proceeding from God's love, as ordered by His wisdom, and as designed for our profit.

As the bee sucks honey out of the bitter herb, so faith may extract much good from afflictions. Faith can turn water into wine, and make bread out of stones. Unbelief gives up in the hour of trial and sinks in despair; but faith keeps the head above water and hopefully looks for deliverance. Human reason may not be able to understand the mysterious ways of God, but faith knows that the sorest disappointments and the heaviest losses are among the "all things" which work together for our good. Carnal friends may tell us that it is useless to strive any longer; but faith says, "Though He slay me, yet will I trust in Him" (Job 13:15). What a wonderful promise is that in Psa. 91:15, "I will be with him in trouble: I will deliver him." Ah, but faith alone can feel that Presence, and faith alone can enjoy now the assured deliverance. It was because of the joy set before Him (by the exercise of faith) that Christ "endured the cross," and only as we view God's precious promises will *we* patiently endure *our* cross.

Sixth, the Christian is to "endure" chastisement *hopefully.* Though quite distinct, the line of demarcation between faith and hope is not a very broad one, and in some of the things said above we have rather anticipated what belongs to this particular point. "For we are saved by hope: but hope that is seen is not hope: for what a man *seeth,* why doth he yet *hope for?* But if we hope for that we see not, then do we with patience wait for it" (Rom. 8:24, 25). This passage clearly intimates that "hope" relates to *the future.* "Hope" in Scripture is far more than a warrantless wish: it is a firm conviction and a comforting expectation of a future good. Now inasmuch as chastisement, patiently and believingly endured, is certain to issue in blessing, hope is to be exercised. "When He hath tried me, I shall come forth as gold" (Job 23:10): that is the language of confident expectation.

While it be true that faith supports the heart under trial, it is equally a fact—though less recognized—that *hope* buoys it up. When the wings of hope are spread, the soul is able to soar above the present distress, and inhale the invigorating air of future bliss. "For our light affliction which is but for a moment, worketh for us a far more exceeding and eternal weight of glory: *while* we look not at the things which are seen, but at the things which are unseen" (2 Cor. 4:17, 18): that also is the language of joyous anticipation. No matter how dark may the clouds which now cover thy horizon, ere long the Sun of righteousness shall arise with healing in His wings. Then seek to walk in the steps of our father Abraham, "who against hope, believed in hope, that he might become the father of many nations" (Rom. 4:18).

Seventh, the Christian is to "endure" chastisement *thankfully.* Be grateful, my despondent brother, that the great God cares so much for a worm of the earth as to be at such pains in your spiritual education. O what a marvel that the Maker of heaven and earth should go to so much trouble in His son-training of us! Fail not, then, to thank Him for His goodness, His faithfulness, His patience, toward thee. "We are chastened of the Lord (now) that we should not be condemned with the world" in the day to come (1 Cor. 11:32): what cause for praise is this! If the Lord Jesus, on the awful night of His betrayal, "sang a hymn" (Matt. 26:30), how much more should we, under our infinitely lighter sorrows, sound forth the praises of our God. May Divine grace enable both writer and reader to "endure chastening" in this sevenfold spirit, and then will God be glorified and we advantaged.

"If ye endure chastening, God dealeth with you as with sons." This does not mean that upon our discharge of the duty enjoined God will act toward us "as with sons"; for this He does in the chastisements themselves, as the apostle has clearly shown. No, rather, the force of these words is, If ye *endure* chastening, then you have the evidence in yourselves that God deals with you as sons. In other words, the more I am enabled to conduct myself under troubles as becometh a child of God, the clearer is the proof of my Divine adoption. The new birth is known by its fruits, and the more my spiritual graces are exercised under testing, the more do I make manifest my regeneration. Furthermore, the clearer the evidence of my regeneration, the clearer do I perceive the dealings of *a Father* toward me in His discipline.

The patient endurance of chastenings is not only of great price in the sight of God, but is of inestimable value unto the souls of them that believe. While it be true that the sevenfold description we have given above depicts not the spirit in which all Christians *do* receive chastening, but rather the spirit in which they *ought to* receive it, and that all coming short thereof is to be mourned and confessed before God; nevertheless, it remains that no truly born-again person continues to either utterly "despise" the rod or completely "faint" beneath it. No, herein lies a fundamental difference between the good-ground hearer and the stony-ground one: of the former it is written, "The righteous also shall hold on his way" (Job. 17:9); of the latter, it is recorded, "Yet hath he not root in himself, but dureth for a while: for when tribulation or persecution ariseth because of the Word, immediately he is offended" (Matt. 13:21).

A mere suffering of things calamitous is not, in itself, any evidence of our acceptance with God. Man is born unto trouble as the sparks fly upwards, so that afflictions or chastisements are no pledges of our adoption; but if we "endure" them with any measure of real faith, submission and perseverance, so that we "faint not" under them—abandon not the Faith or entirely cease seeking to serve the Lord—then do we demonstrate our Divine sonship. So too it is the proper frame of our minds and the due exercise of our hearts which lets in a sense of God's gracious design toward us in His chastenings. The Greek word for "dealeth with us as with sons" is very blessed: literally it signifies "he *offereth Himself* unto us:" He proposeth Himself not as an enemy, but as a Friend; not as toward strangers, but as toward His own beloved children.

"But if ye be without chastisement, whereof all are partakers, then are ye bastards, and not sons" (v. 8). These words present the reverse side of the argument established in the preceding verse: since it be true, both in the natural and in the spiritual realm, that disciplinary dealing is inseparable from the relation between fathers and sons, so that an evidence of adoption is to be clearly inferred therefrom, it necessarily follows that those who are "without chastisement" are not children at all. What we have here is a testing and discriminative rule, which it behoves each of us to measure himself by. That we may not err therein, let us attend to its several terms.

When the apostle says, "But if ye be without chastisement, whereof all are partakers," it is obvious that his words are not to be taken in their widest latitude: the word "all" refers not to all men, but to the "sons" of whom he is speaking. In like manner, "chastisement" is not here to be taken for everything that is grievous and afflictive, for none entirely escape trouble in this life. But *comparatively* speaking, there are those who are largely exempt: such the Psalmist referred to when he said, "For there are no bands in *their* death: but their strength is firm. *They* are not in trouble as other men; neither are they plagued like other men" (Psa. 73:4, 5). No, it is God's *disciplinary* dealings which the apostle is speaking of, corrective instruction which promotes holiness. There are many professors who, whatever trials they may experience, are without any Divine *chastisement* for their good.

Those who are "without chastisement" are but "bastards." It is common knowledge that bastards are despised and neglected—though unjustly so—by those who illegitimately begot them: they are not the objects of that love and care as those begotten in wedlock. This solemn fact has its counterpart in the religious realm.

There is a large class who are destitute of Divine chastisements, for they give no evidence that they receive them, endure them, or improve them. There is a yet more solemn meaning in this word: under the law "bastards" *had no right of inheritance*: "A bastard shall not enter into the congregation of the Lord" (Deut.23:2): No cross, no crown: to be without God's disciplinary chastenings now, means that we must be excluded from His presence hereafter. Here, then, is a further reason why the Christian should be contented with his present lot: the Father's rod upon him now evidences his title unto the Inheritance in the day to come.

CHAPTER NINETY

Divine Chastisement

(Heb. 12:9)

The apostle Paul did not, like so many of our moderns, hurry through a subject and dismiss an unpleasant theme with a brief sentence or two. No, he could say truthfully, "I kept back *nothing* that was profitable unto you." His chief concern was not to please, but to *help* his hearers and readers. Well did he know the tendency of the heart to turn away quickly from what is searching and humbling, unto that which is more attractive and consoling. But so far from acceding to this spirit, he devoted as much attention unto exhortation as instruction, unto reproving as comforting, unto duties as expounding promises; while the latter was given its due place the former was not neglected. It behooves each servant of God to study the methods of the apostles, and seek wisdom and grace to emulate their practice; only thus will they preserve the balance of Truth, and be delivered from "handling the Word deceitfully" (2 Cor. 4:2).

Some years ago, when the editor was preaching a series of sermons on Heb. 12:3-11, several members of the congregation intimated they were growing weary of hearing so much upon the subject of Divine chastisement. Alas, the very ones who chafed so much at hearing about God's rod, have since been smitten the most severely by it. Should any of our present readers feel the same way about the writer's treatment of this same passage, he would lovingly warn them that, though these articles may seem gloomy and irksome while prosperity be smiling upon them, nevertheless they will be well advised to "hearken and hear *for the time to come*" (Isa. 42:23). The sun will not always be shining upon you, dear reader, and if you now store these thoughts up in your memory, they may stand you in good stead when your sky becomes overcast.

Sooner or later, this portion of Holy Writ *will apply* very pertinently unto each of our cases. God "scourgeth *every* son whom He receiveth." None of the followers of "The Man of sorrows" are exempted from sorrow. It has been truly said that "God had one

Son without sin, but none without suffering." So much depends upon *how* we "endure" suffering: the spirit in which it be received, the graces which are exercised by it, and the improvement which we make of it. Our attitude toward God, and the response which we make unto His disciplinary dealings with us, means that we shall either honour or dishonour Him, and suffer loss or reap gain therefrom. Manifold are our obligations to comport ourselves becomingly when God is pleased to scourge us, and many and varied are the motives and arguments which the Spirit, through the apostle, here presents to us for this end.

In the verse which is now to be before us a further reason is given showing the need of the Christian's duty to meekly bear God's chastenings. First, the apostle had reminded the saints of the teaching of Scripture, v. 5: how significant that he began with that! Second, he had comforted them with the assurance that the rod is wielded not by wrath, but in tender solicitude, v. 6. Third, he affirmed that God chastens all His children without exception, bastards only escaping, vv. 7, 8. Now he reminds us that we had natural parents who corrected us, and we gave them reverence. Our earthly fathers had the right, because of their relationship, to discipline us, and we acquiesced. If, then, it was right and meet for us to submit to their corrections, how much more ought we to be in subjection unto our heavenly Father when He reproves us.

"Furthermore, we have had fathers of our flesh, which corrected us, and we gave them reverence: shall we not much rather be in subjection unto the Father of spirits, and live?" (v. 9). The opening "Furthermore" is really humbling and searching. One would think sufficient had been said in the previous verses to make us be submissive under and thankful for the tender discipline of our God. Is it not enough to be told that the Scriptures teach us to expect chastisements, and exhort us not to despise them? Is it not sufficient to be assured that these chastisements proceed from the very heart of our Father, being appointed and regulated by His love? No, a "furthermore" is needed by us! The Holy Spirit deigns to supply further reasons for bringing our unruly hearts into subjection. This should indeed humble us, for the implication is clear that we are *slow* to heed and bow beneath the rod. Yea, is it not sadly true that the older we become, the more need there is for our being chastened?

The writer has been impressed by the fact, both in his study of the Word and his observation of fellow-Christians, that, as a general rule, God uses the rod very little and very lightly upon the babes and younger members of His family, but that He employs it more frequently and severely on mature Christians. We have often heard older saints warning younger brethren and sisters of *their* great danger, yet it is striking to observe that Scripture records not a single instance of a young saint disgracing his profession. Recall the histories of young Joseph, the Hebrew maid in Naaman's household, David as a stripling engaging Goliath, Daniel's early days, and his three youthful companions in the furnace; and it will be found that all of them quitted themselves nobly. On the other hand, there are numerous examples where men in middle life and of grey hairs grievously dishonoured their Lord.

It is true that young Christians *are* feeblest, and with rare exceptions, they *know* it; and therefore does God manifest His grace and power by upholding them: it is the "lambs" which He carries in His arms! But some older Christians seem far less conscious of their danger, and so God often suffers them to have a fall, that He may stain the pride of their self-glory, and that others may see it is *nothing* in the flesh—standing, rank, age, or attainments— which insures our safety; but that *He* upholds the humble and casts down the proud. David did not fall into his great sin till he had reached the prime of life. Lot did not transgress most grossly till he was an old man. Isaac seems to have become a glutton in his old age, and was as a vessel no longer "meet for the Master's use," which rusted out rather than wore out. It was after a life of walking with God, and building the ark, that Noah disgraced himself. The worst sin of Moses was committed not at the beginning but at the end of the wilderness journey. Hezekiah became puffed up with pride near the sunset of his life. What warnings are these!

God thus shows us there is no protection in years. Yea, added years seem to call for increased chastenings. Often there is more grumbling and complaining among the aged pilgrims than the younger ones: it is true their nerves can stand less, but God's grace is sufficient for worn-out nerves. Often there is more occupation with self and circumstances among the fathers and mothers in Israel, and less talking of Christ and His wondrous love, than there is among the babes. Yes, there is much need for all of us to heed the opening "furthermore" of our text. Every physician will tell us there are some diseases which become more troublesome in middle life, and others which are incident to old age. The same is true of different forms of sinning. If we are more liable to certain sins in our youth, we are in greater danger of others in advanced years. Undoubtedly it is the case that the older we get, the more need there is to heed this "furthermore" which prefaces the call of our being in subjection to the Father of spirits. If we do not need more grace, certain it is that we need as much grace, when we are grown old as while we are growing up.

The aged meet with as many temptations as do young Christians. They are tempted to live in the past, rather than in the future.

They are tempted to take things easier, spiritually as well as temporally, so that it has to be said of some "ye *did* run well." O to be like Paul "the aged," who was in full harness to the end. They are tempted to be unduly occupied with their increasing infirmities; but is it not written "the Spirit also *helpeth* our infirmities"! Yet, because this is affirmed, we must not think there is no longer need to earnestly *seek* His help. This comforting word is given in order that we *should* frequently and confidently pray for this very thing. If it were not recorded, we might doubt His readiness to do so, and wonder if we were asking "according to His will." Because *it is* recorded, when feeling our "infirmities" press most heavily upon us, let us cry, "O Holy Spirit of God, do as Thou hast said, and help us."

In this connection let us remind ourselves of that verse, "Who satisfieth thy mouth with good things: so that thy youth is renewed *like the eagle's*" (Psa. 103:5) The eagle is a bird renowned for its *longevity,* often living to be more than a hundred years old. The eagle is also the high-soaring bird, building its nest on the mountain summit. But *how* is the eagle's youth *renewed?* By a new crop of feathers, by the rejuvenation of its wings. And that is precisely what some middle-aged and elderly Christians need: the rejuvenation of their spiritual wings—the wings of faith, of hope, of zeal, of love for souls, of devotedness to Christ. So many leave their first love, lose the joy of their espousals, and instead of setting before younger Christians a bright example of trustfulness and cheerfulness, they often discourage by gloominess and slothfulness. Thus God's chastenings increase in severity and frequency!

Dear friend, instead of saying, "The days of my usefulness are over," rather reason, The night cometh when no man can work; therefore I must make the most of my opportunities while it is yet called day. For your encouragement let it be stated that the most active worker in a church of which the editor was pastor was seventy-seven years old when he went there, and during his stay of three and a half years she did more for the Lord, and was a greater stimulus to him, than any other member of that church. She lived another eight years, and they were, to the very end, filled with devoted service to Christ. We believe that the Lord will yet say of her, as of another woman, "She hath done what she could." O brethren and sisters, especially you who are feeling the weight of years, heed that word, "Be not weary in well doing, for in due season, we shall reap, if we faint not" (Gal. 6:9).

"Furthermore, we have had fathers of our flesh which corrected us and we gave them reverence." It is the duty of children to give the reverence of obedience unto the just commands of their parents, and the reverence of submission to their correction when disobedient. As parents have a charge from God to minister correction to their children when it is due—and not spoil them unto their ruin—so children have a command from God to receive parental reproof in a proper spirit, and not to be discontented, stubborn, or rebellious. For a child to be insubordinate under correction, evidences a double fault; the very correction shows a fault has been committed, and insubordination under correction is only adding wrong to wrong. "We gave them reverence," records the attitude of dutiful children toward their sires: they neither ran away from home in a huff, nor became so discouraged as to quit the path of duty.

From this law of the human home, the apostle points out the humble and submissive conduct which is due unto God when He disciplines His children: "Shall we not much rather be in subjection unto the Father of spirits?" The "much rather" points a contrast suggested by the analogy: that contrast is at least fourfold. First, the former chastening proceeded from those who were our fathers according to the flesh; the other is given by Him who is our heavenly Father. Second, the one was sometimes administered in imperfect knowledge and irritable temper; the other comes from unerring wisdom and untiring love. Third, the one was during but a brief period, when we were children; the other continues throughout the whole of our Christian life. Fourth, the one was designed for our temporal good; the other has in view our spiritual and eternal welfare. Then how much more should we readily submit unto the latter.

"Shall we not much rather be in subjection unto the Father of spirits?" By nature we are not in subjection. We are born into this world filled with the spirit of insubordination: as the descendants of our rebellious first parents, we inherit their evil nature. "Man is born like a wild ass's colt" (Job 11:12). This is very unpalatable and humbling, but nevertheless it is true. As Isa. 53:6 tells us, "we have turned every one to *his own* way," and *that* is one of opposition to the revealed will of God. Even at conversion this wild and rebellious nature is not eradicated. A new nature is given, but the old one lusts against it. It is because of this that discipline and chastisement are needed by us, and the great design of these is to bring us into subjection unto the Father of spirits. To be "in subjection unto the father" is a phrase of extensive import, and it is well that we should understand its various significations.

1. *It denotes an acquiescence in God's sovereign right to do with us as He pleases.* "I was dumb, I opened not my mouth: because thou didst it" (Psa 39:9). It is the duty of saints to be mute under the rod and silent beneath the sharpest afflictions. But this is only possible as we see the hand *of God* in them. If His hand be not seen in the trial, the heart will do nothing but fret and fume. "And

the king said, What have I to do with you, ye sons of Zeruiah? so let him curse, because the Lord hath said unto him, Curse David. Who shall then say, *Wherefore* hast thou done *so?* And David said to Abishai, and to all his servants, Behold, my son, which came forth of my bowels, seeketh my life: How much more now may this Benjamite do it? let him alone, and let him curse, for *the Lord* hath bidden him" (2 Sam. 16:10, 11). What an example of complete submission to the sovereign will of the Most High was this! David knew that Shimei could not curse him without God's permission.

"This will set my heart at rest,
What my God appoints is best."

But with rare exceptions many chastenings are needed to bring us to this place, and to keep us there.

2. *It implies a renunciation of self-will.* To be in subjection unto the Father presupposes a surrendering and resigning of ourselves to Him. A blessed illustration of this is found in Lev. 10:1-3, "And Nadab and Abihu, the sons of Aaron, took either of them his censer, and put fire therein, and put incense thereon, and offered strange fire before the Lord, which He commanded them not. And there went out fire from the Lord, and devoured them, and they died before the Lord. Then Moses said unto Aaron, This is it that the Lord spake, saying, I will be sanctified in them that come nigh Me, and before all the people I will be glorified. And Aaron *held his peace.*" Consider the circumstances. Aaron's two sons, most probably intoxicated at the time, were suddenly cut off by Divine judgment. Their father had no warning to prepare him for this trial; yet he "held his peace!" O quarrel not against Jehovah: be clay in the hands of the Potter: take Christ's yoke upon you, and learn of Him who was "meek and lowly in heart."

3. *It signifies an acknowledgment of God's righteousness and wisdom in all His dealings with us.* We must vindicate God. This is what the Psalmist did: "I know, O Lord, that Thy judgments are *right,* and that Thou *in faithfulness* hast afflicted me" (119:75). Let us see to it that Wisdom is ever justified by her children: let our confession of her be, "Righteous art Thou, O Lord, and upright are Thy judgments" (Psa. 119:137). Whatever be sent, we must vindicate the Sender of all things: the Judge of all the earth cannot do wrong. Stifle, then, the rebellious murmur, What have I done to deserve such treatment by God? and say with the Psalmist, "He hath not dealt with us after our sins, nor rewarded us according to our iniquities" (103:10). Why, my reader, if God dealt with us only according to the strict rule of His justice, we had

been in Hell long ago: "If Thou, Lord, shouldest mark ("impute") iniquities, O Lord, who shall stand?" (Psa. 130:3).

The Babylonian captivity was the severest affliction which God ever brought upon His earthly people during O. T. times, yet even then a renewed heart acknowledged God's righteousness in it: "Now therefore, our God, the great, the mighty and the terrible God, who keepest covenant and mercy, let not all the trouble seem little before Thee, that hath come upon us, on our kings, on our princes, and our priests, and on our prophets, and on our fathers, and on all Thy people, since the time of the kings of Assyria unto this day. *Howbeit* Thou art *just* in all that is brought upon us: for Thou hast done *right,* but we have done wickedly" (Neh. 9:32, 33). God's enemies may talk of His injustice; but let His children proclaim His righteousness. Because God is good, He can do nothing but what is right and good.

4. *It includes a recognition of His care and a sense of His love.* There is a sulking submission, and there is a cheerful submission. There is a fatalistic submission which takes this attitude—this is inevitable, so I must bow to it; and there is a thankful submission, receiving with gratitude whatever God may be pleased to send us. "It is *good* for me that I have been afflicted; that I might learn Thy statutes" (Psa. 119:71). The Psalmist viewed his chastisements with the eye of faith, and doing so he perceived the love behind them. Remember that when God brings His people into the wilderness it is that they may learn more of His sufficiency, and that when He casts them into the furnace, it is that they may enjoy more of His presence.

5. *It involves an active performance of His will.* True submission unto the "Father of spirits" is something more than a passive thing. The other meanings of this expression which we have considered above are more or less of a negative character, but there is a positive and active side to it as well, and it is important that this should be recognized by us. To be "in subjection" to God also means that we are to walk in His precepts and run in the way of His commandments. Negatively, we are not to be murmuring rebels; positively, we are to be obedient children. We are required to be submissive unto God's Word, so that our thoughts are formed and our ways regulated by it. There is not only a suffering of God's will, but a *doing* of it—an actual performance of duty. When we utter that petition in the prayer which the Saviour has given us, "Thy will be done," something more is meant than a pious acquiescence unto the pleasure of the Almighty: it also signifies, may Thy will be *performed* by me. Subjection "unto the Father of spirits," then, is the practical owning of His Lordship.

Two reasons for such subjection are suggested in our text. First, *because the One with whom we have to do is our Father.* O how profoundly thankful we should be that the Lord God stands revealed to us as the "Father"—our Father, because the Father of our Lord and Saviour Jesus Christ, and *He* rendered perfect obedience unto Him. It is but right and meet that children should honour their parents by being in complete subjection to them: not to do so is to ignore their relationship, despise their authority, and slight their love. How much more ought we to be in subjection unto our heavenly Father: there is nothing tyrannical about Him: His commandments are not grievous: He has only our good at heart. "Behold, what manner of love the Father hath bestowed upon us, that we should be called the sons of God" (1 John 3:1), then let us earnestly endeavour to express our gratitude by dutifully walking before Him as obedient children, and no matter how mysterious may be His dealings with us, say with the Saviour, "The cup which My Father hath given Me, shall I not drink it?" (John 18:11).

The particular title of God found in our text calls for a brief comment. It is placed in antithesis from "fathers of our flesh," which has reference to their begetting of our bodies. True, our bodies also are a real creation on the part of God, yet in connection therewith He is pleased to use human instrumentalities. But in connection with the immaterial part of our beings, God is the immediate and alone Creator of them. As the renowned Owen said, "The soul is immediately created and infused; having no other father but God Himself," and rightly did that eminent theologian add, "This is the fundamental reason of our perfect subjection unto God in all afflictions, namely, that our very souls are His, the immediate product of His Divine power, and under his rule alone. May He not do as He wills with His own?" The expression "Father of spirits," refutes, then, the error of traducianists, who suppose that the soul, equally with the body, is transmitted by our parents. In Num. 16:22 He is called "the God of the spirits of all flesh" which refers to all men naturally; while the "Father of spirits" in our text includes the new nature in the regenerate.

The second reason for our subjection to the Father is, *because this is the secret of true happiness,* which is pointed out in the final words of our text "and live." The first meaning of those words is, "and be happy." This is clear from Deut. 5:33, "Ye shall walk in all the ways which the Lord your God hath commanded you, that ye may *live,* and that it may be well with you, and that ye may prolong your days in the land which ye shall possess:" observe the words "prolong your days" are added to "that ye may live," which obviously signifies "that ye may be happy"—compare Ex. 10:17, where Pharaoh called the miseries of the plagues "this death." Life ceases to be *life* when we are wretched. It is the making of God's will our haven, which secures the true resting-place for the heart. The rebellious are fretful and miserable, but "great peace have they which love Thy law and nothing shall offend them" (Psa. 119:165). "Take My yoke upon you," said Christ, "and ye shall find rest unto your souls." Alas, the majority of professing Christians are so little in subjection to God, they have just enough religion to make them miserable.

"Shall we not much rather be in subjection unto the Father of spirits *and live?*" No doubt words of this verse point these to a designed contrast from Deut. 21:18-21, "If a man have a stubborn and rebellious son, which will not obey the voice of his father, or the voice of his mother, and that, when they have chastened him, will not hearken unto them: Then shall his father and his mother lay hold on him, and bring him out unto the elders of his city, and unto the gate of his place.... And all the men of his city shall stone him with stones, *that he die.*" "The increase of spiritual life in this world, and eternal life in the world to come, is that whereunto they (the words "and live") tend" (J. Owen).

CHAPTER NINETY-ONE

Divine Chastisement

(Heb. 12:10)

Would any Christian in his right mind dare to pray, Let me not be afflicted, no matter what good it should do me? And if he were unwilling and afraid to pray thus, why should he murmur when it so falls out? Alas, what a wide breach there is, usually, between our praying and the rest of our conduct. Again; if our rescuer dislocated our shoulder when pulling us out of the water in which we were drowning, would we be angry with him? Of course not. Then why fret against the Lord when He afflicts the body in order to better the soul? If God takes away outward comforts and fills us with inward peace, if he removes our wordly wealth but imparts to us more of the true riches, then, instead of having ground for complaint, we have an abundant cause for thanksgiving and praise. Then why should I fear to enter the dark shaft of tribulation if persuaded that it leads to the gold mines of spiritual experience.

In Scripture, afflictions are compared to fire that purges away the dross (1 Pet. 1:7), to the fan which drives away the chaff (Matt. 3:12), to a pruning-hook which cuts off superfluous branches and makes more fruitful the others that remain (John 15:2), to physic that purges away poisonous matter (Isa. 27:9), to plowing and harrowing the ground that it may be prepared to receive good seed (Jer. 4:3). Then why should we be so upset when God is pleased to use the fire upon us in order to remove our dross, to employ the fan so as to winnow away the chaff, to take the pruning-hook to lop off the superfluities of our souls, to give us physic to purge out our corruptions and filth, to drive the plow into us so as to break up our fallow ground and to destroy the weeds which grow in our souls? Should we not rather rejoice that He will not leave us alone in our carnality, but rather fit us to become partakers of His holiness?

A little child requires much coaxing (at times, something more!) in order to make him take his medicine. He may be very ill, and mother may earnestly assure him that the unpleasant potion will bring sure relief; but the little one cries out, "I cannot take it, it is so nasty." But adults, generally, need not have the doctor argue and plead with them: they will swallow the bitterest remedy if convinced that it will do them good. The application of this to spiritual matters is obvious. Those Christians who are but spiritual babes, fret and fume when called upon to endure Divine chastisement, knowing not the gains they will receive if it be accepted in the right spirit. But those who have grown in grace, and become *men* in Christ, who know that all things work together for good to them that love God, and who have learned by experience the precious fruits which issue from sanctified afflictions, accept from God the bitterest cup, and thank Him for it.

But alas, many of God's people are but infants experimentally, and need much coaxing to reconcile them to the cup of trial. Therefore is it needful to present to our consideration one argument after another. Such is the case here in Heb. 12: if one line of reasoning does not suffice, perhaps another will. The Christian is very sceptical and takes much convincing. We have heard a person say to one who claims he has done, or can do, some remarkable thing, "You must *show me* before I will believe you." Most of us are very much like that in connection with spiritual things. Though the Scriptures assure us, again and again, that chastisement proceeds from our Father's love, and is designed for our good, yet we are slow, very slow, to really believe it. Therefore does the apostle here proceed from one consideration to another so as to assure the hearts and establish the faith of his afflicted brethren upon this important subject.

O that our hearts might be so taught by the Spirit, our understandings so enlightened, our faith so strengthened by Him, that we would be more grateful and increasingly thankful for the merciful discipline of our Father. What a proof of His love is this, that in His chastening of us, His object is to bring us nearer Himself and make us more like His blessed Son. The more highly we prize health, the more willing are we to take that which would cure our sickness; and the more we value holiness (which is the health of our souls) the gladder shall we be for that which is a means to increase the same in us. We are on a low plane of spiritual experience, if we do nothing more than simply "bow" to God's hand. Scripture says, "Giving *thanks* always, for *all* things unto God and the Father in the name of our Lord Jesus Christ" (Eph. 5:20); and again it exhorts us "Rejoice in the Lord alway" (Phil. 4:4). We are to "glory in tribulation" (Rom. 5:3), and *we shall* when we perceive more clearly and fully what blessed fruits are brought forth under the pruning knife.

"For they verily for a few days chastened us after their own pleasure; but He for our profit, that we might be partakers of His holiness" (v. 10). This is a continuation of what was before us in the previous verse. A further reason is given why Christians should be "in subjection unto" their heavenly Father, when His correcting rod is laid upon them. Not only is it becoming for them so to do, because of the relationship which exists between them: but it is also meet they should act thus, because of the gains they receive thereby. The consideration which the apostle now presents to the attention of the afflicted saints is really a double one. First, the chastisement we received from our earthly parents had reference mainly to our good in this life, whereas the disciplinary dealings of our heavenly Father looks forward to the life to come (2 Cor. 4:17). Second, the chastisement of our earthly parents was often a matter of their caprice and sometimes issued from irritability of temper, but the rod of our heavenly Father is wielded by infinite goodness and wisdom, and has in view our well being.

We regard the words "for they verily *for a few days* chastened us" as referring not so much to the brief season of our childhood, but more to the fact that our parents had only our *temporal* interests in view: whereas God has our *eternal* welfare before Him. "The apostle seems to bring in this circumstance to contrast the dealings of earthly parents with those of God. One of the circumstances is, that the corrections of earthly parents had a much less important object than those of God. They related to this life — a life so brief that it may be said to continue but a "few days." Yet, in order to secure the benefit to be derived for so short a period from fatherly correction, we submitted without murmuring. Much more cheerfully ought we to submit to that discipline from the hand of our heavenly Father which is designed to extend its benefits through eternity" (A. Barnes).

The added words "after their own pleasure" or "as seemed good" to them, points another contrast between the disciplinary dealings of our earthly parents and those of our heavenly Father. In their infirmity, sometimes the rod was used upon us in a fit of anger, rather than from a loving desire to reform our manners. "Meaning that it was sometimes done arbitrarily, or under the influence of passion. This is an additional reason why we should submit to God. We submitted to our earthly parents, though their correction was sometimes passionate, and was designed to gratify their own pleasure rather than to promote our good. There is much of this kind of punishment in families; but there in none of it under the administration of God. *'But He for our profit:'* never from passion, from caprice, from the love of power or superiority, but always for our good" (A. Barnes).

Now the particular contribution which our present verse makes to the subject of chastisement is, the apostle here makes known the general end or design of God in the same, namely "our profit." And let it be pointed out that whatsoever He purposes must surely come to pass, for He will make the means He employs effectual unto the accomplishment of His end. Many are the blessings comprehended and various are the fruits produced through and by means of Divine chastisement. This word "for our profit" is a very embracing one, including the development of our characters, the enrichment of our spiritual lives, a closer conformity to the image of Christ. The same truth is found again in the "that we might be partakers of His holiness:" that our lusts might be mortified, our graces vivified, our souls sanctified. Whatever be the form, degree, or duration of our afflictions, all is ordered by infinite wisdom so as to secure this object. But to particularize: the benefits of Divine chastisement —

1. *It weans us from the world.* One of the greatest surprises of the writer's Christian life in connection with his fellow-saints has been, not their ignorance, nor even their inconsistencies, but their *earthliness,* their reluctance to leave this world. As "strangers and pilgrims" we should be longing and yearning for our Heavenly Home; as those who are away from Him whom they love best, we should desire to *"depart* and be with Him" (Phil. 1:23). Paul did. Christ has promised to return for His people, yet how few of them are daily crying, "Even so, come, Lord Jesus." How rarely we hear them saying, in the language of the mother of Sisera, "Why is His chariot so long in coming? why tarry the wheels of His chariot?"

"And all the trials here we see
Should make us long to be with Thee."

Scripture speaks of this world as a "dry and thirsty land, where no water is" (Psa. 63:1), and God intends for us to *prove* this in our experiences. His Word also affirms that this world is a "dark place" (2 Pet. 1:19), and He means for us to discover that this *is* so.

One would think that after the soul had once seen the King in His beauty, it would henceforth discover no attractions elsewhere. One would suppose that once we had quenched our thirst at the Fountain of living waters, we would no more want to drink from the unsatisfying and polluted cisterns of this world. Surely now that we have experienced a taste and foretaste of Heaven itself, we shall be repelled and nauseated by the poor husks this world has to offer. But alas! the "old man" is still in us, unchanged; and though Divine grace subdues his activities, still he is very much alive. It is because of this that we are called on to "crucify the flesh with its affections and lusts." And this is not only an unpalatable, but a very hard task. Therefore does God in His mercy help us: help us by chastenings, which serve to loosen the roots of our souls downward and tighten the anchor-hold of our hearts Heavenward.

This God does in various ways. Sometimes He causes us to lose our confidence in and draw us away from fellowship with worldings by receiving cruel treatment at their hands. "Come out from among them, and be ye separate" is the Lord's word to His people. But they are slow to heed; oftentimes they must be *driven out*. So with worldly pleasures: God often makes the grapes of earthly joys bitter to our taste, so that we should no longer seek after them. It is earthly disappointments and worldly disillusionments which make us sigh for our Heavenly Home. While the Hebrews enjoyed the land of Goshen they were content: hard and cruel bondage was needed to make them ready to leave for the promised land. We were once familiar with a Christian who had formed a habit of meeting each worldly difficulty or trial to the flesh by saying, "This is only another nail in my coffin." But that is a very gloomy way of viewing things: rather should the children of God say after each trial or affliction, "That severs another strand in the rope which binds me to this world, and makes me long all the more for Heaven.

2. *It casts us back the more upon God.* By nature we are filled with a spirit of independency. The fallen sons of Adam are like wild asses' colts. Chastisement is designed to empty us of our self-sufficiency, to make us feel weakness and helplessness. If "in their affliction they will seek Me early" (Hos. 5:15), then surely afflictions are for our "profit." Trials and troubles often drive us to our knees; sickness and sorrow make us seek unto the Lord. It is very noticeable in the four Gospels how rarely men and women that were in health and strength sought out Christ; it was trouble and illness which brought them to the great Physician. A nobleman came to Christ—why? Because his son was at the point of death. Jairus sought out the Master—why? Because his little daughter was so low. The Canaanitish woman interviewed the Lord Jesus—why? On behalf of her tormented daughter. The sisters of Lazarus sent a message to the absent Saviour—why? Because their brother was sick.

Afflictions may be very bitter, but they are a fine tonic for the soul, and are a medicine which God often uses on us. Most vividly is this illustrated in Psa. 107—read carefully verses 11 to 28. Note that it is when men are "brought down," when they are "afflicted," when they are "at their wits' end" that they "*cry* unto the Lord in their trouble." Yes, it is "trouble" which makes us turn unto the Lord, not in a mechanical and formal way, but in deep earnestness. Remember that it is the "effectual *fervent* prayer of a righteous man that availeth much." When you observe that the fire in your room is getting dull, you do not always put on more coal, but simply *stir* with the poker; so God often uses the black poker of adversity in order that the flames of devotion may burn more brightly.

Ah, my brethren, all of us delight in being made to lie down in the "green pastures" and being led beside the "still waters;" yet it would not be for God's glory nor for our own highest good to luxuriate spiritually at all times. And why not? Because our hearts would soon be more occupied with the blessings rather than with the Blesser Himself. Oftentimes the sheep have to be brought into the dry and desolate wilderness, that they may be made more conscious of their dependency upon the Shepherd. May we not discern here one reason why some saints so quickly lose their assurance: they are occupied more with their graces or comfortable feelings than they are with the Giver of them. God is a jealous God, and will not tolerate idols in the hearts of His people. A sense of our acceptance in Christ is indeed a blessed thing, yet it becomes a hindrance if it be treasured more highly than the Saviour Himself.

3. *It makes the promises of God more precious to us.* Trouble often acts on us like a sharp knife which opens the truth of God to us and our hearts unto the truth. Experience unlocks passages which were otherwise closed. There is many a text in the Bible which no commentator can helpfully expound to a child of God: it must be interpreted by experience. Paul wrote his profoundest epistles while in prison; John was "in tribulation" on Patmos when he received the Revelation. If you go down into a deep well or mine in the daytime, you will then see the shining of stars which were not visible from the earth's surface; so God often brings us low in order that we may perceive the shining beauty of some of His comforting assurances. Note how Jacob, in Gen. 32, pleaded God's promises when he heard that Esau was approaching with four hundred men! The promises of resurrection mean far more unto Christians when some of their loved ones have been removed by death.

"When thou passest through the waters, I will be with thee; and through the rivers, they shall not overflow thee: when thou walkest through the fire, thou shalt not be burned" (Isa. 43:2) means far more to afflicted souls than it can to those who are not under the rod. So, too, the many "fear not" promises are most valued when our strength fails us and we are ready to sink under despair. As the late C. H. Spurgeon was wont to say, "There are some verses written, as it were, in a secret ink, which must be held before the fire of adversity before they become visible." There are many passages in Job, the Psalms, and the Lamentations of Jeremiah which do not appeal to one while the sun is shining; but which, in times of adversity, are like the welcome beams of the moon on a dark night. It was his painful thorn in the flesh which taught Paul the blessedness of that text, "My grace is sufficient for thee: for My strength is made perefct in weakness" (2 Cor. 12:9).

4. *It qualifies us to sympathize with others.* If we have never trod the vale of sorrow and affliction we are really unable to "weep with those that weep." There are some surgeons who would be more tender if they had suffered from broken bones themselves. If we have never known much trouble, we can be but poor comforters to others. Even of our Saviour it is written, "For in that He Himself hath suffered being tempted He is able to succour them that are tempted" (Heb. 2:18). Bunyan could never have written the book which he did, unless God had permitted the Devil to tempt and buffet him severely for so many years. How clearly is all this brought out in 2 Cor. 1:4: "Who comforteth us in all our tribulations, *that we* may be able to comfort them which are in any trouble, *by* the comfort wherewith we ourselves are comforted of God." Luther frequently said, "Three things make a good preacher: prayer, meditation, and *temptation.*"

5. *It demonstrates to us the blessedness and sufficiency of Divine grace.* "My grace is sufficient for thee, for My strength is make perfect in weakness" (2 Cor. 12:9). But in order to *prove* this, we have to be brought into the place of severe testing and trial, and made to feel our own incompetency and nothingness. Brethren, if you have prospered in business all your lives, and have always had an easy time financially, then it is probable you know very little about God's strength being perfected in your weakness. If you have been healthy all your lives and have never suffered much weakness and pain, then you are not likely to know much about the strength of God. If you have never been visited with trying situations which bring you to your wits' end, or by heart-rending bereavements, you may not have discovered much of the sufficiency of Divine grace. You have *read* about it in books, *or heard* others speak of it, but this is a very different thing from having an *experimental* acquaintance of it for yourself. It is much tribulation which brings out the sufficiency of God's strength to support under the severest trials, and demonstrates that His grace *can* sustain the heart under the heaviest losses.

It is in the stormiest weather that a captain gives most heed to the steering of his ship; so it is in seasons of stress and grief that Christians pay most attention to, "Let us therefore come boldly unto the Throne of Grace, that we may obtain mercy and find grace to help in time of need" (Heb. 4:16). If Israel had journeyed directly to Canaan, they would have missed the tender care of Jehovah in the wilderness. If Lazarus had not died, Martha and Mary would not have received such a demonstration of Christ as the Resurrection and the Life. And if *you,* my brother, my sister, had not been cast into the furnace of affliction, you would not have known the nearness and preciousness of His presence with you there. Yes, God intends us to *prove* the reality and sufficiency of His grace.

6. *It develops our spiritual graces.* This is clearly set forth in that familiar passage Rom. 5:3-5: "We glory in tribulations also: knowing that tribulation worketh patience; and patience, experience; and experience, hope; and hope maketh not ashamed." This "rejoicing" is not in tribulations considered in themselves, but because the Christian knows they are appointed by his Father, and because of their beneficial effects. Three of these effects or spiritual graces thus developed are here mentioned. First, tribulation worketh "patience." Patience never thrives except under buffetings and disappointments: it is not even called into exercise while things are going smoothly and pleasantly. Sanctified tribulations call into activity that strength and fortitude which is evidenced by a submissive endurance of suffering. The patience here referred to signifies deliverance from murmuring, refusing to take things into our own hands (which only causes additional trouble), a contented waiting for God's time of deliverance, and a persevering continuance in the path of duty.

Second, patience worketh experience, that is a *vital* experience of the reality of what we profess; a personal acquaintance with that which before we knew only theoretically; an experience of the sufficiency of Divine grace to support and sustain; an experience of God's faithfulness, that He *is* "a very present help in trouble"; an experience of the preciousness of Christ, such as the three Hebrews had in the furnace. The Greek word for "experience" also means "the obtaining of proof." The patient submission which tribulation works in the saint *proves* both to him and to his brethren the reality of his trust in God: it makes manifest the fact that the faith which he professes is genuine. Instead of his faith being overcome, it triumphs. The test of a ship is to weather the storm; so it is with faith. Real faith ever says, "Though He slay me, yet will I trust in Him." Third, experience worketh hope. This is a grace which anticipates the future. While circumstances are as we like them, our outlook is mainly confined to the present: but sorrows and trials make us long for the future bliss. "*As* an eagle stirreth up her nest . . . *so* the Lord led Israel" (Deut. 32:11, 12). God removes us from our comfortable resting places for the purpose of teaching us to use the wings of hope.

7. *It brings us into fellowship with the sufferings of Christ.* The cross is the symbol of Christian discipleship. Like the scars which the wounded soldier prizes above all other distinctions, so our sufferings are the proof of our oneness with Christ (Rom. 8:17). Not only so, they make us appreciate the more what He endured for us. While we have plenty, we cannot properly estimate or appreciate the poverty which our Saviour endured. While we enjoy a comfortable bed we cannot truly sympathize with Him who "had not where to lay His head." It is not till some familiar friend, on whom we counted, has basely betrayed our trust, that we can enter into something of what the Saviour suffered through the perfidy of Judas. It is only when some brother has denied you, that you begin to understand what Christ felt, when Peter denied Him. As we, in some small measure, obtain an experimental acquaintance with such trials, it makes Christ increasingly precious to us, and enables us to appreciate the more all that He went through on our behalf. In a coming day we are going to share His throne; now we are privileged to taste His cross.

If, then, trials and tribulations, under God, produce such delightful fruits, then *welcome* chastisements that are for "our profit." Let the rains of disappointment come if they water the plants of spiritual graces. Let the winds of adversity blow if they serve to root more securely in grace the trees of the Lord's planting. Let the sun of prosperity be eclipsed if this brings us into closer communion with the Light of life. Oh, brethren and sisters, however distasteful they are to the flesh, chastisements are not to be dreaded, but welcomed, for they are designed to make us "partakers of God's holiness."

CHAPTER NINETY-TWO

Divine Chastisement

(Heb. 12:11)

One reason, perhaps, why so little is written to-day upon Divine chastisement, and why it so rarely forms the theme of the pulpit, is because it suits not the false temper and sentiments of this superficial age. The great majority of the preachers are men-pleasers, and carefully do they trim their sails to the breezes of popular opinion. They are paid to speak "smooth things" and not those which will disturb, to soothe consciences rather than search them. That which is unpalatable, mournful, solemn, dread-inspiring, is sedulously avoided, and attractive, cheerful, and comforting subjects are substituted in their stead. Hence, not only is it now rare for the preacher to dwell upon the eternal punishment of the wicked and bid the unsaved flee from the wrath to come, but Christians hear very little about the Father's rod, and the groans it occasions, or the fruits it afterwards produces. Fifty years ago a faithful servant of God wrote:

"One of the platitudes of the present day is, that religion is not a gloomy, but a cheerful thing. Although it is easy to see what was meant by him who first opposed this assertion, either to morbid and self-assumed gloom, or to the ignorant representation of the world; yet as it is generally understood, nothing can be less true. Blessed are they that mourn. Woe unto you that laugh. Narrow is the way. If any man will serve Me, let him take up his cross, and follow Me. He that seeketh his life shall lose it. Although the Christian anoints his head and washes his face, he is always fasting; the will has been broken by God, by wounding or bereaving us in our most tender point; the flesh is being constantly crucified. We are not born to be happy either in this world or in our present condition, but the reverse—to be unhappy; nay, to try constantly to be dead to self and the world, that the spirit may possess God, and rejoice in Him.

"As there is a false and morbid asceticism, so there is also a false and pernicious tendency to cover a worldly and shallow method of life under the phrase of 'religion being joyous, and no enemy to cheerfulness.' To take a very simple and obvious instance. What is meant by a 'cheerful, pleasant Sunday?' No doubt men have erred on the side of strictness and legalism; but is a 'cheerful Sunday' one in which there is much communion with God in prayer and meditation on God's Word, much anticipation of the joys of Heaven in praise and fellowship with the brethren? Alas! too many understand by a cheerful Sunday a day in which the spiritual element is reduced to a minimum" (Adolph Saphir).

Alas, that conditions have become so much worse since then. The attractions of the world, and everything which is pleasing to the flesh, have been brought into thousands of "churches" (?) under the plea of being "necessary if the young people are to be held." Even in those places where the bars have not thus been let down, where the grosser forms of worldliness are not yet tolerated, the preaching is generally of such a character that few are likely to be made uneasy by it. He who dwells on the exceeding sinfulness of sin, who insists that God will not tolerate unjudged sin even in His own people, but will surely visit it with heavy stripes, is a "kill joy," a "troubler of Israel," a "Job's comforter"; and if he persists in enforcing the precepts, admonitions, warnings, and judgments of Holy Writ, is likely to soon find all doors closed against him. But better this, than be a compromiser; better be deprived of all preaching engagements, than miss the Master's "Well done" in the Day to come.

"Now no chastening for the present seemeth to be joyous, but grievous: nevertheless, afterward it yieldeth the peaceable fruit of righteousness unto them which are exercised thereby" (v. 11). In this verse the apostle concludes his discussion of that theme which is now so unwelcome to the majority of professing Christians. Therein he brings to a close all that he had said concerning those disciplinary afflictions which an all-wise God brings upon His people in this life, His gracious design in the same, and the duty incumbent upon them to receive these in a right spirit. He sums up his argument by balancing the good over against the evil, the future over against the present, the judgment of faith over against the feelings of the flesh.

Our present text is added to what has been said in the previous verses for the purpose of anticipating and removing an objection. After all the comforting and encouraging statements made, namely, that chastisements proceed not from enemies but from our Father, that they are sent not in anger but in love, that they are designed not to crush but "for our profit"; carnal sense and natural reason interposes an objection: "But we find no joy under our afflictions, instead much sorrow. We do not *feel* that they are for our profit; we cannot *see* how they can be so; therefore we are much inclined to doubt what you have said." The apostle grants the force of the objection: that for the present, chastening *does* "seem to be grievous and not joyous." But he brings in a double limitation or qualification: in reference to outward sense, it only "seems" so; in reference to time, this is only for "the present." Having made this concession, the apostle turns to the objector and says, "Nevertheless." He reminds him that, first, there is an "afterward" beyond the present moment, to be borne in mind; second, he presses on him the need of being "exercised thereby"; third, he assures him that if he is so exercised "peaceable fruit" will be the happy issue. There are four things told us in the text about chastisement as it is viewed by human reason.

1. *All that carnal reason can perceive in our chastenings is* BUT SEEMING. All that flesh and blood can discover about the nature and quality of Divine afflictions is but their outward and superficial appearance. The eye of reason is utterly incapable of discovering the virtue and value of sanctified trials. How often we are deceived by mere "seeming"! This is true in the natural sphere: appearances are proverbially deceptive. There are many optical illusions. Have you not noticed some nights when the sun is sinking in the west, that it is much bigger than at its zenith? Yet it is not so in reality; it only "seems" to be so. Have you stood on the deck of a ship in mid-ocean and, while gazing at the horizon, suddenly been startled by the sight of land?—the outline of the coast, with the rising hills in the background, there clearly defined? Yet after all, it was but "seeming"; it was nothing but clouds. In like manner, you have read of a mirage seen by travelers in the desert: away over the sands, they see in the distance green trees and a shining pool of water; but this is only an optical delusion, effected in some way by the atmosphere.

Now if this be so in connection with natural things, the "seeming" *not* being the actual, the apparent *not* being the reality, how much more is it true in connection with the things of God! Afflictions are *not* what they "seem" to be. They appear to work for our ill, and not for our good; so that we are inclined to say, "An enemy hath done this." They seem to be for our injury, rather than our "profit," and we murmur and are cast down. So often *fear* distorts our vision; so often *unbelief* brings scales over our eyes, and we exaggerate the dimensions of trials in the dark and dim light. So often we are selfish, fond of our fleshly ease; and therefore spiritual discernment falls to a low ebb. No, chastenings for the present do not *seem* to be joyous, but "grievous"; but that is because we view them through our natural senses and in the light of carnal reason.

2. *Carnal reason judges afflictions in the light of the PRESENT.* The tendency with all of us is to estimate things in the light of the *now.* The ungodly are ever ready to sacrifice their future interests for present gratification. One of their favourite mottos is, "A bird in the hand is worth two in the bush:" it may be to the slothful, but the enterprising and diligent would rather be put to a little trouble and secure the two. Man is a very short-sighted creature, and even the Christian is often dominated by the same sentiments that regulate the wicked. The light of the *now* is generally the worst in which to form a true estimate of things. We are too close to them to obtain a right perspective, and see things in their proper proportions. To view an oil painting to the best advantage, we need to step back a few feet from it. The same principle applies to our lives. Proof of this is found as we now look back upon that which is past. To-day the Christian discovers a meaning, a needs-be, a preciousness, in many a past experience, and even disappointment, which he could not discern at the time.

The case of Jacob is much to the point, and should guard us against following his foolish example. After Joseph had been removed from his doting father, and when he thought he had lost Simeon too, viewing things in the light of "the present," he petulantly said, "All these things are against me" (Gen. 42:36). Such is often the mournful plaint which issues from our short-sighted unbelief. But later, Jacob discovered his mistake, and found that all those things had been working together for good to himself and his loved ones. Alas, we are so impatient and impetuous, so occupied with the present, that we fail to look forward and by faith anticipate the happy sequel. Then, too, the effects which afflictions have upon the old man, *disqualify* us to estimate them aright. If my heart is palpitating, if my mind is agitated, and my soul is cast down, then I am in no fit state to judge the quality and blessedness of Divine afflictions. No, chastenings *for the present do not* "seem to be joyous, but grievous;" that is because we take such a short-sighted view of them and fail to look forward with the eyes of faith and hope.

3. *To carnal reason afflictions never seem "joyous."* This logically follows from what has been before us under the first two points. Because carnal reason sees *only* the "seeming" of things, and because it estimates them *only* in the light of "the present," afflictions are not joyous. Nor does God intend that, in themselves, they should be. If afflictions *did* "seem" to be joyous, would they be chastisements at all? It would be of little use for an earthly parent to whip his child in such a way as to produce only smiles. Such would be merely a make-belief; no smart, no benefit. Solomon

said, "It is the blueness of the wound which maketh the heart better;" so if Divine chastisements are not painful to the flesh and extort a groan and cry, what good end would they serve? If God sent us trials such as we wished, they would not be chastenings at all. No, afflictions do not "seem" to be joyous.

They are not joyous in *the form* they assume. When the Lord smites, He does so in a tender place, that we may feel the smart of it. They are not joyous in *the force* of them. Oftentimes we are inclined to say, If the trial had not been quite so severe, or the disappointment had not been so great, I could have endured it. God puts just so much bitter herbs into our cup as to make the draught unpleasant. They are not joyous in *the time* of them. We always think they come at the wrong season. If it were left to our choosing, they would never come; but if we *must* have them, we would choose the time when they are the least grievous; and thus miss their blessing. Nor are they joyous in *the instruments* used: "If it were an enemy, then I could have borne it," said David. That is what we all think. O if my trial were not just *that!* Poverty I could endure, but not reproach and slander. To have lost my own health would have been a hard blow, but I could have borne it; but the removal of that dear child, the light of my eyes, how can I ever rejoice again? Have you not heard brethren speak thus?

4. *To carnal reason afflictions ever seem to be "grievous."* Probably the most grievous part to the Christian is that he cannot *see* how much a loss or trial can possibly benefit him. If he could thus see, he *would* rejoice. Even here we must walk by faith and not by sight. But this is easier said than done; yea, it can only be done by God's enabling. Usually, the Christian altogether fails to see why such a trouble is sent upon *him;* it seems to work harm and not good. Why this financial loss, when he was giving more to the Lord's work? Why this breakdown in health, when he was being most used in His service? Why this removal of a Sabbath school teacher, just when he was most needed? Why was my husband called away, when the children most required him? Yes, such afflictions are indeed grievous to the flesh.

But let it be pointed out that these reasonings are *only* "seeming." The Christian, by grace, eventually triumphs. Faith looks up at the cloud (though it is often very late in doing so) and says, The chastisement was not as severe as it might have been, certainly it was not as severe as I deserved, and truly it was nothing in comparison to what the Saviour suffered for me. O let faith expel carnal reason, and say, "For our light affliction, which is but for a moment, worketh for us a far more exceeding and eternal weight of glory." But note carefully that this is only "*while* we look not at the things which are seen, but at the things which are not seen"

(2 Cor. 4:17, 18). For much in the above four points the writer acknowledges his indebtedness to a sermon by C. H. Spurgeon on the same verse.

"Nevertheless, afterward it yieldeth the peaceable fruit of righteousness unto them which are exercised thereby." This is what the apostle sets over against the estimate of carnal reason and the feelings of our natural senses. Medicine may not be a pleasant thing to take, but if it be blest by God, the renewed health it gives is good compensation. The pruned vine at the end of the winter presents a sorry appearance to the eye, but its heavily-laden branches in the autumn vindicate the gardener's efforts. Did not the "afterward" prove to Jacob that his doleful reasonings were quite unwarranted? Job squirmed under the rod, as well he might, but was not his end more prosperous than his beginning? Thank God for this "Nevertheless afterward."

Yet this "afterward" is also a very searching word: it is one which should pierce and test each of us. Have we not all passed through sorrow? Can any of us look back on the past without recalling seasons of deep and heavy affliction? Has no sword pierced our souls? no painful sacrifice been demanded of us? But, my reader, do these experiences belong to the *past* in every sense? Have they gone, disappeared, without leaving any *effects* behind them? No, that is impossible: we are either the better or the worse because of them. Then ask yourself, *What* fruits have they produced? Have your past experiences hardened, soured, frozen you? Or have they softened, sweetened, mellowed you? Has pride been subdued, self-pleasing been mortified, patience developed? How have afflictions, chastisements, left us? *What* does the "afterward" reveal?

Not all men are the gainers by afflictions; nor are Christians so always. Many seek to flee from trials and troubles, instead of being "exercised" thereby. Others are callous and do not yield: as Heb. 12:5 intimates, they "despised" the chastenings of the Lord. There are some who imagine that, when visited with affliction, it is a display of courage if they refuse to be affected. They count it weakness to mourn over losses and weep over sorrows. But such an attitude is altogether un-Christian. Christ wept and again and again we are told that He "groaned." Such an attitude is also foolish to the last degree, for it is calculated to counteract the very design of afflictions, and only calls for severer ones to break our proud spirits. It is no mark of weakness to acknowledge that we *feel* the strokes of an *Almighty* arm.

It is the truest wisdom to humble ourselves beneath "the mighty hand of God." If we are among His people, He will mercifully compel us to acknowledge that His chastenings are not to be despised and made light of. He will—and O how easily He *can* do it—continue or increase our afflictions until He *tames* our wild spirits, and brings us like obedient children into subjection to Himself. What a warning is found in Isa. 9:9-11. "And all the people shall know, even Ephraim and the inhabitants of Samaria, that say in the pride and stoutness of heart, The bricks are fallen down, *but we will* build with hewn stones; the sycamores are cut down, *but we will* change them into cedars. *Therefore* the Lord shall set up the adversaries of Rezin against him, and join his enemies together." This means that, because the people had hardened themselves under the chastening hand of God, instead of being "exercised" thereby, that He sent sorer afflictions upon them.

The ones benefitted by the Father's chastenings are they who are "*exercised* thereby." The Greek word for "exercised" was borrowed from the gymnastic games. It had reference to the athlete stripping himself of his outer clothing. Thus, this word in our text is almost parallel with the "laying aside of every weight" in v.1. If afflictions cause us to be stripped of pride, sloth, selfishness, a revengeful spirit, then "fruit" *will be* produced. It is only as we *improve* our chastenings, that we are gainers. The natural effect of affliction on an unsanctified soul is either to irritate or depress, which produces rebellion or sinking in despair. This is the result of hardness of heart and unbelief. Even with regard to the Christian it is true that, only as he views them as proceeding from his Father in order to bring him into subjection, and as he is "exercised thereby," he is truly profited.

1. The *conscience* needs to be "exercised." There must be a turning unto the Sender of our trials, and a seeking from Him of the meaning and message of them. "There was a famine in the days of David three years, year after year; and David *inquired* of the Lord" (2 Sam. 21:1)! So should we when the providences of God frown upon us. There must be an honest self-examination, a diligent scrutiny of our ways, to discover what it is God is displeased with. Careful investigation will often show that much of our supposed godly zeal in service is but the result of habit, or the imitating of some eminent saint, instead of proceeding from the heart, and being rendered "unto the Lord."

2. *Prayer* has to be "exercised" or engaged in. It is true that painful afflictions have a tendency to stifle the voice of supplication, that one who is smarting under the rod feels little inclination to approach the Throne of Grace, but this carnal disposition must be steadily resisted, and the help of the Holy Spirit definitely sought. The heavier our load, the more depressed our heart, the sorer our anguish, the greater our need to pray. God requires to be sought unto for grace to submit to His dealings, for help to improve the

same, for Him to sanctify unto our good all that perplexes and distresses us.

3. The grace of *meekness* must be "exercised," for "a meek and quiet spirit" is of "great price" in the sight of Him with whom we have to do (1 Pet. 3:4). Meekness is the opposite of self-will and hardness of heart. It is a pliability of soul, which is ready to be fashioned after the Divine image. It is a holy submission, willing to be moulded as the Heavenly Potter determines. There can be no "peaceable fruit of righteousness" until our wills are broken, and we have no mind of our own. How much we need to heed that word of Christ's, "Take My yoke upon you, and *learn of Me,* for I am meek" (Matt. 11:29).

4. *Patience* must be "exercised." Rest in the Lord, and wait patiently for Him" (Psa. 37:7): "wait" for *His* time of deliverance, for if we attempt to deliver ourselves, we are very likely to plunge into deeper trials. Fruit is not ripened in a day; nor do the benefits of chastisements appear immediately. Patience must have her perfect work if the soul is to be enriched by afflictions. In the interval of waiting, allow nothing to deter your plodding perseveringly along the path of duty.

5. *Faith* must be "exercised." *God's* hand must be seen in every trial and affliction if it is to be borne with meekness and patience. While we look no further than the malice of Satan, or the jealousy, enmity, injustice of men, the heart will be fretful and rebellious. But if we receive the cup from the Father's hand, our passions will be calmed and the inward tumult stilled. Only by the exercise of faith will the soul be brought into a disposition to quietly submit, and digest the lessons we are intended to learn.

6. *Hope* must be "exercised." As faith looks upward and sees *God's* hand in the trial, hope is to look forward and anticipate the *gains* thereof. Hope is a confident expectation of future good. It is the opposite of despair. Hope lays hold of the promised "Afterward," and thus it sustains and cheers in the present. Hope assures the cast-down soul "I shall *yet* praise Him for the help of His countenance" (Psa. 42:5). "But the God of all grace, who hath called us unto His eternal glory by Christ Jesus, *after* that ye have suffered a while, make you perfect, stablish, strengthen, settle you" (1 Pet. 5:10).

7. *Love* must be "exercised." It is the Father's *love* which chastens us (v.5); then ought not we to love Him in return for His care and patient training of us? Instead of doubting His wisdom or questioning His goodness, there should be an affectionate gratitude flowing out to the One who is seeking nought but our welfare. "We can never find any benefit in chastenings, unless we are *exercised* by them, that is, unless all our graces are stirred up by them to a holy,

constant exercise" (John Owen)—how different that, from the fatalistic inertia of many hyper-Calvinists!

What we have sought to bring out above is the fact that spiritual "fruit" *is not* the natural or spontaneous effect of affliction. Nay, have we not observed that few of those who suffer severe financial reverses, heavy domestic bereavements, or personal bodily pain, are, spiritually, the gainers thereby. Yea, do we need to look any further than ourselves, to perceive how little we have learned by and profited from past trials? And the cause is plain: we were *not duly exercised* thereby. May this word abide with each of us for the future.

What is meant by "the peaceable fruit of righteousness"? If we took this expression by itself, it would signify *the effects of* righteousness, the fruit which righteousness itself brings forth. But in our text it is chastenings or afflictions which are specifically mentioned as producing this fruit. It is the Spirit tranquilizing and purifying the heart. "Righteousness" in our text is parallel with "His holiness" in v. 10. It may be summed up in the mortification of sin and the vivification of vital godliness. It is called the "*peaceable* fruit" because it issues in the taming of our wild spirits, the quieting of our restless hearts, the more firm anchoring of our souls. But this only comes when we truly realize that it is the Father's *love* which has afflicted us. May the Spirit of God grant us all "exercised" hearts, so that we shall daily search ourselves, examine our ways, and be stripped of all that is displeasing to Him.

CHAPTER NINETY-THREE

A Call to Steadfastness

(Heb. 12:12, 13)

The didactic (teaching) portions of Scripture are very much more than abstract statements of truth: they are designed not only for the instructing of the mind, but also for the influencing of the heart. This is far too little recognised in our day, when the craving for information is so often divorced from any serious concern as to the *use* to be made of the same. This, no doubt, is one of the evil fruits borne by the modern school-methods, where instead of seeking to *draw out* (the meaning of the word "educate") and develope the mind of the pupil, he is made to "cram" or fill his head with a mass of facts and figures, most of which are of no service to him in the later life. Not such is God's method. His method of instruction is to set before us moral and spiritual principles, and then show us how to *apply* them in a practical way; inculcate a motive, and thereby call into exercise our inward faculties. Hence, the test of Christian knowledge is not how much we understand, but how far our knowledge is affecting our lives.

It is one thing to possess a clear intellectual grasp of the doctrines of grace, it is quite another to experience the grace of the doctrines in a spiritual way. It is one thing to believe the Scriptures are the inspired and inerrant Word of God, it is another for the soul to live under the awe of their Divine authority, realising that one day we shall be judged by them. It is one thing to be convinced that Jesus Christ is the Son of God, the King of kings and Lord of lords, it is another to surrender to His sceptre and live in personal subjection to Him. What does it profit me to be convinced that God is omnipotent, unless I am learning to lean upon His mighty arm? What avail is it to me that I am assured of God's omniscience unless the knowledge that His eye is ever upon me acts as a salutary restraint to my actions? What does it advantage me to know that without holiness no man shall see the Lord, unless I am making the acquirement of holiness my chief concern and aim!

That which has been pointed out above has to do with no obscure and intricate subject which lies far above the reach of the rank and file of the common people, but is plain, self-evident, simple. Alas, that our hearts are so little impressed by it and our consciences so rarely exercised over it. When we measure ourselves by *that* standard, have we not all of us much cause to hang our heads in shame? Our intellects are stored with Scripture truth, but how little are our lives moulded thereby. Our doctrinal views are sound and orthodox, but how little we know experimentally of "the truth which is after godliness" (Titus 1:1). Has not the Saviour much ground for saying to both writer and reader, "Why call ye Me, Lord, Lord, and *do not* the things which I say?" (Luke 6:46). O that we may be duly humbled over our sad failures.

The above reflections have been suggested by the *use* which the apostle makes in our text of the subject he had been discussing in the previous verses. His opening "Wherefore" denotes that he was now going to make a practical application unto those whom he was writing to of the exposition just given of the truth of Divine chastisement. In this we may see him following out the course he pursued in all his epistles, and which the servants of God are required to emulate to-day. No matter what was the doctrine under consideration, the apostle always turned it to a practical end, as his oft-repeated "Therefore" and "Wherefore" intimate. Was he contending for the Christian's emancipation from the ceremonial law, then he adds, "Stand fast *therefore* in the liberty wherewith Christ hath made us free" (Gal. 5:1). Was he opening up the glorious truth of resurrection, then he concludes with "*therefore* . . . be ye steadfast, unmoveable, always abounding in the work of the Lord" (1 Cor. 15:58). Was he setting forth the blessed hope of Christ's return, then he finishes with "*Wherefore* comfort one another with these words" (1 Thess. 4:18).

It is this which urgently needs to be laid to heart—*the use* we make of the precious truths which the Most High has so graciously revealed to us. That is (partly, at least) what the Saviour had in mind when He said, "Take heed therefore *how* ye hear" (Luke 8:18)—see to it that your hearts are duly affected, so that the truth will regulate all your conduct. It is not sufficient that I assume a reverent demeanor when attending the means of grace, that I pay close attention to what I hear: it is the assimilation of the same, so that I go forth and live under the power thereof, which is the all-important matter. The same is true of our reading; it is not the book which adds to my store of information, or which entertains and thrills, but the one which stirs me up to godly living, which proves the most helpful. So it is with our response to the Scriptures, it is not how many difficult passages do I have light upon, nor how many verses have I memorized, but how many of its commands and percepts am I honestly endeavouring to obey.

This is the keynote struck by the apostle in the verses which are now to engage our attention. He had thrown not a little light on the distressing circumstances in which the Hebrews then found themselves, namely, the bitter persecution they were encountering at the hands of their unbelieving countrymen. He had pointed out that so far from their afflictions being exceptional, and a warrantable ground for consternation, they were, in some form or other, the common portion of *all* God's people, while they are left in this scene. He had set before them some most blessed truths, which were well calculated to strengthen their faith, comfort their hearts, and raise their drooping spirits. He had given an exposition of the subjection of Divine chastisement, such as must bring peace and consolation to all who mix faith therewith. He had silenced every objection which could well be made against the duty to which he had called them. And now he presses upon them the practical profit to which they must turn the doctrine inculcated.

"Wherefore lift up the hands which hang down, and the feeble knees; And make straight paths for your feet, lest that which is lame be turned out of the way; but let it rather be healed" (vv. 12, 13). Here we have, first, the conclusion drawn from the preceding premises. Second, the several duties enjoined. Third, the reason by which they are enforced. The duties are expressed in figurative language, yet in such terms as the meaning is not difficult to perceive. The enforcing reason or motive for compliance is taken from the evil effects which a non-compliance of one's duty would have upon others, which plainly inculcates the importance and value of personal example, and the influence which it exerts upon our fellows.

"Wherefore" means, in view of what has been said: because of the preceding considerations a certain course of conduct ought to follow. There is, we believe, a double reference in this opening "wherefore," namely, an immediate and a remote one. Immediately, it connects with the preceding verse, the most important word of which is "exercised." The apostle was alluding again to the well-known Grecian "Games." In the gymnasium, the instructor would challenge the youth to combat. He was an experienced man, and knew how to strike, guard, wrestle. Many severe blows would the combatants receive from him, but it was part of their training, preparing them for their future appearance in the public contests. The youth whose athletic frame was prepared for the coming great venture, would boldly step forward, willing to be "exercised" by his trainer; but he who shirked the trial and refused to encounter the master, received no help at his hands; but the fault was entirely his own.

This, it seems to us, is the figure carried forward in our text; "Now no chastening for the present seemeth to be joyous, but grievous: nevertheless afterward it yieldeth the peaceable fruit of righteousness unto them which are *exercised* thereby. *Wherefore* lift up the hands which hang down." The Christian who gives way before trial, who sinks under affliction, who sulks or repines beneath persecution, will bring forth none of the "peaceable fruit of righteousness." If he "faints" under chastisement, if his hands become idle and his legs no longer capable of supporting him, a profitable use cannot be made of the tribulation through which he is called upon to pass. Then let him pull himself together, gird up the loins of his mind and "*endure* hardness as a good soldier of Jesus Christ" (2 Tim. 2:3). Let his attitude be, Now is the time of my training, so I will seek to play the man; I will seek grace from God to muster all my faith and courage and valiantly wrestle with whatever opposes and oppresses me.

More remotely, our opening "Wherefore" looks back unto *all* that has been said in the previous verses. Heb. 12 opens with a stirring call for God's people to persevere in the course of Christian duty, to go forward in the spiritual life, no matter what impediments might stand in their way; to "run with patience (or perseverance) the race which is set before us," drawing strength from the Christ for enablement ((vv. 1, 2). Then he anticipated an objection: We are being sorely oppressed, tempted to renounce our profession, hounded by our unbelieving brethren. To this he replies, Consider your Master, who went before you in the same path of suffering (v.3.). Bear in mind that your lot has not become extreme: ye have not yet been called upon to experience a martyr's death (v. 4). Furthermore, you are losing sight of that scriptural exhortation, "My son, despise not thou the chastening of the Lord" (v. 5). This led the apostle to open to them, in a most precious manner, the whole subject of Divine chastisement. Let us present a brief summary of the same.

The trials through which the children of God are called upon to pass are not Divine punishments, but gracious discipline designed for their good. We are expressly bidden "not to faint" beneath them (v. 5). The rod is wielded not in wrath, but in tender solicitude, and is a manifestation not of God's anger but of His love (v. 6). Our duty then is to "endure" chastening as becometh the children of God (v. 7). To be without chastisement, so far from being an evidence of our spiritual sonship, would demonstrate we were not sons at all (v. 8). Inasmuch as we gave reverence to our earthly parents when they corrected us, how much more ought we to be in subjection to our heavenly Father (v. 9). God's design in our afflictions is our "profit," that by them we might become increasingly "partakers of His holiness" in an experimental way. Though these chastenings are unpleasant to flesh and blood, nevertheless "the peaceable fruit of righteousness" issues therefrom when we are suitably "exercised thereby" (v. 11).

Now from these considerations a very obvious conclusion is drawn, and by them a bounden duty is enforced. In view of the "great cloud of witnesses" by which we are encompassed (v. 1), seeing that the saints of other days—in themselves as weak, as sinful, as much oppressed by the world as we are—fought a good fight, kept the faith, and finished their course, let us gird ourselves for the contest and strain every effort to persevere in the path of duty. In view of the fact that our Leader, the Captain of our salvation, has left us such an example of heroic endurance (v. 3), let us earnestly seek to follow His steps and acquit ourselves like men. Finally, because God Himself is the Author and Regulator of our trials—the severest of our chastenings proceed from a loving Father, seeking our good—then let us not be cast down by the difficulties of the way nor discouraged by the roughness of the path; but let us nerve ourselves to steadfastness in the faith and fidelity to our Redeemer.

Thus the coherence of our opening "Wherefore" is perfectly obvious and the duty it presses so plain that there cannot be misunderstanding. In view of all the above-mentioned considerations, and particularly in view of the fact that the most precious fruits issue from afflictions when we are duly "exercised" by them, then let us not be dejected in our minds nor faint in our spirits by reason thereof. As the champions in the public "Games" used their hands and arms to the very best of their ability, and as the runners in the races used their legs and knees to the best possible effect—and in case their hands and knees began to fail and flag, exerted their wills to the utmost to rouse up their members to renewed effort—so should we be very courageous, zealous and active, and in case our hearts begin to fail us through multiplied discouragements, we must marshal all our resolution and strive prayerfully and manfully against giving way to despair.

"Wherefore lift up the hands that hang down." The duty here enjoined is set forth in figurative language, but the meaning is none the less obvious because of the graphic metaphors used. The apostle transferred unto members of our physical body the condition in which the faculties of our souls are liable to fall under certain trials. For the hands to hang down and the knees to become feeble are figurative expressions, denoting the tendency to abandon the discharge of our Christian duty because of the opposition encountered. For the hands of a boxer or fencer to hang down means that his arms are become weary to the point of exhaustion; for the knees to be feeble signifies that through the protracted exertions of the runner his legs have been debilitated by their nervous energy being spent. The spiritual reference is to a decay in the Christian's courage and resolution. Two evils produce this: despondency as to success—when hope is gone effort ceases; weariness in the performance of duty.

This same figure is employed in other passages of Scripture. In Ezek. 7:16, 17 we read, "But they that escape of them shall escape, and shall be on the mountains like doves of the valleys, all of them mourning, every one for his iniquity. All hands shall be feeble, and all knees shall be as weak as water:" here the reference is to that inertia which is produced by poignant conviction of sin after a season of backsliding. Again, in Ezek. 21:7 we are told, "When they shall say unto thee, Wherefore sighest thou? that thou shalt answer, For the tidings, because it cometh: and every heart shall melt, and all hands shall be feeble, and every spirit shall fail, and all knees shall be as weak as water:" where we behold the paralyzing effects of consternation in view of the tidings of sore judgment. But in our text the reference is to the disheartenment caused by fierce opposition and persecution. Despair and becoming weary of well doing are the two evils in all our afflictions which we most need to guard against. It is failure at this point which has led to so many scandalous backslidings and cursed apostacies. Such an exhortation as the one before us intimates that the Hebrews had either already given way to an enervating spirit of gloom or were in great danger of so doing.

Now "It is the duty of all faithful ministers of the Gospel to consider diligently what failures or temptations their flocks are liable or exposed to, so as to apply suitable means for their preservation" (J. Owen). This is what the apostle is seen doing here. In view of the lethargy of the Hebrews he exhorts them to *"lift up* the hands which hang down, and the feeble knees." The word "lift up" signifies not simply to elevate, but to "rectify" or set right again, restoring them to their proper state, so as to apply them to duty. It was a call to steadfastness and resolute perseverance: be not dejected in your minds nor faint in your spirits by reason of the present distress, nor be so terrified of the threatening danger as to give up hope and be completely overwhelmed. Under sore trial and affliction, persecution and the prospect of yet sorer opposition, the temptation is for the heart to sink within us and the path of duty to be forsaken.

"Wherefore lift up the hands which hang down, and the feeble knees:" literally, "hands which are loose" or slack, dangling inert; "feeble knees" is still stronger in the Greek, being almost the equivalent of palsied knees — enervated knees which need bandages to brace them. In view of which he calls them to arouse themselves, to stir up all their graces unto exercise, to refuse taking the line of least resistance, to renew their courage and bear up under their trials. Resolution will accomplish much to stimulate jaded nerves and flagging energies. The Christian life, from start to finish is a struggle, a fight, an unceasing warfare against foes within and without, and only he who endures to the end shall receive the crown of life. To give way to dejection is harmful, to sink into despair is dangerous, to quit the discharge of our duties is the fore-runner of apostasy.

But the question arises *how* are we to set about this particular task? To say that we are helpless in ourselves affords no encouragement; in fact to affirm that the Christian is utterly impotent is to deny that there is any vital difference between himself and those who are dead in sins. Christians in their greatest weakness have *some* strength, some grace, some spiritual life; and where there is some life, there is some ability to stir and move. And God is pleased to assist where there is *sincere endeavour*. The believer is responsible to arm his mind against discouragements by considering God's design in them, and the blessed fruits which issue from trials and afflictions when we are duly exercised by them. Of what value is a clear intellectual grasp of the nature and end of Divine chastisements unless it produces a practical effect upon the heart and life? Let the distressed saint ponder anew the blessed considerations set before him in Heb. 12: 1-11 and find in them motives and incentives unto renewed courage, fidelity and perseverance.

Let the hope of ultimate victory nerve you. Look forward to the goal: the determination to reach home is a powerful stimulus to a weary traveller. Earnestly endeavour to counteract every disposition to faintness and despondency by viewing your trials and persecutions as a part of God's discipline for your soul: then submit to them as such, and seek to get them sanctified to your spiritual profit. Remember that you cannot fight with hands hanging down, nor run the race set before us if your knees give way; so summon all your resolution to remain steadfast in the discharge of every duty God has appointed and assigned you. Rest in the love of your heavenly Father, assured that all of the present distress is designed for your ultimate good, and this will reinvigorate the soul. Finally, seek grace to lay hold of and plead the promise, "They that wait upon the Lord shall renew their strength" (Isa. 40:31).

It is to be noted that this exhortation is couched abstractly. It is not "lift up *your* hands," which would restrict it individually; nor is it "lift up the hands of those who are dejected," which would limit the exhortation to a ministry unto others. Worded as it is there is a *double* reference: it is a call to the individual Christian to persevering activity, and it is an exhortation for him to seek the well being of his fellow-Christians. That our text *has* a reference to our seeking to encourage and strengthen fellow-pilgrims is clear from a comparison of Job 4:3, 4 and Isa. 35:3, 4, with which I Thess. 5:14 may be compared. The best way for the individual Christian to strengthen the hands of his feeble fellows is by setting before them a worthy example of faith, courage, and steadfastness. In addition, he is to pray for them, speak words of encouragement, remind them of God's promises, relate to them His gracious dealings and powerful deliverances in his own life.

"And make straight paths for your feet." The previous verse concerns the inward frame and spirit of the believer's mind; this one has respect to his outward conduct. As Barnes has well pointed out, the term used here signifies "straight" horizontally, that is level and plain, all obstacles are to be removed so that we do not stumble and fall—cf. Prov. 4:25-27. The word for "paths" is derived from one meaning "a wheel" and signifies here "the marks made by a wheel"—it is paths marked out for others, leaving the tracks which may be followed by them. The reference, then, is to the believer so manifesting his course that his fellows may see and follow it. The Christian course is *exemplary,* that is, it is one which impresses and influences others. How very careful should we be then as to our conduct!

Here, then, is an exhortation unto the Christian to see well to his *walk,* which means the regulating of all his actions by the revealed will of God, to be obedient unto the Divine precepts, to follow not the ways and fashions of an evil world, but to cleave to the narrow way, and turn not aside from the Highway of Holiness. "It is our duty not only to be found in the ways of God in general but to take care that we walk carefully, circumspectly, uprightly and diligently in them. Hereon depends our own peace, and all our usefulness toward others. It is a sad thing when some men's walk in the ways of God shall deter others from them or turn them out of them" (J. Owen).

"And make straight paths for your feet." A most timely word for us today when iniquity abounds and the love of many waxes cold, when the poor and afflicted in Zion stand in need of all the godly encouragement they can obtain. We are surrounded by a "*crooked* generation," both of professing and profane, whose evil ways we are but too apt to learn; we are beset on every hand by temptations to turn aside into what Bunyan termed "By-path Meadow," to enter paths which God has prohibited, to feed on pride and indulge our lusts. How the heart of the mature Christian aches for the lambs of Christ's flock, and how it behooves him to walk softly and carefully lest he put some stumblingblock in their way. Solemn indeed is "As for such as turn aside unto their crooked ways, the Lord shall lead them forth with the workers of iniquity" (Psa. 125:5), and also "They have made them crooked paths: whosoever goeth therein *shall not know peace*" (Isa. 59:8).

"Lest that which is lame be turned out of the way." The word "lest" is a translation of two Greek words, "that not." It is a word of caution and prevention, warning each of us that carelessness as to our own walk is likely to have an ill effect upon weaker Christians. The word "lame" is transferred from the body to some defect of our graces which unfits the soul for the discharge of Christian duty: one who is lame is ill-capacitated to run in a race, and one who is lacking in courage, zeal, and perseverance is ill-fitted to fight the good fight of faith. Walk carefully then, my brother, if for no reason than for the sake of the feebler saints. Backslidden Christians are the plague of the church: inconsistencies in God's people spread discouragements among weak believers.

There are always some "lame" sheep in God's earthly flock. While there are some Christians with strong and vigorous faith, so that they "mount up with wings as eagles, run and are not weary," and make steady progress in practical holiness, all are not so highly favoured. In most families of any size there is one frail and sickly member; so it is in the various branches of the Household of Faith. Some are constitutionally gloomy, temperamentally vacillating, physically infirm, and these have a special claim upon the strong. They are not to be snubbed and shunned: they need an example of cheerfulness set before them, wise counsel given to them, their arms supported by prayer and love's solicitude for their good. Whatever is weak in their faith and hope, whatever tends to dishearten and discourage them, should be carefully attended to, so far as lies in our power. A stitch in time saves nine: many a sheep might have been kept from falling into the ditch, had one with a shepherd's heart gone after it at the first sign of straying.

"But let it rather be healed." "Heal" signifies to correct that which is amiss. It is the recovering of a lapsed one which is here in view. Instead of despising sickly Christians, exercise love's sympathy toward them. While we should be thankful if God has granted us healthy graces, we must beware of presumption: "If a man be overtaken in a fault, ye which are spiritual restore such an one in the spirit of meekness; *considering thyself*, lest thou also be tempted" (Gal. 6:1). To those groaning under the burden of sin, tell them of the sufficiency of Christ's blood. To those fearful about the future, remind them of God's faithfulness. To those who are despondent, seek to cheer by citing some of God's precious promises. Study the holy art of speaking a word in season to the needy. You will be of great value to the church if you develop a spirit of compassion and the gift of lifting up those fallen by the wayside."

CHAPTER NINETY-FOUR

A Call to Diligence

(Heb. 12:14)

The connection between the verses which were before us on the last occasion and that which is now to engage our attention is not apparent at the first glance. There the apostle made a practical application to his readers of the important considerations he had been setting before them in the preceding verses, calling them unto the duty of steadfastness. Here there is a lively exhortation unto the pursuit of peace and holiness. The relation between these exhortations and those which follow, is more intimate than a number of pearls strung together, rather is it more like that of the several members of our physical body, which are vitally joined and dependent upon one another. Failure to observe this fact results in loss, for not only do we fail to appreciate the living connection of one part with another, but we lose the motive and incentive which they mutually supply. It is the business of the teacher to point this out, that we may be duly affected thereby and rejoice together in the perfect handiwork of God.

"From his exhortation unto patient perseverance in the profession of the Gospel under sufferings and affliction, the apostle proceeds unto a prescription of practical duties; and athough they are such as are absolutely necessary in themselves at all times, yet they are here peculiarly enjoined with respect to the same end, or our constancy in professing the Gospel. For no light, no knowledge of the truth, no resolution or courage, will preserve any man in his profession, especially in times of trial, without a diligent attention unto the duties of holiness and Gospel obedience. And he begins with a precept, general and comprehensive of all others" (J. Owen).

The connection between Heb. 12:14, etc., and vv. 12, 13, is threefold. First, the diligent pursuit of peace toward our fellows and of holiness toward God are timely aids unto perseverance in the faith and in consequence, powerful means for preservation from apostasy. The one is so closely joined to the other that the former cannot be realised without an eager striving after the latter. Second, inasmuch as love toward our neighbour ("peace," with all that that involves and includes) and love toward God ("holiness") is the sum of our duty, it is impossible that we should devote ourselves unto their cultivation and exercise so long as we are permitting afflictions and persecution to paralyze the mind: the spirit of resolute determination must possess us before we can develop our spiritual graces. Third, oppression and suffering provide an opportunity for the exercise and manifestation of our spiritual graces, and are to be improved by us to this very end. "If the children of God grow impatient under afflictions, they will neither walk so quietly and peaceably towards men nor so piously toward God as they should do" (Matt. Henry).

The first thing which needs to be borne in mind as we approach each verse of this epistle is the special circumstances of those immediately addressed, and to perceive the peculiar pertinency of the apostle's instruction to those who were so situated, for this will the better enable us to make a correct application unto ourselves. Now the Hebrews were living among a people where their own espousal of Christianity had produced a serious breach, which had stirred up the fierce opposition of their fellow-countrymen. The attitude of these Hebrews towards Christ was neither understood nor appreciated by the unbelieving Jews; so far from it, they were regarded as renegades and denounced as apostates from the faith of their fathers. Every effort was made to poison their minds against the Gospel, and where this failed, relentless persecution was brought to bear upon them. Hence, it was by no means an easy matter for them to maintain the *spirit* of the Gospel and live amicably with those who surrounded them; instead, they were sorely tempted to entertain a bitter spirit toward those who troubled them so unjustly, to retaliate and avenge their wrongs. Here, then, was the need for them to be exhorted "follow peace with all men!"

Now while it be true that Christians are now, for the most part, spared the severe suffering which those Hebrews were called upon to endure, yet faithfulness to Christ is bound to incur the hostility of those who hate Him, and will in some form or other issue in opposition. There is a radical difference in nature between those treading the narrow way to Heaven and those following the broad road to Hell. The character and conduct of the former condemn and rile the self-pleasing disposition and flesh-indulging ways of the latter. The children of the Devil have no love for the children of God, and they delight in doing whatever they can to annoy and aggravate them; and nothing gives them more pleasure than to see successful their efforts to tempt them to compromise or stir up unto angry retaliation. Thus it is a timely injunction for *all* believers, in any age and in any country, to strive earnestly to live in peace with all men.

"Follow peace with all men." This is a very humbling word that Christians require *to be told* to do this. Its implication is clear: by nature men are fractious, wrathful, revengeful creatures. That is one reason why Christ declared "it must needs be that offences come" (Matt. 18:7)—"must" because of the awful depravity of fallen human nature; yet forget not that He at once added, "But woe to that man by whom the offence cometh." It is because of this contentious, envious, revengeful, spirit which is in us, that we need the exhortation of our text, and in view of what is recorded in Scripture, even of saints, its timeliness is the more apparent. Have we not read of "the strife" between the herdsmen of Abraham and Lot which caused the patriarch and his nephew to part asunder? Have we not read of the discords and fightings between the tribes of Israel issuing in their kingdom being rent in twain? Have we not read of the "contention" between Paul and Barnabas which issued in their separating? These are solemn warnings, danger-signals, which we all do well to take to heart.

" It is the duty of Christians to be at peace among themselves, to be on their guard against all alienation of affection towards each other; and there can be no doubt that the maintenance of this brotherly-kindness is well fitted to promote steadfastness in the faith and profession of the Gospel. But in the words before us there seems to be a reference not so much to the peace which Christians should endeavour to maintain among themselves, as that which they should endeavour to preserve in reference to the world around them. They are to 'follow peace with *all* men.'

"They live amidst men whose modes of thinking, and feeling and acting are very different from—are in many points directly opposite to—theirs. They have been fairly warned, that 'if they would live godly in this world, they must suffer persecution.' They have been told that 'if they were of the world, the world would love its own; but because they are not of the world, therefore the world hateth them.' 'In the world,' says their Lord and Master, 'ye shall have tribulation.' But this, so far from making them reckless as to their behaviour towards the men of the world, ought to have the directly opposite effect. If the world persecute them, they must take care that this persecution has in no degree been provoked by their improper or imprudent behaviour. They must do everything that lies in their power, consistent with duty, to live in peace with their ungodly neighbours. They must carefully abstain from injuring them; they must endeavour to promote their happiness. They must do everything but sin in order to prevent a quarrel.

"This is of great importance, both to themselves and to their unbelieving brethren. A mind harassed by those feelings which are almost inseparable from a state of discord is not by any means in the fittest state for studying the doctrines, cherishing the feelings, enjoying the comforts, performing the duties of Christianity; and, on the other hand, the probability of our being useful to our unbelieving brethren is greatly diminished when we cease to be on good terms with them. As far as lies in us, then, if it be possible, we are to 'live peaceably with all men' " (John Brown, 1872).

"Follow peace with all men." The Greek word for "follow" is a very emphatical one, signifying an "earnest pursuit:" it is the eager chasing after something which flies from one, being used of hunters and hounds after game. The Christian is to spare no effort to live amicably with all men, and no matter how contentious and unfriendly they may be, he is to strive and overtake that which seeks to flee from him. *Peace* is one of the outstanding graces which the Christian is called upon to exercise and manifest. All things pertaining to the Church are denominated things of *peace.* God is "the God of peace" (Heb. 13:20), Christ is "the Prince of peace" (Isa. 9:6), a believer is designated "the son of peace" (Luke 10:6), and Christians are bidden to have their "feet shod with the preparation of the Gospel of peace" (Eph. 6:15).

In this term "follow," or pursue, the apostle continues to preserve the central figure of the entire passage, introduced in the first verse of our chapter, of the running of a race: the same word is rendered "I press forward" in Phil. 3:14. Peace may be elusive and hard to capture, nevertheless strive after it, run hard in the chase thereof, for it is well worth overtaking. Spare no pains, strain every nerve to attain unto it. If this exhortion be duly heeded by us then Christians are plainly forbidden to embroil themselves or take any part in the strifes and quarrels of the world: thus they are hereby forbidden to engage in politics, where there is little else than envy, contention and anger. Still less may the Christian take any part in war: there is not a single word in all the N.T. which warrants a follower of the Prince of peace slaying his fellowmen. "Depart from evil, and do good; seek peace, and pursue it" (Psa. 34:14).

The word "follow" or pursue does not imply the actual obtainment of peace: the most eager hunters and hounds often miss their prey. Nevertheless, nothing short of our utmost endeavours are required of us. "If it be possible, as much as lieth in you, live peaceably with all men" (Rom. 12:18): with fellow-Christians, with those who are strangers to Christ (Eph. 2:19), with our enemies (Matt. 5:44). Few things more adorn and beautify a Christian profession than exercising and manifesting the spirit of peace. Then let us prayerfully strive to avoid those things which occasion strife. Remember the old adage that "It takes two to make a quarrel:" therefore see to it that *you* provoke not others. Give no encouragement to those who love contention; refrain from all argument—the things of God are too holy: debating is a work of the flesh. To "follow peace with all men" presupposes *righteousness* in our dealings with them, for we most certainly are not entitled to expect them to treat us amicably unless we give unto each his due, and treat others as we would have them treat us.

Do not merely be placid when no one irritates you, but go out of your way to be gracious unto those who oppose. Be not fretful if others fail to render the respect which you consider to be your due. Do not be so ready to "stand up for your rights," but *yield* everything except truth and the requirements of holiness. "If we would follow peace, we must gird up our loins with the girdle of *forbearance*: we must resolve that as we will not give offence, so neither will take offence, and if offence be felt, we must resolve to forgive" (C. H. Spurgeon). Remember we cannot successfully "pursue peace" if the heavy burden of *pride* be on our shoulder: pride ever stirs up strife. Nor can we "pursue peace" if the spirit of *envy* fills the heart: envy is sure to see faults where they exist not, and make trouble. Nor can we "pursue peace" if we are loose-tongued, busybodies, talebearers.

Even when opposed, our duty is to be peaceful toward those who persecute—a hard lesson, a high attainment, yet Divine grace (when earnestly sought) is "sufficient" even here. Remember the example which the Saviour has left us: and cry mightily unto God for help to emulate the same. "When He was reviled, He reviled not again; when He suffered, He threatened not" (1 Pet. 2:23): He prayed for God to forgive His very murderers. "With all lowliness and meekness, with longsuffering, forbearing one another in love" (Eph. 4:2). Ah, *there* are the prerequisities for the procuring of peace—the lack of which being the cause of so much confusion, strife and war. If *love* reigns our skirts will be clear, for "Love suffereth long, and is kind; love envieth not; doth not behave itself unseemly; seeketh not her own, is not easily provoked; thinketh no evil, beareth all things, believeth all things, hopeth all things, endureth all things" (1 Cor. 13:4-7).

"Follow peace with all men." This includes even more than we have intimated above: the Christian is not only to be a peacekeeper, but he should seek to be a peace-maker: such have the express benediction of Christ—"*Blessed are* the peacemakers: for they shall be called the children of God" (Matt. 5:9). Seek, then, to restore amicable relations between those who are at enmity and be used of God as a medium of their reconciliation. Instead of fanning the flames of dissension or driving the wedge of division further in, endeavour to cool them by the water of the Word, and by a gracious demeanor and wise counsel seek to smooth out difficulties and heal wounds. "And the fruit of righteousness is sown in peace of them that make peace" (James 3:18). "Peaceable men do sow a seed that afterward will yield sheaves of comfort into their own bosoms" (T. Manton).

"Follow peace with all men *and holiness.*" First, the cultivation of peace is a great *aid unto* personal and practical holiness: where discontent, envy, and strife dominate the heart, piety is choked. The two things are inseparably connected: where love to our neighbour is lacking, love to God will not be in exercise. The two tables of the law must not be divorced: God will not accept our worship in the house of prayer while we entertain in our heart the spirit of bitterness toward another (Matt. 5:23, 24). "If a man say, I love God, and hateth his brother, he is a liar: for he that loveth not his brother whom he hath seen, how can he love God whom he hath not seen?" (1 John 4:20). O my reader, if we imagine that we are sincere in our quest after holiness while striving not to live peaceably with all men, we are cherishing a vain deceit.

"Some who have aimed at holiness have made the great mistake of supposing it needful to be morose, contentious, faultfinding, and censorious with everybody else. Their holiness has consisted of negatives, protests, and oppositions for oppositions sake. Their religion mainly lies in contrarieties and singularities; to them the text offers this wise counsel, follow holiness, but also follow peace. Courtesy is not inconsistent with faithfulness. It is not needful to be savage in order to be sanctified. A bitter spirit is a poor companion for a renewed heart. Let your determination principle be sweetened by tenderness towards your fellow-men. Be resolute for the right, but be also gentle, pitiful, courteous. Consider the meekness as well as the boldness of Jesus. Follow peace, but not at the expense of holiness. Follow holiness, but do not needlessly endanger peace" (C. H. Spurgeon, on text, 1870).

"Follow peace with all men, *and holiness.*" By a harmless, kind, and useful behaviour toward their unbelieving neighbours the people of God are to conduct themselves. They must avoid that which fosters bitterness and strife, and make it manifest they are followers of the Prince of peace. Yet in pursuing this most needful and inestimable policy there must be no sacrifice of principle. While peace is a most precious commodity nevertheless, like gold, it may be purchased too dearly. "The wisdom which is from above *is first pure,* then peaceable" (James 3:17). Peace must not be severed from holiness by a compliance with any evil or a neglect of any duty. "First being by interpretation king of righteousness, and after that also King of peace" (Heb. 7:2). "Peace has special relation to man and his good, holiness to God and His honour. These two may no more be severed than the two tables of the law. Be sure then that peace lacks not this companion of holiness: if they cannot stand together, let peace go and holiness be cleaved unto" (W. Gouge).

There may be the former without the latter. Men may be so determined to maintain peace that they compromise principle, sacrifice the truth, and ignore the claims of God. Peace must never be sought after a price of unfaithfulness to Christ. "Buy the truth *and sell it not*" (Prov. 23:23) is ever binding upon the Christian. Thus, important though it be to "follow peace with all men," it is still more important that we diligently pursue "holiness." Holiness is devotedness to God and that temper of mind and course of conduct which agrees with the fact that we are "not our own, but bought with a price." Peace with men, then, is not to be purchased at the expense of devotedness to God: "infinitely better to have the whole world for our enemies and God for our friend, than to have the whole world for our friends and God for our enemy" (John Brown).

The Christian is not only to be diligent in his quest for peace, but he is to be still more earnest in his pursuit after personal and practical holiness. Seeking after the good will of our fellows must be subordinated unto seeking the approbation of God. Our chief aim must be conformity to the image of Christ. If He has delivered us from wrath to come, we must endeavour by all that is within us to *follow Him* along the narrow way which leadeth unto Life. If He be our Lord and Master, then He is to be unreservedly obeyed. To "follow" holiness is to *live* like persons who are devoted to God—to His glory, to His claims upon us, to His cause in this world. It is to *make it evident* that we belong to Him. It is to separate ourselves from all that is opposed to Him. It is to mortify the flesh, with its affections and lusts. It is to "cleanse ourselves from all filthiness of the flesh and of the spirit" (2 Cor. 7:1). It is a life task from which there is no discharge while we remain in the body.

To urge us the more after holiness, the apostle at once adds "without which no man shall see the Lord"—"which" is in the singular number, showing that the antecedent is "holiness." The believer may fail to "follow peace with all men," and though he will suffer loss thereby and bring himself under the chastening rod of his Father, yet this will not entail the Loss of Heaven itself. But it is otherwise with holiness: unless we are made partakers of the Divine nature, unless there be personal devotedness to God, unless there be an earnest striving after conformity to His will, then Heaven will never be reached. There is only one route which leads to the Country of everlasting bliss, and that is the Highway of Holiness; and unless (by grace) we tread the same, our course must inevitably terminate in the caverns of eternal woe.

The negative here is fearfully emphatic: "without which (namely, "holiness") no man shall see the Lord"—in the Greek it is still stronger the negative being threefold—"not, without, no man." God Himself is essentially, ineffably, infinitely holy, and only holy characters shall ever "see" *Him*. Without holiness *no* man shall see Him: no, no matter how orthodox his beliefs, how diligent his attendance upon the means of grace, how liberal he may be in contributing to the cause, nor how zealous in performing religious duties. How this searching word should make everyone of us quail! Even though I be a preacher, devoting the whole of my life to study and labouring for the good of souls, even though I be blest with much light from the Word and be used of God in turning many from Satan to Christ, yet without holiness—both inward and outward—I shall never see the Lord. Unless the earnest pursuit of holiness occupy all my powers, I am but a formal professor, having a name to live while being spiritually dead.

Without holiness men are strangers to God and cannot be admitted to His fellowship, still less to His eternal habitation. "Thus saith the Lord God; No stranger, uncircumcised in heart, nor uncircumcised in flesh shall enter into My sanctuary" (Ezek. 44:9): such as have no holiness within and without, in heart or in life, cannot be admitted into the sanctuary. If God shut the door of His earthly sanctuary against such as were strangers to holiness, will He not much more shut the doors of His celestial tabernacle against those who are strangers to Christ? "For what fellowship hath righteousness with unrighteousness? and what communion hath light with darkness? and what concord hath Christ with Belial?" (2 Cor. 6:14, 15).

Unholy persons have fellowship and are familiar with Satan: "Ye are of your father the Devil, and the lusts of your father ye will do" (John 8:44); and again "The whole world lieth in the Wicked one" (1 John 5:19). It would be awful blasphemy to affirm that the thrice holy God would have fellowship with those who are in covenant with the Devil. O make no mistake upon this point, dear reader: if you are not walking after the Spirit, you are walking after the flesh: if you are not living to please Christ, you are living to please self; if you have not been delivered from the power of Darkness, you cannot enjoy the Light. Listen to those piercing words of the Redeemer, "Except a man be born again, he cannot see the kingdom of God" (John 3:3), and the new birth is holiness begun, it is the implantation of a principle of holiness in the heart, which is the life task of the Christian to cultivate.

The "holiness" referred to in our text is *not* imputed holiness, for we cannot be exhorted to "follow after" that! No, it is personal and practical holiness, which is not attained by standing still, but by an earnest, diligent, persistent pursuit after the same. "It will be well for us to remember that the religion of Jesus Christ is not a matter of trifling, that the gaining of Heaven is not to be achieved by a few half-hearted efforts; and if we will at the same time recollect that all-sufficient succour is prepared for us in the covenant of grace we shall be in a right state of mind: resolute, yet humble, leaning upon the merits of Christ, and yet aiming at personal holiness. I am persuaded that if self-righteousness be deadly, self-indulgence is indeed ruinous. I desire to maintain always a balance in my ministry, and while combating self-righteousness, to war perpetually with loose living" (C. H. Spurgeon).

But for the comfort of the poor and afflicted people of God, who find sin their greatest burden and who grieve sorely over their paucity of holiness, let it be pointed out that our text does not say "without *the perfection of* holiness no man shall see the Lord." Had it done so, we would not be writing this article, for then the editor had been entirely without hope. There is none upon earth who is fully conformed to God's will. Practical holiness is a matter of growth. In this life holiness is but infantile, and will only be matured in glory. At present it exists more in the form of longings and strivings, hungerings and efforts, rather than in realisations and attainments. The very fact that the Christian is exhorted to "follow" or pursue holiness, proves that he has not yet reached it.

"Without holiness no man shall *see the Lord*" spiritually, not corporeally: with an enlightened understanding and with love's discernment, so as to enjoy personal communion with Him. "If we say that we have fellowship with Him, and walk in darkness, we lie, and do not the truth" (1 John 1:6): how clear is that! "The pure in heart shall see God" (Matt 5:8): see Him in His holy ordinances, see His blessed image reflected, though dimly, by his saints, see Him by faith with the eyes of the heart, as Moses, who "endured as seeing Him who is invisible" (Heb. 11:27); and thus be prepared and capacitated to "see" Him in His unveiled glory in the courts above. O to be able to truthfully say, "As for me, I will behold Thy face in righteousness: I shall be satisfied, when I awake, with Thy likeness" (Psa. 17:15). How we should labour after holiness, using all the means appointed thereto, since it is the medium for the soul's vision of God.

CHAPTER NINETY-FIVE

A Call to Examination

(Heb. 12:15)

We had first thought of giving a brief exposition of this verse at the close of the preceding article. But we felt this would scarcely satisfy some of our more critical readers. Nor is it our custom to dodge difficulties, and this presents a real difficulty unto not a few. Those Arminians who are ready to grasp at a straw have appealed to it in support of their favourite tenet "falling from grace." On the other hand, it must be acknowledged that the replies given by Calvinists thereon have often been unsatisfactory. It seems therefore that a more careful consideration and fuller elucidation of its contents are called for. Following, then, our usual practice, we shall endeavour, as God assists, to bring out the meaning of its several terms and apply them to our consciences and lives.

The following are the points upon which our attention needs to be concentrated. First, the connection between our present verse and its context. Second, the duty enjoined: "looking diligently." Third, the danger to be avoided: "lest any man fail of the grace of God." Fourth, the evil warned against: "lest any root of bitterness springing up trouble you." Fifth, the resultant consequence if the evil be tolerated: "and thereby many be defiled." In considering these points it will have to be carefully ascertained what it is about which we are here exhorted to be "looking diligently." What is signified by "lest any man fail of the grace of God," and if that be the correct translation, or whether the Greek requires us to accept the marginal alternative of "falling from the grace of God." And finally, what is denoted by the "root of bitterness springing up." May wisdom be granted us from on High.

First, then, *the connection* between our present verse and its context. We will first consider its more general and remote relation, and then its more specific and immediate. The link between Heb. 12:15 and that which precedes may be thus exhibited: if the afflictions which fidelity to Christ occasion and the chastenings of the Father are not duly improved by professing Christians they are almost certain to become a serious stumbling-block in the way of personal piety, yea, a temptation to apostasy itself. This, we believe, is the first reference in the "looking diligently." Unless professing Christians are duly "exercised" (v. 11) over God's disciplinary dealings with them, they are very apt to misconstrue them, chafe against them, call into question the Divine goodness, and sink into a state of despair, with its accompanying inertia.

What has just been pointed out above receives confirmation from the verses which immediately follow, for vv. 16 and 17 are obviously a continuation of our present text. There we find a solemn exhortation against apostasy itself, pointed by the awful case and example of Esau. Here we are warned against that, which if neglected, has a fearful tendency unto apostasy. Most of us know from painful experience how easily we become discouraged when things do not go as we want, how ready we are to "faint" (v. 5) when the rod of adversity is laid upon us, how real is the temptation to compromise or forsake the path of duty altogether when trials multiply or opposition and persecution is all that our best efforts meet with. Real, then, is our need for heeding this exhortation "Looking diligently lest any man fail of the grace of God."

It is unspeakably solemn to note that in the case of Esau his temptation to sell his birthright—apostatize—was occasioned by his *faintness,* for we are told that he said to Jacob, "Feed me, I pray thee, with that same red pottage, for I am faint" (Gen. 25:30). And is it not when we are faint in our minds, cast down by the diffculties of the way, disheartened by the lack of appreciation our efforts meet with, and crushed by one trial on top of another, that Satan bids us give up the fight of faith and "get what pleasure we can out of life" by indulging the lusts of the flesh? Looked at thus our text points out the *spring* of apostasy—"failing of the grace of God;" the *nature* of apostasy—a "root of bitterness springing up;" and the *result* of apostasy—"many be defiled."

Considering now the more specific and immediate connection of our verse with its context. First, unless the hands which hang down be lifted up and the feeble knees strenghtened (v. 12), there will be a "failing of the grace of God;" and unless straight paths are made for our feet and that which is "lame" be prevented from "turning out of the way" (v. 13), then a "root of bitterness" (an apostate) will spring up, and in consequence, "many will be defiled." Second, in v. 14 we are exhorted to "follow" two things, namely, "peace" and "holiness;" while in v. 15 we are warned to avoid two things, namely, "failing of the grace of God" and suffering "a root of bitterness to spring up." The opening "Looking diligently" clearly denotes that our avoidance of the two evils of v. 15 turns or is dependent upon our earnest pursuit of the spiritual graces inculcated in v. 14.

We are now ready to contemplate the duty which is here enjoined: "looking diligently." This is a call to examination: first, to self-examination. Its immediate force is derived from the closing words of the preceding verse, where the solemn and searching statement is made that "without which (namely 'holiness') no man shall see the Lord." No matter though I am in fellowship with the people of God, a member of a scriptural church, a regular attender upon the means of grace, a firm believer in all the doctrines of the Word; yet, if I have never been sanctified by the Spirit of God, if I am not diligently and earnestly cultivating practical holiness, both of heart and life, then I shall never enter Heaven, and enjoy the beatific vision. Hence the pertinency and urgency of this exhortation, "*Looking diligently* lest any man fail of the grace of God." There is far too much at stake to remain in uncertainty upon such a vital matter, and only the religious trifler will disregard this imperative summons.

The call to careful self-examination receives its urgency from the very great danger there is of *self-deception.* Sin darkens the understanding, so that man is unable to perceive his real state before God. Satan "hath blinded the minds of them which believe not" (2 Cor. 4:4). The deep-rooted pride of our hearts makes us think the best of ourselves, so that if a question is raised in our hearts, we are ever prone to give ourselves the benefit of the doubt. A spirit of sloth possesses us by nature, so that we are unwilling to go to the trouble which real self-examination calls for. Hence the vast majority of religious professors remain with a head knowledge of the Truth, with outward attention to forms and ceremonies, or resting on a mere consent to the letter of some verse like John 3:16, refusing to "make their calling and election *sure.*"

God has warned us plainly in His Word that, "There is a generation that are pure in their own eyes and yet is not washed from their filthiness" (Prov. 30:12). He has set before us those who say "I am rich, and increased with goods, and have need of nothing," and who know not that they are "wretched, and miserable, and poor, and blind, and naked" (Rev. 3:17). And let it be duly noted that *those* were in church association, and that at a time before the last of the apostles had left the earth. Christ has told us that "*Many* will say to Me in that day, Lord, Lord, have we not prophesied in Thy name? and in Thy name have cast out devils? and in Thy name done many wonderful works?" yea, that they affirm "we have eaten and drunk in Thy presence" (Luke 13:26); yet will He answer them "I never knew you: depart from Me, ye that work iniquity" (Matt. 7:23). How such words as those should make *each of us* tremble! How it behooves us to be "Looking diligently lest any man fail of the grace of God." Alas that such words

—written first to those who had been addressed as "holy brethren, partakers of the heavenly calling" (3:1)—should, for the most part, fall upon unheeding ears.

The fact is, that our diligence and honesty in self-examination will largely be detemined by the value which we set upon our soul and its eternal interests. Alas, the vast majority of professing Christians to-day are far, far more concerned about their bodies than their souls, about carnal pleasures than spiritual riches, about earthly comforts than heavenly consolations, about the good opinion of their fellows rather than the approbation of God. But a few—and O *how few*—are made serious, become in deadly earnest to examine well their foundations and test every inch of the ground they stand on. With them religion is not something to be taken up and laid down according to their fitful moods. *Where will they spend* ETERNITY is their all-absorbing concern. Every other interest in life sinks into utter insignificance before the vital consideration of seeking to make sure that they have "the root of the matter" in them.

O my reader, can you be satisfied with the cheap, easy-going religion of the day, which utterly ignores the clamant call of the Son of God "Agonize to enter in at the strait gate" (Luke 13:24)? Can you rest content with the "smooth things" now being proclaimed from wellnigh every pulpit, which assures those who are at emnity with God they can become Christians more easily than a youth can join the army, or a man become a 'free mason' or 'odd fellow'? Can you follow the great crowd who claim to have "received Christ as their personal Saviour" when no miracle of grace has been wrought in their hearts, while the Lord Himself declares "Strait is the gate, and narrow is the way, which leadeth unto Life, and *few* there be that find it" (Matt 7:14)? Dare you rest upon some "decision" made when you were deeply stirred by some anecdotes addressed to your emotions? Have you nothing more than some change in your religious views or some reformation in your outward ways to show that you are "a new creature in Christ Jesus"? Slight not, we beseech you, this pressing word, "Looking diligently lest any man fail of the grace of God."

But the word "Looking diligently" has a wider signification than self-examination: it also points out our duty toward each other. The Greek term means "overseeing," exercising a jealous care for one another. This seems to have misled Owen and several others who confined the exhortation unto "the body of the church or society of the faithful" in their mutual relation. But as Spurgeon pointed out on the text, "In the church of God each one should be on his watchtower for himself and for others. The first person who is likely to fail in the church is *myself*. Each one ought to feel that: the beginning of the watch should therefore be at home." Our text is very similar to the exhortation found in Heb. 3:13, 14, which is first unto the individual and then to the assembly—"Take heed, brethren, lest there be in any of you an evil heart of unbelief, in departing from the living God. But exhort one another daily."

Earnestly endeavouring to look well unto my own going, it is then both my duty and privilege to exercise watchfulness over others. "How many persons might be saved from backsliding by a little oversight! If we would speak to the brother kindly and considerately, when we think he is growing a little cold, we might restore him. We need not always speak directly to him by way of rebuke, but we may place a suggestive book in his way, or speak generally upon the subject. Love can invent many ways of warning a friend without making him angry, and a holy example will also prove a great rebuke to sin. In the church we ought to bear one another's burden, and so fulfil the law of Christ, exercising the office of bishops over one another, and watching lest any man fail of the grace of God" (C. H. Spurgeon).

How little of this loving solicitude for the spiritual wellbeing of our fellow-pilgrims is in evidence to-day! How little earnest and diligent praying for one another! How little faithfulness in counselling, warning, exhorting! Probably one principal reason for this is the hyper-touchiness of so many professing Christians in this generation. No matter how tactfully the counsel be tendered, how faithfully the warning be given, or how lovingly the rebuke be administered; no matter though it be given by an experienced senior to one he is on familiar terms with, yet in nine cases out of ten his efforts are resented, and he is told—by attitude if not in words—to "mind his own business." Never mind, even if a single ear be gained and a single soul helped, it is worth the disappointments of being repulsed by the others. Only one leper out of the ten appreciated Christ's kindness!

"Lest any man fail of the grace of God." This is the clause which has occasioned controversy: though really it affords no warrant for it, nor will the Greek permit of the marginal rendering. The root word which is here rendered "fail" occurs many times in the N.T., but never once has it the force of "fall from." It means "to lack" or "be deficient of." In Rom. 3:23 it is rendered "come short of," in Luke 15:14 to "want," in 2 Cor. 12:11 "come behind," in Matt. 19:20 "lack," in Phil. 4:12 "suffer need," in Heb. 11:37 to be "destitute." Thus there is no room for uncertainty as to the meaning of this exhortation: "Looking diligently lest any man fail—come short of, be deficient in, lack—the grace of God."

But to what does " the grace of God" here refer? That is not quite so easy to answer, for sometimes "grace" is to be regarded objectively, sometimes subjectively; in some passages it refers to the free favour of God, in others to His benevolent operation within the heart, in still others to the effects produced thereby. In our present passage, it seems to the writer, to be used more abstractly, having a comprehensive scope as it is applicable to widely different cases. We feel it safest to regard the clause thus, for God's commandment is "exceeding broad" (Psa. 119:96), and very often a single word has a twofold or threefold reference, and therefore we need to be constantly on our guard against *limiting* the meaning or restricting the application of any utterance of Holy Writ. According to our light we will endeavour to show some of the different cases to which this exhortation belongs.

"By 'the grace of God,' God's favour and acceptance in Christ, as it is proposed and declared by the Gospel, is intended. Herein all spiritual mercies and privileges, in adoption, justification, sanctification and consolation, do consist. For these things, proceeding from the love, grace, and goodness of God in Christ, and being effects thereof, are called the grace of God. The attaining and participation of these things, is that which in the faith and profession of the Gospel, men aim at and design; without which, both the one and the other are in vain. This grace, under all their profession of the Gospel, men may fail of, and this is the evil cautioned against" (J. Owen).

Men may "fail of the grace of God," then, by *not submitting* themselves to the terms of the Gospel. Those terms are repugnant to the natural man: they are distasteful to his carnal lusts, they are humbling to his pride. But it is at the former of these two points that the majority "fail." The Gospel calls upon sinners to repent, and they cannot do that with sincerity unless they throw down the weapons of their rebellion against God. The thrice holy God will pardon no man so long as he is determined to please himself and continue in a course of sinning. Again; the Gospel calls on sinners to receive Christ Jesus as *Lord*: to give Him the throne of their hearts, to bow to His sceptre. The holy Redeemer will save no man who is unwilling for Him to "rule over" him (Luke 19:14).

Second, to "fail of the grace of God" is to be satisfied with *something short of* Divine grace communicated to and ruling in the heart. It is to be contented with a religious substitute for it. How many are deceived by "a form of godliness" who know nothing of its "power" (2 Tim. 3:5). How many mistake a head-knowledge of the Truth for a miracle of grace wrought in the heart. How many substitute outward forms and ceremonies for an experimental acquaintance with the substance of them. How many confuse an external reformation of life with the Divine regeneration and transformation of the soul. Alas, of how very many does it have to be said, "He feedeth on ashes; a deceived heart hath turned him aside, that he cannot deliver his soul" (Isa 44:20). O how few there are who know "the grace of God *in truth*" (Col. 1:6). Do *you*, my reader? *Do* you?

"Some have maintained an admirable character to all appearance all their lives, and yet have failed of the grace of God because of some secret sin. They persuaded even themselves that they were believers, and yet they were not truly so; they had no *inward* holiness, they allowed one sin to get the mastery, they indulged in an unsanctified passion, and so, though they were laid in the grave like sheep, they died with a false hope, and missed eternal life. This is a most dreadful state to be in, and perhaps some of us are in it. Let the prayer be breathed, 'Search me, O God, and know my heart: try me, and know my thoughts: and see if there be any wicked way in me, and lead me in the way everlasting.' Are ye earnest in secret prayer? Do ye love the reading of the Bible? Have ye the fear of God before your eyes? Do you really commune with God? Do you truly love Christ? Ask yourselves these questions *often*, for though we preach the free Gospel of Jesus Christ, I hope as plainly as any, we feel it to be just as needful to set you on self-examination and to excite in you a holy anxiety. It ought to be often a question with you 'Have I the grace of God, or do I fall short of it? Am I a piece of rock crystal which is very like the diamond, but yet is not diamond?' " (C. H. Spurgeon).

Third, multitudes "fail of the grace of God" by *not persevering* in the use of the outward means. They are very earnest and zealous at first, but become careless and slothful. "There are some persons who for a time appear to possess the grace of God, and for a while exhibit many outward evidences of being Christians, but at last *the* temptation comes most suitable to their depraved tastes, and they are carried away with it. They fail of the grace of God. They appear to have attained it, but they fail at last; like a man in business who makes money for a time, but fails in the end. They fail of the grace of God—like an arrow shot from the bow, which goes straight towards the target for a time, but having too little impetus, fails to reach the mark. There are some who did run well, what doth hinder them that they should not obey the truth?" (C. H. Spurgeon).

Finally, genuine Christians themselves "fail of the grace of God" by *not improving* that which God has already bestowed upon them. Faith has been imparted to them, but how little they exercise it. There is an infinite fulness in Christ for them, but how little do they draw upon it. Wondrous privileges are theirs, but how little do they use them. Light has been communicated to them, but how little do they walk in it. They fail to watch and pray lest they enter into temptation (Mark 14:38). They fail to cleanse themselves from all filthiness of the flesh and spirit (2 Cor. 7:1). They fail to grow in grace and in the knowledge of the Lord Jesus (2 Pet. 3:18). They fail to keep themselves from idols (1 John 5:21). They fail to keep themselves in the love of God (Jude 21). And by so failing, their peace is disturbed, their joy is diminished, their testimony is marred, and frequent chastenings are brought upon them.

"Lest any root of bitterness springing up trouble you." This is the evil warned against. Observe how abstractly this also is worded: it is not "lest any root of bitterness spring up *in* you," or "*among* you," but simply "springing up." The reference, we believe, is again a double one: first to the individual himself, and then to the corporate company. This second "lest" is obviously related intimately to the first: if we "fail of the grace of God" then "a root of bitterness springing up" is to be surely expected. Nor can there be any doubt as to what is signified by this figure of a "root of bitterness springing up"—the uprising of evil is evidently that which is in view. This is what we are here to guard against: failure to do so will bring "trouble" upon us and occasion a stumblingblock to others.

The first thing to be noted here is the expression "root of bitterness." Now the root of a tree is that part of it which is underground, hence the reference is to that which is *unseen.* It points to *indwelling sin,* which continues in a man even after he is regenerated. That is why the Christian is exhorted, "Let not sin therefore reign in your mortal body, that ye should obey it in the lusts thereof" (Rom. 6:12). And if *that* is to be obeyed, then it is imperative we heed the word "Keep thy heart with all diligence, for out of it are the issues of life" (Prov. 4:23). Every stirring of sin within is to be resisted, every defiling effect of it confessed to God. If the weeds be not kept down, the flowers and vegetables will be choked. If the Christian fails in the work of *mortification* then the cultivation of his graces will be arrested.

"Lest any root of bitterness springing up." The "springing up" is the appearance of its stalk above the ground. It is the open manifestion of sin in the life, issuing from an *unmortified* lust in the soul, which is here in view. What is unjudged before God in secret usually ends in becoming open before men. "Be sure your sin will find you out" (Num. 32:23) is a solemn word for each of us on this point. "Lest *any* root" emphasizes the need of constant watchfulness against *every* sin, for many branches and sprigs are ready to issue from the main trunk of indwelling corruption. Our safeguards are to yield ourselves *wholly* to God without reserve at any point, to be well instructed in practical godliness, to preserve a tender conscience, to be more distrustful about ourselves, to cultivate closer daily communion with God, to fix our affections upon things above.

"Lest any root *of bitterness* springing up." By nature, sin is pleasant and delightful to us, but in the end it "biteth like a serpent and stingeth like an adder" (Prov. 23:32). Particularly is this the case with the Christian. God will not long suffer him to indulge his lusts, without making him taste the bitter consequences of the same. The lashings of his conscience, the convictions of the Spirit, the wretchedness of his soul, will cause him to say, "He hath filled me with bitterness, He hath made me drunken with wormwood" (Lam. 3:15). As our text says, "lest any root of bitterness springing up *trouble*." That which is contrary to God's holiness and offends His majesty, He makes a source of trouble to us, either in our minds, bodies, estates, or families. "And many be defiled:" sin is like leaven—its influence spreads: "evil communications corrupt good manners" (1 Cor. 15:33).

The second half of our text also refers to the local church: in it there is, no doubt, an allusion to Deut. 29:18. Great watchfulness needs to be exercised and a strict discipline maintained therein. Unregenerate professors are ever seeking to creep into the assembly of the saints. If God's servants sleep, the Enemy will sow his tares among the wheat. When the suspicion of church officers is aroused, prayer for discernment and guidance is called for. Where the one suspected breaks out in corrupt doctrine or in loose living, he is to be dealt with promptly. Delay is dangerous. The allowance of a "little leaven" will soon corrupt the whole lump. At no point does the local church fail more deplorably to-day than in its refusal to maintain Scriptural discipline.

CHAPTER NINETY-SIX

A Warning Against Apostasy

(Heb. 12:16, 17)

The verses which we are now to consider are among the most solemn to be found in the Word of God. They present a most pointed warning against apostasy. They bring before us what is to all tender consciences a terror-provoking subject, namely, *sin for which there is no forgiveness.* It is indeed to be deplored that recent writers have dealt with it like they do with most matters—very superficially or quite erroneously. Either they have limited themselves unto two or three passages, ignoring many others directly relating to the theme, or they have wrongly affirmed that no one can commit "the unpardonable sin" during this present dispensation. On the other hand, most of the old writers seem to have devoted their efforts to re-assuring weak and fearing Christians that *they* had not committed this awful offence, rather than in making any attempt to define the character of the transgression itself.

The subject is admittedly a difficult one, and we believe God has permitted a measure of obscurity to rest upon it, and that in order to deter men from rashly venturing too near the brink of this terrible precipice. It therefore becomes us to approach it in fear and trembling, with modesty and humility, seeking grace and wisdom from on High to deal with it in a faithful, clear, and helpful manner. For this is no easy thing, if we are to avoid error and preserve the balance of truth. Two extremes have to be guarded against: a blunting of its fearful point so that the wicked would be encouraged to continue trifling with God and sporting with their eternal destiny, or failing to write with sufficient definiteness so that awakened and contrite sinners would not be delivered from sinking into despair beneath Satan's lying misuse of it against them.

Before turning to the positive side it seems necessary to briefly point out wherein they seriously err, who insist that no one ever sins beyond the possibility of Divine pardon during this present era of grace. There are quite a number of passages in the N.T. epistles which clearly show the contrary. In 2 Thess. 2:11, 12 we read, "For this cause God shall send them strong delusion, that they should believe a lie; that they all might be damned who believed not the truth, but had pleasure in unrighteousness." In Heb. 6:4, 6 it is said of some that " it is impossible to renew them again unto repentance." In Heb. 10:26, 27 it is said, "For if we sin wilfully after that we have received the knowledge of the truth there remaineth no more sacrifice for sins, but a certain fearful looking for of judgment and fiery indignation, which shall devour the adversaries;" while in 1 John 5:16 we are expressly informed "there is a sin unto death." In our judgment each of these passages refers to a class of offenders who have so grievously provoked God that their doom is irrevocably sealed while they are yet here upon earth.

Against the testimony of the above scriptures an appeal has often been made to, "The blood of Jesus Christ His Son cleanseth us from *all* sin." But the Word of God does not contradict itself, and it is an evil practice which cannot be too strongly condemned to pit one passage against another: any attempt to neutralize one text by another is handling the Truth deceitfully. With regard to 1 John 1:7 three things need to be pointed out. First, the precious blood of Christ was never designed to cleanse from every sin—was it designed to cleanse Judas from his betrayal of the Saviour! Its application is no wider than its impetration: its virtue does not extend beyond *the purpose for which* it was shed. Second, it does not say "the blood of Jesus Christ His Son cleanseth from all sin;" instead, it is strictly qualified: "cleanseth *us* from all sin," that is, God's own people. It is dishonest to appropriate these words to unbelievers. Third, the promise is further limited in the preceding clause, "But *if* we walk in the light as He is in the light."

Nor do we at all agree with those writers who, while allowing that "the unpardonable sin" may be committed during this present dispensation, yet affirm it is a very rare occurrence, a most exceptional thing, of which only one or two isolated cases may be found. On the contrary, we believe that the Scriptures themselves clearly intimate that *many* have been guilty of sins for which there was no forgiveness either in this world or the world to come. We say "sins," for a careful and prolonged study of the subject has convinced us that "the unpardonable sin" is *not* one particular act of committing some specific offence, like maliciously ascribing to Satan the works of the Holy Spirit (which, no doubt, is one form of it), but that it varies considerably in different cases. Both of these conclusions of the present writer will receive illustration and confirmation in what follows.

The first human being who was guilty of unpardonable sin was Cain. He was a professor or outward worshipper of God, but because Abel's offering was accepted and his own rejected, he waxed angry. The Lord condescended to expostulate with him, and went so far as to assure him that if he did well he would not lose his pre-eminence as the firstborn. But so far from doing well, he persisted in wickedness, and his enmity against God was evidenced by his hatred of His child, ending in the murder of him. Whereupon the Lord said unto him, "The voice of thy brother's blood crieth unto Me from the ground. And now art thou *cursed* from the earth . . . A fugitive and a vagabond shalt thou be in the earth" (Gen. 4:10-12). To which Cain answered, "Mine iniquity is greater than it may be forgiven" (Gen. 4:13, margin).

The record of Gen. 6 makes it clear that a whole generation of the world's inhabitants had transgressed beyond all hope of remedy or forgiveness. "And God saw that the wickedness of man was great in the earth, and that every imagination of the thoughts if his heart was only evil continually. And it repented the Lord that He had made man on the earth. And the Lord said, I will destroy man whom I have created from the face of the earth" (Gen. 6:5-7), which was duly accomplished by the Flood. The whole of mankind in the days of Nimrod sinned so grievously (Rom. 1:21-23) that "God gave them up" (Rom. 1:24-26), for His Spirit "will not always strive with men."

A whole generation of the Hebrews were also guilty of "the great trangression." In Ex. 23:20, 21, we read, "Behold, I send an Angel before thee, to keep thee in the way, and to bring thee into the place which I have prepared. Beware of Him, and obey His voice, provoke Him not; for He will *not pardon* your transgressions: for My Name is in Him." Alas they heeded not this solemn word: "our fathers would not obey, but thrust Him from them, and in their hearts turned back into Egypt" (Acts 7:39). Consequently the Lord said, "Wherefore I was grieved with that generation, and said, They do always err in their heart, and they have not known My ways. So I sware in My wrath, They shall not enter into My rest" (Heb. 3:10, 11).

It seems evident to the writer that there have been some in every age who have gone beyond the bounds of Divine mercy. Passing by such individual cases as Pharaoh, Balaam, and Saul, we would observe that the Pharisees of Christ's day—the bulk of them at least—were guilty of sin for which there was no forgiveness. It is clear from John 3:2 that they recognised Him as "a Teacher come from God" and from John 11:47 that they could not gainsay His miracles. Nay more, it is plain from Mark 12:7 that they *knew* the righteousness of His claims: "But those husbandmen said among themselves, This is the Heir: come, let us kill Him." Thus they acted with their eyes wide open, sinning against their own confession, against light and knowledge, against the strong conviction His miracles produced, and against His holy life spread before them. Therefore did Christ say to them, "I go My way, and ye shall seek Me, and shall *die in your sins*: whither I go, ye cannot come" (John 8:21).

"Keep back Thy servant also from presumptuous sins; let them not have dominion over me; then shall I be upright, and I shall be innocent from the great transgression" (Psa. 19:13). Here the unpardonable sin is denominated "the great transgression." It is called such because this is what a bold and audacious defiance of God necessarily culminates in, unless sovereign grace intervenes. "Presumptuous" sins are committed by those who, while professing God's name and avowing a claim upon His mercy, persist in a known course contrary to His Word. Such rebels, presuming upon God's patience and goodness, are mocked by Him, being suffered to go beyond the bounds of His forgiveness. It is also called "blasphemy against the Spirit" (Matt. 12:31), "resisting the Spirit" (Acts 7:51), "doing despite unto the Spirit of grace" (Heb. 10:29). The "new testament" or "covenant" is "the ministration of the Spirit" (2 Cor. 3:8), which far exceeds in glory the legal dispensation. To be guilty of the great transgression is to sin wilfully against and to speak maliciously of the Holy Spirit, who is revealed and promised in the Gospel; it is a quenching of His convictions, resisting His enlightenment, defying His authority.

It is called "a sin unto death" (1 John 5:16) because its perpetrator is now out of the reach of the promise of eternal life, having made the Gospel, which is a proclamation of Divine grace unto those who will submit themselves to its requirements, a "savour of death unto death" to himself. He was convicted by it that he was legally dead, and because of his impenitence, unbelief, hard-heartedness, and determination to go on having *his own* way, he is left spiritually dead. Unto others God grants "repentance unto life," (Acts 11:18), but when once "sin unto death" has been committed, it is "impossible to renew again unto repentance" (Heb. 6:4-6). By his opposition to the Gospel and refusal to receive Christ's "yoke," the guilty rebel has trampled under foot the blood of God's Son, and as *that* alone can procure forgiveness, there is now no pardon available for him.

The very fact that it is designated "*a* sin unto death" rather than "*the* sin unto death" confirms what we said in a previous paragraph, namely, that it is not some specific offence but rather that the particular form it takes varies in different cases. And herein we may perceive how the *sovereignty* of God is exercised in connection therewith. God allows some to go to greater lengths of wickedness than others: some evil-doers He cuts off in youth, while other workers of iniquity are permitted to live unto old age. Against some He is more quickly and more strongly provoked than others. Some souls He abandons to themselves more readily than He does others. It is *this* which renders the subject so unspeakably solemn: no man has any means of knowing how soon *he may cross the line which marks the limits of God's forebearance with him.* To trifle with God is hazardous to the last degree.

That the sovereignty of God is exercised in this matter appears very clearly from the cases of those whom He is pleased to save. What fearful crimes Manasseh was guilty of before Divine grace renewed him! What dreadful sins Saul of Tarsus committed ere the Lord Jesus apprehended him! Let the writer and the reader review their own unregenerate days: how dreadfully did we provoke the Majesty on high; how long did we persevere in a course of open rebellion; against what restraints, privileges, light and knowledge, warnings and entreaties, did we act! How many of the godless companions of our youth were cut off in their guilt, while we were spared. Was it because *our* sins were less crimson? No, indeed; so far as we can perceive, our sins were of a deeper dye than theirs. Then why did God save us? and why were they sent to Hell? "Even so, Father, for so it seemed good in Thy sight" *must* be the answer.

A sovereign God has drawn the line in every life which marks the parting of the ways. When that line is reached by the individual, God does one of two things with him: either He performs a miracle of grace so that he becomes "a new creature in Christ Jesus," or henceforth that individual is *abandoned* by Him, given up to hardness of heart and final impenitency; and *which* it is, depends entirely upon His own imperial pleasure. And none can tell how near he may be to that line, for some reach it much earlier in life than others—according as God sovereignly decreed. Therefore it is the part of wisdom for each sinner to promptly heed that word "Seek ye the Lord *while he may be found*" (Isa. 55:6), which plainly denotes that soon it may be too late—as Prov. 1:28-31 and Matt. 25:8-12 plainly show.

This solemn distinction which God makes between one case and another was strikingly shadowed out under the law. We refer to a remarkable detail concerning the *jubilee* year, a detail which seems to have escaped the notice of those who have preached and written on the subject. Those in Israel who, through poverty, had sold their possessions, had them restored at the year of jubilee: see Lev. 25:25-28. That was a wondrous and beautiful figure of the free grace of God towards His people in Christ, by which, and not because of anything of their own, they are restored to the Divine favour and given a title to the heavenly inheritance. But in connection therewith there was *an exception,* designed by God, we doubt not, to adumbrate that which we are here treating upon. That exception we will briefly notice.

"If a man sell a dwellinghouse in a walled city, then he may redeem it within a whole year after it is sold; within a full year may he redeem it. And if it be not redeemed within the space of a full year, then the house that is in the walled city shall be established forever to him that bought it throughout his generations: *it shall not go out in the jubilee*" (Lev. 25:29, 30). We cannot now attempt an exposition of this interesting passage or dwell upon its leading features. No part of the "land" could be sold outright (see v. 23), for that was the free gift of *God's* bounty—there can be no failure in Divine grace; but houses in the city were the result of *their* labour—human responsibility being in view. If the house was sold and not repurchased within a year, it passed *beyond the reach of redemption,* its forfeiture being irrevocable and irrecoverable! Symbolically, the "house" spoke of security under the Divine covenant, for in all generations God in covenant has been the "dwelling-place" of His people (Psa. 90:1). To part with his house typified a professor selling himself to work presumptuous wickedness (1 Kings 21:20), and so selling his soul, his God, his all. To such an one the Spirit will never "proclaim liberty" of the Jubilee, for Satan holds him fast, and Divine justice forbids his discharge: when God "shutteth up a man, there can be *no opening*" (Job 12:14).

In view of all that has been before us, how softly we should tread, how careful we should be of not provoking the Holy One! How earestly we should pray to be kept back from "presumptuous sins"! How diligently should the young improve their privileges: how they should heed that warning, "He that being often reproved hardeneth his neck, shall suddenly be destroyed, and that *without remedy*" (Prov. 29:1)! How careful we should be against adding sin to sin, lest we provoke God to leave us unto final impenitency. Our only safeguard is to heed the voice of the Lord *without delay,* lest he "swear in His wrath" that *we* "should not enter into His rest"! How we need to beg God to write those words upon our hearts, "Take heed, brethren, lest there be in you an evil heart of unbelief, in departing from the living God" (Heb. 3:12), for there is no hope whatever for the apostate.

A word now unto those with tender consciences that fear *they* may have committed sin for which there is no forgiveness. The trembling and contrite sinner is the farthest from it. There is not one instance recorded in Scripture where any who was guilty of "the great transgression" and had been given up by God to inevitable destruction, ever repented of his sins, or sought God's mercy in Christ; instead, they all continued obstinate and defiant, the implacable enemies of Christ and His ways unto the end. While there be in the heart any sincere valuing of God's approbation, any real sense of His holiness which deters from trifling with Him, any genuine purpose to turn unto Him and submit to His requirements, any true fearing of His wrath, *that* soul *has not* been abandoned by Him. If you have a deep desire to obtain an interest in Christ, or become a better Christian; if you are deeply troubled over sin, if your heart grieves over its hardness, if you yearn and pray for more tenderness of conscience, more yieldedness of will, more love and obedience to Christ, then you have *no cause* to suspect you have committed "the unpardonable sin."

"Lest there by any fornicator, or profane person, as Esau, who, for one morsel of meat sold his birthright. For ye know how that afterward when he would have inherited the blessing, he was rejected: for he found no place of repentance, though he sought it carefully with tears" (Heb. 12:16,17). These verses continue what was before us in the preceding one, and complete the series of exhortations begun in v. 12. As we pointed out at the close of the previous article, the ultimate reference in v. 15 is first a warning against that which if disregarded would end in apostasy. and second, a caution against suffering one who evidences the symptoms of an apostate to remain in the assembly—its language being an allusion unto Deut. 29:18. That warning and caution is now exemplified by citing the fearful example of Esau, who, though born among the covenant people and receiving (we doubt not) a pious upbringing, committed a sin for which there was no forgiveness, and became an apostate.

First of all, two particular sins are here warned against: "fornication" and "profanity," each of which is "a root of bitterness," which if permitted to "spring up" will cause "trouble" to the guilty one and "defile many" with whom he is associated. Both "fornication" and "profanity" are opposed unto the *holiness* exhorted unto in v. 14. Fornication is a sin against the second table of the Law, and profanity a breach of its first table. As in v. 14 the apostle had enjoined the Hebrews to "follow peace" which has respect to *man* and "holiness" which regards our relation to *God,* so now he forbids two sins, the first of which would be committed against man, the second against God. The two sins go together, for where a course of moral uncleanness is followed, profanity almost always accompanies it; and on the other hand, profane persons habitually think lightly of immorality. The forsaking of either sin by sincere repentance is exceedingly rare.

The term "profane" has a more specific meaning and a wider application than it is commonly accorded in our speech to-day. "Holy things are said to be profaned when men take off the veneration that is due unto them, and expose them to common use or contempt. To 'profane' is to violate, to corrupt, to prostitute to common use things sacred, either in their nature or by Divine institution. A profane person is one that despiseth, sets light by, or condemneth sacred things. Such as mock at religion, or who lightly regard its promises and threatenings; who despise or neglect its worship, who speak irreverently of its concerns, we call profane persons, and such they are, and such the world is filled with at this day. This profaneness is the last step of entrance into final apostasy. When men, from professors of religion, become despisers of and scoffers at it, their state is dangerous, if not irrevocable" (J. Owen).

An instance of this evil is given in Esau, and a fearfully solemn case his is, one which would warn us not to put our trust in *external* privileges. "He was the firstborn of Isaac, circumcised according to the law of that ordinance, and partaker of all the worship of God in that holy family; yet an outcast from the covenant of grace and the promise thereof" (Owen). The particular offence with which he is here charged is that "for one morsel of meat" he "sold his birthright." Now the birthright or privilege of the firstborn carried with it the following things: the special blessing of his father, a double portion of his goods, dominion over his brethren, and priestly functions (Num. 3:41) when the father was absent from home. The "birthright" was regarded as a very special thing, being typical of the primogeniture of Christ, of the adoption of saints, and of a title to the heavenly inheritance. All of this Esau despised.

The historical account of Esau's sin is recorded in the closing verses of Gen. 25: the heinousness of it is exhibited in our text. Esau preferred the gratification of the flesh rather than the blessing of God. He relinquished all claims to the privileges contained in and annexed to his being the firstborn, for a trifling and temporary enjoyment of the body. Alas, how many there are like him in the world to-day. What vast numbers prefer carnal pleasures to spiritual joys, temporal advantages to eternal riches, physical gratification to the soul's salvation. By calling Esau "profane," the Holy Spirit reveals that he placed no higher value upon sacred things than he did upon those which were common. That which he received at the price of his wickedness is termed "meat," to indicate that satisfying of the flesh was his motive; and a "morsel," to emphasise the paltriness of his choice.

The enormity of the sin of "profanity" is determined by the sacredness of the objects to which it is opposed: let the reader carefully compare Lev. 18:21; 21:9; Neh. 13:17; Ezek. 22:26. The "profane" are guilty of trampling God's pearls beneath their feet. To spurn the Scriptures, to desecrate the Sabbath, to revile God's servants, to despise or ridicule the Gospel, to mock at the future state, are all so many forms of this unspeakable wickedness. As helps against it we would mention the need of being well instructed from the Word, so that we may know *what are* "holy" things. To bring our hearts to realise the superlative excellency of holiness. To meditate seriously and frequently upon God's indignation against those who slight what He highly esteems.

"For ye know how that afterward, when he would have inherited the blessing, he was rejected: for he found no place of repentance, though he sought it carefully with tears" (v. 17). This takes us back to the closing section of Gen. 27, where we learn the consequences which his sin entailed. Isaac had pronounced the patriarchal benediction upon Jacob, which, when his brother learned thereof deeply agitated him: "He cried with a great and exceeding bitter cry" (Gen. 27:34). It was then that his "tears" were shed: but they proceeded not from anguish of heart because he had sinned so grievously against God, rather did they flow from a sense of self-pity—they expressed his chagrin for the consequences which his *folly* had produced. Similar are the lamentations of probably ninty-nine out of a hundred so called "death-bed repentances." And such will be the "weeping and wailing" of those in Hell: not because *God* was so slighted and wronged by them, but because of the eternal suffering which their sins have justly resulted in.

Esau's "tears" were of no avail: "he was rejected." His appeal *came too late*: Isaac had already bestowed the blessing upon Jacob. It was like an Israelite seeking to recover his property eighteen months after he had sold it: see again Lev. 25:30. Isaac, who was a prophet of God, His mouthpiece, refused to be moved by Esau's bitter wailing. In like manner, the Lord says of those who have sinned away the day of grace "They shall call upon Me, but I will not answer; they shall seek Me early, but they shall not find Me" (Prov. 1:28); and "Therefore will I also deal in fury: Mine eye shall not spare, neither will I have pity: and though they cry in Mine ears with a loud voice, *yet will I not hear them*" (Ezek. 8:18). O what point that gives to the call "Seek ye the Lord while He may be found, call ye upon Him *while He is near*" (Isa. 55:6). Reader, if you have not yet genuinely responded to that call, do so at once; delay is fraught with the utmost peril to your soul.

The apostle was here addressing professing Christians, and the fearful case of Esau is set before them (and *us!*) as a warning against departing from the Narrow Way, of exchanging the high privileges of the faithful for the temporary advantages of a faithless world. The doom of the apostate is irretrievable. To lightly esteem, and then despise, sacred things, will be followed "afterward" by bitter regret and unavailing anguish. To reject the terms of the Gospel in order to gratify the lusts of the flesh for a brief season, and then suffer forever and ever in the Lake of Fire, is the height of madness. No excuse could palliate Esau's profanity, and nothing can extenuate the wickedness of him who prefers the drudgery of Satan to the freedom there is in Christ. Esau's rejection by Isaac was the evidence of his reprobation by God. May it please the Lord to use this article to *search the heart* of every reader.

CHAPTER NINETY-SEVEN

The Inferiority of Judaism

(Heb. 12:18, 19)

As there are certain parts of a country which offer less attraction than others unto tourists and sight-seers, so there are some portions of Scripture which are of less interest to most readers and writers. As there are some scenes in Nature which can be taken in at a glance while others invite a repeated survey, so there are verses in each Epistle which afford less scope than others unto the teacher. That is why almost every preacher has a sermon on certain favourite texts, whereas other verses are neglected by nearly all pulpits. But the expositor has not the same freedom to follow his inclinations as the textual sermonizer: unless he shirks his duty, he must go through a passage verse by verse, and clause by clause. Still more so is this the case with one who essays to write a commentary upon a whole book of the Bible: he is not free to pick and choose, nor yield to his personal preferences, but must give the same attention and enlargement to one part as to another.

The above reflections have occurred to the editor as he has pondered the verses which next claim our consideration in Heb. 12. Their contents are not likely to make much appeal unto the ordinary reader, for there seems little in them which would be relished either by those who have an appetite for "strong meat" or by those preferring the "milk" of babes. Our passage neither sets forth any of the "doctrine of grace" nor presents any practical exhortation for the Christian life. Instead, it alludes to an historical incident which was chiefly of interest to the Jews, and multiplies details from the same which would be tedious unto the average churchgoer of this untoward generation. Nevertheless, it is a part of *God's* Word, and as it lies in our immediate path through this Epistle we shall not ignore or turn from it. As the Lord enables, we shall endeavour to give it the same attention and space as what has preceded it.

The passage upon which we are about to enter (which reaches from 12:18 to the end of the chapter) has been variously interpreted by different conmmentators. One class of more recent writers have, it seems to us, been far more anxious to read into it their own pet theory regarding the future, than to interpret these verses in accord with the theme of the Epistle in which they are found. It would indeed be strange for the apostle to introduce here a reference to some future "millennium:" the more so in view of the fact that he has studiously avoided the use of the future tense—note the emphatic "ye *are* come" (v. 22) and "but *now*" (v. 26). If due attention be paid unto the main line of the apostle's argument in this treatise, then there should be no difficulty in arriving at a correct understanding—of the substance of it, at least—of this portion of it.

As we pointed out so frequently in the earlier articles of this series, the immediate and principal design of the apostle in this Epistle, was to prevail with the Hebrews in persuading them unto a perseverance in their profession of the Gospel, for therein they appear at that time to have been greatly shaken. Therefore does he warn them, again and again, of the various causes and occasions of backsliding. Principal among these were, first, an evil heart of unbelief, the sin which did so easily beset them. Second, an undue valuation of the excellency of Judaism and the Mosaical church-state. Third, wavering under the afflictions and persecutions which fidelity to the Gospel entailed. Fourth, prevalent lusts, such as profaneness and fornication. Each of these we have considered in the preceding sections.

The principal argument which the apostle had urged unto their constancy in Christianity, was the superlative excellency, glory, and benefit of the Gospel-state into which the Hebrews had been called. This he has accomplished and proved by setting forth the person and office of its Author, His priesthood and sacrifice, with all the spiritual worship and privileges belonging thereto. Each of these he compared and contrasted with the things that corresponded unto the same during the O.T. dispensation. Thereby he set over against each other the type and the antitype, the shadow and the substance, and by so doing made it unmistakably evident that the new economy was immeasurably superior to the old, that all the ordinances and institutions of the law were but prefigurations of those spiritual realities which are now revealed by the Gospel.

Having insisted so largely and so particularly on these things in the preceding chapters and brought his arguments from them to a plain issue, he now recapitulates them as a whole. In the passage which is now to engage our attention the apostle presents a brief scheme of the two states or economies (designated as "testaments" or "covenants"), balancing them one against another, and thereby demonstrating the conclusive force of his central argument and the exhortations which he had based upon it, unto constancy and perseverance in the faith of the Gospel. It is no new argument which he here proceeds with, nor is it a special amplification of the warning pointed by the example of Esau; still less is it a departure from his great theme by a sudden excursus into the realm of eschatology. Instead, it is a forcible summary, under a new dress, of all he had previously advanced.

The central design, then, of our passage as a whole, was to present one more and final antithesis of Judaism and Christianity. The contrast here drawn is virtually parallel with the one instituted in Gal. 4 between Hagar and Sarah, the figure of two "mounts" being used instead of the two women. The great honour and chief privilege of the Judaical Church-state whereon all particular advantages did depend, was their coming to and station in mount Sinai at the giving of the Law. It was there that Jehovah revealed Himself with all the insignia of His awe-inspiring majesty. It was there that they were taken into covenant with the Lord (Ex. 24), to be His peculiar people above all the world. It was there that Israel was formed into a national Church (Acts 7:38). It was there that they had committed unto them all the privileges of Divine worship. It is that very glory which the Jews boast of to this day, and whereon they rest in their rejection of the Gospel.

It was necessary, then, for the apostle to make direct reference unto that upon which the unbelieving Hebrews based all their hopes, and to which they were appealing in their efforts to get their believing brethren to apostatise from Christ. His argument had neither been complete nor conclusive unless he could undermine their confidence in the foundational glory of Judaism, take off their hearts from unduly admiring, and show that it had been succeeded by that which "excelleth." He therefore directs attention to those features in connection with the giving of the Law, which so far from being calculated to win the affections, inspired with dread and terror. He points out a number of items which by their very nature intimated that the Divine communications vouchsafed at Sinai were not the full and final unveiling of the Divine character, such as the souls of awakening sinners longed for.

Our introduction has been a somewhat lengthy one, though briefer than that of J. Owen, which we have closely followed in the last paragraphs; yet we deemed it necessary. The details of our present passage cannot be viewed in their true perspective until they are rightly focused in the light of our Epistle as a whole. The *scope* of the passage must first be determined, before we are ready to examine its several members. This calls for time and real *study,* yet only as this preliminary work is properly executed will we be preserved from those errors which are inevitably fallen into when a passage is treated hurriedly and superficially. This is only another way of saying that, the foundation must be well and securely laid, if it is to bear successfully the superstructure which is raised upon it. Alas that such foundation-labour is so little appreciated to-day.

"For ye are not come unto the mount that might be touched, and that burned with fire" (v. 18). The apostle here returns to his central theme by an easy and natural transition. He had just been dehorting from back-sliding, pointed out by the solemn case of Esau. Now he urges unto constancy by appealing to the privileges they enjoyed. As Calvin well put it, "The higher the excellency of Christ's kingdom than the dispensation of Moses, and the more glorious our calling than that of the ancient people, the more disgraceful and the less excusable is our ingratitude, unless we embrace in a becoming manner the great favour offered to us, and humbly adore the majesty of Christ which is here made evident. And then, as God does not present Himself to us clothed in terrors as He did formerly to the Jews, but lovingly and kindly invites us to Himself, so the sin of ingratitude will be thus doubled, except we willingly and in earnest respond to His gracious invitation."

"For ye are not come unto the mount that might be touched." The principal design which the apostle here had in hand was to set forth, in its most attractive form (see vv. 22-24), that evangelical state where-unto the Hebrews had been called and into which they had entered. This he first does *negatively,* by describing the Church-state under the O.T., from which they had been delivered. Thus, before the "Ye are come" of v. 22, he introduces this "For ye are not come." Two things were thereby noted: that order or system to which their fathers belonged, but from which *they* had been freed by their responding to the Gospel call. They were no more concerned in all that dread and terror, and their consideration of that fact supplied a powerful motive to their perseverance in the Christian faith.

Freely granting that a great privilege was conferred on their fathers at Sinai, the apostle observes "that it was done in such a way of dread and terror, as that sundry things are manifest therein: as, 1. That there was no evidence in all that was done of God's being reconciled to them, in and by those things. The whole representation of Him was of an absolute Sovereign and a severe Judge. Nothing declared Him as a Father, gracious and merciful. 2. There was no intimation of any condescension from the exact severity of what was required in the law or of any relief or pardon in case of transgression. 3. There was no promise of grace in a way of aid or assistance for the performance of what was required. Thunders, voices, earthquakes and fire gave no signification of these things. 4. The whole was hereby nothing but a glorious ministration of death and condemnation (as the apostle speaks: 2 Cor. 3:7) whence the conscience of sinners were forced to subscribe to their own condemnation, as just and equal.

"5. God was here represented in all outward demonstrations of infinite holiness, justice, severity and terrible majesty on the one hand; and on the other, men in their lowest condition of sin, misery, guilt and death. If there be not therefore something else to interpose between God and men, somewhat to fill up the space between infinite severity and inexpressible guilt, all this glorious preparation was nothing but a theatre set up for the pronouncing of judgment and the sentence of eternal condemnation against sinners. And on this consideration depends the force of the apostle's argument; and the due apprehension and declaration of, is a better explanation of vv. 18-21 than the opening of the particular expressions will amount to; yet they also must be explained.

"It is hence evident, that the Israelites in the station of Sinai, did bear the persons of convicted sinners under the sentence of the law. There might be many of them justified in their own persons by faith in the promise; but as they stood and heard and received the law, they represented sinners under the sentence of it, not yet relieved by the Gospel. And this we may have respect to in our exposition, as that which is that final intention of the apostle to declare, as is manifest from the description which he gives of the Gospel-state, and of those that are interested therein" (J. Owen).

"For ye are not come unto the mount that might be touched." It is both pathetic and amusing to read the various shifts made by some of the commentators to "harmonize" the opening words of our text with what is said in Ex. 19:12, "Thou shalt set bounds unto the people round about, saying, Take heed to yourselves, that ye go not up into the mount, *or touch* the border of it: whosoever toucheth the mount shall surely be put to death." Some have pleaded that the little "*not* be touched" was inadvertantly dropped by a copyist of the Greek manuscript. Others insist our verse should be rendered, "Ye are come to a mount not to be touched." But the only "discrepancy" here is in the understanding of the expositors. The apostle was not making a quotation from Exodus, but rather describing, negatively, that *order of things* unto which the Gospel had brought the believing Hebrews. In so doing, he shows the striking contrast between it and the order of things connected with the giving of the Law.

"For ye are not come unto the mount that might be touched." The simple and evident meaning of this is: The Gospel has not brought you unto that which is material and visible, palpable and touchable by the physical senses, but only what is spiritual and can only be apprehended by faith. A "mount" is a thing *of the earth;* whereas the glory of Christianity is entirely celestial. The passage which most clearly interprets this clause is found in our Lord's discourse with the woman at the well: "Jesus saith unto her, Woman, believe Me, the hour cometh, when you shall neither in this mountain, nor yet at Jerusalem, worship the Father . . . . But the hour cometh, and now is, when the true worshippers shall worship the Father *in spirit and in truth*" (John 4:21, 23). Judaism was the Church's kindergarten, in which its infantile members were instructed, mainly, through their bodily senses. Christianity has introduced a far superior order of things.

"For ye are not come unto the mount that might be touched," then, is a figurative way of saying that Christ has opened a way into something infinitely superior to a system which, as such, had nothing better than "a *worldly* sanctuary" and "*carnal* ordinances" (Heb. 9:1, 10). The Greek word for "come" in our text is that technical or religious term which had been used repeatedly by the apostle in this Epistle to express a *sacred access* or coming to God in His worship: see 4:16, 7:25, 10:1—last clause "comers thereunto." Mount Sinai was a material thing, exposed to the outward senses, and was an emblem of the entire order of things connected with Judaism. As such, it was in complete contrast from that order of things brought in by Christ, which is wholly spiritually, invisible, and celestial. The one was addressed to the bodily senses; the other to the higher faculties of the soul. Spiritually speaking, Romanists and all other Ritualists are occupied with "the mount that might be touched"!

"And that burned with fire." In their most literal sense those words allude to what transpired at Sinai. In Ex. 19:18 we read, "And mount Sinai was altogether on a smoke, because the Lord descended upon it in fire." But it is with their figurative purport we are more concerned. In Scripture "fire" is the symbol of Divine wrath and judgment. As we are told in Deut. 4:24, "The Lord thy God is a consuming fire, a jealous God," and the "jealousy" of God is, His holy severity against sin, not to leave it unpunished. With respect unto the law which He there gave—for Deut. 33:2 declares "from His right hand went a fiery law"—it signified its inexorable sternness and efficacy to destroy its transgressors. Thus, the "fire" denoted the awful majesty of God as an inflexible Judge, and the terror which His law strikes into the minds of its violators with expectations of fiery indignation.

This was the first thing which the people beheld when they came to Sinai: God as a "consuming fire" presented to their view! Thus it is in the experience of those whom God saves. For many years, it may be, they lived in a state of unconcern: they had no heart-affecting views of the majesty and authority of God, and no pride-withering apprehensions of the fearfulness of their guilt. But when the Spirit awakens them from the sleep of death, gives them to realise *Who it is* with whom they have to do, and whose anger burns against sin; when the Law is applied to their conscience, convicting them of their innumerable offences, their hearts are filled with dread and misery as they perceive their undone condition. There the law leaves them, and thence they must be consumed, unless they obtain deliverance by Jesus Christ.

And that was exactly what, by Divine grace, these believing Hebrews *had* obtained. The Redeemer had "delivered them from the wrath to come" (1 Thess. 1:10). They were now as secure in Him as Noah was in the ark. The fire of God's wrath had spent itself on the person of their Substitute. God was now reconciled to them, and henceforth they had an inalienable standing before Him—not as trembling criminals, but as accepted sons. To them the word was "For ye have not received the spirit of bondage again to fear; but ye have received the Spirit of adoption, whereby we cry, Abba, Father" (Rom. 8:15). No, as Christians, we have nothing more to do with the mount "that burned with fire," but only with "the Throne of Grace." Hallelujah! Alas that so many Christians are being robbed of their birthright. If Romanists and Ritualists are guilty of being occupied with "the mount that might be touched," then those who are constantly presenting God before His people in His dread majesty—instead of as a loving Father—are taking them back to the mount "that burned with fire."

"Nor unto blackness and darkness." Here again the literal allusion is unto the awe-inspiring phenomena which attended the giving of the law. There was "a thick cloud upon the mount, . . . mount Sinai was altogether on a smoke" (Ex. 19:16, 18). Different commentators have resorted to various conjectures in their efforts to "harmonize" the "blackness and darkness" with the "fire:" some suggesting the one was followed by the other after an interval of time, others supposing the "darkness" was over the camp and the "fire" at the summit of the mount. But such theorisings are worthless in the face of Deut. 5:22-23, "The Lord spake unto all your assembly in the mount out of the midst of the fire, of the cloud, and of the thick darkness . . . ye heard the voice out of the midst of the darkness, for the mountain did burn with fire." The fact is this "fire" was *supernatural*: as that of Babylon's furnace *burned not* while the three Hebrews were in it (Dan. 3), this *glowed not*—increasing the terror of its beholders because it emitted no light!

If the above explanation be deemed "far fetched," we would appeal to the corroborating correspondency in the experience of those who have been saved. Was it not a fact that when we were shut up under guilt and terrified by the representation of God's severity against sin, we looked in vain for anything in the Law which could yield relief? When the glory of God's holiness shined into your conscience and His law was applied in convicting and condemning power, did you perceive His *merciful design* in the same? No, indeed; at that time, His gracious purpose was covered with "blackness," and "darkness" filled your soul. You perceived not that the law was His instrument for flaying your self-righteous hopes (Rom 7:10) and "a schoolmaster unto *Christ*" (Gal. 3:24). Your case appeared hopeless; and despite the fiery power of the law, you knew not how to "order your speech (before God) by reason of darkness" (Job 37:19).

"And tempest:" under this term the apostle comprises the thundering, lightnings, the earthquake which were on and in mount Sinai (Ex. 19:16, 18) all of which symbolized the disquieting character of so much that marked the Mosaic economy—in contrast from the peace and assurance which the Gospel imparts to those who believingly appropriate it. The order here agrees with the experience of those whom God saves. First, there is an application of the "fiery law," which burns and terrifies the conscience. Second, there is the blackness and darkness of despair which follows the discovery of our lost condition. Third, there is the agitation of mind and turmoil of heart in seeking help by self-efforts and finding none. The soul has no light and knows not what to do. The mind is in a tumult, for no escape from the law's just course seems possible. Not yet has Christ appeared to the distressed one.

"And the sound of a trumpet." This too, we believe, was a supernatural one, emitting ear-splitting tones, shrill and loud, designed to inspire both awe and fear. It signified the near approach of God. It was to summon the people before Him as their lawgiver and Judge (Ex. 19:17). It was the outward sign of the promulgation of the Law, for immediately upon the sound of it, God spoke unto them. It was a pledge of the final judgment, when all flesh shall be summoned before God to answer the terms of His law. Experimentally, it is the imperative summons of the Word for the soul to answer to God's call. Those who neglect it, will have to answer for the whole when they receive the final summons at the last day.

Those who answer it now, are brought into God's presence in fear and trembling, who then reveals to them Christ as an all-sufficient Saviour.

"And the voice of words." This is the *seventh* and final detail which the apostle here noticed. The "voice of words" was articulate and intelligible, in contrast from the dull roar of the thunder and the shrill tones of the trumpet. Those "words" were the ten commandments, written afterward on the two tables of stone: see Deut. 5:22 and the preceding verses. Those "words" were uttered by the voice of the Lord God Almighty (Ex. 20:1), concerning which we are told, "The voice of the Lord is powerful; the voice of the Lord is full of majesty; the voice of the Lord breaketh the cedars" (Psa. 29:4, 5) etc. It was God declaring unto His Church the eternal establishment of His Law, that no alteration should be made in its commands or penalties, but that all must be fulfilled.

" Which voice they that heard entreated that the words should not be spoken to them any more." This reveals the terror-stricken state of those who were encamped before Sinai. There was that on every side which inspired awe and dread: Nature itself convulsed and supernatural phenomena attending the same. This was intended to show the people that God had ascended His awful tribunal as a strict Judge. But that which filled them with intolerable consternation was the voice of God Himself speaking immediately to them. It was not that they refused to hear Him, but that they desired Him to speak to them through Moses, the typical Mediator. Experimentally, the sinner is overwhelmed when the voice of God in the law comes in power to his conscience.

CHAPTER NINETY-EIGHT

The Inferiority of Judaism

(Heb. 12:20, 21)

The Divine law was, for the substance of it, originally written in the hearts of mankind by God Himself, when their federal head and father was created in His own image and likeness. But through the fall it was considerably marred, as to its efficacious motions in the human heart. The entrance of sin and the corruption of our nature largely silenced its authoritative voice in the soul. Nevertheless, its unchanging demand and dread penalty were secured in the consciences of Adam's depraved posterity. The law is so inlaid with the principles of our moral nature, so engrafted on all the faculties of our souls, that none has been able to completely get from under its power. Though the wicked find it utterly contrary to their desires and designs, and continually threatening their everlasting ruin, yet they cannot utterly cast off its yoke: see Rom. 2:14, 15. Hence it is that, even among the most degraded and savage tribes, a knowledge of right and wrong, with some standard of conduct, is preserved.

Not only was the impression of the Divine law upon the human heart largely—though not totally—defaced by Adam's apostasy, but from Cain unto the Exodus succeeding generations more and more flouted its authority, and disregarded its requirements in their common practice. Therefore, when God took Israel into covenant relationship with Himself and established them into a national Church, He *restored to them His law,* in all its purity, majesty, and terror. This He did, not only to renew it as a guide unto all righteousness and holiness, as the only rule of obedience unto Himself and of right and equity amongst men, and also to be a check unto sin by its commands and threatenings, but principally to declare in the Church *the eternal establishment of it,* that no alteration should be made in it, but that all must be fulfilled to the uttermost before any sinner can have any acceptance with Him.

As the Law was the original rule of obedience between God and mankind, and as it had failed of its end through the entrance of sin, the Lord had never revived and proclaimed it in so solemn a manner at Sinai, had it been capable of any abrogation and alteration at any time. Nay, He then gave many *additional evidences of its perpetuity and abiding authority.* It was solely for the promulgation of His law that the presence of God appeared on the mount, attended with such dreadful solemnity. The Ten Commandments were the *only* communication which God then gave directly unto the people themselves—those institutions which *were* to be repealed at a later date (the ceremonial laws) were given through Moses! Those ten commandments were spoken directly unto the whole nation with a Voice that was great and terrible. Later, they were written by His own finger on tables of stone. Thus did God confirm His law and evidence that it was incapable of dissolution. How it has been established and fulfilled the Epistle to the Romans makes known.

The *different forms* which the Lord's appearances took in O.T. times were always in accord with each distinct revelation of His mind and will. He appeared to Abraham in the shape of a man (Gen. 18:1, 2), because He came to give promise of the Seed of blessing and to vouchsafe a representation of the future incarnation. To Moses He appeared as a flame in a bush which was not consumed (Ex. 3), because He would intimate that all the fiery trials through which the Church should pass would not consume it, and that because *He* was in it. To Joshua He appeared as a man of war, with drawn sword in His hand (Josh. 5:13), because He would assure him of victory over all his enemies. But at Sinai His appearing was surrounded by terrors, because He would represent the severity of His law, with the inevitable and awful destruction of all those who lay not hold of the promise for deliverance.

The *place* of this glorious and solemn appearing of the Lord was also full of significance. It was neither in Egypt not yet in Canaan, but in the midst of a great howling desert. Only those who have actually seen the place, can form any adequate conception of the abject dreariness and desolation of the scene. It was an absolute solitude, far removed from the habitation and converse of man. Here the people could neither see nor hear anything but God and themselves. There was no shelter or place of retirement: they were brought out into the open, face to face with God. Therein He gave a type and representation of the Great Judgment at the last day, when all who are out of Christ will be brought face to face with their Judge, and will behold nothing but the tokens of His wrath, and hear only the Law's dread sentence announcing their irrevocable doom.

Sinai was surrounded by a barren and fruitless wilderness, wherein there was neither food nor water. Accurately does that depict the unregenerate in a state of sin: the Law brings forth nothing in their lives which is acceptable to God or really beneficial to the souls of men. The Mount itself produced nothing but bushes and brambles, from which some scholars say its name is derived. From a distance that vegetation makes an appearance of some fruitfulness in the place, but when it be more closely examined it is found that there is nothing except that which is *fit for the fire.* Thus it is with sinners under the law. They seem to perform many works of obedience, yea, such as they trust in and make their boast of; but when they are weighed in the Divine balance, they are found to be but thorns and briars, the dead works of those whose minds are enmity against God. Nothing else can the law bring forth from those who are out of Christ: "*From Me* is thy fruit found" (Hos. 14:8) is His own avowal.

Nor was there any water in the desert of Horeb to make it fruitful. Pause, my reader, and admire the "wondrous works" (Psa. 145:5) of God. When we are given eyes to see, we may discern the Creator's handiwork as plainly in the desolate wastes of Nature as in the fertile fields and gardens, as truly in the barren and forbidding mountains as in the fruitful and attractive valleys. He whose fingers had shaped the place where His Son was crucified as "a place of *a skull*" (Matt. 27:33), had diverted from the desert of Horeb all rivers and streams. That water upon which the people of God then lived, issued from the smitten rock (Ex. 17:6), for it is only through Christ that *the Holy Spirit is given*: see John 7:28, 39, Acts 2:33, Titus 3:5, 6. They who reject Christ have not the Spirit: see Rom. 8:9, Jude 19.

We may further observe that, the appearing of the Lord God at the giving of the Law was on the top of a high mountain, and not in a plain: this added to both the glory and the terror of it. This gave a striking adumbration of the Throne of His majesty, high over the people, who were far below at its base. As they looked up, they saw the mount above them full of fire and smoke, the ground on which they stood quaking beneath their feet, the air filled with thunderings and lightnings, with the piercing blasts of the trumpet and the voice of the Lord Himself falling on their ears. What other thought could fill their minds than that it was "a fearful thing" to be summoned to judgment before the ineffably Holy One? O that the preachers of our day could say with him who had experienced the reality of Sinai in his own soul, "Knowing therefore *the terror of the Lord,* we persuade men" (2 Cor. 5:11).

The Lord's appearing on mount Sinai was only a *temporary* one—in contrast with His "dwelling" in Zion (Isa. 8:18). This shadowed-forth the fact that the *economy* there instituted was but a transient one—though the *Law* there promulgated is eternal. Those, then, who turn unto Sinai for salvation are left entirely unto themselves. "God dwells no more on Sinai. Those who abide under the law (as a covenant, A.W.P.) shall neither have His presence nor any gracious pledge of it. And all these things are spoken to stir us up to seek for an interest in that blessed Gospel-state which is here proposed to us. And thus much we have seen already, that without it there is neither relief from the cure of the law, nor acceptable fruit of obedience, nor pledge of Divine favour to be obtained" (John Owen, whom we have again followed closely in the above paragraphs).

Before turning to the final lines in the graphic picture which the apostle gave of the appearing of the Lord at Sinai, let us again remind ourselves of his principal *design* in the same. The immediate end which the apostle had before him, was to persuade the Hebrews to adhere closely to the Gospel, his appeal being drawn from the evident fact of the superlative excellency of it to the law. In particular, he was here enforcing his former exhortations unto steadfastness under afflictions, to an upright walk in the ways of God, to the following of peace with all men, and to persevere diligently that they failed not of the grace of God. This he does by pointing out that ancient order of things *from which they had been delivered,* for such is the force of his opening words "ye are *not* come unto" etc. (v. 18).

"For they could not endure that which was commanded" (v. 20). Having mentioned in the preceding verses seven things which their fathers came unto at Sinai, the apostle now describes *the effects* which those startling phenomena produced upon them. The first was, the people "entreated that the word should not be spoken to them any more" (v. 19), the reason being "for they could not endure" it. The display of God's terrible majesty, the distance from Him they were required to maintain, and the high spirituality of the Law then promulgated, with its fearful penalty attending the least infraction of it, completely overwhelmed them. So it is still: a view of God *as a Judge,* represented in fire and blackness, will fill the souls of *convicted* sinners with dread and terror. No matter how boldly and blatantly they have carried themselves, when the Spirit brings a transgressor to that Mount, the stoutest heart will quake.

When God deals with men by the Law, He shuts them up to Himself and their own conscience. As we pointed out in an earlier paragraph, God gave the Law to Israel neither in Egypt nor in Canaan, but in a desert, a place of absolute solitude, remote from the commerce of men. There the people could neither see nor hear anything but God and themselves. There was no shelter or place or retirement: they were brought out into the open, face to face with Him with whom they had to do. So it is now: when God has designs of mercy toward a sinner, when He takes him in hand, He brings him out of all his retreats and refuges, and compels him to face the just demands of His Law, and the unspeakable dreadful manner in which he has hitherto disregarded its requirements and sought to hear not its accusations.

When the Law is preached to sinners — alas in so many places today that which gives "the knowledge of sin" (Rom. 3:20) is entirely omitted—it usually falls upon the ears of those who promptly betake themselves to various retreats and reliefs for evading its searching and terror-producing message. They seek refuge in the concerns and amusements of this life in order to crowd out serious and solemn thoughts of the life to come. They listen to the bewitching promises of self-pleasing, "the pleasures of sin for a season." Or, they put far forward in their minds the "evil day," and take security in resolutions of repentance and reformation before death shall come upon them. They have many other things to engage their attention than to listen to the voice of the Law; at least, they persuade themselves it is not yet necessary that they should seriously hearken thereto.

But when God brings the sinner to the Mount, as He most certainly will, either here or hereafter, all these pretenses and false comforts vanish, every prop is knocked from under him: to hide away from his Judge is now impossible. "Judgment also will I lay to the line, and righteousness to the plummet: and the hail shall sweep away the *refuge* of lies, and the waters shall overflow the *hiding* place" (Isa. 28:17). Then it is that the sinner discovers that "the bed is shorter than a man can stretch himself on it: the covering narrower than he can wrap himself in it" (Isa. 28:20). He is forced out into the open: he is brought face to face with his Maker; he is compelled to attend unto the voice of the Law. There is neither escape nor relief for him. His *conscience* is now held to that which he can neither endure nor avoid. He is made to come out from behind the trees, to find his fig-leaves provide no covering (Gen. 3:9-11).

As the stern and inexorable voice of the Law enters into his innermost being, "piercing even to the dividing asunder of soul and spirit, and of the joints and marrow, and is a discerner of the thoughts and intents of the heart" (Heb. 4:12), the poor sinner is paralyzed with fear. The sight of the Divine Majesty on His throne, overwhelms him: the terms and curse of the Law slay his every hope. Now he experiences the truth of Rom. 7:9, 10, "For I was alive (in my own estimation) without the law once; but when the commandment came (applied in power to the conscience by the Spirit) sin revived (became a living, raging, cursed reality) and I died (to all expectation of winning God's approval). And the commandment, which was unto life, I found unto death." Like Israel before Sinai, the sinner *cannot endure* the voice of the Law. The Law commands him, but provides no strength to meet its requirements. It shows him his sins, but it reveals no Saviour. He is encompassed with terror and sees no way of escape from eternal death.

That is the very office of the Law in the hands of the Holy Spirit: to shatter the sinner's unconcern, to make him conscious of the claims of the holy God, to convict him of his lifelong rebellion against Him, to strip him of the rags of his self-righteousness, to slay all hope of self-help and self-deliverance, to bring him to the realization that he is *lost,* utterly undone, *sentenced to death.* "Which voice they that heard entreated that the word should not be spoken to them any more; for they could not endure that which was commanded" (Heb. 12:19, 20). When the Holy Spirit applies the Law in power, the sinner's own conscience is obliged to acknowledge that his condemnation is *just.* And there the Law leaves him: wretched, hopeless, terror-stricken. Unless he flies for refuge to Christ he is lost forever.

Reader, suffer us please to make this a personal issue. Have *you* ever experienced anything which corresponds, in substance, to what we have said above? Have you ever heard the thunderings and felt the lightnings of Sinai in your own soul? Have you, in your conscience, been brought face to face with your Judge, and heard Him read the fearful record of your transgressions? Have you received by the Law such a knowledge of sin that you are painfully conscious that every faculty of your soul and every member of your body is defiled and corrupt? Have you been driven out of every refuge, and relief and brought into the presence of Him who is ineffably holy and inflexibly just, who "will by no means clear the guilty" (Ex. 34:7)? Have you heard that dread sentence "*Cursed is* every one that continueth not in all things which are written in the book of the law to do them" (Gal. 3:10)? Has it brought you down into the dust to cry, "I am lost: utterly, hopelessly lost; there is *nothing* I can do to deliver myself"? The ground must be ploughed before it can receive seed, and the heart must be broken up by the Law before it is ready for the Gospel.

In addition to the other terror-producing elements connected with the institution of Judaism, the apostle mentions two other features. "And if so much as a beast touch the mountain, it shall be stoned, or thrust through with a dart" (v. 20). To increase the reverence which was due to the appearing of Jehovah on Sinai, the people were required to keep their distance at the base of the mount, and were strictly forbidden an approach beyond the bounds fixed to them. This command was confirmed by a penalty, that every one who transgressed it should be put to death, as a disobedient rebel, devoted to utter destruction. This restriction and its sanction was also designed to produce in the people awe and terror of God in His giving of the Law.

That to which the apostle referred is recorded in Ex. 19:12, 13, "Take heed to yourselves, that ye go not into the mount, or touch the border of it: whosoever touchest the mount shall be surely put to death: There shall not a hand touch it, but he shall surely be stoned, or shot through; whether it be beast or man, it shall not live." As Owen well suggested, the prohibition respecting the cattle of the Israelites not only made the more manifest the absolute inaccessibleness of God in and by the Law, but also seemed to intimate the uncleanness of *all* things which sinners possess, by virtue of their relation to them. Everything that fallen man touches is defiled by him, and even "the *sacrifice* of the wicked is an abomination to the Lord" (Prov. 15:8).

The punishment of the man who defiantly touched the Mount was death by stoning, that of a beast by stoning or being thrust through with a dart. In either case they were slain at a distance: no hand *touched* the one who had offended. This emphasized the heinousness of the offence and the execrableness of the offender: others must not be defiled by coming into immediate contact with them — at what a distance ought we to keep ourselves from everything which falls under the curse of the Law! How the whole of this brings out the stern *severity* of the Law! "If even an irrational animal was to be put to death in a manner which marked it as unclean — as something not to be touched — what might rational offenders expect as the punishment of their sins? and if the violation of a *positive* institution of this kind involved consequences so fearful, what must be the result of transgressing the *moral* requirements of the great Lawgiver?" (John Brown).

"And so terrible was the sight, that Moses said, I exceedingly fear and quake" (v. 21). The apostle now turns from the people themselves, and describes the effect upon their leader of the terror-producing phenomena that attended the institution of Judaism. Here was the very man who had dared, again and again, to confront the powerful monarch of Egypt and make known to him the demand of God, and later announced to his face the coming of plague after plague. Here was the commander-in-chief of Israel's hosts, who had boldly led them through the Red Sea. He was a holy person, more eminent in grace than all others of his time, for he was "very meek, above all the men which were upon the face of the earth" (Num. 12:3). Now if *such* a man was overcome with dread, how terrible must be the severity and curse of the Divine Law!

Furthermore, let it be carefully borne in mind that Moses was no stranger to the Lord Himself: not only was he accustomed to receive Divine revelations, but he had previously beheld a representation of the Lord's presence at the bush. Moreover, he was the Divinely-appointed intermediary, the mediator between God and the people at that time. Yet none of these privileges exempted him from an overwhelming dread of the terror of the Lord in the giving the Law. What a proof is this that the very best of men cannot stand before God on the ground of their own righteousness! How utterly vain are the hopes of those who think to be saved by Moses (John 9:28)! Surely if there be anything in all the Scriptures which should turn us from resting on the Law for salvation, it is the horror and terror of Moses on mount Sinai.

"And so terrible was the sight, that Moses said, I exceedingly fear and quake." The fact that there is no record given in the O.T. of this particular item, occasions no difficulty whatever unto those who believe in the full inspiration of Holy Writ. Nor is there any need for us to have recourse unto the Romish theory of "unwritten tradition," and suppose that a knowledge of the terror of Moses had been orally preserved among the Jews. That which had not been chronicled in the book of Exodus, was here revealed to the apostle by the Holy Spirit Himself, and was now recorded by him for the purpose of accentuating the awfulness of what occurred at Sinai; and this, that the Hebrews should be increasingly thankful that Divine grace had connected them with so different an order of things.

The scope and design of the whole of our passage should now be obvious to the reader. The purpose of the apostle was to show again how inferior Judaism was to Christianity. This he here does by taking us back to Sinai, where Judaism was formally instituted by the appearing of Jehovah at the giving of the law, and where the Mosaic economy was established by a covenant based thereon. All the circumstances connected with its institution were in most striking accord with the leading features and characteristics of that dispensation. At that time the nation of Israel was in a waste, howling wilderness, standing in speechless terror at the foot of the

Mount. There Jehovah manifested Himself in His awful holiness and majesty, as Lawgiver and Judge; the people at a distance fenced off from Him. How profoundly thankful should Christians be that *they* belong to a much more mild and gracious order of things!

Sinai was "the mount that might be touched" — a symbol of that order of things which was addressed to the outward senses. The "blackness and darkness" which covered it was emblematic of the *obscurity* of spiritual things under the Mosaic economy, a thick veil of types and shadows hiding the substance and reality now revealed by the Gospel. The people being fenced off at the base of the mount denoted that under Judaism they had no way of approach and no access into the immediate presence of God. The thunderings, lightnings and fire, expressed the wrath of God against all who transgress His righteous Law. The "tempest" was a sign of the instability and temporariness of that dispensation, in contrast with the peace which Christ has made and the permanent and eternal order of things which He has brought in. The utter consternation of Moses gave clear proof that *he* was not the perfect and ultimate Mediator between God and men. All of which plainly intimated the need for something else, something better, something more suited unto lost sinners.

CHAPTER NINETY-NINE

The Superiority of Christianity

(Heb. 12:22-24)

"But ye are come unto mount Sion, and unto the city of the living God, the heavenly Jerusalem, and to an innumerable company of angels, to the general assembly; the Church of the firstborn, which are written in Heaven; and to God the Judge of all, and to the spirits of just men made perfect, and to Jesus the Mediator of the new covenant, and to the blood of sprinkling, that speaketh better things than that of Abel" (12:22-24). In these verses the apostle completes the last great contrast which he draws between Judaism and Christianity, in which he displays the immeasurable superiority of the latter over the former. Though there may not be in them much of personal interest to some of our readers, yet we feel it incumbent upon us to give the same careful attention to this passage as we have to the previous sections of this epistle.

The central design of the apostle in vv. 18-24 was to convince the believing Hebrews of the pre-eminence of the new covenant above the old, that is, of the Gospel-economy over the Legal. To this end he first directed attention to the awful phenomena which attended the institution of Judaism, and now he sets before them the attractive features which characterizes Christianity. Everything connected with the giving of the Law was fearful and terrifying, but all that marks the Evangelical system is blessed and winsome. The manifestation of the Divine presence at Sinai though vivid and truly magnificent, was awe-inspiring, but the revelation of His love and grace in the Gospel prompts to peace and joy. Those pertained to things of the earth, these concern Heaven itself; those were addressed to the senses of the body, these call into exercise the higher faculties of the soul.

When going over vv. 18-21 we sought to make clear the *figurative* meaning of their contents. Though there be in them an allusion to historical facts, yet it should be obvious that it is not with their literal signification the apostle was chiefly concerned. As this may not be fully apparent to some of our readers, we must labour the point a little — rendered the more necessary by the gross and carnal ideas entertained by some Bible students. Surely it is quite plain to any unbiased mind that when he said, "For ye are not come unto the mount that might be touched, and that burned with fire" (v. 18) the apostle had reference to something else than a mountain in Arabia. There would be neither force nor even sense in telling Christians "Ye are not come to mount Sinai" — why even of the Hebrew believers it is improbable that any of them had ever seen it.

If, then, the words "For ye are not come unto the mount that might be touched" refer not to any material mount, then they must intimate *that order of things* which was formally inaugurated at Sinai, the moral features of which were suitably symbolized and strikingly adumbrated by the physical phenomena which attended the giving of the Law. This we sought to show in the course of the two preceding articles. Now the same principle of interpretation holds good and must be applied to the terms of the passage upon which we are now entering. "But ye are come unto mount Sion" no more has reference to a natural mountain than "We have an altar" (Heb. 13:10) means that Christians have a tangible and visible altar. Whatever future the earthly Sion may yet have, it is the antitypical, the spiritual, the Heavenly Sion, which is here in view.

One of the hardest tasks which sometimes confronts the careful and honest expositor of Holy Writ is to determine when its language is to be understood literally and when it is to be regarded as figurative. Nor is this always to be settled so easily as many suppose: the controversy upon the meaning of our Lord's words at the institution of the holy "Supper," "This is My body" shows otherwise. It had been a simple matter for Him to say "This (bread) *represents* My body," but He did not — why, is best known to Himself. Nor does this example stand by any means alone: much of Christ's language was of a figurative character, and more than once His own apostles failed to understand His purport — see Matt. 16:5-7; Mark 7:14-18; John 4:31-34 and 21:22, 23.

No, it is by no means always an easy matter to determine when the language of Scripture is to be regarded literally, and when it is to be understood figuratively. In previous generations perhaps there was a tendency to "spiritualize" too much: whether that be so or no, certainly the pendulum has now swung to the opposite extreme. How very often do we hear it said, "The language of Scripture means just what it says, and says just what it means". Many believe that such a declaration is very honouring to God's Word, and suppose that anything to the contrary savours strongly of

"Modernism." But, surely, a little reflection will soon indicate that such a statement needs qualifying, for there is not a little of the language of Scripture which *must* be understood other than literally.

To say nothing about many poetic expressions in the Psalms (such as "He maketh me to lie down in green pastures"), and symbolic language in the Prophets (like "then will I sprinkle clean water upon you . . . I will take away the stony heart out of your flesh"), take such a saying of our Lord's as this: "There is no man that hath left house, or brethren, or sisters, or father, or mother, or wife, or children or lands, for My sake and the Gospel's, but he shall receive a hundredfold now in this time, houses, and brethren, and sisters, and mothers, and children and lands, with persecutions" (Mark 10:29, 30) — the impossibility of *literalising* such a promise appears, for example, in a man's receiving or having a hundred mothers. Now if *that* statement is not to be interpreted literally, why should an outcry be raised if the writer presents good reasons for interpreting *other* verses figuratively?

After reading the above, some may be inclined to say, "All of this is very bewildering and confusing." Our reply is, Then you must have sat under very superficial preaching. Any well-instructed scribe would have taught you that there is great variety used in the language of Holy Writ, and often much care and pains are required in order to ascertain its precise character. That is one reason why God has graciously provided "*teachers*" (Eph. 4:11) for His people. True, the path of duty is so plainly defined for us that the wayfaring man (though a fool) need not err therein; but that does not alter the fact that in order to ascertain the exact significance of many particular expressions of Scripture, much prayer, and comparing passage with passage, is called for. The Bible is not a lazy man's book, and the Holy Spirit has designedly put not a little therein to stain the pride of men.

Now much help is obtained upon this difficulty by recognising that many of the things which pertain to the new covenant are expressed in language taken from the old, the antitype being presented under the phraseology of the type. For instance, when Christ announced the free intercourse between Heaven and earth which was to result from His mediation, He described it to Nathanael in the words of Jacob's vision: "Hereafter ye shall see heaven open, and the angels of God ascending and descending upon the Son of man" (John 1:51) — not that the Lord Jesus was ever to present the appearance of a ladder for that purpose, such as the patriarch saw in his dream, but that spiritually there would be a like medium of communication established and the agency of a like intercourse maintained. In a similar manner, the death of Christ is frequently spoken of under the terms of the Levitical sacrifices, while the application of His atonement to the soul is called the "sprinkling of His blood on the conscience."

Not until we clearly perceive that most of that which pertains to the new economy is exhibited to us under the images of the old, are we in the position to understand much of the language found in the Prophets, and many of the expressions employed by our Lord and His apostles. Thus, Christ is spoken of as "our Passover" (1 Cor. 5:7) and as Priest "after the order of Melchizedek" (Heb. 6:20). Paradise is described as "Abraham's bosom" (Luke 16:22). The N.T. saints are referred to as "the children of Abraham" (Gal. 3:7) as "the Israel of God" (Gal. 6:16), as "the Circumcision" (Phil. 3:3), as "a chosen generation, a royal priesthood, a holy nation, a peculiar people" (1 Pet. 2:9), and that "Jerusalem which is above is free, which is the mother of us all" (Gal. 4:26). Such terminology as this should amply prepare us for "ye are come unto *mount Sion,*" and should remove all uncertainty as to what is denoted thereby.

"But ye are come unto Mount Sion." In these words the apostle commences the second member of the comparison between Judaism and Christianity, which completes the foundation on which he bases the great exhortation found in vv. 25-29. In the former member (vv. 18-21) he had described the state of the Israelitish people (and the Church in it) as they existed under the Legal economy, taken from the terror-producing character of the giving of the Law and the nature of its demands: "they could not endure that which was commanded . . . and so terrible was the sight, that Moses said, I exceedingly fear and quake." But now the apostle contrasted the blessed and glorious state into which believers have been called by the Gospel, thereby making manifest how incomparably more excellent was the new covenant in itself than the old, and, how infinitely more beneficial are its privileges unto those whom Divine grace gives a part therein. No less than eight of these privileges are here enumerated — always the number of *a new beginning.*

"That in the dispensation of the fulness of times he might gather together in one all things in Christ, both which are in heaven, and which are on earth; even in Him" (Eph. 1:10). These words throw light on the passage now before us: all the *spiritual* things of grace and glory, both in heaven and in earth, have been headed up in Christ, so that they all now centre in Him. By His mediatorial work the Lord Jesus has repaired the great breach which the sin of Adam entailed. Before sin entered the world there was perfect harmony between Heaven and earth, man and angels uniting in hymning their glorious Creator: together they formed one spiritual society of worshippers. But upon the fall, that spiritual union was broken, and not only did the human race (in their federal head) become alienated from God Himself, but they became alienated from the holy spirits which surround His throne. But the last Adam has restored the disruption which the first Adam's sin produced, and in reconciling His people to God, He has also brought them back into fellowship with the angelic hosts.

Now because God has gathered together in one, recapitulated or headed up, "all things in Christ both which are in heaven and which are in earth," when we savingly "come" to Christ, we at the same time, "come" to all that God has made to centre in Him; or, in other words, we obtain an interest or right in all that is headed up in Him. Let the reader seek to grasp clearly this fact: it is because believers have been brought *to Christ* that they "are come unto Mount Sion, and unto the city of the living God, the heavenly Jerusalem, and to an innumerable company of angels!" By their initiation into the Gospel state, Christians are also inducted into and given access unto all these privileges. Christ and His mediation are specifically mentioned at the close of the various privileges here listed (v. 24), to teach us it is on *that* account we are interested in them and as the reason for our being so interested.

Yes, it is to *Christ* and Him alone (though not, of course, to the exclusion of the Father and His eternal love or the Holy Spirit and His gracious operations) that the Christian owes every blessing: his standing before God, his new creation state, his induction into the society of the holy, his eternal inheritance. It was by Christ that he was delivered from the condemnation and curse of the law, with the unspeakable terror it caused him. And it is by Christ that he has been brought to the antitypical Sion and the heavenly Jerusalem. Not by anything he has done or will do are such inestimable blessings made his. Observe how jealously the Spirit of Truth has guarded this very point, in using the passive and not the active voice: the verb is "ye *are* come" and not "ye *have* come." The same fact is emphasized again in 1 Pet. 2:25 — "ye were as sheep going astray; but *are* (not "have") now returned unto the Shepherd and Bishop of your souls" — because of what the Spirit wrought in us, we being entirely passive.

"But ye are come unto Mount Sion." We need hardly say that this language looks back to the "Zion" of the O.T., the variation in spelling being due to the difference between the Hebrew and Greek. It is in fact to the O.T. we must turn for light upon our present verse, and, as usual, the *initial* reference is the one which supplies us with the needed key. The first time that "Zion" is mentioned there is in 2 Sam. 5:6, 7, "And the king and his men went to Jerusalem unto the Jebusites the inhabitants of the land . . . thinking David cannot come in hither. Nevertheless, David took the stronghold of Zion: the same is the city of David." The deeper significance of this appears when we carefully ponder *its setting*: Zion was captured by David when Israel had been thoroughly tried and found completely wanting. It occurred at a notable crisis in the history of the nation, namely, after the priesthood had been deplorably corrupted (1 Sam. 2:22, 25) and after the king of *their* choice (Saul) had reduced himself (1 Sam. 28:7) and them (1 Sam. 31:1, 7) to the lowest degradation.

It was, then, at a time when Israel's fortunes were at a low ebb, when they were thoroughly disheartened, and when (because of their great wickedness) they had the least reason to expect it, that God graciously intervened. Just when Saul and Jonathan had been slain in battle, when the Philistines triumphed and Israel had fled before them in dismay, the Lord brought forth the man of *His* choice — David, whose name means the "Beloved." Up to this time the hill of Zion had been a continual menace to Israel, but now David wrested it out of the hand of the Jebusites and made it the stronghold of Jerusalem. On one of its eminences the temple was erected, which was the dwellingplace of Jehovah in the midst of His people. "Zion," then, stands for the highest revelation of Divine *grace* in the O.T. times.

Zion lay to the south-west of Jerusalem, being the oldest and highest part of that ancient city. It was outside of the city itself and separate from it, though in Scripture frequently identified with it. Mount Zion had two heads or peaks: Moriah on which the temple was erected, the seat of the *worship* of God; and the other, whereon the palace of David was built, the *royal* residence of the kings of Judah — a striking figure of the priestly and kingly offices meeting in Christ. Zion, then, was situated in the best part of the world — Canaan, the land which flowed with milk and honey; in the best part of that land — in Judah's portion; in the best part of his heritage — Jerusalem; and in the best part of that metropolis — the highest point, the "city of David." Let the interested reader carefully ponder the following passages and observe the precious things said of Zion: Psa. 48:2, 3; 50:2; 132: 13, 14; 133:3.

"Zion is, first, the place of God's habitation, where He dwells forever: Psa. 9:11; 76:2. Second, it is the seat of the throne, reign and kingdom of Christ: Psa. 2:6; Isa. 24:23. Third, it is the object of Divine promises innumerable: Psa. 125:1; 128:5, of Christ Himself: Isa. 59:20. Fourth, thence did the Gospel proceed and the law of Christ come forth: Isa. 40:9, Micah 4:2. Fifth, it was the object of God's especial love, and the place of the birth of His elect: Psa. 87:2, 5. Sixth, the joy of the whole earth: Psa. 48:2. Seventh, salvation and all blessings came forth out of Zion: Psa. 14:7; 110:2; 128:5. Now these things were not spoken of nor accomplished towards that Mount Zion which was in Jerusalem absolutely, but only as it was *typical* of believers under the Gospel; so the meaning of the apostle is, that by the Gospel believers do come to that state wherein they have an interest in and a right to all the blessed and glorious things that are spoken in the Scriptures concerning and to Zion. All the privileges ascribed, all the promises made to it, are theirs. Zion is the place of God's especial gracious residence, of the throne of Christ in His reign, the object of all promises. This is the first privilege of believers under the Gospel. They come to Mount Zion, they are interested in the promises of God recorded in the Scriptures made to Zion; in all the love and care of God expressed towards it, in all the spiritual glories assigned to it. The things spoken of it were never accomplished in the earthly Zion, but only typically; spiritually, and in their reality, they belong to believers under the new testament" (John Owen).

The contrasts between Sinai and Sion were very marked. The former was located in one of the dreariest and driest places on earth, a "howling desert"; the other was situated in the midst of that land which flowed with milk and honey. The one was ugly, barren, forbidding; the other was "beautiful for situation, the joy of the whole earth." Sinai was enveloped in "blackness and darkness," while Sion signified "sunny" or "shone upon." God came down on Sinai for only a brief moment, but He dwells in Sion "forever." On the former He appeared in terrible majesty; in the other He is manifested in grace and blessing. At Sinai the typical mediator trembled and quaked; on Sion Christ is crowned with glory and honour.

"But ye are come to Mount Sion." By this, then, we understand, first, that in being brought to Christ, the believer comes to the antitypical, the spiritual, Sion. Second, more specifically, we understand by this expression that believers are come to *the Throne of Grace*. Just as, originally, the historical Sion was *a menace* to Israel, so while we were under the curse of the law God's throne was one of *judgment*. But, just as David (the "Beloved") secured Sion for Israel and it became the place of blessing, where God abode in grace, so as the result of Christ's work the Throne of Heaven has become the Throne of Grace, He being Himself seated thereon. Third, in its wider scope, it signifies that believers have a right or title to all the good and glorious things spoken of and to Sion in the O.T.

"And unto the City of the living God, the heavenly Jerusalem," by which we understand Heaven itself, of which the earthly Jerusalem — the seat and centre of the worship of God — was the emblem. From earliest times the saints were taught by the Holy Spirit to contemplate the future blessedness of the righteous under the image of a splendid "City," reared on permanent foundations. Of Abraham it is declared, "He looked for a city which hath foundation, whose Builder and Maker is God" (Heb. 11:10). The force of that statement is best perceived in the light of the previous verse: "By faith he sojourned in the land of promise, as in a strange country, dwelling in tents with Isaac and Jacob, the heirs with him of the same promise." Abraham was given to realize that Canaan was but a figure of his everlasting heritage, and therefore did he look forward to (v. 10), "seek" (v. 14), and "desire a better Country, that is, a heavenly" (v. 14). The eternal Abode of the blessed is there called both a "City" and a "Country."

Many are the allusions to this "City" in the Psalms and the Prophets: we single out a few of the more prominent ones. "There is a river (The Spirit), the streams (His graces) whereof shall make glad the city of God, the holy place of the tabernacles of the Most High" (Psa. 46:4). "Great is the Lord, and greatly to be praised in the city of our God, in the mountain of His holiness" (Psa. 48:1). "Glorious things are spoken of thee, O city of God" (Psa. 87:3). "He led them forth by the right way, that they might go to a city of habitation" (Psa. 107:7). "We have a strong city; salvation will God appoint for walls and bulwarks" (Isa. 26:1). It is to be noted that in several passages the "City" is mentioned with particular reference to "Zion," for we can only have access to God via the Throne of Grace: John 14:6.

The "City of the living God" intimates the *nearness* of the saints to God, for Jerusalem was adjacent to Zion — *their* homes and dwellings were near to *His*. This figure of the *"city"* is also found in "Ye are no more strangers and foreigners, but *fellow-citizens* with the saints, and of the household of God" (Eph. 2:19)—see too Rev. 3:12. It is designated "the heavenly Jerusalem" in contrast from the earthly, the "Jerusalem which is above is free, which is the mother of us all" (Gal. 4:26). It is referred to again in Heb. 13:14. A "city" is a place of permanent residence, in contrast from the moving tent of the wilderness. In Bible times a "city" was a place of safety, being surrounded by strong and high walls; so in Heaven we shall be eternally secure from sin and Satan, death and every enemy. A city is well stocked with provisions: so in Heaven nothing is lacking which is good and blessed.

"But ye are come unto . . . the City of the living God, the heavenly Jerusalem." "The apostle herein prefers the privileges of the Gospel not only above what the people were made partakers of at Sinai in the wilderness, but also above all that they afterwards enjoyed in Jerusalem in the land of Canaan. In the glory and privileges of that city the Hebrews greatly boasted. But the apostle casts *that* city in the state wherein it then was, into the *same* condition with Mount Sinai in Arabia, that is, *under bondage,* as indeed it then was (Gal. 4:25); and he opposeth thereunto that 'Jerusalem which is above,' that is, this heavenly Jerusalem. This the second privilege of the Gospel-state, wherein all the remaining promises of the O.T. are transferred and made over to believers: whatever is spoken of the city of God or of Jerusalem that is *spiritual,* that contains in it the love or favour of God, it is all made theirs; faith can lay a claim to it all.

"Believers are so 'come' to this city, as to be inhabitants, free denizens, possessors of it, to whom all the rights, privileges, and immunities of it do belong; and what is spoken of it in the Scripture is a ground of faith to them, and a spring of consolation. For they may with consolation make application of what is so spoken to themselves in every condition. A 'city' is the only place of rest, peace, safety and honour, among men in this world: to all these in the spiritual sense we are brought by the Gospel. Whilst men are under the law they are at Sinai — in a wilderness where is none of these things; the souls of sinners can find no place of rest or safety under the law. But we have all these things by the Gospel: rest in Christ, peace with God, order in the communion of faith, safety in Divine protection, and honour in our relation to God in Christ" (John Owen).

CHAPTER ONE HUNDRED

The Superiority of Christianity

(Heb. 12:22-24)

"But ye are come unto" etc. (v. 22). These words do not, in fact cannot, mean, that in some mystical sense believers are "in spirit" projected into the future, to something which will only be actualised in the future. The Greek verb has a specific significance in this Epistle, as may be seen by a careful reference to 4:16, 7:25, 11:6: "to come unto" here means *to approach as worshippers.* In the verses now before us we are shown the high dignity and honour of that spiritual worship which is the privilege of Christians under the Gospel dispensation. When they meet together in the name of the Lord Jesus, as His people, and with a due observance of His holy institutions, they "are come unto," have access to, the eight privileges here enumerated: they draw nigh by faith to Heaven itself, to the antitypical holy of holies. But this is possible only to *spiritual* worshippers.

They who are strangers to experimental spirituality soon grow weary even of the outward form of worship, unless their eyes are entertained with an imposing ritual and their ears regaled by appealing music. This is the secret of the pomp and pageantry of Romanism — now, alas, being more and more imitated by professing Protestants; it is to attract and charm religious worldlings. Ritualists quite obscure the simplicity and beauty of true Gospel worship. Man in his natural estate is far too carnal to be pleased with a worship in which there is nothing calculated to fire the imagination and intoxicate the senses by means of tangible objects. But they who worship in spirit and in truth can draw nigh to God more joyously in a barn, and mingle their praises with the songs of Heaven, than if they were in a cathedral.

How vast is the difference between that spiritual adoration which issues from renewed hearts and that "form of godliness" which is associated with altars and candles, choirs and surpliced ministers! Only that is acceptable to God which is produced by the Holy Spirit through sinners washed in the blood of the Lamb. Under grace-magnifying and Christ-exalting preaching, the spiritual senses of real Christians are exercised; as they behold the Saviour's glories in the glass of the Gospel, as they hear His voice, they have an inward impression of His presence, they taste afresh of His goodness, and His name is to them as ointment poured forth, perfuming their spirits. In this joyous frame, their hearts are drawn Heavenwards, and their songs of praise mingle with those of the holy angels and the spirits of just men made perfect.

"But ye are come unto Mount Sion." David, after having taken Mount Zion from the Jebusites, made it the place of his residence, so that it became "the city of the great king." There he reigned and ruled, there he issued his laws, and thence he extended the sway of his peaceful sceptre over the whole of the holy land. From that circumstance, Mount Zion became the great type of the kingdom of God, of which the Lord Jesus Christ is the Head and Sovereign. As David ruling upon Mount Zion in the palace built there as his royal seat, issuing his commands which were obeyed all over the land, so our blessed Redeemer has been exalted according to God's promise "Yet have I set My King upon My holy hill of Zion" (Psa. 2:6 and cf. Heb. 2:9); and there sitting as King in Sion, issues His mandates and sways His peaceful sceptre over the hearts of His obedient people.

"And unto the City of the living God, the heavenly Jerusalem." Most of the older writers understood these terms to refer to the Church, but we think this is a mistake, for the Church is referred to, separately, in a later clause. As pointed out in the preceding article, we regard this language as signifying Heaven itself, as the residence of God and the eternal abode of His people. "The living God" is the true and only God, the Triune Jehovah, the Fountain of all life, the One who is "from everlasting to everlasting," without beginning or end: this title is given to each of the eternal Three—Matt. 16:16, 1 Tim. 4:10, 2 Cor. 6:16, cf. 1 Cor. 3:16. As "Zion" was the seat of David's throne, so "Jerusalem" was the dwelling place of Jehovah in the midst of His covenant people. "Jerusalem" signifies "the Vision of Peace," and in Heaven the "sons of peace" (Luke 10:6) will behold the glory of God in the face of the Prince of peace.

"And to an innumerable company of angels." This is the third great privilege enjoyed by the worshippers under the Christian economy: having mentioned the place to which Divine grace has brought believers, the Holy Spirit now described the *inhabitants* of the heavenly Jerusalem. The angels, who are worshippers of God and His Christ, are perhaps mentioned first because they are in closer proximity to the Throne, because they are the original denizens of Heaven, and because they are greatly in the majority. The reference is, of course, to the holy angels who kept their first estate and sinned not when some of their fellows apostatised. They are "the elect angels" (1 Tim. 5:21), and although they have not been redeemed by the atoning blood of the Lamb, it appears highly probable that they were *confirmed* in their standing by the incarnation of the Son, for God has united in Christ both elect men and elect angels (Eph. 1:10), that He might be "the Head of all principality and power" (Col. 2:10).

"Ye are come unto . . . an innumerable company of angels." This sets before us a further contrast between that which characterises Christianity, and what obtained under the Mosaic economy—that is, so far as the Israelitish nation as a whole was concerned. It is clear from several passages that "angels" were connected with the giving of the Law, when Judaism was formally instituted. We read, "the Lord came from Sinai and rose up from Seir unto them; He shined from mount Paran, and He came with ten thousands of saints: from His right hand went a fiery law for them" (Deut. 33:2): and again, "The chariots of God are twenty thousands, even thousands of angels: the Lord is among them, as in Sinai" (Psa. 68:17). But while many "thousands" of the heavenly hosts attended Jehovah upon Sinai, this was very different from the "innumerable company" with which we are connected, namely the "ten thousand times ten thousand, and thousands of thousands" of Rev. 5:11. And even to the many thousands of angels at Sinai the Nation *did not* "come": instead, they were fenced off at the foot of the mount.

Redeemed sinners who have fellowship with the Father and the Son by the Holy Spirit, are of one spirit with all the heavenly hosts, for there is a union of sentiment between them. Christians have been brought into a state of amity and friendship with the holy angels: they are members of the same family (Eph. 3:15), are united under the same Head (Col. 2:10), and joined together in the same worship (Heb. 1:6; Rev. 5:9-14). We are "come unto" them *by a spiritual relation,* entering into association with them, sharing the benefits of their kind offices, for "are they not all ministering spirits, sent forth to minister for them who shall be heirs of salvation?" (Heb. 1:14). The angels are "*fellow* servants" with believers "that have the testimony of Jesus" (Rev. 19:10). Wondrous fact is this that sinners of the earth, while here in this world, have communication with the angels in Heaven, for they are constantly engaged in the same worship of God in Christ as we are: Thus there is perfect oneness of accord between us.

As we pointed out in the preceding chapter, the Church's spiritual union with the holy angels—being united together in one spiritual society and family—is due to the atoning work of Christ, who by putting away the sins of His people has restored the breach made by Adam's fall and "reconciled *all* things unto Himself" (Col. 1:20). Hence we believe that in the verse now before us there is not only a contrast drawn between Judaism and Christianity, but that its ultimate reference is to the immense difference brought in between the offence of the first Adam and the righteousness of the last Adam. Upon the transgression of Adam we read "So He drove out the man: and He placed at the east of the garden of Eden cherubim, and a flaming sword which turned every way, to keep the way of the tree of life" (Gen. 3:24). There God made His "angels spirits, and His ministers a flame of fire" (Heb. 1:7) to execute His vengeance against us; but now these same angels are our associates in worship and service.

God is "the Lord *of hosts*" (Psa. 46:7), myriads of holy celestial creatures being in an attendance upon Him—"*an innumerable* company of angels:" how this should help us to realise the majesty and grandeur of that Kingdom into which Divine grace has brought us. In this expression we may also discern a word to encourage our trembling hearts in connection with our wrestling against the "hosts of wicked spirits" (Eph. 6:12): numerous as are the forces of Satan assailing us, an "*innumerable* company of angels" are defending us! This was the blessed truth by which Elisha comforted his fearing servant "they that be with us are more than they that be with them" (2 Kings 6:16, 17). "When the thought of Satan and his legions brings fear, we ought to comfort ourselves with the assurance that more in number and greater in power are the loving and watchful angels, who for Christ's sake regard us with the deepest interest and affection" (A. Saphir).

Before turning to the next item a word should be said in refutation of the blasphemous error of Romanists concerning our relation to the angels. They teach that we are "come unto" the angels with our prayers, which is one of their empty superstitions—there is not a word in Scriptures to countenance such an idea. Though it be true that the angels are superior to us in dignity and power, yet in communion with God we are their equals—"*fellow*-servant" (Rev. 22:9), and, as Owen pointed out, "Nothing can be more groundless than that fellow-servants should worship one another"—the worshipping of angels is *condemned* in Col. 2:18, Rev. 22:8, 9. Well did Owen also point out, "It is the highest madness for any one to pretend himself to be the head of the church, as the pope does, unless he assume also to himself to be the head of all the angels in Heaven," for we belong to the same holy society.

"To the general assembly." This expression occasions some difficulty, for in the first place it is not quite clear as to what the Spirit specifically alludes unto. In the second place, the Greek word (*pangueris,* a compound one) occurs nowhere else in the N.T., so that we are not able to obtain any help from its usage in other passages. In the third place, it is not very easy to decide whether this clause is to be linked with the one immediately preceding or with the one following it. In its classical usage the Greek word was employed in connection with a public convocation, when all the people were gathered together to celebrate a public festival or solemnity. Most of the commentators link this word with what follows: "To the general assembly and church of the firstborn," understanding the reference to be unto the ("general") union of believing Jews and believing Gentiles in one Body. Personally, we think this is a mistake.

First, such language would be tautological, for if the "general assembly" points to the middle wall of partition being broken down, and converted Jews and Gentiles being joined together in one Body, *that* would be "the Church." Second, the denomination "church of the firstborn" takes in *the totality* of God's elect and redeemed people of all ages. Third, there is no "and" between the "innumerable company of angels" and the "general assembly," as there is in every other instance in these verses where a *new* object is introduced. Personally, we regard this third expression as in apposition (the placing together of two nouns, one of which explains the other) to the former, thus: "unto an innumerable company of angels—the general assembly." There are various ranks and orders among the angels: principalities and powers, thrones and dominions, seraphim and cherubim, and the "general assembly" of them would be the solemn convocation of all the angelic hosts before the throne of God—compare "A fiery stream issued and came forth from before Him: thousand thousands ministered unto Him, and ten thousand times ten thousand stood before Him: *the judgment* (a special convocation) was set, and the books were opened" (Dan. 7:10).

No doubt this amplifying expression (of the "innumerable company of angels") also emphasizes another contrast between the privileges of Christianity and that which obtained under Judaism. Perhaps the contrastive allusion is a double one. First, from the general assembly of Israel at Sinai, when the whole of the nation was then formally assembled together—in fear and trembling. Second, to the general assembly of all the male Israelites three times in the year at the solemn feasts of the O.T. Church (Ex. 34:23, Deut. 16:16) which was called "the great congregation"

(Psa. 22:25, 35:18, etc.)—in joy and praise. But each of these were on earth, by men in the flesh; whereas Christians, in their worship, unite with all the holy hosts of Heaven in blessing and adoring the Triune God.

"And Church of the firstborn, which are written in heaven": that is, to the entire company of God's redeemed. "This is that church whereunto all the promises do belong; the church built on the rock, against which the gates of hell shall not prevail; the spouse, the body of Christ, the temple of God, His habitation forever. This is the church which Christ loved and gave Himself for, which He washed in His own blood, that He might sanctify and cleanse it with the washing of water by the word, that He might present it to Himself a glorious church, not having spot or wrinkle or any such thing, but that it should be holy and without blemish (Eph. 5:25-27). This is the church out of which none can be saved, and whereof no one member shall be lost" (J. Owen).

This is the only place in the N.T. where the election of grace is designated "the Church of the firstborn ones" (plural number in the Greek). Why so here? For at least three reasons. First, so as to identify the Church with Christ *as* the "Heir of all things" (Heb. 1:2). The prominent idea associated with the "firstborn" in Scripture is *not* that of priority, but rather excellency, dignity, dominion, and right to the inheritance. This is clear from "Reuben, thou art my firstborn, . . . the excellency of dignity, and the excellency of power" (Gen. 49:3); and again "I will make Him My firstborn, higher than the kings of the earth" (Psa. 89:27). For the "firstborn" and the "inheritance" see Gen. 27:19, 28, 29 and cf. Heb. 12:16; Deut. 21:16; 1 Chron. 5:1. Second, this title intimates the Church's glory is superior to that of the celestial spirits: redeemed sinners and not fallen angels are God's "firstborn ones." Third, this points a further contrast from Judaism: Israel was God's "firstborn" (Ex. 4:22) among the nations of the earth; but the Church is His "firstborn" among the inhabitants of Heaven!

The Church is raised to the highest created dignity: superior privileges and a nobler dignity of sonship pertain to its members than to the holy angels. This is solely due to their union with Christ, the original "Firstborn": Psa. 89:26, 27; Rom. 8:29; Heb. 1:6. Christians have been made "kings and priests unto God" (Rev. 1:6), which compromises the whole right of the inheritance. The entire election of grace, by God's gratuitous adoption, are not only members of His family, but "heirs of God and joint-heirs with Christ" (Rom.8:17), and thus given an inalienable title to the heavenly inheritance. This was equally true of the saints of all generations from the foundation of the world, yet a much clearer and fuller revelation thereof has been made under this Christian economy: "which in other ages was not made known unto the sons of men, *as it is now* revealed unto His holy apostles and prophets by the Spirit" (Eph. 3:5).

"Which are written in Heaven," announcing that they are genuine Christians—in contrast from mere professors, whose names are recorded only upon the church-scrolls of earth. Just as the registering of men's names on the rolls of corporations, etc., assures them of their *right* to the privileges thereof (for example, to vote—which we believe is something that no child of God should do), so our names being written in Heaven is the guaranty of our title to the celestial heritage. It was to this Christ referred when He said, "Rejoice because your names are written in heaven" (Luke 10:20). The apostle Paul also speaks of those "whose names are in the book of life" (Phil. 4:3): that Book of Life (cf. Rev. 3:5 and 13:8) is none other than the roll of God's elect, in His eternal immutable designation of them unto grace and glory. "Written in Heaven" points another contrast from Judaism: the names of Jews (as such) were only written upon the synagogue scrolls.

"And to God the Judge of all." The reference here is not (as some recent writers have supposed) unto the person of Christ, but rather unto God the Father in His rectoral office as the high Governor of all. Does this seem to spoil the harmony of the passage? had we not much preferred it to read "and to God our Father"? No, coming to "God the Judge of all" in nowise conflicts with the other privileges mentioned: it it a vastly different thing to be brought before a judge to be tried and sentenced as a criminal, from having a favourable access to him as our occasions and needs may require. Such is the meaning here: we are come not only to the heavenly Jerusalem, to an innumerable company of angels, to the Church, but also the supreme *Head* of the heavenly society—the Author and End of it.

"And to God the Judge of all," that is, the Majesty of Heaven itself. It was God as Judge who appointed Christ to death, and it was God as Judge who accepted His sacrifice and raised Him from the dead. To God as "Judge" believers have been reconciled and by Him they were justified (Rom. 8:33). Concerning Christ our Exemplar, we read "when He suffered, He threatened not, but committed Himself to Him *that judgeth righteously*" (1 Pet. 2:23). The apostle reminded the saints that "it is a righteous thing for God (as "Judge") to recompense tribulation to them that trouble you" (2 Thess. 1:6). Now it was as Judge that God ascended His awful tribunal at Sinai, and *that* the people could not endure: but Christians draw nigh to Him with holy boldness because His law has nothing against them—the requirements of His justice were fully met by Christ. How great is the privilege of that state which enables poor sinners, called by the Gospel, to approach the Judge of all upon His "bench" or throne without fear! Only by *faith* is this possible.

"And to the spirits of just men made perfect." It is blessed to note that this comes immediately after mention of "the Judge of all"—to show us the saints had nothing to fear from Him, "for there is therefore now no condemnation to them which are in Christ" (Rom. 8:1). The reference is to the O.T. believers, who have passed through death: that N.T. saints are "come" to *them* is clear from Eph. 2:19. Of course that "made perfect" is relative and not absolute, for their resurrection and full glorification is yet future. As Owen defined it: first, they had reached the end of the race wherein they had been engaged, with all the duties and difficulties, temptations and tribulations connected therewith. Second, they were completely delivered from sin and sorrow, labour and trouble, which in this life they had been exposed to. Third, they had now entered their rest and reward and were, according to their present capacity, in the immediate presence of God and perfectly happy.

"And to Jesus the Mediator of the new covenant:" His personal name is used here because it is *in this character* He *saves* His people from their sins—compare our exposition of 9:15-17. Here again a contrast is drawn from that which obtained under the old covenant. Moses was the middle person between Israel and God: chosen by the people (Ex. 20:19, etc.) and appointed by Him to declare His mind unto them; unto him they were all baptised (1 Cor. 10:2). But Moses was merely a man, a fallen descendant of Adam: he delivered God's law to the people, but was incapable of magnifying and making it honourable by a perfect personal obedience. Nor was he that "surety" of the covenant unto God for the people, as Christ was; he did not confirm the covenant by offering himself as a sacrifice to God, nor could he give the people an interest in heavenly privileges. How far short he came of Christ!

By being brought unto "Sion," Christians are come to all the mercy, grace and glory prepared in the new covenant and presented in the promises of it. Herein lies the supreme blessedness and eternal security of the Church, that its members are taken into *such* a covenant that they have a personal interest in the Mediator of it, who is able to save them unto the uttermost. This is the very substance and essence of Christian faith, that it has to do with *the Mediator of the new covenant,* by whom alone we obtain deliverance from the old covenant and the curse with which it is accompanied. It is both the privilege and wisdom of faith to *make use of* this

"Mediator" in all our dealings with God: He it is who offers to God our prayers and praises and brings down the favour of God upon His people.

"And to the blood of sprinkling, that speaketh better things than that of Abel." The blood of Christ is referred to thus in allusion unto the various sprinklings of blood Divinely instituted under the old covenant, the three most signal instances of which are recorded in Ex. 12:22; 24:6-8; Lev. 16:14, the principal reference here being to Ex. 24, where the old covenant was thus ratified. All of those instances were eminent types of the redemption, justification and sanctification of the Church by the blood of Christ. The specific thing denoted by the "sprinkling" (in contrast from its "shedding") is *the application to believers* of its virtues and benefits. The more the Christian exercises repentance toward God and faith toward our Lord Jesus Christ, the more will he experience the peace-speaking power of that precious blood in his conscience. The blood of Christ "speaketh" to God as a powerful Advocate: urging the fulfillment of the Mediator's part of the everlasting covenant, His perfect satisfaction to Divine justice, the full discharge from condemnation purchased for His people.

The contrast here is very impressive: the blood of Abel called for vengeance (Gen. 4:10), whereas the blood of Christ calls for blessing to be bestowed on those for whom it was shed. Even the blood of the wicked if unrighteously shed, calls to God for it to be recompensed. But Abel was a saint, the first martyr, and *his* blood cried according to the worth that was in him, for "precious in the sight of the Lord is the death of His saints." If then the blood of a saint speaks so forcibly to God, how infinitely more powerfully must the blood of *"the King of saints"* (Rev. 15:3) plead! If the blood of a single member of Christ's Body so speaks to God, what will the blood of the Head Himself! Moreover, Abel's blood only cried to God "from the ground," where it was shed, but Christ's blood speaks in Heaven itself (Heb. 9:12).

CHAPTER ONE HUNDRED ONE

The Call to Hear

(Heb. 12:25, 26)

"See that ye refuse not Him that speaketh: for if they escaped not who refused Him that spake on earth, much more shall not we escape, if we turn away from Him that speaketh from Heaven" (v. 25). In these words we find the Holy Spirit moving the apostle to make a practical application unto his readers of what he had just brought before them in the previous verses. The degree or extent of the privileges enjoyed, is the measure of our responsibility: the richer the blessing God grants us, the deeper is our debt of obligation to Him. "For unto whomsoever much is given, of him shall be much required; and to whom men have committed much, of him they will ask the more" (Luke 12:48): it was of this principle and fact the Hebrews were now reminded.

The apostle had just completed drawing his final contrast between Judaism and Christianity (vv. 18-24), in which he had again shown the immeasurable superiority of the latter over the former, and now he uses this as a basis for an exhortation unto faith and obedience, or faithfulness and perseverance. Herein we have another example of the apostolic method of ministry: all their teaching had a *practical* end in view. Their aim was something more than enlightening the mind, namely, the moving of the will and ordering of the walk. Alas that there is so little of this in present-day teaching and preaching. The design of the pulpit now seems to be entertaining the people, and rarely does it go further than instructing the mind—that which searches the conscience or calls for the performance of duty, that which is solemn and unpalatable to the flesh, is, for the most part, studiously avoided. May it please the Lord to grant His servants all needed grace for deliverance from a compliance with this "speak unto us *smooth* things."

The grander the revelation which God is pleased to make of Himself, the more punctual the attendance and the fuller the response which He requires from us. In the verses which are now before us we find the apostle improving his argument by pointing out the weighty implications of it. Therein he returns to his main design, which was to urge the professing Hebrews unto steadfastness in their Christian course and conflict, and to steadily resist the temptation to lapse back into Judaism. This deeply important and most necessary exhortation he had urged upon them again and again; see Heb. 2:1, 3; 3:12, 13; 4:1; 6:4-6; 10:26-29; 12:1, 15. Therein the servant of God may learn another valuable lesson pointed to by the example of the apostle, namely, how God requires him to go over the same ground again and again where the *practical duties* of the Christian are concerned, and hesitate not to frequently repeat the *exhortations* of Holy Writ! This may not increase his popularity with men, but it will meet with the Lord's approval; and no faithful minister can have both!

"See that ye refuse not Him that speaketh." The Greek word for "see" is rendered "take heed" in Heb. 3:12; the word for "refuse" signifies "deprecate"—do not disregard, still less reject. Now not only is this argument based upon the statement made in the preceding verses, but *the motive* for complying with it is to be drawn therefrom. It is because we "are not come unto the mount that might be touched and that burned with fire" (v. 18), that is, unto that order of things wherein the Divine righteousness was so vividly displayed in *judicial* manifestion; but because we "are come unto mount Sion," which speaks of pure *grace,* that we are now thus exhorted, for holiness ever becometh God's house. It is in the realisation of God's wondrous grace that the Christian is ever to find his most effectual incentive unto a godly walk; see Titus 2:11, 12.

"See that ye refuse not Him that speaketh," which is the negative way of saying "*Hear* Him"—*Heed* Him, by believing and yielding obedience to what He says. This exhortation looks back to "I will raise them up a Prophet, from among their brethren, like unto thee, and will put My words in His mouth: and He shall speak unto them all that I shall command Him. And it shall come to pass, that whosoever will not *hearken* unto My words which He shall speak in My name, I will require it of him" (Deut. 18:18, 19); cf. Acts 3:22; 7:37. This is what the apostle now reminded the Hebrews of: take heed that ye hear Him, for if you fail to, God will consume you with His wrath. A similar charge was given by God after Christ became incarnate: "This is My Beloved Son, in whom I am well pleased: *hear ye Him*" (Matt. 17:5).

"This is the foundation of all Gospel faith and obedience, and the formal reason of the condemnation of all unbelievers. God hath given command unto all men to hear, that is, believe and obey His Son Jesus Christ. By virtue thereof, He hath given command unto others to preach the Gospel unto all individuals. They who believe them, believe in Christ; and they who believe in Christ through Him, believe in God (1 Pet. 1:21), so that their faith is ultimately resolved into the authority of God Himself. And so they who refuse them, who hear them not, do thereby refuse Christ Himself; and by so doing, reject the authority of God, who hath given this command to hear Him, and hath taken on Himself to require it when it is neglected; which is the condemnation of all unbelievers. This method, with respect unto faith and unbelief, is declared and established by our Saviour: 'he that heareth you, heareth Me; and He that despiseth you, despiseth Me; and he that despiseth Me, despiseth Him that sent Me:' Luke 10:16" (John Owen).

"See that ye refuse not Him that speaketh"—note carefully the *present* tense: not "that spoke." Christ is still speaking through His Gospel, by His Spirit, and instrumentally through His own commissioned servants, calling upon all who come under the sound of His voice to serve and obey Him. There are many ways in which we may "refuse" to hear and heed Him. First, by neglecting to read daily and diligently the Scriptures through which He speaks. Second, by failing to attend public preaching where His Word is faithfully dispensed—if so be we live in a place where this holy privilege is obtainable. Third, by failing to comply with the terms of His Gospel and yield ourselves unto His authority. Fourth, by forsaking the Narrow Way of His commandments and going back again to the world. Fifth, by abandoning the truth for error, which generally ends in total apostasy. How we need to pray for an *hearing ear,* that is, for a responsive heart and yielded will.

"For if they escaped not who refused Him that spake on earth. much more shall not we escape, if we turn away from Him that speaketh from Heaven." In these words the apostle continues to emphasize the contrast which obtains between Judaism and Christianity. What we have here is an echo from the keynote struck in the opening words of our epistle: "God, who at sundry times and in divers manners spake in time past *unto the fathers* by the prophets, hath in these last days spoken *unto us* by His Son" (1:1, 2). It is in the light of that statement our present verse is to be read and interpreted. The *Speaker* throughout is one and the same, namely, God (the Father), but the mouthpieces He employed differed greatly: under Judaism He spoke through mere men, the "prophets," but in connection with Christianity He speaks in and by His own beloved "Son."

This difference in the respective mouthpieces employed by God was in accord with and indicative of the relative importance of the two revelations given by Him. Judaism was but a religion for earth, and a temporary arrangement for the time being: accordingly, human agents were God's instruments in connection therewith. But Christianity is a revelation which concerns a *heavenly* calling, heavenly citizenship, a heavenly inheritance, and exhibits *eternal* relations and realities: appropriately, then, was the everlasting Son, "the Lord from Heaven," the One by whom its grand secrets were disclosed. "No man hath seen God at any time; the only begotten Son, which is in the bosom of the Father, He hath declared Him" (John 1:18). The primary reference there is a *dispensational* one. Under Judaism God dwelt behind the veil; but under Christianity "we all with unveiled face" behold, as in a glass, "the glory of the Lord" (2 Cor. 3:18). Under the old covenant men were unable to go in to God; but under the new covenant God has, in the person of Christ, come out to men.

But blessed and glorious as is the contrast between Judaism and Christianity, equally solemn and terrible is the contrast between *the punishment* meted out to those who refuse God's revelation under each. God speaks now from a higher throne than the one He assumed at Sinai: that was on earth; the one He now occupies is in Heaven. Therefore it must inevitably follow that the guilt of those who refuse to heed Him to-day is far greater, and their punishment must be the more intolerable. Not only do higher privileges involve increased obligations, but the failure to discharge those added obligations necessarily incurs deeper guilt and a heavier penalty. *This* is what the apostle presses here, as he had in "For if the word spoken by angels (at Sinai) was steadfast, and every transgression and disobedience received a just recompense of reward; how shall *we* escape if we neglect so great salvation?" (2:2, 3). If, then, we in any wise fear God's vengeance or value His favour how it behooves us to most seriously heed the grace proffered in the Gospel!

Though Christianity has in it far less of what is terrifying than had Judaism and far more in it which exhibits the grace and mercy of God, nevertheless, apostacy from the one cannot be less terrible in its consequences than was apostacy from the other. There is as much to be dreaded in disregarding the authoritative voice of God now as there was then; yea, as we have pointed out, the rejection of His message through Christ involves a worse doom than despising of His word through Moses and the prophets. "He that despised Moses' law died without mercy under two or three witnesses: of how much *sorer* punishment, suppose ye, shall he be thought worthy who hath trodden under foot the Son of God?" (Heb. 10:28, 29). True, God does not now speak amid thunderings and lightnings, but rather by a tender appeal to our hearts; yet the rejection of the latter is fraught with more direful consequences than was the refusal of the former.

Alas that this weighty truth is so feebly apprehended to-day, and so little emphasised by the pulpit. Is it not a fact that the idea now generally prevailing is, that the God of the N.T. is far more amiable and benevolent than the God of the O.T.? How far from the truth is this: "I change not" (Mal. 3:6) is the Lord's express avowal. Moreover, it is under the new covenant (and not the old) that we find the most awe-inspiring and terror-provoking revelation of the righteous wrath of a sin-hating God. It was not through Moses or the prophets, but by the Lord Jesus that the everlasting fires of Hell were most vividly depicted: He it was who spoke the plainest and the most frequently of that fearful place wherein there is "wailing and gnashing of teeth." If Christ was the One to most fully reveal God's love, He was also the One who most fully declared His wrath.

"They escaped not who refused Him that spake on earth." No, even though they had enjoyed such unparalleled privileges. They had been brought out of the house of bondage, delivered from the enemy at the Red Sea, ate of the heavenly manna and drank of the water from the smitten rock; yet we are told "But with many of them God was not well-pleased: for they were overthrown in the wilderness" (1 Cor. 10:5). The apostle had already reminded the Hebrews that it was of them God had declared, "They do always err in their heart, and they have not known My ways. So I sware in My wrath, They shall not enter into My rest" (3:10, 11). And this was because "they *refused* Him that spake" to them. They were disobedient at Sinai, where, so far from submitting to the Divine authority to have " no other gods," they made and worshipped the golden calf. They were unbelieving at Kadesh Barnea, when they listened to the scepticism of the ten spies.

"Much more shall not we escape, if we turn away from Him that speaketh from heaven." Again we say, how greatly at variance with this is the idea which now obtains so generally. The great majority of professing Christians suppose there is much *less* danger of those bearing the name of the Lord being severely dealt with under the milder regime of Christianity, than there was for renegades in the days of Moses. But our text says, "much *more* shall not we escape!" Though it be true that Christianity is essentially a system of *grace,* nevertheless the requirements of *holiness* and the claims of *justice* are not thereby set aside. The despisers of grace must be and will be as surely punished as were the despisers of Law; yea, "much more" so because *their* sin of refusal is more heinous. It is "the wrath of the Lamb" (Rev. 6:16) which the despisers of the

Gospel—its invitations and its requirements—will have to reckon with: so far as mount Sion excels mount Sinai so will the punishment of Christ-scorners exceed that of those who despised Moses.

Ere passing on to our next verse we must anticipate a "difficulty" which our passage is likely to raise in the minds of some readers: How are we to harmonize the eternal security of the saints with this "much more shall not *we* escape if we turn away from Him that speaketh from Heaven?" Alas, that such a question needs answering: those who frame it betray a lamentable ignorance of *what* the "security of saints" consists of. God has never promised any man to preserve him in the path of self-will and self-pleasing. Those who reach Heaven are they who follow (though stumbling by and with many falls) the only path which leads there, namely, the "Narrow Way" of *self-denial.* Or, to put it in another way, the only ones who escape the everlasting burnings are they who *heed* Him that speaketh from Heaven, for "He became the Author of eternal salvation unto all them that *obey* Him" (Heb. 5:9).

The writer believes firmly in the blessed truth of "the eternal security of the saints," but by no means all who profess to be Christians are "saints." This raises the question, how may I know whether or not I am a saint? The answer is, By impartially examining myself in the light of Holy Writ and ascertaining whether or no I possess *the character and conduct of* a "saint." The Lord Jesus said, "My sheep hear My voice, and I know them, and they follow Me" (John 10:27). A "saint" or "sheep" of Christ, then is one who *hears* HIS voice above all the siren voices of the world, above all the clamourings of the flesh, and gives evidence that he does so by *following* Him, that is, by heeding His commandments, being regulated by His will, submitting to His Lordship. And to them, and to none other, Christ says, "And I give unto them eternal life, and they shall never perish, neither shall any man pluck them out of My hand" (John 10:28).

Should it be asked, But was not the apostle addressing the "saints," "sheep," "holy brethren, partakers of the heavenly calling" (3:1) here in Heb. 12:25? And if so, *why* did he present before *them* such an awful threat? First, these solemn words were addressed to *all* who come under the sound of the Gospel, and the response made by the hearer or reader serves as an admirable *test.* The proud and self-confident, who rely wholly upon a profession made by them years ago, ignore it to their own undoing, supposing those words have no application to *them;* whereas the lowly and self-distrustful lay it to heart with trembling, and are thereby preserved from the doom threatened. Second, in the preservation of His people from destruction God uses warnings and threatenings, as well as promises and assurances. He keeps His people in the Narrow Way by causing them to heed such an exhortation as this, "Be not high-minded, but fear; for if God spared not the natural branches, take heed lest He also spare not *thee*" (Rom. 11:20, 21).

What is meant by *turning away from* "Him that speaketh from Heaven"? First, it describes the attitude of that large class who come under the sound of the Gospel and dislike its exacting terms: Christ is far too holy to suit their carnal hearts, His call for them "to forsake all and follow Him" pleases not their corrupt nature; so He is "despised and rejected" by them. Second, it depicts the conduct of the stony-ground hearers, who under the emotional appeals of high-pressure evangelists "receive the Word with joy," yet have "no *root*" in themselves, and so they quickly "fall away:" the scoffings of their godless companions or the appeal of worldly pleasures are too strong for them to continue resisting. Third, it denotes the lapse of those who having "escaped the pollutions of the world through the knowledge of the Lord and Saviour Jesus Christ are again entangled therein and overcome" so that "the latter end is worse with them than the beginning" (2 Pet. 2:20). Fourth, it announces the apostasy of those who, under pressure of persecution, renounce the Faith.

"Whose voice then shook the earth: but now He hath promised, saying, Yet once more I shake not the earth only, but also heaven" (v. 26). There are some points about this verse and the one immediately following which are far from easy to elucidate, yet their main purport is not difficult to determine. In ceasing to "speak on earth" and in now "speaking from Heaven" God gave therein intimation that the old covenant had been *supplanted* by the new: that He had done with Judaism and established the "better thing" in its place. This was what the pious Hebrews found so hard to perceive, for Judaism had been instituted by God Himself. Nevertheless, He only designed it to fulfill a temporary purpose "until the time of reformation" (9:10), and that time had now arrived. It was to demonstrate and establish this important fact that God moved His servant to write this Epistle.

Once more we would call attention to the method employed: Paul did not simply press his apostolic authority, though that had been sufficient of itself; instead, he referred his readers to *the written Word of God,* quoting from Haggai—in this too he has left an admirable example for all ministers of the Gospel to follow: the words of God Himself are far more weighty than any of ours. At every vital stage of his argument the apostle had referred the Hebrews to the O. T. Scriptures. When he affirmed that Christ was superior to the heavenly hosts, he quoted, "Let all the angels of God worship

Him" (1:6). When he warned of the danger of apostacy, he referred them to Psa. 95 (3:7-11). When he insisted that Christ's priesthood excelled Aaron's, he cited, "Thou art a priest for ever after the order of Melchizedek" (7:17). When he declared that the old covenant was an imperfect and temporary one, he reminded them that Jeremiah had foretold the "new covenant" (8:8-10).

When he dwelt upon Christ coming to earth with the express purpose of supplanting all the Levitical sacrifices by offering Himself unto God, the apostle showed that Psa. 40 had fore-announced (10:5-7) this very truth. When he called upon the Hebrews to walk by faith, he quoted Hab. 2:4, and then devoted the whole of the 11th chapter to illustrate the fact that all of the O.T. saints had so walked. When he admonished them for fainting under the chastening rod of God, he bade them remember the exhortation of Prov. 3:11 (12:5). When he would prove to them the inferiority of Judaism to Christianity, he dwelt upon the Exodus record of the terrifying phenomena which accompanied the appearing of the Lord at Sinai, where He entered into covenant with their fathers (12:18-21). And now that he affirmed that God no longer spake to them "on earth," but rather "from Heaven," he appeals again to their own Scriptures to show this very change had been Divinely predicted.

What an amazing knowledge of the Scriptures Paul possessed! and what a splendid use he made of it! He did not entertain his hearers and readers with anecdotes or by relating some of the sensational experiences through which God had brought him, still less did he descend to "pleasantries" and jokes in order to amuse them. No, he constantly brought them face to face with the Holy Word of the thrice Holy God. And that, by grace, is the unvarying policy we have sought to follow in this magazine: not only do we sedulously avoid any cheapening of the glorious Gospel of Christ, but we endeavour to furnish a proof text for every statement we make; for we ask no one to believe any doctrine or perform any duty on *our* mere say-so. Some may complain that there is "too much repetition" in our articles, or that they are "too introspective," or "too Calvinistic," but their quarrel is not with us, but with Him whose Word we expound and enforce.

"Whose voice then shook the earth: but now He hath promised, saying, Yet once more I shake not the earth only, but also heaven" (v. 26). The simplest and surest way of discovering the meaning of this verse and the force of citing Hag. 2:6, is to keep in mind the particular design which the apostle had before him. That was twofold: to enforce the exhortation he had just given in the previous verse, and to continue emphasising and demonstrating the superiority of Christianity over Judaism. We will consider its terms, then, from each of these viewpoints. First, Paul emphasizes the terribleness of turning away from God in Christ: if He who "shook" the earth is to be feared, much more so is He who "shakes" Heaven! Then let us beware of ignoring His voice: by inattention, by unbelief, by disobedience, by apostasy.

"Whose voice then shook the earth" is a figurative reference to God's omnipotence, for His "voice" here has reference to the mighty power of God in operation: let the reader carefully compare Psa. 29:3-9, where he will find the wondrous effects of Providence ascribed to the "voice" of God. In particular, the apostle here alludes to the declaration of God's authority and the putting forth of His great strength at the time the Law was given: Sinai itself was convulsed, so that "the whole mount quaked greatly" (Ex. 19:18). Yet more than the earthquake is included in the words of our text: the entire commotion involved, with all the particulars enumerated in Heb. 12:18-21, is comprehended therein. It is designated "shook the *earth*" because it was all on the earth, and involved only earthly things—it did not reach to Heaven and eternal things.

"But now He hath promised, saying, Yet once more I shake not the earth only, but also Heaven." This clause has presented a hard riddle to the commentators, and scarcely any two of them, ancient or modern, agree in the solutions they have offered. Personally, we think they created their own difficulties. First, through failing to perceive that the "but *now*" is to be understood in connection with *the subject* the apostle was then discussing, and not as something God was *then* promising to make good in the future. Second, through failing to give proper attention and weight to the term "promised," which is surely enough to show that the final destruction of this scene (when the doom of the wicked will be sealed) cannot be the subject of which Haggai was prophesying. Third, through a slavish adherence to literalism—recent writers especially—which caused many to miss the meaning of "the earth" and "Heaven" in this passage. But these are points of too much importance to dismiss hurriedly, so we must leave their consideration till the next article.

CHAPTER ONE HUNDRED TWO

The Passing of Judaism

(Heb. 12:26, 27)

It is exceedingly difficult, if not quite impossible, for us to form any adequate conception of the serious obstacles presented to the mind of a pious Jew, when any one sought to persuade him that Judaism had been set aside by God and that he must turn his own back upon it. No analogy or parallel exists in our own experience. It was not merely that the Hebrews were required to turn away from something which their ancestors had set up, and around which twined all their own sentiments and affections of national patriotism, but that they were called upon to abandon a religious system that had been appointed and established by Jehovah Himself. That institution, a theocracy, was unique, sharply distinguished from all the idolatrous systems of the heathen. It was God's outstanding witness in the earth. It had been signally honoured and favoured by Him. It had existed for no less than fifteen centuries, and even when Christ appeared, He acknowledged the temple—the centre and headquarters of Judaism—as "My Father's House."

We cannot but admire the tender grace of God in the gentle and gradual way in which He "broke the news" to His people, little by little preparing their minds to receive the truth that His purpose in Judaism had been completely accomplished. Intimations were given through the prophets that the order of things with which they were connected would give place to another and better. To the same effect the Lord Jesus dropped one hint after another: as, for example, when He pointed out that the old bottles were incapable of receiving the new wine, or when He declared, not that which enters into a man defileth him (as the ceremonial law had taught!) but that which issues from the heart, or when He announced "The hour cometh when ye shall neither in this mountain, nor yet at Jerusalem, worship the Father" (John 4:21; and finally, when He solemnly affirmed "Behold, your house is left unto you desolate" (Matt. 23:38).

The rending of the temple veil by a Divine hand was full of deep meaning for those who had eyes to see. The word given through

Stephen that "the Most High dwelleth not in temples made with hands" (Acts 7:48), was another clear ray of heavenly light on the same subject. The conversion of Saul of Tarsus, and the commissioning of him as an apostle to the Gentiles, intimated the direction in which the stream of Divine mercy was now flowing—it had burst the narrow banks of Judaism! The vision granted to Peter (Acts 10) and his message to Cornelius (v. 35), was a further advance along the same line. The important decision of the apostles and elders of the Church at Jerusalem in Acts 15:23-29 not to bind the ceremonial law upon the Gentile converts, was another radical step in the same direction.

Yet Jerusalem still survived, the temple was yet intact, and its services continued. Moreover, the leaders of the Nation had rejected Christ and denounced Christianity as a device of Satan. Many of the Jewish Christians were sorely puzzled and deeply exercised, for the Roman yoke had not been removed. As yet the followers of Christ were but few in number, and for the most part, poor and despised. The Hebrew believers were being hotly persecuted by their unbelieving brethren, and God had made no manifest interposition on their behalf. They were therefore almost ready to conclude that, after all, they had made a dreadful mistake in forsaking the religion of their fathers, and that the sore afflictions they were passing through were a Divine judgment upon them. It was to allay their fears, to more thoroughly instruct their minds, to establish their hearts, that God moved the apostle to write this particular epistle to them—the great theme of which is a display of the immeasurable superiority of Christianity over Judaism, and its chief design being a call to perseverance and a warning against apostasy.

But even in this epistle the apostle did not come right out and say plainly "God has discarded Judaism." No, the path of *faith* is never an easy one. Faith can only thrive while it *fights* (1 Tim. 6:12). There must be that which deeply exercises the heart if the soul is to be kept in the place of complete dependence upon God! Nevertheless, God always grants sufficient light unto a truly exercised soul to indicate the path which is to be followed; He always provides a foundation for faith to rest upon. Though He may not remove the chief obstacle (as He did not for the Hebrews while the temple still stood!) and grant a complete solution to our difficulties, yet He graciously furnishes the humble soul sufficient help to circumvent them. Thus it was in this epistle. *Though no explicit statement is made* that God had done with Judaism, yet sufficient proof was furnished that He *had* set up something better in its place. This comes out again and again in almost every chapter, notably so in the passage now before us.

What has been pointed out in the last paragraph presents a principle and a fact which it is deeply important for true Christians to lay hold of to-day. Not a few of the Lord's people are now confronted with similar problems, which if not so acute as the Hebrews faced, are just as real to them: problems relating to church-fellowship, baptism, the Lord's supper, Sabbath observance. For thirty years a situation existed in Israel which produced two parties, neither of which could convince the other; and, as usual, the larger party was in the wrong. On the one hand was the long-established Judaism, which contained the great majority of the Nation; on the other hand was the handful of God's faithful servants with the few who had sufficient grace to receive their teachings and walk by faith. Had the latter been regulated by ancient custom, or by mere numbers, or by the logic of circumstances (the outward providences of God), they had missed God's will for them and had "forsaken their own mercy" (Jonah 2:8).

The little company of converted Hebrews who had left Judaism for Christ were faced with a perplexing and trying situation. No doubt in the case of many of them, their loved ones still adhered reverently and vigourously to the religion of their fathers. Nor could either party convince the other of its error by a simple and direct appeal to Holy Writ. Each side had some Scripture to support it! Nowhere in the O.T. had God *expressly said* that He would yet do away with Judaism, and nowhere in the N.T. had He *openly declared* that He had now set Judaism aside. No, dear reader, *that* is rarely God's way! In like manner, Christendom is now divided on various points both of doctrine and of duty, and each side is able to make out a real "case" by an appeal to Scripture, and often, neither can cite one decisive verse proving the other to be wrong. Yet *one is* wrong! Only by earnestly waiting *upon God* individually can *His* mind be discovered.

But *why* has God ordered things thus? Why are not the Scriptures so worded that there would be no room for controversy? *To try our hearts.* The situation which confronted the converted Hebrews was a real test as to whether they would be followers of *men* or pleasers of *God.* The self-righteous Pharisees could appeal to a long-established system of religion in justification of their rejection of Christ; and there are those in Christendom to-day who vindicate their adherence to what *God* has never commanded and which is dishonouring to His Son, by an appeal to a long line of godly men who have believed and practiced these very things. When others seek to show that an *opposite* course is required by Scripture, they profess to be "unable to see" what is quite clear to simple and humble souls, and ask for some verse which expressly *forbids* what they are doing; which is like those who, in the face of His miracles, said, "If Thou be the Christ tell us *plainly*" (John 10:24).

No doubt it *had* made matters much easier for the Hebrews if the apostle said plainly, "God has completely finished with Judaism:" *that* had "settled the matter" for hesitating ones who were halting between two opinions—and poor fallen human nature loves to have things *so* "settled" that there may be an end to perturbation of mind and exercise of heart. Moreover, the converted Hebrews would then have had a clear proof-text which *must* have silenced those who differed from them—and we love to have a verse which will close the mouths of those who agree not with us, do we not? Or, God could have allowed the Romans to capture Jerusalem and destroy the temple thirty years sooner than they did: *that* also had "settled the matter"—yes, and left the Hebrews to walk by sight, instead of by faith! Instead, He gave them this epistle, which called for prayer, study, meditation, and for *more prayer*.

Let us now very briefly review the line of the apostle's argument in 12:18 and onwards. First, he informs the believing Hebrews "Ye are not come unto the mount that might be touched" and which was so "terrible" that even Moses quaked "exceedingly" (vv. 18-21): no, Divine mercy had delivered them from that system. Second, Paul assures them "But ye are come unto mount Sion (vv. 22-24): God had brought them unto an order of things where the Throne of Grace predominated. It is ever the Lord's way to reserve the best wine for the last. Third, the apostle reminds them that increased privileges involve additional obligations, and that failure to discharge those obligations incurs greater guilt; therefore does he urge them to take heed unto God speaking to them in the person of Christ, warning them that failure so to do would bring down upon them the Divine wrath more surely than did the disobedience of Israel of old (v. 25).

"Whose voice then shook the earth: but now He hath promised, saying, Yet once more I shake not the earth only, but also heaven" (v. 26). This verse has occasioned much difficulty to the commentators, scarcely any two of them (ancient or modern) agreeing in their interpretation of it. Many of them suppose that the ultimate, if not the prime, reference in the quotation here made from Haggai relates to the final destruction of the earth and the heavens connected with it, as it is described in 2 Pet. 3:10-12. But to suppose that Paul here made a declaration which concerned the then far-distant future, is not only to break the unity of this passage, but is to charge him with making a quotation which had no real relevancy to the immediate subject he was discussing. In pondering

Heb. 12:26-29 our first concern must be to trace the connection with the context.

Now in the context the apostle had been treating of two things: the immeasurable superiority of Christianity over Judaism, and what this involved concerning the responsibility of those who were the subjects of this higher and grander revelation. These same two things *are still before* the apostle in the closing verses of our chapter: he *continued* to show how immeasurably the new covenant excells the old, and he *continued* to enforce the pressing call which he had made in v. 25. First, he had intimated the vast difference which obtained between the *mouthpieces* which God employed in connection with the two revelations (v. 25): namely, "Moses" (10:28) and "His Son" (1:2). Second, he had shown the great disproportion between those two teachers, by pointing out the respective *positions* they occupied (v. 25). "Moses' seat" (Matt. 23:2) was "on earth," whereas Christ speaks as seated upon His mediatorial throne "from Heaven."

Two things were intimated by God in the different seats or positions occupied by the messengers He had employed. First, inasmuch as He now spake through the Son from Heaven, God denoted that He had finished with Judaism, which was entirely a thing of the earth. Second, that Christianity was of Divine origin, and had to do solely with celestial things. From one angle, this call in Heb. 12:25 was very similar to that exhortation "If ye then be risen with Christ, seek those things which are above, where Christ sitteth on the right hand of God. Set your affection on things above, not on things on the earth" (Col. 3:1, 2). Before their conversion, the affections of the Hebrews had been centred upon the temple—notice how the disciples, just before the crucifixion, came to Christ "for to show Him the buildings of the temple" (Matt. 24:1); but *they* were to be "thrown down!"—Christ had returned to Heaven, and thither their hearts must follow Him. Thus, the *heavenly* calling (Heb. 3:1), heavenly citizenship (Phil. 3:20), heavenly inheritance (1 Pet. 1:4), instead of the earthly concerns of Judaism, were now to engage the hearts and minds of the regenerate in Israel.

Next, in the verses now before us, the apostle brings out the vastly different *effects* produced through the two messengers. *This* is the *central* fact in vv. 26, 27: the Voice "from Heaven" produced proportionately greater *results* than did the voice which spake "on earth." God through Christ speaks more powerfully and effectually than He did through Moses. Let us be careful not to lose sight of this *general* idea when pondering the details. A much greater and more far-reaching "shaking" was produced by the latter than was the case with the former. We believe that Matthew Henry was on the right track when he said, "It is by the Gospel from heaven that God shook to pieces the civil and ecclesiastical state of the Jewish nation, and introduced a new state of the church, that cannot be removed, shall never be changed for any other on earth, but shall remain till it be made perfect in heaven." The apostle is still supplying proof that the Hebrew believers were no longer connected with Judaism, but were come to the antitypical Zion.

"Whose voice *then* shook the earth." Here is the connecting link with the context: the "then" referring to the instituting of Judaism. "But now He hath promised, saying, Yet once more I shake not the earth only, but also heaven." The "but now" is not so much a time-mark as it is an adverbial expression, relating to *the theme* under immediate discussion, namely, the establishment and super-excellency of Christianity. Thus, to show once more the infinitely surpassing and glorious effects of power and majesty which issued from the voice of Christ, speaking from heaven by the Gospel, and so as to give a more lively representation of the same, the apostle compares them with the greatly inferior effects that accompanied the deliverance of the Law. As the right understanding of this "But now" has an important bearing upon all that follows, we subjoin the comments of another thereon.

"The word *now* does not denote the period when the promise was made, but the period to which the promise referred, which was *now,* opposed to *then* when the Law was established. It was equivalent to 'But with regard to the present period, which is the commencement of a new order of things, He has promised, saying.' This use of the word *now* in the apostle's writings is common: Rom. 3:21; 16:26 etc." (John Brown). There is, then, an opposition of the "But now" to what occurred at the "then" at the beginning of the verse. It is to be carefully noted that Paul *did not* say "He hath now promised," i.e. that in the apostle's day God had announced He was going to do something in the far-distant future; instead, it is "But now He hath promised:" the "now" relating to the *fulfilment* of what Haggai had foretold, and not to some promise given through the apostle.

"But now He hath promised, saying." This "saying" which the apostle at once quotes from Haggai he styles a "promise," and that for at least three reasons. First, because what was but a prophecy in Haggai's day had received its actual accomplishment in the apostle's time, in connection with the establishment of Christianity. Second, because this was therefore something for *faith to lay hold of,* and that is what he was seeking to persuade the Hebrew believers to do. Third, to prevent any misconception on *our* part:

had the apostle been pointing out that the prophecy of Haggai contained a yet deeper meaning and more ultimate reference, even to predicting the final destruction of this world and all its works, he had surely been very far from designating such an unparalleled Divine judgment as that, by the term "promise!" A "promise" always refers to something that is *good,* and never to a calamity!

"Whose voice then shook the earth: but now He hath promised, saying, Yet once more I shake not the earth only, but also heaven." Let us now inquire, *What is denoted* by this "shaking" of earth and heaven? This is a figure which is used in the O.T. quite frequently to express *a great change,* produced by the providences and power of God in the affairs of men. "God is our refuge and strength, a very present help in trouble. Therefore will not we fear, though *the earth be removed,* and though the mountains be carried into the midst of the sea" (Psa. 46:1, 2), which is explained in "The heathen raged, *the kingdoms were moved*: He uttered His voice, the earth melted" (v. 6). "Thou hast made *the earth* to tremble: Thou hast broken it: heal the breaches thereof, for it shaketh" (Psa. 60:2): what is signified by that metaphorical language is indicated in the next verse, "Thou hast showed *Thy people* hard things: Thou hast made us to drink the wine of astonishment." "Therefore I will *shake the heavens,* and the earth shall remove out of her place" (Isa. 13:13)—language which signifies a tremendous commotion among the nations—compare Joel 3:16. Such vivid imagery is common in the Prophets.

"He stretched out His hand over *the sea,*" which is interpreted in the next sentence "He shook *the kingdoms*" (Isa. 23:11). "Behold, the Lord maketh *the earth* empty, and maketh it waste, and turneth it upside down" (Isa. 24:1)—words, we need hardly say, which are not to be taken literally. "At His wrath *the earth* shall tremble," explained in the following clause, "and *the nations* shall not be able to abide His indignation" (Jer. 10:10). "Arise, contend thou with the mountains: and let the hills hear thy voice. Hear ye O mountains, the Lord's controversy, and ye strong foundations of the earth" (Micah 6:1, 2): such language is not to be understood literally, as the next clause shows "For the Lord hath a controversy with *His people.*" "For the powers of heaven shall be shaken" (Luke 21:26). Even Mr. Darby admitted (in his "Synopsis"), "This shaking of all things—whether here (Heb. 12:26, 27) or in the analogous passage in 2 Pet.—evidently goes beyond Judaism, *but has peculiar application to it*"—italics ours.

"Whose voice then shook the earth." The immediate reference is to Sinai at the time the law was given. But, as we have seen, that material mount was emblematic of the entire economy which was then established. Thus the "shaking" of the "earth" denoted the great outward *change* which took place in the days of Moses. The *external* state of Israel was then greatly altered. They were organised into a kingdom and church-state (Acts 7:38), into a theocracy. Yet glorious as was that change, it reached not to "heaven," that is to say, it affected not their *inner* man and was not concerned with *spiritual and eternal* relations. "The economy established at Sinai, *viewed by itself,* was a temporal covenant with a worldly nation, referring to temporal promises, an earthly inheritance, a worldly sanctuary, a typical priesthood, and carnal ordinances" (J. Brown).

"But now (in relation to Christianity) He hath promised, saying, Yet once more I shake not the earth only, but also heaven." The careful reader will observe that the prophet had said, "I will shake the heavens, and the earth, and the sea, and the dry land" (Hag. 2:6), whereas the apostle was moved by the Holy Spirit to word it—for the sake of his emphasis—"I shake not the earth only, but also heaven," hence a shaking of *both* "earth" and "heaven" was here in view. "The voice in heaven produces more extensive and more permament effects. It shakes both earth and heaven—effects a change both on *the external and spiritual* circumstances of those who are under it; and it effects a *permament* change, which is to admit of no radical essential change forever" (J. Brown).

Though a great change had been produced in connection with the giving of the old covenant, a far greater change had been effected in the establishing of the new covenant. *That* had affected but one nation only, and that, merely in its external and temporal circumstances: *this* reaches unto God's people among all nations, and affects their spiritual and eternal interests. It was reserved for God's *Son* to bring this about, for in all things *He* must have the preeminence. A much greater commotion and convulsion in human affairs has been brought in by Immanuel, yea, it was then as though the very universe was shaken to its centre. In order to the establishing of that kingdom of Christ's which shall never be moved, there were tremendous revolutions, both in connection with Judaism and the idolatrous systems of the heathen—"These that have turned the world upside down" (Acts 17:6) was the charge preferred against the apostles.

Now as the great change in the temporal affairs of Israel at the instituting of Judaism had been adumbrated by the quaking of Sinai, so the far greater alterations introduced by the establishing of Christianity were also shadowed forth in the various physical phenomena and angelic appearances. "At His birth a new star appeared in the heavens, which filled the generality of men with amazement, and put those who were wise to diligent inquiries about it. His birth was proclaimed by an angel from heaven, and celebrated by 'a multitude of the heavenly hosts.' In His ministry the heavens were opened, and the Holy Spirit descended on Him in the shape of a dove. These things may answer that mighty work in heaven which is here intimated. On the earth, wise men came from the east to inquire after Him; Herod and all Jerusalem were shaken at the tidings of Him. In the discharge of His work He wrought miracles in heaven and earth, sea and dry land, on the whole creation of God. Wherefore in the first coming of Christ the words had their literal accomplishment in an eminent manner.

"Take the words metaphorically for great changes, commotions and alterations in the world, and so also were they accomplished in Him and His coming. No such alteration made in the world since the creation of it as was then, and in what ensued thereon. All the 'heavens' of the world were then shaken, and after a while removed: that is, all their *gods* and all their worship, which had continued from time immemorial, which were the 'heavens of the people,' were first shaken, and then utterly demolished. The 'earth' also was moved, shaken and changed: for all nations were stirred up, some to inquire after Him, some to oppose Him, whereon great concussions and commotions did ensue; till all the most noble parts of it were made subject to Him.

"But, as we observed before, it is the dealing of God with *the church,* and the alteration which He would make in the state thereof, concerning which the apostle treats. It is therefore the 'heaven' of Mosaic worship and that Judaical church-state, with the 'earth' of their political state belonging thereunto, that are here intended. These were they that were 'shaken' at the coming of Christ, and so shaken as shortly after to be removed and taken away, for the introduction of the more heavenly worship of the Gospel, and the immovable evangelical church-state. This was the greatest commotion and alteration that God ever made in the 'heaven' and 'earth' of the church. This was far more great and glorious than the shaking of the 'earth' at the giving of the law. Wherefore, not to exclude the senses before mentioned, which are consistent with this, and may be respected in the prophecy as *outward signs* and indications of it, *this* is that which is principally intended in the words, and which is proper to the argument in hand" (John Owen).

"And this word, Yet once more, signifieth the removing of those things that are shaken, as of things that are made, that those things which cannot be shaken may remain" (v. 27). This is the apostle's inspired commentary on Haggai's prophecy. He points out that the "yet once more" denoted there had previously been a great change wrought in Israel's fortunes, and also that now another radical alteration had been made therein. He insists that the "shaking" was in order to effect a *removal* of what was only transient, and that the great change was only in order that that which is unchangeable might remain—*that the permanent might be fixedly established.*

CHAPTER ONE HUNDRED THREE

The Establishing of Christianity

(Heb. 12:27)

The Divine incarnation was not some sudden, isolated, and unexpected event. The advent of our blessed Lord, and with it the dawn of Christianity, marked a climax and consummation. The world was prepared through long processes for the coming of the One and the preaching of the other: from Eden to Bethlehem the centuries were preparing for the appearing of Immanuel. As the processes of creation fitted the earth for man to live upon it, so all history paved the way for the birth of the God-man. The Holy Scriptures focused the Divine preparation in one race, yet all peoples shared in the process: outside of the elect nation God was at work, and all streams converged to a single centre. The march of events was both slow and complicated, yet eventually the stage was fully set and a suitable background made for the appearing of the promised Saviour.

"*When the fulness of time was come,* God sent forth His Son, born of a woman" (Gal. 4:4). This signifies much more than that the time appointed by the Father had now arrived when He would put an end to the Mosaic economy and replace the shadows and types by the substance and Antitype. It denoted that conditions were peculiarly suitable for the introduction of a new and enlarged dispensation, that everything was now ripe for the execution of God's great purpose. All the foundations had been laid. The long night of preparation had now run its course. The chrysalis was ready to burst its bonds; the fields were white unto the harvest; the olive tree was ready for the grafting of other branches into it (Rom. 11). The "fulness of time" intimates both ripeness of opportunity and consummation of need. The advent of God's Son to this earth and the proclamation of the Gospel far and wide, not only introduced a new era, it also marked the climax of the old.

In its relation to the immediate context this expression, "the fulness of time," signifies that the Church on earth had been prepared for the coming of God's Son by having now outgrown the conditions of her childhood and minority, making her feel the irksomeness of the bonds upon her and to long for the liberty of maturity. The legal economy was merely a "schoolmaster unto Christ," and it had now served its purpose. The old economy had decayed and waxed old, and was "ready to vanish away" (Heb. 8:13). Aged Simeon was a representative of that godly remnant who were "waiting for the Consolation of Israel," for there was a Divinely prepared company that then "looked for redemption in Jerusalem" (Luke 2:25, 38). The favoured Nation as a whole had lost its liberty, being under the yoke of the Romans, and seemed on the point of relinquishing its mission; the need for the fulfillment of the Messianic prophecies was real and pressing.

There was a remarkable combination of circumstances tending to prepare the world for the Gospel, and a fearful climax in the world's need of redemption. The break up of old heathen faiths and the passing away of the prejudices of antiquity, disposed men for a new revelation which was spiritual, humane, non-provincial. The utter failure of Pagan religion from immorality, and of Pagan philosophy from its impotency to cure that immorality and the miseries it entailed, called loudly for some new Faith, which should be both sure and powerful. The century immediately preceding our Lord's advent was probably the most remarkable in all history. Everything was in a state of transition; old things were passing away; the fruit of the ancient order was rotting upon the tree, though without yielding the seeds of a new order. There were strange rumours afloat of coming relief, and singular hopes stirred the hearts of men that some Great One was about to appear and renovate the world.

"The fulness of time was come." First, *the world had reached its climacteric of sin.* History has given a faithful record of the terrible moral conditions which obtained among men in the century that immediately preceded our Lord's advent. At Rome, which was then the metropolis of the world, the Court of Caesar was steeped in luxury and licentiousness. To provide amusement for his senators six hundred gladiators fought a hand to hand conflict in the public theatre. Not to be outdone, Pompey turned five hundred lions into the arena to engage an equal number of his braves, and "delicate ladies" sat applauding and gloating over the blood that flowed. Children were the property of the state, to be disposed of as was deemed best for the public interests. The aged and infirm were banished to an island in the Tiber. Marriage was wholly a matter of sensual caprice; divorce was so frequent, it was customary for women to count them by the number of rings worn on their fingers. About two thirds of the entire civilized world were slaves, their masters having absolute power over them.

Conditions in Greece were even worse. Sensual indulgence and every species of cruelty were carried to the highest pitch. Gluttony was an art. Fornication was indulged without restraint. Parents were at liberty to expose their children to perish from cold and hunger or to be eaten up by wild beasts, such exposure being practised frequently, and passed without punishment or censure. Wars were carried on with the utmost ferocity: if any of the vanquished escaped death, slavery of the most abject kind was the only prospect before them; and in consequence, death was considered preferable to capture. "The dark places of the earth were filled with the habitations of cruelty" (Psa. 74:20). The world had reached its climacteric of sin, and this provided a dark background from which could shine forth the Light. Oftentimes a disease cannot be treated until it "comes to a head." In view of the above conditions, the world was ready for the appearing of the great Physician.

"The fulness of time was come." *The world had reached its consummation of want.* It had been predicted of old that the Messiah should be "the Desire of all nations:" to this end there must be a complete exposure of the failure of all human plans for deliverance. This time had arrived when Christ was born. Never before had the abject misery and need of humanity been so apparent and so extensive. Philosophy had lost its power to satisfy men, and the old religions were dead. The Greeks and Romans stood at the head of the nations at the time our Lord appeared on earth, and the religious state of those peoples in that age is too well known to require any lengthy description of it. Polytheism and Pantheism were the popular concepts: innumerable deities were worshipped, and to those gods were attributed the most abominable characteristics. Human sacrifices were frequently offered upon their altars.

Judaism was also fully ripe for the accomplishment of Messianic prophecy. Sadduceeism had leavened the ruling classes and affected the nation with rationalism and sceptism. Phariseeism, which represented the ideas and ideals of the popular party, was too often only formal and hypocritical, and at best was cold and hard, "binding heavy burdens" and laying on men's shoulders a load which they refused to touch with their fingers (Matt. 23:4). The nation was under the government of Rome, and was thoroughly discouraged. Was there, then, no eye to pity, no arm to save? Was God unmindful of the tragic condition of mankind? No, blessed be His name, the "fulness of time was come:" a platform was then ready on which the glories of Divine grace might be exhibited, and now arose "the Sun of righteousness with healing in His wings" (Mal. 4:2).

"The fulness of time was come." *The needed preparations were completed,* and the high-water mark was reached. Side by side with the preliminary movements in Israel, Divine providence had also been at work in heathendom, making ready the world for the dawn of Christianity. Political conditions were singularly favourable for the coming of the Gospel. Most of the then known earth was within the bounds of the Roman empire. Everywhere the Romans went good roads were made, along which went the soldier, and after him the merchant and scholar. In a short time commercial intercourse fused various peoples. Previously, old national distinctions had bound up religious prejudices, each country having its own gods, and any attempt to foist a foreign religion upon a nation was bitterly resented. But national barriers were now broken down by Roman prowess and international intercourse, and religious exclusiveness was greatly weakened. All of this facilitated the task of the missionaries of the Cross. The Roman roads became highways for the evangelists, and Roman law afforded them protection.

Parallel with the growth of the Roman empire was the spread of Grecian culture. The Grecian tongue was the one most extensively used as the language of learning: all educated people were supposed to understand it. This was a most suitable medium by which the Christian messengers could speak to a great multitude of peoples, without enduring the tedious delay of learning new languages. In Syria, Egypt, Phrygia, and Italy, as well as Greece and Asia Minor, the heralds of Christ could make themselves understood everywhere by using the common tongue employed by all teachers of that day. Moreover this language was so delicately modulated as to surpass all other forms of speech in its capacity for expressing *new* ideas. It was therefore exactly what was needed for the setting forth of a new revelation to the world at large.

It was the same with Judaism. Now had arrived the time for the fulfilment of its mission: the giving to the world of the O.T. Scriptures, and the realisation of the Hope which they presented. Judaism was to give birth to Christianity: out of the old soil the new order was to spring. The position of the Jews at that time wonderfully faciliated the spread of the Gospel, for they were already dispersed abroad everywhere. In the days of Augustus there were forty thousand Jews at Rome, and by the time of Tiberius double that number. The Jewish synagogues furnished a means of communication between Christian gospellers and the heathen world. A synagogue was to be found in almost every town throughout the Roman empire, and to it the evangelists first went; and thus a suitable language was provided for communicating with all peoples, and centres of work were to be found in every city.

In such a striking conjunction of favourable providences we cannot but behold and admire the controlling hand of Him who worketh all things after the counsel of His own will. They served to greatly lessen the severe shock which the displacing of the old order of things and the introduction of the new order was bound to bring, for the claims of Christ are of a very radical nature and His demands revolutionizing. Even so, the establishing of Christianity is spoken of as a *shaking* of "not the earth only, but also heaven" (v.26): though such language be figurative, nevertheless it refers to that which was intensely real and drastic. Our assertion that the last clause of v. 26 is *not* to be understood in a material sense (as is now widely supposed), calls for some further expository remarks thereon, particularly concerning its setting here, its original, and its connection.

At v. 25 the apostle began an exhortation which was based upon what had ben pointed out in vv. 18-24, and which he re-enforces by additional considerations. The exhortation consists of a call to hear and heed God's message to us through Christ. God is the Author of Old and New Testaments alike: in the former He spoke through Moses and the prophets; in the latter by the Son, His final Spokesman. The manifestation which God made in Christ and the message He has given us through Him, completes the revelation of His will. This final message was declared neither by man nor angel, but by the only begotten Son. Then let us beware of treating *such* a revelation in a manner ill-fitting its high character. The superior dignity of the Messenger and the supreme importance of His message must ensure severer punishment to those who despise and reject Him.

The urgency of this call for us to hear Christ is intimated by pointing out that since those who had disregarded God's message through Moses escaped not, a far worse punishment must be the portion of those who turn a deaf ear unto Him speaking through the Son (v. 25). The superiority of God's revelation by the Son to the message given through Moses was evidenced by the phenomena which attended each, and the different effects which followed their appearing: the Voice "from heaven" (by Christ) produced proportionately greater results than did the Voice which spake by Moses, "on earth." The Voice through each produced a "shaking," but that through the latter was far more extensive than that through the former (v. 26). In proof of this declaration the apostle quoted and commented upon a striking prediction found in Haggai, the pertinency and scope of which we would now consider. For a better understanding thereof we will turn to its original setting.

In chapter 1 Haggai *rebukes* the indifference of the Jewish remnant (who had returned to Palestine from the Babylonish captivity) for their neglect to rebuild God's house. This stirred them up to proceed therewith. In chapter 2 the prophet *comforts* them. The rebuilding of the temple had then proceeded far enough for it to be made manifest that in its *outward* glory it was far inferior to Solomon's. A great lamentation ensued, and the prophet asks, "Who is left among you that saw this house in her first glory? and how do ye see it now? is it not in your eyes in comparison of it as nothing?" (2:3). The people greatly feared that Jehovah had deserted them, and to re-assure them Haggai declared, "Yet now be strong, O Zerubbabel, saith the Lord; and be strong, O Joshua, son of Josedech, the high priest; and be strong all ye people of the land, saith the Lord, and work: for I am with you, saith the Lord of hosts: according to the word that I *covenanted* with you when ye came out of Egypt, so My Spirit remaineth among you: fear ye not" (2:4, 5); and then it was that he set before them the grand hope of the Messiah's appearing.

"For thus saith the Lord of hosts, Yet once, it is a little while and I will shake the heavens, and the earth, and the sea, and the dry land; And I will shake all nations, and the Desire of all nations shall come: and I will fill this house with glory, saith the Lord of hosts. The silver is Mine, and the gold is Mine, saith the Lord of hosts. The glory of this latter house shall be greater than of the former, saith the Lord of hosts: and in *this* place will I give peace, saith the Lord of hosts" (Hag. 2:6-9). Here was a message of comfort to the sorrowing remnant of the prophet's day, and from it the apostle quotes in Heb. 12.

The first thing we would note in the above prediction is the statement "*a little while* and I will shake," which makes it evident that the "shaking" *did not* look forward to the final and universal convulsion of nature at the end of time; rather was the reference to that which preceded and was connected with the establishing of Christianity, which was comparatively an impending event in Haggai's day. Second, the "shaking" was not to occur in the material world, but in the political and religious realms, as is clear from the closing verses of this very chapter. "I will shake the heavens, and the earth" (v. 21) is at once defined as "and I will overthrow the throne of kingdoms, and I will destroy the strength of the kingdoms of the heathen" (v. 22)—this commenced shortly afterwards, for the axe lay at the root of the Persian empire. Third, there was the express promise that the glory of the temple built in Haggai's day should exceed that of Solomon's.

That third item needs to be very carefully weighed by us, for it is of great importance. *This* was the chief point of *comfort* in Haggai's prediction. His fellows were deeply distressed (see Ezra 3:12) at the comparative meanness of the house of God which they were erecting, but he assures them it should yet possess a glory that far excelled that of Solomon's. That greater glory was not a material one, but a *spiritual*: it was expressly said to be the coming to it of "the Desire of all nations." It was by the appearing of the Messiah that the *real* "glory" would accrue unto the second temple, and that must be while *it* still stood! Haggai's temple was enlarged and beautified by Herod three hundred years later, but the original structure was never destroyed, so that it continued one and the same "house;" and to *it* Christ came! The "little while," then, of Hag. 2:6 was parallel with the "suddenly" of Mal. 3:1.

The fourth and last thing was "and in this place will I *give peace*, saith the Lord of hosts" (2:9). That also was *spiritual*: referring to the peace which Christ should make "through the blood of His cross" (Col. 1:20) between God and His people, and the amity which should be established between believing Jews and believing Gentiles (see Eph. 2:14-16) in the same worship of God. *This* was the principal work of Christ: to put away sin (which was the cause of enmity and strife) and to bring in peace. Finally, the manner in which all this was to be effected was by a great "shaking," not only in the midst of Israel, but also among the Gentiles. Observe carefully the "yet once" of Hag. 2:6: there had been a great "shaking" when the first covenant was instituted, but there would be a still greater at the establishing of the new covenant. Thus the "yet once" signifies, first, once more; and secondly, once for all—finally.

Now from the above prophecy of Haggai Paul quotes in Heb. 12:26. The apostle's object was a double one: to supply additional proof for the superiority of Christianity over Judaism, and to give further point to the exhortation he had made in v. 25. Evidence is here given from the O.T. to show that the voice of God speaking by Christ had produced far greater effects than His word had through Moses. The contrasts, then, between the old and new covenants, and the excelling of the latter over the former, may be summed up thus: the one was connected with Sinai, the other brings us unto Sion (vv. 18-24); the one was inaugurated by Moses, the other by the Son; the one was God speaking "on earth," the other "from heaven;" the one "shook the earth," the other "heaven" itself (v. 26); the one is "removed" the other "remains" (v. 27); therefore, HEAR *the Son!*

How far astray, then, are those commentators who suppose that Haggai's prophecy refers to the final judgment at the last day, when the whole fabric of nature shall shake and be removed! First, such a terrifying event was altogether alien to the scope of Haggai's purpose, which was to *comfort* his sorrowing brethren. Second, such a prediction had been entirely irrevelant to the apostle's scope, for he was comparing not the giving of the law with the Day of Judgment, but the giving of the law with the promulgation of the Gospel by Christ Himself; for his whole design was to exhibit the pre-eminence of the Evangelical economy. Third, nor would such dreadful doom be designated a "promise" (Heb. 12:26). Fourth, the apostle clearly intimated that Haggai's prophecy was now fulfilled (v. 28). Finally, there is no reason whatever why we should regard the shaking of heaven and earth here as a *literal* one: it was *spiritual* things of which the apostle was discoursing—such as issue in that unshakable kingdom which believers receive in this world.

Let us admire *the striking appropriateness* of Haggai's prophecy to the purpose the apostle then had in hand. Haggai's prediction concerned the person and appearing of Christ: "The Desire of all nations shall come." There it was announced that God would do greater works than He had performed in the days of Moses (Hag. 2:5-7). God shook Egypt before He gave the law, He shook Sinai at the giving of it, He shook the surrounding nations (especially in Canaan) just after it. But in "a little while" He would do greater things. The prophet's design was to fix the eyes of the Jews upon the *first advent of Christ,* which was their great expectation, and to assure them that their temple would then possess a glory far excelling that of Solomon's. Meanwhile, God would overthrow "the throne of kingdoms and destroy the strength of the heathen" (v. 22), as the forerunning signs of Christ's advent during the short season which intervened before His appearing.

How pertinent and well-suited, then, was Haggai's prophecy to the subject Paul was developing! That prediction had been fulfilled: Christ had come and made good its terms: conclusive proof of this is found in the *changing* of the verb—the prophet's "I will shake" being altered to "I shake," for the apostle regarded the "shaking" as present and *not future.* A "promise" had been given that a greater work of Divine power, grace and glory should be wrought at the appearing of the Messiah than what took place in connection with the exodus from Egypt and the giving of the law, and this was now accomplished. How clearly and how forcibly did this demonstrate the *pre-eminency* of the new covenant above the old: so far as the glory of the second temple excelled that of the first was Christianity superior to Judaism! Finally, how well did this "shaking" of heaven intimate the permamency and finality of Christianity, for the shaking was in order that the unshakable might abide (v. 27).

It now remains for us to weigh *the comment* which the apostle made upon this citation from Haggai: "And this word, Yet once more, *signifieth* the removing of those things that are shaken, as of things that are made, that those things which cannot be shaken may remain" (v. 27). Incidentally, let it be pointed out that here we have a helpful illustration of the province and task of *the teacher*: in expounding God's Word he not only compares passage with passage and defines the meaning of its terms, but he also indicates what legitimate *inferences and conclusions* may be drawn, what its statements *imply* as well as directly affirm. This is exactly what the apostle does here: he *argues* that the word "once" (used by the prophet) not only signified "once more," but that it also denoted the setting aside of the order of things previously existing.

There is a fulness in the words of Holy Writ which can only be discovered by prolonged meditation and careful analysis. The prophecy of Haggai had said nothing expressly about the "removing" of anything, yet what was not stated explicitly *was* contained therein implicitly. The apostle insists that a "removing" was implied in the terms of Haggai's prediction. The very fact that God had "shaken" the Mosaic economy to its very foundations — the preaching and miracles of Christ (and later by His apostles) had caused thousands to leave it, the Lord's denunciation of the religion leaders and His exposure of their hypocrisy had undermined the confidence of the masses, while the rending of the temple veil by a Divine hand had clearly and solemnly signified the end of the Levitical system—was plain intimation that He was on the eve of setting the whole aside, and that, for the purpose of setting up something better in its place; what that something is, we must leave for our next chapter.

N. B. Had some of our twentieth century Christians been present they would have taken issue with the apostle and said, "Paul, you are taking undue liberties with the Word of God, which we cannot consent to. The Holy Spirit through Haggai spoke of a "shaking," whereas *you* change it to "removing." Had the apostle replied,

"I am simply pointing out what the prophet's language clearly implies, drawing an obvious inference from his statement." The rejoinder would be, "We do not need to do any *reasoning* upon the Word. Moreover, any simple soul can see that shaking and removing are very different things, and had the prophet *meant* the latter he would have said so, and not used the former." An expositor of Scripture often encounters such quibbling to-day: it is worse than ignorance, for it deceives not a few into supposing that such slavish adherence to the letter of Scripture (being occupied with its *sound,* instead of seeking its *sense*) is *honouring* the same.

CHAPTER ONE HUNDRED FOUR

The Kingdom of Christ

(Heb. 12:28)

We hope that we made clear in the preceding articles the general idea contained in the citation from the O.T. which the apostle made in Heb. 12:26, namely, that under the proclamation of the Gospel there would be a more radical and far-reaching effect produced, than was the case at the giving of the Law, thereby manifesting the superiority of the one over the other. The more specific meaning of Haggai's prediction (2:6) was that the *Jewish* church and state would be dissolved, for both the ecclesiastical and civil spheres of Judaism ("heaven and earth") were "shaken." Its wider significance comprehended the convulsions which would be produced in *heathendom* (the "sea" of Hag. 2:6, and cf. vv. 21, 22). The great design of God in the Divine incarnation was the setting up of *Christ's kingdom,* but before it could be properly established there had to be a mighty shaking in order that the shadows in Judaism might give place to the substance, and that sinners among the Gentiles be made spiritual.

The appearing of the Messiah introduced and necessitated a total dissolution of the entire Judaic economy: the Levitical institutions being fulfilled in Christ, they had now served their purpose. This was solemnly signified by the Divine rending of the temple veil, and forty years later by the total destruction of the temple itself. But in the meanwhile it was difficult to persuade the Hebrews that such was the case, and therefore did the apostle clinch the argument he had made in 12:18-24 and the exhortation he had given in v. 26 by quoting a proof-text from their own Scriptures. Haggai's language that the Lord would "shake the heavens" referred, as we have seen, *not* to the starry heavens or celestial planets, but to the Judaical constitution under the ceremonial law—called the "heavens" because they typed out heavenly things! Ultimately God would "shake" and remove all dominions, thrones and powers which were opposed to the kingdom of Christ—as, for example, He later did the Roman empire.

"Wherefore we receiving a kingdom which cannot be moved" (v. 28). The design of the Holy Spirit in the whole of this passage (12:18-29) was to enhance in the Hebrews' estimation the supremacy and excellency of Christ's kingdom, which His Gospel has "brought to light," and of which the believers have been given the right and assurance, for it was *to make way for* the establishment of Christ's kingdom that those mighty "shakings" occurred. Paul insists that God's "shakings" were in order to "remove" that which hindered the manifestation and development of Christ's kingdom. Here, then, is further proof that, so far from Haggai's prophecy looking forward to the universal convulsion of nature at the last day, it has already had its fulfillment: believers *now* actually obtain the fruit of that "shaking," for they "receive" the unshakable kingdom, namely the kingdom of Christ which cannot be moved. We trust this is now so plain to the reader that further effort on our part to establish the same is unnecessary.

But not only did the prophecy of Haggai announce the superiority of Christianity over Judaism and the necessary setting aside of the one for the other, but it also clearly intimated *the finality* of the Christian dispensation. This is plain from the words of 12:27, "yet once more." According to modern dispensationalists Paul *should* have said, "yet *twice* more," for their view is, that just as the Mosaic dispensation was followed by the Christian, so the Christian will be succeeded by a revived and glorified Judaism in "the Millennium." But "*once* more" means once only, and then *no* more. Christianity is the *final* thing which God has for this earth. The *last* great dispensational change was made when the Gospel was given to all the world: hence Peter could say, "the *end* of *all* things is at hand" (1 Pet. 4:7), for God has now spoken His last word to mankind. Hence also John said, "It *is* the *last* hour" (1 John 2:18), which had not been true if another dispensation is to follow the one we are now in.

"And this word, Yet once more, signifieth the removing of those things that are shaken, as of things that are made, that those things which cannot be shaken may remain" (v. 27). Here the apostle *explains* Haggai's "Yet once it is a little while (cf. the "now" of Heb. 12:26) and I will shake the heavens" etc. When Paul refers to the things shaken and removed "as of things that are *made,*" he was far from adding a superflous clause: it emphasised again the contrast he was drawing. The phrase "as of things that are made" is elliptical, needing the added words "made" (by hands) to bring out its sense. Everything connected with Judaism was made by human hands: even the tables of stone on which were inscribed the ten commandments, God commanded Moses to "hew"

(Ex. 34: 1), while the tabernacle and all connected with it was to be "made" according to "the pattern" God showed him (Ex. 25:8, 9). In sharp and blessed contrast, the immaterial and spiritual things of Christianity are "*not* made with hands" (2 Cor. 5:1), but are "made *without* hands" (Col. 2:11).

"Wherefore we receiving a kingdom which cannot be moved let us have grace whereby we may serve God." The apostle here draws an inference from what had just been pointed out concerning the shaking and removing of Judaism and the establishing of Christianity. First, here is a great privilege into which Christians have entered, namely, *a spiritual state* under the rule of Jesus Christ—whom God hath anointed and set as king upon His holy hill of Zion (Psa. 2:6)—here called a "kingdom." Second, the essential character of this kingdom, in contrast from all others, namely its immoveability—its finality and permanency. Third, the way of the believer's participation of it: we "receive" it. "This kingdom, then, is the rule of Christ in and over the Gospel-state of the church, which the apostle hath proved to be more excellent than that of the Law" (John Owen). This kingdom we must now consider.

At the beginning of human history God's kingdom was realised on this earth, so that there was no need to pray, "Thy kingdom come." God's kingship was established in Eden, and all the blessings that flow from subjection to His dominion were then enjoyed. The supremacy of God was gladly and spontaneously acknowledged by all His creatures. But sin entered, and a radical change ensued. Man repudiated the kingship of God, for by transgressing His commandments Adam rejected His sovereignty. By so doing, by heeding the suggestions of the Serpent, the "kingdom of Satan" (Matt. 12:26) was set up in this world. Shortly afterwards, God established His mediatorial kingdom, Abel being its first subject.

Since the Fall there have been two great empires at work on this earth: the "world" and "the kingdom of God." Those who belong to the former own not God; those who pertain to the latter, profess subjection to Him. In O.T. times the Israelitish theocracy was the particular sphere of God's kingdom on earth, the domain where His authority was manifested in a special way (Judges 8:23, 1 Sam. 12:12, Hos. 13:9, 10, etc.). But subjection to Him, even there, was, on the part of the Nation as a whole, but partial and brief. The time soon came when Jehovah had to say to His servant, "They have not rejected thee, but they have rejected Me, that I should not *reign over* them" (1 Sam. 8:7). Then it was that the Lord appointed human kings in Israel as *His representatives,* for while the Sinaitic convenant (Ex. 19:6) continued in force Jehovah remained their King—it was the "*King* which made a marriage feast for His

Son" (Matt. 22:2)! Though Saul, David, and his successors, bore the regal character, and thus partly *obscured* the Divine government, yet it was *not abolished* (see 2 Chron. 13:8). The throne on which Solomon sat was called "The throne of the kingdom of the Lord" (1 Chron. 28:5).

Through Israel's prophets God announced that there should yet be a more glorious display of His government than had been witnessed by their fathers of old, and promised that His dominion would take a more *spiritual* form in the establishing of the Messianic kingdom. This became the great theme of the later predictions of the O.T., though the nature and character of what was to come was necessarily depicted under the figures and forms of those material things with which the people were familiar and by those objects of Judaism which were most venerated by them. The setting up of the spiritual and immoveable kingdom of Christ was the issue and goal of all the prophets declared: see Luke 1:69, 70 and cf. Dan. 2:44. "The Lord reigneth, He is clothed with majesty; the Lord is clothed with strength, wherewith He hath girded Himself: the world (i.e. the "world to come" of Heb. 2:5, the *new* "world" brought in by Christ) also is established, that it *cannot be moved*" (Psa. 93:1, which is parallel with "we receiving a kingdom which *cannot be moved*" (Heb. 12:28).

But though it had been clearly revealed through the prophets that the Lord Messiah would be a King and have a universal empire, yet the bulk of Abraham's natural descendants entertained a grossly mistaken conception of the true design of Christ's appearing and the *real nature* of His kingdom, and this mistake produced a most pernicious influence upon their tempers and conduct when the gracious purpose of His advent was fulfilled. The sense which *they* affixed to the Messianic prophecies was one that flattered their pride and fostered their carnality. Being ignorant of their *spiritual needs* and puffed up with a false persuasion of their peculiar interests in Jehovah's favour on the ground of their fleshly descent from Abraham (John 8:39, 41), the lowly life and holy teaching and claims of the Lord Jesus were bitterly opposed by them (John 8:48, 59; Luke 19:14).

Though God had made many announcements through Israel's prophets that the Messiah would occupy the regal office, yet clear intimation was given that *He* would be very different from the monarchs of earth (Isa. 53:2). Though the Messiah's dominion and reign had been described under material symbols, yet was it made plain that *His* kingdom would *not* be "of this world." Through Zechariah it was announced, "Behold, Thy King cometh unto thee: He is just and having salvation: *lowly,* and riding upon an ass, and upon a colt the foal of an ass" (9:9). How different was *that* from the imposing splendour assumed by earth's sovereigns! what a contrast was His ass from their magnificent chariots and state-coaches! How plainly did the poverty and meanness of Christ's regal appearance intimate that *His* kingdom was *not* of a temporal kind! The Maker of heaven and earth, the Lord of angels, disdained such things as are highly esteemed among men.

The fatal mistake made by the Jews respecting *the true nature* of the kingdom of the Messiah lay at the foundation of all the opposition with which they treated Him, and of their own ultimate ruin. How it behooves *us,* then, to prayerfully seek *right* views of Christ's kingdom, and to resist everything which tends to secularize His holy dominion, lest by corrupting the Evangelical Economy we dishonour the blessed Redeemer, and be finally punished as the enemies of His government. As the main cause of the Jews' infidelity was their erroneous notion of a *temporal* kingdom of the Messiah, so the principal source of the corruption of Christianity has been the attempt made by Rome and her daughters to turn the spiritual kingdom of Christ into a temporal one, by uniting church and state and seeking to extend it by earthly means.

In John's Gospel (which gives the *spiritual* side of things more than do the first three Gospels, being specially written to and for believers), there is a most significant word after the account of our Lord's regal entry into Jerusalem on the back of an ass: "These things *understood not* His disciples at the first: but when Jesus was glorified, then remembered they that these things were written of Him" (John 12:16). So prejudiced were the apostles by the erroneous teaching of the Pharisees, that even they did not rightly apprehend *the nature of* Christ's kingdom till *after* His ascension. They, too, were looking for a *material* kingdom, expecting it to appear in external pomp and glory; and hence they were at a complete loss to apprehend those scriptures which spoke of Christ's kingdom as of a mean and lowly appearance. Well did Matt. Henry say, "The right understanding of the spiritual nature of Christ's kingdom of its powers, glories, and victories, would prevent our misinterpreting and misapplying of the Scriptures that speak of it."

Alas, how blind men still are as to *what* constitutes the true *glory* of Christ's kingdom, namely, that it is a spiritual one, advanced by spiritual means, for spiritual persons, and unto spiritual ends. "To subdue hearts, not to conquer kingdoms; to bestow the riches of His grace to poor and needy sinners, not, like Solomon, to heap up gold and silver and precious stones; to save to the uttermost all that come unto God by Him, not to spread ruin and desolation over countless provinces (as did Ceasar, Charlmagne, Napoleon—A.W.P.); to be surrounded with an army of martyrs, not an army of soldiers; to hold a court where paupers, not princes, are freely welcome" (J. C. Philpot). Only those favoured with true spiritual discernment will be able to perceive *what* the real honours and glories of the Lamb consist of.

The Mediatorial King must of necessity have a kingdom: even at His birth He was proclaimed as "Christ *the Lord*" (Luke 2:11), and the first inquiry made of Him was "where is He that is born *King* of the Jews?" (Matt. 2:2). Christ's Kingship and kingdom follow from a twofold cause. First, His sovereignty *as God* is essential to His Divine nature, being underived, absolute, eternal, and unchanging. Second, His sovereignty *as Mediator* is derived, being given to Him by the Father as the reward of His obedience and sufferings. It has two distinct aspects: first, in its wider and more general application it embraces all the universe; second, in its narrower and more specific administration it is restricted to the Church, the election of grace. In addition to these distinctions, it is important to note Christ never affirmed that the setting up of His kingdom on this earth was in any way dependent upon the attitude of the Jews toward Him: no, the eternal purpose of God was never left contingent upon the conduct of worms of the dust.

"When the Jews refused Jesus as the Messiah, He did not say that the founding of the kingdom would be postponed until His second coming, but He did say the kingdom should be taken from them and given to the Gentiles!" (W. Masselink, "Why the Thousand Years?"). "Jesus saith unto them, Did ye never read in the scriptures, The Stone which the builders rejected, the same is become the Head of the corner: this is the Lord's doing, and it is marvellous in our eyes? *Therefore* say I unto you, The kingdom of God shall be taken from you and given to a nation bringing forth the fruits thereof" (Matt. 21:42, 43). Moreover, every passage in the epistles which speak of Christ's kingdom as a *present* reality, refutes the theory that His kingdom has been postponed until His second advent: see Col. 1:13, Rev. 1:9—Christ's kingdom existed in the days of John, and he was *in* it! Christ is *now* "the Prince of the kings of the earth" (Rev. 1:5). He has already been "*crowned* with glory and honour" (Heb. 2:9).

In consequence of the entrance of sin, God has set up a kingdom in antagonism to the kingdom of Satan. It is essentially different from the kingdoms of the world, in its origin, nature, end, method of development and continuance. It is essentially a kingdom of righteousness, and its central principle is the loyalty of heart of its subjects to the King Himself. It is not a democracy, but an absolute monarchy. The special agency for the extension of it is the organized churches of Christ with their regular ministry. By His providential operations the Lord Jesus is working in every sphere and causing all the historic movements of peoples and nations, civilised and uncivilised, to further its interests and advance its growth; though at the time of such movements this is hidden from carnal sense. Its consummation shall be ushered in by the return of the King, when His servants shall be rewarded and His enemies slain.

"There is but one kingdom or spiritual realm in which Christ reigns forever, and which in the end shall be eternally glorious in the perfect glory of her King; yet in Scripture there are three distinct names used to set forth the excellencies and the blessedness of that realm in various aspects, namely, the Kingdom, the Church, and the City of God" (A. A. Hodge). Of the three terms the word "kingdom" is the most flexible and has the widest range in its N.T. usage. It designates, first, a *sphere* of rule, a realm over which the government of Christ extends. It signifies, second, a *reign* or the exercise of royal authority. It denotes, third, the *benefits* or blessings which result from the benevolent exercise of Christ's regal authority. "For the kingdom of God is not meat and drink"—the reign of Christ does not express itself in that kind of activity; "but righteousness and peace and joy in the Holy Spirit" (Rom. 14:17)—*these* are the characteristics of His realm.

That Christ's kingdom is of an altogether *different* nature and character from the kingdoms of this world is clear from His own teaching: "But Jesus called them to Him, and saith unto them, Ye know that they which are accounted to *rule over* the Gentiles exercise lordship over them; and their great ones exercise authority upon them. But so shall it not be *among you*: but whosoever will be great among you, shall be your *minister;* and whosoever of you will be the chiefest, shall be *servant* of all. For even the Son of Man came not to be ministered unto, but *to minister,* and to give His life a ransom for many" (Mark 10:42-45). And again, "My kingdom is not of this world" (John 18:36): observe He did not say "My kingdom is not *in* this world," but "not *of* it." It is not a provincial thing, nor a political institution; it is not regulated by territorial or material considerations, nor is it governed by carnal policy; it is not made up of unregenerate subjects, nor is it seeking mundane aggrandizement. It is purely a *spiritual* regime, regulated by *the Truth.* This is seen from the *means* He used at its first establishment, and His appointments for its support and enlargement—not physical force, but gracious overtures.

Some men who are fond of drawing innumerable distinctions and contrasts under the guise of "rightly dividing the Word of Truth," draw a sharp line between the kingdom of God and the kingdom of Christ. But this is clearly confuted by "hath any inheritance in the kingdom of Christ and of God" (Eph. 5:5), and again "the kingdoms of this world are become the kingdoms of our Lord and of His Christ" (Rev. 11:15 and cf. 12:10). Its spiritual nature is plainly seen from Jehovah's statement, "they have rejected Me, that I should not reign over them" (1 Sam. 8:7): His throne and sceptre was an *invisible* one. In like manner when the Jews said of Christ, "We will not have this Man to reign over us" (Luke 19:14), they intimated that they were unwilling to surrender their hearts to His moral sway. So too when Paul said, "But I will come to you shortly, if the Lord will, and will know, not the speech of them which are puffed up, but *the power*. For the kingdom of God is not in word, but in power" (1 Cor. 4:19, 20) he obviously meant, "the spiritual power thereof felt in your hearts."

The reign of Christ has a twofold application. First, He sustains the relation of a gracious Sovereign to His redeemed people, ruling them in love, maintaining their interests, supplying their needs, restraining their foes; training them for His service now and for the glory awaiting them in Heaven. Second, He is the moral Governor over the world, for however unconscious they may be of His operations, all men are controlled by Him and their schemings and actions over-ruled for His own ends. Even earth's potentates are obliged to obey His secret will: "*by Me* kings reign, and princes decree justice" (Prov. 8:15); "The king's heart is in the hand of the Lord, as the rivers of water: He turneth it whithersoever He will" (Prov. 21:1). His government over the world, yea, over the entire universe, is administered by a wisely adapted series of means, appointed and directed by Him.

It is important to recognise this twofold scope of Christ's reign. To the Father He said, "As Thou has given Him power over *all flesh,* that He should give eternal life to *as many as Thou hast given Him*" (John 17:2). The kingdom of Christ as it is spiritual and inward is peculiar to the elect, but His kingdom as it is judicial and outward is universal. The two things are distinguished again in Psalm 2: "Yet have I set My King upon My *holy hill of Zion*" (v. 6), and "Ask of Me, and I shall give Thee *the heathen* for Thine inheritance, and the uttermost parts of the earth for Thy possession" (v. 8). Christ is not only "King of saints" (Rev. 15:3), but He is also "King of nations" (Jer. 10:7). He reigns over all mankind, and those who do not submit themselves to Him as Redeemer, shall yet stand before Him as Judge. "Thou shalt break them with a rod of iron; Thou shall dash them to pieces like a potter's vessel" (Psa. 2:9): this speaks of the judiciary acts of His power. Joseph in Egypt typed out the same: the power of all the land was made over to him (Gen. 41:43), but his brethren had a special claim upon his affections.

Now this kingdom of Christ, considered in its spiritual and inward aspect, believers are said to "receive," that is, they participate in its privileges and blessings. As Christ's kingdom is "not of the world" but "heavenly" (2 Tim. 4:18), so its subjects are not of the world but heavenly. From the Divine side, they enter by means of the Spirit's quickening, for "except a man be born again, he cannot see the kingdom of God" (John 3:3). From the human side, they enter when they throw down the weapons of their rebellion and take Christ's yoke upon them, for "except ye be converted, and become as little children, ye shall not enter into the kingdom of heaven" (Matt. 18:3). It was when we transferred our allegiance from Satan to Christ that it could be said, "The Father hath delivered us from the power of darkness, and hath translated us into the kingdom of His dear Son" (Col. 1:13). They who have received the Gospel into an honest and good heart have been admitted into and made participants of the kingdom of Christ.

"Wherefore we receiving a kingdom which cannot be moved." In seeking to define more closely the "we receiving," let us remember the threefold meaning of the term "kingdom." First, it signifies that we are admitted into that *realm* or sphere where Christ is owned as Supreme. Second, it signifies that we have surrendered to the *reign* or sceptre of Christ, for Him to rule over our hearts and lives. Third, it signifies that we now participate in the *blessings* of Christ's government. This word "receiving" also denotes that we have this kingdom *from Another*: "walk worthy of God, who hath *called you unto* His kingdom and glory" (1 Thess. 2:12); "hath not God *chosen* the poor of this world, rich in faith, and *heirs* of the kingdom?" (James 2:5); "Come ye blessed of My Father, inherit the kingdom *prepared for you* from the foundation of the world" (Matt. 25:34); all bring out this thought.

In affirming that this is a kingdom "which cannot be moved" the apostle emphasised once more the great superiority of Christianity over Judaism, and also showed wherein the kingdom of Christ differs from all the kingdoms of earth, which are subject to commotions and convulsions. This "kingdom which cannot be moved" is but another name for "those things which cannot be shaken" that "remain" of v. 27: it is the substance and reality of what was typed out under the Mosaic economy. "We have received a kingdom that shall never be moved, nor give way to any new dispensation. The canon of Scripture is now perfected, the Spirit of prophecy is ceased, the mystery of God is finished: He hath put His last hand to it. The Gospel-church may be made more large, more prosperous, more purified from contracted pollution, but it shall never be altered for another dispensation; they who perish under the Gospel, perish without remedy" (Matt. Henry).

CHAPTER ONE HUNDRED FIVE

The Final Warning

(Heb. 12:28, 29)

"Wherefore we receiving a kingdom which cannot be moved, let us have grace whereby we may serve God acceptably, with reverence and godly fear. For our God is a consuming fire." A brief analysis of these verses reveals the following weighty points. First, the inestimable blessing which believers have been made the recipients of: a kingdom which is eternal. Second, the obligation devolving upon them: to serve God with true veneration and pious devotedness. Third, the warning by which this is pointed: because there can be no escape from the Divine wrath which overtakes apostates. In his helpful commentary J. Brown pointed out that "to receive an immoveable kingdom is but another mode of expressing what is meant by 'ye are come to mount Sion' (v. 22). It is another descriptive figurative mode of expressing that the privileges and honours under the new covenant men obtain by the faith of the truth as it is in Jesus." In support of this: "they that trust in the Lord shall be as mount Zion: they shall *never be moved*" (Psa. 125:1).

Now there is a twofold "kingdom" which believers have "received:" a kingdom of grace, which is set up in the heart of the saint, where Christ reigns as supreme Sovereign, and a kingdom of glory, prepared for us in Heaven, where we shall reign as kings with Christ forever. John Owen insisted that the former only is here intended, Ezekiel Hopkins threw the emphasis almost entirely upon the latter; personally we believe that *both* are included, and shall expound it accordingly, condensing the main points from each of these writers.

Christians are already possessors of the kingdom of *grace,* for Christ has established His dominion over them. Though He sits personally upon the Throne of heaven, yet He rules in believers by His spirit (who has received commission from Him), and also by His Word energized in them by the Spirit. The *interest* of believers in this kingdom is called their "receiving" it, because they have it by gift or grant from their Father: Luke 12:32. First, they receive its doctrine, truth, and law: they own its reality and submit to its authority: Rom. 6:17. Second, they receive it in the light, grace, and spiritual benefits of it: they enjoy its privileges of righteousness, peace, and joy: Rom. 14:17. Third, they receive it in its dignities and securities: they are kings and priests unto God (Rev. 1:6), and so safe are they as to be "kept by the power of God through faith" (1 Pet. 1:5). Fourth, they receive it by a supernatural initiation into its spiritual mysteries (1 Cor. 4:20), the glory of which is immediate access to God and heart enjoyment of Him.

The privileges which Christians receive by their believing the Gospel are inconceivably grand. They are in the kingdom, the kingdom of God and Christ, a spiritual and heavenly kingdom; enriched with inexhaustible treasures of spiritual and celestial blessings. Christians are not to be measured by their outward appearance or worldly circumstances, but rather by the interest they have in that kingdom which it was their Father's good pleasure to give them. It is therefore their privilege and duty to conduct themselves and behave as those who have received such wondrous privileges and high dignities from God Himself: far should they be from envying poor millionaires and the godless potentates of this earth. *Our* portion is infinitely superior to the baubles of time and sense. Though the world knows us not, unto God we are "the excellent of the earth" (Psa. 16:3), the crown-jewels of His Son, those whom angels serve or minister unto. O for grace to conduct ourselves as the sons and daughters of the Almighty.

In what sense or senses has the believer "received" the kingdom of *glory?* First, by the immutable Word of Promise. To the believer the promise of God is as good security as the actual possession. The poor worldling cannot understand this, and he regards the confidence of the Christian as naught but fanaticism. But the simple trusting soul already possesses the kingdom of glory because God has infallibly assured him "in black and white" of the possession of it. It is the immutable Word of Promise which gives him the right and title *to* the inheritance, and therefore as it now belongs to him by right and title, he may well call it *his*. When God has promised any thing, it is all the same to a believer whether He saith it *is* done or it shall be done.

Second, the believer has "received" the kingdom of glory by grace giving him the *earnest* and *firstfruits* of it. The comforts and graces of the Spirit are referred to again and again under these figures: appropriately so, for an "earnest" is a part (an instalment) of what is agreed upon, and the "firstfruits" are a sample and pledge of the coming harvest. Now grace and glory are one and the same in essence, differing only in degree: grace is Heaven brought down into the soul, glory is the soul conducted to Heaven. Grace is glory commenced, glory is grace consummated. Probably one of the meanings of "Light is sown for the righteous" (Psa. 97:11) is, the "light" of everlasting life and bliss is now in the graces of regenerated souls as in their seed, and they shall certainly bud and blossom forth into perfect fruitage.

Third, the believer has "received" the kingdom of glory by *the realisation of faith.* "Faith is the substance of things hoped for, the evidence of things not seen" (Heb. 11:1). Here is a spiritual grace which brings distant things near and gives to the future a present reality. Faith brings into the soul what lies altogether outside the reach of our natural senses. It is a supernatural faculty which is quite beyond the ken of the natural man. Faith beholds what the eye cannot see, it grasps that made without hands; it supplies demonstration or proof of that which the infidel scoffs at.

Fourth, the believer has "received" the kingdom of glory by *the embraces of hope.* In Scripture, the grace of "hope" is something far better than a vague longing for something we do not yet possess: it is a sure expectation, a definite assurance of what God has promised. Hope supplies a present anticipation of the future realisation. Faith believes, hope enjoys those things which God has prepared for them that love Him. Therefore hope is called the "anchor of the soul . . . which entereth into that within the veil" (Heb. 6:19), for it lays hold on that glory which is there laid up for us. Hope is *the taster* of our comforts, and excites the same delight and complacency as the fruition itself will impart—the same in kind, though not in degree.

The particular property of this kingdom which is here emphasized by the Holy Spirit (in accordance with the thought of the context) is, that it "cannot be moved"; therein does it differ from all other kingdoms—here, as everywhere, does our blessed Redeemer have the "pre-eminence." Owen pointed out that, "No dominion ever so dreamed of eternity, as did the Roman Empire; but it hath not only been shaken, but broken to pieces and scattered like chaff before the wind: see Dan. 2:44; 7:14, 27"—so terribly so, that to-day, the closest students of history are unable to agree as to its actual boundaries. But nothing like that shall ever happen to the Saviour's dominion: therefore do we read of "the *everlasting* kingdom of our Lord and Saviour Jesus Christ" (2 Pet. 1:11). No internal decays can ruin it; no external opposition shall overthrow it. Yet the language of our verse goes even further than that: *God Himself* will not remove it.

"That which is here peculiarly intended is, that it is not obnoxious unto such a shaking and removal as the church-state was under the old covenant; that is, God Himself would never make any alteration in it, nor ever introduce another church-state or worship. God hath put the last hand, the hand of His only Son, unto all revelations and institutions. No addition shall be made unto what *He* hath done, nor alteration in it: no other way of calling, sanctifying, ruling, and saving of the church, shall ever be appointed or admitted; for it is here called an immoveable kingdom, in opposition unto that church state of the Jews which God Himself first shook, and then took away—for it was ordained only for a season" (John Owen). Here again we perceive the superiority of Christianity over Judaism: the one was mutable, the other immutable; the one was evanescent, the other eternal; the one was founded by Moses, the other is established by Him who is "the same yesterday, and to-day, and forever."

The fact that Christ's kingdom is an "everlasting" one (2 Pet. 1:11), that it shall "never be moved" (Heb. 12:28), and that "of His kingdom there shall be no end" (Luke 1:33), has occasioned difficulty to some, in the light of "then cometh the end, when He shall have *delivered up* the kingdom to God, even the Father" (I Cor. 15:24). But the difficulty is at once removed if we bear in mind the distinctions pointed out in our last article. The sovereign dominion whch Christ has over all creatures as a Divine person, is something of which He can never divest Himself. Likewise, that dominion over His own people which belongs to Him as the incarnate Son, is also eternal: He will remain forever the Head and Husband of the Church; nor can He relinquish the Mediatorial office. But that dominion to which He was exalted after His resurrection, and which extends over all principalities and powers (John 17:2, Matt. 28:18), *will be* relinquished when its design is accomplished: this is clearly seen in the remaining words of 1 Cor. 15:24, "When He shall have *put down* all rule and all authority and power. For He must reign till He hath put all enemies under His feet." Thus, the "kingdom" which Christ delivers up to the Father is that rule of His over His *enemies*.

The immovability and eternality of Christ's kingdom holds good of it equally whether we consider it in its present grace aspect or its future glory aspect, for we have received "a kingdom which cannot be moved." The kingdom of grace is so Divinely fixed in the heart of believers that all the efforts of sin and all the attacks of Satan are unable to overthrow it: "the foundation of God standeth *sure*" (2 Tim. 2:19); "being confident of this very thing, that He which hath begun a good work in you *will* finish it" (Phil.

1:6). It is absolutely impossible that one of Christ's sheep should perish: in the day to come He will exclaim, "Behold I and the children which God hath given Me" (Heb. 2:13). If this be true of the kingdom of grace, then much more so of the kingdom of glory, when sin shall be no more and Satan shall never again tempt the redeemed.

Now from the glorious nature of this "kingdom" the apostle proceeds to draw an inference or point a practical conclusion: "Wherefore we receiving a kingdom which cannot be moved, let us have grace whereby we may serve God acceptably." As J. Brown pointed out, to "receive a kingdom" is to be *invested with royalty,* to be made kings and priests unto God (Rev. 1:6). Since, then, royalty is the most exalted form of human life, the most dignified honour known upon earth, how it behooves us to seek from God that aid which shall enable us to "walk worthy of the vocation wherewith we are called." Once again we are reminded of the inseparable connection between privilege and duty, and the greater the privilege the stronger the obligation to express our gratitude in a suitable and becoming manner: not merely in emotional ecstasies or fulsome words, but by obedience and worship, that we may "serve God acceptably with reverence and godly fear."

The commentators differ considerably as to what is denoted by "let us have grace," yet it seems to us, its meaning is quite simple and obvious. Its signification may be ascertained by three considerations involved in what immedately follows. First, this "grace" is essential unto the serving of God "acceptably" and, as we shall see, this "service" has a principal reference to our worshipping of Him. Second, this "grace" is the root from which proceeds "reverence and godly fear," so that it must point to something more than simple *gratitude* for what God has already done for us—which is how many of the writers limit it. Third, this "grace" is imperative if we are not to be consumed by Divine wrath—the "consuming fire" of v. 29. We therefore understand this expression to mean, let us *persevere* in the faith and duties of the Gospel, whereby we are alone enabled to offer acceptable worship to God; let us endeavour after an *increase* of Divine aid and succour; let us strive after a continual *exercise* of the grace He has given us; let us seek to bring our hearts more and more under its sanctifying power.

We believe the key to our present passage is found in Ex. 19:10, 11, 15. Under the old covenant the way and means in which Israel was to make a solemn approach unto God in worship was specifically defined: they were to reverently prepare themselves by purification from uncleanness and separation from fleshly indulgences. That was an outward adumbration of the *spiritual* purity which God now requires from us both internally and externally. Because God has revealed Himself in Christ in a far more glorious manner to us than He manifested Himself before Israel at Sinai, we ought to earnestly endeavour after a more eminent preparation of heart and sanctification of our whole persons in all our approaches to the Most High. There must be in us the spiritual counterpart of what was shadowed out in them ceremonially. The fear of God was wrought in Israel by the terrors of His law: though our fear be of another kind, it ought to be none the less real and effectual in us to its proper ends.

The great end in view is, that "we may serve God acceptably." In this particular epistle the Greek word used here signifies that service unto God which consists in His *worship,* in prayer and praise, and the observance of all the institutions of Divine worship. For example, "in which were offered both gifts and sacrifices, that could not make him that did *the service* perfect, as pertaining to the conscience" (9:9); and again, "We have an altar, whereof they have no right to eat which *serve* the tabernacle" (13:10); while in 10:2 the word is actually rendered "worshippers." Nor is this meaning of the Greek word peculiar to the Hebrews epistle: "She was a widow of about four score and four years, which departed not from the temple, but *served* God with fastings and prayers night and day" (Luke 2:37); "who change the truth of God into a lie, and worship and serve the creature more than the Creator" (Rom. 1:25). The specific reference, then, is had unto the worship of God acording to the Gospel, as superseding the institutions under the old economy. Needless to say, such worship cannot proceed from any who are not walking in Gospel obedience.

Now it is in order to our being so fitted for the Divine service that we may worship God *"acceptably,"* that the exhortation comes, "let us have grace." There is a double reference: that our persons may be acceptable, and that our worship may be pleasing in His sight. An intimation is hereby given that there may be a performance of the duties of Divine worship when neither the persons who perform them, nor the duties themselves, *are* accepted by Him. So it was with Cain and his sacrifice, as it is with all hypocrites always. The principal things required unto this acceptance are, first, that the persons of the worshippers be accepted in the Beloved. Second, that the actual performance of worship must, in all the duties of it, be in strict accord with what God (and none other) has appointed. Third, that our spiritual graces be in actual exercise, for it is in and by *this,* in the discharge of all our religious duties, that we give glory unto God. How can our worship be pleasing unto Him if we be in a backslidden state?

That which is here specifically singled out as necessary unto our worship being acceptable is, that we serve God "with reverence and godly fear." As J. Owen wisely pointed out, these "may be learned best from what they are *opposed unto.* For they are prescribed as contrary unto some such defects and faults of Divine worship, as from which we ought to be deterred, by the consideration of the holiness and severity of God as is manifest from the next verse, 'for our God is a consuming fire.' " The sins from which we ought to be deterred by a consideration of these Divine perfections are, first, the want of a due sense of the awe-inspiring majesty of Him with whom we have to do. God provided against this evil under the old economy by the terror wrought in the people at the giving of the Law, by the many restrictions interposed against their approaches to Him (none being allowed to enter the holy of holies), and by all the outward ceremonies appointed; and though all these are now removed, yet a deep spiritual sense of God's holiness and greatness should be retained in the mind of all who draw nigh to Him in worship.

Second, the lack of a due sense of our own vileness, and our infinite distance from God both in nature and state, which is always required to be in us. The Lord will never accept the worship of a pharisee: while we are puffed up with a sense of our own importance and filled with self-righteousness or self-complacency, He will not accept our approaches unto Him. And nothing is more calculated to hide pride from us and fill our hearts with a sense of our utter insignificance as a sight and realisation of the ineffable purity and high sovereignty of God. When Isaiah beheld Him "high and lifted up," he exclaimed "Woe is me! for I am undone" (Isa. 6:5); when Job beheld the Almighty, he cried, "Behold, I am vile" (40:4).

Third, carnal boldness in a formal performance of sacred duties, while neglecting an earnest endeavour to exercise grace in them, which is something which God abhors. O the daring impiety of worldly professors taking upon their polluted lips the ineffable name of God, and offering unto Him "the sacrifice of fools" (Eccl. 5:1). What a marvel it is that He does not strike dead those blatant and presumptuous souls who vainly attempt to deceive Him with their lip service while their hearts are far from Him. It is to prevent these, and other like evils, that we are here exhorted to worship God "with reverence and godly fear," that is, with a holy abasement of soul, having our minds awed by a sense of the infinite majesty of God, our hearts humbled by a consciousness of our vileness and our creaturely nothingness.

No exhortation in this epistle is more needed by our perverse generation than this one. How this imperative requirement "with reverence and godly fear" rebukes the cheap, flippant, irreverent "worship" (?) of the day. O what unholy lightness and ungodly familiarity now marks the religion of Christendom: many address the great Deity as though they were His equals, and conduct themselves with far less decorum than they would show in the presence of an earthly monarch. The omission of bowing the head in silent prayer when we take our place in the congregation, the vulgar glancing around, the unseemingly whispering and chattering, the readiness to smile or laugh at any remarks of the preacher's which may be wrested, are all so many instances of this glaring and growing evil. "God is greatly to be feared in the assembly of the saints, and to be had in reverence of all about Him" (Psa. 89:7).

The Greek word for "reverence" is rendered "shamefacedness" in 1 Tim. 2:9. This, in extraordinary instances, is called a "blushing," a "being ashamed," a "confusion of face" (Ezra 9:6; Dan. 9:7); yet, the essence of it, ought always to accompany us in the whole worship of God. "Godly fear" is a holy awe of the soul when engaged in sacred duties, and this from a consideration of the great danger there is of our sinful miscarriages in the worship of God, and of His severity against such heinous offences. God will not be mocked. A serious soul is hereby moved unto watchfulness and diligence not to provoke so great, so holy, so jealous a God, by a neglect of that reverence and godly fear which He requires in His service, and which is due unto Him on account of His glorious perfections. If the seraphim veil their faces before Him (Isa. 6:2). how much more should we do so!

"For our God is a consuming fire" (v. 29). This is the reason given why we must serve God with reverence and fear. The words are taken from Deut. 4:24, where they are used to deter Israel from idolatry, for that is a sin God will not tolerate. The same description of God is here applied by the apostle unto those lacking grace to worship Him with the humility and awe which He demands. If we are graceless in our persons, and devoid of reverence in our worship, God will deal with us accordingly. As a fire consumes combustible matter cast into it, so God will destroy sinners. The title "our God" denotes a *covenant* relationship, yet though Christians are firmly assured of their interest in the everlasting covenant, God requires them to have holy apprehensions of His majesty and terror: see 2 Cor. 5:10, 11.

The twin graces of love and fear, fear and love, should be *jointly* active in the believer, and it is in preserving a balance between them that his spiritual health largely consists. So it is here: observe the remarkable conjunction: "our God," in covenant relationship, our Father; and yet "a consuming fire," to be trembled at! The first is to prevent despair from considering God's ineffable purity and inflexible justice; the latter is to check a presumptous irreverence unto which a one-sided occupation with His grace and love might embolden us. Thus, the principal exhortation "let us have grace whereby we may serve God acceptably" is urged by two widely different motives: because we have "received a kingdom" and because God is a "consuming fire." Carnal reason would ask, If we have received a kingdom which cannot be moved, why should we fear? But if God be such "a consuming fire" how can we ever expect such a kingdom, since we are but a stubble? But the Spirit-taught have no difficulty in perceiving why the apostle joined together these two things.

The Christian's interest in His favour, is no warrant for casting off a solemn fear of God: though He has laid down His enmity against him, He has not cast off His majesty and sovereignty over him. "Even those who stand highest in the love and favour of God, and have the fullest assurance thereof and of their interest in Him as *their* God, ought, nothwithstanding, to fear Him as a sin-avenging God and a consuming fire" (Ezek. Hopkins, 1680). Though God has taken His redeemed into intimate nearness to Himself, yet He requires that they always retain a due apprehension of the majesty of His person, the holiness of His nature, the severity of His justice, and the ardent jealousy of His worship. If we truly dread falling under the guilt of this awful sin of irreverence, our minds will be influenced unto godly fear. The grace of *fear* is in nowise inconsistent with or an impediment to a spirit of adoption, holy boldness, or godly rejoicing: see Psa. 2:11, Matt. 28:8, Phil. 2:12.

"Let us have grace whereby we may serve God acceptably," for without it there will be neither "reverence" nor "godly fear." Without Divine aid and unction we cannot serve God at all, for He accounts not that *worship* which is offered by graceless persons. Without grace in actual operation we cannot serve God acceptably, for it is in the *exercise* of faith and fear, love and awe, that the very life and soul of spiritual worship consists. O how earnestly do we need to seek an increase of Divine "grace" (2 Cor. 9:8; 12:9), and keep it operative in all duties of the worship of God: that in view of His awful wrath, we may have a dread of displeasing Him; in view of His majesty our hearts may be humbled; and in view of His love, we may seek to honour, please and adore Him. "Sanctify the Lord of hosts Himself; and let Him be your fear, and let Him be your dread" (Isa. 8:13 and cf. Matt. 10:28).

CHAPTER ONE HUNDRED SIX

Brotherly Love

(Heb. 13:1)

Most of the commentators regard the final chapter of Hebrews as an appendix or postscript, containing sundry exhortations which have no direct relation to the body of the epistle. Personally, we regard it as a serious mistake, due to lack of perspicuity, to ignore the organic connection between the central theme of the apostle and the various duties which he here inculcates; rather do we agree with Owen that in these closing verses there is exhibited an exemplification of "that Divine *wisdom* wherewith he was actuated in writing of the whole, which the apostle Peter refers to in 2 Pet. 3:15" The more an anointed mind meditates on this fact, with the faith and reverence which the Holy Scriptures call for, the more will the Divine inspiration of this portion be revealed. It is a great pity that so many writers become slack when they reach the final chapter of an epistle, seeming to imagine that its contents are of less importance and value than those of the earlier ones.

Unless we carefully bear in mind the *order* which the apostle was moved by the Holy Spirit to follow in this treatise, we shall fail to learn some most vital and valuable lessons concerning the proper method and manner of setting forth the Truth of God before the souls of men. Not only is the teacher of God's Word to hold fast the system of doctrine contained therein (introducing no speculations of his own), to preserve a due balance of Truth (not allowing personal preference to make him a hobbyist), but in order for his ministry to be most acceptable to God and profitable to his hearers or readers he must adhere strictly to *the order of Scripture;* for if the context and connections of a passage be ignored, there is great danger of perverting it, for its proper emphasis is then lost and the chain of Truth is broken. Let preachers especially attend closely to the remarks which follow.

A careful reading through of our epistle at a single sitting will reveal the fact that throughout the first twelve chapters not a single moral or ecclesiastical duty is inculcated. It is true that here and there the apostle breaks in upon the orderly development of his thesis, by urging an exhortation unto obedience to God and perseverance in the faith, or by interspersing a solemn warning against the fatal consequences of apostasy; nevertheless, never once does he formally press upon the Hebrews any of the duties enjoined by the second table of the Law—those were reserved for his closing words. The course followed by the apostle was, first, to set forth the glorious person, offices, and work of Christ, and then, having laid a firm foundation for faith and obedience, to exhort unto evangelical and moral duties. As we deem this a most essential consideration we subjoin a paragraph from that master exegete, John Owen.

"He prescribes by his own example, as he also doth in most of his other epistles, the true order and method of preaching the Gospel; that is, first, to declare the mysteries of it, with the grace of God therein, and then to improve it unto practical duties of obedience. And they will be mistaken, who in this work propose unto themselves any other method; and those most of all, who think one part of it enough without the other. For as the declaration of spiritual truths, without showing how they are the vital quickening form of obedience, and without the application of them thereunto, tends only unto that knowledge which puffeth up, but doth not edify; so the pressing of moral duties, without a due declaration of the grace of God in Christ Jesus, which alone enables us unto them, and renders them acceptable unto God, with their necessary dependence thereon, is but to deceive the souls of men, and lead them out of the way and off from the Gospel."

The Divine mysteries unfolded and the great doctrines expounded in the Holy Scriptures are not mere abstractions addressed to the intellect, devoid of valuable fruits and effects: where they are truly received into the soul and there mixed with faith, they issue, first, in the heart being spiritually moulded thereby and drawn out Godwards, and second, they issue in practical results manward. If the Gospel makes known the infinite love and amazing grace of God in Christ, it also directs unto the performance of spiritual and moral duties. So far from the Gospel freeing believers from the duties required by the Law, it lays upon us additional obligations, directs to their right performance, and supplies new and powerful motives to their discharge.

So much, then, for the *general* relation of the contents of Heb. 13 to what has preceded it; now for the more *specific* connection. So far from there being a radical break between Heb. 12 and 13 the closing verses of the former and the opening ones of the latter are closely linked together. There the apostle had mentioned the principal duties which believers are to perform Godwards, namely, to "hear" (v. 25) and to "serve Him acceptably" (v. 28); here, he tabulates those duties which are to be performed manwards. He begins with what is really the sum and substance of all the rest, brotherly love: first, the loving of *God* with all our heart, and then our *neighbour* as ourselves. Adolph Saphir pointed out another link of connection which is not so evident at first sight: having just reminded the Hebrews that "things that are made" shall be shaken and removed (12:27), he now exhorts them to "let that *abide* which is of God, which is eternal, even *love.*"

"Let brotherly love continue" (13:1). The first application in the case of the Hebrews would be, See to it that your having become Christians does not make you behave in a less kindly manner unto your brethren according to the flesh, the Jews. True, they are occasioning great provocation by their enmity and persecution, yet this does not warrant your retaliating in a like spirit, rather does it provide opportunity for the exercise and manifestation of Divine grace. Remember the example left by your Master: the Jews treated Him most vilely, yet He bore patiently their revilings; yea continued to seek their good—then do you follow His steps. Most blessedly did the writer of this epistle emulate his Lord, and practise what he here inculcated: see Rom. 9:1-3 and 10:1.

This lower application of our text holds good for any of us who may, in our measure, be circumstanced similarly to the Hebrews. Since yielding ourselves to the claims of the Lord Jesus, our relations and friends may have turned against us, and, stirred up by Satan, are now opposing, annoying, ill-treating us. In such a case the word comes to us "Let brotherly love continue." Avenge not yourself: answer not railing with railing: but exercise a spirit of true benevolence, desiring and seeking only their good. "If thine enemy hunger, feed him; if he thirst, give him drink: for in so doing thou shalt heap coals of fire on his head. Be not overcome of evil, but overcome evil with good" (Rom. 12:20, 21).

"Let brotherly love continue." The higher reference is, of course, to that special and spiritual affection which is to be cultivated between and among God's children. "He calls love *brotherly,* not only to teach us that we ought to be mutually united together by a peculiar and inward feeling of love, but also that we may remember that *we cannot be Christians without loving the brethren,* for he speaks of the love which the Household of Faith ought to cultivate one towards another, as the Lord has bound them closely together by the common bond of adoption" (John Calvin). Matt. Henry well pointed out, "the spirit of Christianity is a spirit of love." The fruit of the Spirit is love (Gal. 5:22). Faith worketh by love (Gal. 5:6). "Everyone that loveth Him that begat loveth him also that is begotten of Him" (1 John 5:1). Love to the brethren is both the first indication and fruit of the Christian life (Acts 16:33) and the final aim and result of Divine grace (2 Pet. 1:7).

It is to be noted that these Hebrew believers were not exhorted "let us *have* brotherly love," but "let brotherly love *continue.*" Thus the apostle's language clearly supposes that they already had love for each other, that he approvingly notices the same, and then calls upon them for a continuance of it. Like his Master, Paul combines exhortation with commendation: let all His servants do so wherever possible. He had already reminded them "God is not unrighteous to forget your work and labour of *love,* which ye have showed toward His name, in that ye have ministered to the saints, and do minister" (6:10); and "Ye endured a great fight of afflictions; partly whilst ye were made a gazingstock both by reproaches and afflictions; and partly, whilst ye *became companions* of them that were so used" (10:32, 33). But the apostle felt there was danger of their brotherly love decaying, for there were disputes among them concerning the ceremonies of the Mosaic law, and wrangling over religious differences bodes ill for the health of spiritual affection. He therefore puts them on their guard, and bids them live and love as "brethren."

"A love hath its foundation in *relation.* Where there is relation, there is love, or there ought so to be; and where there is no relation, there can be no love, properly so called. Hence it is here mentioned with respect unto a brotherhood . . . . This brotherhood is religious: all believers have one Father (Matt. 23: 8,9), one elder Brother (Rom. 8:29), who is not ashamed to call them brethren (Heb. 2:11); have one spirit, and are called in one hope of calling (Eph. 4:4), which being a spirit of adoption interesteth them all in the same family (Eph. 3:14, 15)"—John Owen. Brotherly love we would define as that gracious bond which knits together the hearts of God's children; or more definitely, it is that spiritual and affectionate solicitude which Christians have toward each other, manifested by a desiring and endeavouring after their highest mutual interests.

This duty was enjoined upon His disciples by the Lord Jesus: "A new commandment I give unto you, That ye love one another; as I have loved you, that ye also love one another" (John 13:34). It was to this word of Christ that His apostle referred in "Brethren, I write no new commandment unto you, but old commandment which ye had from the beginning. The old commandment is the word which ye have heard from the beginning. Again, a new commandment I write unto you, which thing is true in Him and in you" (1 John 2:7, 8 and cf. 3:11). Some have been puzzled by his "I write no new commandment unto you . . . . Again, a new commandment I write unto you," yet the seeming ambiguity is easily explained. When a statute is *renewed* under another administration of government it is counted a "new" one. So it is in this case. That which was required by the Law (Lev. 19:18) is repeated by the Gospel (John 15:12), so that absolutely speaking it is not a new, but an old commandment. Yet relatively, it *is* "new," because enforced by new motives (1 John 3:16) and a new Pattern (1 John 4:10, 11). Thus, "Let us do good unto all men, *especially* unto them who are of the household of faith" (Gal. 6:10), because the latter have peculiar claims upon our affections, being created in the same image, professing the same faith, and having the same infirmities.

The maintenance of brotherly love tends in various ways to the spiritual blessing of the Church, the honour of the Gospel, and the comfort of believers. The exercise thereof is the best testimony to the world of the genuineness of our profession. The cultivation and manifestion of Christian affection between the people of God is a far more weighty argument with unbelievers than any apologetics. Believers should conduct themselves toward each other in such a way that no button or pin is needed to label them as brethren in Christ. "By this shall all men know that ye are My disciples, if ye have *love one to another*" (John 13:35). It should be made quite evident that their hearts are knit together by a bond more intimate, spiritual, and enduring than any which mere nature can produce. Their deportment unto each other should be such as not only to mark them as fellow disciples, but as Christ says,, "*My* disciples"—reflecting *His* love!

The exercise of brotherly love in not only a testimony unto the world, but it is also an evidence to Christians themselves of their regeneration: "We know that we have passed from death unto life because we love the brethren" (1 John 3:14). There should be a word of comfort here for those poor saints whose souls are cast down. At present they cannot "read their title clear to mansions in the sky," and are afraid to cry "Abba, Father" lest they be guilty of presumption. But here is a door of hope opened to Christ's *little* ones: you may, dear reader, be afraid to affirm that you love *God*, but do you not love *His people?* If you do, you must have been born again, and have in you the same spiritual nature which is in them. But *do I* love them? Well, do you relish their company, admire what you see of Christ in them, wish them well, pray for them, and seek their good? If so, you certainly love them.

But not only is the exercise of Christian love a testimony unto the world of our Christian discipleship, and a sure evidence of our own regeneration, but it is also that which *delights God Himself.* Of course it does! It is the product of His own grace: the immediate fruit of His Spirit. "Behold, how good and how pleasant it is for brethren to dwell together in unity!" (Psa. 133:1) is what the Lord Himself declares. This also comes out very sweetly in Rev. 3. There we find one of the epistles addressed to the seven churches which are in Asia, namely, the Philadelphian, the church of "brotherly love," for that is the meaning of the word "Philadelphia," and in *that* epistle there are *no censures* or rebukes: there was that there which refreshed the heart of the Lord!

But our text refers not so much to the existence and exercise of brotherly love, as it does to its *maintenance*: "Let brotherly love *continue*" or "abide constant" as some render it, for the word includes the idea of enduring in the face of difficulties and temptations. That which is enjoined is perseverance in a pure and unselfish affection toward fellow-Christians. Brotherly love is a tender plant which requires much attention: if it be not watched and watered, it quickly wilts. It is an exotic, for it is not a native of the soil of fallen human nature—"hateful and hating one another" (Titus 3:3) is a solemn description of what we were in our unregenerate state. Yes, brotherly love is a very tender plant and quickly affected by the cold air of unkindness, easily nipped by the frost of harsh words. If it is to thrive, it must needs be carefully protected and diligently cultivated.

"Let brotherly love continue:" what a *needful* word is this! It was so at the beginning, and therefore did the Lord God make it a fundamental in man's duty: "thou shalt love thy neighbour as thyself." O what strife and bloodshed, suffering and sorrow had been avoided, had this commandment been universally heeded. But alas, sin has domineered and dominated, and where sin is regnant love is dormant. If we wish to obtain a better idea of what sin is then contrast it with its opposite—*God.* Now God is spirit (John 4:24), God is light (1 John 1:5), God is love (1 John 4:8); whereas sin is fleshly, sin is darkness, sin is hatred. But if we have enlisted under the banner of Christ we are called unto a warfare against sin: against fleshliness, against hatred. Then "let brotherly love continue."

Yes, a most needful exhortation is this: not only because hatred so largely sways the world, but also because of the state of Christendom. Two hundred and fifty years ago J. Owen wrote, "It (brotherly love) is, as unto its lustre and splendor, retired to Heaven, abiding in its power and efficacious exercise only in some corners of the earth. Envy, wrath, selfishness, love of the world, with coldness in all the concerns of religion, have possessed the place of it. And in vain shall men wrangle and contend about their differences in faith and worship, pretending to design the advancement of religion by an imposition of their persuasions on others: unless this holy love be again re-introduced among all those who profess the name of Christ, all the concerns of religion will more and more run into ruin. The very name of a brotherhood amongst Christians is a matter of scorn and reproach, and all the consequents of such a relation are despised."

Nor are things any better to-day. O how little is brotherly love in evidence, generally speaking, among professing Christians. Is not that tragic word of Christ receiving its prophetic fulfilment: "because iniquitiy shall abound, the love of many shall wax cold" (Matt. 24:12). But, my reader, Christ's love has not changed, nor should ours: "Having loved His own which were in the world, He loved them *unto the end*" (John 13:1). Alas, have not all of us reason to hang our heads in shame! Such an exhortation as this is most needful to-day when there is such a wide tendency to value light more highly than love, to esteem an understanding of the mysteries of Faith above the drawing out our affections unto each other. Here is a searching question which each of us should honestly face: Is my love for the brethren keeping pace with my growing (intellectual) knowledge of the Truth?

"Let brotherly love continue." What a *humbling* word is this! One had thought that those bound together by such intimate ties, fellow-members of the Body of Christ, would spontaneously love each other, and make it their constant aim to promote their interests. Ah, my reader, the Holy Spirit deemed it requisite *to* call upon us to perform this duty. What sort of creatures are we that still require to be thus exhorted! How this ought to hide pride from us: surely we have little cause for self-complacency when we need *bidding* to love one another! "Hateful and hating one another" (Titus 3:3): true, that was in our unregenerate days, nevertheless the *root* of that "hatred" still remains in the believer, and unless it be judged and mortified will greatly hinder the maintenance and exercise of Christian affection.

"Let brotherly love continue." What a *solemn* word is this! Is the reader startled by *that* adjective?—a needful and humbling one, but scarcely a "solemn." Ah, have we forgotten the context? Look at the verse which immediately precedes, and remember that when this epistle was first written there were no chapter-breaks: 12:29 and 13:1 read consecutively, without any hiatus—"our God is a consuming fire: let brotherly love continue!" The fact these two verses are placed in immediate juxtaposition strikes a most solemn note. Go back in your mind to the first pair of brothers who ever walked this earth: did "brotherly love continue" with them? Far otherwise: Cain hated and murdered his brother. And did not *he* find our God to be "a consuming fire"? Most assuredly he did, as his own words testify, "My punishment is greater than I can bear" (Gen. 4:13)—the wrath of God burned in his conscience, and he had a fearful foretaste of Hell before he went there.

But it may be objected to what has just been said, The case of Cain and Abel is scarcely a pertinent and appropriate one, for they were merely *natural* brothers where as the text relates primarily to those who are brethren *spiritually*. True, but the natural frequently adumbrates the spiritual, and there is much in Gen. 4 which each Christian needs to take to heart. However, let us pass on down the course of human history a few centuries. Were not Abraham and Lot brethren spiritually? They were: then did brotherly love continue between them? It did not: strife arose between their herdsmen, and they separated (Gen. 13). Lot preferred the well-watered plains and a home in Sodom to fellowship with the father of the faithful. And what was the sequel? Did *he* find that "our God is a consuming fire"? Witness the destruction of all his property in that city when God rained down fire and brimstone from heaven!—another solemn warning is that for us.

"Let brotherly love continue." But what a *gracious* word is this! Consider its implications: are they not similar to " walk worthy of the vocation wherewith ye are called, with all lowliness and meekness, with longsuffering, *forbearing one another in love*" (Eph. 4:1, 2)? That means we are to conduct ourselves not according to the dictates of the flesh, but according to the requirements of *grace*. If grace has been shown toward me, then surely I ought to be gracious to others. But that is not always easy: not only has the root of "hatred" been left in me, but the "flesh" still remains in my brethren! and there will be much in them to test and try my love, otherwise there would be no need for this exhortation "forbearing one another in love." God has wisely so ordered this that our love might rise above the mere amiability of nature. We are not merely to govern our tempers, act courteously, be pleasant to one another, but *bear with* infirmities and be ready to forgive a slight: "Love suffereth long, and is kind" (1 Cor. 13:4).

"Let brotherly love continue." What a *comprehensive* word is this! Had we the ability to fully open it and space to bring out all that is included, it would be necessary to quote a large percentage of the precepts of Scripture. If brotherly love is to continue then we must exhort one another daily, provoke unto good works, minister to each other in many different ways. It includes far more than dwelling together in peace and harmony, though unless *that* be present, other things cannot follow. It also involves a godly concern for each other: see Lev. 19:17 and 1 John 5:2. It also embraces our praying definitely for each other. Another practical form of it is to write helpful spiritual letters to those now at a distance from us: you once enjoyed sweet converse together, but Providence has divided your paths: well, keep in touch via the post! "Let brotherly love *continue*."

"Let brotherly love continue." What a *forcible* word is this, by which we mean, it should drive all of us to our knees! We are just as dependent upon the Holy Spirit to call forth *love* into action as we are our *faith*: not only toward God, but toward each other—"The Lord *direct your hearts into* the love of God" (2 Thess. 3:5). Observe the forcible emphasis Christ placed upon this precept in His paschal discourse: "A new commandment I give unto you, That ye love one another" (John 13:34). Ah, but the Saviour did not deem that enough: "This is My commandment, That ye love one another, as I have loved you" (John 15:12): why that repetition? Nor did *that* suffice: "These things I command you, that ye love one another" (John 15:17). In an earlier paragraph we reminded the reader that the Philadelphian church is the church of "Brotherly love." Have you observed the central exhortation in the epistle addressed to *that* church: *"Hold that fast* which thou hast, that no man take thy crown"? (Rev. 3:11).

"Let brotherly love continue." What a *Divine* word is this. The love which is here enjoined is a holy and spiritual one, made possible "because the love of *God* is shed abroad in our hearts by the Holy Spirit" (Rom. 5:5). For until *then* there is naught but hatred. Love for the brethren is a love for the image of God stamped upon their souls: "every one that loveth Him that begat, loveth him also that is begotten of Him" (1 John 5:1). No man can love another for the grace that is in his heart, unless grace be in his own heart. It is *natural* to love those who are kind and generous to us; it is *supernatural* to love those who are faithful and holy in their dealings with us.

"Put on therefore, as the elect of God, holy and beloved, bowels of mercies, kindness, humbleness of mind, meekness, longsuffering; forbearing one another and forgiving one another, if any man have a quarrel against any; even as Christ forgave you, so also do ye. And above all these things put on LOVE, which is the bond of perfectness" (Col. 3:12-14).

CHAPTER ONE HUNDRED SEVEN

Brotherly Love

(Heb. 13:1-3)

Brotherly love is that spiritual benevolence and affectionate solicitude which Christians have one toward another, desiring and seeking their highest interests. The varied characteristics of it are beautifully delineated in 1 Cor. 13. In the opening verse of Heb. 13 the apostle exhorts unto the maintenance of the same, "Let brotherly love *continue.*" Negatively, that means, Let us be constantly on our guard against those things which are likely to interrupt its flow. Positively, it signifies, Let us be diligent in employing those means which are calculated to keep it in a healthy state. It is along these two lines that our responsibility here is to be discharged, and therefore it is of first importance that due heed be given thereto. We therefore propose to point out some of the main hindrances and obstacles to the continuance of brotherly love, and then mention some of the aids and helps to the furtherance of the same. May the blessed Spirit direct the writer's thoughts and give the reader to lay to heart whatever is of Himself.

The root hindrance to the exercise of brotherly love is *self-love*—to be so occupied with number one that the interests of others are lost sight of. In Prov. 30:15 we read, "The horseleech hath two daughters crying Give, give." This repulsive creature has two forks in her tongue, which she employs for gorging herself in the blood of her unhappy victim. Spirtually the "horseleech" represents self-love and her two daughters are self-righteousness, and self-pity. As the horseleech is never satisfied, often continuing to gorge itself until it bursts, so self-love is never contented, crying "Give, give." All the blessings and mercies of God are perverted by making them to minister *unto self.* Now the antidote for this evil spirit is for the heart to be engaged with the example which Christ has left us. *He* came not to be ministered unto, but to minister *unto others.* He pleased not Himself, but ever "went about doing good." He was tireless in relieving distress and seeking the welfare of all with whom He came into contact. Then "Let this mind be in you, which was also in Christ Jesus" (Phil. 2:5). If brotherly love is to continue self must be denied.

Inseparably connected with self-love is *pride,* and the fostering of pride is fatal to the cultivation of brotherly affection. The majority, if not all, of the petty grievances among Christians, are to be traced back to this evil root. "Love suffereth long," but pride is terribly impatient. "Love envieth not," but pride is intensely jealous. "Love seeketh not her own," but pride ever desires gratification. "Love seeketh not her own," but pride demands constant attention from others. "Love beareth all things," but pride is resentful of the slightest injury. "Love endureth all things," but pride is offended if a brother fails to greet him on the street. Pride must be *mortified* if brotherly love is to flourish. Therefore the first injunction of Christ to those who come unto Him for rest is, "Take *My* yoke upon you, and learn of Me; for I am meek and *lowly in heart.*"

Another great enemy to brotherly love is *a sectarian spirit,* and this evil is far more widespread than many suppose. Our readers would be surprised if they knew how often a sample copy of this magazine is despised by those who have a reputation for being stalwarts in the Faith and as possessing a relish for spiritual things, yet because this paper is not issued by *their* denomination or "circle of fellowship" it is at once relegated to the waste-paper basket. Alas, how frequently is a spirit of partizanship mistaken for brotherly love: so long as a person "believes *our* doctrines" and is willing to "join our church," he is received with open arms. On the other hand, no matter how sound in the faith a man may be, nor how godly his walk, if he refuses to affiliate himself with some particular group of professing Christians, he is looked upon with suspicion and given the cold shoulder. But such things ought not to be: they betray a very low state of spirituality.

We are far from advocating the entering into familiar fellowship with every one who claims to be a Christian — Scipture warns us to "lay hands suddenly on no man" (1 Tim. 5:22), for all is not gold that glitters; and perhaps there never was a day in which empty profession abounded so much as it does now. Yet there is a happy medium between being taken in by every impostor who comes along, and refusing to believe that there are any genuine saints left upon earth. Surely a tree may be known by its fruits. When we meet with one in whom we can discern the image of Christ, whether that one be a member of our party or not, *there* should our affections be fixed. "Wherefore receive ye one another, as Christ also received us, to the glory of God" (Rom. 15:7): it is our bounden duty to love all whom Christ loves. It is utterly vain that we boast of our orthodoxy or of the "light" we have, if brotherly love be not shown by us to the feeblest member of Christ's body who crosses our path.

There are many other things which are serious obstacles to the maintenance of brotherly love, yet we must not do more than barely mention them: the love of the world; failure to mortify the lusts of the flesh in our souls; being unduly wrapt up in the members of our own family, so that those related to us by the blood of Christ have not that place in our affections which they ought; ignorance of the directions in which it should be exercised and of the proper duties which it calls for; forgetfulness of the foundation of it, which is a mutual interest in the grace of God, that we are fellow-members of the Household of Faith; a readiness to listen to idle gossip, which in most instances, is a "giving place to the Devil," who accuses the brethren day and night. But there is one other serious hindrance to the continuance of brotherly love which we will notice in a little more detail, namely, *impatience.*

By impatience we mean *a lack of forbearance.* True brotherly love is a reflection of God's love for us, and *He* loves His people not for their native attractiveness, but for *Christ's* sake; and therefore does He love them in spite of their ugliness and vileness. God is "longsuffering to usward" (2 Pet. 3:9), bearing with our crookedness, pardoning our iniquities, healing our diseases, and His word to us is, "Be ye therefore followers (emulators) of God, as dear children, and walk in love" (Eph. 5:1, 2). We are to love the saints for what we can see *of Christ* in them; yes, *love* them, and for *that* reason — in spite of all their ignorance, perverseness, ill-temper, obstinacy, fretfulness. It is the image of God in them — not their wealth, amiability, social position — which is the magnet that attracts a renewed heart toward them.

"Forbearing one another in love" (Eph. 4:2). False love is glad of any specious excuse for throwing off the garb that sits so loosely and uncomfortably upon it. Ahitophel was glad of a pretext to forsake David, whom he hated in his heart, although with his mouth he continued to show much love. "Forbearing one another in love:" that love which a little silence or neglect can destroy never came from God, that love which a few blasts of malice from the lips of a new acquaintance will wither, is not worth possessing! Remember, dear brother, God suffers our love for one another to be *tried and tested*—as He does our faith—or there would be no need for this exhortation "*forbearing* one another in love." The most spiritual Christian on earth is full of infirmities, and the best way of enduring them is to frequently and honestly remind yourself that *you* also are full of faults and failings.

John Owen pointed out that there are certain *occasions* (in addition to the *causes* we have mentioned above) of the decay and loss of brotherly love. "1. Differences in opinion and practice about things in religion (unless these be of a vital nature they should not be allowed to affect our *love* for each other, A.W.P.). 2. Unsuitableness of natural tempers and inclinations. 3. Readiness to receive a sense of appearing provocations. 4. Different and sometimes inconsistent secular interests. 5. An abuse of spiritual gifts, by pride on the one hand, or envy on the other. 6. Attempts for domination, inconsistent in a fraternity; which are all to be watched against."

We sincerely trust that the reader is not becoming weary of our lengthy exposition of Heb. 13:1: the subject of which it treats is of such deep practical importance that we feel one more aspect of it requires to be considered. We shall therefore elaborate a little on some of the sub-headings which Owen mentioned under *the means* of its preservation. First, "An endeavour to grow and thrive in the principle of it, or the power of adopting grace." The three principal graces—faith, hope, love—can only thrive in a healthy soul. Just so far as personal piety wanes will brotherly love deteriorate. If close personal communion with Christ be neglected, then there can be no real spiritual fellowship with His people. Unless, then, *my* heart be kept warm in the love of God, affection toward my brethren is sure to decay. Second, "A deep sense of the weight or moment of this duty, from the especial instruction and command of Christ." Only as the heart is deeply impressed by the vital importance of the maintenance of brotherly love will serious and constant efforts be made thereunto.

Third, "Of the trial which is connected thereunto, of the sincerity of our grace and the truth of our sanctification, for 'by this we know we have passed from death unto life.'" This is indeed a weighty consideration: if Christians were more concerned to obtain *proof* of their regeneration, they would devote far closer attention to the cultivation of brotherly love, which is one of the chief evidences of the new birth (1 John 3:14). If I am at outs with my brethren and am unconcerned about their temporal and eternal interests, then I have no right to regard myself as a child of God. Fourth, "A due consideration of the use, yea, the necessity of this duty to the glory of God, and edification of the church." The greater concern we *really* have for the manifestative glory of God in this world, the more zealous shall we be in seeking to promote the same by the increase of brotherly love in our self and among the saints: the glory of God and the welfare of His people are inseparably bound together.

Fifth, "Of that breach of union, loss of peace, discord and confusion, which must and will ensue on the neglect of it." Serious indeed are the consequences of a decay of brotherly love, yea, fatal if the disease be not arrested. Therefore does it behoove each of us to honestly and seriously face the question, How far is *my* lack of brotherly love contributing unto the spiritual decline in Christendom to-day? Sixth, "Constant watchfulness against all those vicious habits of mind, in self-love, love of the world, which are apt to impair it." If *that* be faithfully attended to, it will prove one of the most effectual of all the means for the cultivation of this grace. Seventh, "Diligent heed that it be not impaired in its vital acts: such as are patience, forbearance, readiness to forgive, unaptness to believe evil, without which no other duties of it will be long continued. Eighth, fervent prayer for supplies of grace enabling thereunto."

After the opening exhortation of Heb. 13—which is fundamental to the discharge of all mutual Christian duties—the Holy Spirit through the apostle proceeds to point out some of *the ways in which* the existence and continuance of brotherly love are to be evidenced. "Be not forgetful to entertain strangers" (v. 2). Here is the first instance given, among sundry particulars, in which the greatest of all the Christian graces is to be exemplified. The duty which is inculcated is that of *Christian hospitality*. That which was commanded under the old covenant is repeated under the new: "But the stranger that dwelleth with you shall be unto you as one born among you, and thou shalt love him as thyself; for ye were strangers in the land of Egypt: I am the Lord your God" (Lev. 19:34 and cf. Deut. 10:19, etc.). The Greek word for "entertain" is rendered "lodge" in Acts 10:18, 23, and 28:7.

There was a special urgency for pressing this duty by the apostles, arising from *the persecution* of the Lord's people in different places, which resulted in their being driven from their own homes and forced to seek a refuge abroad. "At that time there was a great persecution against the church which was at Jerusalem; and they were all scattered abroad throughout the regions of Judea and Samaria, except the apostles" (Acts 8:1)—some travelled as far as "Phenice and Cyprus and Antioch" (Acts 11:19). Therein did they obey the direction of Christ's that "when they persecute you in this city, flee ye into another" (Matt. 10:23), removing to other parts where, for the present, peace obtained; for the providence of God so directs things it is very rare that persecution prevails universally—hence some places of quiet retirement are generally available, at least for a season. Yet this being forced to leave their *own* habitations required them to seek refuge among strangers, and this it is which gives point to our present exhortation.

Moreover "at that time there were sundry persons, especially of the converted Hebrews, who went up and down from one city, yea, one nation, unto another, on their own charges, to preach the Gospel. They went forth for the sake of Christ, taking nothing of the Gentiles unto whom they preached (3 John 7); and these were only brethren, and not officers of any church. The reception, entertainment, and assistance of these when they came unto any church or place as strangers, the apostle celebrates and highly commends in his well-beloved Gaius (3 John 5, 6). Such as these, when they came to them as strangers, the apostle recommends unto the love and charity of the Hebrews in a peculiar manner. And he who is not ready to receive and entertain such persons, will manifest how little concern he hath in the Gospel or the glory of Christ Himself" (J. Owen).

Though circumstances have altered (for the moment, for none can say how soon the restraining hand of God may be partly withdrawn and His enemies allowed to shed the blood of His people once more—such is even now the case in some parts of the earth), yet the principle of this injunction is still binding on all who bear the name of Christ. Not only are our hearts, but our homes as well, to be opened unto such as are really needy: "distributing to the necessity of saints; given to hospitality" (Rom. 12:13). An eminent and spiritual scholar points out that "the original word hath respect not so much to the exercise of the duty itself, as to the disposition, readiness, and frame of mind which is required in it and to it. Hence the Syriac renders it 'the *love* of strangers,' and that properly; but it is of such a love as is *effectual,* and whose proper exercise consists in the entertainment of them, which is the proper effect of love towards them."

In Eastern countries, where they travelled almost barefoot, the washing of the feet (1 Tim. 5:10), as well as the setting before them of food and giving lodgment for the night, would be included. The word for "strangers" is not found in the Greek: literally it reads "of hospitality not be forgetful"—be not unmindful of, grow not slack in, the discharge of this duty. It is to be observed that one of the necessary qualifications of a bishop is that he must be "a lover of hospitality" (Titus 1:8). Just as worldings delight in entertaining their relatives and friends, so the Lord's people should be eager and alert to render loving hospitality to homeless or stranded Christians, and as 1 Pet. 4:9 says "use hospitality one to another *without grudging*." The same applies, of course, to entertaining in our homes travelling servants of God—rather than sending them to some hotel to mingle with the ungodly.

"Be not forgetful to entertain strangers: for thereby some have entertained angels unawares" (v. 2). The second clause is to be regarded as supplying a *motive* for the discharge of this duty of Christian hospitality. Needless to say these added words do not signify that we may expect, literally, to receive a similar honour, but it is mentioned for the purpose of supplying *encouragement*. The apostle here reminds us that in former days some had been richly rewarded for their diligent observance of this duty, for they had been granted the holy privilege of receiving angels under the appearance of men. How this consideration enforces our exhortation is apparent: had there not been a readiness of mind unto this, a spirit of real hospitality in their hearts, they had neglected the opportunity with which Divine grace so highly favoured them. Let us, then, seek to cultivate the virtue of generosity: "the liberal deviseth liberal things" (Isa. 32:8).

"For thereby some have entertained angels unawares." The special reference, no doubt, is unto the cases of Abraham (Gen. 18:1-3) and of Lot (Gen. 19:1-3). We say "special reference" for the use of the plural "some" is sufficient to bar us from ascribing it to them alone, exclusively of all others. It is quite likely that in those ancient times, when God so much used the ministry of angels unto His saints, that others of them shared the same holy privilege. The real point for us in this allusion is that the Lord will be no man's debtor, that He honours those who honour Him—whether they honour Him directly, or indirectly in the persons of His people. "For God is not unrighteous to forget your work and labour of love, which ye have showed toward His name, in that ye have ministered to the saints and do minister" (Heb. 6:10). This too is recorded for our encouragement and when we have discharged the duty (as opportunity afforded—for God accepts the will for the deed!), if in indigent circumstances we may plead this before Him.

The Scriptures are full of examples where the Spirit has joined together duty and privilege, obedience and reward. Whenever we comply with such commands, we may count upon God recompensing those who exercised kindness unto His people. The cases of Rebekah (Gen. 24:18, 19, 22), of Potiphar (Gen. 39:5), of the Egyptian midwives (Ex. 2:17, 20), of Rahab (Joshua 6:25), of the widow of Zarephath (1 Kings 17:15, 23), of the woman of Shunem (2 Kings 4:8), of the inhabitants of Melita (Acts 28:2, 8, 9), all illustrate this. The resulting gains will more than repay any expense we incur in befriending the saints. Beautifully did Calvin point out that "not merely angels, *but Christ Himself*, is received by us, when we receive the poor of the flock in His name." Solemn beyond words is the warning of Matt. 25:41-43; but inexpressibly blessed is Matt. 25:34-36.

Compassion for the afflicted is the next thing exhorted unto: "Remember them that are in bonds, as bound with them" (v. 3). Love to the brethren is to manifest itself in sympathy for sufferers. Most reprehensible and un-Christlike is that selfish callousness which says, I have troubles enough of my own without concerning myself over those of other people. Putting it on its lowest ground, such a spirit ministers no relief: the most effectual method of getting away from our own sorrows is to seek out and relieve others in distress. But nothing has a more beneficial tendency to counteract our innate selfishness than a compliance with such exhortations as the one here before us: to be occupied with the severer afflictions which some of our brethren are experiencing will free our minds from the lighter trials we may be passing through.

"Remember them that are in bonds." The immediate reference is unto those who had been deprived of their liberty for Christ's sake, who had been cast into prison. The "remember" signifies far more than to merely *think* of them, including *all* the duties which their situation called for. It means, first, feel for them, take to heart their case, have compassion toward them. Our great High Priest is touched with the feeling of their infirmities (Heb. 4:15), and so must we be. At best their food was coarse, their beds hard, and the ties which bound them to their families had been rudely sundered. Often they lay, cruelly fettered, in a dark and damp dungeon. *They* felt their situation, their confinement, their separation from wife and children; then identify yourself with them and have a feeling sense of what they suffer. "Remember," too, that but for the sovereignty of God, and His restraining hand, *you* would be in the same condition as they!

But more: "remember" them in your prayers. Intercede for them, seeking on their behalf grace from God, that they may meekly acquiesce to His providential dealings, that their sufferings may be sanctified to their souls, that the Most High will so overrule things that this Satanic opposition against some of His saints may yet issue in the extension of His kingdom. Finally, do unto them as you would wish them to do unto you were you in their place. If you can obtain permission, visit them (Matt. 25:36), endeavour to comfort them, so far as practicable relieve their sufferings; and leave no stone unturned to seek their lawful release. Divine providence so regulates things that, as a rule, while some of the saints are in prison, others of them still enjoy their liberty—thus allowing an opportunity for the practical exercise of Christian sympathy.

"And them which suffer adversity, as being yourselves also in the body" (v. 3). There is probably a double reference here: first, to those who were not actually in prison, but who had been severely flogged, or were in sore straits because heavy fines had been imposed on them. Second, to the wives and children of those who had been imprisoned, and who would suffer keen adversity now that the breadwinners were removed from them. Such have a very real claim upon the sympathy of those who had escaped the persecutions of the foes of the Gospel. If *you* are not in a financial position to do much for them, then acquaint some of your richer brethren with their case and endeavour to stir them up to supply their needs. "As being yourselves also in the body" is a reminder that it may be *your* turn next to experience such opposition.

John Owen, who lived in particularly stormy times (the days of Bunyan), said, "Whilst God is pleased to give grace and courage unto some to suffer for the Gospel unto bonds, and to others to perform this duty towards them, the church will be no loser by suffering. When some are tried as unto their constancy in bonds, others are tried as unto their sincerity in the discharge of the duties required of them. And usually more fail in neglect of their duty towards sufferers, and so fall from their profession, than do so fail under and on the account of their sufferings." That the apostle Paul practised what he preached is clear from "Who is weak, and I am not weak? who is offended, and I burn not?" (2 Cor. 11:29). For illustrations of the discharge of these duties see Gen. 14:14, Neh. 1:4, Job 29:15, 16, Jer. 38:7, etc. For solemn warnings read Job 19:14-16, Prov. 21:13, Matt. 25:43, James 2:13.

We need hardly say that *the principles* of v. 3 are of *general* application at all times and to all cases of suffering Christians. The same is summed up in "Bear ye one another's burdens, and so fullfill the law of Christ" (Gal. 6:2). The sentiment of this verse has been beatifully expressed in the lines of that hymn so precious in its hallowed memories:

"Blest be the tie that binds
Our hearts in Christian love;
The fellowship of kindred minds
Is like to that above.
We share our mutual woes,
Our mutual burdens bear,
And often for each other flows
The sympathizing tear."

The Lord grant unto both writer and reader more of His grace so that we shall "Rejoice with them that do rejoice, and weep with them that weep" (Rom. 12:15).

CHAPTER ONE HUNDRED EIGHT

Marriage

(Heb. 13:4)

From a prescription of duties towards others, the apostle next proceeds to give directions unto those which concern ourselves, wherein our own persons and walking are concerned. He does this in a prohibition of the two most radical and comprehensive lusts of corrupt nature, namely, uncleanness and covetousness: the first respecting the persons of men in a peculiar manner, the other their conversation or conduct. Acts of moral uncleanness are distinguishable from all other sins which are perpetrated in external acts, in that they are immediately against a man's self and his own person (see 1 Cor. 6:18), and therefore is chastity enforced under the means for preserving the same, that is, marriage; while the antidote for covetousness is given, namely, a spirit of contentment. The connection between Heb. 13:4-6 and 13:1-3 is obvious: unless uncleanness and covetousness be mortified there can be no real love exercised unto the brethren.

As God hath knit the bones and sinews together for the strengthening of our bodies, so He has ordained the joining of man and woman together in wedlock for the strengthening of their lives, for "two are better than one" (Eccl. 4:9); and therefore when God made the woman for the man He said, "I will make him a help meet for him" (Gen. 2:18), showing that man is *advantaged* by having a wife. That such does not actually prove to be the case in all instances is, for the most part at least, to be attributed unto *departure* from the Divine precepts thereon. As this is a subject of such vital moment, we deem it expedient to present a fairly comprehensive outline of the teaching of Holy Writ upon it, especially for the benefit of our young readers; though we trust we shall be enabled to include that which will be helpful to older ones too.

It is perhaps a trite remark, yet none the less weighty for having been uttered so often, that with the one exception of personal conversion, marriage is the most momentous of all earthly events in the life of a man or woman. It forms a bond of union which binds them until death. It brings them into such intimate relations that they *must* either sweeten or embitter each other's existence. It entails circumstances and consequences which are not less far-reaching than the endless ages of eternity. How essential it is, then, that we should have the blessing of Heaven upon such a solemn yet precious undertaking; and in order to this, how absolutely necessary it is that we be subject to God and to His Word thereon. Far, far better to remain single unto the end of our days, than to enter into the marriage state *without* the Divine benediction upon it. The records of history and the facts of observation bear abundant testimony to the truth of that remark.

Even those who look no further than the temporal happiness of individuals and the welfare of existing society, are not insensible to the great importance of our domestic relations, which the strongest affections of nature secure, and which even our wants and weaknesses cement. We can form no conception of social virtue or felicity, yea, no conception of human society itself, which has not its foundation *in the family*. No matter how excellent the constitution and laws of a country may be, or how vast its resources and prosperity, there is no sure basis for social order, or public as well as private virtue, until it be laid in the wise regulation of its families. After all, a nation is but the aggregate of its families, and unless there be good husbands and wives, fathers and mothers, sons and daughters, there cannot possibly be good citizens. Therefore the present decay of home life and family discipline threaten the stability of our nation to-day far more severely than does any foreign hostility.

But the *Scriptural* view of the relative duties of the members of a Christian household, portrays the prevailing effects in a most alarming manner, as being dishonouring to God, disastrous to the spiritual condition of the churches, and as raising up a most serious obstacle in the way of evangelical progress. Sad beyond words is it to see that professing Christians are themselves largely responsible for the lowering of marital standards, the general disregard of domestic relations, and the rapid disappearance of family discipline. As, then, *marriage* is the basis of the home or family, it is incumbent on the writer to summon his readers to a serious and prayerful consideration of the revealed will of God on this vital theme. Though we can hardly hope to arrest the awful disease which is now eating out the very vitals of our nation, yet if God is pleased to bless this article to a few individuals our labour will not be in vain.

We will begin by pointing out *the exellency* of wedlock: "Marriage is honourable:" says our text, and it is so first of all because

God Himself has placed special honour upon it. All other ordinances or institutions (except the Sabbath) were appointed of God by the medium of men or angels (Acts 7:35), but marriage was ordained *immediately* by the Lord Himself—no man or angel brought the first wife to her husband (Gen. 2:22). Thus marriage had more Divine honour put upon it than had all the other Divine institutions, because it was directly solemnized by God Himself. Again; this was the *first* ordinance God instituted, yea, the first thing He did after man and woman were created, and that, while they were still in their unfallen state. Moreover, *the place* where their marriage occurred shows the honourableness of this institution: whereas all other institutions (save the Sabbath) were instituted outside of paradise, marriage was solemnized in Eden itself!—intimating how happy they are that marry in the Lord.

"*God's crowning creative act* was the making of woman. At the close of each creative day it is formally recorded that 'God saw what He had made, that it was good.' But when Adam was made, it is explicitly recorded that 'God saw it was *not* good that the man should be alone.' As to man the creative work lacked completeness, until, as all animals and even plants had their mates, there should be found for Adam also an help, meet for him—his counterpart and companion. Not till this want was met did God see the work of the last creative day also to be good.

"This is the first great Scripture lesson on family life, and it should be well learned . . . . The Divine institution of marriage teaches that *the ideal state* of both man and woman is not in separation but in union, that each is meant and fitted for the other; and that God's ideal is such union, based on a pure and holy love, enduring for life, exclusive of all rivalry or other partnership, and incapable of alienation or unfaithfulness because it is a union in the Lord—a holy wedlock of soul and spirit in mutual sympathy and affection" (A. T. Pierson).

As God the Father honoured the institution of marriage, so also did God the Son. First, by His being "*born* of a woman" (Gal. 4:4). Second, by His *miracles,* for the first supernatural sign that He wrought was at the marriage of Cana in Galilee (John 2:9), where He turned the water into wine, thereby intimating that if Christ be present at your wedding (i.e., if you "marry in the Lord") your life shall be a joyous or blessed one. Third, by His *parables,* for He compared the kingdom of God unto a marriage (Matt. 22:2) and holiness to a "wedding garment" (Matt. 22:11). So also in His teaching: when the Pharisees sought to ensnare Him on the subject of divorce, He set His imprimatur on the original constitution, adding "What therefore God hath joined together, let not man put asunder" (Matt. 19:4-6).

The institution of marriage has been still further honoured by the Holy Spirit, for He has used it as a figure of the union which exists between Christ and the Church. "For this cause shall a man leave his father and mother, and shall be joined unto his wife, and they two shall be one flesh. This is a great mystery, but I speak concerning Christ and the Church" (Eph. 5:31, 32). The relation which obtains between the Redeemer and the redeemed is likened, again and again, unto that which exists between a wedded man and woman: Christ is the "Husband" (Isa. 54:5), the Church is the "Wife" (Rev. 21:9). "Turn, O backsliding children, saith the Lord, for I am *married* unto you" (Jer. 3:14). Thus, each person of the blessed Trinity has set His seal upon the honourableness of the marriage state.

There is no doubt that in true marriage each party helps the other equally, and in view of what has been pointed out above, any who venture to hold or teach any other doctrine or philosophy join issue with the Most High. This does not lay down a hard and fast rule that *every* man and woman is obliged to enter into matrimony: there may be good and wise reasons for abiding alone, adequate motives for remaining in the single state—physical and moral, domestic and social. Nevertheless, a single life should be regarded as abnormal and exceptional, rather than ideal. Any teaching that leads men and women to think of the marriage bond as the sign of bondage, and the sacrifice of all independence, to construe wifehood and motherhood as drudgery and interference with woman's higher destiny, any public sentiment to cultivate celebacy as more desirable and honourable, or to substitute anything else for marriage and home, not only invades God's ordinance, but opens the door to nameless crimes and threatens the very foundations of society.

Now it is clear that marriage must have particular *reasons for the appointment of it.* Three are given in Scripture. First, for *the propagation of children.* This is its obvious and normal purpose: "So God created man in His own image, in the image of God created He him: male and female created He them" (Gen. 1:27)—not both males or both females, but one male and one female; and to make the design of this unmistakably plain God said, "Be fruitful and multiply." For this reason marriage is called "matrimony," which signifies *motherage,* because it results in virgins becoming mothers. Therefore it is desirable that marriage be entered into at an early age, before the prime of life be passed: twice in Scripture we read of "the wife of thy *youth*" (Prov. 5:18; Mal. 2:15). We have pointed out that the propagation of children is the "normal" end of marriage; yet there are special seasons of acute "distress" when 1 Cor. 7:29 holds good.

Second, marriage is designed as a *preventive of immorality*: "To avoid fornication, let every man have his own wife, and let every woman have her own husband" (1 Cor. 7:2). If any were exempted it might be supposed that *kings* would be given dispensation—because of the lack of a successor to the throne should his wife be barren; yet the king is expressly forbidden a plurality of wives (Deut. 17:17), showing that the endangering of a monarchy is not sufficient to countervail the sin of adultery. For this cause a whore is termed a "strange woman" (Prov. 2:16), showing that she should be a stranger to us; and children born out of marriage are called "bastards," which (under the Law) were excluded from the congregation of the Lord (Deut. 23:2).

The third purpose of marriage is for the *avoiding of the inconveniences of solitude,* signified in the "it is not good that the man should be alone" (Gen. 2:18: as though the Lord had said, This life would be irksome and miserable for man if no wife be given him for a companion: "Woe to him that is alone when he falleth, for he hath not another to help him up" (Eccl. 4:10). Someone has said, "like a turtle which has lost his mate, like one leg when the other is cut off, like one wing when the other is clipped, so had man been if woman had not been given to him." Therefore for mutual society and comfort God united man and woman that the cares and fears of this life might be eased by the cheer and help of each other.

Let us next consider *the choice of our mate.* First, the one selected for our life's partner must be outside those degrees of near kinship prohibited by the Divine law: Lev. 18:6-17. Second, the Christian must wed a fellow Christian. From earliest times God has commanded that "the people shall dwell alone, and shall not be numbered among the nations" (Num. 23:9). His law unto Israel in connection with the Canaanites, was, "Neither shalt thou make marriages with them: thy daughter thou shalt not give unto his son, nor his daughter shalt thou take unto thy son" (Deut. 7:3 and cf. Josh. 23:12). How much more, then, must God require the separation of those who are His people by a spiritual and heavenly tie than those who occupied only a fleshly and earthly relation to Him. "Be ye not unequally yoked together with unbelievers" (2 Cor. 6:14) is the clarion order to His saints of this dispensation. *Partnership* of any kind of one who is born again with one in a state of nature is here prohibited, as is evident from the terms used in the next verse—"fellowship, communion, concord, part, agreement."

There are but two families in this world: the children of God and the children of the Devil (1 John 3:10). If, then, a daughter of God marries a son of the Evil one she becomes a daughter-in-law to Satan! If a son of God marries a daughter of Satan, he becomes a son-in-law to the Devil! By such an infamous step an affinity is formed between one belonging to the most High and one belonging to His arch-enemy. "Strong language!" yes, but not too strong. O the dishonour done to Christ by such a union; O the bitter reaping from such a sowing. In every case it is the poor believer who suffers. Read the inspired histories of Samson, Solomon, and Ahab, and see what followed *their* unholy alliances in wedlock. As well might an athlete attach to himself a heavy weight and then expect to win a race, as for one to progress spiritually after marrying a worldling.

Should any Christian reader be inclined or expect to become betrothed, the first question for him or her to carefully weigh in the Lord's presence is, Will this union be with an unbeliever? For if you are really cognizant of and heart and soul be impressed with the tremendous *difference* which God, in His grace, has put between you and those who are—however attractive in the flesh—yet in their sins, then you should have no difficulty in rejecting every suggestion and proposal of making common cause with such. *You* are "the righteousness of God" in Christ, but unbelievers are "unrighteous"; *you* are "light in the Lord," but they are darkness; *you* have been translated into the kingdom of God's dear Son, but unbelievers are under the power of Belial; *you* are a son of peace, whereas all unbelievers are "children of wrath" (Eph. 2:3); therefore "be ye separate, saith the Lord, and *touch not* the unclean; and I will receive you" (2 Cor. 6:17).

The danger of forming such an alliance is *before* marriage, or even betrothal, neither of which could be seriously entertained by any real Christian unless the sweetness of fellowship with the Lord had been lost. The affections must first be withdrawn from Christ before we can find delight in social intimacy with those who are alienated from God, and whose interests are confined to this world. The child of God who is "keeping his heart with all diligence" will not, cannot, have a joy in intimacies with the unregenerate. Alas, how often is the seeking or the accepting of close friendship with unbelievers the first step to *open* departure from Christ. The path which the Christian is called upon to tread is indeed a narrow one, but if he attempts to widen it, or leave it for a broader road, it must be in contravention of the Word of God, and to his or her own irreparable damage and loss.

Third, "married . . . only *in the Lord*" (1 Cor. 7:39) goes much further than prohibiting an unbeliever for a mate. Even among the children of God there are many who would not be suitable to each other in such a tie. A pretty face is an attraction, but O how vain to be governed in such a serious undertaking by such a trifle. Earthly goods and social position have their value here, yet how base and degrading to suffer them to control such a solemn undertaking. O what watchfulness and prayerfulness is needed in the regulation of our affections! Who fully understands the temperament that will match mine? that will be able to bear patiently with my faults, be a corrective to my tendencies, and a real help in my desire to live for Christ in this world? How many make a fair show at the start, but turn out wretchedly. Who can shield me from a host of evils which beset the unwary, but God my Father?

"A virtuous woman is a crown to her husband" (Prov. 12:4): a pious and competent wife is the most valuable of all God's temporal blessings: she is the special gift of His grace. "A prudent wife is from the Lord" (Prov. 19:14), and He requires to be definitely and diligently *sought unto*: see Gen. 24:12. It is not sufficient to have the approval of trusted friends and parents, valuable and even needful as that (generally) is for our happiness; for though they are concerned for our welfare, yet their wisdom is not sufficiently far-reaching. The One who appointed the ordinance must needs be given the first place in it if we are to have *His* blessing on it. Now prayer is never intended to be a substitute for the proper discharge of our responsibilities: we are ever required to use care and discretion, and must never act hurriedly and rashly. Our better judgment is to regulate our emotion: in the body the head is placed over the heart, and not the heart over the head!

"Whoso findeth a wife (a real one) findeth a good thing, and obtaineth favour of the Lord" (Prov. 18:22): "findeth" implies a definite *quest.* To direct us therein the Holy Spirit has supplied two rules or qualifications. First, *godliness,* because our partner must be like Christ's Spouse, pure and holy. Second, *fitness,* "a help, meet for him" (Gen. 2:18), showing that a wife cannot be a "help" unless she be "meet," and for that she must have much in common with her mate. If her huband be a labouring man, it would be madness for him to choose a lazy woman; if he be a learned man, a woman with no love of knowledge would be quite unsuited. Marriage is called a "yoke," and two cannot pull together if all the burden is to fall upon one—as it would if one weak and sickly was the partner chosen.

Now for the benefit of our younger readers, let us point out some of the *marks* by which a godly and fit mate may be *identified.* First, the *reputation*: a good man commonly has a good name

(Prov. 22:1), none can accuse him of open sins. Second, the *countenance*: our looks reveal our characters, and therefore Scripture speaks of "proud looks" and "wanton looks,"—"the show of their countenance doth witness against them" (Isa. 3:9). Third, the *speech,* for "out of the abundance of the heart the mouth speaketh:" "the heart of the wise teacheth his mouth, and addeth learning to his lips" (Prov. 16:23); "She openeth her mouth with wisdom, and in her tongue is the law of kindness" (Prov. 31:26). Fourth, the *apparel*: a modest woman is known by the modesty of her attire. If the clothing be vulgar or showy the heart is vain. Fifth, the *company* kept: birds of a feather flock together—a person may be known by his or her associates.

A word of warning is, perhaps, not quite needless. No matter how carefully and prayerfully one's partner be selected, he will *not* find marriage a perfect thing. Not that God did not make it perfect, but man has fallen since, and the fall has marred everything. The apple may still be sweet, but it has a worm inside. The rose has not lost its fragrance, but thorns grow with it. Willingly or unwillingly, everywhere we must read the ruin which sin has brought in. Then let us not dream of those faultless people which a diseased fancy can picture and novelists portray. The most godly men and women have their failings; and though such be easy to bear when there is genuine love, yet they have to be *borne.*

A few brief remarks now on *the home-life* of the wedded couple. Light and help will be obtained here if it be borne in mind that marriage pictures forth the relation between Christ and His Church. This, then, involves three things. First, the attitude and actions of husband and wife are to be regulated by *love,* for *that* is the cementing tie between Lord Jesus and His Spouse: a holy love, sacrificial love, an enduring love which nought can sever. There is nothing like love to make the wheels of home life run smoothly. The husband sustains to his mate the same relation as does the Redeemer to the redeemed, and hence the exhortation, "Husbands love your wives, even as Christ also loved the Church" (Eph. 5:25): with a hearty and constant love, ever seeking her good, ministering to her needs, protecting and providing for her, bearing with her infirmities: thus "giving honour unto the wife, as unto the weaker vessel, and as being heirs together of the grace of life; that your prayers be not hindered" (1 Pet. 3:7).

Second, the *headship* of the husband. "The head of the woman is the man" (1 Cor. 11:3); "For the husband is the head of the wife, even as Christ is the Head of the Church" (Eph. 5:23). Unless this Divine appointment be duly heeded there is sure to be confusion. The household must have a leader, and God has committed its rule unto the husband, holding *him* responsible for its orderly management; and serious will be the loss if he shirks his duty and turns the reins of government over to his wife. But this does not mean that Scripture gives him license to be a domestic tyrant, treating his wife as a servant: his dominion is to be exercised in love toward the one who is his consort. "Likewise ye husbands *dwell with* them" (1 Pet. 3:7): seek their society after the day's labour is over. That Divine injunction plainly condemns those who leave their wives and go abroad on the pretext of a "call from God."

Third, the *subjection* of the wife. "Wives *submit* yourselves unto your own husbands, as unto the Lord" (Eph. 5:22): there is only one exception to be made in the application of this rule, namely when he commands what God forbids or forbids what God commands. "For after this manner in the old time the holy women also, who trusted in God, adorned themselves, being in subjection unto their own husbands" (1 Pet. 3:5): alas, how little of this spiritual "adornment" is evident to-day! "Even as Sarah *obeyed* Abraham, calling him lord: whose daughters ye are, so long as ye do well, and are not afraid with any amazement" (1 Pet. 3:6): willing and loving subjection to the husband, out of respect for the authority of God, is what characterises the daughters of Sarah. Where the wife refuses to submit to her husband, the children are sure to defy their parents—sow the wind, reap the whirlwind.

We have space for only one other matter, which it is deeply important for young husbands to heed. "Prepare thy work without, and make it fit for thyself in the field; and *afterwards* build thine house" (Prov. 24:27). The point here is that the husband is not to think of owning his own house before he can afford it. As Matt. Henry says, "This is a rule of providence in the management of household affairs. We must prefer necessities before luxuries, and not lay that out for show which should be expended for the support of the family." Alas, in this degenerate age so many young couples want to start where their parents ended, and then feel they must imitate their godless neighbours in various extravagancies. Never go into debt or purchase on the "credit system:" "Owe no man anything" (Rom. 13:8)!

And now for a final word on our text. "Marriage is honourable *in all*" who are called thereunto, no class of persons being precluded. This clearly gives the lie to the pernicious teaching of Rome concerning the celibacy of the clergy, as does also 1 Tim. 3:2, etc. "And the bed undefiled" not only signifies fidelity to the marriage vow (1 Thess. 4:4), but that the conjugal act of intercourse is not polluting: in their unfallen state Adam and Eve were bidden to "multiply;" yet moderation and sobriety is to obtain here, as in all things. We do not believe in what is termed "birth control," but we do earnestly urge *self-control,* especially by the husband, "But whoremongers and adulterers God will judge." This is a most solemn warning against unfaithfulness: those who live and die impenitently in these sins will eternally perish (Eph. 5:5).

CHAPTER ONE HUNDRED NINE

Covetousness

(Heb. 13:5)

In this chapter of Hebrews the apostle makes a practical application of the theme of the epistle. Having set forth at length the amazing grace of God toward His believing people by the provision He has made for them in the Mediator and Surety of the covenant, having shown that they now have in Christ the substance of all that was shadowed forth in the ceremonial law, the tabernacle, and the priesthood of Israel, we now have pressed upon us the responsibilities and obligations which devolve upon those who are the favoured recipients of those spiritual blessings. First, that which is fundamental to the discharge of all Christian duties is exhorted unto: the continuance of brotherly love (v. 1). Second, instances are given in which this chief spiritual grace is to be exemplified: in Christian hospitality (v. 2), and in compassion for the afflicted (v. 3). Third, prohibitions are made against the two most radical lusts of fallen nature: moral uncleanness (v. 4) and covetousness (v. 5), for the indulgence of these is fatal to the exercise of brotherly love.

Having in our last article dealt at length with the merciful provision which God has made for the avoidance of moral uncleanness — the ordinance of marriage — we now turn to the second great sin which is here dehorted against, namely, covetousness. "Let your conversation be without covetousness, and be content with such things as ye have" (v. 5). Here is an evil and its remedy set before us side by side, as was the case in the previous verse, though there the remedy is given before that which it counteracts. We will follow the order of the our present text and consider first the vice which is here forbidden, before we contemplate the virtue which is enjoined: yet it will be helpful to keep them both in mind, for the latter casts light upon the former, enabling us to determine its exact nature as nothing else will.

"Let your conversation be without covetousness." The Greek word which is here rendered "covetousness" is literally "lover of silver," and the R.V. renders our text "Be ye free from the love of money." Now while it be true that the love of money or worldly possessions is one of the principal forms of covetousness, yet we are satisfied that the translation of the A.V. is to be preferred here. The scope of the Greek verb is much wider than a lusting after material riches. This appears from the only other verse in the N.T. where this word occurs, namely, 1 Tim. 3:3, in a passage which describes the qualifications of a bishop: "Not given to wine, no striker, not greedy of filthy lucre; but patient, not a brawler, not covetous." The very fact that a previous clause specifies "not greedy of filthy lucre" makes it clear that "not covetous" includes more than "not a lover of money."

A comment or two also requires to be made upon the term "conversation." This word is limited to-day unto our speech with one another, but three hundred years ago, when the A.V. was made, it had a much more comprehensive meaning. Its latitude can be gathered from its employment in the Scriptures. For example, in 1 Pet. 3:2 we read, "while they behold your chaste conversation:" note "behold" was *not* "hear!" The term then has reference to behaviour or deportment: "But as He which hath called you is holy, so be ye holy in all manner of conversation" (1 Pet. 1:15). It is not to be restricted to that which is external, but includes both character and conduct. The Syriac renders our word "mind," probably because both covetousness and contentment are mental states. "Let your conversation be as it becometh the Gospel of Christ" (Phil. 1:27): this obviously means, Let your affections and actions correspond to the revelation of Divine grace you have received; conduct yourself in such a manner that those around will be impressed by the principles, motives, and sentiments which govern you.

So it is here in our text: let not covetousness rule your heart nor regulate your life. But exactly what is "covetousness"? It is the opposite of contentment, a being dissatisfied with our present lot and portion. It is an over-eager desire for the things of this world. It is a lusting after what God has forbidden or withheld from us, for we may crave, wrongly, after things which are not evil or injurious in themselves. All abnormal and irregular desires, all unholy and inordinate thoughts and affections, are comprehended by this term. To covet is to think upon and hanker after anything which my acquirement of would result in injury to my neighbor. "We *may* desire that part of a man's property which he is inclined to dispose of, if we mean to obtain it on equitable terms; but when he chooses to keep, we must not covet. The poor man may desire moderate relief from the rich, but he must not covet his affluence, or repine even though he does not relieve him" (Thos. Scott).

Now some sins are more easily detected than others, and for the most part condemned by those professing godliness. But covetousness is only too often winked at, and some covetous persons are regarded as very respectable people. Many professing Christians look upon covetousness as quite a trifling matter, while the world applauds it as legitimate ambition, as business shrewdness, as prudence, etc. All sorts of excuses are made for this sin and plausible pretences argued in its favour. It is indeed a very subtle sin, which few are conscious of. In one of his sermons Spurgeon mentions a prominent man who had a great many people come to him to make confession, and this man observed that while different ones acknowledged all sorts of outrageous crimes, he never had one who confessed to covetousness. Few suspect that this is one of the prevailing iniquities of their hearts, rather are they inclined to regard this vice as a virtue.

But the Holy Scriptures are very explicit on this subject. The Divine law expressly declares, "Thou shalt not covet thy neighbour's house, thou shalt not covet thy neighbour's wife, nor his manservant, nor his maidservant, nor his ox, nor his ass, nor anything that is thy neighbour's (Ex. 20:17). "The covetous, whom the Lord abhorreth" (Psa. 10:3). To His disciples Christ said, "Take heed, and beware of covetousness: for a man's life consisteth not in the abundance of the things which he possesseth" (Luke 12:15). The votaries of Mammon are linked with "drunkards and adulterers," and such are excluded from the kingdom of God (1 Cor. 6:10). The covetous are branded with the most detestable character of idolaters (Col. 3:5) — no doubt this is because they who are ruled by this lust *adore* their gold and put their *trust* in it, making a god of it. How we need to pray, "Incline mine heart unto Thy testimonies, and not to covetousness" (Psa. 119:36).

God's Word also sets before us some fearfully solemn examples of the judgments which fell upon covetous souls. The fall of our first parents originated in covetousness, lusting after that which God had forbidden. Thus the very frontispiece of Holy Writ exhibits the frightfulness of this sin. See what covetousness did for Balaam: he "loved the wages of unrighteousness" (2 Pet. 2:15)— the honours and wealth which Balak promised were too attractive for him to resist. See what covetousness did for Achan, who lusted after the forbidden silver and gold: he and his whole family were stoned to death (Josh. 7). Look at Gehazi: lusting after the money his master had refused, and in consequence, he and his seed were smitten with leprosy (2 Kings 5). Consider the awful case of

Judas, who for thirty pieces of silver sold the Lord of glory. Remember the case of Ananias and Sapphira (Acts 5). In view of these warnings shall we call this worst of iniquities "a little sin"? Surely it is something to be trembled at!

Covetousness is an inordinate desire of the heart after the creature; which is a fruit of man's apostacy from the Lord. No longer finding in God the supreme object of his soul's delight and confidence, fallen man loves and trusts in the creature (mere *things*) rather than the Creator. This takes on many forms: men lust after honours, wealth, pleasures, knowledge, for Scripture speaks of "the desires of the flesh *and of the mind*" (Eph. 2:3), and of "filthiness of the flesh *and spirit*" (2 Cor. 7:1). It is the very nature of the depraved heart to hanker after that which God has forbidden and to crave after what is evil, though this spirit may be developed more strongly in some than in others; at any rate, a larger measure of restraining grace is granted to one than to another. These irregular desires and inordinate thoughts are the firstborn of our corrupt nature, the first risings of indwelling sin, the beginnings of all transgressions committed by us.

"Thou shalt not covet" (Ex. 20:17). "The commandment requires moderation in respect of all worldly goods, submission to God, acquiescence in His will, love to His commandments, and a reliance on Him for the daily supply of all our wants as He sees good. This is right and reasonable, fit for God to command and profitable for man to obey, the very temper and felicity of Heaven itself. But it is so contrary to the desires of our hearts *by nature,* and so superior to the actual attainments of the best Christians on earth, that it is very difficult to persuade them that God requires such perfection, and still more difficult to satisfy them that it is indispensable to the happiness of rational creatures, and most difficult of all to convince them that everything inconsistent with this or short of it is sin; that it deserves the wrath of God, and cannot be taken away, except by the mercy of God through the atonement of Christ" (T. Scott).

The most common form of this sin is, of course, the love of money, the lusting after more and more of material riches. This is evident in getting, keeping, and spending. First, *in getting.* To acquire wealth becomes the dominant passion of the soul. An insatiable greed possesses the heart. This exists in varying degrees in different persons, and is demonstrated in numerous ways. That we may be quite practical let us mention one or two. Often this is manifested in a greedy and grasping effort after *inequitable profits* and by paying an *unjustly small wage* to employees, the chief design of its perpetrators being to amass fortunes for their descendants. Yet often these very men hold prominent positions in the churches and "make long prayers," while devouring widows' houses and grinding the face of the poor. Alas, how the Gospel is dishonoured and the sanctuary defiled by such sanctimonious wretches.

Again. Recently we read a faithful article wherein the writer took to task the lies and deceptions practised by many shopkeepers and their assistants in palming off upon the public various forms of merchandise by misrepresenting their quality and value; the writer concluding with a solemn emphasis upon "all *liars* shall have their part in the lake which burneth with fire and brimstone" (Rev. 21:8). As he finished reading the same, this writer asked himself the question, And how far is a greedy and grasping public to blame? Who is largely responsible for this commercial dishonesty? *Who tempt the tradesmen* to mark their wares as "great bargains," "prices much reduced?" Is it not the covetous purchasers? How many to-day are possessed with an insatiable craving after "bargains," buying things "cheap," without any conscientious consideration of the real worth of the article: it is *that* which fosters so much fraud. Let the Christian buy only *what* he needs, and *when* he needs it, and so far as possible only from upright traders, and then he will be more willing to pay according to the value received.

Second, covetousness evidences itself *in keeping*. There is a miserliness which clings to money as a drowning man to a log. There is a hoarding up for self which is entirely reprehensible. "There is one alone, and there is not a second; yea, he hath neither child nor brother; yet is there no end of all his labour; neither is his eye satisfied with riches; neither saith he, For whom do I labour and bereave my soul of good? This is also vanity, yea, it is a sore travail" (Eccl. 4:8). Yes, there are those who are utterly unconcerned about their eternal interests, and labour day in and day out, year after year, in order to add to what they have already accumulated, and who begrudge purchasing for themselves the bare necessities of life. They continue to amass money utterly regardless of Christ's cause on earth or the poor and needy among their fellow-men. There are still those the language of whose actions is, "I will pull down my barns, and build greater; and there will I bestow all my fruits and my goods. And I will say to my soul, Soul, thou hast much goods laid up for many years: take thine ease; eat, drink, be merry" (Luke 12:18, 19).

Third, covetousness also manifests itself in *spending*. If there be those who are niggardly, there are others who are wastrels. If there be those who condemn the miser for his stinginess, often they are guilty in turn of wreckless prodigality. That which ought to be saved for a rainy day, is used to gratify a desire which covets some unnecessary object. But let us not be misunderstood on these points. Neither the possession nor the retention of wealth is wrong in itself, providing it be acquired honestly and preserved with a justifiable motive. God is the One who "giveth thee power to get wealth" (Deut. 8:18), and therefore is His goodness to be acknowledged when He is pleased to prosper us in basket and in store. Yet even then we need the exhortation, "If riches increase, set not thine heart upon them" (Psa. 62:10).

"Not slothful in business" (Rom. 12:11) is a Divine exhortation. So also there is a prudence and thrift which is legitimate, as is clear from, "There is that withholdeth *more than is meet*, but it tendeth to poverty" (Prov. 11:24). So also it is a bounden duty to make provision for those who are dependent upon us: "But if any provide not for his own, and specially for those of his own house, he hath denied the faith, and is worse than an infidel" (1 Tim. 5:8). It is easy to swing to the opposite extreme and become fanatical, and under the guise of trusting God, *tempt* Him. To lay up for a rainy day is quite permissible: see Prov. 6:6-8. Neither idleness nor extravagance are to be condoned. Those who through indolence or prodigality waste their substance and fail in business cannot be too severely censured, for they not only impoverish themselves but injure others, becoming the pests of society and a public burden.

Yet how difficult it is to strike the happy mean: to be provident without being prodigal, to be "not slothful in business" and yet not *bury* ourselves in it, to be thrifty without being miserly, to use this world and yet not abuse it. How appropriate is the prayer, "Remove from me vanity and lies; give me *neither poverty nor riches*; feed me with food convenient for me: lest I be full, and deny Thee, and say, Who is the Lord? or lest I be poor, and steal, and take the name of my God in vain" (Prov. 30:8, 9). Rom. 7:7 shows that it is only as the Spirit applies the Law in power to the conscience that we are taught to see the evil and feel the danger of covetousness; as, at the same time, it serves to check an avaricious disposition and curb inordinate fondness for the creature. That which most effectually strikes at our innate selfishness is the love of God shed abroad in the heart. A generous heart and a liberal hand should ever characterize the Christian.

A few words next upon *the heinousness* of covetousness. This evil lust blinds the understanding and corrupts the judgment, so that it regards light as darkness, and darkness as light. "If I have made gold my hope, or have said to the fine gold, Thou art my confidence; if I rejoiced because my wealth was great and because mine hand had gotten much . . . This also was an iniquity to be punished by the judge, for I should have denied the God that is above" (Job 31:24, 25, 28)—how little this is realized by the guilty one! It is an *insatiable* lust, for when covetousness rules, the heart is never satisfied: "He that loveth silver shall not be satisfied with silver, nor he that loveth abundance with increase" (Eccl. 5:10). It is a *devouring* sin: "the deceitfulness of riches choke the Word" (Matt. 13:22).

So terrible is this sin and so great is its power that, one who is governed by it will trample upon the claims of justice, as Ahab did in seizing the vineyard of Naboth (1 Kings 21); he will disregard the call of charity, as David did in taking the wife of Uriah (2 Sam. 11); he will stoop to the most fearful lies, as did Ananias and Sapphira; he will defy the express commandment of God, as Achan did; he will sell Christ, as Judas did. This is the *mother* sin, for "the love of money is the root of *all* evil." It is a gnawing and fatal sin: "But they that will be (are determined to be) rich fall into temptation and a snare, and into many foolish and hurtful lusts, which drown men in destruction and perdition . . . which while some have coveted after they have erred from the faith, and pierced themselves through with many sorrows" (1 Tim. 6:9, 10).

It is the working of this evil lust which lies at the root of very much of the fearful Sabbath-desecration that is now so rife. It is the greed of gold which causes the railways to run special excursions on the Lord's day, tempting people to leave the city for the country-side or the sea-beach. It is the lure of lucre which prompts thousands of shops to be open seven days in the week. It is the love of money which lies behind the Sunday editions of the newspaper. How the nations of Christendom are heaping up to themselves "wrath against the Day of Wrath!" God will not be mocked with impugnity. Those who believe the Scriptures must perforce expect that soon a far worse war than the last is likely to be sent as a scourge from Heaven upon the present Sabbath profaners.

It was the spirit of covetousness which prompted Israel of old to disregard the fourth commandment. "In those days saw I in Jerusalem some treading winepresses on the Sabbath, and bringing in sheaves, and lading asses; as also wine, grapes, and figs, and all manner of burdens, which they brought into Jerusalem on the Sabbath day: and I testified against them in the day wherein they sold victuals. There dwelt men of Tyre also therein, which brought fish, and all manner of ware, and sold in the Sabbath unto the children of Judah, and in Jerusalem" (Neh. 13:15, 16). Because of their

Sabbath profanation, the sore judgment of God fell upon the nation. "Then I contended with the nobles of Judah, and said unto them, What evil is this that ye do, and profane the Sabbath day? Did not your fathers thus, and did not our God bring all this evil upon us and upon this city? yet *ye bring more wrath* on Israel by profaning the Sabbath" (Neh. 13:17, 18): "Hallow My Sabbaths and they shall be a sign between Me and you, that ye may know that I am the Lord your God. Notwithstanding, the children rebelled against Me: they walked not in My statutes neither kept My judgments to do them, which if a man do, he shall even live in them: they polluted My Sabbaths: then I said, I will pour out My fury upon them" (Ezek. 20:20, 21).

Thus, not only is covetousness a fearful sin in itself, but it is also the prolific mother of other evils. In the poor, it works envy, discontent, and fraud; in the rich, pride, luxury, and avarice. This vile lust unfits for the performing of holy duties, preventing the exercise of those graces which are necessary thereto. It exposes to manifold temptations, whereby we are rendered an easy prey to many spiritual enemies. The more we yield to this evil spirit, the more do we conduct ourselves as though we desired our portion in this world, and look no further than present things, contrary to "while we look not at the things which are seen, but at the things which are not seen" (2 Cor. 4:18). It tends to cast contempt on the mercies which are ours and quenches the spirit of thanksgiving. It turns the heart away from God: "How hardly shall they that have riches enter into the kingdom of God!" (Mark 10:23).

Let us now go deeper and solemnly observe the comprehensiveness of God's searching law, "Thou shalt not covet" (Ex. 20:17). Light is cast upon those words by, "I had not known sin, but by the Law; for I had not known lust ('concupiscence,' margin) except the law had said, Thou shalt not covet or "lust" (Rom. 7:7) — "concupiscence" is an evil desire, an inordinate affection, a secret lusting after something. What the apostle means is, I had never discovered *my inward depravity* unless the Spirit had enlightened my understanding, convicted my conscience, and made me feel the corruptions of my heart. Man ever looks on the outward appearance — and as a Pharisee of the Pharisees Paul's *actions* fully conformed to the Law — but when the Spirit quickens a soul, he is made to realize that God requires "Truth in the *inward* parts" (Psa. 51:6) and cries "Create in me a clean heart, O God, and renew a right spirit within me" (Psa. 51:10).

"Thou shalt not covet." That which is here forbidden is concupiscence, or those imaginations, thoughts, and desires, which precede the consent of the will. Herein we may perceive the exalted holiness of the Divine Law — far transcending all human codes — requiring *inward purity.* Herein, too, we may recognize one of the fundamental errors of Romanists, who, following the Pelagians, deny that these lustings are sinful until they are yielded to, and who affirm that evil imaginations only become sinful when the mind definitely assents to them. But the holy Law of God condemns that which *instigates unto* what is forbidden, condemns that which *inclines toward* what is unholy, and denounces that which inflames with cupidity. All irregular desires are forbidden. Corrupt imaginations and unlawful inclinations that *precede* the consent of the will are evil, being the seeds of all other sins.

Again we say, Herein God's Law differs from and is immeasurably superior to all of man's laws, for it takes note of and prohibits all the hidden desires and secret lustings of the heart. It is this tenth commandment which, above all others, discovers unto us our depravity and shows how very far short we come of that perfection which the Law requires. There is first an evil thought in the mind causing us to think of something which is not ours. This is followed by a longing after or wishing for it. There is then an inward delight by way of anticipating the pleasure that object will give; and then, unless restraining grace intervenes, the outward act of sin is committed — see James 1:14, 15. The first evil thought is involuntary, due to the mind's being turned from good to evil, even though that evil be simply lusting after a new but unnecessary hat! The longing is caused by the heart's being enticed by the delight promised. Then the consent of the will is gained, and the mind plans how to gain the coveted object.

This concupiscence or evil lusting of the heart is called "the law of sin which is in my members" (Rom. 7:23). It is what the older theologians term "original sin," being the fountain of evil within, corrupting all our faculties. Discontent with our lot, envy of our neighbours, yea, even the very "*thought of* foolishness is SIN" (Prov. 24:9). How high is the standard set before us: "Let none of you *imagine* evil in your hearts against his neighbour; and *love* no false oath; for all these are things that I hate, saith the Lord" (Zech. 8:17). Does the third commandment interdict any blasphemous oath upon the lips? then the tenth prohibits any risings of the heart against God. Does the fourth commandment interdict all unnecessary work on the Sabbath? then the tenth condemns our saying "what a weariness is it." Does the eighth commandment interdict every act of theft? then the tenth prohibits our desiring anything which is our neighbour's.

But it is not until after a person is regenerate that he takes notice of the *inward* motions of sin and takes cognizance of the state of his *heart.* Then Satan will seek to persuade that he is not responsible for involuntary thoughts (which come unbidden), that evil desires are beyond our control — infirmities which are excusable. But God says to him "*Keep thine heart* with all diligence, for out of it are the issues of life" (Prov. 4:23), and makes him realize that every lusting after what He has forbidden or withheld is a species of self-will. Therefore we are accountable to *judge* the first inclination toward evil and *resist* the very earliest solicitations. The fact that we discover so much within that is contrary to God's holy requirements should deeply humble us, and cause us to live more and more out of self and upon Christ.

CHAPTER ONE HUNRED TEN

Contentment

(Heb. 13:5, 6)

Discontent, though few appear to realize it, is *sinful,* a grievous offence against the Most High. It is an impugning of His wisdom, a denial of His goodness, a rising up of my will against His. To murmur at our lot is to take issue with God's sovereignty, quarrelling as it does with His providence, and therefore, is a being guilty of high treason against the King of the universe. Since God orders all the circumstances of human life, then every person ought to be entirely satisfied with the state and situation in which he is placed. One has no more excuse to grumble at his lot than has another. This truth Paul instructed Timothy to press upon others: "Let as many *servants* as are under the yoke, count their own masters worthy of all honour, *that* the name of God and His doctrine *be not blasphemed*" (1 Tim. 6:1).

"The wicked are like the troubled sea, when it *cannot rest,* whose waters cast up mire and dirt. There is no peace, saith my God, to the wicked" (Isa. 57:20, 21). The ungodly are total strangers to real contentment. No matter how much they have, they are ever lusting after more. But God exhorts His people, "Let your conversation be without covetousness; and be content with such things as ye have" (Heb. 13:5). As it is their bounden duty to avoid the vice of covetousness, so it is their personal responsibility to cultivate the virtue of contentment; and failure at either point is culpable. The contentment here exhorted unto is something other than a fatalistic indifference: it is a holy composure of mind, a resting in the Lord, a being pleased with what pleases Him — satisfied with the portion He has allotted. Anything short of this is evil.

Discontent *is contrary to our prayers,* and therefore must be most reprehensible. When we truly pray, we desire God to give or withhold, to bestow or take away, according as will be most for His glory and our highest good. Realizing that we know not what is best, we leave it with God. In real prayer we submit our understandings to the Divine wisdom, our wills to His good pleasure.

But to be dissatisfied with our lot and complain at our portion is to exercise the very opposite spirit, indicating an unwillingness to be at God's disposal, and leaning to our own understanding as though we knew better than He what was most conducive to our present and future well being. This is a tempting of God and a grieving of His Holy Spirit, and has a strong tendency to provoke Him to fight against us (Isa. 63:10).

When God *does* fight against us because of this sin, He often gives us what we were discontented for the want of, but accompanies the same with some sore affliction. For example, Rachel was in a most discontented frame when she said to Jacob "Give me children, else I die" (Gen. 30:1). The sequel is very solemn: she *had* children, and died in childbirth: see Gen. 35:16-18. Again, we are told that Israel "lusted exceedingly in the wilderness, and tempted God in the desert. And He gave them their request, but *sent leanness* into their soul" (Psa. 106:14, 15). These cases need to be taken to heart by us, for they are recorded for our learning and warning. God takes note of the discontent of our hearts as well as the murmuring of our lips. "Giving thanks *always* for all things unto God and the Father in the name of our Lord Jesus Christ" (Eph. 5:20) is the standard which He has set before us.

Not only is discontent a grievous sin against God, but it *unfits* the Christian for the discharge of holy duties, preventing the exercise of those graces which are necessary in order thereunto. It silences the lips of supplication, for how can a murmurer *pray*? It destroys the spirit of submission, for complaining is a "fretting against the Lord." It quenches faith, hope and love. Discontent is the very essence of ingratitude, and therefore it stifles the voice of thanksgiving. There cannot be any rest of soul until we quietly resign our persons and portions to God's good pleasure. Discontent corrodes the strings of the heart, and therefore it arrests all happy endeavour.

Discontent is usually over temporal matters, and this is a sad intimation that material things are sought after more eagerly than are spiritual things. It argues a lack of confidence in the care of our heavenly Father to provide for us the things which are needed. "Christian, let me ask thee this question, Didst thou give thyself to Christ for temporal, or for eternal comforts? Didst thou enter upon religion to save thine estate, or thy soul? Oh, why then shouldest thou be so sad, when thine eternal happiness is so safe? For shame, live like a child of God, an heir of Heaven, and let the world know, that thy hopes and happiness are in a *better* world; that thou art denied those acorns which thy Father giveth to His hogs, yet *thou* hast the children's bread, and expectest thine inheritance when thou comest to age" (G. Swinnock, 1650). What cause have we all to be deeply humbled over our sinful repinings, to hang our heads with shame, and penitently confess the same unto God!

Yet notwithstanding both the sinfulness and injuriousness of discontent, many raise various objections *to excuse* the same. Some will plead their personal temperament in self-vindication, alleging that their natural temper makes them uneasy and anxious, so that they are quite unable to submit themselves unto the disposing providence of God. But, my dear reader, the corruption of our nature and its proneness to sin is no excuse for, but rather an aggravation of it, showing how much our hearts are opposed unto God. The more we yield to our natural inclinations, the more power they obtain over us. In such a case as the above we ought rather to be the more importunate with God, begging Him for His grace to restrain the inordinancy of our affections, to subdue our fears, and work in us willingness to acquiesce to His sovereign pleasure.

Others attempt to justify their discontent and uneasy frame of spirit by alleging that the injuries which others have done them ought to be resented, and that not to manifest discontent under them would be to encourage such people unto further insults and trampling upon them. To this it may be replied that while we complain of injuries done to us by men, and are prone to meditate revenge against them, we do not consider the great dishonour that we bring to God, and how much we provoke Him. It is written, "But if ye forgive not men their tresspasses, neither will your Father forgive your trespasses" (Matt. 6:15). Remember that "What glory is it if, when ye be buffeted for your faults, ye shall take it patiently? but if when ye do well, and suffer for it, ye take it patiently, this is acceptable with God. For even hereunto were ye called: Because Christ also suffered for us, leaving us an example, that ye should follow His steps: who did no sin, neither was guile found in His mouth; who, when He was reviled, reviled not again" (1 Pet. 2:20-23).

Others seek to excuse their discontent by dwelling upon the *magnitude* of their trials, saying that their burden is insupportable, so that they are pressed out of measure, above their strength. Even so, none of our afflictions are as great as our sins; and the more we complain, the heavier do we make our burden. Others point to the altogether *unexpectedness* of their trouble, that it came upon them when they were quite unprepared, and that it is therefore more than flesh and blood can endure. But the Christian should daily expect afflictions in this world, at least so far as not to be unprovided for or think it strange he should be exercised by them (1 Pet. 4:12). With some the *drastic change* from affluence to poverty is so great they argue that it is impossible to bear up under it. But does not God say, "My grace is sufficient for thee" (2 Cor. 12:9)?

Yet no excuses are to be allowed to set aside or modify this Divine injunction, "Be content with such things as ye have." But before proceeding further let it be pointed out that contentment is not incompatible with honest effort to enlarge the provision of earthly things for ourselves and those dependent upon us, for God has given us six days out of seven to be industrious. Idleness must not be allowed to cloak itself under the guise of this grace: contentment and indolence are two vastly different things. "This contentment does not consist in a slothful neglect of the business of life, nor of a real nor pretended apathy to worldly interests. It is substantially a satisfaction with God as our portion and with what He is pleased to appoint for us. It is opposed to covetousness or the inordinate desire of wealth, and to unbelieving anxiety—dissatisfaction with what is present, distrust as to what is future" (John Brown).

Contentment is a tranquillity of soul, a being satisfied with what God has apportioned. It is the opposite of a grasping spirit which is never appeased, with distrustful anxiety, with petulant murmurings. "It is a gracious disposedness of mind, arising solely from trust in and satisfaction with God alone, against all other things whatever appear to be evil" (John Owen). It is our duty to have the scales of our heart so equally poised in all God's dealings with us as that they rise not in prosperity, nor sink in adversity. As the tree bendeth this way or that with the wind, yet still keeps its place, so we should yield according to the gales of Divine providence, yet still remaining steadfast and retaining our piety. The more composure of mind we preserve, the more shall we, on the one hand, "rejoice with trembling" (Psa. 2:11), and on the other, "faint not" when the chastening rod falls upon us.

As this spiritual grace of contentment is so glorifying to God, and so beneficial to ourselves, we will endeavour to mention some of the chief *aids* thereto. First, *a realization of God's goodness.* A deep and fixed sense of His benevolence greatly tends to quieten the heart when outward circumstances are trying to us. If I have formed the habit of meditating daily upon God's fatherly care—and surely I am constantly surrounded by proofs and tokens thereof—then I shall be less apt to chafe and fret when His providences cross my will. Has He not assured me that "all things work together for good to them that love God, to them who are called according to His purpose" (Rom. 8:28)? What more then can I ask? O to rest in His love. Surely He is entitled to my confidence in His paternal solicitude. Remember that each murmur implies unthankfulness. Complaining is the basest of ingratitude. If the Lord provides for the ravens, will He overlook the needs of any of His children? O ye of little faith!

Second, *a steady realization of God's omniscience.* A deep and fixed sense of His unsearchable wisdom is well calculated to allay our fears and compose our minds when everything appears to be going wrong with our circumstances. Settle it in your mind once for all, dear friend, that "the high and lofty One" makes no mistakes. His understanding is infinite, and His resources are without measure. He knows far better than we do what is for our well being and what will best promote our *ultimate* interests. Then let me not be found pitting my puny reason against the ways of the allwise Jehovah. It is nought but pride and self-will which complains at His dealings with me. As another has said, "Now if one creature can and ought to be governed by another that is more wise than himself—as the client by his learned counsel, the patient by his skillful physician—much more should we be satisfied with the unerring dispositions of God." Remember that complaining never relieves a single woe or lightens a single burden; it is therefore most irrational.

Third, *a steady realization of God's supremacy.* A deep and fixed sense of His absolute sovereignty, His indisputable right to do as He pleases in the ordering of all our affairs, should do much to subdue the spirit of rebellion and silence our foolish and wicked murmurings. It is not the Almighty's pleasure to give unto all alike, but rather that some should have more and others less: "The Lord maketh poor, and maketh rich: He bringeth low, and lifteth up. He raiseth up the poor out of the dust, and lifteth up the beggar from the dunghill, to set them among princes" (1 Sam. 2:7, 8). Then quarrel not with the Most High because He distributes His gifts and favours unequally; but rather seek grace that thy will may be brought into subjection to His. It is written "Thou wilt keep him in perfect peace, whose mind is stayed on Thee" (Isa. 26:3). Consider how many lack some of the good things which thou enjoyest. "Woe unto him that striveth with his Maker . . . . Shall the clay say to Him that fashioneth it, What maketh Thou?" (Isa. 45:9).

Fourth, *a steady realization of our ill-deserts.* A deep and fixed sense of our utter unworthiness must do much to still our repinings when we are tempted to complain of the absence of those things our hearts covet. If we live under an habitual sense of our unworthiness, it will greatly reconcile us to deprivations. If we daily remind ourselves that we have forfeited all good and deserve all ill at the hands of God, then we shall heartily acknowledge "It is of the Lord's mercies that we are not consumed" (Lam. 3:22). Nothing will more quickly compose the mind in the face of adversity and nothing will so prevent the heart being puffed up by prosperity, than the realization that "I am not worthy of the least of all the mercies" (Gen. 32:10) of God. Just so far as we really preserve a sense of our ill-deserts will we meekly submit to the allotments of Divine providence. Every Christian cordially assents to the truth "He hath not dealt with us after our sins, nor rewarded us according to our iniquities" (Psa. 103:10), then why complain if God withholds from us what He grants to others?

Fifth, *weanedness from the world.* The more dead we are to the things of time and sense, the less our hearts will crave them, and the smaller will be our disappointment when we do not have them. This world is the great impediment to the heavenly life, being the bait of the flesh and the snare of Satan by which he turns souls from God. The lighter we hold the world's attractions, the more indifferent we are to either poverty or wealth, the greater will be our contentment. God has promised to supply all our needs, therefore "having food and raiment let us be therewith content" (1 Tim. 6:8). Superfluities are hindrances and not helps. "Better is little with the fear of the Lord, than great treasure and trouble therewith" (Prov. 15:16). Remember that the contented man is the only one who *enjoys* what he has. "Set your affection on things above, not on things on the earth" (Col. 3:2).

Sixth, *fellowship with God.* The more we cultivate communion with Him and are occupied with His perfections, the less shall we lust after the baubles which have such a hold upon the ungodly. Walking with God produces a peace and joy such as this poor world can neither give nor take away. "There be many that say, Who will show us any good? Lord, lift Thou up the light of *Thy* countenance upon us. Thou hast put gladness in my heart, *more* than in the time that *their* corn and their wine increased" (Psa. 4:6, 7). Walking in the way of God's commands is a real antidote to discontent: "Great peace have they which love Thy law, and nothing shall offend them" (Psa. 119:165). Seventh, *remembrance of what Christ suffered.* "For consider Him that endured such contradiction of sinners against Himself, lest ye be wearied and faint in your minds" (Heb. 12:3). When tempted to complain at your lot, meditate upon Him who when here had not where to lay His head, who was constantly misunderstood by friends and hated by innumerable enemies. Contemplation of the cross of Christ is a wonderful composer of an agitated mind and a querulous spirit.

"Be content with such things as ye have: *for* He hath said, I will never leave thee, nor forsake thee." Here is an enforcement of what has just gone before, a reason for the duties enjoined, a motive supplied for the performance of them. One of the Divine promises is quoted, which if it be duly appropriated by us, we shall be dissuaded from covetousness and persuaded to contentment. Resting on this Divine assurance will both moderate our desires and alleviate our fears. "I will never leave thee nor forsake thee" is a guarantee of God's continual provision and protection, and this rebukes all inordinate desires and condemns all anxious fears. The evils are closely connected, for in most instances covetousness, in the Christian, is rooted in a fear of want; while discontent generally arises from a suspicion that our present portion will prove to be inadequate for the supply of our needs. Each such disquietude is equally irrational and God-dishonouring.

Both covetousness and discontent proceed from unbelief. If I really trust God, will I have any qualms about the future or tremble at the prospect of starvation? Certainly not: the two things are incompatible, opposites—"I will trust, and not be afraid" (Isa. 12:2). Thus the apostle's argument is clear and convincing: "Let your conversation be without covetousness; be content with such things as ye have: *for* He hath said, I will never leave thee nor forsake thee." The "for *He* hath said" is more forcible than "for *God* hath said:" it is the *character* of the One with whom we have to do that is here held up to our view. "He has said"—*who* has? Why, One whose power is omnipotent, whose wisdom is infinite, whose faithfulness is inviolable, whose love is unchanging. "All the efficacy, power and comfort of Divine promises arise from and are resolved into the excellencies of the Divine nature. He hath said it who is *truth,* and cannot deceive" (J. Owen).

And *what is it* that He has said, which, if faith truly lays hold of, will subdue covetousness and work contentment? *This,* "I will never leave thee nor forsake thee." God's presence, God's providence, God's protection, are here assured us. If due regard be paid to these inestimable blessings, the heart will be kept in peace. What more would we have save a conscious realization of the same? O for a felt sense of His presence, for a gracious manifestation thereof to the soul. What were all the wealth, honours, pleasures of the world worth, if He should totally and finally desert us! The comfort of our soul does not depend upon outward provisions, so much as on our appropriation and enjoyment of what is contained in the Divine promises. If we rested more on them, we would crave less of this world's goods. What possible cause or ground for fear remains when God has pledged us *His* continual presence and assistance?

"I will never leave thee nor forsake thee." It is almost impossible to reproduce in English the emphasis of the original, in which no less than five negatives are used to increase the strength of the negation, according to the Greek idiom. Perhaps the nearest approximation is to render it, "I will never, no, never leave thee, nor ever forsake thee." In view of such assurance we should fear no want, dread no distress, nor have any trepidation about the future. At no time, under any circumstances conceivable or inconceivable, for any possible cause, will God utterly and finally forsake one of His own. Then how *safe* they are! how impossible for one of them to eternally perish! God has here graciously condescended to give the utmost security to the faith of believers in all their difficulties and trials. The continued presence of God with us ensures the continued supply of every need.

"For He hath said, I will never leave thee, nor forsake thee." These words were first spoken by Jehovah to the successor of Moses (Josh. 1:5), whose task it was to dispossess Canaan of all the heathen nations then inhabiting it. The fact that the Holy Spirit moved the apostle to apply unto Christians this promise made to Joshua, supplies clear proof that our modern dispensationalists *wrongly divide* the Word of Truth. Their practice of partitioning the Scriptures and their contention that what God said under one dispensation does not apply to those living in another, is here exposed as nothing less than an effort of Satan to rob God's people of a part of their rightful and needful portion. This precious promise of God belongs as truly to me now as it did to Joshua of old. Let, then, this principle be tenaciously held by us: the Divine promises which were made upon special occasions to particular individuals are of *general* use for *all* the members of the household of faith.

What has just been affirmed is so obvious that it should require no further proof or illustration; but inasmuch as it is being repudiated in some influential quarters to-day, we will labour the point a little. Are not the needs of believers the same in one age as another? Is not God affected alike unto all His children?—does He not bear them the same love? If, then, He would not desert Joshua, then He will not any of us. Are not Christians now under the same everlasting Covenant of Grace as were the O.T. saints? then they have a common charter—"For the promise is unto you, and to your children, and to *all* that are afar off" (Acts 2:39). Let us not forget that "Whatsoever things were written aforetime, were written for our learning, that *we* through patience and comfort of the Scriptures might have hope" (Rom. 15:4).

"*So that* we may boldly say, The Lord is my Helper, and I will not fear what man shall do unto me" (v. 6). An inference is here drawn from the promise just quoted: a double conclusion is reached —confidence in God and courage against man. This intimates that we should make a varied and manifold use of the Divine promises. This twofold conclusion is based upon *the character* of the Promiser: because He is infinitely good, wise, faithful, powerful, and because He changes not, we may boldly or confidently declare with Abraham "God will provide" (Gen. 22:8), with Jonathan "there is no restraint to the Lord" (1 Sam. 14:6), with Jehoshaphat "None is able to withstand Thee" (2 Chron. 20:6), with Paul "If God be for us, who can be against us?" (Rom. 8:31).

"So that we may boldly say, The Lord is my Helper, and I will not fear what man shall do unto me." Once more the apostle confirms his argument by a Divine testimony, for he quotes from Psa. 118:6. In this citing of David's language, Christians are again taught the suitability of O. T. language unto their own case, and the permissibility of appropriating the same unto themselves: "*we* may boldly say" just what the Psalmist did! It was in a time of sore distress that David expressed his confidence in the Lord, at a time when it appeared that his enemies were ready to swallow him up; but contrasting the omnipotency of Jehovah from the feebleness of the creature, his heart was emboldened. The believer is weak and unstable in himself, and constantly in need of assistance, but the Lord is ever ready to take his part and render all needed aid.

"The Lord is my Helper" implies, as W. Gouge pointed out, "a willing readiness and a ready willingness to afford us all needed succour." Those whom He forsakes not, He *helps*—both inwardly and outwardly. Note carefully the change from "*we* may boldly say" to "the Lord is *my* Helper:" general privileges are to be appropriated by us in particular. "Man can do much: he can fine, imprison, banish, reduce to a morsel of bread, yea, torture and put to death; yet as long as God is with us and standeth for us, we may boldly say, 'I will not fear what man can do.' Why? God will not see thee utterly perish. He can give joy in sorrow, life in death" (Thos. Manton). May the Lord graciously grant both writer and reader more faith in Himself, more reliance upon His promises, more consciousness of His presence, more assurance of His help, and then we shall enjoy more deliverance from covetousness, discontent, and the fear of man.

CHAPTER ONE HUNDRED ELEVEN

Motives to Fidelity

(Heb. 13:7, 8)

In seeking to ascertain the meaning and scope of the verses which now require our consideration due notice must be taken of their setting, and that, in turn, weighed in the light of the epistle as a whole. In the immediate context the apostle dehorts from covetousness and discontent, reminding his readers that God had said "I will never leave thee nor forsake thee." From that Divine promise he points out two conclusions which faith will draw. First, "The Lord is my Helper." The child of God is in urgent need of an all-powerful Helper, for he has to contend with a mighty foe whose rage knows no bounds. It is a great mercy when we are made conscious of our helplessness, when our conceit is so subdued as to realize that without Divine assistance defeat is certain. What peace and comfort it brings to the heart when the believer is enabled to realize that the Lord is just as truly his "Helper" when chastening him, as when delivering from trouble!

The second inference which faith makes from the Divine promise is, "I will not fear what man shall do unto me." If the Lord will never leave nor forsake me, then He must be " a very *present help* in trouble" (Psa. 46:1). O what a difference it makes to the sorely-tried soul when he can realize that God is not far away from him, but "at hand" (Phil. 4:5). Yes, even if called upon to walk through the valley of the shadow of death, he will be *with me,* and therefore will His rod and staff comfort me (Psa. 23:4). And since the believer's Helper is none other than the Almighty, no real harm or evil can possibly befall him. Why, then, should he dread the creature? His worst enemy can do nought against him without the Lord's permission. The abiding presence of the Lord ensures the supply of every need: therefore contentment should fill the heart. The abiding presence of the Lord guarantees all-sufficient help, and therefore alarms at man's enmity should be removed.

Even in the more general exhortations of Heb. 13 there is a tacit recognition of the peculiar circumstances of the Hebrews, and more plainly still is this implied in the language of v. 6. The Jewish Christians were being opposed and persecuted by their unbelieving brethren, and the temptation to apostatise was very real and pressing. "The fear of man bringeth a snare" (Prov. 29:25). It did to Abraham, when he went down to Egypt, and later on to Gerar, moving him to conceal Sarah's real relation to him. It did to the whole nation of Israel when they hearkened to the report of the ten spies. It did to Peter, so much so that he denied his Master. It did to Pilate, for when the Jews threatened him with "If thou let this man go, thou art not Caesar's friend" (John 19:12), he unwillingly consented to Christ's crucifixion. Fearfully solemn is that word, "But whosoever shall deny Me before men, him will I also deny before My Father which is in Heaven" (Matt. 10:33).

Now it is in view of the trying situation in which the Hebrew saints were placed that we should consider our present passage. The apostle's design was to fortify them against temptations to apostatise, to encourage them unto steadfastness in the Faith, to *so* establish them that even though they should be called on to suffer a violent death, they would yet remain loyal to Christ. Moreover, their enemies were not only intimidating them by open oppression and threats of more dire persecution, but others under the guise of being Christian teachers, were seeking to poison their minds with errors that undermined the very foundations of the Gospel: it was to them that Paul had reference in v. 9. Hence, in vv. 7, 8 the apostle also calls upon the Hebrews to maintain their profession of the Truth in opposition to the lies of these Judaisers.

"Remember them which have the rule over you, who have spoken unto you the Word of God: whose faith follow, considering the end of their conversation. Jesus Christ the same yesterday, and today, and forever" (vv. 7, 8). A number of questions are raised by the terms of our passage. Who are the rulers here mentioned? In what sense or way are they to be "remembered"? What is signified by "following" their faith? What is denoted by the "end of their conversation"? Wherein do these exhortations furnish motives unto fidelity or steadfastness? Why affirm here the Saviour's immutability?

First of all it should be pointed out that the A.V. rendering of the opening clause is misleading, and quite out of harmony with the remainder of the verse. "Those which have the rule over you" is a single word in the Greek. It is a participle of the present tense, but is frequently used as a noun, as is obviously the case here: "your rulers." That their *present* rulers could *not* be intended is quite apparent from several considerations. First, because the Hebrews were called upon to "remember," rather than submit to them. Second, because they are distinctly described as they "who *have* spoken unto you the Word of God." Third, because they were such as had already received "the *end* of their conversation" or conduct in this world. Finally, because there is a distinct precept given with respect to their attitude toward their living rulers in v. 17.

The reference is, of course, to the spiritual rulers, those who had ministered to them God's Word. The persons intended were the officers in the Church, that is, those who guided and governed its affairs. "Overseers" or "guides" is hardly definite or strong enough to bring out the force of the original term, for while it signifies to lead or go before, it also denotes one who is over others, being the word for "governor" in Matt. 2:6 and Acts 7:10. "Your leaders" would be better, though hardly as good as the word actually used in the A.V.—your *rulers.* Those in view were the apostles and prophets, the elders and pastors, who instructed the saints and directed the government of the churches. No doubt the apostle was more specifically alluding to such men as Stephen and James who had been beheaded by Herod (Acts 12:2), men who had sealed the Truth they proclaimed by laying down their lives for it.

"Who have spoken unto you the Word of God": *that* is the mark by which Christian leaders are to be identified—the men whom God has graciously called to ecclesiastical rule are gifted by Him to expound and enforce the Scriptures, for the function of their office is not legislative, but administrative. The Christian leader, though he possesses no arbitrary power, nevertheless is to bear rule, and that, according to the Scriptures. He is not called upon to invent new laws, but simply to declare the will and apply the statutes of Zion's King. There cannot be a properly ordered household unless *discipline* be duly maintained. Alas, if one section of those who profess to be the ministers of Christ have usurped His prerogatives, exalting themselves into ecclesiastical despots, another class have woefully failed to maintain the honour of His House, letting down the bars and inaugurating a regime of lawlessness.

"Remember them which have the rule over you, who have spoken unto you the Word of God." By this criterion are we to *test* the ostensible "guides" and religious leaders of the day. "Beloved, believe not every spirit, but *try* the spirits, whether they are of God: because many false prophets are gone out into the world" (1 John 4:1); and never was there a time when we more urgently needed to measure men by this standard. "Now I beseech you, brethren, mark them which cause divisions and offences contrary to the doctrine which ye have learned; and avoid them" (Rom. 16:17). "If there come any unto you, and bring not *this doctrine,* receive him not into your house, neither bid him God speed" (2 John 10)—no matter how pleasing his personality, soothing his message, or numerous his followers. "For he whom God hath sent speaketh the words of God" (John 3:34): true of Christ perfectly, but characteristic of all whom He calls to the sacred office of the ministry. To speak God's Word is the grand duty of the Christian teacher—not to indulge in philosophical or theological speculation, nor to tickle the ears of men with sensational topics of the day.

The next thing singled out for mention in connection with these spiritual rulers who had preached the Word of God, is their *"faith,"* which the Hebrews were enjoined to "follow." There is some difference of opinion among the commentators as to exactly what is here referred to. "Faith" is a term which has a varying scope in its N.T. usage, though its different meanings are closely applied, and can usually be determined by the context. First, "Faith" is the principle of *trust* whereby the heart turns to God and rests upon His word, and by which we are, instrumentally, saved: "thy faith hath made thee whole" (Matt. 9:22), "by grace are ye saved through faith" (Eph. 2:8). Second, "faith" has reference to that which is *to be believed,* the Truth of God, the Christian Creed: "exhorting them to continue in the Faith" (Acts 14:22), "the Word of Faith which we preach" (Rom. 10:8), "contend for the Faith" (Jude 3). Third, "faith" is used to designate the *fruits and works* that spring from it, because it is their root: "brought us good tidings of your faith" (1 Thess. 3:6), "show me thy faith" (James 2:18), i.e., the effects of it.

The term "faith" is used in still another sense. Fourth, it signifies *fidelity* or faithfulness, as in the following passages: "The weightier matters of the Law: judgment, mercy, and faith" (Matt. 23:23), "the faith of God" (Rom. 3:3), "the fruit of the Spirit is love, joy, peace . . . . faith" or "faithfulness" as in the R.V. (Gal. 5:22). Personally we consider this last meaning of the term to be primary, though not exclusive, significance in our present verse. The reference is not only to the grace of faith which was in them, but to its whole exercise in all that they did and suffered. Amid much discouragement and bitter opposition those Christian leaders had not fainted, but held on their way. Despite temptations to apostatise they had persevered in their profession, remained loyal to Christ, continued to minister unto His people, and had glorified God by laying down their lives for the Gospel. Faithful to their Master, they were fruitful in his service to the end of their course.

The last thing here mentioned of these spiritual rulers is "the end of their conversation," which is the most difficult to define with exactitude. The Greek word here for "end" is not "telos" which signifies the finish or conclusion of a thing, but "ekbasis" which literally means "a going up out of." It is found elsewhere in the N.T. only in 1 Cor. 10:13, where it is rendered "God is faithful, who will not suffer you to be tempted above that ye are able; but will with the temptation also *make a way to escape*, that ye may be able to bear it." "It is not therefore merely an end that is intended; nor doth the word signify a common end, issue or event of things, but an end accompanied with a deliverance from, and so a conquest over, such difficulties and dangers as men were before exposed unto. These persons, in the whole course of their conversation, were exercised with difficulties, dangers and sufferings, all attempting to stop them in their way, or to turn them out of it. But what did it all amount to, what was the issue of their conflict? It was a blessed deliverance from all troubles, and conquest over them" (J. Owen).

"The end of their conversation," then, has reference to their egress or exit from this world of sin and sorrow. It was a deliverance from all their trials, an honourable way of escape from all their difficulties and dangers, an exodus from the land of their Enemy. Yet it seems to us that the particular term used here by the Spirit is designed to carry our thoughts beyond this present scene. What was before the mind of Paul himself as he announces that the time of his departure was at hand? First, he declared, "I have fought a good fight, I have finished my course, I have kept the faith," and then he added "henceforth there is laid up for me a crown of righteousness" (2 Tim. 4:7, 8). As we have said, "ekbasis" signified a "going up out of:" thus the "end of their conversation" also meant a being taken to be forever with the Lord, a sure though future resurrection, and an unfading diadem of glory.

Corresponding to the three things said of their spiritual leaders, a threefold exhortation is given to the Hebrews. They were required to "remember" those who had spoken to them the Word of God," they were bidden to "follow" their faith, and they were enjoined to "consider" the end of their conversation. "Remember" is another word that is given a comprehensive meaning and scope in its Scriptural usage. It signifies that *reverence and submission* which is due a superior, as in "Remember now thy Creator in the days of thy youth" (Eccl. 12:1). It implies the *holding fast* of what has been received, whether instruction, promises, or warnings: "Remember, forget not, how thou provoked the Lord thy God to wrath in the wilderness" (Deut. 9:7). It means *to recall* that which has been forgotten: "When therefore He was risen from the dead, His disciples remembered that He had said this unto them, and they believed the Scripture, and the word which Jesus had said" (John 2:22). It denotes to *meditate upon,* as in "And thou shalt remember all the way which the Lord thy God led thee these forty years in the wilderness" (Deut. 8:2).

Here in our text the "remember" is used comprehensively, as comprising all those duties of respect and esteem, of love and obedience, which they owed to their departed teachers. Nor was such an exhortation needless. Human nature is very fickle, and tragic it is to mark how quickly many a faithful pastor is forgotten. Such forgetfulness is a species of ingratitude, and therefore is sinful. "Now there was found in it a poor wise man, and he by his wisdom delivered the city: yet no man remembered that same poor man" (Eccl. 9:15)—God taxes them with their forgetfulness! "Remember your leaders" includes thankfulness to God for them, speaking well of them, putting into practice their teaching. More specifically it means: treasure up in heart their instructions; call to mind their counsels, warnings, exhortations; gratefully meditate upon their untiring efforts to establish you in the Faith.

"Remember your rulers." How fearfully has this precept been perverted! What terrible superstitions have been invented and perpetrated in this connection: such as religious celebrations on the anniversary of their death, the dedication of "altars" and "chapels" unto their memory, the adoration of their bones, with the ascription of miraculous cures to them; the offering of prayers for them and to them. True, they are to be esteemed very highly in love for their works' sake (1 Thess. 5:13), both while they are with us and after God has removed them from us, but His servants are not to be "remembered" with idolatrous veneration, nor to the dividing with Christ any of those honours which belong alone unto Him. Not carnally, but spiritually are they to be remembered in what they did and taught, so that we are duly affected thereby.

It is at the point last mentioned we may perceive the pertinency of this precept to the apostle's design. His immediate purpose was to fortify them against departure from the Faith. Hence, he bids them "remember your rulers," for if you bear steadily in mind *their* instruction, you will at once perceive the error of the "divers and strange doctrines" which he warns against in v. 9. "The sheep follow Him: for they know His voice, And a stranger they will not follow, but will flee from him; for they know not the voice of strangers" (John 10:4, 5): *that* is the order—if we are heeding the true servants of Christ, we shall neither be attracted nor deceived by the emissaries of Satan. Again; a loving esteem of our teachers and a grateful remembrance of their devoted and laborious efforts to get us established in the Truth, will make us ashamed to go back on their instruction. Finally; to recall their steadfastness will be an encouragement to us when encountering opposition: *they* did not apostatise in the face of extreme peril—shall *we* spurn the example they left us.

And what is the clear implication of this to present-day preachers? Is there not here a searching word for heart and conscience? Is *your* ministry worthy to be stored up in the hearer's minds? Are your sermons worth remembering? The humble-minded will be ready to answer No, there is little or nothing in my simple and homely discourses deserving to be treasured up. Ah, brother preacher, it is not clever analyses of difficult passages which exhibit your mental acumen, nor lofty flights of language which display your rhetorical powers, that is of lasting worth. Rather is it that which makes sin to be more hated, God to be more feared, Christ to be more highly valued, the path of duty more clearly defined, which is what we are to aim to.

"Whose faith follow." This is the next duty we owe unto our spiritual leaders. It is closely allied to the former: we are to so "remember" them as to be effectually influenced in our own conduct. The word for "follow" signifies to imitate: it is used again in "For yourselves know ye ought to follow us: for we behaved not ourselves disorderly among you" (2 Thess. 3:7). "It is such a following as wherein we are fully conformed unto, and do lively express, that which we are said to follow. So a scholar may be said to follow his master, when, having attained all his arts and sciences, he acts them in the same manner as his master did. So are we to follow the faith of these guides" (John Owen). This is the greatest honour which we can do them, and is far more pleasing to God than erecting a marble monument to their memory or dedicating some "church" unto their name.

"Whose faith *follow*." There are many who sit more or less regularly under the ministry of God's servants, and they approve of their doctrine, admire their courage, speak well of them, but *they do not* carry out their principles or emulate their example. The whole force of this second exhortation is that we are to so "remember" our leaders as to be thereby influenced unto the living of a holy life. To "follow" their faith means to ponder their trust in God and pray for an increase of your own. Recall to mind their instructions, and continue thou in the profession and practice of the doctrine they inculcated. Meditate upon their lives, and so far as their works corresponded to their words, imitate their conduct. Copy their virtues, and not their eccentricities. "No mere man, not the best of men, is to be our pattern or example absolutely, or in all things. This honour is due unto Christ alone" (J. Owen).

"Whose faith follow." The *appropriateness* of this exhortation to the situation in which the Hebrews were is also obvious. It is a spiritual stimulus rightly to "remember" our former leaders, for it makes them, in a sense, present again with us. The faculty to recall the past is not only a Divine gift and mercy, but it entails definite responsibilities. As we recall the testimony and toil of our ministers, their loyalty to Christ and devotedness to our interests, we are to be suitably affected thereby. When encountering opposition, we should remember the much fiercer persecution others have suffered before us. When tempted to compromise and sell the Truth, we should think upon the unswerving fidelity of our fathers in the Faith. Should we ever be under heavy pressure to apostatise, we must weigh well the fact that the principles of the faith of our former leaders were adequate to sustain *their* hearts, so that they met death with holy composure, and seek grace to "hold the beginning of *our* confidence steadfast unto the end."

Once more we would pause and notice the solemn implication of this word to those of us who are ministers of the Gospel. Next to pleasing the Lord Himself, our chief care should be to set before our flock such an example of faith and holiness, as that it will be their duty to remember and follow. This is not optional, but obligatory, for God has bidden each of His servants "be thou *an example* of the believers, in word, in conversation, in love, in spirit, in faith, in purity" (1 Tim. 4:12); and again, "In all things showing thyself *a pattern* of good works: in doctrine uncorruptness, gravity, sincerity, sound speech that cannot be condemned; that he that is of the contrary part may be ashamed, having no evil thing to say of you" (Titus 2:7, 8). Alas, how many of the present-day preachers set an example which if followed by their hearers would lead them to perdition. O for grace to let our light "so shine before men, that they may see our good works, and glorify our Father which is in Heaven" (Matt. 5:16).

"Considering the end of their conversation." Here is the third part of our duty toward those whom God has placed in spiritual authority over us. It signifies to observe diligently and thoroughly, so as to have the heart suitably affected thereby. The word for "considering" occurs again only in Acts 17:23, namely, when Paul "beheld" the gods that the Athenians worshipped, so that "his spirit was stirred in him" (v. 16)! Literally, the term signifies "looking up to." The Hebrews were to recall the "conversation" of their deceased teachers, their manner of life, which was one of testimony and toil, fidelity to Christ and love for the souls of His people: a "conversation" of devoted service in the face of many discouragements and much opposition, sustained by trust in the living God; and the Hebrews were to ponder and take courage and comfort from the blessed end or issue of the same.

Thus the three parts of this exhortation are intimately related. The leaders were to be "remembered" in such a manner as to be effectually influenced by the example they had left; they were to be "followed" because their fidelity was Divinely rewarded with a victorious exit from this world. In the last clause the apostle presented a powerful motive to stir up the saints to the discharge of the duty previously described. Consider their "end" that *yours* may morally resemble it: you must adhere to their doctrine and imitate their practice if you are to receive the victor's crown. "Consider what it (their "end") came to: their faith failed not, their hope did not perish, they were not disappointed, but had a blessed end of their walk and course" (J. Owen). Sometimes God permits His servants to-day to bear witness to the sufficiency of the principles of the Gospel to support and comfort on a deathbed.

"Jesus Christ the same yesterday, and to-day, and forever" (v. 8). We will not now attempt to sermonize upon this well-known and precious verse, but rather give a brief exposition of it. The first thing to ponder is the particular book in which this declaration is made, for that throws light on its scope and meaning. Hebrews is the epistle which treats specifically and at length with the great alteration made by God in His dealings with the Church on earth, the revolution which was introduced by the substituting of the new covenant for the old, the passing away of Judaism and the inauguration of Christianity. This had involved many changes of a radical character, a great "shaking" and "removing" (12:27) of "that which decayeth and waxeth old, ready to vanish away" (8:13). It is in view of *that* our present verse is to be interpreted and enjoyed. The temple is destroyed, the ceremonial law is gone, the Levitical priesthood is no more; but Jesus Christ, the Head of the Church, the Mediator between God and His people, *abides unchanged.*

CHAPTER ONE HUNDRED TWELVE

The Heart Established

(Heb. 13:8, 9)

"Jesus Christ the same yesterday, and to-day, and forever" (v. 8). Sir Rob. Anderson and others regarded this as a declaration of the Saviour's Godhead, arguing that "The Same" is a Divine title taken from Psalm 102:27, etc. But why, it may be asked, should the apostle break his line of thought and introduce a formal affirmation of Christ's Deity in the midst of a series of exhortations? Such an interpretation destroys the unity of the passage. Moreover, there was no need for this, for the Redeemer's Godhead had been clearly and fully established in the opening chapter of the epistle. Nor was there any special reason for Paul, at this point, to insist upon the essential immutability of Christ, and that the translators of the A.V. did *not* so understand him is evident from their declining to add the auxiliary verb: "Jesus Christ *is* the same yesterday, and to-day," etc.

"Jesus Christ the same yesterday, and to-day, and forever." These words, as was intimated in the final paragraph of the preceding article, are not to be taken absolutely, but are to be regarded relatively; that is to say, they are not to be considered by themselves alone, but in connection with the precise place they occupy in the Sacred Canon. Every statement of Scripture is positioned by Divine wisdom, and often we miss an important key to interpretation when ignoring the particular location of a passage. The verse before us illustrates the special theme of the book in which it is found. The subject of the Hebrews' letter is the immeasurable superiority of Christianity over Judaism, and here is further demonstration of the fact. Under Judaism, Aaron had been followed by Eleazer, and he, by Eli; but our great High Priest abides forever. Israel's prophets followed each other on the stage of action; but our Prophet had no successor. So too there had been a long line of kings; but Zion's King is eternal.

"The apostle speaks not of the person of Christ absolutely, but with respect unto His office and His discharge of it: he declares who and what He is therein. He is 'the same' in His Divine person: eternal, immutable, indeficient. Being so in Himself, He is so *in His office* from first to last. Although diverse alterations were made in the institutions of Divine worship, and there were many degrees and parts of Divine revelation (1:1), yet in and through them all, Jesus Christ was still the same. In every state of the church, in every condition of believers, He is the same unto them, and will be so unto the consummation of all things; He is, He ever was, all in all unto the Church. He is the Object, the Author and Finisher of faith, the Preserver and Rewarder of all them that believe, and that equally in all generations" (Condensed from J. Owen).

"Jesus Christ the same yesterday, and to-day, and forever." How thoughtlessly is this statement received by many! How carelessly is its setting ignored by most sermonizers! Were we to take this declaration absolutely it would involve us in inextricable difficulties. Ponder its terms for a moment. Did your Lord undergo no radical change when He became incarnate? Did He experience no great change at His resurrection? During the days of His flesh, He was "The Man of sorrows:" is He so now after His ascension? — one has but to ask the question to perceive its absurdity. This statement, then, is to be understood with certain limitations; or rather, it is to be interpreted in the light of its setting, and for that, not a novice, but an experienced expositor is required. Let us consider it, then, in connection with its context.

First, as has already been pointed out, it most blessedly illustrated the special theme of this epistle, for in contrast from so much that was mutable and transitory in Judaism, the Author of Christianity abides essentially the same in all generations. Second, v. 8 supplies an additional and most powerful motive to fidelity. Some of their spiritual guides had already passed away, and in those still left, time and change would swiftly work their sure effects; but the great Head of the Church remained, being alive for evermore. Jesus Christ was the One who had supported their deceased leaders, who had passed through their trials victoriously, and if trusted in, He would sustain *them,* for He was the same gracious and powerful Shepherd of the sheep. He is for *you,* as for them, "the same" Object of faith, "the same" all-sufficient Saviour, "the same" effectual Intercessor. He is "the same" in His loving design and covenant faithfulness. Then cleave to Him with unshakeable confidence.

Third, the blessed declaration of v. 8 lays a foundation on which to base the exhortation which immediately follows. "The only way by which we can persevere in the right faith is to hold to the foundation, and not in the slightest degree depart from it, for he who holds not to Christ knows nothing but mere vanity, though he may comprehend heaven and earth" (John Calvin). The Lord Jesus is the same, therefore, *be ye not unstable* and fickle. Christ is the same teacher: His doctrine does not vary, His will does not fluctuate, nor His purpose alter; therefore should we remain steadfast in the Truth, shunning novelties and refusing all innovations. It is only by "holding the Head" (Col. 2:19), submitting to His will, receiving His doctrine, obeying His precepts, that we shall be fortified against false teachers and persevere unto the end.

Thus, vv. 7-9 are intimately related and together form a complete hortatory passage: so far as we have light thereon, we understand them to mean: Hold fast to the testimony of your former leaders, for they proved the sufficiency of the Truth they proclaimed; Christian doctrine does not vary from day to day, for Jesus Christ is ever the same. The designation used of Him at once intimates that He is *not* here contemplated so much as the second Person in the Godhead, as the Mediator and Head of the Church. He is the same in His identity (Rev. 5:6), the same in His offices, the same in His efficacy, the same in His will; therefore must we refuse to be led away by those who teach anything different. The whole passage is a strong dissuasion against vacillation. The Truth is fixed; the Gospel is everlasting, therefore should we be "steadfast, unmoveable, always abounding in the work of the Lord" (1 Cor. 15:58).

"Be not carried about with divers and strange doctrines: for it is a good thing that the heart be established with grace: not with meats, which have not profited them that have been occupied therein" (v. 9). This is the point to which the apostle had been leading in the previous verses: trust in Christ, and cleave to Him according to the instruction you have received from your fathers in the Faith, and give not ear unto those who would unsettle and seduce you. "Divers doctrines" are those which differ from pure Christianity; "strange" doctrines are those which are foreign or opposed to the Gospel. To be carried "about" by such is for the mind to be unsettled thereby, producing an unsteadiness of conduct. To be immune from this evil the heart has to be established with grace, which, because of its deep importance, calls for a careful inquiry thereinto. "Not with meats" has reference to the efforts of the Judaisers to graft the ceremonial law on to the Gospel, a thing utterly unprofitable, yea, baneful.

"Be not carried about with divers and strange doctrines." It is to be duly noted that the noun is in the plural number. This is in marked and designed contrast from the revelation which *God* has given us. Truth is a perfect unit, but error is multiform. There is but "*one* faith," as there is but "one Lord" (Eph. 4:5), namely, that which was once for all delivered to the saints (Jude 3) in the revelation made of it by Christ and the apostles (Heb. 2:3, 4). Hence, when the Truth is in view, it is always "doctrine" in the singular number, as "the doctrine" (John 7:17), "the doctrine of Christ" (2 John 9) and see Rom. 16:17; 1 Tim. 4:16 etc. On the other hand, where error is referred to the plural number is employed, as in "doctrines of men" (Col. 2:22), "doctrines of demons" (1 Tim. 4:1). The Truth of God is one uniform system and chain of doctrine, which begins in God and ends in Him; but error is inconsistent and manifold.

"Be not carried about with divers and strange doctrines." The very fact that this dehortation was not only given verbally by the apostles to the Christians of their own day, but is also preserved in the written Word of God, clearly intimates that the people of God will always have to contend against error unto the end of time. Christ Himself declared, "Take heed that no man deceive you: for many shall come in My name, saying, I am Christ; and shall deceive many" (Matt. 24:4, 5); and the last of His apostles wrote "try the spirits whether they are of God, because many false prophets are gone out into the world" (1 John 4:1). How unfeignedly thankful we should be that God has put into our hands an unfailing plummet by which we may measure every preacher and teacher. The doctrine of Christ changes not, and whatever proceeds not from it and accords not with it, is alien to the faith of the Church and is to be refused and rejected.

"Be not carried about with divers and strange doctrines." As this dehortation concerned the Hebrew saints the reference was, of course, to the Mosaic institutions, as the remainder of our verse denotes: "for it is a good thing that the heart be established with grace: not with meats, which have not profited them that have been occupied therein." The Levitical law made distinctions of meats, and things of a like nature, which the false teachers were pressing with much zeal. It is plain from such passages as Rom. 14:13-23, 1 Cor. 8, Gal. 4, etc., that determined efforts were being made by the Enemy to corrupt the Gospel by attaching to it parts of the ceremonialism of Judaism. When Paul says "which have not profited *them* that have been occupied therein" he referred *not* to the O.T. saints who had obeyed the Mosaic precepts, but to those who heeded the errorists of his day.

The principle expressed in this dissuasion is as applicable to and as much needed by the saints of each succeeding generation as it was by those Hebrews. It is one of the marks of the Fall that man is fonder of that which is *material* in religion, than he is of what is *spiritual*; he is most prone — as history universally and sadly shows — to concentrate on *trivialities* rather than upon *essentials*. He is more concerned about the details of ordinances than he is of getting his heart established with grace. He will lend a readier ear to novel "doctrines" than to a solid exposition of the fundamentals of the Faith. He will contend zealously for things which contribute nothing to his salvation nor conduce an iota unto true holiness. And the only sure way of being delivered from this evil tendency, and of being preserved from false doctrines, is to buy the Truth and sell it not, and to have the heart established with grace.

"For it is a good thing that the heart be established with grace." What is denoted by this weighty expression? First, what is it for the heart to be "established" and then how it is so established "with grace"? An established heart is the opposite from one which is "carried about," which term is used again in, "that we henceforth be no more children, tossed to and fro, and carried about with every wind of doctrine, by the sleight of men" (Eph. 4:14). It is a poetic expression in allusion to sailing-ships and the impression of the wind upon them. The figure is apt, and suggestive of the nature of strange doctrines, the way in which they are spread, and their effects on the minds of men. In themselves they are light and vain, "clouds which hold no water" (Jude 12): there is nothing solid and substantial in them for the soul. Those who would impose such doctrines on others, generally do so with much bombast and blustering; unless we believe and practice such things, we are denounced as heretics and unsaved (Acts 15:1). The unlearned and unstable are disturbed by them, carried out of their course, and are in danger of making shipwreck of their faith. Hence, an "established heart" is one which is rooted and grounded in the Truth, securely anchored in Christ, rejoicing in God.

The word "grace" is vastly comprehensive and has various meanings in its Scripture usage. Its grand, original, fundamental signification is to express the free, eternal, and sovereign *favour of God toward His people,* for *that* is the spring and source of all the gifts, benefits and blessings we receive from Him. From this infinite fountain of the uncaused favour and special love of God—which is the "good pleasure of His (immutable) will" — proceed all the *acts* of His grace toward, in, and upon the elect. "Who hath saved us, and called us with an holy calling, not according to our works, but according to His own purpose and grace, which was given us in Christ Jesus before the world began" (2 Tim. 1:9). From that blessed ocean of grace proceed our personal and unconditional election in Christ, our union unto Him, interest in Him, relation to Him, together with our being blessed in Him with all spiritual blessings (Eph. 1:3-6). We read of "the grace of God and the gift by grace" (Rom. 5:15): the former of which must mean the favour of God in His own heart towards us, in distinction from all the favours He bestows upon us; while the latter signifies the righteousness of Christ imputed to us, as flowing from the original grace in God.

The operations, breathings, and influences of the Holy Spirit in quickening, enlightening, revealing and applying Christ to us, so that we are put into actual enjoyment of Him and His salvation, are the outworkings of the everlasting Covenant of Grace; therefore it is *all of grace.* The next most common use of the term is inherent or indwelling grace, being used to designate that supernatural work which is wrought in the Christian at his regeneration, whereby he is made alive Godwards and is given a relish for spiritual things: such passages as "He giveth more grace" (James 4:6), and "grow in grace" (2 Pet. 3:18) have respect to grace in the heart. Then too the whole system of doctrine comprehended by "the Gospel" is so designated, for when Paul said to the Galatians, "Whosoever of you are justified by the law, ye are fallen from grace" (5:4) he meant they had forsaken *the truth of grace.* Among the less frequent uses of the term we may note that its transforming effects are themselves called "grace" (Acts 11:23); gifts for preaching bear the title of "grace" (2 Cor. 6:1), as do those virtues wrought in us by the Spirit (2 Cor. 12:9, 10).

"For it is a good thing that the heart be established with grace." By "grace" in this verse we understand, first, *the doctrine of* grace, that is, the truth of God's free favour without us, in His own heart towards us, which is made known to us in the Gospel (Acts 20:24). Concerning this we read, "For the grace of God that bringeth salvation hath appeared to all men" (Titus 2:11) i.e. it has been revealed in His Gospel. The doctrine of grace is also styled, "wholesome words, even the words of our Lord Jesus Christ, and the doctrine which is according to godliness" (1 Tim. 6:3). The doctrine of grace includes all that sacred system of theology, all the fundamentals of the everlasting Gospel of the blessed God, that grand "mystery" of His mind and will which sets forth to us the complete counsel and covenant of the Eternal Three, the record of God concerning His Son, by which He declares that "he that believeth hath everlasting life."

As the whole of the Gospel, with the great salvation contained in it, and the blessings, consolations, privileges and promises of it, were fully, freely, and impartially preached by the apostles, so it was attended with the Holy Spirit sent down from Heaven to the minds and hearts of many who heard it, so that they were brought to a saving knowledge of the Lord, and to a true and actual closure with Him, by means of the Word of Truth. The doctrine of grace as proclaimed by God's accredited servants, and as clothed with the power of the Spirit, is the Divinely appointed means of turning the elect from darkness unto light, from power of Satan into the kingdom of God's dear Son (Acts 26:18). Their understandings are illumined to know from the Gospel that it is God's will to save them through the appointed Redeemer, and they are enabled to personally realize that Christ Jesus came into the world to save sinners.

Second, it is most important and blessed for the heart to be *"established"* with inherent grace: a fact which every one born of God must more or less know and feel. Where the Holy Spirit of God dwells, there sin is known in its guilt and felt in its power, while the effects of the Fall on all the faculties of the soul are experienced. When the Spirit has revealed the super-excellency of Christ, His all-sufficiency as a Saviour, His suitableness as such, this begets some longings after Him, thirstings for Him, desires to be found in Him, and high prizings of His blood and righteousness. But many there are who, though quickened and called of God, have not yet closed in with Christ, cannot say He died for *them,* know not that *their* sins are pardoned. The Spirit has thus far wrought with them that they feel themselves to be vile sinners, justly deserving of the wrath of God; yet they cannot affirm that their names are written in Heaven.

They are emptied of all creature dependency and self-sufficiency. Their hearts are broken and humbled with a true and thorough sight and sense of sin. They have heard of Christ, and of His infinite tenderness and compassion, love and mercy, to sinners like themselves. The Lord the Spirit has brought them so far as to listen attentively to the preaching of the Gospel and the searching of the Scriptures. Though they may be as bruised reeds and smoking flax, incapable of expressing their wants to God, or of describing their case to others, yet they find in the preaching of Christ crucified that which suits them. Though they cannot yet confidently say of Him "who loved *me* and gave Himself for me," nevertheless *they wait on Him* in his ordinances, longing for Him to arise upon them as the Sun of righteousness with healing in His wings. And though such may be called "seekers only," "inquirers after Christ," yet they are blessed: "*Blessed* are all they that *wait for Him*" (Isa. 30:18); "let the heart of them rejoice that *seek* the Lord" (1 Chron. 16:10).

Upon such persons the Lord, in His good time, causes His light of grace to break forth more clearly, shining within them, causing their spiritual faculties to expand, and be exercised more particularly upon "the mystery of the Gospel" (Eph. 6:19) and the doctrine of grace. Thereby their spiritual "senses" (Heb. 5:14) are brought to taste the sweetness of Divine truth, to have a heart relish of it, to derive nourishment from it, to perceive its spiritual excellency. In receiving and digesting it, they are brought to find the doctrine of God's free grace to be wholesome and sustaining. By this means they are "nourished up" (1 Tim. 4:6) unto everlasting life. It is thus the Lord carries on His work in the souls of His people. At regeneration they are filled with joy in Him, and sin is but little felt within. But as the work of grace is deepened, they are made to see and feel their depravity, and their peace is clouded by increasing discoveries of their vileness, which makes way for a growing appreciation of grace.

Inherent grace, then, is a new nature or holy principle implanted by the Spirit at the new birth. It consists in spiritual perceptions, inward apprehensions, spiritual affections, in the souls of those who are born of God, whereby they are fitted for Him and Divine things, enabled to take holy delight in God, to have holy breathings after Him, to hunger and thirst after righteousness, to yearn for a consciousness of Christ's presence, to have a spiritual appetite to feed upon Him as the Bread of Life. Thus, it is most profitable for the saint to have his heart established with inherent grace, for he is the personal subject of it, and it is for this reason that God's people in general are so fond of *experimental* preaching—the tracing out of the work of the Spirit in their hearts—thereby enabling them to set to their seal that God is true, that He has thus far wrought in them to the praise and glory of His grace.

Nor is there any legality in this, for the work of the Spirit, in all its parts and phases, flows as freely from the Covenant of grace as does the work of Christ. Yea, we are expressly said to be *"saved by* the washing of regeneration and renewing of *the Holy Spirit"* (Titus 3:5), which is thus expressed to show that salvation depends equally upon the distinct offices which the Eternal Three are engaged in on behalf of the elect. It is helpful to converse at times with such as are experimentally acquainted with God, and His Son Jesus Christ, and who hold communion with Him by the Holy Spirit. Genuine Christian experience consists principally in this: the Spirit is pleased to open the Scriptures unto us, making them the ground of our faith, giving us to feel their power, making the experience described in them our own, revealing Christ as set forth in the Word to us, and filling our hearts with His love agreeably to what is revealed of it in the Gospel.

The people of God need to be taught and brought to an acquaintance with the real work of God *within* them, with His *method* of strengthening and comforting them, that they may learn the grounds of spiritual assurance. There is a needs be that the heart be established with grace as it respects their ascertaining for themselves that a supernatural work is actually wrought within them, that Christ is in them the hope of glory, that they "know the grace of God *in truth*" (Col. 1:6), and that their works are "wrought in God" (John 3:21) as Christ expressed it. Let us therefore diligently study the work of the Spirit within us, comparing it with the written Word, and carefully distinguishing between natural and spiritual affections, moral refinements and supernatural regeneration. Nor let us forget that the grace of God within us is only discovered to us as the Spirit shines upon His own work in our souls.

It is also good for the heart to be established with the grace as it respects *the doctrine* of it: in the belief of the Father's everlasting love, the Son's complete salvation, and the Spirit's testimony thereof, which strengthens the faith and confirms the hope of the Christian. Confidence before God can be maintained on no other foundation than that of His *grace*. There are seasons when the believer's mind is filled with distress, when the guilt of sin presses heavily on his conscience, when Satan is allowed to buffet him; then it is that he is forced to cry "have respect to the Covenant" (Psa. 74:20). There are seasons when he cannot pray except with groanings that cannot be uttered, being cast down with soul burdens and conflicts, but they only serve to prove to him the deep need of his heart being established with the truth of grace.

Thus, for the heart to be "established with grace" signifies, first, the doctrine of God's free grace *without* us, in His own heart toward us; and second, the blessed operations of the Spirit *within* us. When God's free-grace salvation is brought home to the heart by the Spirit, it produces blessed fruits and consequences in the person to whom it becomes "the power of God" (Rom. 1:16). It is of vast importance to hold forth a clear profession of the doctrine of grace, and it is of incalculable worth to be able to declare a genuine work of grace wrought in the heart by the Spirit agreeably to the truth we profess. The doctrine of grace is the means, in the hands of the Spirit, of begetting faith, promoting its growth, and supporting it. Therefore there is a real need of God's everlasting love and Christ's finished redemption being preached, though they be already known, and their power felt in the heart, because our walk with God and our confidence in Him receive all their encouragement therefrom.

While it is certain that the head must be enlightened with the knowledge of Truth before the heart can experience the virtue and efficacy of it, yet our text speaks of "the heart" so as to emphasise the quickening and operative power of Divine truth, when it is embraced and maintained in the soul. It is good for the heart to be established with grace, for it promotes the believer's spiritual growth, secures his wellbeing, and greatly contributes to his comfort. It is also a preservative against error, an antidote against unbelief, and a choice cordial to revive the soul in seasons of distress.

N.B. For much in the second half of this chapter we are indebted to a valuable sermon by S. E. Pierce.

CHAPTER ONE HUNDRED THIRTEEN

The Christian's Altar

(Heb. 13:10)

There is a saying that "a man usually finds what he is looking for," and there is a sense in which that principle holds good of not a little consulting of the Scriptures. Various kinds of people approach the Scriptures with the object of finding something in them which will countenance their ideas, and no matter how foolish and far-fetched those ideas may be, they generally succeed in locating that which with some degree of plausibility supports them—that is why the scoffer will often counter a quotation from God's Word with, "O you can prove anything from the Bible." It matters not to those who are determined to procure "proof" for their vagaries, that they *"wrest* the Scriptures" (2 Pet. 3:16) either by detaching a sentence from its context and giving it a meaning quite contrary to its setting, or by interpreting literally that which is figurative, or giving a figurative meaning to that which is literal.

Not only does practically every professedly Christian sect make a show of producing Scriptural warrant for its peculiar beliefs and practices, so that Universalists, Annihilationalists, Seventh-day Adventists, quote a list of texts in proof of their errors, but others who do not claim to be "Christian" appeal to the Bible in support of their delusions. It would probably surprise some of our readers did they know how artfully (but wickedly) Spiritists juggle with Holy Writ, appearing to adduce not a little in favour of clairvoyance, clairaudience, trance-speaking, etc., while Theosophists have the affrontery to say that re-incarnation is plainly taught in the Bible; all of which goes to show how fearfully fallen man may abuse God's mercies and profane that which is most sacred.

Nor are Romanists any exception. It is commonly supposed that they have very little concern for Scripture, buttressing their superstitions by an appeal to tradition and ancient customs. It is true that the rank and file of the Papists are deprived of the Scriptures, and are satisfied with "the authority of the church," as sufficient justification for all they believe and do, but it is a big mistake to suppose that her officers are incapable of making a Scriptural defence of their positions. The writer of this article discovered that more than a quarter of a century ago, in his first pastorate. Situated in a mining-camp in Colorado, the only other "minister" in the country was a Romish priest, with whom we got acquainted. He volunteered to give us Scripture for every Popish dogma and practice, and when we put him to the test (as we did, again and again), we were amazed and awed by the subtle manner in which he mis-"appropriated" the Word. It was then we learned the uselessness of "arguing" about Divine things.

The above thoughts have been suggested by the opening words of our present passage: "We have *an altar*." Most fearfully has this clause been perverted by those who have given it a meaning and put it to a use wholly foreign to the design of the Spirit in the passage from which it is taken. Deceived by the mere sound of words, the affirmation has been boldly made that not only did the Israelites in O.T. times have a literal and material altar, but that "we," Christians, also "have," by Divine appointment, "an altar," that is, a material one of wood and stone, and hence the "altar" and "high altar" in many "protestant churches." But an altar calls for *a sacrifice,* and hence the invention of "the mass" or "unbloody sacrifice of the flesh and blood of Christ" offered by the priests. Many who do not go thus far, insist that the table used for the celebration of the Lord's supper should be designated "an altar," and suppose that our text authorises them therein.

That such a conception as the one we have just mentioned is utterly groundless and erroneous may quickly be demonstrated. In the first place, whatever be signified by the "altar" in our passage, it is manifestly opposed to, set in contrast from, the visible and material altar of Judaism, so much so that they who officiated at the latter were debarred from feasting on the former. In the second place, the Jewish altar, like everything else in the tabernacle, was a shadow or type, and surely it would be placing a severe strain upon the imagination to conclude that the brazen altar of old was but a figure of a table now used in our "churches"! Third, sufficient has been advanced by the apostle in the preceding chapters to make it unmistakably plain that Christ Himself—in His person, office, and sacrificial work—is the antitype and substance of all the tabernacle types! Finally, the Spirit Himself has made it quite clear that our "altar" is a *spiritual* one, and that the "sacrifice" we are to offer thereon is a *spiritual* one: see v. 15.

"We have an altar, whereof they have no right to eat which serve the tabernacle" (v. 10). In seeking to ascertain the meaning of this verse, which has needlessly perplexed and been made the occasion of much profitless controversy, it will greatly simplify the expositor's task if he bears in mind that the primary aim of the Spirit throughout this epistle is to set forth the transcendent excellency of Christ over all persons through whom God had, in times past, spoken unto men, and in the vast superiority of His office and work over all the institutions which had foreshadowed them under the old covenant. As the incarnate Son, He is infinitely above all prophets and angels (chapters 1 and 2). Moses, "the servant *in* the house of God" retires before the presence of Christ "the Son *over* His own house" (chap. 3). So in regard to all the Mosaic institutions: *Christ* fulfills everything which they prefigured.

This is quite an elementary truth, yet is it one of basic importance, for error at this point produces most pernicious and fatal consequences. The entire system of worship that Jehovah appointed for Israel was of a typical character, and the reality and substance of it is now found in Christ. *He* is "the great High Priest" of whom the priests under the law, Aaron himself not excepted, were but faint adumbrations. His very body is "the greater and more perfect tabernacle, not made with hands" (9:11). *His* was the sacrifice which fully and forever accomplished that which all the Levitical offerings proclaimed as necessary to redemption, but the repetition of which clearly testified they had never effected. In like manner, Christ is the grand *Antitype* of all the sacred vessels of the tabernacle: He is the true Brazen-altar, Laver, Golden-altar of incense, Candlestick, Table of shrewbread, Mercyseat, and Ark of the Covenant.

That the Lord Jesus *is* Himself the antitype of "the altar of burnt offering" appears by comparing two of His own declarations: "Ye fools and blind: for whether is greater, the gift, or the altar that sanctifieth the gift?" (Matt. 23:19); "And for their sakes I *sanctify Myself*" (John 17:19). Both "the altar that sanctifieth the gift" and "the gift" itself *meet in Him*—just as both the officiating priest and the sacrifice which he offered find their fulfilment in Him. It seems strange that some able writers have quite missed the point of Matt. 23:19 when dealing with its fulfilment and realization in the Lord Jesus. They have made "the altar" to be the wooden cross to which the Saviour was nailed, and that mistake has laid the foundation for a more serious error. No, "the altar" on which "the gift" was laid pointed to the Divine dignity of Christ's glorious *person*, and it was *that* which gave infinite worth to His sacrifice. It was for this reason the Spirit dwelt at such length upon the unique glory of Christ's person in the earlier chapters of this epistle, *before* He opened to us His sacrificial work.

What has just been pointed out above supplies the key to many a lovely O. T. type. For instance, we are told that "Noah builded *an altar* unto the Lord; and took of every clean beast, and of every clean fowl, and offered burnt offerings on the altar" (Gen. 8:20). Very blessed is that. The *first* act of Noah as he came forth from the ark on to the purified earth was not to build a house for himself, but to erect that which spoke of the person of Christ—for in all things He must have the pre-eminence. On that altar Noah expressed his thanksgiving by presenting his burnt offerings, teaching us that it is only by Christ we can acceptably present to God our sacrifice of praise (Heb. 13:15). And we are told that Noah's offering was "a sweet savour unto the Lord," and then we read "and God *blessed* Noah and his sons" (Gen. 9:1), for all blessing comes to us through Christ.

"And the Lord appeared unto Abram, and said, Unto thy seed will I give this land: and there builded he *an altar* unto the Lord, who appeared unto him" (Gen. 12:7). That was equally blessed. This was the *first* act of Abraham after he had left Chaldea, and then Haran where his progress had been delayed for a season, and had now actually entered Canaan. The Lord appeared to him here, as He had first done in Ur, and made promise of the land unto him and his seed; and his response was to set up an altar. And again we read "and he removed from thence unto a mountain on the east of Bethel, and pitched his tent between Bethel on the west, and Hai on the east; and there he builded an altar unto the Lord" (Gen. 12:8). How significant! Bethel means "the house of God," while Hai signifies "a heap of ruins." It was *between them* that Abram pitched his tent—emblematic of the pilgrim character of the saint while in this world, and erected his altar—symbol of his dependence upon and worship of God. It was to this same altar he returned after his failure in going down into Egypt: Gen. 13:3, 4.

Of Isaac we read, "And he builded an altar there, and called upon the name of the Lord" (Gen. 26:25). How beautifully that brings out another aspect of our type: here the "altar" is the place of prayer, for it is only in the name of Christ—the antitype of the altar—that we can present our petitions acceptably to God. Of Jacob we read, "And he erected there an altar, and called it God, the God of Israel" (Gen. 33:20). That was immediately after his Divine deliverance from Esau and his four hundred men—intimating that it is in and by Christ the believer is eternally *secure.* Of Moses we read, that he "built an altar, and called the name of it the Lord my Banner" (Ex. 17:15). That was after Israel's victory over the Amalekites—denoting that it is only by Christ that believers *can overcome* their spiritual enemies. "And Moses wrote all the words of the Lord, and rose up early in the morning, and builded an altar under the hill" (Ex. 24:4)—only by Christ is the Law magnified and honoured.

But it is more especially upon the brazen altar in the tabernacle that our attention needs to be concentrated. A description of it is supplied in Ex. 27:1-8, though other passages should be carefully compared. This altar occupied a place of first importance among the seven pieces of the furniture in the tabernacle, for it was not only the largest of them all—being almost big enough to hold the others—but it was placed "before the door" (Ex. 40:6), just inside the outer court (Ex. 40:33), and would thus be the first object to meet the eye of the worshipper as he entered the sacred precincts. It was made of wood, but overlaid with brass, so that it could withstand the action of fire, which was burning continually upon it (Lev. 6:13). To it the sinner came with his Divinely-appointed sacrifice, wherein the innocent was slain in the place of the guilty. At this altar the high priest officiated on the great day of atonement (Lev. 16).

The brazen altar was the way of approach to God, for it was there that the Lord promised to meet His people: "*There I will meet with* the children of Israel" (Ex. 29:43): how that reminds us of the Saviour's declaration "I am the Way, the Truth, and the Life: no man cometh unto the Father, but by Me" (John 14:6)! This altar was really the basis of the whole Levitical system, for on it the burnt offering, meal offering, peace offering, and sin offering were presented to God. Blood was put upon its horns, sprinkled upon it, round about it, and poured out at its base. It was the chief connecting-link between the people and Jehovah, they being so identified with it that certain parts of the offerings there presented to Him were eaten by them, and hence we read "Behold Israel after the flesh: are not they which eat of the sacrifices *partakers* of the altar?" (1 Cor. 10:18).

This was an altar for all Israel—and for none else!—and their jealousy was promptly stirred if anything seemed to interfere with it. A striking illustration of this is found in Joshua 22. There we read that the two and a half tribes whose inheritance lay on the far side of Jordan erected an altar—"a great altar to see to" (v. 10). When the other tribes heard of this, they were greatly alarmed and severely censured them, for it appeared to deny the unity of the Nation and to be a rival unto the altar for all the people. They were only satisfied when the Reubenites assured them that they had *not* built this altar by the Jordan to offer sacrifices thereon, but for *a witness* (v. 27), declaring, "God forbid that we should rebel against the Lord, and turn this day from following the Lord, to build an altar for burnt offerings, for meat offerings, or for sacrifices, besides the altar of the Lord our God that is before His tabernacle" (v. 29).

We may see again the prominent place which was given to the altar by Israel in the days of Ezra, for when they returned from the captivity, it was the *first* thing they set up—thus signifying they could not approach God or be connected with Him on any other ground. "Then stood up Jeshua the son of Jozadak, and his brethren the priests, and Zerubbabel the son of Shealtiel, and his brethren, and builded the altar of the God of Israel, to offer burnt offerings thereon, as it is written in the law of Moses the man of God" (Ezra 3:2).

In view of its significance, its importance, its hallowed associations, one can readily imagine what it meant to a converted Jew to abandon the altar of Judaism. Unto his unbelieving brethren he would necessarily appear as a renegade of his fathers, an apostate from God, and a fool to himself. Their taunt would be, In turning your back upon Judaism you have lost everything: you have *no altar!* Why, you are worse off than the wretched Samaritans, for they *do* have a place and system of worship on mount Gerizim: whereas you Christians have *nothing!* But here the apostle turns the tables upon them: he affirms that not only do we "*have* an altar," but it was one which those who still identified themselves with the temple and its services had no right to. In turning from Judaism to Christ the believing Hebrew had left the shadow for the substance, the figure for the reality; whereas those who despised and rejected Christ merely had that which was become "weak and beggarly elements" (Gal. 4:9).

The sad failure of the great mass of the Jews, under the Gospel-preaching of the apostles, to turn their affections unto things above, where Christ had passed within the veil, and their stubbornness in clinging to the tangible system at Jerusalem, was something more than a peculiarity of that nation—it exemplified the universal fondness of man for that which is *material* in religion, and his disrelish of that which is strictly *spiritual.* In Judaism there was much that was addressed to the sense, herein too lies the power and secret of Rome's success: the strength of its appeal to the natural man lies in its sensuous show. Though Christians have no visible manifestation of the Divine glory on earth to which they may draw near when they worship, they do have access to the Throne of Grace in Heaven; but it is only the truly regenerate who prefer the substance to the shadow.

"We have an altar." Our altar, unlike that of Judaism, is inside the veil: "whither the Forerunner is for us entered, even Jesus"

(Heb. 6:20), after that He had appeared here upon earth to put away sin by the sacrifice of Himself. To the Christian comes the blessed exhortation, "Having therefore, brethren, boldness to enter into the Holiest by the blood of Jesus, by a new and living way, which He hath consecrated for us, through the veil, that is to say, His flesh; and having a High Priest, over the house of God, *let us draw near* with a true heart in full assurance of faith" (Heb. 10:19–22). What a marvel of mercy, what a wonder of grace that poor fallen sinners, through faith in Christ's blood, may come into the presence of God without a fear! On the ground of Christ's infinite merits, such are *welcome* there. The presence of Christ on High is the proof that our sins have been put away, and in the joyous consciousness thereof we may approach God as worshippers.

But the special aspect in which our text sets forth Christ as "the altar" of His people, is to present Him as the One who furnishes them with that *spiritual meat* which is needed for nourishment and sustenance in their worship and service. The apostle had just said, "Be not carried about with divers and strange doctrines: for it is a good thing that the heart be established with *grace;* not with *meats,* which have not profited them that have been occupied therein" (v. 9), and when he now adds "we have an altar," his obvious meaning is: we have in Christ the true altar, which supplies us with "grace," that better food which really establishes the heart before God. In other words, the Holy Spirit here explains and declares the fulfilment of those words of Christ "My flesh is meat indeed, and My blood is drink indeed: he that eateth My flesh, and drinketh My blood, dwelleth in Me, and I in him" (John 6:55, 56).

Let us now consider our verse a little closer in the light of its immediate context: that there *is* an intimate connection between them is obvious, for in v. 9 the apostle had spoken of "meats" and here he still refers to "eating"! Of the one he had affirmed they "profited not," concerning the latter he mentions those who have "no right" thereto. Over against the "meats which profited not" he had set that "grace" which establishes the heart, and now he contrasts "the altar" from the defunct figures of Judaism. As we have shown in the preceding article, to have the heart "established with grace" signifies two things: first, to be weaned from self-righteousness and creature dependence as to clearly apprehend that salvation from start to finish is of the unmerited and unconditional favour of God; second, to have the Spirit so shine upon His work within that as we diligently examine the same and carefully compare it with the experience of saints as described in the Scriptures, we may be definitely assured that we are born of God.

Having affirmed the vast superiority of the heart being established with grace over being occupied with "meats"—which expression referred directly to the Mosaical distinctions between clean and unclean articles of diet, but in its wider signification was a part put for the whole ceremonial system—the apostle now declares that the Christian is provided with far more excellent food for the soul. The striking force of this is only apparent by a careful study of the Levitical types and by closely following the apostle's argument in the verses which immediately succeed our text. The Jewish altar had not only typed out Christ offering Himself as a sacrifice to God for the sins of His people, but it had also foreshadowed Him as *the life-sustenance* of the true worshippers of God. How remarkably full were the O. T. types, and how much we lose by ignoring the same and confining our reading to the N. T.—no wonder so much in Hebrews seems to be obscure and of little interest to the Gentile.

Of many of the offerings which were laid on the tabernacle altar only parts of them were consumed by the fire, the remaining portions being reserved *as food* for the priests, or for the offerer and his friends—this food being regarded as particularly sacred, and the eating of it as a great religious privilege. For instance, we read, "This is the law of the meal offering: the sons of Aaron shall offer it before the Lord, before the altar. And he shall take of it his handful, of the flour of the meal offering, and of the oil thereof, and all the frankincense which is upon the meal offering, and shall burn it upon the altar for a sweet savour, the memorial of it, unto the Lord. And *the remainder* thereof shall Aaron and his sons *eat*: with unleavened bread shall it be eaten in the holy place" (Lev. 6:14-16). "This is the law of the trespass offering: it is most holy . . . . Every male among the priests shall *eat* thereof . . . . And the flesh of the sacrifice of his peace offerings for thanksgiving shall be eaten the same day that it is offered" (Lev. 7:1, 6, 15). "And the Lord said unto Aaron, Behold, I also have given thee the charge of Mine heave offerings . . . In the most holy place shalt thou *eat* it: every male shall eat it; it shall be holy unto thee" (Num. 18:8-10).

But the Christian has spiritual food far more holy and precious than any Israelite ever had, or even Aaron the high priest was permitted to taste. *Christ* is our food, the "Bread of life" to our souls. He is not only our sacrifice but our sustenance; He has not only propitiated God, but He is the nourishment of His people. It is true that we should by faith, feed upon Him when remembering His death in the way appointed, yet there is no reference in our text to "the Lord's supper," nor is "the Lord's table" ever called an "altar" in Scripture. Moreover it is our blessed privilege to feed upon Christ not only at "Communion seasons," but constantly. And herein appears again the immeasurable superiority of Christianity over Judaism. Israel according to the flesh partook only of the symbols, whereas we have the Reality. They had only certain parts of the offerings—as it were the crumbs from God's table; whereas we feed with Him on the fatted calf itself. They ate of the sacrifices only occasionally, whereas Christ is our daily food.

"We have an altar," namely, Christ, and He is the only altar which *God owns,* and the only one which must be recognized by us. For almost nineteen centuries—since God employed the Romans to destroy Jerusalem— the Jews have been without an altar, and are so to this day. For Romanists to *invent* an altar, and make it both the foundation and centre of their entire idolatrous system, is the height of presumption, and a fearful insult to Christ and the sufficiency of His sacrifice. If those "which serve the tabernacle"—they who continued officiating at Jerusalem in the days when the apostle wrote this epistle—had "no right" to "eat" of the Christian's altar, that is, enjoy and derive benefit from the person and sacrifice of Christ, then, how much less have the pope and his satellites any title to the benefits of Christ while they so wickedly usurp His place and prerogative. That the Lord Jesus Himself *is* our "altar" as well as interceding High Priest also appears from, "Another angel (Christ as 'the Angel of the Covenant') came and stood at the altar, having a golden censer; and there was given unto Him much incense, that He should offer it with the prayers of all saints upon the golden altar which was before the throne" (Rev. 8:3)!

CHAPTER ONE HUNDRED FOURTEEN

Christ Our Sin Offering

(Heb. 13:11, 12)

In the verses at which we have now arrived the apostle once more sets before us the O.T. shadow and the N.T. substance, which emphasises the importance and necessity of *diligently comparing* one portion of the Scriptures with another, and particularly those sections which record those ordinances that God gave unto Israel wherein the person, office and work of His Son were so vividly, so blessedly, and so fully foreshadowed. The study of the types, when conducted soberly and reverently, yields a rich return. Its evidential value is of great worth, for it affords an unmistakable demonstration of the Divine authorship of the Scriptures, and when the Holy Spirit is pleased to reveal how that type and antitype fit in to each other more perfectly than hand and glove, then the hidden harmony of the different parts of the Word is unveiled to us: the minute analogies, the numerous points of agreement between the one and the other, make it manifest that one presiding Mind controlled the whole.

The comparing of type with antitype also brings out the wondrous *unity of the Scriptures,* showing that beneath incidental diversity there has ever been an essential oneness in God's dealings with His people. Nothing so convincingly exposes the principal error of the Dispensationalists than this particular branch of study. The immediate design and use of the types was to exhibit unto God's people under the old covenant those vital and fundamental elements of Truth which are common alike to all dispensations, but which have received their plainest discovery under the new covenant. By means of material symbols a fitting portrayal was made of things to come, suitably paving the way for their introduction. The ultimate spiritual realities appeared first only in prospect or existed but in embryo. Under the Levitical instructions God caused there to be shadowed forth in parabolic representation the whole work of redemption by means of a vivid appeal to the senses: "The law having a shadow of good things to come" (Heb. 10:1).

The passage just quoted warrants the assertion that a spiritual study of the O. T. types also affords a valuable *aid to the interpretation* of much in the N.T. Just as the *doctrine* expounded in the Epistles rests upon and is illustrated by the central *facts* recorded in the Gospels, so much in both Gospels and Epistles can only be fully appreciated in the light of the O. T. Scriptures. It is to be deplored that so many Christians find the second half of Exodus and the whole of Leviticus little more than a record of meaningless and effete ceremonial rites. If the preacher would take his "illustrations" of Gospel truths from the types, (instead of searching secular history for "suitable anecdotes"), he would not only honour the Scriptures, but stir up and direct the interest of his spiritual hearers in those portions of the Word now so generally neglected. *Christ* is set forth as conspicuously in Leviticus as He is in John's Gospel, for "in the volume of the Book" it is written of Him.

The pity is that many of the more sober-minded and spiritual among God's people have been prejudiced against the study of the types, and the valuable use of them in interpreting the N. T., by the untimely efforts of unqualified novices. The types were never designed by the Holy Spirit to provide a field in which young men might give free play to their imagination, or exercise their carnal ingenuity so as to bring out a mystical meaning to the most prosaic facts, and startle their unlearned hearers by giving to trifles a far-fetched significance. The wild allegorizings of Origen in the past should serve as a lasting warning. There are essential principles and fixed rules of interpreting the types which are never to be ignored. The interpreter must concentrate his attention upon central truths and basic principles, and not occupy his thoughts with petty agreements and fanciful analogies. The central and all-important subjects exemplified in the types are sin and salvation, the purifying of the soul, and the dedication of the heart and life to God.

Again; familiarity with the types and the spiritual principles they exemplify is a great help to *the right understanding of prophecy.* A type necessarily possesses something of a prophetical character, for it is a symbolical promise of the ultimate thing yet to appear, and hence it is not at all surprising that in announcing things to come the prophets, to a large extent, availed themselves of the characters and events of past history, making them the images of a nobler future. In the prospective delineations which are given us in Scripture respecting the final issues of Christ's kingdom among men, while the foundation of all lies in His own mediatorial office and work, yet it is through the personages and ordinances of the *old* covenant that things to come are shadowed forth. Thus, Moses spoke of the Messiah as a Prophet like unto himself (Deut. 18:18). David announced Him as Priest after the order of Melchizedek (Psa. 110), while Malachi predicted His forerunner under the name of Elijah (Mal. 3:1, 4:5). Herein are valuable hints for our guidance, and if they be duly observed there will be no more excuse for interpreting "the Son of David" (Matt. 1:1) in a carnal sense, than for literalizing the "we have an altar" of Heb. 13:10.

From what has been pointed out above on the manifold value of the types—which might be indefinitely amplified, especially the last point—it should be quite evident that they greatly err who look upon the types as a mere kindergarten, designed only for the infancy of the Church. The very fact that the Holy Spirit has preserved a record of them in the imperishable Word of Truth, is clear intimation that they possess far more than a local use and temporary purpose. The mind of God and the circumstances of the fallen creature are substantially the same in all ages, while the spiritual needs of the saints are the same now as they were four thousand years ago, and were the same then as they are to-day. If, then, the wisdom of God placed His people of old under a course of instruction through the types, it is our folly and loss if we despise the same to-day. A mathematician still has use for the elementary principles of arithmetic, as a trained musician scorns not the rudimentary scales.

The basic principles underlying the types were made use of by Christ at the dawn of the N.T. era, thus intimating that the fundamental methods employed by God are the same in all generations. Every miracle the Lord Jesus performed was *a type in history,* for on the outward and visible plane of Nature He displayed the Divine power and work which He came here to accomplish in the higher realm of Grace. In every act of healing men's bodily diseases, there was an adumbration to the eye of sense of that salvation which He would provide for the healing of the soul. In the demands which He made upon those whom He healed, a revelation was given of the principles by which His salvation may be procured by us. The *facts* of the Gospels are the key to the *truths* of the Epistles, and the types of the O.T. are the key to the facts of the Gospel. Thus, one part of Scripture is made dependent on the other, just as no member of our body is independent of its fellow-members.

"For the bodies of those beasts, whose blood is brought into the sanctuary by the high priest for sin, are burned without the camp. Wherefore Jesus also, that He might sanctify the people with His own blood, suffered without the gate" (vv. 11, 12). In these verses the apostle supplies a striking illustration and confirmation of what he had just previously affirmed. In the preceding verse he had declared that Christ is the altar of His people—the antitype of all that had been shadowed out by the typical altars of O.T. times —which, as we showed, signifies not only that Christ is their atoning sacrifice unto God, but that He is also the sustenance, the food, for His people. Then followed the solemn statement that those who stubbornly and unbelievingly continued to adhere unto Judaism, deprived themselves of the blessings enjoyed by Christians.

As we have so often pointed out, the Hebrew saints were being urged to return unto the Divinely-instituted religion of their fathers. In v. 9 the apostle presents to them two further dissausives. First, he assured them they now possess the Antitype of all the types of Judaism: why, then, be tempted by the shadows when they possessed the Substance! Second, he solemnly affirms that those who still clung to Judaism cut themselves off from the Christian privileges: they had "no right," no Divine title to "eat" or partake of them. The application of this principle to us to-day is obvious. The same two-fold argument should suffice to draw off *our* hearts from doting upon ritualistic rites and performances: possessing Christ as our great High Priest, having access to the Throne of Grace, such things as bowing to the east, elevating the offering (collection), candles, incense, pictures, images, are needless and worthless, and if the heart be set on them and a saving value be ascribed to them, they effectually exclude us from an interest in Christ's salvation.

In the preceding article we showed how strikingly and blessedly the O.T. types pointed to Christ as the nourishment of His people: only parts of the sacrifices were burnt upon the altar, other portions thereof being allotted to the priests or the offerer and his family. But there was a notable exception to this, unto which the apostle now directs our attention. "For the bodies of those beasts, whose blood is brought into the sanctuary by the high priest for sin, are burned without the camp." The reference is unto the sin offerings. These were slain on the altar in the outer court, but their blood was carried inside the tabernacle and sprinkled before or upon the throne of Jehovah, while their carcasses were utterly consumed outside the camp. This was, of course, while Israel were sojourners in the wilderness and lived in tents but the same order was observed after they entered Canaan and the temple was built in Jerusalem—the bodies of the sin offerings being carried out beyond the walls of the city to be consumed there.

The apostle was referring to such passages as Lev. 4:1-12, where provision was made for an atonement when a priest had unwittingly sinned against any of the commandments of the Lord. He was to bring a bullock unto the door of the tabernacle for a sin offering, lay his hand upon its head (as an act of identification, to denote that the doom awaiting *it* was what *he* deserved), and kill it before the Lord. Its blood was then to be brought into the tabernacle and sprinkled seven times before the Lord, before the veil of the sanctuary, and upon the horns of the incense altar, and the remainder thereof poured out at the base of the brazen altar. The richest portions of the animal were then burned upon the altar, but the remainder of it was carried forth "without the camp," and there utterly consumed by fire. The same order was followed when the whole congregation sinned through ignorance (Lev. 4:12-21), the account closing with "He shall carry forth the bullock *without* the camp, and burn him as he burned the first bullock: it is a sin offering." The reader may also compare Num. 19:3, 9.

But there is no doubt that the apostle was alluding more particularly unto the chief sin offering which was offered on the annual day of atonement, when propitiation was made for all the sins of Israel once a year, described at length in Lev. 16. Concerning the blood of this sacrifice we read, "And he (the high priest) shall take of the blood of the bullock and sprinkle it with his finger upon the mercyseat eastward, and before the mercyseat shall he sprinkle of the blood with his finger seven times" (v. 14). Regarding the bodies of those beasts used on this occasion we are told, "and the bullock for the sin offering, and the goat for the sin offering, whose blood was brought in to make atonement in the holy place, shall one carry forth without the camp: and they shall burn in the fire their skins and their flesh, and their dung" (v. 27). These passages, then, make it quite clear to which particular class of sacrifices the apostle was referring in Heb. 13:10, 11.

The question now arises, Wherein lies *the relevancy* of this allusion to these passages in Leviticus in our present text? What was the apostle's particular design in referring to the sin offerings? It was twofold. First, to substantiate his assertion that they who served the tabernacle had "no right to eat" of the Christian's altar —i.e., had no title to partake of the benefits of Christ, who has, as our next verse shows, died as a sin offering. There was a Divine prohibition which expressly forbade any feeding upon the same: "And no sin offering, whereof any of the blood is brought into the tabernacle of the congregation to reconcile withal in the holy place, shall be eaten: it shall be *burnt* in the fire" (Lev. 6:30). Those, then, who clung to Judaism were cut off from the Antitype's sin offering. Second, to exhibit the superiority of Christianity: those who trust in Christ *eat* His flesh and drink His blood (John 6:54-56).

But let us dwell for a moment on the spiritual significance of this particular detail in the type. It presents to us that feature in the sufferings of Christ which is the most solemn of all to contemplate, namely, His being made sin for His people and enduring the penal wrath of God. "Outside the camp" was the place where the *leper* was compelled to dwell (Lev. 13:46), it was the place where *criminals* were condemned and slain (Lev. 24:14 and cf. Josh. 7:25, 1 Kings 21:13, Acts 7:58), it was the place where the *defiled* were put (Num. 5:3), it was the place where *filth* was deposited (Deut. 23:12-14). And *that* was the place, dear Christian reader, that the incarnate Son, the Holy One of God, entered for you and for me! O the unspeakable humiliation when He suffered Himself to be "numbered with the transgressors" (Isa. 53:12). O the unutterable mystery of the Blessed One "being made a curse for us" (Gal. 3:13). O the unspeakable anguish when the sword of Divine justice smote Him (Zech. 13:7), and God forsook Him (Matt. 27:46).

Yet let it be emphatically insisted upon that Christ remained, personally and essentially, the *Untainted* One, even when the fearful load of the sins of His people was laid upon Him. This very point was carefully guarded by God — ever jealous of the honour of His son — in the types, yea, in the sin offerings themselves. First, the blood of the sin offering was carried within the sanctuary itself and sprinkled before the Lord (Lev. 4:6), which was *not* done with any other offering. Second, "the fat that covereth the inwards" of the animal was burned upon the altar (Lev. 4:8-10), yea, "for a sweet savour unto the Lord," intimating that God still beheld that in His Son with which He was well pleased even while He was bearing the sins of His people. Third, it was expressly enjoined that the carcase of the bullock should be carried forth "without the camp unto a *clean* place" (Lev. 4:12), signifying it was still *holy* unto the Lord, and *not* a polluted thing.

Christ was "as pure, as holy, and as precious in the sight of God whilst groaning under the infliction of damnatory wrath on the accursed tree, as when He was in the bosom of the Father before all worlds — the very same moment in which He was 'bruised' and 'made a curse' for us, being also that in which He offered Himself for us 'an offering and a sacrifice to God for a sweet-smelling savour.' Never was the character of Jesus exhibited in more transcendent excellency; never were His relations to God and to man maintained in greater perfectness than during the time that He suffered for us on the Tree. Never did the Father more delight in and appreciate the excellency of the Son of His love; never did the Son more love and honour and delight in the Father than when He uttered that bitter cry 'My God, My God, why hast Thou forsaken Me?' The very circumstances which placed Jesus, outwardly, in the extreme of distance from Heaven and from God, only proved that there was an essential nearness — an everlasting moral nearness, which not even the fact of His being the Bearer of damnatory wrath could for one moment alter" (B. W. Newton).

The *immediate* reason why none of the Israelites, not even the high priest, was allowed to *eat* any portion of the sin offering, and why its carcase was burnt outside the camp rather than upon the altar, seems to lie in the distinctive nature and special design of this offering. Had the priest eaten of any portion thereof, *that* had given it the character of a peace offering, and had the whole been consumed upon the altar it had too closely resembled the burnt offering. But, as we have pointed out before, the *ultimate* reason and deeper design was to denote that Judaism had to be abandoned before one could "eat" or derive benefit from the Christian's "altar." Herein lies the superiority of Christianity, that *we are permitted* to feed upon a Sacrifice of the highest and holiest kind, receiving therefrom those blessings and benefits which Christ has procured for His people by the shedding of His precious blood.

The apostle, then, has furnished clear proof of what he had asserted in vv. 9, 10, and that from the O.T. Scriptures themselves. There he had said, "it is good that the heart be established with grace," which means for the mind to have such a fixed persuasion of the Truth as to enjoy peace with God, without which there can be no real and solid tranquillity. Then the apostle had said, "Not with meats, which have *not profited* them that have been occupied therein," which must be understood in the light of the previous clause: the ceremonial distinctions of the Levitical law were altogether inadequate for justification and peace with God. Moreover, that sacrifice which made atonement for *sin* provided *no food* for those who offered it, and the heart cannot be established before God where sins are not remitted.

"Wherefore Jesus also, that He might sanctify the people with His own blood, suffered without the gate." Here is the Christian's altar, here is the all-sufficient sacrifice offered once for all upon it, and here is the blessed effect thereof, his sanctification. The opening "wherefore" of this verse called for the line of thought developed in the opening paragraphs of this article. It intimated that it was for the express purpose of meeting the requirements of the O.T. types that the Lord Jesus was "lead as a lamb to the slaughter" and suffered the horrible ignominy of being cast out of the holy city and put to death in the place where the worst of criminals were executed. What honour did the Substance now place upon the shadows! A wide field of study is here suggested to us, and a reverent and patient survey of it will well repay our efforts.

How frequently in the four Gospels has the Holy Spirit assigned as the reason for what Christ did "that the Scriptures might be fulfilled." That expression is *not* to be restricted to Christ's design in accomplishing the terms of Messianic *prophecy* — though, of course, that is included — for it also and often has reference to His so acting in order that *the types* which foreshadowed Him might be realized. The will of God concerning the Mediator had been intimated in the legal institutions, for in them a prefiguration was made of what Christ should do and suffer, and His perfect obedience to the Father moved Him unto a compliance therewith. Consequently, the fuller be our knowledge of the types, the more shall we be able to understand the recorded details of our Saviour's earthly life (particularly of His last week), and the more can we appreciate the motive which actuated Him — complete subjection to the will of the One who had sent Him. That particular which the Holy Spirit notes in our text is but one illustration from many, if we take the trouble to search them out.

"The complete answering and fulfilling of all types in the person and office of Christ, testifieth the sameness and *immutability* of the counsel of God in the whole work of the redemption and salvation of the Church, notwithstanding all the outward changes that have been in the institutions of Divine worship" (John Owen). But it did something else too: it left the unbelieving Jews *without excuse*: Christ's implicit compliance with the types, His complete and perfect production of all that had been foreshadowed of Him, furnished the most indubitable demonstration that He was the promised Messiah, and therefore His rejection by the Nation at large sealed their doom, and was the reason why, a little later, God destroyed their sanctuary, city, and heritage.

"Wherefore Jesus also, that He might sanctify the people with His own blood, suffered without the gate." Christ Himself is the all-sufficient sin-offering of His people. Just as all the iniquities, transgressions and sins of natural Israel were, in a figure, transferred to the typical offering (Lev. 16:21), so all the iniquities, transgressions and sins of the spiritual Israel were imputed to their Surety (Isa. 53:6, 7, 11, 12). Just as the goat bearing the iniquities of natural Israel was sent away "into a land not inhabited" (Lev. 16:22), so "as far as the east is from the west, so far hath Christ removed our transgression from us" (Psa. 103:12). And just as "on that day shall the priest make an atonement for you, to cleanse you, that ye may be *clean from all your sins* before the Lord" (Lev. 16:30), so "The blood of Jesus Christ God's Son *cleanseth us from all sin* (1 John 1:7).

Observe that in strict keeping with the fact that the Redeemer is here contemplated as the antitypical Sin-offering, He is referred to simply as "Jesus," and *not* "Jesus Christ" as in vv. 8, 21, still less "our Lord Jesus" as in v. 20. He is not alluded to in these different ways at random, nor for the mere purpose of variation. Not so does the Holy Spirit order *His* speech: there is nothing haphazard in His language. The various designations accorded the Saviour in the Word are selected with Divine propriety, and nothing affords a more striking evidence of the *verbal* inspiration of the Scriptures than the unerring precision with which they are used. "Jesus" is His *personal* name as man (Matt. 1:21); "Christ" is His *official* title, as the One anointed of God (Matt. 16:16, 20); while "The Lord Jesus" points to His exalted *status and authority* (John 13:13, Acts 2:36). When "Jesus" is used alone, it is either for the special purpose of identification (as in Acts 1:11), or to emphasize the infinite depths of humiliation into which the Son of God descended.

"Wherefore (in fulfilment of the types which had defined the path He should tread), Jesus also (the Antitype, the Just who had entered the place of the unjust, the infinitely Glorious One who had descended into such unfathomable depths of degradation), that He might sanctify the people with His own blood, *suffered* without the gate." This was the particular feature made most prominent in the type, for the sin-offering was not only slain, and its carcase taken outside the camp, but there is was *utterly consumed.* It spoke of Christ as the Sin-bearer enduring the fiery indignation of a sin-hating God, suffering His penal wrath. It spoke of Christ offering Himself to God as a sacrifice for the sins of His people, to make atonement for them, for His blood was shed, and *blood* was never employed under the types except to make atonement (Lev. 17:11). It is, then, by the voluntary and vicarious blood-shedding of their Covenant-head, and by that alone, believers are sanctified.

"That He might sanctify *the people.*" Ponder carefully, my reader, the definiteness of the language here used. Scripture knows nothing of a vague, general, undeterminable and futile shedding of the precious blood of the Lamb. No indeed: it had a predestined, specific, and invincible end in view. That blood was *not* shed for the whole human race at large (a considerable portion of which was already in Hell when Christ died!), but for "the people," each of whom are sanctified by it. It was for "the *sheep*" He laid down His life (John 10:11). It was to gather together in one "the *children of God* that were scattered abroad" that He was slain (John 11:51, 52). It was for "His *friends*" He endured the cross (John 15:13). It was for *the Church* He gave Himself (Eph. 5:25).

CHAPTER ONE HUNDRED FIFTEEN

Outside the Camp

(Heb. 13:12, 13)

Were it not so pathetic and tragic, it would be most amusing if we could obtain and read a complete record of the manner in which our text has been employed by various individuals and groups during the last four hundred years — to go no farther back. The reader would thereby be supplied with a striking illustration of the fact that "There is no new thing under the sun" (Eccl. 1:9) and see how frequently history repeats itself. He would learn too how easily simple souls were beguiled by a plausible tongue and how successfully Satan deceives the unwary by the very letter of Scripture. He would discover how the different *divisive movements* in the ecclesiastical realm — whether in Poland, Germany, Great Britain, or the U.S.A. — all started in much the same way, followed the same course, and, we might add, met with a similar disappointing sequel. To be forewarned is to be forearmed: it is because the rank and file of the people do so little reading, and are so ignorant of religious history, that they so readily fall a prey to those with high spiritual pretensions.

Hebrews 13:13 has ever been a great favourite with those who started "Come out" movements. It has been used, or rather misused, again and again by ambitious Diotrephes, who desired to head some new party or cause. It has been made a sop for the conscience by many a little group of discontented and disgruntled souls, who because of some grievance (fancied or real) against their religious leaders, church, or denomination, forsook them, and set up an independent banner of their own. It is a verse which has been called into the service of all separatists, who urged all whose confidence they could gain to turn away from — not the secular world, but — their fellow-Christians, on the ground of trifling differences. That which these men urged their dupes to forsake was denounced as the God-abandoned and apostate "Camp," while the criticism they have (often *justly*) met with for their pharisaic conduct, has been smugly interpreted as "bearing Christ's reproach."

In his most interesting and instructive work, "The Laws of Ecclesiastical Polity" — a standard work which long found a place in all well-furnished libraries — Richard Hooker, three hundred years ago, described the tactics followed by the Separatist leaders who preceded or were contemporaneous with him. We will give here a very brief digest of the same. First, in seeking to win the people's attention unto their "cause," these would-be Separatists, loudly proclaimed the faults and failings of those in high places, magnifying and reproving the same with much severity, and thereby obtaining the reputation of great faithfulness, spiritual discernment, love of holiness. Second, those faults and corruptions which have their roots in human frailty, are attributed to an unscriptural and evil ecclesiastical government, whereby they are regarded as possessing much wisdom in determining the cause of those sins they denounce: whereas in reality, the very failures they decry will adhere to *any* form of government which may be established.

Third, having thus obtained such sway in the hearts of their hearers, these men now propose *their own* form of church government (or whatever else they are pleased to designate their scheme or system), declaring with a great blowing of trumpets that it is the only sovereign *remedy* for the evils which poor Christendom is groaning under, embellishing the same with an ear-tickling name or designation. Fourth, they now "interpret" (?) the Scriptures in such a way that everything in them is made to favour their discipline, and discredit the contrary. Fifth, then they seek to persuade the credulous that *they* have been favoured with a special illumination of the Spirit, whereby they are able to discern these things in the Word, while others reading it perceive them not. Sixth, assured that they are led by the Spirit "This hath bred high terms of separation between such and the rest of the world, whereby the one sort are termed, The brethren, The godly, and so forth; the other, worldlings, time-servers, pleasers of men not of God" (Hooker, Vol. 1, p. 106).

Finally, the deceived are now easily drawn to become ardent propagators of their new tenets, zealous proselytisers, seeking to persuade others to leave the apostate "Camp" and join them on "the *true* scriptural ground." "Let any man of contrary opinion open his mouth to persuade them, and they close their ears: his reasons they weigh not, all is answered with 'We are of God, He that knoweth God heareth us' (1 John 4:6), as for the rest, ye are of the world" (Hooker). Such was the policy pursued by the "Fifth Monarchy men," the "Brownists," Thos. Cartwright and his following in the sixteenth and seventeenth centuries. Such too was the course taken by John Kelly in Ireland, Alex. Campbell in Kentucky, more than a century ago — the latter founding "the Christian Church," denouncing all others as unscriptural. So that Mr. J. N. Darby followed a well-trodden path!

"Let us go forth therefore unto Him without the camp, bearing His reproach." After mentioning the Christian's altar and the suffering and offering of Christ thereon, the apostle now draws an exhortation unto that duty which is the basis of our whole Christian profession. There are five things in this brief text which call for prayerful consideration. First, the exact force of its "therefore"— requiring us to ascertain the relation of our text to its setting. Second, what is signified here by "the camp," both as it concerned the Hebrews and as it respects us to-day. Third, in what sense we are to go forth from it. Fourth, how in so doing we go unto Christ. Fifth, by what means this duty is to be discharged.

"Let us go forth *therefore* unto Him without the camp." The duty which is here enjoined on the believer is drawn from what had just been declared: "Wherefore Jesus also, that He might sanctify the people with His own blood, suffered without the gate" (v. 12). There were one or two points in that verse which we reserved for consideration in this article. First, with regard to the meaning of "sanctify." We cannot agree with those commentators (among them some for whom we have a high regard) that would here restrict it to "expiate:" we see no reason for this narrowing of its force. Personally, we consider the term has as wide a signification here as elsewhere in Scripture: by His perfect oblation Christ has *separated* His people from the world, *purified* them from all their iniquities, *consecrated* them to God, so that they stand before Him in all the *acceptableness* of their Head.

Many words have a wider scope in Scripture than in ordinary usage, and the expositor needs to be constantly on his guard against narrowing the meaning of important terms. It is blessedly true that at the cross the believer's Surety expiated all his sins, that is, cancelled their guilt, by making reparation to the Law; but it is *the effects of that* which are here in view. The sanctification of His people was the grand object which Christ had in view in becoming incarnate, and that He steadily pursued throughout the whole of His life and sufferings. The Church is now cleansed, set apart, and adorned by His atoning sacrifice. Christ sustained all the transgressions of His people, made atonement for them, removed the same from before God, and washed them from all defilement by His soul travail, bloody sweat, and death; and in consequence, they now stand before the Eye of infinite justice and holiness as everlastingly righteous, and pure.

Herein we may behold once more the outstanding excellency of Christianity above Judaism — something which we must ever be on the lookout for if we are not to miss the principal design of the Spirit in this epistle. These verses abound in details which exhibit the privileges of the new covenant as far surpassing those of the old. First, we have that "establishing of the heart" before God (v. 9) which the natural Israel possessed not. Second, we have "an altar" furnishing the highest and holiest sacrifice of all (v. 10), which they had no right or title to partake of: *their* sin offerings were *burned,* not eaten (v. 11). Third, we have an effectual and abiding sanctification of our souls before God, whereas they had a sanctification which was but external and evanescent "to the (ceremonial) purifying of the flesh" (Heb. 9:13). Fourth, Jesus has sanctified the people "with *His own* blood" (v. 12), which was something that the high priests of Judaism could never do — they offered to God the blood of others, even that of animals.

A further word now on the fact that the Saviour "suffered without the gate," that is, outside of the city of Jerusalem which answered to the camp in the wilderness, wherein the tabernacle was first set up. Sundry things were represented thereby. First, this signified that He was not only a sacrfice for sin, but was being punished for sins, dealt with as a malefactor and dying that death which by Divine institution was a sign of the curse (Gal. 3:13). "They took Jesus, and led Him away. And He bearing His cross went forth (out of Jerusalem) into a place called the place of a skull, which is called in the Hebrew Golgotha: where they crucified Him, and two with Him" (John 19:16-18). This was done by the malice of the Jews, yet their wickedness was "by the determinate counsel and foreknowledge of God" (Acts 2:23), so that it might appear Christ is *the true sin-offering.* Thus, God made the hatred of Satan and his agents to subserve His purpose and accomplish His own will — how the knowledge of this should *comfort* us when the wicked are plotting against us!

Second, in ordaining that His Son should be put to death outside the city of Jerusalem, symbolic intimation was thereby given by God to the Jews that He had *put an end to all sacrificing in the temple,* so far as their acceptance by Him was concerned: now that Christ Himself was laid on the altar, there was no longer any need for those offerings which prefigured Him. The shadow and the substance could not stand together: for the Levitical sacrifices to be continued after Christ's death would denote either that He had *not come,* or that His offering was *not sufficient* to obtain salvation. Third, Christ's going forth out of Jerusalem signified *the end of the church-state of the Jews,* and therefore as He left the city, He announced their destruction: see Luke 23:28-30. Very solemn was this: Christ was no longer "in the Church" of the Jews (Acts 7:38), their house was now left unto them desolate (Matt. 23:38). If, then, a Jew desired to partake of the benefits of the Messiah, he too must leave the camp — the whole temple system.

What a depth and breadth of meaning there is to every action of our blessed Redeemer! what important truths they illustrated and exemplified! How much we lose by failing to meditate upon the details of our Lord's passion! In addition to what had been pointed out above, we may observe, fourth, that Christ's offering Himself as a sin offering to God outside Jerusalem, clearly shows that His sacrifice and its benefits *were not confined* to the elect among the Jews, but extended equally unto the chosen remnant from the Gentiles. It was, then, yet another sign that "the middle wall of partition" was now broken down, that the barrier which had for so long existed between Judaism and the world no more existed. As 1 John 2:2 declared, "He is the propitiation for our sins: and not for ours only, but also for the sins of the whole world" — for an exposition of which see our booklet on "The Atonement."

Thus, the force of the "therefore" in our text is not difficult to determine: because Jesus Himself "suffered without the gate, let us go forth therefore unto Him without the camp, bearing His reproach." But to make it still more simple for the reader to comprehend, let us divide the "therefore" into its component parts. First and more generally, because Christ has left us an example, let us follow His steps. Second, since we partake of the food of our altar, let us use the strength therefrom in a way pleasing and glorifying to Christ. Third and more specifically, if the Son of God was willing to suffer the ignominy of being cast out of Jerusalem in order to bear our doom, surely it would ill-become the sons of God if they were unwilling to go forth and bear His reproach! Fourth, if Christ in obedience to God took the place of being scorned and hated by men, shall we in disobedience to Him seek to be esteemed and flattered by His enemies? Fifth, because Christ has "sanctified" us, let us *evidence* our separation from the ungodly.

"Let us go forth therefore unto Him without the camp, bearing His reproach." The second thing requiring our careful consideration here is what is meant by "the camp." "The apostle, in all this epistle, hath respect unto the original institution of the Jewish church-state and worship in the wilderness. Therefore he confines his discourse to the tabernacle and the services of it, without any mention of the temple or the city wherein it was built, though all that he speaks be equally applicable unto them. Now the camp in the wilderness was that space of ground which was taken up by the tents of the people, as they were regularly pitched about the tabernacle. Out of this compass the bodies of the beasts for the sin-offerings were carried and burned. Hereunto afterwards answered the city of Jerusalem, as is evident in this place; for whereas in the foregoing verse, Christ is said to suffer 'without the gate,' here He is said to be 'without the camp': these being all one and the same as to the purpose of the apostle" (John Owen).

"The camp" of Israel, then, and later the city of Jerusalem, was the seat and centre of the political and religious life of the Jewish church. To be in "the camp" was to have a right unto all the advantages and privileges of the commonwealth of Israel (Eph. 2:12) and the Divine service of the tabernacle. For to forfeit that right, for any cause, for a season, meant that the offender was taken *out of* the camp: Lev. 14:3; 24:14; Num. 5:2; 12:15. Now it was in that camp that Christ had been "despised and rejected" by the Nation. It was concerning that camp He had solemnly declared, "your house is left unto you desolate" (Matt. 23:38). It was from that camp He had suffered Himself to be conducted, when He went forth to the Cross. Thus, at the time our epistle was written, "the camp" signified an apostate Judaism, which would have none of Christ, which *hated and anathematised* Him; and, in consequence, it was the place *abandoned by God,* given up by Him to destruction — for a generation later it ceased to be, even in a material and outward way.

But Judaism as such has long since passed away, what, then, is *its present counterpart?* The question should not be difficult to decide, though it meets with varied answers. Some say "the camp" is Romanism, and call attention to the many striking points of analogy between it and Judaism. Some say it is "the dead and carnal professing church" — from which, of course, *their* denomination is an exception. Others insist that it is "all the man-made sects and systems of Christendom," from which they have withdrawn, only to set up another system of their own, even more pharisaical than those they denounce. But a single consideration is sufficient to dispose of all such vagaries — which have, in the past, misled the writer. Is *Christ Himself* hated and anathematised by either Rome or the deadest and most erroneous portions of Protestantism? The answer is, NO. We must turn to *other* scriptures (like Rev. 18:4 and 2 Tim. 3:5) to learn God's will for us concerning Romanism or the carnal sects, for Heb. 13:13 cannot be fairly applied to either of them. The very name of Christ was abhorred by Judaism, it is *not so* by either Rome or degenerate Protestantism.

Let us not be misunderstood at this point. We are *not* here expressing our views on *the whole subject* of the Christian's separation from what is dishonouring to Christ, nor are we holding a brief for the Papacy and her daughters. Admittedly Christendom is in a far worse state to-day than it was a century ago, and there is very much going on in it with which the follower of the Lord Jesus should have *no* fellowship; but that is a totally different thing from withdrawing from a company where there are many of God's people and where all the fundamentals of the Truth were faithfully proclaimed — think of denouncing Spurgeon's Tabernacle as a part of "Babylon," and refusing to allow those to "break bread" who occasionally attended its services! No; our present object is to define what "the camp" of Heb. 13:13 actually signifies, and then to show how erroneously that term has been applied to something radically different.

As we have said above "the camp" was that degenerate Judaism which had hounded the Lord of glory to death, and which could not be appeased by anything less than putting Him to death as a base malefactor and blasphemer. It is readily conceded that not only may numerous points of analogy be drawn between Judaism and Romanism, but that large sections of degenerate Protestantism now have many things in common with it. But it was *not* its law, its priesthood, its ceremonialism, nor even its corruptions which caused God to give up Jerusalem unto destruction. The "camp" from which the apostle bade his readers "go forth" was a Judaism which had not only rejected Jesus as the Christ of God, denied that He was risen from the dead, but which also insisted that He was a vile impostor, and *reviled His very name*. But so far as we are aware, there is not a single church or company upon earth that professes to be "Christian" of whom *that* can be said!

The fact is, there is nothing upon earth to-day which exactly duplicates the Judaistic "camp" of the apostle's time. Yet there *is* that which essentially corresponds to it, even though externally it differs somewhat therefrom; and that is *the world*—the secular and profane world. Concerning it we read, "the whole world lieth in the Wicked one" (1 John 5:19). Those who comprise it are unregenerate, unholy, ungodly. It is true that one of the effects of Christianity has been to cast a veneer of morality and religious respectability over large sections of the world; though that veneer is now getting very thin. It is true that in some circles of it, it is still fashionable to feign *respect* for Divine things, yet, if the exacting claims of God be pressed upon them, it soon becomes apparent that the carnal mind is enmity against Him. But for the most part, Christ is openly *hated* by the masses, and His name fearfully blasphemed by them. And there it is that we are plainly told, "the friendship of the world is enmity with God: whosoever therefore will be a friend of the world is the enemy of God" (James 4:4).

Our next consideration is, *In what sense* is the Christian to "go forth" from the camp, i.e., from that which is avowedly and actively hostile to Christ? This question needs to be carefully considered, for here too the language of our text has been sadly wrested. Let us bring the point to a definite issue: is it a corporeal or a mental act which is here enjoined? is it by the body or the soul that the duty is performed? is it by our feet or our hearts that obedience is rendered? In other words, is it a "literal" or a metaphorical forsaking of the world which God requires from us? Those who made the serious mistake of supposing that it is the former, have betaken themselves to monasteries and convents. The explanatory and qualifying words of the apostle "for then (if separation from the wicked were to be taken absolutely) must ye needs go out of the world" (1 Cor. 5:10) shows the error of this; contrary also would it be to the spirit of the Lord's prayer, "I pray *not* that Thou shouldest take them out of the world" (John 17:15).

Let us consider the case of the Jews in the apostle's time. When one of them savingly believed on the Lord Jesus Christ was he required to "literally" or physically get out of Jerusalem? No indeed: even the apostles themselves continued to abide there (Acts 8:1)! It was *not* a *local* departure which was intended—though a little later that *was* necessary if their lives were to be preserved (Luke 21:30-32); rather was it a *moral and religious* going forth from the camp. "There was nothing that these Hebrews did more value and more tenaciously adhere unto, than that political and religious interest in the commonwealth of Israel. They could not understand how all the glorious privileges granted of old unto that church and people, should so cease as that they ought to forsake them. Hereon most of them continued in their unbelief of the Gospel, many would have mixed the doctrine of it with their old ceremonies, and the best of them found no small difficulty in their renunciation. But the apostle shows them, that by the suffering of Christ without the gate or camp, this they *were* called unto" (John Owen).

The application of this principle unto us to-day is not difficult to perceive. It may be stated thus: God requires us to forego and renounce all advantages and privileges—whether social, financial, political, or religious—*which are inconsistent with* an interest in Christ, communion with Him, or fidelity to His cause. An illustration of this is furnished in Phil. 3:4-10: those things which Saul of Tarsus had formerly counted gain—his Jewish birth and orthodoxy, his pharisaic strictness and righteousness, his persecution of the Church—he now "counted loss for Christ." The same thing obtains now in heathendom: when a Parsee, Buddhist, Mohammedan (or a Jew, or a Romanist) is truly converted, he has to turn his back upon, relinquish those things which he had hitherto most highly venerated. Love to Christ moves him to now hate those things which are directly opposed to Him.

Now for the fourth point in our text: by going forth from the camp we go "unto Him," or, conversely, by going forth unto Christ we go outside the camp. The two things are inseparable: they are convertible terms. We cannot go *unto,* without going *from,* and we cannot go "from" without going "unto." This is exactly what conversion is: a turning round, a right-about face. It is the heart turning from Satan to God, from sin to holiness, from things below to things above, from "the camp" unto Christ. That which is opposed to the Lord Jesus is renounced for His sake. The world is left, and He is followed. Self-righteousness is dropped that an hand may lay hold of His atoning sacrifice. To "go forth unto Him" is to betake ourselves to Christ in His office as the Prophet, Priest, and King of His Church, and thereby find acceptance with God. It is to cleave unto and own Him under the contempt and opposition of those who despise and reject Him.

To go forth unto Christ without the camp, then, signifies for us to be so enlightened by the Spirit as for the eyes of our understanding to see Him as the promised Messiah, the only Mediator between God and men; to behold the One whom the Jews and Gentiles condemned to a malefactor's death, as the all-sufficient Saviour. It is for the heart to be attracted by the supernal excellencies of His person, to be won by Him, the soul perceiving Him to be "the Fairest of ten thousand." It is for the will to be brought into subjection of Him, so that His yoke is gladly accepted and His sceptre readily submitted to. In a word, it is to heartily approve of Him whom the world still hates, becoming His humble follower, His willing disciple, and gladly enduring for His sake all the ridicule and persecution which fidelity to Him and His cause entails. Like the Gadarenes of old, the professing world now says to Him "Depart out of our coasts" (Mark 5:17), but those who go forth unto Him exclaim, "my Beloved is mine, and I am His" (Song of Sol. 2:16).

CHAPTER ONE HUNDRED SIXTEEN

Outside the Camp

(Heb. 13:13, 14)

In the preceding article we endeavoured to make clear to the reader exactly what was "the camp" from which the apostle exhorted the Hebrews to go forth. The more accurately a term be defined, the less likelihood of its being wrongly employed. It was at this point the present writer failed in an article which appeared in an issue nearly ten years ago—many a sound sermon has been marred by heading it with the wrong text. Dwelling upon many of the incidental analogies which exist between much that now obtains in Christendom and that which marked Judaism of old, we failed to concentrate upon that which was essential and fundamental, and hence, made a wrong application of this particular term "the camp." That which made the Judaism of Paul's day to differ so radically from its worst state in the times of the prophets, was, that it had hated, rejected, and murdered the incarnate Son of God.

It is *that* particular point, the Jews' casting out of Christ, anathematising Him, condemning Him to a malefactor's death, which must guide us when seeking to identify the modern counterpart of that "camp." There is, really, no exact replica on earth to-day of that Judaism which crucified the Lord Jesus: certainly neither Romanism—blasphemous and horrible as are many of its dogmas and practices—nor the most degenerate branches of Protestantism —rotten as some of them are in doctrine and works—can rightly be designated the present-day "camp." No, as we pointed out previously, that which most closely resembles it, that which in principle is essentially like thereto, is the secular, profane *world*. Its unregenerate and ungodly members do not profess to love Christ: the very mention of Him is hateful to them: they desire to banish Him entirely from their schemes and thoughts— except when they take His holy name in vain.

Next, we sought to show *in what sense* the Lord requires His people to go forth "outside the camp," that is, separate themselves from the ungodly, from those who hate and revile Christ. This, as we saw, is not to be understood "literally" or physically, but metaphorically or morally. It is not a local withdrawal from the world, but a religious and spiritual one. In other words, God does not bid His people be fanatics and lead the lives of hermits. Taking refuge in monasteries and convents is the Devil's perversion of this important practical truth. No; the Christian is still left *in* the world, but he must not be *of* it. Its policy and maxims must not regulate him, its pleasures and attractions must not capture his heart, its friendship must not be sought; its politics are no concern of his. In heart and soul-interests he is a stranger here, and is to conduct himself as a pilgrim passing through this scene—"using this world, but not abusing it" (1 Cor. 7:31).

Then we pointed out that in going *forth* from the camp the Christian goes *unto* Christ: it is the twofoldness of act which the word "conversion" connotes. Yet it is not without reason that the Holy Spirit has worded our text as it is: there is a particular emphasis in it which requires to be noted. It is not, "Let us go forth therefore without the camp unto Him," but "*unto* Him without the camp." The difference is something more than verbal. It stresses the fact that *Christ Himself* must be the grand object before the heart, and then the poor baubles of this world will not possess much attraction for us. If He is not, then, though we may become aesthetes, there will be no contentment, still less joy: our case would be like that of many of the Israelites who had "gone forth" from Egypt, yet continued to lust after its fleshpots.

To go forth unto Christ without the camp means for the believer to make a complete break from his former manner of life, to renounce every thing which is opposed to Christ, to relinquish whatever would hinder communion with Him. In a word, the exhortation of our text is only another way of presenting that declaration of our Lord, "If any man will come after me, let him deny himself, and take up his cross, and follow Me" (Matt. 16:24). Sin must be mortified, the flesh with its affections and lusts crucified, the world forsaken, and the example which Christ has left us diligently followed. So, then, going forth unto Him outside the camp is not a single act, done once for all at conversion, but an *habitual* thing, a constant attitude of life. The cross must be taken up by the Christian "daily:" Luke 9:23.

Obedience to this injunction involves "bearing Christ's reproach." The believer is called unto fellowship with Christ: fellowship now with His sufferings (Phil. 3:10), in the future with His glory. That "reproach" assumes different forms and has various degrees in different locations and periods, according as God is pleased to restrain the enmity of the wicked against His people. But in every age and in every place it has been verified that "all that will live godly in Christ Jesus shall suffer *persecution*" (2 Tim. 3:12). That "persecution," that "reproach" of Christ may be cruel afflictions such as the early Christians experienced; or it may take the milder form of sneers, ridicule, and ostracism, which sensitive souls feel keenly. As Christ declared, "The servant is not greater than his Lord. If they have persecuted Me, they will also persecute you" (John 15:20). One reason why God permits this, is because His people are so prone to flirt with the world, and if we will not separate from them, He often causes them to give us the cold shoulder and oppose us.

The flesh shrinks from and desires to escape such opposition. It is natural for us to want to be well thought of and nicely treated by every one. But let the shrinking Christian call to mind what his Master endured for his sake. In the types, the sin-offering was burned without the camp—far off from the holy of holies where Jehovah had His seat—to represent the sinner's final separation from God, his being cast into "the outer darkness," there to suffer the vengeance of eternal fire. And Christ endured the equivalent of *that* on the cross, during those three hours of awful darkness. He bore the fearful load of His people's sins, and was deprived of the comforts of God's presence. For Christ it meant entering the place of distance from God, but for *us* to "go forth without the camp" means going "unto Him"; for Him it entailed enduring the curse, for us it involves nought but Divine blessing! Then let us cleave to Him despite the world's scorn, and stand by His cause on earth no matter what the cost to us.

But let us now consider by what means this duty of going forth unto Christ is discharged. As we pointed out in the preceding article, it is an act of *the soul* rather than of the body which is here in view. But to particularize. First, the soul of the believer goes forth to Christ *by prayer,* for real prayer is the breathing of the heart after Him and turning unto Him. Its first cry is "Lord, save me, I perish." There is the daily request for Him to make Himself more real to the heart, to grant us closer communion with Himself, and to remove those things which hinder the same. There is the asking Him to teach us how to draw from His fulness, to make us more obedient, to conform us more fully to His holy image. "Let Him kiss me with the kisses of His mouth: for Thy love is better than wine" (Song of Sol. 1:2) is the language of one whose heart is "going forth unto Christ outside the camp"—seeking from Him that which is infinitely superior to the best this poor world affords.

Second, it is the motion *of faith.* Christ is the grand Object of faith, and He can only be known and enjoyed now by faith. It was so at our first conversion; it is so throughout the entire Christian course. "The life which I now live in the flesh," said the apostle, "I live *by the faith* of the Son of God (faith in Him), who loved me, and gave Himself for me" (Gal. 2:20). When faith is inactive, there is no going forth of the soul unto Christ, no real prayer, no communion with Him. But when faith is operative the heart turns unto Him as instinctively as the needle of the compass does unto the north. When faith is sickly and listless the things of this world gain power over us: either its pleasures attract, or its cares distract us. But when faith is healthy and vigorous, the soul "mounts up with wings as eagles" and "runs and is not weary." It is *faith* which makes Christ real and precious to the soul. Then let us be more diligent in guarding against those things which weaken and quench it.

Third, going forth unto Christ outside the camp is *the act of hope.* This is the particular spiritual grace which keeps the heart of the believer from falling into abject despair. There are times when he is sorely tried and dismayed: sin rages within, the accusations of the holy Law sting his conscience, and Satan tries hard to make him believe that all is lost—that having abused his privileges, sinned against much light, turned Divine grace into lasciviousness, there is no remedy. So it seems to the cast-down soul: pray he cannot, and as he reads the Scriptures, instead of finding comfort every page condemns him. Then the Spirit applies some promise, and a little encouragement follows: but conscience still smites, and he groans. Now it is that *hope* acts: Christ had mercy on the leper, the publican, the dying thief; He is full of compassion, I will cast myself afresh on His pity. So too hope looks beyond this scene—with all its disappointments, sorrows, and sufferings—and anticipates the time when we shall be "forever with the Lord."

Fourth, going forth unto Christ without the camp is also *the work of love.* The love of God which the Spirit sheds abroad in the hearts of the regenerate is something more than beautiful sentiment: it is an operative principle. Love yearns for the company of the beloved: it cannot find satisfaction elsewhere. Christ is not to be met with in worldly circles, and therefore when the heart of the believer is in a healthy state, it seeks unto its Beloved outside the same. A word from *His* lips, a smile from *His* face, an embrace from *His* arms, is prized above rubies. To sit at His feet and drink from the fountain of His love, is better than heaps of silver and gold. Christ is precious to those whose sins have been removed by His blood, and their affections "go forth" unto Him—not so fervently and frequently as they should, or as they desire; nevertheless, there are seasons in the life of *every* Christian when he is permitted to lean his head upon the Saviour's bosom. Christ's love to His own attracts their love to Him.

Fifth, going forth unto Christ outside the camp is *the surrender of the will to Him*. There is a change of masters: service to the prince of this world is renounced, and the Lordship of Christ accepted. There is an enlisting under His banner, a putting on of His uniform, a submission to His captaincy, and we act according to His will. How different is all of this from what many suppose our text signifies! One may identify himself with those who claim to have gone forth from "all the man-made sects and systems," and yet the heart be quite dead toward God. Or, one may belong to the most orthodox church, subscribe to its doctrines, adopt their language, echo its groans, and have not a spark of grace in the heart. One may separate from all the world's politics, pastimes and pleasures, and have no love for Christ. There must be the exercise of faith, the stirrings of hope, the actings of love, the surrender of the will, and walking in the path of obedience, in order to meet the terms of our text.

"For here have we no continuing city, but we seek one to come" (v. 14). Four questions are suggested by these words: what is their relation to the preceding verse? what is signified by "no continuing *city*"? what is the "one to come" that we seek? how or in what way do we seek it? That there is a close connection between v. 14 and the previous one is obvious from its opening word. Now that connection is twofold: first, v. 14 supplies two further reasons to enforce the duty specified in v. 13—additional to those implied in vv. 10-12; second, v. 14 may also be regarded as explaining and amplifying the language of v. 13.

The connection of v. 14 with v. 13 will be more apparent as we turn to the second question and consider what is signified by "For here have we no continuing city." Obviously, the "city" is used here metaphorically, as a figure of that which is strong and stable: it is that which provides refuge and rest to the great majority of earth's inhabitants. "Change and decay in all around I see" said the poet: there is nothing lasting, durable, dependable in this world. In Gen. 4:17 we read that Cain "builded a city," and where is it?—destroyed thousands of years ago by the Flood. Thebes, Nineveh, Babylon were all powerful and imposing cities in their day, but where are they now? they no longer exist, yea, their very site is disputed. Such is this world, my reader: "the fashion of this world *passeth away*" (1 Cor. 7:31), and one day "the earth also and the works that are therein shall be *burned up*" (2 Pet. 3:10).

The things of this earth are transitory: that which the natural man values so highly, and sells his soul to obtain, soon vanishes away. All that is mundane is unstable and uncertain: *that* is the meaning, in brief, of "here have we no continuing city." There is however an emphasis in these words which we must not miss: it is *not* simply "here *there is* no continuing city" but "here *have we*" none—something which can be predicated of none but believers. True, the worldling has none in reality, but in his imagination, his plans, his affections, he has—he sets his heart upon the things of this world and acts as though he would enjoy them always: "Their inward thought is, that their houses shall continue forever, and their dwelling-places to all generations: they call their lands after their own names" (Psa. 49:11). And how is the instability of everything mundane to affect and influence the Christian? Thus: he is to renounce them in his heart—leave "the camp"—*that* is the connection with v. 13.

"For here have we no continuing city" (v. 14). "A city is the centre of men's interests and privileges, the residence and seat of their conversation. Hereby are they freed from the condition of strangers and pilgrims; and have all that rest and security in this world they are capable. For those who have no higher aims nor ends than this world, a city is their all. Now it is not said of believers absolutely that they belonged to no city, had none that was theirs in common with other men; for our apostle himself pleaded that he was a citizen of no mean city. This is intimated, as we shall see, in the restriction of the assertion: a *continuing* city. But it is spoken on other accounts" (J. Owen). What those "other accounts" are we shall see presently, meanwhile we will consider the more general meaning.

In His providential dealings with them, God often gives His people painful reminders of the fact that "here have we no continuing city." We are prone to be at ease in Zion, to fix our hearts on things below, to settle down in this world. We like to feel that we are anchored for a while at least, and make our plans accordingly. But God blows upon our schemes and compels us to take up the stakes of our tents, saying, "Arise ye, and depart; for *this* is not your rest; because it is polluted" (Micah 2:10). A significant word on this is found in, "As an eagle *stirreth up her nest,* fluttereth over her young, spreadeth abroad her wings, taketh them, beareth them on her wings; *so* the Lord alone did lead him" (Deut. 32:11, 12). Ah, my reader, it is not a pleasant experience to have our earthly "nest" stirred up, to have our rest disturbed, and be obliged to change our abode; but as that is essential if the eaglets are to be taught to use their wings, so it is necessary for the Christian if he is to live as a stranger and pilgrim in this scene.

God has called His people unto fellowship with Christ, and that means something more than participating in His life and receiving His peace and joy: it also involves entering into His experiences—enduring the wrath of God alone excepted. "When He putteth forth His own sheep, He goeth *before* them, and the sheep *follow* Him" (John 10:4). That denotes two things: that we are not called to tread any path which He did not Himself traverse, and that we are to experience something of His sorrows: "Ye are they which have continued with Me in My temptations" or "trials" (Luke 22:28). Now what was Christ's experience in this world? Even as a child He had no rest here: His parents had to carry Him down into Egypt in order to escape the malice of Herod. Trace the record of His earthly ministry, and how long do we find Him abiding in one place? He was constantly on the move. "Jesus therefore being *wearied with His journey* sat thus on the well" (John 4:6), and in some form or other His people are required to drink from that same cup. If the Lord of glory "had not where to lay His head" when in this world, shall we deem it strange that God so often disturbs our rest?

But let us now consider the more specific meaning of our text. First, the Christian has no city on earth which is the centre of Divine worship, whereunto it is confined, as had been the case with Judaism. Herein the apostle points another contrast. After the Israelites had wandered for many years in the wilderness, they were brought to rest in Canaan, where Jerusalem became their grand centre, and of that city the Jews had for long boasted. But it was not to continue, for within ten years of the writing of this epistle, that city was destroyed. How this verse gives the lie to the pretentions of Rome! No, the Christian has something far better than an insecure and non-continuing city on earth, even the Father's House, with its many mansions, eternal in the heavens!

Second, the believer has no city on earth which supplies him with those things which are his ultimate aim: deliverance from all his enemies, an end to all his trials, an eternal resting-place. His "commonwealth" or "citizenship" is "in Heaven" (Phil. 3:20 R.V.). The Christian does not regard this world as his fixed abode or final home. This is what gives point to the preceding exhortation and explains the force of the opening "For" in v. 14. The fact that everything here is unstable and uncertain should spur the Christian to go forth from the camp—in his heart renounce the world. And further, it should make him willing to "bear the reproach of Christ," even though that involves being driven from his birthplace and compelled to wander about without any fixed residence on earth. Finally, it gives point, as we shall see, to the last clause of our text.

"But we seek one to come" (v. 14). In view of what has been before us, it is quite clear that the "one," the City, that we seek, is Heaven itself, various aspects of which are suggested by the figure here used of it. It is an abiding, heavenly, everlasting "City," which the believer seeks, and the same is referred to again and again in this epistle—in contrast from the temporal and transitory nature of Judaism—under various terms and figures. This "City" is the same as the "better and enduring substance" in Heaven of 10:34. It is that "Heavenly Country" of 11:16. It is "the City of the living God" of 12:22, the seat and centre of Divine worship. It is the same as "those things which cannot be shaken" of 12:27. It is "the Kingdom which cannot be moved," in its final form, of 12:28. It is the "Inheritance incorruptible and undefiled, and that fadeth not away, reserved in Heaven for us" (1 Pet. 1:4).

An earlier reference to this grand object of the believer's desire and quest was before us in "he looked for a City which hath foundations, whose Builder and Maker is God" (11:10). Those "foundations" are, first, the everlasting good-will and pleasure of God toward His people, which is the basis of all His dealings with them. Second, God's foreordination, whereby He predestined His elect unto eternal glory, concerning which we are told "The foundation of God standeth sure, having this seal: The Lord knoweth them that are His" (2 Tim. 2:19). Third, the Everlasting Covenant of free, rich, and sovereign Grace, which God entered into with the Head and Surety of the elect, and which is "ordered in all things and sure." Fourth, the infinite merits and purchase of Christ, for "other foundation can no man lay than that is laid, which is Jesus Christ" (1 Cor. 3:11). Fifth, the whole being confirmed by and resting upon the immutable stability of God's promise and oath: Heb. 6:17-20.

In addition to the few brief remarks we made upon the signification of this figure of the "City" when expounding 11:10, we may note the following—bearing in mind those characteristics of a "city" which specially obtained in ancient times. First, a city was a place of safety and security: "let us go to Jerusalem for fear of the army of the Chaldeans, and for fear of the army of the Syrians: so we dwell at Jerusalem" (Jer. 35:11). In Heaven there will be no wicked men to persecute, no Devil to tempt. Second, a city is compact, being the concentration of numerous houses and homes. So of Heaven Christ declared that in it are "many mansions." There will dwell together forever the myriads of holy angels and the entire

Church of God. Third, in a city is stored all manner of provisions and needful commodities; so in Heaven there is nothing lacking to minister unto the delights of its inhabitants.

Finally, as a "city" on earth is the centre of the world's interests and privileges, the resting-place of travellers and those who go abroad, so Heaven will be the grand Terminal to the wanderings and journeyings of the Christian. His pilgrimage is ended, for Home is reached. On earth he was a stranger and sojourner, but now he has reached the Father's House. There he will meet with no hardships, encounter none to whom he is a hated foreigner, and no longer have to earn his daily bread by the sweat of his brow. Unbroken rest, perfect freedom, unassailable security, congenial society, inconceivable delights, are now his portion forever. Faith then gives place to sight, hope to fruition, grace is swallowed up in glory, and we are "forever with the Lord," beholding His glory, bathing in the ocean of His love.

How the anticipation of this should make us set our affection on things above, spur us on to run the race before us, cause us to drop every weight which hinders us in running! How the consideration and contemplation of that "City" should work powerfully in us to look and long, and prepare us for the same! This brings us to ponder for a moment the meaning of "but we *seek* one to come." This, of course, does not signify that the believer is searching after that which is unknown, but endeavouring to obtain it. It is the treading of that Narrow Way which leads to Heaven, and that with diligence and desire, which is hereby denoted. "And God hath prepared a city of rest for us, so it is our duty continually to endeavour the attainment of it, in the ways of His appointment. The main business of believers in this world is diligently to seek after the attainments of eternal rest with God, and this is the character whereby they may be known" (John Owen).

Here, then, is the *use* which the believer makes of the uncertainty and instability of everything in this world: his heart is fixed on the Home above, and to get safely there is his great concern. The word "seek" in our text is a very strong one: it is used in, "after all these things (the material necessities of this life) do the Gentiles seek" (Matt. 6:32)—i.e., seek with concentrated purpose, earnest effort, untiring zeal. The same word is also rendered "labour" in Heb. 4:11: the Christian deems no task too arduous, no sacrifice too much, no loss too great, if he may but "*win* Christ" (Phil. 3:8). He knows that Heaven will richly compensate him for all the toils and troubles of the journey which lead thither. "Him that overcometh will I make a pillar in the temple of My God, and he shall go no more out" (Rev. 3:12).

CHAPTER ONE HUNDRED SEVENTEEN

The Christian's Sacrifices

(Heb. 13:15, 16)

The verses which are now to engage our attention are closely related with those which immediately precede, as is intimated by the "therefore." The links of connection may be set forth thus. First, "We have an Altar" (v. 10); what *use* are we to make of it? the answer is, offer sacrifice thereon. Second, Jesus has sanctified His people "with His own blood" (v. 12). What is to be their *response?* the answer is, draw night to God as joyous worshippers. Third, we must go forth unto Christ "without the camp." What then, is to be our *attitude* towards those who despise and reject Him? The answer is, not one of malice, but benevolence, doing good unto all as we have opportunity and occasion. Such, in brief, is the relation between our present portion and its context.

Calvin suggested, we believe rightly, that the apostle here anticipated an objection which might have been made against what he had previously advanced. In saying that Jesus "suffered without the gate" (v. 11), plain intimation was given that God had done with, abondoned Judaism as such. In bidding Hebrew believers to go forth unto Christ "without the camp," the Holy Spirit signified they must now turn their backs upon the temple and its service. But this presented a serious difficulty: all the sacrifices— those of thanksgiving as well as those of expiation—were inseparably connected with the temple system, therefore it followed that if the temple was to be deserted, the sacrifices also must have ceased. It was to meet this difficulty, and to make known the superior privileges of Christianity, that the apostle penned our text.

If the Christian was debarred from offering any sacrifice to God, then he would occupy an inferior position and be deprived of a privilege which the Jews of old enjoyed, for sacrifices were instituted for the purpose of *celebrating God's worship.* The apostle therefore shows that another kind of sacrifice remains for us to offer, which is no less pleasing to God than those which He appointed of old, even the praise of our lips. Here we are taught what is the legitimate way of worshipping God under the new covenant, which presents another striking contrast from that which obtained under the old. As our "Altar" is not one of wood or stone, brass or gold, but Christ Himself, so our "sacrifices" are not the fruits of the ground or the firstlings of our herds, but the adoration of our hearts and the devotion of our lives. The contrast, then, is between the outward and ceremonial and the inward and spiritual.

The Jews offered to God a slain lamb each morning and evening, and on certain special days bullocks and rams; but the Christian is to present unto God a *continual* sacrifice of thanksgiving. This brings before us a most interesting and blessed subject, namely, those sacrifices of the Christian with which God is well pleased. The first of these was mentioned by David: "The sacrifices of God are a broken spirit, *a broken and a contrite heart,* O God, Thou wilt not despise" (Psa. 51:17). "When the heart mourns for sins God is better pleased than when the bullock bleeds beneath the axe. 'A broken heart' is an expression implying deep sorrow, embittering the very life; it carries in it the idea of all but killing anguish in that region which is so vital as to be the very source of life. A heart crushed is, to God, a fragrant heart. Men condemn those who are contemptible in their own eyes, but the Lord seeth not as man seeth. He despises what man esteems, and values that which they despise. Never yet has God spurned a lowly, weeping penitent" (C. H. Spurgeon).

John Owen pointed out that there were two things in connection with the O.T. sacrifices: the *slaying* and shedding of the blood of the beast, and then the actual *offering* of it upon the altar. Both of these were required in order to the completing of a sacrifice. On the one hand, the mere killing of the animal was no sacrifice unless its blood was placed upon the altar; and on the other hand, no blood could be presented there to God until it had been actually shed. Corresponding to these, there is a twofold spiritual sacrifice in connection with the Christian profession. The first is what has just been made reference to in the paragraph above: the broken heart and contrite spirit of the believer. That signifies evangelical repentance and mortification, or the crucifixion of the flesh, which is the Christian's first sacrifice, answering to the death of the beast before the altar.

The second sacrifice which the believer presents unto God is his offering of *Christ* each day. This is done by an act of *faith*—which is ever preceded by repentance, just as we must feel ourselves to be desperately sick before we send for the physician. As the awakened sinner is convicted of sin and mourns for it before God, pride and self-righteousness are subdued, and he is able to appreciate the

Lamb of God which taketh away the sin of the (elect) world. Christ appears to him as exactly suited to his case and need. He perceives that He was wounded for his transgressions and bruised for his iniquities. He perceives that Christ took his place and endured the penal wrath of God on his behalf. Therefore does he now lay hold of him by faith and present the atoning sacrifice of Christ to God as the only ground of his acceptance. And as he begins, so he continues. A daily sense of defilement leads to a daily pleading of Christ's blood before the throne of grace. There is first the *appropriating* of Christ, and then the *presenting* of Him to God as the basis of acceptance.

Now it is this laying hold of Christ and the offering of Him to God in the arms of faith which corresponds to the second thing in connection with the tabernacle (and temple) sacrifices of old. As the fire fell upon the oblation placed upon the altar, incense was mingled therewith, so that the whole yielded a "sweet savour unto God." Just as the mere slaying of the animal was not sufficient—its blood must be laid upon the altar and fragrant incense be offered therewith; so the Christian's sacrifice of a broken and contrite heart will not by itself secure the favour of God. Essential as repentance is, it cannot purchase anything from God. The broken heart must lay hold of Christ, exercise faith in His blood (Rom. 3:25), and *plead His merits before God.* Only then will our sacrifice of a contrite spirit be a "sweet smelling savour" unto Him.

The third sacrifice which the Christian presents unto God is *himself.* "I beseech you therefore, brethren, by the mercies of God, that ye present your bodies a living sacrifice, holy, acceptable unto God, which is your reasonable service" (Rom. 12:1). That is an act of *consecration.* It is the recognition and acknowledgement that I am no longer my own, that I have been bought with a price, that I am the purchased property of Another. Hence, of the primitive saints we read that they "first gave their own selves to the Lord" (2 Cor. 8:5), surrendering themselves to His sceptre, taking upon themselves His yoke, henceforth to live to His glory; that as they had formerly served sin and pleased self, now they would serve God and seek only His honour. As Christ gave Himself for us, we now give ourselves back again to Him. Hereby alone can we know that we are saved: not only by believing in Christ for the forgiveness of sins, but by yielding ourselves up to His government, as living sacrifices for His use.

The fourth sacrifice of the Christian is that mentioned in our text, namely, "the fruit of our lips"; but before taking up the same let us say a few words on *the order* of what has now been before us. There can be no acceptable sacrifice of praise until we have offered ourselves unto God as those that are alive from the dead, for as Psa. 115:17 declares, "The *dead* praise not the Lord." No, those who are yet in their sins cannot praise God, for they have no love for Him and no delight in Him. The heart must first be made right before it is attuned to make melody unto Him. God accepts not the lip service of those whose hearts are estranged from Him. Of old He complained "This people draw near Me with their mouth, and with their lips do honour Me, but have removed their heart far from Me" (Isa. 29:13), and as Christ affirmed *"in vain* do they worship" Him (Matt. 15:8). Such hypocrisy is hateful to Him.

Nor can any man present himself acceptably to God until he has *believingly embraced Christ.* No matter how willing I am to live honestly in the future, satisfaction must be made for the debts contracted in the past; and nothing but the atoning work of Christ can satisfy the just demands which the Law has against us. Again; how can I serve in the King's presence unless I be suitably attired? and nothing short of the robe of righteousness which Christ purchased for His people can gratify God's holy eye. Again; how could God Himself accept from me service which is utterly unworthy of His notice and that is constantly defiled by the corrupt nature still within me, unless it were presented in the meritorious name of the Mediator and cleansed by His precious blood. We must, then, accept *Christ's* sacrifice before God will accept *ours;* God's rejection of Cain's offering is clear proof thereof.

Equally evident is it, yet not so clearly perceived to-day by a defectively-visioned Christendom, that no sinner can really accept Christ's sacrifice until his heart be broken by a felt sense of his grievous offences against a gracious God, and until his spirit be truly contrite before Him. The heart must be emptied of sin before there is room for the Saviour. The heart must renounce this evil world before a holy Christ will occupy it. It is a moral impossibility for one who is still in love with his lusts and the willing servant of the Devil to appropriate Christ and present Him to God for his acceptance. Thus, the order of the Christian's sacrifices is unchanging. First, we bow in the dust before God in the spirit of genuine repentance; then we appropriate Christ as His gracious provision, and present Him to God for the obtaining of His favour. Then we yield ourselves to Him unreservedly as His purchased property; and then we render praise and thanksgiving for His amazing grace toward us.

"By Him therefore let us offer the sacrifice of praise to God continually, that is, the fruit of our lips giving thanks to His name" (v. 15). This is *an exhortation to duty,* by way of inference from what was declared concerning the Redeemer and the sanctification of the people by His sufferings. Therein we are shown what use we are to make of our Altar, namely, offer sacrifice. The worship which the Christian presents unto God is the sacrifice of praise. Nothing is more pleasing unto Him, and nothing is more honouring to Him, than the praise of a renewed heart. Has He not declared, "Whoso offereth praise *glorifieth Me*"? (Psa. 50:23). How thankful for that statement should those believers be who feel themselves to be poor and feeble. Had God said, whoso shall create a world, or even whoso shall preach wonderful sermons and be a successful winner of souls, or whoso shall give a huge sum of money to missions, they might well despair. But "whoso offereth praise" opens a wide door of entrance to every believer.

And have not the redeemed abundant cause *for* praising God! First, because He has granted them a vital and experimental knowledge of *Himself*. How the excellencies of God's being, character and attributes, thrill, as well as awe, the souls of the saints! Glance for a moment at Psa. 145, which is entitled a "Psalm of Praise." David begins with "I will extol Thee, my God, O King; and I will bless Thy name for ever and ever. Every day will I bless Thee, and I will praise Thy name for ever and ever. Great is the Lord, and greatly to be praised" (vv. 1-3). In the verses that follow, one perfection of God after another passes in review and stirs the soul to adoration. His "mighty acts" (v. 4), the "glorious honour of His majesty" (v. 5), His "greatness" (v. 6), His "great goodness" and "righteousness" (v. 7), His "fulness of compassion" and "great mercy" (v. 8), His "power" (v. 11), the "glorious majesty of His kingdom" (v. 12), His everlasting "dominion" (v. 13), His providential blessings (vv. 14-17), His dealings in grace with His own (vv. 18, 19), His preserving them (v. 20). No wonder the Psalmist closed with, "my mouth shall speak the praise of the Lord, and let all flesh bless His holy name for ever and ever."

If the Psalms be full of suitable petitions for us to present unto God in prayer, and if they contain language well fitted for the lips of the sobbing penitent, yet they also abound in expressions of gladsome worship. "Sing praises to God, sing praises; sing praises unto our King, sing praises. For God is the King of all the earth: sing ye praises with understanding" (Psa. 47:6, 7). What vehemency of soul is expressed there! Four times over in one verse the Psalmist called upon himself (and us) to render praise unto the Lord, and not merely to utter it, but to "*sing*" the same out of an overflowing heart. In another place the note of praise is carried to yet a higher pitch: "Be glad in the Lord, and rejoice ye righteous; and *shout for joy,* all ye that are upright in heart" (Psa. 32:11). Not in any formal and perfunctory manner is the great God to be praised, but heartily, joyously, merrily. "Sing forth the honour of His name: make His praise glorious" (Psa. 66:2). Then let us offer Him nothing less than glorious praise.

The "therefore" of our text intimates an additional reason why we should praise God: because of *Christ* and His so great *salvation.* For our sakes the Beloved of the Father took upon Him the form of a servant, and was made under the Law. For our sakes the Lord of glory entered into unfathomable depths of shame and humiliation, so that He cried "I am a worm and no man" (Psa. 22:6). For our sakes He bowed His back to the cruel smiter and offered His blessed face to those who plucked off the hair. For our sakes He entered into conflict with the Prince of Darkness, and the pains of death. For our sakes He endured the awful curse of the Law, and for three hours was forsaken by God. No Christian reader can reverently contemplate such mysteries and marvels without being stirred to the depths of his soul. And then, as he seeks to contemplate what the shame and sufferings of Christ have secured for him, "Thanks be unto God for His unspeakable Gift," must be the fervent exclamation of his heart.

And observe well, dear reader, how God has allotted to Christ the position of chief honour in connection with our subject. "*By Him* (the One mentioned in vv. 12, 13) let us offer the sacrifice of praise to God." As the Lord Jesus Himself declared, "I am the Way, the Truth, and the Life: no man cometh unto the Father but by Me" (John 14:6). The saints can no more draw nigh unto God apart from Christ, than the sinner can: we are as dependent upon His mediation to render our *worship* acceptable to God, as we were at first for obtaining the *forgiveness* of our sins. As our great High Priest Christ is the "Minister of the Sanctuary" (Heb. 8:2). He meets us, as it were, at the door of the heavenly temple, and we place our spiritual sacrifices in His hands, that He may, in the sweet fragrance of His merits and perfections, present them for God's acceptance. "Another Angel came and stood at the altar, having a golden censer; and there was given unto Him much incense, that He should *offer it with* the prayers of all saints" (Rev. 8:3).

At every point God has made us dependent upon Christ, the Mediator. Only *by Him* can we offer acceptable sacrifices unto God. First, because it is through Christ's bloodshedding, and that alone, that our *persons* have been sanctified, or made acceptable to God—note how in Gen. 4:4 Jehovah had respect first to Abel himself, and then to his offering! Second, because it is through Christ's atonement, and that alone, that a new and living *way* has been opened for us into God's presence: see Heb. 10:19-21. Third, because He bears "the iniquity of our *holy things*" (fulfilling the type in Ex. 28:38), that is, through His perfect oblation our imperfect offerings are received by God: His merits and intercession cancel their defects. Fourth, because as the Head of the Church, He ministers before God on behalf of its members, *presenting their worship* before Him. Thus, "By Him" signifies, under His guidance, through His mediation, and by our pleading His merits for acceptance with God.

What has just been before us supplies further proof of what was pointed out in an earlier paragraph, namely, that it is impossible for the *unregenerate to worship God acceptably.* "The sacrifice of the wicked is an abomination to the Lord" (Prov. 15:8). And why? Not only because he is utterly sinful in himself, but because there is no Mediator to come between him and God. This is brought out strikingly in the O. T. types. Not a single "song" is recorded in the book of Genesis. In Eden our first parents were fitted to sing unto their Creator, and join the angels in ascribing glory and thanksgiving to the Lord. But after the Fall, sinners could only praise on the ground of *redeeming grace,* and it is not until Exodus is reached that we have the grand type of *redemption.* That book opens with Israel in Egypt, groaning and crying in the house of bondage. Next, the paschal lamb was slain, Egypt was left behind, the Red Sea was crossed, and on its farther shore they looked back and saw all their enemies drowned: *"Then* sang Moses and the children of Israel" (Ex. 15:1). Praise, then, is on the ground of redemption.

"By Him therefore let us *offer* the sacrifice of praise." Every word of Holy Writ is inspired of God, and throughout, its language is chosen with Divine discrimination. Therefore it behooves us to carefully *weigh* each of its terms, or we shall miss their finer shades of meaning. Here is a case in point: it is not "let us *render* praise unto God," but "let us *offer* a sacrifice of praise." Christ has made His people "kings and priests unto God" (Rev. 1:6), and here they are called upon to exercise their priestly functions. Thus we are instructed to make a right use of our "Altar" (v. 10). We are not only partakers of its privileges, but we are to discharge its duties, by bringing our sacrifices thereto. The same aspect of truth is seen again in 1 Pet. 2:5, where we read that believers are "an holy priesthood, to offer up spiritual sacrifices, acceptable to God *by Jesus Christ."* Yes, offered "unto God" and not to angels or saints; and, acceptable "by Jesus Christ," and not the Virgin Mary!

This particular expression "let us *offer a sacrifice* of praise to God" not only emphasises the fact that in their worship believers act in priestly capacity, but it also signifies that we now have the *substance* of what was shadowed forth by the Levitical rites. It also denotes that the Christian ought to be as particular and diligent in the discharge of his evangelical duties as the Jew was in the performing of his ceremonial obligations. As *he* was required to bring an offering that was without physical defect, *so we* must bring to God the very best that our hearts can supply: "Bless the Lord, O my soul, and *all* that is within me, bless His holy name." Content not thyself with offering to God a few formal utterances of thanksgiving, still less hurry through thy worship as a task you are glad to get finished; but strive after reality, fervency, and joy in the same.

When the worshipping Israelite approached the tabernacle or temple, he did not come empty-handed, but brought with him a thank-offering. Then "let *us* offer the sacrifice of praise to God." When the saints come together for public worship, it should be not only for the object of having their empty vessels filled and their hungry souls fed, but with the definite purpose of *offering to God* that which will please Him. The more closely we walk with God, and the more intimate be our communion with Him, the easier the performance of this pleasant duty. The more we delight ourselves in the Lord and regale our souls by the contemplation of His perfections, the more spontaneous, fervent, and constant, will be our worship of Him. The more we cultivate the habit of seeing God's hand in everything, and are grateful to Him for temporal blessings, the more will the spirit of thanksgiving possess our hearts and find expression in songs of praise.

This sacrifice of praise is here designated "the fruit of our lips," which is a quotation from Hos. 14:2, where backsliding Israel vows that in return for God's receiving them graciously, they will render to Him "the calves of their lips" — the Hebrew word for "calves" being the same as for "praise." The expression "fruit of our lips" may at first strike us as strange, but a little reflection will reveal its propriety. Isa. 6:5, 6 serves to open its meaning. By nature our "lips" are unclean: "Their throat is an open sepulchre, with their tongues they have used deceit, the poison of asps is under their lips; whose mouth is full of cursing and bitterness" (Rom. 3:13, 14). But by God's applying to us the virtues of Christ's atonement, our lips are *cleansed*, and should henceforth be used in praising Him. "Fruit" is a living thing: the product of the Holy Spirit. When, through backsliding, the heart has cooled toward God and the music of joy has been silenced, cry unto Him "O Lord, *open* Thou my lips, and my mouth shall show forth Thy praise" (Psa. 51:15).

This "sacrifice of praise" is to be offered unto God not merely on the Sabbath, but *"continually."* Have we not more cause to praise God than to pray? Surely, for we have many things to thank Him for, which we never ask for. Who ever prayed for His election, for godly parents, for their care of us in helpless infancy, for their affection, for their faithfulness in training us the way we should go! Does not God daily heap upon us in favours beyond that we are able to ask or think? Therefore we should be more in praising God than in petitioning Him. *"With thanksgiving* let your requests be made known unto God" (Phil. 4:6): ah, is it not our failure in the former which explains why we are so often denied in the latter? "Continue in prayer, and watch in the same with thanksgiving" (Col. 4:2); "with thanksgiving" is as much a command as is the "continue in prayer."

"It is a good thing to give thanks unto the Lord, and to sing praises unto Thy name, O most High" (Psa. 92:1). Yes, it is not only glorifying to God, but it is beneficial to the soul, To cultivate the habit of praising God will preserve the believer from many evils. The trials of life are more cheerfully borne if the spirit of thankfulness to God be kept lively in the heart. A man cannot be miserable while he is joyful, and nothing promotes joy so much as a heart constantly exercised in praising God. The apostles forgot their smarting backs in the Philippian dungeon as they "sang praise unto God" (Acts 16:25). The happiest soul we have ever met was a sister in a London garret (before the days of old-age pensions), who had neither eaten meat or fruit nor had a glass of milk for years past, but was continually praising the Lord.

Mary was offering to God a sacrifice of praise when she exclaimed "My soul doth magnify the Lord, and my spirit hath rejoiced in God my Saviour" (Luke 1:46, 47). That was no mechanical act, but the spontaneous outburst of a heart delighting itself in the Lord. It is not enough that the believer should *feel* adoring emotions in his soul: they must be expressed by his mouth—that is one reason why the sacrifice of praise is defined in our text as "the fruit of our *lips.*" Vocal, articulated praise, is what becomes those who have received the gift of speech: that is why the saints of all ages have expressed their worship in holy songs and psalms. None of us sing as much as we should—how often the worldling shames us! Then let us say with David "I will praise Thee, O Lord, with my whole heart; I will show forth all Thy marvelous works. I will be glad and rejoice in Thee: I will sing praise to Thy name, O Thou Most High" (Psa. 9:1, 2).

CHAPTER ONE HUNDRED EIGHTEEN

The Christian's Sacrifices

(Heb. 13:15, 16)

From the eighth verse onwards (of Heb. 13) the apostle is engaged in setting forth those spiritual duties of worship of which God Himself is the Object. Therein a series of contrasts are drawn between what obtained under the old covenant and that which pertains to the new. The Christian's privileges greatly excel those which belonged to Judaism as such. These superior blessings have been considered by us as we have passed from verse to verse. What is before us in v. 15 supplies a further exemplification of this general principle. The Levitical rites required God's earthly people to provide material offerings: but the Christian's "sacrifices" are entirely *spiritual* in their character. The Israelitish worshipper could not offer his sacrifices to God directly, but had to allow the priests to officiate for him: whereas Christians have themselves been made priests unto God, and therefore may sacrifice to Him *immediately*. The praise-sacrifices under the Law were only presented at particular times and places (cf. the "Feasts" of Lev. 23): but the Christian may, through Christ, offer a sacrifice to God anywhere, at any time—"continually."

"By Him therefore let us offer the sacrifice of praise to God continually, that is, the fruit of our lips giving thanks to His name" (v. 15). More is implied than is expressed. The language of this verse is restricted to the duties of worship and our oral praising of God therein, yet we know full well that He accepts not thanksgiving from us unless it be accompanied by what good old Matthew Henry called "thanksgiving." Thus it is the *entire compass* of evangelical obedience to God which is comprehended here. Those who have been dedicated to Him by the blood of Christ are under the deepest obligations to please and honour Him. The nature of Gospel obedience consists in thanksgivings for Christ and grace by Him, and therefore the whole of it may be suitably designated "a sacrifice of praise." Gratitude and adoration are the animating principles of all acceptable service. Every act and duty of faith has in it the nature of a sacrifice to God, wherein He is well-pleased.

John Owen suggests a threefold reason for the particular language in which the Christian's duty of obedience is here expressed. "1st. The great obligation that is upon us of continual thankfulness and praise to God on account of Christ's atonement. The sum and glory of our Christian profession, is, that it is the only way of praising and glorifying God for His love and grace in the person and mediation of Christ. 2nd. This obligation to praise succeeding in the room of all terrifying legal constraints to obedience, alters the nature of that obedience from what was required under and by the Law. 3rd. Where the heart is not prepared for and disposed to this fundamental duty of praising God for the death and oblation of Christ, no other duty or act of obedience is accepted with God."

In bidding us offer the sacrifice of praise to God *continually,* two things are denoted: freedom from the limitations of time and place as were appointed under Judaism, and diligent perseverance and constancy therein. To abound in fervent praise unto God is the abiding duty of the Christian. But for that there must be the regular exercise of *faith.* Calling into question the promises of God quenches the spirit of worship; doubts snap the strings of our harps; unbelief is the deadly enemy of praise. To praise God continually requires us to be in *daily communion* with Him. It is not to be wondered at that the joy of many believers is so sickly, when we consider how little fellowship they have with the Lord: if there be so little heat around the bulb of their thermometer, how can the mercury rise higher! To praise God "continually" we must cultivate perpetual gratitude, and surely *that* should not be difficult!

"I will bless the Lord at *all* times; His praise shall continually be in my mouth" (Psa. 34:1): at no lower standard than that must we aim. How this meets the lament made by so many Christians. "There seems so very little I can do to express my gratitude unto the Lord." Ah, my brother, you may not be gifted with talents to exercise in public, you may not have much money to give to God's cause, but what is to withhold your offering unto Him a sacrifice of praise, and that "continually"! Is not this God's due? Did Spurgeon express it too strongly when he said, "Praise is the rent which God requires for the use of His mercies." Then shall we rob God? Shall we withhold that in which He delights? Does not God give us abundant cause to praise Him "continually"!

"To show forth Thy loving kindness in the morning, and Thy faithfulness *every* night" (Psa. 92:2). "I will sing unto the Lord as long as I live; I will sing praise to my God while I have my being" (Psa. 104:33). What a word is that for the aged and infirm

Christian! Ah, dear reader, your eyes may have become so dim that you can scarcely read the Sacred page any more, your strength may have become too feeble for you to walk to the house of prayer, but your *lips* can still articulate and express thanksgiving! "I will be glad and rejoice in Thy *mercy*: for Thou hast considered my trouble" (Psa. 31:7): rejoice in His pardoning mercy, preserving mercy, providing mercy. "Who can utter the mighty acts of the Lord? who can show forth all His praise?" (Psa. 106:2). Well did Goodwin close his reflections upon the Psalms of praise by saying, "My brother, let us *pray for* such a heart as this, that the saints of the O. T. may not shame us who are Christians under the New."

It is striking to note that the Hebrew word "bara" signifies "to create," while "barak" means "to praise," intimating that the praising of God is the chief end of our creation. Though nothing can be added to God's essential glory, yet praise promotes His manifestative glory, for it exalts Him before others. In this manner the angels glorify Him for they are the choristers of Heaven, trumpeting forth His praise. An old writer quaintly pointed out that believers are the "temples" of God, and when their tongues are praising Him, their spiritual "organs" are then sounding forth. We read that the saints in Heaven have "harps" in their hands (Rev. 14:2), which are emblems of *praise*. Alas, that so often *our* harps are "hung on the willows" (Psa. 137:2), and murmurings and complaints are all that issue from our mouths. O my reader, be more earnest and diligent in seeking for grace to enable thee to be praising God continually.

"But to do good and to communicate forget not: for with such sacrifices God is well-pleased" (v. 16). Here is the *fifth sacrifice* which the Christian is to offer unto God, namely, that of *ministering to others,* for all the acts and duties of love may fitly be termed "sacrifices." In the previous verse the apostle has shown the great obligation *Godwards* which the sanctification of the Church by the blood of Christ places upon its members, but here he makes known what influence it ought to have upon our conduct *manwards*. Thus, he turns from the first table of the Law to the second, and insists that if redemption places us under additional obligations to love God with all our hearts, it likewise supplies added reasons why we should love our neighbours as ourselves.

The first word of v. 16 is a connective, but the commentators differ as to how it should be translated. Calvin's annotators insist it should be rendered "And"; John Owen suggested "Moreover"; our translators perferred "But." There is no material difference in these variants: if "but" be retained, it is *not* to be taken as exceptional, as though it introduced something adverse unto what had previously been presented. It is clearly a continuation, or an addition to the duty mentioned in v. 15. As some might think that the *entire* duty of the Christian was comprehended in rendering to God that homage and devotion to which He is justly entitled, and that while we attend to that, nothing else need concern us, the apostle *added* "But"—notwithstanding the diligence required in the former duty —forget not to do good unto men and minister to their needs.

Herein we may perceive once more how carefully the Scriptures preserve the *balance* of truth at every point. The Divine Law is a unit, yet was it written upon *two* tables of stone, and the one must never be exalted to the disparagement of the other. True, there is an *order* to be observed: God Himself ever has the first claim upon our hearts, time and strength; nevertheless our fellow-creatures, and particularly our fellow-believers, also have real claims upon us, which we must not ignore. To disregard the second table of the Law, is not only to inflict an injury upon our neighbours, but it is to disobey and therefore to displease God Himself. There is an harmony in obedience, and a failure in any one point disturbs the whole, as is evident from James 2:10, 11. It is for this reason, then, that our verse closes with, "for with such sacrifices God is well-pleased."

It was at this very point that Israel failed so often under the old covenant. Instead of treating their servants considerately, they imposed upon them; instead of ministering to the widow, they robbed her; instead of relieving the poor, they oppressed them. Nevertheless, they were very strict in keeping up their worship of Jehovah! A striking example of this is recorded in the first half of Isa. 58. The prophet was bidden to cry aloud and spare not, but to show the people their sins. They had sought God "daily," "forsook not His ordinances," yea, took "delight" in approaching Him (v. 2). They were diligent in "fasting," yet God *accepted not* their worship, saying "Is not *this* the fast that I have chosen? to loose the bands of wickedness, to undo the heavy burdens, and to let the oppressed go free, and that ye break every yoke? Is is not to deal thy bread to the hungry, and that thou bring the poor that are cast out to thy house? when thou seest the naked, that thou cover him; and that thou hide not thyself from thine own flesh" (vv. 6, 7).

Another solemn example is found in Zech. 7. God challenges them by asking, "When ye fasted and mourned in the fifth and seventh month, even those seventy years, did ye at all fast *unto Me,* even to Me?" (v. 5). Then the prophet cried, "Thus speaketh the Lord of hosts, saying, Execute true judgment, and show mercy and compassions every man to his brother; and oppress not the widow, nor the fatherless, the stranger nor the poor; and let none of you imagine evil against his brother in your heart" (vv. 9, 10). What a strange anomaly human nature presents! How glaring its inconsistencies! Punctillious in the performances of public worship, yet utterly remiss in attending to private duties! Diligent and zealous in keeping the fasts and feasts of the Lord, yet regardless of the needs and cries of their destitute fellows! How is such to be accounted for? Easily: it bolsters up self-righteousness, feeds the idea that the favour of God can be purchased by the creature, and causes such pharisees to be looked up to for their "holiness" (?) by certain superficial people.

Hence it is that the duties of benevolence inculcated in our text are preceded by "forget not," intimating there is a more than ordinary proneness in professors of the Gospel to neglect them. It is *a sinful neglect* which is here prohibited. John Owen suggested four reasons or vicious habits of mind from which such forgetfulness proceeds. First, "an undue trust unto religious duties, as in many barren professors," by which he means those who set a high value upon their religious acts and think to win Heaven thereby. How many there be who contribute liberally to "the church" and yet under-pay their employees and overcharge their customers!—the gifts of such are a stench in God's nostrils.

Second, "from vain pleas and pretences against duties attended with trouble and charge." It is much easier and pleasanter to go to the house of prayer and sing God's praises, than it is to enter the dwellings of the poor and personally wait upon those who are sick. It costs less to put a coin in the collection-plate than it does to feed and clothe the destitute. Third, "a want of that goodness of nature and disposition which effectual grace will produce." The spirit of Christ in the heart will produce consideration and concern for others, and counteract our innate selfishness; but where Christ is absent, the Devil rules the heart. Fourth, "A want of that compassion toward sufferers, which is required of them that are still in the body: v. 3." May God preserve us from all religion that hardens and produces callousness, stifling even "natural affection."

"But to do good and to communicate forget not." "It is the duty of Christians to express their gratitude to God for His goodness to them, through Christ Jesus, by doing good: i.e., by performing acts of beneficence—in feeding the hungry, clothing the naked, relieving the distressed; and in this way communicating to their poor and afflicted brethren of the blessings Providence has conferred on them. While the terms are of that general kind as to express beneficence and the communication of benefits generally, it seems probable that the apostle had a direct reference to doing good by communicating to others *those* blessings for which they were especially bound to give thanks. It is the duty of Christians to do good to their fellow-men by communicating to them, so far as this is competent to them, those heavenly and *spiritual* blessings for which they are bound continually to give thanks to God" (John Brown).

"But to do good and to communicate forget not." That which is here inculcated is *the sacrifice of love* unto our fellows. Two words are used to set forth this duty. First, "do good" which concerns the whole course of our lives, especially with regard to others. Three things are included. First, a gracious propensity or readiness of mind thereto: "the liberal deviseth liberal things" (Isa. 32:8): he does not wait till he is asked, but seeks to be on the alert and anticipate the needs of others. Second, the actual exercise of this benevolent inclination, in all those ways which will be useful and helpful, spiritually and temporally, to mankind. Idealizing and theorizing is not sufficient: there must be the acting out of good will. Third, by buying up all occasions and opportunities for the exercise of compassion and lovingkindness to others.

A spirit of philanthropy and benevolence is to be manifested by well-doing. It is not enough to *be* good; we must *do* good. "My little children, let us not love in word, neither in tongue; but in deed and in truth" (1 John 3:18). "Now there was at Joppa a certain disciple named Tabitha, which by interpretation is called Dorcas: this woman was *full of good works* and alms deeds which she did" (Acts 9:36): her charitable actions are called "good works" because they were profitable and did good to others. Nor is this ministering to the wants of others to be confined unto the members of our own family, or even the limits of our denomination. "As we have therefore opportunity, let us do good unto *all men,* especially unto those who are of the household of faith" (Gal. 6:10)—therein the spirit of Christianity differs from the narrow and clannish spirit of all other religions. God does good unto all men, and we are to be "emulators of Him as dear children" (Eph. 5:1).

"But to do good and to communicate forget not." Christians are "created in Christ Jesus unto good works" (Eph. 2:10), regeneration capacitating them thereunto. Christ gave Himself for us that we should be a people who are "zealous of good works" (Titus 2:14), for by them we honour Him and adorn our profession. No matter what self-sacrifice they entail, nor how ungrateful be the beneficiaries, we are to be diligent and persevering in helping all we can: "But ye, brethren, be not weary in well doing" (2 Thess. 3:13). "For so is the will of God, that with well doing ye may put to silence the ignorance of foolish men" (1 Pet. 2:15). And even though our well doing fails to silence the criticism of those who believe not, yea, if our perseverance therein brings down upon us increased opposition and persecution, yet it is written, "Wherefore let them that suffer according to the will of God commit the keeping of their souls to Him in well doing, as unto a faithful Creator" (1 Pet. 4:19).

The second term used here in connection with the sacrifice of charity is "communicate," which means passing on to others what God has entrusted to us, according as their necessities do require. Literally, the Greek word signifies "having something in common with others." It is the *actual exercise* of that pity for the poor and indigent which is required of us in the distribution of good things unto them, according to our ability. This is an important evangelical duty which the Scriptures repeatedly charge us with: the glory of God, the salvation of our souls, and the honour of our profession, are highly concerned therein. It is striking to note that when he commended the Corinthians for their liberal contributions to the poor saints at Jerusalem, the apostle declared that "they glorify God for your professed subjection unto the Gospel of Christ" (2 Cor. 9:13)—obedience to the command in our text is required by *the Gospel!*

John Owen rightly pointed out that "To be negligent herein is to despise the wisdom of God in the disposal of the lots and conditions of His own children in the world in so great variety, as He hath done always, and will always continue to do." What light that throws on those providential dispensations of God which are often so mysterious and exercising to the hearts of many of His people! Here is an important reason intimated why God blesses a few of His saints with considerable of this world's goods and why many of them have scarcely any at all: it is to provide opportunity and occasion for the exercise of those graces in them which their several conditions call for. By the unequal distribution of His material mercies, the rich have opportunity for thankfulness, charity, and bounty; while the poor are called upon to exercise patience, submission, trust, and humility. Where those graces are mutually exercised, there is beauty, order, and harmony, and a revenue of glory unto God.

Christians are rarely more sensible of God's goodness to them than when giving and receiving in a proper manner. He that gives aright feels the power of Divine grace at work in his heart, and he who receives aright is very conscious of Divine love and care in such supplies: God is near to both. Consequently, to be selfishly callous on the one hand, or proudly independent and scornful of charity on the other, is to impugn the wisdom of God in His disposal of the varied temporal circumstances of His people. No man is rich or poor merely for himself, but rather to occupy that place in the social order of things which God has designed unto His own glory. From what has been before us we may see how that many even of those who believe not are the temporal gainers by the death of Christ and the fruits thereof in the lives of His people.

Many and varied are *the motives* which Scripture employs to persuade the saint unto this duty of ministering unto the needy of His fellows. "He that hath pity upon the poor lendeth unto the Lord; and that which he hath given will He pay him again" (Prov. 19:17). Do we really believe this? Do we *act* as though we did? The Lord allows none to lose by being generous, but repays him with interest one way or another, either to him or his posterity. "He that giveth unto the poor shall not lack; but he that hideth his eyes shall have many a curse" (Prov. 28:27): the selfish man exposes himself to the ill-will of those whom he callously ignores, and brings himself under the providential curse of God. "He that turneth away his ear from hearing the Law (on this matter), even his prayer shall be abomination" (Prov. 28:9)—bear *that* in mind, dear reader, if you wish to have and retain the ear of God.

"Give and it shall be given unto you; good measure, pressed down, and shaken together, and running over, shall men give into your bosom. For with the same measure that ye mete withal it shall be measured to you again" (Luke 6:38). What an inducement is that! how it should stimulate unto liberality those who by nature have a miserly disposition. "Let your light so shine before men, that they may see your good works, and glorify your Father which is in Heaven" (Matt. 5:16): how that should encourage us in the performing of good works! "But this I say, He which soweth sparingly shall reap also sparingly; and he which soweth bountifully shall reap also bountifully" (2 Cor. 9:6): the writer has lived long enough to see many striking examples of both of these classes. "God anointed Jesus of Nazareth with the Holy Spirit and with power: who went about *doing good*" (Acts 10:38). He was ever thinking of others and ministering to them: feeding the hungry, healing the sick, relieving the distressed; and He has left us an example that we should follow *His* steps.

Let it be pointed out, however, that God requires us to use *discretion and discrimination* in the bestowments of charity. There is a class of shiftless idlers who are ever ready to impose upon the compassionate and generous hearted, and make the benevolence of others a reason for their own indolence. It is positively wrong to encourage those who seek to subsist on the liberality of others, instead of earning their own bread. Indiscriminate giving often does more harm than good. It is our bounden duty to go to the trouble of properly investigating each case on its own merits, instead of allowing our sentiment to override our judgment. God Himself has said, "This we commanded you, that if any would not *work,* neither should he eat" (2 Thess. 3:10), and it is sinful for us to *negative* that by giving money to able-bodied loafers.

"For with such sacrifices God is well-pleased." Whatever benefits the Christian bestows on others God regards them as done to Himself, and honours them with the name of "sacrifices." What gracious condescension on His part, that He should dignify our worthless works as to pronounce them holy and sacred things, acceptable to Himself! Rightly, then, did Calvin point out, "When, therefore, *love* does not prevail among us, we not only rob men of their right, but God Himself, who has by a solemn sentence dedicated to Himself what He has commanded to be done to men." How this consideration ought to stir us up to the exercise of kindness towards our neighbour. The more we do so, the more pleasure do we give unto Him to whom we are infinitely indebted. Withhold not thy hand, then, from that which delights thy God.

"For with *such* sacrifices God is well-pleased." There is a twofold emphasis in the word "such." First, it implies a contrast, denoting that God no longer required those ancient sacrifices which He had enjoined until an abrogation of the old covenant. Herein was a clear intimation that Judaism had been set aside. Second, it graciously stresses the fact that, though *we* deem our feeble praises and charitable works as too poor to be worthy of notice or mention, *God Himself* regards those very things as acts of worship that meet with His hearty approbation.

A beautiful illustration of what has just been pointed out is found in Phil. 4. The Philippian saints had sent a gift to the apostle Paul, which he not only gratefully acknowledged, but declared that the same was "an odour of a sweet smell, a sacrifice acceptable, well-pleasing to God" (v. 18). "Beyond this the highest aspirations of a Christian cannot go. It is all he can wish; it is above all that he can think. To have the approbation of good men is delightful; to have the approbation of our own conscience is more delightful still; but to have the approbation of God, this is surely the highest recompense a creature can reach. This approbation is very strongly expressed in the Word: 'God is not unrighteous to forget your work and labour of love, which ye have showed toward His name, in that ye have ministered to the saints, and do minister' (Heb. 6:10). It will be still more illustriously displayed when the Son appears in the glory of the Father, and in the presence of an assembled universe proclaims to those who, as a token of gratitude to God for the blessings of salvation, have done good and communicated: 'For I was an hungered, and ye gave Me meat; I was thirsty, and ye gave Me drink; I was a stranger, and ye took Me in; naked, and ye clothed Me. . . . Inasmuch as ye have done it unto one of the least of these My brethren, ye have done it unto Me:' Matt. 25:35-40" (John Brown).

CHAPTER ONE HUNDRED NINETEEN

Christian Rulers

(Heb. 13:17)

"Obey them that have the rule over you, and submit yourselves: for they watch for your souls, as they that must give account, that they may do it with joy, and not with grief; for that is unprofitable for you" (v. 17). It is quite clear from the balance of the verse that its opening words have reference to religious leaders, and not to civil rulers. Adolph Saphir, who was very far from being a "Nicolaitan" was right when he declared: "Verses 7 and 17 show that there was *a stated ministry,* that there were recognised and regular teachers and pastors in the congregation, whose gifts not only, but whose *office* was acknowledged." It is impossible that any unprejudiced and impartial mind should attentively consider the terms and implications of these verses and come to any other conclusion. The principle of subordination is absolutely essential to the well-being of any society that is to be rightly ordered and conducted—adumbrated even in the organization of our bodies.

In our text the Holy Spirit sets forth the third great duty which is required in our Christian profession, on account of the sacrifice of Christ and our sanctification by His blood. Most comprehensive and all-inclusive are the exhortations found in vv. 15-17. The first respects our *spiritual* obligation, Godwards, rendering unto Him that which is His due (v. 15). The second respects our *social* obligation, rendering unto our needy fellows that which the requirements of charity dictates, according to our ability. The third has respect to our *ecclesiastical* obligation, rendering unto those officers in the church that submission and respect to which they are entitled by virtue of the position and authority which Christ has accorded them. This is a Gospel institution, which can only be disregarded to the manifest dishonour of the Lord and to our own great loss.

Ever since the great Reformation of the sixteenth century, there have been wide differences of opinion among God's people concerning *the local church*: its constitution, its officers, and its discipline. Even where there was oneness of mind respecting the fundamentals of the Faith, godly men have differed considerably in their ecclesiastical views. Numbers of the most gifted of Christ's servants have, during the last three hundred years, written extensively upon the polity and policy of the local church, and though widely varying positions have been taken, and though each claimed to appeal to Scripture only for his authority, yet none succeeded in carrying the majority of professing Christians with him, or of persuading his opponents that *their* system was wrong.

While on the one hand we must admire the wisdom of Him who has *providentially ordered* as great a variety of types in the ecclesiastical sphere as He has in the physical and social—which though *not a rule* for us to walk by, *is* a subject for our admiration; yet on the other hand we cannot but deplore that they who are united on the same foundations and agreed in all the cardinal truths of Holy Writ, should lay such emphasis upon their circumstantial differences in sentiments as to prevent the exercise of mutual love and forbearance, and instead of labouring *in concert* within their respective departments to promote the common cause of Christ, should so often vex each other with needless disputes and uncharitable censures. Far better be silent altogether than contend for any portion of the Truth in a bitter, angry, censorious spirit.

No true Christian will hesitate to acknowledge that Christ Himself is the one infallible, authoritative Legislator and Governor of His Church, that He is the only Lord of conscience, and that nothing inconsistent with His revealed will should be practised, and that nothing He has definitely enjoined be omitted, by those professing allegiance to Him. But however generally acknowledged these principles are, we cannot get away from the fact that the misconstruction and misapplication of them have contributed more to divide the people of God and to alienate their affections one from the other, than any other cause that can be assigned. Surely those who are built upon the common foundation, who are led by the same Spirit, who are opposed by the same enemies, should love as brethren and bear each other's burdens. But alas! a mistaken zeal for Christ's honour has filled them with animosity against their fellow-disciples, split them into innumerable factions, and given rise to fierce and endless contentions.

We quite agree with the godly John Newton, when he said in his "Apologia," nearly two hundred years ago: "Men are born, educated, and called under a great variety of circumstances. Habits of life, local customs, early connections, and even bodily constitution, have more or less influence in forming their characters, and in giving a tincture and turn to their manner of thinking. So that though, in whatever is *essential* to their peace and holiness, they are all led by the same Spirit and mind the same things; in others of a *secondary* nature, their sentiments may, and often do differ, as much as the features of their faces. A uniformity of judgment among them is *not* to be expected while the wisest are defective in knowledge, the best are defiled with sin, and while the weaknesses of human nature which are common to them all, are so differently affected by a thousand impressions which are from their various situations. They *might*, however, maintain a unity of spirit, and live in the exercise of mutual love; were it not that every party, and almost every individual, unhappily conceives that they are bound in conscience to prescribe *their own* line of conduct as a standard to which all their brethren ought to conform They are comparatively but few who consider this requisition to be as unnecessary, unreasonable, and impracticable, as it would be to insist or expect that every man's shoes should be exactly of one size.

"Thus, though all agree in asserting the authority and rights of the Lord Jesus, as King and Head of His Church, the various apprehensions they frame of the rule to which He requires them to conform, and their pertinacious attachment to *their own* expositions of it, separate them almost as much from each other, as if they were not united to Him by a principle of living faith. Their little differences form them into so many separate interests; and the heat with which they defend their own plans, and oppose all who cannot agree with them in a tittle, makes them forget that they are children in the same family, and servants of the same Master. And while they vex and worry each other with disputations and censures, the world wonders and laughs at them."

The position which has been taken by, perhaps, most of the leading writers, was something like this: Get away from the conflicting views of men, and *read the N.T.* prayerfully and impartially, and it will quickly be apparent that the Lord Jesus has not left such an important matter as the constitution of the churches undefined, but rather directed His apostles to leave in their writings a pattern according to which it was His will all His churches in future ages were to be formed, and (according to the particular leanings of each respective writer) that it will be seen the primitive churches were "Congregational," "Baptist," "Presbyterian," or 'Brethren Assemblies," and therefore any other system or scheme is unscriptural, and a presumptuous deviation from the declared will of the Lord.

If, however, the reader cares to take the time and trouble to consult *a number of the writers* in any one of these different schools, he will find that though they are all agreed that a plain and satisfactory model of this "Congregational" church (or "Baptist," or "Presbyterian," or "Brethren Assembly," as the case may be) can easily be collected and stated from a perusal of the N.T.; yet when these same writers attempt to delineate and describe that church, they *differ considerably among themselves* as to the nature and number of its officers, powers and acts which are requisite to the constitution and administration of a Gospel church. There is very far from being that agreement *among themselves* which is certainly to be expected *if* the plan from which they profess to copy be so clearly and expressly revealed in the N.T. as to be binding upon believers in all ages.

It seems, then, that if every detail of the church's government and worship be exhibited in the Scriptures, either in the form of a precept or precedent, yet thus far God has not given sufficient skill to any one so as to enable him to collect and collate the various rules and regulations scattered throughout the Gospels, Acts, Epistles, and the Revelation, and arrange them into a systematic and orderly structure. But that none really takes this principle seriously appears from his own practices. There are a number of things reported of the primitive Christians which few if any companies of Christians to-day make any attempt to emulate. For example, the holding of all earthly possessions in common (Acts 2:44, 45), greeting one another with a holy kiss (1 Cor. 16:20), making provision for their widows when they reach the age of sixty (1 Tim. 5:9), or sending for the elders of the church to pray over and anoint us when we are sick (James 5:14)!

In reply to what has just been said, it will be pointed out that in the days of the apostles the saints were endowed with *extraordinary* gifts, and consequently there were some things practiced by them (in 1 Cor. 14, for example) which are *not* proper for our imitation to-day who have not those gifts. But that very admission *surrenders* the basic principle contended for. To be told that we should study the apostolic churches for *our model*, and then to be informed that some parts of their practice were *not* designed for our emulation, is too bewildering for the ordinary mind to grasp. Moreover, *God* has not told us anywhere *which* of the primitive practices were but transient and which were not. Where, then, is the man or men qualified to draw the line and declare authoritatively in *what respects* the state of the first Christians was hindered from being a pattern for us by the extraordinary dispensations of that generation, and in what cases their actions *are binding* on us now those extraordinary dispensations have ceased?

To the above it will at once be objected: But consider the only other alternative: surely it is most unreasonable to suppose that the Lord has left His people *without* a complete church model for their guidance! Is it not unthinkable that Christ would fail His people in such a vitally important matter as to how He would have them order all the concerns of the churches which bear His name, that He would leave them in ignorance of His will, as to their constitution, officers, order of worship, discipline, etc? If God ordered Moses to make all things in the tabernacle according to the pattern shown him in the mount, and if that pattern was so complete that every board and pin in the house of worship was definitely defined, is it believable that He has made *less* provision for His people today, now that the fulness of time has come? This argument has indeed a most plausible sound to it, and thousands have been misled thereby; but a dispassionate examination of it shows it to be unwarrantable.

In the first place, there is no promise recorded in the N.T. that He *would* do so, and no statement through any apostle that such a church model *has* been provided! In the second place, the history of Christendom clearly indicates *the contrary*. Had such a model been given, it would be as clearly recognizable as the tabernacle pattern, and all who really desired to please the Lord would have responded thereto; and, in consequence, there had been *uniformity* among the true followers of Christ, instead of endless diversity and variety. But in the third place, this *proves too much*. If a Divine model has been given supplying all the details for the ordering of N.T. churches and their worship, as definite and as complete as was given for the tabernacle, then we would have minute regulations concerning the size, shape, and furnishings of the buildings in which we must worship, full directions for the ministers apparel, and so on! The *absence* of those details is clear proof that no model for the churches comparable to the Divine pattern for the tabernacle has been vouchsafed us.

Then what conclusion are we forced to come to? This: a happy medium between the two alternatives suggested by most of those who have written on the subject. If on the one hand we cannot find in the N.T. that which in any wise corresponds to the "pattern" for the tabernacle (and the minute instructions God gave for the temple), on the other hand the Lord has not left us so completely in ignorance of His will that every man or company of Christians is left entirely to do that which is right in his own eyes. In keeping with the vastly different character of the two dispensations, the "liberty" of the Spirit (2 Cor. 3:17) has supplanted the rigid legality of Judaism, and therefore has Christ supplied us with *general principles* (e.g., 1 Cor. 14:26, 40), which are sufficiently broad to allow of *varied* modification when applied to the differing circumstances of His people, situated in various climes and generations —

in contrast from what was prescribed for the *single nation* of Israel of old.

In the N.T. we *are* furnished with a full revelation of all things necessary unto *salvation,* the knowledge whereof man by his own powers could never attain thereunto; yet there is much *lacking there* on other matters which *was furnished* under the old covenant. God not only supplied Israel with the ceremonial law, which was to regulate all their church or religious life, but He also gave them a complete code of precepts for their *civil* government, and no one pretends He has done *this* for Christians! In the absence of that civil code, why should it be thought strange that God has left many minor ecclesiastical arrangements to the discretion of His servants? Unto those who are indignant at such a statement, and who are still ready to insist that the Lord has made known His will on *all* things respecting church and religious affairs, we would ask, Where does the New Testament prescribe what *marriage rites* should be used? or the form of service for a funeral? But enough.

As Richard Hooker pertinently pointed out, "he who affirms speech to be necessary among all men throughout the world, doth not thereby import that all men must necessarily speak one kind of language. Even so the necessity of polity and regimen in all churches may be held, *without* holding any *one* certain form to be necessary in them all." This is far from granting that all the various modes of church government are *equally agreeable* to the spirit and genius of the Gospel, or equally suited to the promotion of edification. Once again we fully agree with John Newton when he said, "In essentials I agree with them all, and in circumstancials I differ no more from any of them than they differ among themselves. They all confess they are fallible, yet they all decide with an air of infallibility; for they all in their turn expect me to unite with *them,* if I have any regard to the authority and honour of the Lord Jesus as Head of the church. But the very consideration they propose restrains me from uniting with any of them. For I cannot think that I should honour the headship and kingly office of Christ by acknowledging Him as the Head *of a party* and subdivision of His people to the exclusion of the rest.

"Every party uses fair sounding words of liberty; but when an explanation is made, it amounts to little more than this: that they will give me liberty to think as *they* think, and to act as *they* act; which to me, who claim the same right of thinking for myself and of acting according to the dictates of my own conscience, is no liberty at all. I therefore came to such conclusions as these: that I would love them all, that I would hold a friendly intercourse with them all, so far as they should providentially come in my way (and, he might have added, so far as they will allow me!); but that I would stand fast in the liberty with which Christ has made me free, and call none of them master; in fine, that if others sought to honour Him by laying a great stress on matters of doubtful disputation, my way of honouring Him should be by endeavouring to show that His kingdom is not of this world, nor consists in meats and drinks, in pleading for form and parties, but in righteousness, peace, and joy in the Holy Spirit; and that neither circumcision is anything, nor uncircumcision, but a new creature, and the faith which worketh *by love*.

This is the course which the writer has sedulously sought to follow for the past ten years, both in connection with this magazine and in oral ministry. But alas! notwithstanding the boasted "broad-mindedness" and "liberality" of this generation, we have found, everywhere we have been the ecclesiastical barriers are as impregnable to-day as they were a century ago, and that no church, circle, or company of professing Christians is prepared to *really* welcome into their midst (no matter what his reputation or credentials) one who is unprepared to join and limit to *their* party, and pronounce all their shibboleths; and that the vast majority are unwilling to read any religious publication unless it bears upon it the label of their particular denomination. No wonder that the Spirit of God is quenched and His power and blessing absent, where such an unchristlike, sectarian, bigoted and pharisaical spirit prevails.

We are not going to prescribe for others; let every man be fully persuaded in his own mind. But as far as the writer is concerned, he values his Christian liberty far too highly to voluntarily shut himself up in any ecclesiastical prison, where he is excluded from fellowship with his brethren and sisters scattered abroad. Of course since sinless perfection is not to be found in any individual on earth, it is not to be expected from any group of individuals. No one denomination or party has all the light. On the one hand, if the reader be a member of a church where unsound doctrine is preached or where no Scriptural discipline is maintained, his course is clear: Eph. 5:11, 2 Tim. 3:5. But if on the other hand, he belongs to any evangelical church which is honestly seeking to honour Christ and where his soul is being fed, then, in our humble judgment, he will be wise to remain there and "obey them that have the rule over him" yet let him *not* look down upon others who differ from him.

In dissenting from the popular view that the N.T. record of primitive Christianity furnishes a complete model of church government, and that the same is an authoritative rule binding upon the Lord's people throughout the entire course of this dispensation, we are far from supposing that we shall carry with us the majority of our readers—by this time the writer ought to be sufficiently acquainted with human nature to prevent any such foolish day dreaming. And in affirming that the N.T. rather supplies us with general rules and principles, which are sufficiently elastic as to allow for *human discretion to be exercised* in the application of them to particular instances of the church's outward conduct, we are quite prepared to face the charge that this statement is a "dangerous" one. Our reply is, that we are affirming no more than what is universally acknowledged concerning the regulation of the details of the life of *the individual believer.*

Is not the Christian daily made to cry unto God for wisdom how to act in his temporal affairs, and that because there are no specific precepts in the Word which prescribe for those particular exigencies? Is he not obliged, after prayerful deliberation, to *use his common sense* in applying the general rules of Scripture to a hundred minor details of his life? So common an occurrence is this and so universally does it obtain among the saints, that there is no need for us to enlarge upon it by illustrating the point—there is no need to *prove* what is self-evident. In view of this simple and obvious fact, why should we be the least surprised that God has ordained that His churches should follow a similar course, for what is a Gospel church but a company of individual believers in organized relationship. If, then, God has not told the individual believer at what hour he should rise on the Sabbath and how many meals he should eat that day, would we expect Him to state how long the minister's sermon is to be, or how many hymns or psalms are to be sung?

"The Lord Christ in the institution of Gospel churches—their state, order, rule, and worship—doth not require of His disciples that in their observance of His appointments they should *cease to be men,* or forego the use and exercise of their rational abilities, according to the rule of that exercise, which is *the light of nature.* Yea, because the rules and directions are in this case to be applied unto things spiritual and of mere revelation, He giveth wisdom and prudence to make that application in a due manner, unto those to whom the guidance and rule of the church is committed: wherefore, as unto all things which the light of nature directs us unto, with respect unto the observation of the duties prescribed by Christ in and unto the Church, we need no other institution but that of the use of the *especial Spiritual understanding* which the Lord Christ gives us for that end.

"There are in the Scripture *general rules* directing us in the application of natural light, unto such a determination of all circumstances in the acts of church-rule and worship, as are sufficient for their performance decently and in order. Wherefore, as was said before, it is *utterly in vain* and useless, to demand express institution of all the circumstances belonging unto the government, order, and worship of the church; or for the due improvement of things in themselves indifferent unto its edification, as occasion shall require. Nor are they capable to be any otherwise stated, but as they lie in the light of nature and spiritual prudence directed by general rules of Scripture." (John Owen).

Nor is this to discredit or disparage the Holy Scriptures. The Testimony of God is true, perfect, and all-sufficient *for the ends for* which it was given; but that Testimony is not honoured but dishonoured by us, if we extravagently attribute to it that which God *never designed* for the same. Rome has erred grievously by declaring that the Scriptures are not sufficient, that "traditions" must be added if we are to have a full revelation of what is absolutely necessary for us to know in this life in order that we may be *saved* in the next. But some Protestants have gone to another extreme, taking the position that the Scriptures contain such a complete revelation of God's will for the regulation of our lives, both as individuals and as churches, that to act according to any other rule (be it the promptings of conscience or the dictates of reason) is presumptuous and sinful.

But to insist that the conduct of the church must have an express warrant from the N.T. *for every detail* of its procedure, and that to act otherwise is displeasing to the Lord, is to go much farther than that which obtained even under the O.T. What commandment from the Lord did the Gileadites have to erect that altar spoken of in Joshua 22:10? Did not congruity of reason—the fitness of things—induce them thereto and suffice for defence of their act? What Divine commandment had the women of Israel to yearly lament for Jephthah's daughter (Judges 11:40)? What "thus saith the Lord" or scriptural precedent did Ezra have for making "a pulpit of wood" (Neh. 8:4), from which he preached to the people? What Divine Commandment had the Jews to celebrate the feast of "Dedication" (John 10:22), nowhere spoken of in the Law, yet solemnized by Christ Himself! To condemn all that is "of human invention" is not only to fly in the face of the judgment of many of the wisest and most godly men, but is to go beyond what the Scriptures themselves permit.

CHAPTER ONE HUNDRED TWENTY

Christian Rulers

(Heb. 13:17)

In the preceding article we have deviated from our usual custom in this series of giving a word by word exposition of the verse before us, deeming it well to first give it a topical treatment. This magazine, small as is its circulation, goes to hundreds of the Lord's people who are found in many different branches of Christendom. Some of them are sorely perplexed by the babel of tongues which now obtains in the religious realm. The high claims so dogmatically put forth by various sects and systems, assemblies and circles of fellowship, bewilder not a few honest souls, who are desirous of doing that which is most pleasing to the Lord. It was with a desire to afford them some help on what is admittedly a most difficult and complicated subject, that according to the light which God has granted us (or withheld from us), we sought to point out some of the fallacies pertaining to the leading positions taken by ecclesiastical writers.

To say that the diverse denominations, even the evangelically orthodox, cannot all be right, and therefore that among them there must be one much more closely in accord with the Scriptures than the others, sounds very feasible; nevertheless, the writer is satisfied that, generally speaking, it has more of error than truth in it. Comparisons are proverbially odious. As no one believer has all the graces of the Spirit equally developed in him, so no one church or denomination has all the Truth. Think of attempting to draw invidious contrasts between Andrew and Peter, Paul and John, as to which was the more Christlike! As well might one set the rose over against the lily of the valley, or wheat against oats. As 1 Cor. 14:10 tells us, "There are, it may be, so many kinds of voices in the world, and *none* of them is without signification." So in the providence of God each particular denomination has filled a place and served a purpose in His plan concerning His cause upon earth.

Nothing is more offensive to God than creature *pride* (Prov. 6:16, 17), and nothing is more to be deplored among those who bear the name of Christ than that a company of them (be it large or small) shall claim "*we* are *the* people"—the people who meet on the most scriptural ground, the people who adhere closest to the Word. A spirit of bigotry ill-becomes sinners saved by grace, while jealousies and contentions, enmity and reviling, among members of the same Family are most reprehensible: "the wrath of man worketh not the righteousness of God" (James 1:20). Differences of opinion are inevitable while we are in the flesh—permitted by God that we should have occasion to be "*forbearing* one another in love" (Eph. 4:2). That form of church government which accords most closely to the N.T., and where every detail is scrupulously correct, would be valueless in the sight of God unless it were conducted in love and its worship was "in spirit and in truth."

Let it be attentively considered that at the dawn of Christianity the first officers of the church were immediately called by Christ (Gal. 1:2), which none now are, nor have any since the decease of those who were so called at the first; that *they* were endowed with extraordinary gifts and power, but Christ has not continued to communicate such to His servants; that those original officers were blest with Divine inspiration and infallible guidance, both in preaching the Gospel and appointing things necessary for the churches, which *none* can rightly pretend unto to-day; that those first officers had a commission giving them authority towards all the world for evangelization and over all churches for their edification which no servant of Christ can claim to-day. How utterly vain, then, is the claim, either unto a "succession" of those officers, or to a perfect emulation of their order of things. Nevertheless, church-rulers—bishops and deacons—were to continue, as is clear from 1 Tim. 3, etc.

Now in every orderly society there must be *rulers,* and in all ages and dispensations the same have been mercifully appointed by God: Moses, Joshua, the judges and kings over Israel, are so many illustrations of this principle. It is the same in this era, nor does the presence of the Holy Spirit render unnecessary rulers in the churches. Christ is not the Author of confusion: but endless confusion and turmoil is inevitable where there are no accredited and acknowledged leaders. True, the rulers Christ has instituted for His churches possess no arbitrary power, for they are themselves subordinate to Him. Their office is that of a *steward* (Titus 1:7), who is neither to lord it over the household nor to be entirely under subjection to it, but to superintend and provide for the family.

Take the chief steward or "lord chamberlain," of his majesty king George, and while it may not be strictly parallel with the position and duties of an official servant of Christ, yet there is sufficient in common for the former to help us understand the latter. While on the one hand the "lord chamberlain" has to be regulated by certain rules and well established precedents, yet on the other hand he is far more than an automaton mechanically acting according to a written code. As one qualified for his position, he is allowed considerable freedom in making many arrangements for the Royal household; nevertheless, he is *not* free to act arbitrarily or follow nought but his own preferences. No, that which regulates him is the well-being of his august master: he plans and arranges so as to please him, to promote his comfort, to serve his interests and honour; and when he is in doubt as to his procedure, consults the king to ascertain his will.

Analagous is the position occupied by the pastor of a local church. "Who then is a faithful and wise servant, whom his lord hath made ruler over his household, to give them meat in due season? Blessed is that servant, whom his lord when he cometh shall find so doing" (Matt. 24:45, 46). Note carefully the following points in this passage. First, the use of *the singular number*: one servant for each local household! Second, that this servant is made "ruler over the" household! Third, that he is given that position for the purpose of supplying them "meat in due season," which, in its wider signification, means to superintend all the arrangements, to care for all its members, to protect and promote their well-being. Christ does not call dolts and idiots to occupy this place, but men endowed with good common sense, to which He graciously adds spiritual wisdom and discernment.

Now the ruler of Christ's household is neither a supreme sovereign or pope, nor a mere figure head without freedom of action. He, in turn, is the servant, responsible to Him, there to uphold His honour, care for those who are precious in His sight, and to whom he must yet render a full account of his stewardship. Therefore, while on the one hand he must act within the bounds of certain general rules and principles prescribed for his conduct, and must not introduce anything which would dishonour his royal Master or be inimical to His interests; yet on the other hand he is required to use his own judgment in applying those general rules to particular cases and to make whatever minor arrangement he deems most for his Master's glory and the good of His household; and when he is in doubt as to his right or best course, it is his privilege to plead and count upon the promise of James 1:5.

To extend our analogy one point further. As the "lord chamberlain" has other servants under him to assist in the discharge of his honourable duties, servants who co-operate with him by carrying out his instructions, so Christ has provided the pastor of a local church with deacons, and, as many think, with "ruling elders" (or where the church is a larger one—as was the case with many of those in apostolic times—with fellow-pastors or "elders"), to help him in his official duties. So that when our text says "obey them that have the rule over you" it takes in *all* the officers of the local church, whatever be the technical names they now go under. These additional church officers not only provide assistance for the chief ruler, but they also serve as a check upon him, for if they be endowed with the qualifications specified in 1 Tim. 3:8-13, they will not be a party to anything which is obviously dishonouring to Chirst.

If it be true (as many students of Scripture have concluded) that the seven epistles of Revelation 2 and 3 furnish a prophetic outline of the ecclesiastical history of Christendom, then it appears that the trend of church government has passed from one extreme to another, from Nicolaitanism (Rev. 2:6, 15), which signifies *the subjugation of the laity,* to Laodiceanism (Rev. 3:14) which means *the domination of the laity.* Nor need this surprise us, for the same change has taken place in the political and social order. It is indeed striking to observe how close is the resemblance between them. The development of Nonconformity and the rapid spread of Independency in the religious world was quickly followed by the rebellion of the American colonies and the formation of Republics in the U.S.A. and in France. Side by side with the growth of a democratic spirit in the churches, has been the spread of "socialism" in the state, the one more and more re-acting on the other.

One of the most radical and far reaching movements of the last century was that which sought to obliterate all distinctions between the clergy and the laity, establishing a network of "assemblies" all over the English-speaking world, wherein there are (professedly) no officers, where a one-man-ministry is decried, and where the Spirit is (avowedly) free to use whom He pleases. This modern movement also claims to be founded entirely upon the Scriptures, yea, insists that all other bodies of professing Christians are the daughters of Rome and form part of that mystical and apostate Babylon from which God commands His people to come out. This movement has also split up into scores of conflicting parties, each claiming to be the only one which truly "represents" the Body of Christ on earth. But enough; let us now come to closer grips with our text.

"Obey them that have the rule over you, and submit yourselves; for they watch for your souls, as they that must give account, that they may do it with joy, and not with grief: for that is unprofitable for you (v. 17). In these words respect is had to be the ministerial office. To bear "rule" intimates both the duty and dignity of Christ's official servants. God has graciously appointed them to subserve His honour by maintaining decency and order in His churches, and because they are necessary and for the good of His people. To obey and submit to their spiritual leaders is what church-members are here exhorted unto. In v. 7 the apostle made known the particular duties unto those of their guides who had finished their course; here he presses upon them their obligations toward those who were still with them in the body. To ignore those rulers or to rebel against their authority, is to despise the One who has appointed them.

"Obey them that have the rule over you, and submit yourselves." It is abundantly clear from these words that in the days of the Apostles there were two distinct classes among God's people, namely, the rulers and those that were ruled, and as this is not merely an historical statement but a specific exhortation, it is equally clear that the same is binding upon Christians throughout the entire course of this dispensation. This, of course, presupposes a settled church state among them, in which the distinctive duties of each class is here distinctly defined, according to the office of the one and the obligation of the other. The duties here prescribed contain a succinct summary of all that relates to church rule and order, for all that concerns its welfare is comprised in the due obedience of the church to its rulers, and their due discharge of their office.

The Greek word for "them that have the rule over you" ("hegeomai") is rendered "chief" in Luke 22:26 and "governor" in Acts 7:10—"and he (Pharaoh) made him (Joseph) *governor* over Egypt and all his house," which sufficiently intimates its scope. They have received power from Christ to preside over His assemblies, to declare His will and execute His laws, to reprove, rebuke, exhort with all authority and longsuffering. They have no arbitrary power except what Christ has given them, yet within the limits He has prescribed, they are *rulers,* and it is the duty of their members to obey them. "It is of equal importance that the office-bearers in a church should not aspire to a higher degree of authority, and should not be content with a lower degree of authority, than that which their Master has assigned them; and that the members of a church should equally guard against basely submitting to a tyranny which Christ has never instituted, and lawlessly rebelling against a government which He has appointed" (John Brown).

J. Owen declared that the twofold duty here enjoined with respect to the ecclesiastical leaders has respect unto the two parts of their office, namely, teaching and ruling: "obey their teaching and submit to their rule." While it be true that their doctrine or preaching is to be obeyed (so far as it accords with the Truth), and that their authority is to be yielded unto as it respects their ordering of the church's life, yet we rather regard the two exhortations as having a *distributive* force, the second amplifying the first. The word "obey" in our text means an obedience which follows a being persuaded: the mind is first carried along with the preacher so that it believes, and then the will acts—note the marginal alternative in Acts 5:36 for "obeyed" is "believed." "And submit yourselves" seems to us to have reference unto the *spirit* in which they were to obey—obedience was not to be merely an outward act, but prompted by submissive hearts.

Thus, we take it that "obey them that have the rule over you" is not to be restricted to their teaching (as Owen defined it), but includes their ruling of the church as well; while the "submit yourselves" has a wider significance than yielding to their rule, referring to the spirit which was to regulate the whole of their obedience. As Calvin well expressed it, "He commands first obedience and then honour to be rendered to them. These two things are necessarily required, so that the people might have confidence in their pastors, and also reverence them. But it ought at the same time to be noticed that the apostle speaks only of those who *faithfully* performed their office; for they who have nothing but the title, nay, who use the title of pastors, for the purpose of destroying the Church, deserve but little reverence and still less confidence. And this also is what the apostle plainly sets forth when he says, that they *watch* for their souls—a duty which is not performed but by those who are faithful rulers."

The duty here enjoined, then, may be summed up in: cultivate an obedient, compliant, and submissive spirit unto your pastors and church officers. To "obey" and "submit" denotes such a subjection as of inferiors to superiors. It is not a servile subjection, but that reverent respect which God requires, a "submission" which issues from love, and which has for its end the honouring of those to whom honour is due. It would therefore include the doing of everything in the power of the members which would make the lot of their rulers easier and lighter, and, of course, would take in the providing for their temporal sustenance. Those rulers are appointed by God, standing in His immediate stead, so that the Lord Christ declared, "Verily, verily, I say unto you, He that receiveth whomsoever I send receiveth Me; and he that receiveth me receiveth Him that sent Me" (John 13:20).

"Obey them that have the rule over you, and submit yourselves." It scarcely needs pointing out that those words are *not* to be taken absolutely, any more than are "Let every soul be subject unto the higher powers" (Rom. 13:1) or "As the Church is subject unto

Christ, so let the wives be to their own husbands in every thing" (Eph. 5:24). Each of these exhortations is qualified by others: the members of a Gospel church are no more required to receive the pastor's teaching when it be flagrantly opposed to Holy Writ, or to submit to any ruling of his which is manifestly dishonouring to Christ and injurious to His people, than they are to yield to a mandate of Nebuchadnezzar if he sets up an image to himself and commands all to fall down and worship it, or if an ungodly husband required from his wife anything contrary to the laws of nature. No, it is not a blind and implicit obedience which is here enjoined for that would be quite contrary to the whole tenor of Gospel obedience, which is "our *reasonable* service."

The subjection required by our text is only unto that *office* established by Christ Himself. If any usurp that office, and under cloak thereof do teach or enjoin things contrary to what Christ has instituted,then no obedience unto them is required by this command. But it is just at this point that most difficulty is experienced to-day. For many years past large numbers of professing Christians have been demanding that the religious leaders should speak unto them "smooth things," yea, prophesy unto them "deceits," declining to listen unto what condemned their carnal and worldly lives and refusing to heed the holy requirements of God. In consequence, He has suffered their descendants to reap the evil sowings of their fathers, by largely withholding "pastors after His own heart," and allowing thousands of unregenerate men to occupy the modern pulpit. Instead of "obeying" and "submitting" to *them,* God requires His people to turn away from and have nothing to do with them.

The true servants of Christ are to be identified by the marks specified in 1 Tim. 3. They are men who are "apt to teach," being qualified by the Spirit to open up the Scriptures and apply them to the consciences and lives of their hearers. They are "not greedy of filthy lucre" nor "covetous," demanding a salary which would enable them to live above the level of their members, and declining to serve if there were no pay attached to it. "Not a novice," with little or no experience in the spiritual ups and downs of God's tried people, but one who has himself tested and proved the reliability and sufficiency of what he recommends to his hearers. He must be a man who is "not self-willed, not soon angry, not given to wine," but "a lover of good men, sober, just, holy, temperate" (Titus 1:7, 8), or otherwise he could not commend what he teaches by *his own example.* The servants of Christ, then, are endued with a measure of the spirit of their Master, and it is by *that* they are to be distinguished from the false.

To refuse obedience and submission unto such, to contemptuously rail against "the one man system," is to despise a Divine institution, for the office of the "pastor" is as much the Lord's own appointment as is the church itself, or the gifts and graces of its individual members. It is true that men will and do abuse the good gifts of God, but if some pastors are arbitrary, are not some members unruly? If there be pride in the pulpit, is there none in the pew? Alas, in this Laodicean and communistic age, when it has become the fashion to "despise dominion and speak evil of dignities" (Jude 8) and when "the child shall behave himself proudly against the ancient, and the base against the honourable" (Isa. 3:5), almost every individual considers himself qualified to judge and direct both civil and ecclesiastical rulers, to prescribe for both state and church, to scrutinize and criticise everything that is being done, and to say what ought to be done. May the Lord have mercy and subdue the turbulent ragings of pride.

"For they watch for your souls." This is adduced as a reason why we should show proper respect unto Church rulers. "The word used is peculiar unto this place, and it denotes a watchfulness with the greatest care and diligence, and that not without trouble or danger, as Jacob kept and watched the flock of Laban in the night" (J. Owen). The true under-shepherds of Christ have no selfish aims, but rather the spiritual and eternal good of those who are entrusted to their care. Many a minister of the Gospel is often awake, burning midnight oil, while the members of his flock are asleep. Many a one can say, "I will very gladly spend and be spent for you" (2 Cor. 12:15). The ministerial office is no idler's one: it makes demands on heart, mind, and nervous energy, such as none other does.

Here, then, is a motive, to move the members to gladly be subservient to their rulers. The more labour any one undertakes for our sake and the more difficulty and danger he incurs for us, the greater are our obligations to him. Such is the office of bishops or elders; and the heavier the burden they bear, the more honour they deserve. Let, then, our gratitude be evidenced by giving them that which is their due. "We beseech you, brethren, to know them which labour among you, and are over you in the Lord, and admonish you; and to esteem them very highly in love for their work's sake. And be at peace among yourselves" (1 Thess. 5:12, 13). Let us also add that, young men aspiring unto the ministerial office need to think twice about entering a calling which demands ceaseless self-sacrifice, unremitting toil, and a love for Christ and His people which alone will sustain amid sore discouragements.

"They watch for your souls as they that must give account" supplies a further motive. They are placed in a position of trust, commissioned by the Lord, to whom they are immediately responsible. They often render an account to Him now, keeping up a constant intercourse with Him, spreading before Him the state and needs of His people, seeking supplies of grace. A full and final account must be rendered of their stewardship in the Day to come. Unspeakably solemn consideration is *that,* and this it is which actuates them, for they "watch for the souls of their church *as* those who must give account." They bear in mind the awful warning of Ezek. 33:5, and seek to heed the exhortation of 1 Tim. 4:16.

"That they may do it with joy, and not with grief." Here is a further reason why church members should give to their rulers that which is due them. If on the one hand nothing is more encouraging to a pastor than for his people to be responsive and docile, it is equally true that nothing is more disheartening and saddening to him than to meet with opposition from those whose highest interests he is serving with all his might. Every Christian minister who is entitled to that designation, can, in his measure, say with the apostle, "I have no greater joy than to hear that my children walk in truth" (3 John: 4).

"For that is unprofitable for you" furnishes the final motive. For the members of a church to so conduct themselves as to be a constant source of grief unto their minister is to despise their own mercies. It not only prevents their receiving his instruction into their hearts, which results in their spiritual barrenness, but it also saps *his* vigour, quenches his zeal, causing him to proceed with a heavy heart instead of with cheerfulness. What is still more solemn and serious, the Lord Himself is highly displeased, and the tokens of His favour are withdrawn, for He is very sensitive of the mistreatment of His stewards. "We cannot be troublesome or disobedient to our pastors without hazarding our own salvation" (John Calvin)—alas that such erroneous ideas of "salvation" now so widely obtain. May the Lord mercifully pardon any thing in these articles displeasing to Him, and graciously add His blessing to that which is acceptable.

CHAPTER ONE HUNDRED TWENTY-ONE

A Good Conscience

(Heb. 13:18, 19)

Hebrews 13:18, 19 is closely connected with the verse which immediately precedes. In our present portion the apostle mentions another duty which believers owe to those who minister unto them in spiritual things, and this is that they should earnestly remember them before the Throne of Grace. The writer of this epistle besought the prayers of the Hebrews, supporting his plea with a declaration of the sincerity and fidelity with which he had sought to discharge his office. The very fact that the true servants of Christ are so conscientious in the performance of their work, should so endear them to those they minister unto that a spirit of prayer for them ought to be kindled in their hearts. They are the instruments through which we receive the most good, and therefore the least we can do in return is to seek to bear them up before God in the arms of our faith and love.

Before we consider this special need of Christ's servants, and our privilege and duty in ministering unto the same, we propose to devote the remainder of this article unto a careful consideration of the particular reason here advanced by the apostle in support of his request, namely, "for we trust we have a good conscience in all things willing to live honestly." This expression "a good conscience" occurs in several other passages in the N.T., and because of its deep importance it calls for our closest attention. Much is said in the Word about conscience, and much depends upon our having and preserving a good one, and therefore it behooves us to give our best consideration to this weighty subject. Not only is it one of great practical moment, but it is especially timely in view of the conscienceless day in which we live. What, then, is the conscience? What is a *good* conscience, and how is it obtained and maintained? May the Spirit of Truth be our Teacher as we seek to ponder these vital questions.

Conscience is that faculty of the soul which enables us to perceive of conduct in reference to right and wrong, that inward principle which decides upon the lawfulness or unlawfulness of our desires and deeds. Conscience has well been termed the moral *sense,* because it corresponds to those physical faculties whereby we have communion with the outward world, namely, the five senses of sight, hearing, touch, taste and smell. Man has an ethical instinct, a faculty or moral sensibility informing and impressing him. "It is far higher in the scale and keener in its perceptions than any mere bodily sense. There is an inner eye, that sees into the nature of right and wrong; an inner ear, sensitive to the faintest whisper of moral obligation; an inner touch, that feels the pressure of duty, and responds to it sympathetically" (A. T. Pierson).

Conscience is that mysterious principle which bears its witness within us for good or evil, and therefore it is the very centre of human accountability, for it greatly adds to his condemnation that man continues sinning against the dictates of this internal sentinal. Conscience supplies us with self-knowledge and self-judgment, resulting in self-approbation or self-condemnation according to our measure of light. It is a part of the understanding in all rational creatures which passes judgment on all actions for or against them. It bears witness of our thoughts, affections, and actions, for it reflects upon and weighs whatever is proposed to and by the mind. That it bears witness of *emotions* is clear from, "My conscience also bearing me witness in the Holy Spirit, that I have great heaviness and continual sorrow in my heart" (Rom. 9:1, 2). So again we read, "Take no heed unto all words that are spoken, lest thou hear thy servant curse thee; for oftentimes also thine own heart (conscience) knoweth that thou thyself likewise hast (inwardly) cursed others" (Eccl. 7:21, 22). Its voice is heard by the soul secretly acquainting us with the right and wrong of things.

That conscience exists in the unregenerate is clear from Paul's statement concerning the Gentiles: "Which show the work of the law written in their hearts: their conscience also bearing witness, and their thoughts the meanwhile accusing or else excusing one another" (Rom. 2:15). Though the heathen never received the Scriptures, as Israel did, yet they had within them that which accused or excused them. There is within every man (save the idiot) that which reproves him for his sins, yea, for those most secret sins to which none are privy but themselves. Wicked men seek to stifle those inward chidings, but are rarely if ever successful. "The sinners in Zion are afraid; fearfulness hath surprised the hypocrites" (Isa. 33:14). Unregenerate men are without faith, yet not without fear: "The wicked flee when no man pursueth" (Prov. 28:1). There is that within man which appalls the stoutest sinner after the committal of any gross evil: his own heart reproves him.

The Creator has gifted the human soul with various faculties, such as the understanding, affections, and will; and He has also bestowed upon it this power of considering its own state and actions, both inward and outward, constituting conscience both a monitor and judge within man's own bosom — a monitor to warn of duty, a judge to condemn for neglect of the same. It is an impartial judge within us, that cannot be suspected of either undue severity or ill-will, for it is an intrinsic part of our own very selves. Conscience anticipates the Grand Assize in the Day to come, for it forces man to pass verdict upon himself, as he is subject to the judgment of God. It is resident in the understanding, as is clear from 1 Cor. 2:11, where the conscience is termed our "spirit."

The presence of conscience within man supplies one of the clearest demonstrations of the existence of God. To this fact the Holy Spirit appeals in Psa. 53. "The fool hath said in his heart, there is no God" (v. 1). Now how does he prove there is a God? Thus, "There were they in great fear, where no fear was" (v. 5). Though there was no outward cause for fear, none seeking to hurt them, yet even those who lived most atheistically were under a fear. An illustration is seen in the case of Joseph's brethren, who accused themselves when there was none other to accuse them: "They said one to another, We are verily guilty concerning our brother" (Gen. 42:21). Though a man should hide himself from all the world, he cannot get away from himself — his heart will pursue and condemn him. Now the very fact that there is such a hidden fear in man after sinning, that their hearts smite them for crimes done in secret, argues there is a God.

This fear is found in the most obstinate sinners, and in those who, because of their high station and power are exempt from human justice. History records how kings and emperors have followed their wickedness without interference, yet even the infamous Caligula trembled when it thundered. It was not a fear that they might be found out by man and punished by him, for in some notable instances this fear prevailed to such an extent that human punishment had been a welcome relief, and failing which they perforce laid violent hands upon themselves. What can be the reason for this, but that they feared a Judge and Avenger, who would call them to account? As the apostle said of the heathen, "They *know* the judgment of God" (Rom. 1:32): there is a witness in their own souls that they are liable to His justice. Mark the fearful consternation of Belshazzar: the paling of his countenance, smiting of his knees, loosing of his joints, when he read the sentence on the palace walls (Dan. 5:6).

"There is nothing in man that more challenges and demands adequate explanation than his moral sense. Conscience is a court always in session and imperative in its summons. No man can evade it or silence its accusations. It is a complete assize. It has a judge on its bench, and that judge will not be bribed into a lax decision. It has its witness-stand, and can bring witnesses from the whole territory of the past life. It has its jury, ready to give a verdict, 'guilty' or 'not guilty,' in strict accordance with the evidence; and it has its sheriff, *remorse,* with his whip of scorpions, ready to lash the convicted soul. The nearest thing in this world to the bar of God, is the court of conscience. And though it be for a time drugged into a partial apathy, or intoxicated with worldly pleasure, the time comes when in all the majesty of its imperial authority this court calls to its bar every transgressor and holds him to a strict account" (A. T. Pierson).

But though the presence of conscience in us bears witness to the existence of a holy, righteous, sin-hating and sin-avenging God, it is scarcely correct to say (as numbers have done) that the conscience is the voice of God speaking in the soul, rather is it that faculty which *responds* to what He says. When Christ declared "he that hath ears to hear let him hear," He signified, him that has a conscience attuned to the Most High, who desires to know His will and submit to His authority. Conscience sits upon the bench of the heart as God's vicegerent, acquitting or accusing. It acts thus in the natural man, but in the regenerate it is a godly conscience, guided in its operations by the Holy Spirit, bearing its testimony for or against the believer according to his character and conduct, Godwards and manwards.

The actual term conscience is derived from "scio" to know, and "con" with. There is some difference of opinion as to the precise application of the prefix, whether it be a knowledge we have in common with God, or a knowledge according to His Law. Really, it is a distinction with very little difference. The "knowledge" is of one individual alone by himself, but this "knowledge *with*" is where two at least share the same secret, either of them knowing it together with the other. Conscience, then, is that faculty which *combines two together,* and makes them partners in knowledge; it is between man and God. God knows perfectly all the doings of a man, no matter how carefully concealed; and man, by this faculty, also knows together with God the same things of himself. Hence we read of "conscience toward God" (1 Pet. 2:19), or as the Greek may also be rendered (see margin of R.V.) "the conscience of God"—having Him for its Author and Object. Conscience is God's vicegerent, acting for and under Him.

Thus, as the very term implies, conscience must have *a rule* to work by: "knowledge together with." It is not only a knowledge, but a knowledge coupled with *a standard,* according to which a process of inward judgment is carried on. Now our only proper rule is the Word, or revealed will of God. That is divided into two parts: what God speaks to man in His holy Law, and what He says to him in His blessed Gospel. If conscience departs from that Rule, then it is a rebellious one, it has ceased to speak and judge for God, and then the light in man is turned into darkness, for the (inward) eye has become evil (Matt. 6:23). In his primitive condition man had only the Law, and the proper work of conscience then was to speak warningly and condemningly in strict accordance with that Rule, and to allow none other. But our first parents listened to Satan's lie, broke the Law, and came under its condemnation.

Wherever we go conscience accompanies us, whatever we think or do it records and registers in order to the Day of accounts. "When all friends forsake thee, yea, when thy soul forsakes the body, conscience will not, cannot, forsake thee. When thy body is weakest and dullest, the conscience is most vigorous and active. Never more life in the conscience than when death makes its nearest approach to the body. When it smiles, acquits, and comforts, what a heaven doth it create within a man! But when it frowns, condemns and terrifies, how does it becloud, yea, benight all the pleasures, joys and delights of this world" (John Flavell). Conscience, then, is the best of friends or the worst of enemies in the whole creation.

Much of our peace of mind and liberty of spirit in this world will be according to the favourable testimony of conscience, and much of our spiritual bondage, fear, and distress of mind will be according to the charges of wrong-doing which conscience brings against us. When the gnawings of conscience are intensified, they become unendurable, as was the case with Cain, Judas and Sapphira, for they supply a real foretaste of the internal torments of Hell. Most probably this is that "worm that dieth not" (Mark 9:44) which preys upon the lost. As a worm in the body is bred of the corruption that is therein, so the accusations and condemnations of conscience are bred in the soul by the corruptions and guilt that are therein; and as the worm preys upon the tender and invisible parts of the body, so does conscience touch the very quick of the soul.

But notwithstanding what has been predicated of the conscience above, it is, nevertheless, *defiled* (Titus 1:15). In the natural man it is exceeding partial in its office, winking at and indulging favourite sins, whilst being strict and severe upon other sins to which a person is not constitutionally prone. Thus we find the conscience of king Saul exceedingly punctillious in a matter of the ceremonial law (1 Sam. 14:34), yet he scrupled not to slay eighty-five of God's priests! The reason why the conscience is so uneven is because it has been corrupted by the Fall: it is out of order, just as a foul stomach craves certain articles of diet while loathing others which are equally wholesome. So it is in the performance of duties: conscience in the natural man picks and chooses according to its own perverted caprice: neglecting what is distasteful, performing what is pleasing and then being proud because it has done so.

Now conscience is either good or evil, and that, according as it is governed by the revealed will of God. Briefly, the *evil* conscience first. This is of several kinds. There is the ignorant and darkened conscience, relatively so and not absolutely, for all (save idiots) possess rationality and the light of nature. This is the condition of the heathen, and alas, of an increasing number in Christendom, who are reared in homes where God is utterly ignored. Then there is the brazen and defiant conscience, which blatantly refuses to be in subjection to God's known will: such was the case with Pharaoh. In the case of Herod we see a bribed conscience, pretending that his oath obliged him to behead John the Baptist. The seared and insensible conscience (1 Tim. 4:2) pertains to those who have long resisted the light and are given over by God to a reprobate mind. The despairing and desperate conscience leads its possessor to lay violent hands upon himself.

At the new birth the conscience is renewed, being greatly quickened and enlightened by the Holy Spirit. Through the exercise of faith the conscience is purified (Acts 15:9), being cleansed by an appropriation of the blood of Christ (Heb. 9:14). A good conscience may be defined, generally, as one that is *set to please God in all things,* for it hates sin and loves holiness; it is one which is governed by the Word, being in subjection to the authority of its Author. Its binding rule is obedience to God, and to Him alone, refusing to act apart from His light. Consequently, the more conscientious the Christian be, the more he refuses all domination (the traditions and opinions of man) which is not Divine, the more likely is he to gain the reputation of being conceited and intractable. Nevertheless, each of us must be much on his guard lest he mistake pride and self-will for conscientious scruples. There is a vast difference between firmness and an unteachable spirit, as there is between meekness and fickleness.

How is a good and pure conscience obtained? Briefly, by getting it rightly informed, and by casting out its filth through penitential confession. The first great need of conscience is *light,* for ignorance corrupts it. "That the soul be without knowledge, it is not good" (Prov. 19:2). As a judge that understands not the laws of his country is unfit to give judgment on any matter that comes before him, or as a dim eye cannot properly perform its office, so a blind or uninformed conscience is incapable to judge of our duty before God. Conscience cannot take God's part unless it knows His will, and for a full acquaintance with that we must daily read and search the Scriptures. "Wherewithal shall a young man cleanse his way? by taking heed thereto according to Thy Word" (Psa. 119:9). O to be able to say, "Thy Word is a lamp unto my feet, and a light unto my path" (Psa. 119:105).

Let us now mention some of the qualities or characteristics of a good conscience. First, *sincerity*. Alas, how little of this virtue is left in the world: what shams and hypocrisy now obtain on every side — in the religious realm, the political, the commercial, and the social. This is a conscienceless generation, and consequently there is little or no honesty, fidelity, or reality. That which now regulates the average person is a temporary expediency, rather than an acting according to principle. But it is otherwise with the regenerate: the fear of the Lord has been planted in his heart, and therefore can he say with the apostle, "We trust we have a good conscience, in *all things* willing to live honestly." A sincere conscience genuinely desires to know God's will and is truly determined to be in subjection thereto. Guile has received its death wound, and the heart is open to the light, ready to be searched thereby.

Tenderness is another property of a good conscience. By this quality is meant a wakefulness of heart so that it smites for sin upon all occasions offered. So far from being indifferent to God's claims, the heart is acutely sensitive when it has been ignored. Even for what many consider trifling matters, a tender conscience will chide and condemn. Job resolved to preserve a tender conscience when he said, "my heart shall not reproach me as long as I live" (27:6). Again; we may understand this characteristic from its opposite, namely, a seared conscience (1 Tim. 4:2), which is contracted by an habitual practice of that which is evil, the heart becoming as hard as the public highway. Pray frequently for a tender conscience, dear reader.

Fidelity. When conscience faithfully discharges its office there is a constant judging of our state before God as a measuring of our ways by His Holy Word. Thus the apostle Paul could say, "Men and brethren, I have lived in all good conscience before God until this day" (Acts 23:1). The favourable judgment which others may entertain of him will afford no satisfaction to an upright man unless he has the testimony of conscience that his conduct is right in the sight of God. No matter what may be the fashions of the hour nor the common custom of his fellows, one whose heart beats true to God will not do anything knowingly against conscience: his language will ever be, "whether it be right in the sight of God to hearken unto you more than unto *God,* judge ye" (Acts 4:19). On the other hand, his frequent prayer is, "Search me, O God, and know my heart: try me, and know my thoughts; and see if there be any wicked way in me, and lead me in the way everlasting" (Psa. 139:23, 24).

Tranquillity. This is the sure reward of sincerity and fidelity, for Wisdom's ways (in contrast from those of folly) "are ways of pleasantness and all her paths are peace" (Prov. 3:17). An offended conscience will offend us, and "a wounded spirit who can bear?" (Prov. 18:14). The Christian may as well expect to touch a live coal without pain, as to sin without trouble of conscience. But a clear conscience is quiet, condemning not, being unburdened by the guilt of sin. When we walk closely with God there is a serenity of mind and peace of heart which is the very opposite of the state of those who are lawless and disobedient, "for the wicked are like the troubled sea, which cannot rest." The tranquillity of a good conscience is an earnest of the undisturbed calm which awaits us on High.

But let it be pointed out that every peaceful conscience is not a good one, nor is every uneasy conscience an evil one. The conscience of some is quiet because it is insensible. "When a strong man armed keepeth his palace, his goods are in peace" (Luke 11:21): that is a quiet evil conscience, because put to sleep by the opiates of Satan. True tranquillity of conscience is to be determined from the other properties: it must issue from sincerity, tenderness, and fidelity, or otherwise it is a seared one. We must consider not how much inward peace we have, but how much *cause*: as in a building, not the fairness of the structure, but the *foundation* of it is to be most regarded. On the other hand, a tender conscience is liable to err through lack of sufficient light, and needlessly write bitter things against itself, which is a "weak conscience" (1 Cor. 8:12); as we may also be troubled by sins already pardoned.

Now a good conscience can only be maintained by constant diligence: "herein do I *exercise myself* to have always a conscience void of offence toward God and men" (Acts 24:16). The apostle made it his daily employment to keep his conscience clear, that it might not justly accuse him of anything, so that he should have the witness in his own heart that his character and conduct was pleasing in the sight of the Holy One. The maintenance of a good conscience is an essential part of personal piety. "This charge I commit unto thee, son Timothy . . . holding faith and a good conscience" (1 Tim. 1:18, 19): that is the sum of personal godliness — faith being the principle of things to be believed by us, conscience the principle of the things to be done. Faith and a good conscience are linked together again in 1 Tim. 1:5 and 3:9, for we cannot hold the one without the other.

If the reader will turn back to Acts 24 he will find that Paul was replying to charges brought against him. In vv. 14-16 he made his defence, giving therein a brief epitome of practical and experimental Christianity. As the foundation he gives an account of his faith: "believing all things which are written"; as the immediate proof thereof — "and have hope toward God"; and then a brief account of his conversation: "herein do I exercise myself to have always a conscience void of offence." A saving knowledge of the Truth, then, is such a belief of the Scriptures as produces an hope of eternal life, which is evidenced by a keeping of the heart with all diligence. The same is enumerated again in "The end of the commandment" (the design of the Gospel institution) is that love which fulfils the Law, issuing from a heart that beats true to God (1 Tim. 1:5).

"Herein do I *exercise* myself": we must make it our constant endeavour. First, by a diligent and daily searching of the Scriptures that we may discover the will of God. We are exhorted "Be not unwise, but understanding what the will of the Lord is" (Eph. 5:17), and this in order that we may ascertain what is pleasing to Him, so that we offend not either in belief or worship. A conscience ill-informed is, at best, a weak and ignorant one. Second, by a serious inquiry into the state of our heart and ways: "Stand in awe, and sin not; commune with your own heart upon your bed, and be still" (Psa. 4:4). We need to frequently challenge and call ourselves to account. If we would have conscience speak to us, we must speak often to it. It is given us for this very reason that we may judge of our state and actions with respect to the judgment of God. Then "Let us search and try our ways" (Lam. 3:40). Take time, dear reader, to parley with yourself and consider how matters stand between you and God. Short reckonings prevent mistakes, so review each day and put right what has come between you and God.

Third, a uniform course of obedience: "Hereby we know that we are of the Truth, and shall assure our hearts before Him" (1 John 3:19). Fourth, by a constant alertness: "Watch and pray, that ye enter not into temptation" (Matt. 26:41). Fifth, by a serious resistance and mortification of sin: cutting off the right hand and putting out the right eye. Sixth, by a sincere repentance and confession when conscious of failure. Seventh, by faith's appropriation of the cleansing blood of Christ.

CHAPTER ONE HUNDRED TWENTY-TWO

Praying for Ministers

(Heb. 13:18, 19)

"Pray for us: for we trust we have a good conscience, in all things willing to live honestly. But I beseech you the rather to do this, that I may be restored to you the sooner." As was pointed out in the opening paragraph of the previous article, this passage is closely connected with v. 17, where believers are commanded to obey their ecclesiastical leaders. Here is mentioned a further obligation of Christians unto those who minister to them in spiritual things, namely, that they should remember them before the throne of grace. A due observance of this exhortation would probably do more than anything else to counteract and countervail a widespread evil: those who plead with God for blessings upon the preacher are far less likely to go around criticising them unto men. A spirit of fault-finding stifles the breath of intercession; countrariwise, a spirit of prayer will curb complaining and gossiping lips.

"Pray for us." The servants of Christ stand in real and urgent need of the prayers of their people. They are but men themselves, ignorant, weak, and erring, and unless they are granted a double portion of the Spirit they are not equipped for their arduous and honourable calling. They are the ones who bear the brunt of the battle, and are the special objects of Satan's attacks. They are often tempted to compromise, to keep back that which, though unpalatable to them, is most profitable for their hearers. In the face of many disappointments and discouragements, they are apt to grow weary in well doing. It is, then, both our duty and privilege to supplicate God on their behalf for daily supplies of grace to be granted them from on High; that they may be delivered from temptations, kept faithful, steadfast and devoted.

It is to be duly noted that this request was made by none other than the writer of this epistle; if, then, the greatest of the apostles stood in need of the intercessory support of his brethren, how much more so the rank and file of God's ministers. How tenderly, how earnestly, and how frequently Paul made this request! Here he adds,

"I beseech you"—language used again in Rom. 15:30, where he besought the saints to strive together with him in their prayers to God. In 2 Cor. 1:11 he speaks of "helping together by prayer for us." A beautiful type of the efficacy of the prayers of God's people to support one of His servants is found in the holding up the hands of Moses (Ex. 17:12), where we are significantly told, "And it came to pass, when Moses held up his hand, that Israel *prevailed*; and when he let down his hand Amalek prevailed."

"Pray for us." We agree with Owen that though the apostle here used the plural number (as was his general custom) that it was for himself alone he made this request: as the "I" in v. 19 intimates. It is a pre-eminently Pauline touch, and, as we pointed out in our second article of this series it supplies one of the many details which serve to *identify* the writer of this epistle. There is no record in the N.T. that any other of the apostles besought the prayers of the Church. Paul did so in no less than seven of his epistles: Rom. 15:30, Eph. 6:19, Col. 4:3, 1 Thess. 5:25, 2 Thess. 3:1, Philemon 22 and here. "He who laboured more than the other apostles, and who was endowed with so many gifts, seems to have had the greatest craving for sympathy, for affection, for communion, and the most vivid conception that God only giveth the increase; that it is not by might nor by power, but by the Spirit of the Lord" (A. Saphir).

"Pray for us": though the immediate reference was to Paul himself, yet obviously the exhortation applies to all the servants of Christ, and is binding upon all to whom they minister. They are the ones, under God, through whom we receive the most good. Oftentimes they are, ministerially, our spiritual fathers (1 Cor. 4:15), our spiritual nurses (1 Thess. 2:7), our guides, counsellors, and nourishers. They are to be esteemed very highly for their work's sake (1 Thess. 5:13), and that esteem is to be evident by our constantly bearing them up before God in the arms of faith and love. To earnestly supplicate the throne of grace on their behalf, is the least return we can make them for their loving labours, sacrificial endeavour, faithful ministrations. There is no doubt that the more diligent the people are in discharging this duty, the more help and blessing are they likely to receive through their labours.

"Pray for us." The apostle was persuaded that all the blessing he needed could be obtained from God, and from Him alone, and that *prayer* was the appointed means of obtaining those blessings. Someone has said that "If the due obedience of the church by all its members, unto the rulers of it, be the best means of its edification and the chief cause of order and peace in the whole body, certainly prayer for its leaders and fellow-members is the appointed channel for obtaining it." Again, by requesting the prayers of the Hebrew Christians, Paul intimated the regard in which he held them as righteous men, whose prayers would "avail much." His request also signified his confidence in their love for him: a heart that tenderly and faithfully sought their good, doubted not the warmth of their affection for him. Prayer for each other is one of the principal parts of the communion of saints.

The apostle supported his plea for the prayers of his readers by a striking and powerful reason; "For we trust we have a good conscience in all things willing to live honestly." In saying "we trust" two things were intimated. First, his becoming modesty: there was no boastful "we know." Second, his assurance, for such language in Scripture does not express a doubt. Thus though there was confidence in his heart toward God, yet he expressed himself in humble terms—an example we do well to heed in this boastful and egoistic age. It is a grand thing when a minister of the Gospel can truly, though modestly, appeal to the faithful performance of his labours as a reason why he may claim the sympathy and support of his people. It is only when he sincerely aims to do the right and maintains a good conscience that the minister can, with propriety, ask for the prayers of his people.

Probably the reason why Paul here made particular reference to his earnest endeavour to maintain a good conscience, was because he had been so bitterly denounced by his own nation, and no doubt (for Satan was the same then as now) the most unfavourable reports about him had been circulated among the Hebrews. He had been cruelly scourged by his own countrymen, and unjustly imprisoned by the Romans, yet he had the witness within his own bosom that it was his desire and determination to always act with integrity. "Though my name be cast out as evil, and though I be suffering as a wrong-doer, yet I appeal to my faithfulness in the Gospel ministry; I do not walk in craftiness nor handle the Word of God deceitfully, nor do I make merchandise of the Gospel: I have genuinely sought to act honourably under all circumstances." Happy the man that can say that.

"For we trust that we have a good conscience." As we pointed out previously, the conscience is that faculty with which the Creator has endowed man, whereby he is capable of judging his state and actions with respect to the judgment of God. Its office is twofold: to reveal sin to us, and to discover our duty, according to the light shining into it. There is a twofold light which men have to illumine conscience: natural reason and Scripture revelation, and the

Spirit applying the same. If the conscience has only the twilight of nature, as is the case with the heathen, it passes judgment on natural duties and unnatural sins, but if it enjoys the supernatural light of the Word, it judges of those sins and duties which can only be known by Divine revelation. It registers a permament record in the soul. The more light we have, the greater is our responsibility: Luke 12:48.

Though the heathen possess not the Law delivered by revelation of God to them, yet they have, in their moral sensibilities, the substance of its precepts written in their hearts: Rom. 2:15. When Paul said he had "lived in all good conscience before God until this day" (Acts 23:1), it was parallel with his "touching the righteousness which is in the law, blameless" (Phil. 3:6): there was a conformity of his outward conduct to the light which he had in his conscience. Thus "those that say there is no use of the moral law to the Christian, may as well say there is no more use of the faculty of conscience in the soul of a Christian. Tear that faculty out of a man's heart, if you will tear out that other, namely, the obliging precepts. Even as if God would annul colours and light, He must also take away and close up the sense of sight" (Thos. Goodwin).

"The spirit of man is the candle of the Lord, searching all the inward parts of the belly" (Prov. 20:27). This moral sense has been rightly denominated the Divine spy in man's soul. Its checks and reproofs are a warning from God: it acts in His name, citing us before His tribunal. It receives its instruction and authority from God, and is accountable to Him and to none other—alas how many are regulated by the customs and fashions of this world, and live upon the opinions and reports of their fellows. Conscience is a part of that light which "lighteth every man that cometh into the world" (John 1:9). In many passages both the "heart" (1 John 3:20) and the "spirit" (Rom. 8:16, 1 Cor. 2:11) signifies the conscience, while in Psa. 16:10 it is called the "reins." In yet other passages it is likened unto the physical "eye" (Luke 11:34-36): as the eye is the most sensitive member of the body and its visual faculty so is the conscience to the soul.

Conscience, then, is God's witness within man: it is the voice of His Law directing and admonishing the heart, conveying to us a knowledge of right and wrong. Its functions are to give testimony and force a moral verdict. Its business is to pronounce upon each action, whether it be good or evil, with the reward or punishment belonging to it, and then by a reflex act it deposes or witnesses that we have done righteously or unrighteously. Yet while conscience convicts of sin, it in no wise helps us to believe the Gospel: on the contrary, its workings withstand faith. No matter to what extent the natural conscience be enlightened, it conduces nothing to faith, nay it is the greatest enemy to it that the heart of man hath. Faith is the gift of God, a supernatural bestowment, something which is the operation of the Holy Spirit, altogether apart from and transcending the greatest height to which the unaided faculties of fallen man can reach unto.

What has just been pointed out above may, at first sight, surprise the reader; yet it ought not. Conscience is fully capable of hearing what the Law says, for it is but the Law written in the heart naturally; but it is quite deaf to what the Gospel says, and understands not a word of it. If you speak to natural conscience about a Saviour and urge it to believe on Him, its answer will be like unto that of the Jews (and it was this principle of conscience which made them so speak), "as for Moses we know that God spake unto him, but as for this fellow (Christ) we know not whence He is" (John 9:29). Talk to a man of the Law, and conscience responds, for it knows what he *ought* to do; but as for the Gospel its voice is that of a stranger to him. Conscience is quite incapable of pointing out the way of deliverance from the condemnation and penalty of sin, yea, "Except a man be born again, he *cannot see* the kingdom of God" (John 3:3).

It is true that the more conscience be enlightened, the more will it discover to us all manner of sins, and rebuke us for them; yet conscience alone will never discover unbelief to us, and convict us of its heinousness—only the immediate light of the Holy Spirit shining in the heart will do that. There are two great sins which lie outside the jurisdiction of conscience to set them upon the heart, ordinarily. First, the guilt of Adam's original transgression, which has been justly imputed unto all his posterity. An instructed conscience may perceive the depravity and corruption of a nature which has resulted from our fall in Adam, but it will not convict of that fatal condemnation we lie under because of our first father's offence. Second, conscience will not acquaint us with our lack of faith in Christ, and that this is *the* sin of all sins; only the special operation of the Spirit upon the quickened heart can accomplish this. Examine those who are most troubled in conscience, and it will be found that none of them are burdened because of their unbelief.

Until conscience be subordinated unto faith, it is the greatest hindrance to believing which the natural man hath. What is the chief obstacle which an awakened and convicted soul encounters? Why, the greatness of his sins, his heart telling him that he is beyond the reach of mercy, and it is naught but the accusations of a guilty conscience which produces that sense of hopelessness in the heart. Conscience brings our sins to light, makes them to stare us in the face, and terrifies us with their enormity. Conscience it is which tells a distressed soul that salvation is far off from such an one as I am. Conscience will set us working and doing, but only in a legal way: so far from leading us into the path of true peace, it will take us farther away from it. Thus it was with the Jews of old, and thus it is still: "For they, being ignorant of God's righteousness, and going about to establish their own righteousness" (Rom. 10:3).

In the case of a Christian, conscience and faith supplement each other in their workings. If conscience convicts of sin or rebukes for the omission of duty, faith eyes the mercy of God in Christ, penitently confesses the fault, and seeks cleansing through the precious blood. "The worshippers once purged should have had no more conscience of sins" (Heb. 10:2) — no more apprehensions of them as standing against us. It is the believer's bounden duty to maintain a good conscience: 1 Tim. 1:19; 3:9, but in order to that there must be a continual judging of ourselves and our ways. The revealed will of God is its only rule, for nothing else can lawfully bind it; therefore it is infinitely better to offend the whole world than God and conscience. "All my familiars watched for my halting, saying, Peradventure he will be enticed and we shall prevail against him," and what was the prophet's response and recourse? This, "But Thou, O Lord of hosts, that triest the righteous and seest the reins and the heart, let me see Thy vengeance on them: for unto Thee have I opened my cause" (Jer. 20:10, 12).

The sole rule to regulate the conscience of the Christian is God's written Word, for "whatsoever is not of faith (and therefore according to the Word: (Rom. 10:17) is sin" (Rom. 14:23); that is, whatsoever is not done from a settled persuasion of judgment and conscience out of the Word, is sin. The *defects* of a good conscience are, first, *ignorance or error*: some children of God are very imperfectly established in the Truth and are much confused as to what is right and wrong in the sight of God, especially in things indifferent, concerning which there is much difference of opinion. They understand not that *liberty* which Christ has purchased for His people (Gal. 5:1), whereby they are free to make a right and good use of all things indifferent—i.e. things not specifically forbidden by Scripture. "Wine that maketh glad the heart of man, and oil to make his face shine" (Psa. 104:15), which goes beyond bare necessities; to which we may add those innocent recreations which refresh mind and body. How to make a proper use of such things is defined in 1 Tim. 4:4, 5.

Second, and closely connected with the preceding, is what Scripture calls a "*weak* conscience" (1 Cor. 8:12), which is due to lack of light, wrong teaching, to personal prejudice and idiosyncrasies. It is often trying and difficult to know how to act towards those thus afflicted: on the one hand, love desires their good, and must be patient with them and refrain from acting recklessly and needlessly wounding them; but on the other hand, their fads and scruples are not to be so yielded to by us that our own spiritual liberty is annulled—Christ Himself refused to bring His disciples into bondage by yielding to the traditions of men (Mark 7:2), even though He knew they were spying for some fault in Him, and would be offended by His conduct. Third, a *doubting* conscience: Rom. 14: 22, 23. Fourth, a *wounded* conscience, whose peace is disturbed by unrepented and unconfessed sins.

The *benefits and blessings* are indeed rich compensation for every effort we make to maintain a good conscience. First, it gives us confidence Godwards. When we have sinned away our peace there is a strangeness and distance between the soul and the Holy One. When our inward monitor convicts and condemns us, the heart grows shy of God, so that we cannot so comfortably look Him in the face. It is only when everything is made right with God, by contrite confession and faith's appropriation of the cleansing blood of Christ, that we can approach the throne of grace with boldness. "Let us draw near with a true heart in full assurance of faith, having our hearts sprinkled from an evil conscience" (Heb. 10:22)—i.e. a conscience which no longer accuses us before God. "If I regard iniquity in my heart (which is inconsistent with a good conscience) the Lord will not hear me" (Psa. 66:18); but on the other hand "If our heart condemn us not, then have we confidence toward God; and whatsoever we ask, we receive of Him, because we keep His commandment and do those things that are pleasing in His sight" (1 John 3:21, 22).

Second, a clear conscience affords his chief relief when the believer is falsely accused and aspersed by his enemies. What unspeakable consolation is ours when we can rightfully appropriate that benediction of Christ, "Blessed are ye when men shall revile you and persecute you, and say all manner of evil against you falsely, for My sake" (Matt. 5:11). This was the case with the apostle Paul: "For our rejoicing is this, the testimony of our conscience, that in simplicity and godly sincerity, not with fleshly wisdom, but by the grace of God, we have had our conversation in the world" (2 Cor. 1:12). Third, a clear conscience vindicates its possessor against the accusations of Satan. The great enemy of our souls is constantly seeking to take away our peace and joy, and we are powerless against his onslaughts when a guilty conscience confirms his charges. But when we can appeal to a pure conscience and expose his lies, then his fiery darts are successfully quenched. The Psalmist was very bold when he said—see Psa. 7:3, 4, 5, 8.

Fourth, a pure conscience gives great advantage to its possessor when he is lawfully reproving others. The admonitions of that Christian whose life is inconsistent have no weight but he who walks closely with God speaks with authority. That man who is upright before God and his fellows, wields a moral force which is felt even by the ungodly. Finally, a peaceful conscience affords unspeakable comfort in a dying hour. When one has the inward witness that, despite many failures, he has sincerely endeavoured to do that which was right before God and unto his fellows, he has an easy pillow to rest his head upon. "Remember now, O Lord, I beseech Thee, how I have walked before Thee in truth and with a perfect heart, and have done that which is good in Thy sight" (Isa. 38:3): that was an appeal to a good conscience by one who was "sick unto death."

Paul's testimony of his having a good conscience consisted in this: "in all things willing to live honestly." A resolute will and a sincere endeavour to act rightly under all circumstances is the fruit and evidence of a good conscience. Being "willing" signifies a desire and readiness, with an accompanying effort and diligence. "In *all* things" takes in our whole duty to God and man, expresses the strictness and exactness of the apostle's course to maintain a conscience "void of offence" (Acts 24:16). What a striking commentary upon this declaration of Paul's is furnished in the account of his manner of life at Ephesus: see Acts 20:18-27. How his devotion, fidelity, and constancy puts to shame the flesh-loving indolence of so many preachers to-day. What strictness of conscience God requires from His servants: as the least bit of grit in the eye hinders its usefulness, so any sin trifled with will trouble a tender conscience.

We are commanded to "Provide things honest in the sight of all men" (Rom. 12:17) : a good conscience respects the second table of the Law equally with the first, so that we owe no man anything and are not afraid to look anybody in the face. Any faith which does not produce an impartial and universal obedience, is worthless. All the mysteries of our most holy faith are mysteries of *godliness* (1 Tim. 1:9; 3:16). But if the Word of God has come to us in word only and not in power, then are we but Christians of the letter and not of the spirit. Alas, how many today are sound in doctrine and have a carnal assurance of eternal life, yet who exercise themselves not to maintain a conscience void of offence. Alas, alas, what a conscienceless age our lot is cast in. How many souls are stumbled by the loose living of the majority of those who now profess to believe the Gospel.

"In all things willing to live honestly." We are exhorted to have our conversation "honest among the Gentiles: that, whereas they speak against you as evildoers, they may by your good works, which they shall behold, glorify God in the day of visitation" (1 Pet. 2:12). The Greek word in our text expresses more than is commonly understood by "honestly," being the same as that used in "He hath done all things *well*" (Mark 7:37). Its real force is "excellently" or "honourably." In his "in all things *willing to* live honestly" the apostle again expresses his humility and truthfulness. A sincere desire and a diligent endeavour so to act is the highest perfection attainable in this life, for we all fail in the carrying out of it. Thus, in all ages the saints have prayed, "O Lord, I beseech Thee, let now Thine ear be attentive to the prayer of Thy servant, and to the prayer of Thy servants, who *desire to fear* Thy name" (Neh. 1:11). It is blessed to be assured by God Himself that "For if there be first a *willing* mind, it is *accepted* according to that a man hath, and not according to that he hath not" (2 Cor. 8:12).

"But I beseech you the rather to do this, that I may be restored to you the sooner" (v. 19). In this verse Paul added a further reason why he desired the Hebrew saints to pray for him. Many things are intimated therein: that he had been with them previously, but circumstances over which he had no control now prevented his return—the best of ministers may be kept from their people (1 Kings 22:27, Jer. 38:6); that he greatly desired to come to them again, which shows that not his *own* comfort (deliverance from prison) but *their good* was uppermost in his mind; that he had strong confidence in the prevalency of prayer and of their affection for him. "When ministers come to a people as a return of prayer, they come with greater satisfaction to themselves and success to the people. We should fetch in all our mercies by prayer" (Matt. Henry).

The language used here by Paul denotes that he believed man's goings are of the Lord, that He disposes the affairs of the Church much according to their prayers, to His glory and their consolation. "That I may be restored to you the sooner" is very striking, showing that Paul was no blind fatalist: if God had decreed the exact hour, how could prayer bring it to pass "the sooner"? Ah, it is utterly vain for us to reason about or philosophise over the consistency between God's eternal decrees and prayer: sufficient for us to be assured from Scripture that prayer is both a bounden duty and blessed privilege. It is God's way to make us feel the need of and then ask for the bestowment of His mercies before He gives them: Ezek. 36:37. We know not if this prayer was answered, nor is it at all material: "according to our present apprehensions of duty we may lawfully have earnest desires after, and pray for such things, as shall not come to pass. The secret purposes of God are not the rule of prayer" (John Owen).

CHAPTER ONE HUNDRED TWENTY-THREE

The Apostle's Prayer

(Heb. 13:20, 21)

"Now the God of peace, that brought again from the dead our Lord Jesus, that great Shepherd of the sheep, through the blood of the everlasting covenant, make you perfect in every good work to do His will, working in you that which is well pleasing in His sight, through Jesus Christ; to whom be glory forever and ever. Amen" (vv. 20, 21). Let us begin by considering the *connection* which these verses have with what precedes: first with their wider context and then with their more immediate. In them there is really a gathering up into a brief but comprehensive sentence of the whole of what had been previously set forth, except that the apostle here *prays* there might be wrought in the Hebrews that unto which they had been *exhorted*. The substance of the whole doctrinal portion of the epistle is included therein, and the apostle now begs God to apply to the hearts of his readers the benefits and fruit of all the important instruction which he had presented to them. These verses, then, form a fitting conclusion, for what follows them is virtually a postscript.

Viewing our text in the light of its immediate context, we perceive a blessed exemplification of the fact that the apostle practised what he preached, for what he had required from his readers he is here seen doing for them. In vv. 18, 19 he had besought the prayers of the Hebrews on *his* behalf, and now we find him supplicating the Throne of Grace on *their* behalf. What a blessed example the chief of the apostles has left unto all whom Christ has called unto public service. If ministers desire the prayers of their people, then let them see to it that *they* are not backward in praying for those God has committed to their charge. This is an essential part of the minister's functions. It is not sufficient that he faithfully preaches the Word: he must also fervently and frequently ask God to *bless* that Word unto those who have heard him. O that all who are called to the sacred office may feelingly exclaim "God forbid that

I should sin against the Lord in ceasing to pray for you" (1 Sam. 12:23).

The verses which are now before us are in the form of an apostolic benediction or prayer. In them is set forth, in a striking and appropriate manner, the Object to whom the prayer was offered, following which is the matter for which supplication was made. In this article we shall confine ourselves unto the former. The Person to whom the apostle prayed is here described first by one of His titles, namely, "the God of peace"; and then by one of His works, the raising of Christ from the dead, and this in turn is ascribed unto the blood of the everlasting covenant. Those who have followed us through this lengthy series of articles may perceive how aptly the apostle reduces his grand exposition of the superiority of Christianity over Judaism unto these three chief heads: the God of peace, the risen Shepherd of the sheep, the blood of the everlasting covenant.

"The God of peace." The varied manner in which God refers to Himself in Scripture, the different appellations He there assumes, are not regulated by caprice, but ordered by infinite wisdom; and we lose much if we fail to weigh diligently each one. It is not for the mere sake of variation in diction, but each distinguishing title is selected in strict accord with its setting. He is spoken of as "The God of patience and hope" in Rom. 15:5, because that is in keeping with the subject of the four previous verses. In Rom. 16:27 He is addressed "To God only wise," because the immediate context has made known the revelation of the mystery wherein His inscrutable wisdom had been veiled. Before considering the significance of "the God of peace," let it be pointed out that it is an entirely Pauline expression, occurring nowhere in the writing of any other apostle—another identifying mark of the penman of *this* epistle. It is found in Rom. 15:33 and 16:20, 2 Cor. 13:11, Phil. 4:9, 1 Thess. 5:23, 2 Thess. 3:16, and here—seven times in all.

"The God of peace." First, this title contemplates God in relation to *His people,* and not mankind in general; yet in His forensic character, that is, in His office of *Judge.* It will be remembered that in that blessed passage where the two covenants are placed in antithesis and Sion is contrasted from Sinai, it is said, "But ye are come . . . to God the Judge of all" (12:23), which is the climacteric feature of the Gospel. The face of the Supreme Judge is wreathed in smiles of benignity as He beholds His people in the face of His Anointed. But it was not always thus. On the morning of creation as God saw us in Adam, our federal head, He viewed us with complacency, as "very good" (Gen. 1:31). But alas! sin came in, a breach was made between the Creator and the creature, and a state of alienation, *mutual alienation*, ensued, for a holy God could not be at peace with sin.

It needs to be clearly recognized that from the beginning God has sustained *other* relationships to man than those of Creator and Benefactor. Adam, and the human race in him, were placed under law, and therefore became subject to Divine government. In consequence of this, God was his Lord, his King, his Judge. While he remained in loyal subjection unto the Divine authority, yielding obedience to the King's laws, His favour was enjoyed, but when he transgressed, all was altered. Sin has not only defiled man, corrupting the whole of his nature, but it has brought him under the curse of the Divine law, and has subjected him to the Divine wrath. Fallen man, then has to do with an offended Judge. This was speedily made evident unto the original rebel, for we read, "therefore the Lord God sent him forth from the garden of Eden, to till the ground from where he was taken. So He *drove out* the man" (Gen. 3:23, 24).

Alas, how little is this most solemn aspect of the Truth preached to-day! Sin has not only vitiated our nature, it has alienated us from God: as it is written "alienated from the life of God" (Eph. 4:18). Man has not only lost the image of God in which he was created, but he had forfeited the favour of God in which he was instated. In consequence of the fall, there is *a mutual antagonism* between God and man. Sin has made a breach between them, so that all the harmony and concord which there was, both spiritual and judicial, has been completely destroyed. Not only is the carnal mind "enmity against God" (Rom. 8:7), "the *wrath of God* is revealed from heaven against all ungodliness and unrighteousness of men" (Rom. 1:18). That God *is* alienated from the sinner and antagonistic to him, is as clearly taught in the Scriptures as is man's enmity against God.

The One with whom fallen man has to do, is his outraged King and offended Judge, and His own Word leaves us in no doubt as to His *judicial* attitude toward the fallen creature. "Thou hatest all workers of iniquity" (Psa. 5:5). "God is angry with the wicked every day" (Psa. 7:11). "But they rebelled and vexed His Holy Spirit: therefore He was turned to be their *Enemy,* He fought against them" (Isa. 63:10). It was for this reason that none other than our blessed Redeemer said, "Fear not them which kill the body, but are not able to kill the soul: but rather fear Him *which is able* to destroy both soul and body in Hell" (Matt. 10:28), which is to be understood not simply of God's absolute power or omnipotency, but also and chiefly of His *judicial power* or rightful authority, as we are His prisoners and obnoxious to His judgments. Why is the modern pulpit so culpably silent upon these and similar passages?

God's holiness burns against sin, and His justice clamours for satisfaction. But is He not also of infinite mercy? Blessed be His name, He *is,* nevertheless His mercy does not override and nullify His other perfections. Grace reigns but it reigns "*through* righteousness" (Rom. 5:21), and not at the expense of it. When therefore God had designs of mercy toward His people—who sinned and fell in Adam, in common with the non-elect—His wisdom contrived a way whereby His mercy might be exercised consistently with His holiness, yea, in such a way, that His law was magnified and His justice satisfied. This grand contrivance was revealed in the terms of the Everlasting Covenant, which was entered into between God and the Mediator before the foundation of the world, but in view of the entrance of sin and the fall of the elect in Adam. Christ undertook to restore the breach which had been made, to effect a perfect reconciliation between God and His people, to make full satisfaction for all the harm which sin had done to God's manifestative glory.

Many, adopting the horrible heresy of the Socinians ("Unitarians"), will not allow that the reconciliation is *mutual*: but God has been reconciled to His people as truly as they to Him. As we have shown above, the Scriptures not only speak of enmity on *men's* part but also of wrath on *God's* part, and that, not only against sin but sinners themselves, and not the non-elect merely, but the elect too, for *we* "were by nature the children of wrath (yes, of "wrath" in addition to depravity!) even as others" (Eph. 2:3). Sin placed God and His people at judicial variance: they the parties offending, He the party offended. Hence, for Christ to effect perfect conciliation, it was required that He turn away the judicial wrath of God from His people, and in order to this, Christ offered Himself a propitiatory sacrifice to God, Himself bearing that wrath which was due to them.

This central truth in the Atonement, now so generally repudiated, was portrayed again and again in the O.T. types. For instance, when Israel sinned so grievously in connection with the golden calf, we find Jehovah saying to Moses, "Now therefore let Me alone, that My wrath may wax hot against them, and that I may consume them" (Ex. 32:10). But notice how blessedly the immediate sequel shows us the typical mediator interposing between the righteous anger of Jehovah and His sinning people, and turning away His wrath from them: see vv. 11-14. Again we read in Num. 16 that upon the rebellion of Korah and his company, the Lord said unto Moses "Get you up from among this congregation, that I may consume them as in a moment" (v. 45). Whereupon Moses said unto Aaron "Take a censer, and put fire therein from off the altar, and put on incense, and go quickly unto the congregation, and make an *atonement* for them; for there is *wrath* gone out from the Lord: the plague is begun." Aaron did so, and we are told, "he stood between the dead and the living, and the plague was *stayed*" (vv. 46, 48).

Surely nothing could be plainer than the above examples, to which many others might be added. All through the patriarchal and Mosaic economies we find that sacrifices were offered for the specific purpose of averting God's righteous wrath, to appease His judicial displeasure, to turn away His anger, the effect of which being expressly termed a "reconciliation:" see Lev. 16:20, 2 Chron. 29:24, Dan. 9:24. Most obviously the Israelites offered not their sacrifices to turn away their own enmity against God. Inasmuch, then, as those O.T. sacrifices were foreshadowings of Christ's oblation, what a turning of things upside-down is it to affirm that the great end of Christ's work was to reconcile sinners to God, instead of to divert God's wrath from us. The testimony of the N.T. is equally plain and emphatic: then let us bow to the same, instead of resisting and reasoning against it.

Of Christ it is said, "Whom God hath set forth *a propitiation* through faith in His blood, to declare (not His love or grace, but) His *righteousness*" (Rom. 3:25). Now a "propitiation" is that which placates or appeases by satisfying offended justice. The force of this verse is by no means weakened by the fact that the Greek word for "propitiation" is rendered "mercyseat" in Heb. 9:5, for the mercyseat was a *blood-sprinkled* one. It was the place where the typical mediator applied the atoning sacrifice for the satisfying of God's justice against the sins of His people. As a matter of fact the Hebrew word for "mercyseat" signifies "a covering," and it was so designated for two reasons: first, because it covered the ark, hiding from view the condemning Law—the tables of stone beneath it; and second, because the blood sprinkled upon it covered the offences of Israel from the eye of offended justice by an adequate compensation. Thus it fittingly portrayed the averting of deserved vengeance by means of a substitutionary interposition.

"For if, when we were enemies, we were reconciled to God by the death of His Son; much more, being reconciled, we shall be saved by His life" (Rom. 5:10). Yes, when we were "enemies," *God's enemies*—obnoxious to His righteous judgment. This term denotes the relation in which we stood to God as the objects of His governmental displeasure and subject to the curse of His law. But we were "reconciled," that is, restored unto His favour, and that, not by the Spirit's work in us subduing our enmity, but by "the death"—the propitiatory sacrifice—of God's Son. That this statement refers to the turning away of God's anger from us and the restoring us to His favour is clear from the previous verse: "Much more then, being now justified by His blood, we shall be saved from wrath through Him." Now to be "justified is the same as God's being reconciled to us, His acceptance of us into His favour, and not our conversion to Him. Being "justified by His blood" points to the procuring cause of our justification, and that blood was shed that we might be "saved from *wrath*." God is now pacified toward us, because His wrath was exhausted upon our Surety and Substitute.

"That He might reconcile both unto God in one body by the cross, having slain the enmity thereby" (Eph. 2:16). "That He," that is, the Mediator, the incarnate Son. "Might reconcile," that is, restore to God's judicial favour. "Both," that is, elect Jews and elect Gentiles. "Unto God," that is, considered as the moral Governor of the world, the Judge of all the earth. "In one body," that is, Christ's humanity, "the body of His flesh" (Col. 1:22)—here designated "*one* body" to emphasise the *representative character* of Christ's atonement, as He sustained the responsibilities and liabilities of all His people: it is the One acting on behalf of the many as in Rom. 5:17-19. "Having slain the enmity thereby," that is, God's holy wrath, the hostility of His law. The "enmity" of v. 16 cannot possibly refer to that which existed between Jews and Gentiles, for *that* is disposed of in vv. 14, 15. "Enmity" is here personified ("slain") as "sin" as in Rom. 8:3. Thus, Eph. 2:16 signifies, that all the sins of God's people meeting on Christ, Divine justice took satisfaction from Him, and in consequence God's "enmity" has ceased, and we are restored to His favour.

Let it not be thought that we are here inculcating the idea that Christ died in order to render God compassionate toward His people. Not so, the Father Himself is the Author of reconciliation: 2 Cor. 5:19. The gracious *means* by which He designed to effect the reconciliation originated in His own love, yet the atonement of Christ was the righteous instrument of removing the breach between us. The term is entirely a *forensic* one, contemplating God in His office as Judge. It concerns our relationship to Him not as our Creator, or as our Father, but as our King. The reconciliation which Christ has effected wrought no change in God Himself, but it *has* in the administration of His government: His law now regards with approbation those against whom it was formerly hostile. Reconciliation means that transgressors have been restored to *the judicial favour* of God through Christ's having closed the breach which sin had made. It was the amazing love of God which gave Christ to die for us, and His atonement was in order to the removing of those legal obstacles which our sins had interposed against God's love flowing out to us in a way consistent with the honour of His justice.

The great controversy between God and His people has been settled. The fearful breach which their sins occasioned has been repaired. The Prince of peace has silenced the accusations of the law and removed our sins from before God's face. Peace has been made — not a peace at any price, not at the cost of righteousness flouted; no, an *honourable* peace. "The God of peace," then signifies, first, the Judge of all is pacified; second, the King of Heaven has been reconciled to us; third, Jehovah, by virtue of His covenant-promises, has received us to His favour — for while He continued offended, we could not receive any gifts of grace from Him. Just as surely as Christ turned away God's wrath from His elect, so does He in due time send the Holy Spirit into their hearts to destroy *their* enmity against God, this being a consequence of the former.

We trust that what is next to be before us will render yet more intelligible and forcible all that has been said above. "That brought again from the dead our Lord Jesus." Here is the grand *evidence* that God is pacified toward us. When God raised Christ from the dead, He showed that He was propitiated, that He had accepted the ransom which had been given for our redemption. Let it be carefully noted that in our present verse it is the Father who is said to raise Christ, and that, in His character of "the God of peace." We will consider these two things separately. There is an *order* preserved in the personal operations of the Godhead. Resurrection was a work of Divine power, and that Divine power belongs in common to Father, Son, and Holy Spirit, who being one and the same God concur in the same work. Yet They concur in a way proper to Them: in all Their personal operations it is ascribed to the Father, as the Fountain of working and Wellhead of all grace, who doth all things *from* Himself, yet *by* the Son and Spirit.

In the grand mystery of redemption God the Father sustains the office of supreme Judge, and hence we read "Let all the house of Israel know assuredly that *God* hath made that same Jesus, whom ye have crucified, both Lord and Christ" (Acts 2:36 and cf. 10:36). So it is in our text: the raising of Christ is there viewed not so much as an act of Divine power, as of rectoral justice. It is God exercising His *judicial* authority which is emphasized, as is clear from the particular terms used. We are ever the losers if, in our carelessness, we fail to note each single variation of language. It is not *who* "raised again," but *"brought again* from the dead our Lord Jesus." The force of that expression may be ascertained by comparing Acts 16:35, 37, 39. The apostles had been unlawfully imprisoned, and when, later, the magistrates bade them go forth, they refused, demanding an *official* delivery; and we are told "they came and *brought them out of prison*" — compare also John 19:4, 13 for the force of this term "brought."

When Christ was in the state of the dead, He was in effect a prisoner under the arrest of Divine vengeance; but when He was raised, then was our Saviour let out of prison, and the word "brought again" suitably expresses that fact. Christ possessed the power to raise Himself — and considering His death and burial from another angle, He exercised that power; but in His official character as Surety, He lacked the necessary *authority*. The God of peace sent an angel to remove the stone from the sepulchre, not to supply any lack of power in Christ, but as the judge when he is satisfied sends an officer to open the prison doors. It was God Himself, as the Judge of all, who "delivered" Christ up for our offences, and it was God who raised Him for our justification (Rom. 4:25). This was very blessed, for it evidences the perfect subjection of the Son to the Father even in the grave: He did not exercise His might and break prison, but waited till God brought Him forth *honourably* from the dead.

Let us next observe the particular office Christ sustained when the God of peace brought Him again from the dead: "that great Shepherd of the sheep." Note, not "the," but "*that* great Shepherd," because Paul was writing to those who were familiar with the O.T.. "That Shepherd" signifies the One who was *promised* in such passages as "He shall feed His flock like a shepherd: He shall gather the lambs with His arm and carry them in His bosom" (Isa. 40:11), "And I will set up one Shepherd over them, and He shall feed them, even My Servant David: He shall feed them, and He shall be their Shepherd" (Ezek. 34:23) — the Object of the faith and hope of the Church from the beginning. Into the hands of our blessed Redeemer God placed His flock, to be justified and sanctified by Him. Let it be duly recognized that a shepherd is not the lord of the flock, but a *servant* to take charge of and care for it: "*Thine* they were, and Thou gavest them Me" (John 17:6) said Christ.

Christ is the "Shepherd of *the sheep*" and not of the "wolves" (Luke 10:3) or the "goats" (Matt. 25:32,33), for He has received no charge from God to save them — how the basic truth of *particular* redemption stares us in the face on almost every page of Holy Writ! There are three main passages in the N.T. where Christ is viewed in this particular character. He is "the good Shepherd" (John 10:11) *in death*, the "great Shepherd" *in resurrection*, and the "chief Shepherd" *in glory* (1 Pet. 5:4). The "great Shepherd" of the sheep calls attention to the excellency of His person, while the "chief Shepherd" emphasizes His superiority over all His undershepherds or pastors, the One from whom they receive their authority. How jealously the Holy Spirit guarded the glory of Christ at every point: He is not only the "Shepherd" but "that *great* Shepherd," just as He is not only High Priest, but our "great High Priest" (Heb. 4:14), and not merely King, but "the King of kings."

"Through the blood of the everlasting covenant." This is obviously an allusion to "As for Thee also, by the blood of Thy covenant I have sent forth Thy prisoners out of the pit wherein is no water" — the grave (Zech. 9:11). What is said of Christ is often applied to the Church, and here what is said of the Church is applied to Christ, for *together* they form "one Body." If, then, *He* was brought back from the dead through the blood of the everlasting covenant, much more shall *we* be. To say that God brought again from the dead "that great Shepherd of the sheep" means, He was raised not as a private person, but as the public Representative of His people. "The blood of the everlasting covenant" was the meritorious cause; as it was "by His own blood He entered in once into the Holy Place" (Heb. 9:12) and that we have "boldness to enter into the Holiest by the blood of Jesus" (10:19), so it is according to the infinite value of His atoning blood that both the Shepherd and His sheep are delivered from the grave.

As Christ (and His people) was brought into death by the sentence of the Law, so from it He was restored by the law's Administrator, and this acording to His agreement with Him before the foundation of the world. This it is which gives additional meaning to the Divine title at the beginning of our verse: He is called "the God of peace" from that compact which He made with the Mediator, concerning which we read, "The counsel of *peace* shall be between Them Both" (Zech. 6:13); "My kindness shall not depart from thee, neither shall *the covenant of My peace* be removed, saith the Lord that hath mercy on thee" (Isa. 54:10). The older commentators were about equally divided as to whether the final clause of our verse refers to that eternal agreement between God and the Mediator or to the new testament or covenant (Matt. 26:28); personally, we believe that *both* are included. The new covenant (about which we hope to have more to say later in our Covenant articles) is proclaimed in the Gospel, wherein is made known the terms on which we personally enter into the peace which Christ has made, namely, repentance, faith, and obedience. The new covenant is ratified by Christ's blood, and it is "everlasting" because its blessings are eternal.

CHAPTER ONE HUNDRED TWENTY-FOUR

The Apostle's Prayer

(Heb. 13:20, 21)

"Now the God of peace, that brought again from the dead our Lord Jesus, that great Shepherd of the sheep, through the blood of the everlasting covenant; make you perfect in every good work to do His will: working in you that which is well pleasing in His sight, through Jesus Christ." Though this be in the form of a prayer yet it presents a succinct summary of the entire doctrine of the epistle. The "blood of the everlasting covenant" stands over against "the blood of bulls and of goats," that "great Shepherd of the sheep," risen from the dead, is in contrast from Moses, Joshua, David, etc., who had long ago died; while "the God of peace" presents a striking antithesis to Jehovah's descent upon Sinai "in fire." Let us briefly consider these three things again, but this time in their inverse order.

"Through the blood of the everlasting covenant." We consider that this clause has a threefold force, that it is connected — both grammatically and doctrinally — with *each of* the preceding clauses. First, it is through the blood which He shed for sinners that Christ became the great Shepherd of the sheep — He was so previously by ordination, but He became so actually by impetration — the sheep were now His purchased property. Second, it was through or because of the atoning blood that God delivered Christ from the grave, for having fully satisfied Divine justice He was fully entitled to deliverance from prison. Third, it was through or by virtue of the pacifying blood of Christ that God henceforth became "the God of peace" unto His people, the whole controversy which their sins raised having been satisfactorily settled. And Christ shed His precious blood in fulfilment of the stipulations of the Everlasting Covenant, or that agreement which He entered into with the Father before the foundation of the world.

"That brought again from the dead our Lord Jesus, that great Shepherd of the sheep." "The Father is frequently said to raise Christ from the dead because of His sovereign authority in the disposal of the whole work of redemption, which is every where ascribed unto Him. Christ is said to raise Himself or take His life again when He was dead, because of the immediate efficiency of His Divine person therein. But more is intended here than an act of Divine power, whereby the human nature of Christ was quickened. The word used is peculiar, signifying a recovery out of a certain state: a moral act of authority is intended. Christ as the great Shepherd of the sheep was brought into the state of death by the sentence of the Law, and was therefrom restored by the God of peace, to evidence that peace was now perfectly made. The bare resurrection of Christ would not have saved us, for so any other man may be raised by the power of God; but the bringing of Christ from the dead through the blood of the everlasting covenant is that which gives assurance of the complete redemption of the Church (condensed from Owen).

"The God of peace." He is such first, because He takes this title from the Covenant itself (Isa. 54:10). He is so second, because as the supreme Judge He is pacified, and that because His law has received perfect satisfaction from our Surety. He is so third, because He is, in consequence, reconciled to us. Having accepted the person, obedience, and soul-travail of Christ, God is at peace with all His people in Him. Because He is at peace with them, He freely pardons all their iniquities and bestows every needed blessing upon them. When God removes from us all penalties and evils, and gives unto us all the privileges and good of the justified (such as the Holy Spirit to break the power and reign of sin in us) it is as the "God of peace" He does so; yea, as the supreme Judge, acting according to the principles of His government constituted in the everlasting covenant, by virtue of the merits of Christ and of our interest in Him.

God is also called "the God of peace" because He is the Author of that tranquillity which is felt at times in the hearts and consciences of His people, as He is also the Lover of that concord which obtains in measure among them upon earth. Owen suggests a further reason why the apostle uses this Divine title here. "He might have also herein an especial respect to the present state of the Hebrews, for it is evident that they had been tossed, perplexed, and disquieted with various doctrines and pleas about the law, and the observance of its institutions. Wherefore, having performed his part and duty in the communication of the truth to them for the information of their judgments, he now in the close of the whole applies himself by prayer to the God of peace: that He, who alone is the Author of it, who creates it where He pleaseth, would, through his instruction, give rest and peace to their minds" (John Owen).

So completely is God appeased that there is a new covenant procured and constituted, namely, the Christian Covenant, called here "the everlasting covenant." First, because it shall never be repealed and continueth unalterable, the called obtaining by it the title and possession of an eternal inheritance (Heb. 9:15). Second, because Christ's atoning blood is the foundation of this covenant, and as the virtue of it never ceaseth, therefore is it made effectual to secure its end, namely, the eternal salvation of sinful men who are converted and reconciled to God. This new covenant is also designated "the Covenant of Peace:" "I will make a covenant of peace with them" (Ezek. 37:26). First, because in the same this peace and reconciliation is published, and offered to us: "The word which God sent unto the children of Israel, preaching peace by Jesus Christ" (Acts 10:36 and cf. Eph. 2:17), because in this covenant the terms of this peace between us and God are stated: God binding Himself to give to sinful men forgiveness of sins and eternal life upon the conditions of repentance, faith, and new obedience.

A most important practical question is, How do we come to be interested in this Divine peace and reconciliation? A threefold answer may be returned: by ordination, impetration, and application. First, by the Father's eternal decree or foreordination, for as to who should enter into the same has not been left to chance; hence, God's elect are termed "the sons of peace" (Luke 10:6). Second, by the Son's impetration or paying the purchase price: "having made peace through the blood of His cross, by Him to reconcile all things unto Himself" (Col. 1:20). Third, by the Spirit's application, who subdues our enmity, bends our stubborn wills, softens our hard hearts, overcomes our self-righteousness, and brings us into the dust before God as self-condemned criminals suing for mercy. It is at our conversions this Divine peace is actually conveyed to us, for it is only then that God's wrath is removed from us (John 3:36) and that we are restored to His favour. Further grace is given us day by day as those already reconciled to God.

A final reason may now be advanced why God is here addressed as "the God of peace," and that is, to afford us valuable instruction in connection with prayer. It is very striking to note that in more than half of the passages where this particular Divine title occurs, it is where He is being *supplicated* — the reader may verify this for himself by consulting Rom. 15:33 and 16:20, 2 Cor. 13:11, Phil. 4:9, 1 Thess. 5:23, 2 Thess. 3:16, and here. Thus, it is employed for the purpose of *encouraging* us in our addresses at the Throne of Grace. Nothing will impart more confidence and enlarge our hearts more than the realization God has laid aside His wrath, and has only thoughts of grace toward us. Nothing will inspire more liberty of spirit than to look upon God as *reconciled* to us by Jesus Christ: "Therefore being justified by faith, we have peace with God through our Lord Jesus Christ: by whom also we have access by faith into this grace wherein we stand" (Rom. 5:1, 2).

"Make you perfect in every good work to do His will, working in you that which is well-pleasing in His sight, through Jesus Christ." Before taking up the coherency of this sentence let us point out the great practical lesson it contains. No matter how diligent the minister has been in his pulpit preparations, nor how faithfully he has delivered his message, his duty is by no means then fully discharged: he needs to retire to the closet and beg God to apply the sermon to those who heard it, to write it on their hearts, to make it effectual unto their lasting good. This is what the great apostle did. In the body of this epistle he had exhorted the Hebrews unto many good works, and now he prays that God will *enable them thereto*. The same thing holds good for those in the pew. It is not enough to listen reverently and carefully, we must also entreat God to bless unto us what we have heard. It is failure at this point which makes so much hearing unprofitable.

Though the apostle's prayer be brief, it is a most comprehensive one. It makes known the *method* by which Divine grace is administered to us. The grand *fountain* of it is God Himself, as He is the God of peace: that is, as in the eternal counsel of His will, He designed grace and peace unto poor sinners, agreeably to His goodness, wisdom, justice and holiness. The *channel* through which Divine grace is communicated, and that in a way suitable in His death and resurrection. God would have us know that while He is Himself the Giver, yet it is our Surety who merited for us every spiritual blessing we enjoy. The *nature* of this Divine grace relates particularly to our sanctification or perfecting, and this is expressed under the two heads of this prayer, namely, the grand end to be ever kept in view, and the means whereby that end is attained.

Having dwelt at some length upon the solemn manner in which the apostle addressed the Throne of Grace, we now turn to contemplate the *import* of his prayer, observing the two things here asked for the Hebrews. The first was that God would "make them perfect in every good work to do His will." This will require us to enquire into the meaning of this petition, to ponder its extensiveness, and then to mark its implications. Different writers have given various definitions to the "make you perfect," though they all amount to much the same thing. Thos. Scott gives "rectifying every disorder of their souls and completely fitting them for every part of His holy service." Matthew Henry enters into more detail: "A perfection of integrity, a clear mind, a clean heart, lively affections, regular and renewed wills, and suitable strength for every good work to which they are called."

Owen rendered it "make you meet, fit and able." And adds "It is not an absolute perfection that is intended, nor do the words signify any such thing, but it is to bring the faculties of the mind into that order so as to dispose, prepare, and enable them, so that they may work accordingly." The Greek word for "make you perfect" is rendered "fitted" in Rom. 9:22, "framed" in Heb. 11:3, and "prepared" in 10:5, where the product of *Divine workmanship* is seen in each instance. In the case before us it is the gracious operations of the Holy Spirit in connection with the progressive sanctification of the believer. Personally, we regard the definition of Scott (given above) as the best: the most accurate and elucidating.

The work of Divine grace in the elect begins when they are born again by the quickening operations of the Holy Spirit, and this work of grace is continued throughout the whole of their remaining days upon earth. Perfection of grace is not attained in this life (Phil. 3:12, 13), yet *additions to* our present attainments in grace are to be diligently sought (2 Pet. 1:5-7). No matter what spiritual progress has, by grace, been made, we are never to rest satisfied with it: we still need to be further strengthened for duties and fortified for trials. A child grows until it becomes fit for all manly actions, yet further progress is attainable after the state of manhood is reached. So it is spiritually. God requires from us the mortification of every lust, and an universal and impartial obedience from us, and therefore we may perceive how perfectly suited is this prayer to our needs.

Next, we turn to consider the *extensiveness* of this petition: "Make you perfect in *every* good work." This comprehensive expression includes, as Gouge pointed out, all the fruits of holiness Godwards and of righteousness manwards. There is to be no reservation. God requires us to love Him with "all our hearts," that we be sanctified in our "whole spirit, and soul, and body," and that we "grow up into Christ in all things." Many will do some good, but are defective in other things — usually in those which are most necessary. They single out those duties which make the least demand upon them, which require the least denying of self. But we shall never enjoy sound peace of heart till we are conformed unto all the revealed will of God: "Then shall I not be ashamed, when I have respect unto *all* Thy commandments" (Psa. 119:6). Then pray daily to be Divinely fitted unto every good work, especially those which you will find the hardest and most exacting.

"To do His will." Here we have a Scriptural definition of what is a "good work:" it is the performing of God's preceptive will. There are many things done by professing Christians which, though admired by themselves and applauded by their fellows, are not regarded as "good works" by the One with whom we have to do; yea, "that which is highly esteemed among men is abomination in the sight of God" (Luke 16:15). Of old the Jews added their own traditions to the Divine commandments, instituting fasts and feasts, so that the Lord asked "who hath required this at your hand?" (Isa. 1:12). We see the same principle at work to-day among the deluded Romanists, with their bodily austerities, idolatrous devotions, arduous pilgrimages, and impoverishing payments. Nor are many Protestants free from self-appointed deprivations and superstitious exercises. It is not the heeding of religious impulses, nor conforming to ecclesiastical customs, but doing the will of God which is required of us.

The *rule* of our duty is the revealed will of God. The "works" of man are his operations as a rational creature, and if his actions are conformed to God's Law, they are good; if they are not, they are evil. Therefore a man cannot be a good Christian without doing God's will. If it be God's will that he should refrain from such an act or practice, he dare not proceed to do it: see Jer. 35:6, Acts 4:19. On the other hand, if it be the revealed mind of God that he should do such a thing, he dare not omit it, no matter how it cross his inclination or fleshly interests: "To him that knoweth to do good, and doeth it not, to him it is sin" (James 4:17). It is not enough that we thoroughly understand the will of God: we must do it; and the more we *do* it, the better shall we understand: John 7:17.

"Make you perfect in every good work to do His will." Various things are clearly implied by these words. First, that we are imperfect or not qualified unto every good work. Yes, even after we have been regenerated, we are still unprepared to obey the Divine will. Notwithstanding the life, light and liberty we have received from God, yet we have not ability to do that which is well pleasing in His sight. This is indeed an humbling truth, yet truth it is: Christians themselves are unable to perform their duty. Though the love of God has been shed abroad in their hearts, a principle of holiness or new "nature" communicated to them, this of itself is not sufficient. Not only are they still very ignorant of God's will, but there is that in them which is ever opposed to it, inclining them in a contrary direction. Nor do the Scriptures hesitate to press this solemn fact upon us: rather is it frequently iterated for the humbling of ourselves before God.

Second, yet our spiritual impotency is not to be excused, nor are we to pity ourselves because of it; rather is it to be confessed to God with self condemnation. Third, none but God can fit us for the performing of His will, and it is both our duty and privilege to ask Him so to do. We need to diligently beg Him to strengthen us with might by His Spirit in the inner man, to incline our hearts unto His testimonies and not to covetousness, to so bedew our souls that we will grow in grace; for the new nature in the believer is entirely dependent upon God. "Not that we are sufficient of ourselves to think any thing as of ourselves; but our sufficiency is of God" (2 Cor. 3:5). If we need Divine grace to think a good thought or conceive a good purpose, much more do we need His strength to resolve and perform that which is good. Therefore did the apostle pray for supplies of sanctifying grace to be given unto the Hebrews, to enable them to respond to the will of God in the duties of obedience required of them.

"Working in you that which is wellpleasing in His sight." This is both in elucidation and amplification of that which has just preceded, intimating how God makes us perfect or fits us unto every good work. The previous petition expressed the grand *end* for which the apostle prayed, namely, the progressive sanctification of his readers; here, he expresses the *means* by which this was to be accomplished in them. This is effected not by moral persuasion and instruction only, but by an actual and effectual inworking of Divine power. So perverse are we by nature, and so weak even as Christians, that it is not sufficient for our minds to be informed by means of an external revelation of God's will; in addition, He has to stimulate our affections and propel our wills if we are to perform those works which are acceptable to Him. "Without Me ye can no *nothing*."

"Working in you that which is wellpleasing in His sight." This respects the gracious operations of the Holy Spirit in the hearts of the regenerate. It presents a striking and blessed contrast between the unsaved and the saved. Of the former we read, "The prince of the power of the air, the spirit that now worketh in the children of disobedience" (Eph. 2:2); whereas of the latter it is said "It is God which worketh in you both to will and to do of His good pleasure" (Phil. 2:13). First, God puts within us the will or desire unto that which is good, and then He bestows His strength to actually perform. These are quite distinct, and the latter is never commensurate with the former in this life. The distinction was clearly drawn by the apostle when he said, "For to *will* is present with me, but how to *perform* that which is good I find not"

(Rom. 7:18): yet even that "will" or desire had been wrought in him by Divine grace.

Only as these two truths are clearly recognized and honestly acknowledged by us — the Christian's spiritual powerlessness, and the efficiency of inwrought grace — will we rightly ascribe unto God the glory which is His due. To Him alone is due the honour for anything good which proceeds from us or is done by us: "By the grace of God I am what I am: and His grace which was bestowed upon me was not in vain; but I laboured more abundantly than they all: yet not I, but the grace of God which was with me" (1 Cor. 15:10). Not only do we owe to God the new nature which He has placed within us, but we are entirely dependent upon Him for the renewing of that new nature "day by day" (2 Cor. 4:16). It is God who worketh in His people spiritual aspirations, holy desires, pious endeavours: "from Me is thy fruit found" (Hos. 14:8). The more this be realized, the more will our proud hearts be truly humbled.

"Make you perfect in every good work to do His will, working in you that which is wellpleasing in His sight." By linking the two sentences together we are taught the most important lesson that there cannot be conformity to the will of God in the *life,* till there be conformity to Him in the *heart.* Herein we see the radical difference between human efforts at reformation and the Divine method. Man concentrates on that which is visible to the eyes of his fellows, namely, the external: "Woe unto you scribes and pharisees, hypocrites! for ye make clean the outside of the cup and the platter, but within they are full of extortion and excess" (Matt. 23:25 and cf. 27). Not so with Him who looketh on the heart: *He* worketh from within outward, fitting us for an obedient walk by effectually exciting the affections and empowering the will. It is thus that He continues and carries on to completion His work of grace in the elect.

Ere passing on to the next clause, let it be duly pointed out that while it is due alone to the gracious operations of the Spirit that we understand, love, believe, and do the things which God requires from us, it by no means follows that we are warranted to lie upon a bed of ease. No, far from it: we are responsible to *use every means* which God has appointed for our growth in grace and practical sanctification. Those who are fondest of quoting "for it is God which worketh in you both to will and to do of His good pleasure," are usually the slowest to emphasize the preceding exhortation: "work out your own salvation with fear and trembling" (Phil. 2:12). We are commanded to give all diligence to add to our faith the other graces of the Spirit: 2 Pet. 1:5-7. Then let us shake off our carnal security and lethargy: use the means and God will bless our endeavors (2 Tim. 3:16, 17).

"That which is wellpleasing in His sight." First, let us endeavour to live day by day in the consciousness that all we do is done in the sight of God. Nothing can escape His view. He observes those who break His law, and those who keep it: "The eyes of the Lord are in *every* place, beholding the evil and the good" (Prov. 15:3). How it should curb and awe us to realize that God is an observer of every action: "in holiness and righteousness *before Him*" (Luke 1:75). Second, let this be our great aim and end: to please God. That is sound piety, and nothing else is. Pleasing man is the religion of the hypocrites, but pleasing God is genuine spirituality. More than once does the apostle inculcate this as the right end: "Not as pleasing men, but God"; "that ye might walk worthy of the Lord unto all pleasing" (Col. 1:10).

Third, let us see to it that all our works are *so ordered as* to be pleasing to God. In order to this our actions must square with the rule of His Word: only that which is agreeable to His will is acceptable in His sight. But more: it is not sufficient that the substance of what we do be right, but it must issue from a right principle, namely, love to God and faith in Christ; "For without *faith* it is impossible to please Him" (Heb. 11:6), yet it must be a faith that "worketh *by love*" (Gal. 5:6)—not as forced, but as the expression of gratitude. Finally, as to the *manner* of this: our good works must be done with soberness and all seriousness: "serve God acceptably with reverence and godly fear" (Heb. 12:28)—as becometh a menial in the presence of His Majesty. Remember that God actually takes delight in such works and those who do them: Heb. 11:4—what an incentive unto such!

CHAPTER ONE HUNDRED TWENTY-FIVE

Divine Exhortations

(Heb. 13:22)

Before taking up our present verse let us offer some further remarks upon the last portions of v. 21, which, through lack of space, we had to omit from the preceding article. The central thing which we sought to make clear in the previous paper was, that, while the believer received at his regeneration a new nature or principle of grace (often termed by the older writers "the *habit* of grace"), yet it is not sufficient of itself to empower us unto the actual execution of good works. At the beginning God *did* place in Adam everything necessary to equip him for the performing of all obedience; but *not so* with the Christian. God has not communicated to us such supplies of grace that we are self-sufficient. No indeed: rather has He placed *in Christ* all "fulness" of grace for us to draw on (John 1:16), thereby making the members dependent on their Head. And, as we shall now see, it is from Christ that fresh supplies of grace are communicated to us.

"Working in you that which is well-pleasing in His sight through Jesus Christ" (v. 21). The "through Jesus Christ" has a double reference: to God's working in us, and to the acceptance of our works. First, in the light of vv. 20, 21 as a whole, it is clear that what is there insisted upon is, that there are no communications of grace unto us from the God of peace except in and by Jesus Christ—by His mediation and intercession. This is a most important point to be clear upon if the Redeemer is to have that place in our thoughts and hearts which is His due: all the gracious operations of the Spirit within the redeemed, from their generation to their glorification, are conducted according to the mediation of the Saviour and are in response to His intercession for us. Therein we may perceive the admirable wisdom of God, which has so contrived things that *each* Divine Person is exalted in the esteem of His people: the Father as the fountain of all grace, the One in whom it originates; the Son, in His mediatorial office, as the channel through which all grace flows to us; the Spirit as the actual communicator and bestower of it.

Second, in our judgment, these words "through Jesus Christ" have also a more immediate connection with the clause "that which is well-pleasing in His sight," the reference being to those "good works" unto which the God of peace perfects or fits us. The best of our duties, wrought in us as they are by Divine grace, are not acceptable to God simply as they are *ours,* but only on account of the merits of Christ. The reason for this is, that Divine grace issues through an imperfect medium: sin is mixed with our best performances. The light may be bright and steady, yet it is dimmed by an unclean glass through which it may shine. We owe, then, to the Mediator not only the pardon of our sins and the sanctification of our persons, but *the acceptance* of our imperfect worship and service: "To offer up spiritual sacrifices, acceptable to God *by Jesus Christ*" (1 Pet. 2:5) states that aspect of truth we are here emphasising.

"To whom be glory for ever. Amen." Here the apostle, as was his custom, adds praise to petition. This is recorded for our instruction. The same principle is inculcated in that pattern prayer which the Lord Jesus has given to His disciples, for after its seven petitions He teaches us to conclude with, "for Thine is the kingdom, and the power, and the glory, for ever and ever. Amen" (Matt. 6:13). There is some uncertainty as to whether the ascription of praise in our text be unto the God of peace, to whom the whole prayer is addressed, or whether it be unto Jesus Christ, the nearest antecedent. Personally, we believe that *both* are included and intended. Both are equally worthy, and both should receive equal recognition from us. In Phil. 4:20 praise is offered distinctively unto the Father; in Rev. 1:5, 6 to the Mediator; while in Rev. 5:13 it is offered unto both.

"And I beseech you, brethren, suffer the word of exhortation: for I have written a letter unto you in few words" (v. 22). We will first give a brief exposition of this verse, and then make some remarks upon its central theme. The opening word is misleading in our Version, for it is contrastive and not connective, being rightly rendered "But" in the R.V. In the preceding verse, the apostle had spoken of *God* working in His people that which is wellpleasing in His sight: here he addresses *their responsibility,* and urges unto diligence on their part. Herein we may perceive again how perfectly Paul ever preserved the *balance* of truth: unto the Divine operations must be added our endeavours. Though it is God who worketh in us both to will and to do of His good pleasure, nevertheless, we are exhorted to work out our own salvation with fear and trembling: Phil. 2:12, 13.

The "word of exhortation" refers, in our judgment, to the entire contents of this epistle. The Greek word for "exhortation" is quite a comprehensive one, including within its meaning and scope direction, admonition, incitation, and comfort. It is usually translated "consolation" or "exhortation," one as often as the other. Manifestly it was very appropriate for the apostle to thus summarize the whole of his epistle, for, from beginning to end, its contents are a most powerful and impressive incitation unto perseverance in the faith and profession of the Gospel, in the face of strong temptations to apostasy. "The word of exhortation is the truth and doctrine of the Gospel applied unto the edification of believers, whether by way of exhortation or consolation, the one of them including the other" (John Owen—and so all the best of the commentators). But let us observe the tactfulness and gentleness with which the apostle urged the Hebrews to attend unto the exhortations that had been addressed to them.

First, he said, "But I *beseech* you." This was "an affectionate request that they would take kindly what on his part was meant kindly" (J. Brown). Paul did not set himself on some lofty pedestal and *command* them—as he might well have done by virtue of his apostolic authority—but placing himself on their level, he tenderly urged them. "This word of exhortation as it comes out of the bright atmosphere of truth, so it comes out of the genial atmosphere of affection" (A. Saphir). Second, he added, "I beseech you, *brethren*," "denoting (1) his near relation unto them in nature and grace, (2) his love unto them, (3) his common interest with them in the case to hand—all suited to give an access unto his present exhortation" (John Owen); to which we may add, (4) it evidenced his commendable humility and lowliness of heart.

Third, he added "But I beseech you, brethren, *suffer* the word of exhortation." This of course implied there were things in this epistle which were *opposed to* their corruptions and prejudices. This also revealed once more the deep solicitude which the apostle had for the Hebrews. He had written to them some pointed warnings and some severe admonitions, and he was deeply concerned that they should not miss the benefit thereof, either through their negligence or because of their natural antipathy. "Probably he records (uses) the word of *exhortation* for this reason: though men are by nature anxious to learn, they yet prefer to hear something new, rather than to be reminded of things known and often heard before. Besides, as they indulge themselves in sloth, they can ill bear to be stirred and reproved" (John Calvin).

Here we may perceive again what a blessed *example* the apostle has left all ministers of the Word. The preacher must be careful to stir up his hearers to seek their own good: "Son of man, I have made thee a watchman unto the house of Israel: therefore hear the Word at My mouth, and give them warning from Me. When I say unto the wicked, Thou shalt surely die: and thou givest him not warning, nor speaketh to warn the wicked from his wicked way, to save his life; the same wicked man shall die in his iniquity, but his blood will I require at thine hand" (Ezek. 3:17, 18). In nothing are our hearers (even the saints) more backward than to appreciate and respond to the word of *exhortation.* Yet exhortation was the apostle's keynote all through this Epistle. God has given His Word to us for *practical* ends, and the faith of God's elect is "the acknowledging of the truth *which is after godliness*" (Titus 1:1). The Holy Scriptures have been placed in our hands that we may be furnished unto all good works, instructed in every duty, fortified against every temptation. No doctrine is rightly understood unless it affects our *walk.* But in pressing unto a compliance with the Divine precepts let us seek grace that we may do it with the fidelity, wisdom, humility, and tenderness that the apostle evidenced and exemplified.

"For I have written a letter unto you in a few words." Strange to say, some have been puzzled by this clause, because most of Paul's epistles are much shorter than this one, and hence they have invented the wild theory that v. 22 alludes only to this final chapter, which Sir Robt. Anderson strangely designated "a kind of covering letter." But the apostle was not here referring *absolutely* to the length of his epistle, but to *the proportion between* its length and the momentousness and sublimity of the theme of which it treats. In comparison with the importance and comprehensiveness of the many subjects which he had touched upon, brevity had indeed marked his treatment throughout. Nothing more than a short compendium had been given of the new covenant, the office and work of Christ, the superiority of Christianity over Judaism, the life of faith, and the varied duties of the Christian.

The principal subject referred to in our present verse is the Divine *exhortations,* which is one of the greatest practical importance and value, yet alas, it is sadly neglected and generally ignored to-day. In Calvin's time men preferred "to hear something new, rather than to be reminded of things known and often heard before," but the present generation is woefully ignorant of those paths of righteousness which God has marked out in His Word, and so far from *often* hearing of many of those duties that God requires us to perform, most pulpits are largely silent thereon, substituting themes and topics which are more agreeable to the flesh, studiously avoiding that which searches the conscience and calls for reformation. Now an "exhortation" is an urging to the performance of duty, an incitation unto obedience to the Divine precepts. In developing this theme, we feel that we cannot do better than follow the order set forth in Psalm 119.

We are there shown, first, the *blessedness* of those who respond to God's claims upon them: "Blessed are the undefiled in the way, who walk in the Law of the Lord. Blessed are they that keep His testimonies, that seek Him with the whole heart" (vv. 1, 2). The Psalmist began *here* because it is essential that we should have a right understanding of what true blessedness consists. All men desire to be happy: "There be many that say, Who will show us any good?" (Psa. 4:6). This is the cry of the world, "Good, good:" it is the yearning of nature for contentment and satisfaction.

Alas, sin has so blinded our understandings that by nature we neither know where real blessedness is to be found nor how it is obtained. So thoroughly has Satan deceived men, they know not that happiness is the fruit of *holiness,* a conscience testifying to God's approbation. Consequently, all, until Divine grace intervenes, seek happiness in riches, honours and pleasures, and thus they flee from it while they are seeking it—they intend joy, but choose misery. "Thou has put gladness in my heart, more than in the time that their corn and their wine increased" (Psa. 4:7)—yes, "*their* corn and their wine:" not only possessed by them, but chosen by them as their portion and felicity. But David found that by treading the highway of holiness, God had put a gladness in his heart to which the pleasures of the worldling could not for a moment compare.

The main difference in thought between the first two verses of Psa. 119, wherein the secret of true happiness is revealed, is this: in the former the outward conduct of the man of God is described; in the latter, the inward principle which actuates him is seen, namely, whole-hearted seeking unto the Lord. As it is out of the heart there proceeds all the evils enumerated by Christ in Matt. 15:19, so it is out of the heart there issues all the graces described in Gal. 5:22, 23. It is for this reason we are bidden, "Keep thy heart *with all diligence,* for out of it are the issues of life" (Prov. 4:23). This is very solemn and searching, for while "man looketh on the outward appearance, the Lord looketh on the heart" (1 Sam. 16:7). Therefore there must be the exercise of faith and of love before our outward conduct can be pleasing unto God.

After affirming and describing the blessedness of those who walk in the Law of the Lord (vv. 1-3), the Psalmist next reminds us that God has *"commanded us* to keep His precepts diligently" (v. 4). First, he sets before us a most attractive inducement to heed the Divine commands, and then we are reminded of God's righteous claims upon us. We are His creatures, His subjects, and as our Maker and Ruler He has absolute authority over us. God's will has been clearly revealed in His Word, and we are obligated to give our best attention and respect thereunto. God will not be put off with anything: He requires to be served with the utmost care and exactness. Thus, it is not left to our caprice as to whether or not we will walk in God's Law—an absolute necessity is imposed.

"O that my ways *were* directed to keep Thy statutes" (v. 5). Awed by a sense of the authority of God, conscious of the propriety of His commanding His creatures, and of the justice of His claims, the Psalmist now felt his own weakness and utter insufficiency, his deep need of Divine grace, to enable him to fulfill his duty. This is one of the marks of a regenerate soul: first he is enlightened, and then he is convicted. Knowledge of the path of duty is communicated to him, and then consciousness is awakened of his inability to walk therein. Holiness begins with holy desires and aspirations: O that I were walking in the Law of the Lord, and keeping His precepts diligently. He realised that in the past, he had followed his *own* ways and paid little or no attention unto God's authority. But now he longs for this to be radically altered.

This panting after a conformity to the Divine will is the breathing of the new nature, which is received at regeneration. A change of heart is ever evidenced by new desires and new delights. "For they that are after the flesh, do mind the things of the flesh; but they that are after the Spirit, the things of the Spirit" (Rom. 8:5). When the love of God is shed abroad in the heart, *our* love goes out to God, and as His love is a regard for our good, so our love for Him is a regard for His glory. Love to God is testified by a longing to be subject to Him: "For this is the love of God, that we *keep His commandments;* and His commandments are not grievous" (1 John 5:3). The more clearly the believer descerns the wisdom, goodness, purity, and holiness of the Divine precepts, the more earnestly does he long to obey them: "O that my ways were directed to keep Thy statutes"—this is the longing of the heart for directing grace.

Passing over the intervening verses, we observe, next, the Psalmist's *prayer for* enabling grace: "Blessed art Thou O Lord: teach me Thy statutes" (v. 12). One of the duties of God's people in connection with the Divine precepts is to turn them into prayer. This is in accord with the new covenant, where precepts and promises go hand in hand. What God requires from us, we may ask of Him. "Why doth God require what we cannot perform by our own strength? He doth it (1) to keep up His right; (2) to convince us of our impotency, and that upon a trial: without His grace we cannot do His work; (3) that the creature may express his readiness to obey; (4) to bring us to lie at His feet for grace" (T. Manton).

Prayer is the expression of our desires, and if we truly long to obey God, then we shall earnestly supplicate Him for enabling grace. The first thing sought is that God would *teach us* His statutes, which has reference to both the outward means and the inward grace. The letter of the Word and the preaching thereof must not be despised, for it is an ordinance which is appointed by God; yet it is only as the Divine *blessing* attends the same that we are truly profited. When the Lord Jesus taught His disciples we are told, that He first opened to them the Scriptures, and then He opened their understandings (Luke 24:32, 35). The inward teaching of the Spirit consists in enlightening the understanding, inflaming the affections, and moving the will, for Divine teaching is ever accompanied by drawing (John 6:44, 45).

The great need for such inward teaching by the Spirit is our *obstinacy and prejudice.* To live for eternity instead of for time, to walk by faith and not by sight, to deny self and take up the cross daily, seems utter foolishness to the natural man. To yield ourselves wholly to God, is to row against the raging stream of our lusts. The old nature has a long start on the new, so that we are confirmed in evil habits, and therefore to act contrary to our natural bent and bias is likened unto cutting off right hands and plucking out right eyes. Moreover, every step we take, yea, attempt to take, along the highway of holiness, is hotly opposed by Satan. Thus, the need is real, urgent, imperative, that we should be Divinely empowered to discharge our duties. None but God Himself can work in us both to will and to do of His good pleasure.

Next we find the Psalmist declaring, "I will *meditate* in Thy precepts, and have respect unto Thy ways" (v. 15). Prayer is vain unless it be accompanied by faithful endeavour on our part. Here is David's hearty resolution and purpose to discharge his responsibility. He knew that he would never have that respect for God's ways of holiness which is their due, unless he made His precepts the subject of his constant thoughts. "As a man thinketh in his heart, so is he." If our minds were constantly engaged with sacred things, the savour thereof would be apparent in our conversation. But the fear of God and a delight for His Word must first be established in our hearts, for our thoughts follow our affections—that which the heart has no relish for, the mind finds irksome to dwell upon. Difficulties in holy duties lie not in the duties themselves, but in the backwardness of our affections.

"I will meditate in Thy precepts and have respect unto Thy ways" (v. 15). The *order* is deeply suggestive: meditation precedes obedient conduct. Meditation is to be far more than a pious reverie: it is an appointed means to God-pleasing conduct: "Thou shalt meditate therein day and night, *that* thou mayest observe *to do* according to all that is written" (Josh. 1:8). Meditation is not for the purpose of storing the mind with curious notions and subtle ideas, but is to be turned to practical use. Observe well, dear readers, it is not "I will meditate in Thy promises" (though that too has its proper place), but "in Thy *precepts*." And why is it so essential that we *should* meditate therein? That they may be fixed more permanently in the memory, that they may make a deeper impression on the heart, and that we should the better discern their manifold application unto the varied duties of our lives.

"I will meditate in Thy precepts." This was no passing fancy with David, like the forming of a New Year's resolution that is never carried into execution. He repeats his determination "I *will* meditate in Thy statutes" (v. 48), and again he declares, "I will meditate in Thy precepts" (v. 78). It is often said that, in this strenuous and bustling age, meditation is a lost art. True, and is not this one of the chief reasons why obedience to God's commands is a lost practice? God complained of old, "My people do not *consider*" (Isa. 1:3): what goes in at one ear, goes out at the other. "When anyone heareth the Word of the kingdom, and *understandeth it not,* then cometh the Wicked one, and catcheth away that which was sown in his heart" (Matt. 13:19): and how can the Word be understood unless it be prayerfully pondered, turned over and over in the mind. "Let these sayings *sink down* into your ears" (Luke 9:44)—by means of serious reflection and steady contemplation thereof.

"Make me to go in the path of Thy commandments, for therein do I delight" (v. 35). Here we find David praying for *compelling grace.* Though he was a regenerate man and delighted in the Divine precepts, he was painfully conscious of the fact that there was still much in him which pulled the other way. The flesh lusted against the spirit, so that he could not do the things which he would. True, Divine grace has placed within the born-again soul an inclination and tendency toward that which is good, yet fresh supplies of grace are needed daily before he has strength *to perform* that which is good. And for this grace God would be sought unto. Why so? That we may learn that power belongeth unto Him alone, and that we may be kept lowly in our own esteem. Were God to send sufficient rain in a day to suffice for a year, no notice would be taken of His acts of providence; and were He to grant us sufficient grace at the new birth to suffice the rest of our lives, we would quickly become prayerless.

It is a very humbling thing to be brought to realize that we must be "*made* to go" in the path of God's commandments, yet sooner or later each believer experiences the truth of it. Godly desires and holy resolutions are not sufficient to produce actual obedience: God has to work in us to *do,* as well as to "will" of His good pleasure. Peter's resolution was strong when he declared that he would not deny Christ, though all others should do so; yet in the hour of testing he discovered that he was as weak as water. We are told of Hezekiah that "God *left him,* to try him, that he might know all that was in his heart" (2 Chron. 32:31); and at times He does this with all His people, that they may discover that without Him they can do *nothing*. When this discovery *is* made, the soul feels the suitability of this prayer, "Make me to go in the path of Thy commandments."

"Incline my heart unto Thy testimonies, and not to covetousness" (v. 36). In these words there is a confession implied, as well as a supplication expressed. There is an acknowledgment that the natural bent of the heart is away from God unto worldly things. That for which he prayed was that the bias of his heart should be turned unto God and His precepts. For the heart to be "inclined" unto God's Word means, for the affections to be so inflamed unto holiness that *the will* is carried after them. Just as the power of sin lies in the love it has for the objects attracting us, so our aptness for godly duties lies in the *love* we have for them. When God says "I will *cause you* to walk in My statutes" (Ezek. 36:27), it means that He will so enlighten the understanding and kindle the affections that the will is inclined thereto.

But let it be said again that, diligent effort *on our part* must be added to praying, for God will not heed the petitions of the slothful and careless. Hence we must carefully note that not only did David beg God to "Incline my heart unto Thy testimonies," but he also declared "*I have inclined* mine heart to perform Thy statutes always" (v. 112). It is our bounden duty to incline our hearts unto God's Law, yet it is only by God's enablement we can do so. Nevertheless, God deals not with us as stocks and stones, but as rational agents. He sets before us motives and inducements which it is our responsibility to respond unto. He appoints means, which it is our duty to use. He bestows blessings, which it is our obligation to improve—*trading with* the pound He has given us. And this David had done. True, it was all of grace, as he had been the first to acknowledge: nevertheless the fact remained he *had co-operated with* grace: working out what God had worked in; and all is vain till that be done.

Our space is exhausted. Does some captious critic ask, What has all the above to do with Heb. 12:22? We answer, much every way. *How* are we to "suffer the Word of Exhortation"? Psalm 119 supplies a detailed answer! By frequently reminding ourselves that compliance therewith is the way of true blessedness; by constantly calling to mind the Divine authority with which it is invested; by owning and bewailing our perverse disinclination thereto; by earnest prayer for enabling grace; by meditation daily thereon; by begging God to make us go in the path of His commandments; by diligent improvement of the grace given.

CHAPTER ONE HUNDRED TWENTY-SIX

Spiritual Freedom

(Heb. 13:23)

Before turning to our present verse we must complete our observations on the one which occupied our attention in the last article, for the practical importance and value of it cannot be over-estimated or over-emphasized. "Suffer the Word of Exhortation." In its local meaning to the Hebrews this expression comprehended the entire contents of the Epistle which Paul had addressed to them, for, from beginning to end, it was in the nature of an earnest entreaty that they would relinquish the now effete system of Judaism, and remain steadfast in the profession of Christianity and the performance of Gospel duties, This was, then, a final word from the apostle that his readers would duly take to heart the message he had delivered to them, that no matter how radically it conflicted with their traditions, sentiments, and prejudices, their eternal welfare depended upon receiving what was worthy of all acceptation. It was an affectionate appeal to them that they would not, through natural disinclination, miss and lose the inestimable value of what he had written.

But this expression "the Word of Exhortation" has a still wider meaning and application for *us*. It may legitimately be taken for the entire Word of God, for what are the Scriptures—considered from one essential viewpoint—but a continuous exhortation? Just as in Rom. 9:9 we read of "the Word of Promise" and in 2 Pet. 1:19 of the more sure "Word of Prophecy," so here the Scriptures are designated "the Word of Exhortation"—the *emphasis* being changed in each case. And just as responding to the Word of Exhortation meant to the Hebrews that they must first *relinquish* something, and then *adhere* to another thing in its place; so it is with us. The Hebrews were called upon to forsake the Christ-dishonouring camp of Judaism and act by faith in the revelation which God had made in His Son; whereas we are called upon to forsake the world and its vanities, to forsake the pleasures of sin and the indulging of our fleshly lusts, and to tread that highway of holiness which alone conducteth unto Everlasting Life. No matter how much the Divine exhortations cross our wills and oppose our corruptions, obedience thereto is absolutely necessary if we are to escape the wrath to come.

In our last article we sought to show *how* we are to "suffer the Word of Exhortation," how we are to *respond* thereto, by making use of what is found in Psalm 119 on this subject, for it is there, more fully than anywhere else in Scriptures, we are taught how the man of God conducts himself with reference to the Divine Law. We briefly touched upon seven things, and pointed out that we are to "suffer" or give the Word of Exhortation that place in our hearts and lives to which it is entitled, by frequently reminding ourselves that obedience thereto is the way of true blessedness (119:1-3), by constantly calling to mind the Divine authority with which it is invested (v. 4), by earnestly praying for enabling grace (vv. 12, 27), by frequently meditating therein (vv. 15, 48, 78), by begging God to make us go in the path of His commandments (v. 35), by praying Him to incline our hearts thereto (v. 36), by our own diligent improvement of the grace which God has already given to us (v. 112): let us now add a few more words upon this last point.

"I have inclined mine heart to perform Thy statutes always, even unto the end" (v. 112). Was this creature boasting? Most certaintly not, any more than Paul was guilty of the same when he declared "I have fought a good fight, I have finished my course, I have kept the faith." It is not unusual for Scripture to ascribe to us what God works in us, and that because of our subservient endeavours to Divine grace, as we pursue the work of God. The soul responds to the impressions which the Spirit makes upon it. God gives us breath, yet we breathe. God supplies food, yet we have to prepare and eat it. God sets motives before us, but we have to respond thereto. God imparts grace, but we must improve it. This is the way to get more: Luke 8:18. It is our duty to heed that injunction "now *set your heart* and your soul to seek the Lord your God" (1 Chron. 22:19); and as Paul "If that I may apprehend (lay hold of) that for which also I am apprehended of Christ Jesus" (Phil. 3:12).

Moreover, there are certain *aids and helps* thereto, which it is our privilege to employ. For example the Psalmist said, "I am a companion of all them that fear Thee, and of them that keep Thy precepts" (Psa. 119:63). We are largely affected and influenced by the company we keep: "Make no friendship with an angry man; and with a furious man thou shalt not go" (Prov. 22:24). We must not expect to love and obey God's precepts if we have fellowship with those who despise them. But communion with godly souls will be a stimulus to our own piety. "He that walketh with wise men shall be wise" (Prov. 13:20). Here too our responsibility is exercised, for we are free to choose our companions. So far as Providence permits, it is our duty to cultivate acquaintance with those who make conscience of obeying God's commands. Pious conversation with them will kindle the spark of grace in our own hearts: "Ointment and perfume rejoice the heart: so doth the sweetness of a man's friend by hearty counsel" (Prov. 27:9).

There is one other thing we would notice in Psa. 119 as it bears upon the subject of obedience to God's commands, and that is, profiting from Divine chastenings, begging God to sanctify to us the various trials through which we pass. "Before I was afflicted I went astray: but now have I kept Thy Word" (v. 67). It is in seasons of temporal prosperity that we are most apt to decline spiritually, and generally we have to pass through deep waters of trouble before we are restored—the snapping dog of adversity is employed to recover the strayed sheep. Afflictions are blessings in disguise when they cool our lusts, wean us from the world, make us realize our weakness, and cast us back immediately upon God. So declared the Psalmist: "It is good for me that I have been afflicted; that I might learn Thy statutes" (v. 71). Then "despise not thou the chastening of the Lord, nor faint when thou art rebuked of Him" (Heb. 12:5).

Ere turning from this subject, let us remind the reader that the Greek word rendered "exhortation" in 13:22 is translated "consolation" in 6:18, for the term not only signifies to entreat and incite, but it also means to relieve and refresh. It may seem strange to some that the same word should have such different forces as exhortation and consolation, yet these two things have a much closer affinity than is generally realized, and this twofold meaning is designed by the Spirit to inculcate an important practical lesson. To despise the Word of Exhortation is to forsake our own comforts, as many a backslidden Christian can testify. Obedience to the Divine precepts carries its own reward now: peace of conscience, tranquility of mind, contentment of heart, and assurance of God's approbation. Divine consolation is secured by heeding the Word of Exhortation!

"Know ye that our brother Timothy is set at liberty; with whom, if he come shortly, I will see you" (v. 23). Following our usual custom we will first raise the question, What is the *connection* between this verse and the context? At first glance there does not appear to be any relation between them, yet further examination seems to indicate otherwise. Some of our readers may deem us fanciful, but it appears to the writer that this historical allusion to the "liberty" of Timothy supplies an *illustrative encouragement* for us to respond to the call contained in the preceding verse. Let us set it forth thus: those who refuse to heed the Word of Exhortation, and instead give free play to their own corruptions, are in the worst servitude of all—the bondage of sin and Satan; but those who yield submission to the commands and precepts of God enter into true spiritual *freedom.*

It is one of the great delusions of the natural man that he is free only so long as he may please himself, supposing that to be placed under the authority of another is to curtail his liberty and bring him into bondage. But that is a putting of darkness for light and light for darkness. For just so far as the language of our hearts be "let us break Their bands asunder, and cast away Their cords from us" (Psa. 2:3) are we tyrannized over by our lusts. In proportion as we follow the inclinations and devices of our evil hearts are we in servitude to sin and Satan. Lawlessness is not liberty, but libertinism, which is the worst bondage of all: "While they promise them liberty, they themselves are the slaves of corruption, for of whom a man is overcome, of the same is he brought in bondage" (2 Pet. 2:19).

Alas, what widespread ignorance and delusion abounds on this subject to-day. Carnal liberty is but moral thraldom. To make this the more evident let it be pointed out, first, that which most infringes upon a man's real liberty is that which most hinders and disables him to prosecute his true happiness. When the things of sense crowd out the things of the spirit, when the concerns of time oust the interests of eternity, when Satan is given that place in our lives which belongs only to God, then we are forsaking our own mercies and come under the most cruel task-masters. Second, that which disorders the soul and puts reason out of dominion, is certain spiritual bondage. When the base prevail over the honourable, it is a sign that a country is enthralled: and when our fleshly lusts, rather than our understanding and conscience, prevail over the will, it is sure proof that we are in spiritual bondage.

Again; consider the great power and tyranny of sin. Sin, in various forms and ways, has such complete dominion over the unconverted that it robs them of all control over themselves and their actions: they are "*serving* divers lusts and pleasures" (Titus 3:3). This is most evident in the case of the confirmed drunkard and the drug addict—what fetters they have forged for themselves, and how helpless they are to break from them! Yet, the bondage of pleasure and worldly pursuits is just as real, if not so apparent. Sin, even in its most refined forms, obtains such a mastery over its victims that they have no command of their affections and still less of their wills, so that they are quite unable to forsake what they themselves believe to be vanity or follow that which they know to be good. "Can the Ethiopian change his skin, or the leopard his spots? then may ye also do good, that are accustomed to do evil" (Jer. 13:23). Therefore do many of them say, "There is no hope: but we will walk after our own devices, and we will everyone do the imagination of his evil heart" (Jer. 18:12).

Now on the contrary, true liberty is to be found in the ways of God, for spiritual freedom is a freedom from sin and not to sin, a freedom to serve God and not self, a freedom to take upon us the easy yoke of Christ and not the despising of it. Genuine liberty is not a liberty to do what we please, but to do what we ought. "Where the Spirit of the Lord is, there is *liberty*" (2 Cor. 3:17); contrariwise, where Satan rules there is captivity (2 Tim. 2:26). Said the Psalmist, "And I will walk at liberty: for I seek Thy precepts" (119:45). Yes, just so far as we walk according to the Divine precepts, are we freed from the fetters of our corruptions. It is that miracle of grace which brings the heart to love the Divine statutes, that sets the heart at rest. "The way of holiness is not a track for slaves, but the King's highway for freemen, who are joyfully journeying from the Egypt of bondage to the Canaan of rest" (Spurgeon).

First, the way of God's precepts is in itself liberty, and therefore God's Law is called "the perfect Law *of liberty*" (James 1:25). How grievously are they mistaken, then, who accuse us of bringing souls into bondage when we insist that the Law is the believer's Rule of Life—the bondage of the Law from which Divine grace delivers, is from the Law as a covenant of works, and therefore from its condemnation and curse; and not from the preceptive authority of the Law. Yet ever since we drank that poison, "ye shall be as gods" (Gen. 3:5), man affecteth dominion over himself and would be lord of his own actions. But Scripture makes it clear that the most dreadful judgment which God inflicts upon the wicked in this world is when He withdraws His restraints and gives them over to do as they please: Psa. 81:12, Rom. 1:26-29.

Real liberty is found in the ways of God because it is there we are directed to attain unto true felicity. The way of sin seems broad and easy to the flesh, yet is it strait and painful to the spirit —"the way of trangressors is hard." Contrariwise, the way of holiness seems strait and narrow to the flesh, yet, because it is life and peace, it is broad and easy to the spirit—all of Wisdom's ways are "ways of pleasantness." He liveth the freest life who liveth under the bonds of duty, who maketh conscience of pleasing God, for it is the Truth which makes us free (John 8:32). The fuller be our obedience, the more completely emancipated are we from the fetters of moral slavery. The only unshackled ones are those who walk with God.

Second, liberty is given to walk in God's ways. At regeneration the soul, hitherto in prison, is set free by Christ (Luke 4:18, John 8:36). "For the Law of the Spirit of life in Christ Jesus hath made me free from the law of sin and death" (Rom. 8:2). Conversion is a change of masters: "But God be thanked, that ye were the *servants of sin,* but ye have obeyed from the heart that form of doctrine which was delivered you. Being then made free from sin, ye became the *servants of righteousness*" (Rom. 6:17, 18). Redemption is a being delivered from the cruel task-masters of Egypt and coming under the Lordship of Christ. In loving, fearing, serving, and praising God the highest faculties of the soul are exercised in their noblest and most regular way of operation. The soul is lifted above the things of time and sense, elevated to occupation with heavenly and eternal things. (For some things in the last few paragraphs we are indebted to Manton's sermon on Psa. 119:45.)

We trust that the reader is now able to perceive the *connection* between the deeper spiritual significance of Heb. 13:23 and the verse which immediately precedes it. The historical allusion to the physical release of Timothy from his imprisonment, coming immediately after the call for us to heed the Word of Exhortation, is to be regarded as *an illustration* of the spiritual freedom which attends our compliance with that Divine injunction. Just in proportion as we yield subjection to the Divine precept, do we enter into and enjoy *real freedom of soul.* If this should seem too fanciful to some of our more prosaic readers, perhaps they will be willing that others should be permitted to exercise their own judgment thereon.

"Know ye that our brother Timothy is set at liberty." "Who this Timothy was, what was his relation unto Paul, how he loved him, how he employed him and honoured him, joining him with himself in the salutation prefixed unto some of his epistles, with what care and diligence he wrote unto him with reverence unto his office of an evangelist, is known out of his writings. This Timothy was his perpetual companion in all his travels, labours and sufferings, serving him as a son serveth his father, unless when he designed and sent him unto any special work for the Church. And being with him in Judea, he was well known unto the Hebrews also, as was his worth and usefulness" (John Owen).

Timothy means "precious to God." His father was a Greek; his mother a Jewess. Nothing is known of the former. That his mother was a true believer we learn from 2 Tim. 1:5, where the apostle makes mention of the unfeigned faith which "dwelt first in thy grandmother Lois, and thy mother Eunice." The expression "unfeigned faith" testifies to the reality and genuineness of it, in contradistinction from the empty profession of others who, without just cause, posed as believers. From the above reference many have concluded that Timothy, in his early days, received a godly training. This is confirmed by "From a child thou hast known the Holy Scriptures, which are able to make thee wise unto salvation through faith which is in Christ Jesus" (2 Tim. 3:15). Apparently the family resided at Lystra.

The first visit of the apostle Paul to Lystra is recorded in Acts 14. There he and Barnabas "preached the Gospel" (v. 7). There too God wrought a mighty miracle through Paul, by healing an impotent man who had never walked, being a cripple from his mother's womb (v. 10). A deep impression was made upon the heathen inhabitants, who could scarce be restrained from doing homage to the apostles as gods. But shortly after, Jews came from Antioch and Iconium and persuaded the people—so fickle is human nature—to stone Paul. The writer believes that he was then actually stoned to death and that God restored him to life. Possibly the following passage refers to that incident: "We would not, brethren have you ignorant of our troubles which came to us in Asia, that we were pressed out of measure, above strength, insomuch that we despaired even of life: But we had the sentence of death in ourselves, that we should not trust in ourselves, but in God which raiseth the dead: who delivered us from so great a death, and doth deliver: in Whom we trust that He will yet deliver" (2 Cor. 1:8-10).

It was during this first visit of Paul to Lystra that young Timothy was converted. This seems clear from the fact that in 1 Tim. 1:2 he refers to him as "my own son in the faith"; while in 2 Tim. 3:10, 11 Paul reminds him now that he fully knew the persecutions and afflictions which befell his spiritual father "at Antioch, at Iconium, *at Lystra.*" The expression "my own son in the faith" signifies that Paul had, ministerially, begotten him through the Gospel (1 Cor. 4:17). The Lystrians had dragged the body of Paul outside the city (Acts 14:19), but he rose up and returned into it. Next day he departed to Derbe, but after preaching the Gospel there, he returned to Lystra, "confirming the souls of the disciples, exhorting them to continue in the faith, and that we must through much tribulation enter into the kingdom of God" (v. 22).

What has been pointed out above explains the fact that when Paul revisited Lystra some three or four years later, Timothy is already spoken of as a "disciple" (Acts 16:1). The second verse intimates how he had acquitted himself during the apostle's absence. During that time he had established a reputation for godliness, not only in Lystra, but in Iconium. He had become well known to the churches at both cities, and was "well reported of." Probably it was this good report which attracted Paul, who then stood in need of a fellow-helper—Barnabas and Mark having in the interval deserted him (Acts 15:39). The commendation of Timothy's "brethren" inclined Paul to select him for a wider work. But there was, however, one hindrance in the way: Timothy was a Gentile, and the Jewish Christians were not yet, generally, prepared to receive an uncircumcised leader. To place him in office as a teacher might arouse prejudice, so Paul, in deference to their scruples, circumcised the young disciple.

Nothing is told us of what it must have cost Eunice to give up such a son: but *God* took notice (Psa. 56:8). From now on Timothy figured prominently in the history of Paul, becoming his companion and fellow-labourer. Two of his epistles were addressed to him, and in six others he is associated with him in the superscription: compare 2 Cor. 1:1. Timothy was with the apostle during his second great missionary tour, accompanied him to Jerusalem, and was with him in his first imprisonment. In 1 Cor. 4:17 we find Paul affirming that Timothy was "faithful in the Lord." Phil. 2:19-22 presents to us a lovely picture of the gracious power of the Spirit triumphing over the affections of the flesh, and the love of Christ constraining unto unselfishness. The apostle was prisoner in Rome, and Timothy, who was there, was very dear unto him; yet was he willing to part with his beloved companion, even in his sorrow and solitariness, He was solicitous for the welfare of the Philippian saints, and having none other he could send, authorized Timothy to visit them.

In referring to Timothy as being "like minded" with himself, Paul gives us an insight into his ability. Not only was Timothy his "own son in the faith" but he speaks of him "as a son with the father, he hath served with me in the Gospel" (Phil. 2:22). Young believers generally become like those with whom they associate most intimately. Blessed is it when we see them growing up to follow the example of godly leaders—"imitators of *us* and of the Lord" (1 Thess. 1:6). How solemnly important it is, then, that the leaders should live so that the younger Christians may not be made to stumble.

From the personal exhortations addressed by Paul to Timothy (in the epistles bearing his name), it seems clear that he was of a sensitive, shrinking, and timid nature. The word in 2 Tim. 1:6 (cf. 1 Tim. 4:12, 14, 16) seems to imply that he was almost ready to give up in despair. The "God hath not given us the spirit of fear"—really "cowardice" (2 Tim. 1:7) and the "be not ashamed" (v. 8) intimate that there was need for the exhortation "fight the good fight of faith" (1 Tim. 6:12) and "endure hardness as a good soldier of Jesus Christ" (2 Tim. 2:3, and cf. 4:5). That he was a man of frail constitution is evident from 1 Tim. 5:23. Yet to Paul he was "his dearly beloved son" (2 Tim. 1:2). Timothy's "tears" (2 Tim. 1:4) over Paul's imprisonment show that he was a man of feeling.

"Know ye that our brother Timothy is set at liberty: with whom, if he come shortly, I will see you" (Heb. 13:23). This supplies one more incidental confirmation that Paul was the writer of the Hebrews' epistle, for it is clear from this verse that Timothy was the one who accompanied him on his missionary journeys—there is no hint elsewhere that Timothy was the fellow-worker of any one else but Paul. The actual incarceration of Timothy is not recorded in the Acts or elsewhere, but it is clear from this verse that he had been restrained, but that he was now free. The imprisonment of faithful ministers is an honour to them, yet is their release an occasion of rejoicing to the saints; and therefore the apostle acquaints the Hebrews of this good news, for he knew how highly they esteemed Timothy. He had not yet returned to Paul himself—apparently having been imprisoned at some other place than Rome, but if God directed him thither, he purposed that they should both again visit the churches in Judea. Whether this hope was realized, we know not.

CHAPTER ONE HUNDRED TWENTY-SEVEN

Conclusion

(Heb. 13:24, 25)

Everything down here comes, sooner or later, to its end. Terrible prospect for the wicked, for there awaits them naught but the blackness of darkness forever. Blessed outlook for the righteous, for then they are done with sin and suffering forever, and only everlasting glory and bliss stretches before them. How would it be with *you,* my reader, if the hand of time were now writing the *final lines* of your earthly history? Did the apostle experience a pang of regret as he arrived at the parting salutation? did his readers? We cannot be sure, but this writer certainly feels sorry that the closing verses are now reached; and we are assured that not a few of those who have followed us throughout this series will feel much the same. For rather more than ten years we have journeyed together through this epistle, and now we have come to the Conclusion.

It is very doubtful if the writer will ever again attempt a task of such dimensions. Be that as it may, he certainly will never be engaged with a more momentous and glorious subject. There is no book in the N.T. of greater importance, and few of equal. First, it furnishes us a sure guide to the interpretation of the O.T., the Holy Spirit moving the apostle to here open up its principal types. Second, it supplies us with a vivid description and explanation of the Mediator's office and work, demonstrating the worthlessness and needlessness of all other intermediaries between the soul and God. Third, it therefore places in our hands the most conclusive exposure of the errors and fallacies of the Papacy. Fourth, it makes clear to us why Judaism has passed away, and how it can never again be restored.

The deep importance of this epistle is intimated by a feature which is peculiar to it, namely, the absence of the writer's name. But let it be noted that he did not conceal himself, for in 13:18-24, especially, Paul made it quite clear to the Hebrews who was the penman of this epistle: he plainly declared himself and his circumstances as one who was well known to them. The true reason why he did *not* prefix his name to this epistle, as to his others, was this: in all his other epistles he dealt with the churches by virtue of his apostolic authority and the revelation of the Gospel which he had personally received from Christ; but in dealing with the Hebrews, he laid his foundation in the authority of the Holy Scriptures, which they acknowledged, and resolved all his arguments and exhortations thereunto.

They who regard the body of this epistle as concerned merely with the refutation of those arguments brought against the Gospel by the ancient Jews, do greatly err. That which the apostle here took up is of vital moment for *each* generation. Human nature does not change, and the objections brought against the Truth by its enemies are, in substance, the same in every age. As the best means of getting rid of darkness is to let in the light, so the most effectual antidote for the poison of Satan is the pure milk of the Word. Only as we are established in the Truth are we fortified against the sophistries of error. In this epistle the apostle deals with the *fundamental* principles of Christianity, and no effort should be spared to arrive at a sound understanding of them. The foundations of the Faith are ever being attacked, and the ministers of Christ can perform no better service than to establish their people in the grand verities of the Faith.

The chief design of the Holy Spirit in this epistle is to set forth the great difference between the *administration of* the Everlasting Covenant before Christ came and since His coming. The following contrasts may be observed. First, the difference between the instruments God used: the "prophets"—His own Son: 1:1, 2. Second, the difference between priesthood and Priesthood: 7:11-17. Third, the difference between surety and Surety: 7:21, 22. Fourth, the difference between the law and the "Oath:" 7:28. Fifth, the difference between mediator and Mediator: 8:6; 9:15. Sixth, between promises and Promises: 8:6. Seventh, between blood and Blood: 9:12-14. Eighth, between sacrifices and the Sacrifice: 9:26. Ninth, between sprinkling and Sprinkling: 9:13, 14. Tenth, between tabernacle and Tabernacle: 9:8, 24. Eleventh, between the "shadow" and the Substance: 10:1 and cf. Col. 2:17. Twelfth, between "country" and Country: 11:9, 16. In all these contrasts the difference is between the Old and N.T. *administrations* of the Everlasting Covenant.

The outstanding contrast between the Old and N.T. regimes is that the one was but evanescent, whereas the other is abiding. Judaism was but preparatory, a temporary economy; whereas Christianity is permanent, ushering in an everlasting order of things. This is intimated in the opening sentence of the epistle: "God hath in these *last* days spoken unto us in His Son:" *finality* has now been reached! — there is no other dispensation to follow this: cf. 1 Cor. 10:11, 1 Pet. 4:7, 1 John 2:19. In keeping with this we may note how frequently the emphasis is laid upon the abidingness and finality of what is here treated of. We read of "He became the Author of *eternal* salvation unto all them that obey Him" (5:9), of "*eternal* judgment" (6:2), that "He is able also to save them for *evermore* that come unto God by Him" (7:25), of "*eternal* redemption" (9:12), of "the *eternal* Spirit" (9:14), of an "*eternal* inheritance" (9:15), of "the *everlasting* covenant" (13:20).

"Salute all them that have the rule over you, and all the saints. They of Italy salute you" (v. 24). It was the custom of the apostle to close his epistle with a warm greeting: not that this was merely a courtesy or pleasantry, for in those days the love of Christians was strong and fervent, both unto the Lord Himself and to His redeemed: "But as touching brotherly love ye need not that I write unto you: for ye yourselves are taught of God to love one another" (1 Thess. 4:9). How radically different things were then from what they now are! Yet only so in degree, and not in essence, for wherever the love of God is shed abroad in the heart, the affections of that soul will necessarily flow unto *all* His people. "We know that we have passed from death unto life, because we love the brethren" (1 John 3:14), which is as true to-day as it was in the first century.

Salute all that have the rule over you." This evinced the apostle's good will unto the ministers and officers of the churches in Judea, as well as according honour to whom honour is due. Mutual amity between the servants of Christ is to be sedulously sought and lovingly maintained. The large-heartedness of the apostle in this important particular shines forth again and again in the N.T. Calvin suggested that the reason why this salutation was sent more particularly unto the rulers of the churches was "as a mark of honour, that he might conciliate them, and gently lead them to assent to his doctrine" — which was so radically opposed to their earlier training. The "rulers" referred to in this verse are, of course, the same as those mentioned in vv. 7, 17.

"And *all* the saints." One lesson here inculated is that the servants of Christ should be absolutely impartial, manifesting equal respect unto the highest and lowest of God's dear people. This clause also condemns that detestable spirit of eclecticism, fostered so much by Rome. The Gospel has no secrets reserved for the initiated only, but the whole of it is the common property of *all* believers. "This epistle, containing strong meat for the perfect, is addressed to the whole congregation. If any part of Scripture was to be kept from the common people, we might fancy it would be this epistle. The writings of the apostles, as well as the prophets, were read in the public assembly; how much more ought it now to be left to every one to read them according to his need" (Bengel).

Believers are here designated "saints" or *separated ones,* which is their most common appellation in the N.T. They are so in a fourfold respect. First, by the Father's sovereign choice, whereby before the foundation of the world, He singled them out from the mass of their fellows, to be the objects of His special favour. Second, by the Son's redemption, whereby He purchased "a peculiar people" unto Himself, thereby distinguishing between the sheep and the goats. Third, by the Spirit's regeneration, whereby He quickens them unto newness of life, thus making them to differ from those who are left in their natural state—dead in trespasses and sins. Fourth, by their own consecration, whereby they surrender themselves unto the Lord, and dedicate themselves to His service. Their saintship is *evidenced* by their lives: devoted to the love, fear, and will of God. Such are the only proper members of a local church, and such are the only true members of the Church of God.

"They of Italy salute you." They did so through the apostle unto the entire body of the Hebrews: knowing of his intention of sending a letter to them, they desired to be remembered to them. "They of *Italy*" if not all of them Gentiles, certainly included many among their number. A most significant detail was this. In the previous verse Paul had referred to sending "Timothy" unto them, and *his* father was *a Gentile*! But still more striking was this word: it was more than a hint that the "middle wall of partition" was already broken down. Certainly "Italy" was "*outside* the Camp" of Judaism: Jerusalem was no longer the centre of God's earthly witness!

"They of Italy salute you." This is very blessed, showing the victory of the spirit over the flesh. "How does Christianity melt down prejudices! Romans and Jews, Italians and Hebrews, were accustomed to regard each other with contempt and hatred. But in Christ Jesus there is neither Romans nor Jews, neither Italians nor Hebrews: all are one in Him. Christians of different countries should take all proper opportunities of testifying their mutual regards to each other. It is calculated to strengthen and console, and to knit them closer and closer in harmony. Proper expressions of love increase love on both sides" (John Brown).

"Grace be with you all. Amen" (v. 25). The epistle closes with the sign-manual of Paul himself. He commonly employed an amanuensis (Rom. 16:22), but *this* sentence was written by his own hand. This particular apostolic benediction was his own distinctive token. "The salutation of Paul with mine own hand, which is the token in every epistle, so I write: that the grace of our Lord Jesus be with you all. Amen" (2 Thess. 3:17, 18). If the reader will turn to the closing verse of each of the other thirteen epistles of this apostle, it will be found that the same token, substantially, is given in each one. This is the more striking for neither James, Peter, John, nor Jude employed it. Thus, this closing "grace be with you all" is conclusive evidence that *Paul* was the writer of this epistle.

"Grace be with you all. Amen." This is the most comprehensive petition that can be presented to God on behalf of His people, either individually or collectively, for it comprises all manner of the blessings of His free favour. Divine grace comprehends and contains all things pertaining to life and godliness. By grace we are saved (Eph. 2:8), in grace we stand (Rom. 5:2), through grace we are preserved. These words signify, Let the favour of God be *toward* you, His power be working *in* you, bringing forth the fruits of holiness. Thus, the epistle closes with prayer! "When the people of God have been conversing together, by word or writing, it is good to part with prayer, desiring for each other the continuance of the gracious presence of God, that they may meet together in the world of glory" (Matt. Henry.) "Grace be *with* you all" denoted their actual participation therein.

And now our happy task is completed. Very conscious are we of our limitations and infirmities. We can but commit our poor efforts to God, pleading the merits of Christ to countervail our demerits, and asking Him to bless that which was pleasing to Himself. Let those who have accompanied us throughout these articles join the writer in asking: do we now better understand the contents of this difficult yet blessed epistle? Have we a deeper appreciation of that grand order of things that has superceded Judaism? Is Christ more real and precious to our souls? Are we more conscious of the sanctifying effects of the doctrine which it inculcates? Are we now paying more diligent heed to its weighty exhortations? Are our souls more deeply impressed by its solemn warnings against apostasy? May Divine grace indeed be with us all.

N.B. The articles comprising this series have been written on land and sea. They were commenced in Australia, continued as we crossed three oceans, resumed in England, considerably added to during the years we spent in the U.S.A., and completed in Scotland and England.